**An Anthology of Labor Economics:**
Readings and Commentary

# An Anthology of Labor Economics:
## Readings and Commentary

*HD*
*4901*
*M28*

**Ray Marshall**
The University of Texas at Austin

**Richard Perlman**
The University of Wisconsin—Milwaukee

John Wiley & Sons, Inc.
New York • London • Sydney • Toronto

*Library of Congress Cataloging in Publication Data:*

Marshall, F      Ray, comp.
    An anthology of labor economics.

    Includes bibliographies.
    1. Labor economics—Addresses, essays, lectures.
I. Perlman, Richard, joint comp.      II. Title.

HD4901.M28              331'.08              78-175794
ISBN 0-471-57298-5


Printed in the United States of America

10 9 8 7 6 5 4 3 2 1

# Preface

We have called this *An Anthology of Labor Economics* because we wish to emphasize that it is not simply a book of readings. Our objective has been to present a unified treatment of labor economics in which our comments are interwoven with selected works of authorities on various topics. We therefore sought a volume that would not be primarily a supplementary text, although it could be used for that purpose, but could serve as the basic instructional aid for a course in labor economics.

Many of the selections reproduced in this volume might be considered "classics" in the sense that they are standard works in labor economics frequently appearing in readings books; however, familiarity and reputation were not the primary considerations for selection. In order to maintain the unity of the work, writings were selected because they made fundamental contributions to theory, presented significant empirical studies closely related to theoretical concepts, dealt with important policy matters, or fit closely with the subject under consideration. Although unity of subject is more difficult to maintain with our approach than with texts written entirely by one or two authors, our book has the advantage of providing the reader with in-depth material written by authorities on each topic. We have strived for cohesion by lacing the selections together with our own exposition.

The dominant theme of this book is the theory and practice of various subjects in labor economics. Although our emphasis is on current problems and issues, we did not limit our selections to recent works but selected writings that dealt with important problems or contained basic theoretical insights regardless of the date of their publication. For example, although Adam Smith wrote long ago, his insights are fresh enough for inclusion in our treatment of modern aspects of the human capital concept.

Our basic procedure is to introduce each selection with a summary of the main points covered, together with our comments on it. The reader thus has a survey of each work as background to the original material. Moreover, some important topics are treated from different points of view by different authors. We are convinced that looking at topics from different angles facilitates learning. We also have included some related readings at the end of each chapter.

The book is divided into four parts, each dealing with an important division of labor economics. Part I, Labor Movements: Theories and Comparisons, analyses some leading theories of labor movements and outlines the movements of Europe, the developing countries, and the United States. Chapter 2, on the United States, discusses the ideology of the American labor movement, labor in the post-World War II period, government regulation of union activities, union responsibility, a profile of the American labor movement at the end of the 1960's, union growth in the South, unionization of agricultural workers, and some perceptions on the American labor movement at the beginning of the 1970's. Since we emphasize the comparative method, the subsequent chapters deal with some of these aspects of labor movements in other countries. Part III also deals with trade unions but in the context of industrial relations and collective bargaining.

Part II, Wages and Employment: Theory and Practice, presents selections and analyses of labor supply and demand, long-run and short-run changes in the labor force, the inadequate demand-structural controversy over the causes of unemployment, the wage-price-unemployment problem, wage structure, and geographic wage differentials. The impact of unions on wages and bargaining theory are presented in Chapters 12 and 13 of Part III.

Part III analyzes industrial relations and collective bargaining. As in all other parts, our basic concern is with theory and practice. This part opens with a survey of contemporary collective bargaining in the United States, followed by discussions of collective bargaining theories, the impact of unions on relative wages, conflict resolution, and collective bargaining by public employees. The discussion of conflict resolution in Chapter 14 deals wth community (racial, university, etc.) disputes as well as with collective bargaining.

Part IV, Human Resource Development, treats various theoretical and practical aspects of programs to improve the productivity and personal incomes of workers. The need for a comprehensive human resource development strategy is stressed. Specific topics deal with manpower economics, investment in education, the economics of poverty, and Negro employment and income.

Although we have tried for a comprehensive treatment, the seemingly boundless scope of the field of labor economics precludes complete coverage of all topics that fall within the discipline. What we have presented, though, should impress the reader with the growing concern of modern labor economics over the interaction of labor problems with other parts of the economy and society. For example, from the manpower area of labor-management relations, collective bargaining techniques have been expanded to apply to community disputes; from a concern with the effect of unions on wages, labor economics now includes formal study of the wage-inflation full employment interrelationships; from consideration of the quantity of labor supply as a function of population and wage levels, more interest is now expressed in the quality of labor with occupation and earnings dependent on education, training, opportunity, and even the level of discrimination.

This outline of the subjects covered in this volume makes it clear that labor economics deals with some important policy questions as well as some significant theoretical issues. An understanding of these issues is important for material well-being, economic growth, and economic stability. Labor problems are therefore important not only for workers and employers, but also for the general public in its role as consumers, voters, and taxpayers. Wage earners are primarily concerned with their incomes, hours, working conditions, and employment security, while to the employer labor problems involve the recruitment and retention of competent workers at wages that will allow them to operate within the limits of their budgetary constraints. The public is concerned with such matters as the education and training of work forces, economic stability, the elimination of poverty and discrimination (because of race, sex, age, and material origin), and the peaceful settlement of industrial disputes—all of which are among the problems considered by labor economics.

The listing of the problems dealt with in this book indicates the extent of the subject, which relates to almost every theoretical and applied area of economics. Indeed, we must at times call on special insights into these problems afforded by sociologists, lawyers, psychologists, historians, political scientists, and specialists in business administration. However, our primary emphasis is on the *economic* behavior of employers, workers, and trade unions; the way in which the interactions of various factors determine the allocation of resources and the rewards of the factors of production; the ways in which the rules of the economic game are influenced by such external forces as law, government, and public opinion; and how these various outcomes affect the economic health and welfare of workers, employers, and the public. Thus, whether the student intends to become a general economist, a labor economist, or a well-informed citizen, we think an understanding of the issues covered in this volume will be of value.


Ray Marshall
Richard Perlman

# Contents

**Part III.**
**Industrial Relations**
**and Collective**
**Bargaining**

An Anthology of Labor Economics:
Readings and Commentary

# 1

# Labor Movements: Theories and Comparisons

Part 1 discusses theories and comparisons of labor movements, a branch of labor economics that has become increasingly important since World War II. Our primary concern is with the labor movement in the United States, but it is useful for the student of labor economics to at least understand the outlines of labor movements in other countries. Moreover, a knowledge of foreign labor movements deepens our understanding of the American scene. For example, the comparative method helps us to understand why the American labor movement is relatively unique among industrialized nations in not having a labor party or advocating some form of socialism. It is also a useful approach because it facilitates an objective analysis of problems, since we can be more dispassionate about the problems of other countries which do not involve us directly. In addition, the comparative method helps us to identify the unity and diversity in causal relationships between various countries, enabling us to see how labor problems are related to institutions and different stages of economic development. It therefore facilitates the evolution and evaluation of theories or statements of causal relationships.

The comparative method also facilitates the formulation of policy on such important problems as wage and price stability, dispute settlement, collective bargaining by government employees, and other matters common to many industrialized systems. We are not suggesting, of course, that policies should be adopted from other countries without first examining the unique national features that might have given rise to those policies. But an examination of foreign experiences can suggest policies that might, with modifications, be applicable to our situation.

Another major objective of Part I is to examine theories of labor movements, which are basic aids in simplifying and understanding certain fundamental cause and effect relationships. Theories of labor movements are systematic interpretations of the origin and behavior of labor organizations and are important because they help us to determine which influences are merely transitory or accidental and which are basic causal relationships. We hope that an examination of some leading efforts to construct such theories will help the reader order his thinking about labor movements.

Chapter I of this part analyzes some theories of labor movements; Chapter 2 discusses the labor movement in the United States in considerable detail; Chapter 3 outlines European labor movements; and Chapter 4 deals with labor in the developing countries.

# CHAPTER 1

## Theories of Labor Movements

Studies of labor movements—or any other activity—are significant not because of specific facts, which may be relevant only to their particular setting, but primarily because they help clarify general principles that make it possible to isolate the main causal forces influencing the movement or activity in question. The main function of a "theory"—or, as some would prefer, a conceptual framework or interpretation—is to outline the basic causal relationships under consideration. It will be observed, however, that the authors of the various "theories" or "interpretations" discussed in this chapter apply different tests to theories and assign them different functions.

### THE TASK OF LABOR THEORIES

In the first selection in this chapter, Professor John T. Dunlop discusses the need for a theory of the labor movement and sets forth the questions that such a theory should answer. He then judges the extent to which some leading theories answer these questions. Since none of the leading theories satisfied him, he outlined "a more generalized and more integrated understanding of the development of the labor movement," which "claims only to facilitate the development of such a theoretical system." In Dunlop's opinion, the "four interrelated factors" that must be examined relative to the long-run determinants of labor movement growth are: (1) technology, (2) market structures and the character of competition, (3) community institutions of control, and (4) ideas and beliefs.

Dunlop argues that before the Wagner Act of the 1930's, the spread of union organization was determined much more by technology and market structures and competition than was true thereafter because that New Deal legislation introduced the representation election supervised by the National

Labor Relations Board, as the primary method of union organization. In this post-Wagner Act context, community institutions and ideas and beliefs become more important. Dunlop outlines some of the ways that ideas and beliefs have influenced the growth of unions in the United States.

As Professor Dunlop emphasizes, his outline is not a theory of the labor movement: he does more to suggest the main questions that such a theory should answer and some of the general factors influencing *unions* than he does to present a formal theory. It should be emphasized, moreover, that the American *labor movement* consists mainly of unions, but in other countries it encompasses *political parties* and other working class organizations and institutions as well as unions. Professor Dunlop's discussion, however, is concerned primarily with unions and not with noneconomic labor organizations. It will be observed, therefore, that there is a distinction between a theory of *labor organization* and a theory of the *labor movement*. The former accounts for the development of trade unions (the economic labor movement) whereas the latter accounts for the political as well as the economic factors.

# The Development of Labor Organization: A Theoretical Framework[1]

## by John T. Dunlop

The facts do not tell their own story; they must be crossexamined. They must be carefully analyzed, systematized, compared and interpreted."[2] This conclusion is an indictment of the all too frequent approach to the development of the labor movement,[3] in which "history" and "theory" are separate and non-permeable compartments.

Under the caption of "history of labor" are chronicled what purport to be collections of fact and sequences of fact. Under the heading of "theory of labor or-ganization" are found "explanations" conjured out of inner consciousness with only occasional and convenient reference to the past. The "history" and "theory" of the labor movement can have little meaning in isolation.[4] But it is particularly the failure of theoretical apparatus that accounts for the lack of greater understanding of the development of the labor movement and the paucity of significant research. Indeed, despite all the epoch-making developments in the field of labor organization in the past fifteen years,

SOURCE Reprinted with permission of the Macmillan Company from *Insights into Labor Issues*, Richard Lester and Joseph Shister, eds. Copyright 1948 by The Macmillan Company.

[1] This essay has benefited from helpful comments by J. A. Schumpeter, A. P. Usher, and Selig Perlman.

[2] Talcott Parsons, *The Structure of Social Action* (New York, McGraw-Hill Book Co., 1937), p. 698.

[3] See E. Wight Bakke, *Mutual Survival, The Goal of Unions and Management* (New Haven, Labor and Management Center, Yale Univ., 1946), p. 12 for a contrast between a "movement" and a "business."

[4] J. B. Bury, *The Idea of Progress* (New York, Macmillan Co., 1932). See the Introduction by Charles A. Beard, pp. ix-xl.

there has been virtually no contribution to the "theory" and scarcely a reputable narrative of this period exists.[5]

This essay constitutes a re-examination of fashions of thinking in theories of the labor movement. It proceeds from the initial conviction that any theory of the labor movement must first establish its criteria. Just what questions is a theory of labor organization supposed to answer? Only after this task has been explicitly recognized can there be critical discussion of the development of the labor movement.

The body of economic theory attempts to explain the allocation of resources.[6] Business cycle theories present systems of propositions to make intelligible the fluctuations of the economic system. In similar terms, what is the *pièce de résistance* of a theory of the labor movement? By what standards or tests is it possible to prefer one theory to another? What behavior must such a theory explain to be judged a "closer fit" than another model?

EXPLANATIONS OF
THE LABOR MOVEMENT

The literature on theories of the labor movement, if carefully analzed, reveals at least four questions which have been the concern of investigators. As far as can be determined, however, nowhere are these questions posed explicitly.

1. How is one to account for the origin or emergence of labor organizations?

What conditions are necessary and what circumstances stimulate the precipitation of labor organization? Why have some workers organized and others not?

2. What explains the pattern of growth and development of labor organizations? What factors are responsible for the sequence and form in which organizations have emerged in various countries, industries, crafts, and companies? Since there is great diversity in the patterns of development, any theory of the labor movement must account for these differences.

3. What are the ultimate goals of the labor movement? What is its relationship to the future of capitalism? What is its role in the socialist or communist state?

4. Why do individual workers join labor organizations? What system of social psychology accounts for this behavior of the employee?

Most writings on theories of the labor movement have in effect been concerned with one or several of these questions. They show a tendency to seek a single and usually oversimplified statement of the development of labor organization. But the labor movement is highly complex and many-sided. The "history" does not readily lend itself to any single formula.

*Frank Tannenbaum*[7]

To Tannebaum "the labor movement is the result and the machine is the major cause."[8] The machine threatens the se-

---

[5] Selig Perlman's *Theory of the Labor Movement* (New York, Macmillan Co.) was published in 1928. See Horace B. Davis, "The Theory of Union Growth," *Quarterly Journal of Economics,* LV (August, 1941), 611–37, and Russel Bauder, "Three Interpretations of the American Labor Movement," *Social Forces* XXII (December, 1943), 215–24.

[6] Frank H. Knight, *Risk, Uncertainty, and Profit* (London, London School of Economics and Political Science, 1963), Preface to reissue.

[7] Frank Tannenbaum, *The Labor Movement, Its Conservative Functions and Social Consequences* (New York, G. P. Putnam's Sons, 1921).

[8] *Ibid.,* p. 29). As a statement of the origin of labor organizations, this view is to be contrasted with that of John R. Commons, "Whatever may have been its origin in other countries, the labor movement in America did not spring from factory conditions. It arose as a protest against the merchant-capitalist system." (*A Documentary History of American Industrial Society* [Glendale, Calif., Arthur H. Clark Company, 1910], Vol. V, p. 23 [with Helen L. Sumner].)

curity of the individual worker and the wage earner reacts in self-defense through a union to attempt to control the machine. The individual worker seeks to harness the machine and to stem the tide of insecurity by which his life is menaced.

He intends little more than this security when joining a union, but ". . . in the process of carrying out the implications of defense against the competitive character of the capitalist system he contributes to the well-being of present-day society—a contribution which represents a by-product of the more immediate and conscious attempt to find security in an insecure world."[9] Tannenbaum sees the labor movement ultimately displacing the capitalistic system by "industrial democracy," "an achievement which is implicit in the growth and development of the organized labor movement."[10]

Tannebaum provides an answer of sorts to at least three of the four questions posed above; he does not examine the pattern of growth of the labor movement. While not concerned with historical detail, Tannenbaum finds the origin of labor organizations in a reaction to the machine (question 1). The labor movement creates a new society (question 3). The individual worker joins the union in self-defense in quest of security (question 4).

### Sidney and Beatrice Webb[11]

A trade union is a "continuous association of wage-earners for the purpose of maintaining or improving the conditions of their working lives."[12] Its fundamental objective, according to the Webbs, is "the deliberate regulation of the conditions of employment in such a way as to ward off from the manual-working producers the evil effects of industrial competition."[13] The labor organization utilizes, in the well-known schema of the Webbs, the "methods" of mutual insurance, collective bargaining, and legal enactment. The labor organization chooses among these "methods" depending on the stage of development of the society. An era of the master system requires the enforcement of common rules against "industrial parasitism"; the existence of trusts makes legal enactment the only effective method in many cases. The assumption by government of responsibility for social risks, such as old age and unemployment, greatly curtails the use of the method of mutual insurance on the part of labor organizations.

In the view of the Webbs, trade unionism is ". . . not merely an incident of the present phase of capitalist industry, but has a permanent function to fulfill in the democratic state."[14] The special function of the trade union is in the democratic administration of industry. While consumers acting through cooperatives or entrepreneurs may determine *what* is produced, the democratic society requires a labor organization to provide for the participation of workers in the conditions of sale of their services. In the type of democratic society the Webbs eventually expected (the little profit-taker and the trust superseded by the salaried officer of the cooperative and by government agencies), the unions would more and more assume the character of professional associations.

The Webbs use the term "theory of trade unionism"[15] not to refer to an-

---

[9] These lines are in italics in the original. *Op. cit.,* p. 32.

[10] *Ibid.,* p. 44.

[11] Sidney and Beatrice Webb, *Industrial Democracy* (New York, Longmans, Green & Co., 1897); and *History of Trade Unionism* (New York, Longmans, Green & Co., 1894). Also see Margaret Cole, *Beatrice Webb* (New York, Harcourt, Brace & Co., 1946), pp. 73–83.

[12] *History of Trade Unionism* (1920 ed.), p. 1.

[13] *Industrial Democracy* (1914 printing), p. 807.

[14] *Ibid.,* p. 823.

[15] *Ibid.,* pp. viii and 795. See footnote 17.

swers to any of the four questions posed in the preceding section but as a statement of the economic consequences of a labor organization, virtually a theory of wages or collective bargaining. The trade union is pictured as having only two "expedients" for the improvement of conditions of employment:[16] the restriction of numbers in the trade and the establishment of uniform minimum standards required of each firm. The Webbs condemned the former monopolist policy. They endorsed the latter application of the Common Rule, for it transfers competition from wages to quality. The device of the Common Rule envisages the graduan improvement in these minimum standards of wages and conditions. It is the duty of the labor organization to strive prepetually to raise the level of its common rules. This process may be carried on by collective bargaining or by the use of legislation.[17] Such is the Webbs' "theory of trade unionism," an economic rationalization for the establishment of minimum standards.

What the Webbs called their "theory of trade unionism would ordinarily be called a theory of the development of the labor movement. While the Webbs made fundamental and pioneer contributions to the study of trade union government and the narrative of labor organization history, they formulated no systematic, conceptual answers to the first two questions posed in the previous section (the emergence of labor organization and the patterns of development). As for ultimate goals (question 3), the Webbs see the labor union as an instrument of the democratization of both the work community and the wider society as a whole.

### Robert F. Hoxie[18]

Hoxie starts from the proposition that wage earners in similar social and economic environments tend to develop a "common interpretation of the social situation."[19] The union emerges when group sentiments have been crystallized. It appears as a "group interpretation of the social situation in which the workers find themselves, and a remedial program in the form of aims, policies, and methods. . . ."[20] To Hoxie, the union constitutes a common interpretation and set of beliefs concerned with the problems confronting the worker and a generalized program of amelioration. Such a persistent group "viewpoint or interpretation"[21] Hoxie calls a *functional* type of unionism. His name has come to be associated almost exclusively with classification of the functional types he suggests (business unionism, uplift unionism, revolutionary unionism, predatory unionism, and dependent unionism) to the detraction of an understanding of his significant contribution.

The account of the origin of labor organizations which Hoxie gives—a crystallization of group viewpoint and programme of action—leads him to question whether the labor movement has any unity: "Seen from the standpoint of aims, ideals, methods, and theories, there is no normal type to which all union variants approximate, no single labor movement which has progres-

---

[16] *Ibid.*, p. 560.

[17] ". . . the whole community of wage-earners . . . may by a persistent and systematic use of the Device of the Common Rule secure an indefinite, though of course not an unlimited, rise in its Standard of Life. And in this universal and elaborate application of the Common Rule, the economist finds a *sound and consistent theory of Trade Unionism,* adapted to the conditions of modern industry; . . ." *Ibid.*, p. 795. (Italics added.)

[18] Robert F. Hoxie, *Trade Unionism in the United States* (New York, D. Appleton & Co., 1921). See the Introduction by E. H. Downey.

[19] *Ibid.*, p. 58.

[20] *Ibid.*, p. 60.

[21] *Ibid.*, p. 69.

sively adapted itself to progessive change of circumstances, no one set of postulates which can be spoken of as *the* philosophy of unionism. Rather there are competing, relatively stable union types . . ."[22]

Since the labor movement is nonunitary, Hoxie rejects interpretations that look upon trade unionism as fundamentally an economic manifestation of changing methods of production or market developments.[23] The fact of different functional types compels Hoxie to renounce any explanation in environmental terms alone. The subjective factor emphasized in the concept of functional types is equally important.

Hoxie provides an answer to the problem of the emergence of labor organization (question 1) in terms of "group psychology." He accounts for the divergent forms of unionism but is comparatively unconcerned with an explanation of historical development. One of the factors affecting the classification of functional types is the program for social action developed by the group. In this sense, Hoxie indicates the different answers that have been posed to the problem of the relation of the labor movement to the future of capitalism (question 3). But there is no sense of historical development. Here again for Hoxie is reticent to generalize to a "labor movement as a whole" from his "functional types."[24]

*Selig Perlman*[25]

Perlman finds that in any "modern labor situation" there may be said to be three factors operative: "first, the resistance of capitalism, determined by its own historical development, second, the degree of dominance over the labor movement by the intellectual's mentality, which regularly underestimates capitalism's resistance power and overestimates labor's will to radical change; and, third, the degree of maturity of a trade union 'mentality'."[26] By this last factor Perlman means the extent to which the trade union is conscious of job scarcity. "It is the author's contention that manual groups . . . have had their economic attitudes basically determined by a consciousness of scarcity of opportunity. . . . Starting with this consciousness of scarcity, the 'manualist' groups have been led to practicing solidarity, to an insistence upon an 'ownership' by the group as a whole of the totality of economic opportunity extant, to a 'rationing' by the group of such opportunity among the individuals constituting it, to a control by the group over its members in relation to the conditions upon which they as individuals are permitted to occupy a portion of that opportunity. . . ."[27]

Perlman suggests that there are three basic economic philosophies, those of the manual laborer just indicated, the businessman, and the intellectual. In the United States a "stabilized" unionism was delayed until the labor movement developed job consciousness, until it came to assert a "collective mastery over job opportunities and employment bargains," until wage earners dissociated themselves from "producers" generally who were imbued with the doctrine of abundance and who organized under the slogan of antimonopoly. The American Federation of Labor constitutes a shift in the psychology of the

---

[22] E. H. Downey, Introduction to *Trade Unionism in the United States,* pp. xxiii-xxiv.

[23] See the discussion under the heading of John R. Commons which follows in the text.

[24] See, however, *op. cit.,* note 3, p. 59.

[25] Perlman, *op. cit.*

[26] *Ibid.,* p. x.

[27] *Ibid.,* p. 4; also see pp. 237–53. The importance attached to job consciousness is the outcome of one of the few explicit statements on the requirements of a theory of the labor movement. "A theory of the labor movement should include a theory of the psychology of the laboring man" (p. 237).

labor movement, a recognition of the scarcity of opportunity.[28]

Perlman apparently gives a certain primacy to the role of job consciousness in the labor movement. In fact a labor organization can be regarded as fundamentally a manifestation of "economic attitudes." Nonetheless, labor history cannot deny a "truly pivotal part" to the intellectual. The character of the labor movement in any particular country must depend on the particular combination of the role of the intellectual, the resistance of capitalism, and the development of job consciousness.

Perlman is seen to treat in one way or another all four criteria posed in the previous section. Labor organizations develop from a concern with the scarcity of job opportunities (questions 1 and 4). The pattern of development of organization in a particular country depends upon the particular combination of the three factors operative in any "modern labor situation" (question 2). The relation of the labor movement to the future of capitalism is peculiarly influenced by the role of the intellectual (question 3).

### John R. Commons[29]

Commons believed that labor history should be understood in terms of the interaction of "economic, industrial, and political conditions with many varieties of individualistic, socialistic and protectionist philosophies."[30] He treats labor history as a part of its industrial and political history.

Commons' thinking on the origin and emergence of labor organization involved an appraisal of the writings of Marx, Schmoller, and Bucher. He posed the problem of explaining the emergence of the labor movement in terms of the growth of new bargaining classes—the wage earner and the employer. He added the gradual evolution of the employee-employer relationship from the merchant-capitalist dealings with a journeyman. The growth of the market separates from the merchant-capitalist the functions of the custom merchant, the retail merchant, and the wholesale merchant. The employer remains.[31]

While Commons recognized that the changing modes of production influenced to some extent the emergence of labor organization, he attached primary importance to the market expansion. "The extension of the market took precedence over the mode of production as an explanation of the origin of new class alignments."[32]

The pattern of uneven growth in the American labor movement Commons attributed to the fluctuations in economic conditions. Periods of prosperity produced organization while depressions saw the labor movement subside or change its form to political or social agitation.[33]

The theoretical system of Commons seems to have been concerned only with the emergence and the pattern of develop-

[28] Perlman disagrees with the Webbs' view that there is a tendency for unionism to give up the principle of restriction of numbers in favor of the device of the Common Rule. *Ibid.*, pp. 295–98. Also see *Labor in the New Deal Decade*, Three Lectures by Selig Perlman, . . . at the ILGWU Officers Institute, New York City, 1943–1945 (Educational Department, International Ladies' Garment Workers' Union, 1945).

[29] John R. Commons, Ed., *A Documentary History of American Industrial Society,* 11 Vols. (Glendale, Calif., Arthur H. Clark Co., 1910–11). In particular see the Introduction, Vol. V, pp. 19–37, written with Helen L. Sumner. Also John R. Commons and Associates, *History of Labor in the United States,* 2 Vols. (New York, Macmillan Co., 1918), in particular Vol. I, pp. 3–21.

[30] Commons and Associates, *op. cit.*, Vol. I, Introduction; p. 3.

[31] *Ibid.*, p. 106.

[32] *Ibid.*, p. 28.

[33] Commons, Ed., *Documentary History* . . . . Vol V, p. 19.

ment of the labor movement (questions 1 and 2 above).

## The Marxist View

To Karl Marx, the trade union was first and foremost an "organizing center."[34] It provided the locus for collecting the forces of the working class. Without organization, workers competed with each others for available employment. "The trade union developed originally out of the spontaneous attempts of the workers to do away with this competition, or at least to restrict it for the purpose of obtaining at least such contractual conditions as would raise them above the status of bare slaves."[35]

The labor organization provided for Marx the focal point for the functional organization of the working class toward a change in the structure of society. Just as the medieval municipalities and communities were the center of organization of the bourgeoisie, so the trade union for the proletariat. Thus, in addition to its original tasks, the trade union was to learn to take on additional duties, to become the center for organizing the working class for its political emancipation.[36]

It is imperative to distinguish the role of the trade union under capitalism from that after the successful revolution of the proletariat. Left to themselves, labor organizations would remain within the capitalistic framework. Lenin has put this point succinctly. "The spontaneous labour movement, able by itself to create (and inevitably will create) only trade unionism, and working-class trade-union politics are precisely working-class bourgeois politics."[37]

In terms of the fundamental questions posed above, it is apparent that Marx and Lenin, insofar as they formulated a theory of the labor movement, were concerned with the origin or emergence of labor organizations (question 1) and their ultimate relationship to capitalistic society question 3).

A critical comparison of these views is beyond the scope of this essay. There are important similarities of analysis and emphasis that appear at once and more that would be evident save for differences in language. A rather sharp cleavage emerges, however, between writers such as the Webbs and Commons, who look upon the labor movement primarily as the manifestation of economic developments, and those, such as Perlman and Hoxie, who choose to emphasize the habits of mind of wage earners. Compare the *key concepts* of "common rule" (Webbs) and "expansion" of the market" (Commons) on the one hand with "job consciousness" (Perlman) and "functional type" (Hoxie, a persistent exponent of the group viewpoint or interpretation). The Webbs and Commons built their models of the trade union out of changes in observable economic institutions. Hoxie and Perlman were imbued with the necessity of a "psychology" of the labor movement and hold the notion that the outlook of the worker upon his world and his destiny is the cornerstone of a model of trade union development.

This cleavage represents a fundamental failure in the formulation of "theories of the labor movement." For certainly, there are significant interrelations between the outlook of members of a community and the economic institutions. Consider, for

---

[34] A. Lozovsky, *Marx and the Trade Unions* (Nev York, International Publishers Co., 1935), p. 15.
[35] *Ibid., p.* 16. (Italics deleted.)
[36] Paul M. Sweezy, *The Theory of Capitalist Development* (New York, Oxford Univ. Press, 1942), pp. 312–13.
[37] V. L. Lenin, *What Is to Be Done?,* Reprinted from *The Iskra Period* (New York, International Publishers, 1929), p. 90.

instance, the shedding of the "producer class" complex of the American labor movement. Commons explains the development in terms of the final development of the national market while Perlman emphasizes that job consciousness and the belief in scarcity of work opportunities had asserted itself. These developments are clearly not independent.

The sections which follow are intended to present a more generalized and more integrated understanding of the development of the labor movement. The next section provides a scaffolding or generalized theoretical framework for an approach to the labor movement.

## THE DETERMINANTS OF LABOR ORGANIZATION

The labor movement, or any similarly complex social organization, may be fruitfully explored by an examination of four interrelated factors: technology, market structures and the character of competition, community institutions of control, and ideas and beliefs.

1. Technology. This term includes not only changes in machinery and in methods of production but concomitant developments in the size and organization of production and distribution units.

2. Market structures and character of competition. The term comprehends the growth of markets, the changes in the locus of financial control as distinguished from the size of production units, the development of buying and selling institutions in both product and factor markets, and the emergence of specialized functions and personnel within these organizations.

3. Wider community institutions. This phrase is intended to include among others the role of the press, radio, and other means of communication in the society, the formal educational system for both general and vocational training, the courts, governmental administrative agencies, and political parties and organizations.

4. Ideas and beliefs. This caption is a short cut for the value judgments and mores that permeate and identify a social system.

Such a comprehensive scaffolding or method of approach does not in itself constitute a theory of the labor movement. It claims only to facilitate the development of such a theoretical system. It compels reflection on the range of mutual influences operative in any society. Such a comprehensive framework of reference assists in asking significant questions; the complex interrelations between the labor movement and any society are sharpened. The labor movement is seen in the context of its "total" environment. This fourfold scheme is set of preliminary tools through which the labor movement may be reconnoitered and analyzed. The facts of labor history may more readily be cross-examined.

It must be emphasized that these four factors are intended not merely to facilitate the cross-sectional study of the labor movement at any one given time but even more to assist in the analysis of the growth and change of the labor movement over time. The interaction among technological and market factors, community institutions, and ideas and beliefs must be used to account for the development of the labor movement.

Social systems or institutions go through periods of relative stability and through other periods of spectacular and tortuous change. Periods of stability may be regarded as involving a certain equilibrium among these four factors. That is, a given system of technology and markets requires or is compatible with only a limited number of community institutions and value judgments and ideas. The converse is equally true; a given system of ideas and community organization is compatible only with particular types of market and technological arrangements. In these terms, equilibrium in the social system may be said to exist when these four groups of factors are compatible one with another. Equilibrium may involve an unchanging condition or rates of change among the factors which are congruous. Change the technology of a system and there are required alterations in the other three factors, or change the value judgments and ideas of a community and there must be changes in market systems and technology.

The actual course of history does not disclose the isolated reaction to the change in a single factor any more than a series of prices reveals directly the unique effects of shifts in demand or movements along demand schedules. A comprehensive theory of a society should indicate the result of varying one of these factors—the others unchanged—when the system as a whole is in initial equilibrium. The actual course of events consists in continuous and inseparable interaction between the secondary effects of the initial change and new impacts on the social system.

The procedure suggested in this section would analyze the labor movement by indicating the change in each of these four factors over the past and the consequent impact on the emergence and the manner of growth of the labor movement. The labor movement is seen as the product of its total environment. As labor organizations grow they become an independent factor affecting the course of their own destiny.

### The Webbs, Hoxie and Perlman

A theory of the labor movement should explain the relationships between various labor organizations and between the labor movement and the environment within which that movement operates. In the second article in this chapter, Professor Bauder discusses the theories of the Webbs in Great Britain and of Robert Hoxie and Selig Perlman, whose work draws mainly from American experiences, although Perlman was a Russian immigrant who also draws from European experiences. Notice that Bauder does not refer to "theories," but to "systematic interpretations," which he considers to be "essential in order to maintain a consistant point of view, to provide criteria for the separation of the important from the unimportant and to determine the relative emphasis to be accorded to each section of the subject." Bauder makes it clear, however, that these interpretations are merely tentative and should be revised in the process of investigation.

Bauder first examines the interpretations presented by the Webbs in their classic *Industrial Democracy*. As he emphasizes, this work, published in 1897, remained ". . . the source from which, directly or indirectly, much theoretical discussion springs. The basic generalization developed [by the Webbs] is that trade unionism has the primary function of determining or influencing the conditions of employment. More remotely unionism is viewed as an extension of basic democratic processes and as a potent force in the improvement of social efficiency."

In attempting to promote the workers' interests, the Webbs saw trade union policies and procedures changing through time as the incompatibility of each program with economic conditions and efficiency requirements caused them to yield to new doctrines. Thus, the trade unions evolved the *doctrines,* or social concepts, relative to labor's place in society: "vested interests," which held that working conditions should never be interfered with for the worse; "supply and demand," under which unions gave up the guild idea of the right to a trade, but instead attempted to promote their members' interests through controlling the supply of labor; and the "Living Wage" or "National Minimum," a national point of view more compatible with the realities of an industrial society, which maintained that conditions conducive to the efficient use of labor are in the best interest of the whole community.

To carry out its doctrines, the labor movement established certain *regulations* or rules: "restriction of numbers," which tended to give way with economic development to the "common rule." "Restriction of numbers" supported the doctrines of "vested interests" and "supply and demand." Various restrictive rules, such as opposition to machinery and exclusion of outsiders from their trades, proved incompatible with industrial technology and efficiency and therefore gave way to the idea of the *common rule,* which "concentrates on the establishment of a standard minimum of conditions of employment and leaves to competition who shall occupy the jobs." The *common rule* was supported by the doctrine of the *Living wage* or the *National Minimum.*

There is a similar transition in the methods or *devices* used to secure trade union rules. Unions ordinarily start with the method of "mutual insurance" in order to provide income to members when they are unable to work or payments to their families in the event of death. Because it requires the workers to rely too much on their own resources, mutual insurance gives way to "collective bargaining," under which unions share both the costs of benefits and the formulation of working rules with employers. However, collective bargaining has the limitation of being applicable only to those covered by it and those matters subject to control by employers, workers, and unions; collective bargaining also might fail to protect the public interest. This device therefore yields to legal enactment. However, as the Webbs emphasize, mutual insurance, collective bargaining, and legal enactment coexist. Clearly, however, the Webbs' analysis foresees the development of a *political* as well as an *economic* labor movement, in keeping with their socialist ideology.

However, in spite of the trend toward "legal enactment," the "common rule," and the "National Minimum," the Webbs considered unions to have the continuing function of protecting workers from the effects of competition (or, as they put it, "higgling in the market") and from bureaucrats in public employment. The Webbs thought the establishment of minimum standards would produce efficiency because employers could not raise profits by reducing labor standards and therefore would have to become more efficient by innovating and selecting only the best workers. Since inefficient employers would not be able to compete, business would be driven to the most efficient producers. Similarly, inefficient workers would become unemployed. However, the legislatively enacted National Minimum would prevent those who could not compete from being totally degraded. The Webbs thus saw an evolution of democracy from political to industrial and finally to social matters.

Although space permits only the barest outlines of the Webbs' theory—which has had a profound impact on labor economies in the United States and

Europe—the reader interested in gaining a better understanding is urged to read the Webbs' *Industrial Democracy*.

Bauder next develops the interpretation of Robert Hoxie, who "begins with the proposition—that everyone possesses a social philosophy and program which for each individual is determined by work-day environment, union tradition, immediate social milieu, national characteristics and heredity." Thus, for Hoxie, the workers' social psychology produces four main *varieties* of unions with several subvarieties: business, uplift, revolutionary (socialistic and quasi-anarchistic); and predatory (hold-up and guerilla).

The last interpretation Bauder discusses is that of Selig Perlman, whose ideas have been extremely influential in the United States. Perlman is the only one of these writers specifically to address himself to a general theory with universal validity. Perlman's theory is based on three essential ideas: the "psychology" of manualists, the resistance power of capitalism, and the psychology of intellectuals who seek to influence labor movements. Since an outline of Perlman's theory is presented below and is analyzed at length in the article by Gulick and Bers, to be discussed in some detail later, we need not treat it very extensively at this point.

Professor Bauder concludes with some comparisons of these three interpretations, which "are not wholly antithetical, yet at many points . . . lead to very different conclusions." One essential difference is whether there are unitary interpretations of labor movements, as developed by Perlman and the Webbs, or whether there are several types as suggested by Hoxie. Bauder shows that some of Hoxie's types are not "basic." Moreover, Perlman, the Webbs, Marx, and others emphasize the differences between political and economic labor movements, especially when the former is "socialistic."

Since his "interpretations," like those of Professor Dunlop, refer primarily to *unions* and not *labor movements* in a broader sense, Bauder rejects "revolutionary unionism" as a basic union type. He admits that a union might adopt a radical program but insists that this is done from the outside. "Radicalism is an exotic flower grafted on a labor stem. The fundamental differences in ideology and program between trade unionism and socialism must inevitably force conflicts and the one or the other must predominate." Of course, a revolutionary ideology might be inconsistent with trade unionism, but it is clearly possible to have a revolutionary *labor movement* in which unions are subordinant to revolutionary leaders. We shall see, moreover, that moderate socialist parties might have differences with trade union movements, but can still coexist as equals with different functions within the labor movement.

To Bauder, the effectiveness of a theory is determined by its ability to explain trade union practices. (Others, such as Gulick and Bers in their article reproduced in this chapter, judge a theory at least partly in terms of its ability to *predict* behavior as well as to *explain* it.) He first applies this standard to the closed shop, a term that the Webbs did not use. To Perlman, the closed shop was a method of job control. However, it should be observed that union security measures generally have been less significant in Europe than in the United States, partly because class consciousness assured European unions of greater membership and allegiance. In the United States, the closed shop has been important to unions because the absence of class consciousness required unions to organize employers as well as workers. Probably the best framework for understanding the role of union security would be a combination of Perlman's theory and Dunlop's factors, because the incidence of various union security provisions is closely related to markets, technology, and beliefs, especially markets and technology. The closed shop, for example, exists mainly in casual occupations where workers use unions as sources of jobs and employers use them as sources of labor.

In discussing union security and jurisdictional disputes, Bauder gives the impression that Perlman's theory comes closer to meeting his test than those of Hoxie and the Webbs. However, it should be observed that the test imposed by Bauder favors Perlman's theory which, as we shall see in greater detail below, grew out of a study of union work rules in the United States, where job control has been more important than it was in England. If, for example, we had made predictability a test or had selected the political effectiveness of a labor movement as conditions to be explained, we might have found the Webbs' theory a better fit. If we use Dunlop's questions as the standard by which to judge a theory, the interpretations of Perlman, Hoxie, and the Webbs all would be inadequate. As Bauder states, moreover, Perlman's theory is too narrow to deal with certain basic aspects of labor movements, such as cooperatives. Again, however, it should be observed that co-ops are much more a part of the European labor movements, which are influenced more by intellectuals, than they are of the narrower American labor movement, which emphasizes job control.

Bauder also questions Perlman's distinction between the psychology of employers and manualists, the adequacy of his concept of job dictatorship, and failure to relate the trade union as an institution more directly to the economy.

It is difficult to apply Bauder's test to a specifiic labor movement because if we only require a theory to explain practices, those practices, which have different importance in different movements, will bias the outcome of the test, especially where some theories have general objectives and others, like the Webbs, refer mainly to the movement being studied. In other words, any *general* theory probably fits specific conditions better than a specific theory derived from the specific conditions other than those against which it was tested. However, it remains to be seen whether Perlman's theory relates primarily to American conditions, as Gulick and Bers argue, or whether it was really general, as Perlman thought it was.

# Three Interpretations of the American Trade Union Movement

## by Russell Bauder

All fruitful discussion of trade unionism must be built around an express or implied systematic interpretation of its nature and significance. This is essential in order to maintain a consistent point of view, to provide criteria for the separation of the important from the unimportant and to determine the relative emphasis to be accorded to each section of the subject. Once such interpretation is achieved, however, it need not possess the finality of ultimate truth. Rather it should serve as an hypothesis subject to constant revision in the process of investigation. Nevertheless in its formulation it aids in pointing the direction to further research. Expressed as a generalization of existing knowledge, such interpretation also becomes an instrument of exposition. Therefore a familiarity with current interpretation of trade unionism makes possible a better understanding of specific events. At the same time the definite exposition of an interpretation makes visible the cords which are used to tie the many aspects of the subject into unity.

Three systematic interpretations have received serious consideration in discussions of American trade unionism to the extent that the greater part of the literature reflects a predominating influence of one or another. The first developed from Sidney and Beatrice Webb's *History of Trade Unionism* and their *Industrial Democracy*.[1]

Later, in 1916, Robert Franklin Hoxie's functional and genetic interpretation ap-

SOURCE Reprinted with permission from *Social Forces,* Vol. 22, No. 2, December 1943.

[1] Sidney and Beatrice Webb, *History of Trade Unionism* (London: Longmans, Green and Co., 1894); *Industrial Democracy* (London: Longmans, Green and Co., 1897). References are to the 1920 edition.

peared.[2] In the meantime Professor John R. Commons was working with a group of students on an American Labor History. Documents were published in 1918, a two-volume history carrying the material to 1890 appeared in 1924 and two more volumes bring the subject up to 1932 were published in 1935. This historical material, together with European data, was systematized, into an interpretation by Professor Selig Perlman in 1928.[3]

# I

Sidney and Beatrice Webb's *Industrial Democracy* was built upon British materials but their similarity to American experience was apparent. Although formulated some forty years ago, this pioneer work remains the source from which, directly or indirectly, much theoretical discussion springs. The basic generalization developed is that trade unionism has the primary function of determining or influencing the conditions of employment. More remotely unionism is viewed as an extension of basic democratic processes and as a potent force in the improvement of social efficiency.

The Webbs explain that trade union objectives are embodied in regulations which fall into two categories. Restriction of Numbers was given major emphasis in earlier trade union experience but this was found to be giving way to the Device of the Common Rule. Underlying the first of these regulatory programs where two social concepts relative to the place of labor in society. First of these was the Doctrine of Vested Interests enunciating the principle that the "conditions of em-

ployment hitherto enjoyed by any section of workmen ought, under no circumstances, to be interfered with for the worse." This idea of a right to a trade rested partly upon gild and mercantilistic tradition and partly upon the existing position of the wage earner. Encroachment upon this established expectation was viewed as a destruction of property.

Direct adherence to this idea would have stereotyped the industrial order by prohibition of all change whether by invention or by new organizational devices. The onslaught of the Industrial Revolution with its great reorganization of processes and occupations led first to Parliamentary renunciation of any right to a trade. In time a new generation of wage earners grew up with no vested interests of their own and therefore opposed to any social doctrine which might exclude them from desirable occupations. At the same time the growing influence of consumers, who opposed any restriction upon developments which would lower their living costs, made this doctrine increasingly untenable. Finally even the trade unionists came to feel that the doctrine of vested interests was out of date.

In surrendering this doctrine of stability, the trade unions generally fell back upon the doctrine of supply and demand —the business principle that the buyer seeks the lowest price for what he buys and the seller seeks the highest price. Trade unions accordingly should market labor at the best possible price. Under the influence of this idea strong unions with great reserve funds sought to control the entire labor supply of an occupation. This policy forced employers to organize

[2] Robert Franklin Hoxie, "The Essence of Unionism" and "The Interpretation of Union Types," *Jour. Polit. Econ.*, XXII, 201–217 and 464–481. Also, his *Trade Unionism in the United States* (N. Y.: D. Appleton, 1917). References are to the 1919 edition.

[3] The works mentioned here are: *A Documentary History of American Industrial Society*, John R. Commons, ed., 11 Vols. (Cleveland: John B. Clark, 1910–11); Commons and Associates, *History of Labour in the United Statse*, 2 vols. (N. Y.: Macmillan, 1918); Vol. III, Lescohier and Brandeis, *Working Conditions and Labor Legislation* (N.Y.: Macmillan, 1935); Vol. IV, Perlman and Taft, *Labor Movements* (N.Y.: Macmillan, 1935; Selig Perlman, *A Theory of the Labor Movement*, (N.Y.: Macmillan, 1928).

to protect themselves against the power of the labor combination. Finally it tended to produce labor and employer alliances designed to exact better returns from the community and to protect themselves from the "unfair competition" of individuals within their own groups.

The device of restriction of numbers was expressed in a wide variety of rules of varying significance. They all produced in practice, however, one fundamental conclusion, namely, that as restrictive devices, they were more detrimental than useful to the trade union program. Consequently union history shows their progressive abandonment.

Among the earliest of these rules were those expressing opposition to new process and machinery. These have given way to a demand that the operatives already in the trade should be given preferential rights to learn the new process. Apprentice regulations, once universal, are being abandoned because it is found they cannot be enforced. Their continuation means weakening of the unions because they result in recruiting the trade from its poorest establishments and from the areas where union organization is weak. Rules excluding women from trades are being surrendered under the compulsion of competition. Rules of jurisdiction, leading to jurisdictional disputes remain based on the doctrine of vested interests, but the road to solution is becoming more apparent. The unions should limit themselves to determining the proper rate for such disputed jobs and with that established, permit the employer to select the worker he wants.

Thus a survey of the restrictive rules of the unions convinces the Webbs that they have proved unworkable and consequently are in the process of being abandoned. In their place another type of regulation, based on "The Common Rule" is receiving increased emphasis. This concentrates on the establishment of a standard minimum of conditions of employment and leaves to competition the determination of who shall occupy the jobs. Underlying this concept is a third doctrine concerning the relation of labor to society which may be called the "Doctrine of the Living Wage" or the "Doctrine of the National Minimum." Briefly this principle is that the best interests of the community will be served by securing through deliberate action those conditions necessary for the continuous and efficient fulfillment of labor functions.

Most important of these common rules is the standard rate, which may be expressed on either a piece or time basis, but in either case represents the minimum rate at which any member of the trade may be employed. The regulation of the normal day has similar import except that the standard in this case is a maximum. Rules of sanitation and safety are minima. These common rules, applicable alike to large bodies of workmen, are essential to collective bargaining. In their absence, the conditions of employment are left to individual bargaining between parties of unequal economic strength, with a resulting tendency towards the serious deterioration of labor standards. This conviction is universal among trade unionists and the device of the common rule is found in the regulations of all unions.

According to the Webbs there are three methods by which rules, whether for restriction of numbers or for common standards may be secured. First in point of time is the Method of Mutual Insurance under which the labor organization builds up reserve funds from dues and pays its members sick, death, and out-of-work benefits. This device not only stabilizes organization by tying the member more closely to his union; it also protects the union rules from the competition of necessitous members. Such out-of-work benefits may even be used to strengthen rules because the union may establish a new standard and support all those members whose employers refuse to accede to the new demand. Mutual insurance has limited application, however, because the benefit structure cannot be actuarially secure and because it provides no means for discussion with the employers.

The Method of Collective Bargaining meets this last limitation. It involves concerted action on the part of workmen who select representatives to deal with the employer on behalf of the entire body. When successful, this method tends to produce organization of employers and to broaden the bargaining area to the greater part of the trade. Through collective bargaining, then, common rules are established which are coextensive with organization. Such an arrangement possesses the great merit of flexibility but has the drawbacks that it makes no provision for protection of the public interest and that there is always the risk of a serious trade stoppage resulting from failure to reach agreement.

Finally there is the Method of Legal Enactment which means attempting to get the legislative body to adopt a law embodying the rule sought by the trade union. Once this is accomplished, the rule is applied throughout the entire country whether the union is strong or weak. The law is not easily changed so it tends to withstand the shock of business depressions. However, pressure for such laws involves long and uncertain agitation. Successes may be anticipated only for those measures which appear to involve a public purpose whereas many common rules are narrow, technical, and significant only for a particular trade. Consequently no union could rely exclusively on legal enactment. Actually the three methods are used concurrently, each in its appropriate area of effectiveness.

From the functions, rules, and methods of unions, the Webbs turn to economic significance. Their basic premise is that the scale of wages is indeterminate within a large area. The lower limit is the point at which many skilled workers will move to other markets and lines and young people will not be attracted to the trade in sufficient numbers. The upper limit is the point beyond which capital and business power will leave the trade for other lines and new capital cannot be attracted.

Within this wide indeterminate area conditions of employment are determined by the higgling of the market, that is by bargaining. The individual worker, however, stands at the apex of an inverted pyramid of bargaining disadvantage. The consumer forces the retailer to lower prices, the retailer puts pressure on the wholesaler, the wholesaler forces the manufacturer, and finally the manufacturer must press down wages and employment conditions. Further, when the workman seeks employment he has disadvantages in the forms of unequal alternatives, unequal market knowledge, unequal bargaining skill and indefiniteness in the labor contract. Only through unionism can these heavy disadvantages be offset and standards be maintained.[4]

Thus through either the device of restriction of numbers or the common rule, degradation to the subsistence level is avoided. Restriction of numbers, however, produces mixed results. On the one hand, it stereotypes processes and lowers the level of productive efficiency. On the other hand, compared with labor competition, it does fence off certain working groups from the general deterioration. In this select circle there is preserved a high level

[4] In this analysis certain conceptual peculiarities should be mentioned. While the Webbs use the idea of marginal workers, they appear always as the most necessitous and least fitted individuals, not as last units of an interchangeable supply. The concept of competition is similarly given a strange content. It is pictured as working always downward. There is no idea of a market price which would operate to protect a seeker of work from his own necessities. Apparently workmen compete for jobs but employers do not compete for labor (unless the common rule is enforced). Apparently also the employer is indifferent to the quality of his labor and reacts only to its price.

of skill, physical health and intelligence unattainable at a subsistence wage.

Quite different is the consequence of reliance upon the device of the common rule. It changes competition from rivalry to work for less to rivalry to do more and to improve quality. When a standard minimum is enforced, employers must improve their efficiency because they cannot increase their profits by lowering labor standards. Therefore they must take care to select only the best workers. They must give attention to invention and the development of new processes and new methods. Further, inefficient producers cannot meet their pegged costs so business is driven to the most efficient producers who are enabled to expand. Among the workmen, concentration of selection of the best puts a heavy stimulus on all to develop their capacities to the full as being the best way to insure employment. Enforcement of the common rule operates as a potent force for social efficiency.[5]

In itself, however, action along trade union lines is insufficient because unionism cannot be universal. As the regulated trades improve in position, the conditions in the unregulated (non-union) trades must grow progressively worse. There the employers are forced to lower standards to meet the competition of the regulated trades. The narrowing market for the product intensifies competition. At the same time the labor supply is kept inferior because the best elements move into the regulated trades. Because of this tendency there must be a legislatively enforced National Minimum for all which will set a bottom to degradation. Standards above this level would then be the proper sphere for trade union action.

If the Webb's interpretation for trade unionism can be summarized in a few sentences, the following are suggestive. Trade unionism is essentially an economic movement to improve wages, hours and working conditions. Collective action, leading to the enforcement of common rules, stays the destructive forces of competition so that labor standards may be raised. This action may be buttressed by legislation. As minimum standards are enforced, competition is redirected from a destructive to a constructive role by making it into a device powerfully directed to the "selection of the fittest."

*Thus, the effect of the Common Rule on the organization of industry, like its effect on the manual laborer, and the brain-working entrepreneur, is all in the direction of increasing efficiency. It in no way abolishes competition, or lessens its intensity. What it does is perpetually to stimulate the selection of the most efficient workmen, the best equipped employers, and the most advantageous forms of industry. It in no way deteriorates any of the factors of production; on the contrary, its influence acts as a constant incentive to the further improvement of the manual laborers, the machinery, and the organizing ability used in industry.[6]*

## II

The Webbs developed an interpretation of trade unionism essentially economic in character, emphasizing union rules and their economic consequences. Robert Franklin Hoxie accepted the basic characteristics of this economic analysis[7] and

---

[5] The Webbs appear to believe that the appearance of unemployment among union members will effectively check any tendency to push labor costs to an uneconomical level. This overlooks the complexity of forces producing unemployment and assumes that a minority out of employment will be able to control a majority who are enjoying better returns from "high" working standards.

[6] Sidney and Beatrice Webb, *op. cit.*, pp. 733–34.

[7] This may be questioned by some. On p. 254, Hoxie writes, "In 'Industrial Democracy' we have found the only worth while systematic attempt at the general interpretation of unionism. To this store of fundamentals I propose to add a little. . . ." On page 283 he states that unions cannot raise wages as a whole. The Webbs believed that wages as a whole can be raised by union action.

concerned himself with the manner in which union groups come into existence and an analysis of their functional characteristics.

Hoxie begins with the proposition that everyone possesses a social philosophy and program which for each individual is determined by work-day environment, union tradition, immediate social *milieu*, national characteristics, and heredity. Many wage earners will have similar philosophies because the causal environmental factors will be common to great numbers, yet no one philosophy or program will be common to all. Individuals, similarly situated socially and economically and not too far apart in their hereditary, psychological make-ups, will tend to unite into self-conscious, like-minded groups which are trade unions of the various functional types.

❂ ❂ ❂

On the basis of this analysis and method of classification, Hoxie isolated four main varieties of unionism with several sub-varieties. *Business* unionism is trade-conscious rather than class-conscious. It accepts the existing economic system and demands only the right to bargain collectively to secure immediate ends for its membership. The railroad brotherhoods, although presenting other characteristics, are suggested as representative of the type.

*Uplift* unionism is essentially idealistic in its viewpoint. It may be trade, class, or society-conscious. Chiefly it aspires to elevate the moral, intellectual, and social life of the workers. Mutuality and democracy characterize its government. Its methods involve collective bargaining but stress chiefly mutual insurance and idealistic plans for social regeneration. The Knights of Labor, although not strictly conformable, is illustrative.

*Revolutionary* unionism is radical in viewpoint and in action. It is class-conscious rather than trade-conscious and it demands a thorough reorganization of society. Two sub-varieties exist in the United States.[8] *Socialistic* unionism ultimately demands state socialism and expects to achieve its goal through class political action, but immediately it may utilize collective bargaining. *Quasi-anarchistic* unionism repudiates both collective bargaining and political action. It looks forward to a state based on free industrial association to be achieved through agitation, direct action, sabotage, and violence. Examples of the respective variants are the Western Federation of Miners and the Industrial Workers of the World.

Finally there is *Predatory* unionism, also with two sub-varieties. Its distinguishing characteristic is its ruthless pursuit of immediate ends. *Hold-up* unionism appears in the outward garb of business unionism. Generally it is boss-ridden and corrupt. Its methods are a combination of collective bargaining and secret bribery and violence. *Guerilla* unionism, alike in its ruthless pursuit of immediate ends and its secret and violent methods differs in that it always operates against the employer and cannot be bought off. Examples offered are respectively, the building trades unions led by men like "Skinny" Madden and the Structural Iron Workers at the time of the McNamara case.[9]

### III

Professor Perlman displays no interest in the purely economic aspects or consequences of trade unionism. His interests are centered on the analysis of union

---

[8] Probably a current exposition of the type would require the addition of a third variant—communistic unionism.

[9] A fifth functional type, *dependent* unionism, including company unions and union label unions has been suggested by followers of Hoxie. *Cf.* Hoxie, *op. cit.*, p. 51 n.

working rules to discover labor "psychology" by which is meant group mentality or outlook. Generalizing union practices he reaches a monistic interpretation of trade unionism based on the common attribute of job control.

Three economic attitudes are distinguished as impinging on labor relations, that of the employer, that of the "manualist," and that of the intellectual. The employer typically views the world in which he lives as one of expanding or abundant opportunity in which there is plenty for all, or at least for all who have the requisite abilities to foresee, grasp, and profit thereby.

In contrast the "manualist" lives in a world of limited opportunity bounded by prospects of a job. He realizes his lack of capacity for taking advantage of the opportunities which come into being and constantly shift in the business world. He has neither the capacity for taking risks nor is he at home in the complexities and negotiations of the business world. At the same time he may feel that the world has been made one of scarcity for him either by nature or by the existing institutional order.

\* \* \*

In attempting to establish this job control, trade unions face not only the opposition of employers who have a fundamental interest in as well as a prescriptive right to job control, but also opposition from intellectuals who are thought of as educated "non-manualists" wanting to do something for labor. The intellectuals would frame labor's program and shape its policies. Whereas the trade union ideology holds the actual workman in its view, the intellectual envisages labor as an "abstract mass in the grip of an abstract force."

While agreeing that labor is being pushed from behind toward an ultimate social goal, vast differences are entertained both as to the nature of the driving force and the goal. The social justice intellectual, such as the Christian socialist or the anarchist, pictures the force as an awakening self-realization and the goal as the self-governing workshop or the free commune. The efficiency intellectual, such as the Fabian, sees labor driven by an unfolding interest in the possibilities of technical and social efficiency leadings to orderliness, economic planning, and State socialism. Finally, to the Marxian or determinist revolutionary, the force is the mode of production which in its development inevitably hurls the labor mass against the capitalist regimé to achieve a proletarian dictatorship and eventually to full communism. Unions must defend their own ideology and program of job control against the infiltrating tactics of these outside groups.

## IV

These interpretations of trade unionism are not wholly antithetical, yet at many points they lead to very different conclusions. A fundamental difference is whether unionism is essentially unitary or a variety of irreconcilable elements. Both the Webbs and Perlman find that a single formula explains trade unionism, the one in terms of wages, hours and working conditions, the other in terms of job control. Hoxie, on the other hand, finds that there is no single thing which is trade unionism but rather it consists of at least five irreconcilable types.

\* \* \*

Other observers have pointed out the ideological conflict between socialism and trade unionism. Thus G. B. Shaw states, "Trade Unionism is not Socialism; it is the Capitalism of the Proletariat."[10] He fur-

[10] G. B. Shaw, *Intelligent Woman's Guide to Socialism and Capitalism* (N.Y.: Brentano's, 1928), 186.

ther shows that the leaders of English socialism were predominantly "upper middle class" as were Marx and Engels.[11] Beyond this he sees a basic conflict between trade unions with strikes and socialism with compulsory social service.[12]

## V

The basic test of an interpretation of trade unionism is not to be found in a close analysis for internal consistency nor in comparison with orthodox social or economic theories. A social movement need not be consistent; it may even be founded on fallacious doctrine. Rather these interpretations must be tested by determining how well they explain trade union practices. Such a test need not run through the entire range of union behavior, but can concentrate on some of the more controversial elements which are difficult to fit into a consistent pattern. Four of these attitudes and practices, the demand for the closed or union shop, the persistence of restrictive practices, anti-intellectualism, and the jurisdictional dispute provide an adequate if incomplete list for this purpose.

The phrase "closed shop" is not used by the Webbs. They do, however, speak of compulsory union membership. The requirement that all eligible employees be members of the union is explained as a device to maintain a solid bargaining front so that the inequities of individual bargaining may be avoided and so that all employees are made co-participants and subject to union discipline.[13] This is also the position taken by Hoxie.[14] It may be mentioned that the closed or union shop is also an organizing device of great effectiveness. . . .

The anti-intellectualism of trade union-

ism is well known and widely remarked.[15] The leadership of American trade unions has risen from the ranks. No "outsiders," no intellectuals, have held major office with any stability except in the American Newspaper Guild. Any professional or academic person who has associated with the trade union movement has had the experience of having the name "theorist," "college professor" or even "intellectual" hurled at him as an epithet. . . .

This unwillingness to admit intellectuals to their councils, to give them leadership responsibilities or to seek and use their technical advice has puzzled many observers, including the Webbs. They attributed it to ignorance. Hoxie would deal with the problem as one of rival union types—a possibility we have already considered. Again to Perlman this is a basic characteristic of unionism arising from the conflict in ideology between the job control of the unions and the attitude of the intellectuals who view labor as "an abstract mass in the grip of an abstract force."

## VI

The position here taken gives an appearance of complete acceptance of Perlman's institutional interpretation of trade unionism. It does appear to offer a more consistent and a richer explanation of union practices than do the other two. There are, however, certain points which are not met by it. The first and most difficult is that the consumers' cooperative movement, which certainly was initially a product of "organic" labor, cannot be fitted within the framework of scarce economic opportunity. This suggests that the interpretation is narrower than is the labor movement as a whole.

[11] *Ibid.*, p. 185.
[12] *Ibid.*, pp. 356–9.
[13] Sidney and Beatrice Webb, *op. cit.*, pp. 206–219; 533–535.
[14] Hoxie, *op. cit.*, pp. 291, 294.
[15] *Cf.* Perlman and Taft, *op. cit.*, p. 7 paragraph 7 and p. 628 paragraph 7; Sidney and Beatrice Webb, *op. cit.*, p. 267.

It has frequently been suggested that Perlman's distinction between the attitudes of the "manualist" and the business man has been overdrawn. Trade associations, cartels, and the entire code structure of the NRA show us a businessman's "psychology" based on limited economic opportunity together with rules, fully as developed as those of the unions, to exert a collective ownership of the market, to regulate occupancy and tenure, and to protect the market opportunity from contraction and from "interlopers." This, however, broadens the scope of the interpretation. If employers adopt the "psychology" of manual labor, they may better comprehend the labor program, but this would not lead to a cessation of industrial friction because the issue of job control would remain. As the history of trade unionism in fascist countries indicates, scarcity conscious employers will not hesitate to suppress trade unions in order to maintain their job control.

At two other points Perlman's interpretation is incomplete rather than inadequate. Starting from his concept of job control, he describes a labor job dictatorship. He sets the stage for a discussion of collective bargaining as a process of joint control with employer and wage earner participation in the making and administering of the rules of the employer-employee relationship but this is not developed. This would lead to a treatment of collective agreements in terms of concessions or "rights" granted to the participants—the employer, the union, and the rank and file—together with joint grievance machinery for administering the rights and legislative provisions for rule making and rule revision.

Finally, trade unionism is an economic institution having a definite relationship to wages, costs, and employment. Its consequences to the economic order are direct. However, Perlman does not proceed from his interpretation of union behavior to a consideration of these consequences. Any complete interpretation of trade unionism must show its relationship to the production and distribution of wealth.

# Chapter I: Toward a Theory of the Labor Movement

## by Selig Perlman

The present book does not claim to give a full history of the several national labor movements, which the author has chosen as the most significant—the British, the German, the Russian, and the American. Rather it gives a survey of the historical development of these movements in order to show the grounds upon which the author, in the course of more than fifteen years of study and research, has arrived at his theory of the labor movement. It is his belief that the present time [1928] affords a unique opportunity for stock taking in the realm of such theory. First, because during the throbbing dozen years just past, filled to the brim with war and revolution, both capitalism and the labor movement have undergone a testing heretofore undreamed of. At no other time in modern history has society shown itself so nearly "with the lid off" as since the Rus-

sian Revolution. Nor has the labor movement ever before been made to render so strict an account to the outside world, as well as to itself, of what its deep-lying purposes truly are, as during the crowded decade which witnessed the successful Bolshevist Revolution, the decisive defeat of Communism in Germany (largely with the aid of the organized labor movement itself), the class war in Britain culminating in the general strike, the progressive metamorphosis of American capitalism into a "welfare capitalism," with the arrest of the growth of American unionism, notwithstanding the economic prosperity —to say nothing of the eclipse of French unionism and of the destruction of any independent labor movement in Fascist Italy. Second, the present appears an opportune time for a reëxamination of the theory of the labor movement, since, even

SOURCE Reprinted with permission from Selig Perlman, *A Theory of the Labor Movement,* New York, Augustus M. Kelly, 1948 (originally published by Macmillan in 1928).

in the eyes of the Communists, the revolutionary era has been succeeded by a "temporary" stabilization of capitalism.

Three dominant factors are emerging from the seeming medley of contradictory turns and events in recent labor history. The first factor is the demonstrated capacity, as in Germany, Austria, and Hungary, or else incapacity, as in Russia, of the capitalist group to survive as a ruling group and to withstand revolutionary attack when the protective hand of government has been withdrawn. In this sense "capitalism" is not only, nor even primarily, a material or governmental arrangement whereby one class, the capitalist class, owns the means of production, exchange, and distribution, while the other class, labor, is employed for wages. Capitalism is rather a social organization presided over by a class with an "effective will to power," implying the ability to defend its power against all comers—to defend it, not necessarily by physical force, since such force, however important at a crisis, might crumble after all—but to defend it, as it has done in Germany, through having convinced the other classes that they alone, the capitalists, know how to operate the complex economic apparatus of modern society upon which the material welfare of all depends.

The second factor which stands out clearly in the world-wide social situation is the rôle of the so-called "intellectual," the "intelligentsia", in the labor movement and in society at large. It was from the intellectual that the anti-capitalist influences in modern society emanated. It was he who impressed upon the labor movement tenets characteristic of his own mentality: the "nationalization" or "socialization" of industry, and political action, whether "constitutional" or "unconstitutional," on behalf of the "new social order." He, too, has been busily indoctrinating the middle classes with the same views, thus helping to undermine an important prop of capitalism and to some extent even the spirit of resistance of the capitalists themselves.

The third and the most vital factor in the labor situation is the trade union movement. Trade unionism, which is essentially pragmatic, struggles constantly, not only against the employers for an enlarged opportunity measured in income, security, and liberty in the shop and industry, but struggles also, whether consciously or unconsciously, actively or merely passively, against the intellectual who would frame its programs and shape its policies. In this struggle by "organic" labor[1] against dominance by the intellectuals, we perceive a clash of an ideology which holds the concrete workingmen in the center of its vision with a rival ideology which envisages labor merely as an "abstract mass in the grip of an abstract force."[2]

Labor's own "home grown" ideology is disclosed only through a study of the "working rules" of labor's own "institutions." The trade unions are the institutions of labor today, but much can be learned also from labor's institutions in the past, notably the gilds.

It is the author's contention that manual

---

[1] Trade unionists and intellectuals use alike the term "labor," which has an abstract connotation. But, to the trade unionists, "labor" means nothing more abstract or mystical than the millions of concrete human beings with their concrete wants and aspirations. And it is in this sense that the author uses it throughout this book.

[2] I use frequently the term "ideology" in imitation of the usage of socialist intellectuals taken over from Napoleon's term applied by him in contempt to the idealists of his day. I find, however, that the term has quite the same meaning as that which scientists call "ideas" and "theory," philosophers call "idealism" or "ethics," and business men and working men call "philosophy." Unionists speak of "the philosophy of trade unionism." If they were "intellectuals," they would call it "theory," "ideology," "ideas," or "idealism," or "ethics," all of which I sometimes include in the term "mentality."

groups, whether peasants in Russia, modern wage earners, or medieval master workmen, have had their economic attitudes basically determined by a consciousness of scarcity of opportunity, which is characteristic of these groups, and stands out in contrast with the business men's "abundance consciousness," or consciousness of unlimited opportunity. Starting with this consciousness of scarcity, the "manualist" groups have been led to practicing solidarity, to an insistence upon an "ownership" by the group as a whole of the totality of economic opportunity extant, to a "rationing" by the group of such opportunity among the individuals constituting it, to a control by the group over its members in relation to the conditions upon which they as individuals are permitted to occupy a portion of that opportunity—in brief, to a "communism of opportunity." This differs fundamentally from socialism or communism, which would "communize" not only "opportunity," but also production and distribution —just as it is far removed from "capitalism." Capitalism started from the premise of unlimited opportunity, and arrived, in its classical formulation, at "laissez faire" for the individual all along the line—in regard to the "quantity" of opportunity he may appropriate, the price or wage he may charge, and in regard to the ownership of the means of production. "Communism of opportunity" in the sense here employed existed in the medieval gilds before the merchant capitalists had subverted them to the purposes of a protected business men's oligarchy; in Russian peasant land communities with their periodic redivisions, among the several families, of the collectively owned land, the embodiment of the economic opportunity of a peasant group; and exists today in trade unions enforcing a "job control" through union "working rules."

But, in this country, due to the fact that here the "manualist" had found at hand an abundance of opportunity, in unoccupied land and in a pioneer social condition, his economic thinking had therefore issued, not from the scarcity premise but from the premise of abundance. It thus resulted in a social philosophy which was more akin to the business men's than to the trade unionists' or gildsmen's. Accordingly, the American labor movement, which long remained unaware of any distinction between itself and the "producing classes" in general,—which included also farmers, small manufacturers, and small business men,—continued for many decades to worship at the shrine of individualistic "anti-monopoly." "Anti-monopoly" was a program of reform, through politics and legislation, whereby the "producing classes" would apply a corrective to the American social order so that economic individualism might become "safe" for the producers rather than for land speculators, merchant capitalists, and bankers. Unionism, on the contrary, first became a stabilized movement in America only when the abundance consciousness of the pioneer days had been replaced in the mind of labor by a scarcity consciousness —the consciousness of joy scarcity. Only then did the American wage earner become willing to envisage a future in which his union would go on indefinitely controlling his relation to his job rather than endeavoring to afford him, as during the anti-monopoly stage of the labor movement, an escape into free and unregulated self-employment, by winning for him a competitive equality with the "monopolist."

In America, the historical struggle waged by labor for an undivided expression of its own mentality in its own movement was directed against the ideology of "anti-monopoly." But in Europe the antithesis to the labor mentality has been the mentality of the intellectual.

Twenty-five years ago, Nicolai Lenin[3] clearly recognized the divergence which exists between the intellectual and the trade unionist, although not in terms of an inevitable mutual antagonism, when he hurled his unusual polemical powers against those in the Social-Democratic Party, his own party at the time, who would confine their own and the party's agitational activities to playing upon labor's economic grievances. He then said that if it had not been for the "bourgeois intellectuals" Marx and Engels, labor would never have got beyond mere "trifling"—going after an increase in wage here and after a labor law there. Lenin, of course, saw labor and the trade union movement, not as an aggregation of concrete individuals sharing among themselves their collective job opportunity, as well as trying to enlarge it and improve it by joint effort and step by step, but rather as an abstract mass which history had predetermined to hurl itself against the capitalist social order and demolish it. Lenin therefore could never have seen in a nonrevolutionary unionism anything more than a blind groping after a purpose only vaguely grasped, rather than a completely self-conscious movement with a full-blown ideology of its own. But to see "labor" solely as an abstract mass and the concrete individual reduced to a mere mathematical point, as against the trade unionists' striving for job security for the individual and concrete freedom on the job, has not been solely the prerogative of "determinist-revolutionaries" like Lenin and the Communists. The other types of intellectuals in and close to the labor movement, the "ethical" type, the heirs of Owen and the Christian Socialists, and the "social efficiency" type, best represented by the Fabians—to mention but English examples, have equally with the orthodox Marxians reduced labor to a mere abstraction, although each has done so in his own way and has pictured "labor" as an abstract mass in the grip of an abstract force, existing, however, only in his own intellectual imagination, and not in the emotional imagination of the manual worker himself.

## Selig Perlman: A Critique

Because of its importance in American labor thought, we have devoted more attention to Selig Perlman's *A Theory of the Labor Movement* than to any of the other theories. Perhaps the most detailed criticism of Perlman has been made by Professors Charles Gulick and Melvin Bers in "Insights and Illusion in Perlman's Theory of the Labor Movement." A summary of Perlman's basic theory, taken from his *A Theory of the Labor Movement*, has also been presented.

Gulick and Bers are concerned with the ability of Perlman's theory to prosper in the face of developments that they consider to be contrary to Perlman's predictions (they implicitly make predictability a test of the theory). They first restate Perlman's basic ideas about the "Trade Union Mentality,"

[3] "The history of all countries attests to the fact that, left to its own forces, the working class can only attain to trade union consciousness,—that is, the conviction that it is necessary to unite in unions, wage the struggle against the bosses, obtain from the government such or such labor reforms, etc. As to the socialist doctrines, they came from philosophic, historic and economic theories elaborated by certain educated representatives of the possessing classes, the Intellectuals. In their social situation, the founders of contemporary scientific socialism, Marx and Engels, were bourgeois intellectuals." Lenin in *What Is To Be Done?*

the Intellectual," and the "Resistance Power of Capitalism," and make it clear that they consider Perlman to have defined his problem away. For example, the "intellectual" is given a precise meaning as considering labor an "abstract mass in the grip of an abstract force" who conceives of schemes that are incapable of achievement. "A gifted scholar is no 'intellectual' if he counsels unionist to forsake broad political action (as in a labor party) and to spend their energies solely on strengthening 'job control." Thus, ". . . the intellectual is defined as a program in opposition to job control unionism rather than as a group of individuals who are engaged primarily in intellectual activity. And capitalism is defined as both a collection of individuals and a social system with a power to survive, which makes it possible to attribute the strength or weakness of the system to capitalists who operate within the system."

Gulick and Bers therefore consider Perlman's three factors to be "identities by definition" that are "inextricably interrelated" rather than "independent forces, each contributing an influence on the developing labor movement." Thus, acceptance of capitalism and the manualist's mentality implies rejection of the intellectual. Gulick and Bers argue that the "degree of intellectual domination of a labor movement" and the "degree of maturity of the trade union mentality" are ". . . polar opposites. . . [and therefore] are 'independent' factors precisely in the same sense in which 'two factors' may be said to determine a man's height, namely, his tallness and his shortness." Similarly, it is not surprising to Gulick and Bers that a capitalist system in which workers were able to improve their conditions through collective bargaining would be one that was acceptable to manual workers.

Gulick and Bers conclude that Perlman's " 'factors' are so defined that attributing a value or strength to any one of them immediately implies, and may define a value for the other two." Moreover, ". . . confusions are inherent [in Perlman's system] because of the indiscriminate merger of an elaborate system of purely descriptive and/or definitional categories with certain explanatory principles and the designation of the resultant mixture as a 'theory' of the labor movement." Gulick and Bers conclude that Perlman's three-factor schema "does not constitute a theory of the labor movement in any meaningful sense. . . . The schema. . . represents. . . an intricate restatement of the questions to which it apparently addresses itself."

The first of these basic questions raised by Perlman is the attitude of the labor movement toward capitalism. Perlman differed from Marxists, who saw the labor movement as a means of destroying capitalism, because Perlman thought mature trade unionists would embrace capitalism. Moreover, Perlman saw capitalism as a strong and stable system, whereas Marxists " 'saw' its weakness and decline." However, Gulick and Bers find the "purely terminalogical" properties of Perlman's definitional system to be such that it "cannot be wrong."

To be a theory, Gulick and Bers argue, Perlman "should explain, for example, why manualists are attracted to 'intellectualist' programs in some instances and *why* they are indifferent to them in others. The three-factor schema does not offer such an explanation." However, according to Gulick and Bers, one element of Perlman's theory—"the 'psychology' of the laboring man himself"—contains an ingredient of a theory, but they clearly reject Perlman's concept as inadequate because it does not explain why a labor movement is what it is. They consider this psychological idea to be circular reasoning because it was derived from observing work rules that reflect a pre-occupation with job control. This logic is not necessarily false, according to Gulick and Bers, but they consider Perlman to have the burden of supplying positive evidence of its correctness.

Gulick and Bers consider Perlman's point about workers accepting capitalism because they "do not see themselves as efficient capitalists" to be "a roaring non sequitur" because the trade unionists could hire managers in a socialist system, much as they elect leaders and hire technical staffs in the unions. Gulick and Bers also question Perlman's idea that businessmen have an "abundance of opportunity" consciousness as contrasted with the workers' concept of "scarcity of opportunity": "It may be asked, for example, what basic difference from the viewpoint of 'opportunity' appraisal can be read from pools, gentlemen's agreements, Gary dinners, and a basing point system on the one hand and efforts to establish a union shop in the industry on the other?"

In addition, Gulick and Bers argue that Perlman's "scarcity consciousness" defines absolutely no role for political action, "either large or small." These writers disagree with Perlman that American labor's pre-AFL intellectualist-inspired antimonopoly programs were dead-end streets. To Gulick and Bers, these programs "made very good sense indeed" in the middle of the 19th century. However, with economic development, the perfection of a money and credit system, and the settlement of the nation's empty western spaces, these "antimonopolist" programs made less sense. Moreover, economic development produced a level of economic well-being that has made the American worker the "labor aristocrat of the world." This well-being, and such factors as their lack of class consciousness, the evolution of a system that promotes collective bargaining as national policy, and economic prosperity, account for the American workers' willingness to accept the system. Gulick and Bers do not agree, however, that acceptance of the system necessarily implies an acceptance of the capitalists or a willingness to give them credit for the workers' material welfare. European labor movements were more political because political democracy did not come early and the workers' economic conditions were much worse than they were in America.

Gulick and Bers conclude, therefore, that the American labor movement has been shaped by coditions in this country and "that there is little that is intrinsically unalterable in the present basic orientation of American labor." They consider Perlman to have directed attention to important questions that his principles did not explain. Their main criticism is that Perlman's "spurious theory of manualist psychology" was unfortunate because it led to a literature that "appears to have contented itself with the 'psychological' facade while the important elements, the further analysis and elaboration of which would have constituted a real achievement, tended to recede into the background." They also complain about Perlman's ardent followers who overlook the theory's weaknesses and "continue to endorse, nay, to laud a 'theory' which is patently contradicted by almost every labor movement outside the United States."

# Insight and Illusion in Perlman's Theory of the Labor Movement

## by Charles A. Gulick and Melvin K. Bers

Twenty-five years have now passed since the first publication of Professor Selig Perlman's *A Theory of the Labor Movement*[1]—one of the relatively few attempts we have "to devise a general theory of the labor movement . . . which will apply to all areas and times." Particularly since 1950 it has been the subject of a number of "rereadings," "reapprais-als," "comments," and "interpretations."[2] Although some of these writings contain reservations, even sharp criticisms, the frequency with which its basic validity has been attested to has again impressed us with the prevalence of the misconceptions associated with that famous work. These misconceptions, which in the course of years have ingrained themselves in the

Publication of critical analyses may seem to be an unkind manner of commemorating the twenty-fifth anniversary of a book universally acknowledged as a significant contribution to the literature of industrial relations. Yet such must be the fate of books and the ideas they contain if free inquiry for understanding and truth is to prevail. Recently, Professor Perlman's *Theory of the Labor Movement* has undergone considerable re-examination, particularly in regard to its applicability to modern unionism. In this article, however, the fundamental tenets of the theory itself are challenged in a searching appraisal.

[1] The book, originally published in 1928 by Macmillan, was reissued in 1949 by Augustus M. Kelley. It will be cited hereafter as *Theory*.

[2] Philip Taft, "A Rereading of Selig Perlman's *A Theory of the Labor Movement*," *Industrial and Labor Relations Review*, Vol. 4 (October 1950), pp. 70–77. "Theory of the Labor Movement: A Reappraisal" in *Proceedings* of the Industrial Relations Research Association, 1950, pp. 139–183. Adolf Sturmthal, "Comments on Selig Perlman's *A Theory of the Labor Movement*," *Industrial and Labor Relations Review*, Vol. 4 (July 1961), pp. 483–496. Industrial Relations Research Association, *Interpreting the Labor Movement*, 1952.

literature of the field, are attributable in part to a failure to penetrate the terminological system in which the theory is cast; more important, however, they reflect a willingness to accept fundamental propositions which, in fact, suffer from fatal deficiencies. But it is the vigor with which these propositions are sometimes defended which evokes in us the fear, to use an idea of Mr. J. B. S. Hardman and the words of Professor R. S. Bauder, that the theory has indeed become an "article of faith in the academic dogma."[3]

If there is a difference between a theory and a faith, it should be most apparent in the former's vulnerability to perverse fact and the latter's ability to prosper in the face of it. The Perlman theory has demonstrated a surprising immunity to empirical shock. Of the four labor movements discussed in the *Theory*, for example, only one is in approximate conformity with the specifications for the "true" labor movement which emerges from the Perlman system. This one is the American, of course, and as we shall demonstrate below, there is ample reason to challenge the theory on the basis of this experience alone. The last half-century of the British experience directly contradicts the Perlman theory. The Russian experience cannot be incorporated in a meaningful way. With respect to the German movement, we may recall the confident assertion based on the analysis in the 1928 *Theory* that "whatever hardships or even crises the future may be holding in store for the

German labor movement,—its experience, both in the past and in recent years, has amply prepared it to cope with them."[4] Five years later the movement had vanished.

Yet it is not primarily an array of the "facts" with which we shall concern ourselves here. What has been most lacking is adequate attention to the basic structure of the Perlman system and to the methods employed in reaching the propositions by now so familiar to students of labor. That too much has been taken for granted in this sphere, we shall demonstrate through a rigorous analysis of the logical foundations of the Perlman theory.

STRUCTURE OF
THE PERLMAN SYSTEM

We understand the essential question to which Perlman sought to provide an answer to be: Why is the labor movement in a given country what it is? Or, put in a more "historical" way, what have been the crucial influences or factors shaping the development and form of labor movements?[5] Perlman reveals his approach in his Preface, where he reports that during the course of his researches,

. . . *three factors emerged as basic in any modern labor situation: first, the resistance power of capitalism, determined by its own historical development; second, the degree of dominance over the labor movements by the intellectual's "mentality," which regularly underestimates*

---

[3] The phrase becomes even more pungent when one recalls the statement on the first page of the preface to the *Theory* that "at bottom, the Marxian theory of the labor movement rests upon a species of faith."

[4] *Theory*, p. 122.

[5] Perlman's elaboration of the answer to this question can easily lead to the conclusion that he posed to himself two additional fundamental questions. One of them may have been: What are, "truly," the "deep-lying purposes" of the labor movement in general? (*Ibid.*, pp. 3, 278, 295, *passim*.) On pp. 295 ff., he lays great stress on his claim that the "misunderstanding" of the basic purposes of "unionism" (usually synonymous to him with "labor movement") has been "best demonstrated by the deans of the scientific students of the labor movement, Sidney and Beatrice Webb." The other may have been: What lies even deeper as the reason why a "mature" labor movement seeks to attain these purposes; that is, what is the "true" psychology of the worker? (*Ibid.*, p. 237.) As indicated, however, we believe that rigid analysis of these two questions permits consideration of them as a part of the elaboration of the answer to the "essential question."

*capitalism's resistance power and over-estimates labor's will to radical change; and, third, the degree of maturity of a trade union "mentality."*[6]

The broad implication of the approach is that different values attributable to the three factors account for the different observed results in the countries under examination. In Russia, for example, Perlman found: (a) the resistance power of capitalism at a low level, (b) a labor movement dominated by the intellectualist "mentality," (c) a low degree of "maturity" of the trade union "mentality." Result: overthrow of the system and establishment of a society framed in terms of the intellectualist mentality. In the United States he found: (a) a very high resistance power of capitalism, (b) a small and diminishing intellectualist influence upon the labor movement, (c) a completely "mature" trade union "mentality." Result: a stable capitalism and a stable job-conscious trade unionism.

## INTERDEPENDENCE OF THREE FACTORS

With these general comments behind us, it is possible to sketch in the basic criticism of Perlman's three-factor system. As he presents them, the factors appear to be independent forces, each contributing an influence upon the developing labor movement; but on closer analysis they are seen to be inextricably interrelated and are, in fact, partly identities by definition. This is illustrated as follows:

1. The "resistance power of capitalism" is enhanced when the greater part of society (especially the greater part of the manualists and their leaders) accepts fundamental capitalist principles, as for examples, the principle of private property, the principle of private initative in economic affairs, and the principle that capitalists "alone . . . know how to oper-

ate" modern economies. But the very acceptance of these principles is a rejection of the "intellectualist" position, which is characteristically anticapitalist. To the extent, therefore, that such principles are accepted by the labor movement, it is not dominated by the intellectualist mentality. Thus, Perlman's first factor is in large measure defined in terms of his second, and vice versa.

2. When the so-called trade union mentality is fully matured, job-consciousness is the rock upon which labor action is based. But making job-consciousness the focus of attention means ipso facto the rejection of class consciousness as the prime basis for action. Further, it is said to imply a limited sphere for political activity. But to state that the likelihood of a concerted political effort by the working class to secure basic social changes is very small is merely to describe one aspect of a well-entrenched capitalism. Thus, Perlman's first factor and his third factor are in part defined in terms of each other.

3. The second and third factors are merely opposite sides of the same coin. This is clear from the very way in which they are stated. The second factor is the degree of intellectualist domination of the labor movement. The third factor is the degree of maturity of trade union mentality. Both are in terms of degree of domination of the labor movement, and since they are revealed to be polar opposites they are "independent" factors precisely in the same sense in which "two factors" may be said to determine a man's height, namely, his tallness and his shortness. When the trade union mentality is fully "matured," the degree to which the intellectualist mentality guides the actions of workers is, *by definition*, nil. Where the intellectualist mentality dominates, the trade union mentality has not "matured." Reference is being made to an objective condition which can be described in terms

[6] *Ibid.*, p. x.

of either the second or the third factor.

4. The factors are not independent of each other even apart from definition. One element of the resistance power of capitalism as described by Perlman is the actual power wielded by the capitalist class and its will to use it in its own interest. When both the power and the will are very strong, it follows that efforts of the working class (or segments thereof) to enlarge its position in society will encounter obstacles and frictions at every turn. Faced with this sort of resistance, it is less than surprising that laborers see something of a "limited-opportunity" world. Nor is it surprising that the path of least resistance—job-conscious unionism—should appear to be the most feasible alternative to large segments of the wage-earning class. Moreover, if the prevailing capitalism should be operating so successfully that at the same time it yielded a rising level of income, shorter hours of work, and a rising social and political status for most members of the working class, it is not difficult to see how a program designed to sweep away the existing order might lack a mass following. Depending upon one's definition and evaluation of the "resistance power of capitalism," there are certain specific implications for the other two "factors."

The relationships exposed above illustrate two important properties of Perlman's formulation. The first is that his "factors" are so *defined* that attributing a value or strength to any one of them immediately implies, and may define, a value for the other two. The three-factor schema therefore represents a unity in a very fundamental sense.[7]

The second is that confusions are inherent because of the indiscriminate merger of an elaborate system of purely descriptive and/or definitional categories with certain explanatory principles and the designation of the resultant mixture as a "theory" of the labor movement.[8] It is necessary to point out that the three-factor schema taken as a whole does not constitute a theory of the labor movement in any meaningful sense, although it appears to pass as one. This is true because the schema is essentially a definitional system which represents, at best, an intricate restatement of the questions to which it apparently addresses itself.

THE BASIC QUESTIONS

What are these questions? The first, and most important, is the basic attitude (as expressed in the program which it follows) of the labor movement toward capitalism as a system. It is with respect to this question that Perlman took issue with Marxist and other theorists; it is upon this question that his attention is clearly focused in the definition of his "factors." Marxist theorists had propounded an answer which designated the labor movement as the primary force for social change. The change anticipated was the overthrow of capitalism by an alienated working class. In the Perlman *terminology*, the Marxists predicted a labor movement dominated by the "intellectual's mentality." Perlman, in challenging the adequacy of the Marxian analysis, cites, on the other hand, a working class which is "content to leave the employer in the unchallenged possession of his property and business." The prediction implicit in the Perlman theory and expressed in the Perlman *terminology* is that of a labor movement dominated by the "trade union mentality."

---

[7] See p. 35 above, where values have been assigned to the "three factors." It should now be clear why the perfectly symmetrical relationships are no coincidence. Like the three witches in *Macbeth*, the "three factors" speak as if with one voice.

[8] Perlman's "theory of the psychology of the laboring man" embodies such an explanatory principle. It will be examined intensively in a later section of this article.

As was pointed out previously and as we have just indicated again, the two "factors" which figure here represent two alternative programs which labor movements *could* adopt. Which of the two outcomes will be realized is, of course, one issue on which Perlman and his rival theorists differ. It is a little weird, therefore, to find *both outcomes* incorporated as "factors" in a "theory" presumably endeavoring to explain why one of the outcomes is to be anticipated.

Let us turn briefly to a second question. Marxists and Perlman also differ in their estimate of the stability of capitalism as a system. Marxists "saw" its weakness and decline. Perlman, writing in 1928, cited its great strength and resilience. The issue, it would seem to us, was clear-cut. It is again somewhat weird, therefore, to find the whole controversy incorporated as a "factor" (the "resistance power of capitalism") in the Perlman "theory." It is, after all, that very resistance power which was at issue.

Some of the confusion is eliminated, however, when it is recognized that the three-factor schema is primarily a system of definitions and not a theory. It is the purely terminological property of such a system that it cannot be "wrong." This explains why Perlman is always able to apply his system of descriptive categories in a way to give the impression that his "theory" is correct. Any "labor situation" of the type in which Perlman was interested can be described in terms of it. Thus, in describing developments in Russia leading up to the 1917 Revolution, he could say that the "resistance power of capitalism" turned out to be weak; whereas, in describing the United States, it was possible to say that the "resistance power of capitalism" turned out to be strong. Similarly, he could refer to the Russian labor movement as dominated by the "intellectual's mentality" and to the American labor movement as dominated by the "trade union mentality." It could also have been said that in Russia the trade union mentality did not "mature," and that in America the labor movement "freed itself" of the domination of intellectuals. One might even go as far as to say that in Russia and in pre-AFL America, manualists had been hypnotized, in some sense, by "intellectuals."[9]

But all of this is mere description. A theory of the labor movement must answer *why* all this occurred. It should explain, for example, *why* manualists are attracted to "intellectualist" programs in some instances and *why* they are indifferent to them in others. The three-factor schema does not offer such an explanation.[10]

SCARCITY CONSCIOUSNESS

Leaving behind the three-factor schema, which does not constitute a theory, we turn now to a consideration of the unique ingredient of the Perlman system which does. The basic proposition is that the most compelling force operating upon the development of labor movements is

[9] This kind of argument by definition would "explain" all "unmanualist" activity. See *Theory,* p. 301, where Marxists are criticized for employing such circular reasoning, and p. 302 where Perlman employs it.

[10] One might be tempted to suggest that an explanation is provided by the broader concept of the "resistance power of capitalism." Thus, if the question addressed is: "What forces cause labor movements to pursue procapitalist or anticapitalist programs?", any force which is designated *might* at the same time be viewed as an element of strength or weakness of capitalism's "resistance power." It should be obvious, however, that the explanatory content is contained in the particular forces isolated and not in the omnibus category within which one might choose to group them. When Perlman cites his three "basic characteristics of the American community," he does offer a partial explanation of the direction taken by the American labor movement. Nothing in the way of explanation would be contributed, however, by designating these "characteristics" as elements of resistance power, although it might be perfectly legitimate to do so.

the "psychology" of the laboring man himself, and that given certain preconditions, this "psychology" will express itself in the type of movement already described as dominated by a "trade union mentality."[11] The general claim is that previous theorists, notably Marxists and the Webbs, have erred because they failed to grasp the nature of this "psychology," and a considerable portion of the *Theory* is devoted to an exposition of its principal qualities. In this section, therefore, we shall examine closely the case for the unique "psychology"—characterizable as "scarcity consciousness"—in connection with the consequences which are said to flow from it.

The scarcity of which manualists are said to be conscious refers to economic opportunity. Important as this concept of economic opportunity is in Perlman's system, his definition, and even more his usage, of it are elusive. There appear to be three distinct types of opportunity, although Perlman does not trouble to draw precise distinctions among them. The first type may be designated as "mass-worker" opportunity. It is with this type that the average wage earner, the rank-and-file manualist, is associated. This is what Perlman has in mind when he refers to "job opportunity." The second type may be called "bright-worker" opportunity and refers to the possibilities of advancement and improvement open to individuals who are somewhat above the average in "ability and ambition," although not blessed with the spark of entrepreneurial genius

or the ownership of much property or wealth. Perlman speaks of opportunities to get ahead by selling "on the commission basis," by entering (very) small business, by climbing into "minor supervisory positions in the large manufacturing establishments," or by migrating from "older to newer and less developed sections."[12] The third type may be called "entrepreneurial" or "producer" opportunity. It refers to the availability of resources and markets and the freedom to link them together. It refers also to land and other assets and the possibility of attaining ownership of them.

These distinctions having been made, it is possible now to pass to a consideration of the "scarcity consciousness of the manualist" which, according to Perlman, "is a product of two main causes, one lying in himself and the other outside." The "inside" cause, corresponding to the manualist's "psychic self-appraisal," is described as follows:

*The typical manualist is aware of his lack of native capacity for availing himself of economic opportunities as they lie amidst the complex and ever shifting situations of modern business. He knows himself neither for a born taker of risks nor for the possessor of a sufficiently agile mind ever to feel at home in the midst of the uncertain game of competitive business.*[13]

Two important points are to be noted in this formulation. The first is that it refers exclusively to entrepreneurial or producer opportunity. The second is that

---

[11] The preconditions are presented by Perlman when he says that ". . . given the opportunity to exist legally and to develop a leadership from among its own ranks, the trade union's mentality will eventually come to dominate." (*Theory*, p. ix.) The specified preconditions were satisfied for the United States so that a prediction of the continuation of a job-conscious movement in this country was as nearly explicit as could be wished. Supporters of the Perlman position have cited the American experience as corroborative of the theory. On the other hand, the preconditions were satisfied in the United Kingdom by the late 19th century but the British experience since then is clearly in conflict with the theory. Much the same can be said of the experience of other movements. The current method of dealing with this problem is apparently to concentrate upon American developments when discussing the merits of the *Theory*. We accept this convention in our examination of the "psychology" of the laboring man.

[12] *Ibid.*, pp. 165–166.

[13] *Ibid.*, p. 239.

the manualist's lack of native ability is *in itself* the creator of scarcity. For it would make little difference whether producer opportunity were abundant or limited in the real world. If it were abundant, the manualist's self-recognized impotence in the face of it contrives to prevent him from exploiting it. He would not know what to do with this welter of resources and potential markets. The "typical manualist," thus shut off from producer opportunity and presumably also from "bright-worker" opportunity (we take this to be implicit in "typical," especially in view of Perlman's comment that the "great mass of the wage earners . . . will die wage earners"),[14] finds himself limited to job opportunity over which he and his fellows seek to impose a control. The control instrument is, of course, the trade union.

The second source of "scarcity consciousness," designated by Perlman as the "outside" cause and evidently representing the conclusions drawn from a "simple survey of accessible economic opportunity," is the manualist's

*. . . conviction that for him the world has been rendered one of scarcity by an institutional order of things, which purposely reserved the best opportunities for landlords, capitalists, and other privileged groups. It may also be, of course, that the manual worker will ascribe such scarcity to natural rather than to institutional causes, say, to a shortage of land brought on by increase of population, or like mediaeval merchants and master workmen, to the small number of customers and the meagre purchasing power of these. At all events, whether he thought the cause of the apparent limitations to be institutional or natural, a scarcity consciousness has always been typical of the manual worker, in direct contrast to the consciousness of*

[14] *Ibid.*, p. 165.
[15] *Ibid.*, pp. 239–240.
[16] *Ibid.*, p. 241.

*an abundance of opportunity, which dominates the self-confident business man.*[15]

This passage, too, refers exclusively to "producer" opportunity, but an additional reason for its "scarcity" is adduced. This time it is attributed to "natural" causes (such as might yield a shortage of land), or to the "institutional order of things" which manualists learn from experience has operated to reserve producer opportunity for others. Barred from producer opportunity for a second reason, manualists are, by another route, led to control of "job opportunity" and hence the creation of a union.

Implicit in all this, of course, is a scarcity of job opportunity. Otherwise there would appear to be little need for unions. A scarcity of job opportunity is appropriately introduced—"the number of jobs available [is] almost always fewer than the number of job seekers"[16]—and the system is complete.

## FUNCTION OF A LABOR THEORY

It should be noticed that what has been provided by this excursion into manualist "scarcity consciousness" is merely a rationale for unionism per se. The larger question to which Perlman addressed himself (and to which anyone professing to offer a "theory of the labor movement" must address himself) remains unanswered. Why is the labor movement in a given country what it is? For the United States, this means that what has to be explained is the appearance and persistence of job-conscious unionism as *the* labor movement. That American unions are job conscious is not a controversial matter. That manualists are conscious of a scarcity of economic opportunity (of any or all types) and that they have been impelled to seize and control the distribution of opportunity available to them—this, too, is not a controversial matter. No one denies these facts. And nothing is "proved" by incessant reference to them.[17] What a *theory* has to explain is why the nature of the American labor movement involves: (1) the renunciation of any broad program of social reorganization designed to improve the status and economic condition of the group involved; (2) the renunciation of political activity in a predominantly "labor" party as a major weapon for the institution of such a program or, at least, for economic betterment of the group involved; and (3), possibly only a corollary of the first item in this series, apparent contentment with the existing framework of economic institutions and relationships, which reserves to another group ("businessmen") the privilege of making many of the crucial decisions for the community as a whole in the vital spheres of output and employment.

## MANUALIST PSYCHOLOGY

Now it is somewhere in the "psychology of the laboring man" that Perlman claims to find support for this type of labor movement. For the manualist "psychology" (usually the *foundation of*, but frequently *synonymous with*, manualist "mentality" or "ideology" in the Perlman terminology) is supposed to yield the "mature" trade unionism which is precisely this type of labor movement. We are obliged to probe further into Perlman's notion of the manualist "psychology."

The first matter to be questioned is the origin of the notion itself. What is it that convinced Perlman that the manualist "psychology" (or "mentality" or "ideology") really is what he describes it to be? His answer is that the "psychology" is to be *deduced* from the system of shop rules (and the like) of labor's own making.

Labor's own "home grown" ideology is disclosed only through a study of the "working rules" of labor's own "institutions."[18]

Immediately the question arises: Is it possible to deduce from labor's "working rules" what Perlman has in fact deduced? Do imposition of collective ownership over limited job opportunities and the disposition of these jobs in accordance with certain traditionally derived equity principles prove or imply anything about psychic predilections for, or antipathy to, capitalism as a system? Do monopoly and subsequent distribution of job opportunity prove or imply anything about manualist attitudes respecting any particular type or extent of political activity?

Undoubtedly what has greatly impressed Perlman is American labor's preoccupation with control over jobs and wage rates to the exclusion of other types of activity, e.g., formation of a labor party, agitation for basic reforms of the social and economic system, and so on. But if this is the main evidence for the existence of a manualist "psychology" of the kind described by Perlman, the theory of the psychology of the working man" boils down to a piece of circular reasoning. The "psychology" is inferred from the observed fact of almost exclusive preoccupation with control of job opportunites and the renunciation of other types of activity. On the other hand, the "psychology" is in turn defined as that which is typically preoccupied with "job control" to the exclusion of other types of activity. This kind of logic chases its tail forever. Of course, it does not follow from this that a "psychology" so deduced is necessarily false. But unless a great deal of *positive* evidence is sup-

[17] British, French, Italian, German, Austrian, Swedish, Australian, Belgian, and Canadian unions (to mention a few) are also "job conscious"; but in all of the nations indicated, job-conscious unionism is only a part of the labor movement.
[18] Perlman, *Theory*, p. 6. Just below the sentence quoted, Perlman proceeds to base the "ideology" on the "psychology" of "consciousness of scarcity of opportunity."

plied, there is little reason to believe it to be correct. Any number of other deductions are equally possible.

## ECONOMIC OPPORTUNITY

As noted above, an adequate theory of the American labor movement must explain why it is that broad schemes of social reorganization have been rejected in favor of a narrowly oriented job-conscious unionism. Perlman's explanation runs largely in terms of the alleged "psychology of the laboring man." In this a serious logical inconsistency is involved. One might wonder, for example, why it is that unionists halt at monopoly of "job opportunity." Why is it that the whole amount of the community's economic opportunity does not present itself to them as suitable for control? This problem is explicitly recognized by Perlman, but his answer is painfully lame. . . .

*Actually, the typical wage earner, when he can express himself in and through his trade union free of domination by intellectuals, who are never too bashful to do his thinking for him, seldom dreams of shouldering the risks of management. Ordinarily he traces the origin of his opportunity not much farther back than the point where it materializes in jobs, and will grasp and support only such union policies as will enable or force the employers to offer more jobs, equally available to all fellow craftsmen, and upon improved terms.*[19]

A footnote to the excerpt quoted makes it clear that the term "risks of management" refers to the risk of loss of privately invested capital. The assertion that the manulist "seldom dreams" of shouldering these risks may be seen to be an expansion of the idea expressed in Perlman's statement of the "inside" source of "scarcity consciousness"; namely, that manualists

are aware of a lack of entrepreneurial ability. Assuming for the moment that they are, it may be asked what the risks of management have to do with the case. The question to be answered is why manualists have not supported a program of socialism and the answer which has been given is that they do not see themselves as efficient capitalists. This is a roaring *non sequitur*. There is no problem of risk in this sense in a socialist system.

If another kind of risk is envisioned, the statement is equally questionable. Perhaps it may be suggested that risk of failure to perform efficiently in a managerial or administrative capacity is implied. But this presents no problem. The average trade unionist "seldom dreams" of managing his own union; yet this does not prevent him from supporting it. He elects someone with the requisite skills to do the managing.

The mere fact that there have been millions of manualist Socialists, manualist anarchists, manualist Communists, manualist syndicalists, and, for that matter, manualist "free homesteaders" throughout the Western world should be sufficient to call into question Perlman's rather glib treatment of this important issue. If American manualists of recent times have been, in the main, supporters of "free enterprise," the reasons are more fruitfully sought in the modern American environment than in their manualism per se. For there is nothing in the concept of "scarcity consciousness" as developed by Perlman which throws any light on this subject.

The weakness of Perlman's case for the particular worker "psychology" he describes is sharply revealed in his distinction between manualist "psychology" and businessman "psychology." Whereas "scarcity consciousness" and (hence) "pessimism" are said to characterize the former.

\* \* \*

[19] *Ibid.*, pp. 246–247.

We submit that neither of these conceptualizations adequately reflects the real world phenomena to which they refer. . . . It may be asked, for example, what basic difference from the viewpoint of "opportunity" appraisal can be read from pools, gentlemen's agreements, Gary dinners, and a basing point price system on the one hand, and efforts to establish a union shop in the steel industry on the other? Both envision a limited opportunity and both represent attempts to monopolize it or to control its distribution.

＊　＊　＊

Yet, Perlman feels there is one. His dictum is that such collusive activity when undertaken by businessmen ". . . has always sprung from the 'head,' but never spontaneously nor from the 'heart'. . . ."[20] But this flows directly from his having *defined* the businessman's "heart" in a way that excludes a propensity for collusion or a yearning for stability. The "heart" defined in this way is nothing more than the "spirit of enterprise"—that idealization which was postulated at the beginning of the argument.

### WAGE EARNERS VS. BUSINESSMEN

. . . The point which we are attempting to establish here (at the cost perhaps of somewhat cavalier treatment of a complex process in the development of capitalism)

is that the essential "psychologies" of wage earner and businessman cannot be split into polar opposites. Each appears to strive for economic or social advancement or self-betterment, and each employs the methods which give promise of achieving this end.

＊　＊　＊

### POLITICAL ACTIVITY

Futher doubt—extremely strong doubt —is cast upon Perlman's position by the vaguely defined role attributed to political activity in "mature" trade unionism. Logical consistency demands that relegation of political action to a secondary or tertiary role in manualist efforts to improve their positions be somehow traceable to the basic "psychology" of the laboring man. Yet, on this score, Perlman provides no causal link. There is nothing in his entire discussion of "scarcity consciousness" —the key to worker psychology—which specifies a definite role for political action, either large or small.[21]

A final criticism of Perlman's attempt to attribute to manualists some deep-lying and unique "psychology" (and thus to establish this "psychology" as an independent force influencing labor movement development) rests upon his treatment of the shift in the orientation of American labor in the period marked by the decline

---

[20] *Ibid.*, pp. 243, 244.

[21] The great flexibility permitted by this treatment is exploited in Perlman's later writings. The mistrust of political activity reflected in the *Theory* was exchanged for a full endorsement of it a decade later when he wrote that "political action [has] ceased to be a blind alley for labour," and that "the political weapon has become the unions' paramount weapon." H. A. Marquand and Others, *Organized Labour in Four Continents* (London, New York, Toronto, 1939), pp. 326, 399. In the same publication Perlman flirted with the prospect of an independent labor party when, with reference to the American Labor Party of New York and Labor's Non-Partisan League in 1936, he wrote, "Thus the time-hallowed 'reward your friends' strategy was skillfully combined with independent political action, leaving either method or a combination of both available for the future" (p. 397). This relatively "extreme" position was abandoned in a subsequent statement. "So far nothing has happened to upset the conviction that pressure politics and control of a major party through infiltration are the real vehicles rather than a political party in competition with the old parties." T. C. T. McCormick [ed.], *Problems of the Postwar World* (New York, London, 1945), p. 42. It must be emphasized that in dealing with the significant changes in American labor activity since 1928 Perlman has made no reference to corresponding changes in the "psychology" of the laborers. If the same "psychology" is compatible with both the pre-1928 and post-1928 activities, of what importance can it be as an *explanation* of these changes?

---

of the Knights of Labor and the rise of the AFL. The transition period is characteristically described by Perlman as an "evolution of the psychology of the American wage earner,"[22] and the completed process is described as the belated "fruition" of job-and-wage conscious unionism. If it be asked why the "psychology" which Perlman says has "always been typical of the manual worker"[23] was not always typical of the American manualist, the only reply which can be made (and the one which Perlman makes) is that the American case was an "exception to the general rule."[24] But an exception, rather than proving the rule, invariably calls the rule into question, and such an important "exception" as this bids fair to refute it. It does no good to refer to pre-AFL labor activity as some kind of perversion of the "true psychology of the working man" or to represent it as having been "mentally tied to a 'foreign' [non-manualist] philosophy."[25] For this is merely to affirm in different words that the American case *was* an exception.

\* \* \*

## ANTIMONOPOLY PROGRAMS

We have no quarrel with Perlman when he refers to the changing economic context in which American workers found themselves in this period and we applaud him when he traces changed labor attitudes to changes in these objective conditions. We had to balk, however, at his attempt to introduce a spurious psychological factor into the analysis. Perlman's characterization of the shift in American labor as the belated realization ("fruition") of the "true" worker "psychology" has caused him to regard the earlier labor orientation as hopelessly misguided. The impression is always to be gathered from his discussion of the pre-AFL period that "antimonopoly" programs were in their very nature dead-end streets for manualists.

\* \* \*

The shift away from "antimonopoly" programs can better be related to underlying changes in the *entire context* in which wage earners found themselves than to any such factor as the suspiciously sudden appearance of a "typical" manualist "psychology." By 1890, land available for homesteading and suitable to the "family farm" had all but disappeared, while between 1880 and 1900 the population increased by half. It was in this period that the United States became established as an industrial power.

\* \* \*

As a result, the traditional "antimonopoly" program was no longer suitable as the primary orientation of American labor, for the ground had been cut from under many of the old objectives. The public domain was now considerably shrunken, and farm produce prices were also considerably lower. Moreover, the technology and organization typifying modern capitalism yielded a scale of operation which tended to make the "cooperative workshop" something of an industrial anachronism. Many of the objectives of the older antimonopolism were thus, in a significant sense, "technologically" obsolescent.

"Antimonopolism," however, encompasses something more than policies designed to ease the flow of members of the working class into "producer" or "entrepreneurial" pursuits. As consumers, income recipients, and citizens, laborers might still have found attractive a program aimed at curbing the concentration of wealth, income, and economic power. Why did a

[22] *Theory*, p. 108.
[23] *Ibid.*, p. 240.
[24] *Ibid.*, n. 2.
[25] *Ibid.*, p. 182.

more modern antimonopolism not come to characterize the later American labor movement? Where was the spirit of rebellion, where the socialistic tone of the European movements?

## CAPITALIST RESISTANCE

For an answer Perlman leans heavily upon what we have already described as a narrow version of the "resistance power of capitalism." He cites the militancy of the American capitalist class.

\* · \* \*

His explanation suggests that American labor was intimidated by the vigorous "presiding class" and that its response was to retreat to a program which left unchallenged the citadels of the going social order. But again, if we may, it is not enough to cite the organized repression of a militant ruling class. What has to be answered is why it was associated in the United States with a labor movement's rejection of broad schemes of social change, whereas in other countries labor movements faced with similar opposition retained their traditional forms?

Precisely in the period 1870–1900, when Gompers and others were reflecting on the significance of "split workingmen's heads" and were being impressed by the "crushing" tactics of "the courts, the Federal Executive, and the ruling forces in the country," modern technology and modern capitalism were taking firm roots in Imperial Germany and Imperial Austria-Hungary; . . . . But German workers and their leaders saw no reason to reconsider their approach. In Perlman's words, this was "a heroic period in the history of the Social-Democracy." By 1890 it had "triumphantly defeated the best police system on the Continent."[26]

## ECONOMIC PROGRESS

The emergence of a "job-conscious" labor movement in the United States was a phenomenon almost unique in labor history. Yet without resorting to an analysis the essence of which is to divide Western humanity into spurious psychological categories it is possible to find an explanation of it.

There is in the American experience one colossal datum which has stood above all the rest. It has been the fact of a tremendously growing level of material well-being yielded by the system as a whole. The truth is that whether resulting from the "free air" of competitive enterprise, or from native "know-how," or from the context of fabulously rich resources in which the whole system has been immersed, the American wage earner has experienced over a seventy-five year period a rate of economic betterment which has made him labor aristocrat of the world.[27]

\* \* \*

The essential point here is that "job-consciousness" must be seen as a *means,* and that only when a job-conscious labor movement is associated with substantial progress toward the attainment of the prevailing income and status goals of most of its constituents does it have an effective claim on their allegiance. In a very general way, this has been the experience in the United States.[28]

\* \* \*

## CLASS CONSCIOUSNESS

Greater attention must be directed to the "lack of a class consciousness among American labor" which is, in fact, a crucial factor. European labor movements, such

---

[26] *Ibid.,* pp. 81 ff.

[27] If one wished to speak in terms of the "resistance power" of American capitalism, would it be possible to cite a more important factor than this?

[28] As all students of American labor history know, there have been significant deviations from this pattern at times.

as those of Germany and Austria, drew much of their strength from a pervasive class consciousness, and the direction almost invariably taken by these movements —broad programs of social reform implemented by strong political party structures—is roughly the opposite of that taken by the "mature" manualist organizations of Perlman's description. It is revealing that Perlman's "mature" labor activity —"job-conscious unionism"—growing out of a "psychology" said to be characteristic of *all* manual groups, should have emerged from a context in which one of the "basic characteristics" is a *unique* lack of class consciousness among the laboring group. The essential absence in the United States of class consciousness, which is, after all, a powerful organizing and mobilizing force, helps to explain the failure of a broadly oriented labor movement to emerge. And it should be observed that this factor, too, is not independent of what we have cited as the colossal datum in the American experience.

❃ ❃ ❃

Although Perlman explains the failure of American labor to develop a political organization partly on the ground that

workers received the franchise so relatively early in our history, he reveals little appreciation of the fact that the struggle to escape from the status of second-class citizens may be, indeed almost surely is, more important for the rise of labor parties in Central Europe than the teachings of "intellectuals."[29]

❃ ❃ ❃

CONCLUSIONS

... We may summarize our analysis of the Perlman contribution in this way. The three-factor schema directs attention to important questions but does not provide the explanatory principles required of a theory. The assertions with respect to the "psychology" of the laboring man do constitute a theory, but it is a fallacious one. Even if taken at its face value, the so-called "psychology" provides only a rationale for unionism; under no circumstances does it actually explain what it is called upon to explain in the *theory*. But it can not be taken at its face value, and as has been demonstrated, it falls apart completely under close scrutiny.

❃ ❃ ❃

### Kerr, Harbison, Dunlop and Myers

The article by Kerr, Harbison, Dunlop, and Myers on "Industrialism and Industrial Man" summarizes a conceptual framework that resulted from numerous studies of labor problems in the course of economic development. All four of these writers are well-known American labor economists, who were thoroughly grounded in the theories of Marx, the Webbs, Perlman, John R. Commons, and others. However, they found that labor movements were less a reaction to "capitalism," as most of these earlier theorists had thought, than workers' reactions to the problems created by industrialization. The nature of the workers' response to industrialization depends on the nature of the institutions upon which industrialization impinges and the leaders or elites who lead the industrializing process. Industrialization tends to erode institutions, producing certain uniformities, but institutional resistance to change makes it possible for certain unique features to continue.

[29] Probably the most illuminating example of his failure to make the connection suggested appears in *Theory*, p. 291, n. 1.

In the course of their study, the authors changed their initial conception of the inevitable "protest" that accompanies industrialization and focused instead on the "web of rules" that inevitably governs the relationship between managers and the managed.

The authors clearly consider industrialization to be an inexorable universal imperative with a basic logic that not only will cause it to sweep the earth, but also to produce certain common characteristics: advanced technology, a wide range of professions and skills, large organizations, and pluralistic societies held together by consensus ideologies.

But there are different roads to industrialism, depending on which elite— dynastic, middle class, revolutionary intellectuals, colonial administrators, nationalists—leads the process. These elites are ideal types, which abstract from reality and rarely appear in pure form, but they are useful conceptual constructs.

The conceptual framework outlined by Kerr, Harbison, Dunlop, and Myers contains other elements besides industrialization and the elites, such as the constraints on industrialization posed by the culture of traditional societies and limited resources. Industrialization is also conditioned by the influence of the time when industrialization begins.

The strategies adopted by various elites to overcome the obstacles to industrialization are particularly important. The labor problems of an industrial society will reflect these strategies as work forces are structured between the managers and the managed and the "web of rules" is adopted which governs the work relationship. The authors also relate labor problems to "the power, position and policies of the managers. . . ; to the development of the industrial working forces; to the impact of industrialization on the worker and his response thereto; and to the making of the rules by workers, managers, and the State."

These writers feel that although workers are "in the end malleable," their "metamorphosis gives rise to many forms of protest." But they disagree with Marx that protest tends to increase with industrialization; instead, they contend that "protest tends to reach its peak relatively early in the transformation and to decline in its overt manifestations as industrialization reaches the more advanced stages. Incipient protest is moderated, channelled, and redirected in the advanced industrial society."

The kind of labor organizations that emerge with industrialization reflect the strategies adopted by the elite. Although previous theorists considered labor movements to be relatively independent forces to remold society, or at least the working environment, Kerr, Harbison, Dunlop, and Myers believe that "in each society the emerging labor organizations adapt themselves rather distinctively to the prevailing environment." These writers also consider workers to be much less important forces in the industrial society than managers and technicians, a reversal of the role assigned labor by Marx and Perlman's "intellectuals." The authors conclude: "Labor organizations, in summary, are essentially reflections of the societies in which they develop. The universal responses of workers to industrialization, and the nature of expressions of their protest, are increasingly moulded to conform and contribute to the strategy of the industrialising elites. Though the leaders of labour seldom rise to dominating positions in a society, they are persons who always warrant recognition."

The road ahead will therefore lead to increasing uniformity because the forces that tend to unify various societies will overcome those that cause diversity. The forces for uniformity are: technology, education, and the compulsion to compare. The worldwide society of the future produced by these factors will be what the authors call "pluralistic industrialism."

# Industrialism and Industrial Man

## by Clark Kerr, Frederick H. Harbison, John T. Dunlop, and Charles A. Myers

*For a number of years scholars associated with the Inter-University Study of the Labour Problems in Economic Development[1] have been investigating the relationships between industrialisation, managerial leadership and wage-earning groups throughout the world. In the following pages the four members of the co-ordinating board of this project have set down their views on the question. After bringing out the features of industrialisation that are common to all nations, the authors analyse the different roads to industrialism and the types of "elite" likely to assume leadership in the process in different circumstances. In conclusion they make certain predictions as to the form of industrial society that will finally emerge.*

Over five years ago the four of us wrote an article for the *International Labour Review* entitled "The Labour Problem in Economic Development: A Framework for Reappraisal."[2] In that article we suggested an "alternate framework" to replace the "traditional analysis" of labour problems in modern industrial society. We argued that it is "the process of industrialisation" rather than "capitalism" which gives rise to labour problems, that industrial systems differ according to the nature and effectiveness of enterprise organisations and of the elites that direct them, and that "one universal response" to industrialisation is "protest" on the part of the labour force as it is fitted into the new social structure. Then, as now, we

SOURCE Reprinted with permission from the *International Labour Review,* Vol. 82, No. 3, September 1960.

[1] Financed in large part by the Ford Foundation under its programme in economic development and administration, this project has drawn on the resources of a number of universities and individual scholars, particularly at Harvard University, Princeton University, the University of California at Berkeley and the Massachusetts Institute of Technology.

[2] *International Labour Review,* Vol. LXXI, No. 3, March 1955.

sought to go beyond the mere description of individual countries; we sought a system of ideas upon which to make generalisations concerning all industrialising societies at all stages of their development.

In the course of the past five years we have learned much from our own studies and travels as well as from those of our colleagues in the Inter-University Study of Labour Problems in Economic Development.[3] The four of us have ourselves travelled on all five continents. . . . On the basis of our own study and that of our colleagues, we have presented in a forthcoming volume our new formulation of labour problems in economic development, and in this article we shall summarise a few of our basic ideas and findings.[4]

We project a future, still long distant, with a world-wide society of "pluralistic industrialism," in which managers and the managed may still carry on their endless tug of war, in which the contest between the forces of uniformity and diversity will continue, but in which persuasion, pressure, and manipulation will take the place of the open industrial conflict of the earlier stages of development.

In this new formulation, moreover, we have been forced to alter considerably some of our earlier concepts. We have become convinced, for example, that "protest" is not such a dominant aspect of industrialisation as we once thought. Indeed, labour protest is on the decline even as industrialisation around the world proceeds at an ever faster pace. Thus, instead of concentrating on protest, we have turned our attention to the inevitable "structuring" of the managers and the managed in the course of industrialisation and to the complex "web of rules" which binds men together in new chains of subordination and creates a network of rights, obligations, and functions of workers, technicians, and managers in the hierarchy of far-flung private and governmental organisations. . . .

## THE LOGIC OF INDUSTRIALISM

Industrialisation has been abroad in the world for only about two centuries. One

[3] The following books, based on the work of the Inter-University Study, have already been published:

Albert Badre and Simon Siksek: *Manpower and Oil in Arab Countries* (Beirut, American University Press, 1960).

Reinhard Bendix: *Work and Authority in Industry*. Ideologies of Management in the Course of Industrialization (New York, John Wiley & Sons, Inc., 1956).

Henry W. Ehrmann: *Organized Business in France* (Princeton, N.J., Princeton University Press, 1957).

Walter Galenson (editor): *Labor and Economic Development* (New York, John Wiley & Sons, Inc., 1959).

Frederick Harbison and Abdelkader Ibrahim Ibrahim: *Human Resources for Egyptian Enterprise* (New York, McGraw-Hill Book Company, Inc., 1958).

Frederick Harbison and Charles A. Myers: *Management in the Industrial World, an International Analysis* (New York, McGraw-Hill Book Company, Inc., 1959).

Heinz Hartmann: *Authority and Organization in German Management* (Princeton, N.J., Princeton University Press, 1959).

Harvey Leibenstein: *Economic Backwardness and Economic Growth*. Studies in the Theory of Economic Development (New York, John Wiley & Sons, Inc., 1957).

Val R. Lorwin: *The French Labor Movement* (Cambridge, Harvard University Press, 1954).

I. McGivering, D. Matthews, and W. H. Scott: *Management in Britain* (Liverpool, Liverpool University Press, 1960).

Charles A. Myers: *Labor Problems in the Industrialization of India* (Cambridge, Harvard University Press, 1958).

John C. Shearer: *High-Level Manpower in Overseas Subsidiaries*. Experience in Brazil and Mexico (Princeton, N.J., Industrial Relations Section, 1960).

James Sydney Slotkin: *From Field to Factory* (Glencoe, Ill., The Free Press, 1960).

[4] Clark Kerr, Frederick H. Harbison, John T. Dunlop, and Charles A. Myers: *Industrialism and Industrial Man* (Cambridge, Mass., Harvard University Press, 1960).

hundred years ago only England had crossed the great divide on the road toward the industrial society. Today, in the middle of the twentieth century, perhaps a third of the world's population lives in countries which are at least partially industrialised. The remaining two-thirds of the world's peoples, spurred by the revolution of rising aspirations, are in the throes of initiating the march toward industrialism. Probably by the middle of the twenty-first century industrialisation will have swept away most pre-industrial forms of society, except possibly for a few odd backwaters. This is the great transformation in the history of mankind on this planet—more basic, more rapid, and more universal than anything that has gone before. The industrial society knows no national boundaries; it is destined to be a world-wide society.

What then are the common characteristics and imperatives which are inherent in this universal society toward which all peoples are marching? First, the industrial society is associated with a level of technology far in advance of that of earlier societies. The science and technology of industrialism is based upon research organisations: universities, research institutions, laboratories and specialised departments of enterprise. . . . Industrial society is also characterised by vast investments in plant, equipment and machinery which demand the accumulation of capital on a massive scale.

Secondly, the industrial system demands in its labour force a wide range of professions and skills. Indeed, the creation of high-level manpower is one of the major problems encountered in the transition to industrialism. And, since science and technology generate continuous change, new skills and occupations are constantly replacing the old. Thus, industrialism requires an educational system functionally related to the skills and professions imperative to its technology. The variety of skills, responsibilities and employment conditions at the work place creates a new ordering or structuring of society. There are successive levels of authority of managers and the managed as well as extensive specialisation of functions at various levels in the industrial hierarchy. And, as part of this structuring process, the working forces are governed by a web of rules which prescribes such things as hiring, compensation, layoffs, promotions, shift changes, transfers, retirements, and discipline in the work place.

Thirdly, industrialism is associated with sizeable organisations. It is mainly an urban society. It is necessarily characterised by large governmental organisations. And the production of goods and services becomes ever more concentrated in the hands of large enterprises, whether they be private or public. In other words, industrial society is "the organisation society."

Fourthly, the industrial society, in order to survive, must develop a "consensus" which relates individuals and groups to each other and provides a common body of ideas, beliefs and value judgments. The working force, for example, must be dedicated to hard work, and its individuals must assume responsibility for performance of assigned tasks and norms. Regardless of how this is achieved the industrial society must secure a pace of work and a personal responsibility exercised by individual workers and managers unknown in economic activity in traditional societies. . . .

For purposes of analysis we have delineated five ideal types of elite which may under varying circumstances and depending upon the pre-industrial society assume leadership in the industrialisation process. Each of these elites has a strategy by which it seeks to order the surrounding society in a consistent manner.

* * *

To be sure, these "ideal types" seldom appear in a pure form; they abstract from reality. The industrialising elite in any particular country characteristically is a mixture of several of these types, but as analytical devices they give a structure to the task of understanding the different forms of industrialisation; they help to explain the strategies involved and the patterns of management-labour relations which emerge.

Each of the industrialising elites develops a strategy toward the changes to be made in the culture of the traditional societies. The critical elements in the cultural environment are the family system, class and race, religious and ethical valuations, legal concepts, and the concept of the national State. . . . The strategy and success of the different industrialising elites are thus affected in part by the strength and rigidity of the pre-industrial culture and in part by the revolution of rising aspirations. But in the end the new culture of industrialism successfully penetrates and changes the old order.

The elites are also confronted by a number of other constraints, no matter what strategy they elect on the road to the industrial society. First, there are the economic limitations in the short period. . . . Secondly, the chronological date at which a country embarks on the industrialising process makes a difference in the course of growth. There are advantages and disadvantages in an early as compared with a late start.

*  *  *

A detailed analysis of the strategies of the different elites in decision-making along the road of industrialisation lies beyond the scope of this article.[5] In general, however, the dynastic elite is prone to be content with a less strenuous pace; it offers continuity between the old and the new. The rising middle class is apt to rely upon the market and upon elected governments to determine the pace of industrialisation;

it offers individual choice. The revolutionary intellectuals rely upon the single-party State as the engine of development; they offer a harsh but high-velocity industrialisation. The colonial administrators gear the pace to the needs and interests of the mother country; but they are doomed to extinction. The new nationalist leaders encounter perhaps the most serious problems in setting the pace. The aspirations of their masses have been stimulated to expect immediate and substantial results from national independence, while the political uncertainties of a new State complicate the problems of accumulating the necessary human and material capital from both within and beyond the national borders.

Given the economic and cultural limitations listed above, the faster the pace of industrialisation the greater is the need to restrict consumption in order to accumulate capital, the more necessary is the resort to direct control by the government, the more drastic is the required reorganisation in agriculture associated with the development of an industrial labour force, the more likely is the resort to a rigid ideology and compulsion in motivating the work force, and the more centralised must be the web of rules to govern the work place. In determining the pace and the rationale of industrialisation, some elites are more consistently ruthless and determined than others.

In summary, the imperatives of industrialisation cause the industrialising elites to overcome certain constraints and to achieve certain objectives which are the same in all societies undergoing transformation. The approaches which they take to these constraints and objectives explain in large measure the diversity among industrialising economies. Using this system of thought, or logic of industrialism, an examination will now be made of the extent and nature of the labour

[5] See *Industrialism and Industrial Man,* op. cit., Ch. 5, for fuller discussion.

problems which are likely to arise during the development process.

## THE MANAGERS AND THE MANAGED

The labour problem of industrialising societies have their origin in the structuring of relationships between the managers and the managed. They both give rise to and emanate from the web of rules which links men together in the new society. They are related to the power, position and policies of the managers of enterprises whether public or private; to the development of the industrial working forces; to the impact of industrialisation on the worker and his response thereto; and to the making of the rules by workers, managers, and the State. Each of these aspects will now be examined briefly.

### The Managers of Enterprise

The managers of enterprises, public and private, and their technical and professional subordinates are part of every industrialising elite. Management is a hierarchy of functions and people. It includes entrepreneurs, managers, administrators, engineers, and professional specialists who hold the top positions in enterprises. So defined, management is crucial to the success of any industrialisation effort. It may be viewed from three perspectives: as an economic resource, as a class and as a system of authority within the enterprise.

As an economic resource, management becomes more important with the advance of industrialisation. The number of persons in the managerial ranks increases both absolutely and relatively in the economy. This is the inevitable consequence of larger capital outlays, the pace of innovation, the use of more modern machinery, the growth of markets, and the increasing complexity of advancing industrial societies. The accumulation of managerial re-

sources, moreover, requires ever-increasing outlays for technical and managerial education, and forces educational institutions to become more functionally oriented to the training of skilled technicians, engineers, scientists and administrators.

As a class, management becomes more of a profession as industrialisation progresses. In the early stages of development, where enterprises may be new or very small, access to the managerial ranks may be largely dependent on family relationships in some societies, or political connections in others. But as the managerial class must inevitably grow larger it becomes less arbitrarily exclusive. As industrial society lays ever more stress upon scientific discovery, technological innovation and economic progress, patrimonial and political managers are swept aside by the professionals.

As a system of authority, management becomes less dictatorial in its labour policies. In all societies, of course, management cherishes the prerogatives of a rule maker. But others, such as the State and the labour unions, also seek and gain a voice in the rule-making process. As industrialisation advances, they tend to limit, to regulate or sometimes even to displace the unilateral authority of management over the labour force. As a consequence, dictatorial or paternalistic direction gives way to a kind of constitutional management in which the rules of employment are based upon laws, decisions of governments, collective contracts, or agreements. In a few situations employer-employee relationships within the firm may develop along democratic lines with joint participation.

The differences in management are related to the stage of industrial development and also to the elites which assume leadership in the society. The dynastic elite, for example, tends to perpetuate a family-oriented and paternalistic managerial system, whereas the middle-class elite introduces a professionalised managerial class more quickly. The revolutionary intellectuals try to prolong the life of political management, while the new nationalist leaders may encourage the development of any or all kinds of management as the occasion demands.

Yet, despite the fact that the ranks of professional management are destined to expand in all industrialising societies, the managerial class has neither the capacity nor the will to become the dominant ruling group. The managers are characteristically the agents of stockholders, of state bureaucracies, or in some cases of workers' councils. Since they are preoccupied with the internal affairs of enterprise, which become ever more complex, the members of the managerial class are prone to become conformists rather than leaders in the larger affairs of society.[6]

*The Development of the Industrial Labour Force*

Most countries have human resources which are available for industrial employment, but no country is endowed with persons possessing the habits, skills, and "know-how" necessary for industrial development. Thus, the industrialising elites, and particularly the managers of enterprises, are required to build a large and diversified industrial labour force. This involves four interrelated processes: recruitment, commitment, upgrading, and security.

Recruitment is the first step in development of the industrial labour force. It is the process of selecting, hiring, and assigning persons to jobs. Commitment is a longer and more intricate process. It consists of achieving the workers' permanent attachment to and acceptance of industrial employment as a way of life. Upgrading is the process of building the skills, the work habits, and the incentives for productive employment. It involves the training and the energising of the working force. Security includes the various facilities which may be necessary to provide worker security both on and off the job.

From our studies and those of others we have concluded that recruitment, commitment, and upgrading of labour forces can be achieved reasonably well in any industrialising society. Industrial man is a product not of a particular climate or ancestry but rather of persistent effort and investment. Despite the allegations to the contrary, man everywhere is adaptable to the industrial system.

The more difficult and persistent problem is that would-be workers are more often pounding on the gates to be let inside the factory system. Surplus labour and chronic redundancy is the more common problem of most of the underdeveloped countries, even in the early stages of industrialisation. Population keeps expanding more rapidly than industrial employment; urban areas become overcrowded; underemployment persists in the rural areas even as industrialisation advances. The rate of population increase tends to fall only after living standards have risen substantially, and this takes time even in those countries making a rapid march toward industrialism. The newly industrialising countries, therefore, are faced with a dilemma—where and how to hold surplus labour. If held on the land, disguised unemployment mounts; if held within the factories, productive efficiency is impaired; if held outside the factories in overcrowded urban areas, the strain on community resources becomes intolerable. Only employment on massive, labour-intensive public works, roads or irrigation systems seems to offer an answer. Certainly, in the face of mounting pressures

---

[6] A comprehensive analysis of management is presented in another book in the Inter-University series: Frederick Harbison and Charles A. Myers: *Management in the Industrial World, an International Analysis,* op. cit.

of population, industrialisation on its own offers no cure.

Here again the elites adopt somewhat different strategies in developing and managing industrial labour forces. The dynastic elite will rely more heavily on paternalistic devices to commit the worker to industrial enterprise; the middle-class will depend upon the labour market; the revolutionary intellectuals will get commitment by ideological appeals, direction of employment, and differential incentives. The dynastic elite is likely to require the employers to provide jobs for all permanent members of the industrial working force, but is unconcerned with employment problems outside the factory gates. The middle-class elite relies upon the forces of the product market to provide jobs in the long run. The revolutionary intellectuals either refuse to admit the existence of mass unemployment or mobilise a redundant labour force on public works projects. And the nationalist leaders tend to adopt any or all means which appear to offer the most satisfactory solution for the time being.

## The Response of the Worker to Industrialisation

Industrialisation redesigns and restructures its human raw materials, whatever the source. Thus, the development of an industrial work force necessarily involves the destruction of old ways of life and the acceptance of the new imperatives of the industrial work community. While the worker is in the end malleable, his metamorphosis gives rise to many forms of protest.

Characteristically, the partially committed labour force may express protest through excessive absenteeism, turnover, theft, sabotage, and spontaneous or sporadic work stoppages. The committed labour force is more likely to organise industry-wide strikes and formal political activity, while day-to-day grievances are presented through disputes machinery or labour courts, largely without stoppages. Marx saw the intensity of protest increasing in the course of capitalist development. We hold a contrary view. Our studies reveal that protest tends to reach its peak relatively early in the transformation and to decline in its overt manifestations as industrialisation reaches the more advanced stages. Incipient protest is moderated, channelled, and redirected in the advanced industrial society.

The elites, of course, must cope with the problem of worker protest, and here again they adopt different policies toward the formation of labour organisations which possess potential economic and political power. And in each society the emerging labour organisations adapt themselves rather distinctively to the prevailing environment. The labour organisations in the dynastic society remain "foreign" to the elite; in the middle-class society, they tend to conform to the product market structure. The revolutionary intellectuals regard labour organisations as instruments of and subservient to the State. The colonial administrators find labour organisations always in opposition, forever pressing relentlessly for national independence. And the labour organisations under the new nationalist leaders are often beset with conflicting and divided loyalties, sometimes conforming to and on other occasions bringing pressure against the new régime.

Most labour organisations, and particularly those in the newly industrialising countries, pose thorny issues for the elites. First, they lay claim to higher wages, while the elites may be preoccupied with capital formation. Secondly, they may strike at a time when work stoppages will be detrimental to production. Thirdly, they of necessity demand redress of worker grievances and complaints, while the nationalist leaders, in particular, may be intent upon achieving beter discipline, a faster rate of work, and more output.

Finally, labour organisations are prone to seek independence and freedom as institutions, while the elites are more concerned with making them politically subservient or insuring that they will be politically neutral or powerless.

Labour organisations, in summary, are essentially reflections of the societies in which they develop. The universal responses of workers to industrialisation, and the nature of expressions of their protest, are increasingly moulded to conform and contribute to the strategy of the industrialising elites. Though the leaders of labour seldom rise to dominating positions in a society, they are persons who always warrant recognition.

### The Rule Makers and the Rules

Industrialisation creates industrial workers, managers, and government agencies. All three are necessarily involved in industrial relations. And, just as industrialisation brings about different economic systems, so does it necessarily develop different "industrial relations systems." Again, according to the nature of the elites and to the stage of development, every industrial relations system fulfils at least three major functions. First, it defines the relative rights and responsibilities of workers, managers, and the State, and establishes the power relationships between them. Secondly, it channels and controls the responses of workers and managers to the dislocations, frustrations, and insecurities inherent in the industrialising process. And thirdly, it establishes the network of rules, both substantive and procedural, which govern the work place and the work community. Industrial relations systems reflect the persistent themes of uniformity and diversity which have been referred to in this analysis. In our book we have described in some detail the factors accounting for this uniformity and diver-

sity, and we have also pointed out how specific rules are dependent upon the stage of development and the nature of the industrialising elites.[7] These rules govern such things at recruitment and commitment, levels of compensation, the wage structure, and procedures for settlement of disputes.

In effect, therefore, the industrial relations system provides the structure and the machinery for the functional relationship between the managers and the managed in any industrialising society. As a system it is related to the economic system with which it operates. Industrial relations systems, therefore, can be logically analysed and usefully compared. They are not unique, isolated institutional arrangements with particular significance only to a particular country. It is thus manifestly possible and desirable to compare labour problems in one country with those in another, and our analytical framework, we feel, offers a method for doing this.

### THE ROAD AHEAD

As industrialisation advances, the forces making for uniformity among different societies become stronger than those perpetuating diversity. With the passage of time, each developing nation moves further from its pre-industrial stage and from its original industrial leaders. As they bring in new recruits from different strata, the various elites become less distinct. The ideological differences tend to fade; the cultural patterns of the world intermingle and merge. The once vast ideological differences between capitalism and communism give way to more pragmatic considerations in the operation of industrial society. Increasingly, the elites all appear in the same light.

The trend toward greater uniformity is attributable to a variety of pressures. Technology in itself is a unifying force.

---

[7] For an even more extended discussion, see John T. Dunlop: *Industrial Relations Systems,* op. cit.

The thrust of progress also serves the cause of uniformity, and gradually there is less difference between the various categories of workers and industries in each country. Education brings about a new equality with the elimination of illiteracy and the development of skills. The State everywhere becomes ever larger and more important. Larger-scale enterprises are common hallmarks of all advanced industrial societies. Finally, the compulsion to compare helps to achieve uniformity. The pressures for progress and participation in a new economic order are enhanced by the world-wide character of industrialisation, by international trade, by travel, by modern means of communication, and by global exchange of ideas.

The road ahead leads to what we call "pluralistic industrialism." The fully developed industrial society in our view will be one in which the struggle between uniformity and diversity continues, a society which is centralising and decentralising at the same time, a dynamic society which, while marked by complex and conflicting pressures, develops a common cultural consensus.

In this pluralistic industrial society the State will not wither away. It will handle the conflict among the differing power elements in the society; it will control collusion by producers against consumers; and it will establish the relationship between members and their organisations. The managers of enterprise, whether public or private, will be professionals, technically trained and carefully selected for their tasks. They will be bureaucratic managers, if private, and managerial bureaucrats, if public. The distinction between managers will be based more upon the size and scope of their enterprises than upon the ownership of the means of production. Occupational and professional associations will range alongside the State and large-scale enterprise as centres of power and influence. And uniting the State, the enterprises and the occupational associations will be a great web of rules established by all three entities, but particularly by the first.

In this society conflict will persist, but it will take the form of bureaucratic skirmishes rather than class war. Groups will jockey for position over the setting of jurisdictions, the authority to make decisions, the forming of alliances, and the granting or withdrawal of support or effort. The great battles of conflicting parties will be replaced by a myriad of minor contests over comparative details. Labour organisations will cease to be parts of class movements urging programmes of total reform, and become more purely pressure groups representing the occupational interests of their members.

In this emerging world-wide society industrial man will be subject to great pressures of conformity imposed not alone by enterprise management but also by the State and by his occupational association. For most people any true scope for the independent spirit on the job will be missing. But, outside his working life, industrial man may enjoy more freedom than in most earlier forms of society. Politically he can have influence. He will enjoy higher living standards, greater leisure, and more education. And, along with the bureaucratic conservatism of economic life, there may be a new Bohemianism in other aspects of man's existence which can give rise to a new search for individuality and a new meaning to liberty.

Technology need not, as Marx thought, reach into every corner of society. Indeed, the conformity to technology may bring a new dedication to individuality. This is the two-sided face of pluralistic industrialism that makes it a split personality looking in two directions at the same time. Utopia, of course, never arrives, but industrial man the world over will probably acquire greater freedom in his personal life at the cost of greater conformity in his working life. Industrialism can and will bring about for him a better existence.

## Related Readings

The articles and chapters in this section, particularly those by Dunlop and Bauder, contain numerous references to theories of labor movements which the interested reader might wish to pursue in greater depth. In addition, the volume edited by George W. Brooks, Milton Derber, David A. McCabe, and Philip Taft on *Interpreting the Labor Movement* (Madison, Wis., *Industrial Relations Research Association*, 1950), has a number of useful articles, particularly "Theories of the Labor Movement," by Philip Taft. Taft examines theories in terms of their ability to answer questions with respect to the origin and behavior of labor movements. Taft considers the ideas of Lujo Brentano, selected Catholic writers, Marx, the Webbs, Robert Hoxie, John R. Commons, Lenin, and Selig Perlman. Taft defends the unions' "philosophy of simple pragmatism" and concludes: "Writers who have developed theories of labor sometimes seized upon certain aspects of union organization and have tended to over-stress particular characteristics. Unions cannot remain permanently anchored in their views and activities. Their survival depends upon their ability to adjust to changing circumstances."

Selig Perlman's son, Mark, has done considerable work on labor union theories, which he defines as "basic interpretations." (Mark Perlman, *Labor Union Theories in America*, Evanston, Ill. and White Plains, N.Y., Row, Peterson, 1958.) In his book, he analyzes five basic theories used to explain American unions. ". . . (1) the Protestant Christian and the Roman Catholic Christian social movements, (2) the Marxian Socialist movements, (3) the environmental psychological descriptive, (4) the neoclassical economics discipline, and (5) the legal and jurisprudential discipline." Perlman's purpose was not "principally to evaluate ideas. Quite the contrary; the purpose is to suggest a range of ideas and to analyze the course of their development."

In "Labor Movement Theories: Past, Present and Future," *Industrial and Labor Relations Review*, Mark Perlman analyzes a number of theories in order "to describe briefly the course which labor theory has taken from its early beginnings and to indicate current and future lines of development."

# CHAPTER 2

# Labor Movements: The United States

Some aspects of the American labor movement were outlined in connection with the discussions of theories of labor movements in Chapter 1. The present chapter goes into greater detail about the characteristics, trends, and problems of the American labor movement.

The specific questions considered include: why the American labor movement is not socialist; a review of American labor history, centered on the important year 1937; a review of the direction of unionism between 1947 and 1967; government regulation of unions; a discussion of the determinants of union responsibility; a profile of the American labor movement in 1970; the problems of agricultural workers; and factors influencing union growth in the south. The chapter concludes with some perspectives on labor and the American economy in the late 1960's. The impact of unions on wages and collective bargaining by public employees will be analyzed in Part III.

## IDEOLOGY OF THE AMERICAN LABOR MOVEMENT

In the first selection in this chapter, Professor Walter Galenson answers in considerable detail the question of "Why the American Labor Movement is not Socialist," a question raised by Dunlop, Perlman, and Gulick and Bers, in Chapter 1. This is a very important question because it points to a unique feature of the American labor movement and requires an understanding of the relationships between economic and political labor movements as well as the societies in which those movements operate.

In a very brief but excellent outline of American labor history, Galenson first discusses various attempts to radicalize American labor, making it readily apparent that the failure of radicalism has not been a result of the workers' lack of exposure to radical ideas. Instead, the explanation lies in certain fundamental conditions in the American environment: the standard of living, the rate of economic growth, the absence of class consciousness, the nature of the American political system, and the success of collective bargaining. Professor Galenson concludes that the present scheme of things in the American labor movement is not necessarily "frozen immutably," but "the forces that in the past shaped the unique character of the American labor movement continue unabated, for the most part." However, the American and European labor movements have been moving together in Galenson's opinion, so that "there is little left today to divide the moderate Socialist unions of Europe from American business unionism. . . . It is high time to recognize that the doctrines of the past have very little to do with the kind of world in which we live today." As noted in Chapter 1, Kerr, Harbison, Dunlop, and Myers agree with Galenson that ideological differences tend to become less important in the course of economic development.

# Why the American Labor Movement Is Not Socialist

## by Walter Galenson

. . . Europeans are. . . puzzled by the American scene. This is quite understandable, however, because the American labor movement and the closely allied movement of Canada are unique in their attitudes toward capitalism. Almost everywhere else, labor is dedicated to some form of collectivism, or at least to a very restricted type of capitalism.

In trying to explain why the American labor movement is different, I will first consider the various efforts that have been made during the past century to steer American labor into more orthodox ideological channels. Against that background, I will then discuss the basic economic, social, and political features of American life which have molded the present system.

### ATTEMPTS TO RADICALIZE AMERICAN LABOR

Many radical ideologies of Europe, as well as some that were native to the United States, have been urged upon the American labor movement at various times in its history. . . .

The first American labor movement of any importance was the Knights of Labor, established in 1869 as a secret society, but converted a decade later into an open trade union federation. Like many of the early European trade unions, the Knights advocated producers' co-operatives as a means of eliminating the exploitation of labor, and the eventual failure of the co-operatives which it sponsored was a major cause of its decline. However, the Knights of Labor was in no sense a revolutionary organization. It was prepared to work within the framework of capitalism provided that the worst abuses were mitigated through collective bargaining and social legislation. One must keep in mind that in the heyday of the Knights, the American worker already enjoyed the

SOURCE Reprinted with permission from *The American Review*, Vol. 1, No. 2, Winter 1961. Published under the auspices of the Johns Hopkins Bologna Center, Largo Trombetti 3, Bologna, Italy.

right to vote and free public education. These demands of early European socialism did not have to be won by revolutionary activity.

The American Federation of Labor, formed in 1886, supplanted the Knights of Labor as the most representative organization of American workers, and it has occupied that status right down to the present day. It was challenged from the left on numerous occasions, but always emerged unscathed. The AFL was led for many years by Samuel Gompers, a cigar maker by trade, who helped establish the pragmatic approach to political and economic problems which has been its hallmark. Gompers, an immigrant from England, had been a student of Socialist doctrine and was not altogether unsympathetic to the Socialist point of view, but his experience as a labor leader convinced him that it had little chance of success under American conditions. He eventually became a staunch foe of socialism, and its major antagonist within the trade unions.

In 1892, the Socialist Labor party, which had been established two decades earlier, fell under the control of Daniel De Leon, a university teacher and a Marxist fundamentalist. Despairing of making headway within the AFL, he gathered together the remnants of the Knights of Labor and some Socialist-inclined local unions in New York to form the Socialist Trade and Labor Alliance. The Alliance never achieved any real organizational success, though its career was attended by a great deal of furor.

A more serious threat to the Gompers leadership came from Socialist-oriented groups within the AFL. At the AFL conventions of 1893 and 1894, they tried to secure endorsement of collective ownership of the means of production as well as other Socialist demands. Although they were unable to gain a majority for their program, the Socialist teamed up with some personal enemies of Gompers to defeat him for the AFL presidency in 1894,

the only time in his long career that Gompers suffered this fate. The moderate Socialists within the AFL continued their efforts to gain control of the organization, and for several decades they were a force to be reckoned with. In 1902, a resolution that would have committed the AFL "to advise the working people to organize their economic and political power to secure for labor the full equivalent of its toil and the overthrowal of the wage system end the establishment of an industrial co-operative democracy" was defeated only by the narrow margin of 4897 to 4171 votes. The Socialists ran their own candidate against Gompers at the 1912 convention, and gained about one-third of the total vote, being supported, among others, by the delegates of the United Mine Workers, the Brewery Workers, the Machinists, and the Typographical Union. However, Socialist party opposition to American participation in the First World War greatly reduced Socialist strength within the AFL.

Another in the series of efforts to build a radical labor movement independent of the AFL came with the formation of the Industrial Workers of the World in 1905. At its inception, it embraced most of the existing left wing groups, including Daniel De Leon's Socialist Labor Alliance and the followers of Eugene V. Debs, perhaps the most popular Socialist leader in American history. (Debs was imprisoned in 1918 for his opposition to the war, ran for the Presidency of the United States from prison in 1920, and polled close to a million votes for the Socialist party.) But the dominant elements in the IWW came from the western part of the United States, which was then in the process of transformation from a frontier to a settled industrial area. The Western Federation of Miners, an organization of metal miners representing workers in Idaho, Colorado, and Utah, provided the IWW with leadership.

The preamble to the IWW constitution

began categorically: "The working class and the employing class have nothing in common"; on this much, the disparate constituency could agree. But differences of opinion soon developed on many issues, including the desirability of political activity within the framework of the capitalist state. Within a few years, Debs, De Leon, and the Western Federation of Miners all withdrew, leaving the IWW in the hands of an uncompromising, direct action group headed by William D. Haywood and Vincent St. John.

The IWW became the spokesman *par excellence* of the migratory workers who at the time constituted a substantial proportion of the labor force in the West. Working in isolated mining camps, in lumbering operations, on large farms, and on the docks of Pacific Coast ports, these men were homeless and rootless, without families, hounded as "hoboes" and "bums" when they were unable to secure work, which was largely seasonal in character at best. Their ideology was a native American syndicalism; its main ingredients were a rejection of capitalism and all its works, and belief in the efficacy of the strike as a means of securing economic gain, and of the general strike in bringing about the eventual overthrow of capitalism. Collective bargaining and the collective agreement were not for them; they were not in one job long enough to make this a feasible procedure, and it was too slow a means of alleviating the poor condition of labor which they faced. The IWW was never very clear about the nature of the Socialist commonwealth which would take over on the great day when all the nation's workers folded their arms and brought capitalism tumbling down. Its job was to prepare for that day by strikes (revolutionary gymnastics), sabotage, and any other means of weakening capitalism.

The formal structure of the IWW was extremely loose. Combined offices and "flop houses," where penniless members could secure a night's lodging and food, were maintained in a number of cities. Dues payments were sporadic, although the members were intensely loyal to the organization and paid when they could. The IWW led some major strikes of metal and lumber workers during the war, and suffered severe repression both by the government and by vigilante action. Hundreds of its leaders were imprisoned, some were lynched by mobs. William D. Haywood fled the country while out on bail awaiting trial, escaped to Russia, and died an unhappy man after having learned that communism had as little use for syndicalism as did capitalism.

While the action of the government undoubtedly hastened the demise of the IWW, its days were numbered in any event by changes in the economic conditions which had led to its creation. The West was settling down; miners, loggers, and longshoremen were acquiring steady employment and families. Their trade unions began to adopt collective bargaining. Nevertheless, the IWW tradition has not entirely disappeared; the Mine, Mill and Smelter Workers' Union, successor to the Western Federation of Miners, and the West Coast Longshoremen's Union are among the few American labor unions still controlled by Communists, while in the organizations of West Coast seamen and lumber workers, one can still detect some trace of IWW psychology.

With the eclipse of the Socialists within the AFL and the IWW outside it, the mantle of opposition fell to the Communist party, which had been formed as a breakaway from the Socialist party soon after the Russian revolution. For some years it followed a policy of "boring from within" the AFL under the guidance of William Z. Foster, an able trade union organizer. However, in 1928 it was directed by the Red International of Labor Unions to establish an independent trade union center, and the outcome was the Trade Union Unity League. While the League was never very large, it served an important function as a training ground for Communist organizers.

But a much more serious challenge to the AFL came from within its own ranks. The AFL had declined steadily in membership and vitality after 1920, and the economic depression that hit the country in 1929 weakened it still further. A group of AFL union leaders blamed the AFL difficulties on too strict adherence to craft union structure, and advocated industrial unionism as the only way in which workers in the mass production industries could be organized.

The Committee for Industrial Organization (which later became the Congress of Industrial Organizations) was a revolt of the unskilled and semi-skilled workers against the craftsmen who controlled the AFL. Like the "new unionism" of Great Britain in the 1890's, or the transformation of Scandinavian unionism a decade later, it reflected the aspirations of the less privileged labor groups to a greater voice in determining labor conditions and their resentment against exclusion from the union movement. The men who led the CIO were not radicals: John L. Lewis, head of the coal miners' union, was a lifelong Republican, while Sidney Hillman and David Dubinsky, who were presidents respectively, of the men's and ladies' garment workers' unions, had some early connection with socialism but had long since lost any sympathy for Marxism. The CIO was not established to remake the social order. Its only goal was to organize the workers in the steel, automobile, electrical equipment, rubber, textile, and other mass production industries.

It is fair to say that the CIO was somewhat to the left politically of the AFL, but it was never under the domination of anti-capitalistic elements. Philip Murray, who succeeded John L. Lewis as president in 1940, was a cautious Scotch ex-coal miner, who had been Lewis' chief lieutenant for many years. Walter Reuther, who became president on the death of Murray, had once been a member of the Socialist party, but turned later to staunch support of the Democratic party.

However, the CIO did have an internal Communist problem of no mean dimensions. With the advent of the United Front policy in 1934, the Communist party dissolved the Trade Union Unity League and turned its attention once more to the AFL. The organization of the CIO afforded it a tremendous opportunity, for there was a great need of trained organizers, and the Communists were only too willing to oblige. Working for little pay and performing arduous and often dangerous jobs, well disciplined Communist groups established themselves in leadership positions. At the height of their power, they controlled half a dozen major CIO unions and had powerful factions in a number of others.

From the outbreak of war in Europe in September, 1939, to the Nazi attack upon the Soviet Union, the Communist-dominated unions were in the forefront of the struggle against American assistance to the democratic nations, and this brought them into sharp conflict with the CIO leadership. But when Russia entered the war, their policy changed over night, and an internal crises was averted. After the war, tensions once more arose with the growing coolness between the United States and the Soviet Union. When in 1948, the Communist unions supported former Vice President Henry Wallace on a third party ticket in an effort to defeat the Democratic candidate, Harry S. Truman, Philip Murray decided that the Communists would have to go, whatever the cost in CIO strength. A number of Communist unions were expelled from the CIO in 1949 and 1950, and in some cases the CIO set up new unions in an effort to hold the members. Communist power in the labor movement declined precipitously thereafter, and today there are not more than 150,000 workers in the few independent unions under Communist control.

Even this does not tell the whole story, for few of the rank and file members are Communists, and many of the leaders have only a tenuous relationship with the Communist party.

By 1955, the issues that had divided the AFL and CIO were gone. The mass production workers were organized into powerful trade unions, and many of the AFL craft unions had expanded their jurisdictions until they were almost indistinguishable from the CIO unions. Both federations supported the Democratic party on the political front. As a result, the AFL-CIO merger was consummated, and this organization remains the only labor federation in the United States at the present time.

Until 1950, there was scarcely a period in which socialism, in one of its many forms, did not play a significant role on the American labor scene. But during the past decade, Communist strength has dwindled into insignificance, and no ideology of the left has arisen to take its place. Nor is there any immediate prospect that one will emerge. Not a single responsible trade union leader advocates an independent labor party, and there are no proponents of government ownership of industry. The trade unions are wedded more firmly than ever to the Democratic party. Prediction of events to come is a hazardous undertaking, but few would quarrel with the observation that the future of American socialism does not seem bright.

## THE DETERMINANTS OF AMERICAN LABOR IDEOLOGY

European socialists have been prone to attribute the pragmatism of American labor to the "backwardness" of the American worker. The late Harold Laski predicted that eventually the American working class would throw off the blinders that prevented it from seeing the truth about class conflict and catch up with the British. In the light of what is happening in

Britain, these views are not as popular as they once were, but there is still enough economic determinism in the European Left to make the thesis seem tenable.

The fact of the matter is that these visions of the future have as little to do with reality as the utopia of Edward Bellamy or the gehenna of George Orwell. The American worker had the alternative of taking the paths pointed out to him by persuasive prophets—Daniel De Leon, Morris Hillquit, Eugene V. Debs, William Z. Foster, William D. Haywood, or Norman Thomas, to name a few. Yet in the final analysis, he chose to follow such proponents of business unionism as Samuel Gompers, William Green, and George Meany, who promised only a little more of the goods of this world each year. This result flowed from the conjuncture of certain fundamental conditions in the American environment.

### The Standard of Living

It should be observed first that there is no necessary one-to-one relationship between living standards and radicalism. In many countries it is among the better paid workers in the metal trades, on the railroads, in the mines, and on the docks, that foci of discontent exist, while the poorer paid textile, service, and farm laborers are quiescent. Yet there does seem to be a general tendency for economic well being and political conservatism to go hand in hand, as European Socialists are beginning to discover.

\* \* \*

The relatively high American standard of living is not difficult to understand. A vast continent, richly endowed with natural resources, was settled by some of the most energetic and ambitious people of Europe. The productivity of labor, both in the factory and on the farm, was high because of its relative scarcity in relation to capital and land. Unemployment was mainly of a frictional or cyclical character, and not the permanent structural unemployment found in many countries. If employment opportunities in an area dried up, the American worker simply moved where jobs were more abundant. He had no ancestral village to tie him down. The phenomenal growth of California in the last two decades attests to continuing high labor mobility. It is as though Western Europe were a single nation and the underemployed peasants of southern Italy could move freely to Great Britain and Sweden.

It has been remarked that it is inequality, rather than absolute living standards, which gives rise to discontent. Karl Marx once observed: "A house may be large or small; as long as the surrounding houses are equally small it satisfies all social demands for a dwelling. but if a palace arises beside the little house, the little house shrinks into a hut." There has always been, and there still is great inequality of income and wealth in the United States. Whether the degree of inequality is greater or less than in Europe is still a matter of statistical debate. But the political consequences of inequality can be quite different, depending upon the absolute base. A small difference in income may be less tolerable to the worker living on the margin of existence than a large difference to the man who is well off. Statistical comparisons cannot convey anything of the resentments felt, respectively, by a worker who, together with his family, occupies a single room and spends his entire income for inadequate food and clothing, and by a worker with a comfortable house, an adequate diet, and money left over for recreation, when each views a millionaire driving by in his limousine.

## The Rate of Economic Growth

The rate of growth of the American economy has been very impressive, even by modern, forced-draught standards. By 1900, American industry was producing four times the volume of goods that had been turned out thirty years earlier. During the next forty years, when the labor movement reached maturity, there was something more than an additional fourfold increase. Since 1940, the increase in manufacturing output has been about 80 per cent.

\* \* \*

Not all American workers shared the fruits of industrial growth. The IWW episode was illustrative of the alienation of a substantial group with poor conditions of labor and low expectations for future improvement. But the great majority maintained their faith in capitalism because within their experience, this system delivered the goods.

## The Absence of Class Consciousness

A hundred and twenty-five years ago, Alexis de Tocqueville wrote: "America, then, exhibits in her social state an extraordinary phenomenon. Men are there seen on a greater equality in point of fortune and intellect, or, in other words, more equal in their strength than in any other country of the world, or in any other age of which history has preserved the remembrance." A great deal has happened since then. Fortunes have been made, permanent aristocracies of wealth created. Investigators have concluded that social mobility is now greater in the United States than in the industrial nations of Europe. But the belief in equality persists. "Such ideological equalitarianism has played, and continues to play, an important role in facilitating social mobility in the United States. It enables the person of humble birth to regard upward mobility as attainable for himself, or for his children. It facilitates his acceptance as a social equal if he succeeds in rising economically. It mitigates the emotional distance between persons of different social rank. And it fosters in any existing elite the persuasion (however mistaken this may be) that its eminence is the result of individual effort, and hence temporary. The point to emphasize is, not that these beliefs are often contradicted by the experience of those who hold them, but that this equalitarian ideology has persisted in the face of facts which contradict it. We would suggest that the absence of hereditary aristocracy has done much to foster this persistence. Americans have rarely been exposed to persons whose conduct displays a belief in an inherited and God-given superiority and also demands that others demonstrate (by deferential behavior) their recognition of this superiority." (Seymour Martin Lipset and Reinhard Bendix, *Social Mobility in Industrial Society,* Berkeley, 1959.)

The ideal of equality carries over strongly into industrial life. The great deference shown to European managers is absent in the American plant. There is in its place a certain camaraderie, reinforced by the fact that if manager and worker should chance to meet outside the factory, they are likely to be indistinguishable in dress and speech. As soon as the British worker opens his mouth, it is clear to which class he belongs. But one can sit around a table with American labor and management personnel and not be at all conscious of any class differences.

It might have been anticipated that the myth of equality would be dissipated by the hard facts of reality. It is neither easy nor usual for an ordinary worker to attain high position in a large corportion. Most American workers have no illusions on this score. Nevertheless, there is no indication that a working class in the European sense is developing. Even the worker solidarity that appeared during the union organizing drives of the 1930's is vanishing under the impact of full employment prosperity.

*　*　*

National and racial divisions among workers have had a particularly deleterious effect upon the growth of American socialism. The immigrants who brought Marxism to the United States often remained cut off from the native American, and confined their activities to fellow workers from the "old country." In 1917, 33,000 out of 80,000 Socialist party members belonged to fourteen semi-autonomous foreign lanuage federations, each with its own newspapers, benifit societies, etc. This situation has been well summarized in the following words: "The immigrants played a dual role in the development of American socialism. They were largely responsible for its birth. They were also largely responsible for stunting its growth. They could transplant the theory of socialism but they could not naturalize it. In the formative years, therefore, an unequal and uneasy relationship existed between foreign-born and native Socialists. The former enjoyed the prestige of intellectual superiority but could not effectively spread the gospel. The latter suffered from a sense of theoretical inferiority but were indispensable in presenting the face of the party to the general public. It was not unusual for the top leadership of local Socialist groups to be native-born while a majority of the rank and file were foreign-born." (Theodore Draper, *The Roots of American Communism,* New York, 1957.)

The Socialist party was never able to shake off its foreign flavor. Once the stream of immigrants from Europe was cut off, it lost its main source of recruits. The chidren of immigrants, anxious to demonstrate their Americanism, turned their backs on socialism. There was lacking the European tradition of handing down a political creed from father to son. Many working class children moved into the ranks of professionals, thus depriving the workers of good leadership material.

A final factor militating against the formation of a cohesive working class in the United States was the character and structure of the AFL. At its formation, the AFL represented a revolt of the skilled trades against the heterogeneous Knights of Labor, which, it was felt, tended to subordinate the interests of the craftsman to those of the general worker. Craft structure continued for many years to be the AFL shibboleth. The theory was developed that because of the fragility of American working class loyalties, only the mutual bond of a common craft could prevent unions from splintering, thus providing an ideological basis for craft selfishness.

* * *

Conflict between the skilled and unskilled was by no means confined to the United States. The same divisive tendencies had to be overcome in many other countries. But in most cases, the problem was resolved at an earlier stage in labor development, before ideology had been hardened into a fixed mold. The new unionism of the 1890's preceded the formation of the British Labor party, and it has been said of the period: "The older (craft) unions had a tradition that you should keep party politics out of labour questions; these new ones were organized by Socialists, and socialism was their aim . . . there was never any question of the new unions supporting any candidates but independent labour men. . . . This was a natural consequence of their lack of an entrenched position in industry; instead, they sought a statutory minimum wage, and compulsory arbitration. It was also a consequence of their not being able to pay enough to provide social insurance for themselves, as the craftsmen did: they had to win the welfare state instead." (E.H. Phelps Brown.) German unions evolved toward an industrial form at a relatively early stage in their development, while in Norway and Sweden, the unskilled workers captured the labor movement before the First World War. Had American mass production industries been organized

thirty years earlier, the political history of American unionism might have been quite different. But powerful employer oposition and indifference of the crafts held the unskilled in check until the catastrophe of the Great Depression unleashed a flood of organization which carried all obstacles before it.

### Political Barriers to Socialism

It is almost a cliché that the tradition of the American two-party system provided an insurmountable obstacle to the establishment of a labor party. But puting the matter this way is merely to beg the question. In Britain, one of the great parties of the nineteenth century, the Liberals, yielded to a newly organized Labour party. In many other countries, the same process occurred as the labor movement asserted its independence. The right question to ask is this: Why did not the Democratic party in the United States yield its paramountcy to a labor party with the rise of the industrial worker?

Apart from the Socialist party, which never outgrew the sectarian stage, there were several twentieth century efforts in the United States to build democratic third parties. The Progressive movement of 1912, in which Theodore Roosevelt split the Republican vote and secured the election of Woodrow Wilson, and the Communist-supported candidacy of Henry Wallace in 1948, which almost succeeded in bringing about the defeat of Truman, were ephemeral efforts which did not have the support of organized labor. The Progressive party of the 1920's was more significant. It rallied beneath its banner a number of Midwestern farmer-labor parties, and received the strong support of the labor movement in Chicago and other major cities. Robert M. La Follette was nominated for the Presidency on the Progressive ticket in 1924, and because the candidates of both the major parties were conservatives, the AFL, for the first and last time in its history, endorsed a third party candidate. La Follette got five million votes, but despite this promising start, the Progressive coalition fell apart, and in 1928 there were again only two major Presidential candidates.

What these abortive efforts indicated, however, was that from the point of view of election mechanics, a national political campaign could be mounted in a short time, and third parties could get on the ballot. Since 1924, there have been several efforts to establish labor parties on a local basis, mainly in New York State, where the American Labor party and the Liberal party received the backing of the garment unions. But none of these has moved into the national picture.

Samuel Gompers, who more than any other man made explicit the non-partisanship of American labor, wrote in 1920: "The effect of a separate political labor party can only be disastrous to the wage earners of our country and to the interests of all forward looking people. The votes that would go to a labor party candidate would, in the absence of such candidate, go to the best man in the field. In no case would he be an enemy of labor. There can be no hope of success of labor party candidates. The effect, therefore, of a political labor party will be to defeat our friends and to elect our enemies. Labor can look upon the formation of a political labor party only as an act detrimental to the interests of labor and exactly in line with that which is most ardently desired by those who seek to oppress labor."

This statement makes clear the basic reason for the opposition of the leaders of American unionism to independent labor action: the firm conviction that there would be no success. American labor leaders are certainly not averse to winning political power; they would like to sit in the Cabinet, and John L. Lewis once envisioned himself as a Vice-Presidential candidate running alongside Franklin D. Roosevelt. When Lewis broached the sub-

ject to Roosevelt, the latter is reported to have replied: "Which place were you thinking of, John?" But they have been realistic enough to realize that such honors, which many European working class leaders have obtained, were unlikely of attainment via the third party route.

Why was this true? For one thing, industrial workers in the United States, the land *par excellence* of industrialization, have never constituted a majority of the population. In 1950, 46 per cent of all those employed were classified as professional, technical, managerial, and clerical workers, while another 15 per cent were in categories not prone to unionization: private household workers, service workers, and farm laborers. By 1958, the non-worker group percentage had risen to 48 per cent, while industrial workers had shrunk to about 37 per cent of the labor force. Thus, even if wage earners were a solid bloc, they would still fall far short of a majority unless they could count on substantial support from white-collar employees, who have shown little inclination to vote labor anywhere. In the past it was the farmers who blocked labor's road to political power. Today it is the growing middle class—white-collar workers, professionals, the self employed—which stands in the way.

Secondly, American workers have never voted in the same automatic fashion as European workers. European Socialist parties first gained working class allegiance by elementary democratic demands for universal suffrage and free public education, which American workers have enjoyed for a century, and which therefore could not be utilized as issues by aspiring labor politicians.

Since 1928, most trade unions have supported the Democratic party on the national level, and have urged their members to vote, in turn, for Alfred E. Smith, Franklin D. Roosevelt, Harry S. Truman, Adlai Stevenson, and John F. Kennedy. But even during the Roosevelt era, when

American workers were united as never before behind a man whom they felt had rescued them from economic disaster, a minority of trade union leaders and workers supported the Republican party. Among the prominent Republican laborites have been Hutcheson père and fils, presidents of the large Carpenters' Union; John L. Lewis; and Dave Beck and James Hoffa of the Teamsters' Union.

Apart from formal union support, a number of cross currents have contributed to the splitting of the labor vote. Many Negro workers, for example, support the Republican party of Abraham Lincoln. Prosperous workers who leave working class urban districts and acquire suburban homes tend to take on the political hues of their middle class neighbors. Religion also enters into the picture on occasion, as in the 1960 Presidential campaign.

The political tactics of American labor have not worked badly. The Democratic party is a loose coalition of various interest groups, rather than the representative of a particular economic sector of the population. It includes some of the most anti-labor elements in the country, from the South; the political machines of the large Northern cities, which at best are neutral on issues of labor interest; and staunch labor supporters from areas in which the trade union movement is strong. By operating within the Democratic party structure, the unions are able to secure for themselves, on a *quid pro quo* basis, much broader influence than they could hope for as minority independents.

This method is not without its dangers. If public opinion turns against the unions, as it did after the 1945-1947 strike wave, and the 1958-1959 corruption exposures, they are left defenseless, since non-labor politicians cannot be expected to brave the wrath of the electorate in support of an unpopular cause. In normal times, however, the unions are able to achieve constant legislative gains, and in periods of economic crisis, the Democratic party has even been transformed into a powerful instrument for major social reform.

### The Triumph of Collective Bargaining

The method of collective bargaining, as opposed to the method of legal enactment, to use the terminology of the Webbs, has proven eminently successful in the United States, contributing in no small measure to a reluctance on the part of workers to rely upon the state. A great many objectives which are essentially social in character have been achieved by private bargaining. One need only cite the proliferation of pension plans, health and welfare schemes, and the guaranteed annual wage.

There is one other area, however, in which American collective bargaining has made inroads to an extent matched in few other countries: that of management prerogatives. Fully as important as wages to the working man in this age of the large, impersonal factory is the assertion of his rights as an individual, on the job as well as off, and a sense of participation in the enterprise to which he devotes so large a part of his life. To this end, almost every country of Western Europe has established labor-management or production committees to promote industrial democracy. On the whole, these committees have not lived up to expectations, but this is another story.

✻   ✻   ✻

THE FUTURE

One need not be rash in making the prediction that traditional socialism has little future in the United States. There are still a few advocates around, but their voices are no longer heard. The Communist party and the various splinter Socialist groups have no influence whatever on political events. The trade unions are committed more firmly than ever to working within the existing two-party system.

Time does not stand still, however, and there is no reason to believe that the present scheme of things is frozen immutably. The American labor movement is moving in directions which are likely to be not displeasing to European Socialists who drop Marxist slogans and face the world with an objective eye. American labor unions are insisting that the federal government assume greater responsibility for the economy, and in particular, that it pursue the goal of a more rapid rate of economic growth. They are demanding governmental assistance to the relatively underdeveloped portions of the country. They oppose high interest rates, and advocate monetary and fiscal policies which will bring about greater equality of income. In general, they favor a greater degree of governmental control over economic affairs.

On the collective bargaining front, American unions will undoubtedly continue to push not only for higher living standards for workers, but also for a greater share in the right to manage. The Automobile Workers have already proposed a kind of bilateral price fixing in the interest of selling more automobiles. The building unions are currently discussing with employers means of speeding technological change in construction. A joint labor-management committee has been created in steel to consider the human relations problems of the industry.

The forces that in the past shaped the unique character of the American labor movement continue unabated, for the most part. Material living standards remain the highest in the world, and they are improving at a fairly rapid rate. Of class consciousness, one can only say that everything is tending to diminish the possibility of developing a closely-knit, cohesive working class. The number of industrial workers is shrinking in relation to other groups, and the unions are fully aware of the fact that even to hold their own, they must somehow attract white-collar employees and professionals. Paradoxically, the only development that may foster manual worker cohesiveness is the tendency of manual wages to rise faster than those of white-collar employees, for the manualists may become concerned about protecting their differentials.

The American labor movement, until the last war, was turned inward, engrossed with domestic problems. The realization has grown that what is happening elsewhere in the world may be at least of equal importance in affecting the welfare of the American worker. Contact with the international labor movement has broadened tremendously. Differences of policy and practice between European and American labor are narrowing as both groups are discovering an urgent common interest in the maintenance of democratic institutions in the newly emerging nations of Africa and Asia.

It is my own observation that there is little left today to divide the moderate Socialist unions of Europe from American business unionism. The former may be puzzled, and even outraged, by some of the internal practices of American unions, while the latter may be repelled by the remnants of an earlier Socialist ideology that still prevails in some of the European movements. But when it comes to practical and economic policies, there are precious few differences remaining. It is high time to recognize that the doctrines of the past have very little to do with the kind of world in which we live today.

## American Labor Before World War II

As Walter Galenson indicates in the following selection, "1937: The Turning Point for American Labor," 1937 was perhaps the single most important year in American labor history. This article presents a brief outline of the American labor movement before 1937. Galenson indicates that in spite of a long history, the American labor movement was very weak in 1937. Prior to that time, membership was limited mainly to skilled trades and the railroad, construction, and printing industries. Industrial workers' organizations had experienced wide fluctuations in membership, growing during periods of prosperity and general depression, and declining in recessions and open-shop periods like the 1920's. The CIO, formed during 1935, challenged the AFL to organize industrial workers, thereby producing twenty years of intense union conflict and considerable increase in union membership as the CIO spurred the AFL to greater organizing activity. The 1937 experience was particularly significant because it represented the first successful assault on some of the main non-union bastions in the United States. Rapid growth in union membership came during two major waves: the first in 1937 and the second during the defense boom of 1940 and 1941 and continuing throughout the war. The 1937 organizing experience in many cases provided the base for the expansion of union membership during World War II.

Galenson discusses a number of reasons for the rapid growth of union membership during 1937. The first of these was the prevailing sentiment among workers and the public for the growth in union organization. This sentiment prevailed in large measure because of the very bad conditions that all but destroyed the workers' beliefs in the efficacy of the capitalist system. A second reason for this rapid membership growth was the economic recovery of that year, which lessened employers' resistance to union organization. Employers were afraid that strikes would damage their profit positions, which were improving for the first time in many years. Organizing also benefited from the emergence of union leaders with a will to organize. Many AFL union leaders had opposed organizing campaigns among industrial workers for fear that their own jurisdictions would be encroached upon or that the influx of many new members might threaten the political strength of established leaders. These leaders were also afraid to incur the financial risks involved in extending membership to unskilled and semiskilled workers.

One of the most important union leaders to emerge during the 1930's was John L. Lewis of the United Mine Workers, whose union had been hard hit by the economic adversities of the 1920's and 1930's, as well as by the open-shop movement of the 1920's. Conditions were so bad among coal miners that the United Mine Workers were able to organize about 95 percent of their jurisdiction in a relatively short period of time. Although its influence is very difficult to evaluate, the United Mine Workers also benefited from favorable attitudes toward unionism by many of the larger coal operators, especially in the north, who saw the union as a stabilizing influence in the industry at a time when economic conditions were very bad because of intense economic competition. Northern coal operators were especially concerned about lower costs in the South. Since wages constituted a large proportion of the total cost of mining coal, these operators hoped collective bargaining would stabilize prices. It is significant that many of the men who helped organize the CIO unions came from the United Mine Workers and that the United Mine Workers put up a large part of the money for the CIO.

The extent of the workers' desperation during these years is indicated by the fact that they were willing to employ the sit-down strike as an organizing device. Although this revolutionary and illegal weapon caused vigorous protest from the press, the courts, and men like the ex-president of Harvard University, it led to the unionization of General Motors, Chrysler, and United States Steel. However, as Galenson emphasizes, other factors influenced the organization of all these companies. The unionization of United States Steel was particularly important because of its size and significance in the American economy. It caused many American employers to conclude that further resistance to the CIO was futile.

A fourth factor encouraging the rapid expansion of union membership during these years was the attitude of the Roosevelt administration, which encouraged the growth of unions partly for economic reasons. It was felt that one of the causes for the depression was the workers' inability to buy the products of industry. The New Deal therefore thought that encouraging the growth of unions not only would be equitable but would help stabilize the economy by maintaining purchasing power.

However, we must be careful not to overestimate the significance of the legislation passed during the New Deal. Although favorable laws undoubtedly did much to spur the growth of unions, the prevailing opinion about organized labor probably was more important than legislation. As Galenson points out, when the recovery of 1937 was cut short by recession, resistance to union growth by employers increased, and the growth of union membership came to a standstill until World War II, when it was again encouraged by the activities of the War Labor Board. The record of the late 1930's makes it abundantly clear that union membership is influenced by a complex constellation of forces, only one of which is legislation. Favorable labor legislation, for example, could not overcome economic adversity during the late 1930's. However, beginning with World War II, and a different approach by the War Labor Board, union membership again increased rapidly. The main distinction between the War Labor Board and the National Labor Relations Board before the war was that the War Labor Board had the power to translate representation elections into contracts, whereas the National Labor Relations Board merely had the power to require employers to bargain with unions; it could not compel them to sign contracts. Even after the passage of the Wagner Act it was necessary for unions to win strikes in order to get contracts from recalcitrant employers. Union organizing therefore continued to depend heavily on economic power.

# 1937: The Turning Point for American Labor

## by Walter Galenson

The American labor movement was one of the pioneers of trade unionism. . . .

On the other side, American employers were second to none in their animosity toward trade unions. Every weapon in the arsenal of repression, including outright violence, was employed in the fight to prevent the organization of labor. Where repression failed, paternalistic schemes were employed; the decade preceding the 1929 crash is often called the era of "welfare capitalism" because of the concerted and successful campaign by employers to hold the loyalty of their employees through profit sharing, pension schemes, company housing, and other unilaterally conferred benefits.

Even before the Great Depression, the American labor movement was very weak. The economic crisis reduced it to a state of impotence. By 1933, the paper membership of the American Federation of Labor had fallen to 2.1 million, from a high of 4.7 million in 1920. Many of these members were not paying dues, others were not covered by union agreements, but were working under open shop conditions. There were about 25 million wage and salary workers in non-agricultural employment in 1933, so that the percentage of organization was very low indeed.

But even this does not tell the whole story. AFofL membership was concentrated in the building trades, the printing trades, and the railroads. During 1933 and 1934, in the flush of enthusiasm that accompanied the election of Franklin D. Roosevelt, coal miners and garment workers flocked to the unions, converting their industries from nonunion to union status almost over night. But the great strongholds of American manufacturing remained untouched. There were practically no organizations among workers in steel,

SOURCE Reprinted with permission from *Festskrift Til Frederik Zeuthen*, Copenhagen 1958; Institute of Industrial Relations, University of California, Berkeley, Reprint No. 120, 1959.

automobiles, industrial machinery, electrical goods, rubber, non-ferrous metals, chemicals, glass, lumber, food processing, and textiles. Of the service industries, truck transportation and wholesale and retail trade were operating largely on a non-union basis. Some of the major centers of heavy industry, such as Pittsburgh, Detroit, and Akron, were proudly "open shop."

Against this unpromising tableau, a great upsurge commenced. Incensed by the inability, and in some cases, the downright unwillingness of the dominant leaders of the American Federation of Labor to tackle the mass production industries, a rebel group within the AFofL formed a new, informal organization late in 1935, the Committee for Industrial Organization. Its thesis was that the craft structure of AFofL unionism was obsolete, and that only through large, industrial unions could the semi-skilled workers who manned manufacturing industry be organized successfully. The craft unions, jealous of their jurisdictional claims, expelled these proponents of industrial unionism from the AFofL, thus giving rise to two decades of bitter fratricidal strife within the labor movement.

The CIO set about the task of organizing the mass production workers in a systematic fashion. Within five years of its formation, it boasted 40 national unions, including some of the largest in the country. On the eve of American entry into the war, it had almost three million members.[1] More significant than quantity was the distribution of the membership. There were CIO unions in almost every branch of manufacturing, although in such industries as chemicals and petroleum, the unions had only a precarious toehold. The former geographical centers of anti-unionism had been converted into union strong-holds.

The great CIO drives were attended by widespread public alarm. But at the same time, there occurred a much less noticed but equally significant forward thrust by the AFofL. Revitalized by the spur of CIO competition, and forced by the logic of events to discard the constraints of craft union structure, the AFofL moved in two directions: to complete organization within its traditional areas of concentration, and into manufacturing. The Carpenter's Union, for example, which had been confined to building construction, branched out into lumber and woodworking. The Machinists' Union left railroad roundhouses and small machine shops for aircraft and shipbuilding. By 1941, the AFofL had 4.6 million members. Total union membership, including AFofL, CIO, and independents, was about 8.3 million, making the labor movement of the United States one of the most formidable in the world.

The rate of union growth during this period was not uniform. There were two major waves, the first in 1937, the second commencing during the defense boom of 1940–1941, and continuing with greater or less intensity throughout the war. The 1937 episode, with which we shall be particularly concerned, was in many ways the more remarkable. It was the first successful assault upon the bastions of heavy industry. Although all the gains achieved in the initial spurt were not held, strong points were retained which led to further expansion when the economic recession of 1937–1939 had dissipated. It is not at all certain that without the 1937 union victories, the defense and wartime periods would have yielded so large a harvest of unionism. Indeed, the organization of American manufacturing might have been permanently forestalled. In any event, the issue was finally decided in 1937, after half a century of preparatory conflict.

---

[1] The CIO claimed five million members in 1941, but this was certainly an exaggeration. The estimate in the text is derived from contemporary CIO publications.

The question of why, within the space of a few months, there should have been such a tremendous burst of energy on the part of those forces seeking to bring the worker into trade unions, sweeping all before it in apparently invincible fashion, has never been explored. There can be no adequate development of the theme within the scope of this brief essay, but I shall attempt to delineate some of the elements which combined to produce the events of 1937.

The principal ingredient which went into the success of the 1937 campaign was the strength of organizational sentiment among American workers. Their belief in the efficiency of capitalism was all but destroyed by the shattering experience of the depression. It was not low wages which were fundamentally at the root of their dissatisfaction, for the CIO made its greatest headway in relatively high wage industries. What workers rebelled against was the insecurity of their employment, the arbitrary character of management decisions affecting their lives, and the speeding up of work by companies seeking desperately to prevent operating losses. A contemporary survey by an agency of the Federal government found:

*One of the psychological problems faced by the automobile worker today is the gamble that he knows he is facing as he goes to work each day. He sees the men waiting at the gate for an interview for employment. If he is feeling badly on a particular day and slows down in his gait, his straw-boss or foreman tells him, 'Step on it. If you don't want the job, there are thousands outside who do,' or, 'Look out the window and see the men waiting in line for your job.'[2]*

The pace of the work was a constant source of resentment, as a close student of automobile labor observed:

*Rebellion against the industry hit the speed-up like a tidal wave at the point when the man in the shop was convinced that the machine had failed to live up to its promise insofar as it affected him . . . automobile labor was pushed to the breaking point. Prodigious new quotas of output were wrung from lines that had been fast and taxing in the 20's . . . the men who tended the lines at the time considered the pace more than their bodies could stand. They could feel the speed-up in their bones. They were convinced that standing up to such a pace was aging and debilitating.[3]*

The economic background was of crucial significance. Industrial activity had risen steadily after the low point of 1932, and the outlook for the future at the beginning of 1937 was optimistic. Corporate profits reached a cyclical peak during the last quarter of 1936 and the first quarter of 1937.[4] The index of industrial production in May, 1937 was six per cent higher than the 1929 peak.

The picture was not without its dark side. Average unemployment in 1937 has been estimated at 20 per cent of the nonfarm labor forn.[5] But severe as this figure appears from our present vantage point, it represented a substantial degree of recovery from the 1933 level of 35.3 per cent unemployment. And the important thing was that expectations were for improvements rather than deterioration in business conditions. For the first time in eight years, firms were looking forward to substantial profits, and investors to dividends. Anything which might impair these

---

[2] U.S. National Recovery Administration, Preliminary Report on Regularization of Employment and Improvement of Labor Conditions in the Automobile Industry, January 23, 1935, p. 51.

[3] Keith Sward, *The Legend of Henry Ford*, New York, 1948, p. 353.

[4] Kenneth D. Roose, *The Economics of Recession and Revival*, New Haven, 1954, p. 204.

[5] National Bureau of Economic Research, *The Measurement and Behavior of Unemployment*, New York, 1957, p. 215.

expectations, including industrial strife, was to be avoided. In this respect, 1937 differed sharply from 1933–1934, when a similar burst of union enthusiasm foundered on the rocks of continued depression.

A favorable economic climate and worker desire to organize were necessary but not sufficient conditions for the successful prosecution of a drive to unionize the nation's industrial workers. Leadership with a will to surmount formidable obstacles, and to give central direction to the movement lest its energies be dissipated on innumerable small fronts, was a prime requisite. The group which controlled the American Federation of Labor did not possess the needed qualities. Engrossed with jurisdictional rivalries and intimidated by a decade and a half of adversity, men like William L. Hutcheson of the Carpenters and Arthur Wharton of the Machinists, who dominated the Executive Council of the AFofL, were not inclined to risk their hard-won treasuries and the modicum of organizational stability they had attained on risky organizational ventures. They counseled a policy of caution and slow advance. Moreover, they feared the effects of industrial unionism. When asked to contribute money for a campaign in steel, Wharton replied:

*It is rather a complex situation to step in and ask us to contribute money to put our organization out of existence where we have a number employed. We think the craft organization is all right . . . I do not feel disposed to obligate my organization in any way in a campaign that has for its purpose eliminating my organization from the jurisdiction belonging to it.*[6]

The mantle of leadership, at this crucial juncture, fell upon John L. Lewis, president of the United Mine Workers of America. There was nothing in Lewis' previous history to make him an obvious choice for the task. A political conserva-

tive, a lifelong adherent of the Republican Party, Lewis had become president of the coal miners' union in 1919. For the next decade, he presided over the decline of the union, resulting from the poor economic status of the industry. He ruthlessly and effectively stifled all opposition to his policies, and by expelling from membership those who disagreed with him, became the organization's absolute ruler. In 1930, the Mine Workers' Union had only 84,000 members out of a labor force of well over half a million men.

Between 1932 and 1935, however, there was a revival of interest in the union among coal miners accompanying the enactment of the National Industrial Recovery Act, which seemed to hold out Federal government protection of the right to organize. By April, 1935, average paid up coal membership had reached 541,000, about 95 per cent of the eligible employees. A treasury of $2,298,000 had been accumulated, a great sum for those days. In essence, what Lewis did was to throw the treasury of the Mine Workers' Union into the organization of steel and other mass production industries.

It soon became evident that if anyone could break the resistance of American employers to unionism, it was Lewis. He was as tough as the most anti-union employer; he possessed great administrative talents and had a flair for dramatizing himself and his cause; a superb orator, he was equally at home on the speaker's platform and before a radio microphone; and above all, he was willing to play for high stakes. Lewis was very much in the tradition of the industrial tycoons who had built American industry, only he operated on the other side of the fence. He had some very able associates, in particular, Sidney Hillman of the Amalgamated Clothing Worker's Union, but the 1937 campaign was very largely his creation.

President William Green of the AFofL

[6] American Federation of Labor, Meeting of the Executive Council, January 29–February 14, 1935.

had urged the creation of a special fund to finance an organizing drive in steel, but received no response within his organization. By way of contrast, the United Mine Workers' Union advanced $1,665,000 to other CIO unions during 1936 and 1937, while contributions by the men's and women's garment workers raised the total to almost two million dollars.[7] The money was used to establish newspapers, print leaflets, hire halls, buy radio time, and above all, to pay for the services of organizers, many of whom were experienced men and women from the coal industry and the needle trades. Philip Murray, vice president of the Mine Workers, became the head of the steel workers' organization. John Brophy, Van A. Bittner, Allen S. Haywood, Adolph Germer, Powers Hapgood, and William Mitch were among the mine union officials who were dispatched to positions of leadership in other industries.

The first great explosion came in the closing days of 1936, in the automobile industry. It took the form of the sit-down strike, in which workers occupied the factories, barricaded themselves, and resisted attempts at forcible eviction by resort to such weapons as automobile door hinges and fire hoses. A sufficient number of key plants of the General Motors Corporation were occupied to result in complete paralysis of the entire system, idling 200,000 employees. Management was utterly shaken, for although there had been some minor sit downs in rubber the previous summer, the extension of this anarcho-syndicalist weapon to the heart of American industry was entirely unexpected. Vice-President William S. Knudsen of GM wrote to the Automobile Workers' Union, in response to its request for a bargaining conference:

*Sit-down strikes are strikes. Such strikers are clearly trespassers and violators of the law of the land. We cannot have bona fide collective bargaining with sit-down strikers in illegal possession of plants. Collective bargaining cannot be justified if one party, having seized the plant, holds a gun at the other party's head.[8]*

\* \* \*

It is difficult even in retrospect to appreciate the revolutionary character of the sit-down strike, a labor weapon that was used with great effectiveness during the first six months of 1937, and then disappeared. Conservatives were outraged by it. A group of citizens headed by A. Lawrence Lowell, president-emeritus of Harvard University, urged immediate federal legislation to curb sit-downs, which were castigated in the following terms:

*Armed insurrection—defiance of law, order, and duly elected authority—is spreading like wildfire. It is rapidly growing beyond control . . . The issue is vital; it dwarfs any other issue now agitating the public mind; it attacks and undermines the very foundation of our political and social structure . . . freedom and liberty are at an end, government becomes a mockery, superseded by anarchy, mob rule, and ruthless dictatorship.[9]*

The willingness of ordinarily law abiding workers to adopt such an extreme course attests eloquently to the degree of their discontent. Not only in the case of General Motors, but again in their fight for recognition by the Chrysler Corporation, did they resort to this weapon, which the United States Supreme Court branded as illegal soon thereafter. However, the desired result was achieved, and by June, 1937, the Union had organized over half

---

[7] United Mine Workers of America, Proceedings of the Thirty-Seventh Constitutional Convention, 1942, pp. 154–155.
[8] *The New York Times,* January 1, 1937, p. 10.
[9] *The New York Times,* March 27, 1937.

a million automobile workers, and established itself firmly throughout the industry, with the sole exception of the Ford Motor Company.

John L. Lewis was the principal union negotiator in both the General Motors and Chrysler strikes. At the same time, he was engaged in secret conversations with Myron C. Taylor, chairman of the board of the United States Steel Corporation, the classic anti-union American firm. Recognition of the Steel Workers' Union by the Steel Corporation electrified the entire country, particularly because the union was generally believed to be weak, and had not called any strikes. What induced so abrupt an about-face by United States Steel is still not clear; among the contributing factors may have been the urgent desire to maintain current profit levels, pressure by the Federal government, and imminent large purchases of steel by the British Government, which insisted upon a guarantee of promt delivery in the interest of its rearmament program.[10] But about its effect there was no doubt; many an American employer concluded that further resistance to the CIO was futile.

The automobile and steel episodes emphasize a fourth factor that aided the unions in 1937: the benevolent attitude toward union aspirations that was characteristic of the Federal government, and many state governments as well. Prior to the Roosevelt Administration, the Federal government had maintained a suspicious neutrality at best, and at worst, antipathy toward labor unions. In 1935, the United States Congress enacted the National Labor Relations (Wagner) Act, which established the principle of collective bargaining as the national labor policy. In April, 1937, much to the surprise of American employers, the Supreme Court held the Wagner Act constitutional, and employers awoke to the fact that they were required by law to bargain in good faith with the representatives of their employees.

It was not only through legislation that the unions were assisted by government, however. The fact that the President of the United States had been elected with strong union support (John L. Lewis had contributed $500,000 to the Democratic Party during the 1936 presidential campaign), and against the strong opposition of the business community, was an important moral element. On the local level, pro-union officials often refused to use police and troops against strikers, and on occasion, aided the unions by forcing struck plants to close. During the steel organizing drive in Pennsylvania, the nation's major steel producing state, the Lieutenant-Governor of Pennsylvania, who had been the secretary-treasurer of the United Mine Workers, spoke at union rallies in towns which had long been barred to union organizers, escorted by the same state police who had broken the great steel strike of 1919. The political activity of the CIO in 1936 paid off handsomely in 1937.

*   *   *

The complete conquest of American industry was forestalled by a sudden, unexpected economic recession. In September, 1937, the most precipitous economic decline in American history began. Between that month and June, 1938, industrial production as a whole fell by 33 per cent, and the production of durable goods by over 50 per cent.[11] Unemployment rose to 26.4 per cent of the non-agricultural labor force.

The recession increased the resistance of employers, for with the expectation of declining prices and profits, there was no longer the same urgency to maintain production. It also reduced the willingness of

[10] For a more detailed discussion of this matter, see Walter Galenson, "The Unionization of the American Steel Industry," *International Review of Social History*, 1956, p. 2.

[11] Roose op. cit., p. 55.

workers to risk their job security in strikes, and made dues collection more difficult. The rout of the Steel Workers' Union in the bloody "Little Steel" strikes during the summer of 1937, in which many lives were lost, heralded the conclusion of the 1937 CIO drive. Major employers which had not been organized, including the Ford Motor Company, Westinghouse, Standard Oil of New Jersey, and Swift and Company, were confirmed in the wisdom of their decision not to follow the lead of the United States Steel Corporation.

The CIO was forced to curtail its activities drastically. The Steel Workers' Union, for example, cut its staff from 437 to 213 full time people. In industry after industry, the unions went on the defensive, and concentrated upon holding the gains they had made earlier in the year. A perusal of contemporary union documents reveals a uniform story of stagnation and decline, following swiftly on the brilliant promise of early 1937.

The American Federation of Labor, which had remained passive throughout the period of the CIO industrial drives, seemingly unable to adjust itself to the fast moving course of events, was less affected by the recession than was the CIO. Its major strength was in sectors of the economy—services and consumer nondurables—which were not hit as hard as heavy industry. Relying upon their greater experience and superior financial resources, AFofL unions took advantage of the loss of momentum by the CIO to launch a counterattack, in which they abandoned the craft structural form and made an all-out effort to attract the semiskilled worker. AFofL unions such as the Teamsters, the Carpenters, and the Machinists began to grow rapidly, and soon the AFofL outdistanced the CIO by a decisive margin, establishing itself once more as the dominant labor federation.

But despite its abrupt end, the CIO drive ranks as the most remarkable episode in the annals of American labor. It left behind a legacy of unionism in heavy industry which proved unshakable during several years of economic adversity, in contrast with the past, when only craft unionism had managed to weather depression. The entire social structure of the country, its basic power relationships, were altered fundamentally over the brief span of six months. The United States had suddenly been propelled into the ranks of those nations in which the voice of organized labor counted.

### Government Regulation of Union Activities

Although union growth in the United States has been caused mainly by economic forces, government regulation has also played an important role. The government's atitude toward unions has changed considerably through time, as Charles Gregory demonstrates in the next selection, "Government Regulation or Control of Union Activities" (from William Haber, editor, *Labor in a Changing America*, New York, Basic Books, 1966). Early labor organizations were controlled mainly through the conspiracy doctrine and the injuntion. According to Gregory, during these early years, ". . . the courts applied a double standard by denying to unions what they let business groups do."

Labor organizations were also regulated by the Sherman Anti-Trust Act of 1890: Under its terms ". . . most union interferences with the movement of goods in interstate commerce" were regarded by the federal courts "as unlawful restraints of trade."

However, the depression of the 1930's caused considerable change in labor policy. The depression not only caused public opinion to shift from employers to unions, but also led to the belief, expressed in the National Labor Relations Act, that economics as well as equity required the establishment of collective bargaining. Collective bargaining was equitable because the government had encouraged the growth of employers' power by permitting them to form "corporate and other forms of business enterprise." At the same time, the government had used its power to prevent the spread of the labor movement. It therefore was equitable to allow workers to organize. Economic considerations were important because there was a prevailing belief that a major cause of the depression was a failure of purchasing power by workers and farmers who sold on competitive markets and bought their supplies from manufacturers who had the power to fix prices. Congress therefore thought that collective bargaining might sustain purchasing power and stabilize economic conditions; it therefore passed the Norris-La Guardia Act in 1932 to make it difficult for employers to use injunctions and "yellow-dog" contracts against unions, and the National Labor Relations Act of 1935 to make it possible for workers to organize and bargain collectively through representatives of their own choosing. Moreover, during the 1930's courts began to hand down decisions more favorable to organized labor.

However, as unions grew during the late 1930's and World War II, public opinion turned against them and Congress passed the Taft-Hartley Act in 1947 and the Landrum-Griffin Act in 1959.

# Government Regulation or Control of Union Activities

## by Charles Gregory

### EARLY JUDICIAL CONTROL OF LABOR UNIONS

Before 1910, the regulation and control of American labor unions was chiefly by judge-made law. Workers who used economic pressure to spread union organization in the early 1800's were held guilty of common-law criminal conspiracy. But this device for controlling unions was abandoned around 1850. Courts soon began to allow peaceful strikes for immediate benefits. But most judges thought that campaigns to extend union organization were unlawful. Actions for damages had become the only recourse in these cases. Then around 1880, state courts developed a far more effective device—the labor injunction. This remedy protected only against the tortious invasion of property rights. But our state courts soon invented theories making most peaceful union self-help pressures unlawful.

The courts had always allowed business combinations to eliminate trade rivals and control markets. No legal wrong was done if they were pursuing self-interest and gain. But if *unions* sought to protect *their* standards by eliminating nonunion employers and workers, the courts held this to be wrongful for the spread of unionization led to monopoly. And though monopoly was not tortious according to common law, the courts declared it to be an illegal purpose for union self-help. This was enough to support the labor injunction. Moreover, peaceful secondary boycotts and organizational picketing were made torts in themselves. Thus the courts applied a double standard by denying to unions what they let business groups do.

### THE LABOR INJUNCTION

The labor injunction was the most ruthless anti-union weapon ever devised. It

SOURCE Reprinted with permission from Chapter 17 of *Labor in a Changing America* edited by William Haber, © 1966 by Basic Books, Inc., Publishers, New York.

was used to protect business only when unions threatened employers with organizing pressures. This remedy was far more effective than other legal sanctions. Criminal prosecutions and damage suits required extensive pleadings, months of waiting, and jury trials. But a judge could issue an injunction without a jury trial. And he could issue a temporary injunction without any trial at all. Thus strikes, picket lines, and boycotts could be smothered before they really got started. Anyone disobeying an injunction was summarily thrown into jail for contempt of court, again without jury trial.

## SHERMAN ANTI-TRUST ACT—1890

As industry grew larger, employers began to produce for markets in other states and buy materials from outside. Then the Sherman Anti-Trust Act was passed in 1890. It was believed to be designed to apply only to business organizations as an anti-trust measure. This act was enforced by indictments, triple damage suits, and injunctions. Under its terms, federal courts soon began to apply it to labor unions and to regard most union interferences with the movement of goods in interstate commerce as unlawful restraints of trade. Unions exerted organizational pressures on nonunion employers by peaceful boycotts. Because they disrupted the interstate movements of goods, the Supreme Court ruled that these boycotts violated the Sherman Act. But clearly they were not restraints of trade at all. The unions were simply trying to improve their conditions of work—not to monopolize the market for goods. They obstructed the transit of goods; but so did train robbers. And nobody would think of suing *them* under the Sherman Act.

But the Supreme Court refused to declare simple strikes unlawful under the Sherman Act merely because they disrupted the flow of goods in commerce.

To show a violation in this area required proof that the strike was intended to unionize the employer—and for the purpose of eliminating competition between union-made and nonunion-made goods in interstate markets. Thus bargaining strikes which also obstructed the flow of goods in commerce would never be violations. Clearly the Supreme Court was using the Sherman Act merely as a device to stop the spread of union organization. And its concern over the movement of goods in commerce was only *incidental.*

## ANTI-INJUNCTION MEASURES: THE CLAYTON ACT OF 1914 AND THE NORRIS-LA GUARDIA ACT OF 1932

At the same time, the labor injunction flourished in common law in federal and state courts. In 1914, Congress passed the Clayton Act to limit use of the injunction against union self-help pressures in labor disputes. Section 6 of the Act declared that the labor of a human being was not a commodity. Section 20 seemed to offer some relief from the courts injunctive process. But this measure was so narrowly construed that injunctions against union organizational drives continued. All that the Clayton Act *actually* did was to allow further injunctive relief against unions under the Sherman Act. In the 1920's, Professor Felix Frankfurter headed an attempt to promulgate a *really* effective anti-injunction law. The result was the Norris-La Guardia Act of 1932. This act defined permissible labor disputes broadly enough to include organizational drives against nonunion employers. It required only that the union have an economic interest in employment conditions at the nonunion plant. Then it described the permissible union self-help techniques—the strike, the secondary boycott, and picketing. Such devices when used in a labor dispute as defined were nonenjoinable in federal courts.

## CHANGING FEDERAL POLICY—NATIONAL LABOR RELATIONS ACT OF 1935

While this act did not legalize organizational pressures, it removed the injunction, employers' only effective defense against unions. Certainly it meant congressional approval of union expansion throughout entire industries by economic self-help. But it left employers free to fight back with economic weapons by discriminating against employees who supported unionism. The National Industrial Recovery Act of 1933 and the amended Railway Labor Act of 1934 had introduced the principle that employees could join unions without employer interference. But in 1935, Congress passed the National Labor Relations Act, or Wagner Act, to replace the NIRA which was ruled unconstitutional. That statute prohibited anti-union conduct by most employers. If an employer interfered with his employees' attempts to organize unions or tried to dominate such unions, if he discriminated against employees for their union interest or refused to bargain with newly formed unions, he was committing unfair labor practices. The National Labor Relations Board, set up under the terms of the Wagner Act, ordered these unfair practices stopped and granted remedies such as reinstatement of employees with back pay. And the federal courts enforced these orders. Thus, Congress proclaimed the national policy of strong affiliated labor unions organized throughout entire industries. In upholding this statute, the Supreme Court greatly expanded the commerce power of Congress to cover virtually all important units of industry and production. Thereafter unions began to form and grow rapidly.

## REPRESENTATIONAL FUNCTIONS OF THE NATIONAL LABOR RELATIONS BOARD

The Labor Relations Board administers an elaborate procedure enabling workers to select or reject unions. Many employers voluntarily recognize unions formed or chosen by their employees. The Board conducts elections when necessary, especially where two or more unions are competing for representational rights. The Board has strict rules governing attempts by outside unions to displace already recognized unions. It will protect an established employer—union contract relationship for three years. Then an outside union may call for an election. To avoid needless conflict, the AFL-CIO has developed no-raiding pacts, administered by an impartial arbitrator. The Board's enormously complicated task of handling these representational matters is a most important aspect of regulating and controlling unions today.

## UNION IMMUNITY FROM ANTI-TRUST LAWS

The anti-injunction and Wagner acts clearly made the expansion of union strength the prevailing national policy. At the same time, the interpretations of the Sherman Act remained unchanged. Under them, union self-help pressures to extend unionism and eliminate nonunionism were still illegal. The Supreme Court should have recognized this contradiction and have overruled its earlier decisions, making organizational strikes and boycotts illegal under the Sherman Act. But what it did in the 1941 Hutcheson Case was to indulge in some judicial sleight of hand. It said that since peaceful union self-help conduct in a broad labor dispute context is no longer enjoinable, it is lawful for all purposes—even under the Sherman Act. It based this incredible inference on Section 20 of the Clayton Act which was rejuvenated by the later Norris-La Guardia Act. In effect, the Hutcheson doctrine removed labor unions from the jurisdiction of the Sherman Anti-Trust Act. However, it could still be applied if the unions' conduct was violent or if they connived with employers to restrain trade.

## PEACEFUL PICKETING
## AND FREE SPEECH—1937–1949

By 1930, a few state courts allowed peaceful organizational picketing and secondary boycotts. But most of them curtailed such conduct by injunctions or criminal statutes. In 1940, however, the Supreme Court declared peaceful picketing to be constitutionally protected free speech. This placed it beyond the power of states to control. Most lawyers accepted the identity of picketing and free speech; but many thought it palpably untenable for even *peaceful* picketing cannot be dissociated from a pattern of coercion. And if it *were* merely free speech, Congress could not regulate it. Fortunately, the Supreme Court withdrew protection from peaceful picketing wherever its compliance would force the picketed employer to commit a crime. Thus, his refusal to sell ice to nonunion peddlers in compliance with picketing demands would be a violation of the state anti-monopoly law. Soon states were freely allowed to circumvent this constitutional doctrine simply by making the union's demands on the picketed employer contrary to public policy.

The Supreme Court then extended the doctrine of federal preemption to prevent states from regulating unions. In the Wagner Act, Congress had guaranteed employees and unions the right to promote their interests by concerted activities, and the states were powerless to impose conflicting controls over union conduct guaranteed protection in federal statutes, except when violence occurred.

## RAILWAY LABOR ACTS—1926 AND 1934

After decades of bitter strikes, the railroad brotherhoods were firmly established. In the 1926 Railway Labor Act, Congress provided mediation and voluntary arbitration of bargaining disputes, with emergency powers vested in the President. This was unsatisfactory since the carriers still interfered with the union organization of their employees. The amended Railway Labor Act of 1934 created boards of adjustment to dispose of grievances and the National Mediation Board to handle all unsettled bargaining and representational disputes. It clarified and enforced the rights of employees and unions to organize and bargain collectively, introducing the principle of majority rule. Moreover, in 1951, Congress permitted the carriers and brotherhoods to contract for the union shop.

Changes in labor relations laws and policies were constant from 1935 to around 1950. But World War II dominated this period. Thus, although there were many strong unions by 1941—unions maintaining a tremendous pressure for higher wages and other concessions—in industries that had never been organized before, and this continued during the war, a war economy could not afford to have strikes. The War Labor Board was created to handle the constantly recurring disputes between unions and employers. Although strikes never were prohibited, the unions made voluntary no-strike pledges that were honored almost 100 per cent.

War Labor Board tripartite panels held hearings on bargaining demands. Sometimes they persuaded the parties to settle. Usually they made recommendations on issues that remained unsettled. The War Labor Board affirmed or modified these, in the end promulgating final contracts. The War Labor Board kept wages at a reasonably stable level, made a sensible compromise on the issue of union security, and refused to include novel items in collective agreements. But most important for the future of labor relations, it added grievance arbitration to thousands of contracts.

\* \* \*

## TAFT-HARTLEY ACT—1947

The intensive strikes for money items and the closed union shop immediately after World War II contributed to Congress' passage of the Taft-Hartley Act in 1947. Title I of this statute is the amended National Labor Relations Act. The original National Labor Relations Act designated only unfair labor practices of employers. Unions were free to exercise any organizational and bargaining pressures. Unions were guaranteed the right to strike, and employees the right to engage in concerted activities. The National Labor Relations Board protected most of this conduct from employers' reprisals. When labor organizations had become very strong, extreme union self-help tactics were regarded as intolerable. This conduct included pressures against employers to force their employees to organize, pressures directly against employees themselves, secondary picketing and boycotting which implicated neutral employers and their employees, and even pressures against employers to ignore National Labor Relations Board certifications of other unions. Most unions sought the closed or union shop.

## UNIONS' UNFAIR LABOR PRACTICES

Congress amended the National Labor Relations Act by defining six unfair labor practices of unions. The first made it unfair for unions to restrain or coerce employees. The second prohibited unions from trying to make employers discriminate against nonunion employees. The third was a union's refusal to bargain in good faith with the appropriate employer. But the fourth was the most elaborate: Subsection A outlawed union secondary labor boycotts; whereas, Subsection B allowed secondary tactics if the union was certified to the employer against whom the pressure was aimed. Subsection C outlawed union attempts to make an employer deal with a union when another union had been certified to him by the National Labor Relations Board. Subsection D made it an unfair practice for unions to engage in work-jurisdiction disputes, where two unions claim the right to do certain work, and each strikes if the employer gives the work to members of the other union.

The fifth unfair labor practice was to prevent excessively large initiation fees under a valid union-shop agreement. In a union shop, an employer is free to hire anyone he pleases, but he must agree to discharge an employee who refuses to join the union or who does not pay his dues. Under the Wagner Act, federal policy accepted the closed union shop if the employer agreed to hire only union members. This is forbidden by the 1947 statute. But employers, now free to hire anybody they please, may make and enforce agreements requiring both new and old employees to join the union. However, Congress deferred to the states in 1947 by specifying that any state was free to forbid agreements making employment conditional on union membership. Now there are about twenty of these so-called right-to-work statutes. A corporation with plants in forty states may have a master contract with one union covering all these plants; but half of these plants might be union shops and half of them not because of local right-to-work laws.

Whether to have union security or right-to-work statutes is a contentious issue. Supporters of right-to-work laws say that they allow employment without paying tribute to unions. Opponents of these acts say they are meant to keep unions weak by denying them financial support from workers who profit by union bargaining gains. They call such nonunion workers free riders. A compromise is the so-called agency shop where an employee pays the equivalent of union dues without actually joining the union. The National Labor Relations Board finds this compromise acceptable; but right-to-work states are in disagreement about the agency shop. Unions want Congress to permit union shops throughout industry as it did on the railroads in 1951.

### Featherbedding

Another union unfair labor practice which was declared unlawful was featherbedding, the device of gaining employment and pay for unnecessary and unwanted services.

\* \* \*

## ORGANIZATION OF GOVERNMENT EMPLOYEES

The 1947 statute contained additional restraints on unions. Strikes by government employees were declared unlawful, and individual offenders are summarily discharged. Government employees have long been allowed to organize, but their use of collective strength in bargaining has always been discouraged. Recently an effective representational procedure was established to enable organization of government employees. And plans are afoot to develop some type of negotiation—possibly with arbitration—to set terms and conditions of work for public employees. Collective bargaining by government workers has become a critical issue in states and municipalities. School teachers, policemen, and firemen, hospital workers, and other public employees also understand and seek to use the advantages of organization. Their strikes would generally be thought to be illegal. Everyone but the public employees themselves seem to think that their services cannot be suspended. Since we all hate to pay higher taxes in order to improve public working conditions, how else can group bargaining be made effective than by the strike? Negotiation with expert mediators might suffice, but eventually arbitrators may have to break the log jams. This is an extreme recourse, but if strikes of public workers are to be forbidden, a substitute must be found. The only answer seems to be some sort of arbitration.

## NATIONAL EMERGENCY STRIKES

In the Taft-Hartley Act, Congress provided a method of controlling national emergency strikes, except those handled under the Railway Labor Act. Whenever the President thinks an industry-wide strike imperils the national health or safety, he sets up an emergency board to investigate and report to him. The President may then direct the Attorney General to have the strike or lockout enjoined. Federal mediators undertake to secure agreement between the parties. If the dispute is not settled in sixty days, the National Labor Relations Board files a supplemental report containing the employer's last offer to the union. The National Labor Relations Board then conducts a secret ballot among the employees to see if they wish to accept the offer. The injunction is then dissolved. If settlement has not been reached, the strike may be resumed. By that time, the President has made a complete report to Congress.

This device has been invoked twenty-four times, and the Supreme Court upheld this procedure in the steel strike of 1959. It declared that by "national health" Congress meant that of the economy as a whole and the general well-being of the country. Another technique used during the war was seizure and public operation of strike-bound plants. The Supreme Court declared that the President has no such power of seizure, however, in the absence of specific legislation granting him such authority. The President has appointed groups to handle disputes between unions and employers under contract with the Atomic Energy Commission or engaged in missile construction. When mediation fails, the appropriate panel takes jurisdiction, requesting the parties to appear and submit their claims. After hearings, the panel makes recommendations disposing of the various demands presented. The parties' submission to this procedure is entirely voluntary, but it has been effective in avoiding disruptive strikes.

## ENFORCEMENT OF COLLECTIVE BARGAINING

Since 1935, a kind of self-government, far more effective than any imposed control or regulation, has evolved in collective bargaining. This is chiefly a result of increased union responsibility. A generation ago, labor unions generally could not sue or be sued. The Wagner Act greatly increased the number of unions and resulting collective agreements, but provided no means for their enforcement. Finally in 1947, Congress provided that the parties might sue each other in the federal courts if the employer operated in interstate commerce. Under this vague provision, the Supreme Court would not let unions directly sue to enforce promises dealing with the terms and conditions of individual employment. Federal courts could enforce promises to unions, however, including commitments to arbitrate unsettled grievances arising under contracts.

## GRIEVANCE ARBITRATION

Since World War II, thousands of collective agreements provided for such arbitration. Now that unions could compel employers to comply with promises to arbitrate, it became possible to enforce provisions dealing with individual terms and conditions of employment. This whole development of grievance arbitration has become one of the most stabilizing controls in modern labor relations. Strikes seldom occur now, except when new agreements are bargained. With longer and longer contract terms, arbitration of unsettled matters arising under them will greatly minimize wasteful disputes.

\* \* \*

## POLITICAL CONTRIBUTIONS BY UNIONS

The Taft-Hartley Act makes it unlawful for unions to contribute money to support political candidates in federal elections. It forbids unions and their officials to demand or accept money from employers and to condone payments to employees where no services are performed. These are largely to prevent bribery and shakedowns.

## REGULATION OF INTERNAL UNION AFFAIRS

Traditionally, courts refused to interfere with the internal affairs of labor unions, treating them like clubs and lodges. They would protect vested property rights of members, but only when remedies within the organization were exhausted. Many unions would not admit Negroes or would only let them join auxiliaries, with no voting rights. But some courts now regard this as a denial of equal protection under the Constitution. The National Labor Relations Board recently revoked the certification of a union that refused to admit or represent Negroes. Unions are under fire where they prevent Negroes from obtaining employment by denying them membership. Since 1959, in the Landrum-Griffin Act, Congress has required unions to file elaborate reports with the government concerning their internal affairs. This statute also grants redress to employees against union officials who deny them the right to participate in union meetings and elections. But its chief concern is to prevent union officials from misappropriating funds. As unions have become more powerful, a greater measure of control has been necessary to insure their fiduciary responsibilities. Furthermore, unions are now sufficiently public in nature so that disclosure of their internal affairs is essential.

\* \* \*

## Union Responsibility

Although "The Price of Union Responsibility," was written in 1948, its basic theme is as valid now as it was then. In this article, Lloyd Fisher, develops the proposition that the American labor movement will be "responsible" when its institutional survival or sovereignty is secure. He emphasizes the process whereby a union is transformed from a protest to a business organization. In his view, a union will become responsible when it has "sovereignty sufficient for the political body to make its rules and to police its membership."

Moreover, according to Fisher, issues of sovereignty, which are essential to industrial peace and stability, are much more difficult to resolve than economic issues, which can be compromised. Therefore, "the basic long-term requirement for industrial peace is much more a political settlement than an economic settlement." Such settlements had, in his judgment, been achieved in Great Britain and Sweden, but not in the United States. (However, as noted in connection with our discussion of European labor movements, nationwide bargaining arrangements that meet institutional needs of unions and employers tend to cause trouble when they become unresponsive to the needs of individual workers in the shop.) Although Fisher clearly considered a secure labor movement essential to political and social stability, he was critical of the American labor movement for relying too much on employers to guarantee union sovereignty instead of building a stronger base among the workers.

# The Price of Union Responsibility

## by Lloyd H. Fisher

One of the more difficult tasks of a democratic society is the reconciliation of irreconcilable objectives. The objectives that give concern are not those of contending pressure groups, for our political institutions are reasonably well designed for this type of reconciliation. The difficult tasks arise when, out of a confusion of means and ends, the public itself makes inconsistent and incompatible demands.

The present demand for labor legislation is a major case in point. Most readers of the political horoscope would agree that there is a considerable body of public sentiment for some kind of restriction upon labor. The object of this legislation, broadly conceived, would be to secure by statute a more responsible labor movement. Its principal means would be to limit the authority and effectiveness of the trade union.

As the term "responsibility" is custom- arily employed, it is intended to describe a complex of desirable moral traits. The responsible union leader is able to commit his union to an agreement and to the observance of that agreement. He may be a formidable adversary at the bargaining table, but the bargain once concluded is a contract and therefore sanctified. He represents his constituents well, and within the common commercial assumptions of a capitalist society, conceding the right of employers to reasonable profit. He believes in a fair day's work for a fair day's wage.

Then too, economists often use the word "responsibility" to denote concern for the effects of a given set of wage demands upon the general economic welfare. A responsible trade union will not make excessive wage demands. We may define "excessive demands" as those which will result in price increases, destruction of

SOURCE Reprinted with permission from the National Conference of Social Work and published in the Proceedings of its Seventy-fourth Annual Meeting by Columbia University Press, New York, 1948.

capital, unemployment, or all three. For present purposes, the term "responsibility" will be employed in its more customary sense of commercial morality, although the two meanings need not be antagonistic.

As unions grow in strength and become securely established in the economic life of the nation, their roles may undergo a substantial change. Arising out of deeply felt grievances and propelled by a widespread sense of injustice and insecurity, the original organizing impulse of most unions was one of protest. But as the union redresses injustice, improves wages, grows in its control of job opportunities, and generally develops an area of sovereignty which is the fundamental quest of the movement in America, its original motivations are frequently attenuated, its broad objectives narrowed, its passion for social justice calmed. The union acquires valuable contracts, treasuries, an apparatus, an officialdom. It has its own laws in the form of a constitution, a grant of territory from its central body, its internal courts, its legislative and excutive functions. From management, an area of economic control has been wrested. In short, it has been transformed from a protest organization to a business organization enjoying a substantial degree of political and economic autonomy and with resources and enterprises of its own.

Characteristically, it is in this phase of development that unions are most responsible, when contracts are most likely to be held sacred, when leadership is most likely to guarantee the performance of membership. The trade union secure in the hegemony over what it claims in jurisdiction, ordinarily unstinted recognition, and job control is most likely to develop the pattern of business responsibility.

The question that must be met by business revolves around a guess as to whether the labor movement, secure in an autonomous position with sovereignty over its constituents, can better be fitted into the structure of a business community than the union whose sovereignty is bitterly contested within the plant, within the community, and within the nation.

In a complex society such as our own the distance between membership and leadership grows daily wider. The separation between ownership and management which occurred long ago in the joint stock corporations has its analogies in the labor union. The separation is not yet so great, but it continues to grow. The union executive can often speak with the same authority that lends so much weight to the statements of a corporation president.

This is true, not so much because of usurpation of power, as because of the growing complexity of our society. The case was clearly stated by Karl Mannheim when he observed that modern man lives increasingly within a smaller and smaller segment of total social experience. What is true resembles less and less what would appear to be true as measured by the daily experiences of the ordinary worker. So a great deal must be delegated to the union leader—not only of the execution and interpretation of policy, but of the interpretation of fact as well.

The labor leader lives partly in the world of management and partly in the world of the worker. He has frequently to choose between the role of militant rank-and-file leader and that of business envoy to management, between the conduct of a military campaign and the negotiation of a commercial treaty.

The public focus on the specific issues involved in disputes over contract renewals obscures the underlying conflict. Wages, hours, and working conditions are important means of labor union action, but they are not its ends. The fundamental quest of the labor movement is for sovereignty in all matters affecting the employment relationship. The conflict which underlies our industrial relations is the contest for the loyalty of the American worker. It is for this reason precisely that neither side will count the monetary cost of strikes too closely.

The essential issue is whether the function of an employer shall be confined to that of the entrepreneur, or whether he must, by the exercise of this function, be a boss as well. Long after the disintegration of the guilds, the word for employer was still "master." Although "master" has now lost its synonymity with "employer," it is still at the borders of this same problem that the battle rages.

The National Association of Manufacturers declared in 1914 that "the real and ideal union is the one between employer and employee." Its platform of December, 1946, and the legislative proposals which correspond to it do not vary substantially from this earlier theme. Measures introduced into Congress include bans on the closed shop, the union shop, preferential hiring, maintenance of membership, secondary boycotts, and, most interesting of all, on industry-wide bargaining. It is reasonably clear that each of these measures is squarely aimed at the political aspirations of the labor movement for sovereignty. The prohibitions against all forms of union security are intended to establish the sovereignty of the individual worker, and the ban against industry-wide bargaining, to deny labor the right to federate into a national state.

The demands of a union are twofold. There are the worker-oriented demands concerning wages, hours, and working conditions. Perhaps even more important are the union-oriented demands for the closed shop, or some variant of it, and the dues check-off.

A modern union is not identical with its membership any more than a corporation is the simple sum of its stockholders, and so it is not unreasonable that the union should have requirements which are distinct and separate from those of its membership. Any experienced management negotiator understands that it is essential to a labor union that gains be made

in its name. The employer who offers an unsolicited wage increase will find it no substitute for an increase bargained for by the union. He will merely have added to the total cost if, indeed, he is not found guilty of an unfair labor practice by the Federal courts.

It is an axiom of management that responsibility must go hand in hand with authority. This is quite as true in industrial relations as elsewhere. If the object is responsible trade union action, the ends will not be served by the proposed attack upon the institutional structure of unionism. The true sources of conservatism, and therefore of responsibility, spring from the institutional requirements of the labor union as a continuing political body rather than from the transitory and more or less accidental composition of its rank-and-file membership. To be responsible, therefore, the prime requirement is sovereignty sufficient for the political body to make its rules and to police its membership.

All political bodies are organized for internal control as well as external aggression. The labor union too has its system of internal enforcement as well as its apparatus for external conflict. The means at the disposal of a well-organized trade union for controlling its membership are at least as great as the facilities of the unorganized employer for disciplining his employees. The union, then, potentially is a means, not only of representing the worker, but of guaranteeing his performance as well. As a sovereign power may guarantee the behavior of its nationals, so the sovereign trade union may pledge the performance of its members.

In the search for industrial peace there are two broad paths discernible. Along one path lies the curbing of the right of association. Senator Joseph H. Ball, of Minnesota, in his measure to outlaw industry-wide bargaining, has proclaimed this course the only liberal alternative. The other path is marked by the deliberate encouragement of association, the conscious use of balance of power as the strategy of industrial peace.

Which way is chosen depends upon how high an evaluation is placed upon the costs of industrial peace. If industrial peace is the paramount objective, the warring parties can best make it. But obviously, the ability to make peace is synonymous with the power to make it, and the power to make peace involves a status, a territory, and a sovereignty that American labor has not yet attained and American industry has never been willing to concede. If there is to be a settlement, labor and management must be strong enough to propose terms and to accept them and, having accepted them, to enforce them. The alternative, if we are not to have nationalization of industry on the one hand or an utterly debilitated labor movement on the other, will be those hundreds of skirmishes, punctuated with occasional major encounters, which have written the recent history of industrial relations in America.

Public emphasis has commonly dwelt on the economic aspects of industrial disputes. These are the body of labor's demands, the current, continuous, and public issues in the majority of controversies that meet the public eye. Yet these are not the most difficult issues, nor are they the deep and fundamental sources of long-continuing discord between management and unions. For these are also the arbitrable issues and the ones which increasingly are submitted to a third party for settlement when the principals fail to agree.

There are, as well, issues which neither management nor labor will submit to impartial determination, which in the long run are even more important to the building and maintenance of industrial peace. These are the issues of sovereignty. Just as a national state holds its sovereignty inviolable, so the great states of Labor and Management hold certain territory inviol-

able. They will bargain over the terms upon which the employment relationship will be based and, if necessary, submit the differences to arbitration. But each reserves an area the propriety of which it will not refer to an outside party. These nonarbitrable issues of industrial relations must be resolved by mutual agreement or by warfare.

The specific issues which are nonarbitrable will vary somewhat from situation to situation, but in the main the outlines are clear. For management, the reservation, central and nonarbitrable, is the right of management to noninterference in the direction of the enterprise. For labor, the equivalent condition is a set of guarantees that the institutional security of the union will not be challenged. Management and labor will interpret the specific contract guarantees necessary to these ends differently, according to the situation. The island bases which labor may regard as necessary to the security of its mainland are often interpreted as bases for attack by management, and the reverse is as commonly true.

The basic, long-term requirement for industrial peace is much more a political settlement than an economic settlement. No single point enunciated by the N.A.M. in its program for industrial peace deals with wages. I have no intention of deprecating the importance of economic settlements. The failure to arrive at economic agreements will produce strikes as certainly as failures of political agreement. But peacemaking institutions for bringing about economic accord are well developed. The successful practice of private, voluntary arbitration has grown markedly in recent years and has excellent prospects of even greater development. None of the machinery for the development of national political agreements exists in America, and the first steps necessary to bring it into existence have been and are being bitterly opposed.

The United States is not without a

history of effort toward political settlement. The Industrial Commission of 1901, the United States Commission on Industrial Relations of 1912, and the President's Industrial Conference of 1919–20 each emphasized the need of finding a *modus vivendi* within which labor and industry could subsist secure in the necessary privileges and immunities. Each of these was without substantial result; and indeed the most ambitious plan, that put forth by the President's Industrial Conference of 1919–20, was roundly attacked by labor as thinly disguised company unionism.

The first War Labor Board, under the chairmanship of former President William H. Taft, reached an emergency settlement of the problems of status by simply freezing union security where it was when the Board took jurisdiction. The Board enunciated the principle that it would neither grant, augment, nor diminish any form of union security then in force.

With the passage of the Railway Labor Act in 1926 and its amendments in 1934, the principle of exclusive representation for purposes of collective bargaining was introduced into law. Under its terms, management was required to deal with a single employee representative of any craft or other appropriate unit, whenever a majority of the appropriate employees so decided.

The National Industrial Recovery Act of 1933 wrote collective bargaining into the law of the land, and the National Labor Relations Act made exclusive representation in collective bargaining mandatory whenever a majority of affected employees so declared in elections conducted by the National Labor Relations Board.

There have been two recent developments of significance. The National War Labor Board achieved a striking measure of success during the war years. It gave to labor a status which by itself it had been unable to achieve—equal representation with industry in the highest industrial tribunal of the land; and, equally impor-

tant, it denied the unorganized worker, not only representation, but likewise access to the judical apparatus of the Board. In this brief period alone, organized labor came into equal sovereignty on a national scale.

The President's Labor-Management Conference of November, 1945, an invitation to labor and management to work out the terms of industrial peace in the postwar world, found both parties unwilling to conclude voluntarily the political settlement which was asked of them.

But all these measures were limited in their achievement. The series of Presidential commissions, culminating in the Conference of November, 1945, were utter failures. The legislative enactments had for their principal objects the strengthening of labor's bargaining power so that, now more nearly equal in power, it might generate the pressure necessary to accomplish a stable settlement. That the NLRA did greatly increase the strength and power of labor is undoubted. The increase in union membership subsequent to its passage offers ample proof. But, primarily, it equipped labor to occupy that restless middle ground between the *pax Romana* and the negotiated peace. The National War Labor Board was unable and unwilling to survive the national emergency even in an attenuated form more appropriate to peacetime.

Periodically, attention is directed to those apparently happier nations across the sea—England and Sweden—where industrial relations are conducted on a higher plane. The outstanding fact in both England and Sweden is that the basic political agreement between industry and labor has been reached, relatively informally in England, formally in Sweden.

The hallmark of a political settlement is the development of strong employers' associations for industry-wide, market-wide, nation-wide, and, on occasion, class-wide bargaining between management and labor. In England and Sweden organization has been met by counter-organization, federation of unions by federation of employers. Local bargaining has virtually disappeared, and interposed between the individual employer and his employees are authoritative bodies of employers and unions able to propose settlements and to enforce them.

The simple significance of the British and Swedish experience is that labor and management have come to terms. These terms are not the wages, hours, and working conditions of the steel industry or the boot and shoe industry, for these will be annually disputed. They are the more fundamental terms of political recognition, and only with political recognition can genuinely diplomatic negotiations take place. British and Swedish industry has long proclaimed a preference for dealing with strong national unions, for the British Tory and the Swedish Conservative know know what many American industrialists do not—that the center of labor is conservative and that militance and radicalism come from the periphery. They know that what strengthens the institutional structure of labor potentially increases its bonds with management.

Such a political settlement will not satisfy the great American quest for moral absolutes and cost-free solutions. But there are no cost-free solutions.

The conservative American industrialist should be calculating the price which he is willing to pay for a conservative and responsible labor movement; for there is every probability that a conservative labor movement can be had at a price that is not too great. The intelligent conservative cannot fail to have noted that the labor movement has in the past rendered valiant service in the campaign for high tariffs. He must have noted the opposition of important sections of organized labor to the public ownership of utilities. It will not have escaped him that labor has sometimes opposed the minimum wage, has stood shoulder to shoulder with industry

in opposition to compulsory arbitration, that the outstanding speech on free enterprise at the President's Labor-Management Conference came, not from the president of the N.A.M., but from the president of the United Mine Workers. Finally, he will have observed that within the labor movement those unions with the greatest institutional security are politically the farthest from the left. All these considerations constitute one account in the ledger.

In the other account are the cost items. A grant of sovereignty cannot be made conditionally. Power thus conceded, however felicitous its use in national affairs, will be used in plant or factory as well. It will abruptly terminate the dream of complete sway for the manager over his enterprise. It may involve the use against the employer of demands too great to resist and too costly to accept. To the extent that the territory of labor is augmented, that of management declines.

In intrinsic terms, the choice ought to be a close one, narrowly balanced and delicately poised. Yet there is little reason to believe that American management will tarry long over the decision. As a matter of fact, the decision has been made and is already embodied in a series of drastic bills. That management has decided to wage such large-scale battle against the sovereignty of the labor union is not evidence of any dearth of intelligent conservatism. It is merely a judgment of the necessity for concession, and a conclusion that labor's bargaining power is not yet great enough to command a political settlement.

It is as reasonable to lay the causes of industrial unrest to the weakness of labor as to its strength. For labor has not earned politically its present area of sovereignty. The hold of the American labor union upon its members seldom extends beyond the employment relationship. The labor movement has developed no consistent political philosophy and has no discernible political ends. It presents not even the most conventional threat of a public ownership movement, let alone nationalization. It has produced no coöperative movement. While it may produce members loyal to union leadership in industrial disputes, it has developed no threat to the sovereignty of business enterprise which needs to be politically compromised. The social activities of the unions abroad in education, recreation, insurance, and civic enterprise are conspicuously infrequent here. The claims of the union upon the loyalty of its membership which are so widely developed throughout the entire social and political life of the working class in England are in America largely confined to the factory or the trade. The union member will follow his leaders into and out of limited industrial battle but not much farther.

The stability of any balance-of-power relationship depends upon an equality of strength and upon the reasonable certainty that neither side can safely assume victory. But no such balance exists. The temporary force that a union can muster in a single spectacular effort, such as a steel strike, a coal strike, or a railroad strike, is illusory, since there are not reserve forces sufficient to protect the legislative flank and rear.

The fault lies in part with the labor movement itself, for the trade union in America has relied extensively upon the employer to guarantee its sovereignty. The principal device has been the closed shop contract or some variant of it. As a substitute for the solidarity of American workers, the union has depended upon the contractual obligation of the employer to dismiss an employee not in good standing in his union. With these major tactical objectives, American labor has not dem-

onstrated the bargaining power to generate the pressure necessary for political settlement. It is therefore of little consequence that settlement might be had upon terms relatively favorable to employers if there is no political necessity for any settlement at all.

When William Green, president of the American Federation of Labor, predicts that American labor will move to the left if its institutional privileges and immunities are taken from it by legislation, he is probably correct. But if he is correct it will not be because of any mass outburst on the part of the rank and file of labor, or for the American worker's loss of confidence in the democratic institutions of capitalism, but because the leadership of American labor may come to believe that it cannot do business with American employers. Then the American employer may come to believe that union responsibility is worth its price.

We must choose whether to rely on the institutions of collective bargaining or to invoke the police power of the State. The first course requires the promotion of strong unions and strong employers' organizations, with authority democratically conferred but adequate to the task. This I conceive to be the Swedish way and the British way and one pattern for the future. The other is to limit freedom of association and to depend upon the State to prescribe the limits of organization, of action, and of contract. But if it is the State rather than the employer with whom labor must bargain, labor will learn how to do this as well, and it will be by political organization rather than economic organization. And political issues are not limited to wages, hours, and working conditions.

# A Profile of the American Labor Movement at the Beginning of the 1970's

"A Profile of the Labor Movement: Its Membership and Leadership," from *Labor and the American Economy* by Derrik C. Bok and John T. Dunlop, outlines the characteristics of union members and leaders in the United States. Their statistics reveal, for example, that the typical union member falls in the middle income group, with very few among the very rich or the very poor. Moreover, union members have education levels slightly higher than the average for the rest of the population. The typical union member also is a blue collar male who is more likely to work in the transportation, construction, manufacturing, or mining industries than he is in government, services, trade, finance, real estate, or agriculture. Geographically, union members are concentrated in the north and far west.

Bok and Dunlop confirm the conclusion that union members in the United States typically lack class bias. Union members reflect prevailing social and political attitudes: they are not significantly more willing to support sweeping social reform and are not significantly more conservative than other groups in our society. With respect to the reasons for the lack of class consciousness among American workers, Bok and Dunlop stress the heterogeneity of the population and "the ideals of class consciousness, individual initiative, and abundant opportunity, a society in which workers enjoyed the right of suffrage and opportunity for a free public education."

Although the statistics are not very reliable, the evidence available to Bok and Dunlop indicates that unions in the United States are not as well organized in terms of the nonagricultural work force as workers in Europe and Australia. The relatively low degree of unionization in the United States can be accounted for by a number of factors, including the greater employer opposition here and the lack of solidarity among Americans.

Other differences between American and European labor movements noted by Bok and Dunlop include the lack of a distinctive political party in the United States, the fact that local unions are relatively stronger here than in other countries, the looser federation here as contrasted with most European labor movements, the larger number of full-time union officials here who typically come up through the ranks, and the relative absence of intellectuals, who are attracted to other labor movements for political or ideological reasons, but not attracted to the business unions of the United States.

## A Profile of the Labor Movement:
## Its Membership and Leadership[1]

## by Derek C. Bok and John T. Dunlop

In 1966, 18.3 million men and women in the United States were paying dues to labor unions.* By 1968, the figure is estimated to have exceeded 19 million. The number of employees subject to collective-bargaining agreements is still larger by three quarters of a million, since not all employees covered by collective-bargaining agreements are required to be union members. The past five years have been a period of marked expansion in the total number of union members, reversing a decline which set in with the recession of 1958. Nevertheless, the labor force has grown so rapidly that union membership in 1968, as a percentage of employment in non-agricultural enterprises, was little more than 28 percent compared to the level of 33–34 percent achieved in the middle 1950's.†

Union members are organized into more than 70,000 local unions, which are in turn affiliated with 190 national or international unions (except for fewer than a thousand locals, with an aggregate of little more than a half million members, that are directly affiliated with the AFL-CIO or in single-firm and local unaffiliated

* This Bureau of Labor Statistics figure excludes approximately 1.4 million members of national and international unions with headquarters in the United States who were in Canada and other areas outside the United States. This figure also excludes many members, who may number over 900,000, exempt from dues payments in whole or in part as provided in union constitutions, by virtue of being unemployed, on strike, retired, apprentices prior to being eligible to membership, or in military service.[2]

† Appendix A of this chapter presents the data on union membership, and union membership as a percentage of nonagricultural employees, for the years 1930–68 in chart form.

unions). Two third of these national unions with more than three quarters of the membership are affiliated with the AFL-CIO, even after the disaffiliation of Walter Reuther and the Auto Workers in 1968.

## THE UNION MEMBER[3]

Union members do not represent a mirror image of the entire adult population, or even the work force, of this country. Instead they are rather heavily concentrated in certain income ranges, educational levels, industries, occupations and regions.

### Income

Unionists fall mainly in the middle-income group, with relatively few members numbered among the very rich or the very poor. In 1965, 69.1 percent of union heads of households had incomes ranging from $5,000 to $10,000. Among households headed by nonmembers, only 43.4 percent fell within this income range. Conversely, only 3.9 percent of union household heads received less than $3,000 during the same year, while 14.2 percent earned more than $10,000. For nonunion households, the corresponding figures were substantially larger; 14.3 percent fell below $3,000, while 21.6 percent earned over $10,000.

### Education

Much the same pattern carries over the area of education. In 1965, 44 percent of all union heads of households had an education that extended through all or part of high school (but not beyond). Only 32 percent of nonunion household heads fell within these categories. At the upper end of the scale, however, the figures were sharply reversed. Only 1.4 percent of all union family heads had received a college diploma and .4 percent had received an advanced degree. Among family heads who were not members of unions, over eight times as many (11.4 percent) had graduated from college, while almost twenty times as many (7.8 percent) had obtained an advanced degree.

### Sex

It is well known that women workers are underrepresented in labor unions. Among employees outside the agricultural sector, only one woman in seven belongs to a union, while one man in every three is a member. To some extent, the difference is explained by the heavy employment of women in clerical and sales occupations and in service industries, where unions have traditionally made little headway. But other causes are probably more important. Women can be among the most loyal, determined union members when their sense of injustice is aroused. In general, however, women outside the professions appear not to place the importance that men do on matters connected with employment; they frequently do not conceive of themselves as remaining in a job for a working lifetime. Thus, even in operative and semi-skilled occupations, which are quite highly organized, women seem to be less inclined to join unions than men.

### Industry and Occupation

Union members are distributed most unevenly among different industries, as the following table reveals:

| Industry | Percentage Organized |
|---|---|
| Transportation, communications, public utilities | 74.7% |
| Construction | 70.9 |
| Manufacturing | 50.0 |
| Mining | 47.2 |
| Government | 14.1 |
| Services | 10.5 |
| Trade | 9.3 |
| Finance, real estate | 2.0 |
| Agriculture | .8 |

These differences are the result of many factors. The variations in the occupational mix of different industries are significant, for unions seem to have much greater appeal in some occupational groups than others. The prevalence of women in certain occupations helps to explain the low rate of unionization in the trade and service sectors. With a few notable exceptions, white-collar workers have traditionally been cool to unions, especially professional and technical employees. On the other hand, blue-collar employees in the skilled and semiskilled categories seem to be the most promising target for unionization.* Unskilled laborers tend to fall between these poles. They are usually more susceptible than white-collar workers, but they are also more apt to be foreign-born, easily replaceable, quickly intimidated by hostile employers, subject to considerable turnover and thus often frustrating to union organizers seeking to attract continuing affiliation. These differences reveal themselves dramatically in figures comparing the rates of unionization among occupations.

## Geography

Union membership is not distributed throughout the United States in proportion to population or employment. In general terms, the extent of union organization—measured as a fraction of nonagricultural employment—is greatest in the east-northcentral and eastern industrial states and on the West Coast. The

| Occupations | Percentage Organized |
|---|---|
| Operatives (semiskilled) | 63% |
| Craftsmen and foremen | 50 |
| Laborers (excluding agriculture) | 38 |
| Clerical | 26 |
| Service | 20 |
| Sales | |
| Managers | } 5–10 |
| Professional and technical | |

* Selig Perlman, writing in the late 1920's, contended that ". . . manual groups, whether peasants in Russia, modern wage earners, or medieval master workmen, have had their economic attitudes basically determined by a consciousness of a scarcity of opportunity, which is characteristic of these groups and stands out in contrast with the businessmen's 'abundance consciousness,' or consciousness of unlimited opportunity. Starting with this consciousness of scarcity, the 'manualist' groups have been led to practicing solidarity, to an insistence upon an 'ownership' by the group as a whole of the totality of economic-opportunity extent, to a 'rationing' by the group of such opportunity among the individuals constituting it, to a control by the group over its members in relation to the conditions on which they as individuals are permitted to occupy a portion of that opportunity—in brief, to a 'communism of opportunity.' "[4]

extent of organization is least in the South, the Southwest and the Middle West plain states. There are, of course, important variations within these groupings.[5] For example, there appears to be some tendency for employees in metropolitan areas to be slightly more highly organized than employees in smaller communities.[6]

The five states with the largest employment—New York, California, Pennsylvania, Illinois, and Ohio—contain 48 percent of the union members while they employ 38 percent of the nonagricultural work force. These five states have 8.7 million union members.

Many more characteristics of union members could be cited. For example, it is interesting to note that the union movement includes about the same proportion of nonwhites as in the nonagricultural work force and that unions contain a disproportionate number of war veterans and Catholics.* But even more important than these demographic factors are the attitudes of union employees on social, political and economic questions. For, in the last analysis, these sentiments will probably have the most direct effects upon the course of union behavior.

. . . the opinions of union members are particularly striking in their lack of any special class bias.[7]

* * *

It is well to compare these findings with the standard theories that popular writers have expressed about the political sentiments of union members. One view, less prevalent now than two decades ago, maintains that union members are, more than the rest of the population, willing to support sweeping social and economic programs.* Another theory has flowered more recently in the wake of repeated claims of "white backlash" in heavily blue-collar areas. According to this opinion, union members were more "progressive" in earlier decades but have become strongly conservative as their wages and conditions have risen to more comfortable middle-class levels.†

Neither of these theories is well supported by the facts. According to recent opinion surveys, union members as a group do not exhibit any special desire for drastic social and economic change.

* * *

Various forces have contributed to this peculiar lack of class sentiment among union members (and other manual workers). One important factor was the extreme heterogeneity of the American labor force in the formative years of industrialization. During this period, a network of language, racial and religious barriers was thrown up by repeated waves of immigration. Particular ethnic groups gained control over different jobs, while recent immigrants and Negro laborers were excluded from the better jobs and later used as strikebreakers by employers. These experiences produced cleavages that kept the labor movement from achieving the

* In 1959, 48 percent of union family heads were war veterans, as compared with 37 percent for nonunion heads. The respective proportions of Catholics are 30 percent and 18 percent. (From the 1959 Survey of Consumers, Survey Research Center, University of Michigan.)
* According to C. Wright Mills, "This is where labor stands: there are labor leaders who are running labor unions, most of them along the main drift; there are left intellectuals who are not running labor unions, but who think they know how to run them against the main drift; and there are wage workers who are disgruntled and ready to do what must be done."[8]
† This view was exemplified by the oft-repeated suggestion during the 1968 Presidential campaign that union members were a leading stronghold of support for Governor George Wallace. In fact, only 15 percent of union members voted for Wallace compared with 13 percent of the total number casting ballots. The 2-percent difference could be ascribed to a variety of factors—e.g., the fact that union members are predominantly male, and males throughout the country were significantly more favorable to Wallace than females.

degree of unity reached in Great Britain and Scandinavia.

Labor organizations in America also grew up in a society that stressed the ideals of classlessness, individual initiative, and abundant opportunity, a society in which workers enjoyed the right of suffrage and the opportunity for a free public education. In this atmosphere, employees were less inclined than workers in Europe to submerge their sense of individuality and identify with a working class.

*　*　*

## THE UNIONS

The American union movement has certain characteristics that give it a special flavor and set it somewhat apart from most of its counterparts abroad.

### Size

Despite all of the concern expressed over labor's power, union membership in America is a smaller proportion of the work force than in any of the other major industrial democracies. . . .*

The low levels of unionization in America can be explained largely by two factors. One important factor is the widespread opposition of employers—an attitude no longer prevalent in Europe save in Italy and France. Although American labor leaders often exaggerate the significance of this opposition, its importance can be seen in the ease with which unions can usually organize blue-collar workers once management has been persuaded to remain neutral. Employer opposition, however, does not wholly explain the stunted growth of the American labor movement. Unionization is proportionately much greater in Italy than in the United States despite widespread hostility from employers, and this has been true even though Italian unions have had to cope with severe internal divisions, less impressive achievements at the bargaining table, and an almost total lack of formal organizing efforts. In other countries, moreover, employers were often

| * Union Membership as Percentage of Nonagricultural Employed Labor Force | | | |
|---|---|---|---|
| | Union Membership (thousands) | Total Number Employed (thousands) | Percentage of Organization |
| Austria | 1,540 | 2,247 | 68.5% |
| Sweden | 2,165 | 3,302 | 65.6 |
| Belgium | 1,700 | 3,407 | 49.9 |
| Italy | 6,320 | 14,242 | 44.4 |
| Australia | 1,475 | 3,448 | 42.8 |
| England | 8,757 | 22,621 | 38.7 |
| Netherlands | 1,430 | 3,978 | 35.9 |
| Germany | 7,996 | 23,733 | 33.7 |
| France | 3,071 | 10,243 | 29.0 |
| United States | 17,299 | 60,770 | 28.5 |

(Australian data are for 1963); data relating to other countries are for 1965.)[9]

Statistical comparisons of union membership among countries should be used with considerable caution, since the meaning of membership varies greatly. In the United States membership is measured by dues payments, but in Europe not only are dues levels much lower, but membership is not reported according to regular dues payments. In addition, it should be emphasized that the political and economic power of the union movement does not bear any simple relation to the proportion of the labor force that is organized; such power depends on several other factors such as the financial strength of the unions, the nature of the party system, etcetera.

openly hostile toward unions in the early stages of organization, but their policies eventually changed because they could not overcome the determination of the unions.[10]

A second factor has been the lack of solidarity among workers in the United States. . . .

*　*　*

### Unions and Politics

The lack of a distinctive ideology among the working people of this country has also had a marked influence on the political activity of American unions. The labor movement in the United States is unique in failing to produce a political party based explicitly on working-class support. Nor have American unions followed the example of many European countries by splitting into rival organizations based upon party lines.

*　*　*

### Strong Local Unions

Unions in this country were generally forced to achieve recognition and establish bargaining relationships on a plant-by-plant basis rather than by agreement with a strong national or regional association of employers. This process encouraged the growth of active local unions in the plant, with important functions to perform. . . .

The impotrance of local unions is reflected in the financial holdings of labor organizations in the United States. At the end of 1966, all union bodies had combined assets of $1,839,000,000, and the combined assets of local unions and intermediate bodies* exceeded those of the international unions. In the same year, local unions had receipts of $1,256,000,000; intermediate bodies net receipts of $14,000,-000 and international unions net receipts of $560,000,000.[11]

*　*　*

### A Loose Federation

At higher levels in the union structure, the labor movement in America has remained markedly decentralized in the sense that the central federation has had relatively little authority over its member unions. In part, this is the result of the lack of a class sentiment strong enough to transcend the attachments of workers to their own separate crafts and occupations. In part, the absence of a strong federation reflected the predominance in our labor movement of bargaining rather than political action, for which a powerful central body would have been more necessary to enable the movement to act in unison in election campaigns and lobbying efforts. . . . The AFL-CIO has acquired some power to investigate and suspend affiliates for corruption or Communist influence, but it has little or no authority over the bargaining and strike policies of its members, nor is it able to control their membership requirements or political activities.

There are other countries, notably Britain and Australia, where the central federation is also rather weak. But the situation is more often to the contrary. . . .

*　*　*

THE NEAR UNIONS

It has been assumed that everyone understands what a union is in this country. But any careful newspaper reader will agree that the definition of "union" has become decidedly vague in recent years.

---

* Locals of the same international union in a metropolitan area or state often form a district council or state council for purposes of bargaining or organizing. Such bodies typically maintain their own financial status. Intermediate bodies may also be composed of a number of locals in the same industry from different international unions.

A decade ago, the National Education Association, an organization of a million schoolteachers and administrators, prided itself on its status as a thoroughly professional association. Today, the teachers affiliated with N.E.A. have embraced the idea of negotiation with school boards and have resorted to strikes and other collective sanctions to achieve their proposals. Professional associations of nurses have come to engage in mass resignations and other forms of economic pressure to achieve collective agreements. In professional athletics, football, basketball, and baseball associations have all sprung up seeking negotiations and uttering ominous threats of stopping play. . . . The near unions tend to have supervisory employees as members; their members are more independent, have higher incomes, and are more responsive to professional concerns than are members of conventional unions. It is unclear whether these organizations are in transition toward more conventional unions or constitute a more permanent form of employee organization.

Although the total size of the near unions is uncertain, their combined membership is certainly greater than two million persons. With the addition of the near unions, the composition of membership in all employee organizations is less heavily concentrated than in the AFL-CIO alone among certain income and occupational groups. It is also more diverse in its goals, its strategies and its political outlook.

THE UNION LEADER

In contrast to the labor movements in other countries, unions in the United States boast a much higher number of full-time officials. . . .* [T]he root of the matter, once again, lies in the decentralized pattern of union organization and labor relations in the United States. For the most part, collective bargaining has not consisted of negotiations with huge industrywide employer associations. The predominant tendency has been to conduct separate negotiations with individual plants and companies. As a result, there are a vast number of contracts to be negotiated. . . . To perform all this work, a host of union officials is required.

Almost all labor leaders have come up from the ranks of the members working in the plants and crafts that the unions represent. Unlike the situation in several other countries, especially in the underdeveloped world, very few of these leaders have backgrounds as lawyers, politicians, editors, professors or intellectuals. Nor are their fathers predominantly found outside the ranks of labor. . . .

. . . In a mobile society without marked class divisions, one might have expected that union leaders would be drawn to a larger extent from different areas of society. But other forces have tugged more strongly in the opposite direction. Intellectuals and professionals are most often drawn to a labor movement as a vehicle for their own political advancement or a

---

* Ratio of officers to members

| United States | 1:300 |
| Denmark | 1:775 |
| Australia | 1:900 |
| Sweden | 1:1700 |
| Great Britain | 1:2000 |
| Norway | 1:2200 |

Seymour M. Lipset, "Trade Unions and Social Structure: II," *Industrial Relations*, February 1962, p. 93.

force for promoting certain political and social ideals. . . . [T]he work of the unions has centered upon the bargaining process and, especially at the lowest levels of the union hierarchy, upon the day-to-day business of administering the working conditions in the shop and factory. . . . To the intellectual or the professional man, however, these matters are not only unfamiliar; they are also of precious little interest.

Emerging as he does from the rank and file, the union leader naturally tends to reflect many of the characteristics of his membership. . . .

The average age of the national officer of a union is fifty-three—about the same as for business executives at the vice-president and president level.

❋   ❋   ❋

# Appendix A

UNION MEMBERSHIP

Chart 1. *Membership of national and international unions, 1930–1966.* *

Chart 2. *Membership as a percent of total labor force and of employees in nonagricultural establishments, 1930–1966.†*

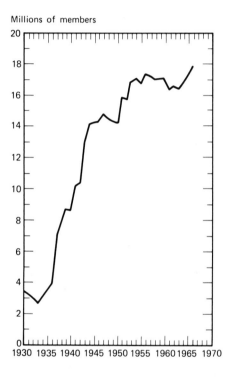

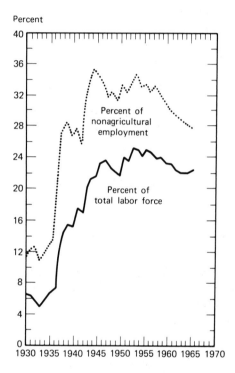

* Excludes Canadian membership, but includes members in other areas outside the United States. Members of AFL–CIO directly affiliated local unions are also included. For the years 1948–52, midpoints of membership estimates, which were expressed as ranges, were used.

† Excludes Canadian membership. The dotted line for the period since 1960 estimates the effect of including membership in "near unions."

SOURCE United States Department of Labor, Bureau of Labor Statistics, *Directory of National and International Labor Unions in the United States 1967,* Bulletin No. 1596, p. 57.

*Do you favor subsidizing the poor through a negative income tax?* (Harris, April 18, 1968)

|  | Total Queried | Union Members | AFL-CIO | Teamsters |
|---|---|---|---|---|
| Favor | 27% | 31% | 21% | 34% |
| Oppose | 60 | 58 | 57 | 57 |
| Not sure | 13 | 12 | 12 | 9 |

*Do you favor a $32 billion program to rebuild the cities?* (Harris, April 15, 1968)

|  | Queried Total | Union Members | AFL-CIO | Teamsters |
|---|---|---|---|---|
| Favor | 34% | 37% | 39% | 23% |
| Oppose | 52 | 51 | 51 | 62 |
| Not sure | 14 | 12 | 10 | 15 |

*Do you favor such a program at the cost of paying $35 more in taxes?* (Harris, April 15, 1968)

|  | Total Queried | Union Members | AFL-CIO | Teamsters |
|---|---|---|---|---|
| Favor | 30% | 30% | 30% | 15% |
| Oppose | 59 | 62 | 62 | 77 |
| Not sure | 11 | 9 | 8 | 8 |

*How much would you like to see the federal government owning and operating essential industries?* (Opinion Research, August 1960)

|  | Nationwide Public Respondents | Union Members Households |
|---|---|---|
| A great deal | 11% | 12% |
| Fair amount | 20 | 20 |
| Very little | 15 | 16 |
| Nothing | 36 | 36 |
| No opinion | 18 | 16 |

❋  ❋  ❋

*President Johnson has proposed that Congress set aside about $3.4 billion for aid in other parts of the world. . . . Would you like to see this amount increased or decreased?* (Gallup, February 17, 1965)

|  | Non-Unionists (2,581) | Union Member (485) |
|---|---|---|
| Increase aid | 5.5% | 8.5% |
| Keep at same level | 32.9 | 36.5 |
| Decrease aid | 49.2 | 46.8 |
| No opinion | 12.4 | 8.2 |

*Would you like to see the Congress pass the (1964) Civil Rights Act?* (Gallup, December 31, 1963)

|  | Non-Unionists (3,214) | Union Members (575) |
|---|---|---|
| Yes | 59.4% | 63.8% |
| No | 32.4 | 27.5 |
| Not sure | 8.2 | 9.7 |

*Have Negroes tried to move too fast?* (Harris, April 15, 1968)

|  | Total Queried | Union Members | AFL-CIO | Teamsters |
|---|---|---|---|---|
| Too fast | 61% | 69% | 63% | 66% |
| Too slow | 9 | 6 | 6 | 4 |
| About right | 20 | 18 | 24 | 11 |
| Not sure | 10 | 6 | 7 | 19 |

❋  ❋  ❋

*Which statement about Vietnam do you agree with most?* (Harris, April 16, 1968)

| | Total Queried | Union Members | AFL-CIO | Teamsters |
|---|---|---|---|---|
| I disagree with our present policy. We are not going far enough. We should go further, such as carrying the war more into North Vietnam. | 21% | 23% | 27% | 31% |
| I agree with what we are doing but we should increase our military effort. | 38 | 41 | 37 | 44 |
| I agree with what we are doing, but we should do more to bring about negotiations, such as stop bombing North Vietnam. | 17 | 21 | 15 | 15 |
| I disagree with our present policy. We should pull out our troops now. | 15 | 10 | 13 | 11 |
| Not sure. | 9 | 6 | 8 | — |

\* \* \*

*Do you tend to feel that people running the country don't really care what happens to people like yourself?* (Harris, May 16, 1968)

| | Total Queried | Union Members | AFL-CIO | Teamsters |
|---|---|---|---|---|
| Yes | 26% | 26% | 22% | 28% |
| No | 67 | 68 | 71 | 64 |
| Not sure | 7 | 6 | 7 | 8 |

*Percentage voting for George Wallace by* ( Harris, November 2, 1968)*

| | Under $3,000 | $3,000– 4,999 | $5,000– 6,999 | $7,000– 9,999 | $10,000 14,999 | $15,000 + |
|---|---|---|---|---|---|---|
| Total | 14% | 14% | 16% | 13% | 11% | 7% |
| Union members | 4 | 9 | 17 | 15 | 11 | 20 |
| Non-union members | 15 | 14 | 11 | 11 | 11 | 5 |

Notes to Chapter II of *Labor and the American Community* by Derek C. Bok, and John T. Dunlop.

[1] This chapter utilizes unpublished statistical data tabulated particularly for the present study. The University of Michigan, Survey Research Center, in connection with its Survey of Consumers in 1959 and in 1966 asked the question, "Do you belong to a labor union?" The statistical data contained in these surveys of households permitted tabulations, which had not previously been prepared, to show the characteristics of heads of households who were union members compared to those who were not union members. There were 2,799 households in the 1959 sample and 2,417 in the 1965 sample. The tabulations which show the characteristics of households in which the head of the household reported being a union member, compared to all other households were prepared for this study under the supervision of Professor Leo Troy of Rutgers University.

It is to be regretted that similar information is not available on an annual basis from the special supplemental information collected each April in the Current Population Survey. An additional question or two on union membership is long overdue. It is hoped that the rich information here reported from the two households studies of the University of Michigan, Survey Research Center will help to persuade the Bureau of the Census and the Bureau of Labor Statistics of the significance of reporting annually such data with the larger sample of C.P.S.

[2] U.S. Department of Labor, Bureau of Labor Statistics, *Directory of National and International Labor Unions in the United States, 1967*, Bulletin No. 1596 (Washington, D.C.: 1968), p. 55; Leo Troy, *Trade Union Membership 1897–1962*, Occasional Paper 92 (New York: National Bureau of Economic Research, 1965), Also see Arthur B. Shostak, *America's Forgotten Labor Organization, A Survey of the Role of the Single-Firm Independent Union in American Industry* (Princeton: Industrial Relations Section, Princeton University, 1962).

[3] The following sources are particularly rele-

* These figures suggest that substantial variations may appear among different subcategories within the total union membership. (The strong support for Wallace among union members with incomes over $15,000, however, must be treated with skepticism, since only a handful of union members were numbered among the 246 persons in this category polled by the Harris organization.)

vant to this section: Ruth Kornhauser, "Some Social Determinants and Consequences of Union Membership," *Labor History*, Winter 1961, pp. 30–61; Gladys L. Palmer, *Labor Mobility in Six Cities* (New York: Social Science Research Council 1954); Angus Campbell, Gerald Gurin, and Warren Miller, *The Voter Decides* (New York: Row, Peterson, 1954), p. 6.

4 Selig Perlman, *A Theory of the Labor Movement* (New York: Macmillan, 1928).

5 U.S. Department of Labor, *op. cit.*, p. 64; Ray Marshall, *Labor in the South* (Cambridge: Harvard University Press, 1967).

6 Kornhauser, *op. cit.*, p. 40. These results appear to be confirmed by the Michigan Survey Research Center results.

7 Robert W. Smuts, *European Impressions of the American Worker* (New York: King's Crown Press, 1953), p. 2. Also see E. Levasseur, *The American Workman* (Baltimore: Johns Hopkins Press, 1900), pp. 444-45.

8 C. Wright Mills, *The New Men of Power, America's Labor Leaders* (New York: Harcourt, Brace, 1948), p. 291. Also see William Z. Foster, *Misleaders of Labor* (New York: Trade Union

Educational League, 1927); the Communist Party analysis saw in the semiskilled and the unskilled the prospects of radical change—"Among them the spirit of class solidarity burns brightest, and that of class antagonism runs strongest." (p. 315.)

9 Statistics compiled from U.S. Department of Labor, *op. cit.*, p. 56; *Directory of Labor Organizations: Europe*, May 1965, pp. xii-xiii; *Directory of Labor Organizations: Asia and Australia*, March 1963, pp. x-xi; and International Labour Office, *Yearbook of Labour Statistics*, 1967, Table 3, pp. 276–95.

10 See T. L. Johnson, *Collective Bargaining in Sweden* (Cambridge: Harvard University Press, 1962), pp. 23–91; Walter Galenson, *The Danish System of Labor Relations* (Cambridge: Harvard University Press, 1952), pp. 7–93.

11 These estimates were prepared by Professor Leo Troy from special tabulations prepared for this study from the financial reports filed annually by labor organizations with the Department of Labor as required by the Labor-Management Reporting and Disclosure Act of 1959.

## Unionization of Agricultural Workers

One of the weaknesses of unionism and collective bargaining is that it does the least for those who need the most help. Because union organizing in the United States depends largely on the ability to win strikes, workers with little economic power, because of low skills and an inability to inflict damage on (or to convey benefits to) employers, have great difficulty getting organized. Although the economic conditions of many low-wage industries are such that workers could in many cases gain very small economic advantages through organization, these workers could nevertheless gain the benefits of participating in the formulation of rules governing their wages, hours, and working conditions if they could replace individual with group bargaining.

Agricultural workers generally have not benefited from welfare and labor legislation. There is little doubt that their relative isolation, their invisibility, and their limited political power—as contrasted with farmers' organizations, which have had inordinate political power—rather than economic considerations account for the public policy discrimination against agricultural workers. It is true that agricultural conditions are not identical with those in other industries, but there is considerable variation even within a given manufacturing industry. Moreover, a major advantage of collective bargaining is its adaptability to a wide range of diverse circumstances. It is sometimes argued that agriculture is unique because the employers' vulnerability to strikes at harvest time would give the workers too much power. However, many nonagricultural employers also have periods of special vulnerability to strikes. Moreover, negotiations need not take place at harvest time, and contracts could include "no strike" clauses. The argument against collective bargaining by agricultural workers also assumes that farm workers would in fact be able to successfully strike employers—an assumption that is by no means certain.

Indeed, history demonstrates that agricultural workers have had great difficulty in organizing. Some successes were achieved in the late 1960's and early 1970's by the United Farm Workers Organizing Committee, AFL-CIO, led by Cesar Chavez, in Arizona and California, but not without a great struggle. The UFWOC's limited success came as a result of a nationwide grape boycott by thousands of sympathizers, and was made possible because the union concentrated on specialty crops in a limited geographic area. It has been much more difficult to organize in basic crops and in places like the Rio Grande Valley of Texas.

In "A New Era for Farm Labor," Varden Fuller analyzes the possible impacts of some recent developments affecting agricultural workers. Various signs indicate that there might be a growing public concern over the plight of these workers. Fuller first examines the consequences of discontinuing the Bracero program, under which Mexican workers were recruited to work in agriculture in the United States, and concludes that there were some labor shortages as a result of the plan's discontinuation but, in the words of the Secretary of Labor ". . . these shortages were substantially less serious than anyone could have predicted in advance." Moreover, in California, higher wage rates followed the end of the Bracero program, but these wages attracted more domestic workers to agriculture and were not inconsistent with the trends prevailing during the time the Bracero program was in effect.

Fuller next examines some of the factors that might encourage union growth (the increasing vertical integration of agriculture, growing union and public support for agricultural unionization, and the removal of the agricultural exclusion provision of the National Labor Relations Act) as well as the forces limiting unionization (small, scattered units, the number of seasonal workers who have not been very responsive to unionization, the high cost of organizing, and the administrative and legal difficulties in applying the NLRA to agricultural workers) and concludes:

> . . . it seems reasonable to expect a new and more broadly supported step forward in the development of farm worker unions and collective bargaining, but under very substantial constraints. Initially, and perhaps for many years, the pattern will be quite spotty. The greatest impact of limited unionization may very well be indirect. Farmers' organizations are already increasing their appeals to members to upgrade employment practices and conditions as a deterrent to union organization.

In 1967, the Fair Labor Standard Act was amended to extend minimum wages to agricultural workers. Fuller expects FLSA coverage to raise wages, reduce regional differentials, and lead to the substitution of capital for labor, especially in low-wage areas. Since many of the agricultural workers likely to be displaced by rising costs and changing technology are not suited by education or training for nonagricultural jobs, many economists question the wisdom of a minimum wage program that displaces them.

With respect to migrancy and manpower utilization, Fuller presents evidence to indicate that a high percentage of farm workers engage in nonfarm work, suggesting the possibility of linkage between agricultural and other industries to eliminate migratory and part-time agricultural employment. However, according to Fuller, the organization and procedures of farm placement in the U.S. Employment Service have contributed to the "estrangement of farm workers from local labor markets." Fuller discusses the upgrading of rural employment and the growing public realization of the need to develop a "viable, diversified rural economy." He suggests replacing the Farm Placement Service with a Rural Industries Manpower Service in order to facilitate the achievement of this objective.

Fuller concludes with a qualified affirmative answer to the question "Is there to be a new era for farm labor?" Since farm employers apparently no longer have access to foreign labor, they will have to become more competitive for labor—both among themselves and against other labor markets. Furthermore, unionization drives are likely to have an impact even if they are not highly successful, since farm employers will be under pressure to improve wages and conditions in order to combat unionism.

# A New Era for Farm Labor?

## by Varden Fuller*

Several recent occurrences suggest the prospect of a new era for farm labor. The years 1965 and 1966 saw the termination of the Bracero program, a national minimum wage for farm labor, and possibly the onset of unionization and collective bargaining.

Furthermore, one gets the impression of substantive changes in attitudes: the public seems less concerned by suggestions that crops will go unharvested or food prices will skyrocket if farmers do not get foreign laborers or if farm wages are raised. There also appears to be a quite abrupt change of posture among the farm placement personnel of the Federal-State Employment Service: throughout the postwar years and until 1964, their concept of mission was heavily dominated by the farmers' need to be assured of an "adequate" labor supply—the definition of adequacy being mainly that of farm employers, or more precisely that of the professionals whom the farmers hired to speak for them. Now placement personnel seem to be concerned as well with the interests of farm workers and in the development and effective utilization of domestic manpower resources. Farm spokesmen still insist that due to the peculiarities of farm employment they must obtain labor under special terms and conditions, but one has the feeling that such statements are made chiefly for the record. The small band of emerging farm labor leadership reflects more poise and assurance than formerly. Meetings and conferences on farm labor in the past did not usually include farm laborers; this is no longer so. And, for the first time in history, a major Presidential commission on farm policy (the Food and Fiber Com-

SOURCE Reprinted with permission from *Industrial Relations,* Vol. 6, No. 3, May 1967.

* Professor of Agricultural Economics, University of California, Berkeley, California.

mission) has labor members and seeks the testimony of farm workers.

Do these events and apparent changes of attitude herald a new era in farm labor? More specifically, is the long-standing and ever-widening gap between farm labor standards and those prevailing elsewhere about to be narrowed, or even eliminated? This article examines the several factors underlying this question and suggests a tentative answer.

## TERMINATION OF
## THE BRACERO PROGRAM

Public Law 78, authorizing government participation of importation of Mexican farm labor under contract, was enacted and approved by President Truman in 1951 as a Korean War emergency measure. With each temporary extension, the opposition of labor unions and "do-good" organizations mounted. The law's supporters would not commit themselves to an arrangement for terminating the program, and when sufficient votes could no longer be marshalled for a further extension in 1964, the program died.

During the fifties there were as many as three or four hundred thousand imported Mexican workers (Braceros) working the fruit, vegetable, cotton, and sugar beet crops in many states. Under more rigorous federal administration the numbers were substantially reduced and the program was increasingly confined to California. The peak employment of Braceros in 1964 was only 72,000, and although seven states were involved. California had nine-tenths of the total.[1] Thereafter, un-

der the authority of the Immigration and Nationality Act (P.L. 414), the Secretary of Labor admitted some temporary contract workers, but in sharply reduced numbers. Mexican workers were admitted to the state of California only—17,000 in 1965 and 7,760 in 1966.[2]

The apprehensions of those who advocated foreign labor and their predictions of disaster throughout late 1964 and most of 1965 were not completely confirmed by events. Trouble did develop for many individual farm employers, but usually not for large groups; nevertheless, the impact was definitely felt in the harvests of California asparagus and strawberries and Michigan pickling cucumbers. Had the development and use of mechanical harvest procedures for California canning tomatoes not been unexpectedly successful, the producers of this crop would have needed a much larger Mexican labor authorization than they received in 1965. In assessing the 1965 experience, the Secretary of Labor concluded:

*Any fair-minded appraisal of the year's experience would require recognition of both the fact that some labor shortages developed which would not have occurred if Public Law 78 had not been repealed (or if Public Law 414 had been more loosely administered) and the fact that these shortages were substantially less serious than anyone could have predicted in advance.*[3]

\* \* \*

[1] *Report on Manpower Requirement, Resources, Utilization, and Training*, U.S. Department of Labor (Washington, D.C.: 1966), p. 132. This report also contains many other details surrounding the ending of the Bracero program.
[2] *Ibid.;* see also, *Farm Labor Developments: Employment and Wage Supplement*, U.S. Department of Labor (Washington, D.C.: October, 1966), p. 5. Relatively small numbers of other nationalities—principally Canadians and British West Indians, who were not covered by Public Law 78—have been admitted for farm employment, mainly on the East Coast. Under more stringent regulation, these also have declined.
[3] *Year of Transition: Seasonal Farm Labor, 1965*, a report of the Secretary of Labor, U.S. Department of Labor (mimeographed, 1966), p. 16.

## UNIONIZATION OF FARM WORKERS

Farm workers have never been covered by national labor relations legislation. Moreover, their heterogeneous composition, mainly temporary employment, and mobility have made unionization difficult. Nevertheless, over the years, there have been many unsuccessful attempts at organization. Outstanding exceptions are the Hawaiian pineapple and sugar industries and the market milk dairies near San Francisco and Los Angeles.

In the past two years, renewed efforts have been made to unionize seasonal farm workers in the San Joaquin Valley grape area of California, and in Texas and Florida. There have been some unusual occurrences. Three California employers accepted a union as a bargaining agent and entered into collective bargaining; another agreed to voluntary elections at which a union won bargaining recognition. Contracts have been negotiated and issues are being resolved by arbitration. These facts suggest that collective bargaining may have gained a foothold in agriculture and will sperad. Whether this is a likely prospect depends on a variety of factors which operate both for and against such a development.

*Vertical integration of agricultural Industry.* Significantly, collective bargaining has been established for farm workers (that is, field or production workers as distinguished from processing workers) only in those companies in which farm production has been allied by contract or by ownership to processing, handling, or manufacturing. Also, in these instances, collective bargaining has already been established in the processing segment. In integrated arrangements, there are many opportunities for established unions on the processing side to influence managements' attitude with respect to field workers. Contractual and ownership integration—sometimes called "agri-business"—is likely to increase, thus certainly improving the outlook for farm unionism.

*Union and Public Support.* The AFL-CIO and its consituent unions are taking more direct, vigorous roles, as are independent unions, churches, groups and organizations based on civil rights, minority groups, and related causes. Urban newspapers are tending to be more sympathetic. For example, the *San Francisco Examiner* editorially supported unionization of farm workers on July 24, 1966. Despite appeals for noninterference from churchmen, local authorities, and community leaders within the affected areas, outside concern and interest shows little evidence of diminishing. External interest and action may reasonably be expected to continue, and if so, they are likely to have considerable influence on the attitudes and actions of both workers and employers.

*Possible Congressional Action.* It is coming to be realized—by people generally and by some farm employers as well—that the NLRA does not benefit union organizers alone. Economic pressure and force are the obvious alternatives to an orderly procedure to test whether employees want to be represented by a union. Senate Bill 1866 of the 89th Congress, introduced in April 1965, would have amended the National Labor Relations Act to remove the present exclusion of farm workers. At hearings held by the Senate Subcommittee on Migratory Labor in late 1965 and early 1966, most farmers' organizations offered testimony opposed to the bill. Nevertheless, the Subcommittee concluded:

*The benefits of the collective bargaining right and procedures of the National Labor Relations Act should be extended to our citizens employed in agriculture. Con-*

*sideration should be given to the possible desirability of new concepts which may be more suitable to a mobile, seasonal agricultural labor force than those afforded by the present Federal labor laws. For example, jurisdiction standards for the National Labor Relations Board could be revised* *to meet the special problems of agriculture. Futhermore, a thorough review of this subject may demonstrate the need for an accelerated election procedure as well as an administrative board which deals exclusively with collective bargaining rights in agriculture.*[4]

Senator Murphy of California in his individual statement as a member of the Subcommittee seems not to disagree seriously with the majority:

*These questions are not insoluble. I have no doubt that the Congress, once alerted to the complexities of the situation, could provide workable guidelines for collective bargaining by farmworkers while at the same time preserving freedom of choice and equality of bargaining power. But the* *situation calls for careful analysis and good judgment, and not a headlong rush to apply to agriculture a legislative scheme which needs special tailoring to avoid a misfit which would be more of a hindrance than a help.*[5]

## FORCES LIMITING UNION GROWTH

Neither the prospect of labor relations legislation nor the forces and influences mentioned above are likely to generate unionization of the type seen in the thirties. On the contrary, the obstacles to unionism seem substantial and no great changes seem likely. Some of the more apparent obstacles are detailed below.

*The Problem of Small, Scattered Units.* Although the size of the average farm has risen rapidly and consistently, employment per unit is not following the same trend—due mainly to the advance of technology. Employment in large numbers per farm unit seldom occurs except in temporary harvest periods. Farms having five or more year-round hired men—usually dairies, stock ranches, or poultry farms—are few and exceptional. Widely separated, small units and close relations with a working employer are obstructive to union organization.

*Seasonal Workers Are Less Responsive to Unions.* Many expect to be in farm work only temporarily and do not regard an improved future in farm labor as a goal worth striving for. Those who are resigned to a future in farm labor—mostly older, less educated, and otherwise handi-capped persons—are typically neither well prepared for nor strongly motivated toward purposeful collective action.

*High Cost of Organization Without NLRA Coverage.* As long as farm labor continues to be excluded from statutory coverage, unions will have to use strikes and other pressures in order to obtain recognition as bargaining agents. Since such measures are expensive and uncertain, organizational efforts are likely to be restricted to the few situations in which the prospects of success appear good.

*Possible Administrative and Legal Difficulties Under NLRA Coverage.* Even if the law was changed, problems would remain. Were farm workers covered under the present legislation, it would be necessary to make considerable changes in court rulings and administrative procedures regarding such matters as appro-

---

[4] *Migratory Farm Labor Problem in the United States,* U.S. Senate Committee on Labor and Public Welfare, Subcommittee on Migratory Labor, 89th Cong., 2d sess., Report 1549 (Washington, D.C.: August 30, 1966), p. 35.
[5] *Ibid.,* p. 163.

priate bargaining units and voter eligibility in order to accommodate these to special farm problems. Lengthy court battles should probably be expected.

On the other hand, if a special law were passed, restricted to agriculture—as suggested by the Senate Subcommittee—the pace would not be likely to be any more rapid. The backlog of administrative experience and court decisions under the NLRA will not be directly relevant, and therefore time will be required to develop new procedures and practices. Either way it goes, taxing demands on the time and resources of the principal parties as well as on the administrative agency would seem to be unavoidable—assuming, of course, that farm employers continue to oppose collective bargaining.

In summary, then, it seems reasonable to expect a new and more broadly supported step forward in the development of farm worker unions and collective bargaining, but under very substantial constraints. Initially, and perhaps for many years, the pattern will be quite spotty. The greatest impact of limited unionization may very well be indirect. Farmers' organizations are already increasing their appeals to members to upgrade employment practices and conditions as a deterrent to union organization.

## THE MINIMUM WAGE IN AGRICULTURE

The Fair Labor Standards Amendments of 1966 . . . apply[s] a national minimum wage to agriculture for the first time. Effective February 1, 1967, the minimum rate [was] $1 an hour; the rate [rose] to $1.15 a year later and to $1.30 on February 1, 1969. Only large employment units are covered and some categories of workers are excluded. . . .

The principal exemption from the new law is coverage for farm employees on farms which, in any quarter of the pre-ceding year, did not use more than 500 man-days (the equal of six or seven men working full time) of agricultural labor. As the consolidation of farms continues, no doubt there will be an increase in the proportion of farms covered. However, the day is far off when the majority of hired farm workers will be effectively covered by present minimum wage legislation.

Nevertheless, the law should have a considerable indirect impact on wages: by raising the lowest rates paid by covered employers, it will encourage other employers to raise their rates so as to preserve established relationships among individual farms and neighboring labor market areas. The present law should reduce regional farm wage differences between North and South and East and West, but it is not likely to eliminate them. It can be expected to accelerate mechanization and other forms of capital-labor substitution more in the low wage regions than in the higher ones.

## FARM LABOR AND MANPOWER PROGRAMS

National policy recognizes that manpower is a resource to be developed and utilized effectively. Both self-employed and hired farm workers are treated comparatively well under the recently enacted man-power and poverty programs. But these programs depend on local initiative and concurrence. Federal and state officials can do little until local leaders ask for help. Given the fact that farm workers characteristically lack cohesion, congregation, and articulation—particularly when contrasted with eligibles in the metropolitan trouble spots—it is not surprising that there have been proportionally few projects under the Manpower Development and Training Act for farm people. However, a general rural manpower service (as I will discuss later) might become the agency through which rural community leaders and agricultural extension personnel could take a more active interest in manpower development.

## MIGRANCY AND SEASONALITY

Whatever else may happen—higher wages, unions, collective contracts, or even unemployment insurance—agriculture will still require large numbers of temporary workers. Mechanization has dramatically reduced seasonal labor requirements in many important crops and undoubtedly will continue to do so. Yet, sharp peaks in employment have been left, and more highly skilled people are required to operate and attend the new equipment. The day is still far off when biologically seasonal crops will be handled by regularly employed, year-round personnel. Meanwhile, traditional solutions to temporary labor needs become increasingly less satisfactory.

Employers can no longer rely on alien contract labor. Within our borders migratory patterns are breaking down and interarea recruitment is becoming less effective. Migratory families settle down once they are given reasonable opportunities for steady work. Now, in an era of concern about poverty and underprivilege, and with community centered antipoverty programs; a new set of forces has come into effect against migrancy. In my view, it is contradictory for government to sponsor simultaneously community war-on-poverty programs and interarea seasonal labor recruitment programs. Manpower training, job development, and fair employment programs may lower the level of underprivilege which has in the past produced seasonal farm laborers. Therefore, farm employers and others concerned might well be advised to seek new arrangements to get seasonal labor.

Over the years, farmers have often been exhorted to diversify their enterprise so as to provide continuous employment for themselves and hired personnel. But the trend has been toward more specialization, not less, It is realistic to expect that as long as seasonal workers are available, specialized farms will continue and seasonal labor requirements will be substantial. Moreover, given the regional diversity in our climates, soils, water supplies, and market proximities, there are advantages in specialization that, in the general interest, ought not to be obstructed.

Therefore, it seems as if seasonal work force needs will have to be satisfied more and more from among the residents of the immediate labor market area; and recruitment—both public and private—will have to depend less on need and disadvantage to create a labor supply. Assuming that these generalizations are valid as to direction even though not specific as to timing or magnitude, they suggest the development of two sources of seasonal labor: (1) persons who are not obligated to support a family and who are not seeking full-year employment—which is a roundabout way of referring to students, housewives, and retired, able-bodied persons; (2) persons who seek full-year employment and are able to combine other part-year employment with farm work in a seasonally complementary way.

What are the possibilities of integrating farm and other employment in rural economies? And what are the possibilities of establishing dependable seasonal patterns of employment which will more systematically utilize persons not regularly in the labor market? There are a priori grounds for believing that possibilities for both are considerable. But before going further into these questions, I wish to examine some of the implications of recent data on farm labor force participation and composition.

## LABOR FORCE PARTICIPATION AND COMPOSITION

National data from the U.S. Department of Agriculture show that of all per-

TABLE 1.  PERSONS DOING SOME FARM WORK, BUT WORKING IN ONLY ONE QUARTER, BY AGE
AND SEX, CALIFORNIA, 1964

| | Males | | Females | |
| | Farm Work Only | Farm and Nonfarm Work | Farm Work Only | Farm and Nonfarm Work |
| Age | | | | |
|---|---|---|---|---|
| 16 and under | 19,000 | 500 | 8,850 | 100 |
| 17–21 | 16,325 | 2,550 | 8,450 | 725 |
| 22–29 | 10,925 | 1,825 | 7,575 | 300 |
| 30–39 | 11,175 | 975 | 10,650 | 525 |
| 40–49 | 10,900 | 1,075 | 7,700 | 300 |
| 50–59 | 8,400 | 475 | 6,375 | 100 |
| 60 and over | 9,900 | 100 | 4,925 | 50 |
| Total | 86,625 | 7,500 | 54,525 | 2,100 |

SOURCE: Based on California State Department of Employment, Research and Statistics, Report 830, No. 2 (November 7, 1966).

sons doing 25 days or more of farm work a year, the majority (three-fifths in 1964-1965) did not do farm work as their chief activity. Some were mainly unemployed; but the largest segment was made up of those not in the labor force most of the year. Moreover, in the postwar years there has been a persistent decline in the proportion of those (employed 25 days or more a year on farms) whose chief activity is farm work. The principal reciprocal of this trend has been the increase temporary use of persons not otherwise in the labor force.[6]

* * *

Because of their surprisingly large numbers, those doing some farm work only in one quarter and not otherwise employed (in California) call for further attention.[7] A ready surmise is that they would be mainly women and minors, but they were not, as Table 1 indicates. It is astonishing to find that some 45,000 males between 22 and 60 years did some farm work (judged by their earnings, not much) and were not in the California labor force more than one quarter. Some of this magnitude is attributable to interstate migrancy, but this could explain no more than a small fraction of the total. Apparently there are quite a large number of adult males in California who are not only casual to farm employment but also to the labor market. In contrast, the brief labor force participation of approximately 40,000 males under 22 years and 56,000 females of all ages is in line with expectations. It is to be noted that relatively few of the short-term farm workers did other than farm work.

The median earnings in Table 2 show that earnings increase more than in pro-

TABLE 2.  MEDIAN EARNINGS BY NUMBER OF QUARTERS OF SOME EMPLOYMENT,
BY SEX, CALIFORNIA, 1964

| | One Quarter | Two Quarters | Three Quarters | Four Quarters |
|---|---|---|---|---|
| Males, farm work only | $ 84 | $397 | $1,121 | $3,181 |
| Males, farm and nonfarm work | 203 | 469 | 1,130 | 2,817 |
| Females, farm work only | 76 | 285 | 640 | 1,590 |
| Females, farm and nonfarm work | 203 | 374 | 847 | 1,580 |

SOURCE: See source for Table 1.

[6] *Rural People in the American Economy*, U.S. Department of Agriculture, Agricultural Economic Report 101 (Washington, D.C.: October, 1966), p. 46.
[7] The data are for 1964 and therefore before the post-Bracero supply response discussed above.

portion to additional quarters worked. The increasing differences imply that with a longer spread of work activity over time, there is a correlated tendency toward intensification of labor force participation on a day-by-day basis. However, as we noted previously, the tendency to more intense participation is frustrated if the worker has to seek employment from numerous employers.

A related matter is the relation between farm and nonfarm employment in the utilization of the labor force. When one looks at the overall median earnings, one sees the great importance of combining nonfarm and farm work:

|  | Males | Females |
|---|---|---|
| Farm work only | $ 681 | $160 |
| Farm and nonfarm work | 1,602 | 838 |

These results are in accord with data from other sources and they have been interpreted as meaning that the best way for a farm worker to improve his income situation is to obtain nonfarm work. National data of the U.S. Department of Agriculture also show that farm workers earn more per day in nonfarm than in farm work.[8] However, in California the data indicate that the principal contribution of nonfarm work toward increased earnings is through additional employment (see Table 2). One-quarter workers who have nonfarm as well as farm work have a definite advantage over one-quarter workers who have farm work only. This advantage diminishes for two-quarter workers, tends to disappear for three-quarter workers, and actually is reversed for four-quarter males. Thus, a combination of farm and nonfarm work appears to improve an in-dividual's chances for more intensive labor force participation and longer term employment. At the same, those who do farm work only and get an equivalent amount of employment are able to earn equal or better incomes.

Nonfarm employment plays a prominent role in the annual work program of many of those who do farm work, especially among workers who are active in at least three quarters (see Table 3). . . .

It has been noted previously that many of the four-quarter California workers are apparently job-to-job casuals. This has a marked effect on the range of earnings, as Table 4 indicates. One would expect that a distribution of earnings restricted to four-quarter male workers would be more closely centered around the medians. Some of the range shown in Table 4 may be attributable to differences in work-

TABLE 3.  PERCENTAGES OF PERSONS DOING SOME FARM WORK WHO ALSO HAD NONFARM EMPLOYMENT, BY SEX, CALIFORNIA

| Quarters of Earnings | Males | Females |
|---|---|---|
| One | 8% | 4% |
| Two | 37 | 29 |
| Three | 49 | 45 |
| Four | 45 | 52 |
| All | 36 | 24 |

SOURCE: See source for Table 1.

[8] *The Hired Farm Working Force of 1965*, U.S. Department of Agriculture, Agricultural Economic Report 98 (Washington, D.C.: 1965), p. 15.

finding abilities and on-the-job performances of individuals; it is not likely that these are the primary causes, however, considering the fact that these were the individuals who presumably were the most successful in piecing together full-year employment from a series of jobs in and out of agriculture.

## LABOR FORCE
## UTILIZATION IN RURAL ECONOMIES

Historically, farm employers with short-term seasonal labor needs have believed that the workers should or would have to come from outside the area—from a "migratory stream," from abroad, or from a special recruitment program. Government and academic people, by identifying migratory streams, have contributed to the notion that such labor is the only feasible solution to seasonal labor needs. The federal farm placement system built its "annual worker plan" on the concept of arranging and expediting continuous migratory movements. Because of these attitudes and the practices associated with them, workers who wished to settle down were not encouraged by employers or by the placement service, and particularly not by local authorities who were apprehensive lest the workers become relief charges.

Another factor contributing to the estrangement of farm workers from local labor markets is the structure of government farm placement. For almost a quarter century, farm placement has been operationally separate from the general federal-state placement system. Farm placement offices are expected to make referrals only to farm employers. Farm placement personnel have the responsibility for recruitment of farm labor as well as placement of those seeking farm work on their own initiative. In recruitment, aside from the specific responsibilities in foreign labor, the major emphasis has been on interarea movements. Local office personnel have characteristically not been expected or even permitted to help workers arrange combinations of seasonal farm and other jobs which would give an approximation of full employment in one area. Individual farm placement officers have occasionally been interested in trying to help farm workers to arrange annual work programs within areas of feasible daily commuting, but the restricted obligations of the placement program have constrained rather than encouraged this.

In my view, there are two major reasons for optimism regarding the development of a "pluralistic" rural economy and a multiple-occupation labor force. First, there is the upgrading of farm jobs and farm workers. These help to remove bar-

TABLE 4.  ANNUAL EARNINGS OF FOUR-QUARTER MALE WORKERS, CALIFORNIA, 1964

| Annual Earnings | Farm Work Only | Work Farm and Nonfarm |
|---|---|---|
| Under $1,000 | 9% | 10% |
| 1,000–1,999 | 18 | 22 |
| 2,000–2,999 | 20 | 23 |
| 3,000–3,999 | 21 | 18 |
| 4,000–4,999 | 16 | 11 |
| 5,000 and over | 16 | 16 |
| Total workers | 92,525 | 76,675 |
| Median earnings | $3,181 | $2,817 |

SOURCE: See source for Table 1.

riers between farm and nonfarm jobs and to create an environment in which workers are willing and able to move between farm and nonfarm work. Second there is the unique set of economic and demographic facts concerning rural areas. Although our rural areas are ceasing to be dominantly agricultural, we have yet to evolve policies which recognize the changes taking place. It is a common assumption that if either self-employed farmers or hired farm workers are redundant to an area, seasonally or permanently, they go somewhere else. And "somewhere else," as we can no longer avoid realizing, has all too often been a jobless, congested city slum.

A nation that has done so much to advance farm technology should have concerned itself long ago with its obligations to the people made redundant by that technology. Even though the historic farm exodus is now well along, it is not too late to apply energy and resources to develop viable, diversified rural economies. Success would bring many benefits, particularly the building up of a stable labor force and an orderly set of employment relations which would help get seasonal farm work done and would provide worthwhile earning prospects.

A Rural Industries Manpower Service, instead of the Farm Placement Service, would be a good starting point. Such a service could be a center for contact and communication. In addition to placement and recruitment, it should help workers arrange annual work programs composed of several short-term jobs in farming and other rural industries. In so doing, some training needs would be encountered, and here too the proposed service might play a vital role by helping to develop appropriate training programs. In combining these activities, manpower service personnel should take the initiative on job development, i.e., informing potential employers of workers' qualifications and availability and soliciting placement or-

ders. Given a rural labor market of diversified skill and an effective manpower service, efforts to encourage the decentralization of industry into rural areas should become more rewarding. Also, the new "growth" industries—particularly recreation, but not excluding health and education—might find rural locations to be practical in such a manpower environment.

We know from the data that have been reviewed here and from other sources as well, that many farm workers show versatility and initiative in working on a series of jobs for different employers, both in and out of agriculture. Nevertheless, both the data on length of employment and on earnings strongly imply that the long-term workers, and especially those participating in the labor force through four quarters, could make a greater manpower contribution and improve their income position if public and private procurement and management practices were to undergo some rationalization. A rural industries manpower service could be a good way to begin. The rationalization could be carried much further if, in addition, farmers would associate themselves for a collective (as opposed to an individual) approach to labor needs, as, for example, they have already done for obtaining and managing Braceros.

CONCLUSION

Is there to be a new era for farm labor? A qualifiedly affirmative answer seems in order. Since farm employers apparently no longer have access to foreign labor, they will have to become more competitive for labor—both among themselves and against other labor markets. Furthermore, unionization drives are likely to have an impact even if they are not highly successful, for farm employers will be under pressure to improve wages and conditions in order to combat unionism.

The critical question is, if unemployment rises again and the antipoverty programs are curtailed, will thousands be thrown into the open-ended farm labor market for whatever they can get, thereby cancelling the forces for improvement? The optimistic view is that the level of unemployment will remain low and the antipoverty effort, including manpower development and training will be sustained; in this case the differences between farm and other employment can be expected to narrow over time.

In a full employment economy, with the borders closed to foreign workers, seasonal labor needs in farming will be met to an increasing extent by local residents, who normally are not in the labor market for more than two or three months a year. Union organization is not likely to have much appeal to such persons, but earnings and working conditions will have to be attractive if they are to be induced into a regular pattern of farm labor force participation. At the other extreme is the small minority of workers who are regularly employed by the same employer throughout the year. This group has comparatively good incomes and often also has fringe benefits—insurance, profit-sharing, paid vacations, and housing. Most of this group are in dairies or other livestock enterprises. Although dairy workers in the Los Angeles and San Francisco areas have had unions and collective bargaining for many years, they have not spread to others in the regularly employed category. For this regular work force, in which the level of skill is relatively high, prevailing conditions already are close to being competitive.

Between these extremes are the large numbers of more than incidental and less than fully employed workers. This is the group which has the most to gain and possibly the most interest in unionization. It is mainly for them that some improvement in public and private manpower policies and programs is important. The evidence is that this group has the initiative and versatility to put bits and pieces of jobs together toward the goal of full-time work. They need some assistance toward a more systematic way of trying to achieve a full year's income. Such assistance would help solve agriculture's manpower needs and, at the same time, the income needs of the workers. In the past, when rural economic activity was confined mainly to farming, occupational and employment diversity was less practical. Now, and in the future, with greater economic diversity in rural areas, increased population, and more rapid transportation, the delineation between farm and nonfarm labor can be expected to become less and less distinct.

Those interested in improving the lot of farm labor should be aware that the demand for labor probably will be highly responsive to rising cost. In spite of the revolutionary reductions in manpower needs that already have occurred, there is much potential for further innovation, such as alteration of plant forms and production technique and improved mechanical substitutes for the human hand. If costs go up, these innovations will be accelerated. Rising labor costs and the latitude of labor-saving possibilities will both add further to the already existing economic and technical pressures on farmers to consolidate into larger enterprises.

For the above reasons, a new era for farm labor is likely to be one in which many of those now in the field will not be present. But this will not be the first such episode in American economic history, nor the last.

## Related Readings

The concluding chapter from *Labor and the American Economy* (New York, Simon and Schuster, 1970) by Derek C. Bok and John T. Dunlop, contains some perspectives on the American labor movement based on a detailed analysis of the relationship between unions and the economy. Bok and Dunlop conclude that unions are among the least understood of the institutions in the American economy and, surprisingly, there seems to be an inverse relationship between education and incomes and the level of understanding of the labor movement. Examples of ideas held by businessmen, which are unsupported by the facts, according to Bok and Dunlop, are that unions cause inefficiency and inflation and that the labor movement is a powerful political force in the economy. On the other hand, the authors believe liberal intellectuals engage in gross oversimplification when they argue that the labor movement has become a part of the establishment, that it is not interested in helping disadvantaged workers, and that it is led by people who are out of touch with dramatic, progressive social events. The authors argue that even though the labor movement has not come forth with many new ideas about how to solve social problems, national union leaders have supported many liberal causes, with the possible exception of the war against poverty, in which the labor movement has played only a modest role.

Although many liberal intellectuals think American unions are conservative because of the nature of their leadership, Bok and Dunlop demonstrate that union members actually are much more conservative than their leaders. The authors therefore believe that liberal critics are wrong when they think that greater control by the membership would cause unions to be more progressive.

> Because of the indifference and opposition of union members, grass-roots democracy threatens to hamper, rather than promote, union programs for social reform. Indeed, the disinterest and hostility of the members undoubtedly help to explain why union efforts to combat poverty, racial discrimination, and other domestic problems, have almost invariably been more impressive at the Federation level than in the local communities.

Bok and Dunlop are also skeptical of the suggestion that charismatic leadership and education will cause union members to be more responsive to the liberal intellectuals' ideals. They argue "neither of these views seems particularly realistic in any society. Very few people have the capacity to give 'electrifying impulses' to millions of others." Moreover, "unlike their counterparts in Scandinavia, American workers have never responded in large numbers to education programs, regardless of the agency presenting them." Therefore, "the job of informing members about social issues is a burden that must fall upon the entire culture; it cannot be discharged by any single institution."

In response to the question of whether unions are worth saving, Bok and Dunlop argue, "of all major institutions in America there is none whose value to society is so widely questioned as the labor organization." Nevertheless, the authors obviously feel, and we agree, that unions are indeed worth saving because they convey many benefits to society: (1) they provide a better means of fixing rules governing wages, hours, and working conditions than would be afforded by government regulations; (2) they have influenced the form of compensation to workers; (3) they have caused fairer treatment for their members; and (4)

> Unions are the most potent organized body to represent the political interests of workers and to a lesser extent of the poor and disadvantaged. One has only to look at the unrepresented segments of our society to see the consequences of remaining unorganized. Consider the legislative accomplishments of veterans who are well organized, and compare them with the plight of the unorganized draftee who receives compensation below the federal minimum wage and suffers needlessly in searching for jobs and pursuing his education because of the uncertainties of the selective service system.

Nevertheless, Bok and Dunlop feel that the labor movement must meet several important challenges if the benefits of collective bargaining are to be preserved. They argue that the labor movement must: be sufficiently responsive to social pressures to avoid government control of collective bargaining; be more responsive to the needs of their members; come to terms with racial discrimination within the labor movement; develop greater respect for unions in the society as a whole; and, most important, develop the knowledge, talent and organizational structure to meet the challenges it faces.

Although the determinants of union behavior are fairly well known to scholars of the labor movement, they are often misunderstood by business groups and the liberal critics of the unions. In part, this misunderstanding results from different value systems, but it also stems from ulterior motives that cause these groups to ascribe considerable power to union leaders. Businessmen exaggerate the union leaders' power because they are accustomed to authoritarian organizations and therefore do not understand the nature of democratic entities like unions. Liberals, on the other hand, often romanticize workers as underdogs and "as a result—until recently at any rate—these critics could seldom bring themselves to blame union shortcomings on the members; instead they concluded that the leaders must somehow be responsible." Bok and Dunlop feel that "because of these tendencies to exaggerate the labor leader, one must take pains to construct a more realistic picture of how the union policy is actually made."

In their view "in the end, union behavior is the product of four broad influences that are constantly interacting upon one another: the desires of the members, the nature and abilities of the leadership, the capacities and opinions of subordinates, and the pressures of the environment."

In order to meet the challenges it faces, the labor movement must adopt an agenda that is different from the ones proposed by their critics and the ones currently being pursued by the American labor movement. Bok and Dunlop argue:

A . . . realistic agenda for union leaders would emphasize . . . : a much
expanded and upgraded program of staff training, a new emphasis on
research, and more effective administration. A continuous program of experimentation to find new programs to meet new needs of their members,
and more imaginative, more carefully planned community programs
(coupled with a restructuring of the local federations to give greater influence to the AFL-CIO). These steps may not seem as dramatic to some
critics as new programs to minimize strikes and overcome racial restrictions, but they are steps which top labor leaders are much freer to take.

The authors conclude that closer relations must be established between unions
and governments, federations, and universities.

Unions face evident risks that they will be taken more and more for
granted by their members, that they will function at a growing disadvantage in dealing with institutions possessing greater knowledge and superior
techniques, and that their social role will be preempted increasingly by
other groups. Should these risks materialize, the prospects are that unions
will become progressively duller bureaucracies, more fatuous at times to
arouse an indifferent membership, and largely ignored in the major developments of the society and rather widely disliked as a necessary evil,
and a source of periodic inconvenience.

In "The Direction of Unionism 1947–1967: Thrust or Drift?" *Industrial and
Labor Relations Review,* vol. 20, no. 4, July 1967, Joseph Shister analyzes some
of the most significant union developments in the postwar period. He begins
by summarizing the conditions of unionism in 1947, and then discusses some
of the factors shaping the American labor movement in subsequent years. With
respect to union membership, Shister points out that growth has been fairly
steady throughout the postwar period with the exception of 1950 to 1953
when there was a significant increase in the extent of union membership.
During that Korean War period, membership increased from 22 to 26 percent
of the work force. Shister also makes it clear that the future of the American
labor movement depends, to a very significant degree, on its ability to organize
such previously unorganized groups as white-collar workers, agricultural workers, and many others in the south.

The term "white-collar" covers many diverse groups with differing pro-
pensities to organize. For example, although professionals have been very
difficult to unionize, many of these workers are affiliated with the AFL-CIO
and others have their own associations, some of which are becoming collective
bargaining organizations. Collective bargaining seems to have a particular appeal for professionals in the rapidly expanding government and nonprofit
sectors where wage increases have lagged behind those in manufacturing.
However, as Shister points out, the unionization of some of these professionals,
particularly the teachers, is influenced by many noneconomic factors.

The organization of white-collar and other government employees has been
encouraged by the federal government's favorable attitude toward collective
bargaining expressed in executive orders 10988, issued by President Kennedy
in 1962, and 11491, issued by President Nixon in 1969. (These will be discussed
in Chapter 15.)

Although agricultural workers have been at the bottom of the economic ladder in the United States, they have also responded very slowly to union organizing efforts. Shister discusses many of the reasons for the difficulties involved in organizing agricultural workers and many others will be discussed later. However, Shister's main conclusion is that because of inadequate legal protection as well as their economic weaknesses, unionization of agricultural workers is not likely to be very significant for some time to come. Although other union leaders are very critical of the Taft-Hartley Act, agricultural workers do not even benefit from its coverage. However, it is not at all clear that Taft-Hartley coverage would do very much to stimulate the growth of unions among agricultural workers. In part, this is because the ability to organize is determined primarily by the ability to win strikes. Taft-Hartley protection could do something to help agricultural workers gain recognition and bargaining rights but it could do very little to help agricultural workers' unions win strikes.

Shister also dispels the popularly held notion that all union organizers have an intense desire to expand unionism to all sectors of the work force. As he emphasizes, the primary incentive for organizing by business unionists is to protect their wages and working conditions from nonunion competition. Where these unions have already organized their jurisdictions, they have very limited incentives to extend unionism to other workers. However, Shister also emphasizes that business unionism might want to expand unionism for political reasons. If these unionists have a need for political allies in order to defend themselves from encroachments by the government, they might be willing to incur the financial cost involved in expanding unionism.

Business unionists have been challenged in the postwar period by social unionists and by intellectuals. The social unionists differ from business unionists not only in their desire to expand unionism to disadvantaged workers but also in such matters as foreign policy. As Shister points out, the traditional business leaders of the AFL-CIO have been staunch defenders of American foreign policy in the postwar period, particularly with respect to a hard anti-Communist line, whereas social unionists like the late Walter Reuther were critical of American foreign policy and felt that communism no longer presented the monolithic threat to the so-called free labor movements of the West. Social unionists were also critical of the AFL-CIO for not doing more to eliminate discrimination within the ranks of organized labor.

Liberal intellectuals have been critical of American unions not only for their lack of social motivation, but also because the labor movement was no longer where the social action was. As a consequence, many of the intellectuals who supported the labor movement during the excitement of the 1930's have left it.

Even though the labor movement's accomplishments have fallen far short of the expectations of liberal intellectuals and social unionists, Shister considers them to be important nevertheless. Moreover, he makes it clear that the labor movement's failure to move faster on the social front is a result, in significant measure, of the fact that the labor movement is a political institution conrolled by its members and the membership is much less interested in social affairs than they are in accomplishing economic objectives.

In discussing the centralization issue, Shister makes it plain that the trend toward greater control by the national union offices results from a variety of factors that "neither the membership nor the leadership could ignore, if they were concerned (as indeed they should have been) with union effectiveness and protecting and enhancing job interest."

Shister next picks up the question of unions' political activity. He concludes, "The changes which have occurred relate, not to the fundamental style of politics, but to the magnitude and intensity of political activity within the same stylistic setting." In other words, the traditional political philosophy of the American labor movement remains unchanged, but there has been a considerable increase in the relative importance of political activity within the labor movement. That is, as government activity becomes more important in an interdependent society, the labor movement obviously has been forced to pay more and more attention to political affairs. However, it retains its traditional approach of not forming a separate political party and of working within the existing political structure.

The labor movement experienced a number of political successes as well as failures in the postwar period. As Shister states, "It has unquestionably had a legislative influence—although how much of an influence is impossible to say with reasonably objective certainty—in the raising of minimum wage standards, the expansion of minimum wage coverage, the liberalization of unemployment insurance and social security systems, the establishment of Medicare, the enactment of Civil Rights laws, the increased federal aid to education, the enactment of the poverty and related programs, the passage of the 1964 federal income tax cut, to mention only some of the more publicized socio-economic measures." On the negative side, the labor movement has had a number of significant political failures; for example, it has not been able to avoid the passage of such anti-union legislation as the Taft-Hartley and Landrum-Griffin Acts and the so-called right-to-work laws in the states. Shister concludes, "In brief, American unionism has been a political influence, but far less than it would have liked to be, or many people believe it is."

Shister points out a number of reasons for the labor movement's political weakness. First, it has been unable to deliver the vote of the union members and their families, in part because voting behavior is determined by many things other than the worker's union membership or the like, and many of these other things have had a much stronger influence than the political and education campaigns of the unions. However, Shister also makes it clear that he considers the labor movement to have been hampered by poor strategy in some of its legislative fights.

Shister concludes with the observation that the present trends in the American labor movement are likely to continue in the foreseeable future. For example, he expects white-collar unionism to continue to grow in the private and public sectors and for union membership to expand in the south, but "short of some serious socio-economic dislocation in the country or dramatic shift in public policy favoring unionization—both of which seem most unlikely in the foreseeable future—we will not witness any great spurts of growth in these sectors comparable to the major spurts of the blue-collar growth in the past." Moreover, Shister does not believe the American labor movement is likely to form an independent political party, or to give major support to the so-called social unionists. He concludes, "Even if social unionism should finally prevail, the picture will not change in the direction that the profits of doom may have predicted. For there is little in that philosophy which necessitates the abolition of the free market, the nationalization of industry, and so forth. It represents, instead, an attempt to make capitalism economically more effective and socially more humane."

On the history of American unions, the standard early work is John R. Commons et al., *History of Labor in the United States* (New York, Macmillan, 1918). A good, short summary of the early trade union movement is Selig Perlman's *History of Trade Unionism*, originally published in 1922 but reissued by Augustus M. Kelley, 1955. Philip Taft's *Organized Labor in American History* (New York, Harper and Row, 1964), and Irving Bernstein's *The Lean Years: A History of the American Workers, 1920–1933* (Boston, Houghton Mifflin, 1960) and *The Turbulent Years: A History of the American Workers 1933–1941* (Boston, Houghton Mifflin, 1970) contain good, longer treatments of American labor history. Lloyd Ulman's *Rise of National Unions* (Cambridge, Harvard University Press, 1955) contains an excellent analysis of the factors responsible for the emergence of national unions, which are the dominant structural types in the United States. Walter Galenson's *The CIO Challenge to the AFL* (Cambridge, Harvard University Press, 1960) is the best study available on the origin of the CIO.

Ray Marshall's *Labor in the South* (Cambridge, Harvard University Press, 1967) contains a history of organized labor in the south and a detailed analysis of the factors influencing union growth. Excellent treatments of the racial practices of American unions are in Sterling D. Spero and A.L. Harris, *The Black Worker* (New York, Columbia University Press, 1931); Herbert R. Northrup *Organized Labor and the Negro* (New York, Harper and Bros., 1944). More recent works include Ray Marshall, *The Negro and Organized Labor* (New York, Wiley, 1965) and Julius Jacobson, ed., *The Negro and the American Labor Movement* (Garden City, N.Y., Doubleday (Anchor Books), 1968).

Good statistical analyses of the growth of American unions are Leo Wolman, *Ebb and Flow in Trade Unionism* (New York, National Bureau of Economic Research, 1936); Leo Troy, *Distribution of Union Membership Among the States*, (New York, National Bureau of Economic Research, 1957); and Irving Bernstein, "The Growth of American Unions," (*The American Economic Review*, June 1954) and "The Growth of American Unions, 1945–1960" (*Labor History*, Spring 1961). In the 1961 article, Bernstein presents a good discussion of the statistical problems involved in measuring union membership; he gives a critical analysis of the so-called "saturationist" position which holds that union growth slowed down after World War II because unions had "penetrated the readily organizable segments of the labor force—male, blue-collar workers employed mainly by large firms in the manufacturing, mining, transportation, and construction industries in the larger urban centers of the North and West" (p. 131).

For a good discussion of union lobbying tactics, which the author argues contributed to the passage of the Landrum-Griffin Act, see Sar A. Levitan "Union Lobbyists' Contributions to Tough Labor Legislation" (*Labor Law Journal*, October 1959).

Everett M. Kassalow, *Trade Unionism and Industrial Relations: An Inter-*

*national Comparison* (New York, Random House, 1969, Ch. 1.) has a good comparison of the background differences in the American and European labor movements. The pros and cons of whether the American labor movement faces a crisis are debated in *The Crisis in the American Trade Union Movement* (The Annals of the American Academy of Political and Social Science, November 1963).

Curtis Aller, *Labor Relations in the Hawaiian Sugar Industry* (Berkeley, Institute of Industrial Relations, University of California, 1957) presents an analysis of the unionization by the International Longshoreman and Warehouseman's Union (ILWU) of the Hawaiian sugar and pineapple industries. The ILWU's success led to the enactment of the Hawaii Employment Relations Act, which recognized the right of agricultural workers to organize. This is one of the most successful organizing experiences of agricultural workers in the United States. Varden Fuller, *Labor Relations in Agriculture* (Berkeley, Institute of Industrial Relations, University of California, 1955) discusses the factors influencing collective bargaining and unionization in American agriculture. Fuller concludes that unionization has been unsuccessful mainly because of a lack of protective labor legislation, the power of farm employers' organizations, and the abundant supply of agricultural labor which lacks a strong industry or area identification. The most comprehensive study of collective bargaining efforts in agriculture before World War II is Stuart Jamieson, *Labor Unionism in American Agriculture* (U.S. Department of Labor, Bureau of Labor Statistics, 1945). One of the most noteworthy recent efforts to organize farm workers is by The National Farm Workers in California. Much of this effort centered around a strike and boycott by grape workers, a colorful and sympathetic account of which is in John Gregory Dunne, *Delano: The Story of the California Grape Strike* (New York, Farrar, Straus and Giroux, 1967). Alexander Morin, *The Organizability of Farm Labor in the United States* (Cambridge, Harvard University Press, 1952) presents a detailed analysis of the differences between union organizing among agricultural and nonagricultural workers. Morin finds farm workers more difficult to organize than nonagricultural industries because of the mobility of the work force, the administrative and financial problems involved in maintaining a union organization, and the lack of protective labor legislation. He points out, however, that agricultural workers are more likely to organize when they are concentrated in a fairly limited area, have some homogeneity as a group, and possess an awareness of their common problems. *Farm Labor Organizing, 1905–1967: A Brief History* (New York, National Advisory Committee on Farm Labor, 1967) discusses the reasons for the exclusion of farm labor from the coverage of the National Labor Relations Act, the unsuccessful attempts of the Southern Tenant Farmers Union in the 1930's to organize agricultural workers in the South, and the success of the International Longshoreman's and Warehouseman's Union in organizing sugar and pineapple plantations in Hawaii. Although the coverage of this pamplet is national, it emphasizes the problems of workers in California.

# CHAPTER 3

# Labor Movements: Europe

## *INTRODUCTION*

Labor movements exhibit some principles that apply generally over a period of time and also apply to specific movements at a particular time. Most labor movements originated after the industrial revolution, during times of adversity for workers. Indeed, in a real sense, the basic ideological conflict of the 19th and 20th centuries has concerned the question of how the labor problems of industrial societies could be resolved. Revolutionaries consider labor problems to be inextricably bound up with the capitalist system and therefore do not believe the workers' problems can be resolved within the framework of that system. Socialists of more moderate persuasions—like the British Labor party and the Social Democratic parties of most Western countries—believe that government ownership and regulation is essential to the solution of labor problems.

These ideological conflicts are reflected in the labor movements of various countries. Indeed, the dominant ideology of a labor movement is likely to reflect the success or failure of political and economic movements within a country. Where political democracy was established without great difficulty—as in Great Britain and the United States—labor movements have been more moderate. Similarly, collective bargaining has gained more support in those countries where it appears to have produced satisfactory results for the workers.

## *UNIONS IN POSTWAR EUROPE*

Since labor movements were responses to specific conditions, it is not surprising that their goals and procedures should change as those conditions change. The effects of some recent trends in European labor movements were analyzed by Arthur Ross. In "Prosperity and Labor Relations in Europe: The Case of West Germany," Ross demonstrates the impact of prosperity following World War II on the German labor movement. In his introduction he shows that the adverse economic conditions that gave rise to European labor movements no longer exist. Widespread unemployment has been replaced by labor shortages, and large corporations with scientific management are becoming much more important. These changes have had a profound impact on European labor movements, which have been characterized by class identifications, strong ideological or religious influences, a high degree of union organization, centralized collective bargaining, limited economic power, wage restraints, fewer prolonged strikes and limited impact of collective bargaining on the personnel practices of individual plants. As a consequence of these traditional characteristics, European countries have had considerable government regulation of employment conditions at the shop level, while centralized collective bargaining provisions have set general instead of particular working conditions.

However, as Ross demonstrates, traditional European collective bargaining procedures have created problems for unions since the Second World War. Because of the failure to set specific wages and working conditions at the plant level, workers see fewer direct benefits from collective bargaining than their American counterparts. In Ross's view, European unions have been weakened by these developments as well as by a continuation of the outmoded "class struggle" ideas upon which their traditional procedures have been based. In order to counteract these tendencies and compete with rival organizations that seek to fill the void at the shop level, European unions have been forced to shift their activities more into the plants. In Germany this has taken the form of attempts to control the government-sponsored works councils, the prevalent form of worker representation at the shop level, and efforts to decentralize wage determination. As might be expected, decentralization would strengthen unions relative to management and therefore is resisted by many companies. The trade union movement has also dropped many of its "previous ideological trappings," and reduced its "emphasis on political action, except for co-determination."

# Prosperity and Labor Relations in Europe: The Case of West Germany[*]

## by Arthur M. Ross

### I. INTRODUCTION

Western European industrial relations became stabilized in their traditional form during an era of frequent unemployment, low wages and subsistence living standards. The dominant purpose was to protect workers and employers against unrestricted wage cutting in the labor market and price cutting in the product market.[1] The principal organizations were the trade unions, strong at the top but weak at the plant level, and the employer association. The leading instrument of protection was the minimum wage, pitched at a level appropriate to smaller and less efficient firms.

The standard technique was the national or regional multi-employer agreement, frequently supplemented by social legislation defining basic terms of employment.

It is well recognized that European economics have entered into a new era. . . . Since the early 1950's they have enjoyed long periods of full employment, with extremely minor trade fluctuations as in 1958. Production has expanded rapidly: in the seven years between 1953 and 1960, industrial output rose 82 per cent in Italy, 80 per cent in West Germany, 68 per cent in France, and 30 per cent in the United Kingdom, as compared

SOURCE Reprinted with permission from *The Quarterly Journal of Economics,* Vol. 76, No. 3, August 1962.

[*] Much of the material in this article was gathered while on sabbatical leave in Europe between January and August of 1961. The present article analyzes developments in West Germany. Subsequent articles will deal with France, Italy, and the United Kingdom.

[1] The classic formulation of this essentially defensive strategy is found in Sidney and Beatrice Webb's *Industrial Democracy* (London and New York: Longmans, Green, 1902), in which collective bargaining is described as the "dyke" protecting the workers' standard of life against the competitive pressures which develop in a cumulative "chain of bargains."

with 19 per cent in the United States.[2] Widespread labor shortages have been experienced; imported workers and seasonal migrants have become important constituents of the labor supply in several countries.

*　*　*

Real earnings have advanced at an unprecedented pace; but more impressive than statistics is the physical evidence of middle-class living standards so clearly visible in homes and stores and on the highways. Television and traffic jams, deodorants and demand deposits have not only undermined European moral superiority regarding American materialism but have also quickened the *embourgeoisment* of the European working class, with great consequences in economic and social life.

It could only be expected that these developments would produce important changes in the established systems of industrial relations (described in Section II), which had arisen under such different circumstances earlier in the century. In Section III of this article I shall attempt to characterize the new tendencies in a general fashion. Section IV, a description of recent developments in West Germany, represents the first step toward verification. An account of one country can be only illustrative and not really probative, however. Additional articles dealing with Italy, France and the United Kingdom, which I plan to publish in the near future, should facilitate a more definite judgment of the hypotheses advanced in Section III.

## II. THE TRADITIONAL SYSTEMS

Let us begin by examining more closely some of the common characteristics of traditional Western European systems of industrial relations. In doing so it will be convenient to indicate the contrasting institutions and practices in the United States.

1.　Belonging to unions has been a customary expression of class identification among large segments of European workers. In 1948, for example, unions had enrolled 49 per cent of nonagricultural employees in the United Kingdom; more than 40 per cent in Holland and Germany; and about 55 per cent in Denmark, Norway, and Sweden. An intensive degree of organization has been attained without benefit of union security clauses. In the United States, on the other hand, only 30.3 per cent of wage and salary earners had enrolled despite the prevalence of union security.[3] One of the principal explanations for this contrast is that white-collar, technical and professional employees have been highly organized in Europe.

2.　European unionism has had strong political, ideological and religious tendencies. There have been close relations between union federations and labor parties; in some cases the union federations have clearly been the junior partner. Two or more federations, representing different ideological strains and affiliated with competing political parties, have been established in several countries. The European unions are strongest at the center and weakest at the local or plant level; in fact they frequently do not have any formal existence or "presence" inside the plant.

3.　European employers, like their workers, have been highly organized. Every European country has had a network of employer associations, federations and confederations to develop economic, social and personnel policies; to negotiate

---

[2] Organisation for European Economic Co-operation (OEEC), *General Statistics* (No. 5, 1961), p. 2. Italy has not enjoyed full employment, because of continued stagnation in the South. Northern Italy has been highly prosperous.

[3] See Arthur M. Ross and Paul T. Hartman, *Changing Patterns of Industrial Conflict* (New York: Wiley, 1960), p. 203.

with unions; to deal with government agencies and to represent employers in other respects. In some countries these organizations have enjoyed a prescriptive monopoly of union-management relationships, to the point where a relationship between unions and individual firms cannot be said to exist. This situation reflects the strength of the cartel principle in European economic life, just as the relative unimportance of employer associations in the United States reflects a deep-rooted economic individualism.

4. It follows naturally that European collective bargaining has been highly centralized as compared with the American brand. Typically collective agreements have been negotiated with national or regional industry associations. A few minimum wage rates for broad skill categories of workers, attuned to the wage-paying capacity of marginal firms in the industrial group, have stood at the center of these agreements. In some countries an even higher degree of centralization has been attained, and a master wage bargain, establishing a wage pattern for the entire nation, has been negotiated between the central confederations of industry and labor. This situation has prevailed in the Netherlands, Denmark, and Sweden.

5. European labor organizations, for the most part, had lesser economic strength than those in the United States. To explain this fact we may point to some of the traditional advantages of American unionists. Until recently output per man-hour has increased more rapidly in this country, creating the possibility of greater economic gains. Only a small proportion of American industrial output has been exported, so that the competitive constraints of the world market have not limited union bargaining power to the same extent as in European trading countries. American unions have had substantial monthly dues, collected quite systematically, and special strike funds permitting them to support prolonged stoppages. Finally, a decentralized bargaining system has permitted American unions to obtain higher wages in those companies with greater ability to pay.

6. Until recently negotiated wage increases have been more restrained in Europe than in the United States. This has resulted from the lesser bargaining power of European unions, mentioned above. Another reason is that in countries with highly integrated bargaining structures, central labor and industry federation have considered it their responsibility to protect the price level and the foreign exchange position. Furthermore the close relations between trade unions and Social Democratic governments may have encouraged restraint in some of these countries.

7. European labor contracts have not involved such substantial control of personnel policies as in the United States. Typical European industry-wide agreements have emphasized minimum wages and fringe benefits, to the extent that the latter are not governed by legislation. In some cases there are provisions dealing with hiring, promotion, job assignments, etc., but the language is necessarily so general that there is little impact at the plant level. Seniority and union security, two crucial concepts in the United States, have had little significance in Europe.

8. Resort to long work stoppages as sustained tests of economic strength between employers and unions has been generally infrequent since the 1930's. A recent study shows that in the United Kingdom, Denmark, Germany and the Netherlands, strikes have not only been quite rare, but typically very brief. Norway and Sweden have also seen very few stoppages, although those few have tended to be long. Exactly the opposite pattern of industrial conflict has been found in France and Italy: widespread incidence of strike activity with extremely brief duration. Thus in European countries strikes have either withered away or else

have been used as massive gestures of protest. In the United States and Canada, on the other hand, the strike persists as a genuine trial of economic force.[4]

9. Finally, in some European countries parliamentary legislation has had a significant influence on employment conditions. Statutory minimum wages (or related determinations such as Wages Council orders in the United Kingdom) have regulated actual wages to a greater extent than in the United States. Fringe benefits such as paid holidays, paid vacations, sick leave and family allowances have been widely subject to legislation. Social insurance has been more comprehensive than in this country, and has generally been left to the state rather than shared between public and private instrumentalities.

There are the general outlines of the "dyke" which Western European countries constructed to provide basic protection against competition in labor and product markets.

## III. IMPACT OF THE NEW ECONOMIC ERA

We may now describe the impact of recent economic changes upon these established systems. Needless to say it is risky to state general propositions concerning societies as different as France and Germany, let us say, or Italy and Sweden.

*  *  *

Thus, although some broad generalizations can be stated, differences in degree and some outright exceptions must be recognized. I do not wish to suggest that the new trends have been encountered everywhere to a uniform degree, but only that they have been widely experienced to one degree or another.

1. "Wage drift"—a tendency for actual wage earnings to increase more rapidly than the official negotiated rates—has been a pervasive and persistent phenomenon in European economies. Wage drift results when the negotiated rates in multi-employer agreements are pitched below the market level in a context of high prosperity and labor shortages. The instruments of wage drift have varied from place to place. They have included plant agreements negotiated with works councils and other local representative bodies; premium wage rates offered voluntarily for the purpose of recruiting or holding manpower in a tight labor market; systematic or specious overtime; job evaluation plans installed locally and bearing little relationship to the industry-wide agreements; and loose incentive rates combined with long runs.

2. Under these circumstances some of the vitality and significance has been drained out of the collective agreements negotiated by trade unions and employer associations. Employee earnings have become partly dissociated from contractual rates, although the link has not been broken entirely. Thus the center of gravity is shifting in Western European relations. What is said and done by unions and employer associations is becoming less important; what goes on in plants and localities counts for more.

3. This may appear as a movement in the direction of American practice, since wages are still determined primarily at the plant or company level in this country. There are crucial differences, however. First, American unions have an existence and an apparatus inside the employing enterprise. European unions have local outposts or branches, but in the majority of countries they do not operate within the gates of the plant. The agencies of representation inside the enterprise include works councils, plant committees, and shop stewards. Relations between trade unions and plant representatives

[4] *Ibid.*, Chap. 3, pp. 15–33.

vary from one country to another but there is frequently a competitive element. Second, wage determination in American plants or companies is the prototype of collective bargaining. In Europe, however, the prevalent juridical concept of collective bargaining, as well as the conventional understanding of the term frequently does not include wage determination at the plant level.[5]

4. The reaction of trade unions to the shift in the center of gravity has been a rather ambivalent mixture of resisting the new trend and attempting to adapt themselves to it. In the latter regard various expedients have been adopted. English unions are striving to gain more control over shop stewards and the shop-steward councils. Italian unions are endeavoring to extend their organization within the plant alongside the elected "internal commissions," and to create a union-management relationship at the plant level. Some of the French unions have obtained collective bargaining contracts in large industrial plants, along the lines of typical American contracts. In Germany the leading trade union has moved to appoint its own delegates within the plant communities, to gain more control over works councils, to become a party to job evaluation plans, and to fashion other instruments to plant-level wage negotiation.

5. Employer associations have sought to "hold the line" on wage increases, but member firms have widely ignored their appeals to preserve the integrity of industry-wide contracts. In general the associations have been unable to impose effective discipline upon the errant members, although the Scandinavian associations are more cohesive than those elsewhere. Both the associations and the member firms are united in their desire to prevent the unions from incorporating the "wage drift" into binding contracts, thus forestalling wage cuts in the event that economic conditions should deteriorate and labor markets become looser. Likewise they stand together in resisting intensive regulation of personnel policies such as is characteristic of American labor contracts.

6. Broad multi-industry and economy-wide wage bargains, as well as industry-wide collective agreements, have felt the impact of prosperity, high profits and labor shortages. In Italy there has traditionally been one contract for a vast conglomeration of industries including basic steel, metal fabrication, shipbuilding, automobiles, electrical machinery and others. In 1960–61 the unions were successful in breaking out of this "metal-mechanical" contract and negotiating higher wages for certain enterprises with superior ability to pay. In Denmark the system of economy-wide wage bargains has been subject to divisive pressures for a number of years. These pressures were too great for the central confederations in 1956 and again in 1961; large strikes took place and the national wage patterns were breached. Employer confederations in both countries are viewing these developments with great concern and demanding that the rules of the game be clarified and stabilized.

7. Trade unions have been encountering serious membership problems in several European countries. These problems resemble those of the American labor movement to some extent. For example, the newer elements in the labor force, particularly young workers and white-collar employees, are frequently apathetic toward unionism. The percentage of wage and salary earners enrolled in unions has been declining in the United Kingdom, Germany, Italy and France. In the latter two countries, many workers remain outside the unions in order to avoid being involved in political and ideological conflicts. There

---

[5] Some countries, including Italy and Germany, have legal definitions of collective bargaining; others, such as the United Kingdom, do not.

are chronic difficulties in collecting dues. Worker indifference results from the fact that earnings exceed negotiated rates; from the experience of many years of full employment and rising wages; from closer contact with plant committees as a form of representation; from the frequent "extension" of collective agreements, by government action, to cover unorganized plants; and from the widespread success of paternalistic employer policies. As class consciousness has declined, some labor organizations have turned their thoughts to the possibility of union security clauses.

8. Furthermore, the prestige and power of the central labor federations has been diminishing, particularly in the United Kingdom, Germany and Denmark. This development is the result of several causes: the dispersion of power in collective bargaining, the declining force of ideology, and a lessening of intimacy between union federations and labor parties.

9. There is a widespread feeling in Europe, particularly among journalists and scholars, that the labor movements are unequal to the challenge of rapid economic, social and technological changes; that they have failed to generate any new ideas and are content to rehearse archaic routines; that they led by plodding, unimaginative and complacent bureaucrats. These opinions are strikingly similar to those current in the United States. In Britain and Denmark the employers are described as being equally unprogressive, but this accusation is not heard in the Common Market countries.

10. Since the 1958 recession wage increases have been accelerating in European countries. Widespread apprehension of inflation has developed in financial and governmental circles, resulting in a series of statements by leading officials urging wage restraint, proposing "wage stops," or advocating that wage increases be limited, in one fashion or another, by the increase in productivity. . . . Most European unions have the same profound

unenthusiasm as American unions over the concept of wage restraint. Whether consultative mechanisms should be created to develop "national wage policy," and how such a policy might be implemented within a collective bargaining system, remain open questions in Europe as in the United States.

## IV. THE CASE OF WEST GERMANY

In illustrating these trends it is appropriate to begin with West Germany, where the new economic era has been most remarkable and most remarked upon.

### A. Background of Labor-Management Institutions

The West German trade union movement is the largest in any industrialized country enjoying free institutions, with the exception of the United States and the United Kingdom. The dominant labor federation is the *Deutsche Gewerkschaftsbund* (DGB), a grouping of sixteen industrial unions with a total membership of approximately 6,400,000. There are smaller federations of salaried employees, civil service officials, and Christian unionists, with about 1,200,000 members in the aggregate. The largest and most militant industrial union is *Industrie Gewerkschaft Metall* (I G Metall), or Metal Workers Union, with 1,800,000 members in the iron and steel, shipbuilding and other metalworking industries. I G Metall is relatively more influential in Germany than any single union in the United States.

Employer associations are extremely strong and pervasive, reflecting the importance of the organizational principle in German economic life. There are hundreds of local and regional associations, and thirty-seven national associations covering major branches of industry such as metal trades, chemicals, coal mining, construction, garments, etc. In addition there are fourteen regional confederations of industry associations. At the top of the pyramid stands the *Bundesvereinigung der Deutschen Arbeitgeberverebände* (BDA), or German Confederation of Employers' Associations. The BDA, although it does not actually participate in collective bargaining, has important policy-making, educational and representative functions in economic and political life.

Collective agreements are usually negotiated for whole industries at the regional level, insofar as workers and employers are organized. The federal Minister of Labor may extend the coverage of a privately negotiated agreement, giving it the force of law in nonunion as well as unionized firms, provided that firms employing more than 50 per cent of the workers in the industry are participants, and that extension is deemed to be in the national interest. Thus, although the Metal Workers' Union has 1,800,000 members, about 3,500,000 workers are affected by its various regional contracts, including one contract covering 800,000 employees of metal-using factories in the Ruhr district (North Rhine Westphalia).

## B. Recent Economic Changes

West Germany's economic growth since 1950 is so well known as to need little documentation. Gross national product tripled in the ensuing decade, rising from 97 billion marks in 1950 to 276 billion in 1960. The average increase in real product was 6.8 per cent per year during the 1953–60 period, as compared with 3.6 per cent in the United States. . . .

Unemployment diminished to the vanishing point while labor shortages became chronic. There were 1,600,000 unemployed workers—10.3 per cent of the West German labor force—in 1950. In May 1961 only 110,000 unemployed—less than one-half per cent of the labor force—were counted. At that time it was estimated that there were five vacancies for every jobless worker.

Although real wages in Germany remain below those in Great Britain, Sweden and various other countries, the rate of increase has been quite extraordinary. Money income per worker rose 132 per cent in the 1950–60 decade; the consumer price index advanced 23 per cent; so that the increase in real income per worker was 88 per cent, despite a reduction in the length of the work week. . . .

We need not stop to consider the role of American aid, Germany's modern capital plant, economic policies, the native diligence of the people, and the steady flow of able young refugees from the East in producing this extraordinary development. Whatever the explanation, it was inevitable that the industrial relations system would be greatly affected. We may now consider how the institutions and practices in the labor market have been altered in recent years.

## C. The Wage Drift

The payment of wage rates in excess of contract minima has been traditional in Germany, but observers are unanimous in reporting that the gap between contractual wage rates and actual hourly earnings has widened greatly in recent years. Statistical demonstrations are difficult to find, however. Although adequate statistics on earnings are available, contractual wage rates are seldom tabulated in comparable form. Some studies compare hourly earnings with hourly wage rates at the plant level, rather than with rates in the industry-wide contracts. Furthermore, some comparisons between increases in negotiated rates and hourly earnings over a considerable number of years tend to miss the true significance of wage drift. In Western Europe negotiated increases frequently represent, to a considerable extent, a "pick-up" or consolidation of wage drift which has already accumulated. For example, the OEEC presents some statistics on earnings of male Germans in manufacturing, mining, construction and energy. Between 1953 and 1960, hourly earnings increased 55 per cent. Negotiated increases accounted for 44 per cent;[6] employment shifts, 1 per cent; and higher social security taxes, 2 per cent. Residual wage drift explained the remaining 7 per cent.[7] It cannot be assumed, however, that labor management negotiations really brought about original increases, not previously installed, totaling 44 per cent. . . .

Table 1 shows gross hourly earnings and contract wage rates among journeymen and skilled workers in various districts, for each of the two years between November 1958 and November 1960. We should note first that the earnings are considerably higher than the contract rates. . . .

Thus the contractual wage rates, which historically have reflected the circumstances of the marginal firm and the fear of unemployment, are now well below the market level as determined by supply and demand in a period of full employment.

\* \* \*

One of the important instruments of wage drift in Germany is job evaluation, sometimes called "analytical wage evaluation." Regional agreements in metal industries include job evaluation, but the listing of job classifications is inadequate and insufficient weight is given to certain elements or factors. For example, an employee who moves red-hot iron in a rolling mill will be classified as semi-skilled. The job description in the regional agreement will yield a rate of perhaps 1.80 marks per hour. At his place of employment the employer will have installed a more realistic evaluation plan, which will give weight

to danger, physical strain and working conditions as well as to level of skills. Consequently the employee's rate will be 3.50 marks rather than 1.80.

## D. The Shifting Center of Gravity in Labor Relations

The reduced importance of regional and national industry-wide agreements raises the question of labor-management relations inside the establishment. Here the crucial fact is that the German labor union does not have a formal existence within the plant. The prevalent form of worker representation at the shop level is not the union but the *Betriebsrat* or works council. . . .

Works council legislation provides a framework of consultation and negotiation on various questions and is designed to preserve industrial peace. There is no doubt that it reflects the employers' desire to keep trade unions out of the plants. According to Heinz Hartmann:

*This legislation laid the basis for a dualism in labor representation which at times flares into a full-fledged rivalry . . . By cooperating with the Betriebsrat management played down the power of trade unions in the company.*[8]

The Works Constitution Act makes a distinction between "social matters," "personnel matters" and "economic matters." The "social matters" include numerous local working conditions which are commonly covered by union-management agreements in the United States: methods of remuneration, established of piece rates, work schedules, vacation schedules, administration of welfare services, industrial discipline, etc. In these matters the works council has a right of "co-decision." A conciliation committee issues a binding

---

[6] It is not clear whether this figure represents the sum of increases in the industry-wide contracts or in plant wage schedules.

[7] See OEEC, *The Problem of Rising Prices* (Paris, 1961), p. 322.

[8] Heinz Hartmann, *Authority and Organization in German Management* (Princeton University Press, 1960), pp. 130–31.

TABLE 1. INCREASES IN GROSS HOURLY EARNINGS AND CONTRACT WAGE RATES, NOVEMBER 1958–NOVEMBER 1960

| District | Gross Hourly Earnings Dpf (performance group 1[a]) Men | | | Increase in % | | Contract Wage Rates Dpf | | | Increase in % | |
|---|---|---|---|---|---|---|---|---|---|---|
| | Nov. 58 | Nov. 59 | Nov. 60 | Nov. 58/59 | Nov. 59/60 | Nov. 58 | Nov. 59 | Nov. 60 | Nov. 58/59 | Nov. 59/60 |
| Schleswig-Holstein | 263.8 | 274.9 | 303.3 | +4.2 | +10.3 | 190 | 194 | 211 | +2.1 | +8.8 |
| Hamburg | 277.1 | 293.9 | 324.7 | +6.1 | +10.5 | 200 | 205 | 222 | +2.5 | +8.3 |
| Bremen, Landbetr. | | | | | | 200 | 217 | 235 | +8.5 | +8.3 |
| Bremen, Werftbetr. | 257.8 | 278.6 | 308.1 | +8.1 | +10.6 | 200 | 213 | 231 | +6.5 | +8.5 |
| Niedersachsen | 258.6 | 286.5 | 320.4 | +10.8 | +11.8 | 192 | 207 | 225 | +7.8 | +8.7 |
| Nordrhein-Westfalen | 271.9 | 285.2 | 319.6 | +4.9 | +12.1 | 195 | 199 | 216 | +2.1 | +8.5 |
| Hessen | 257.6 | 278.8 | 313.1 | +8.2 | +12.3 | 189 | 208 | 226 | +10.1 | +8.7 |
| Rheinland-Rheinhessen | | | | | | 184 | 203 | 220 | +10.3 | +8.4 |
| Pfalz | 236.4 | 256.1 | 290.7 | +8.3 | +13.5 | 192 | 206 | 224 | +7.3 | +8.7 |
| Bayern | 241.3 | 261.1 | 297.9 | +8.2 | +14.1 | 191 | 205 | 223 | +7.3 | +8.8 |
| Wttbg.-Baden[b] | 262.8 | 279.2 | 310.2 | +6.2 | +11.1 | 200 | 205 | 222 | +2.5 | +8.3 |
| Wttbg.-Hohenzollern[b] | 242.9 | 260.6 | 293.3 | +7.3 | +12.5 | 184 | 195 | 211 | +6.0 | +8.2 |
| Sudbaden[b] | 242.7 | 265.2 | 292.4 | +9.3 | +10.3 | 184 | 200 | 216 | +8.7 | +8.0 |

SOURCE: *Die Metallindustrie in der Bundesrepublik Deutschland, Sozialpolitische Daten, Anlage zum Geschäftsbericht 1959/61 des Gesamtverbandes der Metallindustriellen Arbeitgeberverbände.*
[a] Workers classified in "performance group 1" by the federal office of statistics include journeymen and some skilled workers.
[b] Gross hourly earnings in machinery manufacturing, automobiles, electrical apparatus precision equipment, and optical goods.

decision if agreement cannot be reached.

On "personnel matters" such as recruitment, reclassification, transfer and dismissal, the works council has a right of consultation which is less than a right of co-decision. However, there is separate legislation dealing with "socially unjustified" dismissals.

With respect to economic matters," employers and works councils are not ordinarily permitted to negotiate wage agreements, since these are reserved for a higher level of bargaining. In exceptional cases an industry-wide agreement might authorize local wage agreements. The works council does have a right of co-decision "in the event of proposed alterations in the undertaking which may involve substantial disadvantages for the staff or a large section thereof, such as reduction or cessation of operations . . . amalgamation with other undertakings, important changes in the purpose of the undertaking and similar cases. In these matters the management and the works council are to come to agreed solutions. If this is not possible, a mediation process takes place."[9]

In any event works councils and employers are forbidden to initiate work stoppages, and are legally obligated to avoid any actions which might endanger industrial peace in the establishment. The fact that so many important matters are lodged with works councils, rather than unions, and that works councils are forbidden to strike, helps to explain the almost complete disappearance of strikes in Germany during the postwar period.

In discharging their joint responsibilities under the Works Constitution Act, employers and works councils in the larger firms have established a great variety of joint committees to deal with such matters as supplementary pensions, sickness benefits, piece rate systems, distribution of company housing and apprenticeship training.

### E.  Unions and Works Councils

Enough has been said to indicate that the more vital aspects of industrial relations have been shifting into the plants, where trade unions do not have any formal existence. As we might expect, the more aggressive unions are attempting to push themselves within the plant gates and break through the juridical wall which formally separates from the works councils.

I do not mean to suggest that union endeavors to control the works councils are new. On the contrary, these endeavors have been going on since the enactment of the first works council law in 1920. Recent developments have sharpened the issue, however. To some labor organizations the present situation is probably satisfactory; but to others, including the mammoth Metal Workers' Union, it leaves much to be desired.

*On the company level, the trade unions have no organizations that would match . . . the non-union organs . . . German labor unions are not organized in plant locals. Rather their smallest units cover one or more industries in a town or district.[10]*

To maintain relations with works councils has become a principal task of the unions' district branches. Unions frequently describe works councils as "the prolonged arm of the trade union" despite the formal separation of the two bodies. Although the Works Constitution Act does not permit unions to participate officially in works council elections, they generally submit lists of candidates. Apparently these slates are almost always elected—

[9] International Labour Office, Labour-Management Relations Series, No. 6 (Geneva, 1959, mimeo.), pp. 120–21.

[10] Hartmann, *op. cit.,* p. 136.

too often to suit Chancellor Adenauer, who has sought to sponsor a Christian labor movement in competition with DGB. It was astonishing, the Chancellor remarked in June 1961, that DGB, with a membership of (sic) only 5,000,000 out of 21,000,000 wage earners, should have obtained 85 per cent of the mandates in works-council elections. The Chancellor added that "Christian quarters" should ask themselves whether all necessary measures had been taken to enlighten the workers as to the significance of these elections. DGB took offense to these remarks, it was reported.

The aim of penetrating into the works-council structure won encouragement from the German Federal Labor Court in a ruling of December 2, 1960. The Court held that a union could exact organizational loyalty from its members in connection with works-council elections. The case had arisen when the management of a metal plant challenged the validity of an election, on the ground that the Metal Workers' Union had prohibited its members from endorsing slates designated by Catholic unions or other competing organizations. In upholding the election, the Court supported the view of the DGB unions that they should be free to play a major role in works councils despite the formal separation decreed by the Works Constitution Act.

Thus, unions have evidently made progress toward their objective of penetrating within the plant. Nevertheless they are not satisfied with their present position. The desire for more vital participation is illustrated by two programs which the Metal Workers' Union has initiated.

The first is the appointment of shop stewards or "go-betweens" to facilitate and normalize the relations between the union and the works councils. This step is described as necessary because or rivalries between the two organizations. Chairmen of works councils consider themselves too big to take union advice. (The Chairman is often freed from production work and is generally an important functionary in the plant.) One shop steward is elected for every twenty to twenty-five I G Metall members in an establishment. Specific duties of shop stewards include promoting trade union solidarity, influencing membership opinion, drawing up election slates, representing union members in works-council meetings, collecting dues and recruiting new members. IGM spends several million marks annually for educational activities directed toward the shop stewards. Thus, the union is constructing an apparatus inside the plant.

I G Metall's second program is to negotiate more relativistic wage provisions in the industry-wide agreements and to associate itself with the job-evaluation plans which employers and works councils have been adopting. The union recognizes that, wholly aside from the level of wages, the job classifications of the industry contracts are often unrealistic and unsatisfactory in application to specific cases.

* * *

I G Metall would like to improve the classifications, descriptions and wage levels in the industry contracts and to negotiate supplemental job evaluation agreements for each factory. The union has developed what it considers a model job evaluation plan, but has not been successful in getting it adopted. The employers and works councils are more familiar with their own plans and are not anxious for IGM to receive credit for a new system.

* * *

In this connection, it might be noted that I G Metall does have some 800 company agreements. Most of these are with small employers who do not belong to the industry associations. However, the Volkswagen plant with some 60,000 employees, as well as certain large iron and steel companies, are covered by company agreements. I G Metall would like to extend this type of agreement; but even though the union does not insist on negotiating all the way up to actual wage levels, the difficulties are great. They include the resistance of works councils; the opposition of employers, who are stressing solidarity along the lines of Scandinavian associations; and the conservatism of German workers.

## F.  Union and Employer Views on Plant Agreements

There has been considerable discussion of a more decentralized wage system in Germany although, as we have seen, there is strong resistance to any actual change in existing arrangements.

The unions' objective is called *"betriebsnah,"* or "close to the undertaking." They argue that several benefits could be achieved. The gap between negotiated wage rates and workers' earnings could be reduced. Unions could take advantage of the wage-paying capacity of efficient, profitable firms rather than gearing their contracts to the circumstances of the marginal firms. Their appeal to workers would be improved and they could break out of the membership stagnation in which they have been mired for several years.

As presently conceived the new approach includes five main points:

1.  Modernization of job classifications and description in collective agreements.

2.  The *"Effectivklausel"* or binding clause. This would require the employer to increase actual wage payments by the amount of any negotiated wage increases.

3.  Incorporation of fringe benefits into collective agreements. In addition to conventional fringe benefits, employers frequently furnish free transportation, subsidized meals, etc.

4.  Supplemental agreements for individual plants and companies. Such agree-

ments should be based upon *"Rentabilitatslohn,"* i.e., wages in accordances with profitability.

5.  The *"Oeffnungsklausel"* or "opening clause." Unions would be entitled to initiate negotiations in the event of altered economic conditions.

These notions have been strongly opposed by the BDA, the Federation of Metal Trades Associations and other employer groups on numerous grounds: Under present circumstances the employer can act quickly when conditions change; costs can be reduced without the need for bargaining. Premium wages and voluntary social payments would have to be eliminated if they should be transformed into binding obligations. Wages should be uniform within an industry in order to normalize competition. If differences are to exist, they should be voluntary and should serve to attract the necessary manpower.

Further arguments are advanced against the unions' new approach. Shop agreements are permissible in certain exceptional cases but cannot be accepted as a normal procedure, since they reduce the employer's freedom of action and create rigidity. Plant-level bargaining works in the United States because the unions have accepted the free-enterprise system, but this is not always the case with German unions. If shop-level bargaining were to become general, wages would no longer be oriented to the marginal firm. The principle of *"Rentabilitatslohn"* would capture the "profit rents" of the enterprises, which have a regulative function in the economy. The *"Oeffnungskausel"* or opening clause would endanger the "peace obligation" which German labor law imposes upon employers and unions.[11]

Not all employers are opposed to shop-level bargaining. The Metal Workers claim that some employers sympathize with the new approach, but are unable to deviate

---

[11] BDA, *Memorandum über die Solidarität der Arbeitgeber auf dem Gebiet der Lohn- und Tarifpolitik in ihrer wirstschaftlichen und politischen Bedeutung,* 1959.

| Year | Workers Involved | Man-Days Lost |
|------|------------------|---------------|
| 1950 | 79,300 | 380,100 |
| 1951 | 174,300 | 1,592,900 |
| 1952 | 84,100 | 442,900 |
| 1953 | 50,600 | 1,488,200 |
| 1954 | 115,900 | 1,586,500 |
| 1955 | 600,400 | 856,700 |
| 1956 | 52,500 | 1,580,200 |
| 1957 | 45,300 | 1,071,800 |
| 1958 | 202,600 | 782,200 |
| 1959 | 21,600 | 61,800 |
| 1960 | 17,100 | 37,700 |

SOURCES: United Nations Yearbook of Labor Statistics, 1955, p. 401; 1960, p. 522. Germany: *Statistiches Bundesamt: Wirtschaft und Statistik*, Feb. 1961, p. 86.
[a] Saar district included for 1959 and 1960. West Berlin included for 1960.

from the policy of their associations. One employer association recently expressed its willingness to discuss the matter.

## G. Recent Strike Experience

On general principle one might have expected a substantial increase in German strike activity in recent years. High prosperity, labor shortages, and the unions' desire to break out of the industry-wide bargaining system would suggest this result. The fact is, however, that strike activity remained nominal throughout the 1950's. If there was any trend at all, it was downward.

Table 2 shows the number of workers involved in strikes and man-days of idleness in the German Federal Republic, from 1953 to 1960. . . . Since 1955, fewer than 1 per cent of union members have gone on strike in every year except one. (This compared with ratios of 10 to 15 per cent in the United States.)[12] . . . One reason for this situation is the abhorrence of overt social conflict which has characterized postwar Germany and has been noted by so many observers.[13] In this connection the ILO study group mentioned above made the following pertinent observation:

*Germany, in spite of its freedom of collective bargaining has a detailed code of labor laws which regulate the various obligations arising out of the relationship between employer and worker. This may be attributed to a preference on the part of Germans for precision and certainty and for clearly stated legal provisions which would be enforceable by the courts.*[14]

One of the "clearly stated legal provisions" is the "peace obligation" mentioned above. The parties are prohibited from using economic force in connection with any subject covered by the agreement. Inasmuch as the agreement is enforceable in the labor courts, the strike weapon can be used only in situations where no contract exists.

This "peace obligation" differs greatly from the situation in England, where there are numerous unofficial strikes during the period of collective agreements; and from that in France and Italy, where massive

[12] Ross and Hartman, *op. cit.*, p. 205.
[13] *Ibid.*, p. 99.
[14] ILO, *op. cit.*, p. 10.

demonstration stoppages are likely to be called at any time.

Private conciliation procedures developed by labor and management also have the strength of law. Unions and employers associations in major branches of industry have negotiated special agreements providing detailed conciliation procedures. Furthermore, in September 1954, BDA and DGB concluded a model conciliation agreement which was then recommended to all affiliated organizations. The agreement established joint conciliation boards to which unresolved disputes are submitted within a specified time limit. The task of the boards is to assist the parties by diplomatic measures; and if this attempt fails, to suggest a compromise.

Any strike which begins prior to the termination of voluntary conciliation efforts is illegal, and damages can be assessed. Unions have been ordered to pay damages on several occasions because of premature strike action. The most important of these cases was a stoppage of metal workers in Schleswig-Holstein in 1956–57. The courts ruled that the union had violated a five-day cooling-off period required by the conciliation agreement, by laying plans for a strike ballot before the five days had elapsed.

There are further reasons why prosperity, labor shortages and a shift in the center of gravity toward the plant have not brought a renewal of strike activity. Works councils, not legally recognized as bargaining agents, do not have the right to strike. The weakness of the unions at the grass roots has already been described. In the majority of unions a strike may be commenced only after 75 per cent of the union members have voted to sanction it. Finally we should note that the emphasis on restoring Germany's place in the world has inhibited overt expressions of social conflict; and that throughout the postwar period, German labor has continued to place primary emphasis on political and legislative goals, particularly co-determination. Obviously the decision to seek representation on the governing boards of the enterprises is inconsistent with any substantial reliance on the strike as a tactical instrument.

## H. The Condition of the Union Movement

The German trade union movement, like its American counterpart, has encountered serious organizational problems in recent years. In 1953 there were 6,882,000 union members in the Federal Republic, equalling 47 per cent of wage and salary employment. In 1959 total membership had risen to only 7,592,000 despite the vast expansion of the labor force. The intensity of organization has declined to approximately 35–37 per cent.[15]

The DGB, which includes the bulk of trade union members, reported a net gain of only 47,000 between September 1958 and December 1960. During this period the labor force grew by 570,000, so that the expansion of membership was less than 10 per cent of the labor force increase.

Union organizational weaknesses are noted in the majority of advanced Western nations, and undoubtedly some profound and pervasive causes are at work. Two special influences in West Germany may be noted, however. The first is the wage drift. Workers who already receive considerably more than contractual wage rates see no great advantage in joining the union and paying dues. The second is the law on "extension" of contracts, which takes effect within an industry when firms employing 50 per cent of the workers are covered by a collective agreement. The

---

[15] OEEC, *The Problem of Rising Prices, op. cit.,* p. 316; Ross and Hartman, *op. cit.,* p. 202.

result is that large groups of nonunion workers receive the benefit of the agreements.[16]

With workers losing interest in unionism, the question of union security clauses has been cropping up recently. Traditionally German unions have opposed such clauses. The DGB still maintains officially that every worker should have absolute freedom to join a union or remain outside. Furthermore, the union leaders reject the checkoff system, believing that they can maintain closer contact with members through direct collection of dues. During the last two or three years, however, there has been widespread discussion of union security. In 1960 the construction workers union requested that the "agency shop" be granted. Under this arrangement (known in Switzerland as "solidarity contributions") all workers in the industry assist in financing the union, whether they belong or not. The construction employers denied the request, but the demand for union security may be heard more loudly in the future.

The ideological component of German unionism has declined during the postwar period. This reflects in part the political apathy of the membership, but also a deliberate shift in policy.

*When immediately after the war the occupation forces permitted the re-establishment of the trade unions, which they regarded as a safeguard for democracy, the responsible union leaders decided not to repeat the mistakes committed before 1933 when the movement was split up into several ideological and political groups; they agreed on the establishment of a united trade union organization which was to be independent from any political party.[17]*

The German unions say they are independent of the Socialist Party but cannot be neutral. Among the 519 deputies in the federal parliament in 1957, there were 198 trade-union members, mostly Socialists. Nevertheless the relationship between the Socialist Party and the union movement is not so close as in England or Scandinavia.

The decline in ideology is manifested also in the weakening or abandonment of socialist objectives. The DGB (along with the Socialist Party) has been revising its economic program in favor or free-enterprise principles. The Metal Workers' Union, however, retains its militant ideology. In October 1960 the union reaffirmed its position that key industries should be nationalized and should be guided by a central economic plan.[18] It is evident that the Metal Workers' Union stands in the forefront of the German labor movement both in economic and political militancy; but whether time is working on its side is not yet so clear.

The trend away from centralism in industrial relations, the decline of ideology, and the loosening of the connection between the economic and political arms of the labor movement have all acted to undermine the strength and significance of the DGB as a union federation.

\* \* \*

## I. The Problem of Wage Policy

Since 1953 Germany has encountered a creeping inflation not radically different

---

[16] ". . . Since it is only the employers who must be well organized in order to be accepted as representative, and since non-union workers benefit equally from the fruits of collective bargaining, both the necessity for strong union organization and the incentive to become a union member tend to be somewhat reduced. The unions are aware of this and with the advent of full employment in recent years there has been some pressure to have the law amended." (OEEC, *The Problem of Rising Prices, op. cit.,* p. 319.)

[17] ILO, *op. cit.,* p. 15.

[18] *Bericht der Geschäftsführung,* May 1959–June 1961, GDM, pp. 8–9.

from that experienced in the United States. The cost of living index advanced approximately 15 per cent between 1953 and 1960. Actually it is doubtful that this can be considered a wage-push inflation; output per man-hour increased at approximately the same rate as average hourly earnings (between 6 and 7 per cent annually) during this period.[19] Nevertheless there has been considerable discussion of the need for an anti-inflationary wage policy in recent years.

The trade unions helped to inspire this discussion by urging that they were entitled to more generous treatment. They practiced unprecedented wage restraint during a long decade of economic recovery and capital accumulation, the unions held. Now the worker should share more fully in national prosperity, they argued.

Chancellor Adenauer raised the issue of wage policy in rather general terms toward the end of 1957.

\* \* \*

Then Dr. Adenauer, after holding separate talks with leaders of the BDA and DGB, published an open letter in February 1960. He stated in part:

*The will of the nation is to maintain, for the benefit of all of us, stability of purchasing power and of the currency. . . The Memorandum of the Bundesbank indicates the frame which should be respected by the parties. . . In this context I urgently ask the employers to let the public participate in the progress made by reducing prices. . . The unions should contribute to the maintenance of currency stability by keeping their claims within the above-mentioned limits.*[20]

The BDA implored its members that under no circumstances should pay increases exceeding 4 per cent be granted.

This advice was almost universally disregarded.

\* \* \*

There is no doubt that this wage movement represented, in considerable part, the recognition and incorporation of increases which had already been granted in local plants. In other words, previous wage drift was legitimized at the same time as original increases were initiated. Of course, additional wage drift was also accumulating from month to month, so that it would be difficult to disentangle the original and secondary elements.

\* \* \*

The DGB has reacted negatively to the proposition that wages should be tied to productivity. Among the grounds for dissent are that such a policy would tie the hands of unions; that wage control cannot be discussed in isolation from price control; and that labor should have a higher proportion of total income. In addition to rehearsing these familiar propositions, the unions have expressed the fear that attempts will be made to abolish free collective bargaining and impose an authoritative "wage policy" in 1962.

Within the employer community there have been urgent discussions of wage policy for several years. These discussions have been carried on within a rather constrained context: the fact that each employer association is autonomous in its collective bargaining decisions; the knowledge that individual employers are offering considerably more than contractual wage rates; the desire to have the government's moral support while avoiding direct controls.

In 1955 BDA established a special committee for co-ordination of wage policy, instructing the committee to "outline the

[19] OEEC, *The Problem of Rising Prices, op. cit.,* p. 329.
[20] *Ibid.,* p. 350.

limits" with respect to wages and working hours.[21]

In June 1959 a memorandum on "Solidarity of Employers in the Sphere of Wage and Collective Bargaining Policy" was circulated to the affiliated associations. The memorandum rules out centralized, economy-wide wage agreements, on the ground that differences among regions and industries were too great to be overcome. Regional interindustrial agreements are suitable in exceptional cases, e.g., white collar workers, but not as a general rule. Agreements at the shop level contradict the principle of solidarity. Legislation on working hours, paid vacations, etc., would not be helpful because unions could always demand more favorable conditions in collective bargaining. Thus the memorandum returns to the established practice of wage policy by industry. The appropriate geographical area to be covered by an industry contract depends on circumstances and cannot be defined in any general fashion. Solidarity must therefore be achieved within a framework of industry contracts.

\* \* \*

The issuance of the Blessing Memorandum in January 1960 was praised by BDA as "the first step towards an objectivization of wage policy." A number of comments were added, including the following: (a) The principles of the Blessing Memorandum are not too rigid as a basis for wage policy. (b) Workers should not receive cost-of-living increases in addition to productivity increases, because of the inflationary consequences. (c) Nothwithstanding the gap between contract rates and actual earnings, the contract rates should not be increased by more than 4 per cent because such increases are incorporated into earnings. (d) Neither should

earnings be advanced more rapidly than productivity. (e) If contract rates increased more slowly than productivity in previous years, the deficiency cannot be remedied in the future. It is too late to redistribute income which has already been distributed. (f) If some workers do not receive a contractual increase in a given year, others are not thereby entitled to receive more than their share. The contracts covering the first-mentioned group will eventually expire, and their actual earnings will probably keep on rising in the meantime. (g) Productivity and profits in a particular industry cannot replace average productivity as the objective criterion.[22]

Whether all these propositions were logically defensible, and whether 4 per cent was a proper estimate of average productivity growth in Germany, need not be debated here. Suffice it to say that BDA closed up any possible loopholes in the Blessing Memorandum. As we have seen, however, the impact on wage determination was negligible during the subsequent two years.

## J. Conclusion

In Section III of this article the impacts of the new European economy upon labor-management relations were sketched out in general terms. It was emphasized, however, that these tendencies have not developed to the same extent in every country: first, because the industrial relations systems were different to begin with; and second, because the economic changes have been of varying magnitude.

In West Germany production has increased at an extraordinary rate; the labor market has been extremely tight; incomes have risen rapidly; middle-class living standards have spread widely.

[21] BDA, *Gesamtüberblick aus dem Jahresbericht 1956* (Bad Godesberg, 1956), pp. 12–13.
[22] BDA, *Lohn- und Tarifpolitik. I: Die Beteiligung der Arbeitnehmer am wirtschaftlichen Fortschritt,* 1960.

Under these circumstances the traditional multi-employer agreements have declined in significance. Worker earnings have risen far above the minimum rates in such agreements. Although sizeable increases are regularly negotiated by the national unions and the employer associations, these increases partially represent a consolidation of previously accumulated wage drift.

This shift in the center of gravity has tended to move the employer associations off the center of the stage; yet the associational principle remains important in German life. Employer groups have retained sufficient strength to preserve the works council system as the dominant form of plant representation, and to obtain favorable wage policy pronouncements from the government.

The trade-union movement has responded to the new situation by dropping many of its previous ideological trappings; by reducing the emphasis on political action, except for co-determination; and by fortifying its efforts to control the works-council apparatus. But even though union candidates are usually elected, works councils continue to pursue an independent policy and union position inside the plant remains weak. Additional union problems include partial dissociation from wage developments; apathy among workers; a decline in the intensity of organization; and inability, for all practical purposes, to conduct successful strikes.

The stability of this balance of forces, in which the individual firm continues to enjoy great autonomy, depends on the maintenance of German prosperity. A drastic change in the economic situation would increase the relative strength of the trade unions, the employer associations and the government.

In two other articles not reproduced in this volume, Professor Ross applies his conceptual framework to Great Britain, Italy, and France. ("Prosperity and British Industrial Relations," *Industrial Relations*, Feb. 1963, p. 63; "Prosperity and Labor Relations in Western Europe: Italy and France," *Industrial and Labor Relations Review*, October 1962.) Although there are many similarities, the following significant differences are evident: British unions were better organized than those of the other countries studied; strike frequency had been rising in Britain; British unions were not as centralized, were characterized by more diversity in structural types, and industial unions were less important; British employers were not as well organized as their German or Italian counterparts; British collective bargaining was less centralized; and the British shop stewards were not as removed from the centralized collective bargaining system as was true of various continental government-sponsored agencies, like the German works councils. As Ross observes: ". . . the British bargaining institutions, as compared with those on the continent, reflect a longer historical development, a more solidly established union movement, less paternalism and authoritarianism on the part of employers, and generally a greater diversity of practice" ("Prosperity and British Industrial Relations," p. 69). As a consequence, "political and economic changes impinging on labor-management relations have been less drastic than on the Continent." Moreover, the rates of economic growth and technological change were considerably lower in Britain during the 1950's and 1960's than they were on the Continent.

Nevertheless, postwar Britain has been characterized by affluence and full employment, with significant implications for industrial relations. As in other countries, many important issues have not been covered by industry-wide agreements. Although power "has gravitated to the working level," shop relations tend to be "disordered and poorly organized," with resulting "chaotic internal wage structure, insurgency and irresponsibility on the part of the shop stewards, and frequent resort to unofficial strikes in the absence of systematic grievance and arbitration procedures. The British trade unions are in trouble: they are unpopular with the public, their organizing campaigns are not successful." (*Ibid.* pp. 93–94.)

The economic policies of the British Labour government created strains between the British Trades Union Congress (TUC) and its affiliates and the TUC and the Labour party. A major area of disagreement has been over the government's desire to restrict wage increases in order to achieve economic stability and the unions' desire to use their economic power to raise wages. Ross concludes ". . . the British industrial relations system, as it now stands, is inadequate to deal with the new pressures created by technological, economic, and social changes" (*Ibid,* p. 94). For a further discussion of European and American wage-price problems, see Chapter 8.)

The Italian labor movement has some characteristics that distinguish it from the British and German, but has had similar problems as a result of postwar prosperity. The Italian labor movement is split ideologically between the dominant Communist-controlled Confederazione Generale Italiana del Lavoro (CGIL), the Christian Democratic Confederazione Italiano Sindicati der Lavoratori (CISL), and the Unione Italiana del Lavoro (UIL) allied with the Saragot Socialists. As in Germany, prosperity has caused some changes in industrial relations, especially in the more prosperous north: a wage drift has caused actual wages to be disassociated from those negotiated in the centralized agreements, unions have attempted to decentralize wage determination and "extend their organizations inside the plants, where works councils and paternalistic policies are still dominant" ("Prosperity and Labor Relations in Western Europe: Italy and France," p. 69), and the political ties between the unions and the parties have been "loosening somewhat."

Although France and Italy have had similar labor movements—both characterized by internal ideological splits with dominant Communist-controlled federations and weak collective bargaining systems—less change occurred in France than in Italy in the postwar period. "Ideology and politics remain the principal preoccupations of the [French] labor movement. There is no significant trend toward plant unionism; in fact, not even works councils are functioning in the majority of establishments. The industrial relations system remains highly centralized, and, while some significant plant-level agreements were negotiated in larger enterprises during the 1950's this development did not spread very far." (*Ibid.*)

How do we account for the differences between France and Italy? Ross suggested a number of explanations: unions have been too weak in France to "exercise any significant initiative"; the class-warfare orientation of the dominant Communist-controlled CGT has been much more rigid than that of the CGIL in Italy; the Christian CFTC and the Socialist FO in France prefer centralized agreements, which they think best protect their members' long-term interests; the smaller size of French firms and employer opposition to bargaining have made collective bargaining more difficult; the French government under General Charles DeGaulle sponsored union-management cooperation, which competes with unions for establishing rules governing wages, hours, and working conditions; and the Algerian War diverted attention from economic reform.

The studies by Ross and others on European labor movements make it apparent that although European and American labor movements are converging, wide differences continue between European countries and between Europe and the United States.

### Worker Participation in Management

The comparative method is useful because it demonstrates those causal relationships that tend to be universal and those that are unique to each country. In Part II we shall examine some comparative analyses of wage-price or incomes policies. Comparisons of various aspects of labor movements between countries are made in Part I. However, special attention also is given in this section to worker participation in industry, a question that has received a great deal of attention in Europe, but surprisingly little in the United States.

One of the main labor problems of an industrial society is how to provide for worker participation in the formulation of rules that affect their working lives. The problem comes about, of course, because the large-scale capital requirements of modern industry make it difficult for workers to acquire the necessary capital to go into business for themselves. They therefore become dependent on owners and managers for their jobs. Hence, it is not surprising that industrialization led to demands for industrial democracy in an effort to give workers some control over decision making. However, worker participation has various definitions, including ownership and control by workers, participation on boards of directors, participation on management committees, participation on plant committees, or regular collective bargaining procedures. Sometimes these joint committees are required by law and sometimes they are purely voluntary organizations as in Great Britain.

In "Workers' Control of Industry *in Europe*," Frederic Meyers makes it clear that the demand for workers' control of industry is based on a wide spectrum of Socialist and Christian thought with a long history in Europe. However, the most intensive worker control movement has taken place since World War II, and in Western Europe, the Works Council movement has been particularly important in Germany, as Ross noted in his article. Indeed, the demand for worker participation in Germany extends to joint participation on the boards of directors of steel and coal companies under a law of 1951 and in other industries by a general law passed in 1952. As Meyers emphasizes, moreover, although the works' councils elected by employees within plants have a variety of functions, their real power is primarily in the social, personnel, and economic area. In many countries the works councils have competed with regular collective bargaining procedures but, as Meyers points out, in Germany, there has been a curious blend of the concept of bargaining and the concept of cooperation, whereby the works council is the grievance mechanism through which the collective bargaining contract is enforced.

In Belgium, the works councils are chosen in governmental-conducted elections, but their powers are very narrowly circumscribed by law; in only two areas did the councils have determinative functions: the unimportant one of determining vacation schedules and the somewhat more important one of managing the social welfare programs of the enterprise. The latter might include as examples, canteens, recreation programs, and relief funds normally financed from fines levied on disciplinary measures." The procedures with respect to works councils in France are similar to those in Belgium, the councils being elected under a law requiring the representation from manual workers, technicians, white-collar workers, supervisors, and employers. Moreover, "the French councils have the power to manage only the social welfare functions of the enterprise."

The British joint council movement, unlike the works councils on the Continent, is wholly voluntary. This movement stems primarily from the recommendations of the so-called Whitley Committee of 1917. At that time, the establishment of joint committees was designed to promote cooperation for wartime production.

For a variety of reasons, Meyers concludes, the works council movement has not been too successful in accomplishing its objectives. In Belgium and France, employers have actively opposed the encroachment of the councils on management's functions. "Only in Germany where the councils have well-defined functions and powers and where employers are probably more pragmatic in their attitudes than in France and Belgium, have the councils been much more than peripheral appendages to the managerial function. Even in Germany the accomplishment and form for the councils have been disappointing."

Another impediment to the success of the works councils has been the incompatibility of their objectives. As Meyers emphasizes, these organizations attempt to mix the philosophies of conflict and cooperation. In the conflict role, the employees' representatives are supposed to fight for improvements in the worker's conditions, while in their cooperative role, the representatives are supposed to increase productivity. Although these objectives are not always incompatible, they frequently are, causing considerable difficulty for the representatives. Moreover, the works councils have sometimes actively competed with the trade unions and at other times have been taken over by them. In either case, they seem to have been much more successful in carrying out the conflict role than in cooperating with employers for improvements in productivity. Indeed, as Meyers points out in his concluding section, there seems to be some inverse correlation between the strength of the works councils and the strength of collective bargaining.

Even though the accomplishments of the works councils have been disappointing, Meyers makes it clear that there is very little labor movement support for abolishing them. This is true because various factions within the labor movements see benefits in the councils, although these differ from faction to faction. Meyers concludes that although the works councils perhaps have not made much difference economically, they have significant political implications. The economic effects have been limited by the fact that:

The established norms of business behavior are not easily and suddenly altered. The pre-existing ethic of business impinges on, and forces some conformity from labor managers, as well as the reverse.

In terms of political activity, the story may be different. It is hard to see the Krupp enterprises, with trade-union appointed members of the board of directors, diverting corporate funds to wholly reactionary policital movements. That is to say, the German government is probably freer now to pursue social reform, including extensions of comanagement, than at any past time.

# Workers' Control of Industry in Europe

## by Frederic Meyers

American trade unions are almost unique in the world labor movement in their willing acceptance of the basic capitalistic institutions of private property.

### ANTICAPITALISM IN EUROPEAN UNIONS

Virtually all foreign labor movements have a formal commitment, at least ideologically, to some kind of change in the forms of property holdings. They envisage basic changes that would alter the techniques by which decisions about employment relationships would be taken, and, more fundamentally, would shift the locus of control over *all* industrial decisions.

Some foreign labor movements seek economic organization along familiar orthodox socialist lines, with productive property held by the State. The State, in turn, would be controlled by representatives of the working class, and the terms of employment would be set by negotiation between particular bodies of workers and representatives of the general interests of workers. General industrial policies would be made through managerial forms designed and controlled by the socialist State.

Classical British guild socialism, the revision of Vandervelde in Belgium, and French anarchosyndicalism would vest the property rights to productive enterprise in the continuing body of workers using the tools in each enterprise. These, rather than the State, would be the owners, and at the same time the employed; hence, no conflict and no negotiation would be necessary to divide the product of individual enterprise, though of course conflicts of interest might still remain between individuals and perhaps between enterprises.

SOURCE Reprinted with permission from (*Southwestern*) *Social Science Quarterly,* 39 (September 1958), pp. 100–111.

The "Christian" labor movements of Europe, finding their ideological inspiration in the social doctrines of the Catholic Church, and especially in the encyclicals Quadragesimo anno and Rerum novarum, though expressing a devotion to the institution of private property in general, seek significant alterations in the rights concomitant with ownership.

\* \* \*

The *Program* of the International Federation of Christian Trade Unions makes a clear and sharp distinction between private property in consumers' goods—which is to remain limited "only by the rights of fellow-men and the precepts of charity"— and property in capital goods—which *may* be limited by necessary but not general nationalization, or collective ownership, and *must* be subject to joint management of workers and employers.[1]

Even the German Christian Democratic Party, the party of Adenauer and Ludwig Erhard, in the period before the lessening of influence from its working-class left, adopted in Ahlen in 1947 a program containing the following:

*The capitalistic economic system has not proved suitable to the political and social life interests of the German people. After the terrible political, economic and social collapse resulting from criminal power policies, only an organization new from the ground up can succeed.*

*The content and goal of the social and economic reorganization can no longer be capitalistic power and profit seeking, but only the welfare of our people.*[2]

These several ideological streams converge in immediate demands for some form of industrial comanagement. For the "Christian" trade unionists, the appropriate form and extent of comanagement is an ultimate goal; for the socialists of various stripes and for the anarchosyndicalists,

it is a way station on the road to full "workers' control."

Though the idea of workers' control— or its halfway step, comanagement—is a very old one, providing for some form of participation by the worker in management, apart from collective bargaining, is relatively new in the four countries here to be considered as examples—France, Belgium, Germany, and Britain and, for that matter, anywhere in Europe. This extension of the idea of control is not, however, limited to these four; it is to be found in virtually every Western European country. In Eastern Europe, the Jugoslavian workers' councils and their powers distinguish the Jugoslavian economy markedly from those of the other Communist countries.

## THE WORKS-COUNCIL MOVEMENT

Voluntary joint councils in France date back to 1885, but they were few and the movement did not spread quickly. In Belgium, the idea was discussed prominently after the First World War but did not take hold then. In Germany, legal provision for voluntary councils came with the *Arbeiterschutzgesetz* of 1891. Later, a law of 1920 created certain compulsory councils, but with an extremely limited function. In Britain, the voluntary "joint consultative committees" became quite common after the appearance of the "Whitley Report" during the First World War, but the "Whitley Council" movement did not gain rapid ground until the Second World War.

But after the Second World War, the movement did spread very rapidly. The provisional government of General de Gaulle in France, perhaps to take the steam out of a spreading movement toward real comanagement, adopted an ordinance providing for compulsory establishment of works councils with limited

---

[1] *Program of the International Federation of Christian Trade Unions* (Utrecht, n.d.).
[2] "Das Programm von Ahlen" (Christliche Democratische Union, 1947).

powers in large enterprises. The 1945 law was amended in 1946[3] to expand its scope and to strengthen the councils somewhat. In Belgium, an act of 1948 became effective in 1950,[4] generally providing for the compulsory establishment of works councils in establishments employing fifty or more persons. In Britain, though no legal provision for compulsory comanagement in private industry appeared, voluntary "Whitley Councils" became more common after a postwar decline in the wartime Joint Production Committees; in the nationalized industries, the governing boards were either mandated or advised to establish joint consultation.

The movement proceeded much the furthest in Germany. There, in 1952, works councils with extensive powers were made compulsory in most industry.[5] And in addition, equal worker participation on the boards of directors of coal and steel companies was provided in the *Mitbestimmungsrecht* of 1951.[6] [and in other industries by a general law the following year].

Since the German works-council movement has made the most headway, perhaps it would be well to start with a brief description of it. The scope of the law is most extensive. It applies to all industrial enterprises employing as many as five employees eligible to vote for works councilors, and to all agricultural and forestry enterprises employing ten. The works councilors are elected by the employees, with discrete representation for manual and for white-collar workers. Under German law, any employee may be nominated or elected, but in plants where unions are active, they ordinarily present slates, and the vast majority of works councilors have been elected from union slates. It should be noted that the organizing of white-collar workers has proceded much further

in fact throughout the Continent, than in the United States.

The functions of the council are categorized into four general types: general, social, personal, and economic. General functions include, particularly, the receiving of financial, production, technical, and other information about the enterprise, the giving of which is compulsory. On the basis of this information the council may propose general measures in the interest of the enterprise and its personnel, but these proposals are largely advisory.

The social, personal and economic functions are those in which the council has real power. In these areas, its powers are "codeterminative" rather than merely "cooperative." Social functions include the management of all welfare programs of the enterprise, carrying on trade instruction, determining vacation schedules, the time and place of wage payment, etc. Personal functions include recruitment, job assignment, transfer and discharge. Economic functions include such things as manufacturing and work methods, production programing, alterations in plant layout, and the introduction of new techniques. In certain of these matters, statutory criteria are laid down for the making of these decisions by council and employer.

The works council is conceived of legally as a body co-operative with the employer; yet understandings with the employer are reduced to writing in the form of a quasi-contract or plant agreement, enforceable in the labor courts. The "plant agreement" (*Betriebsvereinbarung*) is to be distinguished from the collective agreement (*Tarifvertrag*) in that the parties to the former are the works council and the employer, whereas the parties to the latter are the union and the employer or employer federation. The plant agreement *may* deal with matters normally the sub-

---

[3] *Ordinance of 22 Feb. 1945;* Law of May 16, 1946.
[4] Law of September 20, 1948.
[5] "Betriebsverfassungsgesetz," *Bundes Gesetzblatt*, Teil I, No. 43, pp. 681–695.
[6] Law of May 21, 1951.

ject of collective bargaining, yet it may also go well beyond the ordinary scope of collective agreements reached at arm's length, and with the possible use of coercive measures.

Collective agreements are normally concluded in Germany between regional or national associations of employers and national unions. The law is that provisions of the collective agreements supersede those of plant agreements. Yet the curious blend of the concept of bargaining and the concept of co-operation is illustrated by the fact that the works council normally is the grievance processing mechanism through which the collective agreement is enforced.

In addition to the works council, worker participation in management is carried into the internal management of the German corporation. Under the general law of 1952, employees directly elect one-third of the members of the boards of directors of German corporations except the mining and steel companies. Two of these must be employees of the company in question, but the others, if any, may be trade-union functionaries with no present or prior connection with it. Workers thus have at least a nominal voice in the top executive power. But since employee representation is a minority one, and further, since effective management is carried on not by the board of directors but by an executive committee of full-time executives, employee representation probably means at present only that employees may have access to information and may check, by threat of publicity or legal action, extreme abuses of power.

In the coal and steel industry, employee representation in top management is carried further. Employees designate a number of directors equal to those designated by stockholders, with a neutral chairman chosen by joint agreement. In addition, the labor director, who is a member of the executive committee that wields effective power, cannot be designated without the assent of the directors representing the employees.

In Belgium, the works council is elected, in government-conducted elections, solely from slates presented by the unions. Since there are dual unions in Belgium, there is real competition for representation, but no councilor may be elected except from a slate presented by some union. In this respect, the works councils in Belgium are legally tied more closely to the labor movement than are those in Germany. However, the works council functions for the enterprise, and the councilor is legally representative of the body of employees in the plant, rather than a representative of his union, when he acts in the capacity of works councilor. However, he has a second function; he is also the grievance representative of the wokers in the plant for enforcing the terms of the collective agreement. In this respect, there is again a curious admixture of the concepts of conflict and co-operation, with the grievance process being grounded in the notion of the advocacy of diverse interest, and the work-councilor function being grounded in a concept of mutuality.

The functions assigned to the Belgian works councils are, by law, severely limited. In only two areas do the councils have determinative functions: the unimportant one of determining vacation schedules, and the somewhat more important one of managing the social-welfare programs of the enterprise. The latter might include, as examples, canteens, recreation programs, and relief funds normally financed from fines levied as disciplinary measures. The employer is required to furnish the works councils with rather complete financial information, and that he does so is assured by the appointment of financial inspectors by the State. The council is empowered to give advice to the employer on a wide range of questions, and generally to watch over his observance of law and regulation in which the employees have an interest. But these functions are largely advisory. In both Germany and Belgium, the councils preempt certain areas of decision-making in behalf of employees, deal co-operatively with the employer, or advice him. The structure of these councils presumes a bilateral *co-operation.*

In France, the employer, under the law requiring the establishment of councils, is merely one of several interest groups integrally composing the council. By French law, works councils are composed of representatives elected from slates proposed by the unions of manual laborers, technicans, white-collar workers and supervisors, and by the employer or his designee. The employer representative, on questions concerning which the council has definitive power, has only one vote— equal to that of any other councilor.

As in Belgium, the French councils have the power to manage only the social-welfare functions of the enterprise. The employer must provide them with such financial information as is presented stockholders; they may send two delegates, without vote, to all meetings of boards of directors; and they may have a certified accountant examine the books. They may advise on the disposition of profits, and they are to be consulted on virtually all significant economic decisions, including price policies.

In Britain, the joint-council movement has been wholly voluntary, though in one nationalized industry the governing board has been mandated and in the others it has been recommended that they establish some form of joint consultation, legally distinguished from "conciliation," i.e., collective bargaining. Consequently, though the consultative movement is fairly widespread, its scope is less than that in the other three countries considered.

The British movement is still based primarily upon the recommendations of the Whitley Committee of 1917. Its philosophy made of the councils bipartite bodies, with worker representatives to be designated by the unions where such existed. Their functions were to be wholly consultative, and their scope limited to matters not the appropriate subjects of collective bargaining, where the latter was practiced. During the war, the consultative councils were primarily joint-production committees. Since the war, their activities have expanded to include various social functions, but in many industries they still include functions important with respect to production.

They are commonly consulted about introducing new techniques, layoffs necessitated by declining output, safety and health, etc. They also serve as a means of communicating suggestions from workers to management concerning production and efficiency.

## EVALUATION OF THE MOVEMENT

There are, of course, numbers of possible criteria upon which the success of works-council movement could be evaluated—some of them conflicting. There is little doubt that, in their own terms, they have not fulfilled expectations. In Belgium and France, their acceptance by the employer has been most extremely reluctant. In Belgium, employers have gone so far as either to eliminate social welfare programs or to transfer them to autonomous corporations to avoid their management by works councils. In France, employers, with occasional exceptions, have with great energy and ingenuity resisted "encroachment" by councils on the management function. Lorwin reports that often the employer has kept the council "dangling on his generosity to bail it out of recurring deficits on the cafeteria, crèche, or vacation colony, so that it is most 'reasonable' about making any economic demands."[7] Only in Germany, where the

---

[7] Val R. Lorwin, *The French Labor Movement* (Cambridge, Harvard University Press, 1945), p. 266.

councils have well-defined functions and powers and where employers are probably more pragmatic in their attitudes than in France and Belgium, have the councils been much more than peripheral appendages to the managerial function. Even in Germany the accomplishments and form of the councils have been disappointing.[8]

Part of the difficulty stems from the attempt to admix the philosophies of conflict and co-operation, a paradox which seeps out into the formal structure and function and underlies the whole problem. The question has been posed for both French and Belgium councils: are they duel or dialogue?[9]

In terms of the objectives of the labor movements, the achievements of the councils have been most fractional, whether viewed from the co-operative philosophy of the "Christians," or the syndicalist philosophies and those of the socialists. Yet, for differing reasons, all the labor movements would oppose abolishing the councils; indeed, they support with great vigor an extention of the movement.

Roman Catholic criticism is directed primarily toward the restriction of function. Accepting the concept of the council as a co-operative body, Catholicism would make the council the basic managerial organization of the enterprise, to which would be entrusted the whole of the managerial function, either integrating employers into it, as in France, or making decisions jointly with employers, as in Belgium or Germany. To the Catholic labor movements, then, the works councils are a first step on the road to full comanagement; it remains only to expand their function and perfect the form. Catholics would also extend the council structure to the industry and the economy. Such a formal structure already exists in Belgium, but largely without function.

The socialists of varying stripes see the primary usefulness of the councils to be to train people from the working class in managerial skills and techniques. The present forms of the council are not regarded as particularly suitable for the functions they perform but valuable as training schools for working-class industrial managers. Thus, even the Communist-dominated C.G.T. in France expends a great deal of effort in electing works councilors and in training them in schools and through the publication of an excellent technical journal devoted to the problems of works councils. Ultimately, perhaps, they are regarded as a going managerial structure to whom enterprise management might be turned over. Undoubtedly many convinced socialists have learned a great deal about the intricacies of enterprise management through their participation in joint councils.

Despite these criticisms and disappointments, and despite the generally low scholarly assessments of the achievements of the movement thus far, it may have significant potentialities. Such movements, once begun, never return to their starting places. They have a way of developing and turning into problem-solving directions, carrying along both advocates and opponents into unforeseen institutional change.

Except in France, the labor movements in the countries with which we are concerned are both strong and politically effective. Even in France, though the labor movements are weak, no government can presently be formed without the consent of the Socialists, who, though they have no integral connection with any segment of the trade-union movement, listen programmatically to the trade-union federation, *Force-Ouvrière*. Also, it is probably true that no government can be formed

---

[8] See Edwin F. Beal, "Origins of Codetermination," *Industrial and Labor Relations Review*, Vol. 8, No. 4 (July, 1955), especially p. 497.

[9] Marcel David (ed.), *La Participation des Travailleurs à la Gestion des Entreprises Privées* (Paris, Dalloz, 1954).

without the consent of the M.R.P., whose left wing has its anchor in the "Christian" trade-union movement. It is probably true, therefore, that the works-council movement is not likely to regress in the near future; it might conceivably make progress. It might be noted, incidentally, that trade-union participation in management has been applied to the nationalized industries in France, where union representatives as such sit on the managing boards, along with representatives of government, consumers, and persons chosen for their technical proficiency. . . .

In Germany, resistance to further extension of the principle of comanagement has hardened within C.D.U., the party of Adenauer. Nevertheless, the left wing of that party, with strong support from the Socialists, extended the principle of *Mitbestimmung* to holding companies in the iron and steel industry as late as 1956.[10] Backtracking seems highly unlikely, and with the emergence of a two-party system, as seems to have been the result of the 1957 elections, the United States pattern of both the right and left parties shifting toward center might well be repeated. If so, the extension of *Mitbestimmung*, which already has strong support within C.D.U., might well become the accommodation between the classical socialists, Christian Social Democrats, and political necessity.

Curiously, it is only in Britain, the ideological home of guild socialism, that there are but few political forces which might push the joint-consultation movement further. The Labour Party, in its nationalization programs after the war, deserted the old slogan of "worker control." The management of nationalized industries was entrusted to independent management boards, which, though they drew personnel from the labor movement, drew them as competent individuals who then severed their former connection, rather than as representatives of a movement or class. This managerial structure was devised with full support from the labor movement, which drew back from the divided responsibility that participation in management might have entailed. Only the Communists in the British labor movement are critical of the managerial structure of nationalized industry on the ground that workers are inadequately represented. . . .

## IMPLICATIONS OF THE MOVEMENT

The movement toward greater participation of the worker in management, if futhered, would have significant implications. European capitalism has never closely resembled American capitalism, any more than European unionism has closely resembled American unionism or European democracy, our democracy. Rights of property in productive goods have, in Europe, carried a different connotation of control than in the United States, and have included the right to combination—antitrust legislation being regarded as an invasion of property rights. Decartelization of Germany failed, not only because it conflicted with German tradition but with British and French tradition as well. The British common-law doctrine of conspiracy, on which our antitrust laws are based, never played a significant role in British business law, either in the nineteenth century or after.

In the period of growth and the growing regulation of "big business," the important conflict of interest, in the American mind, was that between consumer and business, a conflict that could reasonably be resolved by protecting the forces of competition. Protection of the right to bargain collectively was subsequently integrated into this schema in that it opposes two powerful negotiants in the labor market. The resulting bargain might then approx-

[10] *Bundesgesetzblatt,* Teil I, No. 38 (1956).

imate what would result if multitudinous weak negotiants met. These controls over the centers of economic power, together with general fiscal and monetary controls, are generally regarded as sufficient to protect the consumer interest and that of functional groups with conflicting claims on national income.

In Europe the conflict that submerged all others in the general consciousness was that of class. As suffrage was extended and workers became politically more effective, the concessions made in terms of economic policy took forms intended to moderate *this* conflict. The most notorious case, and one of the earliest, was that of the German social reforms of Bismarck. The hypothesis is here advanced that one of the modern expressions of this phenomenon is the trend toward the increased participation of the worker in management of private enterprises.

Historically speaking, unfettered private property as a basic social institution has had only momentary meaning. Western "capitalisms"—in which the exercise of control over "private" property by non-property-holding social groups, through state power, state-required recognition of nonpropertied groups, or state-permitted group coercion—have departed far from an absolute conception of property.

Classical economics worked out with rigorous logic the kind of society likely to result when the center of economic decision-making lay with profit-seeking property-holders. It is even able to accommodate itself to a society in which group coercions are limited to face-to-face market activities. But the changes in the kinds of business decisions made when they are expressions of the interests of nonproperty-holding groups may be so fundamental as to require a quite different portraiture of society. The American form of collective bargaining may be a real and significant challenge to these "managerial prerogatives." But defenses to this kind of challenge in Europe may be out-flanked by the workers' council movement. In Britain, the greater success of collective bargaining as a managerial technique may explain the relative weakness of joint consultation.

What difference does an extensive participation of the worker in management likely entail? Not an easily answered question. The answer depends in part on the structural forms of the participation, for these forms determine in some measure the constituency and the interests to whom the worker-manager is answerable. If he is effectively answerable to a constituency representing worker interest as a single social group, his managerial terms of reference are likely to be quite different from those resulting from his answerability to a single-plant constituency. . . .

Alternatively, if employees of a particular plant or enterprise exercise control through their power of removal or failure to renominate works councilors, the policies of those councilors are likely to be quite different from those in a situation where control over councilors is exercised by national unions or national federations of unions. Most forms of works councils recognize the discrete interest between white-collar and manual workers by providing separate representation.

For these reasons, among others, it is impossible to predict the way an economy in which managerial functions are shared by workers would operate. Whatever the structural forms of worker participation, the exercise of the managerial function would follow different criteria and achieve different results from those in which property-holders are in sole control of the decision-making process. It is quite clear, in other words, that the resulting social form would differ both from its European antecedents and from a society of enforced competition or State-sponsored countervailing market power.

It may be said that too much has been made here of what is still a peripheral shift in managerial power. Many observers have argued that even in the German iron, steel, and coal industries—where co-management has proceeded furthest—managerial behavior is not significantly different from what it was before 1933. In terms of price and output decisions, the evidence of different managerial criteria is not immediately apparent. But particular instances do exist. And it may take time for general changes to be worked. The established norms of business behavior are not easily and suddenly altered. The pre-existing ethic of business impinges on, and forces some conformity from, labor managers, as well as the reverse.

In terms of political activity, the story may be different. It is hard to see the Krupp enterprises, with trade-union appointed members of the board of directors, diverting corporate funds to wholly reactionary political movements. That is to say, the German government is probably freer now to pursue social reform, including extension of comanagement, than at any past time.

The works-council movement is still in its infancy, but its significance is better grasped in Europe than in the United States. European scholars have devoted much attention to the problem,[11] while Americans, focusing attention on the one hand almost wholly on the spectacular German development in coal and steel, and, on the other hand, on the weaknesses in collective bargaining, may have missed the more pervasive aspects of what may become a broad social movement. It is a movement with most significant implications for a most significant variable in the course of economic development—control over the industrial decision-making process.

### Related Readings

Good studies of European labor movements are too numerous to list in full. However, a number of them are particularly useful. Walter Galenson, ed., *Comparative Labor Movements* (New York, Prentice-Hall, 1952) is old, but has good selections on Great Britain (Allan Flanders), Scandinavia (Walter Galenson), Australia (Kenneth F. Walker), Germany (Philip Taft), France (Val R. Lorwin), Italy (John Clark Adams), and Russia (Isaac Deutcher). An excellent summary of the structure of European labor movements and a discussion of the problems of democracy and trade unionism in general is found in Walter Galenson's *Trade Union Democracy in Western Europe* (Berkeley, University of California Press, 1961).

A recent work on comparative labor movements, which relies heavily on the comparative method to analyze labor movements and such topics as national incomes policies, unionization of white-collar workers and public employees, worker participation in management, and the relations between unions and political parties, is Everett M. Kassalow's *Trade Unions and Industrial Relations: An International Comparison* (New York, Random House, 1969).

We also have found Adolph Sturmthal's books *The Tragedy of European Labor* (New York, Columbia University Press, 1943) and *Unity and Diversity in European Labor* (Glencoe, Ill., Free Press, 1953) to be particularly useful in understanding broad political, social, and economic developments in European labor movements. For a very thorough account of the evolution of workers councils and their operation in France, Germany, Yugoslavia, and Poland, see Sturmthal's *Workers Councils* (Cambridge, Harvard University Press, 1964).

Although the article "Crosscurrents in Workers Participation," by Milton

---

[11] See particularly, David, *op. cit.*, and the bibliography cited therein.

Derber in *Industrial Relations*, February 1970, was published twelve years after Frederic Meyers' article, Derber confirms many of Meyers' conclusions. The main theme of Derber's article is that the growing interest in workers' participation is not matched by very many successful worker participation programs. Derber based his article on his observations in England, Israel, and Australia and, to a very limited extent, in Iran and India. With respect to Britain, he concludes: "The recent English experience then, is one of expanding worker participation in the collective bargaining sphere, but little or no affirmative involvement in other aspects of management." In Israel, worker participation is very highly developed and has been pushed for ideological reasons, but the results have been mainly negative. The programs in Israel "appeared to have been frustrated by resistance and apathy on the part of both managers and workers." ". . . the concept of workers participation in management is less developed in Australia than in any other Western country of my knowledge."

Summarizing, for all countries, Derber gives the following reasons for the gap between rhetoric and action with respect to worker participation: opposition from professional managers who consider worker participation an encroachment on their professional jurisdictions; lack of strong motivation by workers to engage in worker participation so long as their needs are being satisfied by other means; resistance to worker participation by many enterprises because of the time it requires for decision making; and problem-solving difficulties created by worker participation because it is hard to find uniform solutions for every level of the decision-making process. Thus, although there is considerable ideological and intellectual interest in worker participation, Derber finds little enthusiasm for it by either workers or management in concrete situations. Moreover, he confirms Meyers' observations that cooperation and conflict are very difficult to reconcile by workers' representatives. As a result of these difficulties, Derber concludes that the questions of worker participation in management is far from resolved and is currently in a state of flux.

In the symposium from which Derber's article was taken, George Strauss and Eliezer Rosenstein, in a paper entitled "Workers Participation: A Critical View," summarize the issues raised in the symposium and pose some questions for further consideration. Their thesis mainly is that:

> (1) participation in many cases has been introduced from the top down as symbolic solutions to ideological contradictions; (2) its appeal is due in large part to its apparent consistency with both socialist and human relations theory; (3) in practice it has only spotty success and chiefly in the personnel and welfare rather than in the production areas; nevertheless, (4) its chief value may be that of providing another forum for the resolution of conflicts as well as another means by which management can induce compliance with its directives.

In other words, Strauss and Rosenstein conclude that worker participation can be a useful adjunct to collective bargaining, but thus far has not been a successful substitute for it.

# CHAPTER 4

# Labor Movements of Developing Countries

The labor movements of developing countries have considerable significance for economic development as well as for political and social stability.
But the pressures facing these trade unions and the environments in which they
operate cause them to be very unlike the labor movements in the more industrialized countries of Europe and North America. In the industrial countries
of the West, trade unions are likely to be more independent of political leaders
and to place more emphasis on collective bargaining and economic gains for
their members. The labor movements of the developing countries, on the other
hand, have greater difficulties establishing collective bargaining relations with
employers, partly because their leaders are likely to be intellectuals whose
talents and interests incline them toward political activities rather than collective bargaining. In some cases like India, Indonesia, Ghana, and Israel, the
labor movements were vehicles to establish political independence. Collective
bargaining is also impeded by the workers' limited bargaining power, caused
by labor surpluses and limited skills.

But the main obstacles to collective bargaining in the developing countries
are imposed by political leaders who consider collective bargaining to be
incompatible with industrialization. The basic argument is that the use of
economic and political power by unions to increase consumption promotes
economic instability and diverts resources from capital formation. Political
leaders in these countries therefore are likely to insist that unions play a
*productionist* role until the economy gets developed, at which time they can
become more *consumptionist*. The insistence on a productionist role for trade
unions has been advanced by leaders with a wide variety of political persuasions. Countries led by dictatorships have greater power to hold down consumption through centralized planning and the military power of the state.
Countries that try to follow democratic procedures have greater difficulty, but

their industrializing elites also ordinarily insist on a productionist role for unions. We might note in passing that where labor movements have been used to help countries achieve independence, political leaders have encouraged consumptionist roles for the labor movement before independence and productionist roles in the new nations.

## THE PRODUCTIONIST POSITION

Asoka Mehta, writing from India, outlines a productionist position in his article "The Mediating Role of the Trade Union in Underdeveloped Countries." He discusses the reasons for weak unions in the underdeveloped countries and makes the point that economic development strengthens unions. He argues for a partnership between government and unions to promote economic development, and contends that state enterprises should be model employers, though they often have the same attitudes as private employers. Moreover, "as active partners in economic development, the trade unions should assist the State in removing the defects and streamlining the machinery for socialist patterns of society." He then outlines the specific things unions should do to restrain consumption and encourage productivity, moderate their political activities to make them compatible with economic development, cushion the shocks that workers experience when they move from rural to urban areas, and facilitate the workers' psychological adjustment to urban industrial environments.

# The Mediating Role of the Trade Union in Underdeveloped Countries

## by Asoka Mehta

In this paper I propose a role for the trade unions in underdeveloped countries which is at variance with trade union practices in the West. In the West, unions have either been political adjuncts for the Communist or Socialist parties, as instruments for power, or more usually, economic institutions to raise wages and protect the workers against the authority of the employer.

Neither of these roles is possible, I believe, in underdeveloped countries. There the chief problem is economic growth, and therefore, the major question for unions is subordination of immediate wage gains and similar considerations to the development of the country.

### I. NEW FACTORS, NEW METHODS

A majority of unions in the underdeveloped countries restrict their activities to collective bargaining within the legal framework provided by national legislation on industrial relations. Most of the Asian countries have provided statutory machinery for collective bargaining.[1] Over-reliance of trade unions on Government machinery, however, is partly responsible for their weakness. In industrially advanced countries like the United Kingdom, the United States, and Sweden, the State's role is limited to setting up the machinery, within which the representatives of employers and employees negotiate and conclude collective agreements. In the underdeveloped countries, however, the industrial relations machinery gives the State an indirect weapon to control labor-management relations. . . .

The desire of trade unions to play a

SOURCE Reprinted with permission from *Economic Development and Cultural Change,* Chicago, University of Chicago, October 1957.

[1] For texts of the industrial legislation in Asia, see International Labour Office [Indian Branch], *Asian Labour Laws* (1951), New Delhi. A summary appears on pp. 211–234 of the book.

decisive role in the economic growth of an underdeveloped country can only succeed if they are independent. No amount of State protection or employers' goodwill will enable unionism to develop on right lines. Trade union movements in Asian countries suffer from various inherent defects, which must be removed before the unions undertake their rightful responsibilities in the economic growth of the country. The main defect of Asian trade unions are their unsound finances, low and irregular membership, faulty administrative and accounts work, lack of experience and maturity among union leaders, influence of outsiders, exploitation for political purposes, rivalry and multiplicity of unions, loose structure at various levels, absence of welfare work, and heavy reliance on Government machinery.

No doubt some of these defects are due to the difficulties created by Asian economies, namely, illiteracy and poverty, unemployment and underemployment, indebtedness, growth in population, migratory character, and caste and communal considerations. An improvement in these factors, which have been so far kept outside the ken of trade unions, will enable the unions to strengthen themselves. It will then be possible to have regular paid membership, to engage full-time leadership of career unionists, to grant adequate welfare benefits to its members, to wield efficiently and profitably the weapon of collective bargaining, and to exert sufficient political influence to get enacted legislation for the improvement in labor conditions.

. . . The role of the trade union, therefore, must be different from what it was under foreign rule. It is their interest and in the interest of the country to render active cooperation in all development plans which aim at the prosperity of the country.

## II. THE ROLE IN PLANNING

Economic development by planning means state control over industries, because primarily it becomes the responsibility of the Government to promote, assist, and regulate the development of industry in the national interest.

\* \* \*

What should be the trade union's attitude to this development, and what role should they play under the circumstances? Unfortunately the attitude toward labor problems of the State managers is much the same as that of private employers. Workers' expectation of getting a better deal are frustrated, and this is manifested in more strikes in the public sector. The profit motive is still there, because an ever-developing economy is in need of more money. The bureaucrats who manage the State industries bring in additional evils of red-tapism, routine, and impersonal attitude. The failure of nationalism is not so much due to the defect in the principle but to the way in which the matter has been handled by the state officials, who managed the industries, without any industrial and business experience.

As active partners in economic development, the trade unions should assist the State in removing the defects and streamlining the machinery for socialist patterns of society. They should explain to their members the implication of State Economy and urge the necessity of proving nationalization a success, by making the public sector profitable. In State-owned industries, there should not be any clash of interests between the manager and the managed, and full scope can be given to the joint consultation in industry and to workers' participation in management. The State, on the other hand, must be a model employer, and its present tendency of trying to get exemption from the provisions of various labor Acts should be discouraged. Government factories can be an ideal laboratory for experiments in wage incentives, productivity studies, job analysis and job evaluation, training methods, and time and motion studies. Trade unions can fully cooperate with the State in such constructive activities.

## III. RESTRAINTS ON CONSUMPTON

Traditionally, economists have treated trade unions mainly as economic institutions. Hence it is no wonder that the economic and industrial functions predominate even today, in spite of the realization of the changing significance of trade unionism. The economic and industrial functions of the classical pattern are revealed by these three aims: raising the levels of wages; improvement in working and living conditions; and organization of unskilled masses of labor.

The efforts of trade unions of advanced countries to share in high industrial profits is understandable in view of the fact that by their claims they lower capital-output ratio and increase the labor-output ratio proportionately. In underdeveloped economies, no such bases exist for such legitimate claims. Inflationary pressures or deflationary situations are sudden in such economies, since they are subject to extraneous fluctuations. The lack of incentives and the backward techniques of production mean that the consumption, saving, and investment functions do not work with the same tempo as in developed countries.

In these particular circumstances, the role the trade unions can most usefully play may be as follows:

1. Observing self-imposed wage restraint on all levels;
2. Educating their members to give up extra-spendthrift habits of the labor class;
3. Encouraging small-savings among the classes;
4. Increasing the labor productivity through propaganda;
5. Settling the differences through the legally instituted machinery based on the principles of conciliation and/or arbitration;
6. Helping the displaced labor thrown out of employment as a result of rationalization by inducing them to take training in new skills in the institutions set up by the Government or State management;
7. Initiating cooperative action in the enforcement of minimum wages;
8. Inducing the labor class to effectively participate in social security and provident fund schemes; and
9. Sharing in the profits on an acceptable basis which, while apportioning a significant percentage of profit to labor, will leave sufficient incentive to the management to plow the profits back into the industries they own.

The economic implications of such trade union behavior are two-fold: (1) to restrict consumption, and (2) to bring about an increase in the desired levels of production. The restriction on consumption is most vital since any undue increase in the demand for consumers' goods or semi-necessities manufactured indigenously or imported from abroad may put an immediate pressure on the price-level as a result of demand outpacing the supply. Owing to the general physical bottlenecks that prevent the supply equating with demand, the pressure pushes the prices high enough to disturb the price-cost basis of a development plan. With a view toward holding the levels of income, price, and cost, the restriction on consumption is most essential. Such a restriction, moreover, is essential from another point of view, viz., in raising the size of savings necessary for capital formation.

The policy implications of the trade unions, in this context, therefore, assume major significance. In brief, the action of trade unions in the developing stages should be to forego the ideas of immediate gains at any cost.

This raises the broader question of whether the trade unions should follow policies favoring production or consumption. The trade unions in the West follow policies which favor consumption and are against production. The trade unions in the developing economies face the same choice today. But there is no difficulty in making the choice, if the choice is to be determined within the objectives of economic development. The economic picture of the underdeveloped economies shows that the general purchasing power of the population is low, the resources undeveloped, the techniques of production backward, and the efficiency of monetary controls ineffective due to lack of capital and stock markets and low state of banking. In such circumstances, any attempt to increase consumption of the population is likely to generate inflationary pressure, and with a resort to deficit financing, the gap between money in circulation corresponding to flow in production may assume menacing proportions. This danger becomes more apparent when one considers the physical bottlenecks leading to artificial shortages. The pressure, moreover, may lead to reduction in exports due to rising costs of commodities and the frittering away of resources on foreign imported goods. A reliance on consumption in a backward economy thus brings to the forefront in the accentuated form the cumulative shortages, increasing prices, increasing capital output ratio, and general inflation.

\* \* \*

## IV. POLITICAL ROLE

As I have stated earlier, there has been a tendency on the part of political parties to exploit the trade unions for political ends. Doubless the unions have certain legitimate political functions, and it may be undesirable to restrict their activities only to economic and industrial fields. Workers, when they accept employment under contract, do not cease to be citizens, and as members of the community have every right to exercise their civic and political rights. If they look up to the union for advice and guidance in these matters, it cannot be denied. Besides, the trade union method of legal enactment allows the unions to urge labor representation in legislatures and to get progressive labor laws enacted. Some Asian trade union laws allow establishment of a political fund for limited political activities, e.g., payment of expenses for election to legislature of a candidate, or for maintenance of a member of the legislature.

These are legitimate functions. But fighting the elections on specific issues forming the Government or the opposition, agitation and propaganda on political problems and similar issues should be left outside the trade union field. This demarcation is particularly necessary in underdeveloped countries, where unionism is apt to be radical in its orientation, in view of poor labor conditions and the impatience of workers with the seeming inability of the method of collective bargaining to secure for them immediate betterment.[2] The results have been the tendency to divert resources from investment to consumption, political influence of outsiders or non-workers in the labor movement, inability of the rank and file to rise to leadership, growth of trade unions by political shades, and growing labor indiscipline

---

[2] Walter Galenson and Harvey Leibenstein, "Investment Criteria, Productivity and Economic Development", *Quarterly Journal of Economics*, Vol. LXIX, No. 3 (August 1955), pp. 343–370.

among workers even in relation to their unions.[3]

These aspects could be tolerated in a colonial economy for political reasons, but trade unions in a free democratic country on its path of economic development can hardly afford such activities. One of their primary functions should now be to mitigate the feeling of distrusts by the workers of the legally constituted Government and to assist it in implementing the development plans.

## V. CUSHIONING THE URBAN SHOCK

One of the disquieting features of the aftermath of the Second World War has been the rapid growth of . . . cities . . .

. . . The main cause of overcrowding in cities is the large scale migration from rural areas, leading to urban concentration which is often linked with industrialization. The blending of the two populations with different cultures and outlook has been difficult often and has created certain political, economic, and social problems. Responsible governments have tried to slow down or canalize the flow of humanity on three grounds: the decisive influence of industrialization, the long-term advantages of economic expansion, and the immediate dangers of over-hasty development.[4] The general consensus however, is against Government control, particularly when people leave their rural surroundings for economic living. Either the Government should provide for them at least a mean subsistence living in their villages, or it should solve the problems created by the migration in cities.

\* \* \*

The immigrants from villages pose a special problem for trade unions. They create or aggravate various social problems like slums, sex-disparity, family questions, crime, delinquency, prostitution, gambling, alcoholism, unfair competition, etc. Their social adjustment in the settled population patterns must be smoothed, and the trade unions can assist the State in this task. One of the main ways in which the problem can be solved is the provision of industrial housing. It is possible for trade unions to float cooperative housing societies for their members and thus canalize the flow of immigrants.

## VI. PSYCHOLOGICAL READJUSTMENTS

In a developing economy, factors like migration create certain important psychological problems, which are generally overlooked by trade unions and the State. Normally the persons who leave their villages for cities in search of employment are young and able-bodied men and their migration upsets the balance between the young and the old and between the sexes. The cream of the country-side is attracted towards the towns, leaving in the rural areas the children and the woman, the old and the infirm. The impact of the migration at the other end is more disastrous. Most of the migrants are new to the cities and to the industries and they swell the unskilled sector of the industrial labor force.

\* \* \*

Industrial labor in the sense of a stable, reliable, and disciplined group that has cut the umbilical cord connecting it with the land and has become suitable for utilization in factories is not abundant but extremely scarce in a backward country. The newcomers are normally taken in "marginal" occupations. . . .

[3] For illustration regarding indiscipline see Morris David Morris, "Labour Discipline, Trade Unions and the State in India", *Journal of Political Economy*, Vol. LXIII (August 1955), pp. 293–308.

[4] Pierre Wigny, "Migratory Movements in Underdeveloped Countries in the Course of Industrialization", *International Labour Review*, Vol. LXVIII, No. 1 (July 1953), pp. 1–13.

The greatest psychological effect created on the mind of the migrant worker is the result of the new nature of work. . . . Accustomed to work in a comparatively free atmosphere, the migrant worker is annoyed with the rules and regulations, in the framing of which he had no hand, and he is inclined to protest. His resentment turns to hostility in the impersonal atmosphere of the factory, and he comes to believe that the employer treats him no better than a machine, as merely a means of production.

The role of trade unions in these circumstances must be to help the villager adjust himself to the city life. A newcomer should not feel lost in the city. He should be assisted in his job hunt and later on he should feel accustomed to the labor discipline, demanded by modern industrialization and structuring.

With the assistance of other parties like the State and the employers, trade unions can successfully meet this demand of industrialism. They can find convenient tools in cooperative societies, training courses, and housing projects. A disciplined, stable, contented and loyal indus-

trial force can then emerge, from which trade unions can draw their strength.

Economic development means change—changed methods of doing things; changed equipment and other resources with which to work; changed habits of consumption, saving, and investment; changed relationships to other people; changed availabilities of goods and services; and often changed attitudes, motivations, and ways of life.[5] The extent and rate of change depend on many factors, including the personality and cultural characteristics of the society; if these characteristics are unfavorable, economic development may take place slowly, if at all. The trade unions, as social organizations of workers, should try to prepare the workers for these inevitable changes on the path of economic growth. Some of the culture changes may not follow the Western pattern, or they may relate only indirectly to economic growth and modern technology.[6] In any case, it remains the responsibility of trade unions to cultivate among workers fine traits of personality and culture and noble qualities like honesty, integrity, and loyalty to the cause of unionism.

## A Critique of the Productionist Position

Some labor economists disagree with the main thrust of Asoka Mehta's position on the role of unions in developing countries. They feel that in a democratic society unions cannot afford to take the restrictive role Mehta assigns them. These economists rest their case on a fundamental principle of unionism: to be viable in the long run, a labor organization must give its members the feeling that the union is producing as much as it can for them. Under certain circumstances, unions might exercise restraint. According to Adolf Sturmthal, in "Unions and Economic Development": ". . . unions cannot exist, for long periods of time, as social welfare agencies—which is what Asoka Mehta in effect suggests they become—and even less as instruments of wage restraints."

Sturmthal draws a number of interesting parallels between developing and industrialized countries. The first is the opposition to collective bargaining by the countries that are now industrialized when they were less developed eco-

---

[5] Samuel P. Hays, Jr., "Personality and Cultural Problems of Point IV", in *The Progress of Underdeveloped Areas*, Bert F. Hoselitz, ed., Chicago, 1952, pp. 206–207.

[6] Morris E. Opler, "The Problem of Selective Culture Change", in *ibid.*, pp. 126–134, gives many Indian examples of such cultural changes.

nomically. Indeed, today the strongest opposition to unions in the United States is in those areas of the country like the south that are less developed economically.

The other parallel concerns wage restraints. Just as political leaders call for wage restraint in the developing countries to promote industrialization, the leaders of the more economically advanced countries of Western Europe and the United States are calling on unions to exercise wage restraint in order to keep wages within the bounds of productivity and thus prevent inflation (see Chapter 8). Sturmthal feels that, in the long run, wage restraints will not be compatible with the realities of the pressures on union leaders in the developed or the underdeveloped countries. He quotes approvingly from Walter Galenson, who argues: "Free trade unions in a democratic society must ordinarily appeal to the worker on an all-out consumptionist platform." To do otherwise would mean abdication to others—especially demogogues and Communists—who would promise to use the unions' full powers to advance the workers' interests.

Sturmthal and Galenson also argue that unions have some positive benefits for economic development. Even if unions cause economic growth to be less rapid than it would be otherwise, they provide for political, social, and economic stability by providing vehicles through which workers can participate in decisions in the plant and at the national level.

Sturmthal concludes, however, that the question of the effect of union wage pressures on economic development remains open pending further research.

# Unions and Economic Development

## by Adolf Sturmthal

Is there on balance an advantage or a disadvantage for a nation to be a late-comer in the process of industrialization? This question has been, in recent years, the subject of extensive and unresolved debate among economic historians. One of the most interesting sub-topics of this argument is that of the role of unions in economic development. Some of the pioneer countries in the process of industrialization—England, France, the United States, the North-German Confederation —succeeded in delaying the emergence of effective unions for some time by legislative, administrative, or judicial devices. The Combination Acts in England, the "Loi Le Chapelier" in France, the "criminal conspiracy" doctrine under the common law in the United States, the suppression of any effective workers' combination in the North-German Confederation, and the anti-Socialist laws of Bismarck are examples of this phenomenon. What has been called the "take-off" period was, as a consequence, in these countries, relatively undisturbed by aggressive unions. Late-comers, however, find themselves in a world in which unionism is increasingly regarded as an essential attribute of a modern democratic society. They are therefore confronted with what appears as a choice between permitting some measure of effective unionism and delaying economic growth, or suppressing democracy altogether for the sake of maximum development; they have to adopt permissive or totalitarian methods of dealing with labor unions, in the words of Karl de Schweinitz.[1]

Expressed in more general terms, the

SOURCE Reprinted with permission from *Economic Development and Cultural Change*, January 1960.

[1] "Industrialization Labor Controls and Democracy," this journal, vol. VII, No. 4, July 1959. Similar conclusions are arrived at by John Dunlop, "The Role of the Free Trade Union in a Less Developed Nation," *American Labor's Role in Less Developed Countries,* Report on a Conference held at Cornell University, October 12–17, 1958, Ithaca, N.Y., no date.

problem is that of fitting labor unions into the process of economic development in its early stages. It is only in the latter period, when there is not yet a "bargaining margin" of national income available, that the problem presents itself with the pessimistic connotations often presented. Stated very simply, the problem is this: unions fundamentally favor consumption; economic development requires keeping aggregate consumption down in order to free resources for investment. Effective unions, whatever else they may do, thus tend to delay, reduce, or prevent altogether the growth of investment. If maximum growth is to be obtained, they must be suppressed by totalitarian methods and replaced by bodies which, in the guise of labor unions, are in fact agencies of a growth-conscious government rather than representatives of the workers. This is the price at which high rates of economic growth can be secured. While milder forms of control may sometimes suffice, their very mildness will at least slow up the process of growth. The dangers which effective unionism involves for economic growth are, in this view fundamentally so great, that where industrialization calls forth "too strong a protest for the security of growth objectives," governments will turn away from "permissive" controls of the labor movement. Totalitarianism becomes the requirement for economic development, since high growth rates frequently engender strong or revolutionary labor protest.

There is no claim, as far as I can see, that this outcome is inevitable, but the implication is clear that the establishment of totalitarian controls is more probable in the world today than that of permissive control systems. In its sophisticated version this theory does not attempt to describe the totalitarian system as one pole and a "democratic" solution of a perfectly "free" labor movement as the alternative. For labor protest must be controlled under all circumstances in early economic development and the problem is only the degree to which it must be subdued and the forms in which this is done, without endangering economic growth. But the significance of these differences in degree, and the way in which the solution of this problem affects all our lives, are obvious.

An attempt to escape from this dilemma is represented by Asoka Mehta's paper on "The Mediating Role of the Trade Union in Underdeveloped Countries."[2] While taking the existence of unions for granted and conceding that they are desirable, Mr. Mehta looks for assignments for them that would interefere as little as possible with the requiments of rapid economic growth. This approach may be called that of a social engineer trying to fit unions into the mechanism of early economic growth so as to make them as harmless as possible. The questions left unanswered in my mind are whether genuine unions could be restricted over the long run to such limited tasks without being kept down by sharp controls, and whether, if existing unions were forced to accept such limitations, new workers' organizations would not arise to attempt to satisfy the demand for higher living standards.

Another method of investigating this problem is presented by Walter Galenson in the introductory chapter to a volume, *Labor and Economic Development*.[3] His method is essentially the comparative analysis of what the various case studies presented in the volume show to be the common labor problems of early industrialization. This list contains a wider

[2] *Economic Development and Cultural Change*, Vol. VI, No. 1, October 1957.

[3] Walter Galenson, ed., *Labor and Economic Development*, New York: John Wiley and Sons Inc., 1959. The volume contains chapters on India (Charles A. Myers), Japan (Robert A. Scalapino), Egypt (Frederick H. Harbison), French West Africa (Elliot Berg), the British West Indies (William H. Knowles).

range of issues than merely that of establishing the place and function of labor unions in the "take-off" period. Problems of the formation of an industrial force, its training and commitment to industrial work, the nature of labor-management relations, are included in the scope of these studies; but the essential problem is that of trade unionism, and the main feature of Galenson's and his contributors' approach is realism. In a developing economy, sooner or later, a trade union movement will emerge. What are its characteristics?

Probably the most reliable prediction that can be made is that these labor movements will not behave like US unions. For business unions of the American type to arise conditions must exist that are unlikely to occur in underdeveloped areas. Among them are relatively high and fairly rapidly rising incomes, so that labor-management conflicts are mainly concerned with the distribution of the yearly increment of the national product rather than with shifts in the shares of different social groups in a given national income. A relatively static national income is, however, precisely the typical situation in underdeveloped countries, and even when national income grows, little of the increment is available for consumption if growth is to become cumulative and self-perpetuating. Another condition for the presence of business unions is the acceptance by the great majority of the workers of the social and political fundamentals of the society in which they live. In the nineteenth century this condition was only rarely met. Even British labor ultimately rebelled against the class stratification of the traditional society, in spite of its relatively greater elasticity than that of most continental European countries. Only in the United States, of all major countries, has there been for a long time a sufficiently large measure of social acceptance of manual labor to permit the full flowering of business unionism. In a few countries, class stratification and discrimination

were widely accepted as God-ordained. Since World War II, however, in most areas of the world, where social and, even more, political discrimination against manual labor exists, it is felt by intellectuals and workers to be unbearable and wholly unjust. The removal of discriminatory institutions is one of the principal assignments of the labor movement. The American labor movement, arising in a country of labor shortage and finding its definitive form long after the Jacksonian era, could devote itself wholeheartedly to a narrow range of economic problems. Most of the labor movements that now come into being in the underdeveloped countries devote a good deal of their attention to the establishment of a higher degree of social and political equality. Economic advancement is not neglected, but it is felt to be dependent upon the achievement of progress in the struggle against discrimination; or else both economic and social advances are regarded as two related fronts in the same war.

* * *

Thus from the angle of US experience, political unionism or unionism with an elaborate—and usually radical—political ideology has usually been regarded as a weak and ineffective form of labor action subject to dissensions and involved doctrinal quarrels. Yet there is hardly a single labor movement in an underdeveloped country which is apolitical and carries as small an ideological freight as American labor. American labor has traditionally kept intellectuals out of its ranks; indeed, its anti-intellectual bias has been one of its most conspicuous traits—even though in that respect it is not as unique as in its almost singleminded concentration on collective bargaining. Labor movements arising in the early phase of industrialization, on the other hand, are almost always led by intellectuals and most often created by them. Indeed, given the low educational level of the workers, the discrimination to which they are exposed, and frequently, their own lack of self-confidence, it is almost inevitable that "outside leaders" be at the head of the movement for long periods.

Any attempt to reshape the labor movement during the early phases of industrialization after the pattern of one movement in one country of highly advanced industry with an almost unique political and social history and a long tradition of labor shortage is thus bound to fail. All efforts to influence these movements and to keep them out of Communist control must allow for their being fundamentally different from the American labor movement, if these efforts are to be successful.

How far, in this diversity, can unions be made to go in furthering or at least not resisting the processes of economic growth? Galenson's excellent discussion of this problem starts with the recognition that unions "are integral parts of the productive mechanism." Their role in the process of economic growth is by no means uniformly negative. The contribution that unions—at least reasonably responsible unions—can make to the establishment and maintenance of discipline in the plant is of greatest importance, for unions are more effective in this field than employers. It is true that unions in the early stages of industrialization are not always responsible organizations—their position is insecure, their membership often illiterate and rarely well-informed on union matters; on the other hand, they are often part of a great nationalist movement and are, therefore, susceptible to an appeal to patriotism, and their leadership is dedicated to the cause of building a modern nation. But while unions may exert responsibility in enforcing discipline in the plant, it would be idle, in Galenson's view, to expect from them responsibility in their efforts to obtain higher living standards for their members. It is at this point that Galenson most clearly parts company from Asoka Mehta.

Unions derive their power from the defense of the interests of their members. These may be political or social interests at any given time, rather than economic interests. The unions may, in certain situations, sacrifice short-term interests in favor of considerations relating to somewhat longer periods, particularly when the majority of the members has been made aware of the long-run union strategy involved. But unions cannot exist, for long periods of time, as social welfare agencies —which is what Asoka Mehta in effect suggests they become—and even less as instruments of wage restraint. True, grievance handling may be one of the cornerstones of the union structure, and unions effectively handling the complaints of their members can afford, at times, to be less aggressive in collective bargaining without losing their influence or membership. But the suggestion that unions delay for a whole period—the "takeoff"—their mission of raising their members' standard of living can only result in these unions ceasing to exist as genuine unions —whatever their name—and, if circumstances permit, new organizations will come into being to perform the function which the original unions no longer fulfill. In a divided world, this prospect can hardly be entertained with equanimity.

This debate has some parallels in the recent discussions on union wage policy under full employment. When unemployment drops below a certain critical level, wage rates tend to increase more rapidly than productivity. As a result labor costs per unit of output rise, driving up prices. One of the most popular solutions to this problem, advocated in many slightly differing versions, is that the unions exert self-restraint in their demand for wage increases. This is intended not merely as a way of meeting a temporary emergency, but as a long-term solution to a long-term problem. The three most startling implications of this policy are: (1) union members are expected to pay dues to an organization which regards the prevention of "excessive" wage increases as one of its assignments. (2) In the absence of unions the workers may well obtain higher money —and perhaps temporarily also real— wages than by ways of collective bargaining. (3) Employers seeking to attract or hold manpower in a tight labor market may offer wage rates above those set in the contract, and thereby not only defeat the unions' sacrifice, but also demonstrate to the workers that management is more eager to pay hgher wages than the union is to obtain them.

The parallel is fairly obvious. While union self-restraint may be an effective way of dealing with temporary emergencies in the process of growth, it is unlikely that unions could long survive the adoption of a more or less permanent policy of wage-restraint. This is not to deny that such a policy might be in the best long-run interests of the country and the workers themselves, even though the longer the run considered, the more dubious that proposition appears for the individual worker. But in any case it is impossible to conceive of unions being established and maintained under the difficult conditions of early industrialization while they tend to restrain the workers from attempts to improve their desperately low standard of living.

It is possible to drive the parallel one step further: for some workers' categories, particularly skilled workers, the operations of the labor market during the "take-off" period may easily produce wage improvements, even in the absence of union pressure. Can it reasonably be expected that the union, in this situation, act as a brake upon wage increases obtainable without its intervention?

All these problems must be examined not simply in the light of economic models, but primarily as issues of political economy. The underdeveloped countries, and particularly their labor movements, are the main target of Communist organizing and propaganda activities. In some parts of the world—e.g., Latin America—nationalistic unions as well—e.g., of the Peronist variety —compete with democratic and Communist-inspired unions for the allegiance of the rising industrial working class. Labor unions that can be convincingly accused of being ineffectual in the struggle for improved living standards will have little chance to survive in this highly competitive struggle. Their sacrifice will have been in vain. They will be destroyed and their membership taken over by more combative unions less concerned with the long-run aspirations of the nation, or at least by unions that succeed in appearing to be more effective in the defense of the immediate interests of the workers. Democracy, or better, the hopes for an evolution toward democracy, may well be the main losers in the process. A nationalistic or Communist totalitarian regime may emerge and settle the issue by the establishment of most rigorous labor controls.

In the words of Walter Galenson: "Free trade unions in a democratic society must ordinarily appeal to the worker on an all-out consumptionist platform. No matter how much 'responsibility' the union leader exhibits in his understanding of the limited consumption possibilities existing at the outset of industrialization, he cannot afford to moderate his demands. To do so would mean abdication to the irresponsible demagogue or to the Communist machine, neither of which has any compunction about outbidding him in promises."

Does this mean that the problem cannot be resolved? Are we confronted with a choice between rapid economic growth and totalitarian controls on one hand, and the existence of reasonably free and reasonably democratic unions together with a low rate of economic progress or even stagnation on the other hand? Two kinds of answers seem to me possible—one on the level of analytical reasoning, the other by reference to the ways of life of the world in which we exist.

To begin with the latter: a great many social problems cannot be resolved in any clear-cut manner. They remain unresolved, but may be reduced in their acuity to a degree that makes tolerable our failure to solve them fundamentally. They continue to produce tensions in our social fabric and as such may exert a not undesirable stimulus. In practical terms: union leaders may be able to delay the struggle for a wage increase or accept a compromise that would postpone the date on which such an increase becomes effective. Such a delay or slowing up of the progress of consumption might, in certain situations, be suffiicient to provide the resources for the initial investment push. In other cases, immediate satisfaction of urgent consumption demands might be necessary to prevent political or social upheavals. In that situation the increase of consumption is the price to be paid to avert a further deterioration of the prospect for economic growth.

It is not at all obvious, in the latter case, whether in the absence of the union the situation would be more favorable for economic growth. Not only would the danger of unrest persist, but it is not unlikely that competitive unions would arise—in the middle of the twentieth century labor organizations have become the rule rather than the exception. The contradiction between union pressure for higher wages and the need to free resources for investment in the interests of economic growth is not resolved, but it is possible, in many circumstances, for a society to provide accommodation for the contradiction and to function effectively on this basis. This is the more possible as other union functions assist the growth process—maintenance of plant discipline, assistance to rural workers in their adaptation to the urban environment, and training and transmission of skills are examples. We may not obtain maximum rates of growth in this way—whatever that means—but a tolerable compromise may avert the danger of being thrown back by unrest and political

upheaval. A mixture of Asoka Mehta and de Schweinitz, plus a certain slowing-up of economic growth below the undefinable maximum rate, might do the trick.

This brings us to the second answer: even union pressure on wages need not be all detrimental for economic development. The theoretical model from which this conclusion is derived is a mechanical and static model. In a more dynamic approach, union pressure on wages may—within certain limits—become an instrument of economic development.

In early industrialization, competition is usually very weak. With sparse transportation systems and protected by tariff walls and exchange regulations, industrial firms normally enjoy quasi-monopolies on their local markets. Traditional social values tend to make the competitor appear as a kind of interloper; public opinion rejects the ethics of a competitive market society. The drive for the improvement of methods and products in such a society is exceedingly weak. Union pressure on wages, by threatening to reduce the profit margin, may, under the circumstances, represent a desirable stimulus for management. Indeed, it may be the only major pressure of this kind until more firm and better communications develop, tariffs are reduced, exchange controls are weakened, and public opinion grows more sympathetic toward the implications of a competitive market economy.

Union pressure upon wages, however, will perform this function merely under certain conditions which we can outline only briefly in this space. One is that the increase in wage costs not be granted in such a way that cost increases can be passed too easily to the consumers of the product. This may require a monetary or fiscal policy endangering economic growth. Another condition necessary in order for this mechanism to work is that the wage pressure and the consequent increase of costs not become so heavy as to be discouraging for management and investors. Union wage demands must not be so large as to make it impossible for management to re-establish reasonable profit margins by feasible devices within a foreseeable time.

Given these and other conditions, the opposition between normal union behavior and the needs of economic growth appears less acute than most of the literature would seem to indicate. The question remains, of course, as to the extent to which these conditions exist in reality. There seems, at first sight, little reason to be optimistic in this respect. But the question is open. . . .

### Related Readings

Good general discussions of labor in the developing countries can be found in Walter Galenson, ed., *Labor in Developing Countries* (Berkeley, University of California Press, 1962) and *Labor and Economic Development* (New York, Wiley, 1959). The 1962 book has chapters on Pakistan; Indonesia; Brazil, Argentina, and Chile; Israel; and Turkey. The 1959 book has chapters on India, Japan, Egypt, French West Africa, and the British West Indies. Galenson's introductions present good, short comparisons of all of these countries. Although these studies confirm the difficulties involved in establishing unions and collective bargaining in the developing countries, Galenson concludes:

". . . independent trade unionism and satisfactory economic development are by no means antithetical. On the contrary, we believe that independent unions can make a major contribution to development by giving the individual worker a sense of personal dignity and a means of redressing his grievances. It is quite understandable for government leaders who are concentrating on the achievement of economic goals in the face of what must sometimes appear to be impossible odds to be impatient with intractable, irresponsible representatives of workers. There is an ever-present temptation to silence them and to substitute paternalism for bargaining and conflict. But the price may be very high indeed: the loss to the nations of the creative energies of free men who feel themselves masters of their own fates rather than cogs in a vast, imprsonal machine."

(*Labor In Developing Countries*, p. 10.)

A good comparative analysis of labor in the developing countries may be found in Everett M. Kassalow, *Trade Unions and Industrial Relations: An International Comparison* (New York, Random House, 1969, Part Two). In addition to generalizations on forces shaping unionism in new countries, the nature of political unionism and the economic setting and problems, Kassalow discusses labor movements in Kenya, Algeria, India, and Mexico.

# II

---

# Wages and Employment:
# Theory and Practice

Even in this core theoretical section of labor economics, there is evidence of changing interest and content, based on new experiences, so clearly marked in the other applied parts. Although the first chapter, on supply and demand, covers mainly traditional theories, new subjects include modern concepts of alternative uses of time, other than the conventional work-leisure choice, and an explanation of the forces affecting the labor supply of married women. Here are examples of theory keeping up with practice, specifically the more varied uses of non-market work time and the substantial growth of women in the labor force.

For years, analysts have noted and tried to explain the long-run controversy of the labor force participation rate. The second chapter, besides discussing this phenomenon, presents the changes in analysis of cyclical variation in the labor force. Thus, studies with reference to the inflow and outflow of secondary workers during the depression, and over long periods of economic strength, have led to new approaches to the behavior of marginal labor force participants during dips and swells from a high-level economic base.

Similarly, the third chapter studies the problem of unemployment from a prosperity perspective. The inadequate demand-structural controversy disputes the causes of a modest rise in low-level unemployment, modest at least in comparison with the sharp drop during the Great Depression.

The entire subject matter of the fourth chapter, on the inflation-unemployment reduction "trade off," is comparatively new. The effect on prices from a movement toward full employment with the implication that the reduction in unemployment is itself an explanatory variable, has only recently been studied. This is a case, though, in which theory seems to lag behind experience, since studies indicate that the pattern of rising prices with falling unemployment is by no means a new one.

The skill differential, the subject of the fifth chapter, received consideration from Adam Smith. But only recently have theorists of the magnitude and movements in the differential expressed their arguments with reference to the human capital aspect of labor supply and demand, which Smith himself thought crucial to understanding wage differences based on skill differences.

It would be overstating a case to argue that recent studies of industrial and geographical differentials, presented in the last chapter, reflect new theory in response to changing experience. In fact, these differentials persist, and newer works refine the data that show continuing patterns of wage differences. The studies explain these differentials on the basis of market imperfections and nonmarket elements, factors that also prevent the formulation of a definite wage theory, which is a weakness in the discipline of labor economics that is discussed in this section's first chapter.

# CHAPTER 5

# Labor Supply and Demand

If it were not that decisions on labor supply and demand involve people, the subject would be no more than an application of the fundamental theory of the pricing of production factors. In fact, complete economic principles texts include sections on labor supply and demand in their analysis of factor pricing and, to be sure, at least note the complications to the pure theory that the human quality of the labor service introduces.

In regard to supply, labor does not have the same simple theoretical goal of other factors: to maximize money income or profits. Economic goals become less rigid because the worker, unlike other factors, cannot separate his services from himself; consequently, labor involves effort, so that extra labor income must be weighed against the time and energy cost of work. No such considerations confuse decisions on the supply of other factors. Firms supply machines and materials with no extra effort to the supplier if additional units are produced in response to profit-maximizing motives.

Furthermore, suppliers of labor, being tied to their services, take an interest in their working conditions. Thus, it does not always follow that workers will seek employment in firms paying the highest wage for their services, or that competition will equalize wages in all labor's alternative uses, given differences in work atmosphere.

Workers combine, in unions, to supply their services as a group. This leads to further complication in determining labor supply in that the individual worker's income-effort goals are subsumed in the union's wage-employment policy. The supply price of labor in a union situation evolves from an agreement reached over conflicting union wage goals and management profit-maximizing motives. It can be said that producer monopolies gauge their pricing decision on purchasers' reactions, but certainly the give-and-take between unions and management, analyzed in bargaining theories of wages, is more immediate and focused.

In regard to labor demand, deviation from the conventional theory of the demand for productive factors resulting from the human element in labor services is less sharp. Firms may pay more than necessary because they wish to be known as "good" or "high-wage" employers, a thought that never enters their minds as users of machines or materials. But whether, in general, firms have profit maximization as an exclusive goal has long been subject to question. The marginal productivity theory of wages, which simply treats labor like other factors of production, is still the only systematical formal wage theory. It has been discredited by some and questioned by many, but it has yet to be replaced.

In its first section, this chapter presents the basis of individual labor supply theory. Later chapters enlarge on supply theory and practices allowing for group (union) decision making and consideration of the worker as a human resource rather than as a bundle of productive services.

The second section discusses the issue of the applicability of marginal productivity theory to labor demand and the pricing of labor services. Not only does the failure to follow profit maximization practices strictly reduce the application of marginal principles but, in addition, the influence of institutional forces makes wage setting somewhat independent of basic market supply and demand elements.

## Individual Labor Supply

*Supply of Labor and Demand for Leisure.* Conventional theory studies the individual supply of labor in response to different wage levels through its complement, the demand for leisure. This demand, in relation to its price (in this sense, the wage rate), differs significantly from the demand for the usual good or service in that it is uncertain whether more leisure would be demanded (less labor supplied) when its price (wage rate) fell.

For the usual good, a decline in price would ordinarily lead to an increase in the quantity demanded because both income and substitution effects would influence demand in the same direction—to acquire more of the good. The substitution effect arising because the good becomes relatively cheaper than other goods would lead the buyer to purchase more of it instead of other goods. The income effect, in most cases slight, especially if the good is not an important budget element, would operate to increase the purchase of all goods, including the one in question, as real income—spending power—rose with the decline in price of one good.

For a decline in the price of leisure, however, income and substitution effects tend to exert opposite forces. With a decline in wages, the price of leisure falls and, as with other goods and services, the substitution effect works to raise the demand for leisure, which has become relatively cheaper than other "goods." But the fall in wages in itself reduces income, thus tending to decrease the demand for leisure and increase the supply of market work effort. Whether the quantity of leisure demanded increases with a decline in the wage rate depends on whether the substitution effect is stronger than the income effect.

In Figure 5–1, the demand curve for leisure is drawn under the assumption that the substitution effect exceeds the income effect for all relevant wages.

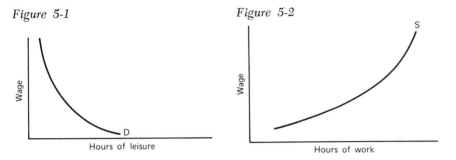

*Figure 5-1*

*Figure 5-2*

Translating this leisure-demand curve into an individual market labor supply schedule, under the simplified assumption of a dichotomous work-leisure time opportunity, yields Figure 5–2.

But it would be unusual for the substitution effect to dominate at all wages, that is, for the labor supply schedule to be positively sloped over its entire range. More conventionally, the labor supply curve is drawn with a backward bend. This signifies that as wages rise and work effort is increased and leisure is reduced, a point is reached at which, with little leisure and much income, the worker would choose to take a wage increase in added leisure as well as in more income. But the increase in income would then be proportionately less than the increase in wages; the income effect would, at these higher wages, outweigh the substitution effect on the demand for leisure.

The nature of the individual supply curve varies for different workers, depending on the relative strength of the demand for income and leisure, but the supply curve may also change direction for a given worker at different wages. Lionel Robbins' well-known article on labor supply, in effect, offers a geometrical presentation of the backward-bending curve, but in the text, Robbins states that "we cannot predict *a priori* what the effects of a change . . . in wage rates will be."

# On the Elasticity of Demand for Income in Terms of Effort

## by Lionel Robbins

1. It is a generally accepted proposition of theoretical economics that the effects of a change in the terms on which incomes from work can be obtained depend upon the elasticity of demand for income in terms of effort.[1] If the elasticity of demand for income in terms of effort is greater than unity, then the effects of a tax or a fall in wage rates will be a diminution of work done and the effects of a bounty or a rise in wage rates will be an increase in work done. If it is less than unity, then the opposite movements are to be expected.

2. These propositions are capable of demonstration by the familiar geometrical constructions of either $(a)$ unit or $(b)$ integral demand curves. The only difference between the constructions relevant here and those of commodity price analysis is that the prices exhibited will be, not money, but effort prices.

$(a)$ Thus, if we employ the unit demand apparatus, we measure quantity of income demanded along $OX$ and the effort price of income along $OY$. The curve $dd^1$ exhibits the conditions of demand, and the quantity of work done for any given income will be shown by a rectangle formed by erecting perpendiculars on $OX$ and $OY$ to cut any point of equilibrium $(P)$ in $dd^1$. If e.g. the effort price of income is $OE_1$ then the quantity of income which will be earned will be $OI_1$, and the amount of work done will be $OE_1P_1I_1$.

The effects of a change in the terms on

SOURCE Reprinted with permission from *Economica*, Vol. 10, June 1930, pp. 123–129.

[1] See Dalton, *Public Finance*, Second Edition, pp. 100–108, or Robertson, *Banking Policy and the Price Level*, Chapters I and II *passim*. It is possible, of course, to reformulate this proposition in terms of the elasticity of supply of effort, and for some purposes it is convenient to do so. But there is much to be said for exhibiting all psychological variables as phenomena of demand. See Wicksteed, *Commonsense of Political Economy*, Book II, Chapter IV, and "The Scope and Method of Political Economy," *Economic Journal*, 1913, pp. 1 *seq*.

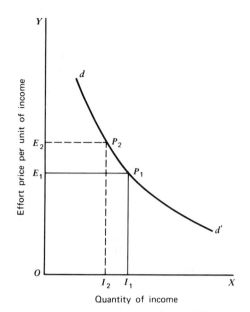

Quantity of income

which income can be obtained can be shown by shifting $E$. Let us suppose for instance the imposition of a uniform income-tax which shifts $E$ from $E_1$ to $E_2$. Then the quantity of income earned will shift to $I_2$ and the change in the amount of work done will be shown by the differ-

Along $OX$ we continue to measure quantity of income. Along $OY$, however, we measure the total amounts of effort which will be expended for different quantities of income. (That is to say, what was a rectangle on the unit apparatus has become a line on this apparatus.) $Od$ is the

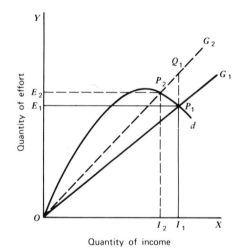

Quantity of income

ence between $E_1P_1I_1O$ and $E_2P_2I_2O$. If in this region $dd^1$ shows an elasticity greater than one this difference will be negative (i.e. less work will be done). If it is less than one the difference will be positive (i.e. more work will be done).

(b) The integral apparatus shows the same result with even greater clarity.

total demand curve. The terms on which income can be obtained will evidently be an angular magnitude, the tangent of the angle $G_1OX$. Thus in the case depicted if the terms on which income can be obtained are represented by $\tan G_1OX$ we get equilibrium at $P_1$ with $OI_1$, income earned for an expenditure of $OE_1$ effort.

Now suppose a tax imposed. We may represent this by swinging $OG$ to the left. (To get $OI_1$ before, it was necessary to expend $I_1P_1$ effort. Now it is necessary to expend $I_1Q_1$.) Equilibrium is re-established at $P_2$ with $OI_2$ income earned and $OE_2$ income expended. Since, in this region, $Od$ shows an elasticity less than unity, $OE_2$ is greater than $OE_1$ (i.e. more work is done).

3. The propositions thus analysed are purely formal in character. They explain what will happen if the conditions of demand are of a certain nature. To discover what the conditions of demand are in any particular case, it is generally supposed that we must rely upon observation. We cannot predict *a priori* what the effects of a change in taxation or of a change in wage rates will be; we must ascertain the probable elasticity of demand for income in terms of effort of the taxpayers or wage-earners concerned.

4. In recent years, however, propositions have been advanced which suggest that formal analysis enables us to predict that the elasticity of demand in the case of effort demand for income must always be less than unity—that is to say that the imposition of a tax will always have the effect of making a man work more, and a rise in his wage rates will always make him work less. If these propositions were true, they would obviously be of the highest *practical* importance—the effect on output of higher taxation need have no terrors for needy Chancellors of the Exchequer—and since they have been advanced by authorities no less eminent than Professor Pigou and Professor Knight, they clearly deserve the very closest attention.

5. The arguments of both the authorities mentioned involve in one form or another implicit appeal to the "law" or assumption of the declining marginal utility of units of income. Now *prima facie*

it is difficult to see how this "law" or assumption justifies the inferences which appear to be based on it. *The assumption that, as income increases, the utility to an individual of additional units declines, justifies us indeed in inferring that the curve which exhibits the condition of demand for income in terms of effort will slope downwards, but it does not seem to justify the assumption that this curve must always cut a rectangular hyperbola negatively (i.e. that it must show an elasticity less than one at all reaches).* The assumption or "law" lays it down that the final degree of utility diminishes, but it does not *prima facie* say anything about the *rate* of diminution.

6. But let us examine more closely the actual arguments concerned. Professor Knight's is the more general and will be taken first.

Professor Knight's argument concerns the effect of a change in wage rates. "In so far as men act rationally," he argues,[2] ". . . they will at a higher rate divide their time between wage earning and non-industrial uses in such a way as to earn *more money* but to work *fewer hours*." And he justifies this proposition by the following reasoning. "Suppose that at a higher rate per hour or per piece, a man previously at the perfect equilibrium adjustment works as before and earns a proportionately higher income. When, now, he goes to spend the extra money, he will naturally want to increase his expenditure for many commodities consumed and to take on some new ones. To divide his resources in such a way as to preserve equal importance of equal expenditures in all fields he must evidently lay out part of his new funds for increased leisure; i.e. buy back some of his working time or spend some of his money by the process of not earning it."

At first sight the argument appears overwhelmingly convincing, sufficient

[2] *Risk, Uncertainty, and Profit,* pp. 117–18.

even to overcome the reflection of common sense that, if it were true, it would follow that it would always be futile to offer rational men permanently higher wages if it was desired to elicit a permanently increased supply of work. But closer inspection seems to reveal a flaw. Professor Knight's argument assumes that the prices of the commodities constituting real income are unaltered. This is presumably true so far as money prices are concerned. But the relevant conception in this connection is not *money price* but *effort price*, and a change in the rate at which money income can be earned, money prices remaining constant, *constitutes* a change in the effort price of commodities. *The money price is the same but the effort price is diminished.* And, that being the case, the question whether more or less effort is expended on commodities is obviously still an open one. It depends on the elasticity of demand for income in terms of effort.

This may sound abstract, but if it is thought of in concrete terms, it becomes very simple. If real income be conceived as consisting of a flow of one commodity, say, bananas, and the process of producing bananas as an exchange of effort for income, then it is surely clear that, if for some reason the effort price of bananas (real income) diminishes (a change equivalent to a rise in money wage rates), it is entirely a matter of elasticity of demand for bananas (real income) whether more or less effort is given for them, just as, if the money price of bananas changes, it is entirely a matter of elasticity whether more or less money is given for them.

The same objection can be put yet another way. In Professor Knight's example leisure is purchased by sacrificing income. We may therefore conceive—as he does—of *a real income price of leisure*. Now when the money rate of wages rises (commodity prices remaining the same) the real income price of leisure (the cost of leisure in terms of real income sacrificed) rises. And when the price of leisure (or anything else) rises it is not at all clear that more will be bought even out of an increased real income. Again it is all a matter of elasticity.

\* \* \*

In Robbins' first figure, Effort Price per Unit of Income, measured along the Y-axis, is simply the reciprocal of the wage rate. Thus the movement from $E_1$ to $E_2$ represents a decline in wages. If the $dd'$ curve is elastic over this range, then the area $OI_2P_2E_2$ would be less than that of $OI_1P_1E_1$, indicating a fall in total effort. If such were the case, the labor supply schedule would be positively sloped over the wage $E_1E_2$, with supply (effort) falling as wages decreased and rising as wages increased. In fact, if $dd'$ follows the customary path of a demand curve, being elastic at its upper reaches and inelastic as it approaches the X-axis, the curve would indicate a backward-bending labor supply curve, with individual labor supply expanding and then contracting as wages rose.

Robbins' second figure demonstrates that he has just this type of labor supply curve in mind. There the slope of the rays $OG_1$, $OG_2$, etc., equals Quantity of Effort divided by Quantity of Income, which again is the reciprocal of the wage rate. Thus, flatter rays represent higher wages. Note that the curve $Od$ rises and then falls. This means that the quantity of effort increases with higher wages, as flatter rays drawn from $O$ to the curve intersect it at higher points, until the highest point on the curve is reached. After this point, flatter rays, representing higher wages, meet the curve at successively lower points, indicating a decline in labor effort at higher wages.

In effect, then, Robbins has given a geometrical presentation of a backward-bending supply schedule. His curves lead him to this result, but there is no necessary reason for them to assume this pattern. Nevertheless, Robbins' contribution has importance as an early presentation of the idea that the direction of the individual labor supply schedule for a given worker may change over a relevant wage range.

*Quality Differences in Hours of Work and Leisure.* Modern theories of labor supply modify the tacit classical assumption of uniform quality of leisure and work hours by explaining how quality differences in time spent in leisure pursuits or work effort influence the nature of the worker's labor supply schedule. It has long been recognized that more arduous work would require a higher wage to bring forth the same supply of labor as for a more pleasant job requiring similar skill and training. But, in general, quality differences in work and leisure hours have only recently been incorporated into the derivation of labor supply schedules.

Consider the case of premium pay for Sunday work. Higher wages must be paid the work force for Sunday work, not because the nature of the job changes on Sunday, but because, to the worker, Sunday hours of leisure have a greater value than weekday leisure hours.

Then there is the case of the night shift. These workers must be paid more than day workers for the same job to compensate for the unpleasantness of night work compared with the day shift and/or to compensate for the preference for nighttime leisure hours. In any case, the substitution effect of a wage increase is weaker for a particular worker for night work. This means that the same worker would have a backward bend to his labor supply curve, with effort being reduced at higher wages, at a lower wage, if he worked at night than if by day.

By the same reasoning, if two jobs differ only in prestige, workers in the lower prestige job would tend to reduce their labor supply as wages rose at a lower wage than those attached to the higher prestige occupation. In an interesting application of this principle, Rottenberg, in the following paper notes that the tendency for workers not to take advantage of full-schedule income opportunities in sugar field work reflects the low prestige associated with this type of labor, rather than a characteristic preference of Antiguans for leisure over work in general.

The low prestige of cane field work weakens the substitution effect of a wage increase on the demand for leisure. Rottenberg's study seems to emphasize that quality differences in work and leisure hours may account for differences in responses to wage increases among occupations.

# Income and Leisure in an Underdeveloped Economy

## by Simon Rottenberg

... At some point in the scale of prices for labor, the utility derived from additional increments of income is assumed to be disproportionately smaller than the disutility incurred from additional increments of work. At that point, and for a range of prices beyond it, the neoclassical doctrine tells us that the worker has a preference for leisure over income and that each successive rise in the price offered for his services will bring forth successively less effort.

The point at which the curve takes its negative slope is not the same for all persons; it must be somehow related to the aspirations which the worker has for income and to the intensity of his desire for leisure. If his income aspirations are strong or his desire for leisure weak, the point of backward turning is high on the price scale. Contrariwise, if his income aspirations are weak or his desire for leisure strong, the point of backward turning is low.

The logic of the doctrine thus requires that each person have a maximum aspiration, which he fixes for himself, for income acquired through effort. For, if the desire for income were without limit, the curve would have a positive slope for its full length to the point where effort is limited by sheer physical capacity and would, thereafter, be vertical to the base, where the graph is plotted according to the traditional schema, with the price of labor on the $y$-axis and the supply offered on the $x$-axis.[1] The aspiration for income, however, need not be constant over time

SOURCE Reprinted with permission from *The Journal of Political Economy,* Vol. 60, April 1952, pp. 95–101.

[1] "Suppose, for instance, that an individual did not wish to earn more than a given money income. If his wage was such that he could obtain this money income without an unreasonable effort, any increase in his wage would result in a decline in the number of hours for which the worker would work. At the higher wage, he could obtain the income of his heart's desire by working fewer hours than at a lower wage" (Kenneth E. Boulding, *Economic Analysis* [New York and London, 1941], p. 227).

for the same person, nor need it be uniform among different persons.

The point at which an individual begins to be insensitive to income incentives will be partly affected by the cultural influences that play upon his character. A man who has been brought up in a community which places a high value on work, which is "consumption conscious," and which attaches prestige to the possession of material goods will not begin to offer less labor until there is a large increase in the price for his services or until the price is very high. On the other hand, a man who lives in a society which values leisure and which attaches no social stigma to living at a close-to-subsistence level will begin to offer less labor when small increases occur and when the price is very low.[2]

These conditions of quick backward turning are said to be particularly characteristic of the people of the underdeveloped economies. It has long been believed to be true of the people of the British West Indies. The ideas that the British West Indian has a large preference for leisure over work and that his wants are small have been advanced by the planter communities of the islands for many years and have been written into Royal Commission and other public reports. In this system of beliefs, the West Indian worker does not respond to income incentives. A small rise in the wage rate, it is said, induces him to exert less energy at work and to reallocate his time between leisure and work in favor of leisure. Similarly, an increase in the wages of some trades, others remaining unchanged, does not cause workers to transfer to the advantaged trades. The report of the Economic Policy Committee of Jamaica, published in 1945, for example, has been paraphrased as saying: "Many [West Indian] workers [do] not want to work for wages regularly five or six days a week all the year round. . . . They prefer to have a lower standard of living and more leisure; they are not educated to appreciate a higher standard of living, and would rather take life more easily than add to their material comforts.' "[3]

If the doctrine is correct that West Indian labor is indolent and incapable of being moved by earning opportunities to exert energy at work beyond what is necessary to achieve income for support of life at very low levels, the likelihood of successful development of the Caribbean economy is small. If the doctrine is true, an important objective of public policy ought to be to raise the level of aspiration for income and for the goods and services for which income exchanges.[4]

---

[2] Marshall's position was that the individual supply curve of labor is generally positively sloped and that the backward turn is "the exception to the rule." "The longer a man works, or even is on duty, the greater is his desire for a respite . . . while every hour's additional work gives him more pay, and brings him nearer to the stage at which his most urgent wants are satisfied; and the higher the pay, the sooner this stage is reached. It depends then on the individual, whether with growing pay new wants arise . . . or he is soon satiated with those enjoyments that can be gained only by work, and then craves more rest, and more opportunities for activities that are themselves pleasurable. No universal rule can be laid down; but experience seems to show that the more ignorant and phlegmatic of races and of individuals, especially if they live in a southern clime, will stay at their work a shorter time, and will exert themselves less while at it, if the rate of pay rises so as to give them their accustomed enjoyment in return for less work than before. But those whose mental horizon is wider, and who have more firmness and elasticity of character, will work the harder and the longer the higher the rate of pay which is open to them: unless indeed they prefer to divert their activities to higher aims than work for material gain. . . . We may conclude that increased remuneration causes an immediate increase in the supply of efficient work, as a rule; and that the exceptions to this rule, just noticed, are seldom on a large scale, though they are not devoid of significance" (Alfred Marshall, *Principles of Economics* [8th ed.; London, 1938], pp. 528–29).

[3] T. S. Simey, *Welfare and Planning in the West Indies* (London, 1946), pp. 133–34.

[4] Any public policy which is calculated to sharpen the aspirations of backwards peoples for goods, to make income-earning a more powerful lever, to introduce the competitive spirit, and to make them over in our puritan image, so that they, too, will look upon the leisurely as social pariahs, is fraught

An attempt to assess the correctness of the thesis that leisure is preferred to work at low standards of acquired income was made in the island of Antigua, one of the Leeward Islands of the British West Indies.

Antigua is a small island of 108 square miles (69,000 acres). Its population is now estimated to be about forty-five thousand, almost all of whom are of Negro descent. The conjunction of a high and stable birth rate and a constantly falling death rate has resulted in a high rate of natural increase of over twenty per thousand of population, so that, with opportunities for emigration now virtually shut off, the population increases by about one thousand per year. The people live at levels of extreme poverty, measured by the standards of the developed areas of the world. At current prices (1951), roughly estimated calculations of national income indicate that per capita income is less than $100 (United States) per annum.

The economy of Antigua is dominated by sugar, and has been throughout the three centuries of its history, although, from time to time, Sea Island cotton has played an important role. These two commodities now constitute close to 100 per cent of all exports. Other exports, principally rum, are of negligible importance. With the exception of ground provisions grown for local consumption, gravel taken from local quarries, charcoal used for fuel, and fish taken from the sea, almost all things consumed in Antigua are brought from abroad, either in finished form or as raw materials for such small-scale, or cottage, industries as furniture-making and tailoring or for the construction industry. For a community such as Antigua, there-fore, which, in general, consumes things which it does not produce and produces things which it does not consume, the volume and value of exports are of enormous importance in determining the standard of living. Since agriculture is overwhelmingly the island's important activity, the value of the sugar crop greatly affects the level of consumption in the island.

The history of the land-tenure pattern of Antigua shows a trend in the direction of concentration at one end and dispersion at the other. In the early years of the sugar industry's history, most cane in Antigua was cultivated on a considerable number of owner-operated estates, many of which ground their cane in small mills located on the estate. The difficulties occasioned by the falling price of sugar, emancipation of the slaves, severance of natural trade relations with the Americans at the opening of the Revolutionary War, removal of the preference enjoyed by the West Indies against East Indian sugar, and protection of the beet-sugar industries of Europe from the competition of lower-cost sugar cane producing areas led to the abandonment of land, the sale and resale of land at losses, the foreclosure by banks, merchants, or other forms of moneylenders of mortgages encumbering the estates, and the splitting of large estates into small plots which were rented to peasant operators. In 1943 a corporation was formed to amalgamate most of the remaining private estates still engaged in cultivating cane. This corporation now owns about 18,000 of the island's 69,000 acres, of which 9,000 acres are arable. Of this, 7,800 acres are worked by the corporation itself and 1,200 acres are rented to peasants on small farms. Peasants also work

with danger. The backward peoples may very well be socially more stable as they are. To make a revolution among them, destroying value-systems which are ancient and rooted, may do enormous harm. But this is the risk to be run and, possibly, the price to be paid for economic development. In the backward areas, now, people live badly; they are malnourished, badly housed, ill and diseased. To improve their conditions of life, either more of them must work, they must work more hours, and they must produce more in each hour of work; or they must be a charge on the people of the developed areas. Our traditions must become theirs, or they must remain poverty-stricken, or the world's well-to-do must move a never ending flow of gifts to them. There is no other way out.

plots rented from the few private estates which remain and plots on government land settlements. The "Census of Agriculture of the Leeward Islands" of 1946 counted in Antigua 3,196 farms of one acre or more and 2,285 small plots of less than one acre.[5] A large proportion of these are devoted to the growing of sugar cane. In 1947, which was a typical recent year, the corporation delivered 110,000 tons of cane; other (private, non-corporation) estates, 15,000 tons; and peasants, 45,000 tons, to the single cane-grinding mill which is closely associated with the corporation through common shareholders.[6]

The planter thesis that the Antiguan worker is voluntarily underemployed because he prefers leisure to income at low living levels can now be discussed more meaningfully within this framework of the fundamental characteristics of the Antiguan economy. Planters of the community lament their inability to find sufficient workers to take the cane crop off the fields within an optimum time period and the unwillingness of workers to perform certain classes of tasks at all. Workers who do accept employment, according to the planters, refuse to work full work weeks but prefer to work relatively few days each week. This has been the traditional opinion of the planter community for many years. A report of 1891, for example, says:

*The number of people is, on the whole, quite sufficient for the sugar estates, but the difficulty is for the planter to obtain that regular labor upon which his operations depend. The labor difficulty was the cause of the abandonment of estates in the past years. . . . All evidence shows that there is plenty of work and wages for the*

*Antiguan laborer, if he would, more largely than he does, take advantage of the opportunity.[7]*

The belief, thus, that Antiguan workers have small fixed wants which are capable of being satisfied with relatively few hours of work is inferred in part from the fact that many wage workers in the cane fields of the island work less than full work weeks. This is taken to prove that the West Indian puts a high premium on leisure. Workers are able to do this because field workers in the cane industry assimilate the situations of contractors rather than of wage workers. For most occupational classes payment is by the task rather than by the hour. Workers report for work when they please, work the number of hours that suits their convenience, work at a pace set by themselves, and are paid for the tasks they perform. In part, also, the inference is drawn from the fact that workers prefer work of some kinds for which wages are low to work of other kinds which pay higher wages. This is taken to prove that the West Indian's desire for income is weak.

The facts from which the thesis is drawn are correct. It is true that wage workers in the cane fields put in short work weeks. Examination of the pay lists of four randomly selected estates for one out-of-crop week of 1949 and one in-crop week of 1950 revealed that, in both weeks, about 40 per cent of all workers worked for three days or less during the week and about 70 per cent worked for four days or less. A survey of employment in Antigua for a week of July, 1950, showed that almost 40 per cent of all wage workers in the cane fields worked less than thirty hours during the week.[8] It is also true that workers

[5] "Census of Agriculture of the Leeward Islands, 1946" (unpublished).

[6] *Report of the Commission Appointed To Enquire into the Organization of the Sugar Industry of Antigua* (London, 1949), p. 14.

[7] Vere Langford Oliver, *The History of the Island of Antigua* (London, 1894), p. clviii, quoting C. W. E. Eves, *The West Indies* (London, 1891).

[8] Simon Rottenberg, "Report on Unemployment in the Presidency of Antigua" (unpublished, 1951). The short work week in the cane fields is not exclusively occasioned by the free decisions of workers

frequently reject high-earning trades in favor of others with less earning power. Some unskilled occupational categories in the agricultural phase of the sugar industry, for which payment is by results, give higher average hourly earnings than most other unskilled classes of work. In spite of this, there is a tendency in the community for workers to eschew this work. Only 6 per cent of the unemployed surveyed in mid-1950 said they were seeking work in agriculture, although about 45 per cent of all employed persons are in agriculture and a high proportion of all opportunities for work is in this sector of the economy.

Yet, although the facts of the short work week and the rejection of higher-earning employments are true, there are ways in which they can be interpreted other than as evidence of a strong desire for leisure and a weak desire for income. It seems to be clear that the unwillingness of workers to spend the full weeks at work is confined, generally speaking, to the cane industry. In sugar-milling, in construction, and in the trades and services, workers turn up for work regularly and do not absent themselves without cause. There are no discernible qualitative differences between cane-field workers and wage workers in other industries. All have felt the same cultural influences, and there does not seem to be any reason to conclude that there is a differential among them with respect to aspirations or incentive effects. Similarly, the higher-wage work which is rejected is always cane-field work or work in agriculture on other crops. The explanation for the difference in willingness to work between sugar-cane-estate workers and other wage workers must therefore be sought in some factor other

than aspiration for income and the goods for which income exchanges or intensity of desire for leisure. Other causes do, in fact, suggest themselves.

Cane-field work for wages in Antigua (and elsewhere in the West Indies) ranks low in the occupational prestige scale of the community. This was quantitatively verified by asking one thousand adult persons to express an occupational preference for their male and female children (real or hypothetical) in a list of nine occupations for each sex. In an economy in which sugar-cane field labor offers an enormously high proportion of the total number of job opportunities, only 1.5 per cent of the interviewed persons chose cane-field jobs for male children and less than 1 per cent chose this work for female children. Four out of every five unemployed persons told interviewers that they were looking for work outside of agriculture.

The flight from the cane fields is not new in the West Indies. A St. Croix (American Virgin Islands) newspaper, for example, reported in 1883:

*From the time of slavery it was the habit, when a fairskinned slave was born and reared, to bring up the same as house-servant or tradesman. Among the owners themselves the saying was current, "Too light to work in the field"; the result of this peculiar notion has been that our field hands, up to this day [1882] are almost exclusively blacks, that fieldwork is considered a disgrace, an imposition on the black race and the parents consequently do all they can to withhold their children from this occupation. . . . Poor whites here would rather starve than work in the field, such occupation being considered beneath them.*[9]

about the allocation of time between work and leisure. In some cases it results from the assignment of short-work-week tasks by the estate managers and in other cases from the stoppage of reaping operations by the managers when the cutting of cane exceeds the capacity of the available railway cars used for transporting cane to the mill or when cutting exceeds the grinding capacity of the mill. It is true, however, that, these cases aside, workers also frequently choose a short week.

[9] *St. Croix Avis,* July 19, 1882, quoted in Albert A. Campbell, *St. Thomas Negroes* (Evanston, Ill., 1943), p. 24.

The desire to escape from the cane fields and the search for prestige exert a powerful and pervasive influence in the Antiguan community. They create labor-force immobilities by causing workers to have occupational reservations which dampen the influence of relative wages as a regulator of resource allocation. The short work week in the cane fields and the rejection of cane-field work are more rationally explicable in these terms than in terms of low-level-income aspirations or preferences for leisure.

Other forms of occupational reservations in Antigua also depress the effects of differential prices in inducing movement of labor between jobs. Within the cane industry, male workers are known to be cutters or cartmen or loaders (all reaping crafts), and they will hold out for work in their own occupational classification. Sometimes a worker will refuse to perform some classes of work for wages, but he will be willing to do the same kind of work to assist, without wages, a peasant neighbor in harvesting his crop. Some kinds of cane-field work are recognized to belong to women or children. Such work is considered to be unfit for men; men performing these tasks are so ridiculed by others that they are unwilling to accept these jobs. Outside the cane fields, men will frequently consider that they are of a particular artisan's trade and they will reject work in other categories, sometimes holding so strongly to their reservations that they are willing to pay the price of unemployment.

That Antiguan workers sometimes reject classes of employment cannot be taken as clear evidence that they are satisfied with little income and that they have a high propensity to allocate time to leisure instead of to work. The refusal of employment ought rather to be interpreted as evidence of occupational immobility created by compartmentalization of the labor force and by custom, tradition, and community values. The facts of West Indian experience from which the conclusion has been drawn that the individual supply curve of labor turns backward when the price of labor is low do not seem to confirm that conclusion at all.

The Antigua inquiry raises a fundamental question about the meaningfulness of the price–labor supply function for communities, such as this one, in which occupational immobilities are enforced by intrenched cultural traditions. The degree of influence exerted by earnings in bringing forth a supply of labor, either in the form of additional workers or in the form of additional hours of work from the individual worker, will vary from one place to another and from one time to another in the same place and will be affected by cultural and psychological factors operative in a community. Marshall, with his characteristic perceptive understanding, saw this, when he said:

*The attractiveness of a trade depends on many other causes besides the difficulty and strain of the work to be done in it on the one hand, and the money earnings to be got in it on the other. . . . We must take account of the facts that one trade is healthier or cleanlier than another, that it is carried on in a more wholesome or pleasant locality, or that it involves a better social position.*[10]

Despite this parenthetical note, most writers treat both the aggregate supply of labor in a particular trade and the supply of labor offered by an individual as though they were mainly functions of price. Where social-prestige factors intensify occupational reservations, however, price changes and relative prices may have a negligible influence on labor supply.

In these circumstances, movement between jobs and the number of hours worked or energy exerted at work may

[10] Marshall, *op. cit.*, pp. 556–57 (italics added).

be more powerfully affected by the value-system of the community than by the price of labor in different trades. Where this is true, the expression of labor supply as a function solely of price gives the economist a dull analytical tool which obscures perception of the really significant relationship.

In "Hours of Work and Hours of Leisure," Lewis expands on the effect of quality differences in work and leisure on labor supply. Earlier in his paper, though, he presents an interesting commentary on the confusion that exists concerning the general nature of the individual supply curve. Many writers have pointed to the long-term trend of higher wages and shorter hours as evidence that the typical American worker has a negative sloped labor supply curve over the relevant wage range. Lewis' argument suggests that although the evidence reveals that the long-run supply curve seems to be negatively sloped, this might not be the case for the short run. It is the short-run curve that more directly relates the response of labor supplied to a specific wage increase.

Lewis explains the long-run trend as a result of the concomitant increase in property and wage increase over time. The property income gain reinforces the income effect of a wage increase (as would a general increase in earning assets or wealth), tending to tip the scales against the substitution effect of wage increases. This leads to the long-run decline in labor supply as wages have risen. But in the short run, in response to a wage increase, with other factors remaining constant, the labor force could still increase its supply of hours without this behavior being inconsistent with the long-run evidence. In short, the long-term trend of hours reduction and wage increase sheds no light on the behavior of short-run schedules, since the elements that determine the long-term trend—specifically the concomitant property income increases—do not operate with a given change in the wage rate.

Moving to Lewis' discussion of leisure hours themselves, he notes that even if workers had no time preference for leisure, that is, even if there were no quality differences between leisure hours in youth and those toward the end of the customary work life, workers would prefer to take leisure in later years. This decision is based on the assumption of declining productivity and earning power with age, which makes an hour's leisure less costly at the end of the work span.

Introducing quality differences in leisure hours into the work-leisure choice probably strengthens the tendency to defer leisure. Considering the inroads of age on health, strength, and general well-being, at the margin an hour's time off from work would tend to be more greatly appreciated by an older than by a younger worker. Expressed differently, the distaste for the last hours of work probably increases with age, thus reducing the substitution effect of a wage increase for later years and making the labor supply curve for an older worker generally steeper if not negative at any given wage.

Leisure can be deferred but it cannot be stored. Thus, workers in the prime of their productivity and earning power may defer their leisure until it is less costly, toward the end of their work life. But those at the earliest stages of their work life, whose earning power because of inexperience is still low, cannot store their leisure for use at a later date when it will not be relatively cheap.

Further explanation for the preference for work among those for whom leisure has not become more expensive because of greater earning power are the added experience to be gained from additional work hours and the probable weak desire or need for leisure among the young and vigorous.

On the subect of quality differences within leisure hours, Lewis mentions the worker preference for consecutive hours of leisure, and for leisure "at home" as opposed to leisure "on the job" in the form of rest periods, coffee breaks, etc. He emphasizes the marginal relationship in these choices in that workers do not prefer all leisure time at home.*

The same marginal aspects influence our distribution of all types of leisure time. When we say we prefer bowling to all other forms of leisure activities, we mean that we prefer the first hours of bowling to other leisure-time activities. But the fact that we don't spend all our leisure time bowling indicates an increasing marginal rate of substitutions of bowling time for other leisure time as we increase our bowling time.

* On the matter of preference for more hours off during the day as contrasted with more days off, Lewis' discussion seems to give too little importance to employers' preferences on this issue. The tendency for shorter hours per day may not only reflect a "slight preference" of workers for this form of leisure instead of more whole days off, but also the wish of employers to maintain daily operations with a given work force.

# Hours of Work and Hours of Leisure

## by H. G. Lewis

In this paper *the shorter work week is a synonym for the declining trend in the fraction of a worker's lifetime devoted to market (labor force or breadwinning) activities* or, equivalently, for *the increasing fraction devoted to non-market (leisure) activities.* The problem of explaining this long-run trend, however, is but one of many problems that fall under the heading "the per capita demand for leisure" or "the per capita supply of hours of work." There are in addition other "time series" variations (seasonal and cyclical, for example) in hours of work as well as many types of cross-sectional "differentials" in hours of work that also demand explana-tions consistent with that for the long-run trend.

\* \* \*

Our approach is orthodox: mainly the theory of the demand for leisure viewed as a consumption good. Let us review quickly the main elements of this theory. Assume a two-commodity world—leisure (time) and "wage goods"—and, to begin with, abstract from the problem of the allocation of a worker's consumption of leisure over his lifetime. Each worker, facing a given market price of leisure in terms of wage goods (real wage rate per hour) and with a given real property income, is viewed as allocating his total income[1] be-

SOURCE Reprinted with permission from *Proceedings of the Ninth Annual Meeting of the Industrial Relations Research Association,* 1956, pp. 196–206.

[1] His real property income plus his real earnings calculated at a zero rate of consumption of leisure time. Furthermore, this total real income should be interpreted as long run or "permanent" income in the sense used by Friedman and Kuznets; see their *Income from Independent Professional Practice* (New York: National Bureau of Economic Research, 1945) pp. 325–338 and 352–364. See also Fried-man's *A Theory of the Consumption Function* (to be published by the National Bureau) chapters II and III for further discussion of the distinction between "permanent" and "transitory" components of income and consumption.

tween leisure and wage goods in such a way as to maximize his utility.

Thus given the worker's tastes, his consumption of leisure and thus his hours of of work supplied, both measured in hours per unit period of time, depend upon his estimates of his long-run or permanent real wage rate and real property income prospects. His demand function for leisure (or labor supply function) has the familiar properties: the substitution effect of a rise in the real wage rate is a reduced consumpton of leisure per head (increased hours of work supplied per head); the income effect of a rise in the real wage rate or in real property income is an increased rate of consumption of leisure per head (reduced supply of hours per head) if leisure is a normal commodity. Market or group demand functions for leisure also have these properties though they may also depend upon the distribution of tastes, real wage rates, and real property income.

Now let us put this theory to work on the problem of the long-run trend. Assume, I think reasonably, that tastes for leisure are very stable in the long run. In the United States in the last half century both the real wage rate per hour and real property income per head have had strong upward trends. Thus each successive generation has been able to estimate higher real wages and real property income prospects than its predecessors. The rise in real wage rate prospects tends on the one hand to produce substitution effects raising the hours of work supplied per head and, on the other hand, income effects lowering the hours of work supplied per head (if leisure is a normal commodity) and the rise in real property income prospects also tends to produce income effects in the same direction. It is apparent that if this theory is to be consistent with the long-run data, leisure must be a normal commodity; one, indeed, for which the long-run income effects outweigh the long-run substitution effects.

That hours of work on the average for the economy as a whole have tended to change relatively slowly and smoothly is quite consistent with this theory, for the hours of labor supplied per head are made to depend chiefly upon long-run or permanent real wage rate and real property income prospects which will tend to be relatively little affected by short-run ("transitory") variations in real wage rates and real property income.

I have said nothing thus far about the *demand* for hours of work per head—that is, about employers' preferences (arising either from the employers' personal tastes or from technological considerations) regarding the hours of labor per capita of their employees. Assume to begin with that at each real wage rate employers are completely indifferent with respect to the hours of work schedules of their employees, though, of course, they are not indifferent with respect to the total of the man-hours of all of their employees taken together. Thus at any given real wage rate, the demand schedule of each employer and, indeed, of all employers together will be infinitely elastic with respect to the hours of work *per employee* and to all other aspects of the hours of work schedules of employees (such as the timing of the hours during the day or week and the like).

Given this assumption about employers' preferences regarding the hours of work schedules of their employees, the equilibrium market real wage rate must be the same for all employers. In particular there will be no "equalizing" real wage rate differentials compensating for the non-pecuniary disadvantages of the hours of work schedules provided by some employers relative to those provided by others, for, indeed, there will be no such non-pecuniary advantages or disadvantages.

For explaining the global facts on the long-run trend of hours of labor in this country (and for understanding many of the cross-section differentials in hours of work as well), it would only complicate the theory, I believe, without substantial gain in interpreting the data, to bring into the theory employer demand schedules for hours of work per employee that are not infinitely elastic.

There are some observed phenomena, however, that cannot be explained with so simple a theory: premium rates for overtime, for night work, and for work on Sundays and holidays, for example. Suppose, therefore, that employers do have preferences, even strong ones, for some hours of work schedules for their employees over other schedules and that therefore they are prepared to offer higher wage rates (premium rates) per hour to employees to induce them to conform to the preferred schedules. Nevertheless it may still be true that these employer preferences will not produce equalizing wage rate differentials. Significant equalizing differentials will appear only if in their absence the number of workers supplying their labor services to employers in particular hours of work schedule categories were not equal to the number demanded by employers for these categories at the going real wage rate.

The crucial test of the importance of employers' preferences in the analysis of hours of work per head data is in the size of equalizing premium rates for hours of work schedules less preferred by employees and in the proportion of the labor force working at these rates. I submit that on this test employers' preferences have played only a minor role in the long-run trend of hours of work in this country. It is probably true that a larger proportion of the total man-hours worked per year in the U. S. is now paid at premium rates than in 1900, though it is questionable that the proportion would be substantially higher than in 1900 in the absence of such legislation as the Fair Labor Standards Act.[2] The main fact, however, is clear: the fraction of total man-hours that is worked at premium rates is relatively small.

Let me summarize the preceding discussion in the language of a supply-demand model: On the supply side there is a stable, negatively inclined long-run schedule relating average hours of work per head to the average real wage rate. On the demand side there is, to a first approximation, an infinitely elastic schedule involving the same variables. With the long-run growth of the economy, the demand schedule has moved upward along the real wage rate axis tracing out the observed hours of work-real wage rate points on the stable long-run supply schedule (except during periods of substantial unemployment or effective legislation affecting hours of work per head when the points are off the supply schedule).

* * *

Thus far my comments have dealt mainly with the long-run decline in the over-all fraction of an average worker's lifetime devoted to market activities. I turn now to some aspects of the "form" of this decline.

First, let us go back to the theory of the individual worker's demand for leisure. He has to determine not only the fraction of his life that he will devote to leisure activities but also the distribution of his consumption of leisure over his lifetime. Because of the phenomena of aging and of learning by experience, the marginal cost of leisure will tend to vary from one age to another. In particular, it is characteris-

[2] I suspect that the term *penalty* rate is at least as accurate descriptively for the last decade and a half as the term *premium* rate: employers pay these rates in significant part not to recruit workers reluctant to work longer hours without a special price incentive, but because the public and, perhaps, to some extent unions have sought to restrain workers from working as many hours as they would like and employers would offer them at prevailing wage rates, in order to ration employment generally or particular attractive union employment opportunities.

tic of persons in almost all pursuits that, if they live long enough, they will reach an age after which the productivity increasing effects of experience are more than offset by the productivity decreasing effects of growing old. Thus the marginal cost of leisure will tend to be relatively low in old age.

Two other factors also work to make the real marginal cost of leisure relatively low in age. One is the interest rate. The other, important only in recent years, is the Federal Old Age Insurance program. This program from the beginning has contained in one form or another an "earnings test" under which insurance benefits are a negatively inclined function of income earned during benefit years. The earnings test tends to make the real marginal cost of leisure time less than the real wage rate per hour.

The rising long-run trend of the real wage rate in the United States is a factor working in the opposite direction partially offsetting the interest rate factor.

Now assume that leisure time is a commodity for which workers have no time preference.[3] Then if the marginal cost of present leisure in terms of future leisure were unity, the individual worker would plan to consume his leisure at a constant rate over his lifetime. We observe, however, that the marginal cost of leisure tends to be relatively low in old age—the marginal cost of present (in youth) leisure in terms of future (in old age) leisure tends to be greater than unity. Under these circumstances the worker will plan to distribute his consumption of leisure disproportionately toward his old age.

Available data indicate that the disproportionately high rate of consumption of leisure time in old age shows itself mainly in retirement from the labor force. Thus the long-run decline in "hours of work" will be registered in part in a decline in labor force participation. This expectation is confirmed by Census data which show a decline of approximately eight to ten percent since 1900 in the proportion of the United States adult male population in the labor force (or if not in the labor force, in school).

It is apparent that future leisure is not a perfect substitute for present leisure, for if that were true, then on the preceding line of reasoning the shorter work week would have taken *only* the form of reduced labor force participation. In fact, of course, the work "week" has fallen also for those in the labor force and this decline has taken several forms. I turn now to examine this variety.

First, why is it that for the great majority of adult males the working hours tend to be bunched rather than spread out over the "waking" hours of the day? That "mixing business and pleasure tends to spoil both" goes far toward explaining the phenomenon. It is apparent, however, that mixing the two does not completely spoil both, for a good many factory workers do have rest periods, office workers coffee breaks, and business managers and professional workers their long lunch "hour." Casual observation indicates, indeed, that there is more mixing of pleasure with business among salaried workers and the self-employed who do not work on a fixed schedule of hours than among hourly-rated "factory" workers who "punch a time clock." This can be rationalized as the result of the higher cost of mixing leisure with work for those whose work activities are highly complementary than for those whose working hours need not be meshed closely with those of fellow workers.

The preceding line of reasoning does not explain, however, why males consume leisure time in larger proportion "at home"

---

[3] By "no time preference" I do not mean a constant rather than a diminishing marginal rate of substitution of present for future leisure, but that the marginal rate of substitution is unity at a rate of consumption of present leisure equal to that for future leisure.

than "at work." Hence assume not only that leisure time is not homogeneous by place of consumption, but also that "at home" leisure is preferred to "at work" leisure.[4] The mixing of "at home" leisure with "at work" work, moreover, will tend to be expensive for most workers because of the travel involved. Thus both the tendency to mix little leisure with work and the tendency to consume leisure at home can be explained as the result of the preference for "at home" leisure over "at work" leisure and the minimizing of the travel costs involved in consuming leisure away from one's place of work.

Furthermore, there are likely to be differences among workers in their relative preferences for "at home" leisure over "at work" leisure that will be correlated with the facilities offered in work places for the consumption of leisure. Thus is it really surprising that professors, for example, tend to consume more leisure time in their university surroundings than factory and mine workers do in factories and mines?

Both of the alternate hypotheses advanced to explain the "bunching" of hours of work during the day imply that the relative costs of any considerable mixing of pleasure and business during the day are high and the returns in satisfaction relatively low, particularly for "factory and mine" workers. This implication is supported by the long-run trend data which indicate that the fraction of the increased consumption of leisure per head since 1900 taken in the form of rest periods, coffee

breaks, and the like has been small, probably no larger than five percent.

The preference for "at home" leisure over "at work" leisure together with the minimizing of the costs of travel and of travel time has another implication: that the reduction in hours of work per head since 1900 would have come about through reducing the number of days worked per year rather than the number of hours worked per day. In fact, however, about half of the reduction came from reduced hours per day. These long-run data suggest that individuals not only are not indifferent between non-consecutive and consecutive leisure time—between 14 hours of leisure distributed equally over the days of the week and 14 hours allotted to a single day, but also that there may be a slight preference for the former over the latter. That this preference is slight is indicated by: (1) about half of the reduction in hours of work per head did come about through fewer days per year; (2) the "non-working" days of the week are consecutive (Saturday and Sunday[5]); and (3) vacations of two weeks or more are now common.

The shortening of the work week thus has come about in a variety of ways: a smaller fraction of lifetime years in the labor force; more holidays not worked; longer vacations; fewer working days in the week;[6] shorter working days; and to a minor extent, more frequent rest periods during the working hours. The relative cost and taste factors that underlie the

---

[4] I mean by lack of *homogeneity* among two kinds of leisure, that there is a diminishing rather than constant marginal rate of substitution of one for the other. A *preference* for one kind of leisure over another means that at equal rates of consumption of the two the rate at which one is substituted for the other is less than one unit of the more preferred to one unit of the less preferred.

[5] That Sundays and holidays are preferred over other days for the consumption of leisure is confirmed by the premium rates commonly paid for work on these days and the relatively small fraction of the labor force that does work on these days. The same kind of evidence confirms the preference for day work over night work. If workers actually preferred to work at night, employers would not have to pay night shift premiums.

[6] Notice in this connection that the alternatives are not simply, for example, five days vs. four days. A four and three-quarter day "week" for example can be obtained by having a four day week, say, every fourth week and five-day weeks the rest of the time. It is very clear, indeed, that additional "holidays" are a means of reducing the number of "days per week" in a gradual fashion without resort to "half-days" of work.

division of workers' leisure over their life-
times, I believe, tend to be quite stable.
Thus I hazard the prediction that in the
next half century the proportions in which
increased consumption of leisure per head
is divided among these forms will differ
fairly little from the proportions observed
in the last fifty years.

### Nonmarket Labor Supply

Lewis' paper introduces the concept of quality differences in work and leisure
hours, but later studies emphasize the need for revising and modifying the entire concept of a two-dimensional work-income–leisure preference schedule.
The classification of all nonmarket work hours as "leisure," with the implication
that these hours give varying degrees of "pleasure" as opposed to the "pain" of
market (paid) work, is indeed artificial. There are many groups of nonmarket
work hours that are closer to market work hours in the sense of effort they entail than they are to leisure. For example, much of the time spent in housework
and in commuting to and from work can be considered as nonmarket labor
rather than leisure.

Why a worker chooses nonpaid labor at all over the opportunity for more
market-labor income only reflects that the two are not perfect substitutes for
each other. It is not that nonmarket labor may in itself be any less distasteful
than market labor, but the positive benefits associated with the various forms
of nonmarket labor cause substitution to be less than perfect. The housewife
performs household duties because they are necessary for the maintenance of
a stable home life; the commuter exerts uncompensated effort in traveling because he likes the benefits of suburban living.

For each of them, however, a reduction in the time cost of nonmarket labor
would lead to a substitution, at least in part, of market labor. But if, as is
usually the case, there is a money cost to the reduction in time cost, the decision becomes more complex. For example, the housewife may reduce the time
cost of housework by using appliances in the performance of many of her
duties. Whether the family would buy appliances to free her for market work
depends on the cost of the appliances, the time saved, the wage she could earn,
and her own and her family's leisure–work-income preference schedule.

These complications influencing labor supply are incorporated by Jacob
Mincer ("Labor Force Participation of Married Women: A Study of Labor Supply") in his theoretical resolution of the apparent paradox between cross-
sectional and time series labor force behavior of wives. What seems paradoxical
is that while many moment-of-time studies, cited by Mincer, indicate a strong
inverse relationship between husbands' income and labor force participation
of wives, over time, as husbands' and family incomes have been rising steadily,
wives' labor force participation has been increasing significantly.

In the detailed statistical portions of his paper, not presented here, Mincer
finds that the positive influence of higher wages is a stronger force leading
wives into the labor force than is the negative influence of higher husbands'
incomes (wages) drawing them out. This explains the long-run growth in labor
force participation of these women while both their husbands' and their own
wages have been increasing.

At a point in time, however, the level of the husband's income appears to be the dominant influence, leading to the negative relationship between this level and the wife's participation. The influence of the wage level of the wife herself is smothered by two factors that do not operate in the long run.

The first factor is the loose relationship between the earnings of husbands and the earnings of their wives. Thus, since the level of wives' earnings is not closely related to their husbands' earnings, whatever influence the level of their own earnings have on their participation would not be strongly felt; participation would then be closely related to the level of husband's earnings. Over time, however, wives' earnings have risen at least as much as their husbands', so the greater influence of wives' own earning levels would outweigh the negative effect of their husbands' higher earnings on labor force participation.

The second factor concerns the relationship between wives' participation and "transitory" and "permanent" family income. When "transitory" or short-term family income is below the "permanent" or expected long-run level, the wife will tend to work, since family consumption patterns are geared more to long-run than short-run income levels. Similarly, when "transitory" exceeds "permanent" income, the tendency will be for the wife not to work, since current income without her contribution would meet family consumption goals. Since Mincer finds "transitory" and "permanent" income only weakly correlated, this means that at any moment a high current income would tend to exceed permanent income and vice versa for a low current income. Thus, in cross-sectional data, labor force participation of wives would be negatively correlated with that of their husbands, if for no other reason than that the higher the current level of husbands' earning, the more likely that transitory income would exceed current income. Over time, the effect of this transistory-permanent income differences washes out as the two levels approach each other; the element fortifying the negative relationship between husbands' earnings levels and wives' participation would be absent.

In all this resolution of the paradox lies the important finding that wives' participation in the labor force is strongly correlated to their own earnings potential, or wage level. That is, wives have a positively sloped labor supply curve, at least insofar as participation in the labor force, if not in hours offered, is concerned, over effective wage ranges. In the theoretical section of his paper, presented here, Mincer offers an explanation for this behavior which is based on his abandonment of the conventional two-dimensional work-income–leisure context for determining the nature of the labor supply schedule.

# Labor Force Participation of Married Women: A Study of Labor Supply

## by Jacob Mincer

### INTRODUCTORY: STATEMENT OF THE PROBLEM

On the assumption that leisure time is a normal good, the standard analysis of work-leisure choices implies a positive substitution effect and a negative income effect on the response of hours of work supplied to variations in the wage rate. An increase in the real wage rate makes leisure time more expensive and tends to elicit an increase in hours of work. However, for a given amount of hours worked, an increase in the wage rate constitutes an increase in income, which leads to an increase in purchase of various goods, including leisure time. Thus, on account of the income effect, hours of work tend to decrease. In which direction hours of work change on balance, given a change in the wage rate, cannot be determined a priori.

It depends on the relative strengths of the income and substitution effects in the relevant range. The single assumption of a positive income elasticity of demand for leisure time is not sufficient to yield empirical implications on this matter.

An empirical generalization which fills this theoretical void is the "backward-bending" supply curve of labor. This is the notion that on the average the income effect is stronger than the substitution effect, so that an increase in the wage rate normally results in a decreased amount (hours) of work offered by suppliers of labor. Extreme examples of such behavior have been repeatedly observed in under-developed countries. On the American scene, several kinds of empirical evidence apparently point to the same relationship:[1] the historically declining work week in in-

SOURCE Reprinted with permission from *Aspects of Labor Economics,* National Bureau of Economic Research, Princeton, N.J., Princeton University Press, 1962, pp. 63–97.

[1] The pioneering works of research and interpretation in this area are well known. See: Paul H. Douglas, *The Theory of Wages,* Macmillan, 1934; John D. Durand, *The Labor Force in the U.S.,* Social Science Research Council, 1948; Clarence D. Long, *Labor Force under Changing Income and Employment,* Princeton University Press for National Bureau of Economic Research, 1958.

dustry; historically declining labor force participation rates of young and old males; an inverse relation between wages of adult males and labor force participation rates of females by cities in cross sections; an inverse relation between incomes of husbands and labor force participation of wives, by husbands' incomes, in budget studies. Similar phenomena have been reported from the experience of other modern economies.

The secular negative association between the length of the work week, participation rates of males, and rising real incomes is clearly consistent with the backward-bending supply curve.[2] Whether this is also true of cross-sectional data on males is a question which has as yet received little attention. Superficially, the cross-sectional behavior of females seems similarly capable of being rationalized in terms of a backward-bending supply response, or at least in terms of a positive income elasticity of demand for leisure. Such views, however, are immediately challenged by contradictory evidence in time series. One of the most striking phenomena in the history of the American labor force is the continuing secular increase in participation rates of females, particularly of married women, despite the growth in real income. Between 1890 and 1960 labor force rates of all females fourteen years old and over rose from about 18 per cent to 36 per cent. In the same period rates of married women rose from 5 per cent to 30 per cent, while real income per worker tripled.[3]

The apparent contradiction between time series and cross sections has already stimulated a substantial amount of research. The investigation reported in this paper is yet another attempt to uncover the basic economic structure which is, in part, responsible for the observed relations.

The study starts from the recognition that the concepts of work, income, and substitution need clarification and elaboration before they can be applied to labor force choices of particular population groups, in this instance married women. The resulting analytical model, even though restricted to two basic economic factors, seems capable of explaining a variety of apparently diverse cross-sectional behavior patterns. It also, in principle, reconciles time series with cross-section behavior, though further elaboration is needed for a proper explanation of the former. The empirical focus of the paper is a reinterpretation of old cross-section materials, and an investigation of newly available data generated by the 1950 BLS Survey of Consumer Expenditures.

## CONCEPTUAL FRAMEWORK

### Work

The analysis of labor supply to the market by way of the theory of demand for leisure time viewed as a consumption good is strictly appropriate whenever leisure time and hours of work in the market in fact constitute an exhaustive dichotomy. This is, of course, never true even in the case of adult males. The logical complement to leisure time is work broadly construed, whether it includes remunerative production in the market or work that is currently "not paid for." The latter includes various forms of investment in oneself, and the production of goods and services for the home and the family. Educational activity is an essential and, indeed, the most important element in the productive life of young boys and girls. Work at home is still an activity to which women, on the average, devote the larger part of

[2] For a rigorous statement, see H. Gregg Lewis, "Hours of Work and Hours of Leisure," *Proceedings of the Industrial Relations Research Association,* 1957.
[3] Based on Long, *The Labor Force,* Table A-6; and *Employment and Earnings,* Bureau of Labor Statistics, 1960.

their married life. It is an exclusive occupation of many women, and of a vast majority when young children are present.

It is, therefore, not sufficient to analyze labor force behavior of married women in terms of the demand for leisure. A predicted change in hours of leisure may imply different changes in hours of work in the market depending on the effects of the casual factors on hours of work at home. Technically speaking, if we are to derive the market supply function in a residual fashion, not only the demand for hours of leisure but also the demand for hours of work at home must be taken into account. The latter is a demand for a productive service derived from the demand by the family for home goods and services. A full application of the theory of demand for a productive service to the home sector has implications for a variety of socioeconomic phenomena beyond the scope of this paper.

*Family Context*

The analysis of market labor supply in terms of consumption theory carries a strong connotation about the appropriate decision-making unit. We take it as self-evident that in studying consumption behavior the family is the unit of analysis. Income is assumed to be pooled, and total family consumption is positively related to it. The distribution of consumption among family members depends on tastes. It is equally important to recognize that the decisions about the production of goods and services at home and about leisure are largely family decisions. The relevant income variable in the demand for home services and for leisure of any family member is total family income. A change in income of some family member will, in general, result in a changed consumption of leisure for the family as a whole. An increase in one individual's income may not result in a decrease in *his* hours of work, but in those of other family members. The total amount of work performed at home is, even more clearly, an outcome of family demand for home goods and for leisure, given the production at home. However, unlike the general consumption case, the distribution of leisure, market work, and home work for each family member as well as among family members is determined not only by tastes and by biological or cultural specialization of functions, but by relative prices which are specific to individual members of the family. This is so, because earning powers in the market and marginal productivities in alternative pursuits differ among individual family members. Other things equal (including family income), an increase in the market wage rate for some family member makes both the consumption of leisure and the production of home services by that individual more costly to the family, and will as a matter of rational family decision encourage greater market labor input by him (her). Even the assumption of a backward-bending supply curve would not justify a prediction of a decrease in total hours of work *for the particular earner*, if wages of other family members are fixed.

Recognition of the family context of leisure and work choices, and of the home-market dichotomy within the world of work, is essential for any analysis of labor force behavior of married women, and perhaps quite important for the analysis of behavior of other family members, including male family heads. For the present purpose of constructing a simple model of labor force behavior of married women it will be sufficient to utilize these concepts only insofar as they help to select and elucidate a few empirically manageable variables to represent the major forces of income and substitution contained in the market supply function.

*Work Choices*

Let us consider the relevant choices of married women as between leisure, work at home, and work in the market. Income is assumed to have a positive effect on the demand for leisure, hence a negative effect on total amount of work. With the relevant prices fixed, increased family income will decrease total hours of work. Since the income effect on the demand for home goods and services is not likely to be negative,[4] it might seem that the increased leisure means exclusively a decrease in hours of work in the market. Such a conclusion, however, would require a complete absence of substitutability between the wife and other (mechanical, or human) factors of production at home, as well as an absence of substitution in consumption between home goods and market-produced goods. Domestic servants, laborsaving appliances, and frozen foods contradict such assumptions. Substitutability is, of course, a matter of degree. It may be concluded therefore that, given the income elasticity of demand for home goods and for leisure, the extent to which income differentially affects hours of work in the two sectors depends on the ease with which substitution in home production or consumption can be carried out. The lesser the substitutability the weaker the negative income effect on hours of work at home, and the stronger the income effect on hours of work in the market.

Change in this degree of substitutability may have played a part in the historical development. At a given moment of time, the degree of substitutability is likely to differ depending on the content of home production. Thus substitutes for a mother's care of small children are much more difficult to come by than those for food preparation or for physical maintenance of the household. It is likely, therefore, that the same change in income will affect hours of market work of the mother more strongly when small children are present

than at other times in the life-cycle.

While family income affects the total amount of work, the market wage rate affects the allocation of hours between leisure, the home, and the market. An increase in the real wage rate, given productivity in the home, is an increase in prices (alternative costs) of home production as well as of leisure in terms of prices of wage goods. To the extent of an existing substitution between home goods and wage goods such a change will lead to an increase in work supplied to the market. Again, the strength of the effect is a matter of the degree of substitution between wage goods and home production.

*Temporal Distribution of Work*

In a broad view, the quantity of labor supplied to the market by a wife is the fraction of her married life during which she participates in the labor force. Abstracting from the temporal distribution of labor force activities over a woman's life, this fraction could be translated into a probability of being in the labor force in a given period of time for an individual, hence into a labor force rate for a large group of women.

If leisure and work preferences, long-run family incomes, and earning power were the same for all women, the total amount of market work would, according to the theory, be the same for all women. Even if that were true, however, the *timing* of market activities during the working life may differ from one individual to another. The life cycle introduces changes in demands for and marginal costs of home work and leisure. Such changes are reflected in the relation between labor force rates and age of woman, presence, number and ages of children. There are life-cycle variations in family

[4] Fragmentary cross-sectional data on food preparation at home indicate a negligible income elasticity. The demand for other home goods and services (including care of children, and their number) may be more income elastic.

incomes and assets which may affect the timing of labor force participation, given a limited income horizon and a less than perfect capital market. Cyclical and random variations in wage rates, employment opportunities, income and employment of other family members, particularly of the head, are also likely to induce temporal variations in the allocation of time between home, market, and leisure. It is not surprising, therefore, that over short periods of observation, variation in labor force participation, or turnover, is the outstanding characteristic of labor force behavior of married women.

To the extent that the temporal distribution of labor force participation can be viewed as a consequence of "transitory" variation in variables favoring particular timing, the distinction between "permanent" and current levels of the independent variables becomes imperative in order to adapt our model to family surveys in which the period of observation is quite short.

＊　＊　＊

In Mincer's model, the wife allocates her time among market work, nonmarket (nonremunerative) housework, and leisure. If the two types of work were perfect substitutes, with respect to the degree of dissatisfaction they entail, then at her maximum position she would work at home the number of hours such that the cost of a reduction in one more hour's work at home would just equal the hourly wage she would earn on the market. Abandoning the unrealistic assumption of perfect substitutability for all levels of hours of work, even if she could reduce her housework hours at a constant cost per hour that was less than the hourly wage rate, she would not reduce her housework to zero. This follows because some of the time spent in housework satisfies family consumer wants only indirectly related to the chores themselves. For example, although hourly rate for a baby-sitter remains constant, the family might feel that if a small child spends every waking hour with a sitter and none with her mother, family well-being—at least the child's—may suffer. Similarly, though the cost per unit of frozen foods may not be related to the quantity bought, family harmony might be disrupted if every meal consisted of TV dinners. Expressed in economic terms, the ratio of the marginal disutility of an extra hour's market work for that of the last hour's housework increases as market work increases relative to housework. At equilibrium, this ratio would equal the ratio of the wage rate to the cost of an hour's reduction of housework.

Mincer is not too concerned with the static situation, but examines the effect of a wage increase. Since, as he points out, the income effect of a wage increase raises the demand for home goods and services, it would seem that the tendency for increased leisure that follows from the normal income effect would be satisfied by a tendency toward a reduction in market labor. But this conclusion would ignore the possibility of substitution of market work for housework made possible by the purchase of goods and services to replace the wife in housework. That is, home production may be maintained, at a cost.

The effect of a wage increase is to disturb the equilibrium position described above. If before the ratio of the marginal disutility of an hour's more market work to an hour's more home work were just equal to the ratio of the hourly wage rate to the money cost of an additional hour's reduction in homework, the increase in wages would raise the latter ratio above that of the former. There would tend to be a substitution of market work for home work until equality between the two ratios was restored. Equality would be reached as market work increased at the expense of home work because the ratio of the marginal disutility of market work to home work would rise as hours of market work rose and home work declined. (In families with small children, this ratio would tend to rise precipitously, making for but a small substitution of market work for home work before equilibrium was restored.) In addition, the marginal cost of reducing home work by additional hours might tend to increase.

Considering first the income effect of the wage increase, leisure hours would increase assuming, of course, that leisure is a "normal" good; one whose consumption increases with an increase in income. Thus, from the income effect alone, the total of work hours, home and market work combined, would decline. Accordingly, the substitution of market work for home work described above would refer to an increase in the share of work hours performed in the market compared to that in the home. The number of market hours from the income effect alone might decline, but this decline would be less than it would have been were there no substitution of market work for home work in the total work mix. Thus, the important influence of the substitution is to weaken the negative income effect on market hours in making the increase in leisure related to this effect at least partly supplied by a reduction in nonmarket (home) work.

As for the substitution effect of the wage increase, there is the usual influence to substitute market work for leisure as the price of leisure increases.

Combining income and substitution effects, if, without the possibility of substituting market for home work, the wife's labor supply curve were positively sloped (that is, the substitution effect outweighed the income effect so that supply of market labor increased while leisure hours declined), then the possibility of market work for home work substitution would only accentuate the tendency for market labor to increase.

But the significant contribution of Mincer's model refers to the case in which without this substitution the labor supply curve would be negatively sloped because the conventional income effect outweighed the substitution effect. In this case, substitution of market work for home work weakens the conventional income effect and allows for increase in both leisure and market work.* Thus, the effect of the substitutability of market for home work increases the probability that the labor supply curve for wives will be positively sloped. This is the focus of Mincer's theoretical model, which his statistical study substantiates.


## The Marginal Productivity Theory and Labor Demand

Marginal principles simply explain a firm's profit-maximizing behavior. Theoretically, under perfect competition, firms employ labor units of a given, equal productivity until the value of the marginal product (price times marginal product) of the last unit hired equals the uniform wage. Allowing for monopoly in the product market and monopsony in the labor market, the

---

* By similar reasoning, if (omitting the substitution possibility) the labor supply curve were positively sloped, with market work increasing and leisure declining, then substitution of market for home work, instead of only for leisure, may allow leisure as well as market work to increase.

equality for profit maximization becomes the equality between the marginal value product (addition to total revenue of the last unit) and the marginal cost of the last worker hired (with supply curve of labor to the firm being positively sloped).*

In any case, whether under competitive or noncompetitive conditions, the demand schedule for labor is downward sloping, with the quantity of labor demanded rising with a decline in wages. Regardless of the degree of competition in the product market, marginal physical product falls with an increase in the variable factor, labor, and in a monopolistic product market, the monetary contribution of the additional worker falls further because of a decline in product price with increased output

Marginal principles apply for profit-maximizing firms even when wages are set by collective bargaining. In a free labor market, the wage would be determined by the marginal contribution of the last worker available. With a collectively bargained wage, the level of employment would be the variable, dependent on the wage set, but again, the profit-maximizing firm would employ workers up to the point where the marginal contribution equals the (established) wage. The firm might make less profit when it had to bargain with the union over wages, but if it were maximizing profits, it could make the best of an inferior situation by equating marginal labor costs and revenues.

In fact, a facetious policy maker could recommend wage increases as the best means of raising labor productivity. At higher bargained wages, the firm would equate marginal labor cost and revenue by using less labor, thereby raising the marginal product of the existing work force. But unions are not happy to have their wage gains accompanied by a decline in employment of their covered workers. Success in retaining the work force may indicate inelasticity of demand for labor, indivisibilities in factor utilization, or the willingness of firms to make less than maximum profits, even at a worsened position because of union wage pressure.

*Weaknesses in Marginal Theory.* If the last two conditions apply, marginalism loses much of its strength as a meaningful theory, that is, one that explains present conditions and also serves as a basis for prediction of future behavior under given circumstances. Factor indivisibility would prevent wage substitution among factors in response to differential cost changes not based on accompanying relative productivity changes. Factors become more substitutable in the long run but, at least for the short run, firms cannot bring their factor marginal costs and revenues into equality. Expressed differently, short-run profit maximization cannot strictly apply marginal principles, leaving, say, employment decisions in response to a wage increase a priori uncertain. Of course, the same uncertainty arises when firms do not even strive to maximize profits.

Even if marginal principles are faithfully followed, they can only uniquely determine a labor demand schedule in a given setting under the assumption that the labor group in question is of equal quality or efficiency. If there are efficiency differences among a given group of workers, then the concept of

---

* The assumption of a positively sloped supply curve to the *firm* is not inconsistent with a negatively sloped *individual* labor supply curve. The worker who would offer less labor at higher wages would still be inclined to offer his services to the highest bidder for any given level of work effort.

marginal productivity loses its significance and there is no reason for wage equality within the group. When all are of different efficiency, each worker in effect becomes a unique factor of production.

The fact that workers have the same occupational classification does not necessarily mean they are of equal efficiency (capable of producing the same output from a given quantity of supporting factors.) John T. Dunlop, in his introductory paper to an international conference on wage determination, notes the vast wage range for particular occupations in the same local labor market. Efficiency differences, Dunlop suggests, could explain only a small part of these differences. He cites other elements which, though perhaps more important, also operate against the significance of marginal principles in wage determination.

# The Task of Contemporary Wage Theory

## by John T. Dunlop

... Wage theory has tended historically to disintegrate on the supply side. As has been noted, in the course of refinement of the wage fund theory and the supply function associated with marginal productivity, the supply function tended to be pushed outside the analytical system. The amount of labour supplied and the wage rate came to be determined by social custom or institutional considerations. The wage rate came to be given for purposes of economic analysis. In a sense, the pivotal task of wage theory is to formulate an acceptable theory on the supply side.

It is not satisfactory to treat wage determination in terms of a single rate. In the past there have been various devices to reduce wage setting to the problem of a single rate. A single unskilled or common labour rate is envisaged into which all skilled labour may be translated as consisting of so many "units" of unskilled labour. This classical convention was followed by both Marx and Keynes. A single wage rate, out of the whole structure, is regarded as an index or barometer for all other rates. But all wage rates do not move together either in the short run nor in the long period. The wage structure is not completely rigid over time. Moreover, the determination of the wage level and the wage structure are closely interrelated.

Wage theory must operate with the concept of wage structure—the complex of rates within firms differentiated by occupation and employee and the complex of interfirm rate structures. The concept of wage structure for the purpose of the present analysis is a central concept; the analysis of wage determination will be approached through the wage structure. Indeed, instead of reducing wage setting to the problem of a single rate, the task of analysing wage determination is

SOURCE Reprinted with permission from John T. Dunlop, Ed., *The Theory of Wage Determination,* New York, Macmillan, 1964, pp. 3–27.

rather the problem of the setting and variation in the whole structure or complex of rates. While the general level of wage rates can be thought of changing apart from variations in structure, in fact they are not dissociated. Changes in the wage level, associated with changes in output levels in the system, are necessarily associated with changes in wage structure. The interrelations between the wage level and the wage structure is itself a major area of inquiry.

A distinction is to be made between the wage structure within a plant, firm, or other grouping in which wage differentials are set by the same authority and the complex of interfirm or group structures set by a number of different agencies. From the point of view of the individual decision makers, the first wage structure is internal while the second is external. One of the central problems of wage analysis is to indicate the interrelations between the internal and external wage structure.

The analysis that follows utilizes two concepts which require explanation: job clusters and wage contours.

## JOB CLUSTERS AND WAGE CONTOURS

A job cluster is defined as a stable group of job classifications or work assignments within a firm (wage determining unit) which are so linked together by (a) technology, (b) by the administrative organization of the production process, including policies of transfer and promotion, or (c) by social custom that they have common wage-making characteristics. In an industrial plant which may literally have thousands of jobs, each wage rate is not equally related and dependent upon all other wage rates. The internal wage structure, the complex of differentials, is not rigidly fixed for all time. Neither do relative rates change in random relation to each other. The internal wage rate structure is to be envisaged as divided into groups of jobs

or job clusters. The wage rates for the operations and jobs within a cluster are more closely related in their wage movements than are rates outside the cluster.

Thus a tool-room in a plant would ordinarily constitute a job cluster. The training and skill of the machinists are similar for those who operate the various specialized machines—lathes, shapers, cutters, and so on. Their work is closely interrelated in the productive process. They may work apart from others. They may have a common promotion and transfer pattern. The wage rates within the tool-room are more closely related with each other than they may be with the rates for other employees in the power plant, on production lines, in the maintenance crew, in the office, or in the sales force. The wage structure of a plant is to be envisaged as comprised of a limited number of such job clusters, each with a number of rates.

From the analytical point of view these job clusters are given in the short period by the technology, the managerial and administrative organization of the wage determining unit, and by the social customs of the work community. Thus, the employees on a furnace or mill may constitute a job cluster (technology); so may employees in a department (administrative organization) or the women in an office (social custom). Wage theory, for the short period, does not seek to explain these job clusters. For the longer period, it is essential to show that the scope of a job cluster within a rate structure may be expanded, restricted, or divided as a consequence of changes in the technology, administrative organization, or social customs in the plant.

The job cluster can be examined in more detail. Ordinarily, a job cluster will contain one, or in some cases several, key rates. The cluster consists of the key rate(s) and a group of associated rates. The key rate may be the highest paid, or the top step in a promotion ladder, or the job at which a large number of workers are employed. Typically, these key rates show relatively less change in job content over time. They are often relatively more standardized as between firms than other jobs. These key rates are those which managements and unions typically have in mind and explicitly discuss in considering the internal wage structure.

The smallest building block in the wage structure is thus the job cluster comprised of a key rate, or several such rates in some cases, and a group of associated rates. The internal wage structure of the plant (wage-determining unit) consists of a number of job clusters. Such is the anatomy of the internal wage structure.

It is not to be presumed that the forces which determine the wage rate for a group of jobs in a cluster are confined within a firm. The "exterior" plays a very important rôle. The "exterior," including the "market," cannot operate directly on a thousand slightly differentiated jobs. The key rates play a decisive rôle in relating the exterior to the internal rate structure. Indeed, the key rates are affected by the exterior, and adjustments in these rates are transmitted to other rates within the plant, cluster by cluster.

A wage contour is defined as a stable group of firms (wage determining units) which are so linked together (a) by similarity of product markets, (b) by resort to similar sources for a labour force, or (c) by common labour market organization (custom) that they have common wage-making characteristics. The wage rates of a particular firm are not ordinarily independent of all other wage rates; they are more closely related to the wage rates of some firms than to others. A contour for particular occupations is to be defined both in terms of the product market and the labour market. A contour thus has three dimensions: (a) particular occupations or job clusters, (b) a sector of industry, and (c) a geographical location. The firms which comprise a contour constitute a particular product market; they

also may be located in one labour market or scattered throughout a region or the country as a whole.

Thus, in the United States, the basic steel contour for production jobs consists of the producers of basic steel products scattered in various communities throughout the country. The wage rates of the jobs in these firms, in their blast furnace, steel works, and rolling mill operations move together. Some other operations and occupations of the same companies, such as cement mills or shipping, are typically excluded from the basic steel contour. While there are a variety of submarkets, and each basic steel producer may have some specialized features to its product market or locality in which it hires labour, none the less the basic steel wage contour is sharply defined and distinguishable from others.

A contour may be confined to a locality in its labour market dimension. Thus, newspapers in New York City constitute a contour for wage-setting purposes. The rates for various occupations in one newspaper are closely related to those in other newspapers in that city. Specialized product markets, for other types of printing or publishing, are a part of still other wage contours.

A contour refers to particular ranges of skill, occupations, or job clusters. Not all types of labour hired by a firm will have wage rates determined in the same contour. Thus, a firm employing a professional chemist, a pattern-maker, and a clerk may be expected to be part of three quite different contours. A construction firm hiring boilermakers, operating engineers, labourers will be a part of the construction product market in each instance, but three separate wage contours are involved. The boilermaker's rate is set over the largest geographical area while the labourer's rate is likely to be confined to a single locality.

A wage contour can be explored in further detail. In the ordinary case a wage contour contains one, or in some instances several key bargains. The contour is comprised of the rates for the key firm(s) and a group of associated firms. The key bargain may be set by the largest firm, the price leader, or the firm with labour relations leadership. Thus, in the basic steel contour, the wages determined by the U.S. Steel Company generally have been followed by all other firms in the contour. In this case the other basic steel producers have customarily followed the "pattern" almost immediately. In other cases more time may elapse before a change by the followers. Some firms may follow only at a distance, altering even the terms of the key settlement in some minor respects.

A wage contour then can be envisaged as a grouping of firms, for a given range of occupations, in which some firms are very closely related to the leaders. Other firms are less directly associated. At the exterior of the contour, furthest from the key rates, the firms may only remotely follow the leadership.

A variety of devices have been developed which relate wages determined by the key bargain to those of other firms in the contour. The existence of a common expiration date or the sequence of anniversary dates is reflective of the relations within a wage contour. Some firms commit themselves in advance to pay the wages of others; many commit themselves to consider a change when a "wage movement" has developed in the industry (contour). Specialized product markets or sources of labour supply or skill requirements may mean that a particular firm, remote from the "centre" of the contour, will modify the "pattern" established at the key bargain in some respects.

The firms which comprise a wage contour may be organized into a formal employers' association rather than appear to make wage decisions without a common organization. In an association not all firms actually have equal weight in making decisions; wage leaders exercise their same functions, although an association may mean that all wages are changed at the same time. In many instances an association constitutes only a formal difference from wage leadership conditions that would be evident without an employer's organization.[1]

Wage-making forces are envisaged as concentrated on the key rates in the job clusters. These rates "extend" out from the internal structure of the firm to the "exterior" and constitute the focal points for wage-setting forces among firms within the contour. The key rates in the job clusters constitute the channels of impact between the exterior developments in the contour and the interior rate structure of the firm. Moreover, in an analogous way, the key bargains constitute the focal point of wage-setting forces within the contour and constitute the points where wage-making forces converge that are exterior to the contour.

A theory of wages is not required to treat each wage rate in the system as of equal importance. The view of the wage structure outlined above singles out a limited number of key rates and key bargains for analysis. These particular rates are selected, at least in the short run, by the anatomy of the wage structure which is given by (a) the technology and administrative arrangements of firms; (b) the competitive patterns in product markets; and (c) the sources of labour supply.

The concepts of job cluster and wage contour are analogous. In each case a group of rates surrounds a key rate. The concepts seek to relate the internal and the external wage structure; they focus attention on the mechanics by which the

---

[1] While the impact of labor organization upon wage rates is frequently discussed in current literature, the question of the effect of employer organization upon wage rates is seldom explored. Frequently, a formal employer organization only sharpens relations already apparent. The wage contour is more sharply defined at the "edges."

internal structure through job clusters are influenced by external developments in the wage contour. Wage theory cannot reduce all structure to a single rate; the limited number of strategic rates depicted by the job clusters and wage contours are to be the focus of wage theory.[2]

WAGE STRUCTURE
IN THE SHORT RUN

The concepts developed in the preceding section can be applied to a particular case. The attached table shows the union scale for motor-truck drivers in Boston for July 1951. Each rate shows the wage scale established between the union and an association or group of employers engaging in selling transportation services. Some small part of the differences in wages may be attributed to variations in the skill or work performed; some small differences may be related to differences in the length of the work week and the timing of contract expiration during a year. But the teamsters who work at these various rates are essentially similar and substitutable. Essentially the same disparity in rates is found in most other cities, with a high similarity in the relative ranking of rates for various branches of the trade.

In a significant sense, the case constitutes a kind of critical experiment. One type of labour performing almost identical work, organized by the same union, is paid markedly different rates by different associations of employers in the truck transportation industry. Why the wide range in wage rates? Are the disparities temporary? Do they arise from "friction" or "immobilities" in the labour market? Are they primarily the consequence of a monopolistic seller of labour discriminating among types of employers? I believe the answer to these several questions is in the negative.

Basically each rate reflects a wage contour. Each is a reflection of the product market. Within any one contour the wage rates will tend to be equal. As among beer distributors, construction firms, ice deliverers, or scrap iron and metal haulers, there will tend to be few differences in rates. But there are sharp differences in rates as among contours. Fundamentally the differences in the product market are reflected back into the labour market.

But what are the mechanics? Why do not teamsters all move to the higher paying contours? Or, why do not the employers in the higher paying contours set a lower rate since similar labour seems to be available to other contours at lower rates? In a perfect labour market (a bourse) such changes toward uniformity would tend to take place.

Part of the explanation is to be found in the historical sequence of growth of the trucker's wage scale as indicated in the preceding section. Newer and expanding industries or contours, such as oil, have had to pay higher wages to attract labor in the evolution of wage scales. Part of the explanation is derived from the fact that this historical structure of wages has conditioned the labour supply so that the relative rates among contours are regarded as proper. A minor part of the explanation lies in the fact that these wage rates are influenced by the wages of the group of workers these employees tend to be associated with in work operations. Teamsters hauling oil and building materials come in contact with high-paid employees in their work operations, while laundry and scrap drivers have more direct contact with lower-paid employees. A larger emphasis is to be placed on the fact that competitive conditions permit higher pay at the

[2] For an imaginative discussion on the concept of labour market, see Clark Kerr, "The Balkanization of Labor Markets," *Labor Mobility and Economic Opportunity* (1954), pp. 92–110. The present discussion would add to that of Professor Kerr the emphasis that the scope of product markets is reflected back into the labour market defining the scope of wage setting.

TABLE 1.   UNION SCALE FOR MOTOR-TRUCK DRIVERS[a]

(Boston, July 1, 1951)

|  | $ |
|---|---|
| Magazine | 2.25 |
| Newspaper, day | 2.16 |
| Oil | 1.985 |
| Building construction | 1.85 |
| Paper handlers, newspaper | 1.832 |
| Beer, bottle and keg | 1.775 |
| Grocery, chain store | 1.679 |
| Meat-packing house, 3–5 tons | 1.64 |
| Bakery, Hebrew | 1.595 |
| Wholesale | 1.57 |
| Rendering | 1.55 |
| Coal | 1.518 |
| Garbage disposal | 1.50 |
| General hauling | 1.50 |
| Food service, retail | 1.475 |
| Ice | 1.45 |
| Armored car | 1.405 |
| Carbonated beverage | 1.38 |
| Waste paper | 1.38 |
| Linen supply | 1.342 |
| Movers, piano and household | 1.30 |
| Scrap, iron and metal | 1.20 |
| Laundry, wholesale | 1.20 |

[a] Bureau of Labor Statistics, *Union Wages and Hours: Motortruck Drivers and Helpers* (July 1, 1951), Bulletin 1052, pp. 9–10.

top of the list. Demand is more inelastic and wages tend to be a lower proportion of the sales revenue. But why do the firms pay more, simply because they can afford to do so? If the union is brought into the explanation as a decisive factor, then an explanation can simply be made in terms of the union acting as a discriminating seller as among different industries. While this factor may be significant in some cases, the type of wage spread is so general, apart from the union, that the principal explanation should lie elsewhere.

In periods of tightness in the labour market the various contours are able to bid for labour, and a differentiated structure of rates reflecting the product market contours and competitive conditions tends to be established. For a variety of reasons these differentials are not readily altered in a looser labour market. There are costs involved in making a wage change or changing a differential among sectors. Newer and expanding employers using the same type of labour have to pay more

to attract a labour force, and a differential once established by a contour is not easily abolished.

For these various reasons the structure of the product market tends to be mirrored in the labour market. The differentials are not transitory; they are not to be dismissed as imperfections. The differentials are not basically to be interpreted as a range of indefinite or random rates, although a community with a wide variety of firms in different product markets may present the impression of random rates. The wage contours and their relative rates reflect the basic nature of product and labour markets.

The arguments developed above can be applied to most of the cases of interfirm wage differentials that have been reported. There are some differences in wage rates which reflect differences in job content; there are differences in costs and earnings in the way firms administer the same wage structure, and there are differences in methods of compensation (incentive and time rates). These factors account for some of the statistically observed variations in wage rates. The theoretically significant differences for similar grades of labour are those which reflect different product market competitive conditions.

\* \* \*

Dunlop notes the deficiency of marginal productivity principles as a theory of wage determination. At best, that is, if firms follow strict policies of profit maximization, they explain the labor demand schedule. Marginal productivity ignores labor supply considerations and, to express this weakness simply, could determine wages only if a given work force had a perfectly inelastic labor supply schedule. Dunlop calls the formulation of a labor supply theory a "pivotal task" of wage theory.

Unions, in effect, establish a perfectly elastic supply schedule. But the wage set at which the covered membership will work results from collective bargaining. Therefore, marginal productivity becomes, at most, a theory of employment rather than an explanation of wage determination.

Dunlop agrees that unions play a role in establishing wage differentials within a particular occupation in a given market area (in his example of the wage pattern for Boston truck drivers). But he gives a greater role to the product market and other forces that establish different wage contours for workers of the same occupation. Whether because of union wage bargaining or conformity to wage patterns established across occupational lines, as long as there are imperfections on the labor supply side, wage differentials among firms in the same industry and among the same type of workers in different employment settings will tend to arise, with marginal productivity principles playing a reduced role in wage determination.

### Related Readings

In his "Comment" on Mincer's paper, *Aspects of Labor Economics*, pp. 98–105, Clarence D. Long presents a careful review of Mincer's findings and a concise explanation of his theoretical model.

Long, in Chapter 7 of his compendious *Labor Force Under Changing Income and Employment* (Princeton, N.J., Princeton University Press, 1958), offers explanations for the increase in female labor force participation over time, an increase that he found to be unexpected in the light of the generally negative cross-sectional correlation between family income and female participation found in many studies. Among the dynamic forces accounting for increased participation, Long notes the increased use of appliances and manufactured food in the home, the decrease in family size, the rising level of female earnings, improved employment opportunities for women and expanded female education.

All of these factors fit into Mincer's model to explain the upward trend in the labor force participation of females (wives) over time. The increase in hourly earnings is the primary force, given a positively sloped labor supply curve, that increases participation. In addition, improvements in appliances and other substitutes for the wife's work in the home have lowered the cost of substitution of market work for homework. Further, the reduction in family size, in effect, increased the disutility saved from an extra hour less of home work. This lowered the ratio of the marginal disutility of an extra hour's market work to that of the last hour of homework and induced more market labor at current wages. Finally, both an expansion of female opportunities in general and advantages in female education undoubtedly widened job alternatives for wives, who, by selecting jobs with favorable nonpecuniary aspects reduced the disutility of the last, or an additional hour's work.

In another study of underdeveloped economies, Elliot Berg, "Backward Sloping Labor Supply Functions in Dual Economies—The African Case" (*Quarterly Journal of Economics*, Vol. 75, August 1961), found individual supply schedules for low-wage labor to be negatively sloped. Berg does not compare differential labor force response to jobs with similar wages but of varying prestige, as does Rottenberg. He did find, though, that the market labor supply increased with higher wages as more workers offered market labor in place of nonremunerative home labor.

M. Blaug, *Economic Theory in Retrospect* (Homewood, Ill., Richard D. Irwin, 1962, pp. 291–293), summarizes earlier theories of labor supply. These theories often considered only part of the influences on labor supply. For example, the notion of a backward-bending supply curve held by earlier theorists was usually based on the assumption of a declining marginal utility of money. Thus, as the wage increased, the marginal dollar earned eventually became worth less than the effort required to earn it. This reasoning entirely ignored the substitution effect, that the marginal unit of effort would secure more dollars at higher wages.

In *The Theory of Wages* (Oxford, Basil Blackwell, 1966, Chapter III), K. Rothschild presents a clear exposition of the conventional analysis of the short-run labor supply schedule, based on the work-income–leisure decision.

J. R. Hicks, in *The Theory of Wages* (New York, Macmillan, 1936), presents a thorough advanced exposition of the marginal productivity theory. Hicks also reviews and comments on Marshall's explanation (in his *Principles of Economics*) of factors affecting the elasticity of labor demand. Allan Cartter, in *Theory of Wages and Employment* (Homewood, Ill., Richard D. Irwin, 1959), traces the development of the theory in the early literature and, in addition, emphasizes its weakness as an explanation of wage determination because of its omission of labor supply elements.

Richard A. Lester, "Shortcomings of Marginal Analysis for Wage-Employment Problems" (*American Economic Review*, Vol. 37, March 1946), and Fritz Machlup, "Marginal Analysis and Empirical Research" (*American Economic Review*, Vol. 37, September 1946), dispute the application of marginalism in firms' wage-employment decisions. Lester, on the basis of questionnaire responses, concluded that firms did not adhere to marginal principles. Machlup points out that many of the responses actually indicated consideration of marginalism, if not strictly a substitution of capital for labor as an answer to a wage increase. To the extent firms tried to maximize profits they behaved like marginalists. But in admitting that firms base business decisions partly on nonpecuniary goals, Machlup's defense of marginalism is weakened.

Many writers have noted that firms do not always aim for profit maximization. Criticisms of marginalism based on this behavior are made by Melvin Reder, "A Reconsideration of the Marginal Productivity Theory" (*Journal of Political Economy*, Vol. 55, October 1947), and Robert A. Gordon, "Short-Period Price Determination in Theory and Practice," (*American Economic Review*, Vol. 38, June 1948).

# CHAPTER 6

# Long-Run and Short-Run Changes in the Labor Force

Although the labor force participation rate of women has been increasing over time, the rate for the labor force as a whole has remained remarkably stable in the long run. In the short run, however, there has been marked variation in the overall rate, related to the level of employment and economic conditions. These short-run variations have important influences on efforts to achieve full employment and on policy decisions to attain this goal. The tendency for the labor force to expand and contract in phase with prosperity and recession about a high economic level dampens variations in the unemployment rate. Although this pattern softens recessions, at least with respect to the employment rate, it also retards the movement toward full employment during prosperity.

## LONG-RUN STABILITY IN LABOR FORCE PARTICIPATION

Clarence Long, in his exhaustive study of labor force participation, *The Labor Force Under Changing Income and Employment* (Princeton, N.J., Princeton University Press, National Bureau of Economic Research, 1958), theorizes that long-run stability has been achieved, not through coincidental offsetting increases by some groups and declines in others, but by a systematic interrelationship between the growth and decline in the particular segments of the labor force. Hours of work have declined for all types of workers, whether classified by occupation, industry, or sex. Thus the constancy in the labor force participation rate, at about 57 percent of the noninstitutional population 14 years of age and over, indicates that gains in productivity over the years have been taken in the form of increased output and shorter hours, but not in any net reduction in the relative number willing to work, which causes relative stability in the long-run manpower potential.

In a theory of stability of the labor force, what is needed first is an explanation of why the increase in female participation more or less balances the decline in participation of young and older men. Then, an explanation is also needed for the tendency for increases in leisure to take the form of shorter hours rather than a reduction in participation. If this were not the case, then even if there was a direct relationship between the reduction in labor force participation of men and the increase in that of women, this substitution would be at less than a one-in to one-out ratio with the overall rate declining.

In his study, Long found stability in the overall rate in the United States and in four other countries over a long period of time, with a decline in participation of older and younger males being matched by an increase in female participation. In the (major) portion of Chapter 13 of *The Labor Force Under Changing Income and Employment*, presented here, Long offers an explanation for the equality of the counterbalancing movements of younger and older men and women, as increased leisure under the influence of higher incomes took the form of shorter hours instead of reduced participation. Elements in Long's hypotheses would seem to apply in the future as well as in the past, and suggest continued stability in the overall rate.

As for the systematic relationship in the substitution of women for older and younger men, Long argues that women both pushed some men out of the labor force and replaced those who left voluntarily. In the case of younger men, both forces operated. Changing technology made educated and trained women more suitable than untrained young men to work force needs of employers. At the same time the younger men were leaving the work force in increasing numbers to devote their time to more education and training than to gainful employment. As for older men, although Long did not note a trend of increased voluntary retirement in response to expanded social security or other income maintenance programs, he believed that the same characteristics of better education and training, as was the case for the displacement of younger men, served as the basis of employer preference for women. In both cases, reduction in family size and improved substitutes for home work formerly provided by women increased the supply of women available to meet employer demands for their services.

# The Labor Force Under Changing Income and Employment

## by Clarence D. Long

### WHY DID FEMALE PARTICIPATION RISE WHILE MALE PARTICIPATION DECLINED?

The great increases in female participation were not demonstrably associated with changes either in real disposable incomes of equivalent adult males or in the ratio of female to male earnings. Any judgments as to what did cause female participation to rise in the amounts and at the times it did must be highly tentative. . . . The hypothesis is that the increases in female participation over 60 years were due primarily to four factors:

1. The release of many women from the home as a result of the great decline in the ratio of the civilian population to the number of working-age females. The decline was due to a reduction in the birth rate and a rise in the female survival rate; and it occurred in a way that enabled millions of females, previously needed at home, to enter the labor force.

2. Labor saved in own home housework with the extended use of household appliances and the purchase of food and clothing formerly produced at home. The saving was probably too fragmentary and too scattered among females to have been responsible for many full-time female additions to the labor force. It was doubtless a marginal or contributing factor in many cases, though it most likely resulted in a higher standard of leisure and of family care. Still it was quantitatively important and, if it does not explain why females increased in the labor force, it may at least help to explain why their participation did not decline as income increased over time.

3. The expanding employment opportunities for females, arising with the

SOURCE Reprinted with permission from *The Labor Force Under Changing Income and Employment*, Princeton, N.J., Princeton University Press for the National Bureau of Economic Research, Princeton, 1958, pp. 267–277.

extensive development of clerical occupations and service industries, and occurring
*pari-passu* with the great increase in
educational attainment of the average
female, which qualified her for such employment.[1] This factor might not have
moved women into the labor force if they
could not have been spared at home, but
it provided the demand.

4. The shorter workweek, making it
easier for females to hold jobs and still
carry out their household responsibilities
which, though lightened, demanded a
good deal of time and energy on the part
of many women. (Reductions in the workweek were closely timed to the increase in
female participation in the four countries
for which data on hours were available.)

If declining household and child-care
responsibilities, rising educational attainment, and shrinking hours of work had
something to do with the increasing tendency of women to seek gainful jobs, we
are led to the next link in the relationship
between female participation and labor
force behavior—that the large-scale entrance of females (chiefly aged 20–64)
may in turn have been an active influence
on the withdrawal of young and elderly
persons.

It has been seen that men 45 and older
reduced their participation by sizable
amounts, and men 65 and older by far
more—even more than young men and
teen-age boys. This decline has not been
closely related to the rise in real incomes
(at least, since 1930), or to the extension
of pensions and of social security (at least,
before 1940), or to any discoverable deterioration in average physical ability to
work (compared with men of the same
age in earlier decades). It does not seem
assignable to changes in self-employment
opportunities, to rapidity of technological
advance, or to the level of unemployment.

There is a possibility that it has been due
to a tightening in company rules and practices against hiring or keeping older workers; but it has not been definitely established that these rules have been more
extensive than several decades ago when
elderly men were in the labor force in
much larger proportions. *In any case it
seems doubtful that employers would
have been so ready to part with this source
of labor supply unless there had been new
sources, namely women, available to take
its place.*

Is it possible that the older men were to
a large extent displaced by the entrance
of better trained women, available at
lower wages? There is some circumstan-
tial support for such a thesis. At both the
1940 and 1950 censuses the participation
of men was closely related at a moment-of-
time to the amount of their education; for
men with education *below* high school,
years of schooling seemed far more important than age in determining participation. A great decline occurred between
1910 and 1950 in the number of years of
school completed by elderly men relative
to the number completed by women 20–
24 or 25–44. And a strong moment-of-time
tendency was observable at the 1940 and
1950 censuses for women with education
*above* high school to be in the labor force
in larger proportions, the more years of
schooling they had achieved.

Why would the influx of women into
the labor force displace elderly men rather
than depress the relative wages of
women? Far from declining, the ratio of
wages of women to those of men *rose*,
but it might have risen even more—as a
result of far better education and greatly
expanded job opportunities for females in
industry—had it not been held down by
the very great rise in the ratio of females
in the labor force.

[1] The increase in female education was both absolute and relative to the educational attainment of
older men, whose schooling was limited by the lack of adequate schools at the times and in the places
of their upbringing, by their disinclination to attend, or by their parents' financial requirements.

How to explain the relation between the influx of women and the decline in participation of young people? As to young males the decline occurred in all five countries and in both recent and early periods, and was reflected fairly closely in greater school attendance in the countries for which data were available. Some of the rise in school attendance may have been cultural and institutional in origin and may have happened regardless of increases in income or in the female labor force. But many teen-agers may have stayed in school as a result of being squeezed out of the labor force by mature, better trained women. Employed sisters, mothers, and wives would also have helped to pay for the education of brothers, sons, and husbands.[2] Similarly, many elderly men have retired at earlier ages because of financial help from working daughters or wives and, in some cases, because their female dependents have become self-supporting.

## AN ATTEMPT TO EXPLAIN THE STABILITY OF THE OVER-ALL LABOR FORCE IN VIEW OF THE DECLINING HOURS OF WORK

But even if the declining participation of males was systematically interrelated with the rising participation of females, we should still have to explain why the two tendencies offset each other so completely as to leave the combined rate nearly stable. Have there been some economic or social forces at work to maintain the almost unchanging over-all rate despite rising income? We examine a number of possible explanations.

One explanation might be that man's aspiration tends to rise as fast as his income, so that instead of increasing his leisure, he strives for the things, e.g. better houses and cars, that a higher income can provide. Then, too, people live and spend competitively and their standard of living goes up with their income.

But in actual fact people have also increased their leisure: this leisure has taken the form of less working hours for the average labor force member.

\* \* \*

We therefore inquire why increased leisure, in the long run, took the form of a reduction in hours and not in over-all participation? Stated in another way, why did the participation of males fall just enough to be offset by the increase in the participation of females? In particular, why didn't the labor force participation of men 25–64—the primary working ages—decline substantially instead of only mildly?[3] Possibly shorter hours offered a line of less resistance than withdrawal from the labor-force—especially among primary workers. Several considerations may suggest this.

In the first place, while the total labor force has remained almost constant in relation to the population, the average number of workers per household has fallen from about 1.75 in 1900 to 1.38 in 1950, as shown in the table on the next page.

This development has been the result of young and elderly men and women setting up separate and independent households. It is no doubt a reflection of the increasing well-being. But it also means that the way people have been choosing to live has made it more difficult for the labor force proportion to decline. There were no data on the distribution of families by numbers of workers in 1900; but in 1930, 1940, and

[2] Surveys made by various unions covering several thousand women members disclosed that up to a fourth of those who were married and separated or divorced gave the education of children as one of their chief reasons for working.

[3] Actually, the decline was balanced by the rise in the relative number of men of that age in the population, which resulted in increases—ranging from slight to substantial—in the ratio of male workers 25–64 to the total labor force 14 and older of both sexes in four of the five countries. Only in Canada was there even a slight decline in the ratio.

|  | 1900 | 1930 | 1940 | 1950 |
|---|---|---|---|---|
| Labor force 14 and older (millions) | 28.1 | 48.7 | 52.8 | 60.1 |
| Private households (millions) | 16.0 [a] | 29.9 | 35.1 | 43.5 |
| Labor force per household (average) | 1.75 | 1.63 | 1.51 | 1.38 |

SOURCE: Labor Force: Appendix A. Households: *Census of 1900* (Special Reports), *Supplementary Analysis and Derivative Tables*, p. 379; *Census of Population, 1930,* Vol. VI, *Families,* pp. 7, 10; *Current Population Reports.* Bureau of the Census, Series P-20, No. 33, p. 15. The word "households" used in 1950 is synonymous with "families" at earlier dates.

[a] Source for 1900 data gave the distribution of all households, including quasi-family groups, by the number of persons per family. A percentage distribution of private families was computed after deducting all quasi-family groups from total families with seven or more members.

Note: Data were unavailable for 1910 and 1920.

1950 almost seven in every ten families had only one worker or none at all.[4] Over two families in every ten had two working members; for these families a complete withdrawal of one worker, perhaps an elderly person or a youth, without replacement by another, perhaps a woman, might have meant an inconveniently large loss of income. And the fewest families— one out of every ten—have in recent decades included three or more workers. These were the only households moderately able to adjust to the withdrawal of one member from the labor force.

It can be argued, of course, that a person need not withdraw permanently from the labor force in order to reduce participation and increase leisure. A woman might work only nine months instead of a full year, a schoolboy during the Christmas holidays but not in the summer; a family head might take an unpaid vacation or advance his retirement. Such reductions are often inconvenient or dangerous. Many breadwinners, and even secondary workers, might jeopardize their jobs by taking unpaid vacations; and the failure to seek new employment immediately after losing a job might destroy the only

chance of finding one or result in a prolonged period of unemployment. For most persons an easier and safer way to more leisure is through a shorter workweek. Also, the new leisure can be spread over the year instead of being concentrated in undue amounts in certain months.

More important, the psychological demand for leisure is surely a personal affair. If rising income made people desire more leisure, it is likely that all the members of any family wished to share in any additional leisure. A shorter workweek for all could better satisfy this wish than the withdrawal of one member of the household from the labor force.

Has the expectation been realized? Or is it not true that reductions in the participation of males and increases in the participation of females have redistributed a large part of the burden of work from males (especially youths and older workers) to females (especially women 25–64)? So far as participation is concerned, there certainly has been such a shift. But so far as the total burden of work—gainful and ungainful—is concerned, several other factors must also be considered.

[4] *Census of Population, 1930,* Vol. VI, *Families,* p. 8; *Current Population Reports,* Bureau of the Census, Series P-50, Nos. 5, 29. The 1940 data given in the P-50 reports are based on sample returns from the 1940 census. The 1950 estimates are based on data from monthly sample surveys.

An appreciable increase in 1940 and 1950 in the number of households with no workers was probably due mainly to the rise in the element of pensions, old age charity, social security, and perhaps personal savings—developments which have enabled many elderly men and women to set up or retain separate households after retirement.

There are no separate statistics on full-time hours for males and females. However, the great relative transfer of female workers since the turn of the century has been from long-hour occupations, such as domestic service and farm labor, into short-hour occupations, such as clerical work. The unskilled category, including laborers and servants, was the largest employer of females in 1910 but it was only the third largest in 1940 or 1950; the category of clerical and kindred work was the third largest employer of females in 1919 and in 1940 and 1950 it was the largest. On the assumption that reductions in hours were the same for males and females in each of the countries—in the United States they must have been at least as much for females as for the whole labor force—male and female participation were multiplied by the length of the full-time workweek. For males, the weekly hours of labor force participation per 1,000 male population 14 and older showed a decline of 41 per cent in the United States during 1890–1950, 27 per cent in Britain during 1911–1951, 17.5 per cent in Canada during 1911–1941, and 28.7 per cent in Germany during 1895–1950. For females, the decline in hours seemed typically to have more than offset the increase in participation, with the result that over the same periods hours of female participation fell 5 per cent in the United States, 14 per cent in Britain, and 7 per cent in Germany. Only in Canada was an increase manifested, but it had occurred up to 1941, a war year. If hours of participation fell during the next decade to the levels of the United States, they were about the same in 1951 as in 1911.

The above computations suggest that the total time females devoted to gainful work may have run counter to the great rise in their labor force participation. Nevertheless, there was probably a relative redistribution of gainful work from males to females, since the declines for females were in all cases much smaller than those for males. Is such a development consistent with the premise that if people desire more leisure as an effect of rising incomes it is likely that all members of a family wish to share in this leisure?

The answer requires that account be taken of a second factor: the burden of *nongainful* work in the home. Illustrative computations in Chapter 7 indicated that a great decline in the size of families and the advance in technology for the home could easily have resulted in more leisure for the average housewife.

These developments still do not amount to an easing in the woman's burden of work as great, relatively, as that apparently realized by a man from reductions in both hours and labor force participation. But females may be more likely to work close to home and therefore spend less time in commuting, as suburbanization pushes the population farther from their jobs.[5] And males very likely now bear a much greater part of the burden of home housework, shopping, and the many chores that go with "do-it-yourself" projects—painting, repairing, and so on. If these two developments could be measured in hours, it is possible that the reduction in total gainful and nongainful effort has not been very different between males and females.[6]

There still remains the question of why at least some workers or families might not have chosen to continue on a longer workweek and either not take the new leisure or take it in reduced participation. The answer is plain. Even had certain workers preferred an undiminished workweek (to allow one or more persons in their families to withdraw altogether from the labor force), their wishes could

[5] There are no statistics which reveal whether the time spent in traveling longer distances by auto has been greater or less than the time formerly spent traveling shorter distances by bus or trolley.

[6] Nothing has been said here about school attendance, for the number of males and females in school has been much the same to the extent that statistics can be relied upon.

scarcely have prevailed, unless they had been willing and able to hold a second job. For, if the great majority were able to win reduction in hours, the shorter work-week would have had to be standard for all workers in a factory or store.

So the shorter workweek may have offered a more convenient, flexible, and equitable "package" in which to obtain additional leisure evenly distributed among workers and over time as incomes rose gradually. Once working hours are reduced, all sorts of obstacles arise to prevent a revision upward. They tend to be frozen into laws on maximum hours and overtime pay; they become inherent in union agreements and factory shifts. Workers gradually buy or rent houses at distances that involve extensive commuting, and the pace of the work itself may increase so that a return to a longer work-week could be accommodated only by relaxing the intensity of effort. Even the employer himself may come to prefer the shorter week and to view a return to a longer week with little enthusiasm.

It would seem highly probable that the demand for leisure has been powerfully and irrevocably shunted toward fewer weekly hours of work and more rest periods and holidays for most persons, and not toward a downward trend in the proportion of population who work in a given week. In bringing about the past reductions in the workweek, the role of the unions, while considerable, has not been the dominant one. In the future, however, unions are likely to be much more important in initiating and pressing for shorter hours. For unions are far stronger now than during the years when most of the reductions occurred. Whether the demand for leisure arises from higher incomes or from the lack of demand for labor, a curtailment in the length of the workweek or additional rest periods, sick leaves, holidays, and vacations is likely to be more acceptable to unions than reductions in the size of the labor force, if only because the former means the possibility of getting higher than proportional wages for overtime at certain seasons of the year and in times of war emergency, or because declines in the labor force mean a loss of union membership and revenue from dues. It appears that any drop in labor supply will continue to take the form of fewer hours and perhaps less effort per hour, and that the over-all labor force will continue to stay rather close to its present and past percentages of working age population.

* * *

### Changes in Labor Force Composition

Both Long's findings and his explanation of the results emphasize that overall stability in labor force participation is achieved by equalizing shifts in composition of the participation of women, and younger and older men. Meanwhile the bulk of the labor force, prime-aged males, remained relatively constant over the long run at a participation rate well over 90 percent. The shifting groups comprise what has come to be called the "secondary work force." Not only are there compensating shifts in the secondary force in the long run but there are also changes in their combined participation in the short run. Before studying these short-run variations in labor force participation, it will be helpful to examine the data to which Long's analysis applies. Furthermore, the figures and projections on changing composition of the labor force, not only by sex but also by broad occupational and industry groupings, and educational attainment, will quantify what has been called the nation's "manpower revolution," the continuing pronounced movement of the labor force, since about 1950, away from men, from the unskilled, uneducated, and from production work, toward women, the skilled, the educated, and toward professional, service, and clerical work, all these changes occurring within a framework of constancy of the overall participation rate.

Table 1* shows this overall stability along with the relative shift from men to women, and the continuing secular movement away from agriculture.

The participation rates separated by age and sex, in Table 2, clearly show the trends discussed by Long, with women replacing very young and older men in the work force over the past quarter of a century.

Note that, unlike the pattern for men, female participation has increased for all age groups, although the greatest relative gains were made among young and middle-aged women.

Turning to the labor force behavior of wives, in Table 3 the data show sharper increases for married women than for females in general, with a relative increase of 80 percent for the former (from 27.0 to 39.6 percent) and only 34 percent for the latter (from 31.8 to 42.7 percent). Moreover, the greatest relative gains in participation occurred among those with young children. Thus the marked trend has been for expanded work participation among those women who showed the least inclination to work in the past—wives, and especially those with young children (the younger the children, the greater the relative increase in market work by mothers).

Over the 11-year period, 1958–1969, the trend of occupational distribution featured mainly relative gains for white-collar workers and a loss for farm workers, with blue-collar and service workers more or less holding their share of the work force.

It is interesting to note, from Table 4, that the white-collar share increased about as much for men as for women. This increase for men resulted from the gains in male professional and technical employment. For women, on the other hand, the greatest relative increase took place among the clerical workers.

Table 5 shows the rapid expansion in educational levels of the work force over less than a 20-year span. By 1969, about two-thirds of the work force were high school graduates, and over the period covered, the number with some college exceeded 50 percent.

Labor force projections made by the Department of Labor show a general continuation of the existing trends in the labor force participation and composition. Table 6 projects stability in the work force up to 1890 with only a slight relative gain for women compared to men.

More pronounced are the expected continuation of the occupational trends. Table 7 shows a gain for professional and technical employment at twice the overall increase for the 1965–1975 period.

The farm work population is projected to continue its decline. Employment of service and clerical workers is expected to show a greater relative increase than overall employment, while laborers should show a percentage decline in employment.

Educational attainment of the work force is projected to continue its ex-

---

* Source: All tables are from *Manpower Report of the President,* U.S. Department of Labor, March 1970.

TABLE 1. EMPLOYMENT STATUS OF THE NONINSTITUTIONAL POPULATION 16 YEARS AND OVER, BY SEX: ANNUAL AVERAGES, 1947–69

[Numbers in thousands]

| Sex and Year | Total Noninstitutional Population | Total Labor Force, Including Armed Forces | | Civilian Labor Force | | | | | | Not in Labor Force |
|---|---|---|---|---|---|---|---|---|---|---|
| | | Number | Percent of Noninstitutional Population | Total | Employed | | | Unemployed | | |
| | | | | | Total | Agriculture | Nonagricultural Industries | Number | Percent of Labor Force | |
| Both sexes | | | | | | | | | | |
| 1947 | 103,418 | 60,941 | 58.9 | 59,350 | 57,039 | 7,891 | 49,148 | 2,311 | 3.9 | 42,477 |
| 1948 | 104,527 | 62,080 | 59.4 | 60,621 | 58,344 | 7,629 | 50,711 | 2,276 | 3.8 | 42,447 |
| 1949 | 105,611 | 62,903 | 59.6 | 61,286 | 57,649 | 7,656 | 49,990 | 3,637 | 5.9 | 42,708 |
| 1950 | 106,645 | 63,858 | 59.9 | 62,208 | 58,920 | 7,160 | 51,752 | 3,288 | 5.3 | 42,787 |
| 1951 | 107,721 | 65,117 | 60.4 | 62,017 | 59,962 | 6,726 | 53,230 | 2,055 | 3.3 | 42,604 |
| 1952 | 108,823 | 65,730 | 60.4 | 62,138 | 60,254 | 6,501 | 53,748 | 1,883 | 3.0 | 43,093 |
| 1953 | 110,601 | 66,560 | 60.2 | 63,015 | 61,181 | 6,261 | 54,915 | 1,834 | 2.9 | 44,041 |
| 1954 | 111,671 | 66,993 | 60.0 | 63,643 | 60,110 | 6,206 | 53,898 | 3,532 | 5.5 | 44,678 |
| 1955 | 112,732 | 68,072 | 60.4 | 65,023 | 62,171 | 6,449 | 55,718 | 2,852 | 4.4 | 44,660 |
| 1956 | 113,811 | 69,409 | 61.0 | 66,552 | 63,802 | 6,283 | 57,506 | 2,750 | 4.1 | 44,402 |
| 1957 | 115,065 | 69,729 | 60.6 | 66,929 | 64,071 | 5,947 | 58,123 | 2,859 | 4.3 | 45,336 |
| 1958 | 116,363 | 70,275 | 60.4 | 67,639 | 63,036 | 5,586 | 57,450 | 4,602 | 6.8 | 46,088 |
| 1959 | 117,881 | 70,921 | 60.2 | 68,369 | 64,630 | 5,565 | 59,065 | 3,740 | 5.5 | 46,960 |
| 1960 | 119,759 | 72,142 | 60.2 | 69,628 | 65,778 | 5,458 | 60,318 | 3,852 | 5.5 | 47,617 |
| 1961 | 121,343 | 73,031 | 60.2 | 70,459 | 65,746 | 5,200 | 60,546 | 4,714 | 6.7 | 48,312 |
| 1962 | 122,981 | 73,442 | 59.7 | 70,614 | 66,702 | 4,944 | 61,759 | 3,911 | 5.5 | 49,539 |
| 1963 | 125,154 | 74,571 | 59.6 | 71,833 | 67,762 | 4,687 | 63,076 | 4,070 | 5.7 | 50,583 |
| 1964 | 127,224 | 75,830 | 59.6 | 73,091 | 69,305 | 4,523 | 64,782 | 3,786 | 5.2 | 51,394 |
| 1965 | 129,236 | 77,178 | 59.7 | 74,455 | 71,088 | 4,361 | 66,726 | 3,366 | 4.5 | 52,058 |
| 1966 | 131,180 | 78,893 | 60.1 | 75,770 | 72,895 | 3,979 | 68,915 | 2,875 | 3.8 | 52,288 |
| 1967 | 133,319 | 80,793 | 60.6 | 77,347 | 74,372 | 3,844 | 70,527 | 2,975 | 3.8 | 52,527 |
| 1968 | 135,562 | 82,272 | 60.7 | 78,737 | 75,920 | 3,817 | 72,103 | 2,817 | 3.6 | 53,291 |
| 1969 | 137,841 | 84,239 | 61.1 | 80,733 | 77,902 | 3,606 | 74,296 | 2,831 | 3.5 | 53,602 |

| Male | | | | | | | | | | |
|---|---|---|---|---|---|---|---|---|---|---|
| 1947 | 50,968 | 44,258 | 86.8 | 42,686 | 40,994 | 6,643 | 34,351 | 1,692 | 4.0 | 6,710 |
| 1948 | 51,439 | 44,729 | 87.0 | 43,286 | 41,726 | 6,358 | 35,366 | 1,559 | 3.6 | 6,710 |
| 1949 | 51,922 | 45,097 | 86.9 | 43,498 | 40,926 | 6,342 | 34,581 | 2,572 | 5.9 | 6,825 |
| 1950 | 52,352 | 45,446 | 86.8 | 43,819 | 41,580 | 6,001 | 35,573 | 2,239 | 5.1 | 6,906 |
| 1951 | 52,788 | 46,063 | 87.3 | 43,001 | 41,780 | 5,533 | 36,243 | 1,221 | 2.8 | 6,725 |
| 1952 | 53,248 | 46,416 | 87.2 | 42,869 | 41,684 | 5,389 | 36,292 | 1,185 | 2.8 | 6,832 |
| 1953 | 54,248 | 47,131 | 86.9 | 43,633 | 42,431 | 5,253 | 37,175 | 1,202 | 2.8 | 7,117 |
| 1954 | 54,706 | 47,275 | 86.4 | 43,965 | 41,620 | 5,200 | 36,414 | 2,344 | 5.3 | 7,431 |
| 1955 | 55,122 | 47,488 | 86.2 | 44,475 | 42,621 | 5,265 | 37,354 | 1,854 | 4.2 | 7,634 |
| 1956 | 55,547 | 47,914 | 86.3 | 45,091 | 43,380 | 5,039 | 38,334 | 1,711 | 3.8 | 7,633 |
| 1957 | 56,082 | 47,964 | 85.5 | 45,197 | 43,357 | 4,824 | 38,532 | 1,841 | 4.1 | 8,118 |
| 1958 | 56,640 | 48,126 | 85.0 | 45,521 | 42,423 | 4,596 | 37,827 | 3,098 | 6.8 | 8,514 |
| 1959 | 57,312 | 48,405 | 84.5 | 45,886 | 43,466 | 4,532 | 38,934 | 2,420 | 5.3 | 8,907 |
| 1960 | 58,144 | 48,870 | 84.0 | 46,388 | 43,904 | 4,472 | 39,431 | 2,486 | 5.4 | 9,274 |
| 1961 | 58,826 | 49,193 | 83.6 | 46,653 | 43,656 | 4,298 | 39,359 | 2,997 | 6.4 | 9,633 |
| 1962 | 59,626 | 49,395 | 82.8 | 46,600 | 44,177 | 4,069 | 40,108 | 2,423 | 5.2 | 10,231 |
| 1963 | 60,627 | 49,835 | 82.2 | 47,129 | 44,657 | 3,809 | 40,849 | 2,472 | 5.2 | 10,792 |
| 1964 | 61,556 | 50,387 | 81.9 | 47,679 | 45,474 | 3,691 | 41,782 | 2,205 | 4.6 | 11,169 |
| 1965 | 62,473 | 50,946 | 81.5 | 48,255 | 46,340 | 3,547 | 42,792 | 1,914 | 4.0 | 11,527 |
| 1966 | 63,351 | 51,560 | 81.4 | 48,471 | 46,919 | 3,243 | 43,675 | 1,551 | 3.2 | 11,792 |
| 1967 | 64,316 | 52,398 | 81.5 | 48,987 | 47,479 | 3,164 | 44,315 | 1,508 | 3.1 | 11,919 |
| 1968 | 65,345 | 53,030 | 81.2 | 49,533 | 48,114 | 3,157 | 44,957 | 1,419 | 2.9 | 12,315 |
| 1969 | 66,365 | 53,688 | 80.9 | 50,221 | 48,818 | 2,963 | 45,854 | 1,403 | 2.8 | 12,677 |

TABLE 1 (Continued)

| Sex and Year | Total Noninstitutional Population | Total Labor Force, Including Armed Forces | | Civilian Labor Force | | | | | | Not in Labor Force |
|---|---|---|---|---|---|---|---|---|---|---|
| | | | | | Employed | | | | | |
| | | Number | Percent of Noninstitutional Population | Total | Total | Agriculture | Nonagricultural Industries | Number | Percent of Labor Force | |
| Female | | | | | | | | | | |
| 1947 | 52,450 | 16,683 | 31.8 | 16,664 | 16,045 | 1,248 | 14,797 | 619 | 3.7 | 35,767 |
| 1948 | 53,088 | 17,351 | 32.7 | 17,335 | 16,618 | 1,271 | 15,345 | 717 | 4.1 | 35,737 |
| 1949 | 53,689 | 17,806 | 33.2 | 17,788 | 16,723 | 1,314 | 15,409 | 1,065 | 6.0 | 35,883 |
| 1950 | 54,293 | 18,412 | 33.9 | 18,389 | 17,340 | 1,159 | 16,179 | 1,049 | 5.7 | 35,881 |
| 1951 | 54,933 | 19,054 | 34.7 | 19,016 | 18,182 | 1,193 | 16,987 | 834 | 4.4 | 35,879 |
| 1952 | 55,575 | 19,314 | 34.8 | 19,269 | 18,570 | 1,112 | 17,456 | 698 | 3.6 | 36,261 |
| 1953 | 56,353 | 19,429 | 34.5 | 19,382 | 18,750 | 1,008 | 17,740 | 632 | 3.3 | 36,924 |
| 1954 | 56,965 | 19,718 | 34.6 | 19,678 | 18,490 | 1,006 | 17,484 | 1,188 | 6.0 | 37,247 |
| 1955 | 57,610 | 20,584 | 35.7 | 20,548 | 19,550 | 1,184 | 18,364 | 998 | 4.9 | 37,026 |
| 1956 | 58,264 | 21,495 | 36.9 | 21,461 | 20,422 | 1,244 | 19,172 | 1,039 | 4.8 | 36,769 |
| 1957 | 58,983 | 21,765 | 36.9 | 21,732 | 20,714 | 1,123 | 19,591 | 1,018 | 4.7 | 37,218 |
| 1958 | 59,723 | 22,149 | 37.1 | 22,118 | 20,613 | 990 | 19,623 | 1,504 | 6.8 | 37,574 |
| 1959 | 60,569 | 22,516 | 37.2 | 22,483 | 21,164 | 1,033 | 20,131 | 1,320 | 5.9 | 38,053 |
| 1960 | 61,615 | 23,272 | 37.8 | 23,240 | 21,874 | 986 | 20,887 | 1,366 | 5.9 | 38,343 |
| 1961 | 62,517 | 23,838 | 38.1 | 23,806 | 22,090 | 902 | 21,187 | 1,717 | 7.2 | 38,679 |
| 1962 | 63,355 | 24,047 | 38.0 | 24,014 | 22,525 | 875 | 21,651 | 1,488 | 6.2 | 39,308 |
| 1963 | 64,527 | 24,736 | 38.3 | 24,704 | 23,105 | 878 | 22,227 | 1,598 | 6.5 | 39,791 |
| 1964 | 65,668 | 25,443 | 38.7 | 25,412 | 23,831 | 832 | 23,000 | 1,581 | 6.2 | 40,225 |
| 1965 | 66,763 | 26,232 | 39.3 | 26,200 | 24,748 | 814 | 23,934 | 1,452 | 5.5 | 40,531 |
| 1966 | 67,829 | 27,333 | 40.3 | 27,299 | 25,976 | 736 | 25,240 | 1,324 | 4.8 | 40,496 |
| 1967 | 69,003 | 28,395 | 41.2 | 28,360 | 26,893 | 680 | 26,212 | 1,468 | 5.2 | 40,608 |
| 1968 | 70,217 | 29,242 | 41.6 | 29,204 | 27,807 | 660 | 27,147 | 1,397 | 4.8 | 40,978 |
| 1969 | 71,476 | 30,551 | 42.7 | 30,512 | 29,084 | 643 | 28,441 | 1,428 | 4.7 | 40,924 |

TABLE 2. LABOR FORCE PARTICIPATION RATES [1] FOR PERSONS 16 YEARS AND OVER, BY SEX AND AGE: ANNUAL AVERAGES, 1947-69

| Sex and Year | Total, 16 Years and Over | 16 and 17 Years | 18 and 19 Years | 20 to 24 Years | 25 to 34 Years | 35 to 44 Years | 45 to 54 Years | 55 to 64 Years | 65 Years and Over | 14 and 15 Years |
|---|---|---|---|---|---|---|---|---|---|---|
| Male | | | | Labor Force Participation Rate | | | | | | |
| 1947 | 86.8 | 52.2 | 80.5 | 84.9 | 95.8 | 98.0 | 95.5 | 89.6 | 47.8 | 27.7 |
| 1948 | 87.0 | 53.4 | 79.9 | 85.7 | 96.1 | 98.0 | 95.8 | 89.5 | 46.8 | 27.5 |
| 1949 | 86.9 | 52.3 | 79.5 | 87.8 | 95.9 | 98.0 | 95.6 | 87.5 | 46.9 | 27.4 |
| 1950 | 86.8 | 52.0 | 79.0 | 89.1 | 96.2 | 97.6 | 95.8 | 86.9 | 45.8 | 28.7 |
| 1951 | 87.3 | 54.5 | 80.3 | 91.1 | 97.1 | 97.6 | 96.0 | 87.2 | 44.9 | 27.7 |
| 1952 | 87.2 | 53.1 | 79.1 | 92.1 | 97.7 | 97.9 | 96.2 | 87.5 | 42.6 | 25.9 |
| 1953 | 86.9 | 51.7 | 78.5 | 92.2 | 97.6 | 98.2 | 96.6 | 87.9 | 41.6 | 24.6 |
| 1954 | 86.4 | 48.3 | 76.5 | 91.5 | 97.5 | 98.1 | 96.5 | 88.7 | 40.5 | 24.7 |
| 1955 | 86.2 | 49.5 | 77.1 | 90.8 | 97.7 | 98.1 | 96.5 | 87.9 | 39.6 | 24.0 |
| 1956 | 86.3 | 52.6 | 77.9 | 90.8 | 97.4 | 98.0 | 96.6 | 88.5 | 40.0 | 26.6 |
| 1957 | 85.5 | 51.1 | 77.7 | 89.8 | 97.3 | 97.9 | 96.4 | 87.5 | 37.5 | 25.1 |
| 1958 | 85.0 | 47.9 | 75.7 | 89.5 | 97.3 | 98.0 | 96.3 | 87.8 | 35.6 | 23.8 |
| 1959 | 84.5 | 46.0 | 75.5 | 90.1 | 97.5 | 97.8 | 96.0 | 87.4 | 34.2 | 24.2 |
| 1960 | 84.0 | 46.8 | 73.6 | 90.2 | 97.7 | 97.7 | 95.8 | 86.8 | 33.1 | 22.3 |
| 1961 | 83.6 | 45.4 | 71.3 | 89.8 | 97.8 | 97.7 | 95.6 | 87.3 | 31.7 | 21.8 |
| 1962 | 82.8 | 43.5 | 71.9 | 89.1 | 97.4 | 97.7 | 95.6 | 86.2 | 30.3 | 21.6 |
| 1963 | 82.2 | 42.7 | 73.1 | 88.3 | 97.3 | 97.6 | 95.8 | 86.2 | 28.4 | 20.9 |
| 1964 | 81.9 | 43.6 | 72.0 | 88.2 | 97.5 | 97.4 | 95.8 | 85.6 | 28.0 | 20.8 |
| 1965 | 81.5 | 44.6 | 70.0 | 88.0 | 97.4 | 97.4 | 95.6 | 84.7 | 27.9 | 21.4 |
| 1966 | 81.4 | 47.0 | 69.0 | 87.9 | 97.5 | 97.3 | 95.3 | 84.5 | 27.0 | 21.6 |
| 1967 | 81.5 | 47.5 | 70.9 | 87.5 | 97.4 | 97.4 | 95.2 | 84.4 | 27.1 | 22.2 |
| 1968 | 81.2 | 46.8 | 70.2 | 86.5 | 97.1 | 97.2 | 94.9 | 84.3 | 27.3 | 22.1 |
| 1969 | 80.9 | 47.7 | 69.6 | 86.6 | 96.9 | 97.0 | 94.6 | 83.4 | 27.2 | 22.0 |
| Female | | | | | | | | | | |
| 1947 | 31.8 | 29.5 | 52.3 | 44.9 | 32.0 | 36.3 | 32.7 | 24.3 | 8.1 | 11.2 |
| 1948 | 32.7 | 31.4 | 52.1 | 45.3 | 33.2 | 36.9 | 35.0 | 24.3 | 9.1 | 12.2 |
| 1949 | 33.2 | 31.2 | 53.0 | 45.0 | 33.5 | 38.1 | 35.9 | 25.3 | 9.6 | 11.8 |
| 1950 | 33.9 | 30.1 | 51.3 | 46.1 | 34.0 | 39.1 | 38.0 | 27.0 | 9.7 | 12.7 |
| 1951 | 34.7 | 32.2 | 52.7 | 46.6 | 35.4 | 39.8 | 39.7 | 27.6 | 8.9 | 11.9 |
| 1952 | 34.8 | 33.4 | 51.4 | 44.8 | 35.5 | 40.5 | 40.1 | 28.7 | 9.1 | 11.1 |
| 1953 | 34.5 | 31.0 | 50.8 | 44.5 | 34.1 | 41.3 | 40.4 | 29.1 | 10.0 | 10.8 |
| 1954 | 34.6 | 28.7 | 50.5 | 45.3 | 34.5 | 41.3 | 41.2 | 30.1 | 9.3 | 11.3 |
| 1955 | 35.7 | 28.9 | 51.0 | 46.0 | 34.9 | 41.6 | 43.8 | 32.5 | 10.6 | 11.3 |
| 1956 | 36.9 | 32.8 | 52.1 | 46.4 | 35.4 | 43.1 | 45.5 | 34.9 | 10.9 | 12.9 |
| 1957 | 36.9 | 31.1 | 51.5 | 46.0 | 35.6 | 43.3 | 46.5 | 34.5 | 10.5 | 12.5 |
| 1958 | 37.1 | 28.1 | 51.0 | 46.4 | 35.6 | 43.4 | 47.9 | 35.2 | 10.3 | 12.1 |
| 1959 | 37.2 | 28.8 | 49.1 | 45.2 | 35.4 | 43.4 | 49.0 | 36.6 | 10.2 | 12.9 |
| 1960 | 37.8 | 29.1 | 51.1 | 46.2 | 36.0 | 43.5 | 49.8 | 37.2 | 10.8 | 12.6 |
| 1961 | 38.1 | 28.5 | 51.1 | 47.1 | 36.4 | 43.8 | 50.1 | 37.9 | 10.7 | 13.1 |
| 1962 | 38.0 | 27.1 | 50.9 | 47.4 | 36.4 | 44.1 | 50.0 | 38.7 | 9.9 | 13.2 |
| 1963 | 38.3 | 27.1 | 50.6 | 47.6 | 37.2 | 44.9 | 50.6 | 39.7 | 9.6 | 11.8 |
| 1964 | 38.7 | 27.4 | 49.3 | 49.5 | 37.3 | 45.0 | 51.4 | 40.2 | 10.1 | 12.0 |
| 1965 | 39.3 | 27.7 | 49.4 | 50.0 | 38.6 | 46.1 | 50.9 | 41.1 | 10.0 | 12.2 |
| 1966 | 40.3 | 30.7 | 52.1 | 51.5 | 39.9 | 46.9 | 51.7 | 41.8 | 9.6 | 13.5 |
| 1967 | 41.1 | 31.0 | 52.3 | 53.4 | 41.9 | 48.1 | 51.8 | 42.4 | 9.6 | 14.7 |
| 1968 | 41.6 | 31.7 | 52.5 | 54.6 | 42.6 | 48.9 | 52.3 | 42.4 | 9.6 | 14.8 |
| 1969 | 42.7 | 33.7 | 53.5 | 56.8 | 43.8 | 49.9 | 53.8 | 43.1 | 9.9 | 14.8 |

[1] Percent of noninstitutional population in the labor force.

Long-Run and Short-Run Changes in the Labor Force    239

| Date | Total | No Children Under 18 Years | Children 6 to 17 Years Only | Children Under 6 Years | | |
|---|---|---|---|---|---|---|
| | | | | Total | No Children 6 to 17 Years | Children 6 to 17 Years |
| | | | Number in Labor Force (Thousands) | | | |
| April 1948 | 7,553 | 4,400 | 1,927 | 1,226 | 594 | 632 |
| April 1949 | 7,959 | 4,544 | 2,130 | 1,285 | 654 | 631 |
| March 1950 | 8,550 | 4,946 | 2,205 | 1,399 | 748 | 651 |
| April 1951 | 9,086 | 5,016 | 2,400 | 1,670 | 886 | 784 |
| April 1952 | 9,222 | 5,042 | 2,492 | 1,688 | 916 | 772 |
| April 1953 | 9,763 | 5,130 | 2,749 | 1,884 | 1,047 | 837 |
| April 1954 | 9,923 | 5,096 | 3,019 | 1,808 | 883 | 925 |
| April 1955 | 10,423 | 5,227 | 3,183 | 2,012 | 927 | 1,086 |
| March 1956 | 11,126 | 5,694 | 3,384 | 2,048 | 971 | 1,077 |
| March 1957 | 11,529 | 5,805 | 3,517 | 2,208 | 961 | 1,247 |
| March 1958 | 11,826 | 5,713 | 3,714 | 2,399 | 1,122 | 1,277 |
| March 1959 | 12,205 | 5,679 | 4,055 | 2,471 | 1,118 | 1,353 |
| March 1960 | 12,253 | 5,692 | 4,087 | 2,474 | 1,123 | 1,351 |
| March 1961 | 13,266 | 6,186 | 4,419 | 2,661 | 1,178 | 1,483 |
| March 1962 | 13,485 | 6,156 | 4,445 | 2,884 | 1,282 | 1,602 |
| March 1963 | 14,061 | 6,366 | 4,689 | 3,006 | 1,346 | 1,660 |
| March 1964 | 14,461 | 6,545 | 4,866 | 3,050 | 1,408 | 1,642 |
| March 1965 | 14,708 | 6,755 | 4,836 | 3,117 | 1,404 | 1,709 |
| March 1966 | 15,178 | 7,043 | 4,949 | 3,186 | 1,431 | 1,755 |
| March 1967 | 15,908 | 7,158 | 5,269 | 3,480 | 1,629 | 1,851 |
| March 1968 | 16,821 | 7,564 | 5,693 | 3,564 | 1,641 | 1,923 |
| March 1969 | 17,595 | 7,853 | 6,146 | 3,596 | 1,756 | 1,840 |
| | | | Labor Force Participation Rate | | | |
| April 1948 | 22.0 | 28.4 | 26.0 | 10.8 | 9.2 | 12.7 |
| April 1949 | 22.5 | 28.7 | 27.3 | 11.0 | 10.0 | 12.2 |
| March 1950 | 23.8 | 30.3 | 28.3 | 11.9 | 11.2 | 12.6 |
| April 1951 | 25.2 | 31.0 | 30.3 | 14.0 | 13.6 | 14.6 |
| April 1952 | 25.3 | 30.9 | 31.1 | 13.9 | 13.7 | 14.1 |
| April 1953 | 26.3 | 31.2 | 32.2 | 15.5 | 15.8 | 15.2 |
| April 1954 | 26.6 | 31.6 | 33.2 | 14.9 | 14.3 | 15.5 |
| April 1955 | 27.7 | 32.7 | 34.7 | 16.2 | 15.1 | 17.3 |
| March 1956 | 29.0 | 35.3 | 36.4 | 15.9 | 15.6 | 16.1 |
| March 1957 | 29.6 | 35.6 | 36.6 | 17.0 | 15.9 | 17.9 |
| March 1958 | 30.2 | 35.4 | 37.6 | 18.2 | 18.4 | 18.1 |
| March 1959 | 30.9 | 35.2 | 39.8 | 18.7 | 18.3 | 19.0 |
| March 1960 | 30.5 | 34.7 | 39.0 | 18.6 | 18.2 | 18.9 |
| March 1961 | 32.7 | 37.3 | 41.7 | 20.0 | 19.6 | 20.3 |
| March 1962 | 32.7 | 36.1 | 41.8 | 21.3 | 21.1 | 21.5 |
| March 1963 | 33.7 | 37.4 | 41.5 | 22.5 | 22.4 | 22.5 |
| March 1964 | 34.4 | 37.8 | 43.0 | 22.7 | 23.6 | 21.9 |
| March 1965 | 34.7 | 38.3 | 42.7 | 23.3 | 23.8 | 22.8 |
| March 1966 | 35.4 | 38.4 | 43.7 | 24.2 | 24.0 | 24.3 |
| March 1967 | 36.8 | 38.9 | 45.0 | 26.5 | 26.9 | 26.2 |
| March 1968 | 38.3 | 40.1 | 46.9 | 27.6 | 27.8 | 27.4 |
| March 1969 | 39.6 | 41.0 | 48.6 | 28.5 | 29.3 | 27.8 |

[1] Percent of civilian population in the labor force.

**TABLE 4. EMPLOYED PERSONS 16 YEARS AND OVER BY OCCUPATION GROUP AND SEX: ANNUAL AVERAGES 1958-69[1]**

| Sex and Year | Total Employed | White-Collar Workers | | | | | Blue-Collar Workers | | | | Service Workers | | | Farm Workers | | |
|---|---|---|---|---|---|---|---|---|---|---|---|---|---|---|---|---|
| | | Total | Professional and Technical | Managers, Officials, and Proprietors | Clerical Workers | Sales Workers | Total | Craftsmen and Foremen | Operatives | Nonfarm Laborers | Total | Private Household Workers | Other Service Workers | Total | Farmers and Farm Managers | Farm laborers and Foremen |
| Both sexes | | | | | | | Percent Distribution | | | | | | | | | |
| 1958 | 100.0 | 42.6 | 11.0 | 10.8 | 14.5 | 6.3 | 37.0 | 13.4 | 18.1 | 5.5 | 11.9 | 3.1 | 8.8 | 8.5 | 4.9 | 3.6 |
| 1959 | 100.0 | 42.7 | 11.0 | 10.7 | 14.4 | 6.5 | 37.1 | 13.2 | 18.3 | 5.6 | 11.9 | 3.0 | 8.9 | 8.3 | 4.7 | 3.6 |
| 1960 | 100.0 | 43.4 | 11.4 | 10.7 | 14.8 | 6.4 | 36.6 | 13.0 | 18.2 | 5.4 | 12.2 | 3.0 | 9.2 | 7.9 | 4.2 | 3.5 |
| 1961 | 100.0 | 43.9 | 11.7 | 10.8 | 15.0 | 6.4 | 36.0 | 13.1 | 17.8 | 5.1 | 12.2 | 3.1 | 9.5 | 7.5 | 4.1 | 3.4 |
| 1962 | 100.0 | 44.4 | 12.0 | 11.1 | 15.1 | 6.2 | 36.1 | 13.0 | 18.0 | 5.1 | 12.6 | 3.0 | 9.5 | 6.9 | 3.9 | 3.1 |
| 1963 | 100.0 | 44.2 | 12.2 | 10.8 | 15.1 | 6.1 | 36.6 | 13.2 | 18.4 | 5.0 | 12.8 | 3.0 | 9.8 | 6.4 | 3.5 | 2.9 |
| 1964 | 100.0 | 44.5 | 12.3 | 10.7 | 15.3 | 6.1 | 36.6 | 13.0 | 18.6 | 5.0 | 12.8 | 2.9 | 9.9 | 6.1 | 3.3 | 2.7 |
| 1965 | 100.0 | 44.8 | 12.5 | 10.3 | 15.7 | 6.3 | 36.9 | 13.0 | 18.8 | 5.2 | 12.6 | 2.8 | 9.8 | 5.7 | 3.1 | 2.6 |
| 1966 | 100.0 | 45.4 | 12.8 | 10.2 | 16.2 | 6.2 | 37.0 | 13.2 | 19.0 | 4.8 | 12.6 | 2.6 | 10.0 | 5.0 | 2.9 | 2.2 |
| 1967 | 100.0 | 46.0 | 13.3 | 10.1 | 16.6 | 6.1 | 36.7 | 13.2 | 18.7 | 4.8 | 12.5 | 2.4 | 10.2 | 4.8 | 2.6 | 2.1 |
| 1968 | 100.0 | 46.8 | 13.6 | 10.2 | 16.9 | 6.1 | 36.3 | 13.2 | 18.4 | 4.7 | 12.4 | 2.3 | 10.1 | 4.6 | 2.5 | 2.0 |
| 1969 | 100.0 | 47.3 | 13.8 | 10.2 | 17.2 | 6.0 | 36.2 | 13.1 | 18.4 | 4.7 | 12.2 | 2.1 | 10.1 | 4.2 | 2.4 | 1.9 |
| Male | | | | | | | | | | | | | | | | |
| 1958 | 100.0 | 36.5 | 10.4 | 13.6 | 6.9 | 5.7 | 46.8 | 19.4 | 19.4 | 8.0 | 6.4 | .1 | 6.3 | 10.4 | 7.0 | 3.4 |
| 1959 | 100.0 | 36.8 | 10.5 | 13.5 | 6.9 | 5.9 | 47.0 | 19.2 | 19.7 | 8.1 | 6.3 | .1 | 6.2 | 10.0 | 6.7 | 3.3 |
| 1960 | 100.0 | 37.4 | 10.9 | 13.6 | 7.2 | 5.8 | 46.5 | 19.0 | 19.6 | 7.9 | 6.5 | .1 | 6.4 | 9.6 | 6.1 | 3.5 |
| 1961 | 100.0 | 38.1 | 11.3 | 13.7 | 7.1 | 5.8 | 46.0 | 19.2 | 19.2 | 7.5 | 6.7 | .1 | 6.6 | 9.3 | 5.9 | 3.4 |
| 1962 | 100.0 | 38.5 | 11.7 | 14.2 | 7.1 | 5.5 | 46.1 | 19.1 | 19.5 | 7.5 | 6.7 | .1 | 6.6 | 8.6 | 5.6 | 3.1 |
| 1963 | 100.0 | 38.2 | 11.9 | 13.8 | 7.0 | 5.5 | 46.9 | 19.4 | 20.1 | 7.4 | 6.9 | .1 | 6.8 | 7.9 | 5.1 | 2.9 |
| 1964 | 100.0 | 38.4 | 12.0 | 13.9 | 7.0 | 5.5 | 47.0 | 19.2 | 20.3 | 7.5 | 7.0 | .1 | 6.9 | 7.6 | 4.8 | 2.8 |
| 1965 | 100.0 | 38.3 | 12.1 | 13.4 | 7.1 | 5.7 | 47.7 | 19.3 | 20.7 | 7.7 | 6.9 | .1 | 6.8 | 7.1 | 4.5 | 2.6 |
| 1966 | 100.0 | 38.6 | 12.4 | 13.3 | 7.1 | 5.7 | 48.0 | 19.9 | 20.8 | 7.3 | 7.1 | .1 | 7.0 | 6.4 | 4.2 | 2.2 |
| 1967 | 100.0 | 39.0 | 13.0 | 13.3 | 7.2 | 5.5 | 47.8 | 20.1 | 20.4 | 7.2 | 7.0 | .1 | 7.0 | 6.2 | 3.9 | 2.2 |
| 1968 | 100.0 | 39.7 | 13.4 | 13.6 | 7.1 | 5.7 | 47.4 | 20.2 | 20.1 | 7.1 | 6.9 | .1 | 6.8 | 6.0 | 3.8 | 2.1 |
| 1969 | 100.0 | 40.1 | 13.8 | 13.8 | 7.0 | 5.5 | 47.7 | 20.2 | 20.2 | 7.2 | 6.7 | .1 | 6.6 | 5.6 | 3.6 | 2.0 |
| Female | | | | | | | | | | | | | | | | |
| 1958 | 100.0 | 55.1 | 12.3 | 5.0 | 30.1 | 7.6 | 17.1 | 1.1 | 15.5 | .5 | 23.2 | 9.4 | 13.8 | 4.7 | .6 | 4.1 |
| 1959 | 100.0 | 54.9 | 12.1 | 5.1 | 29.9 | 7.8 | 16.9 | 1.0 | 15.4 | .5 | 23.5 | 9.0 | 14.4 | 4.8 | .6 | 4.2 |
| 1960 | 100.0 | 55.3 | 12.4 | 5.0 | 30.3 | 7.7 | 16.6 | 1.0 | 15.2 | .4 | 23.7 | 8.9 | 14.8 | 4.4 | .5 | 3.9 |
| 1961 | 100.0 | 55.6 | 12.4 | 5.1 | 30.5 | 7.6 | 16.4 | 1.0 | 15.0 | .3 | 24.2 | 9.0 | 15.2 | 3.9 | .6 | 3.3 |
| 1962 | 100.0 | 56.1 | 12.7 | 5.0 | 30.9 | 7.5 | 16.3 | 1.0 | 15.0 | .4 | 24.0 | 8.8 | 15.2 | 3.6 | .6 | 3.0 |
| 1963 | 100.0 | 55.8 | 12.8 | 4.8 | 30.9 | 7.3 | 16.5 | 1.0 | 15.1 | .4 | 24.1 | 8.6 | 15.5 | 3.5 | .6 | 3.0 |
| 1964 | 100.0 | 56.1 | 13.0 | 4.6 | 31.2 | 7.3 | 16.7 | 1.0 | 15.3 | .4 | 23.9 | 8.4 | 15.5 | 3.3 | .6 | 2.7 |
| 1965 | 100.0 | 57.0 | 13.2 | 4.5 | 31.8 | 7.5 | 16.7 | 1.1 | 15.2 | .4 | 23.2 | 7.7 | 15.5 | 3.1 | .6 | 2.5 |
| 1966 | 100.0 | 57.6 | 13.4 | 4.5 | 32.6 | 7.2 | 17.1 | 1.0 | 15.7 | .4 | 22.7 | 7.2 | 15.5 | 2.6 | .5 | 2.1 |
| 1967 | 100.0 | 58.4 | 13.7 | 4.4 | 33.2 | 7.1 | 17.0 | 1.0 | 15.3 | .5 | 22.3 | 6.5 | 15.8 | 2.3 | .4 | 1.9 |
| 1968 | 100.0 | 59.1 | 13.9 | 4.5 | 33.8 | 6.9 | 16.9 | 1.1 | 15.3 | .5 | 21.8 | 6.1 | 15.8 | 2.1 | .3 | 1.8 |
| 1969 | 100.0 | 59.4 | 13.8 | 4.3 | 34.3 | 6.9 | 17.1 | 1.2 | 15.4 | .5 | 21.6 | 5.5 | 16.1 | 2.0 | .3 | 1.7 |

[1] Data for persons 16 years and over are not available prior to 1958. The lower age limit for the inclusion of persons in labor force statistics was raised from 14 to 16 years of age beginning with the publication of data for 1967, and revisions of occupational data were not possible back to 1947.

These data from 1958 forward are revised from those first published after the age minimum was raised. More exact adjustments for 14- and 15-year-olds were developed in 1969 than were available earlier (see the December 1969 issue of *Employment and Earnings* for a more detailed explanation). The occupational data by color shown in table A–10 are consistent with these revised data.

TABLE 5. YEARS OF SCHOOL COMPLETED BY THE CIVILIAN LABOR FORCE 18 YEARS AND OVER, BY SEX AND COLOR, SELECTED DATES, 1952–69

| Sex, Color, and Date | Total, 18 Years and Over (Thousands) | Percent Distribution | | | | | | | | Median School Years Completed |
| | | Total | Elementary | | High School | | College | | School Years Not Reported | |
| | | | Less than 5 Years[1] | 5 to 8 Years | 1 to 3 Years | 4 Years | 1 to 3 Years | 4 Years or More | | |
| **Both sexes** | | | | | | | | | | |
| *Total* | | | | | | | | | | |
| October 1952 | 60,772 | 100.0 | 7.3 | 30.2 | 18.5 | 26.6 | 8.3 | 7.9 | 1.2 | 10.9 |
| March 1957 | 64,384 | 100.0 | 6.1 | 26.8 | 19.1 | 29.1 | 8.5 | 9.0 | 1.4 | 11.6 |
| March 1959 | 65,842 | 100.0 | 5.2 | 24.8 | 19.5 | 30.3 | 9.2 | 9.5 | 1.6 | 12.0 |
| March 1962 | 67,988 | 100.0 | 4.6 | 22.4 | 19.3 | 32.1 | 10.7 | 11.0 | (2) | 12.1 |
| March 1964 | 69,926 | 100.0 | 3.7 | 20.9 | 19.2 | 34.5 | 10.6 | 11.2 | (2) | 12.2 |
| March 1965 | 71,129 | 100.0 | 3.7 | 19.6 | 19.2 | 35.5 | 10.5 | 11.6 | (2) | 12.2 |
| March 1966 | 71,958 | 100.0 | 3.3 | 18.9 | 19.0 | 36.3 | 10.8 | 11.8 | (2) | 12.2 |
| March 1967 | 73,218 | 100.0 | 3.1 | 17.9 | 18.7 | 36.6 | 11.8 | 12.0 | (2) | 12.3 |
| March 1968 | 75,101 | 100.0 | 2.9 | 16.8 | 18.2 | 37.5 | 12.2 | 12.4 | (2) | 12.3 |
| March 1969 | 76,753 | 100.0 | 2.7 | 15.9 | 17.8 | 38.4 | 12.6 | 12.6 | (2) | 12.4 |
| *White* | | | | | | | | | | |
| October 1952 | (3) | 100.0 | 5.2 | 29.3 | 18.7 | 28.3 | 8.8 | 8.5 | 1.2 | 11.4 |
| March 1957 | (3) | 100.0 | 4.3 | 25.8 | 19.0 | 30.8 | 9.0 | 9.7 | 1.2 | 12.1 |
| March 1959 | 58,726 | 100.0 | 3.7 | 23.6 | 19.4 | 32.0 | 9.7 | 10.2 | 1.4 | 12.1 |
| March 1962 | 60,451 | 100.0 | 3.3 | 21.4 | 18.8 | 33.5 | 11.3 | 11.8 | (2) | 12.2 |
| March 1964 | 62,213 | 100.0 | 2.7 | 19.8 | 18.5 | 36.0 | 11.1 | 11.9 | (2) | 12.2 |
| March 1965 | 63,261 | 100.0 | 2.7 | 18.9 | 18.4 | 36.8 | 11.0 | 12.2 | (2) | 12.3 |
| March 1966 | 63,958 | 100.0 | 2.3 | 17.8 | 18.3 | 37.7 | 11.2 | 12.5 | (2) | 12.3 |
| March 1967 | 65,076 | 100.0 | 2.2 | 16.9 | 18.1 | 37.7 | 12.4 | 12.8 | (2) | 12.3 |
| March 1968 | 66,721 | 100.0 | 1.9 | 16.1 | 17.4 | 38.6 | 12.8 | 13.2 | (2) | 12.4 |
| March 1969 | 68,300 | 100.0 | 2.0 | 15.1 | 16.9 | 39.7 | 13.0 | 13.4 | (2) | 12.4 |

[1] Includes persons reporting no school year completed.
[2] Data for persons whose educational attainment was not reported were distributed among the other categories.
[3] Not available; data published as percent distribution only.

TABLE 6. TOTAL POPULATION,[1] TOTAL LABOR FORCE, AND LABOR FORCE PARTICIPATION RATES, BY SEX AND AGE, 1960 TO 1980

[Numbers in Thousands]

| Sex and Age | Total Population, July 1 | | | | | Total Labor Force, Annual Averages | | | | | Labor Force Participation Rates, Annual Averages (percent) | | | | |
|---|---|---|---|---|---|---|---|---|---|---|---|---|---|---|---|
| | Actual | | | Projected | | Actual | | | Projected | | Actual | | | Projected | |
| | 1960 | 1965 | 1970 | 1975 | 1980 | 1960[2] | 1965 | 1970 | 1975 | 1980 | 1960 | 1965 | 1970 | 1975 | 1980 |
| **Both Sexes** | | | | | | | | | | | | | | | |
| 16 years and over | 121,817 | 131,184 | 141,713 | 153,627 | 165,473 | 72,104 | 77,177 | 84,617 | 92,183 | 99,942 | 59.2 | 58.8 | 59.7 | 60.0 | 60.4 |
| **Male** | | | | | | | | | | | | | | | |
| 16 years and over | 59,420 | 63,608 | 68,485 | 74,127 | 79,824 | 48,933 | 50,946 | 54,960 | 59,356 | 64,061 | 82.4 | 80.1 | 80.3 | 80.1 | 80.3 |
| 16 to 19 years | 5,398 | 6,880 | 7,587 | 8,302 | 8,510 | 3,162 | 3,831 | 4,280 | 4,664 | 4,824 | 58.6 | 55.7 | 56.4 | 56.2 | 56.7 |
| 20 to 24 years | 5,553 | 6,872 | 8,621 | 9,609 | 10,394 | 4,939 | 5,926 | 7,466 | 8,331 | 9,064 | 88.9 | 86.2 | 86.6 | 86.7 | 87.2 |
| 25 to 34 years | 11,347 | 11,091 | 12,540 | 15,557 | 18,285 | 10,940 | 10,653 | 12,063 | 14,966 | 17,590 | 96.4 | 96.0 | 96.2 | 96.2 | 96.2 |
| 35 to 44 years | 11,878 | 11,962 | 11,303 | 11,068 | 12,496 | 11,454 | 11,504 | 10,930 | 10,703 | 12,084 | 96.4 | 96.2 | 96.7 | 96.7 | 96.7 |
| 45 to 54 years | 10,148 | 10,740 | 11,289 | 11,379 | 10,757 | 9,568 | 10,131 | 10,725 | 10,810 | 10,219 | 94.3 | 94.3 | 95.0 | 95.0 | 95.0 |
| 55 to 64 years | 7,564 | 8,131 | 8,759 | 9,287 | 9,776 | 6,445 | 6,768 | 7,388 | 7,795 | 8,184 | 85.2 | 83.2 | 84.3 | 83.9 | 83.7 |
| 55 to 59 years | 4,144 | 4,421 | 4,794 | 4,990 | 5,296 | 3,727 | 3,929 | 4,339 | 4,516 | 4,793 | 89.9 | 88.9 | 90.5 | 90.5 | 90.5 |
| 60 to 64 years | 3,420 | 3,710 | 3,965 | 4,297 | 4,480 | 2,718 | 2,839 | 3,049 | 3,279 | 3,391 | 79.5 | 76.5 | 76.9 | 76.3 | 75.7 |
| 65 years and over | 7,530 | 7,932 | 8,385 | 8,923 | 9,606 | 2,425 | 2,131 | 2,108 | 2,087 | 2,096 | 32.2 | 26.9 | 25.1 | 23.4 | 21.8 |
| 65 to 69 years | 2,941 | 2,871 | 3,137 | 3,362 | 3,651 | 1,348 | 1,209 | 1,142 | 1,136 | 1,143 | 45.8 | 42.1 | 36.4 | 33.8 | 31.3 |
| 70 years and over | 4,590 | 5,061 | 5,248 | 5,561 | 5,955 | 1,077 | 922 | 966 | 951 | 953 | 23.5 | 18.2 | 18.4 | 17.1 | 16.0 |
| **Female** | | | | | | | | | | | | | | | |
| 16 years and over | 62,397 | 67,578 | 73,228 | 79,500 | 85,649 | 23,171 | 26,232 | 29,657 | 32,827 | 35,881 | 37.1 | 38.8 | 40.5 | 41.3 | 41.9 |
| 16 to 19 years | 5,275 | 6,681 | 7,375 | 8,081 | 8,221 | 2,061 | 2,519 | 2,908 | 3,201 | 3,286 | 39.1 | 37.7 | 39.4 | 39.6 | 40.0 |
| 20 to 24 years | 5,547 | 6,796 | 8,483 | 9,446 | 10,230 | 2,558 | 3,375 | 4,267 | 4,865 | 5,380 | 46.1 | 49.7 | 50.3 | 51.5 | 52.6 |
| 25 to 34 years | 11,605 | 11,267 | 12,680 | 15,582 | 18,232 | 4,159 | 4,336 | 4,894 | 6,124 | 7,347 | 35.8 | 38.5 | 38.6 | 39.3 | 40.3 |
| 35 to 44 years | 12,348 | 12,470 | 11,694 | 11,391 | 12,771 | 5,325 | 5,724 | 5,555 | 5,582 | 6,386 | 43.1 | 45.9 | 47.5 | 49.0 | 50.0 |
| 45 to 54 years | 10,438 | 11,304 | 12,071 | 12,195 | 11,437 | 5,150 | 5,714 | 6,675 | 7,024 | 6,805 | 49.3 | 50.5 | 55.3 | 57.6 | 59.5 |
| 55 to 64 years | 8,070 | 8,835 | 9,741 | 10,558 | 11,279 | 2,964 | 3,587 | 4,267 | 4,826 | 5,337 | 36.7 | 40.6 | 43.8 | 45.7 | 47.3 |
| 55 to 59 years | 4,321 | 4,736 | 5,252 | 5,577 | 5,983 | 1,803 | 2,209 | 2,705 | 3,023 | 3,362 | 41.7 | 46.6 | 51.5 | 54.2 | 56.2 |
| 60 to 64 years | 3,749 | 4,099 | 4,489 | 4,981 | 5,296 | 1,161 | 1,378 | 1,562 | 1,803 | 1,975 | 31.0 | 33.6 | 34.8 | 36.2 | 37.3 |
| 65 years and over | 9,115 | 10,225 | 11,186 | 12,248 | 13,481 | 954 | 976 | 1,091 | 1,205 | 1,340 | 10.5 | 9.5 | 9.8 | 9.8 | 9.9 |
| 65 to 69 years | 3,347 | 3,427 | 3,755 | 4,122 | 4,580 | 579 | 585 | 653 | 717 | 797 | 17.3 | 17.1 | 17.4 | 17.4 | 17.4 |
| 70 years and over | 5,768 | 6,798 | 7,431 | 8,126 | 8,901 | 375 | 391 | 438 | 488 | 543 | 6.5 | 5.8 | 5.9 | 6.0 | 6.1 |

1 These population data (and those in table E-4) differ from the figures shown in the preceding table and elsewhere in this report because they are based on earlier population estimates and projections.

2 These data differ from the figures for the same age groups published in section A because they are based on different population estimates.

SOURCE: Population data from the U.S. Department of Commerce, Bureau of the Census, Current Population Reports, Series P-25: for 1960, No. 241; for 1965, unpublished estimates; for 1970–80, No. 286, Series B. All other data from the U.S. Department of Labor, Bureau of Labor Statistics.

TABLE 7. ACTUAL AND PROJECTED EMPLOYMENT FOR PERSONS 16 YEARS AND OVER, BY OCCUPATION GROUP, 1960 TO 1975

| Occupation Group | Actual 1960 | | Actual 1965 | | Projected[1] 1975 | | Number Change (Millions)[2] | | Percent Change[2] | |
|---|---|---|---|---|---|---|---|---|---|---|
| | Number (thousands) | Percent Distribution | Number (thousands) | Percent Distribution | Number (millions) | Percent Distribution[2] | 1960–65 | 1965–75 | 1960–65 | 1965–75 |
| Total employment[3] | 65,777 | 100.0 | 71,088 | 100.0 | 87.2 | 100.0 | 5.3 | 16.1 | 8.1 | 22.7 |
| Professional and technical workers | 7,474 | 11.4 | 8,883 | 12.5 | 12.9 | 14.8 | 1.4 | 4.0 | 18.9 | 45.2 |
| Managers, officials, and proprietors | 7,067 | 10.7 | 7,340 | 10.3 | 9.0 | 10.4 | .3 | 1.7 | 3.9 | 23.3 |
| Clerical workers | 9,759 | 14.8 | 11,129 | 15.7 | 14.8 | 16.9 | 1.4 | 3.6 | 14.0 | 32.5 |
| Sales workers | 4,216 | 6.4 | 4,497 | 6.3 | 5.6 | 6.4 | .3 | 1.1 | 6.7 | 25.0 |
| Craftsmen and foremen | 8,560 | 13.0 | 9,222 | 13.0 | 11.4 | 13.0 | .7 | 2.1 | 7.7 | 23.1 |
| Operatives | 11,950 | 18.2 | 13,336 | 18.8 | 14.7 | 16.9 | 1.4 | 1.4 | 11.6 | 10.5 |
| Service workers | 8,031 | 12.2 | 8,936 | 12.6 | 12.0 | 13.8 | .9 | 3.1 | 11.3 | 34.4 |
| Nonfarm laborers | 3,557 | 5.4 | 3,688 | 5.2 | 3.6 | 4.1 | .1 | —.1 | 3.7 | [4]—2.4 |
| Farmers and farm laborers | 5,163 | 7.8 | 4,057 | 5.7 | 3.2 | 3.6 | —1.1 | —.9 | —21.4 | —21.6 |

[1] These projections of civilian employment assume 3 percent unemployment whereas the projections of total labor force shown in the preceding tables are consistent with 4 percent unemployment. The lower unemployment assumption implies a slightly larger labor force; e.g., the total labor force in 1975 at 3 percent unemployment would be about 92.6 million as compared with 92.2 million at 4 percent unemployment.
[2] Based on data in thousands.
[3] Represents total employment as covered by the Current Population Survey.
[4] Employment is projected at about the level of the past decade; however, because 1965 employment was unusually high, reflecting a sharp increase in manufacturing, the projected percent change from 1965 indicates an apparent decline.

pansion. All in all, if the projections are accurate, the labor force needs will place a further demand for skills, education, and training, with opportunities narrowing for the undereducated and untrained, except in some service industries. The "manpower revolution" is becoming a long-term way of work life.

### Short-Run Participation

Looking at the short-run behavior of work-force membership, conflicting forces lead to contradictory theories and interpretations of the data regarding the behavior of labor force participation during recessions and high prosperity. All students of the issue agree that participation of prime-aged males is essentially unaffected by the level of business activity, so that it is the magnitude of the secondary work force that forms the subject of controversy.

In a depression, job opportunities are scarce, and to the degree that the secondary work force responds to the level of job availability, the unfavorable climate for finding work would act to reduce their participation. This is known as the "discouraged worker" effect—the tendency for those with a slighter attachment to the work force to move towards housework, school, or retirement, and away from a probably futile search for work. At the same time, the loss of family income, experienced by unemployment or reduced hours of the principal breadwinner, tends to induce the participation of secondary workers in job search in order to, at least partially, restore family income and maintain consumption standards. This is known as the "additional worker" effect.

The fact that views differ as to which influence is greater, or whether they are more or less offsetting, can only reflect uncertainty regarding the data, or use of different time periods to substantiate the theory. In any case, the issue is more than academic in that the effect of policy measures to stimulate the economy would have differing effects on the level of unemployment, depending on whether the "additional worker" or "discouraged worker" influence prevailed.

If the labor force increased as the depression deepened because additional workers began seeking jobs to supplement dwindling family income, then when recovery set in, the labor force would decline as the pressure for supplemental family income relaxed. Thus, under such a pattern, advancement of the economy from bad times would be accompanied by a greater decline in unemployment than the rise in employment.

This means that insofar as unemployment reduction is a major goal of recovery, its achievement would be easier the more significant the "additional worker" role in the labor force. Alternatively, though, any tendency for the economy to recede toward very low levels would be accompanied by an even steeper rise in the level of unemployment. In short, the movement of "additional workers" into and out of the labor force, being out of phase with the economic cycle, would lead to wider fluctuation in unemployment than in employment levels or in economic conditions in general.

Obviously, the situation would be reversed if the secondary work force were composed mainly of those more sensitive to job availability than to family income levels, the "discouraged worker" of bad times. Then the labor force participation of secondary workers would be in phase with the cycle, the fluctuations in unemployment would be less than those of employment, and recovery in the economy would find the accompanying reduction in unemployment retarded by the reentry of formerly "discouraged" secondary workers into the labor force.

W.S. Woytinsky, in *Additional Workers and the Volume of Unemployment in the Depression,* offers the most noted presentation of the "additional worker" argument. The beginning section of this work, discussed here, contains Woytinsky's conclusions and method of estimating the volume of "additional workers."

In the depressed 1930's, Woytinsky estimated the "additional workers" at from 10 to 25 percent of the work force. Thus the unemployment level during the period would increase by from 1100 to 1250 for every 1000 increase in the usual work force.

Woytinsky's indirect method of estimation of the secondary work force's contribution to unemployment by comparing household with individual unemployment rates, and one-worker with multiple-worker family unemployment rates, has been subject to the criticism that multiple-worker households contain secondary workers who are always more susceptible to unemployment than primary workers. To test Woytinsky's hypothesis requires a comparison of relative unemployment rates between good years and bad for single- and multiple-worker families to find whether the spread increased as the economy worsened.* Study of only depression years with noncontinuous data did not permit Woytinsky to make this test.

Using a different method for testing the two theories, Long, in Chapter 10 of *The Labor Force Under Changing Income and Employment,* found that there was no significant change in overall labor force participation in the census year 1940, a depressed year, from moderately depressed 1930 and 1950. This finding suggested the hypothesis that the "additional worker" entering the labor force and the "discouraged worker" leaving more or less offset each other.

Woytinsky claimed that the "additional worker" hypothesis applies only to severe depressions. The logic of this limitation suggests that when cuts in family income are severe and protracted, the need to find work for any member of the household overcomes whatever reluctance may impede the attempt to search for scarce work by family members not customarily in the labor force. Implied in this view is that under less than severely depressed conditions, the pressures for family income from the secondary worker, being on the average less significant, would be balanced by the normal reluctance of marginal workers to enter the labor market when jobs are scarce.

In his study of the milder post-World War II recessions, W. Lee Hansen, in "The Cyclical Sensitivity of the Labor Supply," included here, finds relative constancy in total supply during the period. Entrances into the labor force in recessionary periods were balanced by withdrawals of "discouraged" workers. Hansen feels that his findings support Long's position, that forces which tend

---

* Even this test assumes constant relative rates between primary and secondary workers over the cycle.

to increase and decrease the participation of secondary workers during recessions tend to offset each other. But he concludes that the mildness of the postwar recessions might have been an important factor explaining "the failure of individuals to respond in substantial numbers to increases in the level of unemployment, either by entering the labor force to seek employment or by withdrawing because no jobs can be found."

# The Cyclical Sensitivity of the Labor Supply

*by W. Lee Hansen*

Recent detailed investigations indicate that the percentage of persons in the civilian labor force remains relatively constant in the long run and is only slightly responsive, if at all, to changes in income and employment. However, there is as yet considerably less agreement on the short-run, cyclical behavior of the aggregate labor supply, particularly as it affects the level of unemployment when aggregate demand declines. Much of the discussion centers on precisely how the labor force attachment of "fringe" workers—students, older workers, and especially housewives —varies with changes in the level of business activity.[1] Although a number of hypotheses have been advanced to suggest the kinds of changes that may occur and

the reasons for such changes, the evidence offered in support of these hypotheses thus far has been inconclusive. Hence, in this paper an attempt is made to examine some rather neglected labor force data— the "gross change" data—in an effort to evaluate for the postwar period the validity of two of these hypotheses in particular.

## TWO HYPOTHESES

The disagreement as to how the supply of labor varies in the short run may be illustrated by citing two of the hypotheses offered to explain the higher than "normal" unemployment levels during recent recessions. Some commentators conjec-

SOURCE Reprinted with permission from *American Economic Review*, Vol. 51, June 1961, pp. 299–309.

[1] As an example, Wool states that ". . . the systematic inclusion within the labor force of 'fringe' groups has resulted in a high degree of seasonality in the labor force totals . . . and has tended to make the series relatively sensitive to cyclical changes in the level of labor demand." For a recent discussion of the role of fringe or secondary workers, see Wilcock.

tured that as unemployment mounted, a large-scale and presumably temporary influx into the labor force of fringe workers who hoped to augment family incomes exaggerated the magnitude of unemployment. Others disagreed, maintaining that the unemployment totals were understated because of the rapid withdrawal from the labor force of "discouraged" work seekers, i.e., those who finally gave up their unsuccessful search for work. Two other hypotheses relate to periods of prosperity but they are not examined here.[2]

That the level of unemployment in depressed periods may be greatly affected by entry into and exit from the labor force is by no means a recent notion. Its origins go back to the 1930's, when Woytinsky advanced his so-called "additional worker" theory, holding that in periods of depression the ranks of the unemployed are swelled by the entrance of family members seeking jobs because of the unemployment of the primary earner in the family. But, later, Long suggested that even though additional work-seekers may appear in the market in periods of slack demand, their influence upon the unemployment totals will be offset, either completely, or in large part, by those who become too discouraged to continue looking for work. Although these hypotheses were originally designed to throw light on the depression-unemployment experience of the 1930's, their plausibility has caused them to be extended to the recent recessions as well.

Which of these hypotheses is correct is of considerable importance in formulating antirecession policies. If fringe workers do enter the labor force but fail to find employment, thereby increasing the number of unemployed in depressed periods, it seems likely that the pressures for prompt

and large-scale offsetting action by the government to alleviate these conditions will be accentuated. Yet, if this offsetting action should be designed to cope with total recorded unemployment, it may needlessly overshoot the mark. This would occur because as primary workers become re-employed the additional work-seekers are likely simply to withdraw from the labor force. If, however, the influx of additional workers counterbalances the outflow of discouraged workers, no such problem arises.

The kind of evidence required to test these two hypotheses cannot be found in the aggregate labor force statistics; for these statistics provide no indication of the size and pattern of the flows of individuals into and out of the labor force and into and out of employment and unemployment. They cannot tell, for example, how much of any increase in unemployment arises from the disemployment of workers and how much should be ascribed to the enry into the labor force of fringe workers. Nor do they indicate how many of the previously unemployed have been re-employed and how many others have dropped out of the labor market completely.

What is needed are data on gross changes in the labor supply which show the gross movements from month to month of individuals into and out of the labor force and into and out of the employed and unemployed categories. Through casual observation alone, one cannot help being aware of these continuing movements. Young persons graduate from school and seek permanent jobs; others withdraw from the labor force to marry or retire; some people intermittently hold part-time jobs; and still others change jobs or become temporarily unemployed. The way in which these gross

[2] These hypotheses are: (1) fringe workers are attracted in the labor force and hence into employment because of the ease with which they can find jobs; and (2) rising incomes of primary wage-earners enable fringe workers to withdraw from the labor force and employment because it is no longer necessary for them to supplement the family income.

changes vary differentially in response to cyclical changes in demand will determine net changes, and through these the absolute levels of the labor force, employment, and unemployment.

Gross change data are derived from the monthly Current Population Survey conducted by the Bureau of the Census (since 1959 under contract with the Bureau of Labor Statistics). They reflect changes in the labor-force status of individuals within the civilian noninstitutional population from one month to the next. Changes are expressed as "additions" to and "reductions" in the labor force and its components, employment and unemployment. In the case of unemployment, the relationship can be put as follows:

$$U_1 + DE + \underbrace{A}_{H+S+O} - RE - \underbrace{R}_{H+S+O} = U_2$$

where $U_1$ and $U_2$ represent the numbers of unemployed in two successive months. $DE$ is the disemployed, $A$ is the additions to unemployment from outside the labor force, $RE$ is the re-employed, and $R$ is the reduction in unemployment owing to withdrawal from the labor force. In each case the additions ($A$) and reductions ($R$) are classified by prior or subsequent status, respectively, i.e., keeping house ($H$), in school ($S$), or "other" ($O$).[3] These changes are measured by comparing the labor-force status of respondents who are in the sample for two consecutive months. Despite certain deficiencies, the regularity of the patterns observed suggests that these data can be of use in an analysis such as this.[4]

Regular publication of these data began in May 1948 and continued through December 1952. Since that time the data have not been published regularly.[5] The principal reason for this lapse is that the Bureau of the Census, and since July 1959 the Bureau of Labor Statistics, have been examining intensively certain of the estimation problems and biases in the data. However, unpublished data for the period beginning in early 1954 through 1959 have been made available for use in preparing this paper.[6]

## THE IMPACT OF GROSS CHANGE MOVEMENTS ON UNEMPLOYMENT

Before the gross change data are examined, the behavior of the civilian labor force and the level of unemployment from 1948 through 1959 should be briefly reviewed. From 1948 through 1959, the civilian labor force grew from 61 to 69 million persons, while unemployment ranged from yearly averages of 1.9 to 4.7 million persons, with wider variations observable in specific months.[7] During this period, the civilian labor force as a percentage of the civilian noninstitutional population over age 14 remained relatively constant, ranging from 57.9 to 58.9

---

[3] Unfortunately, the "other" category is otherwise undefined; usually about one-third of both additions and reductions are moving from or into the "other" category.

[4] Besides the usual conceptual difficulties and problems of reliability associated with labor force data, biases may appear because less than the full sample is used. For example, only about 65 per cent of the total sample is common to both months; 25 per cent drop out because of sample rotation, and the remaining 10 per cent are not successfully interviewed, primarily because they moved into or out of a sample household between the two interview dates. In addition, because of the gross nature of these data, errors of response may loom rather large and are unlikely to cancel out. Furthermore, the data provide no indication of multiple moves by individuals within periods; only the initial and final status are reflected in the data. Nor can monthly gross changes be cumulated to give gross changes for the year because some individuals change their status several times.

[5] Some more recent, but incomplete, data have appeared.

[6] Data for 1953 and the first month of 1954 are not available because of the difficulties of making them comparable with earlier and later data.

[7] These figures and those given below are based upon the "new definitions."

| Line No. | Category | 1948–49 | | 1953–54 | | 1957–58 | | 1959 |
| | | Peak Nov. '48 | Trough Oct. '49 | Peak Oct. '52 | Trough Apr. '54 | Peak July '57 | Trough Apr. '58 | Peak [a] Oct. '59 |
| --- | --- | --- | --- | --- | --- | --- | --- | --- |
| 1 | Unemployment | 4.2 | 7.1 | 2.8 | 5.9 | 4.3 | 7.2 | 5.8 |
| 2a | Gross additions to unemployment | 1.9 | 2.9 | 1.6 | 2.4 | 2.1 | 3.1 | 2.9 |
| 2b | Gross reductions in unemployment | 1.6 | 2.8 | 1.6 | 2.4 | 2.4 | 3.1 | 2.8 |
| 3a | Gross additions to unemployment from outside the labor force | 0.5 | 0.8 | 0.6 | 0.8 | 0.8 | 1.2 | 1.1 |
| 3b | Gross reductions in unemployment owing to withdrawals from the labor force | 0.5 | 0.7 | 0.6 | 0.8 | 0.8 | 1.0 | 1.0 |
| 4a | Gross additions to unemployment from keeping house | 0.2 | 0.3 | 0.3 | 0.4 | 0.4 | 0.3 | 0.5 |
| 4b | Gross reductions in unemployment owing to withdrawals to keeping house | 0.2 | 0.3 | 0.3 | 0.4 | 0.4 | 0.5 | 0.5 |
| 5 | Line 3a/Line 2a | 0.3 | 0.3 | 0.4 | 0.3 | 0.4 | 0.4 | 0.4 |
| 6 | Line 3b/Line 2b | 0.3 | 0.3 | 0.4 | 0.3 | 0.3 | 0.3 | 0.4 |
| 7 | Line 4a/Line 2a | 0.1 | 0.1 | 0.2 | 0.2 | 0.2 | 0.1 | 0.2 |
| 8 | Line 4b/Line 2b | 0.1 | 0.1 | 0.2 | 0.2 | 0.2 | 0.2 | 0.2 |

[a] See footnote 10.
SOURCE: Derived from gross change data and unpublished data for 1954 through 1959. Data are seasonally adjusted.

per cent, excepting 1956 when it reached 5.93 per cent. Unemployment, meanwhile, varied from 1.6 to 3.8 per cent of the civilian labor force. Examination of the annual data shows that changes in the percentage unemployed are not directly associated with changes in the percentage of people in the civilian labor force. This lack of association occurs despite the influence of three recessions, the Korean war, and alternating periods of "full" employment.[8]

What kind of impact do gross change movements exert on the level of unemployment and what is the significance of these movements for the hypotheses under consideration?

Table 1 presents some rough measures of the pattern of cyclical changes in unemployment and in the gross change rates. All rates were calculated from seasonally adjusted figures and then smoothed by a three-month moving average.[9] The National Bureau dating of cyclical peaks and troughs is used, with two exceptions. Because of the unavailability of gross change data for July 1953, the most recent prior data, for October 1952, are substituted. As a concluding date for the analysis, data for the most recent month available, October 1959, are used.[10]

Line 1 shows the unemployment rate (unemployment as a percentage of the civilian labor force) in peak and trough

[8] For other comments on the stability of the labor force participation rate, see Long and Rees.

[9] The basic data were seasonally adjusted by the author. In computing the rates, gross changes from month 1 to month 2 were divided by the civilian labor force, or, where applicable, the civilian noninstitutional population over age 14 for month 1. The rates were subsequently smoothed because of the large standard error of estimates for month-to-month (net) changes, particularly when the size of the changes is so small (absolutely).

[10] This is not to imply that October 1959 represented a cyclical peak but, rather, a reasonably high level of economic activity.

months, while lines 2a, 3a, 4a, 2b, 3b, and 4b show gross additions to and reductions in unemployment (also as percentages of the civilian labor force) for various labor-force categories. A cursory examination of the rates in lines 2a, 3a, and 4a reveals that they fluctuate with changes in the level of unemployment. This is to be expected of gross additions to unemployment (2a) because with high or low unemployment a larger or smaller proportion of the work force is in the process of becoming disemployed. However, it is apparent that additions to unemployment from outside the labor force (3a) which average about 40 per cent of total additions to unemployment, also fluctuate with unemployment. This clearly indicates that such movements are sensitive to changes in the level of economic activity. (The differences between lines 2a and 3a indicate the rate of additions to unemployment from employment.) Of additions to unemployment from outside the labor force, roughly 50 per cent are housewives (4a); and here again, this rate fluctuates with the unemployment rate. However, the pattern is not quite as consistent as that displayed by the other series (2a and 3a). But when the additions in 3a and 4a are expressed as ratios of total additions to unemployment (2a), these additions constitute a fairly stable proportion of gross additions to unemployment, after due allowance for rounding (lines 5 and 7).

This portion of the evidence relating to gross additions supports the additional worker hypothesis inasmuch as a larger proportion of people flow into the labor force with a rise in unemployment. But, what about the evidence concerning gross reductions?

As can be seen by the rates in lines 2b, 3b, and 4b, reductions from each unemployment status almost completely offset the additions (lines 2a, 3a, and 4a, respectively), with the result that the ratios of withdrawals of unemployed from the labor force (3b) and of the unemployed who became housewives (4b) relative to reductions in total unemployment (2b) also show considerable stability (lines 6 and 8). Once agains, the differences that do appear arise in large part from rounding.

The combined evidence on both additions to and reductions in unemployment where movement is to or from outside the labor force suggests that Woytinsky's hypothesis—that the influx of additional work-seekers raises the unemployment level in periods of high or rising unemployment—is not supported by the data for much of the postwar period. On the contrary, whatever increases in additions did occur were effectively canceled out by increases in reductions, in precisely the manner suggested by Long's hypothesis. Consequently, the Woytinsky hypothesis must be rejected while Long's is supported by the data.[11]

\* \* \*

POSSIBLE EXPLANATIONS

What explains the failure of individuals to respond in substantial numbers to increase in the level of unemployment, either by entering the labor force to seek employment or by withdrawing because no jobs can be found? Three factors appear relevant: (1) the mildness of the postwar recessions, (2) the availability of unemployment compensation and of consumer-held cash assets, and (3) the relative unavailability of large supplies of "additional workers." Let us consider these points.

\* \* \*

How do the various hypotheses about short-run labor supply behavior stand up

---

[11] The data, however, provide no direct evidence on the motivations of the increased numbers of people seeking jobs or discontinuing seeking jobs.

in view of this investigation? Obviously, the separate "additional worker" and "discouraged worker" flows do occur, as suggested by Woytinsky and Long respectively. However, Long's version, which includes both kinds of flows and assumes that they tend to be offsetting, is far more consistent with the experience of the last decade or so than the cruder version of Woytinsky. Still this is not to suggest that under conditions of severe recession or deep depression the inflows and outflows can be expected to balance out as they have in the past.

Some may still argue that the data are too rough to detect the type of movements suggested, especially in view of the mildness of recent recessions. Despite the many shortcomings of the data, seemingly regular and consistent patterns do occur, suggesting that they can be relied upon in an analysis of this kind. Accordingly, it is to be hoped that publication of these data will soon be resumed.

As Hansen explains it, however, the relatively low and briefly held unemployment peaks acted to reduce the inflow of "additional workers" as did the other two elements he cited as forces stabilizing labor force participation—the availability of sources of income maintenance during unemployment and the shortage of potential "additional workers" by the 1950's. Presumably, if the recessions were deeper, these factors would have been less influential in retarding the inflow of "additional workers," and the labor force would have increased. Long's findings, however, of labor force participation stability in 1940, certainly a depressed year by any standard, indicates that a depression would have to be very severe indeed for the "additional worker" theory to be substantiated.

### The Expandable Labor Force

In more recent years, with the economy generally strong, at least in comparison with the 1930's, studies of changes in labor force participation in response to changes in unemployment have focused on the potential expansion of the labor force as the economy moves even closer toward full employment. There is general agreement that the tendency is for expansion and not stability nor contraction of the participation of secondary workers, and the studies deal mainly with the magnitude of the expansion.

The theoretical basis for expansion stems from the greater strength of increased job availability and rising wages pulling secondary workers into the labor force than that of the negative influence of higher earnings of the principal family worker. The fact that the positive labor force response, at least of wives, to higher wages and job availability exceeds the negative reaction to higher husbands' income has already been noted, particularly with reference to Mincer's paper of the previous section.

Note the lack of parallelism with the magnitude of the forces during a deep depression. Then, presumably, the secondary worker is driven into the labor force by the long-term sag of family income to a greater degree than he is driven out by discouragement over the slim probability of finding work. That is, the effect of family income on labor force participation of secondary workers is greater positively at very low economic levels than it is negatively at very high levels.

"Hidden unemployment" of the "expandable labor force" are terms that express the number who are currently not in the labor force but who would enter were the economy to expand and the level of employment to increase; these factors create serious policy problems. The presence of "hidden unemployment" indicates that the actual count of the number unemployed understates the number who would want to work were jobs available. In fact, there is a movement to include the hidden unemployment in official statistics on the employed. More significantly, policy measures to reduce unemployment would face a treadmill effect as the labor force increased when jobs became more generally available and employment increased as a result of economic expansion.

Even if the "hidden unemployed" were comprised mainly of secondary workers whose contributions to family income were not crucial to the maintenance of satisfactory consumption standards, their entrance into the work force with the strengthening of the economy might contribute to the unemployment of some primary workers. The reduction in unemployment would be dampened by their entrance but, more significantly, they might replace primary workers on employment rolls.

The amount of "hidden unemployment" depends on the differential between current measured unemployment and the "full employment" unemployment level, a term expressing the level of frictional unemployment. Since the "hidden unemployed" enter the work force's counted members as the level of actual unemployment falls, their number moves directly with the difference between actual and "full employment" unemployment levels.

There are many thorough recent statistical studies of the magnitude of the "expandable labor force." Again, as in the case of studies of labor force participation changes during generally depressed conditions, these studies center on the behavior of the secondary work force, given the cyclical as well as long-run stability of participation of prime-aged males. Thus, women and younger and older males who enter the labor force, in response to improved job opportunities comprise the expandable labor force.

William G. Bowen and T. A. Finegan present a comprehensible study of the behavior of the labor force under varying levels of the economy. Theirs is a cross-sectional statistical analysis for census years among American cities experiencing differing levels of unemployment.

In the final section, presented here, they isolate the independent influence of unemployment level on labor force participation. First, they estimate the effect of a one percent change in unemployment on participation of each of the subgroups and overall labor force for each of the census years. Then they estimate the volume of the hidden unemployed; that is, the total expansion of the labor force that would occur if the unemployment rate moved from an existing level to a low target level, arbitrarily chosen at four percent.

The volume of "hidden unemployment" is related directly to both the degree of positive response of those outside of the work force to a given reduction in the unemployment rate and to the differences between the existing employment rate to the target rate. Thus, although the sensitivity to participation from a given reduction in unemployment was greater in 1960 than in 1950, the estimated volume of "hidden unemployment" was greater in the earlier year because the unemployment rate was higher then.

# Labor Force Participation and Unemployment

## by William G. Bowen
## and T. A. Finegan

### ESTIMATES OF "HIDDEN UNEMPLOYMENT"

In this concluding section we draw together our findings concerning the relation between unemployment and labor force participation and present estimates of the volume of "hidden unemployment."

The relation between unemployment and labor force participation can be looked at in a number of ways—in terms of effects on participation rates, effects on the absolute size of the labor force, and effects on adjusted unemployment rates—each of which has its uses. Basic to all of these ways of putting the figures together are the net regression coefficients, which are interpreted as indicating the effects of a 1 per cent difference among cities in unemployment rates on intercity differences in participation rates, after the influence of the other independent variables included in the analysis has been taken into account. While these net regression coefficients have already been presented separately for each major labor force group (along with estimates of the effects of the other independent variables used to isolate the influence of unemployment), we thought it would be helpful to assemble all of these coefficients in a single place, and this is what has been done in the top panel of Table 1.

Since there are five major groups and three census years represented in this table, there are fifteen net regression coefficients; and grouping all fifteen in a single table directs our attention to the fact that every one of them has a negative sign (though not all are significant at the 5 per cent level). In short, relatively high

SOURCE Reprinted with permission from Arthur M. Ross, Ed., *Employment and the Labor Market.* Originally published by the University of California Press, reprinted by permission of the Regents of the University of California, 1965, pp. 145–153.

TABLE 1. EFFECTS OF UNEMPLOYMENT ON LABOR-FORCE PARTICIPATION OF MAJOR GROUPS, NET REGRESSION COEFFICIENTS FOR 1960, 1950, AND 1940

| Major Groups | 1960 | 1950 | 1940 |
|---|---|---|---|
| | $b$ | $b$ | $b$ |
| | $(s)$ | $(s)$ | $(s)$ |
| M:14–19 | −1.94 * | −1.63 * | −0.10 † |
| | (0.28) | (0.37) | (0.05) |
| M:25–54 | −0.24 * | −0.24 * | −0.02 |
| | (0.06) | (0.08) | (0.03) |
| M:65+ | −1.62 * | −1.45 * | −0.08 |
| | (0.24) | (0.33) | (0.15) |
| SW:14–19 | −0.73 * | −0.92 * | −0.09 |
| | (0.24) | (0.20) | (0.06) |
| MW | −0.76 * | −0.52 * | −0.54 * |
| | (0.18) | (0.18) | (0.11) |
| | $b$ | $b$ | $b$ |
| Above major groups combined | −0.73 | −0.57 | −0.24 |

| Major Groups | | Notation |
|---|---|---|
| M:14–19 | Males, 14 to 19 years old. | $b$ Net (partial) regression coefficient. |
| M:25–54 | Males, 25 to 54 years old. | $s$ Standard error of the regression coefficient. |
| M:65+ | Males, 65 years old and older. | $b$ Weighted average of the $b$'s for the individual groups, the population of each group serving as its weight. |
| SW:14–19 | Single women, 14–19 years old. | * Significant at the 1 per cent level. |
| MW | Married women, husband present. | † Significant at the 5 per cent level. |

unemployment in a city has tended to be associated with relatively low labor force participation for *all* five of our major groups in *all* of the last three census years. The inference is certainly that high unemployment has, on balance, discouraged labor force participation. A major substantive conclusion of our analysis is that, to the extent that high unemployment has induced some additional family members to enter the labor force, this tendency has been more than offset by the negative effect of high unemployment on labor force participation.

Differential degrees of impact among groups and among census years are, however, at least as striking—and as significant—as this over-all pattern of similarity in direction of impact. In both 1960 and 1950 the labor force participation rates of teen-age males and males aged 65 years and older were much the most sensitive to unemployment; married women and teen-age girls constituted a middle group in

this regard; and, as we would expect, the participation rates of prime-age males were least influenced by unemployment conditions. In 1940, on the other hand, it was the married women whose decisions to participate in the labor force seem to have been most strongly influenced by the over-all level of unemployment.

To be seen in proper perspective, these changes over time in the effects of unemployment on the participation rates of particular labor force groups must be looked at in the context of the pronounced over-all change in the sensitivity of labor force behavior to unemployment rates which has occurred between the pre- and post-World War II census years. When we focus on differential effects among census years, the finding that stands out is the much stronger impact of intercity differences in unemployment on the labor force participation rates of *all* groups in both 1950 and 1960 than in 1940. In 1940 the net regression coefficients were generally small, and the only coefficient significant at the 1 per cent level was the coefficient for married women; in both 1950 and 1960 the net regression coefficients for every group except married women were much larger than in 1940, and all ten coefficients were significant at the 1 per cent level.

To provide a single, over-all measure of the impact of unemployment conditions on labor force participation rates, we constructed a weighted average for each census year of the five major-group regression coefficients. These overall regression coefficients are presented in the bottom panel of Table 1, and they indicate that, whereas in 1940 an unemployment rate 1 per cent above average was associated with an over-all participation rate about *¼ of 1 per cent* below average, in 1960 an unemployment rate of 1 per cent above average was associated with an over-all participation rate about *¾ of 1 per cent* below average. The fact that the over-all regression coefficient was also higher in 1960 than in 1950 gives some impression of an upward trend over time in the sensitivity of labor force participation to unemployment, but results for only three census years can hardly be said to constitute sufficient evidence.

Conjecture as to the existence of a trend leads to a more general unanswered question of considerable importance: *why* were intercity differences in participation rates in the postwar census years more sensitive to unemployment conditions than they were in 1940? There are any number of possible explanations. At one extreme there are *ad hoc* explanations for the sharp increases in the regression coefficients of particular groups—for in-

stance, we suggested earlier that changes in the relation between school enrollment and work have had much to do with the teen-ager regressions. And there are also more general considerations—what were the effects of the high absolute level of unemployment in 1940 and of the even higher rates of unemployment in preceding years? Did the fact that the demand for labor was increasing rather briskly in 1940, in at least some metropolitan areas, lessen the discouraging effects of the high levels of unemployment? How, if at all, does the structural unemployment debate tie in here? In this paper, which is already long, we do no more than pose the questions; and we confess that, at this state of our work, we have no strong evidence in support of any particular answers.[1]

We turn now to another way of looking at our results—this time in terms of estimates of "hidden unemployment." This phrase has become rather popular in recent years, and we use it in its usual sense of a measure of the number of persons who at present are counted as not in the labor force, but who would be in the labor force if labor market conditions were more favorable. To conform again with general practice (and lacking any better bench mark), we use a 4 per cent unemployment rate as our norm. Thus, our estimates of hidden unemployment for a particular year indicate the numbers of additional persons who we estimate would have been in the labor force, had the over-all unemployment rate been 4 per cent rather than whatever it actually was.

Estimates for each of our five major groups for 1960 and 1950 are presented in

---

[1] It has been suggested (by Gertrude Bancroft and Albert Rees) that counting persons on public emergency work in 1940 among the unemployed may be throwing off our results. We have run all of the 1940 regressions treating these persons as employed rather than unemployed, and the general tenor of the results remains much the same—that is, the net regression coefficients for unemployment in 1940 are still much lower than in 1950 or 1960.

TABLE 2. ESTIMATES OF "HIDDEN UNEMPLOYMENT" FOR FIVE MAJOR GROUPS, 1960 AND 1950
(Thousands of persons and per cent of population group)

| Major Groups | "Best" Estimate | | "Lower" Estimate | | "Higher" Estimate | |
|---|---|---|---|---|---|---|
| | 1960 | 1950 | 1960 | 1950 | 1960 | 1950 |
| M:14–19 | 116 | 112 | 99 | 87 | 132 | 137 |
| | (2.3%) | (3.3%) | (2.0%) | (2.5%) | (2.7%) | (4.0%) |
| M:25–54 | 66 | 95 | 50 | 64 | 82 | 127 |
| | (0.3%) | (0.5%) | (0.2%) | (0.3%) | (0.4%) | (0.6%) |
| M:65+ | 92 | 98 | 78 | 75 | 105 | 120 |
| | (1.9%) | (2.9%) | (1.7%) | (2.2%) | (2.2%) | (3.6%) |
| SW:14–19 | 41 | 61 | 27 | 48 | 54 | 74 |
| | (0.9%) | (1.8%) | (0.6%) | (1.5%) | (1.2%) | (2.2%) |
| MW | 257 | 241 | 197 | 158 | 319 | 325 |
| | (0.9%) | (1.0%) | (0.7%) | (0.7%) | (1.1%) | (1.4%) |
| Above major groups combined | 572 | 607 | 451 | 432 | 692 | 783 |
| | (0.9%) | (1.1%) | (0.7%) | (0.8%) | (1.1%) | (1.5%) |

*Notes:* "Hidden unemployment" is defined as the *difference* between (1) the number of persons that *would have been* in the civilian labor force during the designated census week if $U$ had been 4.0 per cent, as predicted by the net regression of $L$ on $U$, and (2) the number of persons who *actually were* in the civilian labor force that week. The estimates are based on a $U$ for the urban civilian labor force of 5.2 per cent in the census week of 1960 and 6.0 per cent in the census week of 1950.

Our "best estimate" of "hidden unemployment" is based on the assumption that the *true* regression coefficient ($B$) for $U$ equals the calculated net regression coefficient ($b$) for $U$. Our "lower estimate" assumes that $B = b-s$, where $s$ is the standard error of $b$. Our "higher estimate" assumes that $B = b + s$.

Estimates for combined groups are the sums of estimates for individual groups.

Table 2.[2] To illustrate the methods used in obtaining these estimates, let us consider the derivation of one particular figure: our "best" estimate of hidden unemployment for urban teen-age males in 1960. This figure was derived by multiplying the net regression coefficient for this group ($-1.94$, as shown in Table 1), expressed as a percentage, by the population of this group (4,972,000 in 1960) to obtain an estimate of the number of additional teen-agers (96,400) who would have been in the labor force, had the unemployment rate been 1 per cent lower than the prevailing rate. To reach our norm of 4.0 per cent, however, the unemployment rate would have had to be 1.2 per cent lower than it actually was (the official rate in 1960 having been 5.2 per cent), and so we had to multiply the 96,400 figure by 1.2 to obtain the figure of 116,000 shown in Table 2.

It must be emphasized that what we are doing here is using cross-sectional regression coefficients (based on intercity differences) to estimate the effect of different unemployment rates on over-all (all-city) participation rates. The crucial assumption is that an over-all decrease of 1 per cent in the unemployment rate would have had the same relative effect on labor force participation rates as a difference of 1 per cent in unemployment rates between representative cities did have on the relative labor force participation rates in those cities. As the consumption function literature illustrates, this method of estimation can be seriously defective; however, the use of time series estimators can also be dangerous (for

[2] No estimates for 1940 are presented in this table or the tables that follow. Because of the high over-all level of unemployment in 1940 (15.4 per cent in the urban sector), we could present estimates of the predicted size of the labor force at 4 per cent unemployment only by applying our 1940 net regression coefficients well outside the range of unemployment rates for which we had any observations. (The city with the lowest unemployment rate in 1940 was Charlotte, N. C., and it had a rate of 7.9 per cent.)

other reasons). In the present context, it is not as yet clear to us whether cross-sectional estimates are likely to be strongly biased in one direction or the other—or at all. Hence, all we can do at this stage is warn the reader to be sure to interpret the hidden unemployment estimates given here in this light. Later on we hope to have much more to say on this subject, and to be able to report some progress in reconciling the cross-sectional and time series results.

One last comment concerning methods: in Table 2 we present "lower" and "higher" estimates of hidden unemployment as well as "best" estimates. The purpose of this is to provide the reader with a range of results based on the standard errors associated with the individual regression coefficients. The "lower" estimate is based on the assumption that the true regression coefficient for each group was one standard error less than the actual coefficient, and the "higher" estimate is based on the assumption that the true coefficients were all one standard error larger than the actual coefficients.[3]

So much for procedures. The results reported in Table 2 are instructive in a number of respects. First, with regard to over-all orders of magnitude, our best estimate of total hidden unemployment for our five major groups in urban areas is 572,000 for 1960 and 607,000 for 1950.

The estimate for 1950 exceeds the estimate for 1960 because the over-all unemployment rate exceeded the 4 per cent target rate by considerably more in 1950 than in 1960. If the difference between the actual and target unemployment rates had been the same in both years, and 1960 estimate of hidden unemployment would have been larger than the 1950 estimate because (a) as Table 1 showed, the over-all net regression coefficient was larger in 1960; and (b) the population base was larger in 1960. The fact that we do arrive at such a substantial estimate of hidden unemployment for 1950 (1.2 per cent of the urban population of our five major groups) suggests that unemployment-related omissions from the labor force count are by no means a phenomenon peculiar to the 1960's.

It should also be noted that the (generally) larger net regression coefficients in 1960 had (generally) smaller standard errors; as a result, the lower and higher estimates in 1960 differ by smaller amounts from the best estimates than is the case in 1950. That is, the best estimates for 1960 are (generally) more reliable than the best estimates for 1950.

The other substantive finding in Table 2 that deserves emphasis is the great contribution which the married-women category makes to the total volume of hidden unemployment in both 1960 and 1950. We shall return to this point shortly, when we compare the volume of hidden unemployment in 1960 among a larger number of labor force groups.

Table 3 presents the Table 2 results in a different format.

Here the "best" estimates of hidden unemployment are translated into "adjusted" unemployment rates by adding the volume of hidden unemployment for each group to both the unemployment numerator and the labor force denominator. We do not call our "adjusted" unemployment rate the "true" rate, because we are well aware that there are other important adjustments that could also be made to the reported figures to bring them closer into line with ordinary conceptions of the unemployment rate as a measure of underutilization. For instance, anything pur-

---

[3] Since it would seem unlikely that the true coefficient for every group would differ in the same direction from the actual coefficient, the interval between the over-all "lower" and "higher" estimates is, no doubt, wider than one would find if he took ±1 standard error from an over-all net regression coefficient. That is, the odds are greater than 68 out of 100 that the "true" over-all estimate of hidden unemployment falls within the lower-higher interval.

TABLE 3. IMPACT OF "HIDDEN UNEMPLOYMENT" ON RATES OF UNEMPLOYMENT OF
FIVE MAJOR GROUPS IN THE URBAN LABOR FORCE, APRIL, 1960, AND APRIL, 1950

| Major Groups | April, 1960 | | April, 1950 | |
|---|---|---|---|---|
| | Reported Rate [a] | Adjusted Rate [b] | Reported Rate [c] | Adjusted Rate [b] |
| M:14–19 | 12.0 | 17.2 | 15.5 | 21.7 |
| M:25–54 | 4.0 | 4.3 | 5.6 | 6.1 |
| M:65+ | 6.3 | 11.8 | 6.6 | 12.6 |
| SW:14–19 | 8.7 | 11.7 | 7.2 | 12.4 |
| MW | 5.1 | 7.7 | 4.5 | 8.2 |
| Above groups combined | 4.9 | 6.4 | 6.0 | 7.9 |

[a] Unemployment rate reported by the *Census of Population* for 1960.

[b] Calculated by adding our "best estimates" of hidden unemployment to the "reported" labor force and unemployment totals for the designated urban groups.

[c] Estimates based on data in the 1950 *Census of Population* and in the *Monthly Report on the Labor Force* for April, 1950. Since both unemployment and labor force participation were underreported to a substantial degree by the 1950 *Census*, it was necessary to develop corrected estimates of both for each of the five major groups of the urban, noninstitutional population. These estimates attempt to correct for the underreporting of visible unemployment: they do not include any "hidden unemployment" as we have defined it.

porting to be a fully adjusted rate would certainly have to take account of part-time work (both in terms of persons on part time who want full-time employment and persons wholly unemployed who want only part-time jobs).

Our adjustment procedure produces an "adjusted" unemployment rate of 6.4 per cent in 1960 (compared with an actual rate of 4.9 per cent) and an adjusted rate of 7.9 per cent in 1950 (versus an actual rate of 6.0 per cent). Even more striking are the differences between the actual and adjusted rates for older males and for

teen-age males. The adjusted older male unemployment rate is nearly twice as high as the actual rate in both 1950 and 1960. Adjusting the male teen-ager rate raises it to 17.2 per cent in 1960 and 21.7 per cent in 1950. In fact, the only group whose unemployment rate is not substantially affected is prime-age males.

Our comparative discussion of the 1960 and 1950 census years in terms of the five major groups is now complete.

✻   ✻   ✻

The writers note that, at least for cross-sectional data, there is a trend for increased volatility in the labor force from one census period to the next. That is, the labor force tends to expand more for a given reduction in unemployment. They do not offer a hypothesis to explain this trend.

Furthermore, they raise the question of the relationship between the "expandable labor force" and the structural unemployment debate. Since this controversy forms the substance of the following chapter, and structural unemployment also plays a part in the wage-inflation issue to be discussed below, it is fitting here to explain how the entry of the "hidden unemployed" into the labor force under improving economic conditions tends to aggravate the structural unemployment problem.

The tie between the expandable labor force and the worsening of structural disequilibrium relates to the fact that additional workers enter the labor force not necessarily in response to particular job openings, but to a general improvement in job availability. Assuming that the "hidden unemployed" who enter the labor force under such a stimulus, young and older men and women with loose labor force attachment, tend to have less training than prime-aged males, at any movement toward a given, low level of unemployment, the labor force will become more heavily weighted with the unskilled. If the increase in overall labor demand accompanying the strengthening of the economy is balanced for all labor classifications from the unskilled to the highly skilled, then the unemployed will be more heavily weighted with the classes to which the new entrants belong, the unskilled ones. That is, the unemployed will comprise more of those who are unable to fit existing job openings, which is the crux of the structural problem.

A simple numerical example may clarify this sequence. Assume that there are two labor classifications of equal size, the skilled and the unskilled, with an equal unemployment rate of 4 percent. If there is an increase in labor supply only in the unskilled as the economy moves to the 2.5 percent unemployment level, the skilled rate would become, say, 2 percent, and the unskilled 3 percent. This, of course, assumes not only a balanced growth in demand for labor of both types but also an elasticity of labor supply of the hidden unemployed with respect to the unemployment rate of —.67. Employment of both groups increases by 2 percent and supply of the unskilled increases by 1 percent with the overall unemployment reduced by 1.5 percent. Relevant to the structural issue, the two groups now have differential unemployment rates.

## Related Readings

In a review article of Long's *The Labor Force—Under Changing Income and Employment*, Sanford Cohen, "The Supply Curve of Labor Re-Examined" (*Industrial and Labor Relations Review*, Vol. 13, July 1959, pp. 64–71), expresses a skeptical view of Long's hypothesis that the balanced long-run entrance of women and exit of older and younger men from the labor force are closely interdependent. He wonders how this theory explains the great increase of women in "the historically female occupations, and the elderly male exodus from the historically male occupations."

A. J. Jaffe and Joseph Froompin, *Technology and Jobs* (New York, Praeger, 1968), and Howard R. Bowen and Garth L. Mangum, *Automation and Economic Progress* (Prentice-Hall, Englewood Cliffs, N.J., 1966), study the effect of technological change on the "manpower evolution."

Dan D. Humphrey, *Journal of Political Economy*, Vol. 48 (June 1940), pp. 412–419, questions Woytinsky's reliance on higher unemployment among multiple-worker families during depressions as a validation of the "additional worker" hypothesis. Humphrey notes that these families have characteristically higher rates than single-worker families and that Woytinsky's data do not permit finding whether the differential between the rates increases as the economy worsens. Woytinsky, himself, in *Employment and Earnings in the United States* (New York, Twentieth Century Fund, 1953, pp. 327–323), agrees that "additional workers" would swell the labor force only during depressions and in boom periods. But when he states that "Employment should be considered as adequate when the labor force is reduced to a minimum . . . ," he would be forced to argue that the 1940 labor force, which Long found to be relatively low, would reflect an "adequate" employment level, a year with a greater than 10 percent unemployment rate.

Although statistical studies measuring the volume of "hidden unemployment" are relatively recent, both the term and its policy implications have long received consideration. In his "Correction of Census Bureau Estimates of Unemployment" (*Review of Economics and Statistics*, Vol. 32, February 1950, pp. 50–55), Russell Nixon argues that official unemployment statistics should be supplemented by including in the work force not only those actively in the labor force but also those more passively available for work. These latter would be calculated from an estimation of the full employment work force. Reflecting the view of the time, Sumner Slichter (*Review of Economics and Statistics*, Vol. 32, pp. 74–77), in his February 1960 "Comment" on Nixon's paper, questions whether those available for but not seeking work should be counted in unemployment. He writes: "Certainly the people who are having a hard time to decide whether to work or not to work can hardly be said to constitute a social problem."

In "The Relation of Labor Force to Employment" (*Industrial and Labor Relations Review*, Vol. 17, April 1964, pp. 454–469), Alfred Tella estimates the expansion of the labor force by sex as the unemployment level falls. He finds the relative expansion of female workers substantially greater than that for males, even though the male group, of course, includes some secondary workers. In "Labor Force Sensitivity to Employment by Age and Sex," (*Industrial Relations*, Vol. 4, February 1965, pp. 69–83), Tella breaks the data into age-sex groupings and finds a more pronounced labor force sensitivity in the young male and older male classes than in prime-aged males. Glen Cain, "Unemployment and the Labor-Force Participation of Secondary Workers" (*Industrial and Labor Relations Review*, Vol. 20, January 1967, pp. 275–297), in a cross-sectional study of metropolitan areas in 1960, also finds participation by secondary workers—in this case, both young and older males and females—to be inversely related to area unemployment rates.

Kenneth Strand and Thomas Dernburg, "Cyclical Variations in Civilian Labor Force Participation" (*Review of Economics and Statistics*, Vol. 46, November 1964, pp. 378–391), find the same relationship. They also conclude that on balance when the economy weakens, the "discouraged worker" effect outweighs the "additional worker" influence in that the labor force diminishes, although the shrinkage is retarded as the recession lengthens. But this pattern does not necessarily refute Woytinsky's additional worker theory in that the period studied, 1953 to 1962, did not include any deep depressions. In another paper, "Hidden Unemployment 1953–62: A Quantitative Analysis by Age and Sex" (*American Economic Review*, Vol. 56, March 1966, pp. 71–95), Dernburg and Strand, find, as did Bowen and Finegan, that the labor force participation sensitivity to changing unemployment levels has been increasing over time.

Jacob Mincer, "Labor Force Participation and Unemployment: A Review of Recent Evidence," in *Prosperity and Unemployment*, Robert A. Gordon and Margaret S. Gordon Eds., Wiley, 1966, pp. 73–112, carefully summarizes the contribution of these and other studies that measure "hidden unemployment." Mincer hypothesizes that the trend of growing responsiveness of the labor force to the business cycle can be explained by the increasing number of "intermittent workers." These are women in the labor force who have a loose attachment to it and the growing number of males, at both ends of the age band, who can move from retirement to work or combine school and work or leave school for work as employment opportunities expand.

In a study of the English labor force, Laurence C. Hunter, "Cyclical Variations in the Labor Supply: British Experience, 1951–1960" (*Oxford Economic Papers*, Vol. 15, July 1963, pp. 140–153), finds a pattern parallel to that of the American experience, with the work force expanding and contracting with the cycle, reducing the amplitude of unemployment swings. But Hunter also notes that British recessions were too mild to put the "additional worker theory" to a fair test.

# CHAPTER 7

# Unemployment: The Inadequate Demand–Structural Controversy

The simplest form of the inadequate demand theory of unemployment states that unemployment exists because the current level of production generated by total demand is insufficient to attain full employment. Expressed in this way, the structuralist would not care to dispute the argument. He would agree that if spending were increased enough, full employment could be reached. To him the issue is the amount by which spending would have to be increased to reach the full employment goal. More precisely, he would worry about the inflationary pressures that arise in an economy pushing towards full employment.

Lord Beveridge's often quoted condition of full employment of "having always more vacant jobs than unemployed men," * provides a basis for explaining the fundamental difference between the two schools of thought regarding the nature of unemployment and the consequences of its reduction. If unemployment were at, say, 1.5 million and vacancies slightly above this number, then by most criteria the economy would be at a full employment level. That is, those out of work, at about 2 percent of the work force, could be assumed to be frictionally unemployed, able to fill existing openings but out of work either as a result of temporary choice, unawareness of openings, or being in transition between jobs. But under Beveridge's definition, if there were, say, 5 million out of work, with slightly over 5 million vacancies, employment would also be full, but the unemployment level would then be over 6 percent, certainly above socially tolerable limits.

* William H. Beveridge, *Full Employment in a Free Society*, New York, Norton, 1945, p. 18.

# THE STRUCTURALIST ARGUMENT

Thus, Beveridge's definition equates full employment with a level of demand such that the number of unemployed could be at the frictional level if the work force were able to fit employers' needs. The surplus of unemployed, in this example, those unable to fill the existing vacancies, would comprise the structurally unemployed. If demand were to increase further, even structuralists would agree that many of the surplus would find work, but inflationary pressures would be created as the economy expanded. In short, the structuralist argument narrows to the view that the presence of structural discrepancies between existing capacities of the work force and job requirements increases the level of demand required to attain a given low level of unemployment

Structural unemployment exists when a number of the currently unemployed are unable to fill existing openings. Inability, at this point, may be expressed simply as not fitting the standards set by the employer for filling a specific job opening (whether or not these standards may be arbitrary, unrealistic, and even unfair is a matter to be discussed in the last chapter, on discrimination). As such, the hypothesis is based on the presence of labor bottlenecks. Since bottlenecks do not occur in bad times, the controversy only applies to our post-World War II economy with its relatively mild recessions. Although the dispute over whether a move toward full employment would meet resistance in the form of structural bottlenecks arose in the mid-1950's, the issue is still important today and the dispute still very much alive, in view of our inflation-prone economy.

Thus, the presence of structural unemployment at any time, requires that vacancies arise in some occupations, or areas, as counterparts to the labor surpluses elsewhere in the economy. These surpluses consist of workers, above the frictional level of unemployment, who are unable to fit the existing openings. Not only must an excess of vacancies exist in some sectors but, of course, there must also be a surplus of workers in others. It would be a very tight national labor market, indeed, that had no surpluses in any particular labor markets, one in which every sector's unemployment was at, or below, its frictional level. Thus, while structural unemployment becomes an issue only in relatively good times, when bottlenecks appear in many sectors of the economy, at least theoretically, if the economy is very strong, structural unemployment may again become insignificant because of the absence of substantial labor surplus sectors. But under these conditions, unemployment itself is not an important economic problem, so that the structural issue may be considered relevant in an economy approaching full employment. In fact, one definition of full employment may hold that this state is reached when there are no significant areas of labor surplus, when the various sectors are at their frictional unemployment level. The relationship between vacancies and labor surplus points out the difficulty of measuring the structural component of any unemployment level. Specifically, what is needed is an accurate vacancy count. Without knowledge of the volume of vacancies in the labor shortage areas, there is no way of estimating the share of the structural component in total unemployment. For example, in an economy of two sectors of equal size, if there is an unemployment rate of 4 percent in one sector and unemployment at the frictional level, say 2 percent, with more vacancies than idle workers in the other sector, this is evidence of structural unemployment. But how much structural unemployment depends on the number of excess vacancies in the latter sector. At a maximum, the entire above-frictional level of unemployment in the first sector can be considered structural in nature. But the structural component would be lower if the excessive vacancies in the second sector were less than the labor surplus in the first. In any case, vacancy data are needed for measuring the volume of structural unemployment.

Structuralists recognize that structural unemployment can be suppressed, that bottlenecks can be somehow widened or circumvented. Specifically, less suitable workers can be employed to fill openings and demand can be diverted toward goods that can be produced by otherwise surplus labor. To the extent that these measures have been taken, the price level at any given (low) unemployment level would be higher than if the labor bottleneck had not tended to appear. But this series of past occurrences does not relate to the central policy question of the effects on the price level of efforts to reduce a given level of unemployment.

If structural elements are present, that is, if bottlenecks would tend to appear as the economy strengthens, then the move toward full employment, if made through an increase in aggregate demand, would force inflationary pressures additional to those that are usually associated with the quickening of expenditures. These would be the pressures associated with using less suitable labor as substitutes for unavailable but more efficient workers in production, and diversion of demand to those goods that can be produced by would-be labor surpluses as prices rose rapidly for goods produced by the scarce workers.

The structuralist need make no value judgment regarding the wisdom of curing unemployment through increases in aggregate demand when structural elements are present. He only points out that the inflationary "cost" is greater than if full employment were reached through widening bottlenecks by educating and training workers to fit openings. Considering the time required for widening bottlenecks in this way, a structuralist might agree that easing a recession through inflationary increases in aggregate demand is worth the cost; he wishes, though, to emphasize that this cost will arise. Thus the policy maker wishes to know if structural problems will arise if the economy is pushed toward full employment in deciding whether the gain of a given drop in unemployment would be worth the consequent rise in prices. The seriousness of potential structural bottlenecks would serve as a guide to the intensity of the consequent inflation.

On the other hand, if none of current unemployment were structural in nature, a policy to widen nonexistent bottlenecks through (re)training or education would not alleviate the unemployment problem, and would lead to an unhappy group of workers who were trained for jobs for which there were no openings. No one would suggest that a policy of employment through retraining should be carried out to alleviate current unemployment that was obviously not structural in nature, that is, when the absence of significant shortages would be easily noted. But emphasis on retraining to accompany a growth in aggregate demand to anticipate future bottlenecks might be frustrating for the newly trained if the market for their new skills became no tighter than for their old.

In summary, structural imbalance, representing merely differential unemployment rates for different labor types or sectors of the economy, can become structural unemployment, a component of total unemployment, only when the overall unemployment rate is low. Then segments of the labor market may have an excess of vacancies over unemployment. This important relationship between structural imbalance and structural unemployment, as well as the need for reducing structural unemployment in facilitating the move of an expanding economy toward full employment, is clearly presented in the following paper by Richard Musgrave.

# Demand Versus Structural Unemployment

## by Richard A. Musgrave

The "structural" aspect of the unemployment problem is important for two reasons. For one thing, the cost of unemployment (be it measured as GNP lost or, preferably, in terms of social distress caused) depends on the incidence of unemployment, as well as on total numbers. For another, appropriate policies to reduce total unemployment may depend on the composition of the unemployment. My concern here is with this second aspect only.

Specifically, I am concerned with the comparative effectiveness of reducing total unemployment (1) by measures to raise aggregate demand, be it via tax reduction, expenditure increase, or monetary expansion, and (2) by measures to improve the employability of the unemployed via retraining, education, placement and other labor market policies. This comparative effectiveness, I take it, is the crux of the debate between the "aggregate demand" and "structural" schools.

The basic economics of the matter are quite simple, and may be represented with the aid of Figure 1. On the vertical axis we measure price, and on the horizontal axis we measure output which, for present purposes, also reflects total employment. For a given level of money expenditures or GNP we have the simple identity $E = PN$, where E is money expenditures, P is the level and N is units of output or employment. Plotting this we obtain the constant expenditure curve (rectangular hyperbola) $E'$. Also, at any time there exists in the economy something like a supply schedule (a great-uncle of the Phillips curve), such as shown by SS, which records the levels of P and N that will be reached as the level

SOURCE Reprinted with permission from *Unemployment in a Prosperous Economy,* William G. Bowen and Frederick H. Harbison, Eds., Princeton, N.J., Princeton University Press, Industrial Relations Section, 1965, pp. 93–97.

271

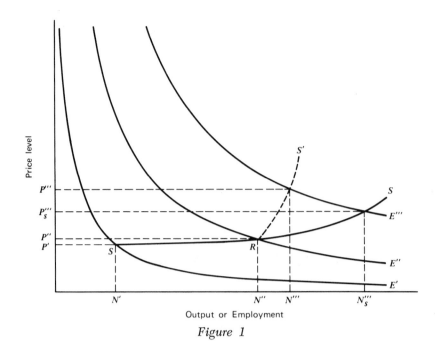

*Figure 1*

of expenditures is increased above the prevailing base.

Suppose the initial expenditure line is E′ the initial output or employment is N′ and the initial price level is P′. Suppose also that N′ involves a "high" level of unemployment and excess capacity in the economy. We would expect that an increase in the expenditure level from E′ to E″ within, say, one year, will result in a substantial increase in output (from N′ to N″) and very little rise in price (from P′ to P″). Also, we would expect that if the rate of increase in E is sufficiently large, say to E‴, the additional demand will press hard on available factors and be reflected largely in increased prices rather than in increased output. Since the adaptability of the economy to an increase in demand is a function of time, the slope of SS will be the steeper, the faster the shift to a higher expenditure level is made.[1] Let us suppose we deal here with a one-year period.

What does the "structural unemployment" thesis have to do with all this? A great deal, because it argues that the SS schedule to the right of the prevailing expenditure level is steep, so that increased expenditures would be frittered away largely in rising prices rather than increased output and employment. This steepness of the SS schedule results because of mismatch between the composition of the unemployed and the composition of the incremental demand for labor induced by a rising expenditure level. In other words, the severity of the "structural" problem is measured by the slope of the SS schedule. The more severe the mismatch, the steeper is the slope and the less effective are aggregate demand measures.

Consider now what happens if "structural" measures are undertaken. Suppose we are at R and launch a large program for retraining, labor mobility, etc.; and, to make my point clear, let me suppose further that this program is financed by taxes so as to neutralize its aggregate

[1] Limited availability of resources, however, will result in an eventual upward slope even if the increase is very gradual. Note also that we are dealing here with the bottleneck cause of the price level-employment relation. The administered wage-price policy aspect (cost-push inflation) is a different matter, and may well be related to the *level* of employment, rather than the rate of increase in outlays.

demand effect. Suppose also that, in the absence of the program, the supply schedule would be as shown by the steeper RS' curve. Due to the program, a better fit between incremental labor supply and demand is obtained, bending the curve downwards to the lesser RS slope. Movement from E'' to E''' now raises employment to $N_s'''$ not only to N'''; and the rise in prices is to $P_s'''$ only and not to P'''.

The structural program is successful in paving the way for the increase in E to do its job. But note that introduction of the program alone does not move us away from N''. For this to come about, we must also have a shift in the E schedule, i.e., an increase in the expenditure level. Even without this, the program may be useful in redistributing unemployment and this may be important in reducing the distress caused by a given level of unemployment. Nevertheless, this constitutes employment diversion, to borrow a term from international trade, not employment creation. For employment creation to come about, we would have to assume not only that labor cost will fall in response to the structural program but also that prices will decline in consequence, a condition which I would reject as rather unrealistic. Structural measures may (and eventually will) be necessary; but they are not a sufficient condition for raising total employment.

Consider now whether the tax cut has been successful as the Council claims, or a failure as Professor Killingsworth suggests. To be sure, the cut did not lower unemployment to 4 percent. This result should not have been promised if, indeed, it was. What the cut did do—and this, it seems to me, is what matters—was to bring about a substantially higher level of expenditure and (with prices nearly constant) output and employment then would have prevailed otherwise. During 1964, GNP rose by $38 billion and employment by 1.5 million, while the price level was nearly stable. Whether 50 or 75 percent of this

gain was due to the tax cut, does not matter; but surely, the cut did make a substantial contribution.

Given this fact, the success of the tax cut is not vitiated by the circumstance that the labor force and productivity grew more rapidly than anticipated. Indeed, these developments showed that structural restraints were less serious than expected. Output and employment rose just as anticipated and this, I repeat, is what matters. The movement, in other words, was of the N' to N'' type, and structural impediments were not a factor. Far from having failed, the experience suggests that a larger cut might well have been called for to do the job fully. At the same time, we only know that actual structural programs were adequate (as evidenced by the absence of price rise), for the actual tax cut. A greater structural effort might have been needed to have the same result for a larger cut.

However this may be, the interesting issue now is not what might have been done in the past, but what should be done in the future. The question to which the assembled labor market experts should address themselves, is this: Comes January 1966, will we be in a position such as shown by N', in which case the number one requirement will be further strengthening of aggregate demand? Or, will we be at N'', with the further path as indicated by RS', in which case it is essential that expansionary measures be accompanied at once by more adequate structural programs?

My hunch is that we shall be closer to N' than N'', given the feasible scale of expansionary policy. Nevertheless, an increased concern with structural measures will be needed sooner or later, and the sooner the more seriously the 4 percent goal (or better) is taken. The combined policy of demand expansion and structural improvement may then take the form of deficit spending on structural programs. The two approaches may thus be combined, but there is no reason why the level of spending needed for structural programs should just match that needed for demand expansion. Other program adjustments, be they tax or expenditure changes will be needed as well. The extent to which the tax or expenditure side should be relied upon in these other adjustments, poses a further interesting structural question; but it has nothing to do with that of "structural unemployment" vs. "aggregate demand" which is considered here.

Musgrave's Figure 1 puts the structural-inadequate demand issue in concise form. It should be noted that he assumes that although there might be structural imbalance in the labor force up to Employment ON″, at price level RP″, at point R, there is no structural unemployment. Thus, he can validly argue that any structural measures would only result in "employment diversion" as structural imbalance is reduced by a "structural program," presumably retraining or relocation measures. These would serve merely to bring regional and/or occupational unemployment rates closer together.

But with a given expansion of spending, the degree to which output and employment would increase would be determined by the extent of potential structural unemployment and the success in widening bottlenecks through structural measures. These alternatives are depicted by the two extensions of the supply curve RS beyond R. With structural unemployment present, the increase in demand would tend to be more dissipated in rising prices rather than rising output, as would be the case if structural bottlenecks did not appear as spending increased. Thus the only inflationary pressures would be those usually associated with rising demand for goods and productive factors.

The trend toward verticality of Musgrave's RS′ curve understates the possibilities for output and employment to expand, albeit in an inflationary manner, from an increase in spending even when structural bottlenecks appear. As was mentioned above, demand may be diverted toward goods that can be produced by surplus labor as the price of goods produced by scarce labor increase more rapidly. Then there are the opportunities for factor substitution, in production, of surplus workers for the more suitable unavailable ones.

Furthermore, Musgrave's conclusion that the expansion that closely followed the tax cut of 1964 revealed that structural elements "were less serious than expected," because prices were relatively stable during the period, may be debated. Prices were stable through 1965, the time the paper was written, but the inflation beginning in 1966 might be considered a lagged manifestation of structural bottlenecks. Musgrave's "hunch" that the economy was closer to N′ than N″ after 1966 was not verified by later events.

**The Inadequate Demand Argument**

The Council of Economic Advisers has been the chief proponent of the inadequate demand view of unemployment, that the economy can move toward full employment without facing inflationary pressures created by labor bottlenecks, or that the structural component of a given level of unemployment is low. Their view was expressed in Council reports prior to and following the tax cut of 1964. To repeat the structuralist position, those who believe the bottleneck element in increasing labor demand to be strong did not, as a matter of principle, argue against the tax cut, but only claimed that the inflationary pressure generated by increased demand would be augmented by the appearance of structural bottlenecks.

Some economists, with a seemingly less polemic viewpoint, suggest that both demand-stimulating and structural measures (retraining, relocation, etc.) are needed to expedite the movement of the economy toward full employment. Increased spending in general would be complemented by structural measures which, by widening incipient bottlenecks, would translate additional spending into expanded output and employment rather than into higher prices. But this is really not a neutral view, but the core of the structural argument, of incipient if not actual bottlenecks. Given budgetary limitations under which policy makers operate, the structuralist only asks that some money be diverted from spending in general into structural measures. Presumably, there is a cost to these measures, or else there would be no reason not to adapt them, and the whole controversy would deal with the single question of whether they would be effective.

Structural problems exist or arise, or they do not. If they do, then widening bottlenecks would be favored over an equal expenditure in undirected additional increases in demand, insofar as inflation represents a social cost. If they do not, then there would be no basis to the structural argument.

There are two additional facets to the structural argument besides supporting a balanced program of increased (government) spending or a tax cut and structural measures. First, the structuralist warns that structural measures take time to be effective in widening bottlenecks that appear with rising demand. Then, if structural elements arise, even if counteracting measures are adoped, prices will rise in the short run from labor bottlenecks unless dampened by monetary measures. Second, perhaps the conscious program to move toward full employment may be initiated at a low enough unemployment rate so that bottlenecks are already present, and structural unemployment forms a substantial part of the overall volume. Then the need for structural measures would be all the more pressing. In fact, the level of unemployment would itself be reduced by the first group of workers being made suitable for job openings through their adoption.

The Council of Economic Advisers' strong inadequate-demand position, with the complementary vigorous denial of the structural argument, was forcefully expressed by its chairman, Walter Heller. He gives a clear presentation of the Council view in his testimony, representing the Council, before the Subcommittee on Employment and Manpower of the Senate Committee on Labor and Public Welfare.

# Statement to U.S. Senate

## by Walter Heller

### II. THE PERSISTENT PROBLEMS OF STRUCTURAL UNEMPLOYMENT

The tax cut would thus increase demand to levels consistent with a 4-percent rate of unemployment. It would ease our most pressing unemployment problems. But no one can assume that our worries about unemployment would then be over. Some of its most distressing and inequitable aspects would remain.

\* \* \*

Experience (which we will review later in this statement) clearly shows (1) that the unemployment rate will decline for every major category of workers and (2) that the sharpest declines will occur where the incidence of unemployment is the highest: among teenagers, the Negroes, the less-skilled, the blue-collar groups generally.

But even so, the unemployment rates of many groups will still be intolerably high.

Back in 1957, for instance, when the average unemployment rate was just over 4 percent for the whole economy, the rates were much higher for many disadvantaged groups and regions—e.g., 10.8 percent for teenagers, 8.0 percent for nonwhites, 9.4 percent for unskilled manual workers, and 11.5 percent for workers in Wilkes-Barre–Hazleton, Pennsylvania.

These *high specific unemployment rates, which persist even when the general rate falls to an acceptable level,* are the essence of the problem of structural unemployment. Even a fully successful tax cut cannot solve problems like these by itself. They require a more direct attack.

To reduce the abnormally high and stubborn unemployment rate for Negroes requires a major improvement in their education and training and an attack on racial discrimination. To reduce the persistent high rate for the unskilled and the uneducated groups demands measures to

SOURCE Reprinted from Annual Report of the Council of Economic Advisors, 1964, pp. 172–182.

help them acquire skills and knowledge. To reduce excessive unemployment associated with declining industries and technological advance requires retraining and relocation. To reduce high unemployment in distressed areas of Pennsylvania, Michigan, Minnesota, and elsewhere calls for special measures to rebuild the economic base of those communities and assist their workers.

Both the Administration and the Congress have recognized that these measures must be taken concurrently with measures to expand aggregate demand. Coal miners in Harlan County are structurally unemployed *now*, and so are Negro and Puerto Rican youths in New York City. Yet programs to reduce structural unemployment will run into severe limits *in the absence of an adequate growth of demand*, i.e., in the absence of rapid expansion of total job opportunities. Such expansion is needed to assure that retrained and upgraded workers, for example, *will* find jobs at the end of the training period and *will not* do so at the expense of job opportunities for other unemployed workers. As structural programs create new and upgraded skills, they will in some cases fit the participants for jobs that had previously gone begging. But for the most part, the needed jobs must be created by expansion of total demand.

Quite apart from the human significance of structural unemployment, it also has great economic importance. For only as we reduce structural and frictional unemployment can we achieve the higher levels of total output which would be associated with unemployment rates below our 4-percent interim target. The Council emphasized this point in its 1963 *Annual Report* (p. 42), as follows:

*Success in a combined policy of strengthening demand and adapting manpower supplies to evolving needs would enable us to achieve an interim objective of 4 percent unemployment and permit us to push beyond it in a setting of reasonable price stability. Bottlenecks in skilled labor, middle-level manpower, and professional personnel [now] tend to become acute as unemployment approaches 4 percent. The result is to retard growth and generate wage-price pressures at particular points in the economy. As we widen or break these bottlenecks by intensified and flexible educational, training, and retraining efforts, our employment sights will steadily rise.*

Every worker needlessly unemployed represents a human cost which offends the sensibilities of a civilized society. But each worker needlessly unemployed also represents a waste of potential goods and services, which even an affluent society can ill afford. More intensive measures to attack structural unemployment are necessary to reduce the unemployment rate not merely to 4 percent, but beyond.

### III. HAS STRUCTURAL UNEMPLOYMENT INCREASED?

The proceding section addressed itself to structural unemployment as a human and social problem and considered its role in the process of lowering the unemployment rate to and below 4 percent. But it is also appropriate to ask: has structural unemployment increased to such an extent since 1957—the last time unemployment was near 4 percent—that it will impede the expansionary effects of demand-creating measures in general and the tax cut in particular?

An affirmative answer would, we believe, represent a misreading of the facts. As we have already pointed out, there *are* serious structural problems, and prompt action is needed both to root out inequities and hardships they inflict and to help us reach our employment goals. But this conclusion need not—and does not—rest on a belief that there has been a disproportionate surge in structural unemployment since 1957.

A reading of the evidence on this score must focus principally on what happens, over time, to the unemployment rates of particular groups—teenagers, untrained and unskilled workers. Negroes, and other disadvantaged groups and regions—in relation to the total unemployment rate. It would clearly be misleading simply to compare unemployment rates for such groups in a year like 1957, when the total rate was about 4 percent, with the corresponding rates in 1962–63, when the total rate has averaged 5.6 percent. Rather, it is the *relationship* between the total rate and the groups' rates—and its historical development—that reveals whether the structural problem is getting worse or not. And this relationship has been remarkably stable.

The disadvantaged groups almost invariably share more than proportionately —and the skilled and white-collar groups less than proportionately—in both decreases and increases in total employment. In the past, when the over-all unemployment rate has risen (or fallen) 1 percentage point, the rate for nonwhites and teenagers has risen (or fallen) by about 2 percentage points, the rate for unskilled workers by about 2½ percentage points. But the rate for professional and technical workers has risen or fallen by only about one-fourth of a percentage point.

One obvious reason for the disproportionate impact on teenagers is that they are the most recent additions to the labor force. When new job opportunities are few, there is a backing-up at the point of entry. Furthermore, even when they do find jobs, they tend to have the lowest seniority and are therefore first to be laid off. Much the same is true of Negroes. Given existing patterns of discrimination, they are often in marginal jobs or at the bottom of seniority lists. Moreover, when jobs are scarce and labor is plentiful, racial discrimination, where it exists, is more likely to enter into hiring and firing decisions. And at such times, employers are also more inclined to pass over inexperienced and untrained workers and less inclined to press their own efforts to adapt such personnel to their needs via in-service training programs. They tend to be less aggressive in seeking new employees outside their own local labor markets. And labor supply considerations are less likely to determine the location of new plants.

On the other hand, employers do not typically discharge many supervisory and technical personnel when output drops and, as a result, they do not need to expand their employment of such persons proportionately when output rises.

\* \* \*

Thus it is not surprising to find that slackened demand since 1957 has intensified inter-group and inter-regional disparities in unemployment rates at the same time that it raised the total unemployment rate. Nonwhites, teenagers, unskilled and semi-skilled workers have suffered a greater-than-average increase in unemployment since 1957. But these same groups will also benefit disproportionately as demand expands and the over-all unemployment rate declines. This point is illustrated in the table on page 280, which shows how the incidence of unemployment changed during the 1960–61 recession and the 1961–62 recovery.

Studies of changes in the incidence of unemployment among unskilled and semi-skilled blue-collar workers—whose jobs would seem to be highly vulnerable to technological change—can provide important insights into the structural unemployment problem. One would expect an accelerated rate of technological displacement to be reflected in rising rates of unemployment for these groups—relative to total unemployment. One would also expect to find such a relative rise for workers in industries such as manufacturing, mining, and transportation where automation has so far found its widest application.

| | Percentage Points | |
|---|---|---|
| | 1960–61 | 1961–62 |
| Total | 1.1 | −1.1 |
| Teenagers | 1.6 | −1.9 |
| Nonwhites | 2.3 | −1.5 |
| Nonfarm laborers | 2.0 | −2.1 |
| Operatives | 1.6 | −2.1 |
| Manufacturing workers | 1.5 | −1.9 |
| Miners | 2.1 | −3.0 |
| For illustrative purposes: | 3.4 | −3.4 |
| Michigan | 6.9 | −7.8 |
| Wheeling, W. Va. | | |

To test this possibility, we have correlated the unemployment rate in specific occupations and industries with the rate for all experienced workers in the labor force during the 1948–57 period—in other words, for the period before the main structural unemployment upsurge is alleged to have occurred. These correlations were then used to calculate what the occupational and industrial distribution of unemployment *would* have been in 1962 if the old relationships had held. If there had been a substantial increase in structural maladjustments, the actual 1962 unemployment rates for what we may call the "technologically vulnerable groups" should have been *higher* than these calculated rates. But in fact, as Table 1

TABLE 1.  UNEMPLOYMENT RATES IN INDUSTRIES AND OCCUPATIONS MOST VULNERABLE TO TECHNOLOGICAL DISPLACEMENT, 1957 AND 1962

[Percent]

| Industry or Occupation | 1957 | 1962 | Change in Rate, 1957–62 | |
|---|---|---|---|---|
| | | | Actual | Expected [a] |
| All workers | 4.3 | 5.6 | 1.3 | — |
| Experienced wage and salary workers | 4.5 | 5.5 | 1.0 | — |
| Workers in selected industries (goods producing) | 5.4 | 6.4 | 1.0 | 1.3 |
| Mining, forestry, and fisheries | 6.3 | 8.6 | 2.3 | 1.8 |
| Construction | 9.8 | 12.0 | 2.2 | 1.8 |
| Durable goods manufacturing | 4.9 | 5.7 | .8 | 1.4 |
| Nondurable goods manufacturing | 5.3 | 5.9 | .6 | 1.0 |
| Transportation and public utilities | 3.1 | 3.9 | .8 | 1.0 |
| Experienced workers | 3.9 | 4.9 | 1.0 | — |
| Workers in selected occupations (blue collar) | 6.0 | 7.4 | 1.4 | 1.7 |
| Craftsmen, foremen, and kindred workers (skilled) | 3.8 | 5.1 | 1.3 | 1.3 |
| Operatives and kindred workers (semi-skilled) | 6.3 | 7.5 | 1.2 | 1.6 |
| Laborers, except farm and mine (unskilled) | 9.4 | 12.4 | 3.0 | 2.6 |

[a] Calculated by use of correlations of (*a*) unemployment rates by industry with the rate for all experienced wage and salary workers, and (*b*) unemployment rates by occupation with the rate for all experienced workers, using data for the period 1948–57 in both cases.

SOURCES: Department of Labor and Council of Economic Advisers.

shows, a majority of the rates are *lower*. For some of these occupations and industries, the actual increase in unemployment was greater than expected, but in most cases it was less. And taking all of the blue-collar occupations and goods-producing industries together, we also find that the rise in actual unemployment was somewhat less than the 1948–57 experience would have suggested.

We do not conclude from this evidence, nor from similar findings by Edward Denison and Otto Eckstein[2] as to the *geographic* distribution of unemployment, that a reduction in structural unemployment has occurred. Similarly, however, we do not conclude that the unusually high unemployment rates experienced by teenagers this year, or the rather low rates experienced by adult males, prove an adverse structural shift. In some labor market areas, imbalances have lessened; in others they have increased. But this does not suggest that the over-all rate of structural unemployment has risen significantly.

One similar piece of evidence relates to job vacancies. Since structural unemployment is a form of joblessness that persists over a protracted period even if unfilled jobs are available, an increase in structural unemployment would be clearly suggested if it were found that the number of job vacancies were rising along with the number of unemployed men.

Unhappily we have no comprehensive and adequate series designed to measure job vacancies in the United States. The Department of Labor currently is proposing experimental work leading toward the eventual establishment of such a series. This is a proposal we strongly endorse, although we share the Labor Department's awareness that such a series involves many technical problems and will

need to be interpreted with care, especially in its early years.

But meanwhile the only available indicator that bears upon the job-vacancy situation is the National Industrial Conference Board's index of the number of help-wanted advertisements published in the classified section of a leading newspaper in each of 33 leading labor market areas. While this series does a good job of reporting what it is designed to report, obviously it provides a comparatively sketchy and imperfect indication of job vacancies. All the same, it is interesting that, after adjustment for changes in the size of the labor force, the help-wanted index was substantially lower in 1960 and 1962 than in 1955–57, when the total unemployment rate was about 4 percent. We have further adjusted the index for changes in the total unemployment rate in order to screen out the effects of slack demand. Even in this form the index fails to rise significantly since 1957—as one would expect it to do if underlying structural unemployment had broadened.

The evidence reviewed above does not yield persuasive indications that structural elements are today a significantly larger factor in our unemployment than in 1957. Nevertheless, it would not be surprising if some particular aspects of structural unemployment have intensified. One would assume that the longer a period of slack persists, the more likely it would be that the detailed structure of skills, experience, and training of the labor force would fail to reflect fully the pattern of job requirements at high levels of employment. High employment in 1967 will call for a somewhat different pattern of jobs than existed in 1957, and a slack labor market does not accurately foretell what that pattern will be. Moreover, there is danger that, after

---

[2] Edward F. Denison, *The Incidence of Unemployment by States and Regions, 1950 and 1960,* and *The Dispersion of Unemployment Among Standard Metropolitan Statistical Areas, 1950 and 1960.* Mimeograph. Otto Eckstein, *The Unemployment Problem in Our Day,* paper delivered before the Conference on Unemployment and the American Economy, Berkeley, California, April 1963.

a long period of slack, new hiring standards, habits of mind, and expectations appropriate to an "easy" labor market will have become entrenched, rationalizing increased discriminations against disadvantaged groups. Thus, after the period of prolonged slack since 1957, there is more need than in the usual "cyclical" recovery for an effective program of specific labor-market policies to assist demand-stimulating policies in tailoring men to jobs and jobs to men.

## IV. SHIFTING EDUCATIONAL REQUIREMENTS AND POSSIBLE SKILLED MANPOWER BOTTLENECKS

In recent weeks—partly before this Committee, partly elsewhere—particular attention has been given to one aspect of the problem of structural maladjustments. This is the question of whether a recent shift in the pace and character of technological change has accelerated the long-term rise in job educational and skill requirements in a way that imposes a new bottleneck on expansion. The issue merits special discussion because of the obstacle to the employment-expanding effects of the tax program that this skilled-manpower bottleneck is alleged to present.

The argument is that the nature of recent technological change has caused a rapid shift in the pattern of manpower demand, pushing down the demand for workers with little training and pushing up the demand for the highly educated. Everyone agrees that the educational level of the Nation's population has continued to advance, causing the supply of highly educated manpower to grow rapidly, and the supply of relatively uneducated manpower to decline. Thus the concern expressed is not about keeping pace with an absolute increase in job educational requirements—which have been rising right along—but about being unable to keep pace with an abrupt recent rise in such requirements.

It is feared that as demand increases, there will not be enough highly educated workers to fill the key technical and professional positions that must be manned if production is to expand to levels consistent with 4-percent unemployment; that, in consequence, expansion of output will be frustrated; and that, because of this, high percentages of the remainder of the labor force—including poorly educated workers—will be left unemployed.

\* \* \*

While there does appear to have been some rise in the demand for highly educated workers relative to their supply during the postwar period *as a whole*, the timing of this change is crucial for purposes of evaluating the bottleneck thesis. Since the economy operated at approximately a 4-percent unemployment rate in the mid-fifties without encountering serious skilled-manpower bottlenecks the key question is whether most of this shift occurred *before* or after the 1955–57 period. Hence a shift in job educational requirements relative to supply that had occurred before those years, and was not serious enough to obstruct expansion then, poses little threat to a new move back toward 4-percent unemployment now.

The available unemployment data seem to show that whatever shift may have occurred in job educational requirements relative to supply *did* occur prior to 1957. Indeed it may have been partially reversed since that time. From 1957 to 1962, for example, the unemployment rate for male workers with an 8th grade education or less rose by about one-half, roughly the same as the rate of overall unemployment. But the unemployment rate for college graduates rose from 0.6 percent to 1.4 percent.

In addition to unemployment rates, the percentages of labor-force participation by groups of different educational attainments also have changed during the postwar period. Here the data currently in hand do not permit us to locate the timing of these changes to the degree that has been possible with the unemployment rates. And so we simply do not know whether here, too, the shift toward greater participation by the well-educated, and lesser participation by the poorly educated, may largely have occurred before 1957.[3]

If, in the absence of information, one assumes that the shift in relative participation rates occurred more recently, one might conclude that there have been some withdrawals from the labor force by poorly educated male workers. Whenever they occurred, they present an obvious challenge to both public and private training programs. But the magnitude of these shifts is easily exaggerated—especially if one fails to make adequate allowance for the improvements in retirement programs during the past dozen years. It is clear that the vast majority of the so-called "losses" of less educated workers from the male labor force were concentrated in the 65-and-older age group.

In any event . . . none of this goes to the real nub of the issue. That nub is the failure of the bottleneck hypothesis to make any allowance for the proven capacity of a free labor market—especially one endowed with a high average level of education and enterprise and expanding programs to improve labor skills and mobility—to reconcile discrepancies between particular labor supplies and particular labor demands.

If relative shortages of particular skills develop, the price system and the market will moderate them, as they always have done in the past. Employers will be prompted to step up their in-service training programs and, as more jobs become available, poorly skilled and poorly educated workers will be more strongly motivated to avail themselves of training,

retraining, and adult education opportunities. Government manpower programs begun in the 1961–63 period will also be operating to help ease the adjustment of specific shortages.

As for the personnel with the very highest skills, many—for the very reason that they are scarce—have been "stockpiled" by their employers and are not working to capacity when business is slack. As business picks up, they will be used more fully—and they will be used more efficiently. As engineers become scarce, and more expensive, their talents will be concentrated on engineering assignments, leaving drafting (for example) for draftsmen, who can be trained more quickly.

Naturally, most college graduates will have jobs no matter how high the unemployment rate in the whole economy, even if they have to work below the level for which they are qualified. If they are already in the supervisory or technical jobs for which they are best qualified, their employers will not have to increase by 10 percent the number of such jobs in order to increase total employment by 10 percent. And to the extent that they are not already in such jobs, they are a hidden reservoir of superior talent.

The highly-educated-manpower-bottleneck argument arrives at its alarming conclusion by projecting to new situations a perfectly static set of educational requirements. The argument makes no allowance for flexibility in the system. Flexibility, of course, is not unlimited. If we were talking about accomplishing a massive increase in output within a few months, manpower bottlenecks might indeed become critical. But we find it unrealistic to believe that they represent a major constraint upon an extra $30 billion of output in what will soon be a $600 billion economy—especially when (a) there are virtually no current signs of tension in either

[3] From data examined since the Testimony was prepared, it appears that the shift toward greater participation by the well educated primarily occurred before 1957; as to the poorly educated, roughly half of the shift toward lower participation occurred prior to and half after 1957.

labor markets or product markets and (b) the demand expansion that will accomplish the closure will be spread over 2 or more years in which continuing new supplies of highly trained manpower will be entering the labor market.

At the beginning of Section III the question was raised whether structural elements in unemployment have grown so much since 1957 that they threaten to impede an economic expansion induced by the tax cut. In Sections III and IV we have examined this question from a number of directions, and we now summarize our answer.

The answer is clear: The evidence we have assembled and the tests we have made do not support the thesis that, overall, the incidence of structural unemployment has increased in importance since we last achieved high employment. There may be some problems that seem more serious today than earlier; but in other areas we have probably progressed.

At the beginning of the section included here, which presents his argument against the structuralist position, Heller comes close to accepting it when he writes that "only as we reduce structural . . . unemployment can we achieve the higher levels of total output which would be associated with unemployment rates below our 4 percent interim target." But he then denies the validity of structuralism through tests that are somewhat apart from the issue.

Heller believes that because the pattern of occupational unemployment after 1957 followed that of the previous decade, the argument of increasing structural bottlenecks is thereby weakened. But the structural argument deals with the seriousness of bottlenecks as the economy strengthens, not as it recedes, as was the case from 1957 to 1962. Furthermore, except for the craftsman group, Heller considers only the unemployment changes for the groups of weakest demand, while the structuralist argument hinges on demand-supply relationships, for the strongest groups, among which bottlenecks may appear.

Again, a structural straw man is attacked when vacancies are asked to rise with increasing unemployment if it is to be inferred that the unemployment rise was partially structural in nature. The structuralist does not expect bottlenecks to appear when the unemployment rate rises, but only when it falls. A fairer test would measure whether vacancies were greater than in the past for a given low level of unemployment.

Heller argues that during the period when structural elements were supposed to have strengthened, after 1957, the growth in the unemployment rate for college graduates from 0.6 percent in 1957 to 1.4 percent in 1962 indicated that supply shifts toward the changes in labor demand had already taken place. But the overall unemployment rate had increased substantially between the two years, so that the rise in unemployment rate would be expected even if the bottleneck problem, which applies only to a strengthening economy, had worsened.

Finally, Heller argues that even if specific labor shortages appear, "the price system and the market will moderate them." But a structuralist would say the same thing. The shortages would be "moderated" by inflation as demand gravitated toward goods and services produced by labor surplus sections as prices rose in the "bottleneck sector," and as producers used available (surplus) labor as a substitute for more suitable but unavailable "bottleneck labor." As for widening bottlenecks through training, retraining, and adult education, this all takes time and if these measures are instituted after the fact of labor shortages, they only validate the structuralist position, which argues the need for these measures as a prerequisite for reducing the inflationary pressures of expansion.

## Structural Imbalance

Another test of the structural hypothesis related changes in unemployment to labor force share of sectors prone to above average unemployment rates. Such a study was conducted by Robert A. Gordon, "Has Structural Unemployment Worsened?" Gordon finds that for the period 1950 to 1962, what he calls the "structural component" had not deteriorated for the special groups studied. From this finding, Gordon concludes that the evidence gives more support to the inadequate-demand than the structural explanation of unemployment.

At the outset, Gordon modifies the old charge against the structuralists—that they believe that structural elements are behind the tendency for business cycles to carry out their stages at higher levels of unemployment. To test the structuralist argument, which is only that movement toward full employment would encounter inflationary pressure from labor bottlenecks and not that these bottlenecks would be a factor in explaining high-level unemployment, Gordon traces the movements of his "structural component." This is a measure of the relationship between the share of unemployment and the labor force for specific, chronically high level unemployment sectors.

# Has Structural Unemployment Worsened?

## by R. A. Gordon

Unemployment in the United States has not averaged below 5.5 per cent of the labor force in any year since 1957.[1] Furthermore, it has shown a distressing tendency to creep upward during the last three business cycles. The inevitable questions result: Why? And what can and should we do about it?

The "why?" has led to a debate, which still goes on, as to how much of the recent high level of unemployment is due to a deficiency of aggregate demand—to a failure of total spending on goods and services to rise at a sufficiently rapid rate —and how much is the result of "structural" changes which make a growing fraction of the labor force unsuited for the jobs that are available. Most of the recent studies that have addressed themselves to this problem come to the conclusion that such structural changes account for little of the net increase in unemployment over the last half-dozen years or so.[2]

Despite these findings, the debate continues, and those who have stressed the structural side of the worsened employ-

SOURCE Reprinted with permission from *Industrial Relations*, Vol. 3, May 1964, pp. 53–77.

[1] The research on which this paper is based is part of the large-scale research and evaluation project on Unemployment and the American Economy being conducted by the Institute of Industrial Relations and the Department of Economics at Berkeley under a grant from the Ford Foundation.

[2] See, for example, *Higher Unemployment Rates, 1957–60: Structural Transformation or Inadequate Demand,* Subcommittee on Economic Statistics of the Joint Economic Committee, 87th Cong., 1st sess. (Washington, D.C.: 1961); the papers by Walter Heller and Otto Eckstein, in A. M. Ross, editor, *Unemployment and the American Economy* (New York: Wiley, 1964); L. E. Galloway, "Labor Mobility, Resource Allocation, and Structural Unemployment," *American Economic Review,* LIII (September, 1963), 694–716; and *Economic Report of the President,* January, 1964, especially Appendix A.

ment picture remain unconvinced that they are wrong.[3] For one thing, there *are* distressingly wide and persistent differences in unemployment rates among different parts of the labor force; we all have become increasingly sensitive to reports of widespread joblessness among youth, Negroes, the unskilled, and so on; and we hear on all sides of the "new industrial revolution" that is "automatizing" production and wiping out hundreds of thousands of jobs formerly held by unskilled and semiskilled workers. Furthermore, it is a statistical fact that fewer workers are employed today in what is loosely called "industry" (manufacturing, the public utilities, transportation, and mining) than in 1957, despite the large increase in real gross national product that has occurred since then.[4] All this suggests that there *must* be something to the structural agreement.

This paper attempts to throw some further light on this debate, both conceptually and factually. The results are striking. Using an approach that is as close to common sense notions as we can achieve, we reach the conclusion that since the mid-fifties—that is, since the American economy last came close to what is generally accepted as full employment—the unemployment situation has not worsened *relatively* for any of the groups on which attention has been focussed in the last few years. Whether we

concentrate our attention on teenagers (before 1963), on blue-collar workers, on the unskilled, on nonwhites, on the least educated, or on workers in the industries supposedly most affected by automation—in none of these cases has the unemployment situation worsened *relatively* when we take account of the rise in total unemployment since the mid-fifties.

We now proceed to define our terms and set out the facts.

## DEFINITION AND MEASUREMENT

It has been said that "The concept of structural unemployment as applied to particular workers or groups of workers is theoretically meaningless and defies empirical measurement."[5] In an important sense, this is so. We cannot identify precisely which of those currently unemployed lost their former jobs for reasons which we call structural. But for present purposes this does not matter.

We start with the essential fact that the labor force is heterogeneous—and heterogeneous in a number of different dimensions. The American data permit us immediately to identify at least six such "dimensions of heterogeneity": age, sex, color, industry of last employment, occupation, and geographical area.[6] Along any one (or some combination) of these dimensions, we can compare unemployment rates for different segments of the labor

---

[3] See, for example, Thomas B. Curtis, *87 Million Jobs* (New York: Buell, Sloan, and Pearce, 1962); also the testimony of W. D. Fackler in *Unemployment Problems,* Hearings before the Special Committee on Unemployment Problems, U. S. Senate, 86th Cong., 1st sess. (Washington, D.C.: October, 1959, pt. 1, pp. 44 ff.; *Employment in the Dynamic American Economy,* Republican Policy Committee of the House of Representatives, in the *Congressional Record* (87th Cong., 1st sess., 1961); and two papers by C. C. Killingsworth, one read at a conference on Employment Security at Michigan State University, October 26, 1963, and the other reproduced in *Nation's Manpower Revolution,* Hearings before the Subcommittee on Employment and Manpower of the Senate Committee on Labor and Public Welfare, 88th Cong., 1st sess. (Washington, D.C.: September–November, 1963), pt. 5, pp. 1461–83. The entire set of the Hearings last cited might also be mentioned in this connection.

[4] See, for example, *A Report on Manpower Requirements, Resources, Utilization, and Training,* U. S. Department of Labor (Washington, D.C.: March, 1963), p. 16. This document will hereafter be referred to as *Manpower Report.*

[5] *Higher Unemployment Rates, 1957–60 . . .* , p. 7.

[6] Actually, we can also get data for a few other dimensions of the labor force, for example, by marital status and education. We shall later give some attention to the distribution of the unemployed by education.

force: white and nonwhite, by age, by occupation, and so on.

If, along any of these dimensions, we discover differences in unemployment rates which persist for long periods of time (through a number of business cycles), we do not have to stretch the ordinary meaning of words to say that there are *structural differentials* in unemployment rates. We are also free to try to measure whether and by how much these differentials have changed.

But now another question arises. Let us consider some one dimension, say, occupation. Let us assume that the unemployment rate for a particular occupation has been increasing relative to the average rate for all workers. But let us assume also that this occupation constitutes a steadily declining fraction of the labor force so that, despite the worsening differential rate, this group represents no larger a fraction of total unemployment than, say, ten years ago. The "structural differential" has widened, but in what sense can we say that there has been an increase in "structural unemployment"?

These questions suggest a simple identity as a basis for studying changes in the composition of total unemployment over time. Let $U$ and $L$ stand for unemployment and labor force, respectively, and let us use the subscript $i$ to represent a particular sector of the labor force when classified in a particular way (for example, by age). Then we can write:

$$\left(\frac{U_i}{L_i} \div \frac{U}{L}\right) \cdot \frac{L_i}{L} = \frac{U_i}{U}$$

This formula says that the ratio of the unemployment rate in one sector to the over-all unemployment rate, weighted by that sector's fraction of the total labor force, is equal to that sector's contribution to total unemployment. We can then study changes over time in the structure of unemployment in terms of (1) the unweighted relative differential rates alone, or (2) the proportional contributions to total unemployment of the different sectors. If, using the second type of measurement, we find changes in the proportional contributions to total unemployment of the different sectors, we can then determine to what extent such changes are to be explained by changes in the relative unemployment rates and to what extent by changes in the proportional size of the different parts of the labor force.[7]

Thus we can speak of changes in either relative unemployment rates or of the changing composition (structure) of unemployment. This is as far as one needs to go if one's primary aim is to sort out the facts. If one insists on going further and constructing a single measure of the extent to which the "structural component" of total unemployment has changed, matters become a bit more difficult, and some degree of arbitrariness enters. A rather straightforward sort of measure might be $(U_i / U) - (L_i / L)$ for some predetermined segment of the labor force—say, teenagers or blue-collar workers or (along whatever dimension we are measuring) all groups having unemployment rates above some predetermined figure in a base year.[8] Use of such a measure should, of course, seek to avoid the influence of purely cyclical changes, which can be done by applying the formula only to years in which over-all unemployment is at a cyclical minimum.

[7] For simplicity, we shall refer to the ratio of one sector's unemployment rate to the national rate as the *relative unemployment rate* for that sector.

[8] This predetermined figure might be the unemployment rate for, say the most favored quarter of the labor force in a past year in which the economy was at what was generally taken to be over-all full employment. The formula could then be applied to the remaining three-quarters of the labor force over a succession of years. Other variants of the suggested formula can also be devised.

We might illustrate this suggestion by looking ahead to Table 3, which applies our initial basic identity to an occupational breakdown of the labor force. By how much has "structural" unemployment among blue-collar workers increased since, say, 1953? In 1953, blue-collar workers accounted for about 56 percent of total unemployment, but for only 40 percent of the labor force. Thus $(U_i/U) - (L_i/L) = .16$. In 1962, the same calculation gives us $.48 - .36 = .12$. Thus, by this definition, the "structural component" of blue-collar unemployment declined relatively rather than increased over the decade.[9]

But this gets us not only ahead of our story but also into an area of definitional controversy which we are seeking to avoid. Let us therefore go back to "sorting out the facts" in terms of the component elements in our simple identity: i.e., changes in relative unemployment rates, in proportions of the labor force, and in proportions of total unemployment. I shall do this for all but one of the six dimensions previously mentioned: i.e., for age, sex, occupation, industry, and color. To these education can also be added. I shall omit the regional dimension both because the regional estimates of total (not merely insured) unemployment have serious defects and because the regional data do not lend themselves readily to the sort of grouping into a few broad categories needed here. (Actually, the monthly household survey was not designed to yield regional data.)

For the dimensions listed, then, let us see what changes have occurred over the postwar period in each of the components of our basic identity. Results are presented for the years 1948, 1953, 1956, 1959, 1962, and in some cases 1963. The first four were the years in which annual average unemployment reached its low point in the successive business cycles since World War II.[10]

UNEMPLOYMENT AMONG YOUTH

. . . There was little if any relative worsening of the teenage unemployment problem from 1948 to 1962—a finding which is in sharp contrast to general impressions. Second, there was, suddenly, an apparent relative deterioration in the teenage position between 1962 and 1963.

For both boys and girls the relative unemployment rate in 1962 was lower than in 1953 or 1956. The fraction of total unemployment accounted for by boys in the 14–19 age group remained fairly constant between 1953 and 1962. The proportion of the labor force accounted for by girls, however, has been rising relatively more rapidly than for boys, with the result that girls in 1962 accounted for a somewhat larger fraction of unemployment than in 1959 or 1953.

*  *  *

[9] This measure might be put in relative rather than absolute terms. Thus we could write $(U_i/U/L_i/L)$ Using this form we find that in 1953 the blue-collar fraction of total unemployment was 1.40 times its share of the labor force. In 1962 this ratio was 1.33.

[10] Annual data for 1962 were the latest available when the calculations for this study were originally made. In the final stages of preparing the paper for publication I added the annual averages for 1963 as they became available, at least where any significant changes seem to have occurred.

The reader should be warned that the data for 1948, 1953, and 1956 are based on the pre-1957 definitions of employment and unemployment and, in general, are less reliable than the later figures because of the smaller samples that were used. Despite some (I think modest) degree of incomparability that is thereby introduced, it has seemed to me important to try to compare the earlier with the later postwar years. The general agreement in the results obtained, however the labor force is classified, is an encouraging sign, although the reader is warned not to place much faith in small differences involving the years 1948, 1953, and 1956.

TABLE 1.  RELATIVE CONTRIBUTIONS TO CIVILIAN LABOR FORCE AND TO UNEMPLOYMENT,
AGE GROUP 14–19, 1948–1963

| Year | Percentage Share of Age Group in | | Difference |
| | Unemployment | Labor Force | |
|---|---|---|---|
| 1948 | 20.1 | 8.6 | 11.5 |
| 1953 | 19.5 | 7.6 | 11.9 |
| 1956 | 20.0 | 7.8 | 12.2 |
| 1959 | 19.0 | 7.9 | 11.1 |
| 1962 | 20.4 | 8.5 | 11.9 |
| 1963 | 23.5 | 8.6 | 14.9 |

Now, combining the figures for the two sexes, let us compare the changes in the teenage share of the labor force with changes in its share of total unemployment. This permits us to use the measure, $(U_i / U) - (L_i / L)$, suggested previously. The figures are given in Table 1.

Again we get the impression that the "youth unemployment problem" (1) showed little relative worsening up to 1962 and (2) did show relative deterioration last year. In 1962, teenagers did not comprise a significantly larger fraction of total unemployment than in 1956 or 1948. (This was particularly so for boys.) And, as we can see from the third column of Table 1, the difference between youth's relative contributions to unemployment and to the labor force showed no net increase between 1953 and 1962. After this decade of comparative stability, the apparent relative deterioration that occurred in 1963 is doubly striking.

These figures, combined with what we know of the present age structure of the population, suggest a double warning for the future. The teenage share of the labor force is now expanding, and it would appear that relative unemployment rates for teenagers may now finally be rising, although we should be careful about generalizing from one year's experience.[11] In the rest of the sixties, the teenage com-

ponent of the labor force will continue to expand more rapidly than the labor force as a whole. By 1970, according to official projections, the 14–19 age group will account for about 10 per cent of the labor force, compared to 8.5 per cent in 1962 and 1963.

Thus, prior to 1963, the youth unemployment problem—taking all teenagers together—had not been one of worsening differential opportunities as measured by unemployment rates. But, by the beginning of the sixties, it was promising to become a more serious problem because of the accelerated increase in the number of teenagers in the labor force. This increase promised to be a problem, not because relative unemployment rates for teenagers had been deteriorating prior to 1963, but because they had been pathetically high throughout the postwar period. It remains to be seen whether the sudden worsening in this relative rate in 1963 will continue or be reversed.

*    *    *

THE PAST AND THE FUTURE

Whether or not the structural problem has worsened significantly in the last few years, some observers express concern about the structural obstacles to attempts —as, for example, through the recently ap-

[11] "Most of the rise [in teenage unemployment] between 1962 and 1963 (about 150,000 altogether) was among 16 and 17 year-olds. Nearly half of these youngsters were seeking only part-time jobs." *Monthly Report on the Labor Force*, December, 1963, p. 13. See also, *Manpower Report*, March, 1964, p. 125.

proved tax cut—to raise total spending "across the board." Thus Killingsworth has argued that a general expansion in demand will quickly run up against "a severe shortage of workers at the top of the educational ladder" and that such bottlenecks will make it difficult or impossible to bring down unemployment rates among the less educated and less skilled to the levels implied by, say, a national unemployment rate of 4 per cent.[12]

Our own tables suggest that we should not ignore Killingsworth's warning. Between 1948 and the mid-fifties, when unemployment tended to be low and economic growth was rapid, *relative* unemployment rates rose for blue-collar and less skilled workers, for nonwhites, and for the least educated. In general, relative rates fell for the more favored groups whose unemployment rates were below the national average to begin with. Does it follow that, as we try to accelerate the expansion in output and employment we shall find that the relatively high unemployment rates come down discouragingly slowly—and that the expansion in total employment is held back by increasingly severe shortages of workers with the scarcest types of education, training, and skills?

This is a problem that should not be ignored. But neither should it be exaggerated. On the whole, I am inclined to accept the position taken by the Council of Economic Advisers on this issue. The economy operated at close to a full-employment level in the mid-fifties without encountering serious bottlenecks of highly educated manpower, and there is little evidence that there has been a marked shift in job educational requirements relative to supply since then. (Indeed, the significant shift in this respect seems to have occurred before 1957.)

More important, as the Council puts it, the bottleneck hypothesis fails "to make any allowance for the proven capacity of a free labor market—especially one endowed with a high average level of education and enterprise and expanding programs to improve labor skills and mobility—to reconcile discrepancies between particular labor supplies and particular labor demands." In tight labor markets, employers are moved to step up their training program; workers are motivated to exploit available training and educational opportunities; and a continuous process of upgrading goes on within the labor force.

So far as those with the highest skills and education are concerned, unquestionably a certain amount of labor hoarding has prevailed in the recent past. Further, a good deal of such highly trained staff is of an "overhead" character; the demand for additional staff should be moderately insensitive to an accelerated rise in output in the short run.

Finally, our supply of educated manpower has been increasing steadily, and a higher educational level brings with it greater flexibility in adjustment to change.

On the whole, I think there is considerable basis for the Council's confidence in what may be called the "forced-draft flexibility" of the labor force under tight labor market conditions. In all probability, however, a price will have to be paid in accelerated wage increase and further upward pressure on prices. But many believe that this is not too high a price to pay for a substantially closer approach to full employment. And the price to be paid can be held down by a vigorous policy of wage and price restraint—by what the Europeans would call an effective "incomes policy." And, needless to say, a much stepped up program of education and retraining will also help.

[12] See his paper, "Automation, Jobs and Manpower," reproduced in *Nation's Manpower Revolution,* pt. 5, p. 1479. The full reference to this set of Senate committee hearings is given in footnote 3.

## SOME CONCLUSIONS

Three broad conclusions stand out as a result of this study. The first merely confirms what we already know: however we classify the American labor force, we find that the incidence of unemployment is distributed very unevenly. There are persistent, structural differences in the incidence of unemployment. In this sense, there is always a structural component in total unemployment.

Our second conclusion offers an answer to the question posed in the title of this paper. On the whole, at least with respect to those "dimensions of heterogeneity" in the labor force that we have examined, structural unemployment has not worsened relatively since the mid-fifties in either of the two senses suggested by our basic identity. The most important qualification to this conclusion suggested by our data arises out of the evidence that the position of teenagers has worsened relatively in the last year or so. (But even here the deterioration has come only very recently, while total unemployment has been at an unsatisfactorily high level since 1957.) A modest modification is also perhaps necessary with respect to education.

With the exceptions noted, the period of high total unemployment in the last half-dozen years has not been characterized by an increasing concentration of unemployment among the groups that are structurally most disadvantaged in seeking jobs. Whether we consider teenagers before 1963, nonwhites, those with the least education, or blue-collar workers, in none of these cases has the unemployment rate since 1956 tended to rise relatively faster than the rate for the whole labor force.

Our third conclusion is implied by the second. The rise in total unemployment in the United States between the mid-fifties and early sixties, it would seem, must reflect primarily the failure of aggregate demand to rise at the rate required by the growth of the labor force and the increase in labor productivity.

❋　❋　❋

Gordon's formula for the "structural differential" might be considered superior to his "structural component" as a measure of the contribution of each sector to structural unemployment. In the former, he weights the ratio of the specific to the overall unemployment rate by the sector's share of the labor force. By doing this, he derives the sector's share of total unemployment which, if the sector is one of unemployment above its frictional level, may contribute to structural unemployment to the degree that there are vacancies in other sectors. This formula notes that the contribution of a sector to total unemployment is determined not only by is own unemployment rate but also by its importance in the labor force.

On the other hand, the "structural component," as presented in its relative rather than absolute form in footnote 9, is nothing more than a comparison of the specific with the overall unemployment rate. As such, it is a measure of "structural imbalance," the degree to which specific unemployment rates differ from the average for all sectors. Although a "structural imbalance" of a particular sector may widen significantly, its contribution to total unemployment may decline if the sector becomes a much smaller part of the total labor force, and then its potential addition to structural unemployment would also become smaller, with the fewer workers involved. In the other groups, besides the teenage one presented here, Gordon also found no significant change in structural imbalance over the period. But does this finding really deny the structural argument? In his conclusion, Gordon states that there has not been "an increasing concentration of unemployment among the groups that are structurally most disadvantaged in seeking jobs" during the latter years of this study, a "period of high total unemployment." But a structuralist would argue that the behavior of specific rates during years when the overall unemployment level is high may not indicate what will tend to happen to relative rates when the economy moves toward full employment. Will bottlenecks then arise which, in the absence of specific antistructural measures, could lead to rising prices? This is the question the structuralist wants answered. Gordon suggests that despite the possible easy adaptation of the labor force to match its skills to industrial needs, under tight labor market conditions, "in all probability, however, a price will have to be paid in accelerated wage increases and further upward pressure on prices. But many believe this is not too high a price to pay for a substantially closer approach to full employment." The structuralist is only interested in the facts, not the normative judgment.

If structural imbalance has not worsened, at overall unemployment somewhat above its frictional level, there is some indication that perhaps structural elements have not become more severe. The closer together the starting point in the move toward full employment finds specific rates, the more likely it is that bottlenecks would not appear until the overall rate was driven down further than would be the case were specific rates widely separated, with incipient bottlenecks in certain sectors. In any case, however, the structuralist would not be convinced that structural unemployment had not worsened until low levels of unemployment were achieved with no more than the normal inflation associated with strengthening of demand for goods and factors.

### Attacking the Structuralist Position

In two lectures, Robert M. Solow, *The Nature and Source of Unemployment in the United States,* argues against the structuralist position. At the outset, he properly scores the crude structuralist view that the high level of American unemployment at the time was mainly a result of imbalance between the unemployed and available job openings, with its implication that employment could be significantly increased without an expansion of aggregate demand.

It is interesting to note, however, that Solow can only cite popular sources and not professional economists for this view. Myrdal's position, as quoted, puts him strongly in the modified structuralist camp. But although he notes that some labor scarcities arise even at relatively high levels of unemployment, Myrdal only claims that the move toward full employment would be accompanied by inflationary pressure caused by growing bottlenecks. He specifically states, as would any modified structuralist, that unemployment cannot be lowered from relatively high levels without demand expansion.

Solow can label as political conservatives those who believe structural imbalance to be the basis of high level unemployment, in that they would deny the need for monetary and fiscal measures to eliminate excessive unemployment. But this label would not fit the modified structuralist who would only claim that the move toward full employment through these measures would be extra inflationary because of structural elements. In fact, he might be a strong "liberal" who advocated their adoption despite the inflationary aspects and who suggested stronger measures that he feels would be needed to reduce unemployment by a given amount.

Undoubtedly, as Solow suggests, the labor and product markets tend to adjust to would-be structural bottlenecks. This adjustment takes the form of higher wages in the labor shortage sector and higher prices for the goods the workers produce. These adjustments reduce unemployment or, more correctly, allow a rise in demand to suppress a current bottleneck, at the cost of higher prices. But this is part of the structural and not the demand-shortage school of thought. Similarly, when Solow claims that "If an increase in demand results in a reduction of unemployment, then evidently at least that much unemployment was not 'structural' in character," he does not allow the structural argument to admit that increased demand can always reduce unemployment, but in an inflationary manner.

In a more pointed attack on the structural position, Solow explains that even the modified structuralist must demonstrate that structural problems have worsened. Since the economy was able to achieve acceptably low levels of unemployment in the past without rising prices, even granted that the structuralist does not argue that high levels of unemployment are characterized by structural bottlenecks, he must claim that the bottleneck problem has become more severe. Only then could structural elements be considered to explain why current moves toward full employment would bring on more inflationary pressure than in the past.

Solow rejects this claim by reviewing studies which show that unemployment imbalances by geographical region, by industry and occupation, and by race are no stronger than in the past. Only the apparent widening imbalance by age and education, presented here, could indicate a growing structural element in overall unemployment. Unfortunately these studies compare periods of relatively high unemployment. The fact that there is no trend of worsening imbalance from one weak period to the next says nothing about the comparison for prosperous periods, which is the crux of the structuralist argument, but it does put the burden of proof on the structuralist to show a widening of bottlenecks between prosperous periods.

## The Nature and Source of Unemployment in the United States

## by Robert A. Solow

### THE STRUCTURAL
### UNEMPLOYMENT THESIS

It is therefore hardly surprising [since unemployment rates are drifting upwards in every phase of the cycle] that in the United States, as in Australia and Denmark, the hypothesis has arisen that the economy suffers primarily from "structural" unemployment that will not yield to—and would indeed frustrate—the standard recipe of expansionary fiscal and monetary policy. This view of the situation has become commonplace among journalists, including those writing for foreign readers. Here is an example that came to hand just as I was preparing this lecture: "American society has been so transformed by the new technology and demographic trends that, under present conditions, the private sector of the economy is no longer capable of providing jobs for our burgeoning work force. The tremendous increase in productivity or output per man-hour over the last four years simply means that increased consumer demand—say, the result of the proposed tax-cut—could be satisfied with little if any increase in payrolls."[1] It would be easy to collect many such statements from the serious press, from Congressional debates, and from trade union and business executives.

In fact, as you will have guessed, I believe this analysis of the problem to be wrong. The evidence, as I hope to show, suggests overwhelmingly that the pace of structural change in the United States has not accelerated recently, and that the chronically high unemployment rate is the sign of chronically weak demand and

SOURCE Reprinted with permission from *The Nature and Source of Unemployment in the United States*, Stockholm, Almquist, 1969, pp. 16–30.

[1] Arnold Beichman in the *Spectator,* Jan. 31, 1964, p. 135.

not of a progressively worse mismatching of the knowledge and skills of the labor force with the requirements of a modern economy. Even so, I might not have used this occasion to argue against the "structuralist" view if it had not recently been adopted by so acute and justly respected an observer of the American scene as Professor Gunnar Myrdal. In his California lectures of exactly a year ago, extended and published in a new book *Challenge to Affluence*, Professor Myrdal lends his prestige as economist and plain-talker to the "structuralist" explanation of American unemployment. He says: "American unemployment is . . . increasingly structural. . . . This structural character of unemployment in America means, first, that already at the present low rate of economic growth and at the present high and rising level of unemployment there is a scarcity of educated and skilled labor which shows up in the high figures for overtime among employees belonging to this elite. A rising trend of business activity would very soon be bottlenecked by a lack of this type of worker, long before the hard core of unemployed—those of an inferior quality—had become absorbed. Expansion simply cannot proceed very far before it meets this physical limitation, which must also have inflationary effects since wages must tend to rise. A balanced employment situation cannot be achieved purely by business expansion."[2]

Although I intend to go on and argue that this view is mistaken, I must make it absolutely clear that Myrdal avoids entirely the policy errors into which other "structuralists" tend to fall. A page before the passage I have already quoted he says, with emphasis: "The first inference to be drawn from the present situation in the labor market of the United States is undoubtedly that business should be given a spurt to expand rapidly. All other measures are otherwise hopeless." That he

sees this is a tribute both to the sureness of his instinct as an economist and to the fact that he is the author of a celebrated book on *The Political Element in the Development of Economic Theory*.

❋ ❋ ❋

Suppose that, as output expands from below-capacity level in response to increased demand, the supply of highly-skilled and perfectly-trained labor in some narrow category approaches exhaustion. Textbook economics does not argue that production must stop expanding. Textbook economics says instead that the wages of skilled workers will rise compared with those of unskilled workers and that the prices of goods and services heavily-weighted with the services of highly-skilled workers will rise relative to those of goods and services produced more with unskilled workers. We know that it is always or almost always possible to make marginal substitutions of somewhat less-skilled for somewhat more-skilled labor here and there in the production process. This is not without cost; but the change in relative wages is supposed, in the textbooks, to make the cost worth incurring. And the change in relative prices is supposed, in the textbooks, both to cover the additional cost and to induce consumers to ease their pressure on those goods and services which have become more costly to produce, and to substitute instead those whose supply is more easily expanded.

Now I am not so naive as to believe that the labor and commodity markets in any advanced economy behave exactly like textbook markets. But I should be very surprised if there were not some of this kind of flexibility to be observed in real-life markets, and the Danish story I quoted to you earlier bears me out quite precisely. But what I find so amusing is that the American defenders of the virtues

[2] *Challenge to Affluence*, pp. 29–30.

of free enterprise against the encroachment of perfectly ordinary compensatory fiscal and monetary policy should be prepared to abandon so lightly one of the chief virtues of the system they claim to be defending. One must be quite clear: the claim that American unemployment is increasingly structural is equivalent to a statement that the labor market (and to some extent commodity markets too) is becoming less and less efficient in its operations.

Of course, if this were a true description of the state of affairs, then the fact that it is used as an argument against strong compensatory fiscal and monetary policy would be beside the point—though perhaps interesting to the student of politics. I propose now to argue that it is, in fact, not true.

## THE "STRUCTURALIST HYPOTHESIS" PRECISELY STATED

The proposition I want to establish is not that there is no structural unemployment in the United States, nor even that there is only a little. It is that there has been no substantial *increase* in the amount of structural unemployment. I have already granted that there is some casual evidence that there may be more structural unemployment in the United States than in some European countries—by which I mean roughly that when, by any reasonable measure, the pressure of general demand is about equally high in the U.S. and in Europe, the unemployment rate will be somewhat higher in the U.S. I think there is little to be gained by trying very hard to define precisely what is to be meant by "full employment" or "structural unemployment". The important thing is to say something about how employment and unemployment will respond to an increase in the general pressure of demand. If an increase in demand results in a reduction of unemployment, then evidently at least that much unem-

ployment was not "structural" in character. If an increase in general demand fails to reduce unemployment, then one may say that such unemployment as remains is "structural". (I don't think one can simply ask whether an increase in demand will begin to generate inflationary wage increases. That is an interesting and important question in itself but it is not what people have in mind when they speak of structural unemployment, unless the wage increases are a symptom of important bottlenecks. But in that case there will be little increase in employment and the criterion I have suggested will suffice.)

The hallmark of rising structural unemployment is a tendency for unemployment to become *more* concentrated in certain groups of the labor force or sectors of the economy. This comes about because the demand for certain kinds of labor (unskilled labor, manufacturing labor, West Virginia labor) falls, compared with the demand for labor generally, while the supply of those kinds of labor fails to fall, or rises, in relative terms. In a sense, structural unemployment is the symptom of a failure of labor mobility. It is a sign of something else as well. Given the circumstances I have just mentioned—falling demand for one category of labor, even at a constant general level of demand, but without fast enough net migration to other parts of the labor market—the result might be not the emergence of concentrated unemployment but falling relative wages. One would expect both consequences to occur in fact. Wage structures are sticky but not completely immovable, even in organized labor markets. They will give at least a little in the fact of growing excess supply. But they may not give enough to provide employment for all those who have not, or not yet, left this weak sector of the labor market. (I hope it is clear that I am not suggesting that cuts in the real wage are a solution for general unemployment, but that a lower relative real wage may mop up some relative unemployment, a quite different matter.) So a rising level of structural unemployment is a sign of some combination of insufficiently rapid labor mobility and insufficiently flexible wage structures. It goes without saying that I would not regard the problem as "solved" if incipient structural unemployment could be converted into chronically low wages in some sectors of the labor market. It is not much better to have people trapped in low-wage employment than in structural unemployment. The solution in either case is to open up new routes of mobility. But for analytical purposes one must see all the dimensions of the problem.

To put the structuralist hypothesis to a test one must try to find—by direct observation or by some kind of statistical adjustment—two or more periods of time when the general pressure of demand was about the same. If it then turns out that in the more recent period the level of unemployment was higher, or more strongly concentrated in certain skill categories or industries or regions, then the conclusion is that there has been an increase in structural unemployment. If the general level of unemployment and its incidence on different groups, or its dispersion among the various groups in the labor force, is about the same in two periods, then there is evidence that the volume of structural unemployment has not significantly changed. The difficult thing is to know when the general pressure of demand is about the same in two separate years. About all anyone can do is to exercise some statistical ingenuity, and this has been done in various ways by the several students of the problem whose results I would like to describe.

## UNEMPLOYMENT AND UNFILLED VACANCIES

One attractive possibility will have occurred to you, but is unfortunately not available for the United States. That is to compare the behavior of unemployment and unfilled vacancies through time. We know, of course, that when unemployment falls the number of unfilled vacancies tends to rise. This fact, as you may remember, has often been made the basis for a definition of "full employment", which is said to exist when the number of unfilled vacancies is at least equal to the number of people unemployed. If this is the case, it is tempting to say that the reason why the number of unemployed workers and the number of unfilled jobs are not *both* lower must be that the unemployed have the wrong qualifications for the available jobs, or are located in different parts of the country, or do not know about the availability of the jobs— in any case, one is tempted to say that they are unemployed for structural or frictional reasons, and not because of an inadequate demand for commodities or for labor. (Even in such circumstances, as you in Sweden know, a further increase in demand can lead to still lower unemployment, and still higher unfilled vacancies, as employers are led to accept somewhat lower qualities of labor, and higher wages induce workers to move.)

For my purpose it doesn't matter whether this is a satisfactory definition of full employment. But the following experiment suggests itself. Imagine two years in which the unemployment rate is the same; if there is a greater number (or, more accurately, a greater rate) of unfilled vacancies in the later year, then one would say that the incidence of structural unemployment must have increased. I can put this a bit differently: you can imagine the economy in any very short period as moving along a downward-sloping curve relating the unemployment rate to the vacancy rate—the higher is one, the lower the other. If, over time, one observes this curve shifting outward, so that a higher vacancy rate is associated with the same unemployment rate or a higher unemployment rate with the same vacancy rate, then the structuralist hypothesis is verified. This statistical device is used by Hancock in the Australian study with which I began this lecture.

An even simpler picture can be read from the monthly OECD publication of "Main Economic Indicators". There you will find time series of unemployment rates and vacancy rates plotted on the same graph, one for each of several countries. When one curve goes up, the other goes down. The points where the two curves cross are points where vacancies and unemployment were exactly in balance. (They correspond to points where Hancock's curve cuts the 45° line from the origin.) It is easy to let the eye follow the crossing points and see if they occur at successively higher or lower unemployment rates (i.e., whether Hancock's curve is shifting outward or inward along the 45° line). To my eye it appears that the locus of crossing-points, taking the period 1950–1963, is approximately horizontal for the United Kingdom, the Netherlands, and Switzerland. For Norway there is no clear pattern, but a horizontal one appears most likely. For France, there are no crossing-points, but one would have to say that the two curves have not shifted relative to one another, so that if there were crossing points they would form a horizontal pattern. For Sweden it is harder to say. There are no other OECD countries for which the required data exist. In no case do the graphs give an impression of increasing structural unemployment.

None of this throws any direct light on the United States. We have no statistics of unfilled vacancies, so no conclusive evidence can be had in this way. I think it would be rather amazing if the United States were the only industrial country in which the structuralist hypothesis were true. I know of no evidence to suggest that the pace of structural change has been faster in the United States than elsewhere during the postwar period, nor that the mobility of the labor force is less or

deteriorating more rapidly. There is one rather unsatisfactory bit of evidence which does suggest that the rate of unfilled vacancies would be no higher or only very slightly higher now than it was a decade or more ago at comparable overall unemployment rates. There exists a time series of the number of help-wanted advertisements appearing in a selected newspaper in each of 33 major labor markets accounting for 44% of nonfarm employment. One can regard this series as a rough indicator of how a comprehensive figure on vacancies would behave if there were one. If the help-wanted index is expressed as a proportion of the labor force and plotted against the unemployment rate, there emerges the kind of downward-sloping curve I spoke of earlier. The economy does indeed travel up and down along the curve as one phase of the business cycle succeeds another. There is no clearly visible tendency for the curve to shift outward—to associate more help-wanted advertising with a given unemployment rate—as time goes on. But I admit that this is a very unsatisfactory source of knowledge, and so I will have to go on to less direct ways of testing the structuralist hypothesis.

✿ ✿ ✿

On the relation between unemployment and educational attainment, Professor Charles Killingsworth of Michigan State University has produced some figures which suggest a kind of imbalance. They show that between April 1950 and March 1962, the unemployment rates for males with amounts of schooling ranging between none and 12 years had increased, while the rate was about constant for those with 13–15 years of school completed, and fell sharply, from 2.2% to 1.4% for college graduates. From this and some other analysis he concludes: ". . . that long before we could get down to an overall unemployment rate as low as 4%, we would have a severe shortage of workers at the top of the educational ladder. This shortage would be a bottleneck to further expansion of employment. . . . We could not get very far below a 5% overall unemployment level without hitting that bottleneck." This is a rather different argument from the one we have been considering so far. The structural unemployment thesis is usually applied to what Myrdal calls the "underclass" of unskilled, low-productivity, often even illiterate members of the labor force. Here we are being told that it is in effect the tail of college graduates that wags the dog of unemployment. I find this new line of argument implausible. In the first place, it would be peculiar if the United States, with its very large proportion of university-trained people, should be unable to reduce its unemployment rate to 4% because it does not have even more, while the other major industrial countries of the world should be able to maintain much lower rates with little difficulty despite a smaller diffusion of university education. In the second place, as Rees has commented, it is natural that when labor markets are generally soft, employers should insist and be able to insist on hiring college graduates for positions which do not really require so much education. A tightening of the labor market would involve a reshuffling of the educated labor force to other kinds of jobs without generating any real bottleneck.

Moreover, there are some difficulties with the figures themselves. I will not bore you with the details, but it may be that the 1950 figures are not directly comparable with the later ones, which come from a different source. But even taking the figures as they stand, they may require a different interpretation. Between April 1950 and March 1957, while the overall unemployment rate was falling by one-third, from 6.2 to 4.1%, the rate for college graduates fell by almost three-quarters, from 2.2 to 0.6%. Between March 1957 and March 1962, while the overall unemployment rate rose back to 6.0%, the rate for college graduates rose more rapidly to 1.4%. Thus it appears that while the balance of supply and demand may have favored highly-educated workers to an unusual extent in 1957, it may actually have been shifting against them slightly in the past 5 years. This interpretation is confirmed by the figures for unemployment among professional and technical workers, an occupational category which is not identical to the group of college graduates. In the years 1948–51, unemployment in this category was rather higher than one would have expected it to be, given the general economic situation. Since then, speaking roughly, the normal situation seems to have been restored. You can imagine that I do not like to say a word against higher education; but I can not honestly attribute the high unemployment rates in the United States to a shortage of my own product. Unless it results from the apparent inability of university courses in elementary economics to produce any impact on the ideas of those who sit through them.

✷　✷　✷

In commenting on Killingsworth's position that bottlenecks in the supply of college graduates contribute significantly to structural unemployment, Solow states that "We are being told that in effect it is the tail of college graduates that wags the dog of unemployment." Whether this description is accurate depends on the volume of surplus labor related to the shortage of college graduates. Truly, if this shortage is not great, *in numbers*, no matter how relatively tight the labor market for college graduates, measured by the difference between openings and their unemployment, this bottleneck would be an unimportant contributor to structural unemployment. But, as Solow notes, vacancy data are needed to measure shortages.

In fact, vacancy data over time are needed to test the structuralist position even when it seems to be substantiated. For example, the structuralist argues that prices would tend to rise more than in the past because of structural elements. Certainly, the relatively low unemployment levels of 1968 were achieved under more inflation than in the past. But this does not necessarily mean that various structural bottlenecks are causing the inflation. Have vacancies increased over this level of a past period of comparable low unemployment? If not, we should look to other causes for the inflation than to worsening structural elements.

### Defending Structuralism

Killingsworth presents the strongest case for the structuralist school. At the outset of the portion of his testimony presented here, he predicts that structural bottlenecks would prevent the economy from advancing to a 4 percent level of unemployment as a result of the 1964 tax cut. His position was vindicated in that the move to low rates was followed, with about a year's lag, by a vigorous inflation.

# Automation, Jobs and Manpower

## by Charles Killingsworth

It is not self-evident from these figures that any part of this creeping unemployment problem is due to automation or other basic changes in the patterns of the economy. There is eminent authority to the contrary. The President's Council of Economic Advisers has repeatedly declared that automation and "structural unemployment" are not responsible for the gradual creep of unemployment above the 4-percent level of 1957. For example, the 1963 report of the Council includes the following passage (p. 25):

*The problems of structural unemployment —of imperfect adaptation of jobs and workers—are persistent and serious, and they are thrown into bold relief by the prolonged lack of sufficient job opportunities over the past 5 years.* But these problems of adaptation have not constituted a greater cause of unemployment in recent years than in earlier periods. *The source of the high unemployment rates in recent years, even in periods of cyclical expansion, lies not in labor market imbalance, but in the markets for goods and services.* [Emphasis not in original.]

This analysis of the unemployment problem—that it is caused primarily by a lagging growth rate—is the basis for the administration's emphasis on a large tax cut as the top-priority item in the program to "get the economy moving again." Chairman Walter Heller of the CEA has repeatedly said that there is a "good prospect" that the tax cut would reduce unemployment to the 4-percent level. (See, for example, "Employment and Aggregate Demand," address delivered in Berkeley, Calif., Apr. 19, 1963.)

I think that it can be demonstrated that the Council is the victim of a half-truth.

SOURCE Reprinted from *The Nation's Manpower Revolution,* U.S. Senate, Subcommittee on Labor and Public Welfare, 88th Congress, 1963, pp. 1475–1480.

The lagging growth rate is only a part of the problem, and it may not be the most important part. I think that it is extremely unlikely that the proposed tax cut, desirable though it is as a part of a program, will prove to be sufficient to reduce unemployment to the 4-percent level. Perhaps it is true that in politics you can't get everything all at once. But I feel compelled to say that my analysis leads me to the conclusion that the administration's economic program is seriously incomplete. It gives woefully inadequate attention to what I regard as a key aspect of the unemployment problem of the 1960's; namely, labor market imbalance.

The Council's position on labor market imbalance, quoted above, rests on meticulous and extensive statistical studies. I am sure that the members of the Council, who are scholars of the highest competence and integrity, are willing to go where the facts lead them. The trouble is that their staff studies have not analyzed the figures which, in my judgment, clearly show a growing problem of labor market imbalance.

Let me preface my own analysis of those figures with a brief restatement of my argument to this point. The fundamental effect of automation on the labor market is to "twist" the pattern of demand —that is, it pushes down the demand for workers with little training while pushing up the demand for workers with large amounts of training. The shift from goods to services is a second major factor which twists the labor market in the same way. There are some low-skilled, blue-collar jobs in service-producing industries; but the most rapidly growing parts of the service sector are health care and education, both of which require a heavy preponderance of highly trained people.

I have already presented some figures showing the changing patterns of demand for labor. These changing patterns of demand would not create labor market imbalance, however, unless changes in the supply of labor lagged behind. We turn now to the figures which show that such a lag has in fact developed.

Table 1 shows the relationship between rates of unemployment and levels of education of males 18 and over in 2 years— 1950 and 1962.[1]

The overall unemployment rate was substantially the same in both years—6.2 in 1950 and 6.0 in 1962. But there was a redistribution of unemployment between these 2 years. The unemployment rates at the top of the educational attainment ladder went down, while the rates at the middle and lower rungs of the ladder went up substantially. The most significant figure in this table, I think, is the

TABLE 1.   EDUCATION AND UNEMPLOYMENT, APRIL 1950 AND MARCH 1962 (MALES, 18 AND OVER)

| Years of School Completed | Unemployment Rates | | Percentage Change, 1950 to 1962 |
| --- | --- | --- | --- |
| | 1950 | 1962 | |
| 0 to 7 | 8.4 | 9.2 | +9.5 |
| 8 | 6.6 | 7.5 | +13.6 |
| 9 to 11 | 6.9 | 7.8 | +13.0 |
| 12 | 4.6 | 4.8 | +4.3 |
| 13 to 15 | 4.1 | 4.0 | −2.4 |
| 16 or more | 2.2 | 1.4 | −36.4 |
| All groups | 6.2 | 6.0 | −3.2 |

[1] The reasons for confining the analysis to males here and in the following paragraphs are explained in the technical note below, which also explains the derivation of the figures.

one showing the very large decrease in the unemployment rate of college graduates.

In a sense, these unemployment figures are only the part of the iceberg that is above the water. For a better understanding of their significance, we must consider also the changes in demand and supply that took place at the various educational levels between 1950 and 1962. Chart 1 shows (for males 18 and over) the percentage changes in the supply of labor (labor force), in the demand for labor (employment), and in unemployment rates at various levels of educational attainment between 1950 and 1962. The left-hand bars show labor force changes, the center bars show employment changes, and the right-hand bars show unemployment rate changes. . . . The three bars at the far right of the chart show these changes for all groups combined; these aggregates obviously conceal some differ-

ences between educational levels which are of cardinal importance.

The bars for the 0 to 7 years of education group show that the number of this group in the labor force declined very greatly from 1950 to 1962; but the jobs held by this group declined even more, so that its unemployment rate went up. The supply of labor with 8 years' of education also decreased, and the demand for this group decreased even more, and its unemployment rate increased by more than the increase in rate for the 0 to 7 classification. We see a different relationship between supply and demand in the 9 to 11 years of education group. Supply increased; demand also increased, but by less than the increase in supply, so that a higher unemployment rate resulted here too. The high school graduates (12 years' of education) fared somewhat better. There was a substantial increase in supply in this group, and demand also kept

*Chart 1. The changing structure of labor force, employment, and unemployment, 1950–1962 (males, 18 and over).*

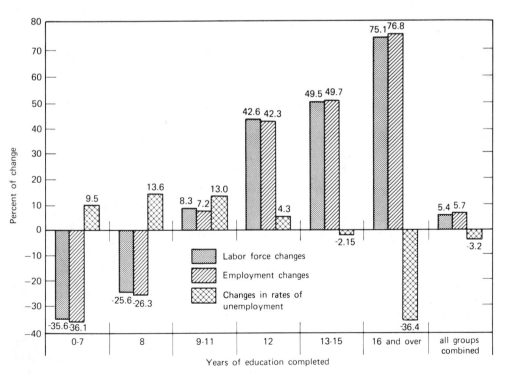

pace, so that this group's unemployment rate went up by less than the rates of the less educated groups. The groups with college training were quite fortunate, especially those with at least 4 years' of college. The supply of men with 13 to 15 years' of education increased by almost 50 percent, but the jobs for them increased by slightly more, so that their unemployment rate (which was already low) went down slightly. The experience of the group with 16 or more years' of education was particularly striking. The supply of men in this group increased by 75 percent, but the jobs for them increased even more than that, so that their unemployment rate went down by more than a third.

It is important to note that all of the improvement in the unemployment situation in 1962, as compared with 1950, was concentrated in the elite group of our labor force—the approximately 20 percent with college training. In all of the other categories, which have about 80 percent of the labor force, unemployment rates were substantially higher in 1962 than in 1950. These figures, I contend, substantiate the thesis that the patterns of demand for labor have been twisted faster than the patterns of supply have changed, and that as a result we had a substantially greater degree of labor market imbalance in 1962 than in 1950.

But these figures do not fully reveal the power of the labor market twist. The "labor force" enumeration includes (with minor exceptions) only those who say that they have jobs or that they have actively sought work in the week preceding the survey. Those who have been out of work so long that they have given up hope and are no longer "actively seeking" work —but who would take a job if one were available—are simply not counted either as unemployed or as members of the labor force. The percentage of a given category of the total population that is "in the labor force" (under the foregoing

definition) is expressed as the "labor force participation rate." It seems probable that worsening employment prospects for a particular group over a long period would force down the labor force participation rate—i.e., would squeeze a number of people out of the labor market altogether, in the sense that they would give up the continuing, active search for jobs. Conversely, it seems probable that improving employment prospects would tend to pull more people into the labor market and thus to raise the labor force participation rate. These two trends are indeed observable since 1950. The squeezing out of people at the lower end of the educational ladder and the pulling in of people at the upper end is another manifestation of the labor market twist. Table 2 presents the pertinent figures for males.

This table tells us that the participation rates at the lower end of the educational scale, which were already relatively low in 1950, had gone much lower by 1962. At the other end of the scale, participation rates had gone up by 1962. (The reason why the increase for college graduates was so small is that even in 1950 their participation rates in the prime age groups —especially 25 to 54—were already quite high, in some categories 98 or 99 percent). Some of the decline in participation rates at the lower end of the scale is due to higher average ages, with a larger proportion in this group (as compared with upper groups) attaining age 65 and voluntarily retiring. But that is by no means the whole story. A detailed comparison by age group as well as by educational level shows that declines occurred at almost every age level in the noncollege category, while there was a rise in participation rates for a majority of the age groups of men with college training.

The important point that I want to make with these figures is that in all likelihood the official unemployment statistics substantially understate the size of the labor surplus of men with limited educa-

| Years of School Completed | Labor Force Participation Rates | | Percentage Change in Rate, 1950 to 1962 |
| --- | --- | --- | --- |
| | 1950 | 1962 | |
| 0 to 4 | 74.6 | 58.2 | −22.0 |
| 5 to 7 | 85.0 | 74.6 | −14.4 |
| 8 | 88.1 | 78.2 | −12.7 |
| 9 to 11 | 92.1 | 88.8 | −3.9 |
| 12 | 94.0 | 90.7 | −3.7 |
| 13 to 15 | 79.6 | 83.0 | +5.4 |
| 16 or more | 92.1 | 92.3 | +0.2 |
| All groups | 87.6 | 83.5 | −4.7 |

SOURCE: The 1950 labor force data are taken from appendix table A1, and population data from the 1950 Census. The 1962 figures are from unpublished data supplied by the U.S. Bureau of Labor Statistics.

tion. If we found jobs for most of those now officially reported as unemployed, the news of improving opportunities would undoubtedly bring back into the labor force many men who are not now counted as members of it. Unfortunately, we cannot count on the same flexibility of supply at the top of the educational scale. Even the most extreme pressures of demand cannot pull the participation rate much above 98 or 99 percent, which (as just stated) is the current rate in some college-trained age groups.

Our overall unemployment rate has now been above 5 percent for more than 5 years, and we cannot be sure what effects a substantial increase in spending by consumers, businesses and Government (i.e., an increase in aggregate demand) would have on the patterns of employment, unemployment, and labor force participation just discussed. Many respected economists believe, as one of them once put it, that the hard core of unemployment is made of ice, not rock, and that it would melt away if overall demand rose high enough. As already noted, the Council of Economic Advisers has virtually guaranteed that the administration's tax cut program —which in its current version would put about $11 billion in the hands of consumers and businesses—would reduce unemployment to an "interim target" rate of 4 percent by 1966. This line of reasoning

assumes (either implicitly or sometimes explicitly) that no serious bottlenecks of labor supply would appear before the achievement of the overall unemployment rate of 4 percent. I seriously question the validity of this critically important assumption under the labor market conditions of today and the foreseeable future.

The benefits of a decline in the overall rate of unemployment appear to be quite unevenly distributed among the educational attainment groups that we have been considering. The year 1957 was the last one in which we had an unemployment rate as low as 4 percent. It is instructive to see how the patterns of unemployment changed from 1950, when the overall rate was above 6 percent, to 1957, and then again to 1962, which had about the same overall rate as 1950. This comparison is made in two forms in Table 3. This table shows the actual unemployment rates for the various educational attainment groups in those 3 years, and it also expresses the unemployment rate for each group in each of the 3 years as a ratio of the rate for all of the other groups combined. (Thus, the 0 to 7 years of education group had an unemployment rate about 50 percent higher than all other groups combined in 1950; its rate was more than double the rate for all other groups in 1957; and its rate was 70 percent higher in 1962.)

Clearly, unemployment at the bottom of the educational scale was relatively unresponsive to general increases in the demand for labor, while there was very strong responsiveness at the top of the educational scale. The percentage unemployment rate for college graduates in 1957 merits close attention. It was an almost incredible 0.6 percent. I have queried the experts in the Bureau of Labor Statistics on this figure, and they assure me that they have no less confidence in it than in the other 1957 figures. Surely a figure as low as that represents what is sometimes called "overfull" employment— i.e., demand which seriously exceeds supply.

Bear in mind that the unemployment rates for the lower educational attainment groups (those with 80 percent of the men) are now higher than in 1950, and that the unemployment rate for college graduates is now substantially lower than in 1950. Also bear in mind that the labor force participation rate figures strongly suggest a large and growing "reserve army"—which is not counted among the unemployed—at the lower educational levels, and that there is no evidence of any such reserve of college-trained men.

Finally, bear in mind the difference between the lower end of the educational scale and the upper end in responsiveness to overall decreases in the unemployment rate.

When you put all of these considerations together, I believe that you are ineluctably led to the conclusion that long before we could get down to an overall unemployment rate at low as 4 percent, we would have a severe shortage of workers at the top of the educational ladder. This shortage would be a bottleneck to further expansion of employment. I cannot pinpoint the level at which the bottleneck would begin to seriously impede expansion; but, on the basis of the relationships revealed by Table 3, it seems reasonable to believe that we could not get very far below a 5-percent overall unemployment level without hitting that bottleneck.

CONCLUSION

The most fundamental conclusion that emerges from my analysis is that automation and the changing pattern of consumer wants have greatly increased the importance of investment in human beings as a

TABLE 3. ACTUAL AND RELATIVE UNEMPLOYMENT RATES BY EDUCATIONAL ATTAINMENT, APRIL 1950, MARCH 1957, AND MARCH 1962 (MALES, 18 AND OVER)

| Years of School Completed | Unemployment Rates | | | | | |
|---|---|---|---|---|---|---|
| | Actual Percentages | | | Relative [a] | | |
| | 1950 | 1957 | 1962 | 1950 | 1957 | 1962 |
| 0 to 7 | 8.4 | 6.9 | 9.2 | 154 | 203 | 170 |
| 8 | 6.6 | 4.4 | 7.5 | 108 | 110 | 132 |
| 9 to 11 | 6.9 | 4.7 | 7.3 | 115 | 120 | 142 |
| 12 | 4.6 | 3.0 | 4.8 | 70 | 67 | 75 |
| 13 to 15 | 4.1 | 2.7 | 4.0 | 64 | 64 | 65 |
| 16 or more | 2.2 | .6 | 1.4 | 34 | 14 | 21 |
| All groups | 6.2 | 4.1 | 6.0 | ([a]) | ([a]) | ([a]) |

[a] The relative unemployment rate is the ratio between the percentage unemployment rate for a given educational attainment group and the percentage unemployment rate for all other groups at the same point in time.

SOURCES: Percentage unemployment figures from appendix table A–3; relative unemployment rates computed from data in appendix Tables 19 and 20.

factor in economic growth. More investment in plant and equipment, without very large increases in our investment in human beings, seems certain to enlarge the surplus of underdeveloped manpower and to create a shortage of the highly developed manpower needed to design, install, and man modern production facilities.

\* \* \*

To my mind, the greatest shortcoming of the administration's program for reducing unemployment is the failure to recognize the crucial need to break the trained manpower bottleneck. I recognize that the administration has recommended what many people regard as very ambitious measures for Federal aid to higher education. But even if these measures were accepted in their entirety, it is most unlikely that they would suffice to break the present and prospective bottlenecks in the supply of highly educated manpower. I am not one who advocates even more billions of dollars in Federal appropriations for higher education. Appropriations for such magnitude almost surely will not be given congressional approval in the foreseeable future. More important, even the largest appropriations within the

realm of remote possibility would leave virtually untouched the most difficult aspect of the financing of higher education. That is the investment that the student, or his parents, must make in his subsistence costs during 4 or more years of training. For most students today, the minimum cost is $5,000.

\* \* \*

I would give a considerably higher priority to the stimulation of investment in human beings than I would to such measures as the proposed tax cut. But I would still rate the tax cut as important. Denying that the tax cut is the "ultimate weapon" against unemployment is not denying that it can make some contribution to the reduction of unemployment. After all, even to get below a 5-percent unemployment rate would be a considerable achievement today. But a really effective attack on the complex problem of unemployment requires a whole arsenal of powerful weapons.

And we don't have all the time in the world. Human history has been described as a race between education and catastrophe. In the past dozen years, education has been falling behind in that race.

\* \* \*

Recall that Heller claimed that the tax cut would lead to a reduction in the unemployment rate to 4 percent, while Killingsworth foresaw a maximum improvement to the 5 percent level. But the difference between the inadequate-demand and structural schools does not hinge on a 1 percent differential in the national unemployment rate. Instead, it centers on the issue of whether improvement in the rate would occur with greater inflationary pressure than in the past. At first view, the structuralist position seems verified. The inflationary market adjustments that permitted the increase in adequate demand to be translated into increased output and employment in the 1966–1969 period represented the structuralist's description of the process toward full employment, not that of the inadequate demand proponent. But the economy was subject to wartime influences, and the rising prices of the period may have simply been an aspect of typical wartime experience rather than a reflection of structural bottlenecks.

Unfortunately, in the absence of vacancy data, Killingsworth is forced to use unemployment figures in statistical support of the structural hypothesis. Comparing 1950 with 1962, two years of almost identical high overall unemployment levels, he finds structural imbalance worsened with higher rates for the high unemployment (low) education levels and lower rates for the low unemployment (high) education levels. Again, without vacancy data, unemployment rates alone tell us nothing about structural components of unemployment, and the use of high unemployment years misses the structuralist test of bottlenecks during business expansion.

But the sectoral employment changes presented indicate that supply changes in response to labor demand shifts were insufficient to reduce structural imbalance. The rates by educational level widened despite increases in supply of the educated and relative decreases in supply of the lesser educated.

It is interesting to note, however, that the unemployment data indicate, that, contrary to Solow's view, the college graduate group is not the tail of the unemployment dog. In 1950, it is true, the college graduate sector was a relatively insignificant component of total unemployment. Then, the unweighted average of the other five educational classes was 6.1 percent and the college graduate group lowered this average to 5.5 percent. But the weighted average for the six groups was 6.2 percent, indicating a preponderance of weighting to the high unemployment lesser educated groups. In 1962, however, the unweighted average of the five other groups was 6.6 percent, with inclusion of the college graduate group, which was now at a lower level than before, reducing this average to 5.8 percent. This was only .2 percentage points below the overall weighted average of 6.0 percent, indicating that the unemployed college graduate group had grown in importance to become almost equal to the average magnitude of the other groups. Moreover, since the college group would constitute the main bottleneck segment in the structuralist argument, perhaps its growing size indicated a larger absolute number of vacancies under tightening labor market conditions. It is this increase in the absolute number that is required to support the view that structural problems have worsened.

It is significant that Killingsworth uses the same unemployment data, that of college graduates, to defend the structural hypothesis that Heller used to attack it. Heller noted the expansion of the rate from 0.6 to 1.4 percent from 1957 to 1962 to suggest that bottlenecks were widening. Killingsworth noted that the reduction from 2.2 to 0.6 percent from 1950 to 1957, as the overall rate fell, indicated a narrowing bottleneck. Without having vacancy data to substantiate his position, he could only argue, intuitively, that "surely a figure as low as that represents what is sometimes called 'overfull' employment—i.e., demand which seriously exceeds supply."

**More Recent Defense of Structuralism**

Although Killingsworth makes telling points for the structural hypothesis, at first, he appears to have erred in his pessimistic prediction that the unemployment rate would not fall below 5 percent after the 1964 stimulation from the tax cut. In fact, the rate fell steadily below 5 percent, below 4 percent, to a low of 3.5 percent for 1969.

But in his recent Congressional statement, parts of which are included here, Killingsworth questions the validity of the unemployment data, specifically the comparability of the post-1965 data with prior figures.

## Rising Unemployment: A "Transitional" Problem?

*by Charles C. Killingsworth*

I believe that the characterization of our growing unemployment problem as "transitional" rests upon assumptions which cannot withstand careful and realistic analysis. Economists generally have accepted a quite superficial explanation of the relatively low unemployment rates of the past five years, and they are now moving to an equally superficial explanation of the current rise in unemployment, and to the advocacy of superficial and inadequate policies for coping with it. The essence of the matter, I believe, is that we never really solved our chronic problem of excessive unemployment which was painfully apparent in the late 1950's and the first half of the 1960's. We simply masked a part of it; temporarily deferred another part of it; and ignored the rest of it. The mask is now slipping and the deferment is beginning to run out, and the

ignored aspect of unemployment has worsened.

### II

The masking of a part of the unemployment problem was the result of two significant changes—one in 1965, the other in 1967—in the definitions used in the monthly surveys which are the basis for the official unemployment statistics. In other words, the yardstick was changed. . . . When we compare current unemployment statistics with pre-1965 figures, it is as if we were comparing measurements in meters and yards while ignoring the difference in the standard of measurement.

If the pre-1965 yardstick for measuring unemployment had been used last month (February), the official report would have shown a national unemployment rate of at least 4.8 per cent, or possibly somewhat

SOURCE Reprinted from Statement for U.S. House of Representatives Select Subcommittee on Labor, March 30, 1970, Detroit, pp. 1–33.

higher, rather than the rate of 4.2 per cent which was actually reported.

What were the changes in definition? In early 1965, the Bureau of Labor Statistics and the Bureau of the Census jointly decided that in making the monthly survey of the labor force, they would henceforth count the enrollees in certain manpower programs as either "employed" or "not in the labor force." The major programs involved at the time were the Neighborhood Youth Corps (the largest), On-the-Job Training under MDTA, Community Action non-professional employment, and College Work Study. Enrollees in these programs were thenceforth counted as "employed." Job Corps enrollees were thenceforth counted as "not in the labor force." In most respects, the largest of these programs are broadly comparable to certain of the work-relief programs of the 1930's and 1940's. Enrollees in those earlier programs (WPA, CCC, NYA) were officially counted as "unemployed," and presumably that established definition had been followed from 1962 to 1965 when the contemporary programs were getting under way. To the best of my knowledge, no public announcement of this change in definition was ever made.

A former staff member of the BLS has made a painstaking study of the effects of this definition change on the official unemployment rate between 1965 and the end of 1967.[1] His principal finding was that the national unemployment rate at the end of 1967 was 0.4 per cent lower than it would have been without the programs and the definition change—that is, the average unemployment rate in the fourth quarter, 1967, would have been 4.0 per cent under the old definitions, rather than the 3.6 per cent that was officially reported. The effect on the 16–21 age group unemployment rate was substantially greater. The reported rate for this group for the fourth quarter of 1967 was 10.8 per cent; under the old definition, it would have been 13.1 per cent, or 2.3 percentage points higher. These estimates are based upon what I regard as highly conservative assumptions, and my rough calculations of the effects of subsequent changes in the enrollments in the pertinent programs and others like them suggest that the 0.4 per cent estimate is almost certainly too low for 1969 and 1970; presently, an estimate of 0.5 or 0.6 per cent would probably be more accurate. But we need not quibble over tenths of a percentage point, except to indicate that the 0.4 per cent estimate is certainly a rock-bottom figure for today.

The set of changes in definition, in 1967, was publicly announced and explained; nevertheless, the changes are generally ignored in making comparisons with earlier figures. The net effect of these changes was to reduce the reported national unemployment rate by about 0.2 per cent. The technical details need not be set forth here, although it is pertinent to note that the effect of these definition changes was considerably greater on the measure of long-term unemployment.[2] This greater effect resulted from the fact that one of the changes was a tightening of the definition of "seeking work."

There is no need to debate here the technical justifications for these changes in definition. Two basic points, however, should be much more widely understood and taken into account than they are. The first is that the significance of the national unemployment rate (and especially some of the detailed rates) as a measure of looseness in the labor market has substantially changed. In practice, one of the major eligibility requirements for the manpower programs mentioned above is the inability of applicants to find

[1] Malcolm S. Cohen, "The Direct Effects of Federal Manpower Programs in Reducing Unemployment," *Journal of Human Resources*, Fall 1969, pp. 491–507.

[2] *Employment and Earnings and Monthly Report on the Labor Force*, February, 1967.

jobs in the regular labor market. Before 1965, the enrollees would have been counted as part of the surplus labor supply—in other words, their failure to find conventional jobs would have been part of the evidence of looseness in the labor market. And the same general point can be made concerning those no longer counted as unemployed under the 1967 changes; before 1967, they too would have added to the measure of looseness in the labor market.

If we are interested in comparing the present state of the labor market with its state in pre-1965 years, we should use the same yardstick. When we do so, it is quite clear that by February, 1970, we already had approximately the same degree of looseness in the labor market that prevailed in the latter part of 1964—looseness that was then expressed in a national unemployment rate which fluctuated around 4.9 to 5.1 per cent. That degree of looseness was recognized then as falling far short of any reasonable definition of "full employment." In the post-Korean recession, we had not reached that degree of labor market looseness until 7 or 8 months after the downturn began.

The second basic point is that failure to take account of these changes in the yardstick for measuring unemployment is one factor that has resulted in a serious overestimate of the effectiveness of fiscal and monetary policy as a remedy for excessive unemployment. I will postpone further development of this point now, but will return to it after examining the effects of the Vietnam War on unemployment.

### III

Now let me explain how we temporarily deferred another part of the unemployment problem during the 1960's. A major expansion in the size of the armed forces was one means. When the Vietnam escalation began in 1965, our armed forces numbered 2.7 million persons; by late 1968, a peak strength of 3.6 million persons was reached—a net increase of about 900,000, most of them young men in the 18–25 age group. In addition, in the fall of 1965, there was a sudden large jump in the number of male enrollees in educational institutions who were full-time students (neither employed part-time nor seeking employment). This increase was about 185,000 larger than would have been expected on the basis of population growth in the relevant age groups; it was unquestionably an effect of draft deferment policies, and was, therefore, a side-effect of Vietnam escalation. It is not hard to demonstrate that virtually all of the additional 900,000 young men who were inducted into the armed forces, and most of the 185,000 draft-deferment seekers, would have been in the labor force had it not been for the Vietnam escalation. It seems reasonable to presume that approximately 1,000,000 young men were thus prevented or deterred from entering the civilian labor force from 1965 on.[3] No doubt some new entrants—younger and older males and females—were attracted into the labor force by the availability of jobs that would otherwise have been filled by the draftees and full-time students. But econometric studies suggest that it is quite conservative to assume that only one new entrant (or re-entrant) would be drawn into the labor force for each two men thus withheld or withdrawn from it, other things remaining constant. Under this assumption, the average size of the civilian labor force during the latter half of the 1960's was about 500,000 *less* than it would have been without the Vietnam buildup. Rather simple calculations show that the net effect of this hold-down of labor force growth was a reduction in the national unemployment rate, which by

---

[3] Of course, some who were drafted in 1965 were discharged in 1967, and so on, but the net number withheld from civilian life was rising until late 1968; and the bulge in college enrollment also persisted.

1967 was at least 0.5 to 0.6 per cent, with a considerably greater effect in the 18–25 male age group.

Another means of temporarily setting aside the unemployment problem was a growth of defense employment which was associated with Vietnam escalation. The U.S. Department of Labor has estimated that from early 1965 to the peak level in 1968, about 1.4 million new jobs had been created in the private sector by Vietnam-related increases in Defense expenditures. (Defense-related civilian employment in government also rose by about 200,000.)

*　*　*

There is another aspect of the matter that the aggregate demand argument ignores. According to some 1967 estimates of the Department of Labor, about 60 per cent of the Vietnam-related increase in defense employment up to that time was in blue-collar jobs, although in 1965 only about 40 per cent of total employment was in the blue-collar category.[4] Defense spending for a Vietnam-type war creates large numbers of assembly-line-type jobs in ammunition factories, aircraft plants, rubber plants, truck plants, and so on (in addition to smaller numbers of high-skilled jobs in these and other industries). Analysis of the employment effects of economic growth *without* a rapidly-increasing military production component shows a quite different pattern of job-creation, with emphasis on service-producing occupations, particularly the highly-skilled ones such as health care and education. Therefore, I conclude that Vietnam escalation played a large role in reversing the secular decline in blue-collar jobs in goods-producing industries which had been a prominent feature of our economy from 1954 to 1965.

## IV

An astonishing feature of almost all discussions of employment and unemployment developments during the past five years has been uncritical reliance on *post hoc, ergo propter hoc* reasoning. The typical analysis has run as follows: "In 1964, just before the great tax cut, the national unemployment rate stood at 5.4 per cent; by 1969, we had achieved a fairly steady rate of about 3.5 per cent; therefore, we now have clear proof that stimulation of aggregate demand, *by itself,* can push the unemployment rate at least as low as 3.5 per cent for a substantial period of time.[5] And this fallacious analysis now leads to the current assertion that the present problem of growing unemployment is "transitional." Stated more fully, the "transitional" argument runs as follows: "Just bear with us while the unemployment rate runs up; this is an unavoidable consequence of the policies that are necessary to defeat the psychology of inflation; but as soon as we have won that psychological victory, we can loosen the screws on monetary and fiscal policy, and the renewed growth of aggregate demand will smoothly and automatically carry us back to a satisfactorily low level of unemployment." . . . The hard fact of the matter, to sum up the argument to this point, is that powerful forces *other* than aggregate demand expansion were at work in the 1965-69 period. The net reduction in the unemployment rate in that period was 1.9 percentage points. The changes in definition (plus manpower programs) were responsible for a minimum of 0.6 points of that reduction; the armed forces expansion and its side effects were responsible for a minimum of another 0.5 points, for

---

[4] Richard P. Oliver, "The Employment Effects of Defense Expenditures," and M. A. Rutzick, "Worker Skills in Current Defense Employment," both in *Monthly Labor Review*, September, 1967, pp. 9–20.

[5] I have presented several specific examples of such analysis by noted economists here and abroad in an article, "Full Employment and the New Economics," *Scottish Journal of Political Economy*, February, 1969, pp. 1–19 at 11.

a total of 1.1 points for these factors—which are, from the analytical standpoint, wholly unrelated to aggregate demand expansion as conventionally defined. Hence, demand expansion as such, *plus* the special structural effects of Vietnam-related increases in defense spending, cannot reasonably be credited with more than 0.8 points of the unemployment rate reduction. In other words, by the most generous estimation procedure that seems reasonable, demand expansion *alone* would have reduced unemployment only to 4.6 per cent in the 1965-69 period. And that degree of demand expansion also was the main factor that produced a politically intolerable rate of inflation.

*  *  *

There is another aspect of our unemployment problem which we have neither deferred nor masked: we have simply treated it with "benign neglect." Through most of the years since World War II, a combination of forces which I have dubbed "the labor market twist" has operated with hardly any general notice. I first called attention to this "twist" in testimony presented to a Senate Subcommittee in 1963.[6] This "twist" has profoundly important implications both for manpower-policy and for welfare policy. I will describe briefly what the twist is, reiterate a key piece of evidence illustrating its operation from 1950 to 1962, and then present evidence showing that its effects were modified very little by the record-breaking economic expansion of the 1960's. Finally, I will suggest some of the general policy conclusions which grow out of the analysis.

The twist thesis is that evolving technology and changing consumption patterns in the U.S. economy have combined to produce exactly opposite effects in the upper and lower sectors of the labor market. At least since 1950, the demand for more-skilled, better-educated workers has grown vigorously and has shown a persistent tendency to outrun the high rate of increase in the supply of such workers. Simultaneously, the demand for less-skilled, less-educated workers has steadily declined at a rate which has consistently run ahead of the shrinkage in the supply of such workers. The result has been chronic looseness in the lower sector of the labor market, coexisting with chronic tightness in the upper sector. And the disparity has grown over time.

Thus, the *average* rate of unemployment for men (18 years of age and older) was virtually the same in 1950 and 1962 —6.2 per cent in 1950 and 6.0 per cent in 1962. Yet the unemployment rates for those subgroups of workers with less than the median education were substantially *higher* in 1962 than in 1950, while the better-educated workers had lower rates in 1962. Furthermore, there was clear evidence of the growth of "hidden unemployment" among the less-educated. A substantial number of them had given up the constant search for jobs and were thus not counted as "unemployed," but instead were classified as "not in the labor force." In other words, detailed comparisons, age group by age group, between 1950 and 1962 showed substantially smaller percentages of virtually all age groups in the lower sector counted as in the labor force in 1962. No such general decline in labor force participation rates was apparent in the upper sector—rather, there was some net increase in participation between 1950 and 1962 (except at age 65 and over). I will not let modesty prevent my stating the important fact that a BLS expert later tested and confirmed my conclusions. He applied the same methodology to data from different sources and for somewhat different time spans; his findings for 1950-60, he re-

<hr/>

[6] "Automation, Jobs and Manpower," Statement before U. S. Senate Subcommittee on Employment and Manpower, *Hearings,* 88th Congress, 1st Session, pt. 5 (September 20, 1963), pp. 1461–1483.

ported, lend "solid support" to the twist thesis.[7]

In 1963, the view which I expressed to this Subcommittee was that tax-cutting alone was not likely to benefit the more disadvantaged members of the labor force nearly as much as the better-educated. This judgment at the time was criticized as excessively pessimistic; but the record of developments in the intervening years shows that I was actually excessively optimistic. I have examined in some detail the data showing the relevant changes from 1962 to 1967—that is, from well before the great tax cut of 1964 until well after it.[8] I will spare you most of the details, and will only summarize some of the salient findings. Understanding is helped, I think, by referring to the "upper half" and the "lower half" of the male labor force. In 1962, the median educational attainment for male workers age 18 and older was 12.2 years; so the lower half was approximately the group without a high school diploma (0–11 years of education) and the upper half was approximately the group with a high school diploma or better (12 or more years of education). From 1962 to 1967, reported unemployment rates in both sectors dropped by roughly the same proportion (slightly more for the upper half than for the lower, but the difference was not large enough to emphasize.) The rate for both subgroups combined dropped from 6.0 per cent in 1962 to 3.1 per cent in 1967. Hence, if one considered only these changes, he might conclude that the benefits of economic growth had been distributed more or less evenly. The relative disparities of 1962 had not been corrected; the unemployment rates for the lower half were still much higher than those for the upper half; but the whole level was much lower. The details are shown in Table 1.[9]

Further analysis clearly shows, however, that sharply different processes were at work in this period in the upper and the lower levels. In the upper half, unemployment rates fell sharply from 1962 to 1967 because demand (as reflected in employment figures) grew more rapidly than either population or labor force. Demand was so strong and opportunities were so abundant and so attractive that extra workers were drawn into the labor force (technically, labor force participation rates generally rose, except for the normal retirement ages). To me, one of the most striking facts about this period of rapid economic growth, with obviously excessive aggregate demand in the later years, is that about 95 per cent of the job growth occurred in the upper half of the labor force. The college-trained group—those with at least one year of college or more—was roughly the top fifth (22 per cent) of the male labor force in 1962; this top fifth got about 40 per cent of the gross increase in jobs in the 1962–67 expansion. Falling unemployment rates in the upper half of the labor force were indisputably the product of rapid economic growth and ebullient demand. (See Table 2.[10])

In the lower half, falling unemployment

---

[7] Denis F. Johnston, "Education and the Labor Force," *Monthly Labor Review*, September 1968, pp. 1–11. Johnston undertook two main comparisons: 1950 with 1960, and 1960 with averages for 1964–67. With regard to the latter comparison, his conclusion was as follows: "On the whole, then, the 'twist' first observed by Killingsworth for the period from the 1950 Census to March 1962 appears to be still in operation despite the recovery since 1962, and has in fact acquired more torque among the older men."

[8] Summarized in my article commenting on Johnston's findings: "The Continuing Labor Market Twist," *ibid.*, pp. 12–17; and elaborated in another article, "Fact and Fallacy in Labor Market Analysis," *Scottish Journal of Political Economy*, February 1970.

[9] Taken from "The Continuing Labor Market Twist," *loc. cit.* The data sources are identified therein. Data for 1969 are not yet available as this is written; data on changes from 1967 to 1968 show no significant alterations in the patterns discussed in this and the next several paragraphs.

[10] *Ibid.*

TABLE 1.  UNEMPLOYMENT RATES BY YEARS OF SCHOOL COMPLETED,
MEN AGE 18 AND OLDER, MARCH 1962 AND MARCH 1967

| Years of School Completed | Unemployment Rate | | Percentage Reduction, 1962–67 |
| --- | --- | --- | --- |
| | 1962 | 1967 | |
| All groups | 6.0 | 3.1 | 48 |
| 0 to 4 | 10.4 | 5.7 | 45 |
| 5 to 7 | 8.5 | 4.7 | 45 |
| 8 | 7.5 | 4.0 | 47 |
| 9 to 11 | 7.8 | 4.6 | 41 |
| 12 | 4.8 | 2.5 | 48 |
| 13 to 15 | 4.0 | 2.2 | 45 |
| 16 or more | 1.4 | 0.7 | 50 |

rates were produced by a very different set of forces and reactions. In the first place, employment *decreased* substantially from 1962 to 1967, and the decrease was greatest for those nearest the bottom. For the subgroup with less than 5 years of education—the functional illiterates—the employment decline was 25.6 per cent in these 5 years. For the whole lower half, the number of jobs decreased by 7.9 per cent. Only in the top layer of the lower half, the subgroup with 9–11 years of schooling, was there a modest increase (2.6 per cent); and much of that must have been attributable to enrollments in the Neighborhood Youth Corps and other manpower programs whose enrollees are counted as "employed." With jobs for the lower half disappearing, how could un-

employment rates fall? Simply because the number of men classified as being "in the labor force" fell even more rapidly than employment.

There is a strong temptation, to which some observers have yielded, to attribute *all* of the labor force shrinkage in this group to population decline and voluntary retirement, and to conclude that the labor force shrinkage has been the independent factor which has *caused* the employment decline. Such reasoning involves reliance on a partial truth to support a wholly erroneous conclusion. Table 3[11] shows the changes, and the rates of change, in the most pertinent figures. The population in what was the "lower half" in 1962 had indeed decreased by 1967, but only by 6 per cent. The rate of labor force decrease

TABLE 2.  EMPLOYMENT BY YEARS OF SCHOOL COMPLETED, MEN AGE 18 AND OLDER,
MARCH 1962 AND MARCH 1967

| Years of School Completed | Number Employed | | Absolute Change, 1962–67 | Percentage Change |
| --- | --- | --- | --- | --- |
| | 1962 | 1967 | | |
| All groups | 42,332 | 45,132 | 2,800 | +6.6 |
| 0 to 4 | 2,171 | 1,616 | −555 | −25.6 |
| 5 to 7 | 4,130 | 3,508 | −622 | −15.1 |
| 8 | 5,895 | 5,254 | −641 | −10.9 |
| 9 to 11 | 8,137 | 8,349 | 212 | +2.6 |
| 12 | 12,308 | 14,946 | 2,638 | +21.4 |
| 13 to 15 | 4,498 | 5,349 | 851 | +18.9 |
| 16 or more | 5,193 | 6,110 | 917 | +17.7 |

[11] Adapted from Table 2 in "Fact and Fallacy in Labor Market Analysis," *loc. cit.*, and the sources cited there.

TABLE 3. LABOR FORCE STATUS OF MALE CIVILIAN POPULATION, AGE 18 YEARS AND OLDER, LESS THAN 12 YEARS OF EDUCATION, MARCH 1962 AND MARCH 1967

[In thousands]

| Category | Year | | Absolute Change, 1962–67 | Percentage Change |
|---|---|---|---|---|
| | 1962 | 1967 | | |
| Population [a] | 28,291 | 26,595 | −1,696 | −6.0 |
| Not in Labor Force | 6,156 | 6,975 | +819 | +13.3 |
| Labor Force | 22,135 | 19,620 | −2,515 | −11.4 |
| Employed | 20,333 | 18,727 | −1,606 | −7.9 |
| Unemployed | 1,802 | 893 | −909 | −50.4 |

[a] Civilian noninstitutional population

was almost double that rate—11.4 per cent—and the absolute number dropping out of the labor force count was about 50 per cent greater than the numerical decline in the population count. Obviously, *some* of the labor force shrinkage was caused by deaths in excess of new accessions. It should be equally obvious that nothing like *all* of the labor force shrinkage is explained by population decrease. An increase in the proportion of men in the 65 and over age bracket, and a higher rate of voluntary retirement[12] account for another part of the labor force shinkage in the lower half. But even these factors, taken together with population decrease, fall far short of explaining all of the labor force shrinkage.

The crucial point here—and it would be hard to overemphasize its significance— is that a large part of the labor force shrinkage in the lower half, and most of the reduction in the reported unemployment total, was caused by a large increase in "hidden unemployment" in this half of the labor force. My estimate of the 1962–67 increase is 734,000 men.[13] The total decrease in *reported* unemployment, 1962–67, was only 909,000 (see Table 3). Therefore, without this massive shift to hidden unemployment, death and voluntary retirement would have reduced the total unemployed by a relatively small amount, and unemployment rates for the subgroups of the lower half would have declined scarcely at all.

❁   ❁   ❁

## VII.

Before proceeding to specific comments about the manpower proposals which this Subcommittee is presently considering, I want to offer some observations concerning probable unemployment developments over the next 15 months and over the longer term as well. I am not a professional economic forecaster, but I have learned one trick of that trade: to guard yourself well with "ifs." That kind of pre-

[12] There has been an increase in the rate of retirements at age 65 at all levels of the male labor market. But this increase has been least for the best-educated and most for the least-educated—suggesting that the same forces which have increased the labor force dropout rate at younger ages among less-educated workers have also affected the decisions of older workers. In other words, it seems quite clear that a substantial proportion of the retirements of older workers in the lower half are really compelled by lack of job opportunities instead of being a matter of voluntary choice.

[13] Assumptions and methodology used in making this estimate are presented in "Fact and Fallacy in Labor Market Analysis," *loc. cit.* The essence of the method is to calculate what the size of the "lower half" labor force would have been if there had been *no* decrease from 1962 to 1967 in labor force participation rates by detailed age and educational attainment classifications, and to compare this hypothetical labor force (cell by cell) with the actual. (Adjustments were made for "normal" increases in voluntary retirement at age 60 and older.) This is a conservative estimation procedure, because in the upper half of the labor force, most participation rates by age *rose* from 1962 to 1967.

caution is particularly in order today, when the experts cannot agree on whether we are in the early stages of a recession or are merely in a slowdown. Some changes in fiscal and monetary policy have already been announced or broadly hinted. Some of the demobilization plans already announced—armed forces reductions and defense spending cutbacks—could be changed. Finally, and especially important, we have had no experience with the new 1967 unemployment definitions in a period of substantial long-term unemployment; and we have little basis for judging the extent to which these new definitions will convert the very long-term unemployed into the hidden unemployed.

Despite all of these uncertainties, I believe that there is a near certainty, in the absence of some new and effective remedies for chronic unemployment, that we will see substantially higher levels of reported unemployment over the next 15 months or so. In that time span, an already loose labor market will have the task of absorbing the normal labor force growth of two million or more workers, and will also have the extraordinary task of redeploying more than a million released servicemen and dismissed defense plant workers. Even if the recent decline in total employment is checked immediately, a resumption of growth is not expected before sometime in the second half of the year. And the slow growth rate that is projected thereafter will not create enough new jobs fast enough to prevent a continuing rise in the reported unemployment rate.

Even if we avoid a major recession, and even if we use the "new" yardstick, there is a strong likelihood that the unemployment rate will be above 5 per cent before the end of this year and will approach 6 per cent by mid-1971. That is the relatively optimistic view. If Milton Friedman is right when he argues that we have already virtually assured a recession by excessively prolonging the "tight money" policy, an unemployment rate of 7 or 8 per cent by mid-1971 would be well within the range of reasonable possibility. That is the relatively pessimistic view.

❉   ❉   ❉

Killingsworth notes that the new methods of measuring the unemployed, mainly by excluding those enrolled in certain manpower programs, accounted for almost one-third of the 1.9 point drop in the unemployment rate from 1964 to 1969.

Furthermore, expansion of the Vietnam War, rather than expansion of aggregate demand, with its accompanying shift of young men from civilian life to the military, and growth in related defense output that absorbed otherwise hard-to-employ blue-collar workers into gainful employment, contributed another .5 points to the overall unemployment drop. Thus the maximum decrease in the rate that could be attributable to normal demand expansion following the tax cut of 1964 was only .8 points, and this small gain was accompanied by the sharpest inflation in recent experience.

Killingsworth then argues that the "labor market twist," his basic structural hypothesis, which he described in his 1963 statement, was just as prevalent six years later. He notes that the more recent changes in labor market demand and supply, specifically during the period of declining unemployment in the late 1960's, showed even reduction for all educational classes, brought about by an increase in demand for the highly educated, and a shrinkage in labor force participation of the lesser educated, with a probable consequent growth in the "hidden unemployed."

In conclusion, therefore, Killingsworth obviously feels that the structuralist position has been vindicated by events. He feels that his earlier prediction that aggregate forces alone would not reduce unemployment below 4 percent has proved correct, even though the reported unemployment rate was less than 4 percent. Moreover, he feels that his analysis of the so-called "labor market twist" indicates the nature of the structural changes that have taken place in the economy. And, although increases in aggregate demand did something to reduce unemployment, they did so only with substantial inflation.

Killingsworth disclaims predictive powers. But his forecast of the unemployment rate for 1970 was substantiated. His even more dismal prediction for 1971 was happily incorrect.


### Structural Unemployment and Wage-Price Flexibility

As has been mentioned above, market changes of an inflationary nature may reduce structural unemployment in a strong economy. Relative wages may rise in the labor shortage sectors leading to further employment among surplus workers, and/or prices may rise in the goods and services produced by the shortage sector diverting demand toward output of the surplus sector workers. The structuralist does not deny such an argument, since the falling unemployment would be accompanied by more sharply rising prices than if structural elements were absent. In fact, the responsibility for continuing unemployment under these flexible conditions could be attributed to the fiscal and monetary authorities who restricted aggregate demand below full employment levels to limit inflation.

But this process assumes a one-sided flexibility only on the part of the scarce labor sectors. The same shifts in demand and production toward the labor surplus sectors could occur if those workers would accept relative wage declines. It is just this unwillingness or inability to have their wages fall sufficiently relative to other sectors that transfers structural imbalance into structural unemployment. There are some who consider that structural unemployment cannot exist in an economy of completely flexible prices and wages.

For example, Clarence Long, in the following paper, argues that the rising level of prosperity unemployment results from the practice of raising effective minimum wages above the productivity gains of the least productive, lowest wage groups. As a result, the supply of these workers exceeds their demand, even in prosperous periods. What is needed, under Long's theory, for relative wage changes to match sectoral productivity growth, and thus avoid creation of labor surpluses in prosperous periods, is for the minimum wage to fall relative to the average, because of the increasing spread in productivity differences. What has occurred, however, has been a rise in the social minimum, a pattern that aggravates the problem of sectoral imbalance.

# A Theory of Creeping Unemployment and Labor Force Replacement

## by Clarence D. Long

## INTRODUCTION

For a generation the theory of what determines unemployment has been the theory of what determines demand. Under the demand theory, unemployment results when total spending falls below the sum needed, at existing prices, to buy all the output the economy can produce at full capacity.

Unfortunately for the demand theory, it has not been able to explain why, in the face of very substantial increases in aggregate spending, unemployment can persist, and even increase. Since 1948 the gross national expenditure has risen more than 90 percent, while the full capacity gross national product of the economy in constant prices has risen about 50 percent (the excess demand having been soaked up by a rise of nearly 30 percent in the price level). There has not been any shortage of aggregate spending; yet peacetime prosperity unemployment has crept generally upward: from 3.85 percent of the labor force during the prosperity period 1947–48; to 4¼ percent during the 30 prosperity months from January 1955 through July 1957; 5 1/3 percent during 1959–60.[1] The period has suffered three complete recessions, when unemployment rose to mod-

SOURCE Reprinted with permission from Address to Catholic Economic Association Annual Meeting, St. Louis, 1960, Reprinted in *Congressional Record,* July 25, 1961, pp. 13430–13434.

[1] In the United States the labor force is currently defined as the sum of all persons reported by the census to be employed or unemployed during a certain specified week, the week which includes the 15th of the month to which the measure refers. The employed category covers all persons 14 and older who have jobs or businesses for pay or profit, including employers and self-employed, unpaid family workers in a store or on a farm who help produce a salable product or service, and employees of nonprofit enterprises and government agencies. The unemployed category includes persons 14 and older who have no job or business of the above-mentioned sort and are seeking such employment during the survey week (or who say they would have sought it had they not been sick or had they not believed that there was no work to be found).

erate peaks, but these peaks have been short lived, so that only a small fraction of the average peacetime unemployment since 1947 has been directly traceable to the business cycle; five-sixths of it has been the kind that prevails even during the good years. The recent problem of unemployment has been not recession unemployment, but the upward creep of prosperity unemployment.

This rise has been accompanied by a great lengthening in the duration of unemployment, by a great increase in the relative burden of unemployment on the colored, especially since 1954, and by especially high unemployment rates in construction, mining and manufacturing, and in blue-collar and manual occupations; since 1954 the blue-collar occupations have borne about two-thirds of the total unemployment, and the white-collar occupations, with over half the labor force and a rising proportion of the labor force, have suffered only one-third. Altogether, the distribution of idleness during the 1950's has been remarkably uneven.

The decade has been characterized not only by creeping unemployment but also by long-term changes in the age and sex composition of the labor force. Over half of the labor force increase for the decade was women 35–64, and the proportion of female workers rose from less than 29 percent of the total labor force in 1950 to nearly 32 percent in 1960, while the proportion of male workers decreased accordingly. Part of this relative decline for males was the continued fall in the labor force participation rates of older men and youths under 25.

These trends raise three questions:

1. What has caused this creeping unemployment?
2. What has caused the relative replacement of the labor force of men and women?

3. What are the prospects for creeping unemployment and labor force replacement in the future?

## A MODEL TO EXPLAIN CREEPING UNEMPLOYMENT

In order to answer these questions, an attempt is made here to develop a theory of creeping unemployment and labor force replacement, and to support it with empirical data. The theory works through two postulates, each serving as the blade of a scissors: First, the greater the opportunity offered to the average worker to improve his personal productivity, the further some of the workers will fall below the average. That is, the faster the march of the average, the greater the lag for the stragglers. We call this the widening productivity spread.

Second, the social minimum wage—the wage below which custom, employer ethics, or law forbids workers to be employed—rises at the same percentage rate as the average wage, and the average wage rises at the same rate as the average productivity. We call this the constant (relative) wage spread.

The widening productivity spread: In recent decades unprecedented opportunities have opened to the average person to improve his personal productivity: better food, sanitation, and medical care, resulting in improved physical strength and well-being; lowered barriers to occupational and geographical movement of workers, enabling millions of workers to aspire to jobs which can bring forth their full productive power; and, above all, more and better education for the average worker.

It is a basic argument of this paper that the greater the average quality of the labor force, the more unfavorable the position of those who cannot improve. Some lack the intelligence to absorb better training and education. Others are deficient in willpower, motivation, or emotional stability. Still others are barred by age, color, or inferior school facilities in their locality. These workers fall behind the average; the higher quality the labor force, the greater the disparity of this group compared with the average. It is much worse to have no education when the average person is a high school graduate, as in 1960, than when the latter has only 8 years of equivalent full-time education, as in 1930.

It is still worse to be an illiterate when the average person has 8 years of education than when he is also an illiterate.

Under capitalistic or mass-production conditions, the pace of work and the job arrangements are geared to the majority of workers. It may be impractical to slow down an assembly line, or to set up a separate and slower assembly line, in order that the weak or slow-witted can find a place. If most workers are literate, firms may not choose to set up special arrangements in order that the illiterate can learn safety rules and other job instructions. In extreme cases this could be true even if the substandard worker were willing to work for nothing.

Even without mass production, it may not be worth while to employ substandard workers if there is a minimum wage which obliges the employer to pay the worker more than his individual productivity justifies.

The social minimum wage: Our second postulate, then, is that there is a social minimum wage below which workers are not employed, because minimum-wage legislation and union wage standards forbid it; because social security and private pensions provide an alternative; and because employers themselves set minimum scales, to head off unionization, to avoid a reputation as a sweatshop, or to maintain employee morale.

This model does not assume that the social minimum rises faster than the average wage (though, if it did, that would accentuate the creeping unemployment); only that the social minimum rises at the same rate as the average wage, that the average wage rises at the same rate as average productivity. The productivity of the stragglers lags behind both the average productivity and the social minimum wage. It becomes unprofitable to hire these stragglers and they become unemployed or leave the labor force. Whether unemployment rises or labor force shrinks depends on whether the stragglers are replaced in the labor force by persons, formerly outside, whose personal productivity rises at a rate equal to, or faster than, the social minimum.

A subsidiary proposition is that the total expenditure of the economy is great enough to buy all the products of the economy at existing prices, and grows at the same annual rate as the full capacity gross national product at constant prices. If aggregate demand should rise at a slower rate than the full capacity output of the economy, we have an additional cause of unemployment. And if it should increase much more rapidly than full capacity output, then, as we show later, it is possible to have an offset to creeping unemployment.

The model assumes that the labor force is divided into nine segments of equal size, each segment increasing its productivity at a different compound percentage rate: the lowest at 1 percent, the next at 1¼ percent, and so on, to the top segment which increases its productivity at the annual rate of 3 percent. Average productivity is the weighted mean for the nine segments. The average wage is assumed to rise at the same rate as the average productivity; thus the same line represents both. The social minimum wage, while below the average wage, is assumed to rise at the same percentage rate.[2] A rise of aggregate demand just fast enough to buy the expanding output of the economy at constant prices is reflected in the rise of both money and real wages at the same rate.

Given these assumptions—a widening dispersion of the productivities of the various segments of the labor force, and an advance of the social minimum wage at the same percentage rate as the average productivity—the lower segment of the labor force tends to lag in its productivity behind the main advance and to become less and less employable at the wage which it insists on getting or which society insists on paying.[3] Thus the tendency toward creeping unemployment and separation from the labor force.

## EMPIRICAL FOUNDATIONS OF THE THEORY

How realistic are our postulates that, as average productivity of the labor force rises, certain segments lag; that average wages rise at the same rate as productivity; and that the social minimum wage rises at least as rapidly as the average wage and average productivity?

The widening productivity spread: The usual statistics on productivity refer only to average output per unit of input. They thus measure the combined product of such inputs as labor, capital, management, and technical knowledge, and cannot indicate the productivity of the individual worker or particular segment of the labor force.[4] For this personal productivity, we need measures of such worker characteristics as age, sex, health, skill and training, occupational and industrial attachment, and education.

In the last two decades a large body of information has developed which establishes a close connection between unemployment and labor force participation on the one hand, and educational attainment, on the other. The strategic factor is not education as such. Education can be regarded as merely standing for intelligence, drive, emotional stability, family affluence, economic opportunity and other factors. These data may not be conclusive—what empirical data ever are? But they do much to support our model.

What do these data show?

First, there has been a close moment-of-time association between education and unemployment. Within a given age and color group, the unemployment rates of urban men varied inversely with years of education. The association was upheld at each of the 1940 and 1950 censuses and may also be observed in the results of the 1959 sample survey. The moment-of-time association was also pronounced in March 1959 among major nonfarm occupations. At one extreme laborers had a median education of 8½ years and unemployment of 11.4 percent. At the other, professional workers had a median education of 16.4 years and unemployment of only 1½ percent. In between, unemployment and education were inversely associated.

Second, there has been a remarkable inverse moment-of-time association between

---

[2] A few students maintain that a more meaningful wage differential is an absolute rather than a percentage differential. If the social minimum wage were to remain below the average wage by a constant absolute differential, it would mean that the social minimum would rise much more rapidly than it does in this theory and therefore have much greater effect in causing creeping unemployment.

[3] In this model we assume that it is the lower productivity segments of the labor force that advance in productivity at a lagging rate. This assumption is made only for simplicity of presentation and is not necessary to the argument. In actual fact, it is likely that some of the higher productivity members of the work force will advance in productivity at lower rates and some of the lower productivity members at higher rates. This will have the effect of narrowing the productivity spread until the two rates of advance cross each other; thereafter the effect will be a widening of the spread.

[4] Even the productivity for individual industries, such as manufacturing and agriculture, are largely the gross result of other factors of the economy, such as better roads provided by government, scientific knowledge provided by universities, improved communications provided by the telephone industry.

education and percentages of men not in the labor force. For men with no education, the not-in-the-labor-force group has been as high as 25 percent of the population of men in the same educational categories. In the case of middle-aged white men, e.g., aged 35–44, the percentage not in labor force fell rapidly with additional education through the eighth grade, then slowly with additional education; for college graduates, the proportion outside the labor force was no more than 2½ percent. In the case of older white men, 55–64, the percentages not in labor force fell more gradually with additional education: beginning at 25 to 32 percent for those with no schooling, and falling to about 15 percent for elementary school graduates, and to 10 percent for college graduates.

For colored men, the slope was more gradual yet. Colored men with no schooling had much smaller percentages not in the labor force than white men of the same age and lack of education. But colored college graduates had somewhat higher percentages not in the labor force than whites in the case of the younger men, and about the same percentages in the case of the men 55–64. In general, education was less of a factor in determining labor force status of colored; but the data were for the urban South, where most jobs open to Negroes were possibly not the kind for which education helped a man to qualify. Also, the social minimum wage was surely lower in the urban South for Negroes than in the urban United States for whites, so that a person with modest qualifications was less apt to be priced out of the market. The economy of the urban South, out of its long experience with Negro labor, has possibly adjusted both in the nature of the job and the level of wages to make a place—humble though it be—for the poorly educated colored man.

So far, the intimate relation of education to unemployment and nonlabor-force status has been demonstrated only in moment-of-time associations. Has education been advancing overtime at different rates for different segments of the labor force, as called for in our model?

The evidence is interesting.

The unemployed have improved much less in education over the past decade than have the employed. In 1950 the unemployed man 18 and older averaged 91.8 percent the education of the employed; in 1959, only 81 percent. In 1950 the not-in-labor-force averaged 92.8 percent the education of the employed; in 1959, only 72.6 percent.

Similar developments have occurred for the various age groups. For the labor force, education rose for each age group from 18–24 through 65 and older. For the not-in-labor-force, education actually fell for several age groups, including 18–24, 35–44, and 45–64.

All these comparisons have been confined to males, because of the complex situation which obtains for female labor force participation relative to husbands' incomes and their own education. Other things equal—age, color, child-care responsibilities, and education—wives are less likely to be in the labor force the higher the incomes of their husbands. But wives of higher income husbands are more apt to have superior education and therefore better job opportunities. These two effects—the income effect and education effect—tend to cancel, but only partially. Thus, women unemployed or not-in-labor-force tend to be inferior in education to the employed women, though the margin —10 or 15 percent—is not as great as in the case of males.

There is, however, a more important comparison. We have seen that women have been entering the labor force in large proportions, replacing the younger and older males and even some of the men of the prime working ages. What has been happening to the education of the employed women, compared to that of the males? Here we find that the female employed had in 1950 25 percent more education that the male not-in-labor-force; in 1952, 41 percent more; and in 1959, 43 percent more. The replacement of older and younger males by women is reflected in the superior education and the more rapidly improving education, of female workers compared to the males.

The statistical basis for the social minimum wage: The other basic postulate which underlies our theory of creeping unemployment—the second blade of the scissors—is that the social minimum wage rises at the same rate as both average wage and average productivity—in other words that the percentage differential between minimum and average wage remains constant, or at least does not widen. What is the evidence that the social minimum wage has in fact kept pace with the average wage during the last decade?

One set consists of the distribution of straight-time hourly earnings of factory production in 1947, 1954, and 1958. The distribution shows that the effective minimum—40 cents in 1947, 75 cents in 1954, and $1 in 1958—not only kept pace with the average (which is all our theory requires) but actually rose faster than the average, from 44 percent in 1947, to 45 percent in 1954, to 50 percent in 1958. The pattern was followed between 1954 and 1958 for each of the major regions, Northeast, South, Midwest, and Far West.

A second set of evidence consists of the distribution of union hourly earnings, on July 1, 1950 and 1958, for the printing trades, the building trades (helpers and laborers), motortruck drivers and helpers, and local transit workers. In the first three cases, both the minimum and the third quartile rose faster than the average. In the fourth, the minimum and third quartile rose slightly less than the average.

A third set consists of the benefit levels in 1950 and 1959 for various social insur-

ance and welfare programs, compared with employment earnings.[5] In the case of old-age and survivors' insurance, average monthly benefits paid to older workers and their wives rose from 21 to 33 percent of monthly earnings of factory workers, and the proportion 65 and older drawing benefits increased from 13 percent in 1948 to 63 percent in 1959 (partly offset by a small decline in the proportion drawing public assistance). In the case of unemployment insurance, average benefits in 1950 were 40.7 percent of net spendable average weekly earnings of factory production workers and in 1959, 41.8 percent. In the case of general public assistance programs, average monthly payments per case in 1950 were 21.1 percent of net spendable average monthly earnings of factory workers and in 1959, 22.0 percent.

## SOME QUESTIONS TO BE ANSWERED

This paper began by reviewing for the past decade the upward creep of prosperity unemployment, with its heavy incidence on the manual and blue-collar worker, on the younger and the older worker, on the colored worker, and on the poorly educated worker. In order to explain these events, a model was constructed on the basis of two postulates: First, a widening productivity spread of the labor force as the average productivity increases, so that in the upward march of productivity certain segments of the labor force lag behind the average; second, a social minimum wage which rises at least as fast as the average wage (in turn assumed to rise as fast as average productivity).

Both postulates seem borne out by the statistics. But certain questions must be dealt with before we can be satisfied with the foundation of our theory.

First, why has there not been much more creeping unemployment? The aver-

---

[5] *Statistical Abstract of the United States*, 1960, pp. 223, 268, 271, 280.

age education of the unemployed has lagged far behind that of the employed; and the social minimum wage has kept pace with, even risen faster than, the average wage and productivity. Yet prosperity unemployment has in recent years been only 1½ higher in percentage of labor force than it was in 1948, a distressing waste but not impressive in comparison with what might perhaps have been expected from differential movements of education and wages.

The explanation is that the poorly educated unemployed have tended to drop out of the labor force, as evidenced by the still greater worsening in the relative education of the not-in-labor-force group.

A second question arises out of the first. If many unemployed have been dropping out of the labor force, why hasn't the labor force been declining as a share of working-age population, instead of remaining approximately constant? What has happened is that their places in the labor force were taken by others, and these others were the better educated women. The superior education of employed female compared with the male not-in-labor-force, and their widening margin of educational superiority during the decade, is consistent with this development.

But what about the social minimum wage of women relative to men? How does this fit into the replacement of men by women over the past decade?

No extensive documentation is needed for the lower pay of women.[6] But have the earnings of women been rising less or more than those of men? On this question the evidence is not plentiful, but recent data for 17 large labor market areas indicate that, in manufacturing, wages of women office workers and industrial nurses rose about the same between 1953–59 as the wages of men in skilled maintenance and unskilled plant work. With employed women enjoying a large and widening superiority in educational attainment over men not in labor force, and working for wages that have been not only lower but show no signs of creeping up on the wages of men, it is not surprising that women have increasingly entered the labor force to take jobs in the expanding clerical, service, technical, and professional occupations; while poorly educated men have left the labor force as they were squeezed from the contracting blue-collar and manual occupations.

A third question concerns the colored workers. Since 1952 rates of unemployment of Negro males have risen and rates of labor force fallen more than the white male rates. Separate data are lacking for the education of colored unemployed, but exist for colored not-in-labor-force. These show that the education of the not-in-labor-force was about the same percentage margin below that of labor force—colored or white—in 1959 as in 1952. If the replacement of Negro males was due to this relatively inferior education, at least there was no worsening during the decade. Why then have their employment rates fallen more than those of white males? The explanation may well be that the colored social minimum wage has risen more rapidly. There is no very direct evidence to support this for recent years, because of the lack of separate wage rates for colored and whites. We can perhaps infer this from the widespread extension of social security and welfare benefit programs. Since 1954 old-age and unemployment

---

[6] W. S. Woytinsky, "Employment and Wages in the United States" (New York: Twentieth Century Fund, 1953, p. 451); also C. D. Long, "The Labor Force Under Changing Income and Employment" (Princeton University Press, 1958), p. 356.

Much of the difference is due to the difference in work that women do. Where they do the same work, the margin is much smaller; perhaps no more than 10 to 20 percent. For example, recent data for 19 large labor market areas disclose that women accounting clerks earned a median of 14 percent less than men accounting clerks of the same grade: "1959 Statistical Supplement," *Monthly Labor Review*, pp. 32–33.

benefits have been extended to more industries and firms, and disability benefits have been provided persons "totally and permanently disabled" beginning at age 50. All of these programs favor the low-wage worker much more than they do the higher wage worker, and therefore the lower wage colored worker more than the higher wage white worker. We also have data on median wage and salary earnings of year-round full-time male workers given separately for white and colored. These show that colored earnings rose from 45 percent of white in 1939 to 63 percent in 1957, to 65 percent in 1959.

A fourth question concerns the farming and rural areas. Separate statistics have not been offered here for these areas, but it can be said that education is poorer in these areas and yet unemployment rates are also lower. What is the explanation for this paradox?

The answer is threefold. Unemployment as a concept is less well-defined for rural areas, because of the large factor of family and self-employment. Much of farming is organized in such a way that education is not important in enabling a person to qualify for wage work. And there is a lower social minimum wage in farm areas; because employers are smaller, community sentiment favoring a minimum wage is weaker, unions are nonexistent, and statutory minimum wage and unemployment insurance protection do not apply to farm labor.

A fifth question concerns the size of demand. We have tried to show that creeping unemployment has resulted even though demand was adequate to buy the full capacity output at constant prices, or even with considerable price rise. However, creeping unemployment need not occur, if the rise of aggregate demand is so rapid as to outstrip the rise in the social minimum wage. This could happen because much of the social minimum is set by wage boards and administrative action and by Federal and State legislation. Such

action takes time, especially since most State legislatures meet in regular session only every 2 years and since resistance to increase is usually offered by employer and tax-paying groups. Even that part of the social minimum which is determined by public opinion and employer conscience may lag during rapid demand inflation, as a result of the money illusion. Creeping unemployment is most apt to occur during periods such as the 1950's when aggregate demand, though it rose fast enough to allow a moderate price inflation, did not prevent the social minimum wage from keeping up with—even gaining on—the average level of wages and productivity.

A sixth question concerns whether creeping unemployment could be due to the immobility of labor in the face of shifting demand. Demands for products, and for manual and blue-collar labor, have been shrinking in mining, manufacturing, transportation, and agriculture, and demand for white collar and service labor has been expanding in the services and trade industries, even in manufacturing. Is it possible that the chief factor has been sheer reluctance or inability to move?

Seeming to favor this argument is the fact that the industries—manufacturing, mining, and agriculture—for which demand has been shrinking relatively have been those in which productivity has been surging ahead; whereas the industries—especially services—for which demand has been expanding relatively have been the industries in which productivity has apparently been lagging. There is also much evidence that people—especially older workers—do not want to move out of the areas of shrinking demand, for example, mining, depressed textile towns, and even agriculture.

Opposing this argument, however, are persuasive considerations.

For one thing, shifts in structure of demand for labor are not entirely autonomous; to some extent they are initiated and stimulated by shifts in the composition of the supply of labor. A plentiful supply of better educated men and women surely stimulated the research and development, the technological innovation; the growth of accounting and recordkeeping, and the other work of the kind so necessary to automation. Undoubtedly shifts in supply and demand interacted to cause the labor market to take the form it did. Stated in another way, the shift in demand for labor is not independent of its cost. The cost is a combined result of both the efficiencies and the prices of different types of labor. Just as the productivity of the better educated made their services relatively cheap, so the steadily advancing social minimum made the services of the uneducated, unskilled, and weakly motivated segments relatively expensive, inducing employers to put in special-purpose machinery and automated systems in order to displace the poorly equipped and over-priced manual labor.

For another thing, while it is true that many of the sectors shrinking in demand and employment are the rapidly rising productivity sectors, the people they are losing are in no way responsible for these increases, except in that their low personal productivity, in comparison with the wages they command, makes it profitable to substitute better methods and machinery in order to get rid of them. Thus, the rapidly rising productivity of the industries they are leaving is due to improving management, additional capital, new technology, and external economies. Even the industries that are giving up manual and blue-collar workers are at the same time taking on well-educated technical and professional workers for research and development and other staff work, and clerical workers for the expanding office work connected with automation.

Still another consideration is that while some of the industries, such as services, which are gaining new workers seem to lag in productivity, the most rapidly expanding employment has been occurring in the technical and professional occupations where productivity cannot be measured and, for all we know, may be rising rapidly —for example, research and development, medicine, and education itself. Indeed the tremendous expansion of the education industry is undoubtedly based on the recognition of the average parent, child, and taxpayer that the great productivity and earning power conferred by education are well worth the expenditure.

A final consideration is that much of the immobility of the workers in industries from which workers should be moving at faster rates but are not is due to two factors. On the one hand, the poor education of these workers gives them very little freedom of choice as to where to move and little information as to where to go. Their immobility is thus closely related to their lagging productivity. On the other hand, the high social minimum wage in their locality relieves the pressure to make a move. High hourly and daily wages make it possible for coal miners to stay on in mining industries so long as they can get 1 or 2 days of work a week. Price supports serve as a social minimum wage, enabling many low-income farmers to hold on in agriculture.

A seventh problem arises from our having attached considerable importance to education as representing the personal productivity of the worker. To what extent is this justified?

Certainly, there has been a close moment-of-time association between annual incomes and years of education completed of persons of any given age, sex, color. In 1939 and 1949, the incomes of white males of a given age, say 35–44, were higher for each higher level of educational attainment, and the same was true for colored males. In 1958, the same pattern was upheld for both races combined (separate data on race not being available). Incomes of colored males were much lower than those of white males of the same education and age group, though it is likely that their quality levels of education were also lower. For whites and colored alike, education has been far more important than age in explaining income difference.

Income has also been related to education over time. Census data show that males of a given age, say 45–54, had larger increases of income from 1949 to 1958 for each higher level of educational attainment: rising from a 26-percent increase for men with 8 years of education, to a 66-percent increase for men of the same age with 4 or more years of college.[7] Shultz estimates that "of the rise in real income per worker from 1929 to 1956 at least half, although it could be substantially more than this," was due to additional education.[8]

It is, of course, true that the moment-of-time comparisons also reflect differences in property incomes and employment. The relationship still holds, however, when property incomes and degree of employment are abstracted. For 1939, years of education were closely related to median wage and salary earnings of native white males and Negro males of various age groups.[9] In 1958, data of the census survey display a good moment-of-time correlation between median wage and salary earning of males employed full time the year round in major nonfarm occupations, and median years of education completed by males 18 and older in those occupations.[10] Not all property income is eliminated when we use wage and salary data. The overeducated dope who inherits a fat job in a family firm will earn a higher wage or salary income than a high quality person who has no family connections. Thus, the high education and high earn-ings of some need not reflect greater personal productivity. However, it is difficult to see how, in occupations outside of firm managers and officials, this would operate on a major scale to invalidate the relation between education, productivity, and earnings.

An eighth problem arises from the question whether productivity is really a personal matter, instead of being set by the job and by the equipment and facilities that go with it?

At first thought, there appears to be much validity to this objection. An individual of very modest personal qualities could be quite productive on an auto assembly line. And however distinguished one's individual qualities, there is surely a limit to one's personal productivity as a barber.

Further thought, however, would seem to weaken this objection or destroy it entirely. With any kind of mobility of capital and labor, workers of superior personal potential are eventually drawn to those industries and occupations which offer the greatest scope for developing their potential. A graduate of the Harvard Business School will not allow himself to be penned up in a barbershop but will seek out areas where his potentialities find greater scope. The advantage of having great drive, education, and ability is that it widens the choice of occupation. Where large quantities of capital and managerial know-how have made it possible to get high output from workers of very modest personal qualities, the employer will not want to hire very superior workers because they will cost too much in wages (since they would be foregoing greater opportunities). Given mobility in the labor market,

[7] Arnold Katz, "Educational Attainment of Workers, 1959, Special Labor Force Reports No. 1," *Monthly Labor Review*, February 1960, Reprint No. 2333, p. 115.

[8] Theodore W. Shultz, *Education and Economic Growth*, University of Chicago, Economics of Agriculture Research Paper No. 6002, Apr. 20, 1960 (mimeographed), pp. 53–54.

[9] Herman P. Miller, *Income of the American People*, New York, John Wiley & Sons, Inc., 1955, p. 67.

[10] Current Population Reports, Consumer Income, Income of Families and Persons in the United States: 1958, series D–60, No. 33, p. 51.

it will pay the employer to hire workers who have just the personal attainment needed and no more. The greater the competition the more this will be true.

But suppose competition in the labor market is limited by unions, so that a given occupation, say, barbering, can, by limiting apprenticeship and establishing quotas on numbers of licenses, gain high wages for workers of little education and ability. To be sure, it is usually difficult in practice to enforce such restrictions, unless there are some scarce qualities called for in a particular job. Nevertheless, it is at least conceivable that unions, by greatly restricting output, can create high marginal value productivity and enforce high wages for poor quality workers. But the unions cannot insure that all these workers get jobs. On the contrary, the restriction of output reduces the number of jobs. The workers thus displaced must offer their services for what they will bring in the nonunion sector, or become part of the problem of creeping unemployment.

A ninth question concerns whether the minimum wage has had any demonstrable effect on employment in particular industries. The Department of Labor and others have conducted a number of studies of the employment effects of raising the minimum wage, under the Fair Labor Standards Act, to 75 cents in 1950, or to $1 in 1956. These studies have applied mainly to the South and have compared employment in certain low-wage industries just before, and just after, the increase in the minimum.[11] A recent study, for example, measured the impact in five industries producing cigars, fertilizer, lumber, men's and children's seamless hosiery, and wooden

containers. It showed that the aggregate employment of these five declined 4½ percent just after the minimum wage increase went into effect, in April 1956, and that employment declined for all but wooden containers—the declines ranging from 3 percent for sawmills to 14 percent for children's seamless hosiery.[12] The report regarded these declines as modest and further indicated that employers attributed only a small part of them directly to the rise in the minimum.

On the other hand, it seems clear that the main employment effects of a minimum wage rise are not realized immediately. The same report revealed that by the end of 12 months (April 1957), there had occurred a further decline of nearly 8 percent—12 percent altogether. One is entitled to wonder what would be the effects after a still longer period—say, 5 years.

The effects of the minimum wage may not only be delayed but also be indirect. Often it is urged that one reason for a reduction in employment is a fall in product demand or a new machine or process. These effects may flow indirectly from the minimum wage. A fall in product demand may be due to a rise in the product price, traceable both to the direct effects of a higher minimum wage and to the indirect effects of higher costs of materials purchased from other industries whose costs have in turn been raised by the minimum. A new machine or process may arise out of research and development in the machinery-making industry and may be inspired by a general climate of desire to eliminate the relatively inefficient and overproofed manual and blue-collar worker. The employer sees merely that

[11] Paul A. Brinker, "The $1 Minimum Wage Impact on 15 Oklahoma Industries," *Monthly Labor Review,* September 1957, pp. 1092–1095; Norman J. Samuels, "Effects of the $1 Minimum Wage in Seven Industries," *Monthly Labor Review,* March 1957, pp. 323–328, April 1957, pp. 441–446; "Effects of the $1 Minimum Wage in Three Seasonal Industries," *Monthly Labor Review,* September 1957, pp. 1087–1091; "Effects of the $1 Minimum Wage: Men's and Boys' Shirt Industry," *Monthly Labor Review,* November 1957, pp. 1339–1342; Louis E. Badenhoop, "Effects of the $1 Minimum Wage in Seven Areas," *Monthly Labor Review,* July 1958, pp. 737–743.

[12] Norman J. Samuels, "Effects of the $1 Minimum Wage in Five Industries," *Monthly Labor Review,* May 1958, pp. 492–501. The rise for wooden containers was 2.1 percent.

here is a new machine that will save labor or turn out a better product and recognizes no close connection between its development and the rise in the minimum wage. Thus the main employment effects of a minimum wage increase are likely to be long run and indirect.

But the statutory minimum wage is, in any case, not the main keystone of the social minimum wage, as we conceive it in this study. Indeed a statutory wage minimum cannot be a firm floor under wages, since it merely prevents a worker from being employed below a certain wage in covered industries. It does not provide a job at the wage or insure a minimum income. Such a minimum income is provided, however, by the various social welfare programs—old-age and survivors' insurance, disability insurance, unemployment insurance, and general relief or charity. It is these programs which provide the real foundation for the social minimum wage; and a full-dress study of their employment effects has yet to be made.

A final question is why creeping unemployment had not been observed long before the 1950's?

It is possible, of course, that creeping unemployment—at least as a temporary phenomenon—has been in existence for a long time, but that it could not formerly be observed, for lack of data. Before 1940, the only national statistics of unemployment covering the whole labor force, and measuring the composition of unemployment, were those reported by the census for 1 month, or 1 day every 10 years. Residual estimates, constructed by subtracting employment interpolations from labor force interpolations, did not show any long-term upward creep.[13] Such estimates, however, were too crude to throw any clear light on unemployment levels and trends. Since 1940, sample surveys have provided monthly estimates of unemployment and its composition, but war and postwar inflations in aggregate demand could have wiped out creeping unemployment during most of 1940–53.

Furthermore, the social minimum wage, while it has doubtless always existed in some degree, did not become important and general until the New Deal of the 1930's, when there were instituted, for the first time, national minimum wage laws, old-age insurance, public assistance, unemployment insurance, and widespread private pension systems; when government began to employ so many people that its relatively generous wage effects for lower echelon workers could be felt in the private sector and when unionism was extended to mass production.

Both these considerations explain why creeping unemployment either did not exist before the 1950's, or could not be detected. Another factor has been labor force dropout and replacement. Labor force replacement has occurred extensively for a half century or longer in the United States, Great Britain, Canada, New Zealand, and Germany. In another place we have shown the importance of the relatively rising educational attainment of women who have replaced the poorly educated young children and older men.[14] The acceleration of this labor force replacement beginning with 1940 is also connected with the upsurge of average education and the consolidation of the social minimum wage that have occurred since that year.

CONCLUDING REMARKS

What do these results suggest for the future? With the tremendous increase in working-age population and labor force that has been projected for the next de-

[13] Stanley Lebergott, "Annual Estimates of Unemployment in the United States 1900–1950," *Measurement and Behavior of Unemployment*, Princeton University Press, 1957, p. 261.

[14] C. D. Long, "The Labor Force Under Changing Income and Employment" (Princeton University Press, 1958), pp. 20–25, ch. 13.

cade, can we look for some combination of a continued upcreep of prosperity unemployment and replacement of the labor force? The answer will, of course, depend on many developments at home and abroad—including fiscal and monetary—not considered in this paper. If those developments should turn out to be not too different, the answer may well be, "Yes." There is likely to be pressure toward strengthening and broadening minimum wage and social insurance legislation, so that there is little prospect of a widening wage spread to match a widening productivity spread.

To be sure, some developments may seem to promise a narrowing of the productivity spread. Federal aid to education will raise its level in rural areas and especially in the South. Negro education will probably improve greatly and should advance closer in standards to white education. Lower barriers to employment of Negroes and older workers, and more job guidance should open up new opportunities for many workers now suffering prosperity unemployment.

On the other hand, these improvements and consolidations may merely alter the identity of the individuals suffering lagging productivity and creeping unemployment, rather than reduce the number. Always there will be some who do not have the intelligence, the motivation, the personality, and the emotional stability to keep up with the average. Many such persons may be holding jobs only because others are prevented from competing with them, and may be displaced if new educational and employment opportunities enable those others now at the lower part of the productivity spread to move up relatively to higher levels. Thus, the productivity spread may continue to widen, because of the innate diversity in the talents and personalities of human beings, despite all efforts to extend advantages to everyone.

Does this mean that it would be wise to jettison the statutory minimum wage and to reduce the social security and welfare benefits that reinforce a rising social minimum?

Many will prefer to wait for far more evidence that creeping unemployment is caused by a constant or narrowing relative wage spread, in the face of a widening productivity spread, than we have been able to marshal in a short paper. Others will perhaps accept the present explanation, but still feel that a social minimum wage is worth the cost of considerable unemployment, because of the protection it gives to the employed. On such matters of policy this paper gives no advice. Our theory of creeping unemployment and labor force replacement is just now being exposed to the weather, and a theory should be well-seasoned before it is used to fashion a plank in a political platform.

❋  ❋  ❋

Long offers two reasons for the growth in structural unemployment based on downward wage inflexibility. First, he argues that the growth is more apparent than real because of the poor unemployment data of earlier years. Second, he points out that pressure to raise social minima was not significant prior to 1940. But these arguments do not explain the growth in prosperity unemployment in the late 1950's compared to the late 1940's.

The title of his paper offers a third, and perhaps stronger reason. Prosperity unemployment has been "creeping" not jumping upwards. A level from about 3 to 5+ percent in economically strong periods can be explained, in harmony with Long's thesis, by a persistent strengthening of pressure to raise legal and social minimum wages.

If wage flexibility would eliminate structural unemployment, it would do no damage to the structural argument. Relative wage increases in the scarce labor sector that take the form of absolute wage increases for these workers would lead to inflation greater than that associated with the normal wage rise that accompanies strengthening demand. This result would be in keeping with structural doctrine.

If relative wage increases for the scarce sector take the form of absolute declines in the labor surplus sectors (again abstracting from the average rise in wages associated with strengthening product and labor markets), both structural unemployment and inflation associated with structural imbalance would be avoided. But this adjustment would be at the expense of the lowest wage earners. As will be noted in the chapter on poverty, the working poor constitute an important segment of those in poverty; a policy that enlarged this group would be socially unacceptable.

Modification of the structuralist argument is required, although a structuralist would then be one who believed that the economy could approach the full employment level only at the cost of higher prices than in the past, or of exacerbation of the current serious poverty-in-the-midst-of-plenty problem.

### Vacancies

As has been noted previously, definitive tests of the structuralist hypothesis require vacancy data. Pilot vacancy counts were made in various areas, in accordance with Labor Department procedures. Vacancy data will have a much wider use than the provision of a basis for testing alternative unemployment hypotheses. They will aid in job placement and improve the operation of the labor market. They will serve as a guide to student and trainee placement and thereby channel investment in education and training toward the more promising fields.

The difficulties in gathering accurate vacancy data have been noted, but in reality each problem has its counterpart in a problem associated with unemployment data. The following Labor Department definition and commentary on conceptual similarity to unemployment data collection points out the parallelism and leads to the hope that in time vacancy data may become as meaningful and useful as our admittedly imperfect unemployment statistics.

# Job Vacancy Statistics

*Job vacancies* are defined as current, unfilled job openings in your establishment which are immediately available for occupancy by workers from outside your firm and for which your firm is actively seeking such workers. Included are full-time, part-time, permanent, temporary, seasonal and short-term job openings.

*"Actively seeking"* is defined as current efforts to fill the job with a worker from outside your firm through: (1) soliciting assistance of public or private employment agencies, school or college placement offices, labor unions, employee groups, business or professional organizations, business associates, friends and employees in locating suitable candidates; (2) using "help wanted" advertising (newspaper, magazine, radio, television, direct mail, posted notice, etc.); (3) conducting recruitment programs or campaigns; (4) interviewing and selecting "gate," "walk-in" or "mail" applicants or workers searched out of applicant files; and (5) opening or reopening the acceptance of applications from prospective candidates.

*Do not include as vacancies* (1) jobs held for employees who will be recalled; (2) jobs to be filled by transfer, promotion, or demotion; (3) jobs held for workers on paid or unpaid leave; (4) jobs filled by overtime work which are not intended to be filled by new workers; (5) job openings for which new workers were already hired and scheduled to start work at a later date; and (6) those jobs unoccupied because of labor-management disputes.

❈ ❈ ❈

SOURCE Reprinted from *Job Vacancy Statistics,* Hearings before the Subcommittee on Economic Statistics, Joint Economic Committee, 89th Congress, Second Session, 1966, pp. 108–109, 105.

## CONCEPTS AND DEFINITIONS

The same job vacancy and reference period concepts and definitions were used on all schedules. The specified reference period was as of the close of business on a given date, which in each instance was a Friday. The Friday of the calendar week which included the 12th of the month was generally used, because that week is the standard reference period used in the household labor force and establishment employment surveys. For the seven area surveys conducted in November, however, the Friday of the following calendar week was used because additional time was needed to prepare for those surveys. The definition of job vacancy, as used in all surveys, is shown at the end of this paper. The most important feature of this definition is that it spells out three conditions which must be met before a job vacancy can be counted. First, the job must be unoccupied; second, the job must be available for immediate occupancy by a new worker from outside the company; third, the job must be the object of management's active search for a new worker from outside the company. These requirements were stipulated to secure conceptual compatibility with the unemployment definition. Just as an individual has to be actively looking for a job to be considered as unemployed so a "bona fide" job vacancy must entail management's positive effort to find a new employee and not merely its intention or desire to hire one. Similarly, like an unemployed worker, a job vacancy must be unoccupied and available for immediate occupation.

For administrative purposes the definition used may be too restrictive in concept, since it excludes those situations in which new workers are currently being sought through positive efforts to fill jobs which, although not immediately available, are expected to become vacant or available in the future. The inclusion of those openings might be particularly useful in connection with employment service operations. To accommodate this use, it might be advantageous to collect data on those openings in the future, but as a separately identified item. A separate breakout would be essential because such expected openings would not be conceptually complemental to current unemployment.

Other questions may be raised in regard to the definition used for job vacancies. Should it include those jobs that are expected to be filled in the future by recall of employees on layoff, or by new workers, already hired, who have not yet started working? Rather convincing arguments can be made both for and against the inclusion of each of these.

\* \* \*

The following simple formulas explain the uniformity in pattern between the two concepts:

Labor Demand — Employment = Vacancies

Labor Supply (Labor Force) — Employment = Unemployed

Note that both terms are residuals, dependent on actual demand and supply conditions.

In order for a job to be vacant, the firm must be actively seeking a worker outside the company. To be unemployed, a worker must be actively seeking work.

Further parallel conceptual problems follow:

To be counted as a vacancy, the job must be unoccupied. That is, for example, if a job is filled through overtime work because of labor shortage, no vacancy exists. If a firm's labor force works short hours because of slack conditions, unemployment statistics will not reflect underutilized labor supply.

Vacancy data are on a current basis and do not reflect search by firms to fill expected future openings. Unemployment counterpart: "hidden unemployment." Workers are not counted as unemployed who would look for work if jobs became more plentiful.

Two further comparable conceptual problems not noted in the above report are:

1. Firms might not list vacancies under very tight labor market conditions because they have little hope of filling them. Unemployment counterpart: the "discouraged worker," not listed as unemployed because he has left the labor force in despair of finding work.

2. Actual vacancy data might misrepresent the direction of labor demand pressure. If firms promote and train from within, the need for additional higher level jobs will be filled from below, so that vacancies appear for lower level jobs. Thus the vacancy data will to this extent not inform guidance counselors, for example, of the need for particular skills. Unemployment counterpart: unemployment data by occupation are of the last job held. To the extent that workers move down the skill ladder in attempts to earn as much income from work as possible, unemployment data in slack times will understate the potential supply at higher level jobs.

### Related Readings

Much of the statistical basis for the inadequate demand position results from the study by James W. Knowles and Edward D. Kalacheck, *Higher Unemployment Rates, 1957–60: Structural Transformation or Inadequate Demand,* Joint Economic Committee, U.S. Congress, Washington 1961. Knowles and Kalacheck find the pattern of sectoral unemployment to be no different, related to the overall level in the early 1960's, from that of the pre-1957 period. As argued here, however, this finding does not necessarily damage the structuralist hypothesis.

Arthur M. Ross, *Introduction to Employment Policy and the Labor Market,* Berkeley, University of California Press, 1965, clearly delineates between the two interpretations of the structuralist school. There is the static view, which is not seriously defended, that *any* given level of unemployment, no matter how high, contains a structural element—vacancies in some sectors and above frictional unemployment levels in others. Then there is the dynamic, or more realistic, view that structural imbalance becomes a factor in overall unemployment as the economy advances toward full employment levels, and that this phenomenon has become more significant than in the past.

In the same volume, Richard S. Lipsey, "Structural and Deficient-Demand Unemployment Reconsidered," Chapter 7, clearly shows that Killingsworth belongs to the latter school, and that he only considered structural imbalance as a growing obstacle to the attainment of full employment. Lipsey further emphasizes that vacancy data would be needed for any worthwhile test of the structural hypothesis and that study of the unemployed alone, whatever the segment, would be a fruitless effort toward finding the importance of structural imbalance in blocking a move toward full employment.

N. J. Simler, "Long-Term Unemployment, the Structural Hypothesis, and

Public Policy" (*American Economic Review*, Vol. 54, December 1964, pp. 985–1001), in general supports the Council's inadequate demand explanation of high level unemployment during the late 1950's to mid-1960's. But the novelty of his presentation lies in his exploration of the interdependence between the two concepts. He suggests that inadequate demand may lead to the emergence or development of structural problems. As workers are laid off for long periods, their skills become outdated and when the economy finally moves upward, the long-term unemployed find that their skills of the past no longer fit current manpower needs.

Long is not alone in suggesting that structural unemployment requires wage and price flexibility. Vladimir Stoikov, "Increasing Structural Unemployment Re-examined" (*Industrial and Labor Relations Review*, Vol. 19, April 1966, pp. 368–376), considers structural unemployment impossible if wages are flexible. In fact, Stoikov implies that the need for relative wage adjustments themselves are indicators of structural disturbance. Harold Demsetz, "Structural Unemployment: A Reconsideration of the Evidence and the Theory" (*Journal of Law and Economics*, Vol. 4, October 1961, pp. 80–92), in supporting the structural hypothesis, sees institutional wage setting, by government through legal minima, and by unions through collective bargaining, as barriers to the relative wage declines required to eliminate sectoral labor surpluses. But as noted in this chapter, there is no margin for wage reductions, in a political or practical sense, for those at the lower end of the wage scale.

Eleanor Gilpatrick, in "On the Classification of Unemployment: A View of the Structural-Inadequate Demand Debate" (*Industrial and Labor Relations Review*, Vol. 19, January 1966, pp. 201–212) and in her comprehensive study *Structural Unemployment and Aggregate Demand* (Johns Hopkins Press, 1966), minimizes the importance of the wage inflexibility theories of Long and others. She notes that this view does not explain chronically high unemployment rates in many less organized and uncovered (by minimum wage law) employment. But these writers would claim that social, if not legal or institutional, minima would prevent wages from falling in these sectors, and that, furthermore, displaced workers covered by the minimum would aggravate labor surpluses in uncovered fields.

Important stimulation to collection of vacancy data in the United States came from the "Gordon Committee" Report, *Measuring Employment and Unemployment*, President's Committee to Appraise Employment and Unemployment Statistics, Washington, 1962. *The Measurement and Interpretation of Job Vacancies*, National Bureau of Economic Research, New York, 1966, presents a compendious treatment of vacancies, including papers on the importance of vacancy data, difficulties in collection, and reports on pilot studies and on foreign data collection methods. In this volume, John T. Dunlop, "Job Vacancy Measures and Economic Analysis," pp. 27–47, notes the tendency for reported vacancies to be concentrated in a few lower skilled jobs in response to labor shortage for higher jobs in firms using their internal labor market. Dunlop also details the various uses of vacancy data. J.C.R. Dow and L.A. Dicks-Mireaux, "The Excess Demand for Labour: A Study of Conditions in Great Britain, 1946–56" (*Oxford Economic Paper*, Vol. 10, February 1958, pp. 1–33), note the parallelism in the conceptual difficulties in collecting vacancy data with those which cloud our unemployment statistics. Richard Perlman, *Labor Theory*, Chapter VIII, New York, Wiley, 1969, reviews the arguments and the literature of the continuing controversy.

# CHAPTER 8

# The Wage-Price-Unemployment Problem

The focus of economic interest reflects the major economic problems of the time. In the past, economists in developed countries were mainly concerned with the issue of full employment and the policies to prevent large-scale unemployment. Since it is more than a generation since the world has been faced with a major depression, concern has shifted to the problems of economic growth and the avoidance of inflation as the economy moves toward full employment from levels of unemployment far less severe than those of the 1930's. This latter issue is of particular interest to students of labor. The problem of wages, unemployment reduction, and price stability has many facets, one of which relates to the structural unemployment issue, discussed in the previous chapter.

Early study of the inflation problem in a high-level economy centered on the underlying causes of price increases. In general, two viewpoints developed: (1) the demand-pull view that strong demand for products is transmitted to the factor market, with prices and costs rising in response to the force of demand, and (2) the cost-push view that factor price rises initiate inflation with producers raising prices to defend profit margins from the inroads of rising costs.

Both views imply a background of prosperous economic conditions. In the case of demand-pull, the assumption of a buoyant economy is obvious. For cost-push, the logic of the argument that autonomous increases in costs, not in response to the stimulation of rising demand, require prosperous conditions, or else the factors that raise their prices would face serious reduction in employment, in the case of wage push, or of output in the case of a profit push. Furthermore, cost-push inflation requires imperfections in the factor (labor) or product markets, depending on whether the push is from labor or business.

If the market for labor were perfectly competitive, the groups raising their wages would become totally unemployed as their wages rose above the market level, while if the product market were perfectly competitive, a rise in particular prices would eliminate sales.

The debate over inflation's causes continues, and the issue is of much more than academic importance. The appropriate policy remedy depends on the nature of the cause. Demand-pull inflation requires a tempering of demand and cost-push requires a reduction in monopolistic pressures toward higher wages and prices. If cost-push forces are at work, and monetary and fiscal checks, classic restraints to demand-pull inflation, are employed, the level of economic activity may be seriously reduced. On the other hand, if the inflation is truly demand-pull in nature, then exhortations to unions or management would be ineffective inflation remedies, and more drastic wage and price controls would suppress but not alleviate inflationary forces.

## THE PHILLIPS CURVE

A new approach to the inflation issue in the late 1950's arose from A. W. Phillips' famous article linking the wage level and, indirectly, the price level to the unemployment rate. The Phillips curve, itself, makes no decision as to the merits of the contrasting inflation viewpoints, but emphasizes the historical negative relationship between unemployment rates and wage and price changes. It leads to the dismal conclusion that a reduction in the unemployment rate, a desirable goal in itself, will inexorably lead to an inflation, actual or suppressed. So widely has the Phillips curve relationship reached even public discussion that since about 1960 policy makers weigh the unemployment reduction-price increase "trade off" in their evaluation of the merits of proposals to strengthen the economy and reduce unemployment.

For a time the administration of the 1960's, as expressed through the Council of Economic Advisers, thought that the signals from the Phillips curve could be muted, and the economy strengthened without inflation by direct, if informal, action against wage and price increases. The anti-inflation Wage-Price Guideposts were designed and advanced for this purpose. They not only received administrative promotion but also academic support as inflation checks. This was especially true in the period immediately following the 1964 tax cuts when prices remained stable while unemployment fell. Since 1966, however, prices rose strongly and steadily, once more following the path indicated by the Phillips curve at low unemployment levels. The principle of the Guideposts, that price rises can be limited by informal means, is still debated, even if the formula itself has been generally discarded.

Phillips' article was the first to present a systematic relationship between wage-price and unemployment levels. But before its appearance, other writers implied a more or less predictable connection between them. In Garbarino's note, presented here, the pattern of wage movements related to the unemployment level are studied to find the level of unemployment at which wage increases exceed 3 percent, adumbrations of Phillips curve analysis.

# Unionism and the General Wage Level

## by Joseph W. Garbarino

The impact of union participation in wage determination has been the subject of increasing concern among economists. Policy makers implementing full employment programs have had to face the task of predicting and coping with the effects of a wage "policy" resulting from a multitude of individual bargains between private groups. Proposed solutions to the problem posed by the possible incompatibility of private collective bargaining and full-employment-without-inflation have been almost as numerous as the writers on the subject. It has been proposed that the maintenance of economic order be entrusted to a variety of forms of compulsory arbitration, to management by the monetary authorities, to a hoped-for development of "social responsibility" by the parties involved, and to the creation of a balance-of-power situation between organized groups.[1]

It is possible to identify a pessimistic and an optimistic group among the writers on the problem. The pessimists feel that union wage policy leads inevitably to price and employment effects which are disastrous for the community.[2] Those holding a more optimistic view feel that the desire and ability of employers to resist wage in-

SOURCE Reprinted with permission from *American Economic Review*, Vol. 40, December 1950, pp. 893–896.

[1] The views of a number of writers are summarized in O. W. Phelps, "Collective Bargaining, Keynesian Model," *Am. Econ. Rev.*, Vol. XXXVIII, No. 4 (Sept., 1948), p. 581 ff. See also W. A. Morton, "Trade Unionism, Full Employment and Inflation," *Am. Econ. Rev.*, Vol. XL, No. 1 (March, 1950), p. 13 ff., Clark Kerr, "Labor Markets, Their Character and Consequences," and Kenneth E. Boulding, "Collective Bargaining and Fiscal Policy," both in *Am. Econ. Rev., Papers and Proceedings*, Vol. XL, No. 2 (May, 1950), pp. 278–91, 306–20.

[2] The most pessimistic prediction seems to belong to Charles Lindblom who sees the end result as inflation and a separation of the labor force into two groups, one privately employed and one publicly employed. *Unions and Capitalism* (New Haven, 1949), p. 155.

creases are underestimated (particularly if proper monetary policy is followed).[3]

The optimists also argue that unionism has not introduced the problem of wage inflation at full employment but may, on the contrary, have minimized it. Their position might be summed up in Kerr's statement: "The problem of undue wage increase under full employment is more the result of full employment than of unionism."[4]

The problem of the future strength and effectiveness of employer opposition to union wage pressures is one of prognostication which will not be attempted at this juncture. Attention will be directed to the second point enumerated above: the relative wage behavior of union and non-union wages under full employment conditions.

It is suggested that the validity of this argument depends on the meaning of the phrase "full employment." Full employment means different things to different people. It has varied from the "more vacant jobs than unemployed men" of Beveridge to more conservative statements couched in terms which represent percentages as high as 5 or 6 per cent of the labor force.[5]

The pertinent question could be stated in a more useful form as follows: "At what level of unemployment is competition for labor in a largely non-union market likely to raise wages significantly?" Some sort of an answer to this question might be suggested by examination of the historical record of wages and unemploy-ment. Data on the percentage of time lost through unemployment are available in a continuous series for the period 1890 to 1946.[6] The Bureau of Labor Statistics has published the results of an attempt to chart the movement of the non-agricultural wage level during the years prior to 1935.[7] The nature of the data precludes very rigorous analysis but some useful generalizations may be developed with a little effort.

The historical record can have nothing to offer our investigation if ambitious definitions of full employment are adopted. Only during World War II did the percentages of time lost by unemployment fall below 3%. The record does, however, show four fairly long periods prior to 1933[8] which were characterized by fairly continuous "low" unemployment.

Data on the level of unemployment and the annual rate of increase in the wage level for these periods are summarized in the table on page 345.

Of the four periods included in Table 1 only the period of World War I and the postwar inflation saw annual increases in wages greater than 3%.

The record gives little help in identifying the critical unemployment percentage at which the rate of wage increase begins to exceed three per cent. In 1916 a fall in unemployment to 4.2% from 13.3% was accompanied by a rise in wages of 7.8%. However, unemployment fell to 4.6% in 1905 from 8.0% in 1904 with only a 2.5% rise in the wage level. The following year a further fall in unemployment to 3.7%

[3] See Kerr, *op. cit.*, p. 289, and Morton, *op. cit.*, p. 28, passim.

[4] Kerr, *op. cit.*, p. 289. Speaking of the "short run," Boulding says, "Unions, paradoxically enough, become devices to prevent money wages rising as fast as otherwise they might have done . . .", *op. cit.*, p. 314.

[5] W. H. Beveridge, *Full Employment in a Free Society* (New York, Norton, 1945), p. 18. Professor Machlup has summarized the meanings assigned to full employment by the various authors in the Twentieth Century Fund's *Financing American Prosperity* (New York, 1945), pp. 395–96.

[6] Stanley Lebergott, "Earnings of Non-Farm Employees in the U.S. 1890–1946," *Journal of the American Statistical Association*, March 1948, Table 2, p. 76.

[7] *Monthly Labor Review*, March 1936, p. 717 ff.

[8] Wage behavior during the pre-1933 period will be accepted as representative of non-union behavior since the general level of non-agricultural wages was probably affected only to a limited extent by the effects of unionism during this time.

TABLE 1.

| Period | Range Per Cent Time Lost Due to Unemployment | Average Per Cent Unemployment | Average Annual Wage Increase Per Cent |
|---|---|---|---|
| I. 1899–07 | 3.7 to 8.4 | 5.8 | 3 |
| II. 1909–13 | 4.8 to 7.0 | 5.9 | 2.7 |
| III. 1916–20 | 3.8 to 6.9 | 4.8 | 20.4 |
| IV. 1923–29 | 4.9 to 10.5 | 7.6 | .9 |

occurred accompanied by only a 3.8% rise in wages. Excluding the 1916–1920 period, the largest year-to-year increase in wages which occurred between 1890 and 1933 was 5.6% in 1907. Although unemployment was at the 5% level or below in seven years (again excluding 1916–20) only in 1907 did wages go up more than 5% in any one year.

The rapid rise in wages which occurred during World War I though unemployment never fell below 3.8% (1917) can hardly be taken as evidence of typical non-union market behavior. During this period a price inflation occurred, the cost of living rose rapidly, and unions doubled their membership. Perhaps most important, drastic changes in the industrial and geographic structure of production took place, accompanied by the need for a considerable over-all expansion of the labor force. It is hardly likely that these last two characteristics would be typical of peacetime full employment periods.

The evidence seems to indicate that unemployment must fall below about 5% in peacetime before non-union markets generate a rate of increase in wages greater than 3%.

Two other periods in the record combine to suggest a further conclusion. During the 1923–29 period an average level of unemployment of 7.6% was accompanied by an annual rate of increase in the wage level of less than 1%. During the period 1890–98 the wage level was almost perfectly stable as unemployment averaged 11.9%. These figures imply that the non-union wage level has been approximately stable at some level of unemployment between 8 and 12%.

There is nothing in the empirical evidence on which to base an estimate of non-union wage behavior at peacetime levels of unemployment below 5%. It appears that the economy of the United States is unlikely to reduce unemployment below say 4%, except in periods of considerable price inflation. Whether this is an inherent characteristic of a private enterprise economy is a moot point which has considerable significance for the setting of full employment goals.

Deductive analysis bears out the implication that a rate of increase in non-union wages of more than 3% is unlikely in the absence of rising prices. The long-run trend of the increase in productivity for the economy as a whole seems to be between 2 and 3% at the most. This means that once near-capacity[9] operation of the economy is approached, annual increases in the general wage level greater than 3% are possible only if prices are rising or non-labor factor returns decreasing. There is a limit to the squeeze which can be put on non-labor shares of income while maintaining full employment under private enterprise. This limit would undoubtedly be reached in a short period.

It seems that the statement that full employment is likely to lead to "undue" wage

[9] Capacity here refers to a point beyond which increases in output sufficient to reduce unit costs through the spreading of overhead are impossible. While output is expanding from low levels, wage increases exceeding the long-run rate of productivity increase may be absorbed without an equivalent increase in unit costs. All this means is that through some part of the recovery and prosperity phase of the cycle substantial wage increases are *possible* at given prices without impairing profit margins.

increases under non-union market conditions would be more accurate if "price inflation" were substituted for "full employment."

The foregoing analysis seems to lead to the following conclusions:

1 There is no evidence that considerable increases in the general wage level would be generated under non-union market conditions except at inflationary levels of employment. This is supported by both inductive and deductive analysis.

2 These levels of employment are unlikely to be realized without a very high contribution to aggregate demand on the part of government. Even with government expenditures at current levels and with a sizeable annual deficit, unemployment is currently (Spring 1950) over the 5% level. Whether the community desire to reduce unemployment below 5% (3 plus million in 1950) is strong enough to accept even a mild price inflation and a larger budget deficit as a consequence is not self-evident. Faced with the implementation of policy, full employment programmers may be well satisfied to measure actual accomplishment against the yardstick of the more modest definitions of full employment. If the private sector of the American economy fails to generate peacetime inflation in the future and if public policy accepts "high level employment" as its aim, the behavior of non-union wage markets would not pose an inflationary problem.

It appears that the argument that union wage policy poses no problem which did not already exist with non-union labor markets is applicable only to a special case unlikely to exist in peacetime. If unionism generates *any* wage increase with unemployment over the 8% level (just under five million in Spring 1950), or if it produces increases larger than 3% at less than the 5% level, a new element will have been introduced into the situation.

Garbarino's implied operational definition of full employment as the level at which competition for labor in a nonunion market is "likely to raise wages significantly" may be criticized because it does not allow for structural unemployment or wage pressure to arise in general while there is still a surplus of labor supply or demand. But in Phillips curve language, he is seeking the level of unemployment at which wages rise more than productivity (3 percent) indicating the presence of inflationary pressure if not actual price increases.

From admittedly sketchy data, Garbarino concludes that prices rose, as wage increases exceeded 3 percent, only as the unemployment rate fell below 5 percent, for the period 1899–1929, and that as a generalization, this pattern would apply to nonunion labor markets at a later date. Furthermore, his prediction (which proved to be quite accurate) that the United States economy could not experience unemployment levels below 4 percent without considerable inflation pinpoints the two unemployment rates so important in the structural debate as well as identifying critical points on the Phillips curve.

Although his prophetic grasp of the Phillips curve methodology represents a significant contribution, Garbarino's implicit assumption regarding the sequence of causation in the wage-price relationship for the period may be questioned. He clearly has a demand-pull model in mind when he argues that in the few periods when wages rose above the 3 percent level, prices which also rose considerably then forced wages up or that " 'price inflation' is likely to lead to 'undue' wage increases under non-union market conditions." It is true that monopolistic union pressure was generally absent during the period covered, but to conclude that workers as a whole were passive wage acceptors during the period would require considerable substantiation. Perhaps wage push was partly responsible for the inflationary interludes.

Similarly, Garbarino is unduly gentle toward the inflationary tendencies of union wage policy when he claims that unions would introduce a "new element . . . into the situation," if wages rose more than 3 percent only when unemployment fell below 5 percent, during the post-1930 "unionized" period, the pattern for the prior period. In fact, this has been roughly the relationship between wages and prices since the 1930's except for the brief "creeping inflation" of the mid-1950's to late-1950's. But unions might have generated a positive inflationary force, offset by changes in other factors affecting prices.

In any case, questioning Garbarino's nonneutral stand regarding inflation's causes does not weaken his main idea of a functional relationship between wage and price changes and the level of unemployment. Neutrality of the Phillips curve is best exemplified in the original Phillips article itself, if not in Phillips' own interpretation of his findings.

# The Relation Between Unemployment and the Rate of Change of Money Wage Rates in the United Kingdom, 1861–1957

*by A. W. Phillips*

## HYPOTHESIS

When the demand for a commodity or service is high relatively to the supply of it we expect the price to rise, the rate of rise being greater the greater the excess demand. Conversely when the demand is low relatively to the supply we expect the price to fall, the rate of fall being greater the greater the deficiency of demand. It seems plausible that this principle should operate as one of the factors determining the rate of change of money wage rates, which are the price of labour services. When the demand for labour is high and there are very few unemployed we should expect employers to bid wage rates up quite rapidly, each firm and each industry being continually tempted to offer a little above the prevailing rates to attract the most suitable labour from other firms and industries. On the other hand it appears that workers are reluctant to offer their services at less than the prevailing rates when the demand for labour is low and unemployment is high so that wage rates fall only very slowly. The relation between unemployment and the rate of change of wage rates is therefore likely to be highly non-linear.

It seems possible that a second factor influencing the rate of change of money wage rates might be the rate of change of the demand for labour, and so of unemployment. Thus in a year of rising business activity, with the demand for labour increasing and the percentage unemployment decreasing, employers will be bidding more vigorously for the services of labour than they would be in a year during which the average percentage unemployment was the same but the demand for labour was not increasing. Conversely in a year of falling business activity, with the demand for labour decreasing and the

SOURCE Reprinted with permission from *Economica,* Vol. 25, December 1958, pp. 283–299.

percentage unemployment increasing, employers will be less inclined to grant wage increases, and workers will be in a weaker position to press for them, than they would be in a year during which the average percentage unemployment was the same but the demand for labour was not decreasing.

\* \* \*

The purpose of the present study is to see whether statistical evidence supports the hypothesis that the rate of change of money wage rates in the United Kingdom can be explained by the level of unemployment and the rate of change of unemployment, except in or immediately after those years in which there was a very rapid rise in import prices, and if so to form some quantitative estimate of the relation between unemployment and the rate of change of money wage rates. The periods 1861–1913, 1913–1948 and 1948–1957 will be considered separately.

1861–1913

Schlote's index of the average price of imports[1] shows an increase of 12.5 per

cent in import prices in 1862 as compared with the previous year, an increase of 7.6 per cent in 1900 and in 1910, and an increase of 7.0 per cent in 1872. In no other year between 1861 and 1913 was there an increase in import prices of as much as 5 per cent. If the hypothesis stated above is correct the rise in import prices in 1862 may just have been sufficient to start up a mild wage-price spiral, but in the remainder of the period changes in import prices will have had little or no effect on the rate of change of wage rates.

A scatter diagram of the rate of change of wage rates and the percentage unemployment for the years 1861–1913 is shown in Figure 1. During this time there were 6½ fairly regular trade cycles with an average period of about 8 years. Scatter diagrams for the years of each trade cycle are shown in Figures 2 to 8. Each dot in the diagrams represents a year, the average rate of change of money wage rates during the year being given by the scale on the vertical axis and the average unemployment during the year by the scale on the horizontal axis. . . .

The crosses shown in Figure 1 give the average values of the rate of change of money wage rates and of the percentage

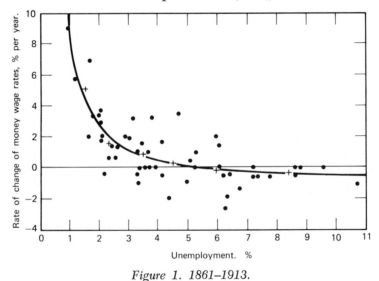

*Figure 1. 1861–1913.*

[1] W. Schlote, *British Overseas Trade from 1700 to the 1930's,* Table 26.

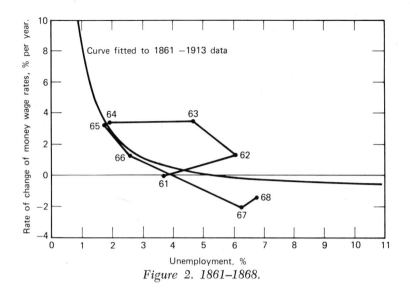

*Figure 2. 1861–1868.*

unemployment in those years in which unemployment lay between 0 and 2, 2 and 3, 3 and 4, 4 and 5, 5 and 7, and 7 and 11 per cent respectively (the upper bound being included in each interval). Since each interval includes years in which unemployment was increasing and years in which it was decreasing the effect of changing unemployment on the rate of change of wage rates tends to be cancelled out by this averaging, so that each cross gives an approximation to the rate of change of wages which would be associated with the indicated level of unemployment if unemployment were held constant at that level.

\* \* \*

From a comparison of Figures 2 to 8 it appears that the width of loops obtained in each trade cycle has tended to narrow, suggesting a reduction in the dependence of the rate of change of wage rates on the rate of change of unemployment. There seem to be two possible explanations of this. First, in the coal and steel industries before the first world war sliding scale adjustments were common, by which wage rates were linked to the prices of the

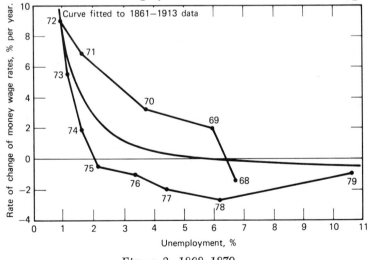

*Figure 3. 1868–1879.*

products.[2] Given the tendency of product prices to rise with an increase in business activity and fall with a decrease in business activity, these agreements may have strengthened the relation between changes in wage rates and changes in unemployment in these industries. During the earlier years of the period these industries would have fairly large weights in the wage index, but with the greater coverage of the statistical material available in later years the weights of these industries in the index would be reduced. Second, it is possible that the decrease in the width of the loops resulted not so much from a reduction in the dependence of wage changes on changes in unemployment as from the introduction of a time lag in the response of wage changes to changes in the level of unemployment, caused by the extension of collective bargaining and particularly by the growth of arbitration and conciliation procedures. If such a time lag existed in the later years of the period the wage change in any year should be related, not to average unemployment during that year, but to the average unemployment lagged by, perhaps, several months. This would have the effect of moving each point in the diagrams horizontally part of the way towards the point of the preceding year and it can easily be seen that this would widen the loops in the diagrams. This fact makes it difficult to discriminate at all closely between the effect of time lags and the effect of dependence of wage changes on the rate of change of unemployment.

At the outset, Phillips assumes that the close curved relationship he finds between the rate of change of money wages and the level of unemployment results from demand-pull forces. He sees wage increases resulting at low levels of unemployment from employers' competition for labor which "bids wage rates up quite rapidly."

But in the same first paragraph, Phillips balances out his reasoning by expressing a cost push sentiment. He explains the leveling off of the Phillips curve at higher unemployment rates as a result of workers "reluctance" to accept wage cuts, despite downward pressure from declining demand.

The most significant aspect of the paper is the finding of long-run stability of the curve. The fitted curve of annual data in Figure 1 shows a distinct, if not close relationship for the period 1861 to 1913. Moreover, other graphs not included here show that the earlier pattern of the wage-change–unemployment level prevailed on balance throughout a century.

Phillips offers explanations for wide deviation from the curve for particular years, but of special interest is his hypothesis regarding cyclical movements of annual data around the curve. Figures 2 and 3 give examples of this cyclical pattern.

The argument is advanced that the so-called Phillips curve "loops" reflect the influence of *change* in the unemployment rate as opposed to the level of unemployment on wages. With rates falling to a particular level, wages would be raised as employers, and perhaps unions, sensed a tightening trend in the labor market, while a rise in the rate to the same level would foster a feeling of pessimism on demanders and suppliers of labor and influence wages negatively.

Certain properties of the curve other than its stability and nonlinearity have economic significance. The curve indicates a constancy of wage pressures for

[2] I am indebted to Professor Phelps Brown for pointing this out to me.

any given level of unemployment. This means that if wages are in an inflationary range in any given year (which in England, for an estimated 2 percent productivity growth, means wages increasing more than 2 percent a year), the inflation will continue year after year if unemployment remains at this level. In other words, the Phillips curve at its highest points does not describe a price increase for a given year but a continuing steady inflation as long as the low level of unemployment is maintained.

The steepness of the curve at low levels of unemployment indicates that there would be less inflation over time if a steady low level of unemployment were maintained than if there were fluctuations around this rate. This suggests that smoothing of the business cycle, which has moved about a relatively low average unemployment rate over the past 20 years, would in itself temper future price increases, at the same low average level. The Phillips curve, for example, tells us that a steady unemployment rate of 4 percent would lead to less inflation than from a rate that fluctuated between 2 and 6 percent.

From the English experience wages begin rising when the unemployment rate falls below about 6 percent and rise above 2 percent, indicating the presence of rising prices, when the unemployment level falls below 2.5 percent. There are two important implications of this finding. First, from low levels of unemployment it is possible for the economy to worsen and the level of unemployment to rise, with wages rising, albeit at a decreasing rate. Furthermore, the rate of wage increase may still be at a pace to indicate rising prices. A look at the basic curve will prove that this is not likely because of the extreme steepness of the British curve at low unemployment rates. But when we examine the Phillips curve for the United States, we find a substantial range of low-level unemployment over which the rate may rise, but the accompanying wage increases, although growing smaller, may still exceed the price stability level.

Second, for British data, and more so for American, wage increases seem to reach the "inflationary rate" at less than full employment, assumed here to be the fractional rate. Most analysts would agree that the frictional unemployment rate for England is something less than 2.5 percent, the rate below which annual wage increases would exceed 2 percent, the assumed annual British productivity growth. This means that inflation arises when there is some slack in the labor market. It could indicate the emergence of demand-pull forces while there was still some excess labor supply, but strongly suggests the possibility of structural bottlenecks and/or union wage pressure as alternative agents of inflation.

### The American Phillips Curve

Phillips' work led to study of the wage-unemployment relationship in other countries. Varying degrees of closeness of fit were found, but the American data led to some interesting similarities and contrasts with the British experience. Two Phillips curve studies of the United States are presented. The Samuelson and Solow paper not only presents a rough estimate of the American Phillips curve but also points out the futility of the demand-pull–cost-push argument. A few of the more common errors in logic and methodology in assigning either cost-push or demand-pull factors as causes of inflation which they note are included here. Bowen and Berry offer a deeper statistical study of the curve and emphasize the differences between the American and British curves.

# Analytical Aspects of Anti-Inflation Policy

## by Paul A. Samuelson and Robert M. Solow

### II

*Truths and Consequences:*
*The Problem of Identification*

The competing (although imperfectly competing) theories of inflation appear to be genuinely different hypotheses about observable facts. In that case one ought to be able to distinguish empirically between cost and demand inflation. What are the earmarks? If I believe in cost-push, what should I expect to find in the facts that I would not expect to find were I a believer in demand-pull? The last clause is important. It will not do to point to circumstances which will accompany any inflation, however caused. A test must have what statisticians call power against the main alternative hypotheses.

Trite as these remarks may seem, they need to be made. The clichés of popular discussion fall into the trap again and again. Although they have been tram-

pled often enough by experts, the errors revive. We will take the time to point the finger once more. We do this because we want to go one step further and argue that this problem of identification is exceedingly difficult. What appear at first to be subtle and reliable ways of distinguishing cost-induced from demand-induced inflation turn out to be far from airtight. In fact we are driven to the belief that aggregate data, recording the *ex post* details of completed transactions, may in most circumstances be quite insufficient. It may be necessary first to disaggregate.

### Common Fallacies

The simplest mistake—to be found in almost any newspaper discussion of the subject—is the belief that if money wages rise faster than productivity, we have a sure sign of cost-inflation. Of course the truth is that in the purest of excess-demand

SOURCE Reprinted with permission from *American Economic Review*, Vol. 50, May 1960, pp. 177–194.

inflation wages will rise faster than productivity; the only alternative is for the full increase in the value of a fixed output to be siphoned off into profits, without this spilling over into the labor market to drive wages up still further. This error is sometimes mixed with the belief that it is possible over long periods for industries with rapid productivity increase to pay higher and increasingly higher wages than those where output per man-hour grows slowly. Such a persistent and growing differential is likely eventually to alter the skill- or quality-mix of the labor force in the different industries, which casts doubt on the original productivity comparison.

One sometimes sees statements to the effect that increases in expenditure more rapid than increases in real output necessarily spell demand inflation. It is simple arithmetic that expenditure outrunning output by itself spells only price increases and provides no evidence at all about the source or cause of the inflation. Much of the talk about "too much money chasing too few goods" is of this kind.

A more solemn version of the fallacy goes: An increase in expenditure can come about only through an increase in the stock of money or an increase in the velocity of circulation. Therefore the only possible causes of inflation are $M$ and $V$ and we need to look no further.

\* \* \*

### The Fundamental Phillips Schedule Relating Unemployment and Wage Changes

Consider also the question of the relation between money wage changes and the degree of unemployment. We have A. W. Phillips' interesting paper on the U. K. history since the Civil War (our Civil War, that is!). His findings are remarkable, even if one disagrees with his interpretations.

In the first place, the period 1861–1913, during which the trade-union movement was rather weak, shows a fairly close relationship between the per cent change in wage rates and the fraction of the labor force unemployed. Due allowance must be made for sharp import-price-induced changes in the cost of living, and for the normal expectation that wages will be rising faster when an unemployment rate of 5 per cent is reached on the upswing than when it is reached on the downswing. In the second place, with minor exceptions, the same relationship that fits for 1861–1913 also seems to fit about as well for 1913–48 and 1948–57. And finally Phillips concludes that the money wage level would stabilize with 5 per cent unemployment; and the rate of increase of money wages would be held down to the 2–3 per cent rate of productivity increase with about 2½ per cent of the labor force unemployed.

Strangely enough, no comparably careful study has been made for the U.S. Garbarino's 1950 note is hardly a full-scale analysis, and Schultze's treatment in his first-class Joint Committee monograph is much too casual. There is some evidence that the U.S. differs from the U.K. on at least two counts. If there is any such relationship characterizing the American labor market, it may have shifted somewhat in the last fifty to sixty years. Secondly, there is a suggestion that in this country it might take 8 to 10 per cent unemployment to stabilize money wages.

But would it take 8 to 10 per cent unemployment forever to stabilize the money wage? Is not this kind of relationship also one which depends heavily on remembered experience? We suspect that this is another way in which a past characterized by rising prices, high employment, and mild, short recessions is likely to breed an inflationary bias—by making the money wage more rigid downward, maybe even perversely inclined to rise during recessions on the grounds that things will soon be different.

There may be no such relation for this country. If there is, why does it not seem to have the same degree of long-run invariance as Phillips' curve for the U.K.? What geographical, economic, sociological facts account for the difference between the two countries? Is there a difference in labor mobility in the two countries? Do the different tolerances for unemployment reflect differences in income level, union organization, or what? What policy decisions might conceivably lead to a decrease in the critical unemployment rate at which wages begin to rise or to rise too fast? Clearly a careful study of this problem might pay handsome dividends.

## III

### A Closer Look at the American Data

In spite of all its deficiencies, we think the accompanying scatter diagram in Figure 1 is useful. Where it does not provide answers, it at least asks interesting questions. We have plotted the yearly percentage changes of average hourly earnings in manufacturing, including supplements (Rees's data) against the annual average percentage of the labor force unemployed.

The first defect to note is the different coverages represented in the two axes. Duesenberry has argued that postwar wage increases in manufacturing on the one hand and in trade, services, etc., on the other, may have quite different explanations: union power in manufacturing and simple excess demand in the other sectors. It is probably true that if we had an unemployment rate for manufacturing alone, it would be somewhat higher during the postwar years than the aggregate figure shown. Even if a qualitative statement like this held true over the whole period, the increasing weight of services in the total might still create a bias. Another defect is our use of annual increments and averages, when a full-scale study would have to look carefully into the nuances of timing.

A first look at the scatter is discourag-

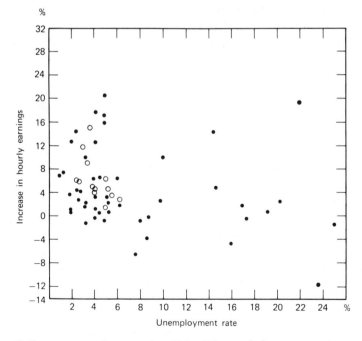

Figure 1. Phillips scatter diagram for U.S. (The circled points are for recent years.)

ing; there are points all over the place. But perhaps one can notice some systematic effects. In the first place, the years from 1933 to 1941 appear to be *sui generis:* money wages rose or failed to fall in the face of massive unemployment. One may attribute this to the workings of the New Deal (the 20 per cent wage increase of 1934 must represent the NRA codes); or alternatively one could argue that by 1933 much of the unemployment had become structural, insulated from the functioning labor market, so that in effect the vertical axis ought to be moved over to the right. This would leave something more like the normal pattern.

The early years of the first World War also behave atypically although not so much so as 1933-39. This may reflect cost-of-living increases, the rapidity of the increase in demand, a special tightness in manufacturing, or all three.

But the bulk of the observations—the period between the turn of the century and the first war, the decade between the end of that war and the Great Depression, and the most recent ten or twelve years —all show a rather consistent pattern. Wage rates do tend to rise when the labor market is tight, and the tighter the faster. What is most interesting is the strong suggestion that the relation, such as it is, has shifted upward slightly but noticeably in the forties and fifties. On the one hand, the first decade of the century and the twenties seem to fit the same pattern. Manufacturing wages seem to stabilize absolutely when 4 or 5 per cent of the labor force is unemployed; and wage increases equal to the productivity increase of 2 to 3 per cent per year is the normal pattern at about 3 per cent unemployment. This is not so terribly different from Phillips' results for the U.K., although the relation holds there with a greater consistency. We comment on this below.

On the other hand, from 1946 to the present, the pattern is fairly consistent and consistently different from the earlier pe-

riod. The annual unemployment rate ranged only narrowly, from 2.5 per cent in 1953 to 6.2 per cent in 1958. Within that range, as might be expected, wages rose faster the lower the unemployment rate. But one would judge now that it would take more like 8 per cent unemployment to keep money wages from rising. And they would rise at 2 to 3 per cent per year with 5 or 6 per cent of the labor force unemployed.

It would be overhasty to conclude that the relation we have been discussing represents a reversible supply curve for labor along which an aggregate demand curve slides. If that were so then movements along the curve might be dubbed standard demand pull, and shifts of the curve might represent the institutional changes on which cost-push theories rest. The apparent shift in our Phillips' curve might be attributed by some economists to the new market power of trade-unions. Others might be more inclined to believe that the expectation of continued full employment, or at least high employment, is enough to explain both the shift in the supply curve, if it is that, and the willingness of employers (conscious that what they get from a work force is partly dependent on its morale and its turnover) to pay wage increases in periods of temporarily slack demand.

This latter consideration, however, casts real doubt on the facile identification of the relationship as merely a supply-of-labor phenomenon. There are two parties to a wage bargain.

## U.S. and U.K. Compared

A comparison of the American position with Phillips' findings for the U.K. is interesting for itself and also as a possible guide to policy. Anything which will shift the relationship downward decreases the price in unemployment that must be paid when a policy is followed of holding down the rate of wage and price increase by pressure on aggregate demand.

One possibility is that the trade-union leadership is more "responsible" in the U.K.; indeed the postwar policy of wage restraint seems visible in Phillips' data. But there are other interpretations. It is clear that the more fractionated and imperfect a labor market is, the higher the over-all excess supply of labor may have to be before the average wage rate becomes stable and the less tight the relation will be in any case. Even a touch of downward inflexibility (and trade-unionism and administered wages surely means at least this) will make this immobility effect more pronounced. It would seem plausible that the sheer geographical compactness of the English economy makes its labor market more perfect than ours in this sense. Moreover, the British have pursued a more deliberate policy of relocation of industry to mop up pockets of structural unemployment.

This suggests that any governmental policy which increases the mobility of labor (geographical and industrial) or improves the flow of information in the labor market will have anti-inflationary effects as well as being desirable for other reasons. A quicker but in the long run probably less efficient approach might be for the government to direct the regional distribution of its expenditures more deliberately in terms of the existence of local unemployment and excess capacity.

The English data show a quite clearly nonlinear (hyperbolic) relation between wage changes and unemployment, reflecting the much discussed downward inflexibility. Our American figures do not contradict this, although they do not tell as plain a story as the English. To the extent that this nonlinearity exists, as Duesenberry has remarked, a given average level of unemployment over the cycle will be compatible with a slower rate of wage increase (and presumably price increase) the less wide the cyclical swings from top to bottom.

A less obvious implication of this point of view is that a deliberate low-pressure policy to stabilize the price level may have a certain self-defeating aspect. It is clear from experience that interregional and interindustrial mobility of labor depends heavily on the pull of job opportunities elsewhere more so than on the push of local unemployment. In effect the imperfection of the labor market is increased, with the consequences we have sketched.

. . . When we translate the Phillips' diagram showing the American pattern of wage increase against degree of unemployment into a related diagram showing the different levels of unemployment that would be "needed" for each degree of price level change, we come out with guesses like the following:

1 In order to have wages increase at no more than the 2½ per cent per annum characteristic of our productivity growth, the American economy would seem on the basis of twentieth-century and postwar experience to have to undergo something like 5 to 6 per cent of the civilian labor force's being unemployed. That much unemployment would appear to be the cost of price stability in the years immediately ahead.

2 In order to achieve the nonperfectionist's goal of high enough output to give us no more than 3 per cent unemployment, the price index might have to rise by as much as 4 to 5 per cent per year. That much price rise would seem to be the necessary cost of high employment and production in the years immediately ahead.

All this is shown in our price-level modification of the Phillips curve, Figure 2. The point A, corresponding to price stability, is seen to involve about 5½ per cent unemployment; whereas the point B, corresponding to 3 per cent unemployment, is seen to involve a price rise of about 4½ per cent per annum. We rather

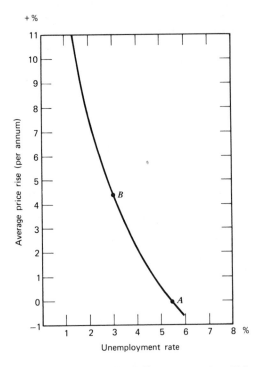

*Figure 2. Modified Phillips curve for U.S. This shows the menu of choice between different degrees of unemployment and price stability, as roughly estimated from last 25 years of American data.*

expect that the tug of war of politics will end us up in the next few years somewhere in between these selected points. We shall probably have some price rise and some excess unemployment.

Aside from the usual warning that these are simply our best guesses we must give another caution. All of our discussion has been phrased in short-run terms, dealing with what might happen in the next few years. It would be wrong, though, to think that our Figure 2 menu that relates obtainable price and unemployment behavior will maintain its same shape in the longer run. What we do in a policy way during the next few years might cause it to shift in a definite way.

Thus, it is conceivable that after they had produced a low-pressure economy, the believers in demand-pull might be disappointed in the short run; i.e., prices

might continue to rise even though unemployment was considerable. Nevertheless, it might be that the low-pressure demand would so act upon wage and other expectations as to shift the curve downward in the longer run—so that over a decade, the economy might enjoy higher employment with price stability than our present-day estimate would indicate.

But also the opposite is conceivable. A low-pressure economy might build up within itself over the years larger and larger amounts of structural unemployment (the reverse of what happened from 1941 to 1953 as a result of strong war and postwar demands). The result would be an upward shift of our menu of choice, with more and more unemployment being needed just to keep prices stable.

Since we have no conclusive or suggestive evidence on these conflicting issues, we shall not attempt to give judgment on them. Instead we venture the reminder that, in the years just ahead, the level of attained growth will be highly correlated with the degree of full employment and high-capacity output.

But what about the longer run? If the per annum rate of technical progress were about the same in a low- and high-pressure economy, then the initial loss in output in going to the low-pressure state would never be made up; however, in relative terms, the initial gap would not grow but would remain constant as time goes by. If a low-pressure economy could succeed in improving the efficiency of our productive factors, some of the loss of growth might be gradually made up and could in long enough time even be more than wiped out. On the other hand, if such an economy produced class warfare and social conflict and depressed the level of research and technical progress, the loss in growth would be compounded in the long run.

A final disclaimer is in order. We have not here entered upon the important question of what feasible institutional reforms might be introduced to lessen the degree of disharmony between full employment and price stability. These could of course involve such wide-ranging issues as direct price and wage controls, antiunion and antitrust legislation, and a host of other measures hopefully designed to move the American Phillips' curves downward and to the left.

In their Phillips curve section, presented here, Samuelson and Solow note the two big differences between the American and British wage-unemployment pattern. First, the American curve has not been stable for as long a period as the British, and second, the American curve lies to the right of the British. That is, both wage stability and price stability, despite a somewhat greater productivity growth rate here, can be attained only at higher levels of unemployment than in England. This poses serious difficulties for policy decisions regarding the unemployment reduction-inflation "trade-off."

The writers link the two differences by suggesting that prior to the shift in the curve it was more closely related to the English. After World War II, the curve shifted to the right as, after relatively long periods of high-level employment, both labor suppliers and demanders agreed on optimistic wages. This means that given wage increases would be sought and granted at higher levels of unemployment than before, in the belief that the labor market on balance was in a tightening trend.

In their explanation of why the American Phillips curve lies to the right of the English, the writers suggest the possibility that the higher level of frictional unemployment may be an important causal factor. But the level of frictional unemployment only tends to affect average wages and prices at very low levels of unemployment, and the American curve lies to the right even for levels clearly above the frictional level.

The problems of disentagling cost-push from demand-pull elements are so complex that even the writers' experiment for testing the effect of a purposeful reduction in demand would not yield conclusive results. If price and wage increases were reduced as demand slackened, the previous inflation might have been of the demand-pull type as Samuelson and Solow suggest, but it might also have been cost-push in nature. As was mentioned above, careful proponents of cost-push agree that these forces operate only during periods of strong demand, and that they are the agent of inflation in that the demand in itself would not have led to "inflationary" wage increases. Therefore, the reduction in demand could have led to a relaxation in cost-push pressures with unemployment still rising, but less than if the cost-push elements had not been present, as the relaxation of, say, union wage demands partially offset the effect of declining demand in increasing unemployment.

The accuracy of Samuelson and Solow's Phillips curve, although roughly drawn, is evidenced by the closeness of their prediction regarding the relationship of price increases to low-level unemployment rates to our actual experience. If anything, they were a little too conservative in their predicted levels of inflation at low unemployment. Our price level in recent years has been rising at about the 5 percent level, but our overall unemployment rate was about a point above the 3 percent level, with which Samuelson and Solow associated this degree of inflation.

At its close, the paper notes that a worsening of structural unemployment would cause a disturbing rightward shift to the curve. The effect of structural unemployment on inflation has already been discussed, and its relationship to the Phillips curve itself will be analyzed after study of Bowen and Berry's paper, which presents closer details of the American curve and its comparison with the English.

### The American and English Curve Compared

Bowen and Berry present a statistical study of the relationship between wage rate changes and both unemployment rates and changes in the rate for particular subgroups, and for the entire range of years 1900 to 1958. The shift and short-run stability of the curve are confirmed by the finding of significance in the correlation over the long period. The shift, however, does not seem to be a persistent one in that the passage of time itself is not an important explanatory variable of the short-period differences.

# Unemployment Conditions and Movements of the Money-Wage Level

## by William G. Bowen and R. A. Berry

### FINDINGS AND INTERPRETATIONS

*The Level of Unemployment as an Explanatory Variable*

To what degree do the United States data support the hypothesis that the rate of change of money wages ($\dot{W}$) is related to the state of the labor market as approx- imated by the level of unemployment ($U$)? The answer to this question depends to a considerable extent on whether one looks at the individual sub-periods or at the entire period between 1900 and 1958 taken as a whole. Correlations for the individual sub-periods are presented in Table 1.

TABLE 1. CORRELATIONS BETWEEN $W$ AND $U$[a]

| Sub-Periods | Simple Correlations $(r_{wU})$ | Partial Correlations $(r_{wU.U})$ |
|---|---|---|
| 1900–1932 (excluding 1915–1920) | −.61 | −.52 |
| 1935–1941 | −.87 | −.83 |
| 1948–1958 | −.34 | −.50 |

[a] These correlations are based on the averaged unemployment methods of aligning the wage and unemployment series. Confidence limits are given in the appendix.

SOURCE Reprinted with permission from *Review of Economics and Statistics*, Vol. 45, May 1963, pp. 163–172.

As this table indicates, the simple correlas between $\dot{W}$ and $U$ are negative in every sub-period and range in value from —.34 in 1948–1958 to —.87 in 1935–1941. The partial correlation coefficients between $\dot{W}$ and $U$, with *changes* in the level of unemployment ($\dot{U}$) held constant, are seen to be very similar to the simple correlation coefficients. The general tenor of the results is not altered by using the first central difference method rather than the averaged unemployment method of alignment, and the evidence as a whole certainly suggests that, within the sub-periods, the rate of change of money wages has been influenced by the level of unemployment.

It is possible to provide at least a rough idea of the extent of the influence by calculating linear regression equations. (The scatter of points does not provide any incentive to experiment with non-linear expressions.) The effect of a 1 per cent change in $U$ on $\dot{W}$ (as calculated by the regression equations given in the appendix) is seen to have varied from —.41 in the 1900–1932 period to —.56 in 1948–1958 to —1.24 in 1935–1941. The number of observations in the two most recent sub-periods—and particularly in the 1935–1941 sub-period—is so limited that it would be foolish to read much importance into these regression coefficients. However, the rather wide range of coefficients does lead one to suspect the lack of any reasonably stable relationship between the level of unemployment and the rate of change of money wages over the period as a whole.

This suspicion is confirmed by the results of direct attempts to correlate $U$ with $\dot{W}$ over the long period. If we combine the data from the three sub-periods, we obtain a partial correlation coefficient ($r_{\dot{W}U.\dot{U}}$) of —.28. If we take the entire period 1900–1958, omitting no years at all, we obtain a partial correlation coefficient of —.20. These coefficients are considerably lower than the corresponding coefficients obtained for the individual sub-periods, and neither of the two long-period coefficients is significant at the 5 per cent level of confidence. It seems reasonable to conclude that the long-period relationship between unemployment levels and annual rates of change of money wages must be described as rather loose—if indeed it makes sense to speak of any statistically significant long-period relationship at all.

The lack of a consistent long-period relationship will not surprise those who have argued that institutional changes in the United States economy over the past 60 years (most notably the development of large industrial unions) have caused upward shifts in the entire unemployment-wage change relationship. It is certainly conceivable that periodic upward shifts in a fairly stable short-period relationship have been responsible for the greater looseness of the long-period relationship.

This is not an easy proposition to prove or to disprove. The testing problem is complicated, first of all, by the possibility that the same structural factors that are alleged to have shifted the unemployment-wage change schedule upward may have simultaneously altered its shape; furthermore, we lack convincing a priori propositions concerning the frequency and timing of any such shifts that may have occurred. As an admittedly rough test of this periodic upward-shift hypothesis, we have introduced time ($t$) an as explanatory variable, along with the level of unemployment.

When the period as a whole is considered, the linear regression equation is:

$$\dot{W} = 6.91 - .51U + .05t$$
(with $t = 0$ in 1900, 1 in 1901, etc.).
$$(R^2 = .04)$$

When the years 1915–1920, 1933–1934, and 1942–1947 are omitted, the equation becomes:

$$\dot{W} = 2.67 - .28U + .07t$$
$$(R^2 = .14)$$

The positive values of the regression co-efficients for $t$ in these two equations do provide some support for the proposition that wages have tended to rise more rapidly at given levels of unemployment as we have moved progressively further into the twentieth century. But the addition of the time variable certainly cannot be said to have removed very much of the loose-ness in the long-period relationships between $U$ and $\dot{W}$. ($U$ and $t$ together explain only 14 per cent of the variation in $\dot{W}$ over the selected group of years repre-sented by the second equation.) The rather weak explanatory power of $t$ un-doubtedly stems, in part, from the pres-ence in the middle of the time series of the years 1935–1941, when wages rose quite rapidly despite high unemployment. In any case, the data do not support the extreme view that during the twentieth century the United States economy has been characterized by a strong, uninter-rupted trend toward ever higher wage in-creases at given levels of unemployment. Money earnings do appear to have risen somewhat more rapidly at given levels of unemployment in the post-World War II period than in the pre-World War I years, but one ought not to exaggerate either the extent or the inexorable character of the change that has occurred.

## Changes in the Level of Unemployment as an Explanatory Variable

One of the most interesting hypotheses to emerge from the Phillips study of United Kingdom data was the view that the rate of change of unemployment ($\dot{U}$), and not just the absolute level of unem-ployment, may have a lot to do with the speed at which money wages rise. The statistical results of our study of United States experience offer consistent support for the "change in unemployment" hy-pothesis.

As Table 2 indicates, the simple and partial correlations between $\dot{U}$ and $\dot{W}$ are as consistently negative in all three sub-periods as the correlations between $U$ and $\dot{W}$ presented earlier.

It is when we calculate long-period cor-relations between $\dot{U}$ and $\dot{W}$ that the con-trast with the correlations between $U$ and $\dot{W}$ becomes especially interesting. Whereas the relationship between the level of un-employment and the rate of change of money wages was markedly weakened when calculations were made for the longer period of time, the long-period cor-relations between *changes* in the level of unemployment and the rate of change of money wages hold up remarkably well. The partial correlation coefficient ($r_{\dot{W}\dot{U}.U}$) is −.63 for the three sub-periods com-bined and −.53 for all years from 1900 through 1958. Both of these coefficients are easily significant at the 1 per cent level of confidence. We conclude that changes in the level of unemployment have had the expected inverse influence on the speed at which money wages have risen during the past half-century taken as a whole and during component sub-periods.

TABLE 2.   CORRELATIONS BETWEEN $\dot{W}$ AND $\dot{U}$[a]

| Sub-Periods | Simple Correlations $(r_{\dot{W}\dot{U}})$ | Partial Correlations $(r_{\dot{W}\dot{U}.U})$ |
|---|---|---|
| 1900–1932 (excluding 1915–1920) | −.56 | −.45 |
| 1935–1941 | −.64 | −.48 |
| 1948–1958 | −.74 | −.78 |

[a] These correlations are based on the averaged unemployment methods of aligning the wage and unemployment series. Confidence limits are given in the appendix.

What theoretical interpretation are we to give to the persistent relationship between changes in the level of unemployment and the rate of change of money earnings revealed by the United States data? The simplest—and in our view the most satisfactory—interpretation is that these statistical results support the hypothesis that changes in the level of unemployment constitute one of the more predictable determinants of the rate of change of money wages.

The basic reason for expecting changes in the level of unemployment to play a role in the wage determination process is that wages are set with an eye to the future as well as with an eye to the present—and changes in unemployment serve as a handy index of future labor market conditions. At a given level of unemployment, employers acting unilaterally are likely to set a higher wage if the trend of unemployment is down than if unemployment is rising and a recession seems to be getting underway. Similarly, wage negotiations between an employer and a union are likely to be influenced to a significant degree by labor market expectations: unions are likely to demand larger wage increases if unemployment seems to be on the wane, and employers are likely to offer less resistance if they foresee a tightening of the labor market in coming months.

Wage decisions are not constantly revised and thus must be attuned to future labor market conditions as well as to the exigencies of the moment—this is especially true of negotiated wage agreements embodied in formal contracts. And, while current changes in unemployment cannot be counted on to produce highly reliable predictions as to future developments (turning points, for instance, will never be detected by this method of prediction), extrapolating the present into the future nonetheless has its uses and its users.

The only objector to this expectations argument known to us is Lipsey. Lipsey challenges the expectations argument on the ground that, if falling unemployment makes employers think they will need more labor in the future, the result will be an increase in competitive bidding which will not only raise wages but which will simultaneously lower the level of unemployment, thus moving the economy along the one basic adjustment curve relating the level of unemployment to changes in money wages.

There seems to be one major difficulty with this argument: expectations as to future labor market conditions (say the expectation of a tightening of labor markets over the next year) may well have a direct influence on current wage negotiations without simultaneously influencing current decisions as to the number of men to be hired. Wage adjustments are, after all, made much less frequently than employment adjustments—for one thing, it is far simpler, from a decision-making standpoint, to hire ten new men than it is to decide upon the precise change to be made in the basic wage schedule applicable to all employees (union approval may also be necessary in the case of a wage change); furthermore, changes in wage schedules are much more irreversible than changes in the number of employees. Consequently, it seems entirely conceivable that a firm engaged in wage negotiations will raise wages now as a protection against the danger of losing employees as job opportunities in general expand, and that the same firm will choose not to hire new men until specific openings actually occur. In the United States economy, wage and employment decisions are not linked together as closely in time as Lipsey's argument suggests.

As an alternative to the expectations hypothesis, Lipsey has presented a hypothesis which depicts economy-wide variations in the rate of change of money wages at given levels of unemployment as a function, not of the rate of change of aggregate unemployment, but of the distribution of aggregate unemployment among local labor markets. This distributional hypothesis in turn depends on another hypothesis—namely, that the reaction function linking levels of unemployment to movements of the money wage level in the typical local labor market is non-linear. The first attempt that we know of to test this local labor market hypothesis has been made by Philip Ross.[1] While Ross' efforts are subject to certain methodological criticisms, it can be reported that he failed to find any consistent relationship—linear or non-linear—between $U$ and $\dot{W}$, or between $\dot{U}$ and $\dot{W}$, at the local labor market level.[2]

Lipsey's distributional hypothesis is appealing on a priori grounds and certainly deserves more testing; but, until such testing is completed, it seems sensible to retain the view that it is expectational considerations that are likely to lead to an inverse relationship between changes in the level of unemployment and changes in the money wage level. In any case, it should be recognized that the expectations hypothesis and Lipsey's distributional hypothesis are by no means mutually exclusive.

There is one final point to be raised concerning the expected relationship between $U$, $\dot{U}$, and $\dot{W}$. One of the most interesting statistical findings reported above was that there is a significant long-period relationship between $\dot{U}$ and $\dot{W}$, but

no significant long-period relationship between $U$ and $\dot{W}$. The point to be made here is that varying amounts of what has come to be called "structural" unemployment may help to explain this statistical finding.[3]

The same total level of unemployment may, of course, at different points in time, include different proportions of "structural" and "cyclical" unemployment. Or, the same amount of cyclical unemployment may, at different points in time, be combined with various amounts of structural unemployment to produce correspondingly different total levels of unemployment.

Now, if we adopt the hypothesis that workers who are structurally unemployed (and thus, by definition, isolated to some extent by geographical or occupational characteristics from the main stream of labor market developments) are likely to have less of a dampening effect on money wage increases than an equal number of cyclically unemployed workers, it follows that the same total level of unemployment can be expected to be associated with different rates of money wage increases as the ratio of structural unemployment to total unemployment varies over time. If there is anything to the popular view that structural unemployment is a higher proportion of total unemployment now than in earlier periods of our history, this may perhaps help explain why wages

[1] "Labor Market Behavior and the Relationship Between Unemployment and Wages," paper delivered at the December 1961 meeting of the Industrial Relations Research Association, to be printed in the *Proceedings*.

[2] There are two major methodological difficulties with Ross' work. First, in the present-day United States economy many wage settlements are determined on a company-wide or even on an industry-wide basis, and the geographic area encompassed by such settlements often extends beyond the boundaries of the standard metropolitan areas used as the units of account in local labor market analysis. Second, Ross does not recognize that causal relationships between money wage levels and unemployment are more likely to run in both directions at the national level. These difficulties are not easy to overcome. Anyone attempting to study local labor market wage phenomena is likely to have difficulty defining the appropriate geographic area and taking account of feed-back effects.

[3] We do not propose to become embroiled in the ongoing debate over the operational meaning of structural unemployment. For present purposes it is sufficient to speak of structural unemployment in the admittedly loose sense of unemployment that is not primarily attributable to a general cyclical decline in aggregate demand, but instead is more closely related to the geographical or occupational characteristics of the unemployed. We recognize that the distinction between "structural" and "cyclical" unemployment is to some extent a distinction of degree, in that a sufficiently strong upsurge of aggregate demand is likely to lead to the employment of even the most chronically unemployed workers.

have gone up more rapidly at given total levels of unemployment in recent years than in some past periods.

The "typical" annual change in total unemployment is, almost by definition, more likely to represent a change in the volume of cyclical unemployment than a change in the volume of structural unemployment (which is presumably of a more "chronic," long-run nature). It is this observation, coupled with the hypothesis mentioned above concerning differences in the wage-determining significance of structural and cyclical unemployment, that suggests one possible clue to the greater persistence of the long-period relationship between *changes* in unemployment and money wage increases than between the level of unemployment and money wage increases. For long-period studies, changes in unemployment may well constitute a more reliable index of active labor market pressures than the level of unemployment, which is more susceptible to inter-period variations in the amount of structural unemployment.[4]

The validity of these speculations concerning the effects of variations in the composition of aggregate unemployment on movements of the general wage level can, of course, be ascertained only by intensive research. We are hopeful that the current interest in refining and decomposing the aggregate unemployment data will lead to investigations along this line.

## COMPARISONS

Precise comparisons of the United States results with the United Kingdom results are not possible for a variety of reasons: the kinds of wage data used differ, unemployment is measured differently in the two countries, the periods studied have not been identical, the same explanatory variables have not been used in all studies, and there have been other differences in procedures. In addition, variations in economic conditions. (some might wish to say variations in economic policies) have produced a substantial number of wage observations for the United States economy in the 3–9 per cent unemployment range, but only very few observations in the same unemployment range for the United Kingdom. On the other hand, the United Kingdom data are replete with observations in the 0–3 per cent unemployment range, while there have been few non-war years in the United States in which unemployment has been this low.

Nonetheless, in spite of these obstacles, there are certain general comparisons between the United States and the United Kingdom results that can be made. First of all, in both the United States and the United Kingdom there is evidence that the magnitude of money wage adjustments has been related to the level of unemployment and to changes in the level of unemployment. The extreme view that money wages must be treated as an exogenous variable, determined primarily by non-market considerations, is not supported by the United States data or by the United Kingdom data.

However, we must quickly add that in neither country can the relation between unemployment conditions and wage changes be said to have been particularly close or consistent over time. The relationships are sufficiently loose to force us to be cautious in estimating the wage implications of alternative sets of unemployment conditions and to encourage us to examine the wage-determining role of factors excluded from this analysis as they interact with unemployment conditions. For the United States economy, $U$ and $\dot{U}$ together "explain" (in the usual

[4] This is the a priori reason (referred to in an earlier footnote) why we might expect to find a more consistent relationship between the rate of wage increase and *absolute* changes in the unemployment percentage than between the rate of wage increase and *percentage* changes in the unemployment percentage—absolute changes are presumably less influenced by the amount of structural unemployment contained in the total level of unemployment than are percentage changes in the unemployment variable.

statistical sense) 50 per cent of the variation in wage changes in the 1900–1932 sub-period (excluding 1915–1920), 82 per cent in the 1935–1941 sub-period, 66 per cent in the 1948–1958 sub-period, 43 per cent when the three sub-periods are combined, and 31 per cent when an equation is fitted to all the data from 1900 through 1958. While entirely comparable estimates of $R^2$ for the British economy are unavailable, we suspect that a number of persons in the United States have a misimpression concerning the tightness of the relationship that has been found between unemployment conditions and the rate of change of money wages in the United Kingdom.[5]

Still another similarity between the United States and the United Kingdom findings is that in both countries wages appear to have risen somewhat more rapidly at given levels of unemployment in the post-World War II period than during earlier periods. It is still too early to tell whether this post-war development represents a once-and-for-all shift in the aggregate relationship between unemployment and the rate of change of wages or whether the relationship is continuing to shift upward over time. Also, there is little definite knowledge concerning the causes of shifts of this kind, although there has, of course, been much speculation.

On the dissimilarity side of the ledger, the United Kingdom studies have suggested the existence of a non-linear relationship between the level of unemployment and the rate of change of money wages, whereas the United States data do not provide any evident support for the use of this type of relationship. However, this comparison may not be too meaningful in that the shortage of United States observations in the under 3 per cent unemployment range may help to explain the lack of an appearance of curvature in the United States relationship.

The work that has been done to date also suggests a more significant dissimilarity between the experience of the United States and the United Kingdom. At given levels of unemployment, wages appear to have risen more rapidly in the United States than in the United Kingdom.[6] Should this apparent difference be attributed to the fact that the official definition of unemployment used in the United Kingdom tends to produce lower unemployment estimates than the official definition used in the United States, to differences in productivity gains between the two countries, to differences in the size and diversity of the economies, to deep-seated differences in institutional arrangements, to variations in the policies followed by public and private bodies, or to still other considerations? For the time being at least, this important set of questions must be consigned to the "unanswered" category.[7]

\* \* \*

---

[5] One of the main criticisms leveled at Phillips by Routh and by Knowles and Winsten was that his paper gave an exaggerated impression of the closeness of the relationship. Lipsey, for selected years within the period since 1919 (which is, of course, the period most nearly comparable to the period used for the United States) has reported an $R^2 = 0.91$ (*op. cit.*, 26). But the high value of this coefficient of multiple determination is due very largely to the strong relationship between $\dot{W}$ and the rate of change of prices ($\dot{P}$). The squared partial correlation coefficients relating $\dot{W}$ to $U$ and $\dot{U}$ are only 0.38 and 0.30, respectively. For reasons mentioned earlier in this paper (and acknowledged by Lipsey), it seems to us to be very dangerous to attach much importance to any single-equation estimate relating wage changes to price changes.

[6] Regardless of the precise procedures used, the United States regression equations predict higher wage increases than the United Kingdom equations over almost all ranges of unemployment.

[7] Information relevant to the first question in this set is contained in an article by Edward Kalachek and Richard Westebee "Rates of Unemployment in Great Britain and the United States, 1950–1960," this REVIEW, XLIII (November 1961), 340–350, which appeared after the completion of this manuscript. Kalachek and Westebee found that intercountry differences in the definition of unemployment and in the normal amount of "frictional unemployment" account, at most, for one half of the spread in unemployment rates between the United States and the United Kingdom during the post-war years.

When changes in the unemployment rate rather than the rate itself are correlated with wage changes, however, the fit is rather close for both the long-run and the shorter subgroups. This finding leads the writers to the "simplest" conclusion that the rate of change in unemployment is a more important determinant of wage changes than the volume of unemployment itself. In accepting the "expectations argument," which states that decreases in the rate will stimulate wage increases in anticipation of tightening labor markets, with opposite effects if the rate increases, they deny Lipsey's claim (which will be found to be at the core of his Phillips curve hypothesis) that rising expectations will increase both wages and employment, resulting simply in an upward movement along the $U$-$\dot{W}$ curve itself. However, they do suggest that increasing structural unemployment may act as the basis for the loose fit of the $U$-$\dot{W}$ correlation, but their previous finding that the curve did not shift to the right uniformly over time seems to deny this.

The writers explain the lack of nonlinearity in the upper reaches of the American curve compared to the English in that the United States has rarely reached those low rates at which, under any hypothesis, expansion must take the form mainly of price increases rather than of output or employment growth. The most important "unanswered" question is the reason why the American curve lies to the right of the English, making it more difficult to pursue a full employment goal without the risks of substantial inflation.

# The Relation Between Unemployment and the Rate of Change of Money Wage Rates in the United Kingdom, 1862–1957: A Further Analysis

## by Richard G. Lipsey

THE RELATION BETWEEN $W$ AND $U$

We shall consider this relationship, first, for a single market, and then for the whole economy, using lower-case letters to refer to the single market variables and capitals to refer to the corresponding macro-variables.

We might analyse the market for any commodity since the argument at this stage is quite general. Since, however, the subject of the present article is the labour market we shall use the terminology appropriate to that market. The usual argument merely states that when there is excess demand, for example $ij$ in Fig. 1, wage rates will rise, while, when there is excess supply, for example $mn$ in Fig. 1,

wage rates will fall. Nothing is said about the speed at which the adjustment takes place. We now introduce the dynamic hypothesis that the rate at which $w$ changes is related to the excess demand, and specifically, the greater is the proportionate disequilibrium, the more rapidly will wages be changing.[1] Thus the hypothesis is $w = f\ [(d - s)\ /\ s]$, which says that the speed at which wages change depends on the excess demand as a proportion of the labour force.[2] Figure 2 illustrates a simple form of this relation, $w = a\ ([(d - s)/s]\ .\ 100)$ according to which if we start with excess demand of, for example, $Oc\ (\ = gh\ /\ w'g$ in Fig. 1), wages will be rising at the rate $cd$, but, if the

SOURCE Reprinted with permission from *Economica*, Vol. 17, February 1960, pp. 3–31.

[1] This is Phillips' hypothesis, *loc. cit.*, p. 283. It is also used extensively, for example, by Bent Hansen, *The Theory of Inflation*, London, 1951.

[2] If we were only concerned with a single market, the hypothesis could be expressed either in absolute or in proportional terms. Inter-market comparisons, however, require a proportionate measure. Consider the elasticity analogy.

excess demand increases to $Oa$ ($= ij / w''j$ in Fig. 1), wages will be rising at the rate $ab$.[3]

There are a number of advantages in including the relations illustrated in Fig. 2 in one's theory rather than having only the ones illustrated in Fig. 1. If it is known that both of the curves of Fig. 1 are shifting continuously (e.g., the demand curve due to cyclical variations in income, and the supply curve due to exogenous changes in the labour force), then no two price-quantity observations will lie on the same curve. It will then be difficult to discover by observation the *ceteris paribus* relations either between supply and price or between demand and price. For the relation in Fig. 2 to be observed it is necessary only that there be an unchanging *adjustment mechanism* in the market, i.e., that a given excess demand should cause a given rate of change of price *whatever the reason for the excess demand*—whether demand shift, a supply shift, or a combination of both. The rate of change of price can be observed directly and, to obtain the relation shown in Fig. 2, it is only necessary to know demand and supply *at the existing market price*; it is not necessary to know what would be demanded and supplied at other prices.

Now if excess demand for labour were directly observable there would be no need to go any further. Unfortunately, this is not the case, at least over a large part of the period under consideration,[4] and it is necessary to relate excess demand to something that is directly observable, in this case the percentage of the labour force unemployed.

Fig. 3 shows the relation between $(d - s) / s$ and the percentage of the labour force unemployed, $u$. When demand is equal to supply (wage rate $Ow_e$ in Fig. 1), there will be jobs available for all those who wish to work at the going wage rate. This is *not* equivalent to saying that there will be no one unemployed, but rather that the number of unemployed will be matched by an equal number of unfilled vacancies. Given that workers change jobs for any reason whatever, and that a finite time is taken to change, zero excess demand must be accompanied by some positive amount of *frictional unemployment*. From this it follows that, when the wage rate is stable (at $Ow_e$ in Fig. 1), there will be some quantity of unemployment ($Oa$ in Fig. 3), the exact quantity being determined by the amount of movement and the time taken to move. Now consider points to the left of $a$ in Fig. 3. The larger is the excess demand the easier will it be to find jobs, and the less will be the time taken in moving between jobs. Thus, unless there is a completely offsetting increase in numbers of persons moving between jobs, an increase in excess demand will cause a reduction in $u$. It is, however, impossible that $u$ could be reduced below zero so that as $(d - s) / s$ approaches infinity, $u$ must approach zero (or some small value $> 0$) asymptotically.[5] Now consider points to the right of $a$. Any increase in excess supply brings an equal increase in the number of persons unemployed. Therefore, to the right of point $a$, there will be a linear relation between $(d - s) / s$ and $u$.[6]

Now in order to obtain the relation be-

[3] The relationship might of course be non-linear, indicating that $w$ increased at either an increasing or a decreasing rate as excess demand increased. The simpler linear relationship is, however, capable of explaining all of the observed phenomena and, in the absence of empirical evidence about the second derivative of $w$, the simpler relationship is assumed.

[4] The difference between unfilled vacancies and unemployed workers might provide a reasonable direct measure of excess demand; but such data are not available for most of the period under consideration.

[5] The following is a simple model which will produce the postulated relationship: *Symbols:* $L \equiv$ labour force $\equiv S$ in Fig. 1, $E \equiv$ number employed, $V \equiv$ number unemployed, $J \equiv$ total jobs available $\equiv D$ in Fig. 1, $N \equiv$ number of unemployed finding jobs, $X \equiv$ proportionate excess demand $\equiv (J-L)/L \equiv (d-s)/s$, $\alpha$ and $\beta$ are two constants.

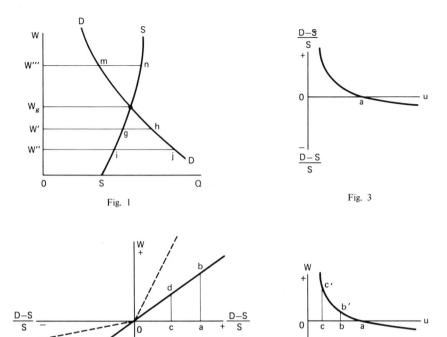

Fig. 1

Fig. 3

Fig. 2

Fig. 4

*Figure 1. Ratios of hourly earnings in 141 occupations to average hourly earnings in manufacturing, 1903 and 1956.*

*Assumptions:* A constant proportion of those employed, $aE$, leave employment per unit of time; the number of unemployed who find jobs depends on the number looking for jobs and the number of jobs available: $N = \beta V (J–E)$.

A constant level of $V$ requires: $aE = \beta V (J–E)$.

But $E = L - V$, so $a (L - V) = \beta V (J - L+V)$.

Expanding: $J = \dfrac{aL}{\beta V} - V+L -\dfrac{a}{\beta}$. But $X \equiv \dfrac{J-L}{L}$.

Eliminating $J$: $X = \dfrac{a}{\beta V} - \dfrac{V}{L} - \dfrac{a}{\beta L}$. ... (1)

Differentiating: $\dfrac{\partial X}{\partial V} = -\dfrac{a}{\beta V^2} - \dfrac{1}{L} <0, \dfrac{\partial^2 X}{\partial V^2} = \dfrac{a}{\beta V} >0$.

Therefore an increase in $X$ is associated with a decrease in $V$ but as $X$ increases $V$ falls at a decreasing rate and, from (1) above, as $X-> \infty$, $V->0$.

[6] There are some reasons for believing that, to the right of $a$ the relation might have a slight curvature which would *increase* as $u$ increased [i.e., $(\partial w/\partial u) <0$ *and* $(\partial^2 w/\partial u^2) <0$]. The excess supply of labour is $[(d–s)/s] . 100$ while $u$ is $[(d–s)/s . 100+F$, where $F$ is the proportion of the labour force frictionally unemployed. If $F$ remains constant as excess supply increases, the relationship between $(d–s)/s$ and $u$ will be linear. If, on the other hand, $F->0$ as $u->100$, then the line relating $u$ to $(d–s)/s$ will *curve* slightly downwards, starting at $u = F$ when $(d–s)/s = 0$ and reaching $u = (d–s)/s$ when excess supply is 100 per cent. If $F$ is small (say 5 per cent.), this curvature will be very slight. A second reason is that people in excess supply may not register as unemployed so that recorded $u$ may not increase as fast as real excess supply. With the data used in this study it is impossible to distinguish between $\partial^2 w/\partial u^2 <0$ for high values of $u$. If, however, it were possible to demonstrate that $(\partial^2 w/\partial u^2) >0$, we should have to abandon the linear hypothesis illustrated in Fig. 2, at least for situations of excess supply.

tween the two observable quantities, $w$ and $u$, we need merely combine Figs. 2 and 3 to obtain the relation illustrated in Fig. 4. The relation between $w$ and $(d-s)$ $/s$ (Fig. 2) is assumed to be linear throughout. The relationship between $w$ and $u$, however, is non-linear to the left of the point $a$ because of the non-linear relation over the range between $u$ and $(d-s)/s$ (Fig. 3) while the relation between $w$ and $u$ is linear to the right of $a$ because of the assumed linear relation over that range between $u$ and $(d-s)/s$ (Fig. 3).

*  *  *

### The Phillips Curve and Structural Unemployment

Lipsey's paper does more than modify Phillips' work. It brings out the role of structural unemployment as a possible prime factor in the inflation process. In the passages of his paper, presented here, inflation is viewed as the consequences of excess demand over supply on an economy or sectoral level.

Changes (increases) in wages are linked linearly to the rate of excess demand for labor. But at low levels of unemployment, below the frictional rate for any sector, excess demand for labor cannot be transferred to an equal reduction in unemployment. Thus, wages and prices may rise in an economy, even if overall unemployment exceeds the frictional rate, if there is some structural unemployment.

Perhaps a numerical example will help clarify Lipsey's hypothesis. Consider a two-sector economy with unemployment rates of 1.25 and 8.75 percent and an overall rate, assuming they are of equal size, of 5 percent. Assume a frictional unemployment rate of 2 percent in each sector. There is excess supply of 6.75 percent in the second sector leading to a certain degree of downward pressure on wages. If there were a .75 percent excess demand in the first sector, that is, if the degree to which unemployment fell below the frictional level, in this case .75 percent (2 percent – 1.25 percent), measured excess demand, then the overall effect would be for a deflationary effect, the same as if unemployment were at 5 percent in each sector. But, and this is the crux of Lipsey's argument, cutting into the frictional base of unemployment by .75 percent in a sector requires more than a .75 rate of excess demand because it takes more demand stimulus to reduce unemployment in a sector below the frictional level than from a level above it to a lower but still higher than frictional rate.

Thus the aggregate labor demand reflected in an overall rate of, say, 5 percent that is comprised of two sectors with one having a rate above the frictional level and the other below it is greater than that when the sectoral rates are equal. In fact, if the sectors with below frictional rates are important enough in the economy, overall demand for labor may exceed supply, leading to average wage increases even if the overall average unemployment rate lies clearly above the frictional level. This is another way of arguing that structural unemployment, described as a situation with labor surplus and deficit sectors, leads to inflation, even when labor demand in total would not be strong enough to do so. In truth, at least for the United States, wage increases exceed productivity gains at a level of overall unemployment estimated by Samuelson and Solow at 5.5 percent, clearly above the frictional rate.

## The Wage-Price Guideposts

Wages tend to rise faster than productivity which, as Samuelson and Solow point out, only means that wage movements are part of the inflationary process and not necessarily the cause of it, during prosperous periods of low unemployment. This predictable condition led the Council of Economic Advisers to enunciate a non- or antiinflationary policy of establishing wage and price Guideposts to keep wages from rising faster than productivity.

As introduced in the 1962 Council report presented here, the Guidepost formula calls for wage increases in each industry "equal to the trend rate of overall productivity increase." The formula calls for "appropriate" price changes in each industry to keep all prices stable. This implies that in each industry the price changes will be opposite and equal to the relative productivity changes. For example, if the overall productivity growth is 3 percent while the industry's productivity increase is 1 percent, the industry's wages will rise by 3 percent in accordance with the Guidepost formula, and prices would increase 2 percent, to match the relative decline in the industry's productivity.

# Guideposts for Noninflationary Wage and Price Behavior

Mandatory controls in peacetime over the outcomes of wage negotiations and over individual price decisions are neither desirable in the American tradition nor practical in a diffuse and decentralized continental economy. Free collective bargaining is the vehicle for the achievement of contractual agreements on wages, fringes, and working conditions, as well as on the "web of rules" by which a large segment of industry governs the performance of work and the distribution of rewards. Similarly, final price decisions lie—and should continue to lie—in the hands of individual firms. It is however, both desirable and practical that discretionary decisions on wages and prices recognize the national interest in the results. The guideposts suggested here as aids to public understanding are not concerned primarily with the relation of employers and employees to each other, but

rather with their joint relation to the rest of the economy.

## Wages, Prices, and Productivity

If all prices remain stable, all hourly labor costs may increase as fast as economy-wide productivity without, for that reason alone, changing the relative share of labor and nonlabor incomes in total output. At the same time, each kind of income increases steadily in absolute amount. If hourly labor costs increase at a slower rate than productivity, the share of nonlabor incomes will grow or prices will fall, or both. Conversely, if hourly labor costs increase more rapidly than productivity, the share of labor incomes in the total product will increase or prices will rise, or both. It is this relationship among long-run economy-wide produc-

SOURCE Reprinted from 1962 Annual Report of the Council of Economic Advisors, pp. 185–190.

tivity, wages, and prices which makes the rate of productivity change an important benchmark for noninflationary wage and price behavior.

Productivity is a *guide* rather than a *rule* for appraising wage and price behavior for several reasons. First, there are a number of problems involved in measuring productivity change, and a number of alternative measures are available. Second, there is nothing immutable in fact or in justice about the distribution of the total product between labor and nonlabor incomes. Third, the pattern of wages and prices among industries is and should be responsive to forces other than changes in productivity.

### Alternative Measures of Productivity

. . . There are a number of conceptual problems in connection with productivity measurement which can give rise to differences in estimates of its rate of growth. Three important conceptual problems are the following:

1. Over what time interval should productivity trends be measured? Very short intervals may give excessive weight to business-cycle movements in productivity, which are not the relevant standards for wage behavior. Very long intervals may hide significant breaks in trends; indeed in the United States—and in other countries as well—productivity appears to have risen more rapidly since the end of the second World War than before. It would be wholly inappropriate for wage behavior in the 1960's to be governed by events long in the past. On the other hand, productivity in the total private economy appears to have advanced less rapidly in the second half of the postwar period than in the first.

2. Even for periods of intermediate length, it is desirable to segregate the trend movements in productivity from those that reflect business-cycle forces. Where the basic statistical materials are available, this problem can be handled by an analytical separation of trend effects and the effects of changes in the rate of capacity utilization.

3. Even apart from such difficulties, there often exist alternative statistical measures of output and labor input. The alternatives may differ conceptually or may simply be derived from different statistical sources. A difficult problem of choice may emerge, unless the alternative measures happen to give similar results.

### The Share of Labor Income

The proportions in which labor and nonlabor incomes share the product of industry have not been immutable throughout American history, nor can they be expected to stand forever where they are today. It is desirable that labor and management should bargain explicitly about the distribution of the income of particular firms or industries. It is, however, undesirable that they should bargain implicitly about the general price level. Excessive wage settlements which are paid for through price increases in major industries put direct pressure on the general price level and produce spillover and imitative effects throughout the economy. Such settlements may fail to redistribute income within the industry involved; rather they redistribute income between that industry and other segments of the economy through the mechanism of inflation.

### Prices and Wages in Individual Industries

What are the guideposts which may be used in judging whether a particular price or wage decision may be inflationary? The desired objective is a stable price level, within which particular prices rise, fall, or remain stable in response to economic pressures. Hence, price stability within any particular industry is not necessarily a correct guide to price and wage decisions in that industry. It is possible, however, to describe in broad outline a set of guides which, if followed, would preserve over-all price stability while still allowing sufficient flexibility to accommodate objectives of efficiency and equity. These are not arbitrary guides. They describe—briefly and no doubt incompletely—how prices and wage rates would behave in a smoothly functioning competitive economy operating near full employment. Nor do they constitute a mechanical formula for determining whether a particular price or wage decision is inflationary. They will serve their purpose if they suggest to the interested public a useful way of approaching the appraisal of such a decision.

If, as a point of departure, we assume no change in the relative shares of labor and nonlabor incomes in a particular industry, then a general guide may be advanced for noninflationary wage behavior, and another for noninflationary price behavior. Both guides, as will be seen, are only first approximations.

The general guide for inflationary wage behavior is that the rate of increase in wage rates (including fringe benefits) in each industry be equal to the trend rate of over-all productivity increase. General acceptance of this guide would maintain stability of labor cost per unit of output for the economy as a whole—though not of course for individual industries.

The general guide for noninflationary price behavior calls for price reduction if the industry's rate of productivity increase exceeds the over-all rate—for this would mean declining unit labor costs; it calls for an appropriate increase in price if the opposite relationship prevails; and it calls for stable prices if the two rates of productivity increase are equal.

These are advanced as general guideposts. To reconcile them with objectives of equity and efficiency, specific modifications must be made to adapt them to the circumstances of particular industries. If all of these modifications are made, each in the specific circumstances to which it applies, they are consistent with stability of the general price level. Public judgments about the effects on the price level of particular wage or price decisions should take into account the modifications as well as the general guides. The most important modifications are the following:

1 Wage rate increases would exceed the general guide rate in an industry which would otherwise be unable to attract sufficient labor; or in which wage rates are exceptionally low compared with the range of wages earned elsewhere by similar labor, because the bargaining position of workers has been weak in particular local labor markets.

2 Wage rate increases would fall short of the general guide rate in an industry which could not provide jobs for its entire labor force even in times of generally full employment; or in which wage rates are exceptionally high compared with the range of wages earned elsewhere by similar labor, because the bargaining position of workers has been especially strong.

3 Prices would rise more rapidly, or fall more slowly, than indicated by the general guide rate in an industry in which the level of profits was insufficient to attract the capital required to finance a needed expansion in capacity; or in which costs other than labor costs had risen.

4 Prices would rise more slowly, or fall more rapidly, then indicated by the general guide in an industry in which the relation of productive capacity to full employment demand shows the desirability of an outflow of capital from the industry; or in which costs other than labor costs have fallen; or in which excessive market power has resulted in rates of profit substantially higher than those earned elsewhere on investments of comparable risk. . . .

Thus, if the Guideposts were followed by all industries, the overall price level would remain stable and the share going to labor and other factors would remain constant on an industry-by-industry basis. Furthermore, with uniform wage changes, the Guideposts would not disrupt the labor market.

But despite their laudable goals and apparent equity, the Guideposts have two serious shortcomings. First, as is emphasized in Friedman's criticism and admitted in Solow's defense of the policy, both presented here, the Guideposts can only operate to thwart cost-push inflation. If demand for goods and labor tend to push wages and prices upward, then to ask labor and management to adhere to the Guidepost formula would be to ask suppliers to deny the rationing role of wages and prices and, in effect, to impose informal and voluntary wage and price controls.

---

# What Price Guideposts?

## by Milton Friedman

### WHY DIRECT CONTROL OF PRICES AND WAGES DOES NOT ELIMINATE INFLATIONARY PRESSURE

An analogy is often drawn between direct control of wages and prices as a reaction to inflation and the breaking of a thermometer as a reaction to, say, an overheated room. This analogy has an element of validity. Prices are partly like thermometers in that they register heat but do not produce it; in both cases, preventing a measuring instrument from recording what is occurring does not prevent the occurrence. But the analogy is also misleading. Breaking the thermometer need have no further effect on the phenomenon being recorded; it simply adds to our ignorance. Controlling prices, insofar as it is successful, has very important effects. Prices are not only measuring instruments, they also play a vital role in the economic process itself.

A much closer analogy is a steam-heating furnace running full blast. Controlling the heat in one room by closing the radiators in that room simply makes other rooms still more overheated. Closing all radiators lets the pressure build up in the boiler and increases the danger that it will explode. Closing or opening individual radiators is a good way to adjust the relative amount of heat in different rooms; it is not a good way to correct for overfueling the furnace. Similarly, changes in individual prices are a good way to adjust to changes in the supply or demand of individual products; preventing individual prices from rising is not a good way to correct for a general tendency of prices to rise.

Suppose that there is such a general tendency, and suppose that some specific price (or set of prices), say, the price of steel, is prevented from rising. Holding

SOURCE Reprinted with permission from *Guideposts, Informal Controls and the Market Place*, George P. Shultz and Robert Z. Aliber (Eds.), Chicago, University of Chicago Press, 1966, pp. 17–39.

down the price of steel does not make more steel available; on the contrary, given that other prices and costs are rising, it reduces the amount that producers can afford to spend in producing steel and is therefore likely to reduce the amount available from current production. Holding down the price of steel does not discourage buyers; on the contrary, it encourages consumption. If the suppressed price is effectively enforced and not evaded by any of the many channels that are available to ingenious sellers and buyers some potential buyers of steel must be frustrated— there is a rationing problem. Chance, favoritism, or bribery will have to decide which buyers succeed in getting the steel. Those who succeed pay less than they are willing to pay. They, instead of the steel producers, have the remainder to spend elsewhere. Those who fail will try to substitute other metals or products and so will divert their demand elsewhere; the excess pressure is shifted, not eliminated.

The situation is precisely the same on the labor market. If wages are tending to rise, suppressing a specific wage rise will mean that fewer workers are available for that type of employment and more are demanded. Again rationing is necessary. The workers employed have less income to spend, but this is just balanced by their employers having larger incomes. And the unsatisfied excess demand for labor is diverted to other workers.

But, it will be said, I have begged the question by *starting* with a general tendency for prices to rise. Can it not be that this general tendency is itself produced by rises in a limited number of prices and wages which in turn produce sympathetic rises in other prices and wages? In such a case, may not preventing the initial price and wage rises nip a wage-price or price-price spiral in the bud?

Despite its popularity, this cost-push theory of inflation has very limited applicability. Unless the cost-push produces a monetary expansion that would otherwise not have occurred, its effect will be limited to at most a temporary general price rise, accompanied by unemployment, and followed by a tendency toward declining prices elsewhere.

Suppose, for example, a strong (or stronger) cartel were formed in steel, and that it decided to raise the price well above the level that otherwise would have prevailed. The price rise would reduce the amount of steel people want to buy. Potential purchasers of steel would shift to substitute products, and no doubt the prices of such substitutes would tend to rise in sympathy. But there is now another effect. Steel producers would hire fewer workers and other resources. These would seek employment elsewhere, tending to drive down wages and prices in other industries. True, wages and prices might be sticky and decline only slowly, but that would only delay the downward adjustments and only at the expense of unemployment.[1]

A textbook example is provided by John L. Lewis and the United Mine Workers. Coal mining hourly earnings rose by "163 per cent from 1945 to 1960. Bituminous coal mining employment dropped from 284,000 to 168,000. By way of comparison, in the same period, manufacturing production hourly earnings rose . . . 122 per cent and manufacturing employment rose."[2] High coal prices undoubtedly put upward pressure on the prices of oil and gas; but the high unemployment put downward pressure on other prices.

The only example I know of in United States history when such a cost-push was

---

[1] Note that even for such a temporary effect, it is not enough that there exist monopolies of business and labor; it is necessary that monopoly power increase; otherwise, relative prices will already have become adjusted.

[2] Yale Brozen, "Guide Lines and Wage Laws: How Should Wage Changes Be Determined?" unpublished paper, p. 8.

important even temporarily for any substantial part of the economy was from 1933 to 1937, when the NIRA, AAA, Wagner Labor Act, and associated growth of union strength unquestionably led to *increasing* market power of both industry and labor and thereby produced upward pressure on a wide range of wages and prices. This cost-push did not account for the concomitant rapid growth in nominal income at the average rate of 14 per cent a year from 1933 to 1937. That reflected rather a rise in the quantity of money at the rate of 11 per cent a year. And the wage and cost-push had nothing to do with the rapid rise in the quantity of money. That reflected rather the flood of gold, initiated by the change in the United States price of gold in 1933 and 1934 and sustained by the reaction to Hitler's assumption of power in Germany.

The cost-push does explain why so large a part of the growth in nominal income was absorbed by prices. Despite unprecedented levels of unemployed resources, wholesale prices rose nearly 50 per cent from 1933 to 1937, and the cost of living rose by 13 per cent. Similarly, the wage cost-push helps to explain why unemployment was still so high in 1937, when monetary restriction was followed by another severe contraction.

\* \* \*

## WHAT HARM WILL BE DONE BY THE GUIDEPOSTS?

Even granted that legally imposed and vigorously enforced wage and price ceilings covering a wide range of the economy would do enormous harm, some may argue that the enunciation of guideposts, their approval by businessmen and labor leaders, and voluntary compliance with them, or even lip service to them, is a palliative that can do no harm and can temporarily help until more effective measures are taken. At the very least, it may be said, it will enable businessmen and

labor leaders to display their sense of social responsibility.

This view seems to me mistaken. The guideposts do harm even when only lip service is paid to them, and the more extensive the compliance, the greater the harm.

In the first place, the guideposts confuse the issue and make correct policy less likely. If there is inflation or inflationary pressure, the governmental monetary (or, some would say, fiscal) authorities are responsible. It is they who must take corrective measures if the inflation is to be stopped. Naturally, the authorities want to shift the blame, so they castigate the rapacious businessman and the selfish labor leader. By approving guidelines, the businessman and the labor leader implicitly whitewash the government for its role and plead guilty to the charge. They thereby encourage the government to postpone taking the corrective measures that alone can succeed.

In the second place, whatever measure of actual compliance there is introduces just that much distortion into the allocation of resources and the distribution of output. To whatever extent the price system is displaced, some other system of organizing resources and rationing output must be adopted. As in the example of the controls on foreign loans by banks, one adverse effect is to foster private collusive arrangements, so that a measure undertaken to keep prices down leads to government support and encouragement of private monopolistic arrangements.

In the third place, "voluntary" controls invite the use of extra-legal powers to produce compliance. And, in the modern world, such powers are ample. There is hardly a business concern that could not have great costs imposed on it by antitrust investigations, tax inquiries, government boycott, or rigid enforcement of any of a myriad of laws, or on the other side of the ledger, that can see no potential benefits from government orders, guarantees of loans, or similar measures. Which of us as an individual could not be, at the very least, seriously inconvenienced by investigation of his income tax returns, no matter how faithfully and carefully prepared, or by the enforcement to the letter of laws we may not even know about? This threat casts a shadow well beyond any particular instance. In a dissenting opinion in a recent court case involving a "stand-in" in a public library, Justice Black wrote, "It should be remembered that if one group can take over libraries for one cause, other groups will assert the right to do it for causes which, while wholly legal may not be so appealing to this court." Precisely the same point applies here. If legal powers granted for other purposes can today be used for the "good" purpose of holding down prices, tomorrow they can be used for other purposes that will seem equally "good" to the men in power—such as simply keeping themselves in power. It is notable how sharp has been the decline in the number of businessmen willing to be quoted by name when they make adverse comments on government.

In the fourth place, compliance with voluntary controls imposes a severe conflict of responsibilities on businessmen and labor leaders. The corporate official is an agent of his stockholders; the labor leader, of the members of his union. He has a responsibility to promote their interests. He is now told that he must sacrifice their interests to some supposedly higher social responsibility. Even supposing that he can know what "social responsibility" demands —say by simply accepting on that question the gospel according to the Council of Economic Advisers—to what extent is it proper for him to do so? If he is to become a civil servant in fact, will he long remain an employee of the stockholders or an agent of the workers in name? Will they not discharge him? Or, alternatively, will not the government exert authority over him in name as in fact?

A second shortcoming of the Guideposts relates to the pricing element in the formula. Although the wage prescription does not introduce a disequilibriating force on the labor market, in that all wages change equally, prices are asked to change in relation to differential productivity movements, in accordance with the pattern described above.

Consider two industries, one with a relative increase and the other with a relative decline in productivity growth compared to the national average. According to the Guideposts, prices should fall in the first industry and rise in the second, with wages rising equally in both. But there is no reason for market demand for each industry's output to follow the determined pricing practice. If, taking just the first industry, demand does not rise in proportion to the price decline, dollar sales will fall and profits will suffer a relative decline. Industries, or firms, cannot be expected to follow a pricing policy dictated by a formula that is only coincidentally consistent with demand conditions for their product.

The Council recognizes the possibility of a failure of Guidepost formula and market demand to mesh. Among its "most important modifications," the policy permits deviation in wages and prices, in weak and strong industries. But if the divergence between Guidepost formula and market realities is widespread, then the formula itself would break down as a guide to actual practice.

Another criticism of the Guideposts is that they tend to harden both existing wage structure and the shares to labor and capital of total output. Solow, in his defense of the Guideposts, answers this criticism by pointing out that, in fact, relative shares have changed very slightly over many years, and that the Guideposts are not expected to be followed so rigidly as to prevent minor changes in relative shares in keeping with historical experience.

But as John T. Dunlop notes in "Guideposts, Wages and Collective Bargaining" (*Guideposts, Informal Controls and the Market Place*, George P. Shultz and Robert Z. Aliber (Eds.), University of Chicago Press, Chicago, 1966), the issue is not past experience but current attitudes. Although the guideposts had some positive effects, they were doomed according to Dunlop, because (1) they were actively opposed by organized labor, most of the business community, and most government and private industrial relations experts: ". . . in our society, the guideposts must command widespread respect and assent among decision makers—which they do not—to be viable" (p. 85); (2) they "are not expressed in criteria that are meaningful to private decision makers. The 'trend rate of overall productivity increase' and the relative rate of an industry's increase in productivity compared to the average are scarcely standards which are meaningful to decision makers on wages and prices . . . wage decisions are typically argued in terms of comparative wages, living costs, competitive conditions, labor shortages ability to pay, specific productivity, job content, and bargaining power" (p. 86); (3) "the guideposts forced the Council of Economic Advisers reluctantly in the direction of becoming an administrative agency. It is ill equipped for that purpose" (pp. 86–87); (4) if the administration of the Guideposts is to be more than "general preachment," a question of due process is involved in determining when to charge specific wage settlements with violations of the Guideposts; and (5) the Guideposts raise "a number of questions of analyses" concerning the "neutrality of the guideposts with respect to the distribution of unions" especially, "if the requisite price reductions do not take place." Nor is it "clear what the 'general guide' for compensation" should be "in the event the price guideposts are not achieved . . ." (p. 89).

A major problem for the Guideposts was their incompatibility with the realities of collective bargaining. Since unions are democratic organizations, it is unreasonable to expect their elected leaders to have the power to raise wages and not do so. Rational leaders will promise to use the union's full power on behalf of the members.

Solow's defense of the Guideposts is on weak ground when he claims that despite their shortcomings, they seem to have served their purposes in restraining inflation in that prices were relatively stable—dspite demand stimulation and unemployment reduction—after appearance of the Guideposts in 1962. As has been noted above, after 1965 prices began rising significantly, despite the continued presence of the Guideposts.

# The Case Against the Case Against the Guideposts

## by Robert M. Solow

### HAVE THE GUIDEPOSTS HAD AN EFFECT ON WAGES AND PRICES?

The most common criticism of dependence on wage-price guideposts is that they simply do not work and have no effect on either wages or prices. Some of these criticisms simply cancel one another: For every employer who complains that unions take the guideposts figure for a floor, there is a union leader who complains that employers take it for a ceiling. Such evidence is worth nothing. Better evidence can be had, but is in the nature of the case uncertain. We may not be able to tell whether the guideposts have had any influence on wage and price decisions: first because there is no way to measure the "intensity" with which the guideposts have been pressed; and second because we have no universally accepted quantitative doctrine about how prices and money wages are determined in the absence of guideposts.

The best such quantitative explanation I know is that of Professor George Perry of the University of Minnesota. He reconstructs the percentage change in hourly wages in manufacturing from one quarter to the same quarter of the next year in terms of four determinants. The determinants are the unemployment rate, the accompanying change in the *Consumer Price Index*, the rate of profit on capital in manufacturing, and the change in the rate of profit. He finds, as you would expect, that wages in manufacturing will rise more rapidly the lower the unemployment rate; the faster the cost of living has been rising, the higher are profits, and the faster they have been rising. The precise relationship is based on the experience of the manufacturing sector from 1948 to 1960; it explains the course of money wages quite well during that period.

When Perry's relationship is used to explain wage changes in manufacturing

SOURCE Reprinted with permission from *Guideposts, Informal Controls and the Market Place,* loc. cit., pp. 41–54.

after 1960, it tells an interesting story. In 1961 and the first half of 1962, wages rose faster than the theory would expect. Beginning with the third quarter of 1962, and without exception for the next fourteen quarters to the end of 1965, wages rose more slowly than the theory would expect. Runs in the residuals are not uncommon, but this run is uncommonly long. Moreover, although the overestimation of wage changes was initially small, it became substantial in 1964 and 1965. In 1965, the annual increase in wage rates was about 1.7 per cent lower than the 1948–60 experience would lead one to expect.

Is all of this difference attributable to the influence of the guideposts? Is any? I don't suppose any definite answer can be given. The timing certainly suggests that the guideposts had something to do with it. But econometric inference is rarely completely solid, and I have no doubt that someone who wanted strongly to resist that conclusion could produce a statistical model giving different results.

What does seem fairly clear is that manufacturing wages have gone up relatively slowly during the past few years, given the unemployment rate actually ruling, the good profits actually earned, and the increase in consumer prices that actually occurred. It is not farfetched to believe that the guideposts might have been an important factor in this structural change.

The object of the guideposts is to stall off premature inflation. Wages themselves are a matter of concern only because they bulk so large in total costs. If the guideposts served only to damp the increase in wages without holding down the price level, then their main result would simply be a transfer of income from wages to profits, and that is not their purpose. So the question arises whether there has been any visible change in price behavior.

All of the obstacles to clear-cut measurement of the wage effects apply equally to the price effects. Moreover, I know of no basic study like Perry's to serve as a starting-point for price behavior. I can report, however, on one small scale and partial experiment.

Year-to-year changes in the wholesale price index for all manufactures, between 1954 and 1965, can be explained moderately well in terms of the McGraw-Hill index of capacity utilization, and the accompanying year-to-year changes in labor costs per unit of output in manufacturing. As one would expect, the price index rises faster the higher the utilization of capacity and the faster unit labor costs increase. If one amends the relation among these variables to allow for a structural shift after 1962, the data suggest that wholesale prices rose about $\frac{7}{10}$ of a point a year more slowly after 1962 than before, for any given utilization rate and change in unit labor costs. (This suggestion just fails of statistical significance, but I suspect that lengthening the period and refining the data would correct that.)

Although this is the most tentative sort of conclusion, it is double-barreled. Even if there were no structural change in price behavior after 1962, it would mean that any reduction or slowdown in unit labor costs achieved through the guideposts was being passed on into prices to the usual extent. If in fact there was a structural change, it means that over and above the effect through labor costs there was a further tendency for prices to rise more slowly than earlier experience would suggest.

There is, as I have said, no firm reason to attribute these shifts in behavior to the guideposts. Nor is there any reason not to.

WOULD THE GUIDEPOSTS FREEZE
THE DISTRIBUTION OF INCOME AND
INTERFERE WITH FREE MARKETS?

It is often remarked—as indeed I remarked earlier—that if wage rates on the average were to rise precisely as fast as productivity, while the price levels were to remain constant, then the proportions of the national income going to labor and to property would stay unchanged. To take some very round numbers, suppose production per man-year were $10,000 and the annual wage $7,500, so that $2,500 went to owners of capital. If productivity and the annual wage were both to rise by that famous 3.2 per cent, and prices were unchanged, then output per man-year would go to $10,320 and the wage $7,740. This would leave $2,580 in property income. Notice that the $320 of new output per man-year has been divided in the same 75–25 proportions as the original $10,000, so that the overall proportional distribution of the national income is undisturbed.

This algebraic fact has led to criticism of the guidepost concept. The argument is not at all about the equity or justice of the current distribution of income. The argument is that the distribution of income—before taxes and transfers—is part of the market process in our economy. Changes in incomes are supposed to guide efficiently the allocation of resources. To freeze the distribution of income in a pattern that may be suitable to current conditions can lead to distortions and inefficiencies if economic conditions change and call for a changed distribution of income.

It seems to me that this argument has no practical weight at all. It is rendered trivial by two facts. The first is that the division of the national income between labor and property incomes is among the slower-changing characteristics of our economy, or of any Western economy. The second is that neither the guideposts nor any other such quantitative prescription can be satisfied *exactly*. Suppose that wage rates do follow the guideposts exactly. Then if the price level, instead of remaining constant, goes up by, say, 1 per cent in a year, the share of wages in national income will fall by 1 per cent—that is, by about ¾ of one percentage point. If, on the other hand, the price level should

fall by 1 per cent, the share of wages in national income would rise by ¾ of 1 percentage point. That may not seem like much, but actually it is quite a lot, more than enough to provide all the flexibility that our economic system is likely to need.

In the twenty years since the end of the war, the proportion of "compensation of employees" to national income has moved about within a narrow range, say from 65 per cent to 71 per cent. There is no reason to suppose that market forces will always want to keep the figure within those bounds, but there is every reason to believe that market forces will never, or hardly ever, want to move the proportional distribution of income very rapidly. As the numerical example shows, if wages adhered to the guidelines, the distribution of income could get from one end of its postwar range to the other in about eight years, with an annual rate of inflation or deflation never exceeding 1 per cent.

There is no practical question, then, of freezing the distribution of income. The normal amount of play in any such policy gives all the room needed for the market to operate. It would be possible to provide formally for more flexibility if that were needed. If the wages guideposts were expressed in terms of a fairly narrow range, say from 3.0 to 3.5 per cent per year, this would serve two purposes. For one thing, it would more nearly express the uncertainty in any estimate of the trend increase in productivity. And secondly, it would permit the outcome to be nearer the bottom or the top of the range, depending on "market forces." Even a steady price level would then permit some drift in the distribution of income.

Even apart from this question of distribution, one hears it said that the guideposts are a dangerous interference in the free market, even a form of price control. At least this criticism is inconsistent with the other one that claims the guideposts to be ineffective. With some ingenuity, one could probably cook up a set of assumptions under which the guideposts had no effect on wage-price behavior, yet managed to do harm to the market economy. But this seems farfetched to me. If they are a real interference with the market, they must be partially effective.

I would contend that it is also farfetched to describe the wage-price guideposts as anything remotely like a system of wage and price controls. But in any case I am not concerned with the way the guideposts have been used by this President or that President, but with the way they were intended. They were intended, as I mentioned earlier, as a device for the education and mobilization of public opinion. The January 1962 Economic Report said:

*Individual wage and price decisions assume national importance when they involve large numbers of workers and large amounts of output directly, or when they are regarded by large segments of the economy as setting a pattern. Because such decisions affect the progress of the whole economy, there is legitimate reason for public interest in their content and consequences. An informed public, aware of the significance of major wage bargains and price decisions, and equipped to judge for itself their compatibility with the national interest, can help to create an atmosphere in which the parties to such decisions will exercise their powers responsibly. . . . The guideposts suggested here as aids to public understanding are not concerned primarily with the relation of employers and employees to each other, but rather with their joint relation to the rest of the economy. (Pp. 185–86.)*

It is no doubt inevitable that an activist President will want to help public opinion along. But that is still a far cry from wage and price control.

Moreover, by both intent and necessity, the guideposts can influence only those wage and price decisions in which the parties have a certain amount of discretion. Atomistic textbook competitors, hav-

ing no discretion, will not be much influenced by either public opinion or the White House. But where there is enough market power, and hence enough discretion, for the guideposts to be a force, there is little or no reason to believe that the "free market" outcome will be in the public interest. The usual presumption against public interference in the market process does not hold. This conclusion does not depend on any very exact evaluation of the amount of competition to which the steel industry, or the aluminum industry, or the tobacco industry, or the United Automobile Workers, or the building trades unions are subject. It is enough that none of them is, and none of them thinks it is, selling against a nearly infinitely elastic demand curve.

Naturally, the fact that a concentrated industry and a strong union may make decisions not in the public interest does not automatically mean that what the guideposts suggest will be better. That question needs to be decided on its merits. Yet, the guideposts are intended to give a summary description of a well-functioning market economy; within limits they can be expected to represent the public interest fairly well. But it is much more important to realize that the public interest does need representation.

It is worth remembering, in this connection, that the guideposts are intended to have an effect on the general level of money wages and prices, not on relative wages and relative prices. Most of the things we expect free markets to accomplish are "real" things, more or less independent of the price level. Ideally, the guideposts should permit markets to allocate resources freely, insuring only that the price level not drift up in the process. The January 1962 Economic Report said: "It is desirable that labor and management should bargain explicitly about the distribution of the income of particular firms or industries. It is, however, undesirable that they should bargain implicitly about general price level." (P. 188.) In practice, one must admit, the guideposts will operate unevenly; relative prices and resource allocation may thus be affected. One can hope that these effects are second-order. . . .

### Modifying the Guideposts

In a move influenced by emerging inflation, the Council tried to tighten the Guideposts' antiinflationary quality in its recommendation for the appropriate productivity standard for the year 1966, as presented in its 1966 report.

In restating the formula, the Council emphasizes that the productivity growth base for any year's wage and price changes should represent a trend value, calculated from a five-year moving average. Since this average was higher in 1966 than in previous years, in the Council's opinion because of "temporarily high productivity gains" of greater efficiency resulting from higher operating rates of prosperity, the Council suggested use of the previous 3.2 percent rate instead of the 3.6 percent rate indicated by the five-year average. By 1967, the Guideposts were abandoned for practical purposes, with wage settlement close to 5 percent at a time when the Guideposts called for 3.2 percent.

# Guideposts for Noninflationary Price and Wage Behavior

## INCREASING IMPORTANCE OF THE GUIDEPOSTS

In the years since 1962, the guideposts have gained increasing significance. The slow and difficult progress in restoring equilibrium in our international balance of payments has underlined the necessity that American goods retain or improve their competitive position in export markets and in our own market. Our goal of balance of payments equilibrium in 1966 and thereafter will permit no retreat from cost-price stability.

During the recent years of still excessive unemployment and idle capacity, strong competition for jobs and markets reinforced a growing sense of responsibility on the part of labor and management. The fuller use of resources achieved last year and the excellent prospects for 1966 may reduce that reinforcement. We now confront the task of reconciling full employment with stable prices.

The record reviewed in previous sections of this chapter makes it clear that the overwhelming majority of private wage and price decisions in recent years has been consistent with the guideposts, whatever the extent to which the guideposts may have consciously entered into the decisions reached. It is clear, however, that in many instances the guideposts have consciously affected these decisions. On numerous occasions, Government officials have specifically reminded unions or managements of the guidepost standards—either publicly or privately, either generally or with reference to specific situations. Several of the more important of these situations have attracted considerable public attention.

In January 1965, the President requested the Council of Economic Advisers to prepare an analysis of steel prices, following certain increases in such prices and at a time when important wage negotiations

SOURCE Reprinted from 1966 Annual Report of the Council of Economic Advisors, pp. 88–93.

were pending. The Report, made public in early May, analyzed the position of the industry and the factors affecting it. It showed that wage and price decisions consistent with the guideposts would be in the interest of both labor and management and of the Nation. Later, the Government helped the two parties to reach a peaceful settlement in the steel wage negotiations. A damaging strike was avoided, and a settlement was achieved within the wage guideposts. According to the best estimates of its cost available to the Government, the settlement averaged 3.2 percent a year, computed over the full 39-month period.

Following the labor settlement, prices on tin plate were raised in October; this was accompanied by a price reduction on a new black plate, which is expected to substitute increasingly for tin plate in many uses. At the year's end, the Bethlehem Steel Company announced a $5 a ton increase on structural steel and pilings. The Council pointed out that such an increase was not justified under the guideposts. In January, the U.S. Steel Corporation announced a smaller increase, accompanying it with price reductions on other steel products.

In October, the Council prepared a guidepost analysis of price increases initiated by producers of primary aluminum; the companies later rescinded these increases.

Also in October, the President, by threatening a veto, persuaded the Congress to enact a pay increase for civil service and postal employees of the Federal Government which was within the guideposts.

These actions and many others clearly reaffirmed the Administration's strong commitment to the guideposts as an essential pillar for price stability.

### THE GUIDEPOSTS RESTATED

1. The general guidepost for wages is that the *annual rate of increase of total employee compensation (wages and fringe benefits) per man-hour worked should equal the national trend rate of increase in output per man-hour.*

2. The general guidepost for prices is that *prices should remain stable in those industries where the increase of productivity equals the national trend; that prices can appropriately rise in those industries where the increase of productivity is smaller than the national trend; and that prices should fall in those industries where the increase of productivity exceeds the national trend.*

Within a given industry, the guideposts allow for individual wage and price adjustments that do not affect the over-all wage or price level of the industry. Increases for some groups of workers or products can be balanced by reductions for others.

Observance of the guideposts would mean that unit labor costs would decline in the industries where productivity gains are above average, and rise in industries where such gains are below the national average. Average unit labor cost in the economy would remain constant. Similarly, the decrease of prices in industries with above-average increases in productivity would offset the price rises in industries with below-average productivity gains. The average level of prices would remain stable.

Adherence to the standards would mean that *all* the participants in the productive processes—employees and owners of invested capital—would share in the over-all gains in productivity created by the growth of capital equipment, improved technology, and a better educated, healthier, and more skilled labor force. This can readily be seen from a simple example. Suppose output in an industry is 1 million units, each selling at $1, for total sales of $1 million. Suppose labor compensation is $600,000. If productivity and wages both rise 3 percent, and employment remains unchanged, production will expand to 1,030,000 units, which, at $1 a unit would raise revenues to $1,030,000. Labor compensation would rise to $618,000. Labor would thus receive 60 percent of the added value, keeping unchanged the share of labor costs in total revenues. If prices of materials and other purchased inputs were unchanged, and the quantities used were expanded in proportion to output, then gross income of owners woud rise in the same proportion as wage income. Thus, the division of income between labor and capital would remain unchanged. And with capital requirements per unit of output unchanged (as has been approximately true), the return per unit of capital would remain unchanged as well.

The actual sharing of gross corporate income between labor and capital has remained virtually unchanged since World War II. There have been repeated short-run swings, with labor's share rising in recession and falling during expansion. Thus, for example, the share of nonwage income rose from 27.2 percent in 1961 to 29.2 percent in 1965. This recent figure is virtually identical with the division of income in 1955 and 1948. The inflationary wage-price spirals of the 1940's and 1950's did not, in fact, change the distribution of income.

Public policy is and should remain neutral with respect to wage and price decisions that attempt to change the distribution of industry's income between labor and capital. But when such decisions lead to inflationary pressure, they properly become a subject of public concern.

## EXCEPTIONS TO
## THE GENERAL GUIDEPOSTS

Some exceptions to the general guideposts are necessary to promote economic objectives. Wage increases above the general guideposts may be desirable

> where wage rates are inadequate for an industry to attract its share of the labor force necessary to meet the demands for its products;

> where wages are particularly low— that is, near the bottom of the economy's wage scales; or

> where changes in work rules create large gains in productivity and substantial human costs requiring special adjustment of compensation.

Because the industries in which unions possess strong market power are largely high-wage industries in which job opportunities are relatively very attractive, the first two of these exceptions are rarely applicable.

On the price side, increases in price above the general guidepost standard may occasionally be appropriate

> to reflect increases in unit material costs, to the extent that such increases are not offset by decreases in other costs and significantly impair gross profit margins on the relevant range of products, or

> to correct an inability to attract needed capital.

The large firms to which guideposts are primarily addressed typically have ready access to sources of capital; moreover, the profits of virtually every industry have risen sharply and are at record levels as a byproduct of the general prosperity in the economy. The second exception is thus not widely applicable in the present environment.

## SHORT-RUN AND TREND
## ELEMENTS IN PRODUCTIVITY AND
## THE GENERAL WAGE GUIDEPOSTS

In the original discussion of the guideposts in the Council's Annual Report of 1962, it was pointed out that, "it is desirable to segregate the trend movements in productivity from those that reflect business-cycle forces." During the last 5 years, the economy has been closing a substantial gap between actual and potential production. This has augmented the yearly productivity gain beyond the long-term sustainable trend. Now that the economy has little gap remaining to close, the trend of productivity gains will be determined only by capital investment, an improving labor force, and technological progress. The temporarily high productivity gains that come from utilizing equipment and manpower more efficiently through higher operating rates are largely behind us.

To assure future stability of unit labor costs, wages should increase no faster than the sustainable trend of productivity.

The original formulation of the guideposts did not specify any particular trend productivity figure, but rather listed various historical averages, covering different time spans and various segments of the economy. Since the economy was just recovering from the second of two recessions in a very short interval, it was difficult to identify the trend productivity rate from the immediately preceding experience. This difficulty was compounded by speculation that the trend rate might be accelerating as a result of faster technological change, particularly the spread of automation.

In the Report of 1964, no single figure for trend productivity was specified, but in a related table the now well-known 3.2 percent appeared as the latest figure in a column labelled "Trend productivity." The figures in that column were described as the "annual average percentage change in output per man-hour during the latest 5 years." A 5-year period was chosen because, at that time, it was sufficiently long to include both the extraordinarily high productivity gains of a year of recovery (1962) and the extraordinarily low productivity gains of a year of recession (1960). Under the conditions of 1964, a 5-year average gave a good approximation of the trend productivity, because, in effect, it averaged out the ups and downs of cyclical productivity swings. These same conditions prevailed in 1964, and the 3.2 percent figure appeared for that year in a

similar table in the 1965 Report. Subsequent revisions of GNP data would have made the 5-year average 3.4 percent in both 1964 and 1965.

Now that the economy is at the end of its fifth year of uninterrupted expansion, a 5-year average no longer gives a reasonable approximation of the true productivity trend. The last recession year drops out of the average, yet the unsustainable productivity gains of a year of recovery and 4 years of improving utilization are retained. If use of the 5-year average were continued this year and in coming years, the figure yielded by the 5-year moving average would rise at this time to 3.6 percent and would undoubtedly fall substantially thereafter.

An analysis of recent productivity movements was presented earlier in this chapter. It is clear from this analysis that 3.6 percent would not be an accurate measure of the true trend of productivity. Rather, it appears that the long-term trend, independent of cyclical swings, is slightly over 3 percent.

For 1966, the Council specifically recommends that the general guidepost for wages of 3.2 percent a year be continued. We make this recommendation in the light of the following additional considerations:

1. With the economy approaching full employment and the crucial test of our ability to reconcile our employment and our cost-price goals at hand, it would be inappropriate to raise the guidepost.

2. The actual productivity gain that can be expected over the next few years is not likely to be above the trend value.

3. The 3.2 percent rate has been consistent with the approximate stability of industrial wholesale prices which has strengthened our competitive position in the world. Now is not the time to abandon that standard.

4. On January 1, employer payroll taxes to finance social security and Medi-

care rose substantially, raising labor costs per hour by an average of two-thirds of a percent. These taxes are not included in the definition of employee compensation for purposes of the guideposts, since the rates and the benefits are determined by law rather than by collective bargaining. Nonetheless, recognition has to be taken of the extraordinary increase in these taxes at this time, which will both raise unit labor costs and yield future benefits to employees. . . .

The Council's hope in reducing the productivity base was to limit wage increases to the lower level and thus temper inflationary pressure. But if, in fact, productivity had grown faster than the 3.2 rate, then if average increases were limited to this value, price stability would be achieved at the expense of labor's share. Certainly, workers with or without union representation would be unwilling to provide this solution to inflation. Prices would have to decline in keeping with the wage increases below productivity growth, to maintain constancy of relative shares. The Council was certainly asking for unusual restraint by suppliers in a situation of rising demand for labor and goods. At present, inflation control by exhortation appears to have failed against the relentless pressure of excess demand.

### Guideposts in Other Countries

Nevertheless, the problem of price stability–full employment and free decision making remains a dilemma for most Western countries. And, although it was opposed by the Nixon administration, the Guideposts issue was raised again in the United States during 1970 when Arthur Burns, Chairman of the Board of Governors of the Federal Reserve System, among others, advocated their use. Moreover, a 1970 report by the Organization for Economic Cooperation and Development "cautiously suggested that the United States resolve its growing difficulties in combining high employment with price stability by installing formal wage and price guidelines" (Clyde H. Furnsworth "22 Nation Group Suggests U.S. Pay-Price Guidelines," *New York Times*, April 27, 1970, p. 1). The OECD report did not consider a so-called "incomes" or guidepost policy to be a panacea, but thought the policy "should be tried in view of the dilemma facing American policy makers—'the risk of a serious downswing with a rapid rise in unemployment' on the one hand and the possibility, on the other hand, that 'the degree of cooling off of the economy acceptable on the basis of social considerations will not produce the expected improvement in price performance.' " (Ibid.)

Since the wage-price problem is common to all industrial societies that permit private wage and price determination, the comparative method provides some insight into the conditions for successful incomes policies.

In "Wage-Price Policies: Some Lessons from Abroad," Lloyd Ulman compares the policies of a number of countries. He raises the question of the curious state of affairs whereby many economists believed the Guideposts were effective while they were ignored and flouted by unions, rejected by management, and disavowed by the Nixon administration.

Underscoring the value of the comparative method, Ulman points out that an examination of the wage-price experience of other countries affords some help in finding our own answers to a number of critical problems. However, Ulman demonstrates that all of the Guidepost objectives are not even theoretically compatible.

# Wage-Price Policies: Some Lessons from Abroad

## by Lloyd Ulman

### THE CHANCES OF UNION SUPPORT

How might incomes policy be made effective? Its ability to curb wage increases depends on its effect on the parties to collective bargaining. Its effectiveness on the labor side would be measured by the extent to which unions can be persuaded to restrain themselves in the exertion of their bargaining power. Its effectiveness on the other side would be measured by the extent to which management can be persuaded to increase its resistance to union demands—and to exercise self-restraint in setting prices. In other words, the potential effectiveness of wage policy is determined by the area of discretion enjoyed by the parties. Why not pitch the bargain at the figure suggested by the wage guidepost or "norm" instead of at some higher figure which might have been otherwise decreed by custom or cussedness? Within the zone of discretion, a norm can take on charisma.

The zone of course is bounded at the top by considerations related to the employer's maximum "ability to pay," or, e.g., his willingness to pay without taking a strike. But it is no less well bounded at the other end by the union negotiator's ability to concede. And his ability to concede is limited by the requirement that a national union settlement not be downgraded by either (a) much larger wage increases won by other unions or (b) exceptionally large wage increases negotiated or freely granted at the plant level. The first condition (a) is best satisfied when bargaining is centralized in the hands of strong union and employer federations, or when the policy is backed by governmental sanctions sufficiently strong to round up the strays. (In some countries legislation provides that, under specified circumstances, the terms of collective agreements must be observed by all firms,

SOURCE Reprinted with permission from *Industrial Relations*, Vol. 8, May 1969, pp. 199–212.

including nonsignatories, in the industries in question. This constitutes a potential sanction against those unions and managements whose settlements exceed the wage policy's norm or ceiling.) Sweden has been regarded, at least until recently, as an example par excellence of a country where private centralization of power in federations—including control over strikes on the union side and lockouts on the management side—has precluded the need for formal governmental income policy. Collective bargaining is less centralized, even at the industry level, in the United States than in Scandinavia, Britain, and The Netherlands. Hence, conditions for union acceptance of guidepost policy here have been regarded as especially unfavorable.

The second condition (b)—that local or sectional wage increases be contained —requires that there be sufficient unemployment, slack, and pressure on profit margins to deter employers from bidding against each other for labor or from yielding to union pressures. This suggests that, up to a point, the higher the level of unemployment, the more successful an incomes policy will be in holding down the rate of wage increase below the rate which might have otherwise been expected at that level of unemployment. On the other hand, the higher the level of unemployment, the more difficult it is to sell workers on an incomes policy as an *alternative* to deflation and unemployment; the British have found this to be the case since the devaluation of 1967. Thus union leaders abroad are presented with an extremely delicate problem. Some will privately agree that they cannot tolerate incomes policy unless there is (as one put it to me) "less overfull employment"; publicly, however, they demand prompt reflationary action by the government as soon as unemployment increases.

How much economic slack would be required to keep down wage drift depends on the extent to which wages and other conditions in the plant are determined by bargaining between the national union and either top management or an employers' association. In this respect, it would appear that the American system of collective bargaining is at some advantage; there is little if any discernible wage drift here. On the other hand, evidence from abroad, especially from Britain, suggests that if bargaining at the industry level is restrained by incomes policy, steam begins to escape from the bottom of the boiler; shop stewards grow more rebellious and exert increasing pressure on management at the plant level.

This potential effect of the policy itself on the locus of union power and on the level of wage determination suggests a more fundamental limitation on the ability of union leaders to conform to incomes policy. Union leaders who do not exceed the norm in their settlements may be on the spot. Those who would otherwise have been content to accept settlements *below* the norm would be under very strong pressure to come up to the officially sanctioned figure. (Thus the policy could raise the lower limit of the bargainers' area of discretion.) Union leaders who negotiate settlements at the guidepost figure are not likely to receive much credit for their efforts from the dues-paying membership. Incomes policy has a built-in disincentive to compliance: it threatens to rob collective bargainers of their raison d'être.

How great a disincentive this is depends in good part on how much unionists in a country are committed to collective bargaining as opposed to more general objectives or political activity. The disincentive to comply with incomes policy is presumably less strong among union movements with socialist traditions and close affiliations with labor parties than it is among American 'business unionists" who are more essentially bargaining animals.

*  *  *

## HAVE INCOMES
## POLICIES BEEN EFFECTIVE?

Statistical evidence as to the effectiveness of the U.S. Guideposts is indirect. In the past, wage increases have been fairly well predictable on the basis of knowledge of unemployment, profits, and past movements in the cost of living. But beginning in 1962, actual wage increases began to fall below expectations; and this led George Perry and others to conclude that the Guideposts must have been effective in reducing wage increases.[1] Moreover, the overpredictions grew rather steadily in magnitude from the end of 1963 until the end of 1966, and this could furnish support for the view that the educational influence of the policy should take some time to reach maximum effectiveness. But the honor of apparently restraining wage behavior was also claimed on behalf of other candidates: the delayed effect of high unemployment levels in the late fifties, reinforced by long-term agreements and "pattern-setting"; the cumulative impact of heightened foreign competition; a belated response to the loss of organizing momentum after World War II; the slowly paced and "balanced" nature of the upswing that began in 1961; growth in the "labor reserves" available to employers as their employment requirements increased, which could damp down the bidding for teenagers, married women, older men, etc.[2] Indeed, the fact alone that, between 1962 and 1965, half of the major negotiated wage settlements—with the notable inclusion of two in basic steel—were *below* Guidepost (3 to 3.5 per cent) levels, suggests that other factors must have been at work.

But the Guideposts might still have contributed to the relatively restrained behavior of employee compensation. Can the analysis of wage and other behavior abroad furnish any useful supplementary evidence on the effectiveness of incomes policies? Statistical evidence most relevant to some hypotheses advanced in the previous sections of this paper is provided by the recent comparative work of a group of Canadian economists, by the work of a compatriot of theirs on wage movements in the United Kingdom, and by a study prepared for the Economic Commission for Europe.[3] Although its value is necessarily restricted by deficiencies in the coverage and quality of data, this evidence can suggest partial and tentative answers to a number of questions.

*Have incomes policies elsewhere appeared to slow down the rate of increase in wage rates?* France, the United Kingdom, and Sweden all experienced very low levels of unemployment compared to the U.S. between the mid-fifties and the mid-sixties and, within their ranges of experience, wages in these three countries appeared to respond more sensitively to unemployment. Nevertheless, the French incomes policy which was inaugurated in 1963 could have conceivably—on the basis

[1] G. Perry, "Wages and the Guideposts," *American Economic Review,* LVII (September, 1967), 897–904; G. Pierson, "Union Strength and the U.S. 'Phillips Curve'," *American Economic Review,* LVIII (June, 1968), 456–467.

[2] For discussion, pro or con, of these considerations see: J. Sheehan, *The Wage-Price Guideposts* (Washington: The Brookings Institution, 1967), pp. 92–95; N. J. Simler and A. Tella, "Labor Reserves and the Phillips Curve," *Review of Economics and Statistics,* XLX (February, 1968), 32–49; O. Eckstein, "Money Wage Determination Revisited," *Review of Economic Studies,* XXXV (April, 1968), 133–143; A. W. Throop, "The Union-Nonunion Wage Differential and Cost-Push Inflation," *American Economic Review,* LVIII (March, 1968), 79–98.

[3] R. Bodkin, E. P. Bond, G. L. Reuber, T. R. Robinson, *Price Stability and High Employment: The Options for Canadian Economic Policy, An Econometric Study Prepared for the Economic Council of Canada* (Ottawa: September, 1966); D. C. Smith, "Incomes Policy," in R. E. Caves and Associates, *Britain's Economic Prospects* (Washington, D.C.: The Brookings Institution, 1968), pp. 104–146; *Incomes in Postwar Europe: A Study of Policies, Growth and Distribution,* Secretariat of the Economic Commission for Europe (Geneva: United Nations, 1967), Chap. 3.

of quite shaky evidence—reduced the rate of wage increase by as much as 2.6 percentage points per year, as opposed to a possible 1.1 to 1.3 point contribution by the U.S. Guideposts. In Britain, according to Professor Smith's estimates, incomes policy appears to have been effective in slowing down the rate of increase in *weekly* wage rates in 1948–1950 (by 2 points), 1961–1962 (1½ points), 1965–1966 (1 point), and 1966–1967 (1¼ to 1½ points). In all but the last period, however, *hourly* rates and earnings did not rise significantly less than expected on the basis of unemployment and price changes; and in 1965–1966, when reductions in the work week were negotiated, hourly earnings actually rose more than expected. In Sweden, a change to centralized bargaining occurred in 1956, but this did not seem to affect the course of wages. What is surprising is that wage increases in West Germany, a country without either a formal incomes policy or a strongly centralized system of collective bargaining, were about 1 point below predicted after 1962. Thus, if France and the United Kingdom can be taken to furnish some evidence of the effectiveness of incomes policy, West Germany's experience is consistent with the hypothesis that other wage depressants might have been at work in the sixties.

*If incomes policy can be effective in slowing down the rate of wage increase, is its influence likely to grow over time, or is it likely to be strongest at the outset (or shortly thereafter)?* The former effect seems to be predicted from the "public education" hypothesis underlying the Guideposts. It seems to have been borne out by the increasing magnitude of the gap between predicted and actual wage increases; but if this gave proof of growing public sophistication and support, it is not easily reconciled with the private repudiation and official abandonment of the policy at the high point of its statistical success. The other view—that policies of wage restraint are more likely to be of only temporary effectiveness—is suggested by the tendency of wage drift to increase and of employer resistance to wane as unemployment falls, by the greater responsiveness of unions to clear and present danger signals than to other incentives to compliance, and by the greater difficulty (or disinclination) in enforcing price restraint than wage restraint. Statistical tests suggest that incomes policies have exerted more of a temporary than a cumulative effect in Britain. These tests did not provide much basis for choosing between the two theories in the case of France; but the wage explosion (of 14 per cent) in 1968 did, since it came when unemployment reached a high point for the decade, after a rise of 40 per cent in the preceding year.

*Has the policy generally borne down as heavily on prices as it has on wages?* In the case of the U.K., as of the U.S., the answer is probably no: prices have not risen more slowly than would have been expected on the basis of changes in wages, import prices, and productivity, except during the British freeze period in 1966–1967.[4] Thus any effect of incomes policy on prices in these two countries was exerted through a prior effect on wages. In France, on the other hand, there is some indirect evidence that the de Gaulle government's price-oriented policy might have been effective in holding down the rate of price increase directly as well as indirectly. These results are consistent with the difference in policy emphasis in the two countries.

*Has incomes policy required compulsion to be effective?* A preliminary econometric analysis by the National Board for Prices

---

[4] R. M. Solow reports that wholesale prices of manufactures might have been expected to rise about .7 of a point more than they did after 1962, in the absence of the Guideposts. See G. P. Shultz and R. Z. Aliber, *Guidelines, Informal Controls, and the Market Place* (Chicago: University of Chicago Press, 1966), p. 47.

and Incomes revealed that the apparent effect of incomes policy on wages was no greater in 1961–1962 and 1966, which were years of "tight control," than in 1948–1950 and 1965, "when the policy was essentially voluntary."[5] When the Dutch unions accepted a reduction in real wages of 5 per cent in 1951, this was regarded as essentially a victory for persuasion. On the other hand, none of the apparent British failures (in 1956 and perhaps in 1965–1966) occurred when the policy was marked by compulsion; and Professor Smith's most clearcut evidence in favor of the effectiveness of *price* policy occurred during the freeze of 1966–1967. It may well be that, with the attrition of incentives to voluntary cooperation, some compulsion is necessary for policy effectiveness. If so, the effectiveness of such policies may be limited in time by the political limitations of compulsion itself. In 1967, the Dutch unions forced the abandonment of a system of prior governmental approval of collective agreements, but they continued to accept the government's right to block wage increases during national economic emergencies—provided prices and other incomes are similarly treated. This is essentially the position of the AFL-CIO—whole hog or no hog, and whole hog "for the duration" only.

\* \* \*

. . . European experience suggests two reasons why incomes policy is not likely to lead to substantial resource misallocation. The first is that labor and product markets are rather imperfect to begin with; indeed, a policy which could distort wages and prices in a perfectly functioning economic system could in principle improve efficiency in an imperfect one. Many British and Northern European economists believe that very great changes in wage structure would be required to move labor out of occupations and regions where it is redundant to fill shortages elsewhere, and that transfers of labor are more likely to be effected through the wasteful intermediary of unemployment. They also believe that institutional arrangements make it very difficult to alter wage structure.[6] Under these conditions wage increases induced by shortages are likely to lever up the general level of wages, rather than to alter wage structures, and to leave the shortages relatively intact. In both Sweden and Britain persistent shortages of skilled labor have been linked to the persistence of traditional wage differentials in the face of changed market conditions. The famous Swedish "active labor market policies"—government-conducted-and-subsidized retraining and relocation programs—were designed as a more efficient substitute for the wage system as well as a complement to the unions' "solidaristic" wage policy which calls for equal pay for the same work.

As noted above, the favorite response of the British Prices and Incomes Board to demands for pay increases based on shortages is to suggest that any pay increases be predicated on the overcoming of shortages through more efficient utilization of existing manpower and/or the negotiation of more appropriate pay structures. It has prescribed the same type of medicine to salaried groups and even self-employed professionals, notably solicitors and architects.

In the area of prices, the British Board has found justification for its interventions in the prevalence of the same conditions which obtain in many labor markets: monopolistic restrictions and operating inefficiency. "It is the very absence in the practical world of such competition in some sectors which makes necessary a

---

[5] National Board for Prices and Incomes, Report No. 77, *Third General Report August 1967 to July 1968*, Cmnd. 3715 (London: HMSO, July 1968), pp. 66–67.

[6] *Wages and Labour Mobility* (Paris: Organisation for Economic Co-operation and Development, 1965).

prices and incomes policy."[7] It should be noted, however, that the Board attributed monopolistic conditions in part to "economies of large-scale production"; the extent of these is a matter of controversy, but it is reasonable to suppose that they are less prevalent in the continental economy of the U.S. Moreover, there is reason to believe that the level of managerial efficiency has been relatively low in the United Kingdom.

It is also true that the short-run movement of prices in both Britain and the U.S. seems to be heavily conditioned by changes in unit costs (wages and productivity); hence the omission of demand factors in price guideposts of both countries is at least not reflected in this version of statistical reality.

The second reason for expecting that the economic costs of incomes policies are likely to be quite limited in practice is that it is more difficult for the policy to affect areas where decision-making is decentralized (e.g., salaried sectors and competitive enterprise) than where it is centralized; and it is in the latter areas where imperfect pricing exists. This differential impact of incomes policy is suggested by the statistical evidence showing the policy's greater impact on wages than on prices. The association between centralization and market imperfections breaks down in some notable instances (e.g., the decentralized U.S. construction sector); but where it holds, the policy tends to be most effective where it is least dangerous.

The foregoing suggests that the net costs of the policy are likely to be considerably lower than its potential or actual gross costs. Consideration of the economic alternatives—more unemployment, more inflation, sharper devaluations—considerably reinforces this impression. The problem boils down to this: Is any loss in efficiency and output due to the policy greater or less than the loss in efficiency and output due to the extra unemployment and unused capacity which would be required without incomes policy?

Incomes policy is also likely to be self-limiting in terms of the loss of freedom which it could impose on the community. Previously, we suggest that a certain amount of compulsory reserve power may be required to backstop cooperation by the trade union movement and that union cooperation might be predicated on union participation in the formulation of public policies, including wage-price policy itself. The U.S. Guideposts were backed neither by legal compulsion nor by union acceptance or involvement. Foreign experience suggests a trade-off: the lesser the degree of legal compulsion, the greater the involvement of the union movement in the formulation and also the administration of the policy. At one extreme is Sweden where the policy is run entirely by the private parties and where the union movement exercises great influence in the Social Democratic Party and Government. The other extreme is represented, at least potentially, by The Netherlands where at the insistence of the unions and management a system of detailed review by a central bipartisan body (the Foundation of Labor) was scrapped, apparently in favor of laissez-faire without guidelines but with retention in the hands of the government of the power to issue full "wage stops" in periods of emergency.

This uneasy trade-off has prompted the criticism (a) that incomes policy inevitably generates governmental interference with private collective bargaining and (b) that it makes for intrusion by private interest groups into areas of general economic policy which should be reserved to the government. Obviously, both types of intrusion can find precedents in advanced political democracies. Most countries have subjected collective bargaining to certain restrictions in the interest of industrial

[7] Cmnd. 3715, *op. cit.*, para. 20.

peace. A Swedish industrialist wryly complained that "Traditionally neither employers nor employees accept what they call 'government interference' in the incomes policy of the organisations, which is indeed a curious atavism in a country where the expansion of state activities in all fields has been evident."[8] The objection to private encroachment in economic policy-making meets most frequently with the reply that the private parties have in effect been making such policy all along, but without regard to the public interest. By raising the levels of wages and prices, the private parties have been obliging the public fiscal and monetary authorities to react to them as best they could. Under incomes policy, the parties are forced to face up to the broader consequences of their own actions.

If the actual degree of compulsion thus far has not been unduly onerous, some observers fear that there is more to come. According to this view, incomes policy is a two-step process. The first step is taken by left-of-center governments to whom the policy is appealing because it appears to be a politically costless way of apparently grappling with the problem of inflation, while blaming the ugly phenomenon on private parties. But then, the government finds that it has given hostage to fortune; having committed itself to curing inflation painlessly, it discovers that a purely voluntary policy is less effective than advertised. The temptation to shore up incomes

policy with a bit of legal compulsion emerges. Moreover, according to this view, recourse to compulsion by a liberal or left-wing party is politically feasible: the unions may not appreciate the move, but they have already been handed a black eye by the policy in its early educational phase, and in any event they cannot shift their political allegiance to a more conservative party. Recent British experience, however, casts doubt on the last proposition. It does not take into account other available options, such as not voting, voting for new political groupings, or refusal to comply with the policy. The decline in Labor's political position in Britain was attributed in part to the unpopularity of compulsory wage restraint. The head of the giant Transport and General Worker's Union made the point succinctly:

*I want to put an equation to you. In my opinion because of this policy we have lost 10 by-elections. If that is the sort of equation we want in our movement—a reduction in wage movement of one per cent for the loss of 10 by-elections—I don't understand it.*[9]

Thus fear of political backlash militates against the onward creep of compulsion. Moreover, it tends to prevent the government from using existing compulsory power to the extent necessary for maximum policy effectiveness. . . .

Ulman's detailed analysis of the experiences of various countries with the Guideposts leads him to a number of conclusions: (1) The Guideposts cannot solve the wage-price problem but can form a useful supplement to other policies. (2) In order to be successful, an incomes policy as Guidepost arrangement is called in England, must have union support and this has been more easily achieved in Europe than the United States because European labor movements have been able to influence public policies more directly through their political parties, thereby giving political as well as economic protection

---

[8] *Financial Times,* November 6, 1968.
[9] *Financial Times,* October 1, 1968.

to their members; have more centralized bargaining arrangements that prevent whipsawing and give greater control to union leaders and management; have a greater external pressure because the importance of international trade presents a "clear and present danger," giving an important incentive for wage-price restraint; and have placed a greater emphasis on wage-leveling to help the disadvantaged. (3) Government monetary policies must be sufficiently restrictive to give employers a will to resist wage increases. (4) "Incomes policy might have had some effect in restraining wage increases, although the statistical evidence is far from conclusive." (5) The unpopularity of Guideposts makes them self-limiting economically and politically, causing their benefits to be greater than their costs.

The weakness of voluntary wage restraints has led to demands for more stringent regulations. It is sometimes assumed that it would be more "rational" to substitute wage and price controls for collective bargaining, making it possible to achieve the objectives of price stability and full employment at the expense of free collective bargaining. Today, a careful listener can hear the sounds policy leaders make when they are about to impose necessary but unpopular measures, in this case formal, legal controls.

From a foreign experience, B. C. Roberts of the London School of Economics gives some insights of the difficulties of wage and price controls in the Netherlands in his article 'National Wage Policy in the Netherlands."

Roberts' article is important not so much for the facts it gives—because these obviously are out of date—but because of the insights it provides into the basic problem of wage and price controls. Roberts describes the operations of the Foundation of Labor (FL) established in 1945 to advise the government of industrial and social policy in the Netherlands. Although legal responsibility for making and enforcing wage policy rests with the Board of Mediators, that organization was required by a 1945 decree to consult with the FL before promulgating any changes. Since wage determination is inextricably bound up with other social and economic policies, in 1950, the Netherlands government created the Social and Economic Council to advise it on broader issues.

# National Wage Policy in the Netherlands

## by B. C. Roberts

### III

The primary objectives which it was hoped would be achieved by the adoption of a National Wage Policy in the Netherlands were (1) the maintenance of economic stability by controlling the general level of wages, and (2) the establishment of equitable and satisfactory wage differentials between different occupations. It was agreed by all parties to the policy that, in principle, wages should be determined in the light of prevailing economic circumstances and estimated future developments. This end was to be secured through the institutional arrangements described, instead of by the pulls and shoves of employers and unions in an oligopolistic labour market. It was also believed that the "crude" forces of supply and demand could be replaced as the determinants of wage relationships by a "rational" calculation based on a sophisticated analysis of occupational differences. How far success in the attainment of these objectives has been achieved will now be examined.

The first step that was taken, when the National Wage Policy was introduced, was the establishment of a national minimum wage for unskilled adult workers at a level that would enable a man to maintain a family of four at a reasonable subsistence standard in the prevailing economic circumstances. Semi-skilled workers' wages were fixed at ten per cent, and skilled workers' wages at twenty per cent above the level set for the unskilled workers. In order to allow for differences in the cost of living the country was divided into five zones and wages were graded accordingly. Thereafter, until 1950, these wage levels were raised by a percentage figure that was approximately equal to the rise in the cost of living. Thus real wages were kept more or less stationary in the immediate

SOURCE Reprinted with permission from *Economica*, Vol. 24, August 1957, pp. 191–204.

post-war years, though a substantial improvement in the standard of living occurred simply because shortages and restrictions on consumption gradually disappeared and rationing was abolished.

The restoration of the Netherlands economy was threatened with a serious check when the Korean conflict began, since the change in the terms of trade brought about by the tense international situation led to a considerable deterioration in the balance of payments.[1] In addition the rearmament programme that was made necessary by the international situation substantially increased the burden of expenditure on defence. Since the economic stability of the country appeared to be in danger the government, with the agreement of the unions and the employers, decided to reduce real wages. This was accomplished by allowing prices to rise in 1951 by ten per cent, but only permitting wages to rise by five per cent. Part of the increase in prices was deliberately brought about by a drastic cut in subsidies and the imposition of taxes on luxury goods and motor vehicles.

These measures were not, however, regarded as adequate to protect the economy from inflation and a substantial reduction in investment was also decided upon. This was tackled by the issue of regulations calculated to reduce gross profit margins. The profits tax was raised and a drive was launched to collect the substantial arrears of taxation owed by private companies. The bank rate was raised by one per cent; a system of quantitative credit controls was introduced; and the capital market was further squeezed by a series of government loans. In addition to these financial measures expenditure on house building was reduced by restrictions on the issue of building licences. The government's policy was consolidated by its own resolution in cutting down the volume of money created on its behalf.

The effect of these determined actions was to check the inflation and to turn, in twelve months, an adverse balance on current account with the rest of the world into a very healthy surplus. Prices, which had risen in 1951 by ten per cent over the previous year, were stabilised, but unemployment, which had been 2.0 per cent in 1950, rose to 3.5 in 1952. In spite of the increase in unemployment and a check to production in 1952, a considerable expansion in output was secured in the following year; the gross national product was 14 per cent greater, at constant prices, in 1953 than it had been in 1950. Wages, however, were successfully limited to an increase which, in 1953, only restored purchasing power to the level of 1950.

By 1953 it was apparent that the crisis was over, though the government was reluctant to relax its stringent policy too quickly lest it should undo the good that had been done. Anxiety about the level of unemployment led it, however, to take steps to encourage more investment, but it continued to resist large-scale wage advances. Pressure for a substantial wage increase mounted, but it was not until January, 1954 that the government finally agreed to a general rise of 5 per cent, and permitted an additional increase of 2 per cent to skilled workers. The unions were not satisfied with the improvement in wages granted; they felt that work-people were entitled to a greater share of the rising tide of prosperity and soon pressed for a further advance. In October, 1954 permission was given by the Board of Mediators for another general wage increase of 6 per cent; this advance was for the first time not based on a rise in the cost of living, but was deliberately intended as an increase in real wages.

[1] Changes in the terms of trade tend to affect Holland to an even greater extent than the United Kingdom, since imports, measured in relation to gross national product, are twice as high as in this country.

Although there was some over-lapping of functions the institutional arrangements seem to have worked reasonably smoothly until the conflicts of 1954. In that year the Foundation of Labour recommended that the powers of the Board of Mediators should be transferred to a standing committee of the Social and Economic Council. Behind this proposal there lay a dispute over the basic principles upon which, up to that stage, wages policy had been determined. Though it was generally accepted in the Netherlands that the control of wage movements by the government had helped considerably in the immediate post-war years, criticism from the employers and a section of the unions began to grow from the end of 1952.[2] Pressure for relaxation might have come earlier had it not been for the economic crisis engendered by the Korean War boom.

It was, perhaps, not unnatural that as memory of the war receded and Holland emerged from the period of reconstruction the unity of opinion upon which the national wages policy was founded should have gradually given way to a hankering for more freedom on the part of the employers. They began to feel that their right to fix wages without the permission of the government should be restored, if not entirely, at least to a much greater extent than had been the case since 1945. Dissatisfaction was also voiced by the Christian trade unions, and even in the "neutral"—mainly socialist orientated—unions, which remained in support of economic planning and the maintenance of a government controlled wage policy, the feeling grew that changes in the system ought to be made.

At first the government was not in favour of the suggestion that the powers of the Board of Mediators should be transferred to the Social and Economic Council; when, however, after an acute conflict, a majority of the Social and Economic Council recommended the adoption of the proposal, the government announced that it was "prepared in principle to move in the direction of transferring powers in the field of wage policy to organised trade and industry as represented in the Social and Economic Council." The Minister of Social Affairs also stated at the same time that the government would instruct the Board of Mediators to consider other fundamental changes in the principles upon which wages had hitherto been determined.

A crisis was reached when, after the two very prosperous years of 1954 and 1955, in which every segment of the economy expanded rapidly, the government, seeking to curb a further rise in wages and prices, again came into conflict with the unions. The unions claimed that the share of wages in the national income had fallen and that on this score they were entitled to a further rise. Faced by this demand the government requested the Social and Economic Council to hold an inquiry into the validity of the argument; it also asked the Council to take into account the fact that controlled house-rents would be allowed to rise in 1957 and that in the same year workers would be called upon to pay old age pension insurance premiums. The Report of the Council confirmed that officially determined wage rates had lagged to some extent, but that earnings per capita had risen by the same amount as the national income per capita. On the basis of the Report it was finally agreed, after prolonged negotiations, which almost ended in the collapse of the Foundation of Labour and of the whole system of wage controls, that a maximum lump sum payment of 3 per cent of the annual wage should be made for the year 1955, and that in addition each industry should be allowed to raise its wages up to a maximum of 6 per cent. When the govern-

---

[2] See B. Zoeteweij, "National Wage Policy: The Experience of the Netherlands", *International Labour Review*, Vol. LXX, No. 2, February, 1955.

ment approved these recommendations in March, 1956, it did so on condition that the lump sum payment was not passed on to prices and also that price increases in respect of the permitted 6 per cent further rise would only be allowed if the increase did not exceed 3 per cent.

In fact, in 1956, industrial wages rose by a little more than 3 per cent over the average of 1955, but by January, 1957, as a result of increases allowed, industrial wage rates had risen by 11 per cent over the level of the previous January. It was expected that much of the increase in wages would be at the expense of profits and there is evidence that to some extent this has occurred. Prices were, on the average, less than 2 per cent above the average of the previous year, but there was a sharp rise at the beginning of 1957; by February of this year the index of retail prices had reached a level of 9 per cent above the figure at which it had stood in January, 1956.

* * *

Thus the Netherlands government has again had to take vigorous steps to restrict the tendency for money incomes to rise faster than the economy can bear. But in order to win the co-operation of the unions it has had to agree to the introduction of direct controls to prevent prices from rising. What is more important is that it has not shirked taking a stiff dose of its own medicine, and it has also indicated that it will not hesitate to introduce further measures to curtail demand if they should prove to be necessary.

IV

The most important feature of the award of March, 1956 was that it modified one of the cardinal principles of the national wage policy as previously carried out. Hitherto wage differentials had been based on a national system of job evaluation and no allowance was made for the ability of one industry to pay a higher wage than another on purely market considerations. In the Report mentioned above the Social and Economic Council recommended that in future it should be possible for enterprises to diverge from compulsory wage regulations, and in effect the 6 per cent. permissive award was also recognition of the need for greater flexibility as between industries.

That the Netherlands authorities should have been compelled to make these concessions to factors they had sought to exclude from consideration in wage determination is an extremely significant event, since it clearly shows the limitations of the assumptions on which the advocates of a national wages policy had based their criticism of free collective bargaining. The abstract conception of social justice which had been at the heart of the attempt to scientifically coordinate wages had not provided either workers or employers with the satisfaction anticipated.

The founders of the Netherlands wage system held the opinion that it was socially and economically undesirable that wage standards should be based upon such differences as might occur in the profitability of enterprise, the supply and demand for labour, the bargaining strength of unions and employers and historical accident and tradition. It was felt that a stable system of wages could only be established on a basis of equity as determined by a scientific calculation of the content of each job, the conditions under which it was performed and the circumstances of the performer. Thus the foundation of the Netherlands wages policy rested upon the notion that work should be rewarded according to social rather than economic criteria.

In order to establish this new basis for fixing wage differentials a committee of experts (Commission for Normalisation) was set up to develop a comprehensive scheme of job evaluation and work classification. The method adopted involved the grading of jobs throughout industry according to a series of factors such as knowledge required, dexterity, care, responsibility, physical effort, risk of accident, etc.[3] Points were then assigned according to the extent to which the factor applied to each job. The next step was to grade each job within a series of broader classifications and to convert the points rating into wages. Each employer had to comply with the basic wage rates as laid down in the regulations, but the detailed application of the standard scheme of job evaluation to particular industries was not made compulsory; its complete adoption was left to the voluntary decision of the employers and unions concerned.[4] Since the wages policy involved not only the control of minimum, but also maximum wages, any change in wage structure had to be ratified by the Board of Mediators. Evasion would have been a comparatively simple matter had the regulations been confined to basic wage rates, and control had, therefore, to be extended to cover every kind of allowance, bonus or payment for overtime and shift work, holiday pay, pension and welfare schemes. Piece rates were permitted so long as they did not exceed rather narrow limits and special arrangements were made for time workers to benefit by an approved system of merit rating. Thus every aspect of wages was subject to regulation, and determined according to a national policy.

The introduction of job evaluation resulted in the breaking down of the main categories of skilled, semi-skilled and unskilled work, on which the broad pattern of differentials was based, into numerous sub-groups. This refinement in the structure of wages does not appear to have made any significant alteration to the differentials between the three main groups. . . . There was a narrowing of the differentials between 1939 and 1947, but thereafter there was little change.

\* \* \*

Neither wage regulation in Holland nor wage restraint in Britain has been a substitute for a disinflationary financial and budgetary policy, but it has been a useful supplementary aid to the more fundamental measures that have been used to check the expansion of demand. The primary lesson to be learnt from the experience of the Netherlands is not that a centralised system of wage control is an effective means of preventing inflation, but that stability can only be achieved by a resolute and persistent control of the factors that lead so easily to an over-rapid expansion of industrial demand. There has been less inflation in the Netherlands because the government, supported by the employers and the unions, has pressed its disinflationary economic policies harder—to the extent of creating more unemployment—than has the British government at any time since the end of the war.

The adoption of a centralised system of wage determination is only compatible with free trade unionism and free enterprise so long as it responds to the economic and political pressures that are generated in a free society. What is altered when wages are determined by a central body is the manner in which collective bargaining takes place. In the Netherlands, bargaining was not eliminated with the establishment of the Foundation of Labour and the Social and Economic Council; it was simply transferred from the industrial to the national level. It is possible, as many supporters of the Na-

---

[3] A. N. van Mill, "Job Classification in the Netherlands", *International Labour Review*, February, 1949.

[4] There are about 200 separate industrial groups for which regulations have been made. In addition the Board has to deal with separate wage schemes for individual enterprises not belonging to an industry covered by a general regulation, and for numerous individual enterprises with exceptions from the general rules of their industry; altogether about 6,000 "individual" cases per annum. M. G. Levenbach, "Collective Bargaining in the Netherlands," *Modern Law Review*, October 1953.

tional Wage Policy in the Netherlands would argue, that this was to the good, since it meant that wages were determined less independently of economic reality than would have been the case under sectional bargaining. However, it is also possible, under the centralised system of bargaining, for the unions to insist on the government adopting, as the price of their acceptance of temporary wage restraint, policies that permit an over-rapid expansion of income at a later stage. Ultimately the outcome of a system of bargaining, whether it be a centralised one like that adopted by the Netherlands, a decentralised one like that of Britain, or an even more decentralised one like that of America, will depend on the power of the contending factions. If the unions are strong and the general economic and political circumstances are favourable, they will be in a position, whatever the formal institutional arrangements through which collective bargaining is carried on, to push wages to levels which in conjunction with investment demand make inflation inevitable. If the unions do not push hard enough the employers will pull the level up themselves.

From the evidence examined it would seem fair to conclude that the centralisation of wage determination in the Netherlands has brought some advantages, but that these have not been as great as the supporters of a national wage policy have often claimed. Neither the problem of inflation nor the problem of wage structure has been satisfactorily solved. The results achieved offer little promise that a similar system, if adopted in Britain, would prove to be the answer to the difficulties that beset this country.

\* \* \*

In order to achieve the primary objectives of its National Wage Policy—economic stability and equitable occupational wage differentials—the Dutch government established a national minimum wage for unskilled adult workers and differentials for semiskilled and skilled workers at 10 and 20 percent above this level respectively. These real levels of wages were maintained until 1950 by cost of living adjustments.

One of the main problems in establishing wage differentials on any fixed differentials is that these might be incompatible with underlying economic and political power relations, which tend to be dynamic. Fixed wage differentials also have difficulty being compatible with employers' manpower requirements. In spite of these problems, the Dutch system worked reasonably well during the ferment associated with the Korean conflict, but came under increasing internal stress when the external threats posed by post-World War II reconstruction receded. With improved conditions, employers wanted greater freedom to determine wages in accordance with labor market conditions and unions wanted to be able to raise wages. As a consequence of disputes over the wage determining process, the government was forced to make concessions which caused wages to rise 11 percent between January 1956 and January 1957. In order to avoid serious inflationary pressures the government adopted some strenuous monetary and fiscal measures, and also had to resort to direct price controls. At the same time, the Social and Economic Council—made up of representatives of unions, employers and the government—recommended greater freedom for employers to diverge from compulsory wage regulations. Roberts concludes:

That the Netherlands authorities should have been compelled to make these concessions to factors they had sought to exclude from consideration in wage determination is an extremely significant event, since it clearly shows the limitations of the assumptions on which the advocates of a national wages policy had based their criticism of free collective bargaining. The abstract conception of social justice which had been at the heart of the attempt to scientifically coordinate wages had not provided either workers or employers with the satisfaction anticipated.

Roberts then proceeds to compare the results of the Netherlands policy with those elsewhere, which ostensibly were based mainly on social rather than economic criteria, and concludes that "the general pattern of differentials. . . does not appear to differ markedly from that which has emerged in other countries."

Although the Dutch curbed inflation more than the British between 1951 and 1957, Roberts contends that the stringent measures taken by the Dutch government to control credit and government expenditures might have played a more important role. Therefore, it is Roberts' position that a policy of centralized wage and price determination "is only compatible with free trade unionism and free enterprise so long as it responds to the economic and political pressures that are generated in a free society." On this basis, he thinks it "fair to conclude that the centralization of wage determination in the Netherlands has brought some advantages, but that these have not been as great as the supporters of a national wage policy have claimed." Certainly, formal controls in the United States would meet as much opposition from economic and political forces, unless the need for their imposition became more evident to wage and price setters and the general public.

## Related Readings

The "creeping inflation" of the 1950's created much concern because, for the first time in our economic history, prices rose significantly in a period during which overall demand was clearly not excessive and the unemployment rate was moderately high. Charles L. Schultze, *Recent Inflation in the United States*, Joint Economic Committee, Washington, 1959, offered a novel and provocative hypothesis based on apparent cost-push considerations. Schultze viewed the inflation as resulting from differential shifts in demand at a time when overall demand was more or less steady. Wages and prices tended to rise in sectors of increasing demand, but the overall rise in prices appeared when sectors losing demand failed to experience equivalent wage and price declines. This wage-price behavior in the declining sector was an expression of cost-push pressure in that demand considerations alone called for declines to offset the increases occurring in the expanding sectors.

Support was offered to the Schultze hypothesis by William G. Bowen and Stanely H. Masters, "Shifts in the Composition of Demand and the Inflation Problem" (*American Economic Review*, Vol. 54, December 1964, pp. 975–984). They found that in the late 1950's and early 1960's when prices were stable, intersectoral demand, admittedly imperfectly measured, was much more uniform than in the Schultze period of comparable overall demand.

More direct support of Schultze's view comes from studies of the roles of unions in wage and price movements. Two American studies, Robert R. France, "Wages, Unemployment, and Prices in the United States, 1890–1932, 1947–1957" (*Industrial and Labor Relations Review*, Vol. 15, January 1962, pp. 171–190), and Kenneth M. McCaffree, "A Further Consideration of Wages, Unemployment and Prices in the United States, 1948–1958" (Ibid., Vol. 17, October 1963, pp. 60–74), conclude that the main influence of unions has been to prevent wages from falling as much as in the past during slack periods. This macroeconomic finding can be applied to Schultze's view that the root of the "creeping inflation" problem is the failure of wages and prices to fall in declining sectors. For the English experience, A. G. Hines, "Trade Unions and Wage Inflation in the United Kingdom, 1893–1961" (*Review of Economic Studies*, Vol. 31, October 1964, pp. 221–252), finds that the degree of unionization was a stronger explanatory variable than the level of unemployment related to wage changes.

But following Lipsey's analysis, demand shift in itself might lead to inflation without the need for cost-push pressures. Nonlinearity in sectoral Phillips curves, at unemployment below frictional levels, or with excess demand present, in some sectors, would lead to the emergence of inflationary forces if strong divergence in sectoral demand rose with overall demand unchanged. The resultant inflation would then be demand-pull in nature, caused by excess labor demand in the expanding sector.

Lipsey's inflation model has been challenged by Phillip Ross, "Labor Market Behavior and the Relationship between Unemployment and Wages" (Proceedings of the 14th Annual Industrial Relations Research Association, 1962, pp. 275–285). Ross found no relationship between wage changes and unemployment levels among local labor markets, with wage changes rather uniform despite wide disparities in unemployment levels. Certainly this seems to deny the presence of sectoral or local Phillips curves. But Lipsey's hypothesis could be modified to allow for greater labor market competition than his presentation of it assumed. Differential levels of unemployment with some sectors below the frictional level—and in Ross' study none of the localities had very low unemployment rates—could be assumed to lead to upward wage pressure that would be transferred throughout the economy through labor market competition and result in a higher overall wage level than would otherwise prevail.

Refinements in the Phillips curve analysis have included additional variables to the wage-estimation equation, mainly because statistical analysis revealed that the simple Phillips curve itself relating wage change to unemployment levels alone did not fit the data too closely. Nicholas Kaldor, "Economic Growth and the Problem of Inflation" (*Economica*, Vol. 26, November 1959, pp. 287–298), suggested that wages would tend to move with profits as unions pressed harder and profitable firms were more susceptible to granting wage increases. In testing Kaldor's theory, Richard G. Lipsey and M. D. Steuer, "The Relation between Profits and Wage Rates" *Economica*, Vol. 38, May 1961, pp. 137–158) found profit changes on balance probably more weakly correlated to wage movements than were unemployment levels. For American data, Ronald G. Bodkin, *The-Wage-Price-Productivity-Nexus* (University of Pennsylvania Press, June 1966), derived similar results, but George L. Perry, *Unemployment Money Wage Rates, and Inflation* (M.I.T. Press, 1966), found a relationship between changes in profits and wage movements.

Related to the shortcomings of the Guideposts, Kelvin Lancaster, "Productivity-Geared Wage Policies" (*Economica*, Vol. 35, August 1958, pp. 199–212), notes that it would be unlikely for labor and product markets to clear by applying a formula that called for equal wage changes, and price changes to respond to differential productivity movements instead of to market forces. Arthur F. Burns, "Wages and Prices by Formula?" (*Harvard Business Review*, Vol. 43, September 1967, pp. 897–904), finds that wages rose less than expected in the years immediately following their appearance, based on preceding wage-unemployment and profit relationships. John Sheahan, *The Wage-Price Guide-posts* (The Brookings Institution, Washington, 1967), reviews other studies similar to Perry's. However, all the studies that find price-stabilizing merit in the Guideposts analyze wage-price movements before the onset of the inflation in 1966. Sheahan also cites the balanced expansion in the 1962–1965 period as an alternative explanation of relative price stability then—shades of Lipsey and Schultze.

In an article that comes to essentially the same conclusions as Lloyd Ulman, E. N. Kassalow ("National Wage Policies: Lessons to Date, Europe and the U.S.A.," Nineteenth Annual *Proceedings* of the Industrial Relations Research Association, 1966) emphasizes the uses and limitations of the comparative method and concludes that "regardless of what data one employs, the results are not supportive of the efficacy of wage policy systems." Moreover, Kassalow agrees with Dunlop and Ulman that "to gain acceptance, a wage control system must allow for participation of labor and management in the decision-making machinery." There also is general agreement, which Kassalow confirms, that wage controls ordinarily lead to demands for control of all other prices. Although productivity is the main factor used, other factors are sometimes used, including the cost of living. Finally, because of the decentralized bargaining system in the United States and the lack of working class solidarity, in the United States as in Britain, "tight wage controls" probably would "require rigid and formal controls, much like those in World War II."

# CHAPTER 9

# Wage Structure–The Skill Differential

Wage flexibility may widen structural bottlenecks and allow rising demand to move the economy toward full employment. But if relative wage adjustments take the form of higher wages for labor shortage jobs or areas instead of wage reductions for labor surplus fields, the mechanism of employment expansion will generate inflation. In the chapter on the economics of poverty, the argument will be advanced that inflationary flexibility of rising wages in the shortage fields is the only feasible adjustment to satisfy the policy goal of limiting the number of the working poor. In part of this chapter, the cyclical behavior of relative wages will be reviewed, and the conclusion reached that they tend to move in a direction that aggravates rather than moderates structural imbalance.

Wages differ among workers in competitive labor markets because of differences in job conditions such as surroundings, prestige, safety, and job security. But by far the greatest variations arise because of differences in value to the employer of the work performed. Apart from differences in talent, experience, motivation, and aptitude for the work, these variations arise from differences in acquired skills, derived from training and education. Thus, differences in investment in the worker are at the source of the skill differential which, in this chapter, serves as the measure of relative wages. Before examining cyclical changes in this differential, which are so important in their relation to the bottleneck problem, long-run variations in the ratio of skilled to unskilled wages, the conventional value used to measure the differential, will be reviewed, because of its intrinsic interest. Furthermore, trends in this differential can be explained by application of the human capital concept, which has greatly increased our understanding of the forces determining economic growth and occupational distribution of the labor force.

## HUMAN CAPITAL

Although refinements of human capital analysis have been introduced into economic theory relatively recently, the concept can be found in *The Wealth of Nations*. Adam Smith, in the passage presented here, explains wage differences partly on the differential costs in acquiring skills.

# The Wealth of Nations

## by Adam Smith

*Inequalities Arising from the*
*Nature of the Employments Themselves*[1]

The five following are the principal circumstances which, so far as I have been able to observe, make up for a small pecuniary gain in some employments, and counter-balance a great one in others: first, the agreeableness or disagreeableness of the employments themselves; secondly, the easiness and cheapness, or the difficulty and expense of learning them; thirdly, the constancy or inconstancy of employment in them; fourthly, the small or great trust which must be reposed in those who exercise them: and fifthly, the probability or improbability of success in them.

\* \* \*

Secondly, The wages of labour vary with the easiness and cheapness, or the difficulty and expence of learning the business.

When any expensive machine is erected, the extraordinary work to be performed by it before it is worn out, it must be expected, will replace the capital laid out upon it, with at least the[2] ordinary profits. A man educated at the expence of much

SOURCE Reprinted with permission from *The Wealth of Nations,* New York, Modern Library, 1937, pp. 100–107.

[1] The foregoing introductory paragraphs would lead a logical reader to expect part I of the chapter to be entitled: "Inequalities of pecuniary wages and profit which merely counterbalance inequalities of other advantages and disadvantages." The rather obscure title actually chosen is due to the fact that nearly a quarter of the part is occupied by a discussion of three further conditions which must be present in addition to "perfect freedom" in order to bring about the equality of total advantages and disadvantages. The chapter would have been clearer if this discussion had been placed at the beginning, but it was probably an afterthought.

[2] Ed. 1 reads "its."

labour and time to any of those employments which require extraordinary dexterity and skill, may be compared to one of those expensive machines. The work which he learns to perform, it must be expected, over and above the usual wages of common labour, will replace to him the whole expence of his education, with at least the ordinary profits of an equally valuable capital. It must do this too in a reasonable time, regard being had to the very uncertain duration of human life, in the same manner as to the more certain duration of the machine.

The difference between the wages of skilled labour and those of common labour, is founded upon this principle.

The policy of Europe considers the labour of all mechanics, artificers, and manufacturers, as skilled labour; and that of all country labourers as common labour. It seems to suppose that of the former to be of a more nice and delicate nature than that of the latter. It is so perhaps in some cases; but in the greater part it is quite otherwise, as I shall endeavour to shew by and by. The laws and customs of Europe, therefore, in order to qualify any person for exercising the one species of labour, impose the necessity of an apprenticeship, though with different degrees of rigour in different places. They leave the other free and open to every body. During the continuance of the apprenticeship, the whole labour of the apprentice belongs to his master. In the mean time he must, in many cases, be maintained by his parents or relations, and in almost all cases must be cloathed by them. Some money too is commonly given to the master for teaching him his trade. They who cannot give money, give time, or become bound for more than the usual number of years; a consideration which, though it is not always advantageous to the master, on account of the usual idleness of apprentices, is always disadvantageous to the apprentice. In country labour, on the contrary, the labourer, while he is employed about the easier, learns the more difficult parts of his business, and his own labour maintains him through all the different stages of his employment. It is reasonable, therefore, that in Europe the wages of mechanics, artificers, and manufacturers, should be somewhat higher than those of common labourers.[3] They are so accordingly, and their superior gains make them in most places be considered as a superior rank of people. This superiority, however, is generally very small; the daily or weekly earnings of journeymen in the more common sorts of manufactures, such as those of plain linen and woollen cloth, computed at an average, are, in most places, very little more than the day wages of common labourers. Their employment, indeed, is more steady and uniform, and the superiority of their earnings, taking the whole year together, may be somewhat greater. It seems evidently, however, to be no greater than what is sufficient to compensate the superior expence of their education.

Education in the ingenious arts and in the liberal professions, is still more tedious and expensive. The pecuniary recompence, therefore, of painters and sculptors, of lawyers and physicians, ought[4] to be much more liberal: and it is so accordingly.

The profits of stock seem to be very little affected by the easiness or difficulty

[3] This argument seems to be modelled closely on Cantillon, *Essai*, pp. 23, 24, but probably also owes something to Mandeville, *Fable of the Bees*, pt. ii., dialogue vi., vol. ii., p. 423. Cp. *Lectures*, pp. 173–175.

[4] The "ought" is equivalent to "it is reasonable they should be" in the previous paragraph, and to "must" in "must not only maintain him while he is idle" on p. 103. Cp. "doivent" in Cantillon, *Essai*, p. 24: "Ceux donc qui emploient des artisans ou gens de métier, doivent nécessairement payer leur travail plus haut que celui d'un laboureur ou manœuvre." The meaning need not be that it is ethically right that a person on whose education much has been spent should receive a large reward, but only that it is economically desirable, since otherwise there would be a deficiency of such persons.

of learning the trade in which it is employed. All the different ways in which stock is commonly employed in great towns seem, in reality, to be almost equally easy and difficult to learn. One branch either of foreign or domestic trade, cannot well be a much more intricate business than another.

\* \* \*

Smith notes job characteristics that lead to what are called compensating wage differences. That is, for work of the same skill level, wages tend to be higher for jobs that are more disagreeable, unsafe, or insecure. But it is his grasp of the role of investment in skills that makes Smith's contribution so advanced for its time. He likens investment in human capital to that of machines in that accumulated wage differences over time for those who undergo education and training defray the cost of their investment and a normal return on it just as investment in physical capital allows a gross return that includes cost and normal profit.

Furthermore, Smith relates the size of wage differences to the magnitude of investments in explaining why skilled factory workers earn more than common labor and why those educated in the professions must earn even more.

In computing rates of return on investment in education or training for a particular occupation, modern studies calculate differences in average annual earnings resulting from the investment. Adam Smith explains that apparently high earnings in some professions are balanced out by the low earnings of those who do not succeed in the field, making for an average that may or may not reflect a high average rate of return on investment in the occupation.

Modern students of human capital suggest that calculated rates on investment in education understate returns to the extent that there are consumption benefits from education. Adam Smith advanced the reward of "public admiration" or prestige as a substitute for monetary rewards in certain fields.

Investment in men and investment in physical capital are linked, under competitive conditions, so that returns on both tend to be equal. Other factors, to be treated in greater detail in the chapter on returns to education enter into the determination of return on human capital, but changes in wage differences between the skilled and unskilled, representing workers who have been the recipient of investment in training and education and those who have not, have an important influence on these returns.

### Long-Run Skill Differential

The long-term trend in the skill differential has followed two distinct patterns. From the turn of the century until about 1950, there was a clear narrowing trend in the skill differential, conventionally measured as the ratio of average wages of a group of skilled occupations to the average for selected unskilled jobs. From 1950 until the 1960's, however, the differential has remained stable. Evidence of stability can be found from foreign data as well as in the United States.

Of the many studies that reveal the historical narrowing trend, that of Paul G. Keat is the most comprehensive. Keat's technique entails examination of the entire occupational wage structure, rather than relative wage movements at the ends of the skill ladder. He finds a clear narrowing trend over the first 50 years of this century with dispersion, measured by the coefficient of variation, narrowing at an average well over 0.5 percent per year for the 141 occupations studied.*

* Technically, it is possible for the dispersion of all occupations to narrow while extremes of the distribution widen, if there is much greater concentration at the center. But the narrowing trend between highest and lowest paid occupations, found in other studies, indicates a pattern of narrowing of wage differences throughout the occupational distribution.

# Long-Run Changes in Occupational Wage Structure, 1900–1956

## by Paul G. Keat

This article will investigate the long-run trend in percentage wage differentials among occupations of different skill levels. Previous studies of this subject[1] have generally concluded that these differentials have been narrowing. Some of these studies concerned themselves with trends within one or a few individual industries while others classified occupations in many industries into two or three broad skill categories. In this article, a composite sample of many occupations in many in-dustries is used. Briefly, my findings confirm those of previous studies on this subject: relative skill differentials have been falling during the period examined.[2]

In the first section of this article, I present several measures of the change in wage dispersion over a period of roughly fifty years. In the second section, I investigate various potential factors which may have been responsible for the overall narrowing of the wage structure.

\* \* \*

SOURCE Reprinted with permission from *Journal of Political Economy*, Vol. 68, December 1960, pp. 584–600.

[1] Stanley Lebergott, "Wage Structures," *Review of Economic Statistics*, XXIX (November, 1947), 274–85; Philip W. Bell, "Cyclical Variations and Trends in Occupational Wage Differentials in American Industries since 1914," *Review of Economics and Statistics*, XXXIII (November, 1951), 329–37; Lloyd G. Reynolds and Cynthia H. Taft, *The Evolution of Wage Structure* (New Haven: Yale University Press, 1956); Harry Ober, "Occupational Wage Differentials, 1907–1947," *Monthly Labor Review*, LXVII (August, 1948), 127–34.

[2] In my dissertation I also investigated the short-run movements in the wage structure. Generally speaking, over the course of a business cycle, the differentials have moved in a direction opposite to the level of business activity. However, throughout these fluctuations, a basic tendency of narrowing can be observed. A period of increasing differentials usually leaves the wage structure narrower than it had been at a previous peak, and a period of narrowing compresses it more than it had been at a previous low point.

Two methods, both expressing differentials in relative rather than in absolute terms, were used to measure changes in wage dispersion. The coefficient of variation was used when a large number of observations was available for a given date. Percentage differences measured dispersion when only a few observations were available.

1. The first test performed involved a list of 141 occupations in seventeen industries.[3] The relative dispersion of hourly wages was compared for 1903 and 1956. The choice of dates was important, since wage differentials may fluctuate with the cycle as well as in trend. To measure the trend, it was necessary to select years which were similar in cyclical position. The initial year, 1903, was a peak year as shown by the reference cycles of the National Bureau of Economic Research. During the period after World War II, the movement of wages was continuously upward, with only small interruptions in business prosperity. Thus any year from 1945 to 1956 was roughly comparable to 1903 in cyclical position; 1956 was selected as the terminal date.

The occupations used in the comparison were largely those with identical or almost identical titles at both initial and terminal dates. The identity of each occupation was confirmed by comparing descriptions of job content wherever possible. These job descriptions also supplied clues to identifying occupations in which content had remained essentially the same, although their titles had changed.

Unfortunately, not many of the identical occupations for which data were available both before World War I and after World War II had data for both 1903 and 1956. For example, 1907 was the earliest year for which union wage rates were published by the Bureau of Labor Statistics for the printing and building trades. For each such occupation, the 1903 and 1956 wages were estimated as follows:

($a$) Let $t_1$ denote the date before World War I at which wage data were available and $t_2$ denote the corresponding date after World War II. Any date $t_2$, 1945–56, was considered acceptable. On the other hand, only 1903, 1907, 1910, 1913, and 1915 were considered acceptable dates for $t_1$; all except 1915 were cyclical peaks, and 1915 was the beginning of the upward movement that continued through World War I.

($b$) let $I$ denote average hourly earnings in all manufacturing industries.[4] Denote by $W$ the occupational wage rate. For each occupation the ratio, $W/I$, was computed for both $t_1$ and $t_2$.

($c$) The 1903 and 1956 values of $W/I$ for each occupation were then estimated as follows:[5]

$$\log\left(\frac{W}{I}\right)_{1903} = \log\left(\frac{W}{I}\right)_{t_1} - \frac{t_1 - 1903}{t_2 - t_1}$$
$$\times \log\frac{(W/I)_{t_2}}{(W/I)_{t_1}}$$

$$\log\left(\frac{W}{I}\right)_{1956} = \log\left(\frac{W}{I}\right)_{t_2} + \frac{1956 - t_2}{t_2 - t_1}$$
$$\times \log\frac{(W/I)_{t_2}}{(W/I)_{t_1}}$$

[3] The list of occupations included fourteen railroad occupations from Interstate Commerce Commission M-300 reports; and twenty-six building and printing trade occupations from Bureau of Labor Statistics union wage-rate surveys; the balance of the occupations was in manufacturing and was obtained from various bulletins and reports published by the United States Bureau of Labor and subsequently the Bureau of Labor Statistics.

[4] Hourly earnings for 1914–56 were obtained from Bureau of Labor Statistics data; for 1903–13 from A. E. Rees, "Real Wages, 1890–1914," in Solomon Fabricant, *Investing in Economic Knowledge* (New York: National Bureau of Economic Research, Inc., 1958), p. 59.

[5] A test was performed on wage data which were available for 1903, 1910, and 1913. The 1910 and 1913 wages were extended to 1903 and checked against the actual figure given for 1903. The results showed that figures so obtained corresponded very closely to the actual figures in a majority of cases. Therefore, the 1910 and 1913 extrapolations were deemed acceptable.

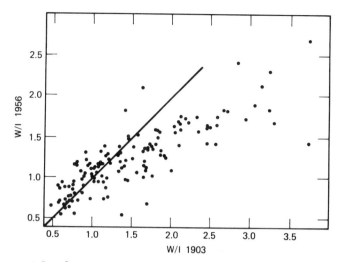

Figure 1. Ratios of hourly earnings in 141 occupations to average hourly earnings in manufacturing, 1903 and 1956.

Figure 1 is a scatter diagram in which 1956 values of $W/I$ have been plotted against the 1903 values. It is apparent that there has been relatively little change between 1903 and 1956 in the rankings. Actually, the Spearman rank correlation coefficient is 0.809; the product moment correlation coefficient is 0.795. The flatness of the scatter to the 1903 axis points clearly to a narrowing of relative wage differentials. The coefficients of variation for $W/I$ (and hence for $W$) for the two years 1903 and 1956 are 0.496 and 0.326, respectively.

In the preceding calculation each occupation was given a weight of 1. Taking account of changes in the numerical importance of various occupations might give a very different picture. Therefore, weights were applied to each of the 141 occupations. The available data are of such nature that the estimated weights

are, at most, rough approximations. Furthermore, several of the occupations are numerically very important, while others are quite insignificant. The building trades, printing trades, and railroad occupations account for a major portion of the employment in the total sample. Since it was impossible to avoid these deficiencies, several tests were used to check the consistency of the results.

In the first instance, the weights were applied to all 141 occupations in three different ways. First the 1903 and 1956 weights were used with their respective years. Then 1903 weights were applied for both 1903 and 1956, and, third, 1956 weights alone were used. Table 1 shows the coefficients of variations and their changes in the three instances. In order to avoid the possible distortion caused by the large number of observations in the predominantly high-paid union trade and

TABLE 1.  CHANGES IN COEFFICIENT OF VARIATION, 141 OCCUPATIONS, 1903–56

|  | 1903 | 1956 | Per Cent Change |
|---|---|---|---|
| 1903 and 1956 weights, respectively | 0.515 | 0.234 | —54.6 |
| 1903 weights | .515 | .341 | —33.8 |
| 1956 weights | 0.369 | 0.234 | —36.6 |

| | 1903 | 1956 | Per Cent Change |
|---|---|---|---|
| *Excluding two unions:* | | | |
| 1903 and 1956 weights | 0.527 | 0.349 | −33.8 |
| 1903 weights | .527 | .352 | −33.2 |
| 1956 weights | .514 | .349 | −32.1 |
| *Excluding two unions and RR's:* | | | |
| 1903 and 1956 weights | .416 | .286 | −31.3 |
| 1903 weights | .416 | .279 | −32.9 |
| 1956 weights | 0.464 | 0.286 | −40.9 |

railroad occupations, additional computations were made. One of these excluded the occupations in two union trades (building and printing); the other excluded these and the railroad occupations. The results are shown in Table 2.

Although there are some differences in the magnitude of the change in the coefficients of variation, the changes are in all cases considerable and consistently in the same direction.

2. The data used in the above estimates were for the United States as a whole. However, the observed narrowing of wage differentials might result from migration of industry from areas with larger wage differentials to areas with smaller interoccupational differences with no change occurring within each region. A rough check on this possibility was made, using the same Bureau of Labor Statistics data where regional wage figures were available. Fewer occupational data were available, and no weighting was used. The results are shown in Table 3. Narrowing of the wage structure appears quite conclusive in the north Atlantic and north-central regions, the rank correlation co-efficient being sufficiently high. In the case of the South, the ranking has changed considerably, casting doubt upon the significance of this particular small sample.

3. To confirm the previous findings, a rough test was performed for each of the industries (or branches of industries) in the original sample, when they included at least five occupations, and for the lumber industry. Wage data were not extrapolated, and no weights were used in computing the coefficients of dispersion. In all but two of these industries the declines in the coefficients of variation were considerable, ranging from 27.0 to 77.5 per cent. The two exceptions were the pulp and paper industry, where partial listing of occupations exhibited a small increase in dispersion, and the blast-furnace part of the steel industry, where the decline in dispersion was minor.[6]

4. From 1914 to 1948 the National Industrial Conference Board published data on average hourly earnings for a large number of manufacturing industries, as well as a composite figure.[7] Average hourly earnings (including overtime and premium pay) are given separately for two groups

[6] As the wages in the southern lumber industry were affected by the minimum-wage acts of 1950 and 1956, statistics from the Bureau of Labor Statistics at dates just prior to and following the enforcement of new minimums were used to compute additional coefficients. The results show that the laws did cause artificial compressions of hourly earnings, from which the wage structure recovered after the passage of time (1950–55). However, the narrowing of differentials between 1903 and 1949 is too large to be ascribed entirely to the 1938 law. In 1949 the earnings of the unskilled were considerably above the 40-cent minimum wage.

[7] M. A. Beney, *Wages, Hours, and Employment in the United States, 1914–1936* (New York: National Industrial Conference Board, 1936). Later data were found in various periodical publications of the National Industrial Conference Board.

TABLE 3. REGIONAL CHANGES IN COEFFICIENT OF VARIATION

| | No. of Occupations | Coefficients of Variation | | Rank Correlation Coefficient |
|---|---|---|---|---|
| | | 1903 | 1956 | |
| North Atlantic (East) | 83 | 0.455 | 0.245 | 0.717 |
| North-central (Lake states) | 53 | .437 | .220 | .630 |
| South | 21 | 0.786 | 0.217 | 0.096 |

of workers: (1) skilled and semiskilled men and (2) unskilled men. Further to confirm my previous findings, two observations (skilled-semi-skilled and unskilled) were taken for each of twenty industries, and the forty observations were arrayed by wage rate. The rank correlation coefficient for the two dates (July, 1914, and July, 1918) is 0.777. The coefficient of variation declines from 0.234 to 0.185, or 22.7 per cent.[8]

5. Although a sample of identical occupations may show a decline in relative wage dispersion, the universe of all occupations may not. A complete universe of occupations for each of 1903 and 1956 is, of course, not available. However, the *Bulletin* of the Bureau of Labor from which the 1903 data were obtained[9] contains data on industries that were not included in the sample of identical occupations, as well as additional occupations in the industries used. Altogether, the 1903 *Bulletin* covered 387 occupations in forty-two industries.

No such unified piece of information is available after World War II. In each of

the years since 1945, the Bureau of Labor Statistics "Wage Structure Series" and later the Bureau of Labor Statistics *Reports* were issued only for selected industries, generally not the same from year to year. Combining the raw data for several years might have been satisfactory, had the level of wages during this period been stable. This, of course, was not the case, so that the data had to be adjusted to a common date.

The year 1946 was used, and twenty industries covered in that year were included. Then industries from succeeding years were added if they did not duplicate those already surveyed in 1946. A total of forty-four industries was obtained.

The average hourly earnings for each occupation in the industries reported in 1947 or later were deflated to July, 1946. The deflators chosen were the average hourly earnings statistics for the industry in question (or the next larger industrial group or closely corresponding industry, if the particular industry was not available) published monthly by the Bureau of Labor Statistics.[10]

[8] While the all-industry data show a narrowing of differentials, almost half of the ratios of skilled-semiskilled to unskilled wages in the specific twenty individual industries shows the opposite tendency. However, the division of all occupations into just two categories makes the entire comparison rather tenuous, and thus the adverse result should not seriously weaken our confidence in the results previously described.

[9] U.S. Bureau of Labor, *Bulletin No. 59: Wages and Hours of Labor, 1890–1904* (Washington: Government Printing Office, 1905).

[10] Table C-1 in the *Monthly Labor Review*. This table presents "gross" hourly earnings, which include overtime and shift premiums. Therefore, they do not correspond exactly to the type of data contained in the occupational distribution. However, it was felt that whatever error could be caused by such discrepancy was minor, in view of the rather rough nature of this test. Only if the proportion of premium payments differed greatly on the two dates used in the comparison could the error thus introduced be serious.

Two deficiences in the method must be pointed out. By deflating all occupations in a given industry by the industry's average wage, it is assumed that the occupational wage structure within the industry remains the same. This, however, cannot be serious. Of the twenty-four industries adjusted to 1946, eleven were dated in some month of 1947 and five more in 1948.

Second, the wage data given in the "Wage Structure Series" and *Reports* are not annual averages. The statistics in each report were collected during a particular month or over a span of two or more months. Thus even the twenty industries surveyed in 1946 are not quite uniform in date. Nevertheless, it would seem that no serious error is introduced. First, eight of the twenty industries were actually surveyed in July, 1946, the date to which the wage data for later years were adjusted. Second, a test was performed on pairs of industries with similar average hourly earnings which were reported at least six months apart in 1946. The coefficient of dispersion was computed for each pair of industries, using both the unadjusted and the adjusted data. No significant difference in dispersion was observed.

In keeping with the procedure used previously, only production workers were included. Both weighted and unweighted coefficients of variation were computed, with the results shown in Table 4. In order to see whether the narrowing in the wage structure results from a change in the wage differentials between male and female workers or whether any distortion is introduced by a change in the proportion of female workers in the samples, separate coefficients were calculated for men and women combined and for male workers alone.

In both weighted and unweighted samples, the cofficient of variation is greater when women are included in the sample. This is as expected, for women tend to be concentrated at the lower end of the wage distribution. However, the decline in the wage structure in the all-male and combined samples is quite consistent. The decline in the unweighted coefficients is 41.9 per cent for the male and female occupations combined and 39.6 per cent for the male occupations alone. In the weighted coefficients, the declines are 26.1 and 25.5 per cent, respectively.

The number of occupations listed in the recent years for each industry is considerably greater than in 1903, and the occupational classifications have probably been subdivided. Subdivision of occupa-

TABLE 4. COEFFICIENTS OF VARIATION IN 1903 AND 1946 FOR A LARGE NUMBER OF OCCUPATIONS[a]

| Year | No. of Industries | Unweighted No. of Occupations | V | Weighted No. of Workers Covered | V |
|---|---|---|---|---|---|
| | | Male and Female Combined | | | |
| 1903 | 42 | 387 | 0.504 | 238,518 | 0.418 |
| 1946 | 44 | 2,531 | 0.293 | 2,328,070 | 0.309 |
| Change (per cent) | ... | ... | −41.9 | ... | −26.1 |
| | | Male Only | | | |
| 1903 | 42 | 326 | 0.428 | 216,472 | 0.388 |
| 1946 | 44 | 1,918 | 0.263 | 1,765,611 | 0.289 |
| Change (per cent) | ... | ... | −39.6 | ... | −25.5 |

[a] SOURCE: Calculated from data of the Bureau of Labor (1903) and the Bureau of Labor Statistics (1946). Occupational weights for industries reported in years other than 1946 were not adjusted for changes in industrial growth.

tions will tend to increase relative wage dispersion. The fact that, despite the subdivision, the coefficient of variation declined substantiates further the earlier finding that skill differentials have narrowed.

*   *   *

## EDUCATION AND TRAINING

The various factors discussed above, if taken together, probably explain only a small fraction of the narrowing that has taken place in occupational wage differentials. Only immigration may be considered as having contributed significantly to the narrowing.

I turn now to education (or training) and to the role that the costs of training may have played in accounting for the change in the wage structure.

First, however, I shall take some of the data used in Section I to establish an index of skilled-unskilled differentials for two widely separated dates. From the original sample of 141 occupations, I computed average hourly wages for skilled and unskilled occupations in ten industries or industry branches, in which specific skilled and unskilled occupations could be identified. A skilled-unskilled wage ratio was obtained for each industry in 1903 and 1956, and the ratios were averaged. The average skilled-unskilled ratio for 1903 was 201 per cent; for 1956, 142 per cent. If it is assumed that these ratios changed at a constant rate, then for the two census years 1900 and 1949, which will be used in subsequent computations, the applicable ratios are 205 and 149 per cent, respectively. These figures are reasonably similar to Ober's 205 and 155 per cent for 1907 and 1947.[11] The coefficient of variation computed for the two pairs of ratios shows a decrease of about 43 per cent.[12]

To isolate the various training factors involved, it is sufficient, I believe, to consider a simple model. Assume that there are only two occupations, A (skilled) and B (unskilled), that differ from each other only in that A requires $d$ years of training, while B requires none. The period $d$ is composed of two parts: school attendance 0 to $d_1$ and on-the-job-training $d_1$ to $d_2$. Assume that persons in B receive earnings of $r$ per year throughout their working lives of $T$ years. During each of the $d_1$ years of their working lives, persons in A receive no wages but incur no direct costs, as they attend free schools. During each of the $d_2-d_1$ years, they pay $f$ per year in direct training costs and receive $r$ per year for whatever work they do during their training. Thereafter, for $T-d_2$ years, they receive $s$ per year. Let $i$ be the private rate of return on A's investment in education and training. Then

$$\int_0^T r e^{-it}dt = \int_{d_1}^{d_2} (r - f) e^{-it}dt + \int_{d_2}^T s e^{-it}dt. \tag{1}$$

Expression (1) can also be written as

$$r(e^{-iT} - 1) = (r - f)(e^{-id_2} - e^{-id_1}) + s(e^{-iT} - e^{-id_2}). \tag{1a}$$

Solve equation (1a) for $D \equiv (s - r)/r$, obtaining

$$D = \frac{(e^{id_2} - e^{-id_1} e^{id_2}) + f/r(e^{-id_1} e^{id_2} - 1)}{1 - e^{-i(T-d_2)}}. \tag{2}$$

---

[11] Ober, *loc. cit.*

[12] The ratio of median annual wages of craftsmen to median annual wages of laborers in 1949, as shown in the 1950 Census, is 161 per cent.

We must now assign values to $f$, $r$, $d_1$, $d_2$, and $T$ for the initial and terminal years. Although the estimates will be based on rather crude data, they may be suggestive of the magnitude, if any, of change in the occupational wage structure accounted for by education and training.

The rate of return from private investment in education has recently been estimated at an upper limit of over 14 per cent.[13]

The years of schooling, $d_1$, in 1949 are approximated by the difference between the median years of school completed by male white craftsmen and male white laborers of median ages in 1950.[14] They are 9.7 and 8.6 years, respectively, or a difference of 1.1 years. There are no similar data for the year 1900. However, it is not unreasonable to assume that the schooling difference was no less in 1900 than it was in 1950; indeed, it could easily have been greater.

We shall consider the second period of training $(d_2—d_1)$ to be equivalent to the length of the apprenticeship period for skilled occupations. A recent publication of the Bureau of Apprenticeship[15] shows the typical years of apprenticeship required in a large number of apprenticeable occupations. By far the largest number of skilled occupations required between three and four years. Slichter[16] points out that the typical period (presumably around 1940, when his book was

published) of apprenticeship in building and metal trades was four to five years. He states also that in the eighteenth century a seven-year period was common. "But the term has been gradually becoming less, and today few unions require an apprenticeship of more than five years."[17] It would thus appear reasonable to use three and a half to four years for 1950. A period greater than four, possibly five, years does not seem unreasonable for 1900. Actually, in subsequent computations we shall test the results by varying the years of apprenticeship.

To establish the direct cost of the training period, we have obtained some earnings data for apprentices at the two dates. It is assumed that the apprentice's alternative was to enter an unskilled occupation and earn the unskilled rate $r$. The cost of apprentice training, $f$, is estimated as the excess of $r$ over the wage of apprentices. This assumption is possibly somewhat crude but should suffice for this test. It is quite possible that persons who entered apprenticeship could have earned a wage higher than $r$. First, they had some additional schooling. Second, they might have been persons of superior ability, who would have commanded higher than unskilled earnings even without additional training. On the other hand, they were younger and thus might have been at lower than average unskilled wages.

A special volume of the 1900 Census

---

[13] In Solomon Fabricant, *Investing in Economic Knowledge* (New York: National Bureau of Economic Research, Inc., 1958), pp. 23–24, G. S. Becker reports on a study of investment in education, presently in progress. The figure quoted in the text refers to the return on investment of private individuals or their families in college education in 1939. In a paper presented at the convention of the American Economic Association in December, 1959, published in "Papers and Proceedings of the Seventy-second Annual Meeting of the American Economic Association" *American Economic Review*, L (May, 1960), 346–54, Becker revised his figure to about 12 per cent. However, as my subsequent computations show, this change does not significantly affect my results.

[14] Computed from data in U.S. Bureau of the Census, *United States Census of Population: 1950: Education, Special Report P-E No. 5B* (Washington: Government Printing Office, 1953), Table 11, pp. 88–107, and U.S. Bureau of the Census, *United States Census of Population: 1950: Occupational Characteristics*, Vol. IV, *Special Report P-E No. 1B* (Government Printing Office, 1956), Tables 6 and 7, pp. 69–92.

[15] U.S. Bureau of Apprenticeship, *Apprentice Training* (Washington: Government Printing Office, 1956), pp. 11–29.

[16] Sumner H. Slichter, *Union Policies and Industrial Management* (Washington: Brookings Institution, 1941), pp. 25–27.

[17] *Ibid.*, p. 25.

provides the data for the initial year.[18] Hourly wage rates for apprentices are given for eight industries. In each of these industries, except one,[19] hourly wage rates of "general hands, helpers and laborers" were available.[20] The average hourly rate was computed for each of the two categories in the eight industries. The results appear in Table 5. The third column in the table shows the ratio of apprentice rates to laborer rates. Only apprentices sixteen years and over are included. However, the Census data for 1910 show that almost 25 percent of the apprentices in that year were under sixteen; probably the younger apprentices would have received lower wages.

From these figures an approximation of $f/r$ is obtained. A simple average of the eight ratios is 72 per cent. If breweries and the furniture industry are omitted, the average ratio is 63 per cent. If each of the individual ratios is weighted by its proportion of all apprentices in the eight industries, an average ratio of 62 per cent obtains; if the proportion of laborers is used as the weight, the average ratio is 67 per cent. It would thus appear that a reasonable range for $f/r$ is 30–40 per cent in 1900.

Some data on the annual earnings of apprentices in 1949 are available in the 1950 Census.[21] Apprentices were classified into three industries—construction, printing, and metal working.[22] Wages of the unskilled were obtained from the laborer category for the same industries.[23] For each pair of occupations in each industry,

TABLE 5. AVERAGE HOURLY WAGE RATES OF APPRENTICES AND LABORERS IN EIGHT INDUSTRIES IN 1900 [a]

| Industry | Average Hourly Wage Rates | | Ratio of Apprentice Rates to Laborer Rates (Per Cent) |
| | Apprentices (Cents) | Laborers | |
| --- | --- | --- | --- |
| Car and railroad shops | 10.3 | 15.1 | 68 |
| Foundries | 8.9 | 14.6 | 61 |
| Iron and steel | 12.1 | 17.1 | 71 |
| Shipyards | 8.6 | 17.1 | 50 |
| Breweries | 17.0 | 18.3 | 93 |
| Printing | 12.3 | 17.7 | 69 |
| Furniture | 11.1 | 10.4 | 107 |
| Wagons and carriages | 8.4 | 14.0 | 60 |

[a] Computed from U.S. Census Office, *Twelfth Census of the United States Taken in the Year 1900, Special Reports: Employees and Wages* (Washington: Government Printing Office, 1903).

[18] U.S. Census Office, *Twelfth Census of the United States Taken in the Year 1900, Special Reports: Employees and Wages* (Washington: Government Printing Office, 1903).

[19] The figures for the iron and steel industry do not contain the "general hands, etc." category. Therefore, data for "other occupations peculiar to the industry" were used. The latter probably include occupations of greater skill than the former category. However, the figure obtained did not appear to be out of line.

[20] The U.S. Bureau of Labor publications during this period contain data for laborer categories in several industries. These data were used in the computations in Section I. However, no comparable apprenticeship data are available in these publications.

[21] U.S. Bureau of the Census, *United States Census of Population: 1950: Occupational Characteristics*, Vol. IV, *Special Report P-E No. 1B* (Washington: Government Printing Office, 1956), Table 22, p. 234.

[22] Apprentices in "other specified trades" and "trade not specified" were included with apprentices in metal-working industries.

[23] Laborers in metal, machinery (except electrical), and transportation equipment industries were combined to arrive at a figure for metal-working industries.

an hourly wage figure was computed to put the wages on the same basis as in 1900.[24]

The average hourly wages for apprentices in the above three industries were $1.29, $1.16, and $1.19, respectively; for laborers, $1.14, $1.35, and $1.39, respectively. The respective ratios were 113, 86, and 86 per cent.

A simple average of the three ratios is 95 per cent. If the individual ratios are weighted by the proportion of apprentices, the average ratio is 96 per cent; weighted by the proportion of laborers, it is 103 per cent. It would appear that a reasonable range for $f/r$ is 0–5 per cent.[25]

The data indicate that apprentices' wages have risen considerably relative to wages of the unskilled. This occurrence appears to be a reasonable consequence of what has been happening in the last fifty years. The increased number of years of school completed may have tended to decrease the number of years required in training, and the additional education may have contributed to lowering the cost of training per year. Further, employees may

have become more efficient in carrying out training programs. All these could have lowered training costs, bringing about an increase in relative wages of apprentices.

The last factor to be estimated is the length of working life, $T$. However, the complete omission of $T$ will not significantly change the final results. A figure in the neighborhood of forty-five years for $T$ appears reasonable. In equation (2), let $i$ be 0.10 and $(T-d_2)$ be 40. The denominator of equation (2) then equals 0.9817. If $(T-d_2)$ is changed to 45, the denominator in equation (2) becomes 0.9889. If $i$ is equal to 0.15, then for $(T-d_2)$ of 40 and 45, we obtain 0.9975 and 0.9988, respectively. These computations give two reasons for omitting the denominator for the purposes of this rough estimate. First, if $T$ is in the neighborhood of 45, even a considerable change in $T$ will have only a minor effect on the estimate. Second, given that $i$ is of the order of 0.10–0.15 (which it appears to be), the denominator of equation (2) is approximately unity.[26]

[24] Hours worked per week and weeks worked per year were obtained from U.S. Bureau of the Census, *United States Census of Population: 1950: Occupational Characteristics*, Vol. IV, *Special Report P-E No. 1B* (Washington: Government Printing Office, 1956), Tables 15 and 17. The hours per year were computed by the formula, $h_y = \overline{h}\,\overline{o} + r_{ho}\sigma_h\sigma_o$, where $h_y$ = hours per year, $\overline{h}$ = average hours per week, $\overline{o}$ = average weeks per year, $r_{ho}$ = correlation between hours and weeks worked, and $\sigma$ = standard deviation. The correlation coefficient, $r_{ho}$, was taken to be 0.77. This figure was obtained by Henry Sanborn, in a doctoral dissertation recently completed at the University of Chicago.

[25] In both years the wage of apprentices has been compared to average unskilled wages. It would have been more appropriate to make the comparison for the two groups at equal ages; the apprentices are, of course, younger. As wages at the beginning of working life are lower than average, the ratio of apprentice wages to unskilled wages has probably been understated. If the age-earnings curve of unskilled workers became flatter during the period 1900–1949, then the figure obtained above would lead to an overestimate of the decline in training costs; if steeper, the decline in training costs would be underestimated. Unfortunately, there are no data available for comparisons of age-earnings curves, as no data at all exist for the early period. Data for a recent period, classified by occupations, are also scant. However, indications are that the age-earnings curve for unskilled workers is relatively flat. Data for four age categories published by the U.S. Bureau of the Census (*Current Population Reports— Consumer Income*, Ser. P-60, No. 11 [Washington: Government Printing Office, 1953], Table B, p. 4) show the following figures for 1951: 25–34 years—$2,361; 35–44 years—$2,291; 45–54 years—$1,985; 55 years and over—$1,919.

[26] Data for working lives of males are available in Stuart Garfinkle, "Changes in Working Life of Men, 1900–2000," *Monthly Labor Review*, LXXVIII (March, 1955), 297–300. In 1900 the expected working life for a man aged twenty (the closest age available in the article to the beginning of working life) was 39.4 years; in 1950, 43.2 years. In 1950, for ages fifteen to nineteen, the expected length of working life was 47.9. These figures strengthen the justification for omitting the denominator from the formula. Actually, had the denominator been calculated, the decline in occupational wage differentials due to education and training would have been greater, although insignificantly, than my computations in Table 6 show.

Equation (2), without its denominator, may be written as

$$D \cong \frac{f}{r}\left[e^{i(d_2-d_1)} - 1\right]$$
$$+ e^{i(d_2-d_1)}(e^{id_1} - 1). \quad (3)$$

Table 6 gives the values for $D + 1$ for a number of pairs of estimates of the effect of education and training. The first $D + 1$ of each pair represents a possible estimate for 1900, the second for 1949. The change in the skilled-unskilled wage ratio for each of the assumptions is shown in the last column. It can be seen that all these ratios cluster around a magnitude of 4/3 except those in which no change in the length of apprenticeship or a relatively low rate of return has been assumed.

At the beginning of the discussion of education and training, the decline in the skilled-unskilled wage rate was computed. The ratios of 1900 and 1949 were 205 and 149, respectively. The ratio of change is 205/149, or approximately 4/3.

The ratio of change in the skill differential is approximately the same as the majority of the ratios obtained in Table 6. Thus, if the values used to measure the effect of education and training are reasonably accurate, the changes in the cost and time of education and training can conceivably explain a large part of the change in the skilled-unskilled wage differential.

The somewhat speculative estimates summarized in Table 6 assumed no change in the internal rate of return on investment in training. A decrease in the rate, of course, would lower the wage differential.[27]

TABLE 6.  SERIES OF ESTIMATES OF EFFECT OF EDUCATION AND TRAINING ON SKILLED–UNSKILLED WAGE DIFFERENTIALS, 1900–1949

| | $i$ | $d_2-d_1$ | $d_1$ | $f/r$ | $D + 1$ | $(D+1)_a/(D+1)_b$* |
|---|---|---|---|---|---|---|
| 1900 | 0.14 | 5 | 1.1 | 0.40 | 1.74 ⎱ | |
| 1949 | .14 | 4 | 1.1 | .05 | 1.33 ⎰ | 1.31 |
| 1900 | .14 | 5 | 1.5 | .40 | 1.88 ⎱ | |
| 1949 | .14 | 4 | 1.1 | .05 | 1.33 ⎰ | 1.41 |
| 1900 | .14 | 5 | 1.1 | .30 | 1.64 ⎱ | |
| 1949 | .14 | 3.5 | 1.1 | .05 | 1.30 ⎰ | 1.26 |
| 1900 | .14 | 5 | 1.1 | .40 | 1.74 ⎱ | |
| 1949 | .14 | 4 | 1.1 | .0 | 1.29 ⎰ | 1.35 |
| 1900 | .14 | 4 | 1.1 | .35 | 1.55 ⎱ | |
| 1949 | .14 | 4 | 1.1 | .05 | 1.33 ⎰ | 1.17 |
| 1900 | .12 | 5 | 1.5 | .40 | 1.69 ⎱ | |
| 1949 | .12 | 3.5 | 1.1 | .05 | 1.24 ⎰ | 1.36 |
| 1900 | .12 | 5 | 1.25 | .35 | 1.58 ⎱ | |
| 1949 | .12 | 3.75 | 1 | .05 | 1.23 ⎰ | 1.29 |
| 1900 | .12 | 5 | 1.1 | .40 | 1.59 ⎱ | |
| 1949 | .12 | 3.5 | 1.1 | .0 | 1.21 ⎰ | 1.31 |
| 1900 | .12 | 5 | 2. | .30 | 1.74 ⎱ | |
| 1949 | .12 | 4 | 1.1 | .05 | 1.26 ⎰ | 1.38 |
| 1900 | .10 | 5 | 1.1 | .35 | 1.42 ⎱ | |
| 1949 | 0.10 | 3.75 | 1.1 | 0.05 | 1.19 ⎰ | 1.19 |

* $(D + 1)_a = (D + 1)_{1900}$; $(D + 1)_b = (D + 1)_{1949}$

[27] This can be seen in Table 6. $D + 1$ for 1900 in the fifth pair of figures is 1.55. If the interest rate for the 1949 figure were to be 12 per cent instead of 14 per cent, $D + 1$ would decrease from 1.33 to 1.26 (the 1949 figure in the ninth pair), and $D + 1_a/D + 1_b$ becomes 1.23.

Several other factors also have been omitted because of scarcity of data:

1. Changes in tastes for skilled occupations relative to unskilled. A shift of tastes in favor of skilled occupations would lower the differential in pecuniary terms.

2. The extent to which those in skilled occupations are a "non-competing" group relative to the unskilled. It has often been said that persons with little capital are at a disadvantage in investing in themselves. As real income has risen in the last half-century, one would expect the disadvantaged group to form a declining fraction of the labor force. This would increase the fraction of the labor force supplying skilled labor at a given wage differential and thus tend to lower the differential.

3. The possibility of changes in job content. The skill required in a specific occupational classification may have become more or less complex during the period of some fifty years. Thus, if a certain skilled occupation required less skill now than it did fifty years ago, *ceteris paribus*, and its wages fell relatively, the occupational wage structure measured by a coefficient of variation would have declined. However, skill differentials as defined in this study may not have been affected. Some of the data used in previous computations would indicate that the possible effect of a change in skill content on the wage structure is not at all clear. Among the industries included in the original sample are some in which changes in job content would not appear to have been great. The southern lumber industry, building, railroad, and printing industries should be included among these. The declines in the coefficient of variation in these industries are distributed throughout the array of ratios. This result, although by no means conclusive, would tend to indicate that changes in skill content have not had an important effect on the occupational wage structure.

Many factors have been offered as explanations for the long-run narrowing trend, among them (1) the development and growth of unions, (2) increase in egalitarian sentiment expressed through minimum wage legislation and general support for equalizing increases, (3) decline in immigration, (4) changing industrial demand away from skilled and toward semiskilled labor, and (5) expansion in education and training. If the first two factors narrowed the differential, they would introduce nonmarket, institutional forces into the determination of relative wages and perhaps distort labor markets, tending to create shortages of skilled labor and surpluses of unskilled. The other three factors would either reduce the supply of the unskilled relative to the skilled or increase the demand for lesser skilled relative to the skilled, in any case tending to raise the relative wages of the unskilled. They may be considered as market forces influencing wage structure to adjust to relative changes in demand and supply.

In the section of Keat's paper not included here, he concludes that unionism was not a significant narrowing factor and that the decline in immigration did act as a compressing force on wage structure. On the influence of unionism, he found no relationship between the degree of unionization and tightening of the occupational wage distribution within industries. In addition, the relatively higher wage increases that occurred in the heavily unionized industries were not found to be an important narrowing factor. Considering the prevalence of craft unionism during much of the period and the uncertainty of whether unions as a whole consider a narrowing of occupational wage differences as a part of their overall wage policy, these findings are not surprising. It is interesting, however, that Keat finds some tendency toward occupational wage equalization among industrial unions.

## Education and the Skill Differential

The relationship between expanded education and training and the skill differential has become a controversial subject. The argument centers on whether the noticeable increase in the level of education has been an autonomous supply phenomenon, autonomous in the sense that the rise in education did not take place in response to a tendency for the returns on education to increase, or whether education has actually expanded in response to factors that raised the returns on schooling. In either case, the skill differential would be subject to narrowing pressure as the overall level of schooling expanded and the number of the trained rose relative to that of the untrained.

The expansion and extension of compulsory education in itself is an autonomous force, but there are indications that laws tightening minimum years of schooling followed rather than led the rise in average years of schooling.

A test of whether expanded education was an autonomous or a responsive factor analyzes returns to education. If it was autonomous, then the consequent narrowing of the skill differential would cause a decline in the rate of return on education. If it was responsive, then the narrowing in the skill differential would result from an increased supply of trained workers that followed a tendency for returns to education to increase; there would be no tendency for the rate of return on investment in schooling to decline. Stability in this rate, discussed in the chapter on education gives support to the "responsiveness" viewpoint. Keat himself argues that a decline in the real cost and time needed to acquire skills explains a large part of the long-term decline in the skill differential. Thus the decline in costs tended to raise the rate of return on training, the number receiving training consequently grew, and the relative increase in the supply of skilled workers lowered the skill differential, without reducing the average rate of return on schooling.

Becker offers a compelling theoretical argument in support of the position that increased schooling, narrowing the skill differential, has been responsive rather than autonomous. Becker, in the brief section of his well-known paper presented here, sees a narrowing trend as a consequence of secular growth in productivity.

# Human Capital

## by Gary Becker

### WAGE DIFFERENTIALS AND SECULAR CHANGES

According to equation (30), the internal rate of return depends on the ratio of the return per unit of time to investment costs. A change in the return and costs by the same percentage would not change the internal rate, while a greater percentage change in the return would change the internal rate in the same direction. The return is measured by the absolute income gain, or by the absolute income difference between persons differing only in the amount of their investment. Note that absolute, not relative, income differ-

ences determine the return and the internal rate.

Occupational and educational wage differentials are sometimes measured by relative, sometimes by absolute, wage differences,[1] although no one has adequately discussed their relative merits. Since marginal productivity analysis relates the derived demand for any class of workers to the ratio of their wages to those of other inputs,[2] wage ratios are more appropriate in understanding forces determining demand. They are not, however, the best measure of forces determining supply, for the return on investment in

SOURCE Reprinted with permission from *Human Capital*, National Bureau of Economic Research, 1964, pp. 52–55.

[1] See A. M. Ross and W. Goldner, "Forces Affecting the Interindustry Wage Structure," *Quarterly Journal of Economics*, May 1950; P. H. Bell, "Cyclical Variations and Trend in Occupational Wage Differentials in American Industry since 1914," *Review of Economics and Statistics*, November 1951; F. Meyers and R. L. Bowlby, "The Interindustry Wage Structure and Productivity," *Industrial and Labor Relations Review*, October 1953; G. Stigler and D. Blank, *The Demand and Supply of Scientific Personnel*, New York, NBER, 1957, Table 11; P. Keat, "Long-Run Changes in Occupational Wage Structure, 1900–1956," *Journal of Political Economy*, December 1960.

[2] Thus the elasticity of substitution is usually defined as the percentage change in the ratio of quantities employed per 1 per cent change in the ratio of wages.

skills and other knowledge is determined by absolute wage differences. Therefore neither wage ratios nor wage differences are uniformly the best measure, ratios being more appropriate in demand studies and differences in supply studies.

The importance of distinguishing between wage ratios and differences, and the confusion resulting from the practice of using ratios to measure supply as well as demand forces, can be illustrated by considering the effects of technological progress. If progress were uniform in all industries and neutral with respect to all factors, and if there were constant costs, initially all wages would rise by the same proportion and the prices of all goods, including the output of industries supplying the investment in human capital,[3] would be unchanged. Since wage ratios would be unchanged, firms would have no incentive initially to alter their factor proportions. Wage differences, on the other hand, would rise at the same rate as wages, and since investment costs would be unchanged, there would be an incentive to invest more in human capital, and thus to increase the relative supply of skilled persons. The increased supply would in turn reduce the rate of increase of wage differences and produce an absolute narrowing of wage ratios.

In the United States during much of the last eighty years, a narrowing of wage ratios has gone hand in in hand with an increasing relative supply of skill, an association that is usually said to result from the effect of an autonomous increase in the supply of skills—brought about by the spread of free education or the rise in incomes—on the return to skill, as measured by wage ratios. An alternative interpretation suggested by the analysis here is that the spread of education and the increased investment in other kinds of human capital were in large part *induced* by technological progress (and perhaps other changes) through the effect on the rate of return, as measured by wage differences and costs. Clearly a secular decline in wage ratios would not be inconsistent with a secular increase in real wage differences if average wages were rising, and, indeed, one important body of data on wages shows a decline in ratios and an even stronger rise in differences.[4]

The interpretation based on autonomous supply shifts has been favored partly because a decline in wage ratios has erroneously been taken as evidence of a decline in the return to skill. While a decision ultimately can be based only on a detailed re-examination of the evidence,[5] the induced approach can be made more plausible by considering trends in physical capital. Economists have been aware that the rate of return on capital could be rising or at least not falling while the ratio of the "rental" price of capital to wages was falling. Consequently, although the rental price of capital declined relative to wages over time, the large secular in-

---

[3] Some persons have argued that only direct investment costs would be unchanged, indirect costs or foregone earnings rising along with wages. Neutral progress implies, however, the same increase in the productivity of a student's time as in his teacher's time or in the use of raw materials, so even foregone earnings would not change.

[4] Keat's data for 1906 and 1953 in the United States show both an average annual decline of 0.8 per cent in the coefficient of variation of wages and an average annual rise of 1.2 per cent in the real standard deviation. The decline in the coefficient of variation was shown in his study (*ibid.*); I computed the change in the real standard deviation from data made available to me by Keat.

[5] For those believing that the qualitative evidence overwhelmingly indicates a continuous secular decline in rates of return on human capital, I reproduce Adam Smith's statement on earnings in some professions. "The lottery of the law, therefore, is very far from being a perfectly fair lottery; and that, as well as many other liberal and honourable professions, is, in point of pecuniary gain, evidently under-recompensed" (*The Wealth of Nations*, Modern Library edition, New York, 1937, p. 106). Since economists tend to believe that law and most other liberal professions are now overcompensated relative to nonprofessional work "in point of pecuniary gain," the return to professional work could not have declined continuously if Smith's observations were accurate.

crease in the amount of physical capital per man-hour is not usually considered autonomous, but rather induced by technological and other developments that, at least temporarily, raised the return. A common explanation based on the effects of economic progress may, then, account for the increase in both human and physical capital.

\* \* \*

Under the simplifying assumption regarding cost structure and technological changes that Becker proposes, there would be a tendency for wages and rates of profit to rise equally. Becker implicitly ties the demand for investment in human capital with that for physical capital. As returns to labor and capital rise, there would be a tendency for the supply of both to increase.

But Becker notes that there has been a secular trend for wages to rise relative to the "rental" price of capital, forcing the rate of return on investment in physical capital down toward its level before the technological improvement took place. Although Becker offers no explanation for this tendency, it could have occurred because of the greater elasticity of supply of capital than of labor; it is a reasonable assumption that the supply of capital can expand more quickly and more strongly than the supply of labor.

Meanwhile, in the labor market itself, with Becker's assumption leading to equal increases in demand for labor of all types, all wages, skilled and unskilled, tend to rise proportionately. Since the absolute differential therefore widens, and costs do not change, the rate of return on a larger stream of absolute income differences rises over the years after education. Now, the rate of return on investment in human capital tends to exceed that on physical capital, which has receded toward its previous level as capital has expanded relative to labor in general. Thus, there is an upward force on the demand for training in response to the differential rates of return. As a result, in time the supply of trained workers rises to that of the untrained, the (percentage) skill differential narrows, and the rate of return on investment in human capital approaches the level for physical capital.

How much of the historical narrowing in the skill differential can be attributed to the expansion of training in response to technological improvement is uncertain. But Becker's argument should not be overused to lead to the position that any absolute increase in the skill differential will induce training and result in a decline in the percentage skill differential. For example, consider the widening of the absolute skill differential and constancy in the percentage difference that might occur with inflation. If all wages and prices increase in the same proportion, the absolute spread between skilled and unskilled wages would then widen. But there would be no change in the rate of return on investment in education to induce expansion of the skilled labor force. In this case along with the growth in the absolute differential, there would be a proportionate rise in the cost of education resulting from the inflation.

Thus, whether a widening of the absolute differential will lead to a narrowing of the percentage skill differential depends on the cause of the widening. If it results from the stimulation to wage increases associated with productivity gains, then this inverse relationship between the absolute and percentage skill differential would arise. But the absolute widening accompanying inflationary wage and price increases would have no effect on the demand for training and the consequent relative supply of skilled and unskilled labor.

Recent stability in the skill differential can be partly explained by a weakening of the narrowing forces. Immigration is at a low volume, but has been so for a long time and is no longer declining; equalitarian sentiment may have pushed down on the wage structure as far as it can against the resistance of market forces.

Changing labor demand may also play a part, as the "new technology" requires a highly trained work force. In fact, stability in the skill differential can be explained by the interaction of changing demand and technological growth. Past increases in productivity have tended to raise all wages, increase the rate of return on investment in training, increase the supply of skilled relative to unskilled labor and therefore tend to narrow relative wage differences. But increased demand for skilled workers would match the increase in supply, neutralizing the effect on the skill differential. But the rate of return on investment in training need not increase in the process even though absolute wage differentials have widened. The demand for education would rise not only in response to the forces accompanying improved productivity but also because of the expanded demand for skilled workers. Prices of educational goods and services would tend to rise as short-run bottlenecks appeared. This process would continue as long as technological advance was accompanied by a relative increase in demand for skilled workers strong enough to raise the cost of education.

### Cyclical Variations in the Skill Differential

Stability in the differential, at least until the mid-1960's, may also be explained on cyclical grounds. The economy had operated at a relatively high, but generally noninflationary, level for over a decade. In general, widening forces on the skill differential tend to be strong during noninflation, near full employment conditions. But the broad issue of the cyclical pattern of the skill differential, especially in its relation to wage flexibility needed to loosen structural stringencies will now be reviewed.

Reder presents a theory of cyclical variation in the skill differential based on employer options in varying hiring standards and wages. He envisions an occupational ladder, with movements up and down dependent on the state of labor demand. The theoretical section of his paper, presented here, deals with tight labor market conditions, but his theory can be applied to depression conditions as well.

# The Theory of Occupational Wage Differentials

## by M. W. Reder

Although data on occupational wage patterns are far from plentiful—and, at best, none too firm—there is a body of such material about which some theoretical speculation (and controversy) has arisen. This paper is an attempt to construct a theoretical model which can be used to interpret the existing data, and to clarify some of the points in dispute. Its first section deals with the structure of the model; the second section uses the model to explain temporal changes in American occupational wage differentials; the third deals with interregional and international differentials, while the fourth considers alternative arguments. Section V attempts to extend the analysis (previously confined to hourly wage differentials) to the differences in annual incomes that are associated with differences in skill.

## I. THEORETICAL CONSIDERATIONS

Economic theory has a ready-to-hand technique for analyzing the wage differentials associated with skill (hereafter called "skill differentials" or "skill margins"); i.e., treat workers of different grades of skill as representing different factors of production, and analyze the behavior of their relative wage rates by means of the theory of related (factor) markets. However, if not carefully used, this mode of analysis can be highly misleading because the wage rates paid for particular jobs are not analogous to factor prices. The skill and other characteristics of workers who apply for given jobs vary with the state of the labor market, and the wage rates paid on given jobs are therefore affected by "quality" variations in the job applicants. As the "quality" variable

SOURCE Reprinted with permission from *American Economic Review,* Vol. 65, December 1955, pp. 833–850.

has not been accorded much attention in wage theory, it will pay us to examine it with some care.

Quality variations in labor markets arise through upgrading and downgrading of members of the labor force relative to the jobs they are to fill. When applicants become scarce, employers tend to lower the minimum standards upon which they insist as a condition for hiring a worker to fill a particular job—and vice versa when applicants become plentiful.[1] These minimal hiring standards may be stated explicitly as age, sex, educational, racial and other prerequisites that must be satisfied as a precondition of hiring. Or they may be the consequence of the unarticulated habits and prejudices of persons responsible for hiring decisions. But whatever the degree of explicitness, minimum hiring (and firing) standards do exist for most jobs in modern industrial communities.

The prevalence of these hiring standards is so widespread as to make it difficult to find situations from which they are absent. Such situations can be found, but they are rare. Their scarcity can be appreciated if it is remembered that jobs without hiring requirements are, by definition, jobs for which selection is nonexistent (*i.e.*, all applicants are taken) or is made by a process unrelated to any social or economic characteristic of the applicants (*e.g.*, by lot). Jobs where selection among applicants is minimal tend to occur where there is no guarantee of minimum earnings and no capital to injure or destroy; *e.g.*, selling on a "straight commission" basis; piecework with no guarantee of minimum earnings and no equipment to damage.[2]

The ability to discriminate among job applicants on the basis of putative differ-

ences in quality implies that variations in relative scarcity of job applicants can be met by varying either (or both) of two determinants of hiring policy; *i.e.*, employers may adjust (1) wage rates; (2) hiring standards; or some combination of the two. There are a number of factors that affect the relative emphasis that a given employer will place upon these two factors. A brief survey of these will clear the ground for the succeeding argument:

1. The employer will be particularly concerned with maintaining hiring standards where there is danger of property loss from incompetent workmen, and the prospective amount of such loss is considerable, relative to the difference in wage cost (per unit of product) between superior and inferior workmen. For example, a processor of gem diamonds is not likely to risk using an inexperienced diamond cutter to save the additional expense of hiring one who is fully qualified. Or if very delicate machinery is to be used, an employer is likely to be insistent upon the workers being fully qualified, even if production must be delayed in order to recruit them. Conversely, among assembly line workers, employers frequently relax hiring standards to speed recruitment.

2. Where agreements among employers against "labor piracy" are operative, expansion of the firm's labor force will tend to be accomplished more by "quality deterioration" and less by wage increases than otherwise. Oligopsonistic agreements in restraint of labor market competition are rarely of a formal nature, but their operation is frequently reported and there is good reason why employers should adhere to them. For if an employer attempts

[1] One set of hiring standards, *A,* is said to be lower than another, *B,* if the job applicants meeting *A* include all who also meet *B,* as well as some who do not.

[2] L. H. Fisher, *The Harvest Labor Market in California* (Cambridge, Mass., 1953) gives an example of this type of situation. In California harvesting almost anybody is accepted for employment. However, they are paid a flat piece-rate per box with no guaranteed hourly minimum; as they use practically no equipment, there is no risk in having them work, and therefore the employer can profitably accept any and all comers, once the decision to begin harvesting has been taken.

to secure more workers in a "tight labor market by raising wages, competing employers are likely to match his increases. And, as knowledge of the wage increase is likely to reach rival employers before it reaches many prospective job applicants, it is unlikely to give the aggressive firm even a temporary advantage.

3. A third factor relates to wage discrimination.[3] If a firm should need additional workers of a particular grade (and cannot obtain them at the going wage rate), it may promote some of its own employees of a lower grade. Promoting workers—new or old—has one advantage over bidding up the wage rate; the increased compensation need be paid only to the promoted workers. But if a wage increase is granted to one worker, others doing similar work—and accustomed to similar rates—must, in practice, get similar increases.

A related advantage of adjusting "quality rather than price" is the greater ease of downgrading workers as compared with lowering wage rates. Shifting workers, reclassifying jobs, etc., are more or less continuous processes, and therefore not subject to the time-lag attendant upon changing contractual prices, i.e., union wage rates. Furthermore, although unions may and do protest against unfavorable job shifts, they are less prone to resist demotions which affect only a few workers at a time than wage cuts which give many workers a common grievance.

4. Frequently the quality of workers can be improved by training. The costs and yields of such training, relative to existing wage differentials between different grades of labor, are the important factors in determining an employer's choice as between raising wage rates and altering hiring standards.[4] Where needed skill can be acquired in a short period and the margin for skill is large, the tendency (ceteris paribus) will be to recruit by changing hiring standards; where the reverse is true, the tendency will be toward raising wage rates.

As workers, once trained, are under no obligation to remain with the employer who bore the cost of their training, employers will not usually invest in such training unless the prospective net gain (if any) from hiring an untrained instead of a trained worker can be realized very quickly. This means, in practice, that employers are reluctant to train workers if it involves a substantial out-of-pocket loss during the training period. Therefore, such training occurs mainly when labor is in such short supply and the demand for output so strong that even the slim marginal contribution of trainees to current output is worth almost as much as their current wage; i.e., such training tends to be concentrated in extreme booms.

In short, there are several important reasons why employers should sometimes prefer to adjust to changes in labor market conditions by altering worker quality[5] together with, or instead of, wage rates. However, both quality and price respond to labor market pressure; the rather notorious stickiness of wage rates is one indication of the importance of quality variation in the labor market.

Now let us examine the implications of

---

[3] I am indebted to my colleague, Tibor Scitovsky, for a discussion of this point.

[4] It should be noted that we speak of an employer's hiring standards with reference only to a particular job or job-type. This implies that promoting workers within the firm is regarded as *hiring* workers for the job to which they are being promoted.

[5] It is important that our use of the term "worker quality" should not be misunderstood. It is not implied, necessarily, that workers currently hired (but not hirable under previous standards) are inferior to those previously hired in any sense except that the employer would previously have rejected them. The *wisdom* of hiring policies—from the employer's own viewpoint—is, in many cases, questionable; hiring policies that involve arbitrary age, race, or sex criteria may not be conducive to profit maximization. Furthermore, one wonders whether investing in on-the-job training—and reducing skill differentials—might not be profitable even when labor is plentiful.

this fact for the behavior of skill margins. To do this let us study the behavior of the wage rates[6] paid to the holders of specific jobs. We assume employers aim at minimizing the total cost of producing their chosen rate of output by adjusting, among other things, the quality of the workers hired for, and the wage rates paid to workers on particular jobs. The wage rates paid (to the holders of particular jobs) will be the higher of (1) the market rate for workers with the characteristics necessary for getting hired and (2) the rate the firm negotiates with the relevant union.[7] Where (2) exceeds (1), the firm is said to have "labor slack" for the given job;[8] labor slack is manifested by the presence of more applicants who meet its hiring standards (for the given job) than it wishes to hire. As a result, a firm with labor slack is compelled to ration the relevant jobs on the basis of "first come, first hired," or in some other way that is of no concern to the *employer*.[9] For simplicity, we shall assume that all firms pay the same wage rate and have similar hiring requirements for similar jobs.[10]

Suppose there should be a general increase in demand for all grades of manual labor of such size that (with given wage rates and hiring standards) labor slack is eliminated from the market for every kind of job. Competition for workers able to meet current hiring standards on the most skilled jobs would then tend to raise their wage rates. However, there would be a brake upon this rise because some workers, previously unable to secure employment in the most highly skilled job categories, would be available at lower rates. Therefore, if the spread between the wage rates of the most skilled and those closest to them in skill should become too large, substitution would tend to occur.[11] This substitution would involve either (1) training the "inferior" workers or (2) altering the production process (and/or product) somewhat so as to facilitate the use of less skilled workers or some combination of the two.[12]

But whatever the process, the substitution of less for more skilled workers reduces (*ceteris paribus*) the supply of persons possessing specified minimum qualifications[13] who are available for jobs requiring less than the highest degree of

[6] By wage rates, we mean straight-time hourly earnings. We abstract from the effect of incentive systems, perquisites and nonpecuniary satisfactions.

[7] It sometimes happens that employers pursue a "generous" wage policy; *i.e.*, they pay a wage rate higher than (1) despite the absence of union pressure. We may treat such behavior as though it resulted from collective bargaining; the employer's conscience serves as the worker's bargaining agent.

[8] The most frequent occurrence of labor slack is where firms reserve jobs for their current holders without attempting to reduce wages, refusing new applicants as well qualified as those presently employed. Similar situations arise where workers, holding lower-paid jobs in a firm, wait for vacancies in better jobs for which they are as fully qualified as the present incumbents. Nevertheless, the reader should not suppose that the presence of labor slack is evidence of employer irrationality; labor slack is often an unavoidable incident in a long-run policy aimed at making a firm an attractive place to work.

[9] It is, of course, possible that the union may be vitally concerned with the method of job rationing adopted.

[10] This assumption is for convenience only. Another assumption, implicitly made, is the absence of monopsony power; this, too, is solely for convenience and could easily be dropped if and when necessary.

[11] This does not require that there be a great deal of worker mobility among firms. Much of this substitution may occur via intrafirm promotions, and the remainder by hiring some new job applicants at higher job grades than they had previously held.

[12] Where there is labor slack, this process of substitution is costless (requiring no adjustment whatever) and inhibits any rise in skilled wage rates.

[13] Including, where relevant, being in an appropriate place on a promotion list. For the sake of brevity, we assume that workers substituted "up the job hierarchy" have hitherto held less skilled jobs than those to which they have been promoted. In some cases this is contrary to fact; jobs sometimes command a premium because of tradition. However, the interrelation among skill and other attributes (education, sex, race, etc.) that are related to labor market premiums is so great as to make it reasonable to assume that a relaxation of hiring standards implies a sacrifice of skill.

skill. This would tend to raise the equilibrium rates paid on these jobs; however, it is possible to substitute less for more skilled workers on these jobs also. This, in turn, reduces the supply of workers holding still less skilled jobs, etc. Now if we assume what is often contrary to fact—full employment and a fixed size of labor force—it follows that the supply of labor for the least skilled jobs could not be increased by attracting those employed on still less attractive jobs (or unemployed). Hence employers wishing to use the cheapest grade of labor would have to scramble for a reduced supply, tending to drive up the wage rate.

It cannot be *deduced* from this consideration that, under the specified conditions, wage rates paid on the lowest grade of jobs would rise proportionately more than the rates on others. But if for other reasons we knew that this did occur, then the relatively greater reduction in the supply of workers available for these jobs would afford an important clue to the explanation of its occurrence. And as we shall see in Section II, skill margins have varied with labor demand in the manner indicated in those cases where the "labor reserve" had been absorbed. Accordingly, we offer the hypothesis that the association of short-period variations in skill margins with the level of aggregate employment is due to the fact that a rise in the level of employment for all grades of labor reduces the supply of labor available for unskilled jobs (at initial wage rates) proportionately more than it reduces the supply available for others. This hypothesis is presumed to hold only when labor demand increases sufficiently to absorb the labor reserve; the operational significance of this proviso will be indicated below.

It is not alleged that there is any particular pattern of variation among the wage rates for skilled and semiskilled jobs. It is alleged only that, under the conditions specified, rates on unskilled jobs are driven up relatively to those on semiskilled (which compete most keenly for labor with the unskilled jobs) and that this, in turn, results in a diminution in the spread between the rates on skilled and unskilled jobs.

But before accepting this hypothesis, it is necessary to consider the effects of unemployment and of a variable size of labor force. It is well known that the business sector of most economies usually possesses a labor reserve in the form of unemployed work-seekers, low-income farm youths, oldsters, juveniles, housewives, etc., who will accept jobs in the business or government sectors of the economy at going wage rates whenever such jobs are available. As the bulk of these persons are available for unskilled jobs, they serve as a replacement for the unskilled workers attracted to better jobs. Therefore, an increase in aggregate labor demand would not be expected to affect skill margins (as far as our hypothesis is concerned), unless the increase were more than sufficient to absorb the entire labor reserve at going wage rates. However, when such large increases do occur, within a short-period (*e.g.*, during both world wars), skill margins would be expected to contract—and they have.[14]

Now let us consider the implications of the labor reserve concept for wage theory. Allegation of the existence of a labor reserve immediately provokes the question, "Why doesn't the unskilled wage rate fall until the labor reserve's members either find employment or cease to desire it?" The answer lies in what we shall, for brevity, call SM (for social minimum). SM is the minimum (straight-time) hourly wage rate at which a business firm or government—as distinguished from a house-

---

[14] The reader should not suppose that the existence of a labor reserve is a special case of labor slack. The workers in the labor reserve may (although they need not) be inferior to those regularly employed.

hold or family farm—can hire an hour of labor. *SM* may be set by statute (*e.g.*, a minimum wage law), by social custom and/or by trade union policy. *SM* is also related, indirectly, to the assistance from social security, friends, family, etc., that a wage earner can obtain. However, when *SM* is not effectively set by statute or union policy, it becomes a very slippery concept. Therefore we shall treat *SM* as established by statute or effective union policy, although its bases are far more complicated than this assumption would suggest.

*SM* is often set higher for men than for women, for workers in the prime of life than for juveniles or aged workers; also, it tends to vary in the same direction as living costs. It is not an absolute minimum rate below which workers are never hired; rather it is a rate below which workers, especially adult males in the prime of life, are not hired by a business firm or government. However, households often hire servants, men and boys for odd jobs, etc., on whatever terms they can obtain them. Also travelers "hire" porters, etc., for tips; and on family farms, the members share in what the "enterprise" earns. Indeed, when there is substantial unemployment, the unemployed have frequently set themselves up as small entrepreneurs (*e.g.*, in garment-making and retail trade). They are able to pay their employees only on some sort of receipts-sharing basis; this implies little more than that wages will not be negative.

In the midst of large-scale unemployment, such attempts at self-help are not likely to be obstructed; but whether substantial businesses can exploit the existence of unemployment to reduce the wage rates they pay their workers below some minimum level depends upon social attitudes. For example, in early 19th century England (under the famous Speenhamland system), workers would frequently eke out a "surviving" by combining parish aid and wages. And, apparently, it was not then considered improper to hire labor that required public assistance in order to survive. But nowadays it would certainly be considered improper, when not illegal, to employ labor at a wage so low that it had to be supplemented by public assistance; and it would be illegal for workers to accept most forms of public assistance while employed. In short, we now have laws and mores that place a floor under the minimum wage rate that a worker need or will accept on a "steady job" with a business firm or government.

Outside the business and government sectors, there is really no effective minimum to wage rates, except reluctance to accept employment at still lower rates. Whether an unemployed worker accepts on offer of a "day's" casual employment depends upon (1) the relative importance of the earnings as compared with his leisure (and shame at working for too little) and (2) his expectation of finding a more attractive employment opportunity during the "day," if he keeps looking. Wage rates paid on odd jobs are rarely recorded; but, we suspect, they are subject to marked short-period fluctuations and considerable dispersion on any given day. In other words, unskilled wage rates have downward rigidity only in the business and government sectors; elsewhere, they are determined in a "classical" manner. Unemployment is, therefore, either voluntary or frictional. However, the frictions (*e.g.*, imperfect communication, intermittent demand, geographical immobility, etc.) that impede the operation of labor markets outside the business and government sectors are far greater than "classical" wage theory would suggest.

            ✿   ✿   ✿

Under full employment conditions, all labor "slack" is taken in. That is, for each occupation, there are no more applicants than the firm wants to hire, at going wages. For firms who wish to expand employment, there are the alternatives of lowering hiring standards, raising wages, or internal training. As standards are lowered along the skill ladder, those with lesser skills can now qualify for jobs just above their previous level. The ranks of the unskilled are filled by the "labor reserve." But as the prosperity swells into a boom the labor reserve becomes exhausted, shortages in unskilled work are aggravated more than for other jobs, which receive added workers as hiring standards are lowered and internal, on-the-job training is expanded. Thus, to the extent that lowered hiring standards and on-the-job training dampen wage increases for the skilled, and the absorption of the labor reserve pushes unskilled wages upward, the skill differential narrows.

Thus, Reder's theory, as he himself acknowledges, serves only to explain the tightening of the skill differential during boom conditions, when the "labor reserve" is completely absorbed into the work force. He considers that only the two World War periods had labor market conditions, with greatest shortages among the unskilled, which met the requirements of his hypothesis.

But what of other stages of the cycle? During the downturn the processes should move in reverse. Hiring standards tighten, training tapers off, and labor supply increases for the lesser skilled down to the lowest level of the unskilled; the labor reserve expands. Downward wage pressure is felt most on the unskilled jobs and the skill differential tends to widen. This phase of Reder's theory was substantiated by the widening of the differential in the short post-World War I depression. But Reder explains the failure of the differential to widen during the Great Depression of the 1930's as based on the pressures of nonmarket forces checking the downward movement of unskilled wages. The growth of industrial unionism, government minimum wage legislation, and general rise in equalitarian sentiment, raised the Social Minimum. To the extent that the differential failed to widen because of this rise in the Social Minimum, unemployment among the unskilled was increased even more than from the effects of the business slowdown alone.

An alternative explanation for the failure of the skill differential to widen during the depression would hold that with unemployment rising so rapidly and steeply for all occupations, each labor class tried to protect its employment levels by matching wage declines for competitive or substitutable labor. Thus, even with less excess supply of skilled workers, accepting Reder's explanation for this condition, the skilled would have matched the wage reduction of the unskilled even if the Social Minimum had not increased. The rise in the Social Minimum then would simply have reduced the need for further decreases in the skilled wage level. The fact that the skill differential did not narrow during this period, despite these forces, gives strength to Reder's hypothesis that the relative supply of unskilled labor increases during depressions.

Reder's theory does not describe the market forces on the differential during periods of "normal" prosperity with some slack in the overall labor market. These are the times, of which the period from the early 1950's to the 1960's was certainly an example, during which the presence of structural unemployment is most probable. Then, on balance, market forces have a neutral effect on the differential. There might be no slack in any occupation, but lowered hiring standards and intensified internal training that dulled wage advances among the skilled and lesser skilled, would be offset, insofar as effect on the skill differential is concerned, by inflow of workers from the Labor Reserve into the labor force. It should be noted that even though the flow of new workers into skilled jobs through rapid training and reduced hiring standards and into unskilled work from the Labor Reserve helps ease labor shortages, without wage increases, the process is still inflationary, because labor efficiency is reduced all along the line. In summary, with market forces having only a neutral effect on the skill differential during prosperous and not boom conditions, nonmarket steps such as a rise in the Social Minimum to narrow differentials would tend to create labor shortages for the skilled and surpluses for the unskilled, which are conditions of structural unemployment.

### Inflation and the Skill Differential

An alternative explanation of boom period narrowing of the skill differential holds that it is not the market force of relative increase in supply of skilled workers that compresses the occupational wage structure, but the tendency for wages of the unskilled to rise more than skilled wages as prices rise at very low unemployment levels. Among explanations for lowest wages to rise faster and higher than wages of those at the top of the skill ladder during inflationary periods are an increase in the Social Minimum expressed by increases in the minimum wage, and the stronger upward pressure on unskilled wages as rising prices threaten subsistence real incomes.

In the short statistical study that follows, Evans concludes that the narrowing of the skill differential is more closely associated with inflation than the tightness of the labor market, as Reder argues. Evans offers no theoretical hypothesis for his finding of the close inverse relationship between the skill differential and the price level during three wartime boom inflationary periods.

# Wage Differentials, Excess Demand for Labor, and Inflation: A Note

## by Robert Evans

Two alternative hypotheses have been used to explain the narrowing of the ratio of skilled to unskilled wage rates[1] during wartime periods in the United States. One relies on real forces, the other on monetary ones. This note seeks to provide one assessment of the relative ability of these hypotheses to account for the reduced margin to skill.

The excess demand for labor hypothesis states that in periods when labor is in short supply, employers dilute job standards, thereby increasing the supply of skilled labor and reducing the supply of unskilled, and that the supply of unskilled can either not be augmented by those not in the labor force or to do so would require a fairly large increase in the wages offered.[2]

The inflation hypothesis says that the wages of the lower paid are raised proportionately more than those of the higher paid on the equitable grounds of maintaining their standard of living.[3]

The years of the Civil War and the First and Second World Wars, the periods to

SOURCE Reprinted with permission from *Review of Economics and Statistics*, Vol. 45, February 1963, pp. 95–98.

[1] The particular portions of the distributions being compared may be important because it is possible that some, but not all, skill margins have changed. For example, if one computes the change in the skill ratio (using medians) for machinists and laborers in the North during the Civil War (calculated from the Aldrich report with firm 35 which hired 1,743 laborers reported in 1860 deleted), there is no apparent change, yet the dispersion of wages (75–25/50) for machinists goes from .099 to .200 and that of laborers from .125 to .277 indicating an increased skill margin for certain groups.

[2] Melvin W. Reder, "The Theory of Occupational Wage Differentials," *American Economic Review*, XLV (December 1955), 838–840.

[3] Wesley C. Mitchell, *A History of the Greenbacks* (Chicago, 1903), 303. See also Gerhard Bry, *Wages in Germany 1871–1945* (Princeton, 1960), 83–85.

which the hypotheses have been previously applied, were associated with declining skill differentials, short-run excess demand for labor, and relatively rapid price rises. For each as a whole, therefore, it is not possible to differentiate between the contending explanations. Yet, both imply that within the periods, years in which the larger changes in the skill differential occur should be characterized by the greater excess demand for labor or the more rapid rise in consumer price indexes.[4] Thus, it follows that simple rank order correlation between year-to-year changes is one appropriate test of the explanatory powers of the different hypotheses.

The skill margin for the Civil War is the ratio of skilled handicraftsmen to unskilled laborers as compiled by Mitchell, and for the World War periods it is the ratio of union wage scales of journeymen to those of laborers and helpers in the building trades. The measure of inflation is the consumer price index and since there is no similarly accepted measure of excess demand for labor, a number of variables, defined in Table 1, are used. The correlations in all cases, save one, are between percentage changes in the variables.

Table 1 presents the basic data for the First and Second World Wars; Table 2, the percentage changes; and Table 3, the rank order correlation coefficients. From Table 3 it is clear that changes in the cost of living provide, by far, the best explanation for the observed year-to-year changes in the skill ratio.

Turning to the Civil War (Table 4), it appears that the inflation hypothesis gives the best result, though it would be desirable if better data on the state of the labor market were available, for it is possible that real wages were chiefly affected by factors other than full employment.

Before accepting the inflation hypothesis, is is desirable to look more closely at the major years of war. This is because some of the years included were not characterized by anything near full employment, and Reder, when he presented the excess demand for labor hypothesis, stressed the need for tight labor market conditions.[5] Looking only at those years for the First and Second World Wars when unemployment was 4 per cent or lower (Table 5), it can be seen that there is a closer correspondence between rising prices and the decreasing skill margin than between the latter and the labor market variables. An alternative to this approach would be to look at the years in which major shifts in the skill margin occurred (Table 6). Again, the conclusion is the same.

In the same way one can examine the experience of the Civil War. Here the major movements in the skill margin are 1862–1863 and 1863–64. These are also the years of maximum prices increases. The decline in the skill ratio between 1862–1863 is probably also consistent with an excess demand for labor hypothesis, for it appears that these years saw a peak tightness in the labor market. This is not so true of 1863–64.[6]

Thus, on the basis of the evidence cited here, the rather strong conclusion is that in terms of aggregate movements, the course of inflation more readily explains the observed changes in the wage differential between skilled and unskilled in the three wartime periods, than does any measure of excess demand in the labor market.

[4] There may exist complex lagged relations which do not show up in the data.
[5] Reder, 842.
[6] Brother Basil Leo Lee FSC, *Discontent in New York City* (Washington, 1943), 203–211. These pages tell of the success of strikes by various workers in 1863 and 1864. Whereas most seem fairly successful in 1863, the same is not true of 1864.

TABLE 1. SKILL MARGINS AND INDICATORS OF EXCESS DEMAND FOR LABOR AND INFLATION IN TWO WARTIME PERIODS

| Year | Skill Margin [a] | Unemployment Rate [b] | Labor Loss Rate [c] | Ratio of Actual to Potential Labor Input [d] | Labor Force Participation Rate [e] | Money Compensation [f] | Real Compensation [g] | Consumer Price Index [h] |
|---|---|---|---|---|---|---|---|---|
| 1914 | 199 | 11.9 | .. | — .04 | .. | $ .220 | $ .616 | 35.7 |
| 1915 | 199 | 14.3 | .. | — 2.42 | .. | .226 | .626 | 36.1 |
| 1916 | 199 | 7.1 | .. | 3.51 | .. | .262 | .675 | 36.8 |
| 1917 | 191 | 7.0 | .. | 5.88 | .. | .316 | .693 | 45.6 |
| 1918 | 183 | 2.1 | .. | 9.24 | .. | .417 | .779 | 53.5 |
| 1919 | 180 | 3.4 | .. | 2.45 | .. | .477 | .774 | 61.6 |
| 1920 | 166 | 5.8 | .. | .88 | .. | .537 | .753 | 71.3 |
| 1921 | 168 | 16.9 | .. | — 1.41 | .. | .464 | .730 | 63.6 |
| 1939 | 170 | 23.8 | .92 | —13.89 | 56.0 [i] | .638 | 1.29 | 49.4 |
| 1940 | 169 | 20.2 | 1.17 | — 9.37 | 56.0 | .670 | 1.35 | 49.8 |
| 1941 | 167 | 13.3 | 2.32 | — .05 | 56.7 | .737 | 1.41 | 52.3 |
| 1942 | 160 | 6.3 | 4.25 | 10.10 | 58.8 | .864 | 1.49 | 58.0 |
| 1943 | 159 | 2.8 | 5.87 | 23.00 | 62.3 | .975 | 1.58 | 61.6 |
| 1944 | 158 | 1.6 | 5.8 | 24.59 | 63.1 | 1.050 | 1.68 | 62.6 |
| 1945 | 154 | 2.5 | 5.8 | 16.09 | 61.9 | 1.060 | 1.66 | 64.0 |
| 1946 | 147 | 5.3 | 4.8 | 1.11 | 57.2 | 1.130 | 1.63 | 69.4 |
| 1947 | 143 | 4.7 | 3.9 | — .35 | 57.4 | 1.300 | 1.64 | 79.5 |

[a] The skill margin is the ratio of union wage scales of journeymen and laborers and helpers in the building trades, from Harry Ober, "Occupational Wage Differentials, 1907–1947," *Monthly Labor Review*, LXVI (August 1948), 130.
[b] The unemployment rate is the per cent of non-farm employees fourteen years and older, from Stanley Lebergott, "Annual Estimates of Unemployment in the United States, 1900–1954," in *The Measurement and Behavior of Unemployment* (Princeton, 1957), 215–216.
[c] The labor loss rate is the annual average of the difference between monthly total separations and layoffs in manufacturing, from Donald Dewey, "Labor Turnover as an Index of Unemployment in the United States, 1919–1958," *Journal of Industrial Economics*, VIII (June 1960), 270.
[d] The ratio of actual to potential labor input is the ratio of actual man-hours divided by potential man-hours assuming a "normal" 4 per cent unemployment rate, from James W. Knowles, "The Potential Economic Growth in the United States," Study Paper 20 prepared in connection with the *Study of Employment, Growth and Price Levels* (Washington, 1960), 26–27.
[e] The labor force participation rate is the ratio of the total labor force as a per cent of the non-institutional population, from *Economic Report of the President, 1961* (Washington, 1961), 146.
[f] Money compensation is the sum of average money earnings and wage supplements for manufacturing, from Albert Rees, "Patterns of Wages, Prices and Productivity," in Charles A. Myers (ed.), *Wages, Profits and Productivity* (New York, 1959), 15–16.
[g] Real compensation is money compensation divided by the Consumer Price Index, 1957 = 100, from Rees, 15–16.
[h] Consumer Price Index, 1957 = 100, from Rees, 15–16.
[i] Estimated.

TABLE 2. PERCENTAGE CHANGES IN SKILL MARGINS AND INDICATORS OF EXCESS DEMAND FOR LABOR AND INFLATION IN TWO WARTIME PERIODS [a]

| Year | Skill Margin | Unemployment Rate | Labor Loss Rate | Ratio of Actual to Potential Labor Input | Labor Force Participation Rate | Real Compensation | Money Compensation | Consumer Price Index |
|---|---|---|---|---|---|---|---|---|
| 1914–15 | 0.00 | + 20.1 | ... | ... | ... | 1.6 | 2.7 | + 1.1 |
| 1915–16 | 0.00 | − 50.4 | ... | ... | ... | 7.8 | 15.9 | + 1.9 |
| 1916–17 | −4.10 | − 1.5 | ... | ... | ... | 2.6 | 20.6 | +23.9 |
| 1917–18 | −4.20 | + 70.0 | ... | ... | ... | 12.4 | 31.9 | +17.3 |
| 1918–19 | −1.70 | + 61.9 | ... | ... | ... | − .7 | 14.3 | +15.1 |
| 1919–20 | −7.80 | + 70.5 | ... | ... | ... | − 2.8 | 12.5 | −15.7 |
| 1920–21 | +1.20 | +191.3 | ... | ... | ... | − 3.1 | −13.6 | −10.2 |
| 1939–40 | − .4 | − 15.2 | +27.1 | ... | 0.0 | 4.6 | 5.0 | 1.8 |
| 1940–41 | −1.2 | − 34.2 | +98.2 | ... | 1.2 | 4.4 | 10.0 | 5.0 |
| 1941–42 | −4.2 | − 52.7 | +83.1 | ... | 3.7 | 5.6 | 17.2 | 10.8 |
| 1942–43 | − .7 | − 63.6 | +38.1 | ... | 5.9 | 7.4 | 12.8 | 6.2 |
| 1943–44 | − .7 | − 42.9 | − 1.2 | ... | 1.2 | 6.3 | 7.6 | 1.6 |
| 1944–45 | −2.6 | + 56.2 | 0.0 | ... | −2.0 | − 1.2 | .9 | 2.2 |
| 1945–46 | −4.6 | +112.0 | −17.3 | ... | −7.6 | − 1.9 | 6.6 | 8.4 |
| 1946–47 | −2.8 | − 11.4 | −18.8 | ... | + .3 | + .6 | 15.0 | 14.5 |

[a] Calculated from data in Table 1.

TABLE 3. RANK ORDER CORRELATION COEFFICIENTS BETWEEN PERCENTAGE YEAR-TO-YEAR CHANGES IN THE VARIABLES

| Test | $r$ [a] 1914–1921 | 1939–1947 |
|---|---|---|
| Skill Margin and Unemployment | .11 | −.40 |
| Skill Margin and Labor Loss | . . | −.11 |
| Skill Margin and Ratio of Actual to Potential Labor Input [a] | .24 | −.14 |
| Skill Margin and Labor Force Participation Rate | . . | −.22 |
| Skill Margin and Real Compensation | .24 | −.57 |
| Skill Margin and Money Compensation | .57 | .31 |
| Skill Margin and Consumer Price Index | .85 | .78 |
| Significance Levels    5 per cent | .714 | .643 |
| 1 per cent | .893 | .833 |

[a] Based on percentage change in skill margin and absolute change in the ratio of inputs.

TABLE 4. SKILL MARGINS, INDICATORS OF EXCESS DEMAND AND INFLATION DURING THE CIVIL WAR

| | Skill Margin [a] | % Change Skill Margin | Consumer Price Index [b] | % Change in Consumer Price Index | Real Wage [c] | % Change in Real Wages |
|---|---|---|---|---|---|---|
| 1860 | 166 | . . | 100 | . . | 100 | . . |
| 1861 | 171 | +3.0 | 101 | 1.0 | 100 | 0 |
| 1862 | 170 | − .6 | 114 | 12.8 | 90 | −10.0 |
| 1863 | 156 | −8.3 | 140 | 22.8 | 84 | − 6.7 |
| 1864 | 147 | −5.8 | 177 | 26.4 | 78 | − 7.2 |
| 1865 | 150 | +2.0 | 176 | − .6 | 87 | +11.5 |
| 1866 | 153 | +2.0 | 168 | − 4.6 | 97 | +11.4 |

Rank order correlation
Skill and Prices (Per Cent) .758
Skill and Real Wages (Per cent) −.55

5 Per cent Level of Significance .829
1 Per cent Level of Significance .943

[a] Ratio of skilled handicraftsmen to unskilled laborers; Table XXVI, from Wesley Clair Mitchell, *A History of the Greenbacks* (Chicago, 1903), 301.
[b] Cost of living, 1860 = 100, from Clarence D. Long, *Wages and Earnings in the United States, 1860–1890* (Princeton, 1960), 156.
[c] Real wages are money wages, Mitchell, 310, divided by the Consumer Price Index.

TABLE 5.   PERCENTAGE CHANGES IN EXCESS VARIABLES AND INFLATION [a]
(YEARS OF 4 PER CENT UNEMPLOYMENT)

| Year | Skill Margin | Unemployment Rate | Labor Loss Rate | Ratio of Actual to Potential Labor Input | Labor Force Participation Rate | Real Compensation | Money Compensation | Consumer Price Index |
|---|---|---|---|---|---|---|---|---|
| 1917–18 | −4.20 | − 70.0 | ... | ... | ... | +12.4 | +31.9 | +17.3 |
| 1918–19 | −1.70 | + 61.9 | ... | ... | ... | − .7 | +14.3 | +15.1 |
| 1919–20 | −7.80 | + 70.5 | ... | ... | ... | − 2.8 | +12.5 | +15.7 |
| 1942–43 | − .7 | − 63.6 | +38.1 | ... | +5.9 | + 7.4 | +12.8 | + 6.2 |
| 1943–44 | − .7 | − 42.9 | − 1.2 | ... | +1.2 | + 6.3 | + 7.6 | + 1.6 |
| 1944–45 | −2.6 | + 56.0 | 0.0 | ... | −2.0 | − 1.2 | + .9 | + 2.2 |
| 1945–46 | −4.6 | +112.0 | −17.3 | ... | −7.6 | − 1.9 | + 6.6 | + 8.4 |

[a] Taken from Table 2.

TABLE 6.   PERCENTAGE CHANGES IN EXCESS DEMAND AND INFLATION IN YEARS OF MAJOR DECLINES IN THE SKILL MARGIN [a]

| Year | Skill Margin | Unemployment Rate | Labor Loss Rate | Labor Force Participation Rate | Real Compensation | Money Compensation | Consumer Price Index |
|---|---|---|---|---|---|---|---|
| 1916–17 | −4.10 | − 1.5 | ... | ... | + 2.6 | 20.6 | +23.9 |
| 1917–18 | −4.20 | − 70.0 | ... | ... | +12.4 | 31.9 | +17.3 |
| 1919–20 | −7.80 | + 70.5 | ... | ... | − 2.8 | 12.5 | +15.7 |
| 1941–42 | −4.2 | − 52.7 | +83.1 | +3.7 | + 5.6 | +17.2 | +10.8 |
| 1944–45 | −2.6 | + 56.2 | 0.0 | −2.0 | − 1.2 | + .9 | + 2.2 |
| 1945–46 | −4.6 | +112.0 | −17.3 | −7.6 | − 1.9 | + 6.6 | + 8.4 |
| 1946–47 | −2.8 | − 11.4 | −18.8 | + .3 | + .6 | +15.0 | +14.5 |

[a] Taken from Table 2.

Although Evans finds a higher correlation between rising prices than falling unemployment with the skill differential, his method does not actually refute Reder's hypothesis. Reder merely argued that labor supply changes would exert stronger upward force on unskilled than on skilled wages during periods of very low unemployment. Thus, even if overall demand slackened somewhat and unemployment rose slightly but remained at a low level, the correlation between unemployment changes and the skill differential would loosen, but there would still be sufficient overall labor market tightness to support Reder's hypothesis.

The issue of the cause of the narrowing of the skill differential during boom periods may not be important because if institutional rather than market forces were at work, there would simply be a greater shortage of skilled than unskilled labor, but probably no structural unemployment. However, in below boom prosperous conditions with the overall unemployment rate above frictional levels, if the skill differential narrowed because of nonmarket forces (say, a rise in the Social Minimum), in response to the inflation that accompanied the relatively low unemployment rates, labor market imbalance would aggravate the inflation.

There have been two inflationary periods in one decade, during 1955–1958 and starting in 1966, at less than boom conditions. In the first period, the skill differential did not narrow. Data are not yet available for the current inflation. But if the differential narrowed because of the general price increase, then relative wage movements would have reduced demand for the unskilled, raised it for the skilled, and created a situation of structural unemployment that would require further inflation to reduce. The path to full employment would have been obstructed by relative wage movements unrelated to labor market demand and supply movements.

Recently, it has become evident that at our comparatively low unemployment levels there is a shortage of trained (skilled) workers and above-frictional unemployment among the unskilled. If relative wages widened, full employment might be more closely approached, albeit in an inflationary manner if the widening takes the form of a greater increase in wages for the workers in short supply than in wage declines for the unskilled. But if nonmarket upward wage pressure tends to raise the wages of the unskilled despite the market signal calling for a relative decline, full employment can only be approached with strongly rising prices, which in themselves lead to relative wage changes that make the goal still more difficult to attain.

### A Human Capital Explanation of the Cyclical Skill Differential

In another theory of cyclical movements of the skill differential, Walter Oi agrees with Reder that market forces will tend to narrow the occupational wage structure in the prosperity phase and widen it during the downswing, but the reasoning that leads him to this same conclusion is quite different. While Reder's theory is based on differential shifts in supply as the economy weakens and strengthens, Oi, in the sections of his paper included here, develops a theory based on cyclical differences in relative labor demand.

# Labor as a Quasi-Fixed Factor

*by Walter Oi*

## I. A SHORT-RUN
## THEORY OF EMPLOYMENT

According to the theory presented here cyclical changes in employment are explained by differential shifts in factor demands and supplies. The first two sections develop a theory of factor demands assuming rigid wage rates. In the next two sections this assumption is relaxed, allowing for variations in factor supplies.

### A. *Nature of the Classical*
### *Short-Run Adjustment Process*

In the classical short-run model certain paths of adjustment are barred to the firm. These barriers usually postulate the presence of fixed factors, short-run changes in output being effected by varying only the remaining factors.

Changes in the amount demanded of any factor are composed of two parts: (*a*) response to changes in the rate of output—the scale effect—and (*b*) response to variations in relative factor prices—the substitution effect. With an assumption of rigid wage rates, the substitution effects may be neglected and attention focused on the scale effects.

Consider a firm faced by a decline in product demand. The adjustment process involves a reduction in output accompanied by a decline in the demand for each variable factor. There is no reason to expect that the demands for all variable factors will be decreased by the same proportion. The reduced demands for variable factors led to an increase in the relative employment of fixed factors. In a sense, the firm now employs too much of the fixed factors and would, therefore, try to substitute fixed factors for variable

SOURCE Reprinted with permission from *Journal of Political Economy,* Vol. 70, December 1962, pp. 538–555.

457

factors. Consequently, those variable factors that tend to be most substitutable for, or least complementary with, the fixed factors will experience the greatest relative declines in demand due to any given decrease in product demand. The converse holds for an increase in product demand. Thus the variable factors that are most substitutable with the fixed factors will exhibit the greatest relative shifts in factor demands.

## B. Demand for a Quasi-Fixed Factor of Production

A quasi-fixed factor is defined as one whose total employment cost is partially variable and partially fixed. In the classical short-run model all factors are classified as either variable or fixed. Each factor may, however, possess a different degree of fixity along some continuum rather than lie at one extreme or the other.

From a firm's viewpoint labor is surely a quasi-fixed factor. The largest part of total labor costs is the variable-wages bill representing payments for a flow of productive services. In addition the firm ordinarily incurs certain fixed employment costs in hiring a specific stock of workers. These fixed employment costs constitute an investment by the firm in its labor force. As such, they introduce an element of capital in the use of labor. Decisions regarding the labor input can no longer be based solely on the current relation between wages and marginal value products but must also take cognizance of the future course of these quantities. The theoretical implications of labor's fixity will be analyzed before turning to the empirical magnitude of these fixed costs.

For analytic purposes fixed employment costs can be separated into two categories called, for convenience, hiring and training costs. Hiring costs are defined as those costs that have no effect on a worker's productivity and include outlays for recruiting, for processing payroll records, and for supplements such as unemployment compensation. These costs are closely related to the number of new workers and only indirectly related to the flow of labor's services. Training expenses, on the other hand, are investments in the human agent, specifically designed to improve a worker's productivity. The effect of training on productivity could be summarized by a production function showing the increment to a worker's marginal value product in the $t$th period, $\Delta M_t$, due to an investment in training of $K$ dollars per worker.[1]

$$\Delta M_t = g(K) . \qquad (1)$$

The total discounted cost, $C$, of hiring an additional worker is the sum of the present value of expected wage payments, the hiring cost, $H$, and training expense, $K$.

$$C = \sum_{t=0}^{T} W_t(1+r)^{-t} + H + K, \qquad (2)$$

where $W_t$ is the expected wage in the $t$th period, $r$ denotes the rate at which future costs are discounted, and $T$ denotes the expected period of employment. The total discounted revenue $Y$, generated by the additional worker is similarly defined as the present value of his expected marginal value products that, in each period, consist of his marginal product without training, $M_t$, and the increment due to his training, $\Delta M_t$.

$$Y = \sum_{t=0}^{T} (M_t + \Delta M_t)(1+r)^{-t} . \qquad (3)$$

Profits will be maximized when the total discounted cost of an additional worker is just equal to the total discounted revenue.

[1] The training activity typically entails direct money outlays as well as numerous implicit costs such as the allocation of old workers to teaching skills and rejection of unqualified workers during the training period.

$$H + K = \sum_{t=0}^{T} (M_t + \Delta M_t - W_t)$$
$$\times (1+r)^{-t}. \tag{4}$$

Equation (4) yields the first implication. In equilibrium a worker's total marginal product, $M_t + \Delta M_t$, must exceed the wage rate, $W_t$, so long as the firm incurs any fixed employment costs. Even under perfect competition wages would be equated to marginal value products if and only if labor is a completely variable factor.

At this point, a digression on the firm's investment in training is in order. The net value of training to the firm is simply the present value of the expected increment in marginal value product, $\Delta M_t$, due to training.

$$V = \sum_{t=0}^{T} \Delta M_t (1+r)^{-t}. \tag{5}$$

An investment in training will prove profitable if the net value to the firm, $V$, exceeds the training expense, $K$. Conceptually training may be categorized as either general or specific. Specific training is defined as that which increases a worker's productivity to a particular firm without affecting his productivity in alternative employments. The time required to adapt workers to the firm's particular production processes, or to its accounting and marketing processes, exemplifies specific training. General training, on the other hand, is defined as that which increases a worker's productivity in several competing employments, as, for example, the training of workers to operate computers or to read railroad tariffs.

Rational behavior implies that the bulk of a firm's investment in training must be devoted to specific training. If train-ing were completely general, all returns would accrue to the worker and none to the firm. Upon completion of general training, the worker would find that his marginal productivity to several firms has been increased. He could now demand a higher wage, either from a competing firm or from his present employer. In either case, the net value of the training to the firm would be reduced to zero. Indeed, a firm could capture these returns only if there were impediments to competition such as imperfect knowledge or binding labor contracts. Thus, no rational firm would underwrite completely general training.[2] If, however, training is specific to a firm, then the worker's alternative marginal product remains unaffected. In this latter case, the firm could weigh the expected returns from this investment against the training cost. To simplify the analysis, I shall assume that the firm bears all specific training costs. As will be shown in section D below, the implications of the theory are not seriously affected by relaxing this assumption.

Returning to the equilibrium condition, it is clear that some expectations model must be formulated since the variables refer to future quantities. Suppose that the firm formulates the following single-valued expectations:

$$W_t = W^*, \; M_t = M^*, \Delta M_t = \Delta M^*$$
$$\text{(for all } t = 0, 1, 2, \ldots T) . \tag{6}$$

Substituting these expected values into equation (4), the equilibrium condition reduces to

$$M^* + \Delta M^* = W^* + \frac{H+K}{\displaystyle\sum_{t=0}^{T}(1+r)^{-t}} . \tag{7}$$

[2] That a firm offers general training to its employees does not necessarily imply that the firm underwrites the general training expense. The worker may bear the training cost by accepting a lower wage than that which he could obtain in some alternative employment.

The concept of a periodic rent, $R$, may be defined as

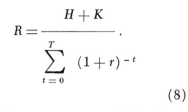

$$R = \frac{H + K}{\displaystyle\sum_{t=0}^{T} (1+r)^{-t}} . \qquad (8)$$

The periodic rent represents the fixed employment costs during each period. It is the surplus that must be earned by each worker in order to amortize the initial fixed employment costs over the expected period of employment, realizing a rate of return of $r$ per cent on this investment. Thus, the equilibrium condition may be rewritten as

$$M^* + \Delta M^* = W^* + R . \qquad (9)$$

In equilibrium, the total expected marginal value product must exceed the expected wage rate by the amount of the periodic rent. The degree of fixity, $f$, of a factor will be defined as the ratio of the periodic rent, $R$, to the total employment cost, $W^* + R$. A value of zero corresponds to a completely variable factor while the degree of fixity, $f$, of a completely fixed factor is designated by a value of unity.

The periodic rent drives a wedge between the wage rate and the marginal value product, the relative magnitude of the wedge being measured by the degree of fixity. In the short run, any fixed employment costs associated with the acquisition of a labor force in prior periods are sunk costs; as such they should not affect a firm's short-run decisions.

Suppose that the firm is initially in a position of long-run equilibrium; that is, the equilibrium condition, equation (9), is satisfied by every factor or grade of labor. For a competitive firm, a decline in product demand is equivalent to a fall in product price, $P^*$.[3] The relevant comparison for short-run profit maximization is that between total expected marginal value product and the expected wage rate, representing the variable component of the total employment cost. Thus the short-run equilibrium condition applicable to cyclical declines in product demands becomes

$$M^* + \Delta M^* = W^* . \qquad (10)$$

The employment of a quasi-fixed factor will only be reduced when $M^* + \Delta M^*$ falls below $W^*$.

For a completely variable factor, the long- and short-run equilibrium conditions, (9) and (10), are equivalent. Any decline in $P^*$ will reduce the demand for a variable factor; with falling employment, the variable factor's marginal physical product will be increased until the equilibrium conditions are again satisfied. The decline in $P^*$ may not be sufficient, however, to warrant a reduction in the demand for some other factor with a higher degree of fixity. In fact, there is, for each quasi-fixed factor, a critical price at which the firm will reduce its demand for that factor. Furthermore, the critical price, in relation to the long-run equilibrium price, will be lower for factors with higher degrees of fixity. Thus, a given decline in $P^*$ may induce a reduction in demand for factors with low degrees of fixity without affecting the demand for factors with higher degrees of fixity.

Consider next, the case of an increase in $P^*$. Beginning at an initial position of long-run equilibrium, there is no reason to expect differential shifts in demand for factors with varying degrees of fixity. Alternatively, in the initial position, the firm may have adjusted to a prior decline in $P^*$. Specifically, assume that the short-run equilibrium condition, (10), is satisfied by each quasi-fixed factor. The de-

[3] The term, $M^* + \Delta M^*$, in eq. (9) denotes the expected marginal value product. For a competitive firm, this is simply the expected product price, $P^*$, times the expected marginal physical product, $X^* + \Delta X^*$.

mand for a factor will be increased if its total marginal product, $M^* + \Delta M^*$, exceeds its total expected employment cost, $W^* + R$. In this latter case, the argument is completely analogous to that for a decline in $P^*$. Each quasi-fixed factor again has its unique critical price at which the demand for it will be increased; these critical prices will be higher for factors with greater degrees of fixity. Thus, a given increase in $P^*$ leads to greater relative shifts in demand for the factors with the lower degrees of fixity.

Up to now, changes in $P^*$ have been treated as if they were known with certainty. The introduction of uncertainty about future product prices reinforces the argument. Suppose that a firm makes appropriate adjustments in factor employments in response to an increase in $P^*$. If the subsequent increase in actual product prices is less than the expected increase, the firm will be obliged to reduce employment. The readjustment due to an error in forecasting product demand necessarily shortens the expected period of employment, thereby increasing the magnitude of the ex post periodic rent.[4] The costs of these readjustments are greater for factors with higher degrees of fixity since the periodic rent comprises a larger share of the total employment costs for these factors. Conversely, consider the case where a reduction in the quantity employed of some factor is greater than that warranted by the subsequent decline in actual prices. The readjustment in this case involves the reemployment of that factor, with additional outlays for hiring and training. One might argue that the firm will simply recall those workers who were previously laid off, thereby avoiding the hiring and training expenses. The Bureau of Labor Statistics data on accessions for the period 1953–58 reveal that only 39 per cent of total accessions in the manufacturing sector were recalls. Even in this case, readjustments are costlier for factors with higher degrees of fixity since the firm cannot be assured that workers who were laid off will be available for recall. If a readjustment in factor employments is required by the subsequent course of actual prices, it will be preferable to make these readjustments in the employment of factors with low degrees of fixity. Such a policy will tend to minimize the costs of readjustments (reversals) in factor employments due to discrepancies between actual and expected product prices.[5]

In summary, certain fixed employment costs are associated with the employment of labor. Firms may invest in hiring—to acquire particular workers—or in specific training to improve labor's productivity. The periodic rent, representing the amortization of these fixed employment costs, drives a wedge between the marginal value product and the wage rate. The relative magnitude of this wedge, measured by the degree of fixity, differs among occupations or grades of labor. In a sense, the periodic rent forms a buffer absorbing short-run variations in a factor's marginal value product. Thus, short-run changes in product demands lead to differential shifts in factor demands, depending on the degree of fixity. Factors with lower degrees of fixity will experience relatively greater shifts in demand as the result of any given short-run change in product demand.

\* \* \*

---

[4] A reduction in the expected period of employment, $T$, increases the periodic rent, $R$, since the initial fixed employment cost of $H + K$ dollars must be amortized over a smaller number of periods. From equation (8), the elasticity of $R$ with respect to $T$ is found to be negative, independent of $H + K$, and less than one in absolute value.

[5] The case where the readjustment involves no reversal in the direction of change in factor employments has not been discussed. This is the case where an increase (or decrease) in employment is less than that warranted by the actual price change. There is no a priori reason why this type of error should lead to differential costs for factors with different degrees of fixity.

## III. ALTERNATIVE HYPOTHESES

In this paper certain aspects of the cyclical behavior of labor markets have been explained by the fixed-cost hypothesis. What are the alternative hypotheses that offer explanations for the same phenomena? The theory that changes in factor employments are due to variations in relative wage rates was considered in subsection IC. This theory was dismissed because it implied changes in factor employments that were contrary to the observed changes.

Another theory is contained in the Reder model.[6] Although Reder's theory is primarily addressed to occupational wage differentials, it implies systematic changes in factor employments. According to Reder, firms adjust to a downswing by raising hiring standards. As a result the average quality of workers in each skill category is improved. The higher standards displace some workers from each skill category. Some of the displaced workers in the higher skill categories are downgraded to lower skill jobs, creating even further displacement of workers in these lower skill categories. The successive bumping effect sifts down through the skill hierarchy of jobs and results in relatively greater unemployment in the low-skill categories. In the upswing, firms adjust by relaxing hiring standards and upgrading workers to higher skill jobs. It is never explicitly stated, but Reder seems to assume that all factor demands shift proportionally. If this interpretation of Reder is correct, there is nothing in his theory that implies differential shifts in employment. The theory is, however, consistent with the emergence of differential unemployment rates since unemployed workers would be classified by their previous occupational status.

There are two possible ways in which differential shifts in employment could be deduced from Reder's theory. First, workers in high-skill jobs could perform the tasks of low-skill jobs while retaining their old job titles. This would appear to be highly unlikely. A second possibility is that hiring standards for high-skill jobs are advanced less than those for low-skill jobs. The elusive nature of hiring standards makes it difficult to test the latter possibility.

As a theory of the cyclical behavior of occupational wage differentials, Reder's theory has an intuitive appeal.[7] If the theory were stated formally, I believe that its basic behavioral relation could be put as follows: the relative rate of change in the wage rate of an occupation, $\Delta W / W$, is proportional to the relative excess demand for or supply of that grade of labor. Algebraically, it may be written:

$$\frac{\Delta W}{W} = k \left( \frac{D - S}{S} \right) \qquad (17)$$

where $k$ is a constant and $D$ and $S$ denote the amounts demanded and supplied of some grade of labor.

In the Reder model the cyclical adjustments involving the upgrading and downgrading of workers generate differential shifts in $S$ for different occupations. In a downswing, the downgrading of workers creates larger excess supplies (in absolute values) in the lower skill jobs. If the same $k$ applies for all occupations—and this must be assumed—the differences in excess supply imply relatively larger declines in the wage rates of low-skill jobs. The fixed-cost hypothesis would also predict a widening of occupational wage differentials in a downswing and a narrowing in the upswing if the behavioral relation (17) holds. Unlike the Reder model, the

[6] M. W. Reder, "The Theory of Occupational Wage Differentials," *American Economic Review*, XLV, No. 5 (December, 1955), 833–52, see esp. pp. 833–40.

[7] Reynolds agrees with Reder's explanation of the cyclical behavior of occupational wage differentials; see L. G. Reynolds and C. B. Taft, *The Evolution of Wage Structure* (New Haven, Conn.: Yale University Press, 1956), p. 364.

fixed-cost hypothesis involves differential shifts in $D$. The advantage of the latter explanation over Reder's theory is that it can simultaneously explain the cyclical behavior of occupational wage differentials and of relative factor employments.

## IV. CONCLUDING REMARKS

The central theme of this paper has been the treatment of labor as a quasi-fixed factor. This concept of labor was suggested by J. M. Clark, who dealt primarily with the social cost of unemployment.[8] The theory of the demand for a quasi-fixed factor generated implications regarding the short-run behavior of labor markets. Differences in the degree of fixity for different occupations imply (1) differential short-run shifts in employment, (2) differences in labor turnover rates, (3) emergence of differential unemployment rates in the cycle, and (4) cyclical variations in relative wage rates. The implications of the fixed-cost hypothesis are, in the main, borne out by the data examined.

The theory of labor as a quasi-fixed factor may also help to explain other phenomena. It is sometimes argued that a firm will maintain its labor force even though the wage rate exceeds the current marginal value product. If the labor has a high degree of fixity, it is to the firm's advantage to maintain its labor force rather than to risk high replacement demands in future periods. Fixed employment costs could also account for a range in indeterminacy in wages frequently mentioned in the literature.[9] In the short run, the specificity of labor to a firm places an upper limit on the wage rate equal to labor's total marginal product; the lower limit is determined by labor's alternative marginal product. Under collective bargaining a short-run wage rate could be set and maintained anywhere within this range.[10]

The classical treatment of labor as a completely variable factor may be adequate for a long-run analysis. To explain the short-run behavior of labor markets, I believe that labor should be viewed as a quasi-fixed factor of production.

Oi points out that, in addition to the wage, there is a fixed labor cost for each worker consisting of his hiring and training costs. Thus, under long-run conditions, the employer reaches an equilibrium position when the marginal value product, including the incremental return resulting from further training undertaken at the company's expense, equals the wage rate plus the fixed employment costs per time period (Equation 9 in his paper.)

For the unskilled worker, there are no incremental returns ($\triangle M$) from training nor are there any training costs ($K$). If hiring costs can be considered as negligible for these workers, then the conventional competitive theory under which the firm in equilibrium equates the marginal value product of the last workers with the wage applies. But for those workers who undergo company training, a degree of fixity enters wage costs and, as Oi expresses it in successive pages, in the section included here, "the periodic rent [the fixed cost element per time period allowing for a competitive return on hiring and training investment costs] drives a wedge between the wage rate and the marginal value product."

[8] *Studies in the Economics of Overhead Costs* (Chicago: University of Chicago Press, 1923), pp. 357–85.

[9] Reynolds and Taft, *op. cit.*, p. 1.

[10] The range of indeterminacy will be wider for factors (grades of labor) with higher degrees of fixity. This range is, however, a short-run phenomenon. The firm would not continue to invest in specific training unless it could recoup the benefits.

In the short run of a cycle, labor is retained if its marginal value product equals its variable cost element, the wage. Since in long-run equilibrium it is greater than the wage, by the amount of the periodic rent, demand and product price must fall somewhat before the firm would lay off a (trained or skilled) worker. Layoffs of the unskilled would begin from an equilibrium position, as soon as the product price and, consequently, the marginal value product started to fall.

The reverse would be true in the expansion phase. Before a firm would hire and, more importantly, train a worker for specialized skills, the expected marginal value product per time period would have to rise above the wage rate by the amount needed to cover the fixed hiring and training costs per time period. Thus the demand for workers who would receive additional company training would increase more slowly than that for unskilled labor as product price rose in the upswing.

In summary, Oi's theory explains why the demand and employment of skilled labor is cyclically less volatile than that for unskilled labor. It is an easy step from an explanation of relative employment changes to that of the behavior of the skill differential. With demand for skilled workers relatively strong in the downswing and weak in the upswing, compared with the unskilled, the skill differential would tend to widen when the economy was weak and to narrow when it was strong.

Oi claims superiority of his hypothesis over Reder's in that it accounts for both relative wage and employment changes, while Reder's theory does not explain the greater cyclical stability of skilled employment that the economy experiences.

But neither theory can account for the fact that after about 1950 the wage differential remained steady during a long period of relative prosperity. With reference to Reder's theory, to repeat, perhaps despite upgrading, quick training, and relaxation of hiring standards, tightness appeared in the skilled labor categories while the economy has not been tight enough to absorb the entire labor reserve, the source of additional unskilled labor.

As for Oi's theory, it should be emphasized that he presents in general an explanation of relative employment changes and only indirectly and inferentially an account of relative wage movements. Although employment of the unskilled may rise faster and further than that of the skilled during the mild prosperity phases of our recent low-amplitude cycles, available supplies of the skilled may still be strained more than those for the unskilled. Assuming non-linearity of wage pressures as labor markets tighten, or specifically to argue, as Lipsey did, that these pressures accelerate when employment is increased by cutting into the frictionally unemployed for labor classes in short supply, although employment of the skilled may have risen less than for the unskilled, market forces would tend to widen the skill differential. This version of the "bottleneck" argument receives substantiation from the fact that in some recessionary years in the 1950's, employment in several skilled classes actually increased. Oi's hypothesis only holds that employment of skilled workers during recession would not fall as much for the unskilled, not that it would actually rise. The increase during bad economic years suggests that in good years, even if the rise in demand for skilled workers was relatively slight, it was partially unfulfilled. All this indicates that efforts to narrow the skill differential, reflections of the rise in the Social Minimum, have perhaps neutralized the widening market forces, leading to a stable differential, aggravating or hardening structural elements, and strengthening the inflationary aspects of measures to approach full employment.


## Related Readings

Two well-known Labor Department studies, Harry Ober, "Occupational Wage Differentials, 1907–1947" (*Monthly Labor Review*, Vol. 71, August 1948, pp. 127–134), and Toivo Kanninen, "Occupational Wage Relationships in Manufacturing" (Ibid., Vol. 76, November 1953, pp. 1171–1178), trace the narrowing of the skill differential over the first half of this century. Philip Bell, "Cyclical Variation and Trends in Occupational Wage Differences in American Industry" (*Review of Economics and Statistics*, Vol. 33, November 1951, pp. 329–337), found, contrary to theoretical expectation, that the differential did not widen during the downswing of the Great Depression, 1929–1933.

Many more recent studies have found a tendency for the differential to stabilize since the early 1950's. Donald J. Blackmore, "Occupational Wage Relationships in Metropolitan Areas, 1961–1962" (*Monthly Labor Review*, Vol. 86, December 1963), using the same measurement technique as in the earlier studies, found constancy in the skill differential over the 1953–1962 decade. Using a slightly different statistical method, Martin Segal, "Occupational Wage Differentials in Major Cities During the 1950's" (*Human Resources in the Urban Economy*, Mark Perlman, Ed., Johns Hopkins Press, 1963, pp. 195–207), found the same stability over the same period, but at a higher ratio of skilled to unskilled wages. For a slightly longer period, 1952–1964, George H. Hildebrand and George E. Delehanty, "Wage Levels and Differentials" (*Prosperity and Unemployment*, Robert A. Gordon and Margaret S. Gordon, Eds., Wiley, 1966), considered that there was a narrowing trend in the differential because the skill wage ratio had fallen in a majority of the metropolitan areas studied. But the differential remained unchanged as measured by the average movement, the method of measurement used in the other studies.

Foreign data reveal the same pattern of stability. H. Günter, "Changes in Occupational Wage Differentials" (*International Labour Review*, Vol. 89, February 1964, pp. 136–155), found no recent changes in the skill differential in Western European countries. Edwin Mansfield, "A Note on Skill Wage Differentials in Great Britain" (*Review of Economics and Statistics*, Vol. 39, August 1957, pp. 348–351), presents data that show that the sharp pre-World War II narrowing trend in the English skill differential had leveled off significantly in the postwar years.

On the influence of inflation in narrowing the skill differential, John R. Hicks, "Economic Foundation of Wage Policy" (*Economic Journal*, Vol. 65, September 1955), argues that inflation strengthens equalitarian sentiment, tending, in Reder's terms, to raise the Social Minimum and lower the skill differential. John T. Dunlop and Melvin Rothbaum, "International Comparison of Wage Structures" (*International Labour Review*, Vol. 71, April 1955, pp. 347–363), interpret their findings of a narrowing in the differentials in Italy, France, and the United States in the immediate post-war period, as reflecting the differential wage pressures, in favor of the unskilled, exerted by inflation.

In his comprehensive review of wage structure theory, Melvin Reder, "Wage Differentials: Theory and Measurement" (*Aspects of Labor Economics*, pp. 257–311), explains why employment of the skilled is more cyclically stable than that of the unskilled, although, as Oi observes, differential employment changes during the cycle do not play a part in Reder's theory. Reder argues that during the downturn, in tightening hiring and retention requirements at all skill levels, firms will have a greater tendency to use workers with broad general skills as operations are curtailed and become discontinuous in some phases of production. Similarly, Louis Salkever, *Toward a Wage Structure Theory*, Humanities Press, 1964, suggests that since the learning process on the job takes longer for skilled than unskilled workers, the sporadic output of recessions would encourage retention of skilled workers who had not yet reached their maximum productivity. This argument, however, comes closer to Oi's human capital approach based on cyclical differences in labor demand by skill level than to Reder's theory involving differential supply shifts.

# CHAPTER 10

# Industrial and Geographical Wage Structures

Economists strive mightily to find some order in the chaos of earnings differences among workers. The first steps in this effort involve classification of labor. Then, differences between and within classes must be analyzed. So far, labor has been discussed in accordance with level of skill; differences in wages by skill have been studied to the degree with which the differences reflect varying embodiments of human capital.

In this section, wage variations among workers of the same skill level or human investment are studied with reference to the strength of competitive labor market forces in equalizing wages for workers of the same skill or occupational classification. Since occupational wage data are limited in scope, the issue is approached indirectly, through examination of industrial and geographical wage levels and movements.

Under competitive labor market conditions, wages for labor of the same type should receive the same wages in all job settings. Translating this condition into industrial wage behavior, each industry will pay labor of the same type the same wage as every other industry. Recognizing that there are barriers to mobility that prevent national wage equalization, this equality is modified to refer to wages within a given labor market. This modification allows for separate study of industrial and regional wage patterns.

## INDUSTRIAL WAGE STRUCTURE

Considering these two classifications separately, and looking first at the industrial structure, it should be stressed at the outset that the competitive tendency for different industries to pay equal wages to labor of the same type is a long-run rather than a short-run condition. Forces that lead to industrial wage differences in the short run, forces that strengthen labor demand in some industries and weaken it in others, may lead to short-run differences in wages that require time for competition in the labor market to equalize wages for perfectly substitutable labor in all its uses.

## The Long-Run Structure

This long-run nature of the competitive model causes serious problems in testing its strength. The usual measure for the long run is a long period of time, but sometimes this practice contains significant error. Specifically, the long run refers to a long enough period of time for a given impulse to work out its effects. But the economy keeps receiving new impulses so that reaction at the end of a long period of time may represent more of a response to recent impulses than final adjustments to the slow process of reaction to an impulse received long ago.

To explain this confusion of a long period with the long run consider the following hypothetical example. In 1900, two industries employing labor of the same type paid the same wages. In 1905, labor demand rose in the first industry, say, because of an increase in product demand. The difference in demand lasted until 1948, and by that time competition had equalized wages in the two industries. But in 1948, labor demand increased in the second industry to the level of the first and in 1949 wages rose in this industry compared to the first, in response to the recent impulse. A long period study of wage movements in the two industries, 1900–1949, would conclude that there was an absence of labor market competition. Wages between them would differ significantly, or would have changed differently even though labor of the same type were employed. This conclusion would miss the intrusion of the short-run change into the long-run process of adjustment. Time series analysis instead of moment-of-time comparisons might reduce this type of error, but not eliminate it as long as individual industries are subject to frequent short-term differential influence on labor demand.

Apart from the conceptual elusiveness of the long-run, industrial wage changes have other shortcomings as an indicator of the strength of competitive labor market forces. In general, the most available data are of manufacturing wages, and important as this large industry group is, manufacturing may not represent labor market conditions for the other 70 percent or so of the work force. Then, wage data are for average hourly earnings or straight time averages, without fringe benefits. The growing importance of these benefits make statistical study of wage rates alone imperfect measures of the pattern of labor returns. Wage studies deal with levels and movements of averages, but most aspects of the competitive hypothesis deal with (unattainable) marginal values. Furthermore, and what is a most serious source of inadequacy of the data, industry wage movements are a poor proxy for changes in wages of labor of the same type. Skill mixes of particular industries may change over time leading to differential wage movements that reflect these changes rather than adjustments in wages of the same type to competitive labor market forces.

Finally, tests of the competitive hypothesis must, by their very nature, be inconclusive. In view of the difficulty of disentangling changes in the industry mix, it is conventionally assumed, tacitly or explicitly, that mixes remain the same over time. Then, if interindustry wage differences were in competitive, long-run equilibrium at the beginning of a long period, with differing wage levels reflecting only differences in industry mix with equal wages for labor of the same type, competitive conditions would lead to an unchanged industrial wage differential at the end of the period. The customary statistical test for this pattern is a negative one, relating comparative wage movements among industries to other economic variables that have short-run impact on the structure and testing the degree of competition by the absence of correlation between interindustry wage changes and specific variables such as changes in unemployment and productivity. This means that a result of insignificant correlation indicates that the competitive hypothesis has not been refuted by the data in question; it can never lead to a positive conclusion that labor market competition operates with strength.

On balance, the data offer this kind of indirect, "negative" support to the competitive hypothesis. The majority of studies show an absence of relationship between long-period employment and wage changes among industries. Insofar as differences in employment represent differences in labor demand, the data thus indicate that, over time, differences in labor demand among industries do not affect the wage pattern among them, in keeping with the operation of labor market competition.

There is also no indication of a long-run functional relationship between wages and productivity changes among industries, further supporting the competitive model which does not allow for differences in wages among industries because of differences in ability to pay.

One relationship that gives strong, indirect evidence of the presence of labor market competition is the significant, long-period, interindustry, negative correlation between productivity changes and product prices. The pattern is for (relative) productivity gainers to experience relative price declines with (relative) productivity losers having relative price increases, with wage movements more or less the same for each. Thus, competition in the labor market transfers differences in productivity into the product market through price changes, rather than allow gains to be distributed among workers in accordance with productivity changes.

## Stability in the Long-Run Structure

A conventional test of the degree of labor market competition involves study of changes in the structure itself. If the labor market were in competitive equilibrium at the beginning of a long period, with equal wages in all industries for the same type of labor, and skill mixes within industries remained unchanged over the period, two heroic assumptions as noted above, differential average wage changes among industries would reflect only different wage experience for particular occupations. Then, if the labor market were also competitive at the end of the period, the industrial ranking by average wages would tend to remain the same, with some shifting arising because of occupational changes in wage rankings with different occupational weight among industries. But in addition, there should be a distinct compression in the whole structure, under competition, because the single important persistent market influence on an industry's average wage level would be the long-term narrowing of the skill differential, with an industry's position in the wage hierarchy greatly reflecting its skill mix. That is, high-wage industries with richer skill mix should move closer to the average, as would low-wage industries with a heavy weight of unskilled labor, over a long period during which the skill differential narrowed.

Cullen's well-known study gives only partial support to the competitive model. Cullen found significant constancy in the structural hierarchy, measured by a significant correlation between wage rankings among manufacturing industries at the beginning and end of a long period, but he did not find the substantial compression that the competitive hypothesis requires.

# The Interindustry Wage Structure, 1899–1950

## by Donald E. Cullen

Table 1 presents one dimension of the structure of average annual earnings in 84 manufacturing industries for the 18 Census years of the 1899–1950 period. The sample from which these correlations were derived includes all the industries for which reasonably comparable earnings data are available for all Census years from 1899 through 1947, and for which comparable data are also available for either 1949 or 1950.[1] Since the *Annual Surveys of Manufactures* for 1949 and 1950 are less comprehensive than the previous full-fledged Censuses, some relatively unimportant industries had to be excluded because they were not covered in either of these two years. Lack of coverage is also the reason why only 70 of

the 84 industries are available for 1949, and only 76 for 1950. Four-digit industries were combined only when necessary to obtain comparable data for earlier years. The 84 industries which met these standards are approximately 20 per cent of the 453 industries covered in the 1947 Census of Manufactures, and in that year they employed 29 per cent of all production workers in manufacturing. Nineteen of the 20 major two-digit manufacturing groups are represented.

The series of rank correlations presented in Table 1 were derived in the usual manner: the ranking of the 84 industries in the base year was compared with their ranking in each of the other indicated years, and coefficients of rank correlation

SOURCE Reprinted with permission from *American Economic Review,* Vol. 46, June 1956, pp. 353–369.

[1] Had 1947 been used as a terminal year, the sample would have been larger but would not have reflected all of the wage changes of the postwar period. On the other hand, the use of data for either 1949 or 1950 alone would have reduced the size of the sample to 70 or 76 industries.

were then computed.[2] Several base years were employed in order to highlight short-run trends.

The over-all impression given by Table 1 is of slow but inexorable change in the interindustry wage structure. Of course, rank correlations are notoriously difficult to interpret in such a context; no one would expect results indicating either perfect rigidity (1.00) or the chaos of pure chance (0.00). Slichter considered the wage structure to exhibit "considerable stability" when his 20-industry sample of unskilled earnings yielded correlations between .7 and .9 for periods of 23 years or less.[3] By this yardstick, the much larger sample used in this study indicates the wage structure to be remarkably stable, for the 1899:1947 correlation of .73 is precisely the same as Slichter obtained for a period (1923–1946) only half as long.

This general impression of stability is borne out by the results of the short-run comparisons in Table 1. For instance, the decade-by-decade correlation coefficients show both a surprising uniformity and a very slow rate of change. The structure in 1919 was also compared with the structure in the 1930's and 1947, since roughly this period was used in those studies which emphasized the rapid rate of change in interindustry wage differentials. The coefficients for 1919:1939 (.83) and 1919:1947 (.85) are even higher than Slichter's for approximately the same years, and again illustrate the misleading impression of the wage structure which is created by a simple listing by industry of percentage or absolute wage changes.

As for the effect of the business cycle on this one dimension of the wage structure, the most significant aspect of the

TABLE 1.  CORRELATION OF STRUCTURE OF ANNUAL EARNINGS IN 84 INDUSTRIES IN CENSUS YEARS, 1899–1950

| Years Compared, 1899 Base | Coefficient of Rank Correlation | Years Compared, Various Bases | Coefficient of Rank Correlation |
|---|---|---|---|
| 1899:1904 | .94 | 1909:1914 | .92 |
| :1909 | .89 | :1919 | .84 |
| :1914 | .87 | 1919:1929 | .88 |
| :1919 | .75 | :1933 | .68 |
| :1921 | .79 | :1939 | .83 |
| :1923 | .77 | :1947 | .85 |
| :1925 | .77 | 1929:1933 | .72 |
| :1927 | .75 | :1935 | .88 |
| :1929 | .75 | :1939 | .88 |
| :1931 | .68 | 1939:1947 | .94 |
| :1933 | .64 | :1949 | .92 [a] |
| :1935 | .72 | :1950 | .88 [b] |
| :1937 | .75 | | |
| :1939 | .74 | | |
| :1947 | .73 | | |
| :1949 | .65 [a] | | |
| :1950 | .66 [b] | | |

[a] 70 industries.

[b] 76 industries.

SOURCE: Supporting data, furnished upon request, from U. S. Bureau of the Census, *Census of Manufactures: 1947*, Vol. II, *Statistics by Industry*, and *Annual Surveys of Manufactures, 1949 and 1950*.

[2] In order to check the comparability of the smaller 1949 and 1950 samples with the full 84-industry sample, the 1899:1947 correlation coefficients were computed for the smaller samples. For this identical time period, the three samples yield these coefficients: .73 (full sample); .69 (1949 sample); and .74 (1950 sample).

[3] Slichter, "Notes on the Structure of Wages," *Review of Economics and Statistics,* Vol. 22 (February 1950), p. 88.

picture which emerges from Table 1 is not the severe jolt dealt by the depression of the 1930's, but the rapidity with which the structure recovered its normal configuration; the structure's rate of change, as measured by rank correlation, was no greater for the 1929–1939 decade as a whole than for most of the other decades during this half century. This resiliency of the wage structure was apparently not even put to the test in the inflationary period following the second world war, although the inflation of the first world war may have temporarily "distorted" wage differentials.

Perhaps a more graphic measure of the type of stability reflected by rank correlation is afforded by an examination of the high-wage and low-wage industries—which have arbitrarily been defined as those in the upper and lower quarter of the wage structure. Of the 21 industries which comprised the high-wage quarter in 1899, 14 were still in the high-wage quarter in 1947. Similarly, 15 of the 21 lowest-paying industries in 1899 were in the low-wage quarter in 1947.

One significant difference should be noted between these high-wage and low-wage industries. Only 3 of the 14 which were high-wage industries at the beginning and end of the 1899–1947 period were in this classification in *all* the 16 Census years of that span; these 3 are printing ink, petroleum refining, and ships and boats.[4] On the other hand, of the 15 industries in the low-wage class in both 1899 and 1947, 10 were continuously in this classification in every intervening Census year: cigars and cigarettes, brooms, paper bags, cordage, confectionery products, corsets, cottonseed oil, textile bags, chewing tobacco, and canning.[5] The low-wage quarter of the wage structure thus appears to have been even more stable than the high-wage quarter—a depressing finding which will be discussed below.

\* \* \*

III. DISPERSION OF THE WAGE STRUCTURE, 1899–1950

Changes in the dispersion of this wage structure can be traced over the past 50 years in Table 2. The first three columns contain data on the dispersion of the structure as a whole, as it existed in each of the 18 Census years. Data in the last two columns pertain only to those industries which constituted the top and bottom quarters of the structure in 1899.

For the structure as a whole, the general impression gained from Table 2 is again one of long-run stability. As measured by the interquartile range, the dispersion of annual earnings about the median fluctuates within narrow limits around 25.0 throughout most of the 1899-1950 period. Similarly, the median earnings of workers in the high-wage industries of each year were quite consistently 50 to 60 per cent higher than the median earnings of workers in the low-wage industries of the same year. The generally steady increase in the dollars-per-year differential is consistent with the results of both of the other dispersion measures. Although a determined trend-spotter might find some significance in the fact that the structure was slightly more dispersed in 1899 and 1904 than in 1949 and 1950, the evidence of the intervening years is strongly against the view that there has been any appreciable long-run narrowing of interindustry wage differentials.

However, it is apparent that the dispersion of this wage structure was repeatedly affected, if only temporarily, by extremes

[4] The 11 other industries which were "high wage" in both 1899 and 1947 are: metal doors, primary nonferrous metals, motor vehicles, locomotives, dressed furs, steel works and rolling mills, steel forgings, carbon black, wire, silverware, grease and tallow.

[5] The 5 other industries which were "low wage" in both 1899 and 1947 are fertilizers, footwear cut stock, pens and pencils, handbags, and matches.

TABLE 2. DISPERSION OF STRUCTURE OF ANNUAL EARNINGS, 1899–1950

| Year | 84 Industries | | | High-Wage and Low-Wage Industries of 1899 | |
|------|-----------------------------------------|--------------------------------|----------------------------------|-----------------------------|----------------------------|
| | Interquartile Range ÷ Median × 100 | High-Low Per Cent Differential [a] | High-Low Dollar Differential [b] | Per Cent Differential [c] | Dollar Differential [c] |
| 1899 | 27.4 | 162 | 209 | 162 | 209 |
| 1904 | 30.0 | 163 | 229 | 162 | 225 |
| 1909 | 25.7 | 159 | 241 | 153 | 216 |
| 1914 | 25.1 | 160 | 277 | 153 | 246 |
| 1919 | 23.5 | 172 | 597 | 155 | 484 |
| 1921 | 21.7 | 155 | 519 | 141 | 391 |
| 1923 | 23.2 | 159 | 577 | 148 | 469 |
| 1925 | 24.2 | 155 | 557 | 145 | 462 |
| 1927 | 25.5 | 153 | 550 | 146 | 477 |
| 1929 | 24.8 | 158 | 597 | 155 | 561 |
| 1931 | 21.1 | 151 | 440 | 133 | 306 |
| 1933 | 22.3 | 153 | 362 | 135 | 252 |
| 1935 | 19.8 | 160 | 463 | 139 | 319 |
| 1937 | 27.9 | 175 | 637 | 163 | 534 |
| 1939 | 30.1 | 175 | 634 | 153 | 474 |
| 1947 | 25.7 | 151 | 1015 | 143 | 868 |
| 1949 [d] | 23.0 | 156 | 1175 | 143 | 943 |
| 1950 [e] | 25.4 | 156 | 1262 | 149 | 1109 |

[a] For each year, the median of the average annual earnings in those industries forming the top quarter of the earnings structure divided by the median of the average annual earnings in those industries forming the lowest quarter of the earnings structure.

[b] For each year, the absolute difference between the medians described in (a).

[c] For each year, the differential between the median earnings in the 21 industries which ranked highest in 1899 and the 21 which ranked lowest in 1899—regardless of the relative position of these industries in subsequent years.

[d] 70 industries.

[e] 76 industries.

SOURCE: Same as Table 1.

of the business cycle. The surprising aspect about these cyclical changes is that they tended to be in the same direction—namely, towards a temporary compression of the structure—in periods of both full employment and depression.

Interindustry wage differentials are expected to narrow during periods of full employment because low-wage industries at such a time "must narrow the gap between their wages and those of industries paying higher wages in order to retain and recruit a work force."[6] As noted in other studies, the clearest example of this tendency is to be found in the experience of the 1940's, when the wage structure was noticeably more compressed than during the late 1930's. On the other hand, the evidence of the period of the first world war is rather equivocal, as shown by the slight contraction in the dispersion of the interquartile range at the same time that the percentage differential was widening between the median earnings of the workers in the top and bottom quarters of the structure.

Interindustry wage differentials might be expected to widen during a depression, since the low-wage industries are then under no pressure to compete with others for workers. Furthermore, Dunlop's study of cyclical wage variation has shown that

[6] J. T. Dunlop and M. Rothbaum, "International Comparisons of Wage Structures," Internat. Lab. Rev., Apr. 1955, LXXI, 359.

in the depression of 1929-1933 wages tended to be reduced in the highly competitive, low-wage industries before they were reduced in the oligopolistic, high-wage industries[7]—a tendency which should also have resulted in a temporary widening of differentials. The evidence of Table 2 is nevertheless to the contrary, showing that the wage structure contracted during the two most severe depressions of the past fifty years—in 1921-1922 and 1929-1933. It is also possible that the narrowing of interindustry differentials from 1904 to 1909 resulted from the sharp recession of 1908, and that differentials were equally compressed in 1914 because of the high unemployment of that year.[8] This interpretation of the 1904-1914 period is difficult to test because Census data were only collected at five-year intervals at that time, and it also fails to explain why the dispersion of 1909 and 1914 became the "normal" dispersion of the wage structure for the remainder of the 1899-1950 period. Finally, it should be noted that interindustry wage differentials actually widened during the recession of 1937-1939.

In spite of the several apparent inconsistencies in the cyclical variations of this wage structure, a generalization might still be hazarded that interindustry differentials have tended to narrow during periods of prolonged full employment (the 1940's, at least until 1947) and periods of very severe unemployment (1921 and 1929-1933). Much less predictable have been the

effects on this wage structure of cyclical movements such as the recessions of 1908, 1914, and 1937, which were characterized by relatively brief periods of unemployment which never reached the proportions typical of a full-scale depression.

The reasons for the unexpected contraction of the wage structure during the early 1930's are not entirely clear. A plausible hypothesis might be adduced from the pronounced tendency for producers' goods industries to be in the high-wage category, and for consumers' goods industries to be low-wage. Accordingly, average annual earnings in the high-wage industries could be expected to suffer a relatively larger drop during a severe depression than earnings in the low-wage industries, thereby compressing the structure.[9] These high-wage industries may also provide the key to an understanding of why interindustry differentials widened, rather than narrowed, during the late 1930's for they were the target of many of the major organizational drives of that era. If earnings in these industries increased more rapidly than in other industries as a result of union pressure, then the structure would naturally have become more dispersed. Although the analysis of variables necessary to test this hypothesis lies outside the scope of this study, it should be remarked that the evidence on the effects of "new unionism" during the 1930's is conflicting at best.[10]

In summary, the results of Table 2 indicate that the dispersion of interindustry

---

[7] J. T. Dunlop, *Wage Determination Under Trade Unions* (New York, 1950), pp. 130–48. The characterization of these two groups of industries as low-wage and high-wage is not Dunlop's but can reasonably be inferred from the listings of these industries on pages 132–43. Dunlop noted differences between the groups in the proportion of labor costs to total costs, as well as differences in product market competition. In their recent 3-country study, Dunlop and Rothbaum explicitly hypothesized that *all* wage differentials tend to widen during periods of unemployment; *op. cit.*, p. 362.

[8] For estimates of unemployment during the early 1900's, see Douglas, *Real Wages*, pp. 445–60.

[9] This hypothesis is not necessarily inconsistent with Dunlop's findings on this period, for he was exclusively concerned with the month-by-month *timing* of wage cuts rather than with either the amounts of these cuts or their cumulative effect over the entire depression period.

[10] For instance, compare the results of A. M. Ross and W. Goldner, "Forces Affecting the Interindustry Wage Structure," *Quart. Jour. Econ.*, May 1950, LXIV, 267, and H. M. Levinson, *Unionism, Wage Trends, and Income Distribution, 1914–1947* (Ann Arbor, 1951), pp. 47–66.

wage differentials exhibited a definite secular stability over the 1899-1950 period, but several of the sort-run changes in this dispersion require further exploration before they can be satisfactorily explained. That these short-run changes have nevertheless failed to alter the basic dispersion of the wage structure is emphasized by the changes which occurred in the 1940's. A comparison of the structure's dispersion in 1937 and 1939 with its dispersion in the postwar years confirms the evidence of other studies that compression undoubtedly did occur during the latter period. However, when this short-run compression is viewed in the context of the entire 1899-1950 period, it emerges as a return of the structure to its "normal" pattern of dispersion which had been disrupted during the 1930's. Interindustry wage differentials in 1937 and 1939 were thus appreciably greater, in relative terms, than in almost any other Census year, and the subsequent narrowing of these differentials served only to return them by 1950 to the spread of the 1920's.

## IV. THE LONG-RUN EQUALIZATION OF EARNINGS

In spite of the relative stability of interindustry wage differentials, the correlation coefficients in Table 1 indicate that there has been a constant, though not rapid, shifting in the relative position of industries within the wage structure. Of particular interest to wage theory is the extent to which this internal movement has resulted in a trend towards the equalization of earnings as between those industries which ranked at the top and bottom of the wage structure fifty years ago. This long-run tendency toward equality is measured in the last two columns of Table 2, in which are listed for the entire 1899–1950 period the percentage and absolute differentials between the median earnings of the 21 industries which ranked highest in 1899 and the median earnings of the 21 industries which ranked lowest in the same year.[11]

It is obvious from Table 2 that median earnings in these two groups of industries have tended to converge relatively, if not absolutely, over the long run, but that this tendency has been so weak that uniformity of earnings has not even been approached. While the high-low spread of the structure as a whole dropped from 162 per cent in 1899 to 156 per cent in 1950, the spread between the two original groups of high-wage and low-wage industries decreased only from 162 per cent to 149 per cent. Similarly, as the absolute high-low differential in the structure as a whole increased from $209 in 1899 to $1262 in 1950, the differential between the two original high-low groups increased only slightly less—from $209 to $1109.

The movement of this differential within the 1899–1950 period presents two interesting aspects. First, most if not all of the narrowing of this differential actually occurred prior to 1921; throughout most of the 1920's, the differential was substantially the same as in 1947–1950. (The same was also true of any compression which occurred in the structure as a whole, slight as that appears to have been.) Second, this differential decreased much more sharply in the early 1930's than the high-low differential for the structure as a whole. Again, the explanation is to be found in the greater volatility of the high-wage industries. In 1929, most of the high-wage industries of 1899 were still at or near the top of the wage structure, but by 1931 the several depression-prone industries in this group—such as locomotives, motor vehicles, and steel works—had plummeted in the structure, to be tempo-

---

[11] This type of comparison was suggested by a similar analysis of the structure of profit rates in R. C. Epstein, *Industrial Profits in the United States* (New York, 1934), pp. 94–113.

rarily supplanted in the high-wage category by such industries as paint, manufactured ice, and glue and gelatin. On the other hand, the majority of the low-wage industries of 1899 not only formed the bulk of the low-wage industries of 1929, but showed little tendency to rise out of that category throughout the depression which followed.

In some respects, the weakness of this tendency toward long-run equalization of earnings is the single most impressive indicator of the stability of the interindustry wage structure. Correlation coefficients are subject to varying interpretations, and the fact that the dispersion of interindustry differentials has remained stable could of course be reconciled with nearly any rate of internal change in the structure. However, it is doubtful that any theory of wage movement—whether based upon the competitive models of Clark and Marshall or the friction-ridden, institutional models of today—would lead one to expect the spread between the high-wage and low-wage industries of fifty years ago to increase fivefold in aboslute terms, or to decrease to such a moderate extent in relative terms, over a span of half a century.

## VI. CONCLUSION

What are the theoretical implications of this persistence of inter-industry wage differentials? At first glance, this might appear to be one more stick with which to belabor neoclassical wage theory, for surely the authors of that theory placed great confidence in the leveling influence of time and competition.[12] While there is probably some truth in this interpretation of persistent wage differentials, it rests upon a debatable equation of stability with rigidity—persistent differentials are

pictured as somehow resisting the eroding effects of competition. Yet, without an analysis of the several variables which presumably influence wage differences (productivity, unionism, competition in the product market, etc.), the stability of this wage structure does not in itself prove the impotence of competitive forces.

It is conceivable, for instance, that the high-wage industries of 1899 tended to retain their relative wage advantage over the long run simply because they tended to maintain a competitive advantage in the product market. As Schumpeter and his followers have pointed out, once an industry has gained a competitive edge, it often has both the means and inclination to retain that edge; the now-familiar chain of reasoning which pictures higher profits as leading to more research, increasing innovation, and higher productivity might well be completed by the addition of expanding employment and higher wages as other characteristics of the consistently successful industry. Regardless of whether this "new competition" thesis can be fitted into the framework of orthodox theory (does the successful industry exhibit higher average or marginal productivity, or both?), the emphasis is the same—the persistence of differentials is attributed to the force of competition (old or new style), rather than to arteriosclerosis of the economic system.

It is therefore apparent that, in the absence of further evidence, the stability of interindustry wage differentials can be accommodated by any or all of the current wage theories. Several of the other studies in this area have attempted to evaluate the major wage determinants believed to be operative and, although these studies have stressed the variability within the structure, none of their results are necessarily inconsistent with the findings of this

[12] For an example of how neoclassicists sometimes framed their analyses in terms of interindustry differentials, see J. B. Clark, *The Distribution of Wealth* (New York, 1899), pp. 80, 282–83.

study. Unfortunately, these studies are so inconsistent with each other in their findings that no convincing explanation of the forces affecting the interindustry wage structure is yet available.[13]

* * *

Cullen's findings of rank correlation of average annual wage levels, the wage value he must use because of data limitation, show a consistent but slight increase in scrambling of the hierarchy over time, with 1899 as the starting date. But with a rank correlation still as high as .69 for the rankings compared with those of 1899 (Table 1), the evidence can be considered to substantiate the point Cullen often makes, that the structure is characterized by long-run overall stability.

In his concluding remarks, Cullen seems to view this stability as evidence against the competitive hypothesis. However, in reality, it is not stability in the structure, but in failure of the structure to compress, under the force of the narrowing skill differential, that most contradicts competitive principles.

Table 2 shows that the percentage spread in average annual wages of the top 25 and bottom 25 percent of the industries shrank from only 163 to 149 percent, from 1899 to 1950, much less than the over 30 percent narrowing of the skill differential for the period. Cullen stresses the importance of this finding in his conclusion that "in some respects, the weakness of this tendency toward long-run equalization of earnings is the single most impressive indicator of the stability of the interindustry wage structure."

Cullen suggests that high-wage industries may have enjoyed long-run strength in the product market, explaining why their wages did not tend to fall toward average levels under the pressure of the narrowing skill differential. If this were the case, then even if labor markets were competitive, continued short-run higher demand for labor of high-wage industries would have prevented the move toward the average industrial wage level which long-run competitive forces would have induced as a result of the decline in the skill differential.

Other factors that might have obscured the effects of labor market competition are the weakness of the data—the use of annual earnings to represent wages, the possibility that the structure was not in competitive equilibrium at the beginning of the period, and possibility that individual industry skill mixes changed substantially over the period. Apart from these elements, there is the conclusion that labor markets did not respond only to competitive forces, that institutional or nonmarket factors tend to determine an industry's position in the wage hierarchy and its relative wage level in resistance to equalizing market forces.

Slitcher also finds stability in the wage structure over time. Confining his study to the movement of male, unskilled labor, he finds a high rank correlation between industry rankings in 1923 with those of 1946.

Slitcher's paper, much of which is presented here, is significant for the wage patterns he finds which, in general, suggest a strong pressure of non-

---

[13] For conflicting conclusions on the effects of unionism and employment change, see the sources cited in footnotes 19 and 21. As for the effects of productivity on wage change, compare the findings of Dunlop, "Productivity and the Wage Structure," p. 350 and Garbarino, op. cit., p. 298, with those of Meyers and Bowlby, op. cit., p. 97 and Backman and Gainsbrugh, op. cit., pp. 60 and 96.

market forces in wage determination. His study, however, is confined to a moment of time. He argues that this cross-sectional approach is superior to study of changes over time in that the structure of any given moment "may reveal some of the long-run influences playing on wages more clearly than the study of changes in the wage structure between two dates." But wage levels at any given time might instead more clearly reflect the effect of recent influences.

# Notes on the Structure of Wages

## by Sumner Slichter

Attention in this study is focused upon the wage structure at a given time rather than changes over a period of time. Comparisons of wage movements through time are useful and interesting, and studies of this sort have been made by Dunlop, Ross, and Garbarino. Examination of the wage structure at a given time is also useful. At any moment the wage structure reflects the accumulated influence of various conditions over a considerable period of time. The conditions affecting the movement of wages in an industry during the last decade may not be the same as those affecting the movement in the previous decade. Hence, the analysis of the wage structure at a given time may reveal some of the long-run influences playing upon wages more clearly than the study of changes in the wage structure between two dates. It has seemed desirable, however, to make comparisons of the stability of the inter-industry wage structure over periods of time, and this has been done.

## III

The results of the study may be summarized as follows:

1. The average hourly earnings of male unskilled workers tend to vary with the average hourly earnings of semi-skilled and skilled workers—that is, where the average hourly earnings of semi-skilled and skilled workers are high, the average hourly earnings of common labor are high and vice versa.

2. Where the proportion of women in an industry is high, there is some tendency (not pronounced) for the hourly earnings of male unskilled labor to be low.

3. In industries where value added by manufacturing per wage-earner hour is high, the hourly earnings of male unskilled labor tend to be high.

SOURCE Reprinted with permission from *Review of Economics and Statistics,* Vol. 22, February 1950, pp. 80–89.

4. In industries where the value product per wage-earner hour is high, the hourly earnings of male unskilled labor tend to be high.

5. In industries where payrolls are a low percentage of income from sales, the hourly earnings of male unskilled labor tend to be high.

6. In industries where income after taxes is a high percentage of sales, the hourly earnings of male unskilled labor tend to be high.

7. The wage structure changes over time, but the changes are fairly slow and the wage structure between industries within a period of twenty or thirty years exhibits only moderate changes. This conclusion, however, might not hold if the unit of observation were the individual firms in a local labor market.

Let us examine these results briefly.

IV

1. *The average hourly earnings of male* *unskilled labor tend to be high where the* *average hourly earnings of male semi-* *skilled and skilled labor are high.* The coefficient of rank correlation among twenty manufacturing industries in 1939 was .7098. Table 1 compares the average hourly earnings of male unskilled labor and male semi-skilled and skilled labor in these industries.

The internal wage structures of the several industries appear to be more or less entities—where for any reason the earnings of semi-skilled and skilled workers are high the earnings of the unskilled workers also tend to be high. In five cases, however (newspaper and magazine printing, book and job printing, leather tanning, chemicals, and lumber and millwork) the difference in rank is large—6 or more.

Among the industries, it is interesting to compare the spread in the ratios between the average hourly earnings of the unskilled workers and the average hourly

TABLE 1.   COMPARISON OF AVERAGE HOURLY EARNINGS OF MALE SKILLED AND SEMI-SKILLED AND MALE UNSKILLED LABOR, 1939

| Industry | Average Hourly Earnings, Male Semi-skilled and Skilled | Rank | Average Hourly Earnings, Male Unskilled | Rank | Deviation |
|---|---|---|---|---|---|
| Printing, newspaper and magazine | $1.104 | 1 | $.623 | 10 | 9 |
| Printing, book and job | 1.024 | 2 | .543 | 12 | 10 |
| Automobile | .976 | 3 | .797 | 1 | 2 |
| Rubber | .967 | 4 | .673 | 3 | 1 |
| Iron and steel | .876 | 5 | .638 | 6 | 1 |
| Electrical manufacturing | .873 | 6 | .669 | 4 | 2 |
| Agricultural implements | .829 | 7 | .654 | 5 | 2 |
| Chemicals | .823 | 8 | .694 | 2 | 6 |
| Paint and varnish | .786 | 9 | .627 | 8 | 1 |
| Foundry and machine shops | .781 | 10 | .629 | 7 | 3 |
| Meat packing | .774 | 11 | .624 | 9 | 2 |
| Lumber and millwork | .746 | 12 | .479 | 18 | 6 |
| Paper products | .735 | 13 | .531 | 15 | 2 |
| Hosiery and knit goods | .707 | 14 | .458 | 19 | 5 |
| Furniture | .706 | 15 | .536 | 14 | 1 |
| Wool | .703 | 16 | .524 | 16 | 0 |
| Paper and pulp | .698 | 17 | .540 | 13 | 4 |
| Leather tanning | .694 | 18 | .557 | 11 | 7 |
| Boot and shoe | .599 | 19 | .434 | 20 | 1 |
| Cotton | .566 | 20 | .494 | 17 | 3 |

SOURCE: National Industrial Conference Board, *The Conference Board Economic Record*, Vol. 11, No. 10, March 28, 1940, pp. 120–34.

earnings of the semi-skilled and skilled workers. Since the degree of skill among the skilled and semi-skilled workers varies from industry to industry, one has no right to expect an approximate uniformity between industries in this spread. Nevertheless, the variation is not large. For 20 industries in 1939, the unweighted average of the average hourly earnings of common labor was 73.1 per cent of the unweighted average of the average hourly earnings of semi-skilled and skilled labor. There was a fairly close concentration around this ratio. In 17 of the 20 industries, the ratio between the average hourly earnings of common labor and the average hourly earnings of semi-skilled or skilled labor was within 10 per cent of the average for the 20 industries; and in 8 cases, within 5 per cent of the average.

The wage policies pursued during the war increased the wages of common labor relative to the earnings of semi-skilled and skilled workers. An unweighted average of the hourly earnings of male unskilled workers in the industries reporting to the National Industrial Conference Board shows that in 1923 the earnings of common labor were 71.6 per cent of the earnings of semi-skilled and skilled workers; in 1929, 72.8 per cent; in 1933, 72.9 per cent; in 1939, 73.1 per cent; in December 1946, 77.1 per cent.[1] The wage policies of the war, however, had little effect upon the tendency for the average hourly earnings of male unskilled labor to be high in those industries where the average hourly earnings of the semi-skilled and skilled are high. In December 1946, the coefficient of rank correlation among the same twenty industries that were compared for 1939 was .6702—only a little less than in 1939.

Why should the earnings of common laborers be high where the earnings of semi-skilled and skilled workers are high? The explanation undoubtedly is that there are certain common influences, such as wage policies, which tend to affect the entire wage structures of plants and to give them a unity. The effect of common influences upon wages throughout the labor force would be shown more clearly if industries or plants could be classified by the average level of skill and responsibility required by the semi-skilled and skilled jobs. As it is, the differences in the average hourly earnings of semi-skilled and skilled workers reflect to considerable extent, not differences in wage policies, but differences in the quality of labor used on the semi-skilled and skilled jobs. Nevertheless, the tendency is quite pronounced for hourly earnings of common laborers to be high where the hourly earnings of semi-skilled and skilled workers are high.

2. *The hourly earnings of male common labor have some (not pronounced) tendency to be low where the percentage of women among the wage earners is high.* The coefficient of rank correlation among 19 industries in 1939 was .4491.

The tendency for the hourly earnings of common labor to be low where the proportion of women in the industry is high, was apparently weakened by the depression. For example, in 1929 the coefficient of rank correlation between the proportion of women among workers and the average hourly earnings of common laborers was .5224, the industries being ranked by the highness of the proportion of women among wage earners and the lowness of the average hourly earnings of male unskilled labor. Possibly the war has still further weakened the relationship, but data on this point are not yet available.

Why is there some tendency for the wages of male common labor to be low in industries where the proportion of women employed is high? Does the employment of women have some more or less direct effect upon either the wages which em-

---

[1] National Industrial Conference Board, *Wages, Hours, and Employment in the United States, 1914–1936,* computed from tables on pages 59–159; *Conference Board Record,* Vol. II, March 28, 1940, computed from tables on pages 115–33; *Management Record,* February 1947, pages 45, 46.

ployers are willing to pay men or the wages which men are willing to accept? Or are the high proportion of women employed and the low wages of men partly the result of common causes?

I believe that each of these last two questions should be answered by "Yes." To some extent the wages of women probably do affect the wages of men. Women are available for lower wages than men. Where women are doing skilled or semi-skilled work, managements are probably reluctant to pay male employees, who are merely doing common labor, as much as or more than semi-skilled or skilled women workers. Under these conditions, employers may content themselves with rather inferior male common laborers in order to keep the common labor scale below the scale for semi-skilled and skilled women. Furthermore, some of the industries which employ a large proportion of women, such as the textile industry, also employ men and are able to offer jobs to both male and female members of families. In such industries the fact that jobs are available for both men and women undoubtedly affects the supply price for male workers.

The industries where a high proportion of workers are women are usually light industries. Some persons are able to accept jobs in either light or heavy industries; others are not strong enough for the heavy industries and must work in the light industries. Consequently, the supply price of labor for the light industries is undoubtedly lower than the supply price for heavy industries. As a result, the tendency for the hourly earnings of male common labor to be low where the proportion of women workers is high is probably in considerable degree explained by the fact that each of these two conditions is likely to be characteristic of industries turning out light products.

3. *Hourly earnings of male unskilled workers tend to be high where the value added by manufacturing per wage-earner hour is high.* The coefficient of rank correlation in 1939 was .9299.

Some correlation between the value added per wage-earner hour and the average hourly wage of male unskilled workers is to be expected because it is from value added that wages are paid. High wages per hour cannot be paid unless the value added per man hour is high. Of course, the value added per wage-earner hour is the average for *all* employees—not merely for common laborers. If a high value added tends to produce high hourly earnings, however, the unskilled laborers may be expected to feel its effects—and this seems to be the case. Although some correlation between the value added per wage-earner hour and hourly earnings of male unskilled labor is to be expected, a correlation of .9299 is so high that it requires an explanation.

"Accepted" wage theory would lead one to expect a high correlation between wages and the *marginal* value added per wage-earner hour. The above high correlation, however, is between hourly earnings and the *average* value added per wage-earner. There are two principal explanations for the high figure. One, of course, is that it is correlation of ranks only; it is quite possible that there is a tendency for the average value added to be high where the marginal value added is high. The second explanation is closely related to the first—a high average value added per man-hour tends to produce high wages (and high earnings) because it produces liberal wage policies. More specific evidence in support of this conclusion will be given when hourly earnings are compared with the ratio of payrolls to income from sales and to profits per dollar of sales.

4. *Hourly earnings of male unskilled workers tend to be high where the value product per wage-earner hour is high.* The coefficient of rank correlation in 1939 was .8297.

The high coefficient of rank correlation

between value product per wage-earner hour and the average hourly earnings of male unskilled workers may seem surprising. A high value of product per wage-earner hour may be the result of two very different causes—either the application of labor to expensive raw materials or a high productivity of labor. The first cause would not be expected to produce high hourly earnings. The meat packing industry, where the deviation between the two ranks is large, is an example of an industry in which the value of product per wage-earner hour is high because labor in the industry is applied to expensive raw materials.

\* \* \*

7. *The inter-industry structure of wages has considerable stability during short or moderately short periods of time.* When the hourly earnings of male unskilled labor in twenty industries in 1923 and 1946 are compared, a coefficient of rank correlation of .7289 is obtained. When the comparison is between 1923 and 1939, the coefficient is .7154; between 1929 and 1939, .8902; and between 1929 and 1946, .8812.

Table 2 compares the average hourly earnings of male unskilled labor in various industries at the several dates.

V

What questions or conclusions of theoretical interest are suggested by the results of this examination of the inter-industry wage structure? One question is: "How important is managerial policy as a determinant of wages?" Others are: "What are the determinants of managerial wage policy?" "What relationship is there between hourly earnings and the price of labor?" "Do the several regularities found in the inter-industry wage structure require any significant modifications of 'accepted' wage theory?"

The results of this study give strong support to the proposition that managerial policy is important in determining inter-industry wage differences. The best evidence in support of this conclusion is supplied by the tendency for the hourly earnings of male unskilled labor to be high where the earnings of semi-skilled and skilled labor are high, where payroll costs are low in relation to gross income, and where profit margins per dollar of sales are high. The tendency for the earnings of male unskilled workers to be low in industries where the proportion of women in the labor force is high is consistent with the view that managerial policy is an important determinant of the level of wages. It can hardly be regarded as strong independent proof, partly because the correlation is not high and partly because the correlation may indicate simply two results of a common cause. The very high correlation between value added per wage-earner hour and average hourly earnings of unskilled labor is best explained by the tendency for a high value added per wage-earner hour to produce liberal wage policies and a low value added to produce niggardly wage policies.

The study shows that two important determinants of wage policy are the size of payrolls relative to gross income and profits per dollar of sales. It is not surprising that managements should watch labor costs most carefully in those industries where payrolls are large relative to gross receipts and where profit margins per dollar of sales are low, and that hourly earnings should be lower in these industries than in others where labor costs are less important or where profit margins are higher. There are probably other important determinants of wage policies, but they are not indicated by the results of this study.

TABLE 2. COMPARISON OF AVERAGE HOURLY EARNINGS OF MALE UNSKILLED LABOR AT SELECTED DATES

| Industry | Earnings | | | | | | | | | | Deviation in Rank | | | |
|---|---|---|---|---|---|---|---|---|---|---|---|---|---|---|
| | 1923 | Rank | 1929 | Rank | 1933 | Rank | 1939 | Rank | July 1946 | Rank | 1923 1939 | 1929 1939 | 1942 1946 | 1929 1946 |
| Printing, newspapers and magazines | .540 | 1 | .486 | 7 | .419 | 8 | .623 | 10 | 1.005 | 9 | 9 | 3 | 8 | 2 |
| Rubber | .522 | 2 | .604 | 1 | .475 | 2 | .673 | 3 | 1.222 | 1 | 1 | 2 | 1 | 0 |
| Automobile | .496 | 3 | .576 | 2 | .505 | 1 | .797 | 1 | 1.161 | 2 | 2 | 1 | 1 | 0 |
| Paint and varnish | .494 | 4 | .476 | 10 | .441 | 5 | .627 | 8 | .959 | 11 | 4 | 2 | 7 | 1 |
| Iron and steel | .484 | 5 | .511 | 5 | .367 | 15 | .638 | 6 | 1.080 | 4 | 1 | 1 | 1 | 1 |
| Chemical | .477 | 6 | .543 | 3 | .469 | 3 | .694 | 2 | 1.082 | 3 | 4 | 1 | 1 | 0 |
| Wool | .470 | 7 | .442 | 17 | .373 | 14 | .524 | 16 | .956 | 12 | 9 | 1 | 3 | 5 |
| Foundry and machine shops | .469 | 8 | .507 | 6 | .432 | 6 | .629 | 7 | 1.068 | 5 | 1 | 1 | 5 | 1 |
| Agricultural implements | .450 | 9 | .512 | 4 | .413 | 9 | .654 | 5 | 1.055 | 6 | 4 | 1 | 3 | 2 |
| Leather and tanning | .442 | 10 | .485 | 8 | .360 | 16 | .557 | 11 | .935 | 15 | 0 | 3 | 4 | 7 |
| Paper and pulp | .442 | 11 | .450 | 15 | .375 | 13 | .540 | 13 | .939 | 14 | 2 | 2 | 3 | 1 |
| Printing, book and job | .442 | 12 | .479 | 9 | .444 | 4 | .543 | 12 | .998 | 10 | 1 | 3 | 3 | 1 |
| Paper products | .435 | 13 | .452 | 14 | .412 | 10 | .531 | 15 | .868 | 19 | 2 | 1 | 6 | 5 |
| Electrical manufacturing | .428 | 14.5 | .474 | 11 | .430 | 7 | .669 | 4 | 1.036 | 7 | 10.5 | 7 | 7.5 | 4 |
| Meat packing | .428 | 14.5 | .471 | 12 | .391 | 12 | .624 | 9 | 1.021 | 8 | 5.5 | 3 | 6.5 | 4 |
| Cotton (north) | .403 | 16 | .362 | 20 | .341 | 19 | .494 | 17 | .890 | 17 | 1 | 3 | 1 | 3 |
| Furniture | .390 | 17 | .447 | 16 | .325 | 20 | .536 | 14 | .900 | 16 | 3 | 2 | 5 | 0 |
| Lumber and mill | .369 | 18 | .454 | 13 | .348 | 17 | .479 | 18 | .948 | 13 | 0 | 5 | 5 | 0 |
| Boot and shoe | .367 | 19 | .438 | 18 | .397 | 11 | .434 | 20 | .577 | 20 | 1 | 2 | 1 | 2 |
| Hosiery and knit goods | .356 | 20 | .385 | 19 | .342 | 18 | .458 | 19 | .872 | 18 | 1 | 0 | 2 | 1 |

SOURCE: National Industrial Conference Board, Wages and Employment in the United States, 1914–1936, pp. 56–185; The Conference Board Economic Record, Vol. II, No. 10, March 28, 1940, pp. 120–32; The Conference Board Management Record, October 1946, p. 339.

Slitcher finds a significant relationship between the industry rankings of unskilled labor and those for semiskilled and skilled labor. That is, industries that pay high wages to their workers having some degree of skill also tend to pay high wages for their unskilled labor. If differences in the skilled wages reflect nonhomogeneity in these labor classes while unskilled labor is more or less similar for all industries, then this relationship suggests that unskilled wages are paid differentially in accordance with internal wage practices of individual industries rather than in response to competitive forces, which would lead to wage equality among the unskilled. High-wage industries seem to pay higher wages for their unskilled labor than required by the labor market for the unskilled as a matter of industry practice. The presence of a consistent, internal wage hierarchy is also revealed by Slichter's finding of a similarity of the skilled-unskilled wage spread among industries.

Slitcher sees less evidence of noncompetitive forces in the fact that unskilled wages among industries tend to be negatively correlated with the proportion of women employed in the industry. In this relationship he reasons that unskilled labor is not necessarily homogeneous when classified in accordance with the number of females in the individual industries. He assumes that unskilled males who perform lighter work, and who thus must accept less pay than the average, are more prevalent in the industries that hire large numbers of females.

Industries that have high profit rates and relatively low labor costs also tend to pay their unskilled workers more. Slichter explains this tendency on the grounds that managements are more restrained in their wage concessions in industries for which profits are low and labor costs high, and more generous where profits are high and labor costs are a relatively small share of total costs. If these influences kept wages apart in the long run, then the labor market would not be considered competitive, but they might separate wages in the short run even under conditions of long-run competitive equilibrium.

Clearly, Slichter's finding of a strong relationship between value added per wage-earner hour and wages, assuming that the value-added data approximate marginal value added, is consistent with short-run labor market competition. If firms (industries) that have a high value added pay high wages, this need not reflect "liberal" company wage policies, as Slichter states, but may simply indicate that labor is paid its marginal value product, the wage it would receive in the short run under competitive conditions. Of course, in the long run, differences in value productivity should be narrowed by relative changes in product prices, and wages for the same type of labor should tend to become equal. Thus, insofar as Slichter's 1940 census data reflect the influence of long-period forces, variations in wages based on inter-industry differences in value added would not be consistent with long-run labor market competition.

### Short-Period Structure Variations

Although in the long run, competition equalizes wages for labor of the same grades, this is not the case for the short run. For the shorter period, differential changes in labor demand for similar labor in its particular employment will induce wage variation. In the long run, wage equality will be restored. In fact, the long run under perfect labor market competition may be defined as the length of time it takes for the labor supply schedule to become infinitely elastic.

This means that long-run wage variations should not be related to economic variables that affect labor demand; more precisely, there should be no variation in wages at all. The strength of short-run competition is more difficult to test. If wages for similar labor vary in accordance with economic factors, such as value productivity or profit rates, short-run competition is indicated. But if no relationship is found, this might indicate either a lack of competition or a rapidly adjusting long-run competitive labor market.

But since there is wide dispersion among wage changes for a short period, a different approach to the issue of factors determining wages, whether competitive or institutional, studies the forces behind wage changes for industries with similar wage differences, rather than the factors explaining wage variation. The two studies, by Maher and by Eckstein and Wilson, strongly support the hypothesis that wage changes, at least in the short run, are strongly related to institutional factors.

Maher notes the similarity of wage movements in the post-World War II period for a group of industries having close institutional ties. He points out the significance of this finding, that these institutional factors—input-output nexus, strong interrelated unions, geographical concentration, high capital intensity—which characterize the "key group" of industries, are not the competitive forces that determine wages.

It is interesting to note that Maher foresees the effectiveness of measures, such as the Wage-Price Guideposts, to blunt cost-push inflation. Wages influenced by institutional forces are determined partly by the suppliers themselves. Thus, for the key group, wages and prices are susceptible to the cost-push forces that are associated with less than perfectly competitive labor markets. Furthermore, as both Maher and Eckstein and Wilson note, there is some "spillover" of wage patterns within the key group into other industries,[*] indicating an expanded potential for cost-push inflation.

One can perhaps extend the chain too far. Extreme administration pressure was placed on the steel industry around 1960 to curtail wage and price increases. With steel an important member of the key group, the question is to what degree steel wage-price rises would be transferred within the group, then outside it, to measure the dampening effect on inflation of effective limitations of cost-push forces in one industry.

[*] Maher's study of the "spillover" effect appears in a section of his paper not included here.

# The Wage Pattern in the United States, 1946–1957

## by John E. Maher

The historic strike in the steel industry in 1959 calls attention to the peculiar importance of collective bargaining negotiations in the basic industries of the United States. For it is widely recognized that a major settlement in these industries has repercussions extending throughout a vast sector of the economy. A major settlement immediately affects the wages (incomes and employment) of large numbers of workers covered by negotiations, and also the costs of production and prices of the employing firm. Furthermore, because of the tendency among other bargainers to adhere to a pattern of wage change, a major settlement eventually influences these crucial variables in a number of related bargaining situations. The pervasiveness of key settlements explains the significance attributed to negotiations in steel and in automobiles, and it is this that largely accounts for the contention by company negotiators in steel in 1959 that their resistance to wage increases was part of a battle against inflation in the whole economy. This pervasiveness of the key bargains also helps us understand the pledges of the AFL-CIO and its affiliates to give millions of dollars to support the striking Steelworkers.

SOURCE Reprinted with permission from the *Industrial and Labor Relations Review*, Vol. 15, No. 1, October 1961, Copyright © 1961 by Cornell University. All rights reserved.

The influence of pattern bargaining on wage movements in American industry during the post-World War II years has long been recognized, but there has been little systematic effort to identify the pattern setters, to trace the pattern, and to analyze its diffusion among bargaining situations outside of the basic pattern-setting group of firms and industries. These tasks are attempted in this article which covers experience during the period, 1946–1957. One of the significant conclusions is that traditional explanations of industrial wage movements have neglected the technical, institutional, and economic interrelationships among the key bargainers, which tend to produce a kind of "demonstration effect" in collective bargaining.

| Year | 1946 | 1947 | 1948 | 1949 | 1950 | 1951 | 1952 | 1953 | 1954 | 1955 | 1956 | 1957 |
|---|---|---|---|---|---|---|---|---|---|---|---|---|
| Wage increase | 18½ | 15 | 11, 12 or 13 | 0 | 10 or 11 | 14 | 8 | 7 or 8½ | 5 | 15 | 10 to 12 | 12 to 13 |

While interpretations of events like the steel strike may vary, there is agreement that economists need to know in more precise terms what the pattern of wage change in the basic industries has been, who the participants were, and to what extent the pattern has spread to bargaining situations outside the basic industries. If these questions can be answered, we may expect to move forward toward a consideration of the impact of pattern bargaining upon the economy as a whole. I venture to suggest that both the theory and measurement of wage changes will be influenced by our understanding of the pattern and that such current issues as "cost-push" inflation will be more successfully treated.

The fact of pattern bargaining has, of course, been long recognized. Arthur M. Ross has perhaps given the most astute appraisal of the phenomenon in his *Trade Union Wage Policy*[1] and in his article, "The External Wage Structure."[2] But the pattern itself has not been defined and measured for an extended time period. Nor has there been a study of the diffusion of the pattern to wage bargains other than in the basic industries. From these gaps in our knowledge it follows that the magnitude of pattern bargaining and its consequences have not been adequately assessed.

## MAJOR PARTICIPANTS IN THE PATTERN

Table 1 presents the pattern of wage changes in selected industries for the years 1946 through 1957. In the next section, we shall explore the details of the wage negotiations from which this pattern is derived.

Table 2 lists the companies and unions whose negotiations will be shown to conform to the wage pattern. It can be seen immediately that the list includes those bargainers upon whom much of government's wage stabilization efforts have depended; especially noteworthy are steel (Little Steel Formula) in World War II and automobiles during the Korean War. Indeed, Kerr has cogently argued that during the latter conflict the Wage Stabilization Board's practice was "to take the top national bargains (especially the UAW-General Motors Agreement) and turn them into governmental policy."[3] But all of these bargaining situations are peculiarly prominent. Thus all eleven of the industries represented may be classed as "potential national emergency industries," and three of them have already been subject to the emergency provisions of the Taft-Hartley Act: meat-packing (1948), nonferrous metals (1951), and steel (1960).

The prominence of these industries and the availability of details of wage negotiation from the Wage Chronology Series of the Bureau of Labor Statistics make these bargaining situations ideally appropriate for study.

### Interrelations of the Key Bargainers

What are the ties that bind these bargaining situations together in such a way

---

[1] Berkeley, 1948, pp. 55–70.
[2] *New Concepts in Wage Determination*, George W. Taylor and Frank Pierson, eds., New York: 1957, pp. 173–205.
[3] Clark Kerr, "Governmental Wage Restraints: Their Limits and Uses in a Mobilized Economy," Proceedings, Fourth Annual Meeting, Industrial Relations Research Association, 1951, p. 14.

TABLE 2. BARGAINING SITUATIONS SELECTED FOR STUDY

| Industry and Company | Union [a] | Avg. Company Employment, 1950–1957 (000's) | Percentage of Workers in Industry Organized [b] | Degree of Industrial Concentration, 1954 [c] |
|---|---|---|---|---|
| Steel | | | 80–100 | .65 (blast furnace) |
| U. S. Steel Corp. | USA (AFL-CIO) | 165 | | .54 (rolling mills and steel works) |
| Automobiles | | | 80–100 | |
| General Motors | | 335 | | |
| Chrysler | UAW(AFL-CIO) | 115 | | |
| Ford | | 165 | | |
| Aluminum | | | 80–100 | [not available] |
| Alcoa | USA (AFL-CIO) AWU (AFL-CIO) | 54 | | |
| Farm machinery | | | 80–100 | n.a. |
| International Harvester | UAW (AFL-CIO) FE-UE (Ind.) | 48 | | |
| Electrical equipment | | | 80–100 | .50 (motors and generators); |
| G. E. | IUE (AFL-CIO) | 112 | | |
| Westinghouse | UE (Ind.) | 57 | | .24 (radios) |
| Rubber | | | 80–100 | .78 (tires); |
| Firestone | | 22 | | .28 (other rubber) |
| Goodyear | URW (AFL-CIO) | 26 | | |
| Goodrich | | 16 | | |
| U.S. | | 32 | | |
| Copper | | | 80–100 | .64 (copper rolling and drawing); |
| Anaconda | | 16 | | |
| Phelps-Dodge | MMSW (Ind.) | 6 | | .90 (copper mining) |
| Aircraft | | | 80–100 | .47 (aircraft); |
| Douglas | IAM (AFL-CIO) | 51 | | .62 (engines) |
| Lockheed | UAW (AFL-CIO) | 29 | | |
| Martin | UAW (AFL-CIO) | 21 | | |
| No. American | UAW (AFL-CIO) | 36 | | |
| Petroleum refining | | | 60–79 | .33 |
| Sinclair | OWU (AFL-CIO) | 9 | | |
| Meatpacking | | | 80–100 | .39 |
| Armour | UPW (AFL-CIO) | 34 | | |
| Swift | MCB (AFL-CIO) | 35 | | |
| Shipbuilding | | | 80–100 | n.a. |
| Bethlehem | SWA (AFL-CIO) | 16 | | |
| Pacific Coast | MTC | 15 | | |

[a] Names of unions have been abbreviated as follows:

USA—United Steelworkers of America (AFL-CIO)

UAW—United Automobile Workers of America (AFL-CIO)

AWU—Aluminum Workers Union (AFL-CIO)

FE-UE—Farm Equipment Division of the United Electrical Workers Union (Ind.). The UAW had replaced the FE-UE as bargaining agent at International Harvester by mid-1955.

IUE—International Union of Electrical Workers (AFL-CIO)

UE—United Electrical Workers (Ind.)

URW—United Rubber Workers (AFL-CIO)

MMSW—Mine, Mill and Smelter Workers (Ind.)

IAM—International Association of Machinists (AFL-CIO)

OWU—Oil Workers Union (AFL-CIO)

UPW—United Packinghouse Workers (AFL-CIO)

MCB—Meat Cutters and Butchers (AFL-CIO)

SWA—Shipbuilding Workers of America (AFL-CIO)

MTC—Metal Trades Council, an organization of former AFL craft affiliates who negotiate together in the Pacific coast shipbuilding industry.

[b] Bulletin No. 909, *Extent of Collective Bargaining and Union Recognition, 1946*, BLS, 1947.

[c] *Statistical Abstract of the United States, 1958*, Table 1027, pp. 786–787. Concentration is based upon the percentage of the value of total shipments in an industry accounted for by the four largest firms.

Industrial and Geographical Wage Structures    491

as to produce conformity to a common pattern of wage change? There are four principal ties: the input-output nexus; the similar internal technological and economic constitution that will produce similar responses to external change; the distribution of the participants; and the institutional channels of communication. Of course, not all of these ties apply equally to all of the bargaining situations.

By the input-output nexus I mean that, with few exceptions, each industry ranks among the largest consumers of the output of one or more of the other industries. Thus, the largest consumer of nonferrous metals is the electrical industry; the largest of rubber and electrical equipment, automobiles; the largest of aluminum, aircraft[4] Since these industries are highly organized by unions and generally dominated by a small number of firms, this industrial interdependence is readily translated into a dependence of firm on firm (and of union on union).

Most of the industries and firms have relatively high capital-output and capital-labor ratios and employ a technology associated with mass production. This grossly similar constitution, together with the fact that the majority produce either capital goods or consumer durables, means that these participants in the pattern of wage change are similarly situated with respect to their sensitivity to fluctuations in general economic activity.

The common ties that I have referred to summarily as "distribution of the participants" are meant to reflect, not only the geographic clustering of the firms in the industrial, northeastern region of the United States and on each coast, but also the concentration of the workers in these industries into a few, large national unions. On the one hand, the geographic clustering implies that these firms must compete in common markets for labor and, perhaps, for other factors of production considered traditionally as having low mobility. On the other hand, concentration of workers within a few large unions suggests that the coordination of bargaining will require that negotiators study and compare the wage movements within and among a few well-defined and highly organized sectors of the economy.[5]

Institutional arrangements affecting bargaining are also important. Almost all of these industries are organized by industrial unions that were once affiliated with the CIO and now with the AFL-CIO. Several of these unions have long competed with each other to represent workers in the various bargaining units. Thus, in the copper industry, the United Steelworkers and the International Union of Mine, Mill and Smelter Workers have competed on various occasions over the years. So, too, have the International Association of Machinists and the United Automobile Workers contested representation in the aircraft industry. Needless to say, the merger of the AFL and CIO has served to diminish conflicts among affiliates. But the very attenuation in this representation struggle has meant that rivalries among the various unions could find outlets more effectively in terms of competition in bargaining. This, of course, is especially true where two or more unions represent workers of the same company.

Leaders of the various unions have also from time to time been engaged in a wider form of rivalry with one another. Thus David McDonald, president of the

---

[4] The industrial classification scheme employed in input-output analysis is not the same as that which describes the industrial position of firms engaged in collective bargaining. Yet a perusal of the distribution of outputs by industry in that analysis is wholly consistent with the statements made above. See W. W. Leontief, *Structure of the American Economy, 1919–1939,* 2nd ed., New York, 1951.

[5] Ten of the fourteen unions listed in Table 2 are among the largest in the country, their average membership in 1958 exceeding 400,000 persons. None of the ten has fewer than 100,000 members and three have about one million. See *Directory of National and International Labor Unions in the United States, 1959,* Bulletin No. 1267 (Washington: Bureau of Labor Statistics, 1959), p. 10.

Steelworkers, and Walter Reuther of the Automobile Workers have traditionally been considered contestant for the position of spokesman for vast segments of the labor movement.[6]

Another characteristic of these industries, one of both economic and institutional significance, is their high degree of industrial concentration (last column of Table 2). The data available show that four companies account for a large share of the total value of shipments in each industry: from about one-fourth in rubber, other than tires, to three-quarters in automobiles. And the particular companies represented in our list of bargains are among the four largest.

## The Logic of Wage Conformity

What do the relationships among the bargainers mean for the study of wages? They mean that the negotiators cannot conceivably negotiate independently of another, since so much of the data "given" to one industry are the variables operated upon by negotiators in another industry. To illustrate: a change in the wages of workers in steel tends to affect the price of a major input to automobiles, namely, steel, and to alter one of the most important bargaining criteria, that is, the wages paid to workers in "comparable" industries. Furthermore, the penalty for a failure of negotiations in steel that results in a strike must be borne eventually by automobile workers because, without continuing steel production, the output of automobiles must cease. Managers, workers, owners, all share interests that cut across these industries. The community of interests has created an ideal situation for what Riesman has called behavior that is "other-directed," that is, the studied conduct of conformity to developing norms. And, as we shall see, bargaining has resulted in this conformity.

Before proceeding to give the substance of those wage negotiations that constitute the pattern, I should anticipate a fundamental question. If the bargainers in the situations just discussed share so many characteristics, what importance is there to the fact of their conformity to a pattern of wage change? What else could have been expected?

The answer is that something quite different could have been expected because the common characteristics referred to above—economic interrelationships, technological and economic structure, distribution, and institutional channels of communication—are *not* sources of influence upon wages that have typically been adduced to explain wage movements (although they are, indeed, related to such other sources). Without attempting a review of the empirical research and theoretical discussion that surrounds this question of what causes changes in wages, we may notice the range of variables and the categories into which they fall. With respect to the employer's derived demand for labor, we notice that changes in (marginal) productivity have been considered crucial. Productivity, in turn, is affected by technological advance, by shifts in the supply functions of other productive factors, and in value terms by changes in the price of output. On the supply side, where workers are organized, we may notice those bargaining criteria made so well known by Slichter: ability to pay, (average) productivity, changes in the wages of workers held to be comparable, movements in the cost of living, and requirements of a minimum budget for a "typical" worker.

\* \* \*

---

[6] Cf. B. Soffer, "The Effects of Cost-of-Living Wage Escalators on General Wage Level Movements," (unpublished Ph.D. dissertation, Princeton, 1956).

Eckstein and Wilson, though writing without prior knowledge of Maher's work, note the same institutional forces on wage changes within the key group (p. 498 Footnote 6). They do not measure the degree of wage change uniformity within the group, as Maher does, but instead extend his analysis to relate the similar changes to the operation of economic forces within their common institutional framework.

# The Determination of Money Wages in American Industry

## by Otto Eckstein and Thomas A. Wilson

HYPOTHESIS 1 (INSTITUTIONAL):
WAGE RATES ARE SET BY A
BARGAINING PROCESS

In much of modern industry, wage rates are determined by contracts reached through collective bargaining, a process which differs mechanically from the classical supply-demand adjustment processes. A theory of wages requires at least a primitive model of the bargaining process, and of the institutional, political and economic forces which it reflects.

No new formal bargaining theory will be advanced here, nor will we apply any of the recent theories, such as those of Zeuthen, Nash, Harsanyi, Schelling or Pen,[1] except to draw on them for general concepts. We view the problem in terms of the utility functions of union leaders and corporate managements, particularly with respect to (1) wage settlements of different amounts, (2) the cost of a strike, and (3) the cost of losing a strike.

HYPOTHESIS 2 (ECONOMIC):
BOTH PRODUCT AND LABOR
MARKET FACTORS INFLUENCE
WAGE DETERMINATION

With labor and product market factors influencing the cost of settlements and of strikes to the bargaining participants, variables pertaining to both markets must affect wage determination. Thus, a union's utility function with respect to the size of

SOURCE Reprinted with permission from *Quarterly Journal of Economics*, Vol. 76, August, 1966, pp. 379–414.

[1] In a general way, our model resembles that of J. Pen in "A General Theory of Bargaining," *American Economic Review*, XLII (Mar. 1952), 24–42. See also his "Wage Determination Revisited," *Kyklos*, XI (No. 1, 1958), 1–28, in which he suggests that bargaining theory be used to isolate strategic variables for statistical analysis. Pen there favors unemployment and consumer prices, although he also mentions profits as a factor.

settlements will shift with economic conditions. Members expect large settlements in good times and make it impossible for union leaders to settle for less. The loss of jobs produced by the wage increases is likely to be greater when unemployment is high, since the degree of control over the labor supply by the union is likely to be weaker when the employers find it easy to get nonunion labor, or to shift the work to regions that are not organized; further, the disutility of any given employment effect is greater since the probability of the laid-off workers being absorbed elsewhere in the industry is smaller. Finally, non-wage benefits, particularly strengthened job security and improvements in the union's security as bargaining agent, are relatively more important under such conditions and unions will be willing to trade off wage gains for them.

Similarly, the disutility to management of large settlements varies with economic conditions.

\* \* \*

HYPOTHESIS 3 (ECONOMIC):
TWO VARIABLES, PROFIT AND
UNEMPLOYMENT RATES, ARE
SUFFICIENT TO EXPLAIN MOST OF
THE VARIATION IN THE RATE
OF INCREASE OF WAGE RATES

The above discussion suggests that a statistical explanation of wage changes must include some labor and some product market variables. One might wish to construct an elaborate system incorporating many variables, such as output and its rate of change, new and unfilled orders, profits and their recent history, and, on the labor market side, unemployment and its change, employment change, vacancy and turnover rates, and all of these variables both for local and national markets. However, there are far too few observations in the history since the rise of industrial trade unions for this approach; also, the variables inevitably are highly correlated with each other; nor is it sound methodology to use more than the necessary number of variables. Two variables have therefore, been singled out, one for each market.

For the labor market, unemployment was chosen.[2] Besides the central role which unemployment plays in determining the division of bargaining power in wage negotiations, it also serves as an appropriate variable in those unorganized labor markets in which the classical supply-demand mechanism applies.[3] All industries contain some unorganized segments, and a statistical analysis must allow for them.

The profit rate was chosen as the strategic variable for the product market. First, it reflects the short-run conditions which affect bargaining power discussed above. Second, it reflects long-run structural characteristics of the product market, such as the degree of monopoly. Finally, although we do not attribute great significance to equity factors in wage determination, the desire of unions to maintain labor's share in industry income and, hence, to insist on large wage increases when profits are high is certainly a real factor.

HYPOTHESIS 4 (INSTITUTIONAL):
WAGE DETERMINATION IN
A GROUP OF HEAVY
INDUSTRIES IS INTERDEPENDENT

Since 1948, wages in several industries, which might be characterized as heavy

---

[2] For evidence of the high correlation between unemployment and other labor market variables, see James W. Knowles and Edward Kalachek, *Higher Unemployment Rates, 1957–1960: Structural Transformation Or Inadequate Demand,* Subcommittee on Economic Statistics of Joint Economic Committee, U.S. Congress, 1961.

[3] Ideally, unemployment should be supplemented by measures of excess demand, such as job vacancy figures. See J. C. R. Dow and L. A. Dicks-Mireaux, "Excess Demand for Labour," *Oxford Economic Papers,* N. S., Vol. 10 (Feb. 1958), for an index using both unemployment and vacancy figures.

industries, moved almost identically. All of these industries are high-wage industries, have strong industrial unions, typically consist of large corporations that possess considerable market power, and are geographically centered in the Midwestern industrial heartland of the continent. For our statistical analysis, the group was defined to include these two-digit industries: rubber, stone clay and glass, primary metals, fabricated metals, nonelectrical machinery, electrical machinery, transportation equipment, and instruments. We call this group the "key group." This list does not define the group perfectly; in each of these two-digit industries some segments do not belong in the group, and conversely, some segments of two-digit industries not included should properly be put inside the group. However, the two-digit industry list is sufficiently accurate for the purpose of the statistical analysis.

The industries in the group are interdependent in a number of ways. First, because of the considerable input-output connections among them, they tend to prosper together. For example, when auto sales are high, rubber, plate glass, and metal fabricating sales are high. When there is much construction, steel and cement fare well. When there is a capital goods boom, machinery, steel, and metal fabricating are prosperous. Second, because of the geographical concentration and perhaps because of some general similarity in the kinds of mechanical skills required, the industries constitute at least a weakly linked labor market. Third, typically a wage pattern is known to exist in these industries. While no one industry is always the leader in establishing this pattern, autos and steel probably play more of a leadership role than the others. But whoever initiates the pattern, it has a very considerable influence on all subsequent settlements in the group. In some instances, the pattern setting and following are quite regular; for example, the cement and aluminum settlements follow the steel settlement, and rubber and plate glass tend to follow the auto settlement.[4]

The political relationships among unions are also close with this group. Some unions are bargaining agents in several industries. Geographic proximity, including proximity of some large plants, makes the members of different unions aware of each others' settlements, and puts pressure on their leaders to achieve as good a settlement as the rest of the group.[5]

The industries outside the group do not exhibit as close patterns of interdependence, although there are considerable spillovers from the key group. On the whole, they are not so well organized,

[4] In the latter case, the possibility of the auto companies going into the rubber or plate glass business makes the wage settlements in these supplier industries inevitably very similar to the auto settlement.

[5] Interdependence of this group has long been recognized by students of labor economies. A fuller account is given by Arthur M. Ross, "The External Wage Structure," in *New Concepts in Wage Determination,* eds. G. H. Taylor and F. Pierson (New York: McGraw-Hill, 1957), pp. 173–205. Ross finds that a group of "hard-goods" industries, which corresponds rather closely to our key group, received virtually identical wage increases over the period 1939–52. Benson Soffer has analyzed some of the interactions within the group in detail in his "On Union Rivalries and the Differentiation of Wage Patterns," *Review of Economics and Statistics,* XLI (Feb. 1959), 53–60.

Dunlop employs the concept of the "wage contour." He defines a contour as a set of bargaining units which are linked via product markets or labor markets, or which have a common labor market organization. Our key group, on these definitions, is a wage contour, and may perhaps be considered the central wage contour in manufacturing. Dunlop stresses the prevalence of these contours all through the economy. Our analysis is confined to manufacturing, which leaves out many of the important wage contours in the economy, and is limited to the two-digit level, at which many smaller contours, even in manufacturing, are not visible.

Ross speaks of "orbits of coercive comparison." The key group appears to be such an orbit, or perhaps should more properly be considered to be two or more linked orbits. See his *Trade Union Wage Policy.*

have lower wages, are dispersed more over the country including the lightly unionized South, and exhibit less interdependence both through input-output connections and through the labor market. Our statistical hypotheses are also tested for these industries on an individual basis, and in some instances, simple hypotheses, including spillovers, do explain wage behavior. In some other cases, unique factors, such as technological changes, changes in the product mix, or large regional movements of the particular industry produce unusual industry wage patterns.[6]

### HYPOTHESIS 5 (INSTITUTIONAL): WAGES ARE DETERMINED IN WAGE ROUNDS

The instrument of wage determination in organized industries is the contract that is negotiated between a union and its employers. Contracts have varied from one year to five years.[7] This institutional arrangement has significant implications. It means that the economic conditions prevailing and expected at the time of the negotiations play a particularly important role in wage determination, and this is true whatever theory of wages one chooses to embrace. A statistical investigation which ignores this crucial factor cannot hope to get very successful results.

Levinson has found that during the postwar period contracts were negotiated in a series of wage rounds.[8] Chronologies of contract settlements show a clustering of settlements in time, and, in the case of the key industries, also in the characteristics of the settlements. These rounds have ranged from one to four years. Once the pattern for a round is set in early key bargains, the movements of wages in the remaining months or years are largely determined until the next round is settled. Thus, to take the most extreme example, the wage settlements of 1955 and 1956 determineed the bulk of the wage movements in the key industries up to 1958. The wages in this four-year period were determined largely by the economic conditions in 1955 and 1956, not by the recession of 1958. While in this instance the result was a particularly large long-term wage increase because of the timing accident, on some other occasion the opposite result might occur.[9]

### THE CENTRAL RESULT ON WAGES: WAGE DETERMINATION IN THE KEY GROUP

These hypotheses form the theoretical basis for the statistical analysis of the rate

[6] As this paper was completed, John E. Maher's "The Wage Pattern in the United States, 1946–1957," *Industrial and Labor Relations Review*, Vol. 15 (Oct. 1961), pp. 1–20, appeared. Maher, on the basis of a detailed analysis of contract terms, also finds the existence of the key group. He explores the interconnections among the unions in the group and cites the same list of reasons as above. His independently derived list of industries is almost identical with our own, which is reassuring. Maher does not seek to explain the changes in the wage pattern of the group from movements of economic variables.

[7] A contract specifies changes in wage rates, not in average hourly earnings, of course. However, recent studies have shown that there has not been much "wage-drift," i.e., changes in hourly straight-time earnings not imposed by contracts, in the United States. See John E. Maher, "Wages: The Pattern of Wage Movements in the United States Since 1945—Its Meaning and Significance," *Review of Economics and Statistics*, XLIII (Aug. 1961), 277–82, especially Charts 1 and 2. Maher finds considerable short-run deviations; they are partly caused by variations in overtime and seasonal factors. . . .

[8] Joint Economic Committee, U. S. Congress, *Staff Report on Employment, Growth and Price Levels*, Dec. 1959, pp. 150–56; Harold M. Levinson, "Postwar Movement of Prices and Wages in Manufacturing Industries," Study Paper No. 21, *Study of Employment, Growth and Price Levels*, Joint Economic Committee, U. S. Congress, Jan. 1960, pp. 7–13, and Levinson, *Collective Bargaining in the Steel Industry: Pattern Setter or Pattern Follower?*, Institute of Industrial Relations, University of Michigan (Ann Arbor, 1962).

[9] The length of wage periods is the result of bargaining with sometimes one side, sometimes the other, pressing for a longer contract and willing to pay a price for it. A guessing game about coming economic conditions seems to be involved. We do not attempt to explain the lengths of the periods; we only identify them.

of increase of wages in the key group. The annual average rate of increase of straight-time hourly earnings in the key group was regressed against profits and unemployment for the five wage rounds since 1948.

The results of this regression, which are striking, are represented in Figure 1. Both profits and unemployment are highly significant; the regression coefficients are several times their standard errors, and the multiple determination coefficient ($R^2$) is .9975. The correlation between the independent variables is fairly low, partly because after-tax profit rates have been affected by changes in tax rates as well as economic conditions, partly because neither profits nor unemployment are perfectly correlated with general prosperity. Thus, even though the correlation has only two degrees of freedom, the fit is so extraordinary that the coefficients are significant at the .99 level. Given the variation in the variables during the period, profits account for 57 per cent of the total explanation, unemployment for the other 43 per cent.

While this result is beyond chance, economists are properly skeptical of any result which is obtained with only two degrees of freedom. Some supporting evidence, based on cross sections and on time series studies of individual industries, will be presented below. But we must stress that the fewness of observations represents historical reality. In the period under study, there were only five or six[10] actual episodes, i.e., five or six points which could be observed. Sample size could conceivably be increased by studying prewar data; however, since industrial unions did not achieve their present position until after World War II, the same mechanism probably would not apply.

The result is consistent with the hypotheses. Both product and factor market variables are important; profit and unemployment appear to be the crucial variables in

wage determination. The bargaining theory is not tested directly, that is the variables could make their influence felt via some other route. However, the fact that an analysis of the key group by wage rounds gives more significant statistical results than time series analyses of annual data, or cross-section analyses of annual or cyclical period data, lends support to the institutional hypotheses which we have adopted.

\* \* \*

## WAGE DETERMINATION OUTSIDE THE KEY GROUP

The profit-unemployment explanation of wage changes was also attempted for the industries outside the key group. Since long-term contracts were less important in these industries a seven-period analysis was used, with periods 3 and 4 subdivided.

Regressions using only industry variables are significant at the .95 level for just three of the eleven industries. To obtain a successful explanation of wage changes in some of these industries, explicit allowance must be made for spillover from the key industries. A regression with key wages and industry unemployment provides statistically significant explanations for eight of the eleven industries, with four of the explanations significant at the .99 level, and similarly for industry profits. Key wages are statistically significant in eight cases; the industry variables are significant in only one and four cases respectively and take on the correct signs in all cases but one in the eight equations. These results are confirmed by a regression using all three independent variables.

Three industries remain without explanation at this stage: chemicals, tobacco and printing. In chemicals, industrial chemicals belong inside the key group; the rest might yield to analysis at a more

[10] A six-period regression was also fitted. Similar results were obtained.

*Figure 1. Wage determination in the key group.*

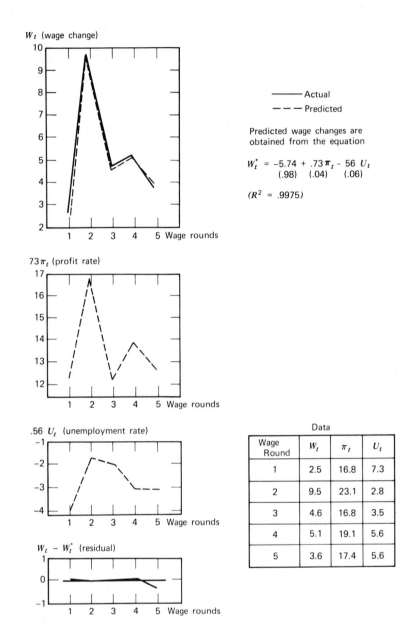

$W_t$ (wage change)

———— Actual

– – – Predicted

Predicted wage changes are obtained from the equation

$$W_t^* = -5.74 + .73\,\pi_t - 56\,U_t$$
$$\quad\quad (.98)\quad (.04)\quad (.06)$$

$(R^2 = .9975)$

$73\pi_t$ (profit rate)

$.56\ U_t$ (unemployment rate)

$W_t - W_t^*$ (residual)

| Wage Round | $W_t$ | $\pi_t$ | $U_t$ |
|---|---|---|---|
| 1 | 2.5 | 16.8 | 7.3 |
| 2 | 9.5 | 23.1 | 2.8 |
| 3 | 4.6 | 16.8 | 3.5 |
| 4 | 5.1 | 19.1 | 5.6 |
| 5 | 3.6 | 17.4 | 5.6 |

Data

detailed level. Printing, a very highly organized industry on a craft union basis, provides a useful illustration that high correlations are not inevitable in the analysis of wages. It is not impossible to get correlations as low as .01!

Even in the industries where the regressions are significant they do not account for all the wage changes by any means. In some of the industries, for example, increases in the minimum wage clearly led to jumps in the average wage in 1956.

Eckstein and Wilson find a close correlation between the profit and unemployment rates and the wage movements of their key group, which comprises a somewhat different set of broader industries than those Maher studied. These are the familiar Phillips curve, and related wage determining variables. It is unfortunate that neither study measures the degree of similarity of a competitive economic variable, such as value productivity changes, to find whether the market force of ability-to-pay also operates on wage changes of the key group.

Eckstein and Wilson present findings in support of the spillover hypothesis in wage movements in the two-digit industry categories outside the key groups. Wage changes in these industries are not closely related to their unemployment and profit rates. The fact that the looseness of fit reflects the tendency to conform to key group wage changes is evidenced by the strengthening of the relationship when key group wage changes are introduced as an explanatory variable for the individual nonkey group wage movements.

## THE GEOGRAPHICAL WAGE STRUCTURE

Moving to geographical wage patterns, perfect competition in the labor market would result in wage equality for the same type of labor between labor markets. In fact this degree of competition would invalidate the concept of local or geographical labor markets making the entire country one unified market.

But wages do differ interregionally. These differences are usually studied with special reference to the relatively low wages of the South. Important aspects of regional wage differences are the problems of measurement and of explaining how they arose and why they persist.

### Measuring Regional Wage Differences

On measurement, the central issue is the establishment of the concept of a regional wage index, a ratio of an area's wage level to a standard, either the wage level of another area or the nation as a whole. The South has lower wages than, say, the North for two basic reasons. First, on the average, southern workers of the same type receive lower wages than those of their counterparts. Second, wages are lower in the South because of the preponderance of low-wage unskilled labor in the South.

These conditions cause ambiguity in the concept of a southern wage index. Should this index measure the ratio of southern to northern wages for labor of the same level, correcting for interarea differences in skill mix or should it measure the ratio of unadjusted average wages of the South to those of the North? If the question is one of the strength of labor market competition, then clearly the first is the relevant index. Under perfect competition, labor mobility would establish wage uniformity beween the regions.

However, if the economic well-being of the area is the issue, then the unadjusted index becomes the appropriate measure. Suppose industries employing large numbers of unskilled labor moved to the South as a partial substitute for labor mobility out of the area in equalizing interregional wages for the same grade of labor. Then wages for perfectly substitutable labor might become equal between the regions, making the adjusted southern wage index equal to 100. But the unadjusted average southern wage level would be well below this value, perhaps even lower than before wages for similar labor became equal. Is this the goal of southern economic development policy?

In earlier studies, regional wage indexes were measured on an industrial basis, correcting for regional differences in industry mix. Thus the southern wage index would be the ratio of the South's average wage level, were it to have the same industrial mix as the non-South, to the average wage of the non-South. This method yields a very imperfect measure of regional wage differences for labor of the same quality, mainly because of possible significant error in the implicit assumption that the skill mix within individual industries is the same for the South as for the non-South.

A much more accurate attempt to measure regional differences in wages for labor of the same type corrects for interregional differences in labor quality. Fuchs makes these corrections in his tight statistical study of the southern wage index. He standardizes for the interregional labor quality differences of age, sex, color, and educational level.

In Table 1, Fuchs shows that, on the average, without adjustment for differences in labor quality, the non-South index is 125, or that southern wages are only 80 percent of the non-South level. Correcting for age, sex, color, and education, the non-South index falls to 117 (Table 3). That is, if the distribution of southern labor with respect to these qualities were the same as that for the rest of the country, southern average wages would rise to 85 percent of the non-South level.

Finally, correcting for the tendency for wages to be higher in larger than in smaller communities, with the South's industry characteristically located in small towns, the non-South index is reduced still further. Table 4 presents a value of 109 for the non-South index, if industrial location were the same in the nation as a whole as it is in the South.

# Differentials in Hourly Earnings by Region and City Size, 1959

## *by Victor R. Fuchs*

### REGIONAL DIFFERENTIALS

Table 1 shows the regional differentials in actual hourly earnings in dollars and in index-number form with the South equal to 100. The figures contain few surprises. Earnings are significantly lower in the South than in other regions; earnings in the West are slightly higher than in the Northeast or North Central divisions. The difference between the South and the rest of the country is much greater for non-whites than for whites; within each color group, the differentials for males and for females appear to be about the same.

Table 2 shows the extent to which regional earnings differences can be explained by differences in color, age, sex, and education. Where the comparison is for a given color-sex group, the effect of differences in age and education is reflected in the "expected" earnings. Labor quality, as measured by these variables,

appears to be somewhat lower in the South than in the rest of the country, and highest in the West. The regional difference is slightly greater for males than for females. In fact, white females in the South have slightly higher "expected" earnings than in the Northeast and North Central.

Table 3 shows that a significant regional wage differential remains after standardizing for color, age, sex, and education. For all non-agricultural employed persons, the differential between the South and the rest of the country is approximately 17 per cent. It is much greater for nonwhites than for whites and is smallest for white males where the differential is of the order of 14 per cent.

It is worth noting that the standardization procedure used here is not the only one available for studying this problem. It would be equally appropriate to stan-

SOURCE Reprinted with permission from *Differentials in Hourly Earnings by Region and City Size, 1959*, National Bureau of Economic Research, Occasional Paper 101, New York, 1967.

503

TABLE 1. AVERAGE HOURLY EARNINGS, NONAGRICULTURAL EMPLOYED PERSONS, BY REGION, 1959

| | South | Non-South | Northeast | North Central | West |
|---|---|---|---|---|---|
| | (Dollars per Hour) | | | | |
| White males | 2.54 | 2.99 | 2.97 | 2.94 | 3.09 |
| White females | 1.56 | 1.83 | 1.84 | 1.75 | 1.97 |
| Nonwhite males | 1.40 | 2.22 | 2.07 | 2.25 | 2.43 |
| Nonwhite females | .92 | 1.50 | 1.55 | 1.40 | 1.56 |
| Total | 2.12 | 2.65 | 2.62 | 2.60 | 2.76 |
| | (Index, South = 100) | | | | |
| White males | 100 | 118 | 117 | 116 | 122 |
| White females | 100 | 117 | 118 | 113 | 126 |
| Nonwhite males | 100 | 159 | 149 | 161 | 174 |
| Nonwhite females | 100 | 163 | 168 | 152 | 170 |
| Total | 100 | 125 | 124 | 123 | 130 |

SOURCE: *U.S. Censuses of Population and Housing: 1960, 1/1,000 Sample.*

dardize by using the actual earnings rates for each color, age, sex, and education cell in each region, weighted by the national distribution of man-hours.[1] When the two standardization procedures yield markedly different results, interpretation is difficult. Fortunately, in this instance the two standardization procedures give very similar results. For white males the difference in results is of the order of 1 per cent. For nonwhite females it goes as high as 2 per cent.

A completely different standardization approach would be to regress hourly earnings of individuals on a group of independent variables with demographic characteristics and geographical location represented by a series of dummy variables. I believe the standardization procedure followed here is easier to manage and to follow because the numerous interactions among the various demographic characteristics and between the demographic characteristics and the geographical variables would require the use of hundreds of dummy variables. Moreover, standardization through regression analysis would require additional calculations in order to obtain geographical differences

in labor quality comparable to those measured by "expected" earnings.

This section has shown that only a portion of the gross non-South/South wage differential is attributable to demographic differences in the labor force. It is sometimes argued that the remainder is largely attributable to differences in city size, rather than to a regional differential at given city sizes. The next section deals with the question of wage differentials associated with city size.

REGIONAL DIFFERENTIAL
ADJUSTED FOR CITY SIZE

. . . the South has a much larger share of its non-agricultural work force outside of Standard Metropolitan Statistical Areas and a much smaller share in SMSA's of 1,000,000 and over than does the non-South. This fact, plus the existence of a significant wage differential across city sizes within regions, suggests the possibility that a substantial portion of the regional wage differential observed in Table 3 is a reflection of the city size effect. Table 4 supports this hypothesis. It summarizes the results by standardizing for city size.

[1] I.e., standardized hourly earnings $= \dfrac{\sum\limits_{c} W_{cr} H_{cu}}{H_u}$

TABLE 2. "EXPECTED" AVERAGE HOURLY EARNINGS, BY REGION, 1959

| | South | Non-South | Northeast | North Central | West |
|---|---|---|---|---|---|
| | (Dollars per Hour) | | | | |
| White males | 2.82 | 2.89 | 2.90 | 2.85 | 2.95 |
| White females | 1.77 | 1.76 | 1.72 | 1.75 | 1.85 |
| Nonwhite males | 1.74 | 1.91 | 1.90 | 1.88 | 2.01 |
| Nonwhite females | 1.16 | 1.24 | 1.19 | 1.21 | 1.31 |
| Total | 2.38 | 2.54 | 2.53 | 2.52 | 2.61 |
| | (Index, South = 100) | | | | |
| White males | 100 | 102 | 103 | 101 | 105 |
| White females | 100 | 99 | 97 | 99 | 105 |
| Nonwhite males | 100 | 110 | 109 | 108 | 116 |
| Nonwhite females | 100 | 107 | 103 | 104 | 113 |
| Total | 100 | 107 | 106 | 106 | 110 |

SOURCE: See Table 1.
NOTE: "Expected" hourly earnings are obtained by multiplying the national average hourly earnings of each color, age, sex, and education cell by the annual hours worked by members of that cell in the region, summing across all cells in the region, and dividing by the total man-hours of the region.

TABLE 3. RATIO OF ACTUAL TO "EXPECTED" HOURLY EARNINGS, BY REGION, 1959

| | South | Non-South | Northeast | North Central | West |
|---|---|---|---|---|---|
| | (Ratio) | | | | |
| White males | .90 | 1.03 | 1.02 | 1.03 | 1.05 |
| White females | .89 | 1.04 | 1.07 | 1.00 | 1.07 |
| Nonwhite males | .80 | 1.16 | 1.09 | 1.20 | 1.21 |
| Nonwhite females | .79 | 1.21 | 1.30 | 1.16 | 1.19 |
| Total | .89 | 1.04 | 1.04 | 1.03 | 1.06 |
| | (Index of Ratio, South = 100) | | | | |
| White males | 100 | 114 | 113 | 114 | 117 |
| White females | 100 | 117 | 120 | 112 | 120 |
| Nonwhite males | 100 | 145 | 136 | 150 | 151 |
| Nonwhite females | 100 | 153 | 165 | 147 | 151 |
| Total | 100 | 117 | 117 | 116 | 119 |

SOURCE: Tables 1 and 2.

The method of adjustment consists of taking the ratio of actual to expected in each city size in each region and weighting it by the share of that city size in national total man-hours. The indexes shown answer the question "What would be the ratio of actual to expected for this region if it had a city size distribution the same as that of the nation as a whole?" Table 4 may be compared directly with Table 3, which shows the indexes of ratios of actual to expected without any adjustment for city size.

Whereas, after adjusting for color, age, sex, and education, the differential between the non-South and the South was of the order of 17 per cent, it is about 9 per cent after city size is also taken into account. City size does make some difference, but does not explain all of the regional differential. It makes the greatest difference in the Northeast, and the least in the North Central. The regional differential continues to be much greater for nonwhites than for whites.

| | South | Non-South | Northeast | North Central | West |
|---|---|---|---|---|---|
| | | (Ratio) | | | |
| White males | .95 | 1.02 | 1.00 | 1.04 | 1.03 |
| White females | .95 | 1.03 | 1.04 | 1.01 | 1.04 |
| Nonwhite males | .85 | 1.15 | a | a | a |
| Nonwhite females | .87 | 1.18 | a | a | a |
| Total | .94 | 1.02 | 1.01 | 1.04 | 1.04 |
| | | (Index of Ratio, South = 100) | | | |
| White males | 100 | 107 | 105 | 109 | 108 |
| White females | 100 | 108 | 109 | 106 | 109 |
| Nonwhite males | 100 | 135 | a | a | a |
| Nonwhite females | 100 | 136 | a | a | a |
| Total | 100 | 109 | 107 | 111 | 111 |

SOURCE: U.S. Censuses of Population and Housing: 1960, 1/1,000 sample.

NOTE: The figure for each region is a weighted average of the ratios of actual to expected for each city size in the region weighted by the U.S. distribution of man-hours by city size for the color-sex group.

a Detailed breakdown within the non-South for nonwhites is not shown because the small sample size makes the results sensitive to choice of standardization procedure.

## SKILL LEVEL AND GEOGRAPHICAL DIFFERENTIALS

In the preceding sections it was shown that there are substantial regional and city size differentials in average hourly earnings after adjusting for color, age, sex, and education. It was also shown that there is a regional differential in standardized wages within city size classes and that there is a very large city size wage differential within regions. This section attempts to answer the question whether these geographical differentials are similar for different groups in the labor force, or whether they vary systematically with education, color, and sex.

Table 5 explores the non-South/South wage differential by city size for the sexes, colors, and educational classes. In each case the index is based on the South equal to 100, and the hourly earnings have been standardized for the demographic characteristics except the one being studied.

Inspection of Table 5 reveals that the standardized regional wage differential tends to vary inversely with skill level.[2] Thus, we observe that the ratio is lower for males than for females and lower for whites than for nonwhites; it also declines with increased years of schooling. This relationship tends to be present at all city sizes, except SMSA's of one million or more.

✽ ✽ ✽

[2] This finding is consistent with results reported in Joseph Bloch, "Regional Wage Differentials: 1907–1946," *Monthly Labor Review,* April 1948, p. 375; Lloyd Saville, "Earnings of Skilled and Unskilled Workers in New England and the South," *Journal of Political Economy,* October 1954, pp. 400–402; and Victor R. Fuchs and Richard Perlman, "Recent Trends in Southern Wage Differentials," *Review of Economics and Statistics,* August 1960, pp. 292–300.

| | | Urban Places | | Standard Metropolitan Statistical Areas | | | | All City Sizes |
|---|---|---|---|---|---|---|---|---|
| | Rural | Under 10,000 | 10,000– 99,999 | Under 250,000 | 250,000– 499,999 | 500,000– 999,999 | 1,000,000 and More | |
| Years of schooling | | | | | | | | |
| 0–4 | 133 | 148* | 204 | 142 | 108 | 118 | 107 | 144 |
| 5–8 | 123 | 121 | 124 | 115 | 117 | 120 | 112 | 126 |
| 9–11 | 119 | 121 | 121 | 114 | 116 | 117 | 105 | 122 |
| 12 | 112 | 106 | 118 | 113 | 100 | 107 | 105 | 113 |
| 13–15 | 105 | 117 | 99 | 98 | 98 | 114 | 102 | 110 |
| 16 and over | 108 | 111 | 93 | 111 | 97 | 90 | 108 | 109 |
| Sex | | | | | | | | |
| Male | 115 | 114 | 112 | 111 | 105 | 109 | 107 | 116 |
| Female | 118 | 121 | 120 | 115 | 112 | 111 | 105 | 120 |
| Color | | | | | | | | |
| White | 115 | 114 | 110 | 110 | 104 | 107 | 105 | 115 |
| Nonwhite | 147 | 153* | 170 | 150 | 158 | 140 | 121 | 147 |
| Total | 116 | 115 | 113 | 112 | 106 | 109 | 106 | 117 |

SOURCE: See Table 1.
NOTE: Earnings standardized by ratio of actual to "expected."
* Fewer than fifty observations in the Non-South.

Tables 2, 3, and 4 show that southern wages are relatively lowest for non-whites. Fuchs notes that this pattern is related to the strong tendency for southern wages to be relatively lowest for unskilled labor. Table 5, which presents wage differences by detailed school levels and by sex and color, unadjusted for other factors, clearly points out this tendency.

In a section not presented here, Fuchs introduces interregional differences in the extent of unionization as an explanatory variable for lower southern wages. The fact that southern industry is less unionized than in other regions seems to explain all the remaining difference in the non-South–South wage differences, since unionism is associated with high wages. However, to the extent that unions tend to represent high wage workers instead of acting as a force to raise wages, the low degree of southern unionism reflects rather than explains low southern wages.

In any case, however, Fuchs' study presents convincing evidence that when differences in labor quality and industry location by city size are taken into account, comparatively little interregional wage difference is left. What remains may be considered as representing barriers to mobility imposed by the costs of moving, such as loss of seniority and pension rights, transportation and job search costs, and the nonmonetary costs of leaving a familiar setting, family, and friends. Perhaps competition has equalized regional standardized wages as much as it can.

### Explaining Lower Southern Wages

Considering the cause of the origin and persistence of the low southern wage index, explanation depends on the type of index under study. Gallaway, in the section of his paper presented here, rightfully questions the explanation of the low standardized southern index as being based on the presence of "excess supply" of (unskilled) labor in the South. If there were a greater labor-capital ratio in the South than in the non-South, if interregional production functions for individual industries were the same, and if capital-labor ratios were the same for each industry with the South just having greater concentration of (unskilled) labor intensive industries, the southern standardized wage index would be about 100. The fact that it is not (and Gallaway's standardized-by-industry-mix index of 85 is identical to Fuchs' value derived from standardization by labor quality for a different time period) indicates that there are differences in capital-labor ratios between industries, the ratio being lower for southern industries.

# The North-South Wage Differential

## by Lowell E. Gallaway

A highly abstracted purely competitive model of a factor market has as an end result an equalization of factor prices throughout the market. Consequently, the persistence of sizeable regional wage differentials in a national labor market calls for an explanation. An often offered one is that there are barriers to the free flow of resources between regions, barriers such as a lack of labor mobility, high moving costs, lack of labor market information, etc. Such an explanation is suggested by Cairnes' concept of non-competing groups[1] and receives support from the findings of the labor market research of Reynolds, Kerr, et al.[2] However, explaining regional wage differentials by such a device is not entirely satisfactory. To a sizeable extent this approach is a question-begging one. While it provides considerable insight into the factors which serve to perpetuate a wage differential, it does not afford much that is helpful with respect to determining the forces which generated the initial differential. After all, the existence of regional wage differentials insistently de-

SOURCE Reprinted with permission from *Review of Economics and Statistics,* Vol. 45, August 1963, pp. 264–272.

[1] J. E. Cairnes, *Political Economy.* (New York, 1874).

[2] See, for example, Lloyd Reynolds, *The Structure of Labor Markets,* Clark Kerr, "The Balkanization of Labor, Markets," in *Labor Mobility and Economic Opportunity* (Technology Press of M.I.T. and John Wiley and Sons, 1954), and Myers and Shultz, *The Dynamics of a Labor Market.* Kerr in his essay summarizes the matter well by suggesting five sources of barriers that tend to isolate certain kinds of labor markets: (1) the preferences of individual workers; (2) the preferences of individual employers; (3) the actions of the community of workers; (4) the actions of the community of employers; and (5) the actions of government. The first two he treats as barriers generated by the exercise of free choice while the last three are deemed to create institutional rules of either a formal or informal character which limit the flow of labor resources between sub-markets.

mands an explanation primarily because it represents a deviation from the expected result of a competitive market. Explaining such a differential by merely pointing out that the market is imperfect is next to no explanation at all. That is tautologically implicit in the conceptualization of the competitive market. If a competitive market eliminates differentials and differentials persist, then the market is obviously not competitive and barriers to the adjustment process must exist in order to perpetuate the differentials.

This suggests that an appropriate point of departure for attempting to explain the existence of regional wage differentials is to accept as a working proposition the assumption that barriers to the free flow of resources between regions do exist. Given this, the task of accounting for regional wage differentials becomes one of determining what forces work to create differentials. Several alternative explanations may be considered. Trade union representatives would argue that regional wage differentials are created by the ability of employers to exploit an unorganized labor force. Others have suggested that an explanation may be found in a more plentiful labor supply or a deficiency of product demand[3] while a fourth possibility is that the production functions vary interregionally so as to produce a lower marginal value product schedule for the workers of one of the regions. In this paper an attempt will be made to shed some light on the nature of regional wage differentials by developing suitable empirical tests for several of the suggested explanations of their causes. As a vehicle for discussion, the best known of the regional wage differentials, the North-South one, will be treated.

## I. THE REGIONAL WAGE DIFFERENTIAL DEFINED

Before attempting to test empirically various explanations of the origin of regional wage differentials, it is necessary to define more precisely what is meant by the term "regional wage differential." In its crudest form it may be taken to mean that the average wage of all workers in one region differs significantly from the average wage of all workers of another region.[4] Such a comparison can be made by computing an index expressing the average wage rate of one region in terms of the average wage rate of another region according to the following expression:

$$W_x = \frac{\Sigma w_x h_x \ \Sigma h_y}{\Sigma w_y h_y \ \Sigma h_x} \qquad (1)$$

where $W$ denotes the index of the average wage rate of a region, $w$ denotes the average hourly work rate, $h$ denotes the number of hours worked, and the subscripts $x$ and $y$ refer to particular regions. Obviously, such a concept of a regional wage differential has shortcomings in that it does not provide a comparison between wages paid for similar types of work. The most striking deficiency lies in its inability to take account of differences in the intraregional industrial mix. This produces incomparabilities on two counts: (1) employments are included in the computation of the average wage rates which are not common to the regions involved, and (2) the differing importance of the employments that are common to the regions is not considered (that is, common employments are weighted differently in computing the average wage rate for different regions). These shortcomings can be corrected by the device of assigning weights

---

[3] See, for example, Victor R. Fuchs and Richard Perlman, "Recent Trends in Southern Wage Differentials," this *Review*, XLII (August 1960), 292–300.

[4] This definition eliminates from consideration regional wage differentials in particular employments. The emphasis in this discussion is upon differences in the general level of wages between regions.

TABLE 1. HOURLY WAGE RATES AND HOURLY WAGE RATES ADJUSTED FOR DIFFERENCES
IN INTER-REGIONAL INDUSTRIAL MIX, EAST SOUTH CENTRAL, SOUTH ATLANTIC,
AND MIDDLE ATLANTIC STATES, 1954

| Region | (Index) Hourly Wage Rate | Hourly Wage Adjusted for Differences Between Regional Industry Mix and Industry Mix of Middle Atlantic States |
| --- | --- | --- |
| Middle Atlantic States | 100 | 100 |
| East South Central States | 79 | 85 |
| South Atlantic States | 79 | 86 |

SOURCE: *Census of Manufactures, 1954.*

to the wage rates for different employments that will make the computed averages comparable between regions. This was accomplished by the use of the following expression:

$$W_x = \frac{\Sigma w_x h_x}{\Sigma w_y h_x} \qquad (2)$$

This expression provides an index for the average wage rate of region $x$ relative to region $y$ by weighting the wage rates of region $y$ by the number of hours worked in the particular employment in region $x$. In brief, it compares the actual wage bill of region $x$ for common employments to what that wage bill would have been if every worker in these employments had been paid at the same rate as his counterpart in region $y$. The results of this procedure are shown in Table 1 which presents comparisons of wage rates in the East South Central and South Atlantic States with those of the Middle Atlantic States for the year 1954. The East South Central and South Atlantic States were chosen as being representative of southern wage conditions while the Middle Atlantic States were selected to represent northern wage conditions. These data indicate that the unadjusted wage differential is in the

neighborhood of twenty per cent and the adjusted wage differential is approximately fifteen percent. Thus, after taking into account the differences in the industrial mix between regions, there still remains a sizeable differential to be explained.[5]

## II. THE MONOPSONISTIC EXPLOITATION ARGUMENT

The contention that the existence of regional wage differentials can be explained by the ability of employers to gain a relative advantage over unorganized workers is merely the familiar monopsonistic exploitation argument. Simply stated, under conditions of monopsony in the labor market it is possible for employers to pay workers a wage that is less than their marginal value product. Assuming similar production functions and a similar demand for the product, this would result in a lower wage and a reduced level of employment in the region with the monopsonistic imperfection. It is possible to determine the implications of this contention by assuming the following production function:

$$O = aC^a L^{1-a} \qquad (3)$$

where $O$ denotes output, $C$ denotes capital

[5] A number of other types of adjustments might be considered, for example, corrections for differences in the sex composition of employment, size of cities, worker skills, and occupational or racial mix of the labor force. These adjustments were not made primarily because the data employed in the paper are presented by industrial classification. Due to this, it was felt that it was necessary to correct the apparent differential only for the factor that would not be present on an industry-by-industry basis, *viz.*, the difference in the industrial mix. The impact of sex composition, size of cities, worker skills, and occupational or racial mix will be reflected in the individual industry differentials, whereas the impact of the differing industrial mix will not.

inputs, and $L$ denotes labor inputs. Now, (3) may be differentiated with respect to the labor input variable to produce:

$$\frac{\partial O}{\partial L} = a(1-a)\frac{C^a}{L^a} \qquad (4)$$

which is also equal to the marginal physical product of labor.

Combining (3) and (4) produces:

$$MPP_L = (1-a)\frac{O}{L} \qquad (5)$$

If both sides are converted to money terms and if it is assumed that the money wage rate is equated with the marginal value product of labor, (5) becomes:

$$w = (1-a)\frac{O'}{L} \qquad (6)$$

where $O'$ denotes total value added by manufacture.

Now, if wages in the southern regions are less than the marginal value product of labor (that is, if monopsonistic exploitation exists) and if the regional product functions are similar,

$$\frac{w_s L_s}{O'_s} < \frac{w_n L_n}{O'_n} \qquad (7)$$

where the subscripts $s$ and $n$ denote South and North, respectively. Since $wL$ is equal to the total wage bill, the monopsonistic exploitation hypothesis can be tested empirically by comparing the ratios of the wage bill to total value added for the various regions.

This was done for approximately 150 separate industrial classifications using the data of the 1954 Census of Manufacturers. An industry-by-industry basis of comparison was selected in an effort to develop comparisons between the ratio of the wage bill to total value added for similar types of work in different regions. Since the Census industry classifications are frequently quite broad in scope, the comparisons were restricted primarily to four-digit Census classifications and occasionally a three-digit classification industry. No two-digit industry classifications were employed. The first results of the computations are presented in Table 2 which shows frequency distributions of the difference between the ratio of the wage bill for production workers to total value added for some 144 three- and four-digit Census classification industries located in the Middle Atlantic and East South Central States and for some 156 industries located in the Middle Atlantic and South

TABLE 2. COMPARISON OF RATIO OF PRODUCTION WORKER WAGES TO TOTAL VALUE ADDED, MIDDLE ATLANTIC, EAST SOUTH CENTRAL, AND SOUTH ATLANTIC STATES, UNITED STATES, 1954

| Ratio of production workers' wages to total value added. Middle Atlantic States, less ratio of production workers' wages to total value added, East South Central and South Atlantic States | Number of Industries | |
|---|---|---|
| | East South Central States | South Atlantic States |
| −33.00 −27.01 | 1 | 0 |
| −27.00 −21.01 | 2 | 0 |
| −21.00 −15.01 | 4 | 2 |
| −15.00 − 9.01 | 7 | 13 |
| − 9.00 − 3.01 | 24 | 23 |
| − 3.00 + 2.99 | 53 | 55 |
| + 3.00 + 8.99 | 30 | 43 |
| + 9.00 +14.99 | 15 | 14 |
| +15.00 +20.99 | 5 | 4 |
| +21.00 +26.99 | 3 | 2 |
| Total | 144 | 156 |

SOURCE: *Census of Manufactures, 1954.*

Atlantic States. A positive difference indicates that the ratio of the wage bill to total value added was less in the East South Central or South Atlantic States and lends support to the monopsonistic exploitation hypothesis. A negative difference does not support the hypothesis. The mean value of the differences presented in the distribution relating the Middle Atlantic and East South Central States is +1.00 percentage points. The significance of this value may be tested by framing the hypothesis that is not significantly different from zero. Such a hypothesis cannot be rejected with any sizeable degree of confidence for there is approximately an eighteen per cent probability that the value differs from zero as the result of chance.[6]

A less clear-cut result is found when the frequency distribution relating the Middle Atlantic and South Atlantic States is considered. This distribution shows a mean difference between the ratios of +1.38 percentage points which indicates a two-and-one-half per cent probability that the mean of the distribution differs from zero as the result of chance.

The results of these data indicate that the validity of the monopsonistic exploitation hypothesis is far from clear. There appears to be more empirical justification for the contention in the South Atlantic States but even here there is room for doubt. After all, a one per cent shift in value added away from workers would produce only a two-and-one-half to three per cent change in wages (the wage bill varies from about one-third to two-fifths of value added). Of course, these results are not entirely conclusive in that the mean differences between the ratio of the wage bill to value added that have been computed weight each type of employment equally. Obviously, some employments are more important in a region than others, and it is possible that the difference between the ratios of the wage bill to

value added would be significantly large if a weighted average of these ratios were computed. This was done, the results confirming the previous findings: the weighted average of the wage bill as a percentage of value added for the Middle Atlantic States is 37.06 per cent as compared with 38.20 per cent for the East South Central States (a difference of −1.14 percentage points) and the same percentages for the Middle Atlantic and South Atlantic States are 36.80 and 35.95 respectively (a difference of +0.85 percentage points). In fact, the weighted averages argue more strongly against the monopsonistic exploitation hypothesis.

\* \* \*

## IV. THE EXCESS LABOR SUPPLY ARGUMENT

A brief discussion of a third explanation of regional wage differentials, *viz.*, the excess labor supply hypothesis, is in order. This argument maintains that regional wage differentials are the result of "too large" a supply of labor. In this form, this explanation of regional wage differentials leaves much to be desired. It is akin to the contention that regional wage differentials are the result of barriers to the free flow of labor between regions, that is, it may well be tautologically implicit in the concept of a free (or at least relatively free) market for labor. If wage differentials exist, fewer workers competing against each other would tend to eliminate the differentials. However, this does not necessarily mean that there is an excess supply of labor. The term "excess supply" must be given more precision before this can be determined. If by excess supply it is meant that there are workers available and willing to work in sufficient numbers to reduce the wage below that in another region, then it may be argued that an excess supply of labor does exist in low wage

---

[6] The standard error of the mean is 0.75 which produces a $T$ value of 1.33.

regions. However, this is an empty definition at best. To define excess supply as existing when differentials exist and then to explain differentials by the presence of excess supply is certainly circular reasoning

A better alternative is to define an excess supply of labor in a relative sense, that is, in terms of the relative supply of the other factors of production. In this sense an excess supply of labor is merely the obverse side of the coin of, say, a relative lack of capital. However, again there is no obviously apparent yardstick by which one can distinguish between an excess supply of labor and a relative lack of capital. Regional wage differentials may just as well result from an excess supply of labor as from a lack of capital. In fact, in the relative sense both are present when there are regional wage differentials and once again the concept of an excess supply of labor becomes ephemeral. One cannot really assess the significance of the relative supplies of the factors of production until the regional production functions have been examined.

## V. REGIONAL PRODUCTION FUNCTIONS

A fourth explanation of persistent interregional wage differentials is that the production functions of the two regions differ in such a fashion as to produce differential marginal value produce schedules for the workers of the two regions. The data derived from the 1954 Census of Manufacturers support this as a possibility. There are marked differences in the average value productivity of workers in the Middle Atlantic States and those in the East South Central and South Atlantic States, differences that apparently cannot be ex-

plained by the exploitation or deficiency of product demand hypothesis. If it is assumed that average and marginal productivity are proportional, an expected wage for the southern workers can be computed by multiplying their actual value added per hour by the ratio of the northern workers' wages to their value added per hour, that is,

$$w'_x = \frac{w_y}{V_y} V_x \qquad (9)$$

where $w'$ denotes the expected wage in a region, $w$ denotes the actual wage in a region. $V$ denotes the value added per hour in a region, and the subscripts $x$ and $y$ refer to particular regions. When this is done, the wage differentials between various kinds of employment are largely accounted for. Table 3 shows data which indicate that when the actual wage of southern workers is subtracted from the expected wage ($w'_x - w_x$) and expressed as a percentage of the northern workers' wage the differentials that remain appear to be randomly distributed about zero. The mean value of these differentials is —0.87 per cent for the East South Central States and —1.93 for the South Atlantic States and the respective standard errors of these means are 1.89 and 1.86.[7] Consequently, the respective means have approximately a 65 and 30 per cent probability that they differ from zero as the result of chance.[8] Thus, the regional wage differences may be accounted for by the differences in average value productivity, which may in turn result from differences in the regional production functions.

Whether this is the case depends on whether a region is operating on a different production function or is operating at a different point on the same production

---

[7] Six observations were omitted from the calculation, three at each extreme of the distribution in an attempt to eliminate some of the uward bias implicit in using a distribution of percentages. Weighted differentials were also calculated for each region. The results were —4.51 per cent for the East South Central and —7.27 per cent for the South Atlantic States.

[8] The respective $T$ values were 0.46 and 1.04.

TABLE 3. WAGE DIFFERENTIALS AFTER STANDARDIZING FOR DIFFERENCES
IN AVERAGE VALUE PRODUCTIVITY, EAST SOUTH CENTRAL AND
SOUTH ATLANTIC STATES, UNITED STATES, 1954

| | Region | |
| --- | --- | --- |
| Differential | East South Central | South Atlantic |
| −80.00 −60.01 | 0 | 2 |
| −60.00 −40.01 | 3 | 3 |
| −40.00 −20.01 | 21 | 22 |
| −20.00 − 0.01 | 50 | 63 |
| 0.00 +19.99 | 46 | 44 |
| +20.00 +39.99 | 12 | 16 |
| +40.00 +59.99 | 4 | 4 |
| +60.00 +79.99 | 2 | 1 |
| +80.00 +99.99 | 0 | 1 |
| Total | 138 | 156 |

SOURCE: *Census of Manufactures, 1954.*

function. This may be empirically tested by considering the following expression:

$$a = 1 - \frac{wL}{O'} \qquad (10)$$

which is a rearrangment of (6). From this expression the values of the exponent $a$ in the production function (1) can be determined for the various regions. Since the values of $a$ are determined by the value of $\frac{wL}{O'}$, it is apparent that the results of the test will parallel those of the monopsonistic exploitation test, that is, the differences in the values for $a$ for different regions by industry will be randomly distributed about zero. This argues for similar production functions for the regions. However, since expression (10) assumes an absence of monopsonistic exploitation and the monopsonistic exploitation test assumed similar production functions, there is the possibility of circularity in the testing of the two propositions. A careful examination of this circularity reveals that there are two possibilities that are consistent with the empirical evidence:

1. both the monopsonistic exploitation and dissimilar production function hypotheses are invalid, or

2. both of the hypotheses are valid.

The latter possibility could result if the lower wage rate resulting from the existence of monopsonistic exploitation were disguised by the presence of a higher marginal value product schedule for labor as the result of differences in the regional production functions. Of course, the marginal value product schedule would have to be enough higher to just offset the impact of the monopsonistic imperfection. While this possibility cannot be ignored, the weight of probability lies with the proposition that both hypotheses are invalid.

VI. CONCLUSIONS

The results of the tests thus far conducted have been largely negative. A series of possible explanations of the origin of regional wage differentials have successively been rejected and, as yet, none accepted. However, by implication it has been established that the capital-labor ratio of the South is less than that of the North. This is a confirmation of what is sometimes known as the "excess" labor supply hypothesis, although, as has been noted, the use of the term "excess" merely reflects a relative lack of capital goods and a relative abundance of labor.

Pursuing this line of argument further,

the different capital-labor mix between North and South itself requires some explanation. Apparently, two factors have contributed to this:

1. The historical accident of southern economic development with its focus on land as a factor of production rather than capital goods which created an initial relative lack of capital.

2. The aforementioned barriers to the free inter-regional flow of the factors of production. These barriers have served to perpetuate the existing imbalance in the capital-labor mix by limiting the flow of labor out of the region and limiting the flow of capital into the region. In the presence of a free flow of either resource an equilibration of both relative and absolute factor prices would have occurred.

The apparent presence of barriers to factor mobility of such strength suggests that the North-South wage differential will be a somewhat permanent feature of our system.[9] Such a possibility raises the question of what are the necessary conditions for a narrowing of this differential. Equation (4) implies:

$$w = a(1-a)\frac{C^a}{L^a} \qquad (4a)$$

Differentiating (4a) produces:

$$dw = a\,a(1-a)\frac{C^a}{L^a}\left(\frac{dC}{C} - \frac{dL}{L}\right) \qquad (11)$$

From this it is obvious that the key factor in determining the changes in regional wage rates is the relationship between the percentage changes in capital and labor inputs. The greater the differential between the percentage change in capital and the percentage change in labor, the greater the change in wages, *ceteris paribus*. Consequently, if the wage differential between North and South were to be narrowed, the differential between the two percentage changes would have to be larger in the South than in the North. In fact, it would have to be sufficiently large to offset the existing differences in the capital-labor ratio. Symbolically, the necessary condition for a narrowing of the North-South wage differential is that:

$$\triangle R_s\,(C^a/L^a)_s > \triangle R_n\,(C^a/L^a)_n \qquad (12)$$

where $\triangle R$ denotes the difference between the percentage changes in capital inputs and labor inputs.

Whether this has been the case in recent years can be tested by employing the data developed in solving (10) for $a$ to obtain estimates of the regional capital stock by industry for the year 1954.[10] Combining these data with those contained in the Annual Survey of Manufactures for new expenditures on capital goods permits the calculation of the percentage rates of change in the capital and labor inputs and the value of the ratio $\frac{C^a}{L^a}$ for the various regions. These may then be used as indicated in (12) to determine whether conditions over the past few years have been conducive to a narrowing of the wage differential. In Table 4 the values of $\triangle R_{ij}$ $(C_{ij}{}^a/L_{ij}{}^a)$ are presented for the Census

---

[9] Fuchs and Perlman, op. cit., note some narrowing of the North-South wage differential but primarily before 1947. The findings of G. H. Borts, "The Equalization of Returns and Regional Economic Growth," *The American Economic Review*, L (June 1960), 319–347 would also seem to support this conclusion.

[10] Simply stated, the technique for arriving at estimates of capital stock by industry and region for the year 1954 consists of solving for capital stock by use of the previously determined value for $a$ and a value for total (United States) capital stock by industry obtained from the estimates of total capital stock in manufacturing for the United States contained in D. Creamer, J. Dobrovolsky, and I. Borenstein, *Capital in Manufacturing and Mining* (Princeton, 1960). Given the 1954 data it is then possible to update the estimates by use of data for new capital expenditures from the Annual Survey of Manufactures and the data describing depreciation allowances by industry for the United States. A detailed description of the technique is contained in the author's "A Note on Regional Capital Estimates by Industry, 1954–1957," *Southern Economic Journal* (July 1962).

TABLE 4. CAPITAL-LABOR INPUT RELATIONSHIPS, BY INDUSTRY AND REGION, 1954–1957

| Industry | Middle Atlantic States $\triangle R\ (C^a/L^a)$ | South Atlantic States $\triangle R\ (C^a/L^a)$ | > or < Mid-Atlantic | East South Central States $\triangle R\ (C^a/L^a)$ | > or < Mid-Atlantic |
|---|---|---|---|---|---|
| Food and kindred products | .0000 | .0017 | > | .0008 | > |
| Tobacco manufactures | .0005 | .0014 | > | .0014 | > |
| Textile mills | −.0012 | .0030 | > | .0042 | > |
| Apparel and related products | −.0013 | .0045 | > | .0009 | > |
| Lumber and wood products | −.0016 | .0060 | > | .0037 | > |
| Furniture and fixtures | −.0002 | .0061 | > | .0008 | > |
| Pulp, paper, and allied products | .0013 | .0145 | > | .0227 | > |
| Printing & Publishing | .0002 | .0014 | > | .0036 | > |
| Chemicals & products | .0000 | .0020 | > | .0011 | > |
| Petroleum and coal products | −.0083 | −.0210 | < | −.0153 | < |
| Rubber products | −.0005 | −.0019 | < | .0005 | > |
| Leather and leather goods | −.0006 | .0089 | > | .0005 | > |
| Stone, clay, and glass products | .0047 | .0144 | > | .0225 | > |
| Primary metal industries | −.0064 | .0202 | > | .0046 | > |
| Fabricated Metal industries | .0002 | .0053 | > | .0053 | > |
| Machinery (except electrical) | .0002 | .0041 | > | .0084 | > |
| Electrical machinery | −.0016 | .0031 | > | .0050 | > |
| Transportation equipment | .0017 | −.0056 | < | −.0058 | < |
| Instruments and related products | −.0004 | −.0025 | < | .0040 | > |
| Miscellaneous manufacturing | .0003 | .0081 | > | .0074 | > |

SOURCE: *Census of Manufactures, 1954* and *Annual Survey of Manufactures, 1955–1957.*

Bureau twenty two-digit classification industries for the period 1954–1957. These data indicate that over this period conditions were such as to favor a narrowing of the North-South wage differential. Comparing the Middle Atlantic and South Atlantic States, it can be seen that in sixteen of the twenty cases $\triangle R_s(C^a/L^a)_s > \triangle R_n(C^a/L^a)_n$. Similarly, a comparison of the Middle Atlantic and East South Central States shows that in eighteen of the twenty industries the same condition existed. Admittedly, the period covered by these data is brief, too brief when the long-run nature of the process of interregional resource movements is considered. However, they may be indicative of the development of conditions which will serve to gradually eliminate the North-South wage differential.

The data of Gallaway's Table 3 support this view. Standardized wage differences are explained by a lower marginal value productivity for labor on an industry-by-industry basis for the South, where more labor relative to capital is used in production. Table 4 shows that over a short period, in-migration of capital and out-migration of labor are acting to equalize capital-labor production ratios interregionally, thus tending to equalize standardized wages among areas.

Gallaway explains the present difference in capital-labor mix for the South as a whole as the historical accident of southern economic development with its focus on land rather than on capital as the most required supporting factor to labor, as agriculture rather than industry was stressed. An alternative argument would note the long-time trend in lower investment in human capital in the South, which resulted in the heavy weight of the unskilled in the labor force.

In any case, further mobility of labor and capital would tend to raise the southern standardized wage index closer to 100. But for the unadjusted southern index to move toward that value requires an upgrading of southern labor through an expansion of investment in education and training to the level of other regions.


## Related Readings

Melvin Reder, "Wage Differentials: Theory and Measurement," *Aspects of Labor Economics*, reviews and comments on studies of the industrial wage structure. Well-known statistical treatments of the relationship between industrial wage changes and economic variables are Solomon Fabricant, *Employment in Manufacturing 1899–1939* (National Bureau of Economic Research, New York, 1942) and *Basic Facts on Productivity Change* (NBER, Occasional Paper No. 63, New York, 1959); John W. Kendrick, *Productivity Trends in the United States* (NBER, Princeton University Press, Princeton, 1961); and W. E. G. Salter, *Productivity and Technological Change* (Cambridge University Press, Cambridge, 1960). Important short-run studies are those of Joseph Garbarino, "A Theory of Interindustry Wage Structure Variation" (*Quarterly Journal of Economics*, Vol. 54, May 1950) and, for Great Britain, E. H. Phelps Brown and M. H. Browne, "Earnings in Industries of the United Kingdom, 1948–1959" (*Economic Journal* Vol. 62, September 1962, pp. 517–549).

Related to Cullen's paper, Pamela Haddy and N. Arnold Tolles, "British and American Changes in Interindustry Wage Structure under Full Employment" (*Review of Economics and Statistics*, Vol. 33, November 1957, pp. 408–414), find the same stability in industrial rankings by wage levels among British industries, for a briefer, more recent period, as did Cullen for American industries.

Benson Soffer, "On Union Rivalries and the Minimum Differentiation of Wage Patterns" (*Review of Economics and Statistics*, Vol. 41, February 1959), explains that the "key group" or "pattern bargaining" theory views wage changes for the group as determined by similar institutional forces making for uniform wage changes despite the presence of nonuniform market forces impinging on the individual industries. Timothy W. McGuire and Leonard A. Rapping, "Industry Wage Change Dispersion and the 'Spillover' Hypothesis" (*American Economic Review*, Vol. 56, June 1966), note the difficulty in assigning causes to wage uniformity, whether the bases of similar wage changes are institutional elements or market forces. Maurice Benewitz and Alan Spiro, "Comment" (on Maher's paper) (*Industrial and Labor Relations Review*, Vol. 16, October 1962, pp. 122–125), argue that Maher has merely chosen the industries that form the center of a wage change dispersion, with scatter occurring under competitive market forces in the short run. But Maher offers institutional reasons explaining why these industries form a similar pattern of wage changes, whether or not they are at the center of the distribution of wage changes. To Kenneth Alexander's, "Comment" (on Maher's paper), ILRR (July 1962), pp. 539–543, that he overstates the impact of key group bargaining on cost-push inflation, Maher replies, *Ibid.*, pp. 543–547, that at least in a significant number of cases—in key group bargaining—"wage changes are not . . . a function of changes in [economic] variables, peculiar to the firms in these negotiations."

A comprehensive survey of the dispute over the differential effect of competitive and institutional forces—unionism in this case—is offered by Clark

Kerr, "Wage Relationships—The Comparative Impact of Market and Power Forces," *Theory of Wage Determination* (Macmillan, London, 1964, Chapter 12).

R. J. Wonnacott, "Wage Levels and Employment Structure in United States Regions: A Free Trade Precedent" (*Journal of Political Economy*, Vol. 72, August 1964, pp. 414–419), points out the statistical problems involved in calculating a regional wage index. Joseph W. Bloch, "Regional Wage Differentials: 1907–46" (*Monthly Labor Review*, Vol. 66, April 1948, pp. 371–377), finds long-run stability in the low southern wage index, with a sharp dip, later corrected, during the depression. Using a different method from those of Fuchs and Gallaway, Martin Segal, "Regional Wage Differences in Manufacturing in the Postwar Period" (*Review of Economics and Statistics*, Vol. 43, May 1961, pp. 148–155), derives slightly lower values for the southern standardized index for 1947 and 1954.

Robert L. Bunting, "A Test of the Theory of Geographic Mobility" (*Industrial and Labor Relations Review*, Vol. 15 October 1961, pp. 75–82, finds that workers do migrate toward areas of "higher net advantage" (higher wages). But Robert L. Raimon "Interstate Migration and Wage Theory" (*Review of Economics and Statistics*, Vol. 44, November 1962, pp. 428–437), finds the pull of greater job opportunity stronger than that of higher wages, although the two influences generally operate together, with higher wages paid by states with greater labor demand. To the extent, though, that a regional wage differential for similar labor does exist, if Raimon's findings apply as the general case, if labor markets were stronger in the South, movement out of the region tending to equalize wages would not occur.

# III

## Industrial Relations and Collective Bargaining

Part III deals with some aspects of industrial relations and collective bargaining. Our concern here is not only with labor organizations, which were analyzed in detail in Part I, but also with the relations between unions, management, government agencies, and other groups. We say "other groups" because one of the trends in industrial relations is the effort to transfer negotiation and dispute settlement techniques from labor-management relations, where they have become fairly institutionalized, to community disputes, where relations are less structured. We shall therefore consider community disputes in connection with our discussion of conflict resolution in Chapter 14.

Besides conflict resolution, Part III analyzes the following topics: contemporary collective bargaining; theories of industrial relations and bargaining; the impact of unions on wages; and collective bargaining in the public sector. The primary objective of this section is to give the reader an understanding of the basic nature of collective bargaining as an institution and to analyze some problems associated with it. As in other parts of this book, our basic approach is to present the theory as well as the practice of our subject.

# CHAPTER 11

# Contemporary Collective Bargaining

## INTRODUCTION

Although unions struggled for many years to gain acceptance before the 1930's, collective bargaining had become institutionalized by the end of World War II. That is, it had become a generally accepted way of formulating some of the rules governing wages, hours, and working conditions. The reasons for this general acceptance are, first, that collective bargaining is widely regarded as a good rule-making system because it is flexible, provides for participation by workers and employers, and is generally considered to be equitable. The system is flexible because it permits rule making by those with the greatest familiarity with the conditions that the rules are designed to cover. Moreover, the rules can be readily adapted to changing circumstances. This system also provides for participation in the rule-making process by workers and employers, giving them both an incentive to abide by the rules resulting from their joint endeavors. People ordinarily seem to be more willing to adhere to rules that they have participated in formulating than they are to directives unilaterally imposed on them.

Not only does collective bargaining promote participation at the job level, but it also makes it possible for workers to participate in the formulation of rules governing the larger society. This is done through labor organizations that speak for them before legislative committees and other public bodies. Indeed, as noted in Part I, many students of collective bargaining argue that the sense of participation in the larger society promotes political, economic, and social stability and therefore is one of the most important benefits of that system to the society as a whole. Finally, collective bargaining is regarded as an equitable system because it equalizes power between workers and employers.

Many people therefore regard collective bargaining as the extension of democracy to the work place.

In spite of its generally accepted advantages, however, collective bargaining is not without its faults. For one thing, this system is not universal because in no country are all workers covered by collective bargaining. Indeed, as we saw in Chapter 2, this system contains an inequitable feature in the sense that those workers who need help the most are unable to gain the benefits of collective bargaining. This is true in large measure because bargaining depends upon economic power and some workers, like unskilled agricultural workers, have been too weak economically to gain the benefits of unionization. Moreover, in many regions of the country, like the South, a complex constellation of forces has kept collective bargaining from covering more than a small fraction of the total work force. Collective bargaining also does not contain sufficient safeguards for the public interest, especially to prevent collusion by unions and employers at the expense of the public, to contain inflationary wage-price practices, and to protect the public from the disruption of services in the event of strikes or other conflicts.

Because of its weaknesses, and perhaps also because it has become a generally accepted institution, collective bargaining has come under increasing attack from many of its former friends, like liberal intellectuals, as well as from its conservative business critics. The selections in this part attempt to deal with these and other aspects of collective bargaining.

## COLLECTIVE BARGAINING IN THE POSTWAR PERIOD

In "Collective Bargaining in the Postwar Period," Robert M. Macdonald summarizes some of the important forces influencing collective bargaining in the United States since the Second World War. He states at the outset that his "essay does not attempt a full-scale evaluation of collective bargaining as such. Rather it aims at providing the background and perspective necessary for understanding and judging the institutions and practices of the modern collective bargaining system."

Although Macdonald demonstrates that the collective bargaining system became fairly firmly established in the United States after World War II, he also shows that collective bargaining has been subject to a wide variety of pressures, especially in the immediate postwar period and following the Korean War, when the system was forced to adjust to many of the problems growing out of wartime conditions. Because of union aggressivesness during the war and poor management, many inefficient industrial relations practices were adopted that could not be sustained in the more competitive times following the Korean War. In order to protect profit margins, management therefore adopted a hard-line bargaining position that intensified labor management conflict.

The resolution of these problems led to many new programs and procedures, some of which "reveal a degree of ingenuity and inventiveness curiously at odds with the claims of critics that collective bargaining has lost its creative impulse." One of these new developments was the long-term contract, which some scholars consider to be inflationary. However, Macdonald concludes that it is very difficult to determine whether the long-term contract is indeed inflationary. The postwar period also saw the widespread introduction of escalator clauses, interest in which seemed to fluctuate with the business cycle. Another innovation was the union-management study committees, which sought to avoid crisis bargaining through continuous study of the issues without the threat of a strike deadline. The postwar period also saw a growth in fringe benefits negotiated in collective bargaining agreements. However, Macdonald believes that the unions' influence on the expansion of fringe benefits is easily exaggerated.

After examining the influence of many environmental factors on collective bargaining, Macdonald concludes that it has not been inflexible, in part because it has been a decentralized system characterized by a high degree of pragmatism; therefore, the collective bargaining system has been highly experimental.

> The flexibility of the bargaining mechanism is revealed in the intricately varied and changing structure of relationships, in the continuous modification of bargaining procedures, and especially in the evolution of the detailed content of collective agreements. In the postwar period, collective bargaining has been instrumental in developing a wide array of income-maintenance and employment-adjustment measures which have added immeasurably to the security and well-being of wage earners and their families.

Although Macdonald is clearly convinced of the benefits of collective bargaining, he concludes:

> This does not mean, of course, that one should condone each and every bargaining practice; for the test is always whether or not the practice achieves a reasonable balance between the competing interests of workers and consumers. Economists are prone to to judge the results of bargaining in terms of the competitive standard. This by itself, however, is too narrow a base for judging the utility of the bargaining system. Collective bargaining performs functions that are indispensable to the maintenance of a humane industrial society. It secures, above all, the workers' commitment to political democracy and a free enterprise economy. Consequently, evaluations of its worth and proposals for its reform, if they are to serve society's interests, must take account of the vital functions fulfilled by the bargaining system.

# Collective Bargaining in the Postwar Period

## by Robert M. Macdonald

In recent years, the collective bargaining system has been the subject of growing criticism for its failure to serve adequately the national interest. Although the criticisms vary widely in content and intensity and are often mixed with attacks on the quality of union leadership, they do reflect a fairly widespread concern that the effects of collective bargaining on the nation's economy are too disruptive to be tolerated much longer. The bill of particulars in this indictment is by now a familiar one and requires no detailed exposition here. In sum, the claim is made that collective bargaining, as currently practiced, has impeded the economy's growth, imparted an upward drift to the general price level, and periodically imperiled the nation's health and safety.

In the past, it is argued, these impediments and disturbances, though troublesome, were at least tolerable. More recently, however, as national and international problems confront the nation with sterner tasks—the need to eliminate poverty and injustice at home, to meet the challenge of foreign competition in domestic and world markets, and to fulfill economic and military obligations abroad —these impediments have become unduly burdensome. It is essential, therefore, that the parties to collective bargaining (principally the trade unions) adapt their methods and results to conform to the im-

In the past two decades, collective bargaining has developed into a major institution of the American economy. Emerging from World War II with large memberships into a period of flourishing business activity, unions have negotiated substantial wage increases and significantly expanded the kinds and amounts of other job benefits. In this article the evolution of bargaining institutions and practices in the postwar period is reviewed, with particular attention to those developments which illuminate the current status of collective bargaining and the probable direction of future developments.

peratives of a new and more demanding environment—either voluntarily through the exercise of self-restraint or involuntarily through the medium of public controls.

. . . [T]his essay does not attempt a full-scale evaluation of collective bargaining as such. Rather, it aims at providing the background and perspective necessary for understanding and judging the institutions and practices of the modern bargaining system. It reviews how bargaining patterns and practices have evolved in the postwar period, examines their current effectiveness, and comments on the prospects for change.

\* \* \*

The discussion makes no claim to being exhaustive. On the contrary, it is limited to those changes which serve to illuminate the current status of collective bargaining practice and the probable direction of future developments. The first part of the article provides a general review of the evolution of bargaining institutions and practices in the postwar period. Subsequent sections examine within this framework the most significant patterns of change in the bargaining system—the development of the structure of bargaining units, the movement toward longer-term contracts, and the elaboration of private compensation systems.

POSTWAR EVOLUTION OF
COLLECTIVE BARGAINING

Although the establishment of unionism on a broad scale dates from the 1930's and the revolutionary labor policies of the New Deal, the development of the modern collective bargaining system, especially in the mass-production industries, is in many ways an accomplishment of the post-World War II period. . . . the prewar years were pre-eminently an organizing period for labor, and such relationships as were established were tentative and based on the most rudimentary forms of agreement.

Consequently, when the war intruded and agencies were organized to settle labor disputes within the framework of the government's stabilization policies, these agencies were forced to impose their settlements on a private bargaining system which had only begun to develop its own institutions and practices.

\* \* \*

Although it was evident at the war's end that serious labor troubles would accompany the removal of controls, it is doubtful that many were prepared for the massive wave of bitter strikes which poured across the nation in 1945–1946, affecting almost every major industry. Eventually, under prodding from the President, agreements were reached and large-scale strife (with the notable exception of the coal industry) subsided; but not before a troubled public, alarmed by the power unions had demonstrated to disrupt the nation's economy, had become convinced of the need for firm controls. This need found expression, of course, in the Taft-Hartley Act, passed in 1947 for the specific purpose of protecting the individual and society against abuses of union power.

UNION-MANAGEMENT
RELATIONSHIPS TAKE FORM

. . . it is remarkable how swiftly the institutions and practices of the modern bargaining system were developed. Satisfactory accommodations, to be sure, were not reached overnight; antagonisms died hard, and there was widespread reluctance on each side to recognize, much less to accept, the legitimacy of the other side's interests and concerns. Too many companies, moreover, purchased peaceful relations at the expense of efficiency, granting concessions in the negotiation and administration of contracts which severely hampered the exercise of management initiative. An unknown but substantial proportion of these concessions were actually the legacy of wartime dealings, but the sources of concession were the same in the two periods.

* * *

Although it is tempting to attribute the loose work standards, costly incentive systems, restrict seniority arrangements, excessive idle-time allowances, and other inefficiencies found to exist in the late forties and early fifties to the importunacies of aggressive unions, at least part of the blame clearly resided with management. Many employers were simply ignorant, shortsighted, or neglectful in their management of the labor-relations function; and through weak bargaining and lax administration, they permitted such practices to proliferate as long as their operations remained profitable.

Not all companies adopted the line of least resistance in their initial adaptation to unionism. On the contrary, a significant number recognized from the outset the revolutionary consequences of collective bargaining for management and the need for radical changes in their methods of decision making and operation.[1] Companies in this group constitute, however, a distinct minority of American business, and they attracted only passing attention from others as long as the post-war inflation continued and profits were easily realized.[2]

. . . The fact remains, nevertheless, that the transformation of the bargaining system in this brief span of years was little short of phenomenal. It was a period, following on prewar and wartime beginnings, that witnessed the systematic development of the collective agreement into an elaborate network of rules for regulating all phases of the employment relationship. These detailed rules covered not only the traditional subjects of wage scales, working hours, job assignments, production standards, layoffs, and the like, but also an increasingly complex array of supplementary wage programs which were radically altering the character of employee compensation systems. In addition, it was a period of experimentation with policies and procedures that would help contain conflict and stabilize relations. Some of the innovations adopted, notably the longer contract term, but also the use of joint committees to explore the more technical aspects of contract issues, were designed to facilitate negotiations. Others, such as the establishment of screening committees of the occasional agreement to promote educational programs in contract administration, were intended to foster the orderly and peaceful resolution of grievance problems. . . .

THE POST-KOREAN WAR PERIOD

The end of the Korean War and the ensuing recession of 1953–1954 marked the finish of the comfortable economic environment in which collective bargaining had flourished for almost a decade. As competition returned in full force to domestic markets, many companies found them-

---

[1] In these companies, organization structures were revamped to accommodate to the rising importance of the industrial relations function, long-range policies were formulated to guide actions in dealing with unions, and procedures were established to ensure that policies were adhered to at all levels of decision making. The importance attached to the administrative function was demonstrated in the upgrading and training of supervisory forces and in the adoption of firm disciplinary policies to be applied consistently in all matters of wrongdoing. It was characteristic of the management of such companies that they understood, even as they deplored, the political character of the union. And from this understanding flowed an awareness that freedom to manage was to be preserved not by appeals to unions to act responsibly but by adherence to policies designed to persuade union leaders and members alike that responsible behavior was simply a matter of self-interest.

[2] It is somewhat ironic, in the light of contemporary criticisms of collective bargaining, that the minority of companies adopting a firm approach were often maligned for their failure to effect a "constructive accommodation" with unionism. Apparently, expert opinion was lulled as much by the ease of profitmaking as were many of the practitioners.

selves in serious financial difficulties and were compelled to embark on programs of stringent retrenchment and reform in order to meet the requirements of the new environment. Their problems, it should be noted, were not all attributable to poor labor standards; nevertheless, for a substantial number of companies, labor costs were badly out of line and improvement of labor practices was clearly a necessary condition for survival.

* * *

If the immediate post-Korean years ushered in a harsher climate for collective bargaining, it was not until the late fifties and early sixties that the full impact of the change was felt. By this time, the American economy was in the doldrums, plagued by excessive and persistent unemployment, a sluggish growth rate, and a continuing deficit in the balance of international payments. Since the achievement of balance-of-payments equilibrium was premised on preservation of the exchange value of the dollar, a primary constraint on policy was the maintenance of price stability. What the economy also needed, however, was a vigorous expansion of aggregate demand in a setting which would encourage the exploitation of technological innovations so as to increase the efficiency of American industry and enhance its position vis-à-vis competitors in world markets. With the policy orientation so firmly settled on the need to contain price increases and foster technological change, it is not surprising that the environment proved uncongenial and even hostile to unions. Policy makers feared that the beneficial effects of expansionary measures would be dissipated by the tendency of collective bargaining to push up prices in advance of the realization of full-capacity output. In addition, there was widespread concern that union insistence on security programs and on the maintenance of outmoded work practices would deprive industry and the nation of the full advantages of technological improvements, thus inhibiting progress and compounding the danger of inflation.

HARDENING POSITIONS

It would be idle to contend that the public's concern with collective bargaining performance during this period was without justification. . . . The dominant social fact of the period was the failure of the economic system to meet the employment needs of the community. This fact alone was sufficient to strain the bargaining process. In the late fifties and early sixties, however, the scarcity of jobs coexisted with rapid economic change—a dual condition which brought the efficiency requirements of employers and the security needs of workers directly into conflict.

The motivations of employers were straightforward enough: hard pressed by domestic and foreign competition and favored by economic circumstance and the climate of opinion alike, they simply found the times propitious for an all-out assault on labor costs. . . . Unions inevitably were placed on the defensive. With unemployment already excessive and employers moving determinedly to curtail labor expenditures, union leaders had no alternative but to conduct a holding operation, attempting to shore up job opportunities against the corrosive influence of technological improvements, mergers, plant relocations, contracting out, and the like. Their concern for security was sharpened, moreover, by the failure of unemployment to decline with the resumption of economic growth.

* * *

In the light of these circumstances, it is small wonder that the parties to bargaining had difficulty composing their differences and that disputes in a number of industries—steel, meatpacking, longshoring, and transportation—were especially bitter and prolonged. The stakes were large and compulsions were based on considerations of survival. . . . Yet, even as the clashes were occurring and as editorials were proclaiming regularly the imminent demise of the bargaining system, the parties themselves were evolving programs and procedures which offered constructive solutions to the problems confronting them. . . .

## NEW PROGRAMS

Some of the programs developed in the period reveal a degree of ingenuity and inventiveness curiously at odds with the claim of critics that collective bargaining has lost its creative impulse. As examples of the diversity of approaches adopted, one need only consider the 1960 Mechanization and Modernization Agreement in the Pacific Coast longshore industry, the 1962 Long-Range Sharing Plan negotiated by the Kaiser Steel Company and the United Steelworkers, and the 1959 Automation Fund agreement entered into by Armour and Company and the Packinghouse Workers and Meat Cutters unions. These programs have in common the reconciliation of employer and worker interests in an environment of rapid change, but they chart widely different courses toward that objective. The original Pacific Coast longshore agreement, renewed with some revisions in 1966, consisted essentially of an exchange of work rules (embodying employee property rights) for an employee-financed trust fund (accumulated at the rate of $5 million annually) to be used for wage guarantees and early retirement and other benefits for fully-registered longshoremen. The Kaiser Long-Range Sharing Plan, on the other hand, combines a formula for sharing with employees any cost savings realized by the company, with provisions for protecting the employment and earnings of workers displaced or downgraded by automation or improved production methods. The Armour Automation Fund, finally, is a fund financed by employer

contributions to provide for the study of labor displacement and the development of programs to minimize the impact of change on the company's work force.

While the Kaiser, Armour, and West Coast longshore agreements are the most dramatic and most publicized examples of recent programs introduced explicity to facilitate change, a wide variety of provisions have been adopted in a large and increasing number of agreements which seek in one way or another to accomplish the same objective. These measures include advance notice of change to the union; the use of natural or controlled attrition to effect reductions in the work force; arrangements for the retraining and relocation of employees displaced as a result of technological or economic change; and provisions for early retirement, severance pay, and supplemental unemployment benefits for discharged or laid-off workers. Taken together, provision of this sort (which appear in difference combinations in the majority of collective bargaining agreements) represent a sensible and equitable solution to a difficult industrial relations problem. Some of these devices are, of course, easily criticized, either on the ground that they reduce the potential cost savings of innovation or because they discriminate in favor of those workers who are already employed; but in a society that makes at best only minimal provision for income maintenance during periods of idleness; is often unwilling or unable to maintain employment opportunities, and has until recently neglected the need for the planned preservation and development of its manpower resources, these private devices have great social value and are probably a small price to pay for freedom to innovate.

## JOINT STUDY POSITIONS

Recent innovations in collective bargaining have not been limited, however, to the development of substantive provisions for dealing with the problems of change. They also extend to bargaining procedures where mechanisms have been devised for the in-depth study of labor relations issues, away from the "crisis" atmosphere of the bargaining table.

\* \* \*

Although the typical joint committee is comprised of union and management representatives only, a few committees have broadened their membership to include neutral experts who may serve in a variety of capacities, ranging from mere advice on technical matters to full-fledged direction of the committee's activities.

The potential advantages of the continuous study committee are obvious. It provides opportunity for rational discussion and fact finding on complicated issues, invites a freer exchange of ideas and information between the parties, and encourages experimentation with novel approaches to both old and new labor relations problems. Furthermore, if competently staffed and conscientiously supported, it can lead to an overall improvement in the quality of union-management relations and to a form of continuous bargaining, wherein critical or urgent issues are studied and disposed of as they arise, rather than being left to accumulate as festering grievances which embitter relations and poison the atmosphere in which regular negotiations are conducted.

\* \* \*

[I]f the continuous study committee is to be allowed to develop its full potential as a mechanism for containing conflict and promoting cooperation, it is essential that the parties devise effective means, consistent with the need to preserve an atmosphere of free discussion, for keeping the rank and file informed on issues before the committee. This is assuredly a challenging assignment, but in view of the crises of confidence which has overtaken union leadership in recent years, it is also an assignment whose successful accomplishment may do much to restore the respect of union members for the integrity and competence of their leaders, to say nothing of restoring the confidence of the public in the collective bargaining system.

## CHANGES IN THE STRUCTURE OF BARGAINING

Accompanying these developments in bargaining attitudes, procedures, and agreements in the postwar period have been significant changes in the structure of the bargaining system.

\* \* \*

Statistical measures of the change in bargaining structure in the postwar period are not available. Nevertheless, the direction of the change is clearly identified in the centralization of decision-making power within union and employer organizations, the expanding size and scope of the bargaining unit, and the loss of independence or autonomy in subordinate units of the bargaining system.

In unions, the centralization of power reflects, in part, the natural urge of elected leaders to gather together the reins of control over the organization's major activities, thus minimizing the opportunities for ambitious rivals to challenge the incumbents. More important, however, it stems from the desire to increase bargaining effectiveness. If the union is to maximize its gains, if it is to develop a strategy for the attainment of long-run objectives, it must impose limits on the independence of component units. Unless it can develop a coordinated strategy and secure a common commitment to specific goals, it is constantly exposed to employer exploitation of its weakest members and hence to the destruction of hard-won standards and of possible gains for its membership as a whole. Even in the absence of bureaucratic tendencies, this need exerts a potent influence on the distribution of decision-making power and is no doubt the major factor responsible for the increasingly important role assigned to the national union in the bargaining process in the postwar years. It underlies the grant of authority to national officials to formulate bargaining demands, to coordinate negotiating strategy, and to pass on the acceptability of all contract settlements within the union's jurisdiction.

On the employers' side, the centralization of decision-making power has been largely a defensive response to the presence of unionism and the consolidation of union bargaining efforts. In the large, oligopolistic firms, whose operations are often highly decentralized and usually widely dispersed geographically, this response has taken the form primarily of centrally directed bargaining policies to which divisional and local plant managements are expected to conform. In the small, competitive firm, on the other hand, the tendency has been to join forces with other firms similarly situated, surrendering discretion in bargaining decisions to the collectivity of firms represented by the association. Regardless of the form it takes, however, the move to more centralized decision making is essentially an effort to combat the whipsaw tactics of the union or to secure otherwise a bargaining advantage.

. . . In small-firm, highly competitive industries, unions have invariably favored multiemployer negotiations as the only effective approach to the attainment and maintenance of high labor standards. In this, moreover, they have found the employers normally compliant, since bargaining on a market-wide basis lends stability to the industry's price structure, permits the pooling of bargaining strength, and provides each small employer with access to expert services in the negotiations and administration of the collective agreement. In the large-firm, oligopolistics industries, on the other hand, unions have pushed for company-wide (multiplant) bargaining, but the majority have abandoned their earlier interest in multifirm negotiations. This change of heart can be traced directly to the realization in the immediate postwar years that "pattern" bargaining on a single-company basis could accomplish superior results.

This procedure allows the union to negotiate first a favorable settlement with any one of a few key companies. The settlement then becomes the "pattern" for major competitors and the "target" for smaller firms in the industry or for firms in related industries. Deviations from the pattern can normally be expected as negotiations move outward from the "power-generating sectors" to smaller firms and to satellite industries. There are limits, however, to the union's willingness to retreat from the patterns, set by the need to preserve the integrity of industry standards and by the size and type of concessions required for a firm's survival.[3] The advantages to the union of pattern bargaining are obvious: The union is free to exert pressure on the employer most likely to yield a favorable settlement; it benefits from the reluctance of any one company to stand a strike while its competitors continue to operate; and it is able to vary the level of settlements in accordance with ability to pay without endangering the maintenance of standards in the industry.

## THE CONTEMPORARY STRUCTURE

There are at present approximately 150,000 agreements in the United States, or roughly one agreement for every one hundred workers represented by labor unions. Since most of these agreements

---

[3] How much deviation in settlements actually occurs is difficult to measure. The "pattern" constitutes only part of the total bargain, covering mainly the adjustment in wages and major benefit programs. There is thus considerable scope for differentiation in non-pattern terms of the contract, and hence, in the cost of settlements, even in the absence of "pattern" deviations as such.

are negotiated with a single employer and cover only a small number of workers, the bargaining structure—judged by the size of the typical negotiating unit—is obviously highly decentralized. Indeed, this is one of the distinctive features of the American bargaining system, for negotiations elsewhere in the world are normally collective on the employers' side and the agreements commonly cover entire industries.

* * *

[D]espite the small size of the typical bargaining unit, it is nevertheless true that workers are heavily concentrated in a relatively small number of large units. Thus, in 1961, the Bureau of Labor Statistics found that 8.3 million workers, or about half the number under union contract, were covered by 1,733 major agreements, i.e., agreements embracing one thousand workers or more each. The nine largest agreements covered 1.9 million workers, or more than a tenth of total union coverage.[4]

. . . Although agreements of each type are to be found in the majority of industries, single-firm bargaining predominates in the manufacturing sector of the economy, whereas multifirm bargaining is the dominant form in the nonmanufacturing sector. With the exception of the railroad industry, where the centralized bargaining system is partly the result of extensive government regulation (and, one might add, the steel industry, where government intervention is more or less a habit), multiemployer agreements are largely confined to the small-firm, competitive industries— food, apparel, printing, furniture, and lumber in manufacturing; and mining, trucking, wholesale and retail trade, hotels and restaurants, services, and construction in non-manufacturing. Clearly, the charater of the industry, especially the size of firms and the degree of competition in product and labor markets, is the primary determinant of bargaining unit arrangements.

## CURRENT DEVELOPMENTS IN BARGAINING STRUCTURE

. . . The principal factor encouraging consolidation is the continuing extension of the market. This is especially evident in the traditional "local-market" industries, where competitive areas are expanding rapidly under the impact of spreading urbanization, improvements in the technology of transportation systems, and the growth of larger companies with facilities located in a number of different communities. The effect of these forces is seen most dramatically in the trucking industry, where the Teamsters union has recently negotiated its first nationwide contract and now enjoys a convention mandate to further centralize its bargaining activities. But the same pressures are also at work in other industries (construction, retail food, baking, etc.), gradually expanding negotiating units and drawing the units in different areas into ever tighter relationships.

Operating in the same direction, but at another level, are the efforts of unions with representation rights in the same company to develop systems of joint or coordinated company-wide bargaining similar to the systems already established by the Meat Cutters and Packinghouse Workers in the meat-packing industry and the Auto Workers and Machinists in the aerospace industry. The aim of this drive, which has gained considerable momentum in recent years under the energetic sponsorship of the Industrial Union Department (AFL–CIO), is, of course, to enhance union bargaining power by eliminating employer opportunities for whipsawing. . . .

Less certain in effect, but nonetheless important, are the group of decentralizing pressures associated mainly with the so-

[4] "Major Union Contracts in the United States, 1961," *Monthly Labor Review,* Vol. 85, No. 10 (October 1962), pp. 1136–1144.

called revolt of the local union memberships. This revolt, stemming from the dissatisfaction of subordinate groups with their role in the bargaining process, manifests itself in a variety of ways. It appears in the growing rebelliousness of the skilled trades in industrial unions, in the demands within company-wide bargaining systems for a stronger emphasis on the resolution of local problems, in the defections of subordinate groups from their parent organizations, in more vigorous election challenges to incumbent administrations, and in the reduced willingness of the rank and file to accept agreements negotiated by their representatives.

A careful analysis of the rise in intra-union conflict, which is gradually reshaping the power structure in a number of unions and bargaining units, would indicate that a multiplicity of factors are at work—many of them unique to individual situations. Much of the turbulence can be traced, however, to three general sources: the expanding scope of the bargaining unit itself, the character of the economic environment in recent years, and government policies that impinge on bargaining behavior.

Enlarging the scope of the bargaining unit enhances bargaining power, but it also magnifies the possibilities of intra-organizational conflict. Where the bargaining unit is narrow in scope—confined, say, to a single occupation in a single plant —the interests of members are likely to coincide and the job of developing internal agreement on objectives is relatively straightforward. As the scope of the unit expands, however, to embrace additional groups—different occupations or different plants—aspirations tend to diverge and even to conflict, and the dif-

ficulty of mediating these conflicts increasingly complicates the task of internal agreement. . . . When a strategic group is sufficiently dissatisfied with the unit's performance, there are but two alternatives: to redistribute power with the unit in favor of the group, or to accept the group's withdrawal. This is the basis of the skilled-trades problem in industrial unions. Here, the progressive disillusionment of the skilled craftsmen with industrial-union policies has forced such unions, under pain of mass defections, to adjust procedures so as to strengthen the representation rights of skilled groups on negotiating committees and accord them a larger measure of bargaining autonomy.

The related problem of discontent among local union memberships is attributable . . . in part also to . . . changes in the economic environment. . . . marked by the coincidence of largescale unemployment and rapid industrial change. Pressed by intensified competition, employers in these years were driven to exploit every means of improving efficiency, . . . Understandably, these circumstances induced anxieties in the majority of workers about job security and fear for the preservation of local working conditions. With local issues dominant in the worker's mind, the company-wide bargaining systems developed in the roomier economic environment of the previous decade and geared primarily to the pursuit of monetary gains were simply found wanting. Hence, the difficulties experienced in the auto negotiations and others in recent years where local unions have refused to accept the signing of the company-wide agreement as a signal that local issues should be dropped or compromised.[5]

Lastly, it is clear that public policy has

[5] The recent election reversals also fit within this pattern, especially in the case of the United Steel workers. Although the issues in this campaign were complex, it is clear nevertheless that the repudiation of the McDonald administration turned in part on its inattention to local unions and local problems, its failure to respond to the special needs of different industry groups (in aluminum, non-ferrous metals, can making, etc.), and its tendency to allow the Human Relations Committee to usurp the prerogatives of the regular negotiating committee—in short, its commitment to an over-centralized structure of authority.

also contributed to the current unrest in unions. The encouragement given to craft-type units under the Taft-Hartley Act, especially since the mid-1950's, has increased the vulnerability of industrial unions to special group pressures. The Landrum-Griffin Act of 1959, by stimulating rank-and-file expression and by diluting leadership control, has had much the same effect. In addition, there is little doubt that the latter act has played a role in the increasing incidence of settlement rejections by local union memberships, though here it must surely share the credit with governmental pressures aimed at securing simultaneously adherence to the wage-price guidelines and peaceful contract settlements. Whatever else these policies may have accomplished collectively they have encouraged fragmentation of the bargaining structure, increased the strains on the bargaining process, and complicated the job of peaceful settlement.

Whether the intensification of intra-union conflict is looked upon with favor or distaste depends on one's point of view. For those long troubled by the atrophy of the local union and the absence of effective dissent within unions, the tensions and adjustments are a welcome tonic that may yet reinvigorate the lifeblood of an ailing, if not aged, institution. For others, however, concerned more with the need to structure institutional relationships so as to minimize the incompatibility of collective bargaining with the national interest, the tendency toward fragmentation or decentralization is a disturbing, and even alarming, trend.

*  *  *

Whatever one's view of the ideal state, however, a realistic assessment of the possibilities for bargaining structure must accept at the outset the inevitability of closer government surveillance of the system's performance. If the vitality of the bargaining process is to be preserved, therefore, one cannot avoid the need to effect uneasy compromises between the right of dissent within unions and the need to establish bargaining relationships which facilitate the orderly settlement of disputes within a framework of shifting national interest constraints.

*  *  *

## LONG-TERM AGREEMENTS AND AUTOMATIC WAGE ADJUSTMENTS

The adoption of the long-term agreement and its gradual spread throughout industry is another major development of the postwar period. Indeed, it has been called the most important single development in bargaining practice since the end of World War II. Long-term contracts were not an innovation of the postwar years, but what distinguished the type of agreement pioneered by General Motors and the United Auto Workers in 1948 was the inclusion of provisions making wage adjustments automatic at scheduled dates in the future. These automatic adjustments were of two kinds: a wage improvement factor designed to raise wages annually in line with economy-wide productivity advances and a cost-of-living escalator designed to maintain real wages (the worker's living standards) against movements in the price level of consumer goods. Interestingly enough, when the GM-UAW agreement was first announced, it evoked little enthusiasm and, indeed, a good deal of criticism in industry circles. Since 1950, however, its influence has become pervasive and its implications for wage policy are now a central concern of economists.

The GM formula, embraced first in 1948 and continued in all subsequent agreements with the UAW, . . . formula represented an attempt by the company to formulate a long-term wage policy, based on productivity and living-cost standards, which would reduce the conflict over wage-setting and hence the risk of government involvement in wage decisions. As Joseph Garbarino points out, the unique feature of the approach was the attempt "to develop a policy on the substance of bargaining, as distinct from a strategy for use in the bargaining process."[6]

. . . . In the fall of 1950, . . . fear of inflation and wage controls occasioned by the Korean War encouraged a number of unions to demand cost-of-living escalator clauses in their agreements. As a result, by September 1952, over three million workers—or almost 20 percent of all workers under contract—were covered by escalator agreements. Automatic wage increases were less popular, covering only half as many workers, most of whom were under the jurisdiction of the UAW. . . . Apparently, the decision to adopt these agreements was partly opportunistic and partly a desire to experiment with long-term policies, signaling the parties' confidence in the government's ability to manage the economy and employer acceptance of the permanency of militant unions.[7] Thus, by the end of the 1950's, some five million workers annually were receiving wage increases scheduled in earlier-year negotiations.

The recession beginning in 1958 produced the usual pattern of abandonment of cost-of-living clauses. Inflation was no longer a threat, many of the employers who had adopted such clauses just prior to the price rise of 1955–1957 were opposed to their renewal, and most unions in any case were more interested in job security issues. As a result, coverage had fallen to only two million workers by early 1966. The elimination of escalator clauses did not affect, however, the increase in multiyear contracts with automatic wage increases. Thus, whereas only 5 percent of collective agreements provided for deferred or scheduled increases in 1954, the proportion had increased to 67 percent by the first half of 1966 and was still rising.[8]

More recently, since prices have resumed their upward trend, union interest has again turned to cost-of-living escalator clauses, . . . Many employers can be expected to resist these pressures or at least to try to modify the impact of escalator clauses by seeking limits on the allowable adjustment, longer adjustment intervals, and the elimination of adjustments to small price variations. . . . Similarly, employers have sought to modify the size of automatic wage increases (sometimes by extending the adjustment interval beyond one year), and they have sought to divert part of the increase to other benefits in an effort to hold down the size of the package. As yet, however, success has been limited, confined mainly to modifications of the cost-of-living clause.

## IMPLICATIONS OF THE LONG-TERM CONTRACT

. . . The most intensive study of this aspect of wage policy concludes that long-term formula agreements of the GM-UAW type (especially where they coexist with agreements bargained annually) probably add to inflationary pressures, partly through their impact on wage behavior in recession periods, and partly through the effect of escalator clauses on the wage-price lag.[9] The argument concerning recessionary wage behavior derives essen-

---

[6] Joseph W. Garbarino, *Wage Policy and Long-Term Contracts* (Washington: The Brookings Institution, 1962), p. 3.

[7] *Ibid.*, pp. 79–80.

[8] Bureau of National Affairs, Inc., *Facts for Bargaining*, Jan. 29, 1965 and July 14, 1966. The Bureau has also reported that the most common term for contracts is three years (47 percent), closely followed by two years (40) percent). Approximately a quarter of these agreements provide for reopening on wage and/or non-wage matters prior to the scheduled expiration date. BNA, *Basic Patterns in Union Contracts*, Sept. 9, 1965, p. 36:1.

[9] Garbarino, *op. cit.*, pp. 163–173.

tially from the judgment that the long-term contract has been a major influence in making "the annual money wage increase virtually ubiquitous for the organized worker in the United States."[10] The wage-price-lag argument rests, on the other hand, on the notion that cost-of-living clauses "help to maintain or intensify an inflationary movement that starts elsewhere in the economy" by facilitating or speeding up the escalation process.[11] These arguments are persuasive, but they have not gone unchallenged. Other economists, for example, have concluded that unions with long-term contracts would probably have negotiated wages at least as high in annual bargaining,[12] or have argued that the only realistic alternative to cost-of-living escalator clauses is higher initial wage increases which *anticipate* the expected price rise, thereby *reversing* the adjustment lag and immediately generating inflationary pressures.[13] How one chooses between these views is a matter of personal judgment, for each rests on quite different assumptions about bargaining behavior and the nature of the inflationary process.[14]

There is, however, another difficulty in questions of this sort which further complicates the issue. Much of the investigation of the inflationary potential of long-term contracts in terms of money-wage effects to the virtual neglect of productivity effects which may also be important. It is universally conceded, for example, that management derives considerable advantage from long-term contracts—avoidance of the costs of annual negotiations, a more stable environment for forward planning, less idle time lost through strikes, etc. But if this is so, and even allowing that management pays some price to the union for these advantages, it surely follows that efficiency effects (as well as wage effects) are relevant data in assessing the inflationary impact of the long-term contract.[15] Similarly, even if one accepts that the multiyear contract has been instrumental in establishing the expectation of annual money-wage increases, so that wage rates do in fact rise more than they otherwise would in recessionary periods, it still does not follow that unit wage costs are affected to the same extent or even in the same direction. For as long as relative bargaining power is unchanged, adjustments that compensate for the incremental wage increase may well occur, and indeed are to be expected, in other employment terms. . . .[16]

As we look to the future, there is no reason to expect that the postwar trend toward non-reopenable, long-term contracts will soon be reversed.

*  *  *

---

[10] *Ibid.*, p. 133.

[11] *Ibid.*, p. 64.

[12] Jack Stieber, "Evaluation of Long-Term Contracts," in Harold W. Davey, *et al.*, eds., *New Dimensions in Collective Bargaining* (New York: Harper and Brothers, 1959), p. 151.

[13] See, for example, Alvin H. Hansen, "Inflation and the New Economics," *Challenge*, Vol. 15, No. 2 (November–December 1966), pp. 6, 41.

[14] Alvin Hansen places strong emphasis on the importance to stability of lagged adjustment to change, hence his preference for the cost-of-living escalator over the anticipatory wage increase. As he notes in his argument in favor of such clauses: "The lag is important. Stability in a market economy is largely a function of lagged adjustments. . . . It makes more sense to make the adjustment *after* the event than to force the issue before the event." *Ibid.*, p. 41.

[15] It could be argued that benefits accruing to the employer must be surrendered *in toto* to the union for the risks the latter runs in agreeing to such a contract. There is no reason, however, for supposing that the arrangement is not mutually beneficial; and indeed the parties' strong and growing preference for this type of contract would indicate that it is.

[16] The importance of looking beyond the wage bargain to the much broader range of terms and practices embraced in the collective agreement has been demonstrated time and again. The "hard-line" approach of management in the late 1950's, manifested in the drive to eliminate restrictive rules and other obstacles to efficiency, was reinforced no doubt by the recognition of serious constraints on the manipulation of wage rates.

## THE ELABORATION OF COMPENSATION SYSTEMS

Collective bargaining has been credited with many of the changes which have occurred in the wage patterns and practices of individual firms during the postwar period: the displacement of personal rate systems by more rational plant wage structures (based on job content analysis); the elimination or reduction of occupational rate differentials among plants in the same company; and to a lesser degree, the shift in some industries from incentive to daywork methods of wage payment. Important as such changes in wage systems have been, however, a more dramatic and more significant development of the last two decades has been the growth and proliferation of supplementary wage practices or, as they are often called, fringe benefits. Few of these practices, as such, are innovations of the postwar period; retirement plans, health insurance programs, paid leave, and even the provision of premium payments all have long traditions, especially for white-collar workers, that predate both the depression of the thirties and the advent of unionism. In addition, many of the specific programs received their initial stimulus in World War II from stabilization policies that were more permissive toward fringe improvements than wage increases. The postwar period is nevertheless distinctive in that it witnessed the rapid extension of such benefits to blue-collar work groups and the more or less continuous revision and elaboration of the programs in successive negotiations.

The spectacular growth of fringe benefits and their current importance in American industry are readily demonstrated. For several years now, the Chamber of Commerce of the United States has conducted surveys of fringe payments by a sample of American firms in the manufacturing and nonmanufacturing sectors of the economy. These surveys show that employer expenditures for fringe benefits in 1,181 companies amounted to 71.5 cents an hour in 1965, or 24.7 percent of payroll. They also show that for eighty-four companies reporting throughout the postwar period, fringe expenditures rose from 22.1 an hour in 1947 to 88.8 cents an hour in 1965, or from 16.1 percent to 28.1 percent of payroll.[17] The Chamber's estimates probably overstate the actual size of fringes for industry as a whole, since the sample is biased toward the larger, more prosperous firms. Nevertheless such additional information as is available confirms that the current level of supplementary payments is 20 to 25 percent of labor compensation, and that this percentage has roughly doubled since the end of World War II.

## UNIONISM AS THE SOURCE OF FRINGE BENEFITS

Most students of industrial relations, while reluctant to assign much influence to unions in the wage and productivity areas, have no hesitation in attributing to unionism the major role in the development of fringe benefits. This conclusion, in our view is worth examining more closely; first, because it hardly seems warranted, and second, and more importantly, because an examination of the issue brings to light certain conceptual difficulties in the measurement of union influence which, if ignored, are likely to distort evaluations of the institution's performance.

The view that unions should be credited as the primary agent in the spread of

---

[17] Chamber of Commerce of the United States, *Fringe Benefits 1965*, Washington, 1966, pp. 9, 27. These figures exclude premium payments from the definition of fringe benefits but include such payments, along with expenditures for vacations and holidays, in the definition of payroll. When premium payments are treated as a fringe expenditure and the payroll base is redefined as "straight-time pay for time worked," the ratio of fringe payments to payroll in 1965 (for all firms in the survey) rises from 24.7 percent to 37.8 percent—or to almost two fifths of straight-time wages and salaries.

fringe benefits derives from the notion that these programs, because of their group nature, are not in the category of provisions likely to be introduced unilaterally by employers and from observance of the aggressiveness of unions in pressing fringe demands at the bargaining table. The reasoning here is surely misleading, however, for it is based on an oversimplified view of the problems of personnel management, a misconception of the nature of the bargaining process, and a failure to take account of the evolving requirements of an industrial system. Space limitations preclude a full discussion, but the considerations that underlie this criticism of the popular view can be briefly stated.

First, the idea that employers, absent union pressures, would have little or no reason to initiate fringe benefits is contrary both to fact and to the logic of efficient manpower management. Most of the types of benefit programs in existence today were originated by employers and usually for sound business reasons—to reduce the costs of turnover and absenteeism, to reward effort and improve efficiency, to take advantage of tax savings, and to aid in the recruitment of workers. The early plans, to be sure, were sometimes selective (or discriminatory) in their application, and benefit levels were invariably modest. But these characteristics reflected, respectively, the specific objectives the plans were designed to achieve and the employers' judgment that most workers preferred the bulk of their compensation in ready cash—a conviction that made a good deal of sense as long as incomes were close to the subsistence level.

Second, . . . [t]he depression brought abrupt changes in the social, political, and economic outlook of the nation, and especially a recognition of the worker's dependence on the vagaries of the labor market and his relative helplessness in coping unaided with the problems of unemployment, ill health, and old age. . . . In that environment, characterized by a growing awareness of workers' needs, sustained prosperity, and relatively tight labor markets, it is surely no more unreasonable to suppose that employers in their efforts to attract, retain, and motivate workers would have experimented with supplementary wage programs (already in existence for white-collar groups) than to assume, as many do implicitly, that they would have approached their personnel needs in a manner reminiscent of the early 1930's.

Third, the bargaining process, as it has developed, does not lend itself easily to employer initiatives. The good-faith bargaining requirement, for one thing, pervents the employer from introducing changes unilaterally. More importantly, however, the adversary nature of the relationship and the natural concern of union leaders that all gains appear as the sole achievement of the union dictate that most employers publicly adopt a firm stance even against proposals which serve their own interests and, under different circumstances, would readily be granted. Curiously enough, employer opposition to wage demands is seldom interpreted as evidence that in the absence of union pressures the course of wages would have been vastly different. Yet employer opposition to negotiated fringes is invariably accepted as a reliable indicator of what would have happened in a non-union market.

Finally, it is clear from even a cursory survey of social systems that the provision of protection against interruptions to income (through accidents, sickness, unemployment, and old age) emerges inevitably in the course of industrialization. Whatever the particular institutions of the labor market, it is everywhere the case that responsibility for the minimum welfare and security of the worker has fallen upon employers and/or government. It appears, therefore, that the real issues in this area relate less to the provision of basic protections as such than to the forms which programs take, the timing of their introduction, and the rate of their liberalization.

These considerations do not deny a role to unions in the development of protective measures against insecurity, but they do suggest that the influence of unionism is easily (and often) exaggerated. They also suggest that issues of this sort should be examined within a broader framework than has hitherto been used—a framework that acknowledges the needs of workers in an industrial society, accepts the realistic alternatives available in meeting these needs, and distinguishes the requirements of the system (the workers' needs) from the specific instrument created to fulfill these requirements (the union).

A similar but stronger conclusion about the effect of unionism on fringes is reached in the recent statistical study of the determinants of fringe expenditures by Robert Rice.[18] For years, proponents of the view that unions were the major influential factor in the development of fringes have claimed the support of government surveys which show that the incidence of benefit plans as well as the level of benefit expenditures are appreciably higher in the unionized sector of the economy. Rice's study, based on these same surveys, demonstrates, however, that variations in benefit expenditures are explained largely by variations in employee-earnings levels, and that the apparent casual relationship between expenditures and union status is a spurious one, reflecting mainly the fact that unionism's main strength is in the high-wage sectors of the economy. The assignment of a negligible role to unionism probably carries the argument too far, for an examination of fringe developments in specific industries makes it diffi-

cult to reject entirely the conclusion that unions were influential in the spread of such private programs as pensions and supplemental unemployment benefits (SUB), at least from the standpoint of timing and the rate of benefit liberalization.[19] The absence of any clear statistical relationship between fringe expenditures and unionization casts doubt, however, on the validity of the claim that unionism has been the major causal factor in the growth of such expenditures.

. . . On problem that needs only be alluded to briefly arises from the fact that many supplemental expenditures, e.g., those for insurance, holidays, and vacations, are employee-related rather than earnings-related. As a result, they do not enter into overtime calculations and thus tend to lower overtime costs relative to hiring costs. This progressive lowering of the effective premium rate has not discouraged workers from seeking overtime; consequently, from the standpoint of establishing a premium rate that is just sufficient to attract the necessary supply of additional hours from a given work force, the newer rates are clearly closer to the optimum. Insofar as social policy (the Fair Labor Standards Acts) is intended to discourage long hours and maximize employment opportunities at given levels of demand, however, the failure to relate contributions more directly to earnings has reduced the policy's effectiveness.

A more critical problem in the financing of fringe benefits arises, however, from the preferential tax treatment accorded employer contributions to private pension and welfare plans. As might be expected, the exemption of employer contributions from both the corporate income tax and the personal income tax has encouraged

[18] Robert Rice, "Skill, Earnings, and the Growth of Wage Supplements," *Papers and Proceedings* of the American Economic Association, May 1966, pp. 583–593.

[19] See Robert M. Macdonald, *Collective Bargaining in the Automobile Industry* (New Haven: Yale University Press, 1963), pp. 56–58. Actually, Rice found that unionization had had a significant effect on the *prevalence* of pension plans (Rice, *loc. cit.*, p. 588). His study did not investigate the effect of SUB separately, for the reason no doubt that plans of this nature have been confined to the auto, steel, rubber, and garment industries and have covered less than two million workers in recent years.

the funneling of increasing amounts of income into private noncontributory programs. Even if one grants, however, that the encouragement of private supplementation of public programs is desirable social policy, the method employed is surely inequitable in that it offers lower effective purchase prices (through greater opportunities for tax avoidance) to higher-income groups who are in many ways least in need of protection. Preferential tax treatment of plan contributions, which amounts in effect to government subsidization of benefits for higher-paid employees, would appear less inequitable perhaps if the benefit levels under public programs were less meager. This is certainly not the case, however; and there is always the danger that the continued rapid expansion of programs at the private level, encouraged by federal tax policy, will divert attention and pressure from the need for substantial improvements in the public programs.[20]

Whether this danger materializes depends on the extent to which our recent stepped-up concern for the disadvantaged represents a basic shift in public attitudes toward the social security system. If Medicare and current proposals for liberalizing the OASDI program are harbingers of a new, more vigorous commitment to the security needs of the nation's citizens, then private plans will perforce accommodate, and private expenditures relative to income, may actually decline. As long as tax policy and consumer preferences remain unchanged, however, total expenditures on security benefits (both public and private) can be expected to rise more rapidly than income, at least to the point where further deferrals offer no tax advantage.

## CONCLUSION

This article has discussed the major changes which have occurred in bargaining patterns and practices in the private sector of the economy in the postwar period. It has shown how developments in the bargaining system are a response both to the internal needs of the parties and to stimuli in the external environment. While an explication of these changes supplies a basis for predicting how the system may behave in the future, it does not provide grounds for assessing the overall effectiveness of bargaining institutions or the social and economic consequences of the bargaining process. Nevertheless, the discussion does have implications which are relevant to any contemporary assessment.

In recent years, rising public expectations, coupled with rapid and pervasive change in the society, have posed a challenge of adjustment for all contemporary institutions—social, economic, and political. It is perhaps understandable, therefore, that many observers of the labor scene have found collective bargaining wanting and excessively rigid in its response to the new environment. Judgments of this sort are based, of course, more on intuitive reasoning than on objective standards; nevertheless, the claim of inflexibility is surely not a valid criticism. Particular bargaining relationships, it is true, warrant censure on this score (measured against accomplishments elsewhere); but the record of the last two decades for the bargaining system as a whole is one of remarkable flexibility and adaptability to new and often trying circumstances. This record of vigorous institutional adjustment reflects, on the one hand, the pragmatic attitudes and policies

---

[20] The need for adequate retirement benefits at the public level is all the more critical when account is taken of recent private and governmental criticisms of existing private pension plans. As matters stand, it is estimated that private pension plans cover only 50 percent of employees and that the relative lack of vesting and portability rights and the tendency to fund past service liabilities over excessively long periods will deprive millions of these covered workers of any opportunity to draw benefits.

which have increasingly characterized the practice of bargaining in the postwar years and, on the other, the decentralized character of decision making which has fostered diversity in rule making and a willingness to experiment with novel approaches to old and new problems. A decentralized structure is not, of course, without disadvantages. It may, for example, make difficult, if not impossible, the task of securing compliance with national-interest objectives of the kind embodied in the wage-price guidelines (assuming compliance would serve the national welfare). It certainly has exacerbated conflict in industries, such as newspaper publishing, construction, and transportation, where unionism is at present too highly fractionalized. Granted these possible shortcomings, however, it is doubtful that any *feasible* alternative system devised to perform the same vital functions of assuring equity and fair treatment to workers in a democratic society would have matched the capacity for adaptive behavior exemplified in the present system.

The flexibility of the bargaining mechanism is revealed in the intricately varied and changing structure of relationships, in the continuous modification of bargaining procedures, and especially in the evolution of the detailed content of collective agreements. In the postwar period, collective bargaining has been instrumental in developing a wide array of income-maintenance and employment adjustment measures which had added immeasurably to the security and well-being of wage earners and their families. Again, it is not difficult to find fault with some of these arrangements—to regret their limited or discriminatory coverage, to deplore their effects on mobility and costs, and to question on occasion their worth to the workers involved. In evaluating the measures adopted and in assessing responsibility, however, one does well to bear in mind the social and economic environment of the postwar years. Until very recently, Americans generally have been willing to tolerate prolonged periods of excessive unemployment, an inadequate system of income-maintenance programs, and an archaic set of manpower (or labor market) institutions. As a result, the burden of providing against insecurity of employment and income has fallen largely on individual workers or on the organizations they have created to protect their interests. In such a context, it is simply unreasonable (and largely irrelevant) to condemn collective bargaining because it is not the *ideal* instrument for solving social problems; for as long as society itself is remiss in providing conditions conducive to the acceptance of change, unions are bound to intervene and to seek in private negotiations measures that ease the burden on their constituents.

This does not mean, of course, that one should condone each and every bargaining practice; for the test is always whether or not the practice achieves a reasonable balance between the competing interests of worker and consumers. Economists are prone to judge the results of bargaining in terms of the competitive standard. This by itself, however, is too narrow a base for judging the utility of the bargaining system. Collective bargaining performs functions that are indispensable to the maintenance of a humane industrial society. It secures, above all, the worker's commitment to political democracy and a free enterprise economy. Consequently, evaluations of its worth and proposals for its reform, if they are to serve society's interests, must take account of the vital functions fulfilled by the bargaining system.

### Related Readings

A very useful general work on collective bargaining, which deals in detail with many substantive collective bargaining issues, is Summer Slichter, James Healy, and E. Robert Livernash, *The Impact of Collective Bargaining on Management* (Washington, D.C., Brookings Institution, 1960). A very good analysis of collective bargaining is presented in Neil Chamberlain's *Collective Bargaining* (New York, McGraw-Hill, 1951). A good critique of industrial relations may be found in Allen Flanders' *Industrial Relations: What is Wrong with the System?* (London, Faber and Faber, 1965). A very useful series of articles on some important collective bargaining issues is presented in John T. Dunlop and Neil W. Chamberlain, eds., *Frontiers of Collective Bargaining* (New York, Harper & Row, 1967).

# CHAPTER 12

# Collective Bargaining Theories

*INDUSTRIAL RELATIONS*

Much of the literature on industrial relations—or the interactions between unions, management and specialized government agencies dealing with union-management relations—is factual and descriptive. Essentially, this field has been the preoccupation of practitioners and scholars concerned with the practical issues involved in collective bargaining or dispute settlement. There have therefore been very few attempts to formulate general theories of industrial relations.

In his *Industrial Relations Systems,* John T. Dunlop formulates such a general theory. In the excerpts from Chapter 10 of this book reproduced here, Dunlop summarizes the ideas that he derived from comparative studies of a number of countries and detailed personal involvement and research in the United States.

The central concept in Dunlop's conceptual framework is an *industrial relations system,* which is a subsystem of, and on the same logical plane with, an economic system. Although a theory of industrial relations overlaps economic theory, industrial relations center on the rules governing the system, while economic theory treats rules as given.

The industrial relations system concerns certain actors (workers and their organizations, managers and their organizations, and specialized government agencies) who interact in the interrelated contexts of "technology, market or budgetary constraints, and the power relations in the larger community and the derived status of the actors." The "contexts" produce common rules in a given industry in different countries. Moreover, the industrial-relations system creates "an ideology or a commonly shared body of ideas and beliefs regarding the interaction and roles of the actors which helps to bind the system together."

In addition to the common rules produced by contexts, conditions in particular national systems produce rules unique to each country. "Thus, almost any rule involves the subtle weaving together of technological and market influences and the special characteristics of the national industrial relations system. The context is a whole."

Dunlop's system is variable and applicable to a wide range of situations, although its inner logic remains the same. He points out that the concept of an industrial relations system makes it possible to integrate wage determination and industrial relations experience. With Dunlop's approach, wages and other forms of compensation are treated as being determined like other rules. His approach consequently has the advantage of showing the relationships between wages and other rules. The concept of an industrial relations system therefore is a useful tool of analysis.

# General Theory of Industrial Relations

## by John T. Dunlop

This volume seeks to present a new way of thinking about industrial-relations experience. It develops a systematic body of ideas for arranging and interpreting the known facts of worker-manager-government interactions; it also provides a set of concepts fitted together that require the collection of new facts, presented in new categories. The rules of the work place and work community become the general focus of inquiry to be explained by theoretical analysis.

. . . A general theory of industrial relations is proposed, not alone to encompass countries with diverse economic and political forms, but also to relate experience in component sectors to a country as a whole.

The central concept is that of an *indus-trial-relations system*. The idea is derived in part from the intuition of practitioners and from the growing number of titles written by careful observers of country-wide industrial-relations practices that use the term "system" without explicit or rigorous definition. These insights suggested that the notion of an industrial-relations system might be a fruitful starting point for more systematic work.[1] Moreover, the analogy of the constructive use of "system" in economics comes readily to mind. While a glance at the world of affairs may belie resort to an idea that denotes order and an inner rationality, economics has developed a rigorous analytical discipline, applicable to a variety of political forms, which highlights the inter-dependence of activity within a system, the response of

[1] Joyce Cary, *Art and Reality*, Cambridge, England, University Press, 1958, pp. 1, 96.

the output of the system to exterior changes and features of long-term development from within a system.

There are, of course, serious pitfalls to the direct transfer of concepts from one field of intellectual activity to another, although the danger is probably the more serious the greater the distance of transfer across fields. Each theoretical edifice for a new discipline must be designed afresh if it is to meet the tests of consistency, style and, most of all, usefulness. Formalism rather than functional design is no less sterile in intellectual model building than in using bricks and mortar.

It is important to be clear about the relations between the study of industrial relations and other social sciences, particularly about its relation to economics. In the United States and Great Britain the study of industrial relations is, in large part, an offshoot of economics, although other fields have made some contributions. In France it appears as if the industrial sociologists have been most concerned with developing the field. In many other countries it is largely the preserve of lawyers. In all countries it has been a crossroads where various specialties have converged. The present purpose has been to present a distinctive analytical apparatus for the study of the industrial-relations aspects of behavior in industrial society.

An industrial-relations system is a subsystem of the social system. It is on the same logical plane as an economic system. Both abstract from many significant aspects of human behavior, and both select a limited number of aspects of behavior for rigorous inquiry. Each takes certain data as given, and each seeks to explain limited features of behavior in terms of a small number of variables within its system.[2] But the two systems are not identical, and the disciplines of economic theory and industrial relations have different major problems and analytical subject matter.

Some parameters that are given in economic theory are variables in industrial relations. The rules on workmen's inspectors in coal mining or apprenticeship in building, to select two examples from Chapters 5 and 6, are treated in economics as data or as given from outside the economic system; they are not to be explained. These rules have the same status in economics as technical (engineering) conditions of production. For industrial relations these particular rules are rather variable to be explained by the operation of the industrial-relations system.

There are other parameters treated as given in industrial relations that are variables in economic theory. The level of economic activity and the rate of economic growth, for example, are treated in the main as given for industrial relations but are variables to be explained in economic theory. Other parameters such as technical (engineering) conditions are treated as given for both disciplines. Still other parameters, notably the setting of rules of compensation and the operation of labor markets, are to be explained within both systems.

The economic system and the industrial-relations system are thus partially overlapping, and the disciplines of economics and industrial relations are closely related although they select different variables and givens from industrial society. Economics centers its attention on the national product (output) and its variation over time, and industrial relations centers its attention on the rules of the system and their variations over time. The national product has certain common-sense meaning, but it is only to be fully understood in terms of the operation of the economic system as a whole. The web of rules likewise conveys a common-sense meaning,

[2] J. Tinbergen, *On the Theory of Economic Policy*, 2d Ed., Amsterdam, North-Holland Publishing Company, 1955, pp. 1–26.

but it also is to be understood in terms of the operation of the industrial relations system in its entirety.

An industrial-relations system is comprised of three groups of actors—workers and their organizations, manager and their organizations, and governmental agencies concerned with the work place and work community. These groups interact within a specified environment comprised of three interrelated contexts: the technology, the market or budgetary constraints and the power relations in the larger community and the derived status of the actors. An industrial-relations system creates an ideology or a commonly shared body of ideas and beliefs regarding the interaction and roles of the actors which helps to bind the system together.

Some rules are more or less directly related to the technological and market context of the system, and other rules are associated more uniquely with the power status of the actors in the larger society. Thus, in coal mining similar rules across countries with diverse economic and political systems were observed relating to workmen's safety inspectors, concessionary coal, housing for miners, wet conditions or high temperatures, the measurement of the working day for underground miners, tools and protective clothing, rights in jobs, and some aspects of compensation, particularly the occupational structure. . . . In building, rules that are similar across countries were observed relating to travel compensation, unfavorable weather, apprenticeship, the protection of standard conditions, layoffs and hirings, tools and some aspect of compensation, particularly the area rate. . . The common elements in these rules across countries were attributed largely to the common characteristics of the technological and market or budgetary contexts. It was recognized that in some cases the explicit international borrowing of rules may have arisen from the migration of workers, managers, and engineering enterprises. But even in these cases the industrial relations climate in the importing country would have to be congenial for the transplanted rule to take root and flourish.

Even within the group of rules attributed largely to the technological and market or budgetary contexts, numerous illustrations were observed of the influence of the national social systems. Thus, the distribution of concessionary coal in accordance with size of family in France and Germany and equally among households in the United States and Great Britain is a reflection of national industrial-relations characteristics in a rule largely oriented toward a common technological and market context. Or the rules relating to travel time and travel expense all draw the distinction between job sites within commuting distance and job sites which require a change in living quarters, but the distances which workers are expected to travel, the means of transport, and a variety of other features of these rules reflect national industrial-relations characteristics. The three-kilometer zone in Geneva and the bicycle allowance in the Netherlands are illustrative. Thus, almost any rule involves the subtle weaving together of technological and market influences and the special characteristics of the national industrial relations system. The context is a whole.

\* \* \*

The context of an industrial-relations system is not alone significant to its substantive rules but also to the internal organization of the hierarchies of workers, managers, and specialized government agencies. The formal organizations, the actual internal operations of all three actors and their interaction are sensitive to the variety of technologies and markets or budgets created by industrial society. The status of the actors will likewise affect the forms and the operations of the separate hierarchies. Consider, for instance, the differences in the internal organization of industrial-relations systems in large industrial plants, in the mobile work places of transportation, and in the shifting sites of construction, and further consider the differences in the internal organization of each in the USSR, the United States, Spain, and Yugoslavia. The scope of the organization of each actor, the specialization of functions, the resort to specialized personnel in rule-making, the degree of centralization in policy making and administration, the matching of corresponding levels of contact in the several hierarchies, the channel of internal communication within each hierarchy, indeed, the whole setup of the actors to produce and to administer rules is responsive to the context of the industrial-relations system.

The concept of an industrial-relations system is deliberately variable in scope; it may be used to characterize an immediate work place, an enterprise, a sector, or a country as a whole. The grouping cannot be arbitrary or capricious; the work places and the actors, at varying levels, that are grouped together must reflect a considerable degree of cohesiveness and formal or informal interdependence. Although the scope of an industrial-relations system is variable, according to the problem at hand, the formal structure of the system and its internal logic is unchanged. The scope of the hierarchies of the actors, their prescribed relations, the actual technology, and markets or budgets and the rules which they establish are different. But the logic of a system does not alter with its scope.

The comparative analysis of industrial relations among sectors within a country is facilitated by use of the notion of a system in the same way that comparisons are made among countries. As the scope of a system is narrowed within a country from a large sector to an industry or to an enterprise, the context naturally changes. The status of the actors is particularly affected. Rulemaking by the actors at the plant level in the engineering industry in Great Britain or the basic steel industry in the United States is, within relatively narrow limits, prescribed by rules established by the national actors for these sectors. The status of the local actors and their degrees of freedom is prescribed at these plant levels in the analogous way that the status of the actors in a national system is defined by its larger community, the full social systems.

An industrial-relations system, within a country, is a device to integrate the study of wage rates and other forms of compensation with industrial-relations experience. One of the major difficulties with the present state of discussions of wage determination is that wages tend either to be completely isolated from industrial relations, as in formal economic theory, or they are treated as a vague response to organized pressures in industrial-relations discussions.

Wage rates and other forms of compensation are here treated as another group of rules of the work place, on the same plane as rules respecting physical working conditions or discharge and layoffs. This procedure has the merit of showing how the forms of the rules on compensation, such as travel pay in building, and underground allowances in some coal-producing countries, are directly related to other rules. Wage rules and other rules are not two separate boxes; there is a single highly interrelated body of rules in an industrial-relations system. The actors are frequently concerned with the internal consistency and the internal interdependence among the rules. It is well known that there are substitutions in bargaining, in national industrial-relations systems with collective bargaining, between wage rules and other rules. The rules on wages are related to other rules on the development of a labor force. The concepts here developed help to break down an artificial barrier between wage rules and all other rules.

The scope of an industrial relations system within a country is directly related to the problems of wage determination. In another connection the idea has been developed of a *wage contour* as a wage-setting unit.[3] The wage contour consists of a grouping of enterprises with uniquely interdependent wage rates and other forms of compensation. Thus, the group of plants in the basic-steel industry in the United States or the engineering sector in Great Britain constitutes a wage contour. The scope of a wage contour can be identified with an industrial-relations system. The study of wage setting and the formation of other rules normally make use of a common grouping of enterprises, although the precise scope of enterprises may vary with some rules.

An industrial-relations system can be used as a tool of analysis as in comparative statics to explore the relationship between changes in elements of the system and changes in rules. A significant change in technology, in the market or budgetary context, in the status of the actors (reflected into the industrial-relations system from the larger community), or in the ideology of the system may be expected to change one or more rules. There is a significant place in the discipline of industrial relations for deductive propositions, checked by empirical testing, relating specified changes in the rules. The following illustrations . . . may better convey this judgment.

The rules in coal mining regarding the measurement of the work day, portal-to-portal, and the rules in countries with hot mining temperatures are to be directly related to the deepening of mines or the lengthening of drifts. The postwar changes in the market position of coal, as compared to conditions in the two decades between the wars, vitally affected the rules prescribing the level of wage rates compared to other industries. A shift from family management to professional management may be expected to create a more explicit body of rules. The change in the ideology of the Yugoslav system in the period 1950–1952 was an independent factor having influence on the complex of rules defining the status of the actors.

An industrial-relations system implies an inner unity and consistency, and a significant change in one facet of the context or the ideology may be expected to displace an old equilibrium (in the comparative statics sense) and to create new positions within the system and new rules.

The concept of an industrial relations system is used most fruitfully as a tool of analysis when a specified system is examined in its historical context, and changes in the system are studied through time. While comparative statics is likely to be fruitful in analyzing the consequences of changes in technology and market or budgetary constraints upon a group of rules, the status of the actors and the unifying ideology or commonly shared beliefs particularly need to be understood historically. (1) The status of the actors in a national industrial relations system is likely to be significantly influenced by the period in world history in which the system was first congealed, or drastically reconstructed following a revolution or a war. (2) The status of workers, managers and governmental agencies in a national system is much affected by the sequence in which the larger community secures independence, starts its industrialization drive and recasts traditional or preindustrial political forms. (3) The status of the actors alters systematically in the course of economic development and varies according to whether the industrializing leaders conform to the ideal types of the dynastic-feudal, the middle class or the revolutionary-intellectual elites. . . .

The main outlines of a national indus-

---

[3] John T. Dunlop, "The Task of Contemporary Wage Theory," in *New Concepts in Wage Determination*, George W. Taylor and Frank C. Pierson, Eds., New York, McGraw Hill Book Company, 1957, pp. 131–134.

trial-relations system emerge at a relatively early stage in economic development. The power context is set early and is much influenced by the industrializing elite. While a national industrial-relations system, and particularly the status of the actors, gradually evolves in a variety of ways with the industrialization process, the main structure and relations of a system congeal early, unless transformed by revolution or the dislocations of war in the larger community. Accordingly the present generation is extremely sensitive in the formation of industrial-relations systems in the large number of countries recently embarked on the road to the industrial society. . . .

### Bargaining Theory

Although bargaining and negotiation theory is applicable to a wide range of conflict situations, our primary concern here is with wage determination. There are a number of bargaining theories that cannot be treated in detail in this chapter. Our main purpose is to present the general outlines of the nature of bargaining between unions and management within the context of economic theory. The reader interested in pursuing this topic at greater length is referred to the suggested related references at the end of the chapter.

Wage determination is, to a significant degree, an interaction of market forces and policy by unions and employers. We say "interaction" because neither of these influences operate in isolation, though policy undoubtedly is more important in the short run and market forces are more significant in the long run. Moreover, the interplay of bargaining forces at any given time is influenced by the bargaining power of the parties, which is, in turn, influenced by such economic factors as business conditions, the elasticities of demand for and supply of labor, market structures, and the strategic position of the parties in markets.

### Bilateral Monopoly

Traditional economic theory has attempted to analyze bargaining between a single union (monopolist) and a single employer (monopsonist) in terms of bilateral monopoly models similar to the one Figure 12–1.

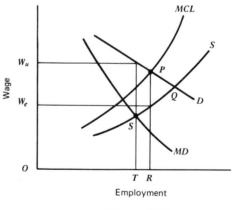

*Figure 12-1*

The employer is aware of his own demand $(D)$ and marginal supply $(MCL)$ curves. $D$ is the employers' marginal revenue product $(MRP)$ curve, showing the contribution of different levels of employment to his total revenue. S is the supply schedule for labor, indicating the wage that must be paid for different amounts of labor. Since increasing wages would cause the employer's total wage bill to rise by more than the increase in the wage of the marginal amount of labor hired, $MCL$ will be above the S schedule. The $MCL$ curve thus shows the change in the employer's total costs associated with various amounts of labor hired. The employer would therefore maximize his profits by equating $MCL$ with $D$ $(MRP)$ at point $P$. If he had power to unilaterally fix the wage-employment relationship, the employer would pay a wage corresponding to point $P$ on the S schedule, or $Ow_e$, and hire a quantity of labor equal $OR$.

The union, on the other hand, to the extent that it operates as a monopolist, is aware of its supply curve, the demand for labor, $D$ (which is the average price of labor to the union and the marginal revenue product to the employer) and the marginal demand curve, which indicates the change in the union's (seller's) revenue from selling different quantities of labor. $D$ is an average revenue schedule to the union (seller) but it is the marginal revenue product curve for the buyer (employer). The S curve is the marginal cost to the union (seller), but the average cost to the employer (buyer). The union as a monopolist would therefore maximize its "profits" by equating S with $MD$ at point $S$. If the union had the power to fix the wage-quantity relationship, it would establish a wage equal $OW_u$ at a quantity of $OT$. In bilateral monopoly, however, neither party has all the power, and therefore the wage will be within the $OW_e$—$OW_u$ range at a quantity between $OT$ and $OR$.

## Union Preference Curves

However, it is difficult to apply the bilateral monopoly analog to unions, because the union does not have a cost outlay corresponding to the costs of a business firm. The union does not buy and sell labor; it merely fixes the terms of the sale. Moreover, the market supply curve of labor represents the preferences of individual workers and, even then, represents opportunity cost rather than cash outlay.

The bilateral monopoly model is therefore inadequate for bargaining purposes. Its main value is to indicate that the union focuses on the inverse functional relationship between employment and wages.

A number of efforts have been made to overcome the inadequacies of the bilateral monopoly model and introduce greater determinacy and relevance into the bargaining situation. Figure 12–2 uses the concept of a union wage-preference curve, instead of the traditional cost schedule. $WP$ shows the path a union would like to follow as demand shifts. $P$ represents the prevailing wage on the labor demand curve $D$. The kink at that point suggests that, with an increase in demand, the union would prefer higher wages to higher employment, but would prefer lower levels of employment to a wage cut if demand shifts downward.

The union's wage preference path, $WP$, is derived from the point of tan-

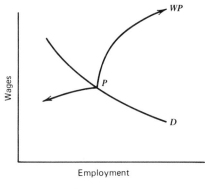

*Figure 12-2*

gency between $D$ and a series of preference or indifference curves, which are presumed to have the shape indicated in Figure 12–3. Although the union prefers to have a higher combination of wages and employment and therefore move to the highest possible preference curve, it is indifferent at a point on a preference curve.

The shape of these preference curves, suggests that in moving along $U_1$ from $P$, it takes a large increase in wages to compensate for a decline in employment and a large increase in employment to compensate for a decline in wages. If $D$ falls to $D_o$, the union's $WP$ equilibrium would therefore be at point $A$ on $U_o$, which is the highest preference curve tangent to $D_o$. However, if demand increases to $D_2$, the union would prefer $R$, which is the highest curve tangent to $D_2$.

But the union does not have complete control of the wage-employment relationship. One limiting factor is the market supply schedule, which shows the range of wages at which workers are willing to offer corresponding amounts of labor (Figure 12–4). Any wage-employment combination to the left of the S schedule is therefore attainable, but any combination to the right, such as indicated by point *0,* is not attainable.

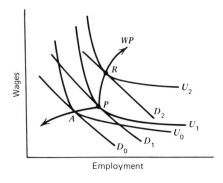

*Figure 12-3*

The union is also limited by the employer's preference curve, which might be as indicated in the following discussion taken from Allan M. Cartter and F. Ray Marshall, "Employers' Goals and Wage Determination." (*Labor Economics:* 1967, Chapter 12).

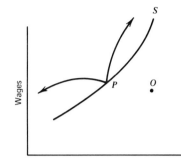

*Figure 12-4*

# The Employer's Bargaining Preferences

## by Allan M. Cartter and F. Ray Marshall

### THE DEMAND FOR LABOR
### AND THE LEVEL OF PROFIT

. . . [W]e need to look more closely at the profit implications of various wage-employment combinations and the relationship of profit levels to the demand schedule. Two axioms can be stated concerning profits and the demand schedule.

First, *at any given level of wages, the most profitable level of employment for the firm is indicated by the corresponding point on the demand schedule.* This can best be seen by looking at a typical diagram showing marginal and average revenue product. In Figure 1 these curves are illustrated, and a horizontal line is drawn at wage level $OW$. At employment level $OQ$, which corresponds to the statement in our axiom, the total return to labor is indicated by the rectangle $OWCQ$, and the return left for other factors of production (including profit) is shown by

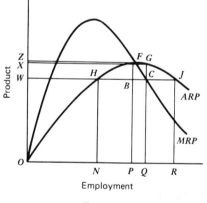

*Figure 1*

rectangle $WXGC$ (that is, by the difference between the wage paid and labor's average revenue product, times the number of workers employed). Any other level of employment at wage rate $OW$ will result in a smaller return for other factors of production, as can readily be seen. For

SOURCE Reprinted with permission from Cartter and Marshall, *Labor Economics: Wages, Employment and Trade Unionism* (Homewood, Ill., Richard D. Irwin, Inc.), pp. 298–303.

example, at employment *ON* or *OR*, there is zero left over for other factors, since points *H* and *J* fall right on the *ARP* curve. At employment level *OP*, there is a slightly larger amount *per worker* left for other factors but a smaller *total* amount (as indicated by rectangle *WZFB*). Thus, if we could think in three-dimensional terms, we could imagine the demand (*MRP*) schedule to be the crest of a hill range, the altitude (the level of profit) declining as one moves to the right or left of any point on the demand schedule. This is why, in the bilateral monopoly case, it was stated that the employer would maximize his return, after the wage had been settled, by adjusting employment to the related point on his demand schedule.

The second axiom is that *the further to the right* (southeastward) *on the demand schedule one moves, the more profitable* (or less unprofitable) *is that position.* In paraphrase, we can say that profits rise as one moves "down" the demand schedule. This is illustrated in Figure 2 by a two-

part diagram. The uppermost graph shows the *ARP* and *MRP* curves; the lower graph indicates the level of net return which would accrue from various wage and employment combinations falling along the labor demand (*MRP*) curve. In the lower diagram, the horizontal line at *O* indicates zero net profit, and *OF* indicates the amount of fixed costs or overhead incurred by the firm. As can be seen, in the early stages where the *MRP* curve is rising, the amount of net return becomes a larger negative figure, reaching its trough at a point corresponding to the peak of the *MRP* curve (*OK*). At *OL*, where the *MRP* and *ARP* curves intersect, the loss is exactly equal to the amount of fixed costs. Losses disappear at a higher level of employment equal to *OM*, and profits are only made if employment (and output) exceed *OM*. Employment level *OL* is equivalent to "the shut-down point" for the firm, in that smaller levels of employment are more costly than shutting the firm down completely and merely incurring the fixed costs. As a consequence, the only relevant part of the demand (*MRP*) curve for labor is the section to the right of employment *OL*, for a firm would not find it advisable to operate to the left of that point.

If we expand the analogy of the demand schedule representing the crest of an imaginary three-dimensional hill, we may also think of the altitude of the hill rising as we move down the demand schedule. . . . Summarizing, we can conclude (1) that a point on the demand schedule is more profitable than any point not on the demand schedule at the same wage level; and (2) that any point further down the demand schedule is more profitable than any preceding point on the schedule.

## EMPLOYER PREFERENCES AND CHANGING DEMAND CONDITIONS

Under completely static conditions, once an employer has maximized his rate

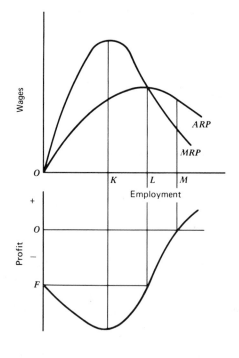

*Figure 2*

of return, there would be no reason for him to alter the level of output, employment, or the wage rate. However, in the real, dynamic world, conditions are always changing. Three types of change may be noted, two of which we shall deal with in this chapter. First, the demand for the final product may rise or fall; second, the efficiency of labor may change (normally it tends to rise over time); and third, the proportions of combining labor and other factors may change by virtue of the employer adding new capital equipment. The first two cases are identical in effect—that is, labor's MRP may rise or fall independently of the entrepreneur's actions—and may be analyzed as a single case.[1]

If the demand for labor rises, how may we expect the employer to react? What are his wage preferences? This can be illustrated in Figure 3 by the two sets of average and marginal revenue product curves. To take an unusual, but clear, case, assume that the existing wage-employment combination lies just at the inter-

section of MRP and ARP—a point at which the total proceeds would go to labor and nothing would be left to cover fixed costs. Now assume that the demand for the product increases, so that the money value of labor's product rises to MRP' and ARP'. If the employer were now to be no better and no worse off than previously, the wage would rise to OW' for approximately the same level of employment. If, on the other hand, the employer could maintain the same wage rate, OW, and expand employment to ON', he would be considerably better off. The total return would now be sufficient to pay the wage bill OWRN' and leave an amount equal to the area of the rectangle OW"SR to pay other factors (including profit).

From Figure 3 we can generalize and say that when the demand for labor increases, maintaining employment and raising wages rate to the new demand curve will give all of the added proceeds to labor, leaving the employer's position unchanged.[2] Alternatively, the maximum advantage which the employer can gain without actually reducing the previously existing wage, is by moving to the right ("due east") to a larger level of employment at the same wage. Thus we can say that the employer's preference is to reach the new demand curve by moving horizontally to the right when demand is rising.

If demand is falling, rather than rising, the picture is reversed. To maintain his profit level, the employer would prefer to maintain the level of employment and reduce wages proportionately. The alternative of maintaining wages and reducing

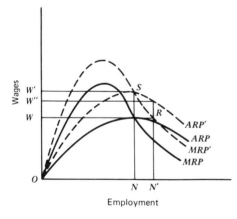

*Figure 3*

[1] A rise or fall in the demand for the final product could also result from a change in sales effort by the firm, a case which falls halfway between cases one and three above. If an increase in advertising expenditures brings about a disproportionate rise in demand, it comes closest to case number one above. Similarly, on-the-job training programs may affect labor's efficiency. Implied here in the second case is the steady improvement in labor efficiency resulting from the social investment in human capital through improved education. The third case we shall leave to a later discussion.

[2] This is true if the elasticity of demand has not changed. If there should be some change in the elasticity of demand, the point on the new demand schedule at which the employer is no better and no worse off may not be precisely above the initial wage-employment combination, but it will be quite close to that point.

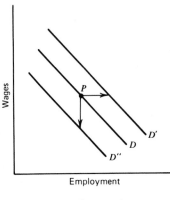

*Figure 4*

employment will mean a substantial reduction in profits. Thus, if we were to illustrate an employer's preference path for wages under conditions of increasing or decreasing demand, it would be as pictured in Figure 4, beginning from some initial point *P*.

## THE RANGE OF WAGE SETTLEMENTS UNDER OPTIMUM CONDITIONS

The maximizing behavior of unions and employers have each been looked at separately; combining them will delimit the boundaries within which an agreement will ideally fall. In overlaying the two wage preference paths, one further assumption will be made in this section,

namely, that each party has accurate knowledge of the level of demand and does not "overshoot" its real preferences by bargaining tactics (a case to be discussed in the next section). Figure 5 illustrates the union and employer wage preference curves, and a hypothetical higher and lower demand schedule than the one existing at the initial point of our analysis.

Looking first at the case of increased demand, the union would prefer to move from *P* to *A*, and the employer would prefer to move from *P* to *B*. We may anticipate, therefore, that the wage settlement will finally fall on the demand schedule *D'* somewhere between *A* and *B*. Similarly, for a decrease of demand, the union would prefer *C* and the employer *E*, and the final settlement is likely to fall between these two points. The shaded areas represent the range of likely settlement.

An economic restraint on the employer's action may be present, however, if the regular market supply curve of labor passes near the original wage-employment combination at *P*. Although the market supply curve was omitted in the previous diagram, Figure 6 illustrates a more likely situation. Here the situation is similar to that in Figure 5, except that the supply curve limits the employer's range of freedom in that the wage-employment combinations at *B* and *E* are unobtainable. The best the employer can hope for, if the

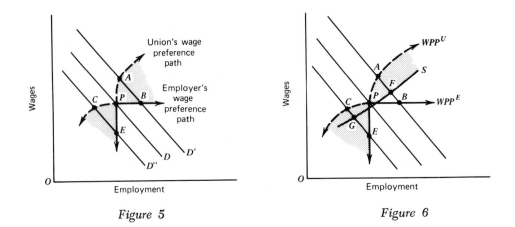

*Figure 5*                    *Figure 6*

demand for labor increases to $D'$, is to settle at point $F$ where the supply and $MRP$ curves intersect; the best he can hope for demand falling to $D''$ is to move to point $G$. Market supply conditions, therefore, tend to narrow the range of conflict between the union and employer, the bargaining range being $AF$ if the demand rises to $D'$ and $CG$ if the demand falls to $D''$.

In summarizing this picture of the likely range of wage settlements, a few general conclusions can be enumerated. First, in the usual bargaining situation, the interests of both union and employer are the same along the upper and lower reaches of the demand schedule. That is to say, neither party wishes to be above point $A$ in Figure 5, and in practice, neither wishes to be below point $B$. (The employer, we recall, would always prefer to be further down the demand curve, but in practice, holding the wage constant is about the best he can hope for when demand is rising—thus $B$ is a practical minimum goal for the employer.) The conflict of in terest lies within fairly narrowly proscribed limits between these points. Second, when demand is increasing, the range of conflict is smaller, the more elastic is the union's wage preference path and/or the more inelastic is the market supply curve of labour.[3] It is possible, although somewhat unlikely, that in times of tight labor supply the range of conflict may disappear entirely, for market supply conditions may dictate an increase in wages approximately equal to what the union would prefer. This situation was generally true in many industries in the 1945–49 period, when wage increases were quite readily granted in unionized areas but when wages rose as fast or faster in unorganized industries. The third conclusion is the reverse of our second, i.e., that the range of conflict when demand is decreasing is smaller, the less elastic is the union's wage preference path and the more elastic is the market supply curve of labor. Thus market pressures are present and show themselves in the position of these curves.

\* \* \*

The employer's preference path is derived from the combination of wages and employment that maximizes his profits. This means that with rising demand, employers prefer to hold wages constant and increase employment, but with declining demand, they prefer to hold employment constant and cut wages as indicated in Figure 4 from Cartter and Marshall.

The use of preference curves and wage preference paths as indicated in Figure 5 and 6 from Cartter and Marshall, is an improvement over the bilateral monopoly model, but it still leaves the wage bargain interminate, somewhere in the range of $A$ and $F$ in Figure. 6.

### Bargaining Models

Bargaining models attempt to make the bilateral monopoly analysis more determinate and realistic, at least theoretically, than the traditional cost, revenue, and indifference approaches presented above. The key concept in most of these bargaining models is that of bargaining power, which may be defined as one's ability to induce an opponent to agree on one's own terms. (See Neil Chamberlain, *A General Theory of Economic Process*, New York, Harper and

---

[3] The *position* of the supply curve is, of course, also important. In the text we assume that the supply curve is in the near vicinity of the wage preference path, so that its elasticity is of prime importance.

Bros., 1955.) Since this concept is defined in terms of one's ability to get an opponent to change, power obviously is related to an opponent's will to resist. Therefore, bargaining power varies with the difference between the parties' objectives. My power over my bargaining opponent is therefore greater if I have an objective that is very close to his. On the other hand, I weaken my position considerably if I assume an objective that is so far from his as to be almost unrealizable.

For unions and employers, the important ingredients of a bargaining theory are (1) bargaining attitude, (2) cost of disagreeing, and (3) cost of agreeing. The cost of disagreeing in the union-management case would be the cost of a strike to both parties. The cost of agreeing is the difference between the parties' basic objectives and the cost of settling at the price under consideration. Obviously, therefore, the greater the distance between a party's wage objective and the wage under consideration, the greater the cost of agreeing on the opponent's terms. We may therefore define a party's bargaining attitude as the ratio between the cost of disagreeing with one's adversary and the cost of agreeing on the adversary's terms. (i.e., Bargaining Attitude = Cost of Disagreeing/Cost of Agreeing). Therefore, whenever the ratio of the cost of disagreeing to the cost of agreeing is less than one, the party will resist settlement because the cost of agreeing would be greater than the cost of disagreeing. Conversely, whenever the result is equal to or greater than one, the union or employer would be willing to accept its adversary's offer, because the cost of a strike is higher than the cost of agreeing on the terms offered.

From this simplified model, it can be seen that negotiations amount to trying to change the other party's bargaining attitude to unity in order to induce him to agree on the terms offered. This can be done either by changing the cost of disagreeing or the cost of agreeing. A union, for example, can attempt to raise the cost of disagreeing as seen by the employer by convincing management that the cost of a strike is greater than it thinks it is. It can do this by demonstrating the solidarity of the workers and their resolve to strike. Similarly, the employer will try to convince the union that the cost of disagreeing as seen by the union is much greater than the union thinks it is. It can do this by indicating that management is willing to hold out during a strike for much longer than the union expects.

Since a party strengthens its bargaining position by moving its objective closer to that of its opponent, compromise is an effective bargaining tactic if it is properly interpreted by one's opponent. For example, the union would strengthen its position by making a wage concession which increases the employer's bargaining attitude, and the employer can strengthen his position by offering a higher wage which comes closer to the union's objective, thereby raising the union's bargaining attitude closer to one. However, there is an obvious danger in this strategy if a compromise is interpreted by one's adversary as a sign of weakness, thereby reducing the ratio of the cost of disagreeing to the cost of agreeing. In any bargaining situation, the ability to bluff and not-bluff is therefore a very important ingredient for the successful outcome of the bargain. A strike not desired by either party could come when one's adversary interprets a bluff as a not-bluff or a not-bluff as a bluff. As will be indicated in Chapter 14, a mediator sometimes can prevent such strikes by helping the parties clarify the real situation.

Bargaining models have several advantages over the traditional bilateral monopoly presentation of economic analysis. These advantages are: explanations of the importance of the power of one party to inflict a penalty on another; the significance of the art of compromise as a policy weapon in bargaining; the importance of time; and the theoretical determinacy possible from the bargaining model.

We say theoretical determinacy because many of the bargaining models depend on variables that cannot be measured and therefore are not determinant in the sense of being operational. The models nevertheless serve a very useful purpose of elucidating the nature of the bargaining process.

In "The Nature of the Bargaining Process," G.L.S. Shackle discusses the questions a bargaining theory should answer and then indicates how economists have attempted to answer those questions. He first raises the question of the determinacy of bargaining models, pointing out that the indeterminacy of the neoclassical bilateral monopoly model and discusses efforts by Hicks, Zeuthen, Pen, and himself to make bargaining determinate. He is particularly impressed by Pen's theory which he terms "one of the most brilliant and most beautiful pieces of theoretical analysis that has been produced in many years past. . . . As a result of his masterly forward stride we now have a theory of bilateral monopoly which can stand comparison with those of perfect or of monopolistic competition." Nevertheless, Shackle is skeptical of Pen's conclusion "that provided the price at which the buyer's net contract ophelimity vanishes is greater than that which annihilates the seller's net contract ophelimity, agreement at some price within the contract zone thus delimited is sure to be attained." Shackle feels that a bargainer might break off negotiations even if the price bargained is within the contract zone if he is afraid of losing face because of having retreated "a long way from his initial claim."

With respect to the question of determinacy, Shackle concludes:

> If our data are restricted to the bargainer's interests in the one particular instance of bargaining, considered in isolation, the price in bilateral monopoly is indeterminate. If we have full knowledge of the parties' expectations and the working rules or functions by which they revise their expectations in the light of fresh data, and of their gambler preferences, the outcome of a bargaining process is in principle determinate. In practice determinacy surely cannot mean that the outcome, except in special cases, could be predicted by a third party, however well informed, in advance of the bargaining. . . .

# The Nature of the Bargaining Process

## by G. L. S. Shackle

SOURCE Reprinted with permission from John T. Dunlop, ed., *Theory of Wage Determination*, New York, Macmillan, 1957.

### QUESTIONS TO BE ANSWERED BY A THEORY OF BARGAINING

In constructing a theory or surveying the theories of others, a set of questions is needed to define the objective of such theories and provide a test of their adequacy. The following list of questions seems to express the purpose of a theory of bargaining:

1. (a) Is the outcome of a bargaining process in any sense determinate, and if so, in what sense?
(b) Is it sometimes determinate and sometimes not, and if so, in what circumstances is it determinate, what are the necessary and sufficient conditions of determinacy?
(c) Is the determinate solution ascertainable in principle otherwise than by the actual carrying through of the bargaining process, for example, by confidential questioning of both parties by a trusted third party?
(d) Are the conditions of determinacy likely to be realized in practice? Or is there something in the nature of bargaining which implies that functions expressing the preferences and intentions of bargainers cannot be treated as stable and invariant throughout the bargaining process and under bargaining pressures? Can the changes of such functions be predicted in advance of the bargaining so as to attain determinacy?

2. In what circumstances will a bargaining process be terminated without agreement? Are the consequences of such a breakdown likely to involve social costs or public injury beyond the private injury or costs entailed to the bargaining parties? If so, what are the remedies?

3. (a) By what means can each party seek to give the ultimately agreed solution

the character he desires? Do these means consist in changing the other party's tastes or his beliefs?

(b) If bargaining involves attempts to change the other party's beliefs, does it for that reason involve deception? If so, is bargaining condemned as a civilized and desirable method of reaching agreed decisions?

(c) What sorts of things does each bargaining party try to conceal from the other, or what are the matters about which each party tries to influence the other's beliefs?

(d) What means does each party use in trying to alter or weaken, or to anchor more firmly, particular beliefs held by the other party?

(e) Is it useful to each bargaining party to render the other party's mental picture "more uncertain"? If Brown cannot confirm Smith in a particular belief which it would be in Brown's interest for Smith to hold, can Brown effect somewhat the same purpose by shaking Smith's faith in all sharply defined relevant beliefs? (In other words, by widening the range of relevant hypotheses to which he attaches low potential surprise.)

4. In the case of "many-track" bargaining (bargaining concerning many variables simultaneously) is it sometimes to the advantage of one bargainer to pretend to attach chief importance to one variable while really attaching more importance to another?

5. In cases where the public is much affected by the outcome of the bargaining or suffers severely from its protraction, can it be made more likely that agreement will be reached or quickly reached either by confining the bargaining to one or few tracks, or by increasing the number of tracks?

6. Where many variables are involved in an essentially unified context of bargaining, can the bargaining be usefully broken down into a series of separate processes each dealing with one variable?

7. In many-track bargaining what aspect or factor is named by the word "procedure," and what part does this play?

8. Is there in bargaining any asymmetry, such that an advantage is enjoyed by the party to whom law, custom, or some inherent feature of the situation assigns the first move? Or is such an advantage enjoyed by the "seller" or by the "buyer"?

The weakness of a list of verbal questions for defining the task of a theory consists in its giving a series of discreet prods in one direction or another instead of a continuous push along the path of a resultant force. The questions unavoidably overlap each other and are partial substitutes; the list can hardly in the nature of things be self-contained in any fundamental sense, for any question or any answer to it may suggest other questions, and there is no guarantee that these will eventually lead back into the nexus and provide us with a closed system where, given a few initial unproven propositions which seem realistic, all that we want to know can be deduced? Another person would produce a different set of questions and even these might be extended and modified. We will now see briefly how economists have tried to answer these questions.

### THE BARGAINING OUTCOME: INDETERMINATE OR DETERMINATE?

"Contract without competition is indeterminate."[1] Thus in 1881 Edgeworth absolved economists from trying to explain how in bilateral monopoly a price is ever fixed. The set of data which for Edgeworth, and for all those after him who discussed the problem in the following fifty years, left the price indeterminate consisted in the interests of the two bar-

---

[1] F. Y. Edgeworth, *Mathematical Psychics,* original edition (1881), p. 20.

gainers, those interests which were directly, intimately, and unmistakably involved in some particular occasion of bargaining. A knowledge of these interests, however exact, would not enable a third party to deduce the price which would be finally agreed on, but would only enable him to name limits between which it must lie, one of these limits being a price which would leave Brown indifferent whether an agreement at that price were made or no agreement made, and the other being a price which would similarly affect Smith. In his brilliant article, "A General Theory of Bargaining,"[2] J. Pen gives the names of Böhm-Bawerk, Sir Arthur Bowley, A. M. Henderson, Marshall, Nichol, Pigou, Stackelberg Stigler and Tintner as having agreed that economic theory appeared to have nothing further to say. The interests of any economic agent depend, of course, upon his tastes and the precise inventory of his resources, and it is these which, from about 1870 onwards, economists have looked upon as the dominant influences on price. The prices of all goods could be deduced if we knew with sufficient detail, for each person in the market, the answers to the questions "What does he like?" and "What does he possess?" It did not occur to most of those who built the beautiful neoclassical structure of static value theory to put upon the same footing as those two questions a third kind of question: "What does he know?" or "What does he believe?" At first sight it is an astonishing paradox of the theory of bilateral monopoly that determinacy should be attainable only by assuming uncertainty in the minds of the bargainers and paying attention to its consequences.

The neoclassics had some intimations of this. Edgeworth quotes[3] from Jevons's *Theory of Political Economy:*

*Such a transaction [viz. in bilateral mo-*

*nopoly] must be settled upon other than strictly economical grounds. . . . The art of bargaining consists in the buyer ascertaining the lowest price at which the seller is willing to part with his object, without disclosing, if possible, the highest price which he, the buyer, is willing to give.*

If Brown hopes to conceal something from Smith, he must be conscious of the possibility that Smith is perhaps concealing something from him, and if Brown has indeed this thought in mind, he is in a state of uncertainty. Would it not have been worth while for the neoclassics to follow up this clue? In their view it would have meant arguing on "other than strictly economical grounds." This choice of location of the boundary of economics was evidently approved by Edgeworth, and in our own day Mr. Sraffa has expressed the view that the arts of bargaining and diplomacy are not subject-matter for economics. Plainly this is a matter of taste or of expediency. Yet how can it be expedient to draw the line where it cuts us off from determinate solutions of our problems?

## HICKS'S THEORY OF
BARGAINING DETERMINACY

Half a century went by before economists attempted any radical improvement on Edgeworth. Professor Zeuthen's *Problems of Monopoly and Economic Welfare* appeared in 1930 and Hicks's *The Theory of Wages* in 1932. Hicks argued thus:[4]

*We can construct a schedule of wages and lengths of strike, setting opposite to each period of stoppage the highest wage an employer will be willing to pay rather than endure a stoppage of that period. At this wage, the expected cost of the stoppage and the expected cost of concession*

[2] *American Economic Review* (March 1952), p. 24.
[3] F. Y. Edgeworth, *Mathematical Psychics,* p. 30.
[4] J. R. Hicks, *The Theory of Wages* (1932), pp. 141–144.

*(accumulated at the current rate of interest) just balance. At any lower wage, the employer would prefer to give in; at any higher wage, he would prefer that a stoppage should take place. This we may call the "employer's concession schedule." . . . Now just as the expected period of stoppage will govern the wage an employer is prepared to pay to avoid a strike, so the wage offered will govern the length of time the men are prepared to stand out. . . . So in their case, too, we can draw up a schedule, a "resistance schedule," giving the length of time they would be willing to stand out rather than allow their remuneration to fall below the corresponding wage.*

Hicks graphs these two schedules as in Fig. 1 and proceeds: "The employer's concession curve and the Union's resistance curve will cut at a point P, and the wage OA corresponding to this point is the highest wage which skillful negotiation can extract from the employer."

It is a question whether Professor Hicks

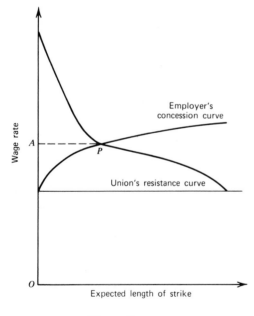

*Figure 1*

[5] J. Pen, "A General Theory of Bargaining," p. 25.

would wish us to interpret this, as Pen does, as a claim that the outcome of the wage bargaining will be determinate at the rate OA. Pen says:[5]

*[I] fail to see why the intersection determines anything. Hicks's reasoning is all about the limits of the contract zone, and explains nothing of what happens between these limits. At the intersection of the curves the contract zone is a single point, so there is no problem at all; but this situation will only be realised by the merest chance. There are no forces compelling the bargainers to the Hicksian point.*

We feel that this criticism is just. But the whole meaning of Professor Hicks's construction is very elusive. Part of the difficulty can perhaps be indirectly expressed by proposing a different construction. In Hicks's diagram the employer's concession curve has a positive slope because the wage rate the employer would agree to rather than suffer a strike of any given length is naturally an increasing function of that length, and the gradient decreases because there is some wage rate byond which it would not pay the employer to continue in business at all. Can we not similarly argue that the longer the strike the trade union members are asked to contemplate, the higher must be the wage rate they hope to gain by it? In that case what we can call the union's inducement curve will also have a positive slope. But this slope will surely increase in steepness from left to right, because the marginal disutility of the length of a strike will be increasing while the marginal utility of the wage will be decreasing. Thus we might arrive at a diagram like Fig. 2. Now if the union knew that the employer would refuse a wage rate greater than $y(x)$ even if he were certain that the result of refusal would be a strike of length $x$ (if, that is to say, it knew the shape of the employer's

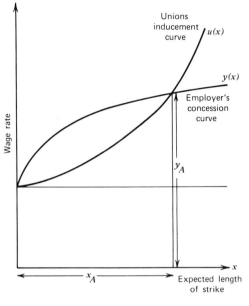

*Figure 2*

concession curve) it would refrain from demanding any wage rate lying on that segment of its inducement curve $u = u(x)$ where $u(x) > y(x)$. Likewise, if the employer knew that the union would face a strike of length $x$ for the sake of a wage rate of $u$, he would concede any $u$ which was less than the corresponding $y$. Thus for any $u(x) < y(x)$ the employer would give way, for any $u(x) > y(x)$ he would refuse. If, then, the forms of the $u$ and $y$ functions were known to both parties and each party knew that the other knew them, agreement would presumably be reached at $y = u$, where $x = x_A$.

But an indispensable and indefensible assumption which underlies this result is, of course, the complete knowledge possessed by both parties. The main object of the employer would plainly be to conceal from the union the fact that the convincing threat of a strike of length $x_A$ could exact from him an agreement to a wage rate $y_A$. On the contrary, he would try to make the union believe that the sure threat of a strike of any given length $x$ would only induce him to concede a wage $y(x)$ less than the union's minimum inducement

$u(x)$ for a strike of that length. For if he could succeed in that purpose he would suffer neither strike nor wage increase, and if he did not know this because he was ignorant or uncertain of the form of $u = u(x)$, nevertheless he might well conjecture something of the sort. The union, for its part, would seek to conceal from the employer the form of $u = u(x)$ and try to make him believe that, for example, a strike of length $x_B > x_A$ could be faced even in order to secure a wage $y_A$. For this might persuade him to concede a somewhat larger wage lying on his concession curve to the right of $x_A$. We must conclude, I think, that in Hicks's theory or in the alternative construction which I have just put forward, suggested by his and obtained from it by substituting my "inducement curve" for his "resistance cure," determinacy of the price is only secured at the sacrifice of the essence of bargaining, namely the interplay of threat, bluff, and deception, the endeavour to trade upon the adversary's uncertainty.

It may now well be asked whether we are justified in criticizing Professor Hicks on the basis of a greatly modified version of his theory. The truth is that it is difficult to proceed upon the basis of his own formulation, for there seems to be something very odd about his "union's resistance curve." It is hard to avoid the suspicion that Professor Hicks started out, in his quest for bargaining determinacy, with the idea at the back of his mind that he needed a Marshallian scissors diagram and that since the employer's concession curve must evidently have a positive slope it would be desirable for the other curve to have a negative slope. Having gone thus far it would be natural to seek a meaning for the other curve which would make it slope downwards to the right, as required for a guaranteed "scissors" intersection. But why is a high wage claim associated with a long strike in the employer's mind and with a short strike in the union's mind? The words "concession" and "resistance" convey a suggestion of some fundamental asymmetry, but they are a red herring. The employer and the union are engaged in a tug-of-war, each is resisting the other, either may be forced to "concede." The sham dynamic aura thrown out by these words must not be allowed to distract us.

Let us simply ask whether the union will be willing to contemplate a long strike in view or hope of a big wage concession or a small one, and the answer seems plain, a big concession. What, then, has gone wrong? Briefly we suggest that with Professor Hicks's "union's resistance curve" (but not with his employer's concession curve) length of strike should be represented, not by the abscissae but by the integrals of that curve in the vertical direction, starting from the horizontal line whose level (at $y_0$ in Fig. 3) stands for the existing wage. Treating this line in Fig. 3 as the horizontal axis, let us cut up the area enclosed by the curve and the two axes into narrow horizontal strips of uniform vertical width. Of these strips, the lowest, whose lower edge is the line at $y_0$, represents by its area the degree of resistance which the union would put up against a proposal to limit the wage increase to the small amount represented by the (vertical) width of this strip. The next strip, somewhat shorter and thus of smaller area, represents the extra effort the union would exert to have the concession pushed up to the amount represented by the combined (vertical) width

of the two lowest strips; and so on. Professor Hicks's "union's resistance curve" is a marginal resistance curve, and its point of intersection with the employer's concession curve has no relevant meaning. Taking $y$, the vertical variable measured from $y_0$, as the independent variable and renaming the horizontal variable as $s$ let us write Hicks's 'union's resistance curve' as $s = s(y)$ and put $z = s\ (y)dy$ for its integral. Then $z$ will be another name for the "length of strike" variable $x$ and the function, say $y = f(z)$, connecting $y$ and $z$ will be the same, except for the constant $y = y_0$, as the union's inducement curve $u = u(x)$. If we assume the inverse of $s = s(y)$, say $y = F(s)$, to have the sort of shape given by Professor Hicks in his diagram (our Fig. 1) to his union's resistance curve, then its integral curve $u = u(x)$ will have a slope very steep near $x = 0$ but rapidly decreasing and then becoming fairly uniform. Such a curve is shown in Fig. 4. This shape for the union's inducement curve differs from what we would suggest, and with this sort of slope the curve might or might not have a point of intersection, other than $x = 0$, $y = y_0$, with the employer's concession curve. But if Professor Hicks had interpreted his union's resistance curve as a "marginal" curve he might not have given it the shape he has. With the sort of shape given to the union's inducement curve $u = u(x)$ in Fig. 2 a satisfactory intersection with the employer's concession curve $y = y(x)$ is almost guaranteed.

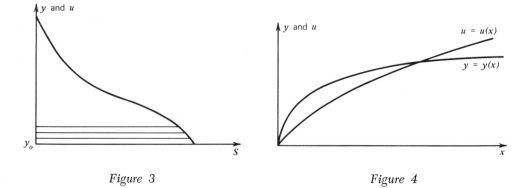

Figure 3                    Figure 4

## ZEUTHEN'S THEORY OF BARGAINING DETERMINACY

Professor Hicks's theory, or our alternative version of it, stands in a sort of no-man's-land marking the boundary, both logical and chronological, between the territory of orthodox theories which declare the price in bilateral monopoly to be indeterminate, and that of theories which make the price determinate by invoking the consequences of uncertainty. The Hicks type of theory can maintain determinacy only by assuming away any elbow-room for bargaining. It stands in the sharpest contrast with "uncertainty" theories, for it assumes that the two bargainers know each other's thoughts and preferences precisely. We pass now to the uncertainty theories, and when we cross the frontier on to this ground the first name is that of Professor Zeuthen.[6]

In the article cited above, Pen summarizes as follows the argument put forward by Professor Zeuthen in 1930.[7]

*At each step in the bargaining process the bargainer must compare the possible advantages and disadvantages. The advantages consist in the attainment of a more favourable price. The disadvantages consist in the possibilities of a conflict. The decisive factors in a bargainer's choice are not only the magnitude of these advantages and disadvantages, but also the bargainer's estimation of their possibility. The latter expectation, designated as the risk of a conflict, is the central factor in Zeuthen's theory.*

Professor Zeuthen[8] considers a trade union whose only object is to make the total wage bill of its members as large as possible and which assumes that the elasticity of demand for labour is zero. At each stage of the negotiation the trade union leaders ask themselves whether it is better to agree on a wage $p$ or to press for a somewhat higher wage $p_n$ at a risk $r$ of precipitating a conflict, that is, a breakdown of the negotiation wherein the $N$ employed members of the union would have a total income of only $S_c$ instead of the income of $pN$ which could be secured by agreeing to a wage $p$. Then by insisting on $p_n$ the trade union stands to gain $N(p_n - p)$, while it stands to lose $pN - S_c$. The trade union will insist on the higher wage $p_n$ so long as

$$(1 - r)(Np_n - Np) > r(Np - S_c).$$

The greatest value of $r$ at which the trade union would still consider it just worth while to press forward is that value, written by Zeuthen $r_{max}$, which would make the two sides of the formula equal, and we have

$$r_{max} = \frac{Np_n - Np}{Np_n - S_c}$$

Zeuthen considers that for the trade union $r_{max}$ will be a decreasing function of $p$, while for the employer, for whom an ex-

---

[6] My first acquaintance with the work of Professor F. Zeuthen on the subject of bargaining and bilateral monopoly was obtained through reading the article here cited by J. Pen, and until I had completed my paper as it stands I had never read any of Professor Zeuthen's own words on this subject, and, in particular, I had never seen his book on *Problems of Monopoly and Economic Warfare*, published in 1930 and now out of print. Professor Zeuthen himself was not able to supply me with a copy of his book (and this disturbed me the more because I have heard it spoken of in terms of the highest praise) but he has now very kindly lent me the manuscript of chapter 57 of his *Economic Theory and Method* (1955), and from this it is even more evident than from Mr. Pen's article that Professor Zeuthen has the distinction of having emphasized as early as 1930 that uncertainty is an essential element of bargaining and that, when we recognize this and analyse its consequences as part of the problem, the bargaining outcome becomes determinate. When writing my chapter on this subject in 1948 (*Expectation in Economics*, 1949), I knew nothing of Professor Zeuthen's long priority in pointing these things out, and hence my omission there of any reference to his work.

[7] F. Zeuthen, *Problems of Monopoly and Economic Warfare* (1930), chapter on "Economic Warfare."

[8] In what follows I have slightly reformulated Professor Zeuthen's argument with an altered notation.

actly parallel formula can be written, it will be an increasing function. There will therefore be some $p$ at which $r_{max}$ is the same value of $r$ for both parties, and Zeuthen believes that at this level of $p$ agreement will be reached. Pen sums the conclusion up as follows: "The outcome of the bargaining is, according to Zeuthen, determined by the equality of the mutual risk of a conflict that the parties dare to accept, and the maximum risk of a conflict that a bargainer will accept equals the quotient of his possible gain and his possible loss." Pen points out, however, that there appears to be no reason why "a bargainer should submit at the moment his adversary accepts the same maximum risk as he does," and accordingly declares that Professor Zeuthen's solution is unacceptable as it stands. However, Pen believes that a real solution is to be found along the path on which Professor Zeuthen has taken the first steps, and he accordingly builds a theory of his own on the basis thus suggested.

## PEN'S THEORY OF BARGAINING DETERMINACY

Pen assumes that any specified price $p$ which might be agreed on between a buyer and a seller would give to the seller a certain ophelimity $S(p)$ and to the buyer a certain ophelimity $B(p)$, and that for each party all the factors or influences which affect the degree of his own satisfaction that he associates with each price are subsumed in the shape of his ophelimity function. In particular, the seller Smith will estimate what quantity the buyer Brown will buy at each price $p$ and Smith will consequently have in mind some particular level of $p$ up to which Smith's profit is an increasing function of $p$ and beyond which, because of Brown's decreasing demand, Smith's profit will be a decreasing function of $p$. Similarly Brown will estimate the quantities that Smith will supply at each $p$ and will have in mind some

$p$ below which these will decrease so rapidly with decrease of $p$ as to outweigh the advantage to Brown of cheapness. Thus Pen argues that the seller's ophelimity function $S(p)$, though no doubt affected by other considerations besides profit, will have a unique maximum at some price $p_s$ and that the buyer's ophelimity function $B(p)$ will have a unique maximum at some other price $p_b$.

Besides the degree of ophelimity $S(p_s)$ which is the greatest the bargaining process can afford him even if he is wholly successful in it, the seller will have in mind another degree of ophelimity specially important to him, namely that degree, positive, zero, or negative, which he would experience in case of "conflict," that is, a breakdown or abandonment of the negotiation without agreement. This degree Mr. Pen calls the seller's "conflict ophelimity" $S_c$. The buyer will similarly have his own conflict ophelimity $B_c$. Now Pen supposes (so we interpret him although he does not says so explicitly) that at any moment of the negotiation some particular price $p$ is, as it were, the immediate, temporary basis or focus of discussion. At any such moment, then, the seller has the choice between agreeing to this price $p$ and thus securing an ophelimity $S(p)$ instead of the inferior ophelimity $S_c$, thus avoiding a loss of ophelimity $S(p) - S_c$ which he would suffer in case of a conflict, or of holding out for the price $p_s$ which will give him his greatest possible ophelimity $S(p_s)$. If he takes this second course he risks a conflict for the sake of a possible improvement $S(p_s) - S(p)$ as compared with the ophelimity he could make certain of by immediate agreement on the price $p$. Further, the seller will have in mind some number $r$ such that $0 \leqslant r \leqslant 1$, which will express his estimate of the risk or probability of a conflict in case he rejects any particular price $p$. If the seller has "neutral risk valuation" he will then decide to reject any $p$ such that $(1 - r)\,[S(p_s) - S(p)] > r[S(p) - S_c].$

As $p$ increases from a level below $p_s$, $S(p)$ will increase and $r$ will increase, so that eventually $p$ will reach a level where

$$(1 - r)[S(p_s) - S(p)] = r[S(p) - S_c],$$

so that

$$\frac{1 - r}{r} = \frac{S(p) - S_c}{S(p_s) - S(p)}$$

or

$$\frac{1}{r} = \frac{S(p) - S_c + S(p_s) - S(p)}{S(p_s) - S(p)}$$

$$= \frac{S(p_s) - S_c}{S(p_s) - S(p)}$$

and

$$r = \frac{S(p_s) - S(p)}{S(p_s) - S_c}.$$

If $p$ reaches this level, the seller will be willing to agree upon it rather than seek to push it higher still. This conclusion is of course only a stage in the complete theory of how the price will be determined, for we have still to consider the buyer. But first Pen seeks to indicate how the seller assigns some particular numerical value to $r$, and here his argument is a little less clear and illuminating than elsewhere. He writes $r$, to which of course the seller can only give a numerical value by his own process of thought and estimation on the basis of such knowledge as he can gather, as a function (called, following Schumpeter, the correspection function) $r_s = F_s[B(p) - B_c]$ of the buyer's net contract ophelimity $B(p) - B_c$, that is, the amount by which the buyer's ophelimity in case the price $p$ is agreed on would exceed the ophelimity he would have if the negotiation were abandoned.

Now from one point of view this seems to me to make a true suggestion: for the meaning which Pen has given to the ophelimity functions implies that the buyer will not in fact permit, if he can help it, a conflict (abandonment of negotiation) to occur at any price less than that which

makes $B(p) - B_c = 0$, and so it is this price, the limit of the contract zone, which the seller really wants to know. If the seller does feel that he knows for certain the exact limits of the contract zone, he will put $r = 0$ for any price within this zone. But from another point of view it seems misleading to write the seller's estimate of $r$ as a function of a price which it is the buyer's chief concern to conceal from him. Pen should have introduced a new symbol to stand for the seller's conjecture of the price which makes $B(p) - B_c = 0$. Introducing the seller's risk valuation coefficient, say $Y_s$, Pen finally writes, as the condition for the seller to agree to a price $p$, the equation

$$Y_s \frac{S(p_s) - S(p)}{S(p_s) - S_c} - F_s[B(p) - B_c] = 0.$$

For agreement to be actually reached, an exactly parallel equation for the buyer,

$$Y_b \frac{B(p_b) - B(p)}{B(p_b) - B_c} - F_b[S(p) - S_c] = 0$$

must simultaneously be satisfied. The bargaining process consists in the efforts made by either party to shift one or several of the four elements, namely, the risk valuation function, the ophelimity function, the conflict ophelimity, and the correspection function, which make up the other party's position, and Mr. Pen's argument implies that, provided the price which reduces to zero the buyer's net contract ophelimity $B(p) - B_c$ is greater than that which reduces to zero the seller's net contract ophelimity $S(p) - S_c$, those efforts will continue until agreement is reached at some price within the contract zone thus defined. This price will be determinate in the sense that it will have to satisfy a pair of equations of the kind described above.

This is evidently a different sort of determinacy from that which economists from Edgeworth onwards who have discussed the problem of bilateral monopoly have had in mind when they asserted that the price would in such circumstances be indeterminate. For the essence of Mr. Pen's theory is that the whole nature of the bargaining process consists in an endeavour of each party to change the form of the functions, or the critical values of variables, which compose the other party's position. Can we meaningfully say that a variable is determinate whose value depends on functions which, as part of the very essence of the matter, are changed as the process of determination goes on?

Pen's theory is one of the most brilliant and most beautiful pieces of theoretical analysis that has been produced in many years past. He makes generous acknowledgments, in particular to Professor Zeuthen; but those who have influenced his construction in any special and important way are very few indeed. As a result of his masterly forward stride we now have a theory of bilateral monopoly which can stand comparison with those of perfect or of monopolistic competition.

A CRITICISM OF PEN'S THEORY

There is only one respect in which we do not feel that Pen's theory is satisfactory beyond all reasonable cavil. He concludes that provided the price at which the buyer's net contract ophelimity vanishes is greater than that which annihilates the seller's net contract ophelimity, agreement at some price within the contract zone thus delimited is sure to be attained. In this matter his results, and those of the writer's own attempt at a theory of the bargaining process,[9] are in collision. I expressed the motive which might lead a bargainer to break off a negotiation even within the contract zone as fear of 'loss of face' through retreating a long way from his initial claim, and the consequent injury to his bargaining power in future. In Pen's theory such a consideration is sup-

posed to influence the shape of the ophelimity functions and be taken account of thus, leaving a "pure" contract zone free, by definition, from the possibility of breakdown. Pen says:[10] "Apart from the sober profit figures there may, even in the case of bargaining business men, be psychological factors behind the ophelimity functions. . . . Sometimes [such a factor] becomes apparent . . . when the bargainer is forced away from a price he has heavily insisted upon, and he fears to 'lose face'. In this case the ophelimity function may show a sharp peak at the price that was claimed before." Here I think there are three points to be made. The first is the minor one that considerations of profit, that is, profit in future negotiations, is surely a large part of the reason for caring about "loss of face." But the main question concerns the meaning of the ophelimity functions. Pen would argue that the shapes of these, and in particular the location of their respective maxima, will be such that there is no room for such a large total concession, by one party or the other, as to cause him "loss of face." Now we have to remember that it is an essential feature of Pen's theory that the shapes of ophelimity functions are altered in the course of the bargaining process, and the question arises whether it is at the beginning, when the bargainers make their intitial claims or take up their initial attitudes, that the contract zone is supposed to be already narrow enough to guard against loss of face to either party, or is it after the shapes have undergone some modification in the course of bargaining? If the former, we must ask how each bargainer can have any idea, especially in advance of hearing the other bargainer's initial "bid," how wide the contract zone is. Does avoidance of breakdown depend on the bargainer who has "second move" and hears the very first bid of all made by

9 *Expectation in Economics* (1949), ch. vi.
10 J. Pen, 'A General Theory of Bargaining', p. 28.

the other before he says anything himself, so that he can set his own aim near enough to the other's to avoid any "loss of face" of his own?

There are two things to be said about this suggestion. 1st, we must notice that it assumes an asymmetry in the bargaining process. The whole contract zone might on this hypothesis be shifted, at the very outset, in favour of the bargainer who first announces a price. Such an asymmetry, I think, may well be a realistic feature but it has been ignored by all writers except those who have approached from the viewpoint of the theory of games. To assume such an asymmetry would introduce a new source of indeterminacy unless we suggest some principle by which one bargainer, say the seller, is always selected as the first announcer of a price. 2nd, there seems to me a more fundamental objection. What reason have we to suppose that the profit to be gained by either party by securing agreement in this particular instance of bargaining must necessarily be sufficient to outweigh considerations of loss of bargaining power, "loss of face," in future negotiations?

Let us turn to the other possibility, that the contract zone is gradually narrowed down by the process of bargaining itself so that the danger of breakdown is avoided. If this is the explanation, then it must be pointed out that when either bargainer allows himself to be persuaded to alter the price at which his own ophelimity function has a maximum, he is in effect making a concession, which if he has already announced a price based on the earlier position of his maximum, he will be known by the other party to have made, so that such a shifting of his ophelimity maximum will involve 'loss of face' and may therefore be impossible. We think, therefore, that unless we consider each particular instance of a bargaining process to be conducted without thought of future instances, we cannot give to the ophelim-

ity functions all the meaning which Pen gives to them.

## BARGAINING ANALYSED IN TERMS OF FOCUS VALUES

In my own attempt at a theory of bargaining, I suppose the seller to be concerned with the following prices:

$m$  his absolute minimum price to accept which would leave him neither better nor worse off than to abandon the negotiation.

$g$  his initial asking price.

$j$  his effective minimum price, the least permitted by some chosen policy.

$v$  the price, unknown to either party until the completion of bargaining, which may ultimately be agreed upon.

Three policies are open to him. The "possible breakdown" policy consists in such a choice of $g$ and $j$ that even if he concedes the whole difference between them he will not "lose face" and be handicapped on subsequent occasions of bargaining. The "possible loss of face" policy consists in resolving to descend from some chosen $g$ whatever distance $g-v$, not greater than $g-m$, may be necessary to secure agreement. The "combined" policy involves accepting the possibility of some loss of face but also in setting some $j > m$ as the limit of his descent.

A bargaining plan consists in a pair of values of $g$ and $j$ chosen together as an entity. The respective outcomes of various bargaining plans are unknown, and the bargainer will determine for each plan that he has in mind a focus gain and a focus loss. For any plan under the "possible breakdown" policy the primary focus gain will be that hypothetical value of $x = v - m$ whose combination of numerical size and of associated potential surprise makes it the most stimulating of the whole range of such hypotheses for which potential surprise is less than the absolute maximum. The primary focus loss of any plan under the "possible breakdown" policy will be the sacrifice of the best hope he could have entertained under the "possible loss of face" policy. For any plan under the "possible loss of face" policy the relevant hypotheses will not be those concerning the gross gain $s = v - m$ but those concerning the net gain $x = s - z$, where $z$ stands for the bargainer's estimate of the time-discounted cash value of the injury he will suffer in future bargaining through the loss of face entailed by his present plan. Since $x$ can thus be either positive or negative, any plan under the "possible loss of face" policy will have one value of $x$ standing for the primary focus gain of this plan and another value of $x$ standing for its primary focus loss. As the final step in choosing amongst bargaining plans, the bargainer may be supposed to go through a mental process which can be represented by his plotting on a "gambler indifference map," for each plan, a point whose co-ordinates are the standardized focus gain and the standardized focus loss of the plan, and adopting the one which lies on the higher indifference curve.

The buyer can be supposed, *mutatis mutandis*, to choose his initial bargaining plan in the same way as the seller. The bargaining process consists in a confrontation of the two initial plans, and the following out of his plan by, say, Smith, until some bid by Brown adds to or alters Smith's conception of what was in Brown's mind. Smith will then make a revised plan; and so on. In my book I concluded the analysis, of which the foregoing is a brief sketch, with the following passage:

*By taking account of the bargainer's attitude to uncertainty, that is, by assuming him to have a given preference system for various gambling situations as these are assessed in his own mind in terms of focus-values, we find, first, that it is by no means certain that agreement will be reached even when the seller's absolute minimum price is below the buyer's absolute maximum price; and secondly, that if exchange does take place, the price, in an important sense, is determinate: it is conceptually knowable in advance, if we are fully informed about the gambler-preference system of each bargainer, and the functions according to which he will draw inferences from a given sequence of "asking prices" or "offered prices" announced by the other bargainer.*

Let us turn back briefly to our list of questions. In answer to questions 1 (a) and (b) there is no real disagreement between the pre-Zeuthenites and the post-Zeuthenites,[11] except that Professor Hicks stands somewhat apart from both. If our data are restricted to the bargainer's interests in the one particular instance of bargaining, considered in isolation, the price in bilateral monopoly is indeterminate. If we have full knowledge of the parties' expectations and the working rules or functions by which they revise their expectations in the light of fresh data, and of their gambler preferences, the outcome of a bargaining process is in principle determinate. In practice determinacy surely cannot mean that the outcome, except in special cases, could be predicted by a third party, however well informed, in advance of the bargaining, as in question 1 (c). Question 1 (d) can now be seen as requiring a distinction between a special meaning of "determinacy," or that which calls for stable functions expressing the preferences and intentions of bargainers, and the more general meaning of "predictable in principle." Pen's theory implies that in the former sense the bargaining outcome is indeterminate, in the latter sense determinate. On question 2 my own analysis suggests that it is where the negotiation is seen as one of a long or endless

---

[11] This is a doctrinal rather than a chronological classification: a pre-Zeuthenite attitude is still taken by some writers.

series of similar negotiations which will be carried on in the future, that fear of future disadvantage through present "loss of face" is most likely to lead to breakdown. In the context of wage disputes this may indeed mean much public injury through prolonged strikes, and a remedy is a pressing need. Pen compresses both tastes and beliefs into the bargainer's ophelimity function, and in answer to question 3 (a) he would say that each bargainer seeks to influence or control both the tastes and beliefs of the other. To try to influence a person's beliefs does not in the abstract or in general imply deception, but in bargaining it plainly may do so. If deception is bad, bargaining is bad.

It is impossible without further extending this chapter to endeavour to link the foregoing survey with the remaining, more specialized questions in our list. The character of that list as a whole seems to suggest why economic theory has been so slow in coming to grips with the problem of bargaining. Perhaps this discussion has served to indicate that an adequate theory of bargaining requires us to study psychological questions which many economists even today regard as outside the proper scope of economics.

### Related Readings

An excellent review of bargaining theory may be found in Allan M. Cartter, *Theory of Wages and Employment* (Homewood, Ill., Richard D. Irwin, Inc., 1959, Chapter 9). Cartter goes beyond reviewing collective bargaining theories and presents some refinements of his own.

A very sophisticated bargaining model was developed by Jan Pen in "General Theory of Bargaining" (*American Economic Review*, March 1952), and *The Wage Rate Under Collective Bargaining* (Cambridge, Mass., Harvard University Press, 1959). Pen uses a formalized game theory model based on simultaneous equations that express the cost of agreeing relative to the cost of disagreeing multiplied by a risk evaluation function from which is subtracted an estimate of one's opponent's will to resist. There is an equation for each party and when each equation is equal to zero each party would be willing to settle at the price under consideration.

# CHAPTER 13

# Impact of Unions on Wages

## INTRODUCTION

The impact of unions on wages has significant implications for economic growth and stability as well as for the distribution of incomes between union and nonunion workers and between labor and other factors of production. It is therefore not surprising that this topic has received considerable attention from economists. The unions' impact might either be on the *general level* of wages and prices, which was discussed in Part II, or on *relative* wages, which is the main topic of this section.

The layman might be surprised to learn that economists doubt that unions have had much impact on wages. In general, this surprise is because the impact has been exaggerated by employers, newspaper editors, and even unions themselves, who take credit for wage increases that might have been caused by increases in productivity and rising general price levels. Since unions negotiate contracts and then wages rise, many assume that the unions *caused* the wages to rise, whereas there would have been some wage increase even in the absence of unions.

Economists, on the other hand, particularly economic theorists, minimize policy decisions, especially in the long run, and emphasize market forces as determinants of wages and employment. The traditional view of classical economics, which carries over to modern economic theorists, is that wages are determined *mainly* by market forces and that the union's impact tends to be exaggerated. (See, for example, the statements of eight leading economic theorists in David McWright, ed., *The Impact of the Union,* New York, Harcourt, Brace and Co., 1951.) The classical view was that market forces were the only determinants of wages in the long run, but after the depression of the 1930's revealed such obvious imperfections in the market mechanism and led to increases in unionization and government regulation of wages and employment, few economists could deny the importance of nonmarket forces in wage determination. Nevertheless, most economists give major emphasis to markets in wage determination, while laymen tend to give greater emphasis to bargaining and policy.

## THE EVIDENCE OF UNIONS' INFLUENCE
## ON RELATIVE WAGES

In "The Influence of Unions on Relative Earnings," from *The Economics of Trade Unions* (Chicago, The University of Chicago Press, 1962), Albert Rees reviews the theoretical and empirical evidence concerning the unions' influence on relative wages, by which he means "comparisons between wages under union and non-union conditions."

Rees begins his chapter with a discussion of the predictions of economic theory, and emphasizes the importance of the concept of the elasticity of demand for union labor. If the demand for labor is relatively inelastic, unions will be able to raise wages without greatly increasing unemployment. The elasticity of demand, on the other hand, is determined by derived demand, which means that the demand for labor is derived from the demand for the final product and the demand for the other factors of production. Rees analyzes the four conditions of inelastic demand developed by Alfred Marshall. "The demand is more inelastic (1) the more essential is union labor to the production of the final product, (2) the more inelastic the demand for the final product, (3) the smaller the ratio of the cost of the union labor to the final cost of the product, and (4) the more inelastic the supply of other factors of production."

Although these predictions of economic theory are fairly straightforward, measuring the impact of unions on wages is much more difficult because of the problems involved in isolating the union's influence. Isolation is difficult, first, because we are dealing with the problem of multiple-causation. For example, unions are influenced by such factors as the ratio of labor cost to total cost and economic conditions which also influence the level of wages. There is a strong positive correlation between the percentage of workers organized in a given industry and wage rates in those industries, but it is difficult to determine whether unions are strong because of the factors that made wages high or whether the wages are high because of the unions. Moreover, empirical investigations of the impact of unions on wages must also deal with the so-called "feed-back problem," which means that there are interactions between union and nonunion sectors that make it difficult to account for causation. For example, an empirical investigation might find very little difference between union wages and nonunion wages because employers in the nonunion sector raise wages in order to avoid unions. In such cases, the union might be responsible for the higher wages in both the union and nonunion sectors, although no difference would appear in an empirical investigation. Wages also might be equalized between union and nonunion sectors because of the tendency for employers to follow wage patterns established in other firms or industries. If the union established a pattern that was followed by the nonunion sector, a measurement of the differences between union wages and nonunion wages would fail to detect the impact of the unions.

In spite of these measurement difficulties, however, a large number of careful empirical investigations have produced some consensus among economists over the relative size of the unions' influence. As Rees explains very carefully, the empirical investigations have been primarily of two types: *cross section* analyses at a given time to determine the differences between union wages and nonunion wages, and *time series* analyses which attempt to study union and nonunion conditions over a period of time.

One conclusion that flows from these studies is that the unions' impact is strongly influenced by business conditions. Unions seem to have their greatest influence during the early stages of a recession or depression, in part, because unions produce a downward rigidity in wage movements. However, if the depression is prolonged, the union influence tends to disappear because not even the strongest unions can withstand the adverse effects of a severe depression. Unions also seem to have an advantage during periods of high employment and stable prices, but the extent of the advantage depends on the strength of the union. As Rees emphasizes, strong unions raise wages by as much as 15 to 25 percent above what they would have been in the absence of unions. The strongest union influence seems to have come from unions of skilled craftsmen and organizations like the United Mine workers. Empirical investigations seem to show that strong industrial unions like the United Steelworkers probably have an impact in the range of 10 to 15 percent when employment is high and prices are stable. However, even during periods of high employment and stable prices, some unions have very limited impact on wages because of adverse economic conditions that make it very difficult for the nonunion sectors to organized or make it difficult for unions to raise wages without generating substantial unemployment.

Rees concludes: "My own best guess of the average effects of all American unions on wages of their members in recent years would lie somewhere between 10 and 15 percent." Rees also concludes that the union's impact on wages is least during periods of rapid and unexpected inflation. "During rapid inflations, demand forces pull up product prices and wage rates in nonunion markets. Agreements fixing wages for a period of time, or even long-term agreements providing for periodic wage increases according to some preagreed formula or schedule can leave unions at a relative disadvantage. The presence of a union, with its power to resist wage cuts at a later date, can also dissuade employers from using wage increases to deal with temporary labor shortages."

Rees next discusses the importance of market structures for the impact of unions on wages. He is skeptical of the argument advanced by some economists that unions will have an advantage in dealing with monopolistic firms. Those who argue that unions have a wage advantage in dealing with firms in monopolistic or oligopolistic product markets base their position partly on a strong positive correlation between market concentration ratios and the degree of unionization, and reason that unions will be able to capture some of the monopoly profit arising in the product market. In this view, such unions will be able to demonstrate benefits to their members through collective bargaining, and therefore will strengthen their positions. However, Rees argues, these findings apply primarily to the manufacturing sector and do not hold for a broader range of industries because "such highly successful and powerful unions as the United Mine Workers, the Teamsters and the building trades unions deal with industries that are highly competitive or would be in the absence of the unions." As he emphasizes, unions in these industries have often helped the employer acquire greater control of the market.

Nevertheless, the conclusion that unions have helped employers in mining, building trades, and transportation gain greater control of the market does not destroy the argument that unions are likely to be more successful in the less competitive markets; a good bit of the success of all these unions results from the fact that they either have helped employers control their product markets, or they occupy strategic positions in the labor and product markets, as is the case with the Teamsters.

In discussing the significance of market structure, it is also important to emphasize the multiplicity of causes influencing both the determination of wages and union strength. To say that there is a strong correlation between market structures and wages is not to deny that other factors might be at work. Moreover, it is important to consider the prevailing institutional arrangements in assessing the importance of market structures on union strength. For example, it is undoubtedly true that before the 1930's unions had much less influence on wage determination in oligopolistic industries than they did after that period. In the institutional setting of the 1920's, large employers were free to use almost all of their economic and political power to prevent unions from organizing their employees. However, after the shifts in public opinion and the passage of favorable legislation during the 1930's, it became much more difficult for these employers to resist unions. Once the oligopolistic employer's power to resist unionization was neutralized, he became easier to organize than competitive firms. In part this was because it was less expensive for the union to organize large firms, but also because the differences between workers and employers in large organizations were likely to be greater than between workers and employers in smaller work units. Moreover, once collective bargaining became accepted public policy, employers who resisted unions ran considerable risk of alienating public opinion.

This is not to argue, however, that in dealing with unions employers conceded larger wage increases than they would have if they had not been organized, although there are a number of influences that might have caused higher wage increases in newly organized oligopolistic firms than would have occurred if those firms had remained unorganized. In the first place, many of these companies had considerable monopsony power in the labor market, so, under traditional economic theory, wages could be raised without reducing employment. The sudden reduction of monopsony power might explain the phenomenon, commonly found in empirical studies, for unions to have a sizeable wage advantage over nonunion firms during the early stages of unionization, but for this advantage to disappear. Obviously, a continuing advantage to firms operating under oligopolistic conditions *would require changes in the extent of monopoly power* through time, which is hardly realistic.

Similarly, in the case of oligopolies where the firms' product and labor demand curves are kinked at prevailing prices, increasing costs will not necessarily reduce employment. In such cases the union might be able to raise wages within the limits of the discontinuity in the marginal revenue product curve without creating unemployment. Indeed, it is conceivable that oligopolistic employers would offer less resistance to wage increases which they might be able to shift to consumers in the form of higher prices. It is even conceivable that oligopolies who raise prices by the same *percentage* amounts as they increase wages could actually profit from a wage increase, depending upon the ratio of labor cost to total cost and the elasticity of demand for the final product.

In his section on relative wages and resource allocation, Rees discusses a number of conditions under which increases in relative wages would not cause employment to be less than it otherwise would have been. We have already mentioned the oligopoly and monopsony cases. Another is the so-called "shock effect" in which rising wage pressures cause employers to become efficient and therefore to absorb more easily the wage increases without reducing employment. However, as Rees points out, there are a number of problems with the shock effect, especially if we assume it to be a continuing phenomenon: "Those labor economists who believe strongly in the importance of shock effects and who see the American labor movement as shot through with monopsony do not believe that unions as a whole have adverse effects on the allocation of labor. Most economists, however, would agree that unions, in-so-far as they have the power to raise relative wages, reduce employment in the union sector and increase it in the non-union sector."

But the argument that union wage policies distort resource allocation does not assume that the labor market would be perfect without union influence. As Rees points out, there are many market imperfections besides the operation of unions. Moreover, he might have pointed out that unions do some things, such as provide better job information and training, which improve the operation of some labor markets. Furthermore, the judgment that "unions make for a worse allocation of labor" implies that a higher gross national product is "better" than such achievements as greater worker participation in the formulation of work rules. Moreover, a larger gross national product in not necessarily "better" for all groups in society.

## LABOR'S SHARE AND THE SIZE DISTRIBUTION OF INCOME

Rees concludes his chapter with discussions of the impact of unions on labor's national income share and on the size distribution of income. With respect to the former, empirical studies are highly inconclusive although, as with relative wages, there are a number of measurement difficulties. However, it is not inconsistent to argue that unions have had an influence on relative wages and no influence on labor's share.

With respect to size distribution, or the proportion of income going to different income levels, Rees concludes:

Perhaps the best summary statement that can be made from the available evidence about the effect of gains on the size distribution of income is that unions have probably raised many higher income workers from an initial position somewhat above the middle of the income distribution to a present position closer to the top. They have narrowed the gap between the best paid manual workers and the very rich, and widened the gap between these workers and the very poor. This effect cannot be completely described by calling it either an increase or a decrease in an equality of income distribution, though it seems closer to the latter than the former.

# The Influence of Unions on Relative Earnings

## by Albert Rees

### PREDICTIONS FROM ECONOMIC THEORY

The discussion of union wage policy in the last chapter dealt with what unions try to do about wages under various circumstances, considered primarily from the point of view of the union as an organization. We now look at the union effect on relative wages from the outside, seeking to find out how well unions achieve their wage objectives and what consequences their impact on wages has.

In judging the consequence of union wage effects, we shall seek to compare the operation of organized labor markets with the operation of unorganized labor markets as they exist in the United States, for it would be unfair to compare the organized market with some theoretical model of a perfect market that has never existed. This effort will involve making implicit judgments about the extent and nature of imperfections, such as lack of knowledge, and barriers to mobility in unorganized markets. In my opinion, such imperfections are pervasive and are important in the short run, but in the long run market forces operate rather effectively.

The term relative wages, which was introduced above, refers to comparisons between wages under union and non-union conditions. Thus a relative wage gain of 10 per cent will mean that union members receive a wage 10 per cent higher than that of comparable non-union workers. At this point little will be said about whether relative gains are made wholly by raising the level of union wages with non-union wages unchanged (which would imply a rise in the general level of wages), or whether they are made in part

SOURCE Reprinted with permission from Albert Rees, *The Economics of Trade Unions,* Chicago, The University of Chicago Press, 1962.

by a reduction in the wage that non-union workers would get in the absence of unions anywhere.

\* \* \*

In particular, these predictions follow from the theory of derived demand developed by Alfred Marshall.[1] The term "derived demand" is used to indicate that the demand for labor is derived from the demand for the final product and the supply of the other factors of production. The more inelastic the demand for union labor, the smaller the effect of a given wage increase on employment and therefore the larger the probable influence of a union on relative wages.

Marshall listed four conditions that affect the demand for union labor. The demand is more inelastic (1) the more essential is union labor to the production of the final product, (2) the more inelastic the demand for the final product, (3) the smaller the ratio of the cost of union labor to the total cost of the product, and (4) the more inelastic the supply of the other factors of production.

Condition 1 means that there should be no good substitutes for union labor in the production process. In the short run, this means that employers should not be able to replace union members with new non-union workers or with supervisory personnel. In the long run, the possibilities for developing labor-saving techniques and processes are an important element in the essentiality of union labor. Condition 2 means that consumers should not reduce their purchases of the final product by a large amount in response to a small increase in its price. This condition can be considered at two levels. If a union has organized all of the firms producing a product in a particular product market, then the condition refers to the market for the product as a whole. It is an advantage to the union to produce a product for which there are no good sub-

stitutes, for then increase in the product price are not likely to cause large reductions in the amount consumed. If the union has not organized all the firms producing the particular product, then we must consider the demand for the product of the union firms. Here the product of the non-union firms will usually be a very good substitute, so that a small rise in the price charged by union firms will cause them to lose a large share of the market. Empirically, this is probably the most important implication of the theory. There have been numerous cases in which the failure of a union to organize all the firms in a product market has left it unable to sustain its wage gains or even its very existence. In the 1920's, the United Mine Workers made very large wage gains in unionized coal fields, but these fields soon lost important markets to the non-union fields, and this led to a rapid decline in the employment of union members. More recently, the union in the hosiery industry has all but disappeared because of similar competition in the product market from non-union firms.

To consider condition 3, that the cost of union labor be a small part of total costs, we return again to the case in which the union has organized the whole product market. Suppose that there is a related product which is a reasonably good substitute for the product of the unionized workers. Ordinarily, this would tend to put the union in a weak position. However, if the union in question represents workers whose wages are a very small part of total cost, then even a large wage increase will have little effect on the price of the product and hence on the volume of sales and employment. For example, let us suppose that the demand for houses is so elastic that an increase in price of 1 per cent will decrease the volume of construction by 2 per cent. Suppose also that the wages of electricans make up 1 per

[1] *Principles of Economics* (8th ed.; New York: Macmillan Co., 1920), pp. 383–86.

cent of the total cost of a new house, and that there are absolutely no substitutes for their services. In this case, an increase in the wages of electricians of 50 per cent would add only one half of 1 per cent to the total price of a house and, despite the high elasticity of demand we have assumed, would reduce the volume of construction by only 1 per cent.[2]

Empirically, the importance of the share of union wages in total cost may lie in the large range of variation in this share among unions. Union wages have at times been as high as two-thirds of total cost in coal mining and can be a small fraction of 1 per cent of total cost for a highly specialized craft union such as pattern-makers. This consideration would lead us to predict that craft unions will in general have more effect than industrial unions on the wages of their members. It should be noted, however, that a craft union has the advantage of being unimportant in total cost only if it bargains as a separate unit, and if unions representing other occupations do not automatically get wage increase as large as those won by the first union. When it becomes certain that increases granted to one craft union will always be extended to the rest, the relevant variable for each union becomes the share of all wages in total cost, and not the share of the wages of its own members. There is no particular reason why the share of all wages in total cost should be smaller for an industry organized on a craft basis than for one organized on an industrial basis.

Condition 4, that the supply of other factors of production be inelastic, means that if the employer tries to economize on union labor by using more of some other factor of production, the price of that factor should rise appreciably in response to his increased use of it. This will be important where condition 1 is not well satisfied.

The elasticity of demand for union labor will limit the wage gains of a union only if the union is concerned about the employment of its members. Of two unions facing identical demand curves, the one most willing to tolerate loss of employment by its members will make the largest wage gains (assuming that the two have equal bargaining skill, and so do the two employers). A union will ordinarily be less concerned about loss of employment among its members where they have good alternative employment opportunities.

Taken together, Marshall's four conditions suggest that there are economic limits imposed on the power of a union to raise wages in a number of different directions. That we do not observe unions with the power to double the wages of their members, or observe them only very rarely and for brief periods, suggests that it is not likely that all the conditions for great union power will be fully satisfied at the same time.

## MEASURING THE IMPACT OF THE UNION

The impact of the union on relative wages has been defined here as the extent to which a union raises the wages of its members and the other workers for whom it bargains above the wages of comparable unorganized workers. This effect can be measured in either of two ways: in cross-section, by comparing the wages of union workers at a point in time with the wages of non-union workers in other occupations or localities, and in time series, by com-

---

[2] In exceptional circumstances, the union is in a better position if it is important in total costs than if it is unimportant. The circumstances are those in which there are relatively good substitutes for union labor in the production process and the demand for the final product is highly inelastic. Here the union has little to fear from raising the price of the final product. If union labor is important, it becomes more difficult for employers to find substitutes for all of it, and the larger the quantities in which they must use the substitutes, the more they drive up their prices. For the original statement of this exception, see J. R. Hicks, *The Theory of Wages* (London: Macmillan and Co., 1935), pp. 241–46.

paring the movement of wages of union workers through time with those of non-union workers. Sometimes the two methods can be combined in a single study. The cross-section method has substantial advantages where wage bargaining takes place in local product markets, some of which are unorganized or only partially organized.

Making useful comparisons is not always easy. If we compare wages in union and non-union plants in the same industry and labor market, we may observe only small differences even where the union is effective, for non-union employers will often be forced to raise wages if they want to prevent the unionization of their workers. Some economists have argued that such considerations vitiate all comparisons between union and non-union wages. This claim, however, is surely too sweeping. A union wage increase will not necessarily affect the wages of non-union workers in other localities or other industries, and if it does have an effect, this effect can be in either direction. In some cases, the union wage increase may be emulated. In others, the effect will operate through the labor market in the opposite direction. The higher wages in the union sector will tend to check the growth of employment in that sector, which will increase the supply of labor to the non-union sector and tend to check increases in non-union wages.

When we begin to make comparisons across localities or industries, new problems arise in defining comparable workers. We would not expect wages in two industries to move in exactly the same way if both were unorganized, for there will be changes through time in the forces governing the size of interindustry wage differentials. Similarly, the wages in the same occupation in two cities will not usually be the same if both are unorganized. There will almost always be some differential whose size is determined by such forces as the age and skill of the workers, the size of the cities, the intensity of the local demand for labor, and the general level of income in the area or region in which the cities are located. In making comparisons between union and non-union wages, there is therefore always a danger of confounding the effect of the union with the effects of other forces that contribute to wage differentials in the absence of unions. These other forces must be carefully considered, and their effects must in so far as possible be removed from the data by appropriate statistical procedures. The resulting estimates of union effect cannot be regarded as exact but should give us the rough order of magnitude of the union effect.

## RESEARCH FINDINGS

Research on the impact of the union on wages has proceeded along two lines. One group of studies has examined a large number of industries simultaneously, classifying them according to the degree of unionization.[3] A second group of studies is based on the intensive examination of the effects of unions on earnings in a single industry.[4] Most of the cross-section studies fall in this group.

---

[3] See Arthur M. Ross, "The Influence of Unionism upon Earnings," *Quarterly Journal of Economics,* February, 1948; Arthur M. Ross and William Goldner "Factors Affecting the Interindustry Wage Structure," *Quarterly Journal of Economics,* May 1950; and Harold M. Levinson, *Unionism, Wage Trends, and Income Distribution* (Ann Arbor: University of Michigan Press, 1951). A new study of this general type is now being conducted by Professor H. Gregg Lewis. His preliminary results were reported in a paper entitled "The Effects of Unions on Industrial Wage Differentials" presented at Princeton, New Jersey, April, 1960, to a conference on labor economics held by the National Bureau of Economic Research.

[4] See Stephen P. Sobotka, "Union Influence on Wages: The Construction Industry," *Journal of Polit-*

Because I shall rely rather heavily in what follows on the estimates made in some of these studies, it is desirable to give some explanation of the estimating techniques that have been used. To use the time-series technique, one must construct a historical wage series for the unionized group going back far enough to include a period in which it was not unionized. It is also necessary to have a comparison or "base" series, often much broader in scope, showing the movement of wages or earnings for a group of workers who remain unorganized throughout the period of the study, or whose extent of unionization is appreciably less. If the workers of the base group are unorganized throughout, the analysis might proceed as follows: Suppose that in the period before the formation of the union under study, the average ratio of wages in the study group to wages in the base group in years of reasonably full employment was 1.20 to 1 and that in the period after the unionization of the study group this average ratio was 1.40 to 1 in comparable years. The estimate of the relative effect of unions on wages would then be approximately 17 per cent.[5] Before the estimate could be accepted, it would have to be determined whether factors other than unionization might account for changes in the ratio. It might also be possible to attach significance to changes in the ratio during the period of unionization.

The cross-section technique refers to a particular year. It can most easily be described for the case in which it is applied to separate local labor markets, in each of which the group under study can be described as entirely unionized or entirely non-unionized. For each market the wages of workers in the study group are divided by the wages of workers in some common base group in which workers are nowhere extensively unionized, such as retail trade, or in which there is little variation in the extent of unionization from place to place. If the base group is nowhere unionized, the estimate is made as follows: Suppose that the average ratio of wages in the study group to those in the base group is 1.40 to 1 in the unionized cities and 1.20 to 1 in the non-union cities. Then the estimate of the relative wage effect of the union in the year studied is again 17 per cent. The purpose of the use of the base group is to eliminate or reduce the effect of differences in wage levels among places that are not the result of unionization.[6]

Having sketched briefly the nature of the research techniques that have been used, I shall now attempt to summarize the findings of this body of research and to make some educated guesses to fill in the gaps. The summary will attempt to indicate both the possible average effect of unions on relative wages, and the range of variation among unions in these effects, though the estimates of the latter kind will be subject to larger errors. Initially, the effects will be stated in terms of the

ical Economy, April, 1953; Joseph Schrer, "The Union Impact on Wages: The Case of the Year-Round Hotel Industry," Inrustrial and Labor Relations Review, January, 1956; Elton Rayack, "The Impact of Unionism on Wages in the Men's Clothing Industry, 1911–1956," Labor Law Journal, September, 1958; Melvin Lurie, "The Effect of Unionization on Wages in the Transit Industry," Journal of Political Economy, June, 1961; and Rush V. Greenslade, "The Economic Effects of Collective Bargaining in Bituminous Coal Mining," (unpublished Ph.D. dissertation, University of Chicago, 1952).

[5] This figure is obtained by dividing 1.40 by 1.20 and subtracting 1.00. The result is then expressed as a percentage by multiplying it by 100.

[6] If the industry or occupation in question is one in which the extent of unionization varies continuously from one market to another, the cross-section technique can still be used. It will then involve estimating a regression equation in which the dependent variable is the ratio of wages in the study group to wages in the base group, and the independent variable is the percentage of workers in the study group who are organized. Ideally, the measure of union effect as we have defined it is the difference in the level of the regression line at zero and 100 per cent unionization, though this measure is subject to error if, for example, either extreme lies outside the actual range of observations. Readers with no background in statistics may safely ignore this footnote and rely on the text.

percentage by which unions raise relative earnings in periods of reasonably full employment and reasonably stable prices.

Strong American unions seem to be able to raise the relative earnings of their members by 15 to 25 per cent. Sobotka's study of the skilled building trades unions, as reinterpreted by H. G. Lewis, suggests a figure toward the high end of this range. It seems probable that craft unions in the printing, railroad, and entertainment industries have at times had effects of this general magnitude, though in recent years declines in demand and technological change may be eroding the power of some of them. Some industrial unions also seem to have effects of this order. Greenslade's study indicates that the United Mine Workers had an effect of at least 20 per cent on relative earnings in 1950–51, and Rayack has estimated that the effect of unionization in men's clothing was about 20 per cent in the early 1920's. Although no study of this type has been made of the teamsters' union, its rapid growth and generally aggresive attitude might lead one to classify it among the strong unions, at least for a large portion of its jurisdiction.

Little research has been done on the effects on earnings of industrial unions in the mass-production manufacturing industries during periods of reasonably stable prices. In the light of what we know about other unions, an effect of 10 to 15 per cent for the strong unions in this group, such as the steelworkers, does not seem unreasonable.

Some recent studies have found periods of stable prices and high employment in which the unions studied had no measurable influence on earnings. The unions for which this was found are of two general types. First, there are those which bargain with firms selling in national product markets and which have failed to organize a substantial majority of the firms in their industry. At the present time, the unions in the textile industry are the best ex-

ample of this situation. Wage increases in the unionized sector that exceed those in the non-union sector give the non-union firms a competive advantage in the product market and therefore have large effects on employment in union firms. The union lacks power because the products of non-union labor are an almost perfect substitute for the products of union labor.

There are other cases in which unions have little or no measurable effect on earnings even though they have organized almost all of the firms in their jurisdictions. Two such cases that have been studied are those of the Amalgamated Clothing Workers and the Amalgamated Association of Street Railway and Motor Coach Operators in the period since World War II. Both of these unions had had substantial effects on the earnings of their members in earlier periods. The relevant common factor is that both unions operate in industries where the demand for the final product has been declining in recent years. The resulting declines in employment and the precarious financial position of many employers have apparently made the unions unwilling to risk further losses in employment by an aggressive wage policy. This attitude is reinforced by the effect of declining employment in raising the average age of union members. Older workers are less mobile and have poorer alternatives in the labor market and will therefore be more concerned with saving their jobs than with higher wage rates.

My own best guess of the average effects of all American unions on the wages of their members in recent years would lie somewhere between 10 and 15 per cent. This is within the range of the estimates being made by H. G. Lewis in his current work covering the whole economy, though his results would not rule out an average effect somewhat higher than this.

The preceding discussion has taken conditions of relatively stable prices and relatively full employment as a norm for measuring union effects on relative wages. We must now ask what deviations from these effects occur under other conditions.

In periods of rapid and unexpected inflation, such as occurred from 1941 to 1948, even the strongest unions seem to have no effect on relative earnings, or to lose most of any effect they previously had.[7] During rapid inflations, demand forces pull up products prices and wage rates in non-union markets. Agreements fixing wages for a period of time, or even long-term agreements providing for periodic wage increases according to some preagreed formula or schedule can leave unions at a relative disadvantage. The presence of a union, with its power to resist wage cuts at a later date, can also dissuade employers from using wage increases to deal with temporary labor shortages.

The sluggishness in wage adjustment created by collective bargaining, which acts to a union's disadvantage in periods of vary rapid price and wage increases, becomes an advantage in periods of recession or in the early stages of a depression. Here union wages may remain fixed while other wages decline, increasing the union's normal effect on relative wages. Such an effect operated in the building and printing industries from 1929 to 1931, as may be seen by comparing their wage movements with those of other industries in which there are a large number of small employers. Because the recessions of the past fifteen years have been comparatively mild, effects of this sort have not been of appreciable importance since 1945. When a depression becomes prolonged and severe, as in 1931–33, the union effect on relative earnings again tends to disappear. Some unions lose their bargaining rights over much of their jurisdictions, some accept wage cuts that wipe out their relative advantages, and

still others preserve the union scale, but permit such substantial amounts of work to be done at wages below the scale that the scale becomes largely a fiction. Fortunately, we have had no opportunity to observe how the stronger unionism of today would adjust to severe depression.

## NON-ECONOMIC LIMITS ON UNION IMPACT

The rough summary of the literature on union effects in the last section suggests that a 25 per cent effect on relative earnings is a large one, one not often exceeded according to the studies made so far. From two points of view, however, this effect may seem rather small. First, it seems small from the point of view of the casual observer, the "man in the street." His offhand impression may be that unions often double the wages of their members. All of his sources of information are biased in the direction of leading him to guess too high. Newspapers and broadcasters give prominent coverage to wage increases resulting from strike settlements or from large-scale negotiations because they are dramatic, while little attention is paid to the gradual upward creep of non-union wages. Small wonder that the public does not suspect that in this race the tortoise sometimes catches up with the hare. The unions themselves tend to take credit for more than their due. Thus a union paper may say to the members, "In 1939 you were earning 70 cents an hour; today you earn $2.50 an hour. This is what your union has done for you." The average reader will not see that much of this increase is due to the rise in the general price level and the increasing productivity of labor, and would thus have taken place even without the union. It might be thought that employers would seek to deny such excessive union claims, but

[7] See Sobotka, *op. cit.*, pp. 139–41, Levinson, *op. cit.*, pp. 33–39 and 47–62, and A. Rees, "Postwar Wage Determination in the Basic Steel Industry," *American Economic Review,* June, 1951.

often they have their own reasons for making similar statements. Employers may exaggerate the union effect on earnings to win support for the position that unions have too much power and should be restrained by public policy.

The rather modest size of measured union effects on relative earnings may also be somewhat surprising from the point of view of economic theory. Surely these are cases where, in the short run at least, the demand for union labor is highly inelastic, so that very substantial increases in relative earnings would have little adverse effect on employment. For some of the highly skilled craft unions, this might be true even over long periods. This suggests that employment effects are not the only force tending to limit the size of union wage gains. Although other possible forces are not dealt with by the received theory, it may be useful to speculate about them.

Workers, employers, and the public undoubtedly have rough ideas about the levels of wages required to get an adequate supply of labor for jobs at various levels of skill. These rough ideas are the basis of the concepts of equity that are so important in explicit discussion of wage differentials. When a union rate is more than about 25 per cent above the nonunion level for similar work, it may be viewed by employers or the public as unfair or unreasonable. Such very high rates will often be accompanied by visible job rationing—conditions of unemployment of qualified workers in times of prosperity, or discriminatory or unduly exacting conditions for entry to employment or union membership. These will increase the sense of unfairness. The result may be stiffened employer resistance to wage demands even when business is good and increased public support for employers in time of dispute.

It would be unreasonable to expect the union or its members to perceive their wage as too high. They may, however, perceive it as "high enough" and prefer to avoid strikes rather than raise it still further. If a union has a high relative wage and still has unexploited bargaining power, it may use this to improve the nonwage conditions of employment. Since these cannot be measured in a single dimension, they are less likely to attract attention and to arouse resentment. The union may also try to force the employer to use more labor at the union wage than he would freely choose to employ—that is, it may force him off of his demand curve to the right. In this context, it is important to note only that it is a way of increasing the income of the membership, assuming that the members have been experiencing some unemployment, without creating a wage that appears unfairly high.

The union studied whose impact on earnings seems to be most in excess of the normal range is the Airline Pilots' Association. This union meets all of the theoretical criteria for expecting a large effect. In addition, the responsibility of its members for the lives of their passenegers serves to insulate it from adverse public reaction to very high earnings. If you tell the average airline passenger that the pilot of a large jet aircraft may earn more than $25,000 a year, he is likely to reply, "Well, you can't pay these fellows too much to suit me." There is, however, no basis for believing that a lower salary would fail to attract enough pilots who were fully qualified in every respect having any bearing on passenger safety. The unusual features of this exception tend to confirm the rule that unions will ordinarily hesitate to set wages palpably above the levels needed to secure an adequate supply of qualified applicants during periods of full employment.

## THE RELATION BETWEEN UNION IMPACT AND MARKET STRUCTURE

In the preceding discussion of union impact, nothing was said about the market organization of the industries with which the unions bargain; that is, about whether they are highly competitive or monopolistic in the sale of their products. Some economists feel that this is a significant variable and that unions make larger gains when they deal with monopolies because they are able to "capture" some of the monopoly profit arising in the product market. It has even been argued that union power is primarily a response to the power of business monopolies—in Galbraith's terms that it is "countervailing" power rather than "original" power.[8]

It is difficult to find support for this position in fact or in theory. Historically, the first unions organized were in industries where most employers were small firms (the outstanding exceptions are the railroads and anthracite mining). In printing, building construction, entertainment, bituminous coal mining, the local service industries, the garment industries, and similar highly competitive industries, we find most of the large craft and industrial unions of the period before 1933. We also find in these competitive sectors most of the unions shown by recent research to have a large effect on relative earnings, though it must be admitted that much of the research has been concentrated on this sector, in part because it lends itself better to the cross-section study.

It is clear that the great financial resources of large firms in such industries as steel, meat-packing, and automobiles were used to help delay the organization of these industries. These firms used their resources to win strikes and to maintain elaborate spy and police systems that prevented unions from getting a secure foothold before the 1930's. This, however, does not meet the argument that once collective bargaining has been accepted in such an industry the union has a special advantage.

The argument that unions have a special advantage in bargaining with a monopolist rests on two kinds of evidence. The first is the conviction of union leaders and students of the day-to-day operation of collective bargaining that unions make larger gains when dealing with monopolistic industries. The second is that three competent statistical studies show a significant correlation between the extent of concentration in the product market (the best available general measure of monopoly power) and wage increases, and two of the three suggest a further correlation between these two variables and the extent of unionization.[9] All three of these studies, and perhaps the more general impression mentioned above, are based on the experience of manufacturing industries. It does seem to be true that in manufacturing, at least in recent years, the most successful unions have dealt with the concentrated industries, though the printing trades unions are an exception. However, this may be because some of the less successful unions in shoes, textiles, and apparel have been dealing with declining or partially organized industries rather than because they were dealing with competitive industries. Moreover, the generalization does not hold when a broader range of industries is considered. Such highly successful and powerful unions as the United Mine Workers, the teamsters, and the building trades unions deal with industries that are highly competitive, or would be in the absence of unions.

[8] See John Kenneth Galbraith, *American Capitalism: A Theory of Countervailing Power* (New York: Houghton Mifflin and Co., 1956), pp. 115 ff.

[9] See Joseph Garbarino, "A Theory of Interindustry Wage Structure Variation," *Quarterly Journal of Economics*, May, 1950; Harold M. Levinson, *Postwar Movement of Prices and Wages in Manufacturing Industries* ("Study Paper" No. 21, Joint Economic Committee, 86 Cong. 2d sess., 1960); and William G. Bowen, *Wage Behavior in the Postwar Period: An Empirical Analysis* (Industrial Relations Section, Princeton University, 1960).

In this discussion, it is important to classify industries as competitive or monopolistic according to their market structure under non-union conditions, since one of the effects of unions in such industries as the building trades and the local service industries may be to create effective cartels in the product market. This possibility is suggested by a number of antitrust cases based on union-employer collusion affecting product prices and the entry of firms into product markets. More study of the nature and importance of such collusion is badly needed.

Professor Melvin W. Reder has pointed out another difficulty encountered by the statitsical studies cited above. All of them correlate wage *changes*, rather than wage *levels*, with the extent of monopoly in product markets. On the assumption that monopoly in product markets is conducive to high wages, one would expect wage levels to be related to the extent of monopoly and wage increases to be related to increases in the extent of monopoly, for if an industry is continuously monopolized, why is not this as much an advantage to the union at the beginning of a period as at the end? The correlations reported by Garbarino, Levinson, and Bowen, unless they happen to depend on the particular time periods covered, suggest an ever increasing differential between the wages paid by monopolists and by competitors for comparable labor. Eventually, such a growing differential would become grossly apparent, and it is not.

On theoretical grounds, there is little reason to believe that it is an advantage to the union to bargain with a monopolist. The possibilities for substituting other factors of production for union labor should not differ systematically according to market structure. The principal apparent difference lies in the price adjustment to a cost increase. A competitive industry will eventually pass all of a cost increase on to consumers in higher product prices[10] and will regain its normal rate of return on capital. In the process the size of the industry will be somewhat reduced. The reduction in industry output and employment will restrain the union's original wage demands if it is foreseen, or postpone or moderate future wage demands if it is not.

A monopolized industry, if it maximizes profits both before and after the increase in costs, may not pass on the full amount of the cost increase in prices and the cost increase will lower monopoly profits. Presumably this is what is meant by the statement that unions can "capture" such profits. But this will be an advantage to the union only if the effects of the price increase on output and employment are smaller for a monopolistic than for a competitive indusrty. Since the maximizing monopoly may add only a portion of the increased cost to product prices, this would seem at first glance to be true. This seeming advantage is offset, however, by the fact that for given demand and cost conditions the monopoly starts with a higher price and a smaller output; these are the necessary consequences of its use of its monopoly power.[11] At this higher price and smaller output, the demand for the product will usually be more elastic; that is, a given percentage price increase will cause a larger percentage reduction in output and employment. This can cancel the advantage to the union of not

---

[10] It is assumed in the text that the industry does not use any highly specialized factors of production other than labor. If it does, some of the wage increase could be shifted backward in lower prices for these specialized inputs. Any changes in costs related to the size of the industry are also ignored.

[11] The assumption that a monopolist and a competitive industry can have identical costs is sometimes questioned on the grounds that the monopolist will reorganize or "rationalize" the industry. For a statement of this objection, see Joan Robinson, *The Economics of Imperfect Competition* (London: Macmillan and Co., 1933), Book IV, Chapter XIV.

having the full cost increase added to prices.[12]

The discussion of the preceding paragraph assumes that the monopolist maximizes money profits, which is the conventional assumption of economic theory. However, there are some plausible models of monopoly behavior that do not involve this assumption. It would be favorable to the union if after the wage increase the monopolist were to raise prices by less than would maximize profits in the long run, but there does not seem to be any mechanism that would lead to this result short of government price controls of a kind we have never had in peacetime. Indeed, the opposite result seems much more probable—that the monopolist will come closer to maximizing profits after the wage increase than before. In the period immediately after World War II, when such concentrated industries as steel and automobiles were charging prices too low to clear the market, negotiated wage increases were used as an occasion to raise prices by more than the direct increase in labor cost. These industries thus took advantage of collective bargaining to move closer to a profit-maximizing position, which in itself is unfavorable to the union.[13]

Nevertheless, it may be an advantage for a union to bargain with an oligopolist when there is excess demand, for if the oligopoly price fails to clear the market both before and after the wage increase, the union need not fear reduction in employment in the short run as a result of reduced consumption of the product. At the new higher price, production will still be at full capacity. In a competitive industry where product markets are continuously cleared, a higher price will always have an adverse effect on consumption, at the very least in causing it to expand at a slower rate.

RELATIVE WAGES
AND RESOURCE ALLOCATION

In the previous discussion of wages, it has been assumed that union-imposed increases in relative wages will cause employment to be smaller than it otherwise would be in the sector covered by the wage increases. This assumption, which follows from the principal propositions of traditional economic theory, deserves more careful examination than it has been given so far, particularly since most unionists and many labor economists deny it.

Let me begin by emphasizing again that the theory does not predict absolute declines in employment wherever unions raise relative wages. If unions raise relative wages in a rapidly growing industry or firm, employment will usually continue to grow, but not as much as it would have otherwise. Several elaborate attempts to measure the employment effect of wage increases have been inadequate because of confusion on this point. Second, employment for this purpose be measured in man-hours and not in men, though for convenience we have been talking about it as though it were always measured in men. A union faced with an employer decision to cut labor input in response to a wage increase can sometimes choose to spread the work in the form of shorter hours rather than to accept layoffs. The prediction does not depend on any one

[12] For a simplified special case it can easily be shown that this offset is exact; that the percentage decline in output is the same for a monopolistic and a competitive industry if the two wage increases, and the two demand curves, and the two cost curves are the same. The case is that in which the demand curves are straight lines, long-run average costs are constant over variations in industry output, and the monopolist maximizes in the long run by equating marginal revenue with long-run average (equals marginal) cost. Readers who do not understand this note and would like to should consult an elementary textbook in economic theory.

[13] See A. Rees, "Wage-Price Relations in the Basic Steel Industry," *Industrial and Labour Relations Review*, January, 1953.

line of response to the increase in relative wages. In some instances the employment effect will operate largely by stimulating the introduction of labor-saving machinery, in some by reducing the sales of the final product, in still others by less obvious kinds of substitutions. It is not even necessary that any employer make a conscious adjustment to the higher wages, provided that the different employers affected start with different proportions of wages to total cost. Under these circumstances, the employers with the smallest proportion of wages to total cost will tend to grow relative to the others because their cost structure has an improved survival value under the changed conditions, and this will tend to reduce the input of labor in the industry as a whole relative to what it would otherwise have been.[14]

The most frequent objection to this theory has been that wage increases improve efficiency, and the greater efficiency makes it unnecessary to reduce employment. Sometimes the introduction of labor-saving machinery is cited as an example of such improved efficiency. Here two cases must be distinguished. The first is that in which the new machinery would have been unprofitable before the wage increase but is profitable afterward. In this case the total costs of production will rise, though the rise will be smaller than if methods of production had remained unchanged. The higher total costs will ordinarily be reflected in product prices, so that employment is reduced both by the change in production methods and by the decreased sales of the product. The guarantee that costs rise in this case is of course contained in the statement that the machinery was unprofitable before the wage increases. Since this case is clearly part and parcel of the original argument for an employment effect, it is surprising to find it cited in rebuttal.

A rather similar line of argument points out that union wage increases will tend to eliminate the least efficient firms, and that this will cause employment to grow in the remaining, more efficient firms. This may indeed result, but it is highly unlikely that the growth of employment in the remaining firms would offset the decline in employment in those that disappear, particularly since the remaining firms will tend to be those that use the least labor per unit of output.

What critics of the theory probably have in mind is the second case, in which the machinery would have been profitable even before the wage increase but the employers did not realize it. In seeking to adjust to the wage increase, they discover their neglected opportunities. In this case total costs and prices could be lower after the wage increase than before, and the larger sales of the product could offset the adverse effect on employment of the change in methods of production. This is one variety of the so-called "shock effect" argument. The argument can turn on improved personnel practices, changes in hiring standards, or reduction of wastes of various sorts rather than on the introduction of new equipment.

Controversy over the shock effect centers on its importance rather than its logical consistency. It can certainly be conceded that few organizations operate continuously at peak efficiency, and that an occasional jolt or crisis can help to bring a firm closer to its best performance level. It may also be conceded that wage increases are probably more effective in helping to improve the efficiency of personnel management or production techniques than are shocks from more remote areas of the firm's operation, such as the introduction of an improved product by a competitor. Such challenges are most likely to be met in kind—product redesign

---

[14] See Armen Alchian, "Uncertainty, Evolution, and Economic Theory," *Journal of Political Economy,* June, 1950.

by product redesign, price cut by price cut, and so on. But this is not sufficient to establish the importance of the shock effect. The degree of inefficiency prior to the wage increase must be very large indeed if the effects of eliminating it will more than offset the entire cost of the wage increase, so that product prices actually fall and sales increase enough to absorb the labor displaced by the more efficient methods. Such large shock effects may be plausible in a few cases where unions are newly established. But it is not plausible to expect them repeatedly as the union wins subsequent wage increases. A gradual upward union push of relative wages seems no more likely to improve efficiency than any of the many other pressures on a firm in a competitive economy.

It should also be noted, as H. Gregg Lewis has pointed out to me, that the shock-effect argument is inconsistent with the observation that unions seek to equalize wages among firms. If union wage increases have such favorable effects on efficiency that unit costs are not raised, then union wage gains should never put a firm at a disadvantage relative to a non-union competitor. The experience of the coal, textile, and hosiery industries, to name but a few conspicuous cases, contradicts this expectation.

There is unfortunately little direct evidence from research on the employment effects of union wage gains. Rayack finds a sharp reduction in the market shares of output and employment of unionized markets in the men's clothing industry in the years 1923–29.[15] Sobotka reports a statistically significant negative correlation for 1939 between the degree of union organization of skilled building trades workers by cities and the ratio of months worked per year between such workers and a base group of non-union workers in the same cities.[16] There is also a careful study of the employment effects of minimum wage laws that finds substantial and consistent effects.[17] The traditional theory and the objections to the theory are the same for legally imposed minimum wages as they are for union-won wage increases.

Apart from the rather scanty published research bearing on this issue, there is at least one important case, that of bituminous coal, in which employment effects seem obvious to casual observation. The United Mine Workers has been mentioned earlier as a union with substantial effects on relative wages operating in an industry in which employment has declined sharply. The recent shifts in demand for bituminous coal have been of a kind that would probably have occurred to almost the same extent in the absence of union wage increases. The crucial point, however, is that there has been a drastic reduction in the amount of labor used to produce a given output. While some of this represents autonomous improvements in technology and some may be the result of shifts in the composition of output by uses, most of it seems to represent the rapid extension, in response to the rising wage, of long-known techniques for saving labor by the increased use of capital. Types of mining that use little labor, such as strip mining, have expanded rapidly even though the union has in effect discriminated against them by financing its generous health and welfare program by a tonnage royalty on output rather than by the usual contribution based on payrolls.

[15] Op. cit., p. 682.
[16] Op. cit., p. 137.
[17] John M. Peterson, "Employment Effects of Minimum Wages, 1938–1950," Journal of Political Economy, October, 1957, and "Employment Effects of State Minimum Wages for Women: Three Historical Cases Re-examined," Industrial and Labor Relations Review, April, 1959. See also the comment by Richard A. Lester on these articles and the reply by Peterson, ibid., January, 1960.

Before we leave the discussion of employment effects, we should consider a special case in which economic theory does not necessarily predict a fall in employment as the result of unionization and the imposition of a union wage scale. This is the case of monopoly in the hiring of labor, usually called labor monopsony. Let us consider first the case of the employer who is the sole user of a certain kind of labor in his labor market. He will find that as he increases his use of this kind of labor, he must raise his wages to attract enough qualified workers. (The same is true of employers as a group in a competitive labor market, but the individual employer in such a market can hire more labor at the going wage.) Our monopsonistic employer will be restrained from expanding employment by the fact that the cost of new employees consists not only of their own wage, but also of the wage increases that must be given to the old employees.[18] If a union now imposes a standard wage slightly above the wage previously paid, the employer finds that the cost of each new worker consists of his own wage alone, and this tends to induce him to employ more workers at the union wage than he employed previously. If the union wage is high enough, this effect will disappear and the ordinary adverse effect of wage increases on employment will reassert itself.

The kind of monopsony considered in the preceding example grows out of the concentration of employment in an area in one employer or a very small number of employers. Such employer concentration is not common in the United States, though it exists in some textile and mining towns.[19] It has probably diminished substantially in recent years as the widespread ownership of cars by industrial workers and the improvement of highways have extended the effective commuting radius to fifty miles or more and have facilitated the permanent movement of labor.

A second kind of monopsony is also possible, that caused by collusive agreement among the employers in an area. Such agreements can set ceilings on wages or wage increases, or more commonly can ban the "pirating" of labor—the hiring of workers already employed in the area without the consent of their present employer. When there is an ample supply of labor in a market, there is usually no need for any such agreements, and when the market is very tight, there is grave doubt that they are effective or enforceable. The anti-pirating agreement can be evaded by workers by the simple expedient of quitting their jobs, which in a tight labor market involves little risk. The firm can evade a maximum wage agreement by lowering its hiring standards and thus making a concealed increase in its wage for new workers. Perhaps collusive monopsony has some impact in labor markets moving from looseness to tightness; perhaps it is largely a ceremony by which the personnel directors of expanding firms avoid giving offense to their colleagues in other firms.

Those labor economists who believe strongly in the importance of shock effects and who see the American labor market as shot through with monopsony do not believe that unions as a whole have adverse effects on the allocation of labor. Most economists, however, would agree that unions, in so far as they have the power to raise relative wages, reduce employment in the union sector and increase it in the non-union sector. This is a worse allocation of labor than would exist with-

---

[18] In the usual terminology of the theory, the marginal labor cost exceeds the wage. The argument does not apply, of course, if the employer can successfully pay lower wages to his original workers than to new workers of the same ability, but such cases must be extremely rare for manual labor.

[19] Estimates of employer concentration have been made by Robert Bunting in an unpublished Ph.D. dissertation, University of Chicago.

out unions, in the sense that a shift of labor toward the union sector could increase the total output of the economy. In the union situation, the same individual might be able to earn $2.00 an hour in non-union employment and $2.20 in union employment, and he might be entirely willing to make the shift if jobs were available in the union sector. That this situation reduces the national output follows from viewing the wage as a measure of what the worker is worth to the employer and to the economy. The union employer is not willing to add another man at $2.20 because the man would not contribute that much to the value of production, but there would usually be some wage just below the union wage at which the worker would be hired and at which he would still be willing to shift. The difference between this wage and the wage in the non-union sector after he has shifted is the measure of the loss in output from having him in the wrong place. In the absence of the union, as more workers shifted the wage differential would tend to disappear, along with the potential gain in output from further reallocation.

The preceding argument does not assume that without unions the mobility of labor would be perfect and everyone would work where he gets the highest income and contributes the most to the national product. Income is not always a good measure of the value of a man's contribution to society, and there are substantial interferences with the optimum allocation of labor quite apart from unions. Perhaps the most important of these is the lack of good information about alternative jobs. The argument only states that the union impact on relative wages adds to these interferences rather than subtracts from them. The orthodox economist does not view the disturbance in allocation created by unions as like the effect of throwing a stone into the glassy surface of a pond, for no such glassy surface ever existed in a real labor market. Rather it is like putting an additional set of snags in a sluggish stream.

The view that unions make for a worse allocation of labor does not necessarily imply an unfavorable judgment of the total effect of unions. There are many other aspects of union activity yet to be considered, and an economy has other and perhaps even more important goals than the most efficient allocation of resources.

## THE UNION INFLUENCE ON LABOR'S SHARE

Many people view trade unions as a device for increasing the worker's share in the distribution of income at the expense of capital; that is, at the expense of the receivers of rent, interest, and profits. Attempts to test this view, which is often expressed by the unions themselves, have led to a number of studies of the effect of unions on labor's share. The studies to date must be regarded as highly inconclusive; no union effect on labor's share can be discovered with any consistency.[20] The ratio of wages and salaries to national income has been rising steadily for a long time. This rise, however, largely reflects the shift of labor from unincorporated business, especially farms (where the labor of the owners or operators is compensated by what appears in the national accounts as profits), to corporate enterprise where all labor is paid by wages and salaries. The statistical adjustments needed to convert the original figures into

---

[20] For a summary of this literature, see Clark Kerr, "Labor's Income Share and the Labor Movement" in G. W. Taylor and F. C. Pierson (eds.), *New Concepts in Wage Determination* (New York: McGraw-Hill Book Co., 1957). For a careful recent study that finds no significant union effect see Norman J. Simler, *The Impact of Unionism on Wage-Income Ratios in the Manufacturing Sector of the Economy* (Minneapolis: University of Minnesota Press, 1961).

estimates of the total labor share, including the share of owner labor, are difficult and the results of different procedures do not usually agree. However, all have the effect of reducing the rise in labor's share and leaving a remainder that shows no particular relation to union power.[21]

* * *

## THE UNION INFLUENCE ON THE SIZE DISTRIBUTION OF INCOME

People are interested in the functional distribution of income (its division between capital and labor) in part because they believe it to be related to the size distribution, the share of income going to people at different income levels. Most people would like to see this size distribution become more equal, at least to the extent of improving the lot of those at the very bottom. The simplest view of the relation between the two distributions is that workers are poor and the receivers of property income are rich. A union that can raise labor's share can then be viewed as a latter-day version of Robin Hood's merry men, with their headquarters removed from Sherwood Forest to a storefront opposite the mill.

Of course, this view of income distribution is much too simple. In fact, there are relatively few employed manual workers at the bottom of the income distribution. Of the 8.7 million families with 1957 incomes under $2,500, only 1.5 million were headed by employed craftsmen, operatives, or non-farm laborers—that is by people in the major occupation groups strongly organized by unions. Perhaps in the absence of unions this number would be somewhat larger, but it seems clear that low wages are no longer a principal

cause of poverty, if they ever were. Almost half of these low income families had heads who were not employed in 1957, and many of these had aged heads, presumably retired.[22] Because large numbers of retired people depend on rents, interest, and dividends for much of their income, it seems probable that income from capital is more important at the very bottom of the income distribution than anywhere else except at the very top.

The union influence on relative earnings implies an influence on the size distribution of income even if there is none on the functional distribution, provided only that the members of effective unions are not equally distributed throughout the size distribution. But this proviso is clearly met, for manual workers are highly concentrated in the middle ranges of the income distribution. To get some idea of the probable union effect on the size distribution, we must look in some detail at the income position of the occupations represented by effective unions.

* * *

Perhaps the best summary statement that can be made from the available evidence about the effect of unions on the size distribution of income is that unions have probably raised many higher income workers from an initial position somewhat above the middle of the income distribution to a present position closer to the top. They have narrowed the gap between the best paid manual workers and the very rich, and widened the gap between these workers and the very poor. This effect cannot be completely described by calling it either an increase or a decrease in the equality of income distribution, though it seems closer to the latter than to the former.

[21] See D. Gale Johnson, "The Functional Distribution of Income in the United States, 1850–1952," *Review of Economics and Statistics,* May, 1954. Johnson finds an increase in labor's functional share of national income from about 68 per cent in 1890 to about 75 per cent in 1952 but notes that almost half of the increase was achieved before 1929, while unions were still weak. See also Irving Kravis, "Relative Income Shares in Fact and Theory," *American Economic Review,* December, 1959.

[22] The statistics in this paragraph are from Robert J. Lampman, *The Low Income Population and Economic Growth* ("Study Paper" No. 12, Joint Economic Committee, 86 Cong. 1st sess.).

## Related Readings

Another review of the problems involved in making empirical investigations, as well as some of the empirical investigations themselves, is by Lloyd G. Reynolds, "The Impact of Collective Bargaining on the Wage Structure in the United States," in John T. Dunlop, Ed., *The Theory of Wage Determination* (New York, St. Martin's Press, 1957). Reynold's study is concerned with "the impact of collective bargaining on relative rates of wages in different localities, occupations, firms, and industries." Reynolds has a particularly good argument for the proposition that "the effects of trade unionism cannot be deduced from first principles and that, on the contrary, simple economic models of union behavior are likely to be quite misleading" (Ibid., p. 219). Reynold's survey leads him to the following hypotheses:

(1) Collective bargaining has reduced occupational differences within particular industries and has probably brought them closer to what they would have been under perfect competiton.
(2) Collective bargaining has reduced interplant differentials, on a national scale in industries characterized by regional or national competition, and on a local basis and local industries. In this respect, also, collective bargaining has probably produced a closer approximation to the competitive wage structure.
(3) Collective bargaining has probably widened interindustry differentials, and in an anti-competitive fashion. Unionism has penetrated most effectively into the relatively high wage industries, and has tended to make the rich richer.
(4) Collective bargaining has probably reduced geographical differentials, but this effect has been weaker than the first three effects, and largely incidental to the reduction to interplant differentials. The reductions of geographical differentials have probably brought the wage structure closer to competitive standards, though unions and a few industries may have overshot the mark. (Ibid., p. 220.)

One of the most thorough studies of the impact of unions on wages is H.G. Lewis, *Unionism and Relative Wages in the United States* (Chicago, University of Chicago Press, 1963). Lewis has a particularly useful analysis of the methodological issues in comparing the relative effects of unions on wages. Based on a survey of some 20 different empirical investigations, as well as his own work, Lewis concludes:

There is much uniformity in the evidence provided by the studies reviewed . . . that the impact of unionism on the average union/nonunion relative wage varied markedly from one date to another. The peak impact of the last forty years occurred, I judge, about 1932–33, near the bottom of the Great Depression. At the peak, the effect of unionism on the average wage of union workers relative to the average of nonunion workers may have been above 25 per cent. In the ensuing inflation, the relative wage effect declined sharply to a level between 10 per cent and 20 per cent, I estimate, by the end of the 1930's.

The decline in the average union/nonunion relative wage effect of unionism continued to about 1947 or 1948 near the peak of the inflation and immediately following World War II. At the trough, the impact of unionism on the average wage of union labor relative to the average wage of non-union labor was close to zero—under five per cent. . . .

The near-zero relative wage effect of unionism observed shortly after World War II did not persist, however, through the following decade. I estimate that in recent years the average union/nonunion relative wage was approximately 10 to 15 per cent higher than it would have been in the absence of unionism. During the 1950's, the extent of the unionization of the labor force was close to 25 per cent. These figures imply that recently the average wage of union workers was about 7 to 11 per cent higher relative to the average wage of all workers, both union and nonunion, than it would have been in the absence of unionism. Similarly, the average wage of nonunion workers is about 3 to 4 per cent lower relative to the average wage of all workers than in the absence of unionism." (Ibid., pp. 4–5.)

# CHAPTER 14

# Conflict Resolution

Conflict resolution is a subject that has implications far beyond collective bargaining. In an interdependent world where conflict is becoming increasingly commonplace, there is a serious need for techniques to resolve disputes. Conflict resolution is important not only in industrial areas, where strikes can lead to low productivity and hardships for companies and workers, but also in areas where conflicts can lead to expensive and time-consuming legal action and, in the international arena, even to wars.

In industrial relations there are two kinds of conflicts of primary interest to us: (1) conflicts arising over the terms of a new collective bargaining contracts, and (2) disputes arising under contracts after they have been agreed to by the parties. The most difficult areas of conflict are those arising over new contract terms, since disputes over the interpretation of contracts are usually resolved by the parties or through arbitration without resort to strikes.

Arbitration is a procedure whereby third parties intervene in disputes and bring about a binding settlement. The arbitrator derives his power from the parties or, in rare cases, from the state if compulsory arbitration exists. Compulsory arbitration means that disputes must be submitted to arbitration, whereas voluntary arbitration means that the parties voluntarily agree to submit the issue to a third party. Collective bargaining agreements commonly contain provisions giving arbitrators the authority to resolve issues arising over the interpretation of existing contracts. It is extremely rare for arbitration to be used to resolve the terms of new contracts because the parties themselves usually insist upon formulating the rules under which they are to operate.

Some observers have recommended compulsory arbitration as a way of resolving labor disputes. However, practitioners of collective bargaining and industrial relations experts uniformly reject compulsory arbitration on the grounds that it would destroy the collective bargaining process by substituting government regulations for collective bargaining. In the view of the critics of compulsory arbitration, collective bargaining is preferable to government regulation because, under collective bargaining, the parties who are to live with the rules participate in their formulation. Moreover, these rules can be much more flexible than government regulations because the parties can readily change contract terms, whereas it would be much more difficult to change government regulations. In addition, it would be very difficult for an outsider to acquire the same knowledge of the conditions under which the parties must work as the parties themselves. It is therefore agreed that compulsory arbitration would destroy collective bargaining by introducing a three-way settlement between the parties and the government. Since one party would ordinarily be able to predict the character of the government's intervention, compulsory arbitration would cause collective bargaining to break down. For example, if unions thought they could get more from the government than they could from management, there would be no need to bargain. On the other hand, employers who thought they could get more from the government would not bargain with unions. Of course, this argument is on the assumption that the outcome of the third-party intervention can be predicted. Nevertheless, compulsory arbitration would destroy the main advantages of collective bargaining by substituting the arbitrator's decision for agreement by the parties.

Although proponents of compulsory arbitration argue that it is preferable to a strike, there is very little professional sentiment in the United States for compulsory arbitration. Consequently, third parties usually intervene in disputes arising over new contracts only through conciliation, mediation, fact finding, or other techniques that do not resort to binding arbitration. Although there is a technical distinction between mediation and conciliation, these forms of intervention are in practice difficult to distinguish between. The technical difference is that under conciliation the third party does not have the power to make a recommendation, whereas the mediator has this power but the parties have no obligation to accept his recommendation.

The article "Mediation and the Role of the Neutral" by Carl Stevens contains an in-depth analysis of the mediation process. According to Stevens, negotiations between the parties is an effort to map out the determinants of the basic power relationships between them without resorting to open conflict. Hopefully, the neutral party can intervene in this process and aid in the containment procedures without distorting the mapping out techniques. Some observers argue that the mediation role is an art that cannot be learned but must be applied according to the circumstances in each case. In this view, there can be no theory of mediation, because the role of the mediator is determined entirely by the talents of certain gifted individuals.

Stevens disagrees with this point of view. It is his belief that collective bargaining is sufficiently rational to make it possible to arrive at some basic principles concerning the conduct of the parties. Moreover, he argues, "unless an investigator has some theories about the agreement process—about why and in what ways the parties do and do not reach their own negotiations—it is difficult to see how he can analyze the contributions of the mediator to the settlement of their conflict."

Stevens defines two kinds of mediation—preventive and dispute. Preventive mediation, as the name implies, is designed to more effectively control conflict in order to prevent disputes, whereas dispute mediation is designed to resolve conflict after it occurs. Stevens is more concerned with the latter.

Stevens distinguishes several stages in the so-called negotiation cycle, pointing out that the role of the mediator is different in different stages. In the first stage, the parties are involved in mapping out the contract zone. "That is the range of outcomes both parties would prefer to a strike." During the middle stages of the negotiation cycle, the parties are actively involved in trying to move their adversaries closer to their own position, and the later stages are when the parties have exhausted these moves and therefore are close to strike deadlines. Although mediators might have a role to play in the earlier stages of the negotiation cycle, Stevens believes that a strong case can be made for late rather than early intervention, because it is at the later stages that the mediator's special professional competence would be most useful.

The bulk of Stevens' article is devoted to the tactics used by mediators to accomplish their primary objectives of helping the parties settle their disputes. These tactics include measures to give each party a more realistic appraisal of their environment and of the intention of the other party. However, as Stevens points out, a more realistic appraisal of the situation does not necessarily lead to conflict resolution. Sometimes the mediator might help produce a settlement through deception which, as Stevens points out, raises some serious moral problems about the nature of the mediation process. Helping the parties acquire a more realistic appraisal of the intentions of their adversaries is important because it can prevent unnecessary strikes, particularly when parties are convinced either that their bluffs will work or that their adversary is bluffing when, in fact, he is not. Under these circumstances the mediator can help resolve conflicts by persuading the parties of the nature of the situation. Similarly, the mediator can help by trying to arrive at the parties' real position which Stevens distinguishes from the parties' final position.

Another tactic used by mediators is proposing alternate solutions to resolve deadlocks. This can come about, for example, where mediators are able to use some ingenuity in affecting compromises that will resolve disputes. Stevens uses the example of the maintenance of membership compromise for disputes over the open and union shops. Mediators also might wish to propose alternate solutions when agreement between the parties is difficult because the deliberations are essentially indeterminate. In such circumstances, the mediator can help resolve the conflict by proposing an alternate solution or playing up a particular settlement that is within the range the parties prefer to no agreement.

Stevens also discusses the importance of separating the parties for separate discussions to permit the mediator to gain a better understanding of the conditions under which they might be willing to settle.

# Mediation and the Role of the Neutral

## by Carl M. Stevens[*]

Most analysis of mediation is essentially descriptive and pragmatic. There is little or no "theory of mediation. . . ."[1]

Until recently an agnosticism has prevailed toward analysis of these problems. For example, some experts in the field have asserted that, for one reason or another, mediation is not susceptible to systematic analysis. They have said that there are "no set rules"; that different mediators get equally good results by different methods; that each case is a law unto itself; and that the very "nature" of the mediation process does not permit generalization.[2]

❊　❊　❊

Some investigations of mediation, which have focused on the personal qualities of the mediator, may lead to the conclusion that the successful mediator is quick of mind and even of temper, has a good sense of humor, and knows and understands the industry and its problems. . . . While these qualities may be a necessary condition for successful performance, they are not also a sufficient condition; a successful mediator must have the specialized skills of conflict management.

Investigations of mediation have tended to focus directly and solely on the process itself. This orientation tends to obscure the fact that analysis of mediation can be most fruitful in the context of a general analysis of collective bargaining. The institution of mediation—including the prospect and availability of, as well as actual, intervention—is an integral part of collective bargaining.[3] That is, unless an in-

* Professor of Economics, Reed College.

vestigator has some theories about the agreement process—about why and in what ways the parties do, or do not, reach agreement in their own negotiations—it is difficult to see how he can analyze the contribution of the mediator to the settlement of their conflict.

* * *

Collective bargaining—like many other human relations—may be involved with nonrationality. If, however, the investigator were to view collective bargaining and the parties to it as dominated by the non-rational, he could not usefully analyze the problems confronted by the mediator.[4] I believe that, although nonrationality must be recognized as potentially important, rationality is sufficiently dominant to make my analysis meaningful. . . .

### The Domain of Inquiry: What Constitutes Mediation?

. . . As comprehended by the Mediation Service, preventive mediation includes involvement by mediators in the following activities: continuing liaison with labor and management officials in a specific industry or company; prenegotiation contract discussions; postnegotiation contract review; joint labor-management committees; labor-management conferences; special consultative and advisory services; and training activities. . . .[5]

[T]he rationale for preventive mediation seems straightforward. Like disputes mediation, it is aimed at more effective control of the conflict inherent in our industrial relations system.

* * *

My primary concern is with disputes mediation as distinguished from preventive mediation. . . . For purposes of this discussion, I have in mind intervention at some stage of a particular set of negotiations in progress—rather than, for example, prenegotiation intervention. However, my disputes-mediation category includes instances of what might be termed "early" intervention—as well as intervention at the time of a deadlock.

## MEDIATION FUNCTIONS AND TACTICS

### Timing of Intervention

. . . In analyzing the timing problem, it will prove helpful to recognize a phenomenon that may be termed the "negotiation cycle." While no two instances of collective bargaining negotiation are precisely the same, a number of investigators have suggested that there tends to be a progression of events, a succession of stages common to many contract negotiations.[6]

. . . This description of the negotiation process implies that the mediator may be expected to serve different functions and may be involved in different tactics depending upon when he enters; his timing may have an important bearing on the appropriateness of his intervention. . . .

Two functions may be selected as characteristic of the early stages of negotiation. Some investigators have suggested that these stages are dominated by the negotiators' roles as delegates: that these stages emphasize interparty conflict as contrasted with greater emphasis upon interpersonal (negotiators *qua* negotiators) interaction.[7]

They have also emphasized that it is important, during the early stages, to perform the information-giving-and-seeking job of blocking out the contract zone—that is, the range of outcomes both parties would prefer to a strike.

The middle stages involve the most active tactical play of the negotiation game. Having determined in a general way where his opposite number stands, each party begins to consolidate his own position and to move his opposite number in a direction favorable to himself. The parties may be viewed as "operating" upon each other by means of various tactics—

such as persuasion, rationalization, bluffs, threats, promises, and so forth.

The later stages precede an impending strike deadline. As the negotiations have proceeded, it is to be hoped that the information picture has cleared somewhat, and that any contract zone has become outlined at least to some degree. Also as the negotiations proceed, the competitive tactics available to each side are being used and may be "used up" by the later stages. For example, threats have been tried, and the results have been pretty well determined. The approach of the deadline tends to eliminate bluff as tactic. One may distinguish a number of special-agreement problems which are likely to confront the parties at or just prior to the strike deadline; some of these will be discussed in subsequent sections.

We may conclude roughly that if the mediator enters the early stages of negotiation, he will be involved primarily with "grandstanding" and with the initial giving and seeking of information. If he enters in the middle stages, he will find himself in the most active tactical phase and may well be actively involved with the tactical operations of the parties themselves. If he enters during the later stages, he will confront one or more of the special agreement problems confronted by the parties and his task will be to help to solve them.

A detailed analysis of the timing problem cannot be undertaken here, but some general implications of the foregoing discussion should be pointed out. An adequate analysis of the timing problem must be referred to some general analysis of the negotiation cycle and of the negotiation functions served by various parts of that cycle. Some discussions of the timing problem imply that the mediator should fill more or less the same functions whether he enters early or late—the significant difference being that the discharge of each becomes easier or harder, depending upon early or late intervention. I have implied that the mediator will serve, at least as regards emphasis, very different functions, depending upon when he enters.

❊   ❊   ❊

## Persuasion I—The Parties' Perception of the Environment

Persuasion is frequently identified as an important mediation tactic. The parties may disagree over the facts—the cost of living, comparative rates, productivity, and so on. The mediator may help them to set the record straight or at least to minimize nonfruitful ways of managing such types of disagreement.

If appeals to the facts in negotiations are usually mere window dressing, serving as rationalizations for the power positions of the parties, then persuasion—in the sense of persuading a party that the facts are other than what he has been contending they are—will not be a potent tactic, in the hands either of the negotiating parties or of the mediator.

Many of the most important "facts" describe the outcome of various courses of action—outcomes that can be known only in terms of probability. Persuasion operating on this front may well modify the parties' appraisal of the power situation. The parties, particularly if they are new to collective bargaining, may underestimate the cost of a strike or a lockout or overestimate the cost of an agreement with their opponent upon the latter's terms; the mediator may assist them to see the realities of the situation. If the parties can be led to agreement in the light of a realistic appraisal of the costs and gains associated with alternative courses of action, the mediator serves a real and important function.[8]

❊   ❊   ❊

An awkward problem may arise if the mediator resorts to persuasion. Does he have a direct interest in bringing the parties to a realistic appraisal of the situation? If his objective is to induce them to agree, a realistic appraisal might in some situations be a means to this end. However, in other situations, bringing them to a nonrealistic appraisal might also be a means to this end: that is, a party might be brought to agreement if he were persuaded to overestimate the cost of a strike, to underestimate the gains to be had thereby, and to underestimate the cost of agreement with the opponent upon the latter's terms. Here the mediator would be abetting the agreement process by deception. (Let me make it clear at this point that, in recognizing this possibility, I in no way intend to advocate that a mediator engage in deception.)

*Persuasion II—Mediator Involvement with the Coercive Tactics of the Parties*

Frequently tactics of coercion are based upon bluff, and mediation tactics may involve the relationship of the mediator to the bluff tactics of the parties. The mediator's involvement in this situation might be quite deliberate. Suppose, for example, that agreement is impeded because one party believes that his bluff about willingness to take a strike, or to continue a strike indefinitely, will prevail and bring the other party to terms. He would make a concession if he did not believe in the strength of his bluff weapon. The mediator might be able to diagnose the bluffing party's true intentions, so advise the opposing party, and then advise the first party that its bluff is no longer effective. At this juncture an awkward problem arises once more. Presumably the mediator does not have a direct interest in eliminating bluff from negotiations. Presumably his objective is to bring the parties to agreement. Elimination of bluff may be a means to this end. It might be, however, that deliberately neglecting so to do will also be a means to this end. Thus the party might capitulate if he did

not suspect that his opponent was bluffing. The mediator, aware that the opponent was bluffing, might neglect to convey this information—or might even undertake to convince the party that this was not the case. . . .

A different negotiation problem is how to "not-bluff" successfully—that is, how one party can successfully convince his opponent that his stated intentions are his true ones. A party intending to strike in a contingency may state his intentions, but the mere statement does not always convince the other. Why should his opposite number believe him? After all, he may be bluffing.

Failure in dealing with this tactical problem may lead to a certain kind of "unnecessary" strike. Suppose that the opponent refuses to concede and reach agreement because he thinks the other's strike threat is a bluff—but he would have conceded if he had known that the threat was real. Of course, if the strike does eventuate, the opponent will learn the truth; but this kind of strike is unnecessary in that, had some other means for conveying the truth been available, it would not have taken place.

Potentially the mediator has a clear-cut contribution to make to this kind of case. He may be able to determine the party's true intentions and so advise the opponent, who may believe the mediator even though he did not believe the party. In using this tactic, the mediator is once more involved with the parties' negotiation game; that is, he is playing a supporting role to not-bluff tactics. It is an interesting question and pertinent to the concept of neutrality whether a mediator's support of not-bluff tactics should be viewed as more privileged or legitimate than his support of bluff tactics.

Perhaps of more importance is the possibility of inadvertent mediator involvement in the tactics of the parties. A mediator in a bluff situation should guard against becoming an unwiting tool of either or both of the parties. A party may have only partially succeeded in making its bluff convincing to the opposite number. If, however, that party can successfully bluff the mediator, he may enlist the mediator as an unwitting ally in his deception.

## A Note Regarding Neutrality

As I have said, I have no intention of advocating that a mediator employ the tactics of deception and coercion. Nevertheless, in an analysis of mediation it is important to draw attention to these possibilities. . . .

Yet, when the mediator intervenes in collective bargaining negotiation, he intervenes in a game of strategy. Surely—and whatever the ultimate conclusions about the mediator's proper function—the mediator's role must be analyzed from this point of view. In their own negotiation the parties operate upon each other through various tactics; and the mediator may find himself involved in any of the aspects of the tactical play.

Discussion with labor and management representatives and with mediators has led me to conclude that these aspects of the mediation situation hold not only in theory but also in actual fact. If this is so, it seems clear that much analysis and discussion of mediation is misleading.

These considerations throw light on the problem of mediator neutrality. Ann Douglas, in discussing the invention of "fictions" about the mediation process, has observed that the claim of neutrality enjoys such widespread credence among mediators that it could almost be said to be a universal in the profession.[9] The "Code of Professional Conduct for Labor Mediators" contains a proviso that presumably relates to the neutrality issue: "Since mediation is essentially a voluntary process, the acceptability of the mediator by the parties as a person of integrity, objectivity,

and fairness is absolutely essential to the effective performance of the duties of the mediator."[10] Although the general thrust of this language is discernible, it is not really very clear as regards particulars. It does not by itself spell out, nor should it be expected to, what particular mediator behaviors and tactics are to be deemed objective, fair or professional.

In Douglas' view, the essential function of this fiction is to shield the mediator from responsibility for the outcome of mediated negotiation, to "purge the mediator of liability for the course of treatment regardless of whether the patient gets well or succumbs." Perhaps this is one facet of mediator neutrality. (Would members of the mediation profession agree?) In any event this line of thought raises some interesting questions about criteria for successful mediation. (Can members of the mediation profession state these criteria?)

Other aspects of the neutrality claim may also be critical. If it is taken to *disclaim* any influence on the substantive outcome of negotiations, then this claim is probably fiction. However, it can be more narrowly construed to imply that the mediator does not deliberately either become involved with the bluff or other tactics of the parties or distort the realities of the negotiation and extranegotiation environment as he sees them—even though doing so might help him achieve his objective of bringing the parties to agreement. Abjuring these tactics still leaves plenty of scope for an active and inventive agent in the negotiation. The "Code of Professional Conduct for Labor Mediators" suggests one significance of neutrality in this context: the acceptability of the institution of mediation by the parties. It seems doubtful that both parties to a dispute would desire to admit a third party known to use such tactics.

A second and somewhat more subtle significance of this version of mediator neutrality has to do with the mediator's neutral posture toward "nature"—the extranegotiation context of the dispute. Within limits, the basic determinants of the outcome of negotiation are the determinants of the basic power relations. Negotiation is a technique for mapping or incorporating these determinants into the outcome, while at the same time containing the conflict short of industrial warfare. It might be argued that the mediator's proper function is to abet the containment process but not to distort the mapping process. He might well distort the latter if he were "non-neutral" and deliberately distorted realities of the negotiation and extranegotiation environment as he saw them; that is, he might distort the legitimate determinants of the outcome.

Closely allied to this, but with a somewhat different implication for motive and function, is that interpretation of neutrality which calls for the mediator to be the servant of the parties rather than, for example, the servant of the public. The mediator intervenes to help the parties achieve their own solution, and an agreement upon one set of terms is as good as an agreement upon any other set so long as it is achieved without resort to direct action.[11]

The "Code of Professional Conduct for Labor Mediators" raises some questions for this particular version of mediator neutrality. Noting that the primary purpose of mediation is to assist the parties to reach agreement, the code goes on to provide: "However, the mediation process may include a responsibility to support the interest of the public that a particular dispute be settled, that a work stoppage be ended, and that normal operations be resumed." In this role the mediator would be a servant of the public as well as of the parties—attempting to protect the former's interest in normal operations rather than in shutdowns.

Some interesting questions about the mediation process and the concept of neutrality are raised by this line of thought. If the mediator is to serve both the parties and the public, does he not have to balance the interests of the one against those of the other? If so, what standards should guide him in maintaining this balance? For example, could a case arise where the public interest was so overwhelming that the mediator might feel justified in somewhat attenuating his neutrality in the interparty sense? Furthermore, it is sometimes pointed out that the public has at least as important an interest in the substantive outcome of collective bargaining as it does in the question whether the outcome is achieved with or without resort to direct action. An instance of this is the public's interest in economic stability. Does the concept of the mediator as partly a servant of the public permit an extension of this part of his cognizance beyond the matter of stoppage versus no stoppage, to other aspects of the public interest?[12]

A somewhat different question, in this same general area, may arise with respect to the mediator's responsibilities to public policy in cases where the parties are attempting to negotiate an illegal agreement, such as one containing prohibited discrimination. Some experts consider that there are instances where the mediator might well be obligated to serve the public interest—as in the case of negotiating an illegal agreement in an important public policy area. But presumably there are other cases where the mediator would not have this responsibility to public policy. The problem is to design a set of principles that would adequately discriminate between the two situations.

## Saving Face and One Function of Rationalization

. . . As Kerr has pointed out, the mere entrance of a mediator into a dispute is in some ways a face-saving device.[13] In an ambiguous situation, the implication that the battle was so hard fought that a mediator had to be brought in may be helpful. More important perhaps, the mediator may share some of the responsibility for the outcome and thereby decrease the responsibility of the parties. He might do this, for example, by making recommendations for a settlement for which he will take responsibility and, if need be, pursuant to this end, public responsibility.

More subtle functions of the mediator in attempting to undo the commitment may be viewed as instances of the negotiation tactic termed "rationalization." For example, if a demand has been wedded to a principle and thereby committed, the mediator might attempt to cut the demand loose by showing that it is not a case in point of the principle. Also, Schelling has suggested that a party attempting to release an opponent from a commitment might confuse the commitment so that party's principals cannot identify compliance with it.[14] The mediator might use the same tactics: he might show that a given standard—cost of living, ability to pay, productivity, comparative rates, etc.—is ambiguous; or that a given package is not really inflationary, thereby providing the party opposing the package on this ground with a set of arguments he can use to show that he miscalculated his commitment.

The foregoing suggestions do not exhaust the possibilities of rationalization. We should note here that to make a useful analysis of the concept of saving face as a mediation tactic, it must be examined in *very particular* terms.

### Proposing the Alternate Solution

. . . This situation involves problems of definition; that is, although the parties want approximately the same terms of settlement, they may have difficulty defining their respective positions in specific institutional terms. It is the function of the mediator to help the parties make their respective definitions, and it requires all a mediator's inventiveness to do this.

Evolution of the maintenance-of-membership provision in collective agreements seems an excellent case of resolution of conflict by definition of a position in equilibrium. Suppose that a management is insisting upon the open shop, while a union is insisting upon the union shop. Each might be willing to compromise his ostensible position, but what kind of shop can be a compromise between the open shop and the union shop? Some shrewdness with respect to the design of institutions may be necessary to come up with an answer to this kind of question—as, for example, by proposing maintenance of membership. Seniority and wage-incentive plans are other areas where institutional complexity may require this particular mediator function.

. . . Once he understands the parties' objectives in more general terms, the mediator may be able to come up with the alternate solution. And once the parties understand their own objectives in more general terms, they may be prepared to accept that alternate.

### Separating the Parties—and More About the Alternate Solution

It is frequently pointed out that separating the parties may be at times a useful mediation technique. Separate caucuses provide forums where the mediator may receive confidential and privileged communications from each party. Also, as Jackson points out in connection with the alternate solution, this technique gives the mediator an opportunity to get each party to adopt the solution as his own, thus avoiding the danger, inherent in making the suggestion to both parties simultaneously, that one party might embrace it and the other feel impelled to oppose it. The control of the communication structure achieved by separating the parties may more generally facilitate attempts at persuasion and also coercion.[15]

In this section I want particularly to draw attention to an aspect of the technique of separating the parties which is less frequently discussed. This aspect relates to the resolution of another of the special agreement problems: how can the parties be brought to agree when their deliberations have become essentially indeterminant?

This is a situation in collective bargaining analogous to the so-called "pure" bargaining game. Suppose there exists a manifest contract zone—that is, a range of outcomes preferred by both parties to no agreement—and both parties know this. This situation is indeterminant in that at least one of the parties would be willing to retreat from each of the potential solutions —those within the contract zone—rather than accept no agreement as the outcome.

Mediation in the face of the manifest contract zone has been recognized as a difficult problem. Kerr remarks:

*A particularly difficult controversy to mediate, strangely enough, is one in which the costs of aggressive conflict to each party are enormous. Then any one of many solutions is better than a strike and the process of narrowing these possible solutions to a single one is an arduous task.*[16]

One possible approach to this problem is along lines suggested by T. C. Schelling.[17] First, Schelling has suggested that the solution to a negotiation of this kind is best viewed as the consequence of convergence of the parties' expectations about what will or must be the outcome. Thus, a party expects a particular outcome within the contract zone to be the solution, because he expects—in spite of the circumstances of the pure-bargaining game —his opposite number to yield no more. If the opposite number shares these expectations with respect to that outcome, then their expectations converge, and that out-

come is the solution. Schelling suggests that the "prominence"—denoting such properties as simplicity, uniqueness, precedent, and so forth—of a particular outcome may serve to establish such expectations.

In addition, there are consequences of what Schelling terms "tacit bargaining." Tacit bargaining refers generally to negotiations in which there is no explicit communication between the players. Collective bargaining is a "mixed" process; that is, it is neither purely competitive nor purely co-operative but combines both elements. There is the possibility that resort to tacit, rather than explicit, bargaining may force elements of co-operation to the fore. Thus, the mediation tactic of converting collective bargaining negotiation into instances of tacit bargaining—for example, by separating the parties—may be helpful in reaching agreement when negotiations have become indeterminant.

Moreover, as I have suggested, in such indeterminant situations it is the prominence of one of the potential outcomes in the contract zone which compels the parties' expectations to converge upon it. This points to another aspect of the mediator's function in this kind of agreement problem. A mediator wishing to use the tacit-bargaining approach may first have to set the situation up by playing an active role—by deliberately contriving to attribute prominence to a particular position.

* * *

## Determining the Real Positions of the Parties

It is sometimes suggested that the mediator's ability to determine the real positions of the parties is a valuable adjunct to his management of a dispute. By a party's "real" position, I mean those terms least favorable to himself that he would be willing to accept rather than to take a strike. By a party's "final" position, I mean the last offer he has put on the table prior to the intervention of the mediator. Now let us suppose that the mediator, wittingly or unwittingly, confronts a problem of the following kind. Although the parties have failed to reach agreement on the basis of their final positions, their real positions—that of each unknown to the other—intersect. In this situation the mediator has potentially a clear-cut role to play. If he can determine the real positions of the parties, he can simply inform them that they are in agreement.[18]

Are the parties likely to reach a deadlock on such a basis? This question should be answered at the level of empirical generalization, and perhaps experienced mediators can throw some light upon it. Analysis of collective bargaining negotiations suggests that such agreement problems are unlikely to arise.

Although space will not permit an elaboration of these points, I may suggest some of the reasons that a party may stand on a final position more favorable to himself than is his real position: (1) to announce his real position (a retreat from an ostensible final position) may be prejudicial in that it may be interpreted as a sign of weakness; (2) an advantage may go to the party who waits for his opposite number to make a last proposal—for example, the party may find that it is more favorable to himself than would have been his own last proposal had he been the first to make such; (3) the party may consider either a strike or mediation a possibility and may wish to "save something" for either eventuality.

One would expect that the nature of this aspect of the mediator's relation with the parties would depend in part upon the way, if any, in which they wish to incorporate him into their own negotiation tactics. For example, one or both of the parties may want deliberately to involve him. Thus, generally a party will consider that it does not serve his own best interests to inform the mediator of his real position. Indeed, it is more realistic to assume that the parties are typically reluctant to reveal their true positions to the mediator. An experienced negotiator has commented that revealing the position in this way "would be just the same thing as publishing it." Thus, if the mediator is to learn the parties' true positions, he will have to infer or deduce them much as if he were himself a party to the negotiations. It is an interesting aspect of the mediation process that the mediator should be expected to play this kind of game.

CONCLUSION

Let me now briefly refer back to the problem of the timing of intervention of mediation with which this discussion opened. A case for late, rather than early, intervention might be constructed on the grounds that the mediator's special professional competence lies precisely in dealing with those special agreement problems that are likely to arise in the later pre-deadline stages of negotiation.

\* \* \*

This does not imply that prenegotiation consultation and concern with the design of bargaining institutions is not important for industrial peace and acceptable substantive outcomes of negotiations. Nor does it imply that persons who are mediators have no role to play in this activity.

Necessity is the mother of social invention, and awareness of necessity on the part of participants in social institutions will prompt them to evolve their own solutions by changing techniques and processes. This is desirable. However—particularly in the case of complex social institutions operating in a rapidly changing environment (such as collective bargaining)—the process of achieving fruitful social innovation might be assisted by the analysis and recommendations of investigators and consultants. Some term other than "mediation" should be applied to such assistance.

*A Note on the Mediator and Voluntary Arbitration*

On this topic Jackson comments:

*A mediator may find an opportunity to suggest that the parties submit their dispute to voluntary arbitration. The mere statement of this alternative is seldom sufficient. If presented at all, it should be accompanied by an attempt to get the parties to agree at least on the items they are willing to arbitrate and to draw up a stipulation of the issues and criteria as guides to the arbitrator.[19]*

Another sense in which the mere statement of this alternative may not be sufficient is involved with the mediator's diagnostic powers in relation to the functions of voluntary arbitration. Under what conditions might it be in the interest of the parties to submit to voluntary arbitration when their own direct negotiations or their mediated negotiations have failed? The mediator who can answer that question has available, potentially at least, a legitimate way in which to induce the parties to arbitrate.

✿ ✿ ✿

## Notes

[1] Shister, surveying recent collective bargaining research, has expressed the opinion that, in light of practical developments in the field, one might reasonably assume that studies of the dynamics of mediation would be most plentiful; but that the exact opposite is true. See Joseph Shister, "Collective Bargaining," *A Decade of Industrial Relations Research—1946–1956*, Neil W. Chamberlain, Frank E. Pierson, and Theresa Wolfson, eds. (New York: Harper & Brothers, 1958), p. 35. See also *Mediation and Mediators: A Summary of Published Materials* (Washington, D.C.: Federal Mediation and Conciliation Service, revised May, 1965).

[2] Of course, not all students of mediation share this agnosticism. See, for example, Appendix II, "Some Suggestions for Social Science Research," in Elmore Jackson, *Meeting of Minds—A Way to Peace through Mediation* (New York: McGraw-Hill Book Company, Inc., 1952). One is struck, however, by Jackson's defensive and almost apologetic tone in suggesting that social science research might contribute something beyond the pragmatic analysis undertaken in the volume.

[3] To avoid misunderstanding, it should be noted that this statement does not say or imply that mediated negotiation is "the same thing" as nonmediated negotiation. See the remarks of Herbert R. Northrup, "Mediation—the Viewpoint of the Mediated," *Labor Law Journal* (October, 1962), p. 833.

[4] Some nonrational behavior can be systematically analyzed—for example, some conflict-choice behavior, which is nonrational in that the choice does not turn, in any direct and simple sense, on maximizing a utility index. Moreover, analysis can suggest some ways of mediating such choice problems—for example, by passing the problem on to a third party who, being himself uninvolved, can come up with a solution. This chapter will undertake no analysis along these lines.

[5] See *Seventeenth Annual Report*, Federal Mediation and Conciliation Service, 1964, pp. 23ff.

[6] See, for example, John T. Dunlop and James J. Healy, *Collective Bargaining: Principles and Cases*, revised edition (Homewood, Illinois: Richard D. Irwin, Inc., 1955), pp. 61ff., for a discussion of the stages of typical contract negotiation. See also Carl M. Stevens, *Strategy in Collective Bargaining Negotiation* (New York: McGraw-Hill Book Company, 1963), whose discussion is organized around the concept of "early" and "later" stages in negotiation. My discussion in various places leans upon and borrows from the analysis developed in this book. The reader should consult it for further discussion of some of my points as well as of related points.

[7] See, for example, Ann Douglas, "What Can Research Tell Us About Mediation," *Labor Law Journal* (August, 1955).

The frequent use of the term "grandstanding" with reference to this stage should not obscure the fact that performance during this stage may be functional for the negotiator's role as delegate. For example, Stagner has pointed out that "ritualistic" attacks upon the employer during negotiation may serve the union officials' "role of spokesman for feelings, demands, hostilities, and insecurities among the workers." See Ross Stagner, *Psychology of Industrial Conflict* (New York: John Wiley and Sons, Inc., 1956), pp. 241–242.

[8] This is a part of what Clark Kerr ("Industrial Conflict and Its Mediation," *The American Journal of Sociology*, November 1954, p. 837) terms "removal of nonrationality." Jackson (*op. cit.*, pp. 32–33) identifies as important aspects of the mediator's persuasion tactic "factual deflation" and "raising doubt in the minds of the parties about positions already assumed."

[9] Douglas, *op. cit.*, p. 550.

[10] See William E. Simkin, "Code of Professional Conduct for Labor Mediators," *Labor Law Journal* (October, 1964).

[11] Edgar L. Warren ("Mediation and Fact Finding," in *Industrial Conflict*, A. W. Kornhauser, R. Dubin and A. Ross, eds. [New York: McGraw-Hill Book Company, 1954], chap. xxii, p. 295) has commented "Unlike the parties, the mediator is not concerned with the content of the settlement. This fact is his greatest strength."

[12] This is a question of some immediate practical significance. The question sometimes arises whether the Federal Mediation and Conciliation Service has any directives from the Labor Department or elsewhere concerning the guidelines that are currently a prominent feature of the Administration's approach to holding the line on inflation. It appears that there are no such formal directives, but some participants in collective bargaining (including third parties) apparently feel that there is informal tension and pressure on this score between the Mediation Service and such bodies as the President's Council of Economic Advisors.

[13] Kerr (*op. cit.*, p. 238) discusses the face-saving function of mediation, including the aspect of sharing responsibility for the outcome.

[14] See Thomas C. Schelling, "Bargaining Communication and Limited War," *The Journal of Conflict Resolution* (March, 1957).

[15] See Bernard Wilson, "Conciliation Officers' Techniques in Settling Disputes" (paper prepared for discussion at the 18th Annual Conference of the Canadian Association of Administrators of Labor Legislation, Quebec, 1959).

[16] See Kerr, *op. cit.*, p. 239. He attributed this point to A. C. Pigou, *The Economics of Welfare* 4th Edition (London: Macmillan and Company Ltd., 1938).

[17] See T. C. Schelling, "The Strategy of Conflict Prospectus," *The Journal of Conflict Resolution* (September, 1958). See also his *The Strategy of Conflict* (Cambridge: Harvard University Press, 1960).

[18] As a way to cope with this agreement problem, the writer has elsewhere suggested the possible utility of a special kind of mediation device: a neutral third party might be continuously informed, during the negotiations, of the true positions of the parties; the sole function of this third party would be to receive this information and to inform the parties of it when they had achieved the necessary conditions for agreement. ("On the Theory of Negotiation," *Quarterly Journal of Economics* [November, 1958].)

[19] Jackson, *op. cit.*, p. 38.

### Collective Bargaining and Community Disputes

The growth of community conflicts, especially over civil rights and student affairs, has led to a search for ways to contain physical conflict in favor of peaceful settlement of differences. Negotiation, mediation, conciliation, and arbitration are natural suggestions because of their effectiveness in the industrial relations field. In "Collective Bargaining and Community Disputes," Theodore Kheel, one of the nation's leading arbitrators and mediators, and a founder of the Institute on Collective Bargaining and Group Relations, discusses the transferability of negotiations and dispute settlement techniques from collective bargaining to community relations.

As Kheel emphasizes, there are many similarities and differences between industrial and community disputes. The differences are particularly important, and stem mainly from the lack of simplicity and structure in community disputes; representation, prerogatives, and recognition problems are especially hard to resolve. In racial disputes, for example, negotiations are very difficult because there are rarely spokesmen for the black communities who are authorized to negotiate with the "establishment," and the parties sometimes have very limited understanding of opposing positions and often have little desire to effect compromises. Some black leaders even argue that the concept of negotiation, because it assumes that fundamental non-negotiable rights will be compromised, is contrary to the interests of blacks. It is also difficult for third parties to mediate race disputes because these conflicts lack the "natural histories" helpful to mediators in other cases.

In order to facilitate mediation, Kheel proposes a Board of Mediation for Community Conflicts in the more populous communities. Such a board would not be "a panacea but . . . a useful addition to other techniques to help contain and conclude community conflicts." Kheel also suggests a number of areas where research can facilitate the application of collective bargaining techniques to community affairs.

The need for a means to resolve disputes involving urban blacks and the poor in general led to the establishment of the Center for Dispute Settlement (CDS) in Washington, D.C. in 1968 by the American Arbitration Association under a grant from the Ford Foundation. In "A New Center for Dispute Settlement," Samuel Jackson discusses the philosophy behind the CDS.

In "Mediation: A Path to Campus Peace," Sam Zagoria, a member of the National Labor Relations Board, concludes: "The techniques of labor-management relations will not cure all student-administration problems but should minimize and deflate many."

# Collective Bargaining and Community Disputes

## by Theodore W. Kheel

Uncontained conflict now threatens to rip the fabric binding our society. The lesson of this past year is clear: We must improve our capacity to accommodate competing claims if we are to resolve community disputes. And we must find a way to resolve such disputes if we are to survive.

In one area of group conflicts, labor and management have developed a system of dispute settlement which, over several decades, has steadily improved its capacity to achieve peaceful accommodations. Even though it comes under attack from time to time, especially when a strike threatens to inconvenience the public, this system of collective bargaining works far better than most people realize, producing agreements and stable relationships in more than 99 percent of all negotiations.

LESSONS PUT TO USE

Collective bargaining is particularly designed for the reconciliation of group differences that are not susceptible to solution through the dictates of law. Although a law can set guidelines, it cannot resolve the claims of competing groups that fall within the framework of these legal standards. In such circumstances, the conflicting demands can be resolved only by an accommodation that is mutually acceptable. The alternative is total defeat for one side or the other, hardly a desirable outcome where claims are legal and interests are legitimate.

Disputes over wages or other financial provisions of a collective bargaining contract cannot be settled by resort to a ready legal standard. Not only is there no legal basis for requiring or not requiring such

SOURCE Reprinted with permission from *Monthly Labor Review,* Vol. 92, No. 1, January 1969.

adjustments, but their variety is so infinite as to make imposition by law an impossibility. Similarly, questions of student participation in university policy or the scope of a local community's role in running the public schools cannot be evolved solely by reference to law. Some other way must be found.

As concerted action by community organizations becomes a more frequent technique, it is worth asking to what extent our experience with collective bargaining and mediation in industrial relations is transferable and useful in such community disputes.

This question has been posed by the newly created Institute of Collective Bargaining and Group Relations, a labor-management organization formed in the belief that there is no viable alternative to collective bargaining in a democratic society. The Institute has two primary objectives: To make collective bargaining work better because obviously there is room for improvement, and to give the public a better understanding of how collective bargaining operates and why it is so important to our society.

The Institute proposes to examine the extent to which the experience of labor and management with collective bargaining can be effectively transferred to other relationships, notably between and among racial, religious, and neighborhood groups. As the Institute has noted, the first national strike took place in 1873 and was marked by violence and strife comparable to, if not greater than, the disorders we have witnessed in our ghettos in recent summers. Nor were the ensuing years peaceful. In the course of time, labor and management, aided by laws to curb extremists, have developed ways of negotiating so that today even the bitterest strike looks like an example of exemplary deportment compared with long-ago struggles. In this development, the Institute believes, there are lessons we can use elsewhere.

## SIMILARITIES AND DIFFERENCES

There are some obvious similarities as well as differences between collective bargaining in labor-management disputes and negotiations in community conflicts. It is important to study these to determine how collective bargaining can be applied to community disagreements.

In both cases accommodation of conflicting interests involves bargaining and therefore communication between groups of people or, more accurately, between their representatives. Collective bargaining depends on "group talk," a technique for communication through spokesmen which is quite different from normal talk among individuals. A representative has a dual responsibility and a dual concern. He must bargain with the other side for the best deal he can get. At the same time, he must make sure that the people he speaks for are satisfied that he has represented their cause effectively. As a result, a group leader may at times exaggerate his position and at other times wish to back down. His flexibility at the bargaining table will often depend on the security of his position within his own organization. The leader with a precarious hold on his followers frequently resorts to greater militancy and intransigence.

Moreover, what is said at the bargaining table must in turn be conveyed to the entire group. If discussion proceeds too quickly, the reporting process breaks down. The traditional media of communication—newspapers, television, and radio—are useful but sometimes misleading channels for informing the rank and file. The news media must report the news as general information for the public, even though their accounts might complicate the reporting functions of participating groups. Timing in communication is critically important for group understanding. In short, there are complications in group relationships not present when two individuals are bargaining solely in their own behalf and have no constituency to whom they must answer in a controversy that does not have widespread public interest.

## ROLE OF LEADERS

Group communications tend to be more difficult if the leadership is inexperienced or insecure. This may be the case even in long established organizations. It was prevalent in the early days of collective bargaining and is now common in community disputes where the leaders have just emerged, asserted power, and find themselves surrounded by others eager to replace them. As a consequence, there is often uncertainty as to who does speak for the community. This will undoubtedly change with time as it has in labor-management affairs, but it is, at present, a reality of existing controversies involving new community organizations which must be taken into account.

Labor organizations in both public and private employment sometimes find themselves faced with dissident groups who may prompt the rank and file to reject agreements reached by their leaders. But such disagreements are for the most part contained within the framework of a single organization. The procedures of the National Labor Relations Act are designed to lead to the selection of a single representative organization, with the exclusive right and obligation to speak for all of the employees in an appropriate bargaining unit. While this does not solve the problems of leadership within the organization, it does confine the area of possible dispute. It is doubtful that the same procedures can be used in community disputes; however, a means of identifying the truly representative leaders must be found.

There are, in addition, other restraints in labor and management affairs which simplify bargaining procedures. The issues tend to be traditional, usually involving financial questions, and the area of appropriate concern for unions in the affairs of companies has been fairly well defined

with the passage of time. As a result, unions today generally recognize the prerogatives that are properly reserved to management; and companies readily negotiate with unions on "wages, hours, and working conditions," the area defined by law as bargainable. Time will probably serve to help identify the proper area of legitimate concern for the participants in community controversies. But the variety is so much greater than in the industrial arena that claims of prerogative will likely continue to be more common and enduring. This merely underscores the importance of finding ways to resolve such disputes.

## MUTUAL ACCEPTANCE

An additional assumption by both unions and companies facilitates bargaining and, indeed, makes accommodation not only possible but inevitable: It is their mutual recognition that an agreement must be reached because they cannot exist without each other. Only in rare instances does the instinct to destroy an opponent appear. Practically all employers today are mainly interested in a settlement they can live with, so that production is not interrupted. Employees also seek an accord, so that their work and pay will not be stopped. Of course, this is an oversimplification of what is a complicated and can still be an antagonistic relationship, understandable only in light of such miscellaneous factors as the psychology of the parties, their past relations, the extent of strike benefits available, the issues in dispute, the role of the international organization and the corporate hierarchy, the state of the job market, and other factors.

The point is that an industrial dispute today is relatively confined in structure, compared with many community conflicts, and is based on mutual acceptance by the participants and on a defined area of negotiation. Moreover, the structure is supported by the legal procedures established for the selection of bargaining representatives and by the important doctrine embodied in the Wagner Act which grants exclusive recognition to the agent picked as spokesman for the employees.

In community conflicts, dozens of rival organizations, groups, and individuals may compete for public support. They may be aligned with certain public officials or programs, or arrayed against them. Groups involved in community disputes are sometimes committed to a rigid accomplishment of their goal. For reasons of ideology or political necessity they sometimes lack sufficient incentive to reach an agreement by accommodation. They think they must seek total victory and total defeat of the adversary, even though accommodation is needed.

Unlike industrial relations, where bargaining is limited by statute to questions of wages, hours, and working conditions, the range of subjects appropriate for bargaining in community disputes is without such limit or definition. The potential for explosion over such emotional issues combined with a less defined structure tends to make bargaining a much more hazardous undertaking. This is frequently exacerbated by the tendency of persons in the community at large to take sides and join in the general clamor, sometimes expressing themselves so emphatically in advertisements, statements, and editorial comments that adversaries become more determined than ever to prevail. This tendency to take sides and to join warring camps is unfortunate. The need for some community leaders to remain neutral and objective is great, and the equities of the opposing sides are not all that clear and unambiguous.

These elements exist in labor-management disputes but they are currently more intense and commonplace in community conflicts. The result is that any attempt to promote careful bargaining or effective mediation must navigate far more treacherous waters than are now present in disputes between workers and their employers, no matter how difficult such disputes may appear to be.

## NEW YORK SCHOOL DISPUTE

There is indisputable need to establish bargaining relationships in community disputes. The conflict of the teachers with local community groups over the decentralization of the vast public school system in New York City in 1968 involved, as finally revealed, though always present, legitimate but overlapping interests that must ultimately be resolved in a bargaining relationship. No one can gainsay the right of local parent groups to a greater voice in educational programs for their children. Nor can anyone deny the right of teachers to protection against arbitrary dismissals or transfers by local officials. The long confrontation in New York City was in large part a result of the failure of all concerned to recognize these legitimate claims and interests from the beginning. Instead, the impression grew that the union was out to stop decentralization and that the local community wanted to destroy the union. Whether or not these were the facts became irrelevant. Each side believed the adversary was out for the kill and acted upon this belief; yet neither could ultimately achieve its objectives without the other.

In the absence of this basic recognition which pervades practically all labor disputes, the conflict steadily worsened, ultimately involving almost everyone in the city on one side or the other. Few were left who could be looked upon as neutrals available to mediate.

The role of public officials was particularly difficult. Should they be mediators or should they become the spokesmen for the point of view they believed to be right? Obviously they should be both, but how a public official, especially the chief magistrate of a community, can pursue both objectives simultaneously is a difficult question to answer. Because settlements *must* be reached and the wounds inflicted by such conflicts must be allowed to heal, the role of public officials is critical. They can be important aids or obstacles to a settlement.

## ROLE OF MEDIATION

In practically all labor disputes, mediation plays a regular and useful role. It is not a substitute for bargaining but an aid to it. It is one of the reasons that labor disputes, regardless of their complexity, are invariably brought to a reasonably balanced conclusion.

Introducing mediation, however, is a difficult mechanical problem even in labor-management disputes, where it is widely accepted. Federal, State, and sometimes city mediation agencies can and do proffer their services in labor disputes. They do so because disputants are reluctant to ask for mediation in the belief that this implies a readiness to make concessions. Inexperienced bargainers in particular feel that they might lose out if they show any sign of weakness. The same obstacle to the introduction of mediation exists in community disputes. In my judgment, a permanent Board of Mediation for Community Conflicts, available to offer its services, should be established in the more populous communities. This will relieve the disputants of the need to request assistance.

One of the most important functions of the mediators is to act as ringmaster, providing a means of communication between the parties. He carries messages from one side to the other, helps each side understand the other's position, and generally keeps the proceedings functioning. Without someone in charge, bargaining can be disorderly; parties may be brought into contact with their opponents at untimely moments, producing unnecessary conflict. There is a time for direct meetings between the parties, but there are also times when it is more productive to keep them apart. The simple matter of assigning rooms and determining the time schedule for separate and joint meetings can be inflammatory unless there is an effective neutral on the scene. This is all the more important in community disputes where there is a loose framework of issues and objectives.

Besides acting as ringmaster, the mediator can help resolve the conflict in other ways. Disputants understandably tend to see the dispute from their own point of view. Robert Burns once asked for the gift of seeing ourselves as others see us. This would be particularly useful in collective bargaining. But there is another gift that is also necessary. It is the gift to see others as they see themselves. In the New York school crisis, the residents of the Ocean-Hill-Brownsville school district had little understanding of how trade unions work, and consequently they could not understand the arrangements that were necessary to resolve union problems. Correspondingly, the union was not properly attuned to the community's demand. There is still much for both sides to learn, and the beginning of the understanding necessary for resolution of such disputes is an awareness of the other fellow's problem.

## NEED FOR RESTRAINT

Through a Board of Mediation, the value of mediation for community disputes can be realized as it has been in labor-management conflicts. It will perform effectively if it is available to assist without having to take sides. Members of the Board should be committed to withhold public statements about the controversy before, during, and after their involvement. Nor should they offer solutions publicly before testing them on the parties privately. Once a mediator takes a public position, his usefulness is drastically diminished, if not eliminated. These restraints are vitally necessary to encourage the disputants to place confidence in the mediators without fearing that their confidence will be abused or their bargaining position prejudiced. It would then be possible for public officials who feel they must take a position on some aspects of the dispute to do so, even though they might thereby diminish their effectiveness as mediators. I do not propose such a Board of Mediation as a panacea but as a useful addition to other techniques to help contain and conclude community conflicts.

Thus, we see that it is not simple to transfer the experience of labor and management to community disputes, but that there are lessons to be learned. Both types of disputes are group controversies, and the means by which groups "talk" with one another have much in common. But to provide a setting in which talks can be fruitful requires two major achievements: A procedure for selecting community leaders and the acceptance of accommodation as the goal of bargaining.

The way in which labor and management select their representatives is infinitely simpler, aided, as it is, by the procedures of the National Labor Relations Act. Such procedures cannot be readily adopted to community disputes, but until some form of leadership selection is established and wins public support, bargaining will be obstructed. At the same time, the instinct to gain a total victory, an impossibility in any long-term relationship, or the fear of losing face in making concessions must be fought. The necessity of reaching an accommodation between claims that are not illegal and interests that are legitimate is imperative, even though the means of doing so is not as well developed. In an industrial dispute, a strike is recognized as an incentive to agree. The disputants know that the strike will ultimately end and that their relationship will be resumed. Thus it is customary for union members to protect the company's machinery during a strike so that it will be in condition when the strike

is over. This same commitment to the eventual settlement must also be generated in community disputes if they are to be resolved.

## RESEARCH OPPORTUNITIES

Since the most readily transferable technique is the process of mediation, I favor creation of a Board of Mediation for Community Disputes as a first step. It is also important to continue the study of labor and management negotiations for the guidance it can provide in resolving other group disputes. We must examine ways to select negotiating representatives in community disputes; the scope of subjects appropriate for bargaining in particular kinds of disputes; the proper role of communications and media; the most effective forms of action by individuals and groups in the community who are not parties to the dispute; and the general problems of bargaining tactics and techniques as they apply to community conflict.

The institutes at major universities that have specialized in labor-management relations should consider expanding their activities to include community relations and group disputes outside the industrial arena. Students of labor-management relations have tended to focus too sharply on substantive issues, questions of a guaranteed annual wage, pension plans, vacations, seniority schedules, and other terms of labor contracts, and not enough on the mechanics of dispute settlement. Even when studies are made of impasse procedures, they are concerned mainly with legislation, or the kind of board to be appointed, or the number of days allocated for the procedures. Inadequate attention has been given to the problems inherent in group relations—problems of communication through representatives, the psychology of the group and individual members of the group, the limitations and difficulties of group leadership, and others.

These subjects should be explored further in labor-management context, and the inquiry should be extended to other group disputes.

Despite the obstacles to the development of effective techniques for resolving community conflict through collective bargaining, there is much that can be gained by such study and little to lose. The need is urgent.

# A New Center for Dispute Settlement

## by Samuel C. Jackson

Seldom in our nation's history . . . have the conflicts between Americans seemed quite so difficult to resolve. The numerous changes in our social order precipitate daily clashes between Americans that defy resolutions by most existing institutions. It is because of this obduracy that the American Arbitration Association recently established the Center for Dispute Settlement. The Center offers arbitration, mediation, negotiation, and factfinding as methods for resolving conflicts that arise daily in our urban centers. We believe that the application of these methods will go a long way toward the just settlement of disputes by private means without government interference.

The underlying premise of the Center's operation is that no procedure now exists to resolve most of the grievances of urban black citizens and the poor of all races in any systematic and equitable manner: Their dispute with the landlord who consistently fails to make repairs or to comply with minimum housing codes; the incessant quarrel with local merchants who "wiggle out" of their responsibility to comply with expressed or implied warranties of their merchandise by transferring the installment note to a loan company; the welfare recipient who is cut off from benefits prior to a hearing; the efforts of the poor to secure their fair share of city services or to influence the city planning that so personally affects their lives—such as the location of a highway through their neighborhood to carry suburban dwellers to and from work, or the urban renewal that violently takes their property and sells it to entrepreneurs who build luxury apartments beyond their ability to rent, or commercial ventures for the affluent; disputes over control of or participation in model cities and poverty pro-

SOURCE Reprinted with permission from *Monthly Labor Review*, Vol. 92, No. 1, January 1969.

grams; disputes regarding school boundaries and efforts of parents to influence local school administrations; the growing incidence of government employees organizing to bargain collectively to improve their working conditions; and their increasing use of work disruption tactics to secure their goals.

Likewise, the Center operates on the assumption that the vast majority of businessmen are dissatisfied with the time-consuming litigation necessary to repossess merchandise sold, to secure a judgment against a delinquent consumer or to evict a tenant. . . . Recognizing that disputes will occur, most businessmen desire that resolution be available more swiftly and economically and without government regulation.

In most instances, the existing legal-judicial system, as viewed by the black citizen or by other ghetto poor, has been weighed and found gravely wanting. The courts as he sees them are complicated, foreign, impersonal, white, expensive, distant, slow, and full of technicalities and red tape. He seldom believes that he can secure justice and doubts if the court personnel, from the lowest clerk to the highest judge, care equally for him as they do for the property-owner or the merchant or lender who is most often involved in their disputes. . . .

These grievances, left unattended, fester without remedy and now more frequently find a voice in civil disruption, rebellions, and riots. Thus, there is need to employ extrajudicial techniques to resolve certain kinds of conflict situations.

Although the context may be new, this need for an extrajudicial means of settling disputes is hardly unique. In labor-management disputes and in disputes over various commercial or insurance contracts, once traditional methods of settlement have poven ineffective, too expensive, or too slow, mediation and arbitration have been substituted successfully. We hope that, in the same way, these methods can work in urban community conflicts.

# Mediation: A Path to Campus Peace?

## by Sam Zagoria

As the drama of American student unrest continues to unfold, parallels between today's campus confrontations and the workers' unrest of the thirties become apparent. This leads to pondering whether some of the procedures used to bring order and stability to labor-management relations may serve to improve student-administration relations.

. . . [E]mployers and workers have found that establishing a formal grievance procedure has several useful effects: It gives individuals a stated method for voicing complaints and in so doing also warns management of problem areas; it gives relief to pent-up irritation; it provides a method for getting the affected parties together in a calm, problem-solving atmosphere and may spell out the several levels of authority to which the issue may be successively appealed. In the course of this procedure the issue is clarified, often

cooled down, meaningful dialogue is made possible, and grievants are made aware that they do not have to create a crisis confrontation in order to be heard. With a grievance procedure established, a worker is assured that he may raise a complaint without jeopardizing his status in the plant. Similar grievance machinery in the university would . . . help achieve these same benefits.

. . . [S]ince colleges are public or at least quasi-public, third-party intervention, when necessary to resolve controversial matters, may not be inappropriate.

It may be desirable to provide some off-campus terminal facilities in the hard-core grievance that cannot be resolved on campus even at the highest levels. One such peacemaker might be the Center for Dispute Settlement. . . . Other possibilities include public boards, outside educational authorities, factfinding commissions and

SOURCE Reprinted with permission from *Monthly Labor Review,* Vol. 92, No. 1, January 1969.

similar dispute-settlement mechanisms. Of course, these third parties are most likely to succeed when they are activated or chosen by both parties.

The traditional techniques of mediation can also serve to bring parties together, to engineer acceptable and sometimes innovative solutions. Many States now have mediation boards or services, and many communities have gifted individuals who, through their experience and standing with the parties, can help guide the disputants to peaceful resolution.

Together, such points of contact and such procedures could provide students and administrators with abundant opportunities to defuse explosive situations, occasionally to face parties with the tempering question, "What would you do about it if you were in my place?" and to demonstrate beyond any possible doubt that problems can be aired, debated, and dealt with without violence.

To some, the foregoing might even suggest resort to compulsory collective bargaining. To others, it may raise the devilment of codetermination. It need not be either. Of the arsenal of techniques in the labor-management field, collective bargaining is probably the least appropriate to the environment of student-university relations. The students lack an authorized exclusive representative. Congress has not given students the right to engage in concerted action with protection against retaliation. In addition, here, unlike a worker-employer dispute, a walkout means financial loss only to the student, for the university has collected the tuition and fees in advance and here the university continues to hold the ultimate weapon—dismissal. The position of the university administration obviously is far different from that of an employer in a labor dispute.

Gradually, as settlements are achieved by one means or another, a body of lore can develop and help define appropriateness of items subject to such mutual discussion; and slowly, the broad outline of student rights as related to faculty and administration rights will emerge. . . .

The techniques of labor-management relations will not cure all student-administration problems but should minimize and deflate many.

### Related Readings

For a pragmatic analysis of the mediation process, see Elmore Jackson, *Meeting of the Minds—A Way to Peace Through Mediation* (New York, McGraw-Hill, 1952). For a good theoretical discussion of negotiations, see Carl Stevens, *Strategy in Collective Bargaining Negotiation* (New York, McGraw-Hill, 1963) and T.C. Schelling, *The Strategy of Conflict* (Cambridge, Harvard University Press, 1960). James Wilson discusses the application of protest strategy to race conflict in "The Strategy of Protest: Problems of Negro Civic Action," *Journal of Conflict Resolution,* September 1961. See also Bernard P. Indik and Georgina M. Smith, "Resolution of Social Conflict Through Collective Bargaining," *George Washington Law Review,* May 1968, and *Industrial Conflict and Race Conflict,* Proceedings of the Industrial Relations Research Association, Spring 1967. Another useful work is W. Ellison Chalmers and Gerald W. Cormick, eds., *Racial Conflict and Negotiations,* Ann Arbor, Mich., Institute of Labor and Industrial Relations and the National Center for Dispute Settlement of the America Arbitration Association, 1971.

# CHAPTER 15

# Public Employees

Collective bargaining is expanding more rapidly among public employees than among workers in any other sector. Indeed, 50 percent of all federal employees were represented by labor organizations in 1971. In part, this membership growth occurred because the governments are employing a larger percentage of the total work force, but it is also a result of the emergence of political and economic conditions conducive to the growth of collective bargaining in the public sector.

The unionization of public employees raises a number of important questions. Since the strike has been an important factor in private bargaining, can strikes be permitted among government employees? If not, how can bargaining take place in cases where managers refuse to yield? If strikes are to be outlawed, what penalties are to be imposed against those who do strike? Are there effective ways to resolve disputes without strikes? If strikes are permitted, would it be practical or equitable to let some workers strike and not others? What are the implications of giving public managers the authority—usually reserved to legislatures—to fix the terms of public employment? What are the implications of employee organizations using political power to appeal directly to political leaders over the heads of administrators? Private employers resist wage increases because of market forces that cause higher costs to reduce profits, but what forces cause public employers to resist wage increases? Is public collective bargaining sufficiently different to require separate machinery to supervise public employee labor relations similar to the role of the National Labor Relations Board in the private sector? What are the prospects for the growth of collective bargaining in the public sector? The selections in this chapter analyze these and other important questions dealing with public employee collective bargaining.

In "The Public Sector," George Hildebrand presents a very penetrating analysis of the implications of collective bargaining by government employees. He first presents some statistics on the magnitude of government union membership and then discusses some of the special features (strikes usually prohibited, the absence of market [but not budgetary] constraints, and the difficulties involved in delegating legislative power to public managers) of collective bargaining in the public sector.

Hildebrand next discusses the extent to which private collective bargaining practices may be transferred to the public sector. His first discussion concerns the special problems involved in the recognition of bargaining agents. This is a very important question because the type of recognition granted to a bargaining agent frequently influences that agent's bargaining power. On the public employer's side, of course, the ultimate authority to grant recognition for bargaining purposes rests with the legislature. At the national level, Congress has been very reluctant to delegate its powers to federal managers. However, President Kennedy, by Executive Order 10988 in 1962, provided for modified collective bargaining in the federal service.

Although federal employees' unions are denied the right to strike, they have exercised considerable political influence. As Hildebrand emphasizes, the political nature of bargaining in the public sector creates special problems:

> In this situation, the elected officials face an unhappy choice. If they refuse to deal and insist upon leaving the bargaining in the hands of their managers, they risk both a strike and political reprisal at the polls. If, however, they succumb to the union's strategy, they inevitably undermine a negotiating position of their own managerial subordinates. In the natural history of this situation, once the elected officials have gone over the heads of their managers to deal directly with the union, what has begun as a variant of private-sector bargaining ends by becoming an extension of machine politics.

Moreover, Hildebrand shows that the injection of the political element causes the bargaining process to undergo a subtle transformation, which raises the question of whether there is a risk that "in such a political situation the settlements negotiated with the unions, while acceptable to the participating labor organizations, might at times produce a severe and unjustified inflation of cost and a marked deterioration in the quality of services?"

In discussing the operation of collective bargaining at the municipal level, Hildebrand discerns four ingredients of apparently successful systems.

> (1) An all-inclusive bargaining unit with exclusive representation permits effective bargaining while it reduces the possibility of leapfrogging by rival unions. (2) The representatives of management can make proposals on money issues because the elected officials are brought into the bargaining process at an early stage, knowing what moneys are probably available and able to make commitments. (3) The negotiated terms are simultaneously incorporated in Civil Service regulations, preventing any possible hiatus there and allowing the city employees, through their union, to help shape the rules under which they are to work. (4) Most important, the practice of reaching a full "family understanding" on the management side, in regard to proposals, counterproposals, and terms of settlements,

greatly reduces the possibility of divide-and-conquer tactics and backdoor deals, which in turn protects the integrity of the bargaining process.

One of the most important issues involved in public employee bargaining is the argument that the doctrine of political sovereignty "obviates any possibility of collective bargaining in the public sector." Strictly interpreted, the sovereignty doctrine amounts to the contention "that it is unlawful for the lawmakers and the Civil Service Commission to share the process of rule-making with a group of employees acting through a union; it is basically a rationale for continued unilateral power."

Although Hildebrand does not accept this rationale, he believes there are some other very important problems in public employee bargaining, particularly the relationship between the civil service regulations and collective bargaining agreements and the problem of leap-frogging by competitive collective bargaining organizations. He therefore feels that in order to accommodate the objectives of the right of employees to be represented by unions of their own choosing and a need for stability in the bargaining relationship, an independent agency must be created to conduct certification and decertification proceedings. Finally, Hildebrand concludes that the sovereignty question poses a serious problem in the conflict between collective bargaining and detailed Civil Service regulations:

> If government collective bargaining is to work, detailed civil service regulations must go. Further, the lawmakers will have to delegate the authority to negotiate to the appropriate executives. In so doing, they will have to back their negotiators fully regarding positions, offers, and counter offers. Above all, it is vital to the integrity of the process that the top authorities be willing to commit themselves to settlements provisionally reached.

Hildebrand next considers the problem of impasses, which comes about because it is generally considered improper to permit government employees to strike. Without the right to strike, it is difficult for many observers to see how public employee conflicts can be resolved. However, Hildebrand rejects the idea that strikes can be legalized on a selective basis, as "unworkable and inequitable." He also rejects a strict sovereignty doctrine as the basis for banning all strikes, arguing that it is too legalistic and would preclude all collective bargaining. He feels, however, that a ban of government employee strikes based upon the special nature of government services is much more persuasive. He concludes:

> On the whole, however, the case for a no-strike policy rests upon essentiality: the large and general potential losses make uninterrupted provision superior to the interests of the bargaining parties. So persuasive is this claim that denial of it immediately compels one to engage in the futile task of trying to sort out exceptions, or to select some permissible strikes that will allow for continued partial operation—say, a particular school, a subway line, or a naval base. In consequence, the ban must be total if it is to be undertaken at all.

However, if strikes are to be banned in the public service, the question of effective penalties must be seriously considered; but experience demonstrates that punitive laws with severe penalties are very difficult to enforce, especially where public officials are vulnerable to reprisal. When this happens, punitive laws become inequitable and self-defeating. "If sanctions are provided, they should be effective as well as equitable. Moreover, they should be coupled with positive incentives, sufficient in most cases to induce the union to give up the strike weapon." Hildebrand sees two main alternatives for sanctions. One is to make the no-strike pledge a condition for recognition, and the other is to permit injunctions and contempt proceedings against striking organizations and their leaders. He suggests a procedure under which a no-strike ban might be implemented, but points out that there are many problems with this procedure. However, the use of injunctions also has weaknesses as well as strong points, causing Hildebrand to conclude: "It seems evident that there is no foolproof solution to the whole problem of sanctions against strikes."

Moreover, even if the strike problem were successfully resolved, there would still be a need for procedures to resolve deadlocked negotiations and other disputes between the parties. Hildebrand rejects compulsory arbitration as a solution to impasses because of the problems involved in delegating legislative powers to the arbitrator: lawmakers are not likely to surrender their powers to appropriate funds and "the delegation of these powers is unsound in principle, because it strikes at the very foundation of representative government." The weaknesses of compulsory arbitration lead Hildebrand to conclude that fact finding with recommendations is a better alternative.

> However, this . . . procedure might still fail to produce the desired agreement. At this point the injunction becomes a final remedy, to be vacated only when settlement is made. There is no dodging the possibility that the employees would be expected to work without a contract, or the ugly problems of preserving continuity of operations. But the chances of traversing this last unhappy mile ought to be greatly reduced if the right to bargain and a procedure for handling impasses that emphasizes continued negotiations are put into effect.
>
> Impasses are a logical possible extension of collective bargaining. In the final analysis, they can be resolved only by the lawmakers, which converts the question to one of straight political bargaining involving diverse interest groups. Thus, the real problem is how fact finding with recommendations can contribute to an equitable and viable decision.

Although the final decision must be made by legislatures, Hildebrand thinks fact finding can be a "useful and even a powerful device," by clarifying basic issues and exposing extreme positions.

Hildebrand's article concludes with a discussion of the relative bargaining power of the parties in the public sector. These power relations are different from those in the private sector, where the discipline of the product market is an important constraint on bargaining. Hildebrand states that even though government services are ordinarily free, public policy makers nevertheless are governed by the budgetary constraints, "because the real resources required to produce the service are scarce, have their prices, and must be paid for." Hildebrand's conclusion is that "It should be clear from this review of the matter that neither side loses all capacity to influence the outcome simply because it lacks the right to engage in economic warfare." And he concludes his article with "some tentative hypothesis regarding the operation of relative bargaining power in the public domain."

# The Public Sector

## by George H. Hildebrand*

For some years experts have been declaring that the American labor movement has been stagnating, if not regressing, largely owing to its failure to penetrate new territory in the labor force.[1] This criticism is valid for the private sector, but in the public sector we find a different situation: a much faster rate of increase in employment than in the traditional centers of union power, and what looks like the beginnings of a real breakthrough for unionism, embracing diverse groups—federal civil servants, municipal employees, schoolteachers, and various unclassified federal, state, and local government workers.[2]

Between 1950 and 1965 the number of employees in government at all levels rose from 6,000,000 to 10,000,000, or by two-thirds. Of the 4,000,000 new government employees, approximately 3,600,000 were in state and local governments, while 450,000 were at the federal level. As of 1965, 76 per cent of all public employment was at the state and local levels, against 68 per cent in 1950. It is estimated that by 1957 total government employment will be 14,700,000—12,200,000 in state and local and 2,500,000 in federal service. The public sector is expected to expand most rapidly in employment.[3]

In 1956, 915,000 government workers belonged to unions. By 1962 this figure had risen to 1,220,000. After the issuance of Executive Order 10988 on January 17, 1962, more than 200,000 federal employees joined unions, bringing the total for the public sector today to roughly 1,500,000. As of 1962 forty-one national unions had members in public employment; twenty-seven were affiliated with the AFL-CIO; while five who confine themselves entirely to the public sector had memberships of over 100,000 each.

\* \* \*

## SPECIAL FEATURES OF COLLECTIVE BARGAINING IN THE PUBLIC SECTOR

Four main elements distinguish collective bargaining for government workers from bargaining in the private sector. One is that the right to strike or to lock out is usually taken away by law or force of public opinion, or is relinquished by the union itself. Several hard questions inevitably arise. Should the strike be entirely ruled out? Is loss of the strike or the lockout fatal to the bargaining power of either party? How can the community deal effectively with strikes when they do occur? What mechanisms can resolve bargaining impasses?

A second distinguishing element is that most of the services provided by government are supplied free. They are financed by taxes and appropriations through the legislature, a board of supervisors, a municipal council, or a board of education.[4] Unlike the private sector, no loss of revenue follows from a work stoppage, an advantage that lowers management's cost of disagreement with the union. At the same time, however, if the service affected is essential and used by many people, public opinion can enter as in influence of major importance as both sides reckon their costs of agreement or disagreement. Furthermore, since the service need not be financially self-liquidating, the management is free of the discipline of having to balance costs against revenues.[5] Costs remain a problem, but taxes and subsidies permit them to be shifted to third parties without fear of the losses that might result from raising prices. Instead the risk takes the form of possible reprisal at the polls.

The third peculiar element is that the "employer" or management immediately involved in collective bargaining may lack final power to reach agreement. Instead, it must gain the consent of higher levels of political authority, initially the executive and ultimately the relevant lawmaking body. Formally this also holds in private enterprise, where the chief negotiator on the management side requires the consent and co-operation of top management and the board of directors; but in this case the power to bargain and to make an agreement can either be granted in advance or quickly obtained, because the power structure is closely linked and cohesive, while the profit motive supplies the necessary unity of interest. By contrast, in the public sector the aim of the ultimate decision makers is re-election, an outcome that depends upon a more diffuse set of interests which in some situations may conflict with those of government managements.

Finally, both at law and by traditional inclination legislative bodies in the United States are ordinarily wont to retain as much of their rule-making jurisdiction as they can. In consequence there is a strong tendency to treat the legislative process that governs the employment relationship in the public service as reserved territory, to be excluded as much as possible from collective bargaining. This approach is also convenient for managements in the public domain, simply because it preserves their power to make unilateral decisions.[6]

\* \* \*

## RECOGNITION, NEGOTIABLE ISSUES, AND BARGAINING PROCEDURE

A key question is to what extent are the practices of the private sector transferable to the public sector. The short answer is that because the public sector is *sui generis*, there are barriers to full-scale importation of private bargaining institutions; although all elements essential to collective bargaining can be used.

One of these elements is recognition of the union as a bargaining agent. Formal procedures are required providing for hearing representation cases, for fixing the boundaries of voting and bargaining units, and for conducting representation elections, which now exist at the federal level and within local units of government in a few states.[7] More critical, however, is the need to ensure the independence and neutrality of the agency empowered to conduct certification and decertification procedures. Acute problems are likely to emerge here, particularly at the local level: pressures by large international unions for political favors in the form of specially carved out bargaining units; pressures from the "employer" side for units designed to serve its special interests; and the possible development of a crazyquilt of jurisdictions reflecting the competing ambitions of rival unions, which would lead to leapfrogging tactics and difficult and costly settlements.

In the public service, recognition has usually been granted in three ways: informally, where the union has the right to present its views but need not be consulted; formally, but where multiple representation is permitted, meaning that the union represents its own members only; and formally, with exclusive representation.[8]

It goes without saying that multiple representation weakens a union's bargaining power. As in some school systems, each recognized union plays the role of a petitioner; it appears before the board of education to plead for changes in terms of employment and leaves it to the board to decide on the recommendations. This is collective bargaining in a primitive form, and in time it is likely to yield to exclusive representation, particularly if a legal procedure is available to resolve representation questions. But even exclusive recognition may involve no more than informal discussions of requests, with the ultimate decision to be left to those public officials who have the vested power to make it. In essence this power must include the authority to levy taxes, to make appropriations, and to fix wages, salaries, and other conditions of work. If discussions or negotiations are to produce any agreement, the persons having such authority must be committed to that agreement. Where this is possible, full collective bargaining becomes a reality.

Who, then, is the real employer in public bargaining? Who are the officials endowed with the legal power to commit a public agency or an enterprise to a collective bargain? The answer is obvious: ultimately the legislative body having competent jurisdiction, although that body may delegate some of its power to subordinate officials.

At the federal level, Congress, of course, is the ultimate authority. So far as the classified service is concerned, Congress has shown no disposition to delegate its power to fix salaries, hours, and benefits. Furthermore, long ago it established the Civil Service Commission to wipe out the spoils system. In consequence the commission administers the merit system for appointments and promotions, deals with problems of occupational structure, promulgates various detailed regulations, and provides a grievance procedure for employee complaints concerning the application of its rules.

However, as of 1961 only 41 per cent of all federal employees were in the classified group, while even within this group there were some blue-collar personnel. The majority of federal workers are assigned to the Post Office and to special establishments of an industrial type, such as Navy yards, military bases, or special corporations such as the Tennessee Valley Authority.[9] Here the practices are quite diverse. In the TVA and the Government Printing Office, for example, full-scale bargaining including money issues has long prevailed.[10] Within the Post Office Department the work force is highly organized. Collective bargaining occurs over a rather limited range of issues, but money questions are handled by special legislation. Accordingly, the real power of the postal unions lies in their political influence with Congress, which is not inconsiderable; but use of such power is not truly collective bargaining. Within the Navy one finds an interesting blend: unions are recognized and are allowed to participate in wage surveys as well as to recommend changes in wage schedules. A system of shop councils was also introduced in 1959; and while it bears some superficial similarity to the employee representation plans of the twenties, there is no explicit bar to exclusive union representation—hence to a type of collective bargaining—in matters affecting work methods, working conditions, and related employee interests.[11]

In the federal scene as a whole, then, the consequence of Executive Order 10988 for the classified personnel is collective bargaining in fact, though truncated in form. Agreements cannot embrace wages, hours, and major benefits. Accordingly, the negotiations concentrate upon personnel policies, rights of individual employees, and rights of the union as an organization. For example, negotiations occur over assignments, schedules, transfers, time off for union representation, job posting, written reasons for refusal of promotion, right of the union to be present at grievance and appellate hearings, voluntary checkoff (since January 1964), "advisory" (nonbinding) arbitration procedure for grievances, and the like.[12] Money issues and other basic rules of the employment relationship continue to be written by Congress and to be translated into detailed regulations by the Civil Service Commission.

It automatically follows that in their natural concern over money questions, unions in the classified service have every incentive to promote their interests before the appropriate Congressional body through political action rather than by collective bargaining.[13] A second inevitable result is that the most effective of these unions are those that represent unclassified personnel. Typically, these are old-line craft organizations whose base is in the private sector, and who deal with agencies to whom Congress has granted the necessary freedom either to engage in full-scale bargaining or to negotiate on a much wider scale. Furthermore, in their development of the relationship these organizations have been unhampered by the constraints and competition of a parallel civil service system.[14]

In municipal bargaining, if the system has passed beyond the petition stage to involve exclusive recognition, well-defined bargaining units, and formal negotiations and agreements, full-fledged collective bargaining can occur. Here the negotiable issues can include wages, hours, fringes, work rules, and virtually all of the private sector subjects.[15] Even more, the "legislature" (the city council) is much more likely to be closely involved in the bargaining relation. The territorial unit is relatively small; the appointed executives who are immediately responsible for representing management can be in close and continuous contact with the mayor and his council; and the latter are in a position to make commitments that they can deliver, because—as in the relation of the British Cabinet to Parliament—the mayor serves in the dual capacity of chief executive and (but not always) majority leader.[16]

* * *

Thus there exists an uneasy and potentially unstable relationship between the managers immediately "in charge" and the elected officials to whom they are responsible and upon whom they depend for their budgets and their jobs. The reason for this instability is that the situation is fraught with "politics," in the nonpejorative sense of the word.

On the one side, the managers normally have a professional interest in operating their agencies effectively and in protecting this function as best they can at the bargaining table, in much the same way as executives do in the private sector. In pursuit of this objective, they are acting on behalf of the interests of two important groups: the users of the service and the taxpayers who pay for it. On the other side, the function of the union is to promote and protect the interests of the employees, who constitute a legitimate "third estate" in this competition of aims. At the same time, however, the managers must depend upon the support of the elected officials in the pursuit of their professional interest.

\* \* \*

In this situation, the elected officials face an unhappy choice. If they refuse to deal and insist upon leaving the bargaining in the hands of their managers, they risk both a strike and political reprisal at the polls. If, however, they succumb to the union's strategy, they inevitably undermine the negotiating position of their own managerial subordinates. In the natural history of this situation, once the elected officials have gone over the heads of their managers to deal directly with the union, what has begun as a variant of private-sector bargaining ends by becoming an extension of machine politics. Such a consummation is not inevitable, but under conducive circumstances, the top political authorities will find it very difficult to resist its thrust—all the more so if they can count upon subsidies from the state and federal governments to help pay for expensive settlements.

Although there need be nothing inherently perilous or unlawful about this outcome, its potential implications do call for careful scrutiny, particularly if we are concerned to protect the interest of third parties. Without doubt a strong case can be made for encouraging the organization of government workers in order to introduce collective bargaining into public service, so that these employees may have a hand in shaping their working environment. But collective bargaining requires

for its very existence the presence of two independent sets of parties who seek to accommodate their conflicting interests through negotiation and joint administration of a contract. In the situation above, however, we have quite a different process and quite a different relationship, because the managerial side has lost its independence through a successful exercise of political power—not bargaining power in the sense—by the union side.

\* \* \*

However, there is another, extremely thorny aspect to the situation. Where the bargaining becomes an exercise of political influence, the underlying rationale for the organization of public employees undergoes a subtle transformation. No longer is the ruling purpose that of bringing about collective bargaining and its attendant benefits. Now the purpose is different: to promote the formation of new interest groups that incidentally can be a reservoir of potential votes and at the same time are a means of influencing the thinking of local government leaders. The primary objective of such influence, of course, is to affect the employment relationship in the public service, although it may well extend beyond its immediate compass. To be sure, such an objective is consistent with traditional democracy.[17] But if the managements of the public services can be captured in this way, a disturbing question arises. Is there a chance that in such a political situation the settlements negotiated with the unions, while acceptable to the participating labor organizations, might at times produce a severe and unjustified inflation of costs and a marked deterioration in the quality of services? There is no obvious answer, but the risk is not to be denied, particularly at the municipal level.

Sound policy requires that this risk be faced, and faced squarely. A whole new set of institutional mechanisms is required to promote the fullest possible use of the bargaining process and yet at the same time to protect the community against irreparably damaging work stoppages and irresponsible settlements. In a later section we shall explore some of the possibilities in this relatively unfamiliar field.

As the experience of Philadelphia shows, municipal collective bargaining can be made to work satisfactorily for the diverse interests affected by the process.[18]

* * *

Four ingredients enable this system to work with apparent success. (1) An all-inclusive bargaining unit with exclusive representation permits effective bargaining while it reduces the possibility of leapfrogging by rival unions. (2) The representatives of management can make proposals on money issues because the elected officials are brought into the bargaining process at an early stage, knowing what moneys are probably available and able to make commitments. (3) The negotiated terms are simultaneously incorporated in Civil Service regulations, preventing any possible hiatus there and allowing the city employees, through their union, to help shape the rules under which they are to work. (4) Most important, the practice of reaching a full "family understanding" on the management side, in regard to proposals, counterproposals, and terms of settlement, greatly reduces the possibility of divide-and-conquer tactics and backdoor deals, which in turn protects the integrity of the bargaining process. For the same reason the bargains reached have a good chance of being responsive to all equities at stake—the city government, the employees and their union, the management groups immediately concerned, the taxpayers, and the users of the services the city supplies.[19]

. . . One general problem remains: the argument that the doctrine of political sovereignty obviates any possibility of collective bargaining in the public sector.

Strictly interpreted, all this contention amounts to is that it is unlawful for the lawmakers and the Civil Service Commission to share the process of rule-making with a group of employees acting through a union; it is basically a rationale for continued unilateral power. . . . even though the rationale itself is not finally persuasive and has been set aside in practice, some key problems remain.

One involves the role of the Civil Service Commission. For classified personnel in any jurisdiction, Civil Service regulations represent the unilateral application of a unitary rule system to workers belonging to diverse occupational groups and performing quite diverse functions. If these workers become organized by occupation or by function, the consequence is multiple-unit bargaining. Since the negotiations must be autonomous for each of groups because the very principle of collective bargaining presumes the possibility of bargaining between the designated parties, there is an inevitable diversity of results. This can be desirable, because the rules so negotiated must be responsive to the specific circumstances. But, except for a few general constraints such as the merit system, the consequence must be a sacrifice of the unitary system established by civil service. For this reason civil service commissions are likely to resist the scope of negotiations as narrowly as possible.

But even if detailed civil service regulations can be supplanted in the evolution of government collective bargaining, another difficult problem is likely to assert itself with full vigor: leapfrogging by the emergent unions. Dissident groups within the ranks of recognized organizations will find it profitable to insist upon extreme demands—all the more so where outside unions seeking to occupy rich new bargaining territory are free to challenge representation rights by outpromising the incumbent organizations. Such circumstances are likely to foster unusually difficult negotiations, costly settlements, spill-over of such settlements as they become "orbits of coercive comparison," and continuing instability of bargaining relations. Perhaps the all-inclusive Philadelphia unit offers a partial solution to these problems, because such units are harder for outsiders to challenge and because intergroup conflicts are internal to the union itself and hence are capable of compromise through the processes of union politics. But even then fratricidal warfare and struggles for "craft severance" are possible.

There is another side to the matter. At law and in principle American employees have the right to be represented by unions of their own choosing. Against this stands the need for stability in the bargaining relationship. The accommodation of both objectives requires an impartial agency to conduct certification and decertification proceedings, guided by carefully defined rules for dealing with questions of unit determinations. The procedure should also provide for exclusive representation rights once an organization can command a majority vote. But if multiple representation is allowed to prevail, it may be desirable to provide for an exclusive check-off for the union with the largest plurality, to foster the transition to exclusive representation. There is also need for a contract-bar rule to fix a specific open period when challenge of representation rights alone can be made.

The remaining problem again poses the sovereignty question, this time in a relevant way. If government collective bargaining is to work, detailed civil service regulations must go. Further, the lawmakers will have to delegate the authority to negotiate to the appropriate executives. In so doing, they will have to back their negotiators fully regarding positions, offers, and counter offers. Above all, it is vital to the integrity of the process that the top authorities be willing to commit themselves to settlements provisionally reached.

## THE PROBLEM OF IMPASSES

By statute, by constitutional interpretations in the courts, and by applications of the common law, strikes by government employees have been declared illegal and made enjoinable in many jurisdictions, from the federal to the local. Three central questions thereupon emerge: What are the grounds for denial of the right to strike? What sanctions, if any, are most likely to be effective in enforcing a ban on strikes? And what special procedures, if any, most promise success for handling impasses or grievances about the interpretation and application of the terms of an existing contract, and about disputes over recognition or over the provisions of a new contract?

### Grounds for Outlawing Government Strikes

There are three typical points of view toward this critical question. At one extreme is the view that there should be no ban whatever. At most the contracting parties would simply pledge to do their utmost to avoid stoppages and related forms of economic warfare. In this view there is no real reason to treat government workers differently from those in the private sector. As in the latter domain, strikes involving critical services or products can be dealt with *ex post*, by injunction procedure, while any statute authorizing collective bargaining would stress the positive elements alone.

This approach has its attractions, but in my judgment suffers from a fatal flaw: it overlooks completely the fact that government is a different kind of institution from a private enterprise, and that public opinion insists strongly upon an explicit ban. If legislation is to permit the wider introduction of collective bargaining into the public service, the *quid pro quo* will have to be sacrifice of the right to conduct economic warfare against the state and its citizens.

A second position regarding the strike would legalize stoppages on a selective basis. If by some standard a particular government service is held to be nonessential, then the union would be free to strike or the management to lock out. Another variant would extend the right to strike even to some essential services, if there were some provision for partial operation. For example, a transit union would be permitted to shut down some subway lines but not others; or bargaining units and their accompanying unions would somehow be fragmented over the system, in hopes of preventing total shutdowns over particular disputes.

This approach seems almost quixotic, for it would be both unworkable and inequitable. Its basic disability is that the range of government services is too complex and includes too many widely used essentials to permit even a hypothetical principle of selectivity. Further, public opinion would certainly be intolerant of any such fine distinction. Finally, it would be basically unreasonable to allow some government unions the advantages of the right to strike as an element in bargaining power while denying it to others.[20]

The third main point of view is to accept as permanent the existing policy that strikes should be outlawed in the public sector as a matter of unitary principle; that there are sound grounds for the principle; and that the basic need today is for new institutions designed to make collective bargaining work effectively in the public domain.

But it would be poor thinking simply to fall back upon established policy without searching for a sound and broadly persuasive rationale for it.

Two broad lines of argument have emerged to justify banning the strike. One relies on the principles of sovereignty alone: public employees must not be permitted to challenge the ultimate right of the elected lawmakers to consider and pass legislation, including laws covering terms for government employees. The other argument appeals to the special character of government services, contending that the right of the public to the continuous provision of these services supersedes the right of organized employees and public managements to resort to economic warfare over any issue.[21]

The argument from sovereignty has the advantage of being simple and direct, but the weakness of being legalistic. Narrowly interpreted, it would preclude collective bargaining as such, since such bargaining in essence is an intrusion upon the lawmakers' ultimate prerogatives. When viewed broadly, it concedes the possibility of collective bargaining, hence some practical delegation of these prerogatives. But once this is granted, the doctrine of sovereignty ceases to be insuperable and no longer serves as a condition sufficient unto itself for banning the strike.

A more persuasive case for the ban can be found in the special nature of government services, many of which are supplied on monopolistic terms: although usually no price is charged, government is their exclusive source. National defense, flood and traffic control, and dispensation of justice are familiar examples. . . . The necessity of these services can hardly be questioned—which is another way of saying that their uninterrupted provision must be assured, in order to avoid the immediate and large losses that otherwise would be imposed upon third parties.

A tougher problem concerns that broad array of government services for which privately supplied alternatives either are or can be made available—for example, police and fire protection, local mass transportation, and even education. Theoretically, the possibility of substitutes for government services reduces their essentiality. But there are two drawbacks: the substitute may be available only at so high a price as to be impractical for most users

—for instance, police and fire protection —so that they really must depend upon government to provide it. Furthermore, even if the service ultimately can be had at a feasible price, it is not available in adequate supply in the short run, because it takes time for private producers to enter the field.[22]

Of course one can think of government services that are exclusively provided, whose use can be deferred without large and immediate losses to the whole public, because the users are a small group. Issuance of building permits is one example. A strike by employees in such a public agency could be borne for some time with no more hardship than is caused by many private-sector construction stoppages. The real reason for extending the strike ban to these marginal government activities is, not their essentiality, but rather the unitary principle that there is no practical and equitable way to allow strikes in some parts of government while forbidding them in others.

On the whole, however, the case for a no-strike policy rests upon essentiality: the large and general potential losses make uninterrupted provision superior to the interests of the bargaining parties. So persuasive is this claim that denial of it immediately compels one to engage in the futile task of trying to sort out exceptions, or to select some permissible strikes that will allow for continued partial operation —say, a particular school, a subway line, or a naval base. In consequence, the ban must be total if it is to be undertaken at all. . . .

### Sanctions Against Government Strikes

. . . [I]t makes little sense to ban strikes against government if that ban is not effectively enforced.

\* \* \*

[H]istory reveals the basic weakness of a punitive antistrike law. Where public officials are vulnerable to reprisal, there is a strong probability that they will not enforce such a measure, despite their sworn oath of office to uphold the laws of their jurisdiction. In consequence weak unions and their members lie under its severe sanctions, while strong ones can escape with impunity. What becomes of equality under the law or even respect for law when this becomes an entrenched practice? Further, such a statute is self-defeating on its own terms: the dismissal of an entire striking work force maintains the effects of the strike itself and of course punishes the innocent along with the guilty. . . .

If sanctions are provided, they should be effective as well as equitable. Moreover, they should be coupled with positive incentives, sufficient in most cases to induce the union to give up the strike weapon. In other words, there has to be a trade-off. The basic inducements are granting the right to collective bargaining, providing an agency for handling election and representation questions, through which recognition can be gained and can be made an obligation of public management, and supplying a workable method for dealing with impasses.

As for sanctions as such, there appear to be two main alternatives: to make a no-strike pledge a condition for initial and continuing recognition, or—which is the same thing—to provide for automatic decertification when the pledge is violated; or to rely upon the injunction and contempt proceedings, backed up by fines against the organization and its leaders.

If abandonment of the strike is made a statutory condition for recognition, as is done in Section 2 of Executive Order 10988 at the federal level, the union thereby binds itself to a desired course of conduct. The same statute would put public officials under mandate to reinforce that desired conduct. The mandate would require that: (1) if a union undertakes a strike, recognition would be withdrawn simultaneously, payment of withheld dues would automatically cease, and the bargaining relationship would be terminated; (2) for a period of, say, two years no recognition would be accorded to any labor organization claiming to represent the employees of the affected bargaining unit; (3) at the end of this period any labor organization could initiate representation proceedings upon a sufficient showing, a representation election would follow, and the winner would be certified; (4) upon certification and tender of a no-strike pledge, the chosen organization, which could well be the former one, would then be formally recognized for collective bargaining; and (5) in consequence of a strike no employees would be dismissed.

Of course, this device involves difficulties, some of them serious. As a deterrent to strikes it has considerable potential strength; but an effective deterrent must be credible. If it is undermined by evasive poststrike "settlements," it will quickly lose its force. This is a real danger. But the basic flaw in this device is that its very terms require a dissolution of the bargaining relationship. Thus any possibility of using a prospective negotiated settlement as an inducement to end a strike is foreclosed.[23] To illustrate, if the union is old and well established, the cessation of collective bargaining might not end an illegal strike; this would pose hard problems of whether and how to resume operations. In such a situation the political temptation to yield would likely be strong. If mass quits were to follow the termination of bargaining relations, the effect would be similar to the strike itself. If, short of this, the employees began "working to the rules" or resorted to a wildcat strike, it would be difficult to prove official instigation. Moreover, the problem of continued provision of the service would reassert itself. Accordingly, what seems to be a simple automatic solution to the strike problem actually turns out to be anything but foolproof.

The main alternative sanction is that traditional protective device extended by the courts to injured parties—the injunction. While it must be admitted that in times past the injunction acquired a shady reputation through its misuse by employers to defeat collective bargaining, the principle itself is an entirely equitable one whose utility in this context can hardly be questioned. The power to enjoin strikes against government may already be ample under both common and statutory law in many jurisdictions. But in some cases—so that the injunction can serve as a credible deterrent to undesired conduct—special legislation may be needed if the courts are to have discretionary power to levy fines against organizations and their leaders for actions in contempt.

Under this approach, if a strike occurs, the affected agency or the attorney general of the state could apply in court for a termination order, and the court would be empowered in its discretion to levy cumulative fines against the organization and its leaders for each day of official stoppage—as was done in the Mine Workers' case. The strength of this device is that it hits at a vital point: the finances of the organization instead of its representation rights. The main advantage of this device is that it allows the bargaining relation to resume once compliance is effected. It also allows the court the necessary discretion for fixing appropriate penalties.

But again there are problems and weaknesses. The injunction can be effective as a deterrent only if its credibility is not destroyed by subsequent full remission of fines when a poststrike settlement is reached. As a method of terminating an illegal strike, it can pose enough uncertainty to hasten its end, but again only if the party applying for the injunction has no power to request full remission of fines upon seeking dissolution of the order. Moreover, the injunction offers no assured protection against wildcat strikes, "working to the rules," or mass quits, although it might be drafted to cope with some aspects of these problems. Finally, if no settlement is ultimately achieved, the continuing effect of the injunction is to require the union members to work without a contract, in what is a *de facto* rupture of the bargaining relationship.

It seems evident that there is no foolproof solution to the whole problem of sanctions against strikes. Indeed, it goes against the grain even to consider the matter, because the strike itself is so closely bound up with our whole tradition of free association. But public opinion is strongly oriented against strikes in the public service and is likely to become even more so with the growth of unions in government. Further, in many jurisdictions this popular view has already found its way into law. At the same time the public is unlikely to tolerate transference of the pluralistic approach now applied to the private sector, where most strikes are permitted after due notice, but strikes for recognition or in behalf of jurisdictional claims are banned; and where major "health and safety" strikes either can be temporarily enjoined or are outlawed. By contrast, the public sector seems to be an all-or-nothing proposition, with the electorate firmly on the side of no strikes at all.

However, it makes little practical sense and carries serious implications for the very concept of ordered liberty under law to impose a strike ban that either lacks any enforcement procedure or provides one that is inherently unworkable. . . .

### Resolution of Impasses

Banning strikes in the public sector does not remove the possibility of disputes. Methods are required for dealing with disputes in a fully equitable way, especially impasses arising from a deadlock in negotiations.

Regarding the private sector, it is now a commonplace that, owing to the provision of workable substitutes, disputes over recognition and jurisdictional claims and over the interpretation and application of contract terms no longer lead to industrial warfare. Jurisdictional strikes have been outlawed, and this has called forth a system of private arbitration in certain industries. Questions concerning recognition and representation have been resolved by statutory creation of impartial administrative machinery. Finally, in most agreements today the parties themselves have provided a grievance procedure with arbitration as the terminal step.

It will not be easy to devise similar solutions for the public sector. What is required is appropriate legislation for the state and local levels, as Executive Order 01988 provides in its own way for the federal service. A few states, such as Michigan and Wisconsin, have already taken this step. However, it must be conceded that some difficult problems do assert themselves. They derive from the sovereign status of the appropriate legislative body. For example, it may be impossible to provide for binding arbitration of grievances, because the award may intrude upon the lawmaking function. A possible solution would be advisory arbitrations, where the officials can comply with an award if no question of law is presented.[24] As for questions involving recognition, there appears to be no bar to setting up the requisite administrative agency, provided that its impartiality can be assured.

But what about disputes arising from contract negotiations? Since economic warfare is ruled out, equity requires some procedure for adjudicating conflicting claims. And in keeping with the over-all purpose of promoting voluntary settlement to the fullest possible extent, the impasse procedure ought to try to minimize coercoin against the parties. For these purposes two standard solutions have been commonly proposed.

One of these is compulsory arbitration. This method, however, contains a fatal weakness, for the terms of an award would be binding upon both parties.[25] In the first place, it is unlikely that the lawmakers either could or would surrender their powers to appropriate funds or to pass upon the basic law of labor relations in the public service. In the second place, the delegation of these powers is unsound in principle, because it strikes at the very foundations of representative government. If this system of government is to be preserved, legislative responsibility and accountability cannot be transferred in their entirety to a *pro tem* appointed board. And finally, the availability of a procedure yielding compulsory awards might well vitiate the bargaining process, by inviting either a strategy of extreme and irresponsible demands or other tactics designed to compel arbitration of the successor agreement.

This leaves us with a single alternative: fact finding with recommendations.

The essentials of the fact-finding technique admit of some variations and are subtle in nature. It is desirable that adequate time be provided for the initial stage of negotiations. If during this period a deadlock should develop, either party would be free to request mediation, or the responsible top public official could initiate such a request. Upon a report by the mediator that his efforts have failed, either party or the top official could request appointment of a fact-finding board to study the issues and prepare recommendations for settlement. In my judgment this board should be composed of neutrals, to increase the probability of a unanimous report. Here it seems desirable to provide for a two-step sequence. In the first step the board would investigate the issues and submit a confidential report to the parties, to give them a further opportunity to reach a settlement. If a settlement were not reached within a specified time, then the second stage would begin: the board would make public its findings and recommendations. Thereupon the struggle for

public opinion would start, interest groups could mobilize, and the whole question would move into the arena of a political decision. Perhaps, too, there should be one last effort to break the deadlock, by appointment of a small *ad hoc* committee which, working quietly and privately, would try to persuade the side that is holding out to accept the board's recommendations. The composition of this committee would depend upon which side was obstructing settlement.

\* \* \*

However, this . . . procedure might still fail to produce the desired agreement. At this point the injunction becomes a final remedy, to be vacated only when settlement is made. There is no dodging the possibility that the employees would be expected to work without a contact, or the ugly problems of preserving continuity of operations. But the chances of traversing this last unhappy mile ought to be greatly reduced if the right to bargain and a procedure for handling impasses that emphasizes continued negotiations are put into effect.

Impasses are a logical possible extension of collective bargaining. In the final analysis, they can be resolved only by the lawmakers, which converts the question to one of straight political bargaining involving diverse interest groups. Thus, the real question is how fact finding with recommendations can contribute to an equitable and viable decision.

In my judgment, fact finding can be a useful and even a powerful device, because it is a means of airing the basic issues, while the ensuing recommendations can guide the parties toward settlement and enlighten the electorate, which in turn can influence the lawmakers toward a sound decision. Extreme positions on either side can be exposed for what they really are. Once fully revealed, they are likely to cause opposing interest groups to form as mobilizers of opinion which can supply some of the necessary if contentious pressure upon elected officials to move toward a responsible determination of their course of action. Of course there is no certainty of decision, but resolution is more likely than if they had no impartial and expert guidance at all. In crisis, lawmaking bodies are under enormous pressure to get a settlement at any price. Moreover, they have no time to study the facts and in general lack the expertise to work out a solution. Fact finding with recommendations is a way to redirect the pressure of opinion and to economize on the legislators' time, while providing them the guidance they need.

Also, as a purely technical matter, the technique of fact finding does not deprive the parties of all opportunity for settlement or the legislators of their authority and discretion, because the recommendations are not binding. Accordingly, the lawmakers remain responsible and accountable for the final decision, in keeping with the principles of representative democracy. And they must discharge that responsibility before the bar of a much fuller public understanding.

By contrast, an award in compulsory arbitration would enable the lawmakers to pass the buck in advance to the tribunal, and to be well insulated from public opinion. In other words, compulsory arbitration deprives the parties of continued opportunity to negotiate, and the law makers of the final responsibility that should be theirs; it also sacrifices the critical stage when public opinion is shaped.

## THE QUESTION OF RELATIVE BARGAINING POWER

What differences do the peculiarities of collective bargaining in the public sector make for the relative bargaining power of the parties? Can we expect continuous inflation of wages and salaries within the public domain, accompanied by ever-decreasing efficiency of the work force?

Or will collective bargaining be ineffective, yielding no more than could be had without it, because usually the strike and the lockout are given up?

To deal with these questions, it is useful to single out the peculiarities again and to consider the independent influence of each on the bargaining process. In so doing, we shall adopt Chamberlain's schematic analysis of relative bargaining power.[26] In his approach, bargaining power is each party's "capacity to secure a specific objective." Accordingly, its power depends in part upon the objective and the costs of agreeing and of disagreeing for each side relative to that objective. Power also depends upon bargaining skill and upon the resources each side may employ to affect the other's costs of agreement and disagreement.[27] To each side, these relative costs depend upon the specific demand. Furthermore, they may change during the course of the bargaining—for example, by shifts in public opinion. Moreover, either party may be able to increase its bargaining power if it can either raise the cost of disagreement to the other party or lower that party's cost of agreement—that is, if it can make it either too expensive to disagree or too attractive not to agree.

Let us now apply this framework to the special factors of public-sector bargaining. The first peculiarity here is that the services of government are mostly distributed without charge; that is, as if they were free. This method of distribution relieves the public management directly involved from concern about the discipline of the product market. It can ignore the private-sector relations between marginal revenue and marginal cost—hence the price-elasticity of demand for the service. Considered alone, this situation lowers the employer's cost of agreeing to the union's terms, which favors the union's position. But against it there is a counter force: the agency suffers no loss of revenue from a stoppage, and this lowers its cost of disagreement as well.

But problems of cost nonetheless remain, because the real resources required to produce the service are scarce, have their prices, and must be paid for. There are only two ways to procure the necessary funds: by taxes and by externally supplied subsidies. Costs of settlement accordingly remain highly relevant to management. The higher the money demands or associated work rules affecting the quantity of manpower, the greater will be management's cost of agreement, and the more likely will be an impasse. So far as a subsidy is available, however, taxes need not be increased. In consequence a subsidy lowers management's cost of agreement and correspondingly strengthens the union's bargaining power.

Consider next those cases in which a price is charged. The factors of revenue and of price elasticity now can enter the bargaining arena. Much will depend upon whether an agency is required by law to make the service pay its own way, as the Chicago Transit Authority must do. In such a case the greater the price elasticity, the greater the potential loss of customers and of revenue, and the higher will be the authority's cost of agreement.[28] However, if the agency is not required to cover costs, it must be able to count upon subsidies, which if forthcoming will lower its costs of agreement and so strengthen the union's bargaining power. If, further, a higher political authority decides to hold the price of the service at a given level, the agency can forget about price elasticity of demand; and the union's bargaining power is increased still further. But this also depends upon the willingness of higher authority to underwrite higher costs. If it is liberal here, the agency's cost of agreement with the union's demands will be lower. If the elected officials are stringent about higher costs, the reverse holds, the union's relative bar-

gaining power is diminished, and an impasse is more likely.

The second factor peculiar to public-sector bargaining is the dependence of top managerial authority upon majority coalitions among the electorate—in short, upon public opinion. What kind of a calculus is that authority likely to make regarding the costs of any agreement it is ultimately required to undertake?

Obviously one element is the magnitude of these added labor costs, for they bear directly upon tax revenues and tax rates. Another vital element is the voting bloc commanded by the union itself, or the union in alliance with other local unions in both the public and the private sectors.[29]

Clearly, one determinant in this political calculus is the scale of the union's demands: the higher they are, the higher are the costs of agreement to the authorities, and the greater is the likelihood of an impasse. But matters do not end here. The proportion of union labor costs to the total budget can be decisive. Provided that it is the only union present, a craft group of city fire fighters can gain a lot, simply because there are no significant tax effects; in other words, the city's costs of agreement are low. By contrast, a massive bargaining unit, as in Philadelphia, will enjoy no such economic advantage. . . .

Thus in some situations it pays to be small. But it need not be a handicap to be large, provided that the labor movement has the necessary political muscle at the polls. If it has, the possibility of political reprisal will raise the costs of disagreement to the top political authority, giving the unions greater bargaining power.[30] But the higher the tax impact the more likely it is that opposition groups will form and attempt to exert some political muscle of their own. In consequence the incumbents have a difficult balancing problem; and the higher the union demands, the higher are the costs of agreeing to them. . . .

The third factor peculiar to the government case is absence of the strike and the lockout. Both weapons have a common purpose: to raise the other party's costs of disagreeing to the first party's terms. But there is no way to determine whether relative bargaining power is made more or less equal in consequence of ruling out of economic warfare, because either side's capacity to get agreement on its own terms depends upon its specific demand. The more one side asks for, the higher the other's cost of agreeing relative to disagreeing, and the smaller the likelihood of the latter conceding. In other words, until the demand is served, there is no way of determining a party's real strength.

\* \* \*

Looking now at the union side, a variety of techniques have emerged for influencing the government employer's costs of agreeing or disagreeing. Short of a formal strike, it may be possible to adopt slowdown tactics, to urge candidates for employment to refuse jobs, or to urge individual employees to quit. While it disavows both the strike and the slowdown, the National Education Association recommends the latter two "sanctions" in successive order to impose costs of disagreement upon school boards. In fact, they have been used with some effect and can be effective because of the comparatively high mobility of many teachers in today's tight markets for their services.

Government unions have other ways as well to influence the bargaining relationship. One is to try to affect public opinion through interviews, advertisements, and radio and television programs. Another is to raise the threat of an impasse. An impasse is likely to lead to some kind of intervention—say mediation, fact finding, or arbitration, all of which create uncertainty about the outcome and thus a degree of risk in refusing to settle. And in contrast to these methods of increasing the agency's costs of disagreeing, a union of public employees can try to reduce the employer's costs of agreeing—for example, by offering tangible measures of co-operation to increase efficiency and so cut down the net cost of settlement.

On reflection, the ultimate weapon of a government union is its political power.

\* \* \*

It should be clear from this review of the matter that neither side loses all capacity to influence the outcome simply because it lacks the right to engage in economic warfare. The final step is to suggest some tentative hypotheses regarding the operation of relative bargaining power in the public domain. All of them are subject to test, in some cases by regression analysis, using indicators such as degree of union organization, quit rates, job application lists, wage comparisons, and wage gains relative to the federal guide posts.

1. If the agency which the union deals has the power to assess taxes to cover deficits or increased costs, the profile of wage costs will be warped upward on comparative test.[31]

2. If the agency with which the union deals has continuing access to subsidies from other jurisdictions, its labor cost profile will be warped upward on comparative test.

3. If a union of strategically situated public employees covers only a small fraction of the municipal labor force and is the only government union in the community, its wage profile will be warped upward on comparative test.

4. Where the labor movement as such is relatively large in a given community and the public employees are highly organized as well, the following implications are suggested:

a. A political alliance will be formed involving organized labor, the mayor, and council majorities.

b. It will be difficult to obtain a "family understanding" within public management for bargaining purposes.

c. The operating managements of particular public agencies will find themselves bypassed by higher political authority and accordingly will lose their independence and, with it, their ability to protect their managerial interests.

d. The comparative wage profiles of the employee groups involved will be warped upward on comparative test, the more so if external subsidies can be had.

5. If the opportunity to bargain over money matters is refused, the unions involved will turn to legislative lobbying to promote their interests.

6. If public-employee unions are formed in a community in which the labor movement is weak and the population mainly residential, city management will emphasize sovereignty and unilateralism, and negotiations are likely to be informal and not binding.

These are hardly more than suggestions and by no means exhaust the list, but at least they have the merit of indicating the high importance of systematic study of collective bargaining in the public domain.

## CONCLUSION

The organization of public workers into unions is already well advanced. The number of employees in the public sector now exceeds ten million and is rapidly expanding, opening highly attractive new territory for the labor movement. The opportunity is being vigorously followed up, and there is keen competition among a broad array of organizations in the struggle to capture new members, bargaining rights, and political influence. It is reminiscent of the rush of events in the private sector during the great breakthrough of 1933 to 1940.

As in those times and in that setting, management again faces a growing challenge to its unilateral power—but now management belongs to the public domain. And there is another difference as well: the lack in many jurisdictions of a basic law for collective bargaining and of administrative machinery for dealing with a host of difficult questions that are already strongly asserting themselves. Moreover, the situation is greatly complicated by some decisive differences in kind between government and private enterprise as employing organizations.

The pressure for collective bargaining in the public domain is certain to grow. To meet it intelligently calls for the design of a whole new apparatus of institutional mechanisms, only part of which can be copied from the private sector.

## Notes

[1] The author has received valuable criticisms of an earlier draft from Alice Cook, Jean McKelvey, Kurt Hanslowe, Robert Doherty, Leonard Adams, and Jesse Simons, none of whom bears any responsibility for the remarks below.

[2] The least organizational advance has been made in state government. Probably the basic reason for this is the presence of strong employee associations, which successfully practice direct lobbying with legislatures and hence prefer to work through civil service statutes and usually oppose legislation to make collective bargaining possible at the state level. For these very reasons state laws to provide for collective bargaining for public workers often have been confined to employees in subordinate government units.

[3] Employment data from *Manpower Report of the President* (March, 1966), p. 198; and *Technology and the American Economy* (Report of the National Commission on Technology, Automation, and Economic Progress, February, 1966), p. 29.

[4] The main exceptions where pricing prevails involve government-operated public utilities—transit, power and light, water, port and highway facilities, and the Post Office; even here recourse to tax subsidies is not uncommon.

[5] If cost-benefit analysis could be widely introduced into government, one of its major contributions would be to provide a surrogate for the profit-making constraint in private enterprise.

[6] Management in the private sector has the same motive but lacks the independent and higher legislative authority to back it up.

[7] For a proposed comprehensive statute embracing these and other matters, see *Report of the Interim Commission to Study Collective Bargaining by Municipalities* (State of Connecticut,

February, 1965). See also *A Policy for Employee-Management Cooperation in the Federal Service* (President's Task Force on Employee-Management Relations in the Federal Service, November 30, 1961); *Final Report* (Governor's Committee on Public Employees' Relations, State of New York, March 31, 1966).

[8] For the federal service under Executive Order 10988, recognition is possible in all three ways, with exclusive representation dependent upon a showing of a majority in the bargaining unit (sections 4, 5, and 6). No union can be recognized that asserts the right to strike against the government, advocates overthrow of the government, practices categorical discrimination regarding admission, and/or in the judgment of the agency head is "subject to corrupt influences or influences opposed to basic democratic principles" (sections 2 and 3[a]).

[9] President's Task Force, *A Policy for Employee-Management Cooperation in the Federal Service, op. cit.*

[10] From 1861 to 1903, the Printing Office actually had a closed shop. In 1924 Congress passed the Kiess Act, which explicitly provides for collective bargaining and even for final arbitration of disputes by a joint committee of the Congress (Wilson R. Hart, *Collective Bargaining in the Federal Civil Service* [New York: Harper & Brothers, 1961], pp. 86–87).

[11] *Ibid.*, pp. 92–96. In 1961, Hart concluded that Navy policy was still more conventional than it was innovative, meaning that it tolerated rather than encouraged independent unionism and sought to retain as many of management's unilateral prerogatives as possible.

[12] *Government Employee Relations Reports*, No. 49 (American Bar Association, Section of Labor Relations Law, Report of Committee on Law of Government Employee Relations, Bureau of National Affairs, August 17, 1964).

[13] Consider, for example, the much-heralded postal agreement, whose substance turns out to be rather trivial compared with a typical contract in the private sector.

[14] However, it need not follow that civil service principles are irreconcilable with collective bargaining in the government domain, or that these principles are undesirable *per se*.

[15] In the usual case, appointment and promotion are by competitive merit; the closed and union shops are forbidden; the voluntary check-off is allowed; there is no right to strike; and binding arbitration of disputes over new contracts is precluded.

[16] In situations involving school districts, the chief negotiator for management may be the superintendent rather than the board of education, although the latter must consent to offers, to counter-proposals, and to the ultimate agreement. But the process may not stop with the board. If the taxing power lies beyond—say, with the council or board of supervisors—then these authorities must be brought in somehow. Indeed, with state and now federal financing also involved, the bargaining process becomes still broader in scope and becomes more and more a matter of political power, in the neutral rather than the pejorative sense of the term.

[17] One is reminded of the political efforts of private street railway companies to obtain franchises in the early part of this century. If neither fraud nor bribery were involved in either case, the principle is identical: the use of political influence to gain a lawful end.

[18] As related by the Director of Personnel (1963). See Foster B. Roser, "Collective Bargaining in Philadelphia," in Kenneth O. Warner, *op. cit.*, pp. 103–115.

[19] The basic rules of the game are incorporated in the city charter. The system forbids strikes and allows no arbitration of impasses, although there is grievance arbitration. The agreements include the voluntary check-off. In accordance with the merit principle, there must be no discrimination between union and nonunion employees. The main weakness of the system is lack of a built-in procedure for dealing with impasses.

[20] Belasco argues that loss of the strike weapon generally is no real loss in fact: most services of government, he says, are nonessential and involve little loss if suspended; the services are usually exclusively supplied, so there need be no attrition of customers; the employees have few or no skills and can easily be replaced; and the producing agency would suffer no revenue loss because the services are unpriced. (James A. Belasco, "Resolving Dispute over Contract in the State Public Service: An Analysis," *Labor Law Journal* [September, 1965], pp. 541–542.) I disagree in whole or in part with all of these reasons, as I will point out.

[21] For a summary of both views, see Arvid Anderson, "The Developing State of Collective Bargaining for Public Employees" (Address before the University of Chicago Conference on Public Employment and Collective Bargaining, mimeographed, February 5, 1965).

[22] In mass transit in central cities, substitutes include walking, the automobile, and perhaps competing nonstruck lines: all three involve congestion and large losses of time and money. For these reasons and the impracticality of building a new, substitute transit system, essentiality is extremely high, as the transit unions well know.

[23] To get around this, the period when recognition is automatically withdrawn might be limited to the duration of the strike, instead of an arbitrary two years. But this weakens the strength of the device as a deterrent. A strong union involved in supply of a critical public service could call short strikes with impunity, using them to create immediate massive crises whose pressures would promote costly and inequitable settlements.

[24] Under the amended New York law governing labor relations in nonprofit hospitals and residential care centers (July 1, 1963), any agreement that fails to provide for final and binding determination of grievances "shall be deemed to include" provisions for their submission to arbitra-

tion, at the request of either party or both parties, under rules to be laid down by the New York State Board of Mediation (Section 716, Sub-Section 2). These awards are made subject to full review by the State Supreme Court (Sub-Section 6).

[25] If they are not made binding, the difference from fact finding with recommendations becomes purely semantic.

[26] Neil W. Chamberlain, *Collective Bargaining* (New York: McGraw-Hill, 1951), pp. 220–221 ff. The following equations illustrate this balance:

1. The bargaining power of the union (U) alone depends upon the relative costs to the public employer (E) of disagreeing (d) vs. agreeing (a) to the union's proposal, or

   Union power $= F \, (Ed/Ea)$

2. Similarly, for the public employer,

   Employer power $= F \, (Ud/Ua)$

3. The relative power of each side then depends upon the following:

   a. If $(Ed/Ea) > (Ud/Ua)$, the power balance favors the union.

   b. If $(Ed/Ea) < (Ud/Ua)$, the power balance favors the public employer.

   c. If agreement can be had, then the cost of agreement to both sides must be equal to or less than the costs of disagreement.

d. If agreement cannot be had, then the cost of disagreement to each must be equal to or less than the cost of agreement.

[27] We are dealing here with a purely formal construction, which has the merit of sorting out clearly the determining factors for relative bargaining power. However, it is doubtful that these variables can be measured empirically.

[28] Municipal power and water services usually have lower price elasticities of demand than does, say, public transit. This lowers the cost to the agency of agreeing to the union's demand and therefore, other things being equal, raises the union's bargaining power.

[29] Assuming that the government union has the support, for example, of the central labor council.

[30] Government unions have used political power to gain advantages directly, bypassing collective bargaining. In San Francisco transit wages are fixed automatically by charter amendment at the average of the two highest properties in the country.

[31] The only study I know of in this whole field is Melvin Lurie, "Government Regulation and Union Power: A Case Study of the Boston Transit Industry," *Journal of Law and Economics,* III (October, 1960), pp. 118–135. His evidence does not invalidate this hypothesis.

In "Federal Labor Relations: 1970," W. V. Gill, Executive Director of the U.S. Federal Labor Relations Council, discusses some of the significant changes brought about by Executive Order 11491, which replaces Executive Order 10988, issued by President Kennedy in 1962. One of the first changes produced by the new executive order was the creation of the Federal Labor Relations Council (FLRC) as an overall administrative policy and appellate body within the U.S. Department of Labor. The FLRC is under the direction of Assistant Secretary of Labor for Labor Management Relations, who is assigned responsibility for decisions subject to the right of appeal to the council itself "on unit and representation issues, unfair labor practice complaints, and alleged violations of the standards of conduct for labor organizations." The executive order also establishes a Federal Service Impasses Panel, which is administratively within the FLRC but has considerable independence in performing its functions. The executive order provides that the Federal Mediation and Conciliation Service will offer to assist the parties in reaching an agreement and provide preventive mediation services as needed to improve labor management relations. The Federal Services Impasses Panel probably will first attempt to use fact finding with recommendations as a basis for getting the parties to engage in further negotiations. However, if no agreement is reached within thirty days, the issue will be referred back to the panel for final determination.

Other changes made by the new executive order eliminate some of the confusion created by Executive Order 10988 by providing for exclusive recognition only. The older executive order provided for informal and formal recognition as well as exclusive recognition, which means that, in a sense, under the older order, a multiplicity of collective bargaining agents were involved in each agency. The establishment of exclusive recognition will reduce the number of separate unions in the federal agencies and "will remove fragmentary and in substantial relationships that are no longer worth the time and expense in view of the extensive coverage by exclusive recognitions."

Moreover, the executive order follows the Taft-Hartley procedure of defining supervisors as management. "A supervisor no longer can be represented by a labor organization nor serve as a labor organization representative."

The executive order adopts a number of procedures designed to strengthen collective bargaining. These include making the refusal to negotiate by agency management or the labor organization an unfair labor practice; providing for the delegation of more authority to local officials; instituting special procedures for resolving negotiability problems; limiting the power of headquarters organizations to nullify local agreements; and providing that the parties may agree to binding arbitration to resolve disputes arising under contracts.

# Federal Labor Relations: 1970

## by W. V. Gill

Labor relations in the Federal service has had a remarkable escalation in public interest and importance this year. The postal strike in March, followed by the air traffic controllers' "sick-out," were events unprecedented in our history. The postal negotiations certainly were high drama, and Congressional enactment of the first phase of the settlement—a $2.5 billion pay raise for civilian and military personnel—put government collective bargaining in the big leagues overnight.

These events naturally have aroused speculation in labor relations circles about their effect on the new Executive Order 11491 and Federal labor relations generally. Obviously, their impact is not inconsequential. . . . My remarks will be limited to the basic changes in Federal labor-management relations brought about by Executive Order 11491 which we are just beginning to implement.

The new Order is second-generation hardware. While it evolved directly from eight years of experience under Executive Order 10988, its new policies and machinery represent in toto a radical departure from the old way of doing business. The growth of Federal unionism since 1962 has been phenomenal. Today, a million and a half employees are represented under exclusive recognition—more than half the entire Federal work force. Exclusive recognition now covers some 90 percent of postal employees, 70 percent of the trades and labor, and 30 percent of the white collar. The changes made by the new Order are aimed at developing arrangements suitable for labor relations of these dimensions in the governmental setting.

I say "developing arrangements" advisedly, because if what we have adopted in E.O. 11491 does not work out well in

SOURCE Reprinted by permission from *Collective Bargaining Today: 1970*, copyright 1971 by the Bureau of National Affairs, Inc., Washington, D.C. 20037.

practice it will be changed. But I repeat "work out well *in practice*"—that doesn't mean the first protest from one side that they lost too much in the realignment of policy, or from the other side that they gained too little, will lead the Council to move immediately for change. It took three years, two task forces and a host of compromises to develop the new Order. I think the Council will want and need more than ideological disagreement with a new policy, or half-hearted testing, before it can conclude that it does not work well and should be changed. . . .

Let me outline for you briefly what I consider to be the most significant changes changes brought about by the new Order.

## CENTRAL AUTHORITY ESTABLISHED

First in importance is the establishment of central authority in the Executive branch to administer the program, make policy decisions, and act as the final arbiter of disputes and impasses between the agencies and the unions. There are three elements of central machinery. At the top is the Federal Labor Relations Council, which is the overall administrative, policy and appellate body for the program. The Assistant Secretary of Labor for Labor-Management Relations is assigned the NLRB-type functions. He makes decisions subject to a limited right of appeal to the Council, on unit and representation issues, unfair labor practice complaints, and alleged violations of the standards of conduct for labor organizations. And a Federal Service Impasses Panel is established to bring about the final settlement of negotiation impasses which cannot be resolved through mediation.

This transfer of authority from the individual department and agency heads to central machinery is, of course, the most fundamental change in the program. It provides third-party, impartial process and finality of decision on the significant issues that arise in the labor-management

relationship, and it gets agency management out of the distasteful and inequitable position of being both a party to disputed matters and also the judge who finally decides the dispute. Central decision-making should have the effect, also, of developing consistent policy doctrine and thereby minimizing the number of disputes in the future.

## EXCLUSIVE RECOGNITION ONLY

Another key change is one that simplifies the arrangements for union recognition. The granting of informal and formal recognition was discontinued effective with the signing of the Order on October 29, 1969. Now only exclusive recognition is granted, and it is granted only on the basis of a majority vote in an election conducted under the supervision of the Assistant Secretary of Labor. All existing informal recognitions, about 1,100 units, terminate July 1, 1970. Existing formal recognitions, about 1,200 units, will be terminated in accordance with instructions to be issued by the Council before next October.

The elimination of informal and formal recognition will reduce the number of separate labor organizations Federal agencies deal with by more than half—from nearly 200 down to about 90. And it will remove fragmentary and insubstantial relationships that are no longer worth the time and expense in view of the extensive coverage by exclusive recognition. There now are 2,640 exclusive units covering 1,477,000 employees.

## SUPERVISORS ARE ON
## THE MANAGEMENT SIDE

A third key change is clarification of the status of supervisors in the labor-management relationship. The Order prescribes an official definition of who is a supervisor —very like the Taft-Hartley definition— and provides clearly that supervisors are part of management. A supervisor no longer can be represented by a labor organization nor serve as a labor organization representative. And, by the end of 1970, all supervisors who are currently in units of formal or exclusive recognition must be taken out. Currently, there are about 80 units of exclusive recognition for supervisors, and several hundred formal and exclusive units in which supervisors are mixed in together with rank-and-file employees.

## NEGOTIATION ARRANGEMENTS STRENGTHENED

The fourth main area of change deals with the scope of negotiations. There are a number of items which, taken together, should do much to strengthen the negotiation process and dignify the worth of a negotiated agreement. *First*, the obligation to negotiate in good faith is stated explicitly and is backed up by making "refusal to negotiate" an unfair labor practice by agency management or the labor organization. I do not need to dwell on the implications of this change. It should have a substantial effect in the Federal program, as it has had in the private sector, when supported by third-party enforcement.

*Second*, while negotiations in the governmental setting are necessarily limited by applicable laws and regulations, agencies have been urged to expand the scope of negotiations in bargaining units below the national level by delegating more personnel policy authority to their local officials, and to make exceptions to general agency regulations where uniformity is not essential in a particular situation. This item is more than a pious platitude. The authority behind it is the requirement—not a new one, but a much more significant one now that there will be third-party enforcement—that in prescribing regulations an agency shall have due regard for the obligation of good-faith nego-

tiations. A labor organization may appeal to the Council for a decision when it believes that an agency's regulations are in violation of this provision.

*Third*, and related to the second, are the special procedures provided for resolving doubts or disagreements at the bargaining unit level over the extent of management's authority to negotiate on a particular matter. This has been one of the most troublesome areas in our experience—the so-called "negotiability issues." In some cases, the issue stems from a lack of clarity in agency delegations of authority to local officials; in others, the meaning of the agency's regulations is unclear in the particular situation; sometimes it is a question of interpretation of pertinent statutes, Civil Service Commission regulations, Comptroller General decisions, and so forth; and quite often—as you would expect—the dispute centers around the meaning of the management rights clauses in the Order and the exclusion from the obligation to negotiate on matters with respect to the mission of an agency; its budget; its organization and staffing pattern; the technology of performing its work; and its internal security practices.

The Order provides special procedures to handle these negotiability issues, rather than using the unfair labor practice route, because our experience has been that these situations are not so much a matter of antagonistic refusal to negotiate as they are an honest doubt or disagreement as to whether a specific proposal is or is not open for negotiation.

The procedures provide initially for referral of the issue, by either party, to agency headquarters for an expeditious determination by the agency head. An agency head's decision as to the interpretation of the agency's own regulations is final. However, as I have mentioned, a labor organization may appeal to the Council if it believes that the agency's regulations, as the agency head interprets them, are in violation of the Order or of laws or regulations of governing authority outside the agency. It also may appeal to the Council if it disagrees with an agency head's decision that a proposal is non-negotiable because it would violate law, regulations of governing authority outside the agency, or the Order.

We believe that the largest volume of the Council's appellate workload will be in this area of negotiability issues.

*Fourth*, there are two changes aimed directly at strengthening the worth of the negotiation process and the standing of the negotiated agreement. Headquarters approval of agreements negotiated at a lower level in the agency is still authorized, but the new Order makes it mandatory for headquarters to approve an agreement if it conforms to law and regulations. Second-guessing on the merits of what has been negotiated is not permitted. The other provision in this area is one which insulates the negotiated agreement from the effect of a change in agency regulations during the term of the agreement unless the change is required by law or authority outside the agency, in which case it overrides any negotiated provision to the contrary as in the past. What has been done here is to ensure that an agency's authority to regulate will not, when the matter is wholly within agency discretion, become in conflict with its obligation to negotiate and stick to its agreements. When the term of the agreement is ended, of course, any renegotiation of the agreement will be subject to agency regulations as they exist at that time.

*Fifth*, the Order makes a major change in the area of negotiated grievance procedures. Instead of the advisory arbitration authorized by Executive Order 10988 —where, in effect, the arbitrator's award was only a recommendation to agency management—the parties may now agree

to the use of binding arbitration. It is possible of course that an arbitrator's award may, on rare occasions, involve seriously improper conduct on his part, or exceed his authority, or be contrary to law—the types of situation where in the private sector a party would go to court to seek relief. In any such situation, the Order provides a right of appeal to the Council to set aside or amend the award.

TERMINAL PROCEDURES
FOR NEGOTIATION IMPASSES

Finally, the new Order takes major steps to try to answer the $64 question: How to settle negotiation impasses fairly and finally where the right to strike or lockout is prohibited by law?

First, the Federal Mediation and Conciliation Service is assigned an official role in the program—the same role it plays in private sector disputes. It will proffer its services to assist the parties in reaching agreement and provide preventive mediation services at other times when needed to improve labor-management relationships.

We have high hopes that by extending its full services to the Federal program, FMCS will be able to speed up the settlement of unresolved negotiation problems. But it was our belief in framing the Order that we needed machinery that would guarantee final settlement of even the toughest negotiation impasses—ones that still defy settlement by the parties after exhausting mediation efforts.

It was for these cases that the Order established the Federal Service Impasses Panel. The Panel is administratively within the Council, but independent of the Council in performing its program functions. The Panel members are being appointed by the President from outside the Government. We expect there will be nine members appointed initially, serving in 3-man panels. The members have been tentatively selected and their appointments are presently in clearance. They are persons of high reputation for impartiality and expertise in labor relations, generally ones who have extensive experience in labor arbitration.

The Panel will determine its own method of functioning. We expect that if it takes jurisdiction of an impasse, its usual procedure will be, first, to use fact-finding with recommendations as a basis for further negotiation or settlement by the parties. However, if they are unable to settle within 30 days, they will report back to the Panel which will consider the remaining issues and direct a settlement.

I am sure you recognize the pioneering step involved in providing for the ultimate action of final and binding decision by the Panel on negotiation impasses. It is our hope that this end-of-the road process, with its uncertainty as well as finality, will help force the parties to an attitude of serious and problem-solving bargaining.

CONCLUSION

I think you will agree that these new policies and machinery represent a very substantial evolution in labor relations in the Federal service. Without any real experience yet with the new processes, I cannot venture a prediction whether they will prove in fact to be effective. We are pioneering in very important areas of public employee unionism, and are investing substantial funds to provide the new third-party machinery needed to make the program work. How well we do only time will tell. Whatever it may tell, and whatever adjustments may be made in the present design as we gain experience, in my judgment Executive Order 11491 stands tall as a landmark initiative by President Nixon to bring equity and justice to Federal labor relations.

In "Collective Bargaining in the Public Sector," E. Wight Bakke makes some predictions about the nature and future of collective bargaining in the public sector. He points out at the beginning of his article that many of the issues involved in collective bargaining by public employees have been pretty thoroughly explored. Although collective bargaining is favorably regarded by the industrial relations profession, it is not accepted by all public employers or even by some public employees. Moreover, although "the peculiar conditions in the public sector, which plague the reasonable resolution of issues pretty well settled in the private sector, have been clarified," there is "no widespread consensus . . . on the best way to meet these issues in the public sector."

Bakke devotes most of his paper to predictions of what lies ahead for public employee collective bargaining. He predicts a rapid and extensive expansion for collective bargaining in the public sector because all of the conditions conducive to the establishment of collective bargaining are currently present in the employee relations of large numbers of public employees. These conditions are (1) "common standard terms, applicable to all members of a sizeable group"; (2) "a relative absence of individual bargaining power where individuals have a unique or outstanding skill or individual worth to the employer, so that it is difficult for the employer to replace that specific individual"; (3) "where production of goods and services is a collective undertaking, that is, where production is such that the contribution of any one individual to the total product is difficult to access"; (4) "where relations between workers and employers become very impersonal"; (5) "where the employer is an organized group and the employees are in fact dealing with other employees who are bargaining for the companies"; (6) "where the group concerns and grievances can be interpreted as personal gripes and complaints"; (7) "Where there is dependence on performance of the results of management activities and therefore management can be held accountable by the workers for performance which influences their own working conditions."

Bakke's second prediction is that collective bargaining in the public sector will become very militant in the foreseeable future. This militancy will be caused by a number of factors, including: the resistance to unionism by employers, which will require them to use militant tactics in order to solve their problems collectively; union rivalry; the ineptness that union leaders are likely to exhibit as they attempt to transfer collective bargaining procedures from the private to the public sector; and the fact that "direct action and coercive mass pressure, once thought to be a tactic used only by laboring people and Communists, is becoming an acceptable approach to desired attainment by upper middle class people." Bakke does not feel that strikes are going to be legitimized in the immediate future, but that they, along with other forms of coercion, will be used extensively. However, he feels that the adoption of impasse procedures and mechanisms will bring greater stability to public employee collective bargaining.

His third prediction is that "the dominant objective of union leaders for some time will be the achievement of collective (that is, of organizational) power." This attempt to maximize collective power will have significant implications for public administration because unions are more likely to be concerned with adopting procedures which maximize their power than they are with the establishment of efficient administration. For example, unions are more likely to be interested in bargaining units which favor them strategically and with common rules, than they are with questions of merit.

Bakke's fourth prediction is that "the combination of political and economic bargaining strategies by unions in the public sector will produce a confusing pattern of collective bargaining interactions between public management and public employees." This confusion will result from unions using indirect presures through politicians to effect the decisions of their immediate employers in those cases where direct negotiations fail to produce the desired results.

Bakke's fifth prediction is that "the civil service concept of personal arrangements and practices is going to suffer and be severely modified." This is true in large measure because the civil service regulations are uniform while labor organizations bargain for particular groups and because civil service rules are determined unilaterally and therefore are incompatible with the concept of collective bargaining.

Bakke's sixth prediction is "that the public is going to pay a big price for what the public employees gain through collective bargaining." This price is going to be paid primarily in the form of higher taxes and the interruption of public services. "Collective bargaining is coming to the public sector before the process of such bargaining in a private sector, on which the former is modeled, has developed an adequate concern for the public interest, save as that interest is served by improvement in the conditions of life and work of union members directly and all workers indirectly."

However, Bakke concludes that "it is always possible, of course, that in the light of the obvious and inescapable impact of industrial relations in public employment on the whole public, to say nothing of the dangers to the life of the unions themselves if the public is pushed beyond its tolerance level, that a pattern of collective bargaining in the public sector will be developed by public employers, public union leaders, and public employees which reveals a higher standard of public responsibility than that previously attained by any section of the labor movement."

# Collective Bargaining in the Public Sector

## by E. Wight Bakke

. . . Next to manpower problems, the field of public employment relations has whipped up more interest among [labor specialists] looking for new fields to explore than any other subject. The important issues have been pretty well defined. Let me just call the role of those issues:

1. The basis for the right of public employees to collectively negotiate their terms of work through representatives of their own choosing has been thoroughly explored and, on the whole, that right is accepted by our profession, although not by all public employers and even some public employees. The heads of those who opposed such a change on the grounds of its incompatibility with governmental sovereignty are bloody but in many cases still unbowed. The hassle over this issue has some similarity to that over managerial prerogatives in the private sector.

But it goes deeper than that and involves the very question as to who shall govern politically. It also involves how far those elected to govern can go in the sharing of the legislative and executive powers and obligations delegated to them by the people.

2. The appropriateness of collective bargaining in the public sector of the sort and style developed in the private sector has been both asserted and denied both thoughtfully and eloquently and even passionately by knowledgeable partisans and presumably unbiased neutrals.

3. The peculiar conditions in the public sector which plague the reasonable resolution of issues pretty well settled in the private sector have been clarified. But we are a long way from being certain about how to handle the following problems in the public sector: (1) the appro-

SOURCE An unpublished address to the Connecticut Valley Chapter of the Industrial Relations Research Association on April 8, 1970.

priate bargaining unit; (2) the practicality of exclusive bargaining representation; (3) compulsory union membership; (4) the need for a Public Employee Relations Board to judge and enforce sanctions on either public employers or unions which refuse to bargain in good faith or commit unfair labor practices; (5) the specification of what constitutes refusal to bargain and unfair labor practices; (6) the determination of the scope of bargainable in relation to mandated issues; (7) the integration of the use and applicability of political and economic power simultaneously; (8) the relation of the bargaining time table to budget submission dates; (9) the kinds of impasse breaking procedures that have a chance to succeed; (10) the right of public employees to strike; (11) the rights of the public to uninterrupted essential services; (12) and the possibility of coupling coercive practices with professional ethics, all have made the subject of research and lively debate.

But no widespread concensus exists on the best way to meet these issues in the public sector. . . . Other than proclaiming the ultimate truth about these matters, what can one say that is new to any one who has kept pace with the mounting attention and debate given to this subject? Very little I'm afraid.

* * *

Well there's one way out of this. If there isn't much that's new to say about the past and present, why not take a flier at the future? . . .

Let me make seven predictions of what lies ahead in this area of collective bargaining in the public sector, and give some of my reasons for such prophecies.

1. *Unionization in the public sector is going to increase rapidly and extensively.* It will increase until public employees participate in determining their conditions of employment through collective bargaining by representatives of their own choice to as great an extent as employees do in the private sector.

2. *Union action in the foreseeable future is going to be militant.* The growth of public employee unionism in the next 15 to 20 years will be accompanied by militancy and by the use of coercive mass force to at least as great, and probably a greater, degree than has accompanied the spread of collective bargaining in the private sector since 1935.

3. *The achievement of collective power is going to compete for attention as an objective of union leaders with the adaptation of unionism to effective public administration and to the improvement of professional performance and the professional status of public employees.* In the development of the collective bargaining process, the effort to gain collective power is going to overshadow for a time, but not permanently, the attainment of professional excellence and improvment of professional performance and responsibility in carrying on the administration of the activities in which public employees find their life work.

4. *The combination of political and economic bargaining strategies and tactics will disturb for some time the pattern of collective bargaining interactions between public management and public employee unions and associations.*

5. *The civil service concept of personnel policy and arrangements is going to suffer and be severely modified.* It may be adjusted, but could be destroyed. The nature of its replacement is not clear.

6. *The public is going to pay a big price for what public employees gain.* The serving of public interest for a time, but not permanently, is going to play second fiddle to the serving of partisan and sectoral interests.

7. *Nevertheless nothing is going to stop the introduction of and spread of collective bargaining into the public sector.* None of the other six developments is going to destroy the desirability and practicability of integrating collective bar-

gaining into the process by which the employment conditions and pay of public employees are determined.

Now to be more specific. I'll postpone for the moment the first prediction about the rapid spread of unionization and collective bargaining in the public sector and move on to the prophecies that are more controversial.

My prediction that unionism in the public sector in the foreseeable future is going to be militant unionism is based on the following observations.

*First Observation* Public employee unionism is in the organizing and recognition seeking stage in a situation which suggests to union organizers that militancy is necessary. In spite of the spread of federal and state executive orders and laws nominally giving the right to organize and bargain, and providing mechanisms for recognition, half of the states have not taken that step and three absolutely forbid it. Even where they have many, the public *managers* have not wholeheatedly accepted their responsibility to recognize those rights and engage in realistic collective bargaining leading to *mutual* consent. Even where they have done so, in most situations they are babes in the woods when it comes to dealing with unions and sharing their decision-making power with union leaders supported by mass solidarity. Union leaders are also going to be inept for some time in adapting the only pattern of barganing they are familiar with, that which has been developed in the private sector, to the peculiarities and necessities of industrial relations in the public sector. Ineptness and inexperience is a certain recipe for producing militant attitudes on both sides. Even as they gain experience the confusion over how far public employers can go and still meet their governing obligations and their ultimate responsibilities to the public is going to produce puzzling uncertainties. Union leaders will perceive hesitation rooted in those uncertainties as

stubbornness, arbitrariness, and buck-passing, that can only be met by a show of strength.

*Second Observation* Added to these volatile factors is jurisdictional conflict between different unions, and between the traditional kind of trade unions and so-called professional associations, particularly in the educational field where nearly one-half of the public employees are concentrated. The impact of this factor will be less if election procedures are quickly established. But even so, the competition for acceptance of one union or association over another is likely to cause the leaders of those organizations to demonstrate their militancy as proof to prospective members that they have most to gain by expressing their preference for the union that will really stand up to management. The so-called associations like the N.E.A. and Civil Service Association have already begun to adopt coercive tactics in order to prove themselves in that way as they compete for members with the more traditional type unions.

*Third Observation* Direct action and coercive mass pressure, once thought to be a tactic used only by laboring people and Communists, is becoming an acceptable approach to desire attainment by upper middle class people. Taxpayers, landlords, students in colleges and high schools, teachers, professors, and even priests as well as Negroes and relief clients are learning the utility of direct and coercive mass pressure as a successful way of getting action on demands that formerly got lost in bureaucratic buck-passing and red tape. And if the militant revolt of the women gains momentum and gets integrated with the tactics of public servants, watch out. Over half of public servants are women.

What I am suggesting is that militant direct and coercive mass action is becoming an "in" thing. In such a social atmosphere militancy will be encouraged.

*Fourth Observation* The use of the

strike by public servants is not going to be legitimized, but the strike or some other form of reduction or withdrawal of services having the same impact on the political fortunes of public officials and the loss of essential goods and services for the public is going to be extensively used nevertheless. The declarations of union leaders equating collective bargaining with negotiations against a strike deadline makes that clear. So does the wildcat unwillingness of the rank and file to listen to their leaders advising a less militant approach as was the case in the mail carriers strike. The record of successes by public employees who have resorted to strikes encourages confidence that, notwithstanding its illegality, it is a method that gets results. The very legal prohibition of strikes poses a challenge to daring leaders to prove that no law can really be enforced on large groups of people who don't voluntarily impose that law on themselves.

I happen to believe that impasse procedures and mechanisms, once they are perfected and generally available, will reduce that development. The adoption by all states of a guarantee of the right to organize and provisions for determinative employee participation through collective bargaining in setting the terms of public employment will reduce the chances of strikes. Also were we to have public enforcement on both public employee unions and public employers of a duty to bargain in good faith on a mutually predetermined set of bargainable issues, the duty and issues defined in terms consistent with the realities of public administration, there would be fewer occasions when public employees would have some justification for their perception that to strike was the only way to get action. And just to be really utopian, if the public was willing to pay the price of assuring public employees of conditions and rewards for work better than, or at least equal to, those attained by workers who *were* free to strike, that

justification would be weakened even more. But we are still a long way from carrying on public employee industrial relations within that kind of institutional framework.

The strike in the private sector is the ultimate protection of workers against unilateralism exercised by employers from their position of relative economic power. It will continue to appeal to public employees as their ultimate protection against unilateralism exercised by their public employers from their position of agents of sovereign governmental power, lacking any substitute guarantee of mutually acceptable finality. In the case of both private and public employment it should be observed, however, that the escape from employer unilateralism by endowing unions with a possibility of exercising unilateralism by virtue of their ability to bring the public to its knees by withholding goods and services essential to life and work, does not provide an acceptable definition of a just or justified system of industrial relations in the public sector.

The third prediction I would make is that the dominant objective of union leaders for some time will be the achievement of collective (that is of organizational) power. That objective will compete successfully for attention and activity with both their efforts to adapt the private sector pattern of union activities to the requirements of effective public administration and the improvement of the professional status of their members.

Let me cite several examples. The union leaders proposal for the determination of the appropriate unit for collective bargaining will be the one in each case which is most strategically favorable to the immediate opportunity to organize and to increase their membership rather than one which is geared to meeting the requirements of effective public administration. Any group of employees which appears ready for organization will be defended as an appropriate unit. The result may well be a fractionalization of bargaining units without reference to their community of interest with a larger universe of public employees or without reference to the obstacles raised to the efficient administration of public services and the equitable allocation of public resources by such a fractionalized pattern of bargaining relations. The definition of the appropriate bargaining unit of employees with respect to whose terms of employment a government executive is expected to negotiate affects his administrative tasks in many ways. It affects the number of employee organizations with which he must deal. It affects the problem of giving equitable treatment to all the employees under his management. It affects the variety of negotiating results that he must somehow integrate into a pattern of employment terms and their budgetary implications which make sense for the whole unit of government. It affects the scope of issues with respect to which it is possible to bargain in a particular unit, for some of the terms of employment must necessarily be the same for all employees in the whole political unit, ra†her than peculiar to the particular fractionalized group. It determines how many chances there are that negotiated terms for one group will result in a sense of injustice or inequity to another. I am not criticizing the unions for pushing for a definition of the appropriate unit which is most likely to facilitate organizing, for right now they are in a situation where there are great differences among employees in different groups in the degree of their predisposition to respond favorably to the organizer's appeal. I am only indicating that the immediate problem is accumulating power for public employee unions is to increase the number of groups they can get organized, and that *this* power objective is at this time, and for sometime in the future, is going to be, most immediately satisfied by defining an appropriate unit as any group apparently amenable to organization regardless of

whether the resulting fractionalized pattern of bargaining units makes sense in the effective administration of public industrial relations or not.

One strategy for the accumulation of union power is the de facto development of group solidarity by means of a substitution of the common rule for the merit system of rewards. The latter system is expected to result in the possibility of professional advancement and transfer and the maintenance of professional standards among those public employees to which the term professional accurately applies. That result may be more fancy than fact. The system itself, therefore, may not be worthy of preservation or even possible of improvement so as to achieve the result. Public employment unions to date have shown very little inclination to try or to modify their approach to solidarity via the common rule approach so that an improved merit system would have a chance of success.

A third example is rooted in the previous prediction I made that militant direct action including job action and the strike will be a continuing instrument of power for public employee unions. Those who participate in such direct action are not going to improve their public image as dedicated professionals. Their experience and perception of the degree to which their public employers accord them that status now may be such that this result appears to be no loss. I won't argue with that. I am also aware of the rhetoric of leaders of public employee unions devoted to expounding their deep concern for and plans to improve the professional status of those who will count on the union to promote that improvement. I hope their rhetoric is rooted in and brought to life by genuine effort. The effort will have to be great to compensate for the loss of status in the public mind of those who gain personally by withholding essential services from the public.

My fourth prediction is that the combination of political and economic bargaining strategies by unions in the public sector will produce a confusing pattern of collective bargaining interactions between public management and public employees. It will be similar to what the situation would be in private industry if the union could go around management and make deals with the board of directors representing the stock holders, and if union had an important voice in electing the board of directors.

There will be an uneasy relationship between the administrative managers of public agencies and the elected legislative and executive officials to whom they are responsible and upon whom they depend for support in the pursuit of their professional interests. Those elected officials have a dominant interest in staying in office. Now the union and its allies in the labor movement, particularly in local and state situations can and often do play a very important part in the electoral process. The working class vote can make the difference in election, non-election, or dis-election. When, therefore, as will inevitably be the case, the union which is ostensibly bargaining with the management administrators bypasses them in the hope of getting a back door deal directly with city hall or the state house a serious modification of collective bargaining as developed in the private sector occurs. The management administrators can find their efforts at reaching a settlement short circuited. This was the kind of situation in New York City which had grown up under Mayor Wagner. Mayor Lindsay, faced soon after his inauguration with the transit negotiations, was not fully aware of this. He was aware of it in last year's transit negotiations.

\* \* \*

Collective bargaining as it is defined by practice in the private sector does not involve back door deals with the board of directors, and these directors are not elec-ted either by the union members and their allies in the labor movement or by the ultimate consumers of their services or goods. Collective bargaining in the private sector assumes the existence of two relatively independent parties, the management and workers represented by their union, trying to accommodate their differences and satisfy their respective interests through negotiation and administration of a contract.

My fifth prediction is that the civil service concept of personnel arrangements and practice is going to suffer and be severely modified. It may be adjustable to collective bargaining, but it could also be destroyed.

The question of what will happen to the civil service system is a serious one. The divergency between the method of ordering industrial relations by a Civil Service Commission administering legislative mandates and by collective bargaining is clear. We are already seeing signs of the incompatibility of the two approaches. The civil service approach assumes a uniform set of terms of employment for a large number of functional groups of classified employees. Selection, performance standards, salary grades, tenure, promotion and transfer arrangements, grievance procedures, vacation rights, pensions, apply across the Board, for example. Under collective bargaining the groups organized are multiple and each organization bargains for and in the interests of its own members. It is foolish to expect that any uniformity in terms will be achieved, and leap-frogging becomes a serious possibility for making the principle of coercive comparison rather than the principle of optimal overall benefit the basis of demands and settlements. A case in point is the achievement by the transit workers in New York of a pension scheme which is not only actuarially unsound for the transit industry there, but has already whetted the appetites of other public service workers in New York City and State. But if uniformly applied it would be disastrous to the financial foundation of the city and state and to any rational allocation of available revenues to essential needs of the public services.

The civil service approach, however, is an arrangement whose terms and form have been unilaterally determined ultimately by the legislative mandates and by detailed commission regulations. It conflicts, therefore, with the principle represented by collective bargaining and of authoritative participation by employees in determining the conditions of and payment for their work. There will be an uneasy effort to maintain both for a time by eliminating mandated items from bargainable issues, and by making the bargaining units as comprehensive as possible. The comprehensive bargaining unit in Philadelphia is an example.

An interesting but exasperating possibility arises in the light of the discussion of the political interests and end run machine politics that get involved in public sector bargaining discussed previously. Will the civil service approach, which grew up in the effort to eliminate spoils system politics from public employment relations, be replaced, as collective bargaining develops in the public sector, by a system of determining employment conditions which re-introduces a spoils system involving not so much individuals as groups of individuals? I would say the answer at this point is indeterminate.

My sixth, and next to last prediction, is that the public is going to pay a big price for what the public employees gain through collective bargaining. This is not to say that the price is unjust or that the results aren't worth it. But the serving of the public interest is going to play second fiddle for a time to the serving of partisan and sectoral interests.

The most obvious price is that tax burdens will increase. No one is going to be able to argue, as some economists have, concerning unionism in the private sector, that the unions only negotiate costly improvements in the economic welfare of their members, which workers would have received anyway by the graciousness of increasing productivity and competition for workers in a free market. And the price for administering a system of industrial relations which includes collective bargaining is not likely to decrease government costs per unit of service unless the unions promote some form of union management cooperation, the nature of and tendency to which do not yet appear on the horizon.

A second cost, at least until the dust of organizing activity settles, is rooted in the predisposition to militancy. The interruption in the flow of public services and goods is going to be costly not only in public inconvenience, but in the cost of substitute services and goods even when these can be had. When they cannot be had, as will usually be the case, the disturbance to the normal operations of income producing enterprise for individuals and organizations will add costs that are far from hidden.

Collective bargaining is coming to the public sector before the process of such bargaining in the private sector on which the former is modeled has developed an adequate concern for the public interest, save as that interest is served by improvement in the conditions of life and work of union members directly and all workers indirectly.

It is always possible, of course, that in the light of the obvious and inescapable impact of industrial relations in public employment on the whole public, to say nothing of the dangers to the life of the unions themselves if the public is pushed beyond its tolerance level, that a pattern of collective bargaining in the public sector will be developed by public employers, public union leaders, and public employees which reveals a higher standard of public responsibility than that previously attained by any section of the labor movement.

When it comes right down to it, I pin my hopes, if not any confident prophecy, for the shape of things to come on that possibility. I'm not nearly as pessimistic as you might be led to believe by the observations I've made. But I like to face squarely the kinds of things that can make my optimism so shallow it never makes contact with reality. These predictions I've made, to the extent they hold up under the battering of time and circumstance, reveal problems to be solved. They do not constitute a case against public employment collective bargaining. And it will take a lot of sweat and even tears as well as rational effort on the part of all of us to solve them, public employers, union leaders, public employees, and those of us in academic life who are trying to make sense out of what is happening and will get involved from time to time in mediation, fact finding and arbitration.

Let me close by returning to my first prediction. Nothing is going to stop the growth of collective bargaining in the public sector.

The first reason is that all the conditions and circumstances that have made employees ready for collective bargaining in sectors where it has been established are present in the employment relations of a critical mass of public employees. You men and women whose career interests are focused in industrial relations know them by heart. Let me name them briefly. The predisposition to organization and collective bargaining becomes manifest under certain conditions.

1. Where there is a necessity for common standard terms applicable to all members of a sizable group. When a group of individual employees work under, and must be provided with, approximately the same pay, benefits, hours, and conditions of work, it is impossible for the individual employee, or employer for that matter, to make any substantial modification for individuals which departs from the common rule. This is not the result of a demand for equality or of bureaucratic rigidity, but of operating necessity. The implication is that standards and rules applicable to the whole group should be negotiated groupwise rather than individualwise.

2. Where there is a relative absence of individual bargaining power, where individuals have a unique or outstanding skill or individual worth to the employer so that it is difficult for the employer to replace that specific individual, that individual normally will rely on his own personal bargaining power. Where the group of employees have, or have the opportunity to demonstrate, few unique qualities which vary greatly from person to person, where within reasonable limits one is replaceable by the others, this individual bargaining power does not exist to the same degree. The implication is that a lack of individual bargaining power can be compensated for by group bargaining power maintaining a solid and united front.

3. Where the goods or service produced are social products in the sense that no one employee's contribution produces the whole, and it is difficult to disentangle for personal evaluation the value of his part in the total process.

4. Where there is an impersonality of relations between employer and employee. When the organization for which the individual's work is large enough so that there are several strata of supervision between the employee and the ultimate decision-making employer, the problem is to find and get to the employer. The implication is that many persons cannot do this individually, but they can do it by collectively focusing their search and dealings in an organizational representative.

5. Where the "employer" is an organized group. When the "employer" is not an individual but in reality another group

of employees (or agents) called management who *are* organized, the implication is that an organized group is needed to deal with an organized group. In the case of a school system the school superintendent and the school board in reality constitute an organized group of employees of the public.

6. Where the group concerns and grievances can be interpreted as personal gripes and complaints. When the effort is made to present effectively personal human and even professional interests as having equal legitimacy and force to organizational and managerial interests, some person has to speak up. Lacking the support of the united front of an organized group, that person is likely to be, and is more often than not, labeled a troublemaker, a center of agitated discontent and disloyalty, and other terms scarcely designed to increase that person's job security. The implication is that organized group support for a group spokesman is essential to provide that spokesman with a regularized role which does not damage his personal security.

7. Where there is dependence for performance results on management. When the product of the individuals in the group is greatly dependent on the policies, decisions, resource supplies, etc. stemming from management, the implication is that such common dependency can best be dealt with through collective representation designed to make such managerial action advantageous to good performance results by members of the group.

8. When there is a community of interest among the employees. As you are all aware, there is a basis for such interest in the case of teachers and many other groups of public employees. Identification with common skills, standards of performance, similarity in type and extent of preparation and training, similarity in status in the eyes of the community, and dependence of individual status on the status of the group as a whole are all elements. When there is such a community of interest, the other bases for collective organized representation are reinforced. If that community of interest is exaggerated by the commonly experienced sense of being left behind more privileged groups, or being as a group taken for granted, the predisposition is increased.

All of these factors apply to large numbers of public employees. Not all of them, but enough to provide large numbers who are ready to listen to the appeal of the union organizer.

The second reason is that there is present in these days a driving interest of labor leaders and the labor movement in giving public employees the union message to listen to. It is not only that unions exist whose operational field is precisely that of public employment, and that they are lead by young, capable, and dynamic, expansion-minded leaders. But the labor movement itself must, if it is to maintain its influence and power in the nation, organize the now predominant portion of the country's employees who are in the white collar, technical, and professional occupations. Large segments of public employees are so classified. Their effective organization and the demonstration that collective bargaining gets results for them would constitute a major breakthrough for a movement whose expansion for a long period had leveled off. The whole movement is behind the drive. I think the trend is irreversible.

### Related Readings

General reviews of collective bargaining by government employees can be found in Michael H. Moskow, J. Joseph Loewenberg, and Edward C.

Koziara, *Collective Bargaining in Public Employment* (New York, Random House, 1970); Sterling D. Spero *The Government as Employer* (New York, Rimson, 1948); Wilson R. Hart, *Collective Bargaining in the Federal Civil Service* (New York, Harper and Bros., 1961); and William D. Zosloo, *Collective Bargaining in the United States Federal Civil Service* (Chicago, Public Personnel Assoc., 1966). The Zosloo study is primarily of labor relations in the federal service since the promulgation of Executive Order 10988. The author concludes "that the difference between private and public employment in regard to collective bargaining is one rather of degree than of kind, and that there are no insurmountable legal or constitutional obstacles to granting civil servants similar, if modified, collective bargaining procedures" (pp. 157–158).

A summary of state public employees collective bargaining and organization may be found in Howard J. Anderson, ed., *Public Employee Organization and Bargaining* (Washington, D.C. Bureau of National Affairs, 1968). This volume deals primarily with the developments in public employee relations in New York, Michigan, Wisconsin, New York City, and Canada. Jean T. McKelvey, "The Role of State Agencies in Public Employee Labor Relations" (*Industrial and Labor Relations Review*, January 1967), discusses the advantages and disadvantages of various procedures for handling disputes at the state and local level. McKelvey also discusses the political influences on the organizational interests and philosophies that have produced the diverse state and local arrangements.

Much of the increase in collective bargaining by government employees has been by teachers. The major studies dealing with collective bargaining by teachers are Michael Moskow, *Teachers and Unions* (Philadelphia, University of Pennsylvania, Wharton School of Finance and Commerce, Industrial Research Unit, 1966); Byron Lieberman and Michael H. Moskow, *Collective Negotiations for Teachers* (Chicago, Rand McNally, 1966), T.M. Stinnett, Jack H. Kleinman, and Martha L. Ware, *Professional Negotiations and Public Education* (New York, Macmillan, 1966); Robert E. Doherty and Walter E. Oberer, *Teachers, School Boards, and Collective Bargaining: A Changing of the Guard* (Ithaca, N.Y., New State School of Industrial and Labor Relations, Cornell University, 1967); and Edward D. Shils and C. Taylor Whittier, *Teachers, Administrators, and Collective Bargaining* (New York, Thomas Y. Crowell Co., 1968).

There have been a number of studies by public agencies dealing primarily with the legal right to strike and presenting statistical information on disputes in the public sector. These include Joseph P. Goldberg, "Labor-Management Relations Laws and the Public Service" (*Monthly Labor Review*, June 1968); Anne M. Ross "Public Employee Unions and the Right to Strike" (*Monthly Labor Review*, March 1969); and Sheila C. White, "Work Stoppages of Government Employees" (*Monthly Labor Review*, December 1969). The article by Sheila White presents the statistics on the increase and work stoppages in public employment between 1958–1968. She indicates that the number of such stoppages increased from 15 in 1958 involving 1720 workers to 254 stoppages in 1968 involving 201,800 workers. The man-days idle from government work stoppages increased from 7510 in 1958 to 2,545,200 in 1968. The bulk of these strikes was at the local government level, where there were 235 strikes in 1968 involving 190,900 workers for a total man-days lost of 2,492,800. Major issues in the strikes were wages and supplementary benefits. Most of these government employee strikes were in education and sanitation and health services. White concludes: "Collective bargaining in the public sector in the present time is a relatively new phenomenon. Neither managers nor employees have yet had time to learn how to negotiate. They have also found it difficult to apply the experience gained in private situations to their situation. As both parties experiment with and develop patterns of bargaining, they will become more proficient at negotiating on a give-and-take basis. And as parity with the private sectors is approached, a major cause of work stoppages in the government service will be removed."

# IV

## Human Resource Development

The new human capital approach to labor supply looks upon the worker as the embodiment of past and current investment applied to his own natural endowment. This concept of the quality of the human productive factor is not meant to consider labor as a dehumanized, inanimate agent, such as land or physical capital (machinery), but to explain differences in earnings and economic status in general as a function of the time and money spent in the development of earning capacity.

Although significant differences appear in the quality of education and training, as a rule the greater amounts spent on these investments in human capital, the higher annual and lifetime earnings. In fact, those with the least investment are at the lower end of the income scale and form the bulk of the poverty class.

Recognizing the importance of greater human investment in the long-term attack on poverty and low income, manpower programs have been instituted to aid in the investment in those who, because of lack of resources or opportunity or perhaps as the result of discrimination, have been unable to acquire the human capital required for earning socially acceptable incomes. The first chapter of this section (chapter 16) describes and evaluates the effectiveness of our various manpower programs in reaching the policy goal of improving the productive quality of our work force.

Chapter 17 discusses the efforts to quantify the economic returns from education and training. There is some question as to the accuracy of measurements and even about the wisdom of attempting to put a dollar value on education. But despite these qualifications, and the uncertainty of whether returns from education at all levels exceed the returns on alternative (physical capital) investment, the data show already that earnings vary directly with the amount of human investment.

Although the long-term gains in raising the incomes of those with little human investment by measures to increase this investment through special programs may be substantial, antipoverty policy must recognize that training takes time and must provide more immediate measures that alleviate poverty even if they do not eliminate its causes. Furthermore, many of the poor not now in the labor force, either because of age or disability, would not be able to receive significant returns from investment in their training and education. Chapter 18 studies the poverty problem, measuring its extent, analyzing its causes, and discussing measures to raise the spending power of the poor, if not their labor-earning capacity.

The last chapter treats the special case of the Negro, who is subject to so many forces leading him into poverty—inadequate financial resources for private human capital investment, limited opportunity, and outright discrimination. The relative weakness in Negro earnings is discussed, then the importance of discrimination in the low economic position of the Negro, and finally measures to alleviate his poverty and upgrade his earnings potential.

# CHAPTER 16

# Manpower Programs*

Efforts to solve some of the nation's pressing domestic programs—especially poverty, unemployment, and racial unrest—led to a proliferation of manpower programs designed to help prepare people for present and future jobs by making the labor market operate mort effectively. Functionally, manpower programs involved efforts to recruit, train, and place workers as well as providing certain supportive services. However, it soon became obvious that the problems that concerned manpower programs were caused by deeply entrenched institutions that did not respond readily to partial solutions. In other words, it became very clear that systematic solutions were required that addressed themselves to economic policies (especially measures to sustain employment and growth), education, and welfare (income maintenance, housing, health, supportive services, child support, etc.) as well as manpower programs.

Although there were some earlier manpower programs—such as apprenticeship, the employment service, vocational rehabilitation, and vocational education—the 1960's saw a rapid increase in the number of training programs. The first of these was the Area Redevelopment Act of 1961, which provided public funds for the economic development of depressed areas. The ARA initially committed $10 million to train 20,000 unemployed workers. The Manpower Development and Training Act of 1962 and the Economic Opportunity Act of 1964 with their amendments were the main new manpower acts during the 1960's. Table 1 presents a summary of federally supported manpower programs in 1969.

---

* Parts of this chapter were taken from F. Ray Marshall and Vernon M. Briggs, Jr., "The Administration of Training Programs," Congress of the United States, Joint Economic Committee, *Federal Programs for the Development of Human Resources*, Washington, D.C., U.S. Government Printing Office, 1968, pp. 165–187.

TABLE 1. SUMMARY OF FEDERAL-SUPPORTED MANPOWER PROGRAMS, 1969

| Program | Agency[a] | Level of Operation Fiscal 1968 (Thousands of Persons) | 1969 Appropriation (Millions of $) | Services Provided | Eligibility Criteria | State and Local Program Administrators or Contractors | Allowances |
|---|---|---|---|---|---|---|---|
| United States employment service | MA | 5,760[b] | 341 | Recruitment, counseling, testing, placement, employer services and limited labor market research | All workers but the bulk unemployed | State employment service agencies | None |
| Vocational education | OE | 4,861[c] | 281 | Vocational education | State determined | State vocational education agencies | None in fiscal 1969 |
| Vocational rehabilitation | SRS | 208[d] | 415 | Medical and psychiatric assistance, prosthetic devices, skill training, education and other services needed to enhance employability | Physically, mentally or "socially" handicapped | State rehabilitation agencies | Provides $25 per week for an individual with $10 per dependent to a maximum of four; limited to special workshop projects |
| Adult basic education | OE | 408 | 45 | Rudimentary education | Over 18 years of age | State education agencies | None |
| MDTA Institutional | MA OE | 125[e] | 397 | Remedial and skill training; basic education | Mostly unemployed, but some upgrading | Public schools or skill centers and private schools | Adult—$10 above average weekly unemployment benefits in state plus $5 for each of 4 dependents Youth—$20 per week |
| OJT | MA | 140[e] | | Subsidies to employers to cover training costs | Same | Employers, state apprenticeship agencies, trade associations, unions, and nonprofit community agencies | None |
| Experimentation and demonstration | MA | —[f] | 30 | Research and wide range of services | Same | Public, nonprofit, or private organizations | Same as institutional |
| Job opportunities in the business sector | MA NAB | 12[g] | 152 | Reimbursement to private employers for extraordinary costs of hiring, training, and retention of disadvantaged workers | Disadvantaged[h] | Local NABs, state employment services, and other public and private organizations and employers | (Regular wages paid to enrollees) |
| NYC In-school | MA | 484[i] | 301 | Work experience including limited counseling and some education | 14–21 years of age, family income below poverty level | Same | $1.25 per hour Maximum 15 hours per week |
| Out-of school | MA | 138[i] | | | Mostly 16–21 | Same | $1.40 to $1.60 an hour Maximum 40 hours per week |
| New careers | MA | 4 | 19 | Training and employment as subprofessionals | Disadvantaged adults | Public or nonprofit institutions | Employment at minimum wage |
| Special impact | MA | 3 | 10 | Investment in low income areas to improve employment opportunities | NA | Public or nonprofit institutions | NA |

| Program | Agency | | | Purpose | Eligibility | Institutions | Allowance or wage |
|---|---|---|---|---|---|---|---|
| Operation mainstream | MA | 13 | 41 | Work experience, limited counseling, basic education, and skill training | Disadvantaged adults (rural area emphasis) | Public or nonprofit institutions | Employment at minimum federal or prevailing local wage |
| Concentrated employment program | MA | 16[j] | 74 | Delivery system for varied manpower activities in target areas | Community action agencies and state employment services | Community action agencies and state employment services | Dependent on program to which CEP enrollee is assigned |
| Job Corps | JC | 65 | 295 | Skill training, conservation work, and basic education | Same as NYC but school dropout | Urban centers—private industry and education institutions Conservation centers—Depts. of Interior and Agriculture and state agencies | $30 to $50 per month plus $50 a month adjustment allowance, half of which can be allotted for family support with matching by Job Corps |
| Work experience and training | SRS | 28 | 20 | Work experience, including limited supportive services and basic education | Public assistance recipients and other needy, including farm families with annual income of less than $1200 | Public welfare agencies, nonprofit agencies, and private employers under special waiver | Basic needs as defined by state |
| Work incentive program | MA SRS | — | 118 | Training, employment, and supportive services designed to make welfare recipients self supporting | AFDC recipients | State employment service, welfare agencies, and other public or nonprofit institutions | Regular welfare grant plus up to $30 per month during training |
| CAP Manpower | CAP | NA | 22[k] | Any service enhancing employment and employability of the poor | Income below poverty threshold | Public, nonprofit, or private organizations | Determined by project |

Source: Sar A. Levitan and Garth L. Mangum, *Federal Training and Work Programs in the Sixties* (Ann Arbor, Mich.: The Institute of Labor and Industrial Relations, The University of Michigan, 1969).

[a] See Key to Agency Abbreviations
[b] Nonfarm placements
[c] Excludes home economics students, 1967 academic year
[d] Rehabilitated during the year
[e] Enrolled during the year
[f] The wide variety of services precludes estimating an operational level
[g] Participants under Labor Department contracts, calendar 1968
[h] Poor persons who do not have suitable employment and who are either (1) school dropouts, (2) under 22 years of age, (3) 45 years of age or over, (4) handicapped, or (5) subject to special obstacles to employment
[i] September 1967–August 1968
[j] Persons receiving CEP assistance not included in other programs
[k] Excludes wages paid to indigenous poor
NA—not applicable

*Key to Agency Abbreviations:*
Department of Health, Education and Welfare
  OE—Office of Education
  SRS—Social and Rehabilitation Service
Department of Labor
  MA—Manpower Administration
Office of Economic Opportunity
  CAP—Community Action Program
  JC—Job Corps
National Alliance of Businessmen—NAB

## THE NATURE OF THE PRESENT FEDERALLY ASSISTED TRAINING SYSTEM

Two completely separate training systems had evolved in the United States by the 1960's. One consisted of the older apprenticeship, vocational education, and vocational rehabilitation programs. Before the 1960's, these systems had few full-time trainees and were narrow in focus, almost unconcerned with the economically disadvantaged, and subject to only minimum federal standards. Similarly, they received little in the way of federal financial assistance. In general, they represented local responses to local needs. Over the years, these training enterprises have each developed strong enclaves of supporters in and out of government.

The other training establishment consists of the remedial undertakings initiated in the last few years. They are the remainder of the programs listed in Table 1. Despite some initial actions to the contrary, they focused sharply on the training needs of the "disadvantaged." For many reasons, the institutional restrictiveness of the older programs caused neglect of concern with the needs of this group. Estimated in 1967 to exceed 13 million real or potential labor force participants, the sheer numbers of disadvantaged dictated that new training activities be created.

The new programs are financed almost entirely by federal funds. They are creatures of the executive and legislative branches of the federal government. The new programs are designed as national solutions to national problems, but despite their broad significance, they too must function within local communities. The federal government can state the target goals and provide the financial inducements for participation but the recruitment, selection, training, and placement must be performed locally. The employment service, school system, political power structure, and private employers cannot be circumvented if meaningful long-run results are to occur.

The two training systems have to date failed to adopt a policy of mutual coexistence. Vocational education supporters regard the new programs as a duplicative infringement on their domain. They argue that, if given anywhere near equal funding, they could adequately meet the training needs of the disadvantaged. Similarly, apprenticeship proponents have viewed some aspects of the remedial programs with a skeptical eye. Fearing the creation of an alternate supply of skilled labor or a fragmentation of existing trades, pressure has been exerted in many localities to assure that the newer programs do not offer training in the apprenticeship trades. Preapprenticeship classes (sponsored under MDTA) have been highly selective in their course offerings. Designed to assist disadvantaged youth to reach entry qualification levels, preapprenticeship has had a mixed reception by the apprenticeship establishment.

By the same token, the newer programs distrust the claims of the older system. Regarding their *raison d'etre* as proof-positive of the failures of the older system, the newer ones have concentrated their attention on the segments of our society that have the greatest need. Unlike the older systems, the remedial programs have not been satisfied to wait for trainees to come to them, but have adopted outreach techniques to inform, encourage, assist, and—where necessary—prod participants into the programs.

Supportive services also have become a vital component of the new programs. It was recognized early in their evolution that lack of skills was only one of a constellation of forces that prevented the wider participation of the disadvantaged in the labor market. With parallel attention given to family, health, education, and transportation needs, higher participation and lower dropout rates could be obtained. The specific types and the magnitude of the supportive services varied widely. With differing target groups, costs between programs are necessarily varied. For this reason, comparisons of training costs between the new programs or with older programs are exercises in irrelevancy.

During the early 1960's, when the national unemployment rate was over five percent, the new manpower programs "creamed," that is, they concentrated on the more accessible groups. In this sense, they served as a new kind of social insurance for the nation. Training slots were filled with semitrained people whose alternative was unemployment. The disadvantaged did not have a choice. As in the past, they were excluded by neglect. But as the national unemployment rate declined, interest turned increasingly toward the disadvantaged. With unemployment rates below four percent, there were few others to accommodate. The semi-skilled were able to find jobs on their own. The disadvantaged could not or—without stimulation—would not. Thus the business cycle has had a notable effect on the composition of the clientele served, as will be demonstrated at length below in the paper on "What Stand-By Measures Should Be Developed to Counteract a Potential Downturn in Employment?"

## THE PROLIFERATION OF MANPOWER PROGRAMS

An important cause of proliferation in manpower programs has been the belief by many poverty and civil rights groups that the established manpower system in the United States was not responsive to the needs of the disadvantaged. The poverty programs, for example, bypassed the states partly because of a conviction that many state governments were controlled by conservative economic interests who were not sympathetic with Great Society programs. Conservatives are more likely to see the costs of these programs than they are the benefits. It is not surprising that civil rights leaders should have been reluctant to agree to the administration of these programs by southern states controlled by avowed segregationists. Similarly, the state-controlled employment services were avoided by the sponsors of many of these programs, even though they are the logical focal points for any manpower program, because they were considered to be more responsive to the needs of employers than to workers seeking jobs. Most state employment offices also had a very unfavorable image among Negroes because they either practiced or permitted discrimination. In short, antipoverty forces felt that poverty was caused and perpetuated by the existing political and economic power structure, and therefore felt that better opportunities for the disadvantaged could be obtained only by creating agencies to combat and compete with existing agencies.

Proliferation also has been fostered by the traditional structuring of committees in the Congress and departments in the federal government. Congressmen and Senators with power on key committees, and with organized constituencies among various training, civil rights, and poverty groups, are interested in seeing to it that the corresponding executive departments get budgets and functions. And bureaucrats obviously have an equal interest in protecting their agencies.

The changing targets of manpower legislation have also caused proliferation of training activities. The most extensive program in terms of dollar expenditures—the Manpower Development and Training Act (MDTA)—is a good example. When passed in 1962, it was designed primarily to help retrain those workers who were faced with obsolescence of their present skills. It made no provision for the correction of educational deficiencies; only a token amount of its funds could be used to assist youths (under 22 years of age); and no supportive services were provided. By 1967, the target group was the "disadvantaged worker." Sixty-five percent of MDTA funds were to be expended on this constituency. While defying an exact definition, the disadvantaged include the long-term unemployed, those with low levels of educational attainment, and those with low family incomes. Their ranks are swollen with the illiterates, those in poor health, the unmotivated and hostile, the unskilled, those with little or no work experience, and a disproportionate number of Negroes, Spanish-speaking Americans, and Indians. To adjust to these client groups, it has been necessary to amend the MDTA several times and to add a host of related legislation. In fact, by late 1967 at least 28 job training programs were in existence, administered by 17 different federal agencies, and authorized by 11 statutes.

## NEED FOR A NATIONAL MANPOWER POLICY

There is an obvious need to coordinate the manpower, economic, and welfare requirements which must be considered in solving the nation's poverty and manpower problems. For example, a major economic policy, enunciated in the Employment Act of 1946, commits the federal government to measures to maintain full employment. The traditional approach to this economic policy has been to rely primarily on monetary and fiscal measures to produce desired changes in income and employment. But the experiences of the 1960's make it abundantly clear that it will be very difficult to achieve and maintain full employment through monetary and fiscal policies alone. especially if we wish to avoid inflation and draw various disadvantaged groups into meaningful jobs. Manpower programs must therefore form an important supplement to traditional economic policy. Monetary-fiscal policies operate primarily to influence aggregate demand, while manpower policies influence the aggregate supply of workers. By removing labor bottlenecks, an active manpower policy could make it possible to achieve lower levels of unemployment without inflation and would facilitate the reduction of the pockets of hard core unemployment which respond very slowly to changes in aggregate demand.

Manpower programs attempt to supplement full employment measures by matching workers to changing job requirements. This requires an effective job information and projection system as well as training and retraining programs to give the necessary skills to disadvantaged groups. Our evolving training policy—which is only one part of the total manpower policy—seems to be that citizens should have an opportunity for training in accordance with their abilities regardless of race, creed, color, age, sex, religion, region, or economic status. It is readily apparent that just as policies to reduce unemployment by changing aggregate demand would be more effective if taken in conjunction with effective manpower programs, manpower programs will be more effective if aggregate demand is adequate. These programs are therefore complementary and not competing.

Education and welfare policies obviously also have an impact on manpower programs. Because basic education is required for the acquisition of most work skills, education is clearly related to training. Moreover, an effective continuing education system at all levels of education and for all age groups is necessary to meet the education and training needs of a dynamic industrial economy. Vocational education, in particular, should be closely related to both education and manpower programs, but in practice has not been close enough to either. Too many school systems regard vocational education as a dumping ground for students who are not doing well with academic subjects. Since most skill training programs have academic prerequisites, inferior education causes the disadvantaged to fall further behind in the economic race. Progressive vocational educators have reduced the gap between "academic" and "vocational" education by injecting appropriate academic subjects into vocational training.

Manpower policies must also be coordinated with welfare programs. It becomes increasingly obvious, as we acquire more experience, that a major impediment to the participation in training and retraining programs by the disadvantaged is the absence of supportive services which middle class Americans take for granted. These services include adequate health care, transportation, child care, income maintenance, psychiatric care, guidance, and other activities. Actual and recommended programs that ignore these supportive needs are likely to have only limited effectiveness. For example, there is an assumption that the provision of adequate incomes through the negative income tax or some other income maintenance system would eliminate poverty and provide an alternative for welfare programs. The argument is that the poor are obviously poor because they do not have money, so giving them money will solve their problems. It is our view that this approach is far too simple and inadequate. Although income maintenance programs like the Nixon administration's Family Assistance Plan might be very significant for rural areas, especially in the South, the modest incomes likely from a negative income tax will not ensure the acquisition of the necessary services by all those who have been trapped for generations by the poverty cycle, particularly in urban areas. This is true in large measure because many poor people would not acquire the services if they had the income. Because of the ravages of years—even generations—of poverty, discrimination, and second-class citizenship, many of the hard core unemployed (or, more properly, unemployable) will require considerable counseling, guidance, and material assistance before they acquire the necessary motivations to participate in training or education programs. Because of the feelings of inferiority forced on minorities, many of them must be made to believe that they have the ability to be trained for productive employment.

Regardless of the particular shape of our welfare policies, however, manpower programs could be more effective if there were realistic programs to care for those who are unable to work. An effective welfare system might make it possible for young people to weigh the alternatives more carefully and might obviate the need for the poor to be forced to make occupational and educational choices that yield relatively high, short-run returns at the expense of long-run earnings. A child allowance program, for example, might be designed to reduce the high school dropout problem, permit teenagers to acquire greater capacities for training, and reduce the teenage unemployment problem. Welfare programs also might be designed to get welfare recipients off welfare rolls and into a training program.

## MANPOWER AND THE "NEW FEDERALISM"

Although the manpower programs of the 1960's were primarily the product of the Kennedy-Johnson administrations, as Sar Levitan emphasizes in "Manpower Programs and the 'New Federalism,'" these ". . . programs have become an integral part of economic policy. . ." and are likely to continue as such, whatever political party gains control of the executive branch of the federal government. This is true because the lessons learned from the past have caused manpower policies to "mature" and have demonstrated the importance of manpower programs for economic and social policy. The Nixon administration has been particularly interested in pushing private involvement in manpower efforts like the JOBS program, the expansion of which, according to Levitan, ". . . was based more on principle than proven effectiveness." Moreover, the Nixon regime is interested in streamlining the administration of manpower programs. But, as Levitan points out, this, like many other aspects of manpower policy, is a bipartisan effort.

One of the most significant social programs of the 1970's is likely to be the Family Assistance Plan (FAP). As proposed in 1970, FAP would require beneficiaries to register if they are over 18 and not otherwise excluded, 16 to 17 years of age and not in school, or are full-time workers. Students, children under 16, wives of family heads, the disabled, and female heads of households with children under six are not required to register. FAP would require registered beneficiaries to accept suitable training or employment or lose their benefits. The plan also provides for day-care facilities for children so that benefit recipients can enter training and employment. Financial incentives would be given under the plan for work and training. FAP would be particularly significant in the South where average family incomes of the rural poor could be more than doubled. However, as Levitan emphasizes, FAP's impact is by no means predictable and, as it has been proposed, it raises some serious questions. Employers might use income supplements as wage subsidies and the plan might prevent families from achieving economic independence. Moreover, FAP does not by itself assure jobs for trainees, which could seriously impair the effectiveness of the work and training features.

## ECONOMIC STABILITY

Clarification of the relationships between manpower and economic policies undoubtedly will be one of the most important manpower problems of the 1970's. The administration's bill provides for a "trigger" mechanism to increase manpower funds 10 percent as unemployment reaches 4.5 percent of the labor force for three consecutive months. However, Levitan believes this is an admirable but inadequate feature.

The discussion paper "What Stand-By Measures Should be Developed to Counteract a Potential Cyclical Downturn in Employment," prepared by the Manpower Administration of the U.S. Department of Labor indicates some of the significant problems involved in using manpower programs as countercyclical devices. As this paper indicates, conceptually the kinds of manpower programs to be used vary with business conditions. As is frequently the case, however, implementation is more difficult than conceptualization, because of such problems as poor data, inadequate ability to predict and time manpower programs, and an insufficient array of manpower programs that can be implemented at the right time. However, this paper has a good treatment of the kinds of manpower projection available for the 1970's. Clearly, moreover, there will have to be considerable refinement of data and programs if manpower policies are to effectively complement other countercyclical activities.

## EVALUATION OF HUMAN RESOURCE DEVELOPMENT PROGRAMS

With the growth of programs designed to promote the development of human resources, considerable attention has been devoted to program evaluation. This attention was based on a realization by policy makers and administrators at every level that program effectiveness, both in terms of administration and efficient use of resources, required careful evaluation to see what effect programs were having on their target populations. However, the problem of evaluation is much more complex than might appear at first glance, because goals must be specified, evaluation techniques must be devised, and measurement problems must be overcome.

As Cain and Hollister indicate in "The Methodology of Evaluating Social Action Programs," there are a number of techniques that may be used to come as close as possible to creating laboratory conditions to gauge program effectiveness. Moreover, the evaluator must be alert to a number of obstacles to effective program evaluation.

Cain and Hollister distinguish various kinds of evaluation. Evaluation may be either in terms of *process* (i.e., how well the program is being executed or administered in achieving its objectives) or *results* (i.e., what effect the program has had on its target population). Results evaluation may either be in terms of *actual* or *anticipated* results. Evaluation in terms of *anticipated* results is very important where experimentation is either difficult or impossible, or where it is necessary to judge a proposed program in terms of its "probable" results. Evaluation of actual results is important in attempting to decide what changes to make in ongoing programs.

Cain and Hollister then discuss various evaluation techniques. One of the most important of these is the use of *control groups*, which may be either large or small. They also stress the problem of replication and some of the technical and theoretical problems involved in the use of *statistical models* for purposes of benefit-cost evaluation.

The authors make it clear that evaluation techniques are important, but that much remains to be done before these techniques are sufficiently refined to make them more useful. Moreover, evaluation techniques are important *tools* for judgment but, in the final analysis, the judgment of the evaluator is very important. The tools can aid judgment, but they cannot substitute for it.

In "Facts, Fancies, and Freeloaders in Evaluating Antipoverty Programs," Sar Levitan emphasizes the need for evaluation, but discusses some of the reasons why programs are undertaken without adequate prior evaluation. In part, this is because administrators are reluctant to have programs evaluated, but it also stems from deficiencies in academic communities. He is particularly critical of the cost-benefit approach and the conformity of various academic disciplines. Levitan appeals for the nonconformists who are needed in order to achieve effective program evaluation.

The selections from the paper by Mangum present an overall critique of federal manpower programs. As he points out, there is no systematic manpower program because various pieces of manpower legislation were passed to meet current crises. He emphasizes the small size of manpower expenditures relative to total need, but points to a number of positive contributions of these programs during the 1961–1967 period. In spite of these contributions, however, he believes that much remains to be done to develop an effective delivery system to make it possible to focus resources on manpower problems.

Mangum's paper evaluates four major manpower programs: MDTA, vocational education, vocational rehabilitation, and the U.S. Employment Service. In spite of its built-in creaming tendencies, Mangum concludes that MDTA institutional (classroom) training reaches a higher proportion of the disadvantaged than on-the-job training (OJT) programs run by quality-conscious employers. Congress has attempted to enrich MDTA programs from time to time "without commensurate increases in budget," forcing the skill centers (where a number of training programs are brought together in one place with their related supporting services) to operate at partial capacity because of inadequate funds.

Until the 1960's the main thrust of public skill training in the United States was through the Vocational Education system operated by the states with federal matching funds. Before 1963, this system had been criticized as being unresponsive to the needs of the disadvantaged and the economy. Although some reforms in the Vocational Education system resulted from the Vocational Education Act of 1963, Mangum argues that the basic character of the system has not changed very much.

The vocational rehabilitation program does very little training itself, preferring to contract training for the physically and mentally handicapped to other agencies. Because it deals with physical and mental—rather than cultural handicaps, which are more emotional—the vocational rehabilitation system has considerably more congressional support than the MDTA program. Moreover, the vocational rehabilitation program has undertaken sufficient evaluation of its activities to be able to demonstrate substantial achievements.

The major manpower agency in the United States is the Employment Service which also has been criticized as being unresponsive to the needs of the economy and the disadvantaged. However, as Mangum points out, the Employment Service also is in transition as a result of its involvement in manpower and poverty programs during the 1960's.

# The Methodology of Evaluating Social Action Programs

## by Glen G. Cain and Robinson G. Hollister

### INTRODUCTION

This paper began as a discussion of methods of evaluating manpower programs. . . . But with the recent emphasis on problems of poverty and the disadvantaged worker, manpower programs have come to involve remedial and general education, to intermesh with community action programs providing a variety of welfare services, and, on a trial basis, to assist in migration between labor markets. . . .

We hold the opinion, apparently widely shared, that existing evaluations of social action programs, (and we are including our own), have fallen short of meeting the standards possible within the disciplines of the social sciences. The reasons for these shortcomings are easy to identify. The programs typically involve investments in human beings, a relatively new era of empirical research in economics.

They are aimed at such social and political goals as equality and election victories, as well as economic objectives concerning, say, income and employment. They often attempt to deliver services on a large enough scale to make a noticeable impact upon the community. And at the same time, they are expected to provide a quasi-experimental basis for determining what programs ought to be implemented and how they ought to be run.

It is not surprising, then, that evaluations of social action programs have often not been attempted and when attempted, have not been successful. Despite this background, we believe that existing data and methods permit evaluations which, while not satisfying the methodological purists, can at least provide the rules of evidence for judging the degree to which programs have succeeded or failed. Spe-

SOURCE Reprinted with permission from Arnold Weber *et al.*, (Eds.), *Public–Private Manpower Policy*, Industrial Relations Research Assn. 1969.

cifically, the theme we will develop is that evaluations should be set up to provide the ingredients of an experimental situation: a model suitable for statistical testing, a wide range in the values of the variables representing the program inputs, and the judicious use of control groups.

The paper reflects several backgrounds in which we have had some experience—from economics, the tradition of benefit-cost analyses; from the other social sciences, the approach of quasi-experimental research; and from a governmental agency, the perspective of one initiating and using evaluation studies. Each of these points of view has its own literature which we have by no means covered, but to which we are indebted.[1]

## TYPES OF EVALUATION

There are two broad types of evaluation. The first, which we call "process evaluation," is mainly administrative monitoring. Any program must be monitored (or evaluated) regarding the integrity of its financial transactions and accounting system. There is also an obvious need to check on other managerial functions, including whether or not accurate records are being kept. In sum, "process evaluation" addresses the question: Given the existence of the program, is it being run honestly and administered efficiently?

A second type of evaluation, and the one with which we are concerned, may be called "outcome evaluation," more familiarly known as "cost-benefit analysis." Although both the inputs and outcomes of the program require measurements, the toughest problem is deciding on and measuring the outcomes. With this type of evaluation the whole concept of the program is brought into question, and it is certainly possible that a project might be judged to be a success or a failure irrespective of how well it was being administered.

A useful categorization of cost-benefit evaluations draws a distinction between a priori analyses and ex post analyses. An example of a priori analysis is the cost-effectiveness studies of weapons systems conducted by the Defense Department, which have analyzed war situations where there were no "real outcomes" and, thus, no ex post results with which to test the evaluation models. Similarly, most evaluations of water resource projects are confined to alternative proposals where the benefits and costs are estimated prior to the actual undertaking of the projects.[2] Only in the area of social action programs such as poverty, labor training, and to some extent housing, have substantial attempts been made to evaluate programs, not just in terms of before-the-fact estimates of probable outcomes or in terms of

[1] As examples of the benefit-cost literature, see Robert Dorfman, ed., *Measuring Benefits of Government Investments* (Brookings Institution, Washington, D.C, 1965), and A. R. Prest and R. Turvey, "Cost-Benefit Analysis: A Survey," *Economic Journal,* December, 1965, v. 75, pp. 683–735. As examples of the evaluation research literature, see Edward A. Suchman, *Evaluation Research* (Russell Sage Foundation, New York, 1967), Donald T. Campbell and Julian C. Stanley, *Experimental and Quasi-Experimental Designs for Research* (Chicago, Rand-McNally, 1966), G. H. Orcutt and A. G. Orcutt, "Incentive and Disincentive Experimentation for Income Maintenance Policy Purposes," *American Economic Review,* September, 1968, v. 58, pp. 754–72, and Harold Watts, "Graduated Work Incentives: Progress toward an Experiment in Negative Taxation," Discussion Papers Series, Institute for Research on Poverty, University of Wisconsin, 1968. For examples of the point of view of officials of governmental agencies, see William Gorham, "Notes of a Practitioner," and Elizabeth Drew, "HEW Grapples with PPBS," in *The Public Interest,* Summer, 1967, No. 8.

[2] There does seem to be a developing literature in which the a priori benefit-cost estimates are compared with the ex post results for water projects. See Maynard Hufschmidt, " 'Systematic Errors' in Cost Estimation in Public Investment," to appear in the Universities-National Bureau of Economic Research Conference volume, *The Economics of Public Ouput.* It may be that similar follow-up studies are being undertaken for defense projects—one can at least say that Congressional committees are determined to carry out their own follow-up evaluations on projects such as the TFX.

simulated hypothetical outcomes, but also on the basis of data actually gathered during or after the operation of the program.

A priori cost-benefit analyses of social action programs can, of course, be useful in program planning and feasibility studies, but the real demand and challenge lies in ex post evaluations. This more stringent demand made of social action programs may say something about the degree of skepticism and lack of sympathy Congress (or "society") has concerning these programs, but this posture appears to be one of the facts of political life.

## PROBLEMS OF THE
## DESIGN OF THE EVALUATION [2a]

### A. The Use of Control Groups

Given the objective of a social action program, the evaluative question is: "What difference did the program make?", and this question should be taken literally. We want to know the difference between the behavior with the program and the behavior if there had been no program. To answer the question, some form of control group is essential. We need a basis for comparison—some base group that performs the methodological function of a control group. Let us consider some alternatives.

*The Before-and-After Study* In the before and after study, the assumption is that each subject is his own control (or the aggregate is its own control) and that the behavior of the group before the program is a measure of performance that would have occurred if there had been no program. However, it is well known that there are many situations in which this assumption is not tenable. We might briefly cite some examples found in manpower programs.

Sometimes the "before situation" is a point in time when the participants are at a particularly low state—lower, that is, than is normal for the group. The very fact of being eligible for participation in a poverty program may reflect transitory conditions. Under such conditions we should expect a "natural" regression toward their mean level of performance if we measure their status in an "after situation," even if there were no program in the intervening period. Using zero earnings as the permanent measure of earnings of an unemployed person is an example of attributing normality to a transitory status.

Another similar situation arises when young people are involved in the program. Ordinary maturation and the acquisition of experience over the passage of time would be expected to improve their wages and employment situation.

There may be some structural change in the personal situations of the participants before and after the program, which has nothing to do with the program but would vitiate any simple before-or-after comparison. We should not, for example, look upon the relatively high earnings record of coal miners or packinghouse workers as characteristic of their "before situation" if, in fact, they have been permanently displaced from their jobs.

As a final example of a situation in which the before-and-after comparison is invalid, there is the frequent occurrence of significant environmental changes—particularly in labor market environments—which are characterized by seasonal and cyclical fluctuations. Is it the program or the changed environment which has brought about the change in behavior? All of the above examples of invalidated evaluations could have been at least partially corrected if the control groups had been other similar persons who were

[2a] In a more extended version of this paper prepared for the Institute for Research on Poverty, University of Wisconsin (Discussion Paper 42–69), we discuss several problems associated with the specification of objectives of programs and how these affect evaluation designs.

in similar situations in the pre-training period.

*Control Groups and Small Group Studies* The particular strength of the small scale study is that it greatly facilitates the desideratum of random assignments to "treatment groups" and "control groups" or, at least, a closely supervised matching of treatment and control groups. Its particular shortcoming is that it is likely to lack representativeness—both in terms of the characteristics of the program participants and in terms of the character of the program. There is first the problem of a "hot house environment" of the small group study. (See discussion of "replicability" below.) Second, a wide range of values of the program inputs (i.e., in terms of levels of a given treatment or in terms of qualitatively different types of treatments) is less likely to be available in a small group study. Third, the small group study may not be able to detect the program's differential effects on different types of participants (e.g., by age, sex, color, residence, etc.,) either because the wide variety of participant types are not available or because their numbers are too small. Finally, it is both a strength and a weakness of the small scale study that it is usually confined to a single geographic location. Thus, although "extraneous" noise from different environments are eliminated, we may learn little or nothing about how the program would operate in different environments.

*Control Groups and Large Group Studies* The large scale study, which involves gathering data over a wide range of environments, customarily achieves "control" over the characteristics of participants and nonparticipants and over programs and environmental characteristics by statistical methods, rather than by randomization or careful matching, individual by individual. These studies have the capability of correcting each of the shortcomings attributed to the small scale studies in the preceding paragraph. But because they are almost impossible to operate with randomization, the large scale studies run afoul of the familiar problem in which the selectivity of the participants may be associated with some unmeasured variable(s) which makes it impossible to determine what the net effect of the treatment is. Since this shortcoming is so serious in the minds of many analysts, particularly statisticians, and because the small scale studies have a longer history of usage and acceptability in sociology and psychology, it may be worthwhile to defend at greater length the large scale studies, which are more common to economists.

Randomization is seldom attempted for reasons having to do with the attitudes of the administrators of a program, local pressures from the client population, or various logistic problems. Indeed, all these reasons may serve to botch an *attempted* randomization procedure. Furthermore, we can say with greater certitude that the ideal "double-blind experiment with placebos" is almost impossible to achieve. If we are to do something other than abandon evaluation efforts in the face of these obstacles to randomization, we will have to turn to the large scale study and the statistical design issues that go along with it.

The fact that the programs vary across cities or among administrators may be turned to our advantage by viewing these as "natural experiments"[3] which may permit an extrapolation of the results of the treatment to the "zero" or "no-treatment" level. The analyst should work with the administrator in advance to design the program variability in ways which minimize the confounding of results with environmental influences. Furthermore, ethical problems raised by deliberately excluding some persons from the presumed

[3] We are indebted to Thomas K. Glennen, Rand Corporation, for his ideas on this point.

beneficial treatments are to some extent avoided by assignments to differing treatments (although, here again, randomization is the ideal way to make these assignments).

It is difficult at this stage, to provide more than superficial observations regarding the choice between small and large-scale studies. It would seem that for those evaluations that have a design concept which is radically different from existing designs or where there is a quite narrow hypothesis which requires detailed examination, a small group study would be preferable. Conversely, when the concept underlying a program is quite broad and where large amounts of resources are to be allocated, the large group approach is probably more relevant—a point argued in greater detail in our discussion of the "replicability criterion."

## B. The Replicability Criterion

A source of friction between administrators of programs and those doing evaluation research, usually academicians, is the failure to agree upon the level of decision-making for which the results of the evaluation are to be used. This failure, which is all the more serious because the issue is often not explicitly addressed, leads to disputes regarding two related issues—the scope of the evaluation study and the selection of variables to be studied. To deal with these disputes, we suggest applying the "replicability criterion." We apply this name to the criterion because of the large number of cases in which evaluations of concepts have been made on the basis of projects which are not likely to be replicable on a large scale or which focus on characteristics of the project which are not within the ability of the decision-makers to control. To take an extreme example, it has sometimes been stated that the success of a compensatory education program depended upon the "warmth and enthusiasm" of the teachers. In the context of a nationwide program, no administrator has control over the level of "warmth and enthusiasm" of teachers.

It is sometimes argued by administrators that evaluations which are based upon samples drawn from many centers of a program are not legitimate tests of the program concept since they do not adequately take into account the differences in the details of individual projects or of differentiated populations. These attitudes frequently lead the administrators or other champions of the program to select, either ex ante or ex post, particular "pet" projects for evaluations that "really count." In the extreme, this approach consists of looking at the successful programs (based on observations of ongoing or even completed programs) and then claiming that these are really the ones that should be the basis for the evaluation of the program as a whole. *If* these successful programs have worked with representative participants in representative surroundings and *if* the techniques used—including the quality of the administrative and operational personnel—can be replicated on a nationwide basis, *then* it makes sense to say that the evaluation of the particular program can stand for an evaluation of the overall program. But we can seldom assume these conditional statements. After all, each of the individual programs, a few political plums notwithstanding, was set up because someone thought it was worthwhile. Of course, some will flop because of poor teachers or because one or more operations were fouled up—but it is in the nature of the beast that some incompetent administrative and operational foul-ups will occur. A strength of summary, over-all measures of performance is that they will include "accidental" foul-ups with the "accidental" successes, the few bad administrators and teachers as well as the few charismatic leaders. As a case in point, consider the success (according to prevailing opinion) of Reverend Sullivan's Operation Industrial Council in Philadelphia with the (as yet) absence of any evidence that the OIC idea has been successfully transferred elsewhere.[4]

Small scale studies of pre-selected particular programs are most useful either for assessing radically different program ideas or for providing the administrator with information relevant to decisions of program content *within* the confines of his overall program. These are important uses, but the decisions at a broader level which concern the allocation of resources among programs of widely differing concepts call for a different type of evaluation with a focus on different variables.

It may be helpful to cite an example of the way in which the replicability criterion should have been applied. A few years ago, a broad scale evaluation of the Work Experience Program[5] was carried out. (The evaluation was of necessity based upon very fragmentary data, but we are here concerned with the issues it raised rather than with its own merits.) The evaluation indicated that on the average the unemployment rates among the completers of the program were just as high as those with similar characteristics who had not been in the program. On the basis of this evaluation, it was argued that the concept of the program was faulty, and some rather major shifts in the design and in the allocation of resources to the program were advocated.[6] Other analysts objected to this rather drastic conclusion and argued that the "proper" evaluative procedure was to examine individual projects within the program, pick out those projects which had higher "success rates," and then attempt to determine which characteristics of these projects were related to those "success rates."[7]

The argument as to which approach is proper depends on the particular decision framework to which the evaluation results were to be applied. To the administrators of the program, it is really the project-by-project type of analysis which is relevant to the decision variables which they control. The broader type of evaluation would be of interest, but their primary concern is to adjust the mix of program elements to obtain the best results within the given broad concept of the program. Even for program administrators, however, there will be elements and personnel peculiar to a given area or project that will not be replicable in other areas and other projects.

For decision-makers at levels higher than the program administrator the broader type of evaluation will provide the sort of information relevant to their decision frame. Their task is to allocate resources among programs based upon different broad concepts. Negative findings from the broader evaluation argue against increasing the allocation to the program, although a conservative response might be to hold the line on the program while awaiting the more detailed project-by-project evaluation to determine whether there is something salvageable in the concept embodied in the program. There will always be alternative programs serving the same population however, and

---

[4] Briefly, the OIC concept combines elements of training, job development (often aided by pressure tactics against employers), and a psychological up-lifting of the participants which is conducted with an ideology of militancy and participatory democracy.

[5] The Work Experience program consisted of public employment of welfare recipients and other adult poor under Title V of the Economic Opportunity Act. Only minimal training was offered, but it was hoped that work-for-pay would by itself provide a "springboard" to self-sustaining employment in the private market.

[6] U. S. Congress, House Committee on Ways and Means, *Community Work and Training Program.* 90th Congress, 1st Sess., House Document No. 96 (Washington, D.C.: U. S. Government Printing Office, 1967).

[7] Worth Bateman, "Assessing Program Effectiveness," *Welfare in Review,* Vol. 6, No. 1, January-February 1968.

the decision-maker is justified in shifting resources toward those programs which hold out the promise of better results.

The basic point is that project-by-project evaluations are bound to turn up some "successful" project somewhere, but unless there is good evidence that that "success" can be broadly replicated and that the administrative controls are adequate to insure such replication, then the individual project success is irrelevant. Resources must be allocated in light of evidence that concepts are not only "successful" on a priori grounds or in particular small-scale contexts but that they are in fact "successful" in large-scale implementation.

## C. The Theoretical Framework—Some Statistical Considerations.

The main function of a theoretical framework in cost-benefit evaluations is to provide a statistical model suitable for testing. In this section a few brief remarks will be made about the statistical design of the evaluation—a lengthier discussion of these matters is taken up in another paper.[7a] In these remarks we will adopt the terminology of regression analysis, which is a statistical method flexible enough to handle an analysis of variance approach or that involved in simply working with cell values in tables. In the regression model, the dependent variable is the objective of the social action program and the particular set of independent variables of most interest to us are those that describe or represent the program, or program inputs. In this discussion the independent variables will sometimes be referred to as "treatment variables."

It may be useful to divide the problems of statistical design into two categories:

First, attaining acceptable levels of statistical significance on the measured effects of the treatment variables; second, measuring those effects without bias. We will not discuss the first problem here except to note that the failure to attain statistical significance of the effect of the treatment variable occurs either because of large unexplained variation in the dependent variable or small effects of treatment variables and these can be overcome with sufficiently large sample sizes. In our opinion, the most serious defect in evaluation studies is biases in the measures of effects of the treatment variables, and this error is unlikely to be removed by enlarging the sample size.

One source of bias is inaccurate measures of the treatment variable, but a more pervasive and more serious problem is the presence of variables, not included in the statistical model, which are correlated with both the dependent variable and the treatment variable. Had the assignment to a program been made on a random basis, the laws of probability would have assured a low correlation (zero in the limit of a large enough sample size) between participation in the program and these omitted variables. In the absence of randomization, we must fall back on statistical controls. At this point our theory and a priori information are crucially important. The requirements are obvious: to identify the variables whose omission leads to biases in the measured effects of the treatment variables and to include them in the model. These variables may be objectively measurable, such as age or education or previous work experience. Or they may be such difficult-to-measure characteristics as ambition, motivation, or an "appealing personality."[8]

---

[7a] See the version of this paper in the Discussion Series of the Institute for Research on Poverty.

[8] An important point to be remembered is that, for any given amount of resources available for an evaluation study, there is a trade-off between an allocation of these resources for increased sample size and allocation for improved quality of measurement, which might take the form of an expanded set of variables, improved measures of variables, or reduced attrition from the sample. Too often we have witnessed a single-minded attachment to larger sample sizes, probably stemming from the analyst's fear

As we know too well, however, our theories are woefully weak in providing us with the correct list of variables for explaining such dependent variables as income change, employment experience, health status, or educational attainment, and we often do not have measures of those we do know about. The latter problem frequently arises because of the unfortunate practice of inviting the evaluator in *after* the program has been run and the data have been collected. Even in the best of situations regarding the availability of objective measures of important variables, if we do not have random assignments we must still admit the possibility that *self-selectivity* or the *selectivity procedures* of the program administrators has introduced a systematic difference between the participants and the nonparticipants. We do not claim, as the purists would, that nonrandom procedures invalidate all evaluations, although there are cases when they undoubtedly have, but the advantages of randomization are immense and we can do a great deal more to achieve this procedure if we can only convince each other of its importance.

Another important advantage of randomization should be mentioned. We have noted that variables which are correlated with both the treatment variable and the dependent variable must be included in the model to measure treatment effects without bias. However, since our information about the effect of the treatment variable necessarily depends on variability in treatments, and since the only variation we can observe within the framework of the statistical model is the residual variation in treatments, that is, variation which remains after the entire set of in-

dependent variables is included, greater efficiency is obtained when the treatment variable is uncorrelated with the other independent variables. In the opposite extreme, if the treatment variables were perfectly correlated with some other variable or combination of variables, we would be unable to distinguish between which of the two sets of factors caused a change. It follows that even in the absence of randomization, designing the programs to be studied with as wide a range in levels and types of "treatments" as possible will serve to maximize the information we can extract from an ex post analysis.

There are reasons in addition to those of statistical efficiency for planning for a wide range of values in the treatment of programmatic variables. One is that social action programs have a tendency to change, rather frequently and radically, during the course of their operation. Evaluations designed to test a single type of program are rendered meaningless because the program-type perishes. But if the design covers a wider variety of programs, then a built-in hedge against the effects of change is attained. Indeed, there is an even more fundamental reason why a wide range of inputs and program types should be planned for, and it is simply this: we seldom know enough about what will work in a social action program to justify putting our eggs in the single basket of one type of program. This evaluation model for a single type of project, sometimes described as the analogue of the "pilot plant," is not the appropriate model for social action programs given our current state of knowledge.[9]

---

that he will end up with "too few observations in the cells" of some only vaguely imagined cross-tabulation. This fear should be balanced by an awareness both of the rapidity with which marginal gains in precision of estimates decline with increases in "medium size" samples and of the extent to which a theoretically justified multiple regression model can overcome some of the limitations which cross-tabulation analysis impose on a given-sized sample.

[9] See the vigorous defense of an experimental method in social action programs in: Guy H. Orcutt and Alice G. Orcutt, *op. cit.*

## D. The Theoretical Framework—Some Economic Considerations.

For operational purposes we will assume that the evaluation of each social action program can, at least in principle, be cast in the statistical model discussed in the previous section, complete with variables representing an objective of the program, treatment variables representing the program inputs, control variables, and control groups.[10] However, the substantive theoretical content of these models—the particular selection of variables and their functional form—must come from one or more of the traditional disciplines such as educational psychology (e.g., for Head Start), demography (e.g., for a family planning program), medical science (e.g., for a neighborhood health center), economics (e.g., for a manpower training program), and so on.

Sooner or later economics must enter all evaluations, since "costing out" the programs and the setting of implicit or explicit dollar measures of the worth of a program are essential steps in a complete evaluation. In making the required cost-benefit analysis, the part of economic theory that applies is the investment theory of public finance economics, with its infusion of welfare economics. The function of investment theory is to make commensurable inputs and outcomes of a social action program which are spaced over time.[10a] Welfare economics analyzes the distinctions between financial costs and real resource costs, between direct effects of a program and externalities, and between efficiency criteria and equity (or distributional) criteria.

We will say very little on the last mentioned distributional or equity question of *who pays* and *who receives*, even though we strongly feel that accurate data on the distribution of benefits and costs is essential to an evaluation of social action programs. However, the task of conducting a "conventional" benefit-cost analysis (where the criterion is allocative efficiency) is sufficiently complex that we believe it preferable to separate the distributional questions.

*Program Inputs* In the investment theory model costs are attached to all inputs of a program and a single number emerges which measures the present value of the resources used. Most of the technical problems faced by the analysts on the input side are those of traditional cost accounting. We will confine our remarks to the two familiar and somewhat controversial problems of opportunity costs and transfer payments, which arise in nearly every manpower program. Both of these problems are most effectively dealt with if one starts by asking: What is the decision context for which these input measures are defined?

The most general decision context—and the one to which economists most naturally refer—is that of the productivity of alternative resources utilizations in society or the nation *as a whole*. In this case, one wishes to measure the cost of inputs in terms of the net reduction in value of alternative socially productive activities caused by the use of the inputs in this particular activity. Now, the value of most inputs in terms of their alternative use will be more or less clearly indicated by their market price, but there are some in-

---

[10] This assumption will strike some readers as too positivistic, too restrictive to "things measurable," and too oblivious to the unmeasurable and subjective variables. Let us say in defense of this assumption only that it is a "working assumption" that permits us to discuss an important region of evaluation which covers the measurable portion, that it is desirable to expand this region and, therefore, to narrow the area left for subjective judgments, and that, in any case, the objective portion is necessary to an improved over-all judgment that spans both measurable and unmeasurable inputs and outputs of a program.

[10a] We bypass here the important question of the choice of a discount rate. Some discussion of this issue is provided in the Institute for Research on Poverty version of this paper.

puts for which this will not be true. The most troublesome cases often concern the time of people. A well known example is the value of the time spent by students in school: since those over 14 or so could be in the job market, the social product (or national income) is less; therefore, an estimate is needed of what their earnings would be had they not been in school. (Such an estimate should reflect whatever amount of unemployment would be considered "normal.") For manpower programs the best evaluation design would provide a control group to measure the opportunity costs of the time spent by the trainees in the program.

Sometimes the prices of inputs (market prices or prices fixed by the government) do not adequately reflect their marginal social productivity, and "corrected" or "shadow prices" are necessary. For example, the ostensible prices of leisure or of the housework of a wife are zero and obviously below their real price. By contrast a governmental fixed price of some surplus commodity is too high.

The definition and treatment of transfer payments also depend on the decision context of the analysis. From the national perspective money outlays from the budget of one program that are offset by reduced outlays elsewhere in society do not decrease the value of the social product. When these outlays are in the form of cash payments or consumption goods, they are called transfer payments. An example is the provision of room and board for Job Corps trainees. Since it must be assumed that someone (their parents, themselves, or some welfare agency) would be meeting the costs of their room and board if they were not in the program, the provision of these services by the program reflects no *net* reduction in the value of

alternative socially productive activities. Whoever was paying these costs before will be relieved of that burden and will spend the money thus saved on other goods and services. If there has been an actual *increase* in the value of food consumed by the trainee or in the quality of his housing, the net increase can be counted as a program input—a cost. But in general, it would be equal to the net increase in the value of food and housing consumed—a benefit.[11] To summarize, if these input costs are simply being *transferred* from one individual or agency to another individual or agency they either represent no real cost of resources of this program or they are a cost which is immediately offset by the benefit it yields to the recipient—remembering that the decision context is the general one which includes all members of society, with no one member receiving any different weight in the calculation of benefits.

In a narrower decision context, the accounting basis may shift; some input costs counted in the broader context are not counted in the narrower one and vice versa. One example of a narrow decision context—a favorite of people in government, but repugnant to most economists —is the vaguely defined "public budget." Alternatively the decision context might be considered that of the "taxpayers' viewpoint" if the program participants and their families are excluded from the group considered as taxpayers. In this context the only costs that are to be counted are those that come from the public budget. Some of the examples we discussed above are now reversed. Presumably, most of the opportunity costs of a student's time spent in school is of no interest to the taxpayer since it is a "cost" which is not directly imposed upon the public budget.

[11] When the program produces an increase in consumption of goods and services, the treatment of these transfer payments can become more complicated if we do not assume that the goods and service have a value to the recipients equal to their cost. See A. A. Alchian and W. R. Allen, *University Economics* (Wadsworth: Belmont, California, 1967, Second Edition), pp. 135–140, for an extended discussion.

(A qualification is that the taxpayer should be interested in the taxes the student would pay if he were working.) By contrast the payments for the cost of room and board to a Job Corpsman, which was considered a transfer payment above, would now be considered an input cost from the "taxpayer's viewpoint." The fact that the trainee or his family is relieved of this burden would be of no interest since it would not be reflected in the public budget. However, if the costs of room and board had been met previously by a public welfare agency, then from the "taxpayer's viewpoint," the costs would not be charged to the Job Corps program.

It is not uncommon to see several decision contexts used in one analysis, and used inconsistently. For example, the post-training earnings improvement from participation in a Job Corps program are considered benefits. We all recognize, of course, that the earnings will be used mostly for consumption by the Job Corps graduate. But in the same study, his consumption during training (room, meals, and spending allowance), is not viewed as conferring benefits to the corpsman.[12] Or is it that the benefits should not count because while in training, he is not considered a member of "our society?" We leave this puzzle to those who prefer these restricted decision contexts. There are other such examples and still other and more narrow decision contexts, such as that of a local government or of the project by itself. But it is probably clear that our preference is for the national or total societal perspective.

*Program Outcomes.* The problems of measurement on the outcome side of the evaluation problem are tougher to handle, and ex post evaluations of social action programs face particular problems because these outcomes are likely to involve behavioral relationships which are not well understood. It is particularly difficult to predict long run or permanent behavioral changes from the short run indicators revealed by the on-going or just completed program.

The outcomes we wish to measure from many social action programs occur months or years after the participants have completed the program. We can use proxy measures, which can themselves be measured during and soon after the program, but follow-up studies are clearly preferred and may in many cases be essential. A good deal depends on the confidence we have in the power of our theories to link the proxies or short-run effects (e.g., test scores, health treatments, employment experience in the short-run, etc.) with the longer run goals (longer run educational attainment, longevity, incomes, or all of these and perhaps other "softer" measures of "well-being"). It is a role for "basic research" in the social sciences to provide this type of theoretical-empirical information to evaluations, but we can also hope that the more thorough evaluation studies will contribute to our stock of "basic research" findings.

The major obstacle to follow-up measures is the difficulty in locating people, particularly those from disadvantaged populations who may be less responsive and who have irregular living patterns. The biases due to nonresponse may be severe, since those participants who are easiest to locate are likely to be the most "successful," both because of their apparent stability and because those who have "failed" may well be less responsive to requests to reveal their current status. One way around the costly problem of tracking down respondents for earnings data is to use Social Security records for participant and control groups. The rights of

[12] For just one of many examples of this type of treatment of transfer payments see, "The Feasibility of Benefit-Cost Analysis in the War on Poverty: A Test Application to Manpower Programs," prepared for the General Accounting Office, Resource Management Corporation, UR-054, December 13, 1968.

confidentiality may be preserved by aggregating the data.

Another problem in measuring outcomes, which also tends to be more talked about despairingly than coped with positively, is the category of external or third-party effects of the program. As a typical illustration consider a youth training program, which not only increases the earnings of the youths, but also reduces the incidence of crime among these groups, which generally benefits the community —e.g. less damage and lower costs of prevention and rehabilitation programs. Another source of third-party effects are those accruing to the participant's family members, including those yet to be born. It is an open question, however, whether the problem for concern is the lack of measurement of these external effects, or the tendency by administrators and others (particularly friends of the program) to exaggerate their likely importance and to count as external or secondary benefits those effects which, while benefiting some people do so at the expense of others.[13]

Concerning training and education programs, in particular, two types of effects that have received scant investigation are "negative effects" and those which affect the structure of communities. A discussion, though little measurement, of such effects has appeared in studies and accounts of public housing, urban renewal, and road building programs.[14] The following list of three potential negative effects of manpower programs can serve as examples.

(a) Programs placing the hard-core poor into jobs have had, according to some reports, disruptive effects in the plant—both because of the behavior of the trainee-participants (e.g., disciplinary problems and high rates of absenteeism) and because of the special treatment which the participants received.

(b) Programs which augment the supply of workers in a particular occupation will have the effect of exerting downward pressure on the wages of existing workers in that occupation. It is worth noting that the workers earning high wages are likely to belong to unions which will block these programs in their field (e.g., the building trades), but that low wage workers (like hospital workers) have little or no power to protect their economic interests.

(c) Programs which engender high hopes among some applicants or entrants may lead to a further alienation and hostility for some of those who are rejected or otherwise refused admission or for those who enter and fail. Admission policies are, in fact, just one example of administrative discretionary behavior that can have considerable separate influence on the positive and negative effects of programs—a point brought out in debates about the relative merits of self-help programs,

---

[13] For a notable exception to the absence of attempted measurement of the type of third-party discussed above, see Thomas I. Ribich, *Education and Poverty* (Washington, D.C.: The Brookings Institution, 1968). Ribich's study also gives us some evidence of the likelihood of relatively small quantitative magnitudes of these effects. A rather free wheeling listing of third-party effects runs the risk of double counting benefits. For example, although other family members benefit from the better education or earnings of the head of the household, we should not forget that had the investment expenditure been elsewhere, even if in the form of an across-the-board tax cut, *other* family heads would have had larger incomes, at least, with resulting benefits to *their* families. In his examination of cost-benefit analysis of water resources developments, Roland N. McKean gives an extended discussion of the pitfalls of double counting. See his *Efficiency in Government Through Systems Analysis* (New York: John Wiley and Sons, Inc., read especially Chapter 9.

[14] An exceptionally good discussion of negative external effects, including disruption of the community structure, is contained in Anthony Downs', "Uncompensated Non-Construction Costs Which Urban Highways and Urban Renewal Impose on Residential Households" which will appear in a Universities-National Bureau of Economic Research Conference volume entitled, *Economics of Public Output*. The literature on urban renewal and public housing is extensive and too well known to require listing here.

transfer payment programs, and welfare and relief programs.[15]

Community effects of a social action program can be viewed as a special type of external effect, since the changes in the community structure or in various community institutions are assumed to be important because of the benefits or costs they ultimately provide for third-party individuals in the community. Thus, we are not proposing that the "community" be viewed as an "entity" separate from the individuals who comprise it. However, a separate focus on measures of community institutional changes appears necessary since the present state of our theories of community organization permit us little scope for anything except qualitative linkages between institutional changes and their effects on individuals in the community. We can, for example, consider better communication between the neighborhood populace and the police, school officials, or the employment service as "good things," either in their own right, as expressions of the democratic ethic, or because we believe that such changes will have tangible effects in safety, school achievement or better jobs.

## INTENTIONAL EXPERIMENTS: A SUGGESTED STRATEGY

Underlying the growing interest in evaluations of social action programs is the enlightened idea that the scientific method can be applied to program experience to establish and measure particular cause and effect relationships which are amenable to change through the agents of public policy. However, traditional methods in science, whether the laboratory experimentation of the physical scientists, the testing of pilot models by engineers, or field testing of drugs by medical scientists, are seldom models that can be directly copied, helpful though they are as standards of rigor.

In particular, evaluation designs patterned after the testing of pilot models, which correspond to "demonstration projects" in the field of social action programs, have been inadequate for both theoretical and operational reasons. The present state of our theories of social behavior does not justify settling on a unique plan of action, and we cannot, almost by definition, learn much about alternative courses of action from a single pilot project. It is somewhat paradoxical that on the operational level the pilot model has failed to give us much information because the design has frequently been impossible to control and has spun off in different directions.

The combination of, first, loose administration of and rapid changes in the operation of individual projects and second, a large scale program with many heterogeneous projects (different administrations, different environments, different clientele, etc.), has led to the interesting view that this heterogeneity creates what are, in effect, "natural experiments" for an evaluation design. For economists, who are used to thinking of the measurement of consumers' responses to changes in the price of wheat or investors' responses to changes in the interest rate, the idea of "natural experiments" has a certain appeal. But what should be clear from this discussion—and others before us have reached the same conclusion—is that a greatly improved evaluation could be obtained if social action programs were initiated in *intentional* experiments.

When one talks of "experiments" in the social sciences what inevitably comes to mind is a small scale, carefully controlled study, such as those traditionally employed in psychology. Thus, when one

[15] For an excellent discussion of many of these issues see Joel F. Handler, "Controlling Official Behavior in Welfare Administration," *The Law of the Poor*, ed., J. tenBroek (Chandler Publishing Co., 1966). (Also published in *The California Law Review*, Vol. 54, 1966, p. 479.)

suggests that social action programs be initiated as intentional experiments, people imagine a process which would involve a series of small test projects, a period of delay while those projects are completed and evaluated, and perhaps more retesting before any major program is mounted. This is very definitely *not* what we mean when we suggest social action programs as intentional experimentation. We would stress the word *action* to highlight the difference between what we suggest versus the traditional small scale experimentation.

Social action programs are undertaken because there is a clearly perceived social problem that requires some form of amelioration. In general, (with the exception perhaps of the area of medicinal drugs were a counter tradition has been carefully or painfully built up), we are not willing to postpone large scale attempts at amelioration of such problems until all the steps of a careful testing of hypotheses, development of pilot projects, etc. have been carried out. We would suggest that large scale ameliorative social action and intentional experimentation are not incompatible: experimental designs can be built into a large scale social action program.

If a commitment is made to a more frankly experimental social action program by decision-makers and administrators, then many of the objectives we have advocated can be addressed directly at the planning stage. If we begin a large national program with a frank awareness that we do not know which program concept is more likely to be most efficacious, then several program models could be selected for implementation in several areas, with enough variability in the key elements which make up the concepts to allow good measures of the differential responses to those elements. If social action programs are approached with an "intentionally experimental" point of view, then the analytical powers of our statis-

tical models of evaluation can be greatly enhanced by attempts to insure that "confounding" effects are minimized—i.e., that program treatment variables are uncorrelated with participant characteristics and particular types of environments.

A less technical but equally important gain from this approach to social action programs is the understanding on the part of administrators, decision-makers, and legislators that if we are to learn anything from experience it is necessary to hold the design of the program (that is, the designed project differentials in treatment variables) constant for a long enough period of time to allow for the "settling down" of the program and the collection and analysis of the data. *A commitment to hold to design for a long enough period so that we could learn from experience is a central element in the experimental approach to social action.*

The idea that social action programs should be experimental is simple, but we cannot be sanguine about the speed with which the full implications of this simple idea will be accepted by decision-makers and the public as a whole. The view that programs can be large scale *action* programs and still be designed as intentional experiments has not been easy to get across, even to those involved in experimental methods in the social sciences, with its mehods of small scale research.

The emphasis on ex post evaluation of the fact that at some level legislators understand that social action programs are "testing" concepts. But it will require more explicit acceptance of the idea that some aspects of programs "tested" in action will fail before the full advantages of the intentionally experimental approach can be realized. It takes restraint to mount a program with a built-in experimental design and wait for it to mature before deciding on a single program concept, but we emphasize that restraint does not mean small scale or limited action.

It is not unfair, we think, to characterize the approach to social action programs that has been taken in the past as one of serial experimentation through program failure. A program is built around a single concept, eventually it is realized that it does not work, so the program is scrapped (or allowed to fade away) and a new program and concept is tried. Certainly serial experimentation through failure is the hard way to learn. An intentionally experimental approach would allow us to learn faster by trying alternative concepts *simultaneously* and would make it more likely that we could determine not only *that* a particular concept failed, but also *why* it failed.

## THE ACCEPTABILITY
## OF EVALUATION RESULTS

It does little violence to the facts to state that few decisions about social action programs have been made on the basis of the types of evaluations we have been discussing thus far in this paper. A major reason for this, we feel, is an inadequate taste for rigor (or an overwhelming penchant for visceral judgments) by administrators and legislators and excessive taste for the purely scientific standards by academics. It often seems that the scholars conspire with the legislators to beat down any attempt to bring to bear more orderly evidence about the effectiveness of alternative programs; it is not at all difficult to find experts who will testify that virtually any evaluation study is not adequately "scientific" to provide a sound basis for making program decisions. There is a reasonable and appropriate fear on the part of academics that sophisticated techniques of analysis will be used as deceptive wrapping around an essentially political kernal to mislead administrators or the public. This fear, however, often leads

to the setting of standards of "proof" which cannot, at present, given the state of the art of social sciences, or perhaps never, given the inherent nature of social action programs, be satisfied. The result generally is that the evaluation is discredited, the information it provides ignored, and the decision-maker and legislator can resume the exercise of their visceral talents.

A first step toward creating a more favorable atmosphere for evaluation studies is to recognize that they will not be final arbiters of the worth of a program. A positive but more modest role for evaluation research was recently stated by Kenneth Arrow in a discussion of the relative virtues of the tradition processes of public decision-making (characterized as an adversary process) and the recently developed procedure of the Programming, Planning, Budgeting System (characterized as a rationalistic or "synoptic process".[16] Arrow advocated an approach in between forensics and synoptics.[17] He illustrated his argument by making an analogy with the court system, suggesting that what was happening through the introduction of the more rationalistic processes was the creation of a body of "rules of evidence." The use of systematic evaluation (along with the other elements of the PPBS) represents an attempt to raise the standards of what is admissible as evidence in a decision process that is inherently likely to remain adversary in nature. Higher standards of evaluation will lessen the role of "hearsay" testimony in the decision process, but they are not meant to provide a hard and fast decision rule in and of themselves. The public decision-making process is still a long way from the point at which the evidence from a hard evaluation is the primary or even the significant factor in the totality of fac-

---

[16] For a more complete discussion of this terminology, see Henry Rowen, "Recent Developments in the Measurement of Public Outputs," to be published in a Universities-National Bureau of Economic Research Conference volume, *The Economics of Public Output.*

[17] Remarks by Kenneth Arrow during the NBER conference cited in the previous footnote.

tors which determine major decisions about programs. Therefore, the fear of many academics that poorly understood evaluations will exercise an inordinate influence on public decisions is, to say the least, extremely premature. But if standards for the acceptance of evaluation results are viewed in terms of the "rules of evidence" analogy, we can begin to move toward the judicious mix of rigor and pragmatism that is so badly needed in evaluation analysis.

The predominant view of the role of "serious," independent evaluations[18] (particularly in the eyes of harried administrators), seems to be that a trial (to continue the analogy) aimed at finding a program guilty of failure. There is a sense in which this paranoid view of evaluation is correct. The statistical procedures used usually start with a null hypothesis of "no effect," and the burden of the analysis is to provide evidence that is sufficiently strong to overturn the null hypothesis. As we have pointed out, however, problems of data, organization, and methods conspire to make clear-cut positive findings in evaluations difficult to demonstrate.

The atmosphere for evaluations would be much healthier if the underlying stance were shifted from this old world juridicial rule. Let the program be assumed innocent until proven guilty through clear-cut negative findings. In more precise terms, we should try to avoid committing what are called in statistical theory Type II errors. Thus, an evaluation which does not permit rejecting the null hypothesis (of a zero effect of the program) at customary levels of statistical significance, may be consistent with a finding that a very large positive effect may be just as likely as a zero or negative effect.[19] "Rules of evidence" which emphasize the avoidance of Type II errors are equivalent to an attitude which we have characterized as "innocent until proven guilty." (We must frankly admit that, like court rules of evidence, this basic stance may provide incentives to the program administrators to provide data which are sufficient only for arriving at a "no conclusion" evaluative outcome.)

As a final conciliatory comment; when we talk about evaluation studies leading to verdicts of "success" or "failure," it should be recognized that we are greatly simplifying and abbreviating the typical results. Most social action programs are so complex in the variety of inputs and the multiplicity of objectives, that simple overall judgments are not likely to lead to quick decisions to dump programs. In combination with more detailed studies, the purpose of the evidence provided by the analysts will instead usually be to suggest modifications in the program—to shift the composition of inputs, perhaps to re-emphasize some objectives and de-emphasize others—and to suggest marginal additions or subtractions in the total scale of the program. It is worth emphasizing these modest objectives because the trust and cooperaiton of program administrators are indispensable to an evaluation of the program.

[18] We mean here to exclude the quick and casual sort of evaluation, mainly "in-house" evaluations, that more often than not are meant to provide a gloss of technical justification for a program.

[19] Harold Watts has stressed this point in conversations with the authors. See Glen G. Cain and Harold W. Watts, "The Controversy about the Coleman Report: Comment," *Journal of Human Resources*, Vol. III, No. 3, Summer, 1968, pp. 389–92, also, Harold W. Watts and David L. Horner, "The Educational Benefits of Head Start: A Quantitative Analysis," Discussion Paper Series, The Institute for Research on Poverty, University of Wisconsin, Madison, Wisconsin.

# Facts, Fancies, and Freeloaders in Evaluating Antipoverty Programs[1]

## by Sar A. Levitan

The Nixon administration has not achieved a reputation for reckless spending, but an outsider might easily gain the impression that the federal government is on a spending spree with little regard for the value of the buck. Even a professional gambler in the habit of taking chances might be surprised to discover that the administration is willing to spend funds when it knows little about the soundness of the plunges it is taking. While the seasoned gambler would base his judgments on tried and true permutations and combinations, the administration rarely has the numbers with which to judge even the success of established ventures.

If you think that I am exaggerating, let me cite a few recent examples to indicate the inadequacy of the available information on the basis of which important judgments are made:

1. The Nixon administration has proposed the expansion of JOBS,[2] raising the annual price tag for this program from $160 million to $420 million. It would be reasonable to assume that such eagerness to spend another quarter of a billion dollars is based on proven success. The fact is that the Labor Department in Washington has little information on the JOBS program, who is being hired, how many are being retained, and whether the government is paying subsidies or providing

SOURCE Reprinted with permission from *Poverty and Human Resources,* Vol. 6, November-December 1969.

[1] This paper was delivered before the American Sociological Association, San Francisco, September 4, 1969, and is based on a review of federal antipoverty and manpower programs, *Programs in Aid of the Poor in the 1970's,* scheduled for publication by The Johns Hopkins Press. The study is funded by a grant from The Ford Foundation.

[2] Job Opportunities in the Business Sector (JOBS) eds.

windfalls to employers for doing what they do naturally, that is, hiring workers. Thus, it is impossible to show that as a result of the subsidies, employers are now hiring more disadvantaged persons than they otherwise would in a tight labor market. And there is little evidence that the Labor Department has taken serious steps to appraise the JOBS program or to collect hard data about its operations.

No partisan implications are intended by these remarks. President Johnson had similar confidence in the JOBS program and was willing to tap the public till for this effort as much as President Nixon— and with even less information about the operations of the program.

2. The administration has decided to continue the antipoverty Community Action Program, though there is no evidence that all or even a majority of the thousand community action agencies should be continued. It's hardly a secret that considerable controversy exists about just exactly what most community action agencies do. Major administration spokesmen have not spoken with one voice about the worth of these programs. Not only are there deep disagreements about the appropriate goals of community action agencies, but there is also relatively little information about the achievements that can be chalked up to the $3.5 billion that have been spent by CAP. Description's of CAA's are reminiscent of the blind men and the elephant. Few social scientists, let alone administration officials, have taken the trouble to examine what is happening in the CAA's. Like the blind men, some felt only the heat generated by controversies enacted with community action programs and others touched only the fat of the pork choppers partaking of the antipoverty dollars.

## WHY ALL THE CONFUSION?

The conventional explanation for "the maximum misunderstanding" about anti-poverty and similar welfare efforts is that billions of dollars are spent on "action" programs while only a few cents are allocated to research or evaluation. If this glib explanation was true several years ago, it is no longer true today. During the 60's, millions have been expended on research, and much more would have been forthcoming if the academic community had made its research relevant to program planning and implementation. Regrettably, the information contained in the hundreds of research manuscripts prepared under government contracts has had little influence on policy makers and has contributed little to determining the course of these programs.

The explanation of the doubtful and minimal impact flowing from government-contracted studies is not difficult to find. Since the money for research is plentiful, why has there been little return for the dollars so invested?

1. Since most administrators who spend the money do not cherish having outsiders pass judgment on the value and effectiveness of their programs, research money is frittered away as much by design as by ineptness. While an administrator worth his salt desires a maximum of information on his program, his enthusiasm for added insights is considerably dampened if he has to share this information with the Congressmen who control his purse strings or the public at large. Officials dealing with national defense programs can hide behind the cloak of national security and classify unwelcome information. The options of other officials are much more limited. In spite of this, many an unfriendly report failed to see the light of day because it was claimed to contain privileged information. This subterfuge has been weakened by the Freedom of Information Act, and for more than two years the Office of Economic Opportunity has had a strict rule that any research reports prepared under contract and dealing

with operations of the agency must become public property within two months after they are submitted to OEO. Other agencies may have less fish-bowl-like policies, but it is becoming increasingly difficult for an administrator to hide the results of research conducted by outsiders. The result is that many administrators would rather not have researchers meddling in activities relevant to program operations.

A case in point is the experience of the Neighborhood Youth Corps over the past five years. Little is known about the program's operation or its value although it has already cost the taxpayer about $1.4 billion. In the early days of NYC, its administrators discovered the popularity of distributing money in communities. Congressmen liked this operation as well as many of their constituents. Those responsible for the program saw little gain from digging for information about the impact of the program and avoided, as much as possible, public studies of the subject. Why rock the boat? After four years and more than a billion dollars, a top Labor Department official admitted to a Congressional committee that not a single NYC project had been discontinued or curtailed because it fell short of achieving program goals. The Labor Department simply did not have the information to justify the termination of a project; the data did not exist.

Recently, Secretary of Labor George P. Shultz has taken note of the doubtful effectiveness of out-of-school NYC and has recommended that its funds be cut. He decided, however, to transfer these NYC funds to the JOBS program—a program on which there is even less data.

Nonetheless, there are indications that top Nixon officials dealing with manpower and antipoverty programs are interested in and will seek public evaluation of the programs. Secretary Shultz has shown a strong interest in hard-nosed evaluation and his academic credentials

on that score are unimpeachable. Donald Rumsfeld, the new Director of OEO, has placed equally strong emphasis on evaluation and research in restructuring OEO.

2. If the demand by administrators for evaluation of programs has been less than enthusiastic, the academic community has appeared no less reluctant to deliver the goods. If the initial Shultz-Rumsfeld eagerness to get the facts withstands the passage of time, there is little evidence that social scientists are eager to meet the challenge.

## WHO IS TO BELL THE CAT?

Several factors contribute to the meager pickings that can be gleaned from academic vineyards in evaluating federal welfare programs.

1. First, while evaluation of social programs requires more than a narrow disciplinary approach, the structure of the academic community awards the brownie points to those who specialize in the mysteries and esoterics of narrow disciplines. There are few incentives for studying real problems or for making research results readily available in simple English.

I can imagine the results if social scientists were given the interesting assignment of discovering the reasons for marrying Racquel Welch:

The economist would conclude that one should marry Miss Welch because of her wealth, the salary she commands, and her potential contributions to the GNP. The political scientist would conduct a survey and find that she scores high on the public opinion polls. The psychologist would discover that she has strong maternal instincts. Finally, the sociologist would conclude from his studies that the reason for marrying Miss Welch is that she interacts well with her environment. All may be correct, but I suspect that no single explanation gives a full or satisfactory answer to the question raised.

2. When it comes to evaluation, my fellow economists tend to put all their eggs in the cost-benefit basket. The results of such analyses are as worthy as discussion in the earlier times concerning the number of angels that can dance on the head of a pin. I'm not concerned here with the inherent weaknesses of the cost-benefit approach or the subjective elements involved in these exercises. The problem with the cost-benefit calculators is not that they get the wrong answers, but that they do not raise the right questions. In connection with welfare programs, we should be more concerned with the ability of an affluent society to redistribute available resources than with whether a dollar spent on the poor adds more than a dollar to the gross national product. Thus, a successful birth control program might actually reduce the gross national product, but it is also a most effective antipoverty effort.

3. Aside from narrow disciplinary hangups, there are practical considerations that prevent me from being sanguine about the prospects for developing academic capability to evaluate on-going welfare programs—at least in the short run. The numerologists have taken over not only my own field of study, but also most other disciplines. And unless there is a regression coefficient upon which a model can be built, a study is not worth the effort. As this is the stuff of which promotions are made, an ambitious young academic is likely to be diverted from devoting time to meaningful evaluation of government programs. Why be concerned about mundane details of on-going programs when academic rewards are derived from conceptualizing about the broad issues and their policy implications? The speculations require little work, and the social scientist will be comforted that his fliers will never be proven wrong because

the conclusions are not likely to be tested, nor will anybody care.

4. A more crass consideration also leads many in the academic community to refrain from contributing their efforts to honest evaluation of government programs. Since campuses are becoming more dependent upon government largesse, the sound academic administrator is likely to shun controversial issues that might rock the boat and diminish his chances for the next grant. Very few Congressmen are likely to become concerned about an arid model which draws data from an imaginary universe, but many are likely to react to a report that the NYC projects in their respective districts or stages are providing no training or that the neighborhood centers supported by federal dollars are organizing rent strikes. Here again the incentives are weighed against evaluation.

## AN APPEAL TO THE MAVERICK

However, I am not without hope. Universities have always been, and still remain, the refuge for non-conformists; in this day and age, doing "one's own thing" is becoming even more fashionable. My appeal to the academic free spirit is that he devote greater attention to public programs and to helping improve the quality of these efforts. Conservatives, liberals, and even militants can play the game. By throwing light on the effectiveness of public programs, conservatives can hope to see programs which do not pay off discontinued. The liberal, on the other hand, can anticipate bringing attention to those programs that do work and thus generate additional dollars for them. Finally, there are kicks for the militant who can always show that we do not live in the best of all possible worlds by pointing to the inadequacies of all the programs.

# Evaluating Federal Manpower Programs

## by Garth L. Mangum

### A. THE NATURE OF FEDERAL MANPOWER POLICY

1. There is no federal manpower policy in the dictionary sense: "a definite course of action selected from among alternatives, and in light of given conditions, to guide and determine present and future decisions." However, there are programs and practices which can be analyzed in aggregate and from which policy emphases can be extracted.

2. Legislation in the 1950's such as the National Defense Education Act and practices of agencies such as the Atomic Energy Commission emphasized manpower as an economic resource, with particular concern for the development of scientific and technical manpower. Spending for such purposes increased during the 1960's and now totals over $5 billion annually. However, the focus of public manpower efforts during the 1960's shifted in another direction.

\* \* \*

1. The relevant manpower programs which emphasize in varying degrees services for the competitively disadvantaged are the Manpower Development and Training Act, the Vocational Education Act of 1963, the Vocational Rehabilitation program and the several manpower components of the Economic Opportunity Act. . . . In addition, the United States Employment Service is included, not as a program but as a major deliverer of services.

2. This array of programs did not emerge as part of any systematic effort to identify and provide each of the services needed by various disadvantaged groups or by all the disadvantaged. Instead individual acts were written, considered, and

SOURCE Reprinted with permission from *Proceedings* of the Twentieth Annual Meeting, Industrial Relations Research Association (1967).

amended in rapid succession to meet current crises, real or imagined, with little attention to their interrelations. Though overall objectives are reasonably clear, the objectives of some of the individual programs are not.[1]

3. The resources and enrollments in all of these programs are too small relative to the size of the labor force and the magnitude of needs to have had an appreciable impact on the problems they were intended to "solve." Remedial programs for the disadvantaged currently enroll an average of only 300,000 people at any point in time—this in an economy where in prosperous 1966, 2.5 million persons were unemployed 15 weeks or more, 850,000 were unemployed over half the year, 1.3 million looked for but did not find any work, 1.3 million males 25 to 64 years of age did not seek work and more than five million persons worked for less than the federal minimum wage.

4. The 1961-67 period is most appropriately viewed as an experimental one during which many things were tried with varying degrees of success and failure. A positive contribution of these efforts was the identification of a number of services which have proven useful in lowering the obstacles to employment and retention of the disadvantaged. A few of these are:

a. Outreach to seek the discouraged and undermotivated and encourage them to partake of available services;

b. Adult basic education, to remedy the lack of obsolescence of earlier schooling and prevocational orientation to expose those with limited experience to alternative occupational choices;

c. Training for entry level skills, for those unprepared to profit from the normally more advanced training which assumes mastery of rudimentary education;

d. Training allowances, to provide support and an incentive for those undergoing training and residential facilities for youth whose home environment precludes successful rehabilitation;

e. Work experience, for those unaccustomed to the discipline of the work place;

f. Job development, efforts to solicit job opportunities suited to the abilities of the disadvantaged job seeker;

g. Relocation and transportation assistance to bring the workers to where the jobs are;

h. Subsidization of private employment of the disadvantaged;

i. Job coaching to work out supervisor-worker adjustments after a job is found;

j. Creation of public service jobs tailored to the needs of job seekers not absorbed in the competitive market.

5. Essential as these services are, they are available through no one program, agency or labor market institution. The various programs are limited in the services they can offer. The budgetary commitments for the various services are not rationally related to need. For instance, there are currently more slots for work relief than for training when training should probably stand above work relief in the hierarchy of remedial services.

6. The administrative capability to deliver these services has yet to be developed. At the local level, there is no single agency or combination of easily accessible institutions where those seeking help can find it. Neither has any community the resources to provide some type

---

[1] Sar A. Levitan and Garth L. Mangum, *Making Sense of Federal Manpower Policy*, Policy Papers in Human Resources and Industrial Relations, No. 2, Institute of Labor and Industrial Relations, University of Michigan, Wayne State University, 1967.

of service to all who need it. A multiplicity of federal funding sources encourages interagency competition at the federal level and a proliferation at the local level placing a premium on "grantsmanship." Coordination has been tried with little success and consolidation of programs has been limited. Existing agencies have changed their orientation and biases but slowly and only under considerable outside pressure. New agencies have yet to learn effective practices. Surprisingly little has been done, considering the number of programs and the level of expenditures, to develop or train capable staffs at any level of government.

7. Administration officials and Members of Congress have been too impatient to await the results of new and existing programs and to allow for restructuring, removal of negative elements, and finally their expansion into effective programs. As a result, there has been an excessive resort to gimmicks and to attempts to devise "instant policies for instant success." The procedure has become a familiar one. New approaches are designed intuitively rather than empirically. They are launched with public relations fanfare, complete with numerical goals and early target dates. Manipulation of numbers to "prove" success then becomes a major staff function until a quiet burial of the goals and targets can be devised. The favored gimmicks of the moment are the CEP approach and private enterprise involvement. Both have promise as part of the manpower policy arsenal of weapons but the experiences of neither to date has earned the warmth with which they are being embraced.

8. For no program are there adequate valid data for evaluation of strengths and weaknesses and no program currently has a reporting system capable of producing such data. Data on the characteristics of enrollees are adequate in some but not all programs. Data on services provided are weak and follow-up data on program results are grossly inadequate and undependable. *Ad hoc* internal evaluations have been made of several programs, either in-house or by contract, but for the most part, their coverage is limited, their data weak and their investigations not probing.

9. Nevertheless, one concludes from observation, available data and piecing together other fragmentary evidence that some programs are at least moderately successful and merit expansion. None is a clearly proven failure, though in several cases the funds could have been better spent elsewhere. Through this necessary experimental process many lessons have been learned, needs probed and useful services identified. Congress has demonstrated a willingness to change and adapt programs in light of administrative experience. Expansion of programs has been slower than anticipated but less because of Congressional reluctance than absence of aggressive Administration requests.

B. PROGRAM EVALUATION

1. *MDTA*[2]

MDTA's *original objective* was to *retrain experienced adult family heads* dis-

---

[2] For detailed evaluation of the Manpower Development and Training program see Garth L. Mangum, *Contributions and Costs of Manpower Development and Training,* Policy Papers in Human Resources and Industrial Relations, No. 5, Institute of Labor and Industrial Relations, The University of Michigan, Wayne State University, 1967. The MDTA reporting system is set up to produce adequate data on trainee characteristics, training occupations, completions and employment experiences of the first post-training year. However, serious under-reporting makes the latter of doubtful validity and makes state-by-state analyses shaky. The OJT reporting is particularly bad. The reporting system is especially poor on costs and the nature of the training given. A mass of data is poured into the computers but there have not been the staff resources and top level interest to see that it was retrieved and analyzed for managerial and evaluative purposes. Nevertheless, more information is available than for other programs.

placed by economic and technological change. As labor markets have tightened, its emphasis has shifted to the disadvantaged. MDTA consists of two distinct components—institutional and on-the-job training (OJT)—which are best evaluated separately.

a. The institutional training program has built-in "creaming" tendencies since its enrollees are primarily those who have sought help from an Employment Service office. Nevertheless, MDTA institutional training is increasing its proportionate enrollment of the non-white, the young, the public assistance recipient, the handicapped and those with 9 to 11 years of education. It has yet to make significant progress in serving those with 8 years of schooling or less and persons over 44 years of age. Over half the institutional enrollees are apparently drawn from families with annual incomes of less than $3000 per year. The institutional training program probably "creams" within each disadvantaged category. However, the 70 to 80 MDTA skill centers clearly reach a more disadvantaged clientele than other MDTA projects and are probably reaching as deeply as any program except perhaps the Job Corps.

b. The OJT program has never served appreciable numbers of disadvantaged and its record has been worsening in all categories. This may in part be due to recent pressures to expand it to one-half of the total MDA enrollment, primarily to get more enrollees within the same fixed budget. Enrollment means employment and employers are quality conscious. The federal administrators of the program in the Bureau of Apprenticeship and Training are experienced at promoting apprenticeship but accustomed to leaving recruitment and selection to employers and unions. To augment the limited BAT staff, OJT slots have been contacted to trade associations who subcontract the training to their members or to community

action agencies, unions and civil rights organizations who subcontract, usually with smaller employers. The trade associations have a quality bias and the community contractors, while they have the right prejudices, lack experience and competence.

c. Overall, the MDT program has a favorable cost-benefit experience. The completers have more stable employment and higher earnings after training when compared with their own pre-training experience and with control groups. Disadvantaged institutional completers still have a more difficult time finding jobs than other completers but have better experience than in the absence of training. The disadvantaged have a difficult time getting into OJT but once in have retention rates not significantly different from those of the non-disadvantaged.

In addition to its contributions to its enrollees, MDTA has had a *positive influence on the Employment Service, on Vocational Education and, to a small degree, on apprenticeship.* There are continuing issues of priority between serving the disadvantaged and non-disadvantaged, the relative effectiveness of institutional and on-the-job training and the appropriate federal, state and local administrative roles. None of these threaten the overall value of the program, however.

*Enrichment of the program's services has been authorized from time to time but without commensurate increases in budget.* Thus the choice has been between richer offerings for fewer and a leaner program for more. The program could be doubled in size within the limits of current administrative and training capabilities. *Skill Centers are currently operating at less than half capacity.* Doubling the MDTA budget with emphasis on expanding the skill center concept and directing OJT more clearly toward the disadvantaged should be a legislative priority in 1968.

## 2. *Vocational Education*[3]

The Vocational Education Act of 1963 was the first major reorientation of federally supported vocational education since its beginning in 1917. Most importantly, it directed a shift in objectives from training for occupational categories to serving the training needs of people. It stressed serving those with academic and socio-economic handicaps who could not profit from the regular programs. Federal funds, which are matched equally by the state, were expanded from approximately $50 million to $200 million per year over a three-year period (and Congress actually appropriated the funds). Construction of "area" vocational schools (those serving a broader area than a single high school), more teacher education and better vocational guidance were encouraged. Closer alliance with the Employment Service was directed in order to relate training more directly to the labor market. Money was also authorized for research and innovative programs.

Some progress has been made, but largely, it would seem, for lack of federal leadership, a promising Act has not had a substantial impact upon the status and content of vocational education. The relative emphasis on agriculture and home economics has declined (though their absolute enrollment has increased), new schools have been built, significant research has been undertaken for the first time, and relationships with the Employ-ment Service in determining job market needs have been improved. About one of each four high school students now enrolls in a federally-supported vocational program but 3 of 5 are still in home economics and agriculture. Another 1 in 6 are in office occupations which were added to the list of federally-supported courses by the 1963 Act. Four-fifths of the reported increase in enrollments since 1964 is accounted for by the addition of office occupations and may not reflect an actual increase in enrollments. Post-secondary and adult courses reach 4 percent of the labor force.

Nothing more than pious hope was provided to encourage the desired shift from an occupational grouping to a people-serving orientation. There has been little meaningful innovation under the Act and a great reluctance to adopt proven experiments demonstrated on projects financed by foundations, OEO and MDTA funds. Training occupations still reflect more the 1917 categories than current labor market needs. Offerings for those with special needs account for less than 1 percent of total expenditures. Programs in rural schools and urban slums are limited and poor—just where they are needed most. This generally dismal picture is belied by some real bright spots but in general change has been slow and minor.

## 3. *Vocational Rehabilitation*[4]

The Vocational Rehabilitation program each year results in the placement in com-

---

[3] See Volume I, *Education for Employment*, of forthcoming report of the Vocational Education Advisory Council. The Vocational Education reporting system is abysmal. Its only real concern has been to see that the states match every federal dollar and that the dollars are spent within the occupational categories prescribed by the Smith-Hughes and George Barden Acts. There is practically no information on student characteristics, training contents and results. The Advisory Council on Vocational Education has been hard put to find any data base for its current evaluation of the results of the 1963 Act.

[4] See Garth L. Mangum and Lowell M. Glenn, *Vocational Rehabilitation and Federal Manpower Policy*, Policy Papers in Human Resources and Industrial Relations, No. 4, Institute of Labor and Industrial Relations, the University of Michigan, Wayne State University, 1967. The Vocational Rehabilitation reporting system is reasonably adequate for managing a rehabilitation program but there is no follow-up information to allow realistic assessment of program results beyond immediate employment. Data are currently inadequate to assess the demographic, economic, and cultural characteristics of the clients but the federal agency is now collecting data on an individual client basis and will soon have data processing capability which should improve the situation.

petitive employment of more disadvantaged persons than MDTA or any of the EOA programs and at lower average costs. However, its clientele have physical and mental handicaps rather than economic or cultural ones and *surprisingly little training occurs.* The federal agency claims a 35 to 1 ratio of benefits to costs which can be deflated, using their data, to 12 to 1. However, *the program is of undoubted worth.* Its particular value is an individualized comprehensive services approach involving a close counselor-client relationship. A rehabilitation plan is mutually developed for each individual and the counselor, in effect, has a blank checkbook to purchase whatever services are needed.

There is some debate among vocational rehabilitation personnel between those who favor physical restoration to eliminate handicaps and those who emphasize training and other services to make employment possible despite existing handicaps. In addition to the basic services, there is an extensive research program, encouragement for innovation and a program of grants to universities and individuals for pre-service and in-service training of rehabilitation personnel. The program has favorable congressional support and expands about as rapidly as the states are willing to meet their 25 percent matching requirement.

### 4. *The United States Employment Service*[5]

The manpower legislation of the past five years has had a substantial impact upon the Employment Service, so much so that the agency is quite different from the Employment Service of 1962. No longer is it restricted to referring qualified workers in response to employer job orders.

Through referral to MDTA, Job Corps and Neighborhood Youth Corps, involvement with vocational educators and community action agencies, and its own Youth Opportunity Centers and Human Resources Development Program, the Employment Service can search out those in need of its services, enhance their employability and even provide public employment.

The Employment Service is very much in transition. By and large, its involvement with the disadvantaged has been under pressure from the national office and in response to competition from community action agencies. Its role and objectives are in a state of confusion. The Department of Labor has become a more aggressive partner in the federal-state system. It has continually added new programs and responsibilities to the Employment Service without commensurate increase in staff and budgets. It has then failed to set priorities among the assignments, all of which cannot be fulfilled adequately and equally with available resources. There is also evidence of failure to seek and achieve consensus before major policy changes. As a result, state and local officials do not share the degree of commitment to many responsibilities exhibited by those in Washington.

*Four policy objectives appear to coexist,* each reflecting stages in the agency's development. Many state Employment Security directors and businessmen still see the agency's primary function to be providing a work test for the payment of unemployment compensation. Most local Employment Service managers probably see their agency as an employer-serving labor exchange. The more progressive aspire to the position of Community Manpower Center, serving all occupational groups and community institutions. Cur-

[5] The Employment Service has detailed data on how many transactions occur but none on who is served, how well and what the results are. A forthcoming report by Garth L. Mangum and Arnold L. Nemore, *Reorientation in the Federal-State Employment Service,* will provide some data and more extensive analysis.

rent federal emphasis is on serving the disadvantaged. Mutually exclusive elements in these objectives are apparent. "Image" with employers probably suffers in direct relation to antipoverty involvement.

Problems of salaries and training remain significant barriers to attracting and retaining competent professional personnel. As long as ES and UI are together in the federal and state bureaus, the Employment Service will remain at the fourth tier in the pecking order of authority and prestige in the Labor Department and in a similar position in state governments.

The time is imminent when the USES budget will have exhausted the revenue potential of its Social Security Act Title III basic funding source. At that time, the issues involved in the ES-UI attachment will have to be faced and the decision will have to be made to switch partially or completely to general Treasury funding.

The Employment Service with its ubiquitous local offices is inevitably the "front line" arm of most manpower programs. It has been pressured by events into broadening its activities in behalf of many it previously could not or did not serve. It has cherished ambition to reach upward to others who have not previously sought its services. Without clear objectives it has no measure to evaluate or be evaluated by its own performance.

## C. SUMMARY

### 1. *Accomplishments*

Needed services have been provided, needy persons have been served and useful lessons have been learned.

The base has been established for a coherent program of remedial services to the competitively disadvantaged.

### 2. *Limitations*

The administrative capability has yet to be developed for efficient delivery of services.

The resources committed are grossly inadequate relative to need.

Solution to the first limitation would greatly increase the chances of solving the second.

# Manpower Programs and the "New Federalism"

## by Sar A. Levitan

As the Nixon administration enters its second year, it is becoming increasingly clear that concern about the demise of the Great Society manpower and welfare programs has been exaggerated and premature. The worriers can relax—indications are that the domestic programs inaugurated during the 1960's will continue into the foreseeable future and some efforts are even likely to expand though others are being curtailed. The administration has now given its blessings to the Office of Economic Opportunity and to most manpower efforts initiated in the 1960's.

Manpower programs have become an integral part of economic policy and welfare programs since the beginning of the 1960's. New manpower programs have been introduced, focusing on the needs of the poorly educated, the unskilled, and the unemployed, and new services have been initiated with varying degrees of success. Overall expenditures on manpower programs have increased about fifteenfold in one decade, with an outlay of $2.8 billion projected for fiscal 1971 (Table 1).

Continued growth at these rates and continued experimentation with new manpower programs and services on a broad scale are unlikely in the immediate years ahead. While the 1960's were years of expansion and innovation, the next few years are likely to be characterized by more limited growth and by the application of lessons learned from earlier experiments. Barring unforeseen changes in the health of the economy, this "maturation" of the manpower effort is dictated by several factors.

First, lessons have been learned from the past. While there is no consensus among manpower experts as to the directions of needed changes, there is general

SOURCE Reprinted with permission from *Conference Board Record* (April 1970).

TABLE 1. FEDERAL OUTLAYS FOR MANPOWER PROGRAMS, FISCAL 1961, 1964, 1966–71*

(Millions)

| | 1961 | 1964 | 1966 | 1967 | 1968 | 1969 | 1970 (Estimates) | 1971 (Estimates) |
|---|---|---|---|---|---|---|---|---|
| *Total* | $184 | $380 | $1,346 | $1,619 | $1,942 | $2,011 | $2,385 | $2,830 |
| Institutional Training | — | 93 | 492 | 566 | 587 | 583 | 658 | 739 |
|   MDTA Institutional | — | 93 | 249 | 221 | 235 | 230 | 233 | 241 |
|   Job Corps | — | — | 229 | 321 | 299 | 236 | 163 | 175 |
|   Concentrated Employment (CEP) | — | — | — | 1 | 25 | 52 | 91 | 103 |
|   Work Incentive (WIN) | — | — | — | — | — | 28 | 118 | 146 |
|   Other relief recipients | — | — | 13 | 18 | 22 | 34 | 49 | 68 |
|   O.I.C. | — | — | 1 | 6 | 5 | 4 | 5 | 5 |
| On-the-Job Training | — | 5 | 27 | 53 | 117 | 176 | 280 | 469 |
|   Jobs in the Business Sector | — | — | — | — | 5 | 46 | 139 | 314 |
|   MDTA-OJT | — | 5 | 27 | 53 | 84 | 79 | 74 | 59 |
|   Public Service Careers | — | — | — | — | 13 | 17 | 25 | 51 |
|   New Careers | — | — | — | — | 13 | 27 | 34 | 37 |
|   WIN and CEP-OJT | — | — | — | — | 3 | 7 | 8 | 9 |
| Work Experience and Work Support | — | — | 333 | 388 | 504 | 416 | 425 | 458 |
|   Neighborhood Youth Corps | — | — | 241 | 253 | 341 | 287 | 312 | 336 |
|     In-school and summer | — | — | 178 | 126 | 198 | 182 | 212 | 215 |
|     Out-of-school | — | — | 63 | 127 | 143 | 106 | 100 | 121 |
|   Concentrated employment | — | — | — | — | 27 | 56 | 59 | 67 |
|   Operation Mainstream | — | — | 10 | 9 | 31 | 37 | 41 | 41 |
|   Work experience and training | — | — | 76 | 120 | 98 | 26 | 1 | — |
|   Foster grandparents | — | — | 5 | 6 | 8 | 8 | 9 | 9 |
|   Work incentive | — | — | — | — | — | 1 | 3 | 5 |
| Job Placement and Support | 126 | 181 | 276 | 306 | 330 | 344 | 390 | 454 |
|   Employment Service | 126 | 181 | 262 | 291 | 312 | 317 | 353 | 388 |
|   CAA Outreach | — | — | 12 | 13 | 16 | 22 | 23 | 23 |
|   Child care | — | — | 2 | 2 | 2 | 5 | 14 | 43 |
| Administration, Research, and Support | 4 | 17 | 65 | 92 | 108 | 124 | 132 | 157 |
|   Administration | 4 | 8 | 47 | 56 | 63 | 73 | 75 | 78 |
|   Research | — | 2 | 6 | 8 | 9 | 8 | 13 | 24 |
|   Experimental and demonstration | — | 7 | 4 | 19 | 25 | 20 | 20 | 19 |
|   Technical assistance | — | — | 1 | 1 | 2 | 10 | 11 | 19 |
|   Labor market information | — | — | 8 | 8 | 8 | 11 | 11 | 14 |
|   Evaluation | — | — | — | — | 1 | 2 | 3 | 4 |
| Vocational Rehabilitation | 54 | 84 | 154 | 215 | 297 | 368 | 500 | 553 |

* Includes only outlays by the Departments of Labor and Health, Education, and Welfare.
NOTE: Details may not add totals because of rounding.
SOURCE: U.S. Bureau of the Budget

agreement about the need to consolidate the categorical programs that proliferated during recent years. There is clear evidence that varying eligibility criteria, overlapping services, and conflicting regulations have undermined the effectiveness of manpower efforts, and that many improvements could be made. Some programs and approaches developed during the 1960's have been clearly ineffective,

and resources should be shifted to the more successful efforts.

Second, and more important in determining the cast of manpower efforts in the next few years, are the attitudes and principles of the Nixon administration. President Nixon has consistently supported the idea that the private sector should take a more active role in manpower programs. The ideology of "New

Federalism" is that centralized administration should be reduced and the role of the state and local government expanded, and that these functions should be transferred as much as possible from the public to the private sector. Translated into more specific terms, the Republican precepts of the present administration favor incentives for the business sector to hire and train the disadvantaged. One-the-job training is preferred over institutional training, private over public employment programs, and "workfare" over welfare.

The political principles of the Republican administration combined with a shift in public priorities—e.g., placing clean air and water over help for the poor—point toward stabilization of manpower expenditures and indicate a changing emphasis among individual programs. The hope is to increase the effectiveness of manpower programs through operational reorganization, and the interaction of these forces in manpower developments over the last year is clearly discernible and will undoubtedly set the tenor for the next few years.

A caveat is in order. As in the past, the current and projected state of the economy will continue to influence the character of the manpower efforts. Sustained growth will mean that jobs will continue to be generated, even for the unskilled. Manpower programs must then concentrate on matching supply and demand through training and placement efforts and on providing work incentives for those who are employable but not presently in the work force. Manpower programs must also focus on the needs of those who are working full time but at wages so low that they remain in poverty. Inflation exercises pressure on all government programs, and manpower programs have felt the pinch of budgetary constraints. But if the level of unemployment should rise, pressures will develop to expand job creation programs and to provide income maintenance to persons forced into idleness.

MANPOWER BUDGETS:
FISCAL 1970 AND 1971

The original budget prepared by the Johnson administration for fiscal 1970 showed an increase in aggregate Federal manpower outlays. The Nixon administration made some cuts in total anticipated expenditures and redesigned the structure of several programs. Outlays for manpower programs in 1970 continued to rise, however, as a result of earlier commitments. But for 1971, the administration recommended a 9.5% boost in new obligational authority compared with a requested increase of 18% a year earlier (Table 2).

The most striking changes during the first year of the Nixon administration indicating program emphasis were the drastic curtailment of Job Corps and the expansion of Job Opportunities in the Business Sector (JOBS). President Nixon had struck out against the costly Job Corps in his 1968 campaign, and many impartial observers of anti-poverty programs questioned whether the results measured by low retention rates and little educational advancement among enrollees justified the high cost of residency. The administration revamped the program by shifting it from the Office of Economic Opportunity to the Department of Labor, closing 59 of 123 centers (presumably the least effective), and replacing them with only four nonresidential centers by February 1970. There is little question that the Job Corps needed reform, though the cuts may have been too precipitous and the administration failed to provide alternative programs for the Job Corps clients.

The expansion of funding for the JOBS program, however, was based more on principle than proven effectiveness. The JOBS program gives subsidies averaging around $3,000 per slot to private firms for

TABLE 2. FEDERAL OBLIGATIONS FOR MANPOWER PROGRAMS, FISCAL 1969–71*

(Millions)

| | 1969 (Actual) | 1970 (Estimates) | 1971 (Estimates) |
|---|---|---|---|
| *Total* | $2,243 | $2,643 | $2,895 |
| Institutional Training | 675 | 667 | 712 |
| MDTA Institutional | 233 | 249 | 255 |
| Job Corps | 257 | 155 | 164 |
| Concentrated Employment | 42 | 96 | 98 |
| Work Incentive (WIN) | 103 | 110 | 118 |
| Other relief recipients | 35 | 52 | 72 |
| O.I.C. | 5 | 5 | 5 |
| On-the-Job Training | 278 | 471 | 525 |
| Jobs in the Business Sector | 157 | 312 | 393 |
| MDTA-OJT | 73 | 68 | 29 |
| Public Service Careers | 19 | 47 | 60 |
| New Careers | 22 | 36 | 34 |
| WIN and CEP | 7 | 8 | 9 |
| Work Experience and Work Support | 431 | 431 | 453 |
| Neighborhood Youth Corps | 327 | 316 | 335 |
| In-school and summer | 203 | 218 | 209 |
| Out-of-school | 124 | 98 | 126 |
| Concentrated employment | 45 | 62 | 62 |
| Operation Mainstream | 41 | 41 | 41 |
| Work experience and training | 6 | — | — |
| Foster grandparents | 9 | 9 | 10 |
| Work incentive | 3 | 3 | 5 |
| Job Placement and Support | 347 | 395 | 460 |
| Employment Service | 317 | 358 | 392 |
| CAA Outreach | 24 | 24 | 25 |
| Child care | 6 | 13 | 43 |
| Administration, Research, and Support | 123 | 158 | 182 |
| Administration | 73 | 74 | 78 |
| Research | 11 | 25 | 40 |
| Experimental and demonstration | 18 | 17 | 16 |
| Technical assistance | 8 | 23 | 26 |
| Labor market information | 11 | 16 | 17 |
| Evaluation | 2 | 3 | 5 |
| Vocational Rehabilitation | 389 | 521 | 563 |

* Includes only obligations by the Departments of Labor and Health, Education, and Welfare and the Office of Economic Opportunity.
SOURCE: U.S. Bureau of the Budget

the hiring and training of disadvantaged workers. By the end of 1969 some 88,000 job placements were claimed under the contract portion of the program, but about three of every five had already terminated. Basic questions remained unanswered about the effectiveness of training offered to enrollees and whether new jobs are really being created for the disadvantaged. Preliminary evidence indicated that in many cases training was meager and the jobs were little different from those traditionally filled by unskilled and deficiently educated workers. Furthermore, difficulties had been experienced in inducing companies to participate in the contract program. Despite these warning signals, the Nixon administration adopted President Johnson's proposal to nearly triple outlays for JOBS for fiscal 1970 compared with the previous fiscal year. (The enthusiasm for the JOBS approach was initially proclaimed by the Johnson administration.) The contract JOBS program did not warrant this emphasis on the basis of proven performance, revealing a strong preference for private sector involvement on the part of President Johnson and President Nixon. By the end of 1969, the administration was forced to concede that the commitment of funds to JOBS was in excess of need and the funds allocated to JIBS were curtailed.

Largely as a result of the sharp cut in the Job Corps and the expansion of JOBS, planned outlays for OJT rose much faster than institutional training. Funds allocated to job creation and work experience in fiscal 1970 remained virtually unchanged from the previous year and the administration planned very little expansion of these programs during fiscal 1971. Promises have also been made to beef up the out-of-school Neighborhood Youth Corps by stressing education and training instead of work experience. But this was to be achieved largely by "savings" from stipends paid to enrollees rather than by adding new funds. Whether youths will participate in the program long enough to benefit by the promised education at reduced income remains to be seen.

## STREAMLINING MANPOWER EFFORTS

A major development in the manpower field is a bipartisan effort to overhaul and streamline existing manpower programs . . . legislative proposals . . . by the administration, . . . aim at consolidating and coordinating the categorical and disparate manpower programs.[1]

\* \* \*

## "WORKFARE" VS. WELFARE

A potentially more significant development affecting manpower efforts is President Nixon's Family Assistance Program. Under this welfare proposal, assistance payments would be made to all low-income families with children, including families with a male head who is employed but earning an inadequate income. A family of four with no other income would thus receive a basic annual payment of $1,600—$500 for each of the first two family members and $300 for each additional member.

The manpower aspects of the family assistance proposal focus upon creating work incentives and helping relief recipients to find employment. Under this plan, the first $720 of a family's annual income would be disregarded, and benefits would be reduced 50 cents on the dollar for earnings beyond this point. It would provide expanded assistance for day care centers, enabling adults in recipient families to work, and it would provide for their remedial training and job placement. In the first year, training and day care expenditures would cost an estimated $600 million of the projected additional total expenditure of $4.4 billion for public assistance.

The manpower components of the family assistance proposal are built on the experience of the Work Incentive Program, which was initiated in 1967 to provide work incentives to recipients of Aid to Families with Dependent Children (AFDC). WIN permits the AFDC mother (most AFDC families are headed by a female) to retain the first $30 of her monthly earnings plus one-third of each additional dollar. The program, however, makes little provision for day care and had

[1] The three major bills introduced in 1969 were Congressman Steiger's Comprehensive Manpower Act (H.R. 10908), Congressman O'Hara's Manpower Act (H.R. 11620), and the Administration's Manpower Training Act (H.R. 13472).

scant success in finding employment for participants in its training program.

The importance of the Family Assistance Program is not that it liberalizes the work incentives of WIN, an obviously needed improvement, but rather that the proposal would extend these incentives plus the guaranteed income to families with an employed head. It is estimated that the families of the 1.8 million currently full-time working poor would be covered by the Family Assistance Program.

The Family Assistance Program takes a necessary step toward bridging the gap between welfare and employment. It recognizes the needs of the many who are employed full time but who work at such meager wages that they continue to live in poverty. And it reflects the national ideology and presidential preference for "workfare" over welfare in attempting to increase employment among welfare recipients and enabling them to earn as much as possible.

Despite emphasis upon the admirable twofold objective of creating work incentives for those already receiving welfare and providing additional income for the working poor, the Family Assistance Program raises serious dilemmas and falls short on its promises to reduce dependency. The program would increase the number of those working and receiving assistance, and the income supplements might increase reliance upon public assistance as a substitute for wage increases and tend to encourage irregular and part-time employment. Under this system, two family heads, each with three dependents, could both receive an annual income of $4,000—although one works full time at an hourly rate of $2, while the other works only half time at the same $2 per hour and makes up the difference with cash supplements, food stamps, and other income in kind available under welfare programs. This system may widen the work choices of low-wage earners, but it may also pre-

vent them from ever achieving economic independence.

Judging from the experience of WIN and the work and training efforts of the 1960's, the provision of training through the Family Assistance Program does not necessarily mean that those trained will secure regular employment. Delivery of training to persons in rural areas is costly. Many poorly educated and unskilled workers are not motivated to undergo training, and there is no indication that there will be jobs for them if they undergo successful training. Perhaps most significantly, the efforts don't contribute to any change in the structure of work and training institutions. A mere transfer of the responsibility for income maintenance from an employer to the Federal government without an increase in wage levels will hardly insure decent employment and income for the working poor.

## AN ECONOMIC STABILIZER

Possibly the most innovative feature proposed by the administration relating to manpower policy provides for a trigger mechanism which would increase expenditures for manpower programs when unemployment rises. Included in the administration's Manpower Training Act, the goal of the provision is to achieve an automatic countercyclical mechanism by increasing expenditures for manpower programs when there is a slack in the economy. Specifically, the administration's manpower training bill proposes an automatic increase of 10% in selected manpower funds when unemployment reaches 4.5% of the total labor force for three consecutive months.

While this provision attempts to integrate manpower programs with overall economic policy and is admirable in principle, it is adequate only as an opener. As any poker player knows, more than an initial investment is necessary to win the game, and the soundest economic principles are not good enough to feed unemployed workers and their families. The administration's proposal is only a teaser and needs additional commitment before it becomes part of an effective economic policy. At the present level of appropriations, an increase of 10% in funds allocated to the selected manpower programs covered by the administration's bill means a boost of about $160 million.

The automatic stabilizer proposed by the administration is supposed to compensate the victims of policies aimed at restraining inflation. The additional funds proposed by the administration are adequate to provide for only a small minority of the prospective victims of the constraining economic policies. According to Labor Department estimates, a rise of unemployment from 3.4% (the level of unemployment at the end of 1969) to 4.5% would, during the course of one year, raise the number of persons unemployed 15 weeks or longer from 2.5 million to 3.9 million, and the number of persons unemployed more than 26 weeks during the year would rise from 1 million to 1.8 million. More than $2 billion would be required, again using the Labor Department's estimates, to absorb all the long-term unemployed under current MDTA or work experience programs.

The resort to temporary countercyclical expenditures to provide income or jobs to the unemployed is not without precedent. In the 1958-1959 recession, Congress provided for Temporary Unemployment Compensation at a total cost of more than $600 million. During 1961-1962, the price tag of the Temporary Extended Unemployment Compensation was nearly $800 million, and an additional $850 million was appropriated to create public works jobs in depressed areas. It is true that in both cases unemployment rose to 6% and even higher, but our experience during the past decade clearly indicates that the government should step in before unemployment reaches such a high level. And

one of the salutary lessons we have learned from the 1960's is that the threshold of public tolerance for unemployment has declined. The administration's proposal to raise manpower funds when unemployment reaches 4.5% is therefore sound, but it is not commensurate with the needs of those who become victims of governmental fiscal and monetary policies.

The government should assume responsibility for those who become unemployed as a result of its policies to reduce inflationary pressures. Without raising here any question about the wisdom of these policies, few would argue that the burden of the resulting unemployment should be placed upon those who can least afford it.

Congress would do well to adopt the administration's proposal of automatically boosting the funds allocated to manpower programs by 10% when unemployment reaches 4.5%. But the plan should be extended by raising manpower funds 10% for each 0.2% increase in unemployment. This would mean that the funds allocated to manpower programs would rise automatically by 50% (about $800 million at present level of appropriations) when unemployment reaches 5.3%, and the funds would double if unemployment rises to 6.3%. This provision, together with another proposal by the administration calling for an automatic extension of unemployment insurance when the number of insured unemployed reaches 4.5% (about equivalent to 5.7% of total unemployment), would provide a measure of automatic aid to the victims of monetary and fiscal policies.

POLICY DIRECTIONS

From this brief review of the major manpower developments and policies proposed during the first year of the Nixon administration, it would appear that if the administration's programs prevail there will be a leveling off of manpower outlays and a consolidation of individual programs. Some overlap and waste will be eliminated and the thrust of manpower policy will be to increase the effectiveness of manpower outlays rather than to increase their magnitude. Political forces will be at work favoring decentralization according to the precepts of the "New Federalism," and expanded involvement by the private sector will be stressed. The predicted policy thrusts are necessitated by a combination of economic conditions and political ideology.

The decentralization dictated by the "New Federalism" concepts can create obstacles to effective administration of Federally-funded programs. Many states and localities lack the technical and professional manpower needed to administer such programs, and the prevailing low salaries paid by most states make it unlikely that they will acquire such talent in the near future. *While decentralization may lead to decisions more adapted to local needs, it may also result in decisions which contradict national objectives, so that guidelines must be carefully drawn.* There must also be explicit recognition of the needs of larger cities, which are often neglected in state programs.

Improved administration alone, however, is not enough to carry out effective programs. It only helps to secure a better return on the funds, but it is no substitute for *adequate appropriations.* During its first year, the Nixon administration stressed economy in manpower programs and avoided making commitments for the expansion of these efforts. This retrenchment, dictated by inflationary pressures, must remain only temporary. Improving the administration of the manpower programs would also justify, indeed dictate, the expansion of additional funds to meet

needs. The National Manpower Policy Task Force put it this way in a unanimous policy statement issued in February 1970:

*As we enter a new decade, we should take advantage of the lessons that have been learned from the vast experimentation of the Sixties. Improving the administration of manpower programs and related services to maximize their impact is just as important at this moment as adding funds, and as the administration of manpower programs is improved, it is essential that funds be further expanded. Considering the extent of need, the additional funds become even more justifiable as the effectiveness of the programs is enhanced.*

Finally, whatever the ultimate fate of the President's Family Assistance Program, it is quite clear that during the years ahead there will be an increasing inter-dependence between public assistance and work-oriented manpower programs. The Family Assistance Program is an overdue recognition that a full-time job is not necessarily a cure for poverty. Some form of income supplement for the working poor is likely to become widespread in the years ahead. There will also be an increasing need to tie in training programs for relief recipients, along the lines designed by WIN, with those for other persons who experience difficulties in securing and holding a job.

The substantive revisions proposed by the Nixon administration will improve the tools in the kit to aid the unskilled, unemployed, and the poor. However, none of the measures is a substitute for existing programs, and it will take more funds than the administration has been willing to commit to implement the proposals.

# What Stand-By Measures Should Be Developed to Counteract a Potential Cyclical Downturn in Employment?

## by U.S. Department of Labor, Manpower Administration

The question as posed is only part of a larger question: In what way can, and should, manpower measures be used as a tool for economic stabilization?[1] The question, and its answer, have been largely by-passed in the United States, where manpower programs, particularly training programs, have been utilized primarily as tools for social welfare, directed toward the poor and disadvantaged, with the *implicit assumption that they will have a positive, or at worst a neutral, effect on the economy.* In times of expanding employment and low unemployment, the assumption is a fair one. While we may not have used our manpower programs most effectively to increase productivity and real GNP, and thus constrain inflation, it

is *probable that the productivity of most trainees does increase, and the employment of those previously unemployed certainly represents a real rise in GNP.* If this is not the economically most efficient use of training and other manpower programs, as envisioned in Western Europe, for example, it can claim credit for advances in social welfare for the trainees and the community at large.

But what is true in an expanding economy is not necessarily so in a period of deflation and cyclical downturn. While employment is increasing, trainees can be placed in jobs either with no, or with temporary displacement of current workers. The same is not true when employment is declining. Even the social welfare

SOURCE Reprinted from the Twenty-Sixth Meeting of the National Manpower Advisory Committee (June 19, 1970).

[1] Probably the best available survey on this question is the paper by Gerald Somers (with Duncan MacRae), "Economic Implications of United States Training Programs," prepared for consideration by the OECD in the fall of 1968.

aspects are threatened in the downturn; the most recently hired, the least efficient, and probably the most needy, are the first to be fired. . . .

Like the beginning student in journalism, let us take the questions one at a time: Who, what, when, where and how?

*Who* As indicated above, the persons most immediately affected by an economic downturn are those who are unemployed. Should these be the first to receive manpower services?

There are at least two ways in which manpower training and mobility programs can be of use to the unemployed and affect the unemployment rate. While a worker is in training, he is not counted as unemployed. This is not merely a cynical manipulation of the unemployment statistics. A worker who requires training, or retraining to meet changing technology, is likely to—and should, from an economic point of view—choose to retrain at the time when the opportunity cost of that retraining is lowest. When it is lowest to the individual, it is also lowest to the economy. The period of training or retraining of an unemployed individual can therefore make a *relatively* cheap contribution to the upgrading of the labor force if a better job results at the end of the training. (For the previously unemployed, an entry-level job is obviously a better job.)

But a period of economic downturn may also provide the opportunity of upgrading the presently employed, at relatively low cost. Again, this makes sense only if there are higher-skill jobs waiting at the end of training. . . .

*What* Clearly unemployment insurance, though temporary in its effect, is another counter-cyclical measure. Mobility programs provide yet another possibility. In the past, mobility programs in the United States have been oriented to geographic mobility. What are the possibilities of occupational mobility within industries, and mobility between industries,

directed to greater productivity as well as to elements of more sustained demand? How do we determine these elements?

*When* The "when" of programs is possibly the most crucial element in manpower planning. If we wait too long, the damage is done. If we move too quickly, we may be needlessly expending limited resources; worse yet, we may be instilling an undesirable inflationary element at a time and place where it may unbalance industrial cost structures.

Unemployment insurance has long had a built-in trigger mechanism. We have proposed a similar trigger for the proposed Manpower Training Act. . . .

. . . On the other hand, the UI trigger has an almost immediate effect, whereas the training programs might require two or three months to build up to an effective level. Similarly, it would be unwise to remove the training stimulus abruptly.

*Where* While the counter-cyclical mechanism envisaged in the proposed Manpower Training Act is triggered by a *national* rate of unemployment, and becomes effective nationally through the state and local financial formula, for it to be effective there should be regional and local differences in the way it operates. The temporary removal of the unemployed from the labor force while they undergo training should be proportionally greater in those areas with the greatest unemployment. If they are to be trained for occupations for which there continues to be a strong demand, their prospective jobs are likely to be in other geographic locations. Thus mobility programs, as well as job matching, become increasingly important if manpower activities are successfully to counter the cyclical downturn of employment.

Here, too, many questions arise. While most areas favor inter-area job matching through computerized job banks or other mechanisms, there may be considerable reluctance to train a worker for a job in another jurisdiction. It is more probable that the jurisdiction in which jobs exist will dip into the more depressed area for prospective employees, move them and train them. A governmental body, which may be accused of "raiding" another jurisdiction for the benefit of employers within its boundaries, can anticipate no "profits," suggesting that this kind of counter-cyclical program may better be operated through a NAB-JOBS-type mechanism than through regular government channels.

*How*  The *How,* and the *How Much* are of course the crucial questions.

The existing repertory of manpower programs is limited, and except for UI, untested in a cyclical downturn. The categorical training and work experience programs, together with the newly developing Public Service Careers program (the public employment parallel to JOBS), limited experience with mobility, and the training programs associated with WIN, comprise the range. For purposes of counter-cyclical activity, vocational education and vocational rehabilitation might also be included, but these would surely be slower to have any effect, the one because of its relatively unwieldy institutional framework, the other because of its limited (and non-cyclically affected) clientele. While the President's new welfare and manpower programs provide for expanded services to the poor, as well as decategorization and decentralization of programs, they do not propose anything radically different in the way of manpower activity which would be directly focussed on counter-cyclical effects. . . .

The *How* question also poses some new, or at least intensified, organizational problems. As we move toward greater decentralization of manpower activities, how do we manage to get early enough action from the states and localities to counteract cyclical downturns? To be truly effective, these actions should be initiated when *local* conditions warrant, not when a national unemployment rate rides up. This might mean the initiation of local action

*before* the trigger mechanism provides the additional funds. Can we develop a flexible enough funding operation to provide for such contingencies—a local certification of manpower "disaster relief" to take effect *before* the disaster hits?

To do the job we also need prompter, more detailed, and more accurate data on employment and unemployment. The government has made great progress in recent years in developing general economic indicators and in relating their leads and lags to the economic cycle, but we do not have adequate predictors in the labor force employment-unemployment data, nor have the latter body of data been adequately related to other lead indicators sufficiently well to provide usable forecasts. . . . Projections of employment demand by industry, occupation, or geographic area are very tenuous, and are generally predicated on the assumption of continuing high levels of employment or general economic activity, and are thus useless for the purpose of planning counter-cyclical manpower measures. Here is the material for countless doctoral theses, though their results may prove late for our needs.

And finally, *How Much?* Manpower programs at present total in the neighborhood of $3 billion yearly, the exact amount depending on how broadly they are defined. This is less than two per cent of GNP. In the event of a cyclical downturn, by how much should manpower programs be increased to an effective counter measure? The trigger mechanism in the Manpower Training Act provides for a 10 per cent increase in the limited categories of funds covered in the Act, at the most $300 million. If our belief is correct that manpower programs judiciously applied have considerable economic leverage, this is still a relatively small amount to give St. George for his dragon-slaying activities.

The level of total expenditures to be made on manpower activities is closely related to two other problems concerning which we have little information: first the optimum level at which such programs can be operated, and second, the necessary start-up time for such activities.

Such evaluations and cost-benefit studies of manpower programs as we have are based on thoroughly inadequate data. Among other conceptual difficulties, analysts have had to assume that average costs are equivalent to marginal costs. Consequently, even for relatively small changes in the size of a program (or a project) we are in the dark as to the shape of the cost curve. Ditto for the benefit curve. But I submit that even if we had accurate knowledge of marginal costs and marginal benefits for our present level of operations, we would have *no* knowledge at all of marginal costs and benefits if we were to increase (or decrease) the scale of our manpower activities by the orders of magnitude which may be necessary if they are to have a counter-cyclical effect. There may well be resulting economics of scale. There may equally well be diseconomies on the benefit side, if a massive increase in manpower activities throws on the market a large number of trainees without jobs to absorb them. (All this is quite apart from the humanitarian and social welfare consequences.) We require new studies and analyses of these programs which will indicate their costs and effects at different *scales* of operation and at different *phases* of the economic cycle. The kind of econometric model in which this kind of analysis can be stimulated may take some years (just as the various production models have taken) to develop, but I am convinced that without such models we will not have the tools to answer our questions concerning optimum scale.

Even if we had such answers, we would have the additional question of start-up time (in relation to the cyclical turn)

with changes in program scale. A small increase or decrease in the size of a project or the number of projects is relatively easy and quick to accomplish; a large one is not. It is easier to increase than to decrease, as our experiences with closing down Job Corps camps and opening up urban Job Corps centers indicates, but it is neither easy nor fast to increase on the scale which may be necessary for manpower programs effectively to counter the cycle. Again comparisons are needed with alternative counter-cyclical devices. (The alternative pay-offs should, of course, not be limited to the immediate counter-cyclical effects; long-term economic and social implications of alternative proposals need also to be explored.)

. . . As a framework for discussion, and to give some quantitative orientation on which to focus, I should like to pose the problem in a slightly different way. We can say that at any time there is a "universe of positions"—jobs available, and a "universe of population"— the labor force. These shift with the cycle, and represent the demand and supply of labor.[2] In the sections to follow, which summarize currently available projections, note that the estimates are based on continuing high levels of economic activity; we have no similar projects for a downturn.

## THE UNIVERSE OF POSITIONS

The universe of positions is roughly equivalent to the demand side of the labor market. The next section of this paper discusses the universe of population, which may be thought of roughly as the supply side of the labor market. In order to determine what programs and services might be needed to meet manpower policy goals in a period of cyclical down-

[2] To keep this paper within reasonable bounds, I am only mentioning in this footnote the cause and effect of the price of labor on the supply of and demand for labor in the various phases of the cycle, and the artificial constraints imposed on the free operation of the labor market by minimum wage legislation, in a period of economic decline.

turn in FY 1971, information on both of these universes is essential.

The BLS [Bureau of Labor Statistics] estimates that if fiscal and monetary policies are followed to achieve an unemployment rate of 3 per cent by 1975, there will be a demand for 88.7 million workers (not counting 2.7 million estimated to be in the Armed Forces), an increase of 22 per cent over the 72.9 million workers employed in 1966. This figure includes all workers in the farm and nonfarm economy, including wage and salary workers, self-employed, unpaid family workers, and domestics. Of this total labor demand, nonfarm wage and salary jobs will amount to about 76 million.

For 1971, with an unemployment rate of 3.5-5 percent, the total number of work positions will be perhaps several million less.

BLS estimates that the rate of wage and salary job growth will continue to be faster in the service-producing industries than in the goods-producing industries. Between 1966 and 1975, manpower requirements in the latter are expected to increase by 6 per cent to 24.5 million. The projected gain in manpower requirements in contract construction (27 per cent) contrasts sharply with nursing, where little change is expected. Manpower requirements in manufacturing are expected to rise by about 3 per cent, or less than one-sixth the rate of increase in total wage and salary employment.

Requirements in the service-producing industries are expected to increase rapidly, but at a slower rate than during the post World War II period. Between 1966 and 1975, requirements in these industries are expected to increase by 26 per cent, reaching about 51.3 million in the latter year.

The larger increase in manpower requirements in the service-producing sector is expected to be in the services and miscellaneous industries group (a growth of 35 per cent). The expected increases in government (29 per cent) and in trade (22 per cent) are greater than for total non-agricultural wage and salary employment (19 per cent). The number of jobs in finance, insurance, and real estate, on the other hand, will increase at about the same rate as total nonfarm wage and salary employment (20 per cent), and manpower requirements in transportation and public utilities are expected to rise only moderately (10 per cent).

Moving from an industry to an occupational breakdown of manpower requirements, BLS sees much greater increases in demand between 1966 and 1975 for service workers (31 per cent) and white-collar workers (28 per cent) than for blue-collar workers (10 per cent). A decline of about 14 per cent is anticipated for farmers and farm workers.

Among white collar occupations, the most rapid advance in requirements will be for professional and technical workers, who may increase nearly twice as fast (39 per cent) as the average for all workers (20 per cent). Requirements for both clerical workers and sales workers also are expected to increase rapidly, about one-fourth, and the need for managers, officials, and proprietors should rise more than one-fifth.

Among blue-collar workers, the most rapid increase in requirements will be for craftsmen (18 per cent), about the average increase for total employment. Requirements for operatives will increase more slowly (7 per cent), and little change is expected in the demand for laborers.

The extent to which these demands for workers in specific industries and occupations will be met is difficult to predict. In general it can be said that in the past the country's school system and the country's employers themselves have met the overwhelming majority of skill-development needs of our economy. It seems reasonable to assume that they will continue to do so in the future.

Nevertheless, there have been, particularly in recent years, shortages in various occupations, industries, and areas of the country. These, too, we can expect to find in our planning period, although the number will decline considerably since we are assuming a cyclical downturn with increased unemployment.

As an indication of the magnitude and nature of these shortages, the Department's job vacancy data for April, 1966 are instructive. The surveys found a total of about 200,000 vacancies in 12 major cities. The population in these cities accounted for about one-sixth of the total U.S. population. Applying this relationship to the job vacancy figures for these cities as a crude measure of the total number of vacancies nationwide, yields a figure of 1,200,000. Roughly the same figure is derived by applying the job vacancy rate (15 per cent) for the twelve cities to the country as a whole. (The job vacancy rate is the number of job vacancies divided by the sum of the number employed plus the number of job vacancies.)

These vacancies were distributed by occupations as follows:

area were apparently related inversely to the unemployment rate.

Under the conditions we have assumed for 1971, the number of vacancies—especially long-term vacancies—would be considerably less. For purposes of this analysis, let us assume the number of vacancies will be about 500 thousand with long-term vacancies accounting for 100-200 thousand.

## THE UNIVERSE OF POPULATION

The population of the United States aged 14 and over is expected to increase from 140.5 million in July, 1966 to 150.1 million in July, 1970, and to 162.8 million in July, 1975. The rate of increase for the nonwhite populations is about half again as great as that for the white population in both periods.

The most noticeable item in comparing time periods is the movement of post World War II baby-boom wave through the age categories. By 1970, most of these will be found in the 20-24 age range, and this category will show a 22 per cent in-

| All vacancies—100 per cent | | | |
|---|---|---|---|
| Professional | 11.6% | Service | 10.6% |
| Semi-professional | 6.4 | Skilled | 16.7 |
| Managerial | 1.3 | Semi-skilled | 22.1 |
| Clerical | 17.0 | Unskilled | 9.3 |
| Sales | 4.7 | Other | .3 |

Not all of these vacancies represent actual shortages. Many are very short-term vacancies, and represent simply normal turnover, much like frictional unemployment. Long-term, hard-to-fill vacancies (30 days or more) comprised about 50 per cent of all vacancies in the April, 1966 surveys. There was some variation in this proportion by occupation, with the skilled category showing 60 per cent; professional, semi-professional and semi-skilled also more than half; unskilled, 36 per cent; and clerical 29 per cent. Variations by

crease over 1966, more than 3 times the rate of increase for the total 14-and-over population. By 1975, this category will show an increase of 12 per cent over 1970, still considerably higher than the total 14-and-over increase of 8½ per cent. (The comparable nonwhite rate will be 22 per cent.) The 25-44 group, however, will then feel the impact of the wave, and the 1970-75 rate of increase will rise to 12 per cent after only a 3 per cent 1966-70 increase.

The teen-age category, which caused

so many concerns during the 1960's as the post World War II wave passed through, will accordingly show smaller gains in the 1970's. Whereas in 1960 this category showed a 22 per cent increase over 1955, and in 1965 a 27 per cent increase over 1960, the 1966-70 increase will be 7 per cent and the 1960-75 increase 9 per cent. The nonwhite increase will be 14 per cent for 1966-70 and 13 per cent for 1970-75.

The total resident labor force of the United States is expected to be more than 85 million in 1970, and more than 91 million in 1975. This represents only a slightly higher rate of growth than that for the over-14 population.

Labor force participation rates are expected to increase moderately in the 14-24 age group, for both males and females, with nonwhites showing the greater increases for both sexes. In the 25-54 age group, females are expected to show moderate increases, while white males show virtually no change and nonwhite males show only a slight increase. In the 55-years and over age group, females are expected to show slight increases, while nonwhite males maintain the same rate, and white males show the beginning of a decrease.

If the unemployment rate in FY 1971 is between 3.5 and 5 per cent, the number unemployed at any one time will be roughly between 3 and 4 million. The number experiencing some unemployment over the course of a year has recently been running 3½-4 times the annual average. Thus, this number can be expected to total between 11 and 15 million, and the number experiencing 15 weeks or more of unemployment over a year would be between 2.5 and 3 million.

There may be some amelioration in the discrepancy between unemployment rates for whites and nonwhites during the planning period and between teenagers and other age groups in the labor force. Regarding the latter, hopefully with the passing of the post-World War II wave, teenage unemployment rates will return

to the lower levels prevailing in the mid-50's. Regarding the white-nonwhite differential, there is less cause for optimism, but we look for enlightened efforts by employers plus such agencies as the Office of Federal Contract Compliance to have some impact on reducing the differential. Older workers will probably continue to have a somewhat higher rate than the average.

We may also expect both a relative and absolute decline in the poverty population by FY 1971. This would continue a long-term trend, which has been accelerated in recent years due to continued high-level economic growth. In 1966, there were almost 30 million people in poverty, in 1967 about 26 million, and in 1968 perhaps about 22–23 million. Assuming a continued high level of economic activity during the planning period, the number of poor persons should drop to about 20 million. The number of poor persons of working age (16-64 years of age) would thus be about 8 million, representing about 4 million household units.

MANPOWER
PROGRAMMING ALTERNATIVES

The material presented in the preceeding two sections suggests the magnitude of the manpower problem which would be presented by a mild downturn in the level of economic activity. Thus, it serves as the setting within which to pose some issues as to *alternative manpower program mixes possible to help meet a recession situation*. It goes without saying, that improvements in basic income maintenance programs, such as unemployment insurance (*e.g.*, increased benefit levels to cover more of the wage loss, and extended duration of benefits) and the welfare system (*e.g.*, supplemental income for the "working poor") would be helpful in cushioning the effects of rising unemployment and in maintaining consumer purchasing power, thus helping to moderate the recession.

One programming alternative is to *identify and provide training to fill specific skill shortages*, Although in a cyclical downturn the chief cause of unemployment is inadequate aggregate demand, there would still be some structural unemployment, roughly 100-200 thousand long term vacancies in the situation suggested above. The upgrading of those newly unemployed with considerable work experience may be the best course to fill these vacancies, although some employed persons may be upgraded, too. To the extent employed persons are moved into job vacancies, their positions in turn become vacant. These vacancies could be filled either by the unemployed with some work experience, requiring no additional training, or by trainees, depending upon geographic location of the vacant jobs and the potential workers.

Clearly, this programming approach would only directly meet the needs of a relatively small number of the workers made jobless as the result of the recession. It also would have some counter-cyclical effect by way of sustaining employment and purchasing power above what it would have been without such manpower programs. It probably would not be of direct assistance to the majority of the newly unemployed or to the "hard core" unemployed—*i.e.,* disadvantaged—who did not have suitable jobs *before* the recession.

While the basis is not available for an estimate of the proportion of the unemployed who would have to be reached during a recession to effectively help "turn it around," it clearly would not be the total of unemployed persons, nor even the total of additional unemployed over the pre-recession level. Nonetheless, the very sizeable number whom it would be necessary to reach could not be trained for existing skill shortages. Some other program approach, or approaches would

be needed for whatever number of them it is found necessary to reach to contribute to economic recovery.

Two possible approaches are: (1) Institutional training for skills projected to be demanded in the post-recession period; and (2) job creation, in the public sector. As indicated earlier, a case can be made for retraining workers in new skills, or refurbishing old ones, during periods of unemployment when the opportunity costs to both the worker and society are lowest. The post-World War II recessions have bottomed fairly quickly, although in the last one full recovery took a long time. But a 12 month training program would probably go a long way toward bridging the recession unemployment gap.

If a downturn stretches over a long period, so that the job situation is such that training slots leading to reasonably anticipated employment opportunities are unavailable, expansion of public job opportunities might be desirable. Such job creation could be patterned after any of the existing "public employment" programs. The post-WW II recession experience has been that the long term employment up-trend in the public sector has hardly been affected by the downturn in total employment (and increased unemployment) which are centered in the private sector. Public sector jobs continue to be available. Consequently, a public employment model such as the new Public Service Careers (the public sector counterpart to the JOBS program) could conceivably be a viable job development vehicle. Alternatively, Federally subsidized employment on needed but unfinanced local and State public services could be developed.

The broad issues posed for contingency planning in this presentation are, first, how to predict on a timely basis the occupations and their locations, which could be expected to be in demand during the recession and what kind of standby training capacity should be maintained to meet them? Second, how to predict the duration of the recession, or more precisely, the timing of the resumption of demand in the post-recession period, by occupation, so that training of the unemployed during the recession could be geared up? Finally, based partly on the predicted duration of the recession and the anticipated level of post-recession demand, how much, if any, job creation should be planned, where, and for what kinds (occupationally speaking) of workers?

### Administrative Effectiveness

In addition to an appraisal of economic or educational effectiveness, programs might be evaluated in terms of administrative effectiveness. In other words, we should not only be concerned with whether the programs are efficient in terms of the benefits derived from the costs incurred or whether effective training techniques are being used but also with the effectiveness of the administrative governmental and private agencies.

Much confusion has resulted from the assignment of similar tasks to different agencies of the federal government and to the sharing of responsibilities between federal, state, and local governments. This proliferation not only creates confusion but also makes it difficult to ascertain whether all needy groups are being reached. Moreover, proliferation permits wasteful duplication of overhead, wasteful use of resources by creating unnecessary delays in reviewing and funding programs, produces rivalries (with competing constituencies) between the various agencies administering the programs, creates irritation by employers who are called upon by competing governmental agencies to perform the same functions, might cause funds to be channeled disproportionately to "operators" who understand the system rather than to the people for whom the programs were designed, and makes it difficult to evolve comprehensive local manpower programs.

It can be argued, of course, that there is no need to coordinate training programs because the problem is exaggerated, or because positive benefits are derived from competition among programs. The argument that the problem is exaggerated rests on two main lines of reasoning. The first holds that existing efforts at coordination have been successful and that the problem has been solved. A second line of reasoning holds that the proliferation of programs creates so much confusion that many people reach the erroneous conclusion that an effective job is not being done. As noted earlier, in the most technical economic sense of that term, we have very little knowledge of the effectiveness of these programs. There is merely an assumption, based largely on unsophisticated analyses, that society and the many people who have gone through these programs have derived benefits that exceed the costs. The benefit-cost studies that have been made seem to support this conclusion, but the authors of these studies are the first to concede that the techniques used are still far too crude to permit precise answers. Ignoring the costs, there can be little doubt that the programs have done some good. But this is not the relevant question. The important point for our purpose is whether or not these duplicating and confusing programs have caused waste, and there is, in fact, almost unanimous support for the conclusion that they have.

It might also be argued, of course, that the confusion and waste accompanying these new programs exaggerates the nature of the *permanent* problem, because waste is inevitable in experimental programs such as these. There is much truth in this argument, but it is equally true that the lack of a rational manpower system will become increasingly important as these programs are more adequately funded. Since the present funding of these undertakings probably permits them to reach less than 10 percent of the target populations, it is possible to have considerable duplication, which is not necessarily wasteful in terms of giving the same services to the same people. (Of course, even this duplication would be wasteful if the release of duplicating administrative costs made it possible to reach more people.)

### Efforts to Achieve Coordination

A key facet of administration of the existing programs is the degree to which they are coordinated with one another. To the extent that they are not properly orchestrated, efficiency of operation is sacrificed.

The need for coordination was, therefore, recognized early in development of training programs. Aside from the hortatory expressions contained in most of the statutes, tangible manifestations of a desire to dovetail programs appeared almost simultaneously with the trend toward program proliferation.

In response to a groundswell of criticism over the congruency of the system, Congress established a public advisory committee in 1966 to offer an impartial judgment. Known as the Committee on Administration of Training Programs (CATP), it was instructed ". . . to determine if there is waste, duplication, and inefficiency in administering these programs as many individual programs . . ."; the final report of CATP was made in early 1968, but its recommendations for change were not very extensive and consequently received very little attention.

In 1967, two new administrative arrangements, the Cooperative Area Manpower Planning System (CAMPS) and the Concentrated Employment Program (CEP), were created. CAMPS seeks to bind together the planning activities of the major federal manpower agencies. The arrangement sprang from efforts begun in 1966 to create a national-state plan for administering training under the Manpower Development and Training Act (MDTA). The objective was to realize through interagency cooperation the maximum possible return from the resources available from a single piece of legislation.

Under the CAMPS arrangement, five participating agencies plan the coming year's activities in concert. Information is exchanged on the needs of target groups, anticipated program resources, and mutual program provisions available to meet the needs of client groups. CAMPS also has a line organizational structure. There is a local area body in designated metropolitan areas; 50 state bodies; 11 regional bodies (which includes all 50 states); and a national body that meets monthly in Washington. At each step, a written manpower plan is developed and forwarded for annual approval.

On paper, CAMPS is encompassing in composition and logical in design. In practice, much remains to be demonstrated before any judgment can be made. Mutual planning is not a per se assurance that coordination will occur.

There is no mechanism to assure that written agreements will be implemented in a nonduplicative and efficient manner. It would seem that all that is needed to perfect CAMPS would be to empower it to enforce its mutual agreements. Yet, such a simplistic notion neglects the fact that it is legally and politically impossible for one agency to be bound to the wishes of others. As a result, mutual consent is its only weapon and voluntarism among government agencies in American history affords little grounds for optimism.

CEP also was inaugurated in 1967, when 20 cities and 2 rural areas were designated as CEP targets. In a nutshell, CEP is an arrangement by which six training programs administered by the DOL are bundled together and offered to a locality in the form of a single contract tailored to its specific needs. Obviously, CEP is not a training program but an administrative project. Since it includes only the programs with which DOL has control, the issue of coordination of these six programs in a city is sharply reduced. The problem of coordination with the programs not included in the CEP project remains as does the entire issue in non-CEP localities. Presumably, however, if the arrangement proves viable it will be replicated on a more extensive scale.

There remains another indication of a movement toward coordination through consolidation. There has been a pronounced trend toward program delegation. Instead of operating a program that it has been legislatively assigned, the agency delegates the administration to another while still retaining the right to participate in the planning and target-setting procedures. Specifically, the Neighborhood Youth Corps, Job Corps, Special Impact, Operation Mainstream, and New Careers, which were originally assigned to OEO, have been delegated to DOL for administration. The Title V program was similarly delegated from OEO to HEW; but in 1967 it too was shifted to DOL. A related instrument of consolidation has been legislative transfer of new programs to old line agencies. For example, the adult basic education program was originally an OEO delegated program to HEW but in 1966 it was legislatively transferred to HEW.

### Solutions

Many solutions have been advanced for the problem of administering manpower programs. Some of these suggestions have wide support and others are more controversial. For example, measures to improve the funding cycle by making grants for longer periods and permitting greater flexibility in transferring funds between agencies and programs would receive wide support. It also would be highly desirable to simplify and streamline the funding process in order to reduce the number of steps and the time required to process applications. To the extent possible information and forms should be standardized.

The suggestion that flexibility be introduced by making unrestricted (block) grants by the Federal government to state and local governments is more controversial, because of the fear that these governments would revert to (or continue) their habit of ignoring the disadvantaged. Nor is there any assurance that state and local governments would not themselves be paralyzed by political stalemates that would complicate the implementation of comprehensive training plans.

The argument in favor of block grants to local governments is that the Federal government's role should be mainly to finance manpower projects and set broad policy objectives, but that the implementation should be by state and local governments.

There have been numerous other coordinating proposals and coordination bodies. The Economic Opportunity Council, the Labor-HEW Coordinating Committee, the Interagency Review Committee for MDTA-Redevelopment Area Projects are a few examples of continuing efforts to seek the elusive goal. The fact is, however, that the objective has not been obtained. Indicative of this fact is the conclusion reached by the U. S. Senate Committee on Labor and Public Welfare, which reported in September 1967 the results of its exhaustive inquiry into the War on Poverty.

> The most meaningful level for coordination is the local community where the unemployed live and work. Yet, a community has a great difficulty in putting together a total manpower system. Some of the Federal program funds go through the States in a variety of special programs—work experience and training, MDTA, the Employment Service, apprenticeship training, vocational education, and vocational rehabilitation. Others go directly to the community, but usually in separate grants—Neighborhood Youth Corps, Nelson amendment, Scheuer amendment, special impact, and various projects financed under community action program.
>
> Of the various unsolved problems in the Federal effort to eliminate poverty in America, coordination stands out. And of all the fields of service, the manpower program is the most badly fragmented and needs the greatest attention.

Another controversial recommendation proposes the federalization of the Employment Service in order to make it a more effective manpower agency. The present state control of the Employment Service makes national coordination very difficult. The effective administration of many state systems is also complicated by low salaries, which make it difficult to recruit and retain competent personnel. The low salaries of state employees who have responsibility for (or more responsibility than) cooperating federal employees also complicates the adoption of comprehensive manpower plans where federal-state cooperation is essential. Greater national control would facilitate the enforcement of national standards at the state level and would encourage better research and labor market information and reporting activities.

A number of arguments might be raised against greater national control of the employment service. Some, of course, will object that this would be a further federal encroachment on states' rights. A more serious objection is that greater federal control would involve some complications because of the diverse state unemployment compensation systems. Indeed, the present salary and personnel differences between the states make little sense because the administration of these state-controlled systems is presently financed entirely by the federal government.

Some observers also argue that the CAMPS system can be strengthened to make it an effective coordinating mechanism and avoid the problems associated with drastic reorganization. Some suggest such things as: giving the state CAMPS power to fund projects as well as to plan them; giving the state CAMPS unrestricted funds to be used for emergencies; making state CAMPS repositories of information on manpower programs; and giving state CAMPS greater flexibility in diverting funds from one agency to another.

The major objection to these suggestions is that they contemplate greater reliance on the state CAMPS, which, it is argued, cannot be relied on to carry out national policy since they are composed of state officials. We feel that this objective has considerable validity, but think the suggestions nevertheless have merit. For one thing, the number of states that would not use the funds effectively is not as great as it once was. Moreover, much opposition to manpower programs has been generated by efforts to bypass the states. We therefore feel that the states should be incorporated more effectively into national manpower policy planning and implementation but that safeguards can be adopted to prevent states from avoiding national policies. Even if these safeguards could not be adopted, we feel that the gains to be obtained from going through the states far outweigh the losses.

Although there are many other specific things that could be done to improve the coordination of federal training programs, the most controversial calls for the incorporation of all manpower programs in a single agency. Levitan and Mangum (Sar A. Levitan and Garth L. Mangum, *Making Sense of Federal Manpower Policy,* University of Michigan-Wayne State University and the National Manpower Policy Task Force, 1967), who have studied manpower programs in considerable detail, have made one of the most widely discussed reports recommending the collection of all manpower agencies in a single agency, preferably the Department of Labor. Although Levitan and Mangum suggest several other alternatives, any of which would permit a workable manpower policy, including improving coordination by increasing Congressional oversight, they prefer the single agency approach because it offers a more fundamental solution. One of these other considerations is that Congress might provide more oversight, but Congress has not done an effective job of overseeing these programs because it has lacked the staff and therefore has relied heavily on executive agencies for data and program evaluation. Levitan and Mangum realize that a single agency would not solve the coordination problem, but they feel it would force Congress and the administration to examine the interrelationships and to confront the problem more squarely than they have previously. By absorbing the budgets of existing programs, a single agency could eliminate duplication and expend funds more economically. This agency would have fewer and better personnel and would make possible the successful application of the Planning-Programming-Budgeting System.

Within a single agency, Levitan and Mangum would divide manpower programs into four functional categories: preparation for employment; placement and supportive services; job creation; and experimentation, demonstration, and research.

It might also be argued that a single agency really would not eliminate administrative chaos, but would actually create additional confusion by establishing still another manpower agency. The single-agency bureaucracy would create confusion, it is argued, by attempting to consolidate too many programs under one roof, making coordination extremely difficult. It also is contended that such a reorganization would involve very difficult choices between "training" or "education" programs. Critics of the single agency approach also argue that manpower policies, most of which are still in the experimental stage, should be given a chance to work before being disrupted by radical reorganization; we should not, it is argued, be like the man who keeps pulling his plants up by the roots to see if they are growing. In this view it would be a mistake to disrupt established administrative lines and develop new administrative lines just as people are learning the ropes with the existing system.

Perhaps the strongest argument—other than political feasibility—against the single-agency proposal is that it would destroy competition between agencies. Competition between the Departments of Labor and HEW and the OEO is supposed to have made the programs more effective. Although competition obviously has its advantages, it need not be destroyed by a single agency, whose responsibility would be to coordinate finances and implement broad national policies. The most meaningful competition in manpower programs is likely to be at the local level. In principle, a single agency could provide competition between programs to accomplish existing tasks. Indeed, such an agency could promote competition between various private and public agencies as an experiment to see which kinds of agencies might do the best job under various conditions. These experiments could be much more carefully controlled by a single agency than they can by the existing complex arrangements. It is also important to avoid confusing competition to see which agency can be most effective with interagency rivalry to see which agency can get more funds and influence. Similarly, program consolidation would actually strengthen the specialization by OEO, DOL, and HEW in their respective areas. OEO and HEW would get out of the manpower field, which they acknowledge to be beyond their areas of expertise and would concentrate on other poverty and welfare programs. We would give the single agency control over adult basic education and remedial education programs, but would encourage the attachment of experts in these fields to local comprehensive skill centers wherever feasible and would otherwise encourage the use of local public schools. It would be much easier for a manpower agency to buy the necessary education services than it would be for an education agency to buy manpower services.

Another approach designed to simplify the administrative structure of manpower programs and make them more responsive to the needs of those they are designed to serve is the "training credit" approach. Patterned after the "G.I. Bill" adopted after World War II, this approach would give certain training rights to individuals which could be redeemed wherever training was offered. This approach would create competition between training agencies as well as to simplify governmental administration. Under this plan, the Federal government or the states would certify the eligibility of individuals and training agencies, but would not operate training programs. Training would be given by a variety of public and private agencies in response to individual demand.

## Related Readings

Because it is so important to discover which programs work and why, man-power experts have devoted considerable attention to techniques for evaluating manpower programs. The economists' favorite approach has been to attempt to compare the benefits and costs of various programs. Burton Weisbrod, in "Conceptual Issues in Evaluating Training Programs" (*Monthly Labor Review*, Vol. 89, October 1966), discusses some of the conceptual issues involved in evaluating training programs from the benefit-cost point of view. He first emphasizes the importance of clearly stated program objectives and then discusses some of the problems involved in determining program benefits. A major methodological problem is to hold everything else constant while measuring the benefits of a program. He discusses the various assumptions that must be made about the level of aggregate employment, because it is necessary to avoid attributing employment effects to training programs that resulted from other causes. One approach might be to design an experiment using control groups or statistical procedures to hold other things constant while measuring the impact of training.

Weisbrod concludes his article with discussions of third party benefits and time patterns. It is important to know whether training programs benefit some people at the expense of others and the time when costs and benefits are attributed to programs. Weisbrod concludes with a statement of the importance of specifying the theoretical ideals for program evaluation: "Under those conditions the strengths and limitations of empirical techniques will be recognized. In the course of time, actual evaluation techniques will more rapidly approach theoretical norms if these norms have been identified than if they have not."

*The Emergence of Manpower Policy* by Garth L. Mangum (Holt, Rinehart and Winston, 1969) contains a very good discussion of the origins and objectives of manpower policy in the United States as well as some evaluations of present programs. The National Manpower Policy Task Force and the Institute of Labor and Industrial Relations, University of Michigan-Wayne State University, have published a number of policy papers dealing with all aspects of manpower programs and policies. The policy papers by Sar A. Levitan and Garth L. Mangum have been particularly useful to policy makers and scholars in the manpower field. Some of these papers were published as a book entitled *Federal Training and Work Programs in the 60's* by the Institute of Labor and Industrial Relations University of Michigan-Wayne State University, 1969.

*In Manpower Needs for National Goals in the 1970's* (New York, Praeger, Inc., 1969), Leonard A. Lecht makes some projections based on the assumption that the nation will move toward implementing several national goals in 16 critical areas dealing with problems of race and unemployment, air pollution, decaying cities, and the problems of the young and the aged. If we attempt to achieve all of these objectives during the 1970's, it is Lecht's conclusion that we would face substantial labor shortages. He therefore calls for planning in both the private and public sectors in order to avoid manpower bottlenecks that will make it difficult to accomplish these important national objectives.

*Toward a Manpower Policy*, Robert A. Gordon, Ed. (New York, Wiley, 1967), contains a series of articles dealing with various aspects of the manpower problem. In a paper entitled "The Role of Manpower Policy in Achieving Aggregate Goals," Lester C. Thurow presents a model that "analyzes linkages between manpower programs and aggregate goals." Thurow deals with the linkages between manpower programs and economic growth, unemployment, income equalization, price stability, and private manpower policies. He relies on a regression equation to establish these relationships, and concludes that "manpower programs are theoretically important, and the potential effects are large enough to make them empirically interesting but actual returns are yet to be calculated."

Another paper in the Gordon volume entitled "The Need for Planning and Coordination" by Joseph A. Kershaw presents a very good discussion of the steps necessary for manpower planning. Kershaw also discusses the question of the needs for coordination of manpower programs and is more skeptical of the values of coordinations than Mangum, Levitan, and others discussed above. Kershaw concludes:

I would argue that some coordination of these programs is clearly necessary, given a federal-state-local situation and a multiplicity of agencies necessarily involved in manpower programs. I would only argue that an excessively tidy administration ought not to be the goal; indeed if we were to achieve it—and there is slight danger of this— the effectiveness of our programs might be impaired to some extent. Program effectiveness and tidy administration may be alternatives; where they are I prefer the former. On the other hand, the need for careful planning seems to me to be clear. Unless we design programs that fit together, are consistent with one another, and are in tune with the external economic conditions under which they must operate, confusion and loss of effectiveness seem the most likely results.

Another very useful source of information on manpower programs is the *Manpower Report of the President* transmitted to the Congress each year by the President. These reports contain a great deal of useful information on manpower programs as well as statistical tables on the labor force, employment, unemployment, manpower programs productivity, gross national product, and other matters related to employment.

For a comparative analysis of training and retraining programs, see Margaret S. Gordon, "The Comparative Experience with Retraining Programmes in the United States and Europe," in Jack Stieber, Ed., *Automation and Advanced Technology* (London, Macmillan, 1966). Dr. Gordon concludes:

In all the Western European countries included in this study, retraining programmes have come to be accepted as a permanent instrument of labour market policy, as useful in tight labour markets as in periods of unemployment. I believe this will gradually come to be true, also, in the United States, and that we could have been better equipped to combat the upward drift in the unemployment rate in the last decade if a retraining program had been adopted much earlier.

Dr. Gordon also concludes:

Perhaps the most interesting and challenging issue relating to retraining policies concerns the extent to which they should be governed by what might be called a criterion of *efficiency* as opposed a criterion of increasing the employability of the more disadvantaged among the unemployed.

She examines this issue within the context of manpower policies in the United States and a number of Western European countries.

# CHAPTER 17

# Returns on Investment in Education

In Chapter 9 we noted that the wage advantage for skilled labor, in equilibrium, was the amount required to make it worthwhile, in an economic sense, to acquire skill. Specifically, this means that the differential must be such as to equate the rate of return on investment in acquiring skills (i.e., investment in education and training) to the rate on alternative, physical capital, investment. In this chapter, problems of measuring returns to education will be studied, and actual estimates presented.

Studies indicate that the rate of return is higher on earlier schooling than later, but even for college, the evidence on balance shows an advantage for education over alternative investments. Thus, despite the great advances in educational attainment over the years, the demand for trained and educated workers has at least been keeping pace with the expansion in supply.

Does education pay? This question has been asked in many recent studies, measuring whether the rate of return on investment in education exceeds that on physical capital. In making their calculations, students of the problem are careful to point out that they only derive an answer in purely economic terms, abstracting from the social improvement from having an educated citizenry and from the psychic and elevating gains from training and disciplining the mind. Nevertheless, critics of the entire approach of evaluating the monetary gains of education are repelled by the thought of putting a monetary value on the benefits of education.

## A CRITIQUE OF THE INVESTMENT CONCEPT IN EDUCATION

In truth, those who analyze the economic returns to education imply that these results have some value in determining individual and policy decisions on education, and despite the impossibility of evaluating the nonmonetary advantages of education, their efforts are more than intellectual exercises. As Neil Chamberlain notes in his strong but sprightly criticism of the tendency toward indiscriminate application of "accounting techniques" in measuring the worth of education, made in his presidential address to the Industrial Relations Research Association, much of which is included here, the finding of low rates of return on a particular education investment might act as a deterrent to the offering and undertaking of that education. The human capitalist could not deny this possibility nor would he wish to do so. In short, as Chamberlain implies, rates are calculated in the expectation that they would have some effect on public policy and private decisions regarding the choice to provide and use particular educational services.

# Some Second Thoughts on the Concept of Human Capital

## by Neil W. Chamberlain

The truth that expenditures on human beings are productive of something more than personal satisfaction or a sense of personal completeness is an important one. An outlay on education can also increase the economic productivity of those instructed, giving rise to a stream of returns higher than what they would otherwise have been. Who would dispute what everyone now accepts as self-evident? Education is thus a form of investment, just like an investment in improved capital equipment. In fact, human beings represent a species of physical capital, just like the machines with which they collaborate. Each gives rise to an ongoing stream of productive services. The value of that stream can be modified by improving the quality of both. In the case of human capital—manpower—such improvement need not be restricted to education:

health and environmental conditioning for example are also likely to play their part.

The basic insight of this approach, as long as it is confined to picturesque analogy, recommends it to anyone concerned with the very important problems of helping individuals to improve their material productivity and societies to expand their GNP. These are worthy aims which require no subtle justification. Material wealth can be instrumental and is often essential in achieving a satisfying life, the "good" life. On the whole, people and societies of affluence are more likely to be liberated in spirit than people and societies frustrated with poverty.

But when the analogy of human capital to other forms of capital is pressed too far, not only does it break down on purely logical grounds but it invites conclusions which are both dangerous to social wel-

SOURCE Reprinted with permission from Industrial Relations Research Association, *Proceedings* of the Twentieth Annual Meeting, Washington, 1967, pp. 1–13.

fare and demeaning to the economics profession. It carries the abstract conception of the disembodiment of labor one stage further than where the Clayton Act controversy left it. If workers are not only suppliers of current services but also capital equipment from whom issue a stream of services whose value depends in part on how they are "tooled up" (educated), then the value of such an investment can be compared directly with the value of other investments. Appropriate—that is, economic—choices can be made depending on relative rates of return on competing investments. Expenditures on education can be laid alongside expenditures on road systems, irrigation projects, public housing or baseball stadia to determine which provides the higher payoff. Social choice can then be governed by the maximizing principle in its simplest form, that more is to be preferred to less.

Some advocates of the investment-in-human-capital approach consider this comparability a victory on the side of human welfare conceived in its broadest, not only material, terms. Aha, they say, if we can induce legislators and city councilmen, and businessmen and other taxpayers, to recognize that education can pay dividends no less than a postal system or power project, or for that matter than a factory or farm, the chances are improved for getting appropriations for schools. Education becomes not only a matter of social welfare but a business proposition.

This use of the analogy as a kind of legislative ploy has a certain appeal because of the undeniable core of truth which the analogy reveals. But there is another side of the matter which is a darker side. As soon as one talks about investments, he invites a consideration of any one investment with the alternative possibilities. And as soon as he speaks of returns on investment the comparison among these runs in terms of relative rates. It is difficult to get away from the accountants' logic. Even Professor Schultz, who in addition to being the pioneer is one of the most sophisticated in this field, has lent his support to this next step. Although he expresses some reservations because not all of the more important forms of capital have been identified, he nevertheless believes that "thinking in terms of the rate of return is fundamental."[1]

Understandably, then, within the last few years there has emerged a series of research studies attempting to measure the rate of return in investment in education, both from the standpoint of an individual making such an investment and from that of a society. In doctoral dissertations the subject has steadily moved up the popularity ladder. There has been able exposition of some of the difficulties encountered in making such estimates, just as the accounting literature over the years has offered excellent analyses of some of the subtleties involved in calculating the actual or expected returns on more traditional forms of business investment. In both cases the user of the resulting measures is put on notice as to their deficiencies, but there is no suggestion that there is anything wrong with the concept itself. If investment occurs, it obviously has, or is intended to have, some return. The return is the measure of its value. In weighing competing investments, one can only weigh competing returns, calculated as rates. How else?

And so, in adopting as we have the conception of human capital, and education as investment in human capital, not as analogy but as categorical identity, we put education in the position of having to *defend* its value in the form of a rate of pecuniary return. We may recognize and allude to certain incommensurable values which it also has, but if it *is* investment in

---

[1] T. W. Schultz, "The Rate of Return in Allocating Investment Resources to Education." *Journal of Human Resources,* Summer 1967, p. 295.

capital we cannot evade the accountants' justifiable insistence that while the incommensurables may be held in mind and may even be allowed to tip the scales, they come on top of the rate of return, which is the fundamental base and basis for decision. Economists have responded to the challenge by turning accountants, and have produced the desired measures —admittedly crude at this stage but hopefully to be refined later. In a way that the calculation of rates of return on business and industrial capital never managed to do, the measurement and refinement of rates of return on human capital have aroused the ardor and zeal of numerous members of the economics profession.

* * *

To calculate a rate of return, it is said, is not the same thing as to make a choice on the basis of comparative rates. It simply provides additional and pertinent information. If it is found that graduate education, for example, gives a comparatively low yield, this does not mean that society cannot invoke any other values it wishes and still invest in graduate education. On the other hand, if it is found that graduate education has a high rate of return, this is either economic reinforcement for a decision which still might have been made on other grounds or possibly persuasive of an investment which might otherwise not have been made.

The logic is a little loose. If the calculated rate has some persuasive effect when it is high, it can equally have a persuasive effect when the yield is "demonstrated" to be low. Why else are rates of return computed? Is investment in human resources the same as investment in inanimate plant and equipment, or is it not? If it is (which seems to be the direction of current thinking, seeking to establish a generic concept which will embrace all forms), then the economic calculus should be expected to have its influence, and the fears I express are justified. If it is not the same

thing, then it stands revealed as analogy rather than identity, with all the dangers of analogical reasoning, including those I have suggested.

But let me pass, for the moment, from this point, which might leave us unprofitably arguing the extent to which values are economic or noneconomic, to one which seems to involve no such classificatory problem. Assuming for the moment that expenditures on education *can* be regarded as an investment, I am concerned with the now widespread notion that a rate of return can then be calculated. Here we are dealing with a matter that can be appraised on purely logical grounds or analytical feasibility.

As I have already noted, perhaps the most frequently cited reason for estimates of rates of return, as for cost-benefit analysis quite generally, is that it contributes to an efficient allocation of resources. The sums which are spent on education are already so great that we should know what we are getting for our money, it is said, or on the other hand it is sometimes held that we might well be investing more in education or at least certain forms of education if we were aware of the high returns deriving from such expenditures. The weighing of one outlay against competing outlays involves a judgment in efficiency of resource use which has been the economist's stock in trade for many generations.

But that preoccupation has always been premised on a stability of tastes and resources and an exclusion of exogenous forces, which is to say, change-creating forces. When one deals with social investments which not only are made under conditions of uncertainty but which are themselves intended to be change-creating, there is no firm basis for calculating their payoff. In the face of futurity and purposiveness (to use two favorite terms of one of our intellectual forebears, John R. Commons) calculations which are geared to the past, however refined analytically, make little sense.

There are two elements here which are distinguishable. Let me first consider the uncertainty elements, based on the inscrutability of the future. Since none of us is gifted with prophetic vision, we cannot foretell whether the future will prove economically wise the decisions we made today. We can only look to the future, keeping the past in mind, and conjecture as to the spectrum of likely effects which may issue from present actions. If judgments of this sort involve efficiency, it is in a very special and peculiar sense, certainly not the traditional marginalist meaning. Any implication that such an exercise leads to efficiency in resorce allocation is crudely misleading.

The future value of investment in educated citizenry, whether one is speaking in terms of marginal or total expenditures, will depend, among other things, on the kind of a world in which such educated individuals will live—a world which will be partially, though not wholly, of their own making but the outlines of which are at best conjectural and speculative. The future values to which these pieces of human capital will give rise individually and collectively cannot in fact be known at the time of the investment in their education.

If the uncertain future of a society turns out to be composed largely of making or resisting war, the future value of a present educational system which stresses extended work in the arts will be quite different—and perhaps significantly less—than the future of a type of education emphasizing discipline and physical culture, chauvinistic ideology, and applied science and technology. If a society invests in the education of an elite leadership, the future value of that education will depend, among other things, on whether the future society will accept that leadership, or, as in the case of the Belgian Congo a few years back, exterminate it.

These are matters which are not now predictable, in any scientific sense, and they cannot be made predictable by the expedient of adopting a "most likely" set of assumptions. For one thing, there seldom exists any agreement even among the experts as to the appropriate assumptions concerning the future, and there is certainly no objective basis for isolating such assumptions. The uncertainty element is inherent in futurity insofar as it relates to human affairs.

In this respect, investment in education is of course subject to the same limitations as other forms of investment. All are subject to the uncertain impact of a changing environment, ruling out the measurability of their returns, in any meaningful sense of that term, and leaving them conjectural no matter how refined the effort at quantification.

But there is a second respect—the element of purposiveness—which afflicts investment in education (and certain other types of public investment, as well) more severely than it does traditional investments in producer goods.

This element of purposiveness may take the form of a conscious effort by those responsible for the investment to change the social environment in which the investment comes to fruition, in ways which are designed to augment the value of the stream of services issuing from it. The public and its political representatives may have a vision of a future which differs from the present, and which the social investment in question is in part intended to help realize, thus itself creating the context which is controlling of its value.

To take a specific example, educational patterns which are aimed at achieving less invidious discrimination among races will add to the stream of values flowing from a better educated Negro population. In the absence of such an influence (whether from education or some other source), the same investment in improved education for Negroes is almost certain to have a lower value, though how much lower is a matter of conjecture which is not rendered any more certain by quantification.

Here we are dealing with a future whose speculative characteristics are due not only to unpredictable exogenous events but also to the unpredictable effects of change-inducing actions by the resource-users themselves, those who are endogenous to the system. Indeterminacy is not only environmental to the decision-makers but embedded in their decisions. The very investment decisions which are made, or related decisions, may modify—perhaps unconsciously but often purposively, and sometimes at cross-purposes—the environment in which those investments come to fruition and which will be partially determinative of their value.

But the purposive element of social investment has an even deeper significance. It may involve not simply an effort to change the environment in ways which uncertainly affect the value of the stream of services to which the investment gives rise. Purposiveness may render literally unmeasurable the values from an investment in a way which has nothing to do with uncertainty, and in this respect the very concept of investment in human capital is especially vulnerable.

A society, or some sector of a society, through its agents, may will to change its characteristics not because this is expected to increase the return from its investment but because a change is wanted for its own sake. Educational expenditures aimed at eradicating invidious interracial discrimination may be made not because this is expected to improve the returns on educational investment in minority groups but because the public has come, for other reasons, to want that kind of a society. And how does one measure the rate of return on that kind of investment in education? How does one measure the satisfactions or utilities people derive from one social environment in contrast to another?

The value of an educated citizenry—national income accounting notwithstanding—is not given solely by the bricks and mortar which a society produces but by the institutions which it creates with the bricks and mortar. If the education provided by a people leads to a more productive economic machine but it comes to fruition in a hierarchic, technocratic, militaristic society, to which it has in some indeterminable but realistic sense contributed, the value of the education must be calculated differently than if the end product is equally productive but along lines which are humanistic and permissive. One does not have to make value judgments to call attention to the existence of such differential values, but he does have to make value judgments if he wishes to "measure" them.

I hope that no one misconstrues that what I am saying is that economists *should* make estimates of the pecuniary value of future states of society which education contributes to making. I hope equally that no one construes that I am suggesting that economists should sell short their major accomplishments in the field of public economic policy by substituting murky philosophizing and shallow sociology for "rigorous" analysis. My concern is rather that the admitted success which economics has enjoyed may illadvisedly encourage more ambitious adventures which purport to be "hard," realistic, and rigorous but which in fact incorporate implicit, murky, and shallow assumptions as to social values without an appreciation of that fact.

If economists want to be "scientific" and therefore quantitative, they are obliged to stick to a short enough run for the phenomena with which they work to stay relatively fixed—where changes are so moderate or incremental as not to invalidate logic based on a continuity of circumstance. If economists want to deal with a farther future, which increasingly involves not only change but change which is planned for, they are obliged to work with other standards than efficiency and with methods that are judgmental and strategy oriented rather than scientific.

In my own judgment, both approaches are desirable. We need efficiency-based decisions to help us achieve as much value as we can from a present which we can reasonably regard as having a steady state, and for such decisions quantitative analysis growing out of the recent past acts as a more reliable guide than guesswork.

But we also need strategic decisions anchored in a future which is planned to be different from the present, towards which we draw ourselves by purposeful action. For this latter category of decisions, including many investment decisions, no amount of quantitative analysis will ever suffice, and guesses—if by that we mean informed judgment—are a better guide than econometrics.

❋ ❋ ❋

Chamberlain questions whether the investment concept fits educational expenses. More strongly, however, he argues that even if it does, accurate rates of return would not be calculated. Apart from the difficulties in measuring strictly economic returns, to be discussed below, Chamberlain cites the confusion to calculation introduced when the purpose of education is to affect social relationships. Difficult as it may be to measure the consumption benefits from education, is it not conceptually impossible to place a dollar value on the benefits of social change? If this cannot be done, how can a public policy unit decide whether a particular educational program designed to affect social relationships, say, reducing racial discrimination, "pays" or whether the returns on this "investment" exceed or fall short of those on other educational projects or unrelated "alternative investments"? In any case, economic decisions on education must be based on marginal conclusions. For an analogous investment, it might be argued that health is so important that no expense should be spared in improving health standards. Yet perhaps without realizing it, we often decide that marginal gains in health are not worth the extra cost. For example, our individual physical state might be improved and our life-span extended if we submitted to a daily thorough physical examination, but only a few would consider this a worthwhile investment considering the time and expense of such frequent testing. No matter what the purpose of an investment, at some point marginal increases in returns are not worth the cost.

Similarly with investment in education, the relevant economic question is not whether there should be education, but whether an additional investment would yield a greater return than an alternative undertaking. Students of the rate of return do not claim that their results entail value judgments. Just because a return is low does not mean that the investment should not be undertaken on other than purely economic grounds. But they consider that the calculations provide information for individuals in making decisions on further education and for governments in providing additional facilities.

Furthermore, serious studies of returns to education acknowledge the crudeness of their calculations and conceptual problems in measurement of the economic gains from schooling. Even if the direct gains could be accurately and unambiguously calculated, the indirect gains provide an immeasureable economic benefit to society. Education and acquired knowledge lead to inventions and technological improvements through development of new business and production techniques. It is safe to say that extensive and intensive education beyond current levels would add to these benefits. Thus, even if the direct measurable gains to further education seemed relatively low, the indirect but non-measurable gains might still make the additional investment worthwhile on economic grounds alone.

### Calculating the Rate of Return

Before reviewing the difficulties involved in measurement of returns, it is fitting to examine the methods of calculation. One approach, called the "present value" method, compares the present value of expected returns, discounted by the average rate of return on alternative investments with the present value of costs of education. If the costs are considered, with some tampering with actuality for the sake of simplicity in calculation, to be incurred all at once at the beginning of the investment decision, then their estimation does not require a discounting procedure. Otherwise, they too would be discounted to find their present value. If the present value of returns exceeds the present value of costs, discounted or not, depending on the time dimension assumed for them, then education would yield greater direct returns than alternative investments.

A more popular approach is called the "internal rate of return" method. In this technique, expected returns are discounted by the constant rate that equates their current value with costs. If this calculated rate exceeds the average rate of return on alternative projects, then the returns to education exceed those on other investments, and education "pays," in the limited economic sense treated here. Note that in either method the value that represents the rate of return on other investments is crucial in the determination of whether investment in education pays. In the present value approach, the rate is used in the estimating equation itself; in the internal method, it serves as the basis of comparison.

It will simplify matters in recounting the conceptual problems in measuring the returns to education by setting down the basic equation of the calculations.

$$C = \sum_{i=1}^{T} \frac{(X_{E_i} - X_{N_i})}{(1 + r)^i}$$

where

$C$ = total costs of the education
$X_{E_i}$ = average annual income in year $i$ of those receiving the education
$X_{N_i}$ = average annual income in year $i$ of those not receiving the years of schooling in question
$r$ = the calculated internal rate of return
$T$ = the number of years in the work life after education.*

* Note that with the time horizon beginning just before education, a more accurate formula would discount $C$ to this time, and $i$ would begin the first year after education was completed. For example, to calculate the rate of return on college education, $C$ would be discounted over a four-year period and $i$ would begin at year five. This, of course, is the method used in all calculations but the simplest equation allows for easier analysis of the difficulties in calculation, the issue here.

Each of these terms will be studied in turn for the problems they pose to those who calculate rates of return on investment in education. In general, only the broad problems will be noted, with the nuances reserved for the papers and comments on them to follow.

*Costs* Whether measuring social or private returns, costs are conventionally considered in two categories, direct and indirect. For calculating private returns, direct costs are those associated with the schooling itself—tuition, books, room and board, and incidentals such as transportation. For calculating social returns, these costs are annual building costs, teachers salaries, and related labor costs. In general, these direct costs cause no special conceptual difficulties; it is just a question of the completeness of the data.

Indirect costs, on the other hand, which are the same in calculating private or social returns, are more difficult to measure. These costs are the foregone income of students while attending school. A much-used estimate considers these earnings to be represented by the full-time earnings of nonstudents of the same age group. A proxy group is needed because, of course, it is impossible to measure what the earnings of students would have been were they not attending school. For those of college age, it might be assumed that students could have earned more than nonstudents because of greater intelligence or because of broader work opportunities since they come, on average, from higher income families.

A serious problem in measurement arises over the question of the relationship between education investment costs and education outlays. Specifically, if education is partly a consumption good, whether during the education process itself and/or afterwards, then part of the outlay on education, whether private or public returns are calculated, does not represent investment costs but simply consumption expenses. To the extent that education represents consumption, the internal rate of return is underestimated, that is, costs are overestimated, and a calculated internal rate found to be below the rate of return on alternative investments might incorrectly indicate that the education in question does not pay.

*Lifetime Earnings Difference* $\sum_{i=1}^{T} (X_{E_i} - X_{N_i})$. Here, conceptual and measure-

ment difficulties are most pronounced. First, the basic equation assumes that the earnings advantage of the educated is attributable to education itself, which is certainly unrealistic. The more sophisticated studies attempt to correct these earnings for the greater intellectual capacity of those who receive (college) education, which would lead to higher income for them whether or not they received higher education. But differences in earning capacity resulting from family wealth or wider and more helpful—with respect to income—contacts defy measurement and prevent accurate downward adjustment to the earnings of the educated to derive the annual income streams that truly reflect income earned as a result of the education received.

Then there are the difficult problems created by the time dimension of the calculations. The income streams, to reflect the internal rate on current investment, the meaningful measure sought to determine whether additional schooling would be profitable, must be expected values. The customary method uses the current, cross-sectional difference of earnings between the educated and lesser educated for all age groups to the end of the normal work life. But there is no reason to assume that these earnings differences will apply to future differences in the income streams. Sometimes a growth factor in the differential is introduced, based on past experience, but this only introduces an educated guess into the calculation. Certainly these future differences, which determine the internal rate of return on current investment in education are unknown.

In addition, the data need to be adjusted by mortality considerations and perhaps by the incidence of unemployment. Both these factors reduce the discounted earnings differences in the basic equation which assumes that the members of both groups, the educated and those who do not receive the education, will live to the end of the normal work life,* and that they will always be able to find work at the average wage for their age group and educational level. As was the case for earnings differences themselves, mortality and unemployment estimates used must assume, perhaps with significant error, that current rates will prevail in the future.

*Rate of Return on Alternative Investments* After the internal rate is calculated, the crucial test of whether education pays measures this rate against the rate of return on other investments. But what is the correct alternative rate? The rate of interest? The average profit rate? A composite average rate? Will the current rate chosen accurately reflect future rates? What factor measures the greater risks and illiquidity of investment in education?

### Problems of Measurement

In a very insightful review of the problems that arise in measuring returns to education, William Bowen discusses many of the above issues—the extent to which differential earnings can be attributed to education, the external economies and social benefits of education, consumption aspects of education, the appropriate "other" rate of return, the use of past data to estimate future values. In the section of his paper presented below, Bowen introduces two new conceptual difficulties—the question of whether earnings measure productivity resulting from education or employer preference for the educated, and the imperfections in the calculation caused by nonmonetary attraction of jobs held by the educated.

---

* Fortunately errors in estimation of the average work life have a negligible effect on the internal rate since discounted earnings far in the future add next to nothing to the total present value of the lifetime earnings stream.

# Economic Aspects of Education

## by William G. Bowen

### "Conspicuous Production" and "Tradition-bound" Wage Structures

The link between relative wages and marginal productivities will be weakened to the extent that employers do not set wages so as to maximize their profits. The phrase "conspicuous production" refers to the possibility that some employers may choose to hire college graduates (and pay the "college graduate" salaries) for jobs which do not really require college training. Instances of this type can no doubt be found in a country such as the United States, but I suspect that we tend to exaggerate the frequency with which bosses insist on paying extra for unnecessary qualifications.[1]

The phrase "tradition-bound wage structures" refers to what may well be a more important variant of non-profit maximizing behaviour. Persons who have studied the so-called "underdeveloped countries" have noted a tendency to continue paying relatively high salaries to educated persons in, say, the Government service, when such a salary policy is no longer necessary from a recruitment stand-

SOURCE Reprinted with permission from *Economic Aspects of Education,* Princeton University Industrial Relations Section, 1964, pp. 17–22.

[1] It may well be that as a higher proportion of the people in a country receive a college education, in order to recruit people possessing a certain level of ability, employers will find themselves forced to recruit college graduates—even though college training may be unnecessary for the job. However, this situation ought not to be confused with the "conspicuous production" case. To the extent that these people are paid higher salaries solely because of their basic ability, employers cannot be accused of non-profit-maximizing behaviour. Actually this kind of situation affords an excellent illustration of the need to avoid attributing higher salaries due to ability differentials to education (as discussed above), but it is quite different from a situation in which an employer pays a college graduate holding a particular job more just because he is a college graduate.

point.[2] In countries where the salary structure is rigid because of status overtones, calculations of monetary returns to education can be very misleading as a guide to educational policy.

### The Non-Monetary Attractions of Jobs Open to Graduates

All occupations have their non-monetary plusses and minuses, and the wage structure presumably adjusts accordingly —occupations which are dirty, hard, or unpleasant in any respect will be characterized by higher earnings than other jobs which require the same kinds of qualifications but which are cleaner, easier, more interesting, have a higher status appeal, and so on. Now, there would be no need to dwell on the existence of these non-monetary attractions if they were of roughly the same order of importance in the case of jobs open to highly educated persons and jobs open to persons with lesser amounts of education. In actual fact, however, it seems clear that non-monetary attractions are much greater in the case of the usual jobs filled by, say, college graduates; hence, non-monetary considerations cannot be dismissed as a neutral factor.[3]

It may also be mentioned in passing that there is likely to be an income effect at work here, and that the higher the real income of a society, the greater the weight that the society as a whole is likely to put on the non-monetary side of occupational choice. The president of an American university remarked not long ago that as real income continues to rise we may well see the day when a garbage collector is paid more than a full professor.

The important question is: how (if at all) should one adjust rates of return to take account of differences in non-monetary advantages? This is a very troublesome question at the conceptual level, as well as at the empirical level, and part of the explanation is that the answer depends on whether one is looking at returns to education from the personal profit or national productivity point of view.

From the standpoint of the individual gain from education (personal profit), it seems clear that we ought to add in a sum approximating the dollar equivalent of the non-monetary advantages. Non-monetary advantages certainly do accrue to the individuals concerned and increase their welfare. At the moment, quantitative estimates are lacking, but my guess is that taking account of this consideration would increase the calculated rate of return on higher education (and especially on graduate education) to a very marked extent.

From the national productivity standpoint, one might think at first blush that a similar upward adjustment is required.[4] But, to the extent that the non-monetary aspects of employment are purely a sup-

---

[2] See, for example, the paper prepared by F. H. Harbison for the O.E.C.D. Conference on Education held in Washington in the fall of 1961.

[3] I grant that attitudes toward the non-monetary attractions of certain jobs vary significantly from one person to the next; and I also grant that my own preferences no doubt influence my judgment on this point. But it still seems safe to say that, if salaries were the same and if qualifications were not a constraint, most people would prefer the kinds of jobs that are in fact open only (or mainly) to holders of degrees. Studies that have been made of popular attitudes towards various vocations support this position. (In a poll conducted for the President's Commission on Higher Education and cited by Harris [*The Market for College Graduates*, 1949, p. 7], a cross-section of Americans ranked occupations by prestige. Virtually all of the top occupations would normally require a college education, while most of those ranked lower would not.)

[4] This seems to be Villard's position (see his criticism of Becker's work in the *American Economic Review*, May 1960, p. 376). Many other writers have said essentially the same thing, and I should add that at one point I too shared this position. As the rest of this discussion indicates, I have now revised my views; I have Ralph Turvey to thank for forcing me to think this problem through more fully.

ply-side phenomenon (that is, affect only the willingness of individuals to take jobs at alternative rates of pay and not the costs incurred by employers in hiring additional men), this is not so. The greater the non-monetary attractions of any occupation, the greater the number of people who will be willing to enter the occupation at a given wage and thus the greater the ability of the employer to hire a given number of people at a lower rate of pay. The extent of non-monetary attractions does determine the position of the supply curve of labour, but this does not alter the fact that the employer will still pay that money wage which will equal the value of the marginal product produced by the last man hired. Suppose that all of a sudden there was a sharp increase in the non-monetary attractions of a particular occupation; the result would be a southeasterly shift of the supply schedule (more people willing to enter the occupation at each possible wage) and a movement along the demand (marginal revenue productivity) schedule to a new equilibrium characterized by a lower relative wage and a larger number of people engaged in the occupation. To put the matter another way, if we compare two occupations for which there are identical marginal revenue productivity schedules but which differ in their non-monetary attractions, we should expect to find a lower wage and a larger number of persons engaged in the more attractive of the two occupations—and the

discrepancy in relative wages would measure the difference in *marginal* productivities.[5]

The above line of argument holds only to the extent that non-monetary attractions are truly "non-monetary" and do not cost the employer anything. This is generally true of such attractions as prestige, but it may not be true of attractions such as subsidized housing, subsidized travel, and long paid vacations. Allowances for "fringe benefits" of this type should be added to the basic wage, and it may be that fringes of this kind are more common in occupations filled by relatively well-educated people. An upward adjustment in the rate of return on education should be made to take account of any such discrepancies that can be shown to exist.

There is one final point—the argument presented here is based on the assumption that persons interested in rates of return on education from what we have called the "national productivity" standpoint are concerned solely with the effects of education on the nation's GNP. If one wishes to work from a broader national frame of reference and look at the effects of education on the total "welfare" of the citizenry, then once again, as in the case of the personal profit orientation, a full adjustment for non-monetary attractions is in order since such attractions most certainly do contribute to the aggregate welfare of the populace.

[5] The reason for going through this much detail (and presenting what will appear to professional economists to be a very elementary exposition) is that there have been some misunderstandings, most of which no doubt stem from mixing together the personal profit and national productivity orientations. A major source of confusion to many persons not trained as professional economists is the fact that the "productivity" of an occupation cannot be thought of as an absolute magnitude but must be expected to vary according to the number of persons engaged in the occupation—and it is the productivity of the last person employed (the marginal productivity) which is relevant for most purposes. The fact that in equilibrium (at the level of employment where it will not pay the employer to add one more man nor lay off one man) the marginal revenue product (and thus the wage) in occupation "A" may be lower than in occupation "B" does not mean that at other levels of employment this same relationship between the marginal productivities would necessarily hold; nor does it mean that if the same number of persons were employed in each occupation the marginal productivity in occupation "A" would still be lower than in occupation "B"—it might or it might not.

Bowen explains "conspicuous production" as the preference employers have for college graduates to fill jobs that could be performed as well by those with less education. In such cases, the college graduate worker would be earning more than his contribution to the firm, in more precise terms, more than his marginal value product. This, of course, assumes he is paid a "college graduate" (relatively high) salary.

This practice requires no adjustment to the private returns to college education, but exaggerates the social returns in that average wage differences between college graduates and the lesser educated overstate the additional contribution to total production resulting from college training.

If this practice were diminished or discontinued, as would be likely under tight labor conditions, the effect would be a lowering of the average college-noncollege wage differential. This would follow as wages for the jobs in which "conspicuous production" was practiced suffered a relative decline as the available supply expanded to include those without a college degree. But the fall in the rate of return on a college degree would tend to be arrested, to the extent potential graduates based their educational effort on economic consideraticns, as fewer students studied for degrees in response to the lower returns. If the internal rate had been at its equilibrium level, equal to the rate on alternative investments, after being lowered by the reduction in job preference for graduates, it would rise up toward that level again as the supply of graduates fell.

As Bowen explains, if there are nonmonetary benefits in jobs which the educated hold, such as higher prestige, more pleasant surroundings, the internal rate understates the actual returns to the people receiving the education and later holding the better jobs. From the national, or social point of view, however, if the nonmonetary benefits entail no labor costs for the employer and thus do not reflect greater productivity, than implied in the wage, the somewhat lowered income per educated worker resulting from their extra supply gives a true picture of the national economic gain from education. Bowen notes, however, that if a broader view of national gain is taken, since the welfare of the educated citizenry is enhanced by nonmonetary benefits, even if output is not raised by these benefits, their effect should be counted as a national contribution. Then, as with the case for private returns, the social returns to education would be greater than indicated by the internal rate.

But this uncertainty really also applies to treatment of the consumption benefits from education which also contribute nothing to measurable national output. Because the better educated enjoy a fuller, more varied life—and this assumption has been disputed—education costs should be reduced by the amount education represents consumption rather than investment, in calculating private returns. In practice, the same procedure is used in calculating social returns, since consumption is a part of output. But no actual goods are involved, and if a narrow economic view is taken that only measures education's contribution to GNP, consumption benefits should be ignored in calculating the social return. In short, consumption benefits are as confusing as nonmonetary work benefits to the calculation of social rates of return on investment in education.

## Measuring Indirect Costs of Education

Undoubtedly the most difficult area of measurement in the tabulation of educational returns lies in the estimation of indirect costs. Mary Jean Bowman analyzes these costs in the section of her perceptive paper presented here.

As she explains, the major conceptual difficulty arises from the fact that these indirect costs, the valuation of student time, can be measured only by what is foregone, labor market income for the time of school attendance, and not by direct money payments. The measure, which Bowman selects as the best estimate of the cost of student time, and which is almost universally adopted in rate of return studies, is "the earnings of those of similar age, prior training and ability who are in employment." But as she explains, even this simple standard leads to conceptual problems in the measurement of the (opportunity) cost of student time.

# The Costing of Human Resource Development

## by Mary Jean Bowman

### I. A GENERALIZED CONCEPT OF COSTS AND ITS DIMENSIONS

. . . A general concept of costs adequate to play the part in explanatory tasks that I would impose upon it would necessarily serve also as a tool for prescriptive purposes in societal decision-making. This must be the case, because only if we analyze the incidence of costs and benefits upon individuals, groups and the society at large can we identify the role of costs in development processes and the reaction of those processes on costs. Therefore, social as well as private costs must be assessed. And it must be possible to fit such a cost concept into a battery of decision models ranging from the micro-behavioural to the societal-normative. In other words, a multi-dimensional extension and specification of the "opportunity-cost" concept is called for.

A generalized concept of opportunity costs can start with a very simple definition: the opportunity costs of choosing a commodity, service or activity "A" (or of already having chosen A) are what the individual or group or society gives up (or gave up) in making this choice. In view of the frequent use of the term "opportunity cost" in connection with the measurement of costs of student time, I should add that I am using it in a generic sense that is independent of whether or not an overt expense is directly incurred. Opportunity costs are whatever the bearer of the costs gives up, including, for example, the other things that the student cannot buy when he spends his money on tuition or school books. In this fundamental sense *"all* costs are opportunity costs."[1]

To clarify the specifications needed to make the concept operational, it is neces-

SOURCE Reprinted with permission from *International Economic Conference on the Economics of Education*, London, Macmillan, 1966, pp. 421–450.

[1] The quote is from Fritz Machlup, whose lucid statement in discussion was much appreciated. I took the liberty of incorporating this phrase in my revision.

sary to set out its most important dimensions. I suggest six, though there is no special magic in this number

1. Who bears the costs—that is, whose foregone alternatives are being examined? This may be a student or his family. It may be a business firm that invests in training some of its employees (an investment that can take many different forms). It may be a unit of government —local, provincial or national. It may be the society as a whole (which is *not* the same thing as the government). The list could be extended.

2. The scale units in which the income alternatives are being measured. By this I refer, for example, to the difference between comparisons of alternatives involving only small marginal shifts in numbers attending college and those involving a large percentage increase in the student body. The scale unit in the first instance can be one man regardless of whether we are concerned with individual or societal costs. However, in the second instance a societal assessment will require definition of the scale unit in larger terms. Although I shall sometimes refer to this dimension as the "level of aggregation," it is essential to distinguish between cases in which a summation of small unit measures to arrive at totals or sub-totals could be justified and those in which the decision problem arises *ex ante* only. *Ex post* aggregations at any level, including those for national income measurement, already incorporate the working out of interdependencies that would have invalidated simple summation of micro *ex ante* estimates.

3. The transferability potential. In a generalized theoretical formulation opportunity costs could be defined to encompass all kinds of foregone satisfactions, but this would get us into a utility quagmire. Moreover, if we incorporated all preferences or satisfactions in the theoretical formulation, the model could have no empirical explanatory value; by definition nothing would be left to explain once all external constraints on action had been specified. For private cost assessments at least, it is more useful to begin by including in "foregone opportunities" only what is marketed or potentially marketable. The non-monetary components of the alternatives then become separate variables to be identified and incorporated into explanatory analysis in their own right. On a broader, societal level, a first approximation can be similar, subject to the scale-unit corrections noted in (2). Political-instiutional pressures and constraints (see dimension (6)) could be envisaged as societal counterparts of the non-transferable components of private opportunity alternatives.

4. The time dimensions of the foregone opportunities. This includes not merely one particular date versus another, but comparisons among time paths, and the sequences of costs. This leads also to consideration of the extent to which present choices condition the range of future alternatives.

5. The knowledge and uncertainty dimensions of opportunity perceptions. Associated with this dimension (or set of dimensions in degrees of knowledge, insurability of risk, seriability of events) are theories of behaviour, along a "satisficing" to opitimizing continuum.[2] There is also the distinction between problems in which the appropriate opportunity-cost measure would refer to the best actually perceived alternative versus those in which oppor-

---

[2] The term "satisficing" is borrowed from Herbert Simon, and his adaptive behaviour model of decision making. The "seriability" view of degrees of uncertainy derives from G. L. S. Shackle but is more fully developed in my introduction to the proceedings of the 1955 symposium on *Expectations, Uncertainty and Business Behavior,* which I edited for the Social Science Research Council (published by the Council, New York, 1957). That symposium includes a simple statement of Simon's theoretical position as well.

tunity cost would refer to an hypothesized optimum that omniscience would identify among the potential alternatives.

6. The institutional constraints assumed. This is a matter of identifying the room for manœuvre or manœuvreability in decision-making at any given level of aggregation and in any given problem context. For example, when examining private costs it is important to consider the cost kinks attributable to rationing of public school places and the quite different kinks that may be associated with child labour laws. When considering action by agencies of government or the alternatives faced by society as a whole, it will often be worthwhile to compare the economic implications of analytical constructs allowing little or no room for institutional manœuvre with those that admit full political-social manœuvreability in pursuit of one or another income maximization goal. Here approach to optimization is associated with removal of constraints, whereas in dimension (5) the optimization is approached via increasing knowledge of alternatives.

With the partial exception of items (1) and (2), all of these dimensions relate to identification of the foregone alternatives appropriately included in a given problem context. The locations of alternatives along each of these dimensions will depend upon how the problem itself is posed. The relative locations are fixed though the absolute locations shift with the terms of the problem. Thus generalization of the opportunity-cost concept requires that it take on a variety of particular forms, while remaining unchanged as a generic concept. So understood the concept is clearly appropriate for use in a wide range of problems in both positive and normative economics; their common feature is that they are or can be set up in the form of "decision" problems.[3]

Finally, it should perhaps be pointed out that opportunity costs are measures of *real* costs, or what is sacrificed. I submit that this is the only empirically operational way of measuring real costs. It does not require any sort of psychological theory with respect to satisfactions or dissatisfactions or the onerousness of labour. On the other hand, if the notion of costs has any meaning at all it must entail something negative; in the opportunity-cost approach this negative value is negative income or purchasing power.

To incorporate in a single paper consideration of all of the many facets of cost theory and assessment along all of their dimensions would of course be quite impossible. I must therefore proceed selectively. First, I attempt to clarify some of the controversy and confusion around the "what is put in" as opposed to "what is forgone," or opportunity cost, views of costs. The last half of the paper then concentrates on the opportunity-cost concept in private dicision models, focusing especially on the time dimensions of relationships between human capital formation in schools and on the job.

## II. WHAT-IS-PUT-IN
*VERSUS* WHAT-IS-FORGONE

Within the past year I have read or heard assertions by economists interested in the economics of education that inclusion of opportunity costs of student time in estimating costs of education was "obviously wrong," or "obviously meaningless"—or equally obviously correct or essential. It would seem that something is not quite obvious after all. We may set aside the disputes over particular empirical measures among those who agree in principle. I have already argued implicitly that there are legitimate objections to the theoretical assumptions within which the

[3] I am using the term "decisions" in the broadest sense, to include passive as well as deliberative choices. Actually, the decisions that best fit theoretical models of rational optimization are not the "genuine" or "crucial" decisions of theories of behaviour in the face of true uncertainty.

opportunity-cost concept has sometimes been confined, but most of the otherwise stultifying assumptions either can be or have been legitimately set aside as the problem and its empirical referents may require. The remaining types of opposition to opportunity costs are conveniently discussed under three headings: (1) classical-Marxist predilections for absolute definitions of "real costs," (2) accounting conventions that include what is paid for in a market transaction but exclude most or all of what is only potentially marketable, and (3) conceptual and pragmatic measurement problems related to levels of cost aggregation and the purposes of such aggregation. A common thread that runs through all of these arguments is a preoccupation with the "what is put in" as against the "what is forgone" approach. This entails a blurring of the distinction between costs as such and value, but in saying this I do not mean to re-introduce the notion of the pain or disutility of labour or "waiting."

### Standardized Real Cost Units

\* \* \*

Those who argue for the what-is-put-in orientation of classical and Marxian standardized unit measures of real costs seem, nevertheless, to distinguish them *in principle* from an opportunity-cost approach. This contrast is sharply illuminated when the tacit assumption of full employment is removed. For simplicity of exposition let us return to a one-factor model but assume (in that most unreal of unreal worlds) that there is some involuntary unemployment of the one factor. In the standardized real-cost unit approach, the cost of producing commodity A is simply the number of units of the factor put into making A; there is no need to consider what, if anything, might have been produced instead. But the opportunity-cost view, which is *defined*, not merely measured, by assessment of alternatives, can-

not evade the problem of how to adjust for the existence of idle resources. I find it somewhat ironic that the defenders of absolute real-cost measures so frequently attack opportunity costs precisely on the grounds that in practice opportunity-cost estimates often ignore unemployment.

### The Importance of Being Paid

Both Marshallian expenses of production and modern national-income accounting at factor prices could be viewed as variants of the what-is-put-in approach to costs; they are more limited variants than the classical or Marxian versions, since they disregard either all or a major part of those factor inputs that do not involve direct monetary payments of some kind. However, so far as Marshall is concerned, it is evident that he did not confound money outlays with "costs" in the more generic sense. Neither do national income accountants. Attempts to compare *per capita* incomes among countries in which the non-market sectors of economic life are substantially different in relative importance have, in fact, included estimates of the value of outputs in the subsistence sectors, whatever may be done about measuring costs. For national-income accounting, the importance of being paid is primarily that it is then easier to be counted; this is not a matter of principle or argument over basic concepts and definitions.

What puzzles me is the position of those who use expense data as the exclusive basis for cost measurement in a variety of purposes and who insist that opportunity (and in practice *any*) measure of costs of student time is fallacious—except, perhaps, when the student receives a stipend. There is a limited context in which the expenses basis for cost assessment can be both meaningful and coordinate with an opportunity-cost measurement. If one is interested only in the costs incurred by the man or agency or government that makes direct payments to buy or hire resources, then by definition only such transactions need concern us. Moreover, these payments are in fact the measure of the opportunities that the man or agency making the payments must forego; they measure very precisely what he could have had if he had chosen to spend the money in some other way. But as soon as we want to go beyond this, to a definition that has wider applications, the weakness of a money-outlay approach must become evident. It is not *in principle* adaptable to assessments of the cost burden on any other person or group. The money wages a worker receives may happen to match fairly well what he foregoes in taking on this job; they will match well if competitive equilibrium prevails. But they are not conceived as costs to him, in any definition. Neither, for that matter, are they what he is worth in the job in which he is employed, though they would approximate that in a purely competitive economy. What meaning, beyond the most superficial description, can be given to the expenses incurred by a government in paying high incomes as sinecures to elitist officials? Or, suppose a free market economy with widespread unemployment; in what sense is the salary of an employed machinist the real or societal cost of his productive contributions? Once we push beyond the surface into more fundamental economic issues it becomes clear that there is nothing hard and unequivocal about "costs" in the form of direct money payments. The latter are subject to every defect that their proponents have charged against empirical assessments of opportunity costs in a market economy, plus the fact that they embody these defects virtually *in principle* and not merely by default in empirical approximations.

Money-outlay measures of costs are also inherently loaded with inconsistencies:

for example, if we were to adhere fully to an overt payments basis of costing, the measured total "costs" of secondary schooling to a society would rise or fall according to whether any given number of students were supported by their families or by transfer payments in the form of philanthropic scholarships or government stipends. If student time is to be regarded as a factor input, the *way* it is paid for should not alter its measured cost. The typical answer in national income accounting has been to exclude stipends as "transfer payments."[4] This is to take the position that student time is *not* a resource input. But this means that virtually all the labour time of young men engaged in constructing factories is counted as investment, whereas the time comparable young men devote to building future human productive capacities is excluded. Evidently the expense-outlay approach to costs is a very limited, *ad hoc* sort of measure. It is arbitrary in what it includes or excludes. It is not adaptable to assess either factor inputs in any "real" sense or the incidence of costs on various individuals or agencies or on the society as a whole. But this brings us up against the complex of problems and conventions involved in national income accounting and cost aggregation.

*Cost Aggregations and National Income*

Definition and estimation of costs at one or another relatively gross level of aggregation have been attempted in response to a diverse array of questions. We might divide these questions in two categories or sets. In the first set are questions that are not in fact cost questions at all. These include: (1) What fraction of total resources has been put into education? (2) How big is the education component of national income at factor prices? (3) What

[4] This sentence replaces a statement in the original version that was decidedly awkward and misleading without further elaboration. Mr. Vaizey referred to this in his comments. I have no argument with him about how conventional national income accounting treats these stipends.

has education contributed to growth in national income? The second set of questions entails examination of alternatives, and hence of the costs of what is foregone. Their prototype is (4) what was or would be the cost of devoting such and such resources to education? By now the reader will realize that I am really posing the question: What was or would be the cost of devoting such and such resources to education (for example) *instead of to other things?*

An initial what-is-put-in perspective is suggested by the way in which the first of the above questions was posed. How should we measure the fraction of total resources that has been put into education? If some independent or absolute standardized factor unit were at hand (as in the single-factor economy) the answer would be simple; cost and value are measured in the same way. But in the complexities of a real world some other answer is required. I suggest that the logic of opportunity-cost assessments when used for this purpose can be only as a proxy measure for what is put in. In this context opportunity cost in some arbitrarily chosen base year would be used throughout; otherwise the measuring stick becomes elastic. Moreover, if the data are available,

we could just as reasonably use a base-year rental value measure of input units, which is essentially what Denison did with his education component of labour quality.[5] Returning to measurement in cost units, if opportunity costs are serving only as proxies or stand-in measures, we may then ask whether it is suitable to adjust for unemployment. My answer would be no. I would use as the best of the possible cost measures of student time the earnings of those of similar age, prior training and ability who were in employment. I would object to adjustment for the rate of unemployment on the grounds that we are measuring resources, not failure to use them. In relegating opportunity-cost assessments to a secondary, stand-in rôle in measuring the proportions of resources devoted to education, the operational criteria for empirical measurement are thus changed. A pragmatic and likely rather than an optimal alternative is the most appropriate reference value and unemployment is treated differently. After all, we are trying to measure what is put in, which is not the same thing as what is foregone in any but the perfect equilibrium state,[6] this is not at its core a cost problem.

＊　＊　＊

For example, there is the question of unemployment. Not only is there usually significant unemployment among nonstudents but, in addition, there is the possibility of unemployment for both the educated and lesser educated after education is completed. (Recall that the lifetime earnings stream of the lesser educated represents the opportunity cost of the educated had they not received the education for which returns are being calculated.) From the social point of view, Bowman suggests that unemployment should not be considered, since "we are measuring resources, not failure to use them." But to estimate private returns, the prospective student should write down his indirect educa-

---

[5] Edward F. Denison, *The Sources of Economic Growth in the United States and the Alternatives Before Us*, Committee for Economic Development, New York, 1962. See also Denison's paper for the OECD Economics of Education Study Group meeting in May 1963.

[6] Fritz Machlup's use of an opportunity-cost estimate of training provided by mothers in the home as a component of his assessment of knowledge production is open to attack on these grounds. There is no reason whatever to assume that his estimate has any relation to the inputs into "knowledge production." See my review article, "Professor Machlup on Knowledge and Reform," *School Review,* Summer 1963.

tion costs by the probability that he would be unemployed as a nonstudent, and adjust his expected future earnings gains from education by the probabilities that he would be unemployed if educated or not. The student must take the economy's inability to provide for long-term full employment as a given condition out of his control.

A similar difference between private and social returns arises from the establishment of legal and social constraints, or what Bowman calls institutional constraints. In calculating private returns from education up to, say, 16 years of age, assuming this is the minimum age for leaving school, foregone earnings are zero, since the student cannot work instead of attending school. But in calculating social costs, it should be acknowledged that young students would have had market earnings alternatives were these constraints not imposed, and putative earnings should be included as opportunities foregone in measuring social costs, and returns, to education.

Bowman, under what she calls the "transferability potential" warns against the "utility quagmire" which ensnares attempts to account for differences in satisfaction from alternative occupations and uses of time. Is school work more pleasant, or less distasteful, than market work that could otherwise be performed? Are there positive consumption benefits in later life from being educated? These are factors which, despite their incapability of measurement, influence the effective rate of return on investment in education. Bowman suggests that it is useful to include in foregone opportunities only marketable, or measureable, factors and to leave the nonmonetary components of alternatives "to be identified and incorporated into explanatory analysis in their own right." But because of the imponderable nature of the nonmonetary components, this analysis must suggest only imprecise adjustments to the rate of return.

## Foregone Earnings

Foregone earnings of students received their first systematic treatment as a cost of education by Theodore W. Schultz, in the section of the paper included here. Schultz clearly states the following assumptions he makes in measuring the contribution of foregone earnings to the capital stock in education, the subject of his paper: (1) School is considered work; the possible consumption benefits of education do not confuse the calculation. (2) Foregone earnings are measured by what students would earn if they worked in the market; the issue of whether they might not have worked or have been unemployed does not enter the calculation of social costs of education. (3) These foregone earnings are measured by the income of nonstudents of the same age group. Schultz is aware that those in high school, and especially college, might have higher potential earnings than the nonstudent, but there is no device for measuring the difference.

# Capital Formation by Education

## by Theodore W. Schultz

* * *

## I. EARNINGS THAT STUDENTS FOREGO

It will be convenient to draw an arbitrary line between elementary and secondary schools and to assume that no earnings are foregone on the part of children who attend elementary schools.[1] Beyond the eighth grade, however, these earnings become important. The time and effort of students may usefully be approached as follows: (1) Students study, which is work, and this work, among other things, helps create human capital. Students are not enjoying leisure when they study, nor are they engaged wholly in consumption; they are here viewed as "self-employed" producers of capital. (2)

Assume, then, that if they were not in school, they would be employed producing (other) products and services of value to the economy, for which they would be "paid"; there is, then, an opportunity cost in going to school. (3) The average earnings per week of those young men and women of comparable age and sex who are not attending school or of students while they are not in school are a measure of the (alternative) value productivity of the students' time and effort. (4) The cost of living of students and non-students may be put aside because they go on whether young people go to school or enter the labor market and are about the same except for minor items, such as books, extra clothes, and some travel in getting to and from school.

SOURCE Reprinted with permission from *Journal of Political Economy,* Vol. 68, December 1960, pp. 571–583.

[1] This assumption is plausible enough in the case of our society at the present time. But back no further than 1900, many of these children were of considerable economic value as workers, and some parents were keeping them from school for that reason.

Estimates of the earnings that students have foregone were made in the following manner: High-school students were treated separately from college and university students. The year 1949 was taken as a base year in determining the "earnings" per week of young people, both males and females, for each of four age groups. Students' foregone earnings were calculated on the assumption that, on the average, students forego 40 weeks of such earnings, and then expressed in earning-equivalent weeks of workers in manufacturing in the United States. The results appear in Table 1; they indicate that high-school students forego the equivalent of about 11 weeks

TABLE 1.   ESTIMATES OF EARNINGS FOREGONE BY HIGH-SCHOOL AND COLLEGE OR UNIVERSITY STUDENTS IN 1949 *

| Age | Median Income (Dollars) (1) | Weeks Worked (2) | Income Per Week (Dollars) (3) | Annual Earnings Foregone in Attending School (Dollars) (4) | In Weeks Equivalent to Average Earnings of Workers in Manufacturing (5) |
|---|---|---|---|---|---|
| 14–17: | | | | | |
| Male | 311 | 24 | 13.00 | 520 | . . . |
| Female | 301 | 20 | 15.00 | 600 | . . . |
| 18–19: | | | | | |
| Male | 721 | 32 | 22.50 | 900 | . . . |
| Female | 618 | 29 | 21.30 | 852 | . . . |
| 20–24: | | | | | |
| Male | 1,669 | 40 | 41.70 | 1,669 | . . . |
| Female | 1,276 | 36 | 35.40 | 1,416 | . . . |
| 25–29: | | | | | |
| Male | 2,538 | 44 | 57.70 | 2,308 | . . . |
| Female | 1,334 | 33 | 40.40 | 1,616 | . . . |
| Per Student: | | | | | |
| High school | . . . | . . . | . . . | 583† | 11 weeks |
| College or university | . . . | . . . | . . . | 1,369‡ | 25 weeks |

* Sources and notes:

Column 1: *United States Census of Population, 1950, Special Report on Education, 1953,* Table 13, except for figures for age group 20–24, which are from Herman P. Miller, *Income of the American People* (New York: John Wiley & Sons, 1955), Table 29. Virtually all the income in these age groups would appear to be from "earnings" according to Miller's Table 34.

Column 2: *United States Census of Population, 1950, Special Report on Employment and Personal Characteristics, 1953,* Table 14. Of the persons who did work in 1949, the Census shows the per cent who worked 1–13, 14–26, 27–39, 40–49, and 50–52 weeks, and, on the assumption that these classes averaged out to 7, 20, 33, 45, and 51 weeks, respectively, these were used as weights.

Column 3: col. 1 divided by col. 2.

Column 4: Assumes that students forego, on the average, 40 weeks of earnings: col. 3 multiplied by 40.

Column 5: *Economic Report of the President, January, 1957,* Table E-25. The average gross weekly earnings for all manufacturing was $54.92: Col. 4 divided by 54.92.

† Students enrolled in high school were approximately half males and half females; 92.7 per cent were allocated to the age group 14–17, and 7.3 per cent to ages 18–19. In making this allocation, it was assumed that those below the age of 14 offset those above the age of 19 (*Statistical Abstract of the United States, 1956,* Table 126).

‡ College or university students were distributed as follows:

| Ages | Males (Per Cent) | Females (Per Cent) |
|---|---|---|
| 14–17 | 3.5 | 5.0 |
| 18–19 | 18.2 | 16.0 |
| 20–24 | 30.6 | 11.5 |
| 25–29 | 14.7 | 0.5 |
| | 67.0 | 33.0 |

These percentages were used as weights in calculating the estimate of $1,369 (based on *Statistical Abstract of the United States, 1956,* Table 126).

and college or university students about 25 weeks of such earnings. These 1949 earnings ratios were applied to particular years between 1900 and 1956; an adjustment was then made for unemployment, as set forth in Table 2.

Two sorts of limitations need to be borne in mind in interpreting and in using these estimates. The first pertains to the *11-week* and *25-week* estimates for the base year 1949; the other is inherent in applying the 1949 relationships to other years.

Many of the young people who did work in 1949 were employed for only a few weeks during the year. It seems plausible that their earnings per week would

be below those of workers of equivalent abilities who worked most or all of the year. To this extent, our estimates are too low.[2] Also, it could be that students rate somewhat higher per person in the particular abilities for which earnings are received than do those not in school who are earning income. To the extent that there are such differences, other things being equal, our estimates of earnings foregone are again too low. On the other hand, some students have held jobs while they were attending school; the earnings they have received from such jobs should have been subtracted from our estimates. Then, too, young people are probably burdened with more unemployment rela-

TABLE 2. ANNUAL EARNINGS FOREGONE BY STUDENTS, ADJUSTED AND NOT ADJUSTED FOR UNEMPLOYMENT, 1900–1956, IN CURRENT PRICES*

| | Average Weekly Earnings, All Manufacturing (Dollars) | Annual Earnings Foregone per Student While Attending | | | |
| | | High School | | College or University | |
| Year | | Unadjusted (Dollars) | Adjusted for Unemployment (Dollars) | Unadjusted (Dollars) | Adjusted for Unemployment (Dollars) |
| | (1) | (2) | (3) | (4) | (5) |
| 1900 | 8.37 | 92 | 84 | 209 | 192 |
| 1910 | 10.74 | 118 | 113 | 269 | 259 |
| 1910 | 26.12 | 287 | 275 | 653 | 626 |
| 1930 | 23.25 | 256 | 224 | 581 | 509 |
| 1940 | 25.20 | 277 | 236 | 630 | 537 |
| 1950 | 59.33 | 653 | 626 | 1,483 | 1,422 |
| 1956 | 80.13 | 881 | 855 | 2,003 | 1,943 |

* Sources:

Column 1: *Economic Report of the President, January, 1957*, Table E-25, and U.S. Department of Labor: and *Historical Statistics of the United States, 1789–1945*, a supplement to *Statistical Abstract of the United States, 1949*, Ser. D, pp. 134–44.

Column 2: For high-school students, col. 1 multiplied by 11; based on Table 1.

Column 4: For college and university students, col. 1 multiplied by 25; based on Table 1.

Columns 3 and 5: The per cent unemployed is based on Clarence D. Long, *The Labor Force under Changing Income and Employment* (a N.B.E.R. study [Princeton: Princeton University Press, 1958]), Appendix C, Table C-1 and, for 1956, Table C-2. Unemployed adult male equivalents in per cent of the labor force were as follows: 1900, 8.2; 1910, 3.9; 1920, 4.2; 1930, 12.4; 1940, 14.7; 1950, 4.1; and 1956, 3.0.

[2] Of males aged fourteen to seventeen who worked in 1959, 44 per cent worked only about 7 weeks (an average) and 19 per cent worked about 20 weeks (average). Similarly, in the case of females aged fourteen to seventeen who worked, 53 per cent worked only about 7 weeks and 21 per cent about 20 weeks (averages). For ages eighteen to nineteen, these figures are smaller, i.e., for males, 24 per cent worked only 7 weeks and 19 per cent about 20 weeks; and for females aged eighteen to nineteen, the two figures are 29 and 23 per cent, respectively. For ages twenty to twenty-four, they are 10 and 12 per cent for males and 17 and 15 per cent for females.

tive to the number employed than is the labor force as a whole.[3] Thus, of the four factors just mentioned, two pull in one direction and two in the other. They may be compensating factors.

There is also the question: What would the earnings of school-age workers have been if all of them had entered the labor market? But the question is not relevant because our problem is not one that entails a large shift in the number of human agents. The elasticity of the demand, either in the short or the long run, for such workers over so wide a range is not at issue. Instead, we want to know what earnings a typical student has been foregoing at the margin. Even so, our estimates of earnings foregone are substantially reduced by the effects of the large shift of students into summer employment,[4] the earning figures that we are using, drawing on the 1950 Census, are heavily weighted by this summer employment. As pointed out above, many who did work for pay worked only a couple of months or so.[5]

The other difficulties stem from applying the 1949 "structural" relationships to other periods, especially to earlier years. The only adjustment that has been introduced is that for movements in unemployment. It is not easy to isolate the changes resulting from legislation. Stigler[6] suggests that "on the whole compulsory school attendance laws have followed more than led the increase in enrollments of children over 14." Child labor laws may have done likewise. In any case, these laws may be viewed as a comprehensive private and public effort to invest in education, the child labor laws having the effect of eliminating some job opportunities.[7]

There is a presumption in favor of the view that high-school students in 1949 were attending school more weeks per year than did high-school students in earlier years. Such evidence as I have been able to uncover, however, suggests that for 1900, 1910, and 1920 most high-school students, including those who were attending secondary preparatory schools, were being instructed so that they could win entrance into a college or university and that these students were attending school about as many weeks per year as high-

[3] *The Economic Report of the President, January, 1960,* Table D-18, gives some figures that appear relevant. They show total unemployed equal to 5.2 per cent of the total employed, whereas for the fourteen to nineteen age group it was 11.8 per cent.

[4] In 1955, for example, 1.2 million individuals aged fourteen to nineteen entered the labor force between May and July, in contrast to about 0.4 million in the ages twenty to twenty-four.

[5] One can know something about the relation of the number of individuals in these age groups who are gainfully employed to the number enrolled in school. As one might expect, in the youngest of the three age groups, the number gainfully employed ( April, 1950) was a little more than one-third the number enrolled in school (October, 1950), whereas for the age group twenty to twenty-four there were fully seven times as many in the gainfully employed group as there were enrolled in school. The figures for 1950 are as follows:

| Ages | Enrolled in School (October) (Millions) | Gainfully Employed or in Labor Force (April) (Millions) |
|---|---|---|
| 16–17 | 3.06 | 1.12 |
| 18–19 | 1.19 | 2.39 |
| 20–24 | 0.96 | 7.09 |
| Total | 5.21 | 10.60 |

[6] George S. Stigler, "Employment and Compensation in Education" ("National Bureau of Economic Research, Occasional Papers," No. 33 [New York, 1950]), p. 8 and Appendix B.

[7] In commenting on child labor laws, Albert Rees has called my attention to the *Census of Manufactures* of 1890, which shows that 121,000 children (males under sixteen and females under fifteen) were employed and that their annual earnings were 31 per cent of those of all manufacturing wage earners. This is a substantially higher ratio than that implied for this age group in Tables 1 and 2. Thus using 11 weeks' earnings foregone for 1900 may understate the investment in high-school education at the beginning of this period.

school students in more recent years. Between the early twenties and the mid-forties, there may have been a small dip in this variable as a consequence of the large increases in high-school enrolment and the fact that high-school instruction was no longer devoted primarily to the preparation of students for college.[8]

The weekly earnings of workers who possess the capabilities of students and who are of that age group may have changed substantially since 1900 relative to the earnings of those employed in manufacturing. But it is not possible even to guess whether their earnings have become more or less favorable relative to the earnings of workers in manufacturing. The age groups that appear in Table 1 represent young people who had had more years of schooling than did the same age groups in 1900. But this would also be true of workers in manufacturing. The fact that the wage ratio between skilled and unskilled workers has narrowed may imply that our estimates of earnings foregone by high-school students during the earlier years are somewhat too high, or more plausible, that the estimates for college and university students are on the low side for those years.[9] It would be exceedingly difficult, however, to isolate the effects of these changes.

## II. COSTS OF THE SERVICES PROVIDED BY SCHOOLS

Ideally, we want a measure of the annual flow of the inputs employed for education. This flow consists of the services of teachers, librarians, and school administrators, of the annual factor costs of maintaining and operating the school plant, and of depreciation and interest. It should not include expenditures to operate particular auxiliary enterprises, such as providing room and board for students, operating "organized" athletics or other non-educational activities. School expenditures for scholarships, fellowships, and other financial aids to students should also be excluded, because they are in the nature of transfer payments; the real costs involved in student time are already fully covered by the opportunity-cost estimates.

Tables 3 and 4 give these costs of schools for elementary, secondary, and higher education. Each table is essentially self-contained, with sources and notes.

## III. TOTAL COSTS OF EDUCATION

The estimates of the costs of elementary education were complete as set forth in column 11 of Table 3, inasmuch as no earnings were foregone in accordance with our assumption.

Table 5 summarizes the principal components entering into the costs of high-school education. A comparison of columns 3 and 6 shows at once the importance of the earnings that students forego relative to total costs of this education. That such foregone earnings should have been a

[8] Unfortunately for our purposes, data for the United States do not separate elementary and high-school attendance. The data are mainly for the five to seventeen age group with two sets of figures: (1) the average number of days that schools were in session and (2) the average number of days attended by each enrolled pupil five to seventeen years of age. These are: 1900, 144 and 99 days, respectively; 1910, 156 and 113 days; 1920, 163 and 121 days; 1930, 173 and 143 days; 1940, 175 and 152 days; 1950, 178 and 158 days; and 1956, 178 and 159 days. Thus there has been a 60 per cent increase in the average number of days that each enrolled student attended schools. This rise, however, has been dominated by changes that have occurred in the attendance of elementary students. In the early years, high-school students were heavily concentrated in states that had already established long school sessions and good attendance records. For example, the average number of days attended by high-school students in a sample of such states was 170 days in 1920; a 1925–26 set of 31 states shows 151 days, and another set of states for 1937–38 shows 168 days, rising to 178 days in 1945–46 and 176 days in 1949–50.

[9] Paul G. Keat, "Changes in Occupational Wage Structure, 1900–1956" (unpublished Ph.D. thesis, University of Chicago, March, 1959), p. 77, estimates the wage ratio of skilled to unskilled workers to have been 205 in 1900 and 149 in 1949.

TABLE 3.  ANNUAL RESOURCE COSTS OF EDUCATIONAL SERVICES RENDERED BY ELEMENTARY AND SECONDARY SCHOOLS IN THE UNITED STATES, 1900–1956, IN CURRENT PRICES*

| | Public Schools | | | | | | Private Schools | | Public and Private Schools | | |
| Year | Gross Expenditures (1) | Capital Outlay (2) | Net Expenditures (3) | Value of Property (4) | Implicit Interest and Depreciation (5) | Total Public (6) | Gross Expenditures (7) | Total Private (8) | Total (9) | Secondary (10) | Elementary (11) |
|---|---|---|---|---|---|---|---|---|---|---|---|
| 1900 | 215 | 35 | 180 | .55 | 44 | 224 | 27 | 28 | 252 | 19 | 233 |
| 1910 | 426 | 70 | 356 | 1.1 | 88 | 444 | 54 | 56 | 500 | 50 | 450 |
| 1920 | 1,036 | 154 | 882 | 2.4 | 192 | 1,074 | 104 | 108 | 1,182 | 215 | 967 |
| 1930 | 2,317 | 371 | 1,946 | 6.2 | 496 | 2,442 | 233 | 246 | 2,688 | 741 | 1,947 |
| 1940 | 2,344 | 258 | 2,086 | 7.6 | 608 | 2,694 | 227 | 261 | 2,955 | 1,145 | 1,810 |
| 1950 | 5,838 | 1,014 | 4,824 | 11.4 | 912 | 5,736 | 783 | 769 | 6,505 | 2,286 | 4,219 |
| 1956 | 10,955 | 2,387 | 8,568 | 23.9 | 1,912 | 10,480 | 1,468 | 1,404 | 11,884 | 4,031 | 7,853 |

* Sources and Notes:

Column 1: Lines 1–6, from *Statistical Abstract of the United States, 1955*, Table 145; line 7 from *Biennial Survey of Education in the United States, 1954–56*.

Column 2: Lines 1–6, from *Biennial Survey of Education in the United States, 1948–50*, chap. 2, Table 1; line 7 from the 1954–56 survey.

Column 3: Obtained by subtracting col. 2 from col. 1.

Column 4: From same sources as col. 2.

Column 5: Obtained by taking 8 per cent of col. 4. The distribution of physical assets is placed at 20 per cent land, 72 per cent buildings, and 8 per cent equipment, following Robert Rude's study, "Assets of Private Nonprofit Institutions in the United States, 1890–1948" (N.B.E.R., April, 1954, not published), Table II-2a. With no depreciation or obsolescence on land, 3 per cent on buildings (more obsolescence than for colleges and universities because of changing local and community populations to which high schools must adjust) and 10 per cent on equipment, and with an implicit interest rate of 5.1 per cent, we have an 8 per cent rate per $100 of assets per year.

Column 6: Obtained by adding cols. 3 and 5.

Column 7: From same sources as col. 1, except that line 1 is based on the same ratio as line 2 between cols. 1 and 7; line 3 is based on the same ratio as line 4; and line 7 is based on the same ratio as line 6.

Column 8: Obtained by taking the percentage that col. 7 is of col. 1 and multiplying by col. 6. The gross expenditures of private schools ranged from 9.7 to 13.4 per cent of that of public schools. This procedure assumes that capital outlays, value of physical property, and imputed interest and depreciation bear the same relationship to gross expenditures for private as for public schools.

Column 9: Obtained by adding cols. 6 and 8.

Column 10: Obtained by allocating the total of col. 9 between elementary and secondary schools on the basis that it costs 88 per cent more per student in secondary than in elementary schools. Expenditures for high schools determined by using George J. Stigler's estimates appearing in *Employment and Compensation in Education* ("Occasional Papers," No. 33 [New York: National Bureau of Economic Research, 1950]), Tables 7 and 12. Enrolment in elementary schools is given as 33, and in secondary schools as 21 per teacher (using average for last five years in Stigler's table); and average salary of elementary-school

teachers in 1938 was $1,876, and of secondary-school teachers it was $2,249. This is as 100 to 120. Accordingly, per student, we have: $\frac{120 \div 21}{100 \div 33} \times 100$

= an index of 188 for teacher salary per student in secondary schools compared to 100 for that in elementary schools. A slightly lower ratio appears in the *Biennial Survey of Education in the United States, 1939–40*, chap. 1, Table 42, n. 1, in which secondary-school costs per student are placed 74 per cent higher than that in elementary schools. There are, however, no estimates in the 1939–40 survey which permit one to determine expenditures per student for elementary and secondary schools.

(Millions of Dollars)

| Year | Gross Expenditures (1) | Auxiliary Enterprises (2) | Capital Outlay (3) | Net Expenditures (4) | Value of Physical Property (5) | Implicit Interest and Depreciation (6) | Total (7) |
|---|---|---|---|---|---|---|---|
| 1900 | 46 | 9 | 17 | 20 | 254 | 20 | 40 |
| 1910 | 92 | 18 | 30 | 44 | 461 | 37 | 81 |
| 1920 | 216 | 43 | 48 | 125 | 741 | 59 | 184 |
| 1930 | 632 | 126 | 125 | 381 | 1,925 | 154 | 535 |
| 1940 | 758 | 152 | 84 | 522 | 2,754 | 220 | 742 |
| 1950 | 2,662 | 539 | 417 | 1,706 | 5,273 | 422 | 2,128 |
| 1956 | 4,210 | 736 | 686 | 2,788 | 8,902 | 712 | 3,500 |

* Sources and notes:
   Column 1: Lines 1–6, from *Statistical Abstract of the United States, 1955,* Table 145; and line 17
from *Biennial Survey of Education in the United States, 1954–56.* These expenditures by public and
private institutions were as follows:

| | Public | Private |
|---|---|---|
| | (in Million Dollars) | |
| 1920 | 116 | 100 |
| 1930 | 289 | 343 |
| 1940 | 391 | 367 |
| 1950 | 1,429 | 1,233 |
| 1956 | 2,375 | 1,835 |

   Column 2: Lines 5–7, same source as col. 1. For the two sets of institutions these were as follows:

| | Public | Private |
|---|---|---|
| | (in Million Dollars) | |
| 1940 | 59 | 93 |
| 1950 | 255 | 284 |
| 1956 | 364 | 372 |

Lines 1–4 were obtained by letting these auxiliary enterprises equal one-fifth of gross expenditures.
   Column 3: Lines 4–7 from *Biennial Survey of Education in the United States, 1954–56,* chap. iv,
Sec. II; lines 1–3 obtained by taking 6.5 per cent of col. 5, lines 1–3.
   Column 4: Obtained by subtracting the sums of cols. 2 and 3 from col. 1.
   Column 5: From *Biennial Survey of Education in the United States, 1948–50,* chap. iv, Sec. II,
Table I, and *1954–56.* These estimates check closely with those of Robert Rude, "Assets of Private
Nonprofit Institutions in the United States, 1890–1948," (National Bureau of Economic Research, April,
1954, not published).
   Column 6: Obtained by taking 8 per cent of col. 5; they assume no depreciation and obsolescence
on land, 2 per cent on buildings and improvements, and 10 per cent on equipment. Following Robert
Rude's study cited above, Table II-2a, these physical assets were distributed 15 per cent to land, 70
per cent to buildings and improvements, and 15 per cent to equipment. Assuming an interest rate of
5.1 per cent, we have per $100 of assets:

| | |
|---|---|
| Interest of all assets | $5.10 |
| Depreciation and obsolescence | |
| On buildings and improvements | 1.40 |
| On equipment | 1.50 |
| Total | $8.00 |

Column 7: Is the sum of cols. 4 and 6.

larger proportion of total costs of high-school education during the earlier years (and a larger proportion of total costs of high-school than of college and university education in all years) comes as a surprise. Earnings foregone while attending high school were well over half the total costs in each of the years; they were 73

TABLE 5. EARNINGS FOREGONE AND OTHER RESOURCE COSTS REPRESENTED BY HIGH-SCHOOL EDUCATION, IN THE UNITED STATES, 1900–1956, IN CURRENT PRICES*

| Year | Number of Students (Millions) (1) | Earnings Foregone per Student (Dollars) (2) | Total Earnings Foregone (3) | School Costs (Millions of Dollars) (4) | Additional Expenditures (Millions of Dollars) (5) | Total (6) |
|---|---|---|---|---|---|---|
| 1900 | .7 | 84 | 59 | 19 | 3 | 81 |
| 1910 | 1.1 | 113 | 124 | 50 | 6 | 180 |
| 1920 | 2.5 | 275 | 688 | 215 | 34 | 937 |
| 1930 | 4.8 | 224 | 1,075 | 741 | 54 | 1,870 |
| 1940 | 7.1 | 236 | 1,676 | 1,145 | 84 | 2,905 |
| 1950 | 6.4 | 626 | 4,006 | 2,286 | 200 | 6,492 |
| 1956 | 7.7 | 855 | 6,584 | 4,031 | 329 | 10,944 |

* Sources

Column 1: *Statistical Abstract of the United States, 1955,* Table 145; and *Biennial Survey of Education in the United States, 1954–56* chap. 2, Table 44.

Column 2: From Table 2, col. 3.

Column 3: Col. 1 multiplied by col. 2.

Column 4: From Table 3, col. 10.

Column 5: Expenditures for books, supplies, extra clothes, and travel to and from school estimated at 5 per cent of total earnings foregone; hence, 5 per cent of col. 3.

Column 6: Cols. 3 + 4 + 5.

per cent in 1900 and 60 per cent in 1956; the two low years were 1930 and 1940, when they fell to 57 and 58 per cent of total costs. During 1950 and 1956 they were 62 and 60 per cent, respectively. Other and more general economic implications of these changes in resource costs

of high-school education will be considered later.

Table 6 provides similar estimates for college and university education. Here, too, earnings foregone by students are exceedingly important (see cols. 3 and 6). In 1900 and 1910 these earnings were

TABLE 6. EARNINGS FOREGONE AND OTHER RESOURCE COSTS REPRESENTED BY COLLEGE AND UNIVERSITY EDUCATION IN THE UNITED STATES, 1900–1956, IN CURRENT PRICES*

| Year | Number of Students (Thousands) (1) | Earnings Foregone per Student (Dollars) (2) | Total Earnings Foregone (3) | School Costs (Millions of Dollars) (4) | Additional Expenditures (Millions of Dollars) (5) | Total (6) |
|---|---|---|---|---|---|---|
| 1900 | 238 | 192 | 46 | 40 | 4 | 90 |
| 1910 | 355 | 259 | 92 | 81 | 9 | 182 |
| 1920 | 598 | 626 | 374 | 184 | 37 | 595 |
| 1930 | 1,101 | 509 | 560 | 535 | 56 | 1,151 |
| 1940 | 1,494 | 537 | 802 | 742 | 80 | 1,624 |
| 1950 | 2,659 | 1,422 | 3,781 | 2,128 | 378 | 6,287 |
| 1956 | 2,996 | 1,943 | 5,281 | 3,500 | 582 | 9,903 |

* Sources:

Column 1: *Statistical Abstract of the United States, 1955,* Table 145; and the *Biennial Survey of Education in the United States, 1954–56,* chap. 2, Table 44.

Column 2: From Table 2, col. 5.

Column 3: Col. 1 multiplied by col. 2.

Column 4: From Table 4, col. 7.

Column 5: Expenditures for books, supplies, extra clothes, and travel to and from school estimated at 10 per cent of earnings foregone; thus 10 per cent of col. 3.

Column 6: Cols. 3 + 4 + 5.

about half of all costs, rising to 63 per cent in 1920 and then falling to 49 per cent in 1930 and 1940. With inflation and full employment, they then rose to 60 and 59 per cent in 1950 and 1956.

## IV. CONCLUDING OBSERVATIONS

When costs of all levels of education are aggregated, the proportion of total costs attributable to earnings foregone has clearly risen over time. This is due to the much greater importance of secondary and higher education in more recent years, a change that outweighs the decline in the foregone-earnings proportion of high-school education alone. For all levels of education together, earnings foregone were 26 per cent of total costs in 1900 and 43 per cent in 1956. Probably the actual 1900 figure should be somewhat higher than this because of foregone earnings of children in the higher grades of elementary school (ignored here), but such an adjustment would not substantially alter the picture.

Between 1900 and 1956, the total resources committed to education in the United States rose about *three and one-half times* (1) relative to consumer income in dollars and (2) relative to the gross formation of physical capital in dollars. Accordingly, if we look upon all the resources going into education as "consumption" based on consumer behavior, our estimates would not be inconsistent with the hypothesis that the demand for education has had a high income elasticity.[10]

If, however, we treat the resources entering into education as "investments" based on the behavior of people seeking investment opportunities, our estimates then are not inconsistent with the hypothesis that the rates of return to education were relatively attractive; that is, they were enough larger than the rate of return to investments in physical capital to have "induced" the implied larger rate of growth of this form of human capital.[11]

Again, it should be stressed that the underlying private and public motives that induced the people of the United States to increase so much the share of their resources going into education may have been cultural in ways that can hardly be thought of as "consumption," or they may have been policy-determined for purposes that seem remote from "investment." Even if this were true, it would not preclude the possibility that the rates of return on the resources allocated to education were large simply as a favorable by-product of whatever purposes motivated the large increases in resources entering into education. If so, the task becomes merely one of ascertaining these rates of return. If, however, consumer and investment behavior did play a substantial role in these private and public decisions, then, to this extent, economic theory will also be useful in explaining these two sets of behavior.

\* \* \*

Schultz also notes that his income data for young workers includes many with but a casual attachment to the labor force who work only a few weeks a year and who, because of their low yearly earnings, thereby give the average earnings for each age group a downward bias as a proxy measure of would-be

[10] A 1 per cent increase in real income was associated with a 3.5 per cent increase in resources spent on education, implying an income elasticity of 3.5, had other things stayed constant. Among other changes, the price of educational services rose relative to other consumer prices, offset perhaps in considerable part by improvements in the "quality" of educational services.

[11] Of course, other relevant factors may not have remained constant. For example, it seems plausible to believe that the grip of capital rationing is much less severe presently than it was during earlier years covered by this study.

full-time market earnings of the student. In fact, the data do not separate student from nonstudent earnings. Furthermore, his method of extrapolating actual weeks worked to 40, to estimate the length of the school year, in order to derive annual foregone earnings (Table 1) omits consideration of the fact that many young people work part-time, at least less time per week than students spend on school work.

Inclusion of student earnings as an offset to foregone earnings, as Schultz suggests should be done, is a questionable practice. This market work of students defrays the expenses of education but does not reduce the opportunity cost of time spent in school.

Schultz raises the question of the effect on earnings of school-age workers if all, or large numbers, had entered the labor market instead of attending school—what Bowman calls the scale effect. Although Schultz is concerned only with marginal changes and can ignore the scale effect, it is interesting to note that it works in both directions. That is, a large exodus from school would presumably lower foregone earnings and increase the difference in the lifetime earnings stream between the educated and lesser educated, both factors raising the rate of return on investment in schooling. On the other hand, a large movement toward school would raise foregone earnings of students and reduce the earnings differences after schooling, both reducing the rate of return on education. In short, the scale effect implies the path of adjustment toward equilibrium of the rate of return on education with that of alternative investments.

Schultz finds that, at least for high school students, foregone earnings have declined over the first half of this century as a share of total costs. He finds this result "surprising" in view of the great increase in manufacturing earnings, especially among the unskilled, whose incomes stand for foregone student earnings. This finding underscores the great increase in direct school costs, certainly substantially raised by the sharp rise in labor costs in educational services, but perhaps also reflected in a significant improvement in the quality of education.

### Estimating Rates of Return

Moving from estimates of school costs, or the amount of investment in education, Gary Becker, in his thorough study of the intricacies involved, estimates the return on college education. The section presented here deals only with the methods and results of these calculations for 1939 and 1949.

Becker's best estimate for 1939 is for a private return of about 14.5 percent for urban, native-born white males, with a somewhat lower rate for 1949. His method entails adjustment for mortality, taxes, growth in the differential, and student earnings. The last two warrant special attention.

# Human Capital

## by Gary Becker

### 1. MONEY RATES OF RETURN TO WHITE MALE COLLEGE GRADUATES

#### Returns in 1939

The effect of education on income could easily be determined if information were available on the income of units differing only in education, for then differences in income could be attributed solely to differences in education. These could be geographical units, as countries or states; time units, as the United States today and, say, fifty years ago; or individuals, as college and high-school graduates in the United States. Unfortunately, units differing in education also tend to differ in other factors that influence incomes. For example, higher-income geographical units also tend to have more physical capital per person, while college graduates tend to be abler than high-school graduates. In other words, the raw information has to be standardized for other factors in order to isolate the effect of education. A few attempts have been made to standardize the information on geographical units, and although interesting qualitative results have emerged, only a limited quantitative analysis has been possible.[1] I decided to exploit the extensive data available for the United States since the 1930's on the earnings and incomes of persons with different amounts of education because they seemed most capable of yielding quantitative, although admittedly rough, estimates of rates of return on education.

SOURCE Reprinted with permission from *Human Capital*, National Bureau of Economic Research, New York, 1964, pp. 70–78.

[1] One recent exception is a study by Zvi Griliches of the effect of education on agricultural output using counties as the unit of analysis (see his "The Sources of Measured Productivity Growth: United States Agriculture, 1940–60," *Journal of Political Economy*, August 1963, pp. 331–336).

| Age | Percentage (1) | Absolute (2) |
|-----|---------------|--------------|
| 23–24 | 4 | 51 |
| 25–29 | 29 | 455 |
| 30–34 | 47 | 949 |
| 35–44 | 56 | 1,449 |
| 45–54 | 59 | 1,684 |
| 55–64 | 53 | 1,386 |
| 18–19 | –108 | –557 |
| 20–21 | –95 | –805 |
| 22 | –46 | –487 |

SOURCE: Basic data from *1940 Census of Population, Educational Attainment by Economic Characteristics and Marital Status,* Bureau of the Census, Washington, 1947, Table 29, p. 148. M. Zeman estimated mean incomes at various age and education classes from the Census data (see his "A Quantitative Analysis of White-Non-White Income Differentials in the United States in 1939," unpublished Ph.D. dissertation, University of Chicago, 1955). These data were adjusted for the underreporting of professional earnings, the underreporting of wages and salaries, and unemployment.

The national data on the incomes of persons at different educational levels provided by the 1940 and 1950 Censuses can be supplemented during the 1950's with smaller surveys. Table 1 shows absolute and percentage differences in mean earnings during 1939 at various age classes between urban, native-white, male college and high-school graduates. Average earnings computed from the 1940 Census were uniformly adjusted upward by 10 per cent because of the underestimation of wages and salaries in the Census data. They were also corrected for the abnormally large unemployment in 1939 so that the data could reflect a more normal economic situation. The adjustment for underestimation raises absolute earning differentials but not percentage ones, while the adjustment for unemployment lowers percentage differentials but does not change absolute ones very much. Since only persons with at least $1 of wages or salaries and less than $50 of other income are covered in the 1940 Census, independent professionals and many other persons were excluded. In order to expand the coverage, the earnings of college graduates were considered to be a weighted average at each age of the earnings of college graduates given by the Census and of independent doctors, lawyers, and dentists given elsewhere, the weights being the number of persons in each group. Both the percentage and absolute differences in columns 1 and 2 of Table 1 are substantial and rise with age, averaging about $1,100 (in 1939 dollars) and 45 per cent, respectively, and rising from $450 and 30 per cent at about age 27 to $1,700 and 60 per cent at about age 50.

Since Table 1 gives the income gains of surviving members of different cohorts, one way to relate costs and returns would be to compare these gains with the college costs of the different cohorts. Another, and for my purposes easier, way would be to compare the costs and returns of a given cohort as it ages over time. Since these data are not directly available, the returns to different cohorts as of the moment in time have to be converted into returns to a given cohort aging over time.

The average earnings of a cohort at any age is a weighted average of the earnings of survivors and of those dying earlier. Obviously the latter earn nothing after they die, so the weighted average can be computed simply by multiplying the earnings of survivors by the fraction surviving. Accordingly, the average earnings in 1939 of different cohorts were multiplied by life table survivorship rates[2] to help convert them into earnings at different ages of a single cohort. Since the same rates were used for high-school and college graduates (although a slightly higher rate should have been used for the latter), percentage earnings differentials were unaffected while absolute ones were lowered, especially at older ages.

The secular growth in real earnings per capita would usually enable the cohort of persons graduating from high school or college in any year to earn more at each age than was earned in that year by persons who had graduated earlier. Earnings received in 1939 have to be adjusted upward, therefore, if they are to represent the earnings of cohorts graduating in 1939. Only part of the substantial rate of growth since 1939 in earnings per capita can be used in the adjustment, however, because much of the growth in earnings resulted from the increase in education itself. Moreover, earnings did not grow at the same rate in all age and education categories. Not being able to make an exhaustive study, I simply assumed that if $d(t)$ were the differential observed in 1939 between cohorts graduating from college and high school $t$ years earlier, the differential $t$ years later for cohorts who had graduated in 1939 would be $d(t) (1 + g)^t$, where $g$ is the annual rate of growth in the differential. The most plausible value for $g$ seems to be about .0125, although results are also presented for $g = 0$ and $g = .02$.[3]

Cross-sectional and cohort earnings also differ in several other respects. For example, the former are much more affected by business cycles, and, consequently, as

already mentioned, the 1939 data had to be adjusted for the depressed economic conditions at that time. An interesting difference can be found in the adjustment for income tax payments required to convert before-tax returns into private returns. In 1939 tax rates were low and so only a minor adjustment need be made to incomes received at that time. A much more substantial adjustment, however, has to be made to the incomes of cohorts graduating in 1939 because they received the bulk of their incomes in the 1940's and later, and taxes have risen substantially during these years. Accordingly, two alternative adjustments have been made: one is simply based on the 1939 tax rates, while the other utilizes the much higher rates prevailing in 1949 to approximate the effects of the different tax rates in the 1940's, 1950's, and 1960's.

### Costs in 1939

Total private costs of attending college can be considered the sum of private direct and indirect costs. The former includes tuition, fees, outlays on books and supplies, and any living expenses beyond what would be incurred when not in college. Average tuition and fees per college student in 1939 and other years can be estimated without too much trouble from data collected by the Office of Education. Books and unusual living expenses can be estimated from other surveys, notably a large national sample taken by the Education Office in 1950's. Private direct costs per student averaged about $173 in 1939, of which 65 per cent of $112 were tuition and fees.

---

[2] They should also be multiplied by labor force participation rates because the 1940 Census only includes persons with at least a dollar of earnings in 1939. Experiments on the 1950 Census data indicate, however, that this adjustment has only a slight effect on the results.

[3] According to E. Denison, national income per capita has grown at a rate of 1.7 per cent per annum from 1929 to 1957 and about 25 per cent of this was due to the growth in years of education (see his *Sources of Economic Growth in the United States*, Committee for Economic Development, Washington, 1962). His Table 33 fixes the contribution of education at more than 40 per cent, but it is clear from his derivation that half of that was due to the increase in the number of days of attendance in each school year, which should *not* be excluded from our adjustment.

Since students earn less than if they were participating full time in the labor force, the earnings foregone are an indirect cost of schooling. The amount foregone depends both on the number of hours spent at school work, and the opportunities for part-time (after school) and seasonal (summer) work. The latter determinant is quite sensitive to business conditions and the age, race, sex, etc., of students, so indirect costs vary more over time and among demographic groups than direct costs do.[4]

Indirect costs were estimated by assuming that the typical person attends college from the age of 18 to 22½ and earns one-quarter of what he could have earned. Four and a half years of college are assumed because the Census group with "16+" years of schooling appears to have that much undergraduate and postgraduate training.[5] The one-quarter assumption is based on the notion that college attendance is a full-time occupation for three-quarters of a year—vacations occupying the remaining quarter—for which notion there is direct evidence provided by several studies. In principle, the potential earnings of first-year college students should be measured by the actual earnings of otherwise equivalent persons who entered the full-time labor force after completing high school, the potential earnings of second-year students by the actual earnings of otherwise equivalent persons who entered the labor force after completing one year of college, and so on. Limitations of data necessitated the use of a simpler, but not too inaccurate, method. The potential earnings of students during the first four years of college were measured by the actual earnings of "equivalent" high-school graduates of the same age, and potential earnings during the last half year of study by the earnings of college drop-outs of the same age.

The bottom half of Table 1 shows absolute and percentage differentials from ages 18 to 22 between the net earnings of college students and high-school graduates. "Net" earnings means that direct college costs have been subtracted from the earnings of college students. The total private cost of attending college for the average urban native-white male in 1939 is roughly measured by the series of absolute differentials. Foregone earnings account for about 74 per cent of the total tuition and fees only about 17 per cent, and other direct costs the remaining 9 per cents. Therefore, if tuition and fees alone were eliminated—if colleges were made "free" in the usual meaning of this term—only a relatively small part of the private burden of attending college would be eliminated. That is to say, even at the private level "free" colleges are not really very free after all!

[4] For the purpose of estimating rates of return, it is only necessary to recognize—as every one must—that students earn less than if they were participating in the labor force. This difference in earnings need not be called a cost of education nor related to direct costs. However, foregone earnings are treated as a cost here and throughout the book, because such a treatment adds to the understanding of the economic effects of education (and other human capital). Moreover, the arguments advanced against doing so cannot withstand close scrutiny. To take one prominent example, John Vaizey, who has written extensively on the economic effects of education, in arguing against the inclusion of foregone earnings, said: ". . . for young people there is no alternative; the law forbids them to work," or ". . . if income foregone is added to education costs it must also be added to other sectors of the economy (notably housewives, mothers, unpaid sitters-in, voluntary work of all sorts) . . ." and "Analytically, too, it would be necessary to adjust the costs by some notional estimate of benefits incurred while being educated . . ." (see his The Economics of Education, Glencoe, 1962, 42–43). Now if foregone earnings are excluded because schooling is compulsory, surely direct costs have to be excluded also. If the foregone earnings of other activities are important, then, of course, they should be treated as costs too (and are in my paper A Theory of the Allocation of Time, IBM Research Paper RC-1149, March 20, 1964). Finally, that benefits are incurred while being educated is no more an argument against the inclusion of indirect costs than against the inclusion of direct costs.

[5] See P. C. Glick and H. P. Miller, "Education Level and Potential Income," American Sociological Review, June 1956, p. 311.

## Rates of Return in 1939

The monetary gain from attending college can be determined from a comparison of returns and costs. A person deciding whether or not college "pays" should discount both the streams of returns and costs in order to incorporate the basic economic fact that $1,000 promised in ten years is worth less than $1,000 available today. Discounting of future income is incorporated into the internal rate of return, which is simply a rate of discount that makes the series of absolute earnings differentials between college and high-school graduates sum to zero.[6] One could also compute the present value of the monetary gain, which is the sum of all absolute differentials *after* they have been discounted at appropriate market interest rates. . . . Both methods are used in this chapter, although greatest attention is paid to the internal rate.

Since the concern is with the gain achieved by cohorts, the data in Table 1 have to be adjusted for mortality, growth, and taxation. Note that both measures of monetary gain use absolute, not percentage, earning differentials, so any adjustment changing the former would change the estimated gain, even if the latter were not changed. Thus the adjustments for mortality and growth do not change percentage differentials, but, as shall be seen,

they do significantly alter the estimated gain. Note further that the rate of return to a cohort can be computed either from the stream of total (cohort) absolute differentials or from the mean (i.e., per capita) differentials. Likewise, the present value of the gain can be computed either from total differentials or on a per member basis from mean differentials. There has been considerable controversy over whether mean or median differentials are the more appropriate measure of the central tendency of returns (and presumably also of costs) to education. Means are clearly more appropriate when calculating *cohort* gains; perhaps medians are better for other purposes.[7]

Table 2 presents several alternative estimates of the private rate of return to the cohort of urban native-white males graduating from college in 1939. The estimates increase a little over 1 percentage point for each percentage point of increase in the secular growth in earnings, and are about 1.5 percentage points lower when the tax rates prevailing in 1949 are used in place of those in 1939. A figure of slightly over 14.5 per cent is probably the best single estimate of the rate. This figure and indeed *all* the estimates indicate a very substantial private gain to white male college graduates.

The dominance of foregone earnings and the relative unimportance of tuition

TABLE 2. Alternative estimates of rates of return to 1939 cohort of native-white male college graduates
(per cent)

| Secular Rate of Growth in Earnings (per cent) | Straight 4 Per Cent Tax Rate (1) | 1949 Actual Tax Rates (2) |
|---|---|---|
| 2 | 16.8 | 15.3 |
| 1 | 15.6 | 14.1 |
| 0 | 14.4 | 13.0 |

[6] The internal rate does not, however, necessarily equate the present values of returns and costs.
[7] Edward Renshaw prefers the median to the mean for reasons I find largely unconvincing. See his "Estimating the Returns to Education," *Review of Economics and Statistics,* August 1960, p. 322.

TABLE 3.  EARNING DIFFERENTIALS BETWEEN WHITE MALE COLLEGE AND HIGH-SCHOOL GRADUATES IN 1949 AT VARIOUS AGES

| Age | Percentage (1) | Absolute (2) |
|---|---|---|
| 23–24 | −16 | −372 |
| 25–29 | +8 | +230 |
| 30–34 | 42 | 1,440 |
| 35–44 | 86 | 3,419 |
| 45–54 | 100 | 4,759 |
| 55–64 | 85 | 4,068 |
| 18–19 | −111 | −1,073 |
| 20–21 | −95 | −1,647 |
| 22 | −59 | −1,324 |

SOURCE: *United States Census of Population: 1950, Special Reports—Education,* Bureau of the Census, Washington, 1953, Vol. IV, part 5, chapter B, Table 12.

can be vividly demonstrated with rate of return calculations. The gain from attending college would, of course, increase if any component of cost decreased. But while the complete elimination of tuition would increase the rate of return to these college graduates only by a little over 1 percentage point, the elimination of forgone earnings would almost double it. Thus, good economic reasons, as well as lack of information and motivation, may prevent poorer high-school graduates from attending even tuition-free colleges. The elimination of foregone earnings, which incidentally has never been tried on a large scale in the United States, should have a much greater effect on their incentive to go to college.

### Rates of Return in 1949

Independent estimates of the rate of return to college graduates can be based on data collected by the 1950 Census. Table 3 presents absolute and percentage differentials between the net incomes of college and high-school graduates in 1949, where net income means that direct costs have been subtracted from the earnings of college graduates at ages 18 to 22½. I tried to approximate the returns and costs of the cohorts of persons graduating from college about 1949 by adjusting these figures for mortality, growth, and taxation.

The mortality adjustment was based on rates prevailing in 1949, and income differentials were again assumed to grow at a little over 1 per cent per annum. The tax adjustment was based on the incidence of the personal income tax in 1949, although a somewhat greater adjustment would be more appropriate as taxes have risen a little since 1949. No adjustment for unemployment is necessary since 1949 was a rather normal economic year.

The private rate of return to the 1949 cohort would be 12.7 per cent if income differentials grew at 1 per cent per annum, and about 1 percentage point higher or lower if they grew at 2 per cent or not at all. Probably the best single estimate is close to 13 per cent, somewhat lower than the 14.5 per cent estimate based on the 1940 Census data. Their general agreement increases the confidence that can be placed in the statistical (as opposed to conceptual) reliability of our calculations.

Is the slight decline between 1939 and 1949 indicative of a general secular decline in the monetary gain from education? . . . I shall only consider whether the apparent decline is spurious owing to a shift in the statistical base. The 1949 data refer to the total incomes of all whites while the 1939 data refer only to the earnings of urban native whites. For obvious reasons, the inclusion of property income raises the estimated return in

1949, although probably not by very much. . . . While the direction and, a fortiori, the magnitude of the effect of the other differences is more difficult to determine,[8] they probably cannot fully explain the apparent decline during the 1940's. . . .

Using cross-sectional data as a basis for estimating future earnings differentials requires adjustment of these data for changes in the differential over time. As was discussed in the chapter on the skill differential, Becker explained how the absolute skill differential, if not the percentage, tends to widen from balanced technological improvement. In this rate of return section, Becker measures the gain in the absolute differential by the annual rate of productivity gain, not attributable to education itself, to avoid double counting.

Note that in Table 2, the rate of return rises the greater the assumed annual growth rate in the absolute differential. This follows, as was also explained above, because increases in the absolute earnings differences raise the rate of return.

Becker's treatment of student earnings follows Schultz's suggested practice in that they are considered as an offset to foregone earnings, and as such are included in the (negative) earnings difference between students and nonstudents during the college years, presented in Tables 1 and 3. This offset is measured by Becker at ¼ of what the student could have earned were he a full-time worker instead of a student-part-time worker.

At first view, this seems a perfect adjustment. If the school year is considered 39 weeks, and if the student worked 13 additional weeks during the summer, or if he chose, during the school year, he would be exerting the same total effort as the nonstudent in 52 weeks of market work. If the data on nonstudent earnings, the proxy for would-be student earnings, were not only annual, as they are, but also for an average of 52 weeks work, which they are not, then the ¼ reduction would be appropriate to estimate foregone earnings of student work. But this adjustment should be made even if the student does not work while going to school, if opportunity costs are to serve as the valuation of student time.

In fact, however, male nonstudents tend toward much less than 52 weeks of work annually. From Schultz's Table 1, the average for 18 to 19 year olds in 1949 was 32 weeks, and for 20 to 24 year olds, only the youngest of whom were of college age, the average was 40 weeks. Schultz, of course, used 40-weeks' earnings at prevailing weekly rates as his foregone earnings measure. It is not clear whether Becker used 40 weeks earnings for his unadjusted value of income foregone by college students, but the Census data are for actual earnings that certainly represented less than 52 weeks work for nonstudents.

Thus, to include student work effort as an offset to school indirect costs would underestimate the opportunity cost of school attendance, if these indirect costs are initially measured by reported annual earnings of nonstudents which represent 40 or less weeks of market work.

Omitting student earnings would raise Becker's estimate of foregone earnings to more than the 74 percent share of total costs he calculates, and would

[8] For example, rural and foreign-born whites generally have less education, lower incomes at each education level, and a lower return from additional education than urban native whites do. The first two factors would increase, the third decrease, the rate of return estimated for 1949.

stress even more strongly his observation that "'free' colleges are not really very free after all!" It also strengthens the importance of his hint that elimination of foregone earnings (perhaps through direct subsidies) which still "has not been tried on a large scale in the United States," would be a policy worth serious consideration for broader development of human resources.

In a well-known study, W. Lee Hansen calculates rates of return for all levels of education, from the first year of grade school through college. His paper, all but a small part of which is included here, begins with a discussion of his methods and assumptions in making the calculations. Little need be said in explanation of Hansen's clear exposition. But it is interesting to note that his estimate of foregone earnings is rather close to Schultz's although they use very different methods.

Schultz expands the Census reported earnings to a 40-week equivalent, while Hansen uses the reported data unadjusted for weeks worked. This would tend to make Hansen's estimates much lower than Schultz's. But Hansen uses mean values, which are much greater than the median earnings of Schultz's calculations.

# Total and Private Rates of Return to Investment in Schooling[1]

## by W. Lee Hansen

The costs of schooling and the money returns resulting from investment in schooling are currently receiving more and more attention by economists, not only because of their possible implications for economic growth, but also because they may help individuals to determine how much they should invest in the development of their own human capital. This note provides some further evidence on these two topics; it presents estimates of internal rates of return based on both total and private resource costs for various

amounts of schooling, from elementary school through college.

The fragmentary treatment of both the costs of schooling and the money returns to schooling found in much of the recent literature provided the stimulus for preparing these internal rate-of-return estimates. For example, Miller calculates lifetime income values by level of schooling.[2] Houthakker estimates, on the basis of alternative discount rates, the present value of income streams associated with different levels of schooling.[3] Shultz provides

SOURCE Reprinted with permission from *Journal of Political Economy*, Vol. 71, April 1963, pp. 128–140.

[1] This paper was completed while the author held a postdoctoral fellowship at the University of Chicago. The comments of T. W. Schultz, M. J. Bowman, L. C. Hunter, and H. L. Miller are gratefully acknowledged.
[2] Herman P. Miller, "Annual and Lifetime Income in Relation to Education: 1929–1959," *American Economic Review*, L (December, 1960), 962–86.
[3] H. S. Houthakker, "Education and Income," *Review of Economics and Statistics*, XLI (February, 1959), 24–28.

estimates of total resource costs of education by broad level of schooling,[4] and Becker and Schultz calculate for several levels of education the expected rates of return, sometimes on a total resource cost basis and at other times on a private resource cost basis.[5] Given this diversity of treatment, it is difficult to obtain an overall picture of the relationship among rates of return to different amounts of schooling or to see the nature of the differences between the rates of return as viewed by society and those viewed by individuals. Moreover, the relationship among the various methods of contrasting the economic gains from education—the lifetime income, the present value, and the rate of return comparisons—has been obscured.

It becomes important to understand what some of these relationships are when society and individuals allocate such a large portion of their resources to schooling. At the societal level, for example, we might be interested in determining whether to allocate more funds to reduce the number of dropouts from high school or to stimulate an increased flow of college graduates. As individuals, we would more likely be concerned with deciding whether to continue or to terminate our schooling, on the basis of the relative costs that will be incurred and the benefits that will accrue. To this end, the comprehensive sets of internal rates of return developed here should be useful as a first approximation in seeking answers to questions of this kind.

At the outset, it should be made clear that the measured rates of return are money rates of return; any other costs and benefits associated with schooling are ex-cluded from consideration. In addition, there are problems of measurement, many of which have not been resolved, that make the estimation of even direct money rates of return difficult. Some of these difficulties are discussed in Part I, which outlines the methods and data employed. Part II presents evidence on rates of return to total and to private resource investment in schooling. Part III contrasts three different methods of measuring the economic gains to schooling, while Part IV offers some concluding comments.

## I. ESTIMATION PROCEDURES

To estimate internal rates of return to investments in schooling, we require data on costs—total resource costs and private resource costs—for various levels of schooling as well as data on age-income patterns by each level of schooling. From these, life-cycle cost-income streams can be established that show for each level of schooling the flows of costs incurred during schooling and the subsequent flows of additional income that can be attributed to that schooling. The internal rate of return is then estimated by finding that rate of discount that equates the present value of the cost outlays with the present value of the additional income flows.

The basic source of income data is the *1950 Census of Population*,[6] which provides distributions of income for males by age and level of schooling in 1949. From these, average income figures can be calculated for each age-schooling category, as shown in Table 1. Although Houthakker had previously presented such figures, his method of estimation pro-

[4] Theodore W. Schultz, "Capital Formation by Education," *Journal of Political Economy*, LXVIII (December, 1960), 571–83.

[5] Gary S. Becker, "Underinvestment in College Education?" *American Economic Review*, L (May, 1960), 346–54; and Theodore W. Schultz, "Education as a Source of Economic Growth" (Economics of Education Research Paper, August 15, 1961) (Mimeographed), and "Education and Economic Growth," *Social Forces Influencing American Education*, ed. H. G. Richey (Chicago, 1961). It should be noted that Schultz uses a short-cut method to derive his rate of return estimates.

[6] United States Bureau of the Census, *1950 Census of Population, Special Report*, P.E. No. 5B, *Education*, Table 12.

| Age | 0 | Years of School Completed | | | | | | | |
|-----|---|---------------------------|---|---|---|---|---|---|---|
| | | Elementary School | | | High School | | College | | |
| | | 1–4 | 5–7 | 8 | 1–3 | 4 | 1–3 | 4+ |
| 14–15 | $ 610 | $ 350 | $ 365 | $ 406 | — | — | — | — |
| 16–17 | 526 | 472 | 514 | 534 | $ 429 | — | — | — |
| 18–19 | 684 | 713 | 885 | 1,069 | 941 | $ 955 | — | — |
| 20–21 | 944 | 1,009 | 1,216 | 1,535 | 1,652 | 1,744 | $1,066 | — |
| 22–24 | 1,093 | 1,227 | 1,562 | 1,931 | 2,191 | 2,363 | 1,784 | $1,926 |
| 25–34 | 1,337 | 1,603 | 2,027 | 2,540 | 2,837 | 3,246 | 3,444 | 4,122 |
| 35–44 | 1,605 | 1,842 | 2,457 | 3,029 | 3,449 | 4,055 | 5,014 | 7,085 |
| 45–54 | 1,812 | 2,073 | 2,650 | 3,247 | 3,725 | 4,689 | 5,639 | 8,116 |
| 55–64 | 2,000 | 2,045 | 2,478 | 3,010 | 3,496 | 4,548 | 5,162 | 7,655 |
| 65 or more | 1,140 | 1,189 | 1,560 | 1,898 | 2,379 | 3,155 | 3,435 | 5,421 |

SOURCE: See nn. 6 and 7.

duces a rather peculiar bias.[7] In addition, Houthakker's data show mean incomes of all males over age fourteen, whether they were receiving income or not. But to the extent that only income recipients are represented in the data shown here in Table 1, most of the males outside the labor force, either because of school attendance (younger males) or retirement (older males), are probably excluded. Exclusion of these groups seems likely to provide better estimates of the age-income profiles, particularly at their extremities.

In order to make the task of estimating the rates of return more manageable, the age-income profiles were assumed to commence at the "average" age of completion of each level of schooling.[8] For those with one to four years of schooling, the average amount of school completed was taken as two years; hence the age-income profile for this group was assumed to be-

gin at age eight. For the next group, those with five to seven years of school, six years of schooling were assumed, so that its age-income profile begins at age twelve. The other level of education groups and the ages at which their age-income profiles were assumed to begin are as follows: eight years, age fourteen; one to three years of high school, age sixteen; four years of high school, age eighteen; one to three years of college, age twenty; and four years of college, age twenty-two. In fact, however, for age groups under fourteen the age-income profiles take values of zero, because no income data are collected for these groups.[9]

Two major cost variants are used in the calculations—one for total resource costs and the other for private resource costs. The rationale and procedures for estimating total resource costs have been set forth by Schultz.[10] Total resource costs in-

[7] The mean income figures used in this study were estimated by weighting the mid-values of each income size class by the numbers of income recipients in each size class, for each age-level-of-schooling category. A value of $20,000 was used for the midvalue of the open-ended class. Houthakker used a "representative" income in his weighting, in order to take account of the skewness. However, such a procedures superimposes the skewness of the entire distribution upon each age-level-of-schooling category; this leads to serious problems, particularly at the younger age levels, where the resulting mean income values will substantially overstate the "correct" values.

[8] This is an oversimplification, but it did not seem worthwhile to deal with this in a more detailed fashion.

[9] It is unfortunate that such data are not collected since the earnings of male workers below age fourteen are assuredly not zero. Thus opportunity costs are understated to some extent.

[10] "Capital Formation by Education," op. cit.

clude (1) school costs incurred by society, that is, teachers' salaries, supplies, interest and depreciation on capital, (2) opportunity costs incurred by individuals, namely, income foregone during school attendance, and (3) incidental school-related costs incurred by individuals, for example, books and travel. Private resource costs include the same three components except that in (1) above, tuition and fees paid by individuals are substituted for society's costs which are normally defrayed through taxation.

In developing the cost figures used in these estimates, whether on a total or a private resource basis, the opportunity costs were taken directly from the age-income profiles of the alternative level of schooling being used in the calculations. For example, at age eighteen the opportunity cost for the person undertaking four years of college is the income that the high-school graduate would obtain from ages eighteen to twenty-one. This procedure made it unnecessary to rely upon indirectly estimated opportunity cost figures and yielded at the same time a more detailed set of opportunity costs by age and level of schooling.[11] In completing the estimates of per student total resource cost, school costs paid by society and school-related expenditures incurred by individuals were derived from Schultz's results.[12] In completing the estimates of private resource costs, the amount of tuition and fees paid per student was obtained from already available estimates.[13] Again, the school-related costs from

Schultz's work were used. While the latter costs have an arbitrary quality to them, they seem to be reasonable.[14] The cost figures, exclusive of opportunity costs, by age and grade are summarized in Table 2.

Lifetime cost-income streams were then constructed for each level of schooling with the help of the appropriate age-income profiles and the age-cost estimates. This was done by taking the difference between the cost-income profile for a given level of schooling and the income profile for the particular base level of schooling used in the comparison. For example, in the case of investment in four years of college, the income profile for the base group, high-school graduates, begins at age eighteen. The cost-income profile for the person who completes four years of college also begins at age eighteen; during the four years to age twenty-one it reflects both school and school-related costs and thereafter the somewhat higher income profile of the college graduate. The cost-income stream, the *difference* between these two profiles, reflects at ages eighteen to twenty-one both school and school-related costs as well as opportunity costs; at ages beyond twenty-one the difference reflects the net income stream resulting from four years of college. An additional adjustment is required to reflect the incidence of mortality; this involves adjusting the net cost-income stream downward to reflect the probabilities that at each age the costs or returns will not be incurred or received,

[11] These opportunity cost figures tend to be slightly lower, on a per student basis, than those of Schultz, which average $583 for high school and $1,369 for college, on an annual basis.

[12] *Ibid.*

[13] Average college tuition and fees amounted to $245 in 1949 (see Ernest V. Hollis, "Trends in Tuition Charges and Fees," *Higher Education*, XII [June, 1956], 70). Actually, a figure of $245 was used; this figure was estimated from data on tuition and fees collected, reported for 1949–50 in *Biennial Survey of Education, 1955–56* (Washington: Government Printing Office, 1957), chap. iv. See sources to Table 2.

[14] Schultz simply assumed that these costs were 5 per cent of income foregone at the high-school level and 10 per cent of income foregone at the college level. The absolute figures derived from Schultz's work were used in these calculations even though the income foregone figures differed somewhat.

| Age | School Level (1) | Total Resource Costs | | | Private Resource Costs | | |
|-----|------------------|-----------------------|------|------|------|------|------|
| | | School Costs (2) | Other Costs (3) | Total (4) | Tuition and Fees (5) | Other Costs (6) | Total (7) |
| 6–13 | Elementary | $201 | . . . | $201 | . . . | . . . | . . . |
| 14–17 | High School | 354 | 31 | 385 | . . . | 31 | 31 |
| 18–21 | College | 801 | 142 | 943 | 245 | 142 | 387 |

* Though these cost data are indicated as being for 1950 in Schultz, "Capital Formation by Education," op cit., they actually apply to the 1949–50 school year. Thus these data may overstate somewhat the costs of schooling relative to the income derived from that schooling.

SOURCE: col. (2), elementary school: Schultz, "Capital Formation by Education," op. cit., Table 3, col. (11), 1950 figure divided by number of elementary-school students in 1950, from Statistical Abstract, 1955, Table 152; high school: Schultz, "Capital Formation by Education," op. cit., Table 5, 1950, col. (4) divided by col. (1); college: ibid., Table 6, 1950, col. (4) divided by col. (1).

Col. (3), elementary school: assumed to be zero; high school: ibid., Table 5, 1950, col. (5) divided by col. (1); college: ibid., Table 6, 1950, col. (4) divided by col. (1).

Col. 4, sum of cols. (2) and (3).

Col. (5), elementary school and high school: assumed to be zero; college: based on average tuition and fee charges, derived from Biennial Survey of Education, 1955–56, chaps. i and iv, after adjusting veteran charges for non-tuition items (see n. 13).

Col. (6), same as col. (3).

Col. (7), sum of cols. (5) and (6).

respectively.[15] Finally, the internal rates of return must be estimated by finding that rate of discount which sets the present value of the cost stream equal to the present value of the net return stream.

When considering private rates of return, it is important to show them on both a before- and after-tax basis. Not only will all rates of return be lower after tax, but also the relative declines in the rates will differ, given the progressivity of tax rates and the positive association between income and educational levels. The differences among the before-tax and after-tax rates could be of considerable importance to individuals in the determination of their own investment planning.

To estimate the after-tax incomes and rates of return, the original income data in Table 1 were adjusted for federal income tax payments; while it probably would have been desirable to adjust for all types of taxes, this could not be done in view of the paucity of data. Subsequently, the rates of return were calculated in the same way as described for the before-tax data. The actual after-tax income figures were obtained by multiplying each income figure by the appropriate ratio of after- to before-tax income, derived from Houthakker.[16] These ratios prove to be almost identical to those that would have resulted had the marginal tax rates been applied to the distributions of income recipients in calculating after-tax income.[17]

[15] Calculated from United States Department of Health, Education, and Welfare, National Office of Vital Statistics, United States Life Tables, 1949–51 (Special Reports, Vol. XLI, No. 1 [Washington, 1954]). No attempt was made, however, to adjust for the incidence of unemployment, largely because of the difficulty of disentangling unemployment from non-labor-force status in the data, which show all males classified by the receipt or non-receipt of income rather than by labor-force status.

[16] Houthakker, op. cit., calculated from Tables 1 and 2, pp. 25–26.

[17] Several of the education-age categories were adjusted for taxes by applying the average effective tax liability by size of income group to the midpoint of the size group to determine the mean tax paid. In general, the average effective tax rate derived for an education-age category was almost identical with that calculated by Houthakker.

Returns on Investment in Education 789

As in most empirical studies the available data prove to be somewhat unlike those that we require, and so the rate of return estimates do not provide a full picture of the profitability of schooling.[18] Therefore, several features of the data and the nature of their effects on age-income profiles, and hence on rates of return, deserve mention before the results are discussed. First, since only income rather than earnings data are available, the income profiles used reflect in part receipts from other assets. On the assumption that the relative income from other assets is a positive function of the level of earnings itself, the impact of this would presumably be to raise the age-income profiles of the higher level of schooling groups. Second, certain problems of "mix" exist within the data. For example, among those with little schooling there may be heavy concentrations of certain minority groups, such as Negroes and Puerto Ricans. If they are effectively discriminated against, then the age-income profiles of the lower level of schooling groups would be depressed below their expected level. On the other hand, at higher levels of schooling the age-income profiles may be raised somewhat by reverse discrimination that favors sons, relatives, and others of higher social-economic status. Third, since those people who complete more schooling ordinarily possess greater intelligence, as measured by intelligence scores, some part of the differential income received might have accrued to them anyway. Although our present knowledge makes it difficult to separate the impact of intelligence and schooling, the observed income differences among the lower and higher levels of schooling undoubtedly overstate, and by increasing amounts, the differentials attributable to schooling.[19] Fourth, all cost elements were considered as investment even though some portions might better be regarded as consumption. To the extent that any of the cost is considered as consumption, the investment costs are overstated.[20] Fifth, all estimates rest on cross-section cost-income relationships and thereby ignore future shifts in the relationships of the cost-income streams. And finally, any number of other factors may impinge on the observed income differentials, in the form of education at home, on-the-job-training, and so forth.

While some would suggest that the presence of such problems seriously limits any conclusions concerning the empirical relationships between income and schooling, it nevertheless seems worthwhile to set forth the rate of return estimates in their crude form.[21] From them some preliminary conclusions about resource allocation can be drawn.

## II. INTERNAL RATE OF RETURN ESTIMATES

### A. The Return to Total Resource Investment

Internal rates of return to total resource investment in schooling appear in Table

Admittedly, the use of the average tax liability ignores the effects of age differences, family size, and so on, but it did not seem worthwhile to adjust for these factors, even to the limited extent that such adjustments could be attempted.

[18] The main criticisms of this whole approach have been expressed most fully and forcefully by Edward F. Renshaw, "Estimating the Returns to Education," *Review of Economics and Statistics,* XLII (August, 1960), 318–24.

[19] Becker, *op. cit.,* has made some adjustments for differences in ability, but his method of doing so is not yet available. Differences in intelligence at different levels of schooling are given in Dael Wolfe, *America's Resources of Specialized Talent* (New York: Harper & Bros., 1954), pp. 142–49.

[20] This point is discussed in T. W. Schultz, "Investment in Human Capital," *American Economic Review,* LI (March, 1961), 1–17.

[21] For another dissenting note see John Vaizey, *The Economics of Education* (London: Faber & Faber, 1962), chap. iii.

| To: | From: Age | Grade | (1) 6 1 | (2) 8 3 | (3) 12 7 | (4) 14 9 | (5) 16 11 | (6) 18 13 | (7) 20 15 |
|---|---|---|---|---|---|---|---|---|---|
| (1) | 7 | 2 | 8.9 | . . . | . . . | . . . | . . . | . . . | . . . |
| (2) | 11 | 6 | 12.0 | 14.5 | . . . | . . . | . . . | . . . | . . . |
| (3) | 13 | 8 | 15.0 | 18.5 | 29.2 | . . . | . . . | . . . | . . . |
| (4) | 15 | 10 | 13.7 | 15.9 | 16.3 | 9.5 | . . . | . . . | . . . |
| (5) | 17 | 12 | 13.6 | 15.4 | 15.3 | 11.4 | 13.7 | . . . | . . . |
| (6) | 19 | 14 | 11.3 | 12.1 | 11.1 | 8.2 | 8.2 | 5.4 | . . . |
| (7) | 21 | 16 | 12.1 | 12.7 | 12.1 | 10.5 | 10.9 | 10.2 | 15.6 |

* All rate-of-return figures are subject to some error, since the estimation to one decimal place was made by interpolation between whole percentage figures.

3. The boxed figures in the diagonal to the right show the rates of return to each successive increment of schooling and can be interpreted as "marginal" rates of return. For example, the rate of return to the first two years of elementary school is 8.9 per cent, to the next four years of elementary school 14.5 per cent and so on to the last two years of college 15.6 per cent. Although the marginals provide all of the necessary information, average rates of return to successively more years of schooling can be derived from the marginals; since the average rates are of some interest, they are also shown in the columns. For example, in column (1) we see that at age six the expected rate of return to investment in two years of elementary schooling is 8.9 per cent; the rate of return to investment in six years of elementary schooling (the weighted average of the two marginals) is 12.0 per cent, and so on to the investment in sixteen years of schooling, which yields a 12.1 per cent of return.

Several features of the configuration of rates of return deserve comment. First, the marginal rates rise over the first few years of schooling, reaching a peak with the completion of elementary schooling. This clearly suggests that rapidly increasing returns to schooling prevail over the early years and that a small initial amount of schooling, the first two years, has relatively little impact on earning power. Second, the trend in the rates is downward thereafter, though it is not smooth by any means. While the rate of return to the first two years of high school drops dramatically, it rises somewhat with the completion of high school. The rate drops once again for the first two years of college, and it then displays a significant rise with the completion of four years of college. At this point one can only speculate as to the reasons underlying these declines.

Evidence such as this on the marginal or incremental rates of return is ordinarily used in discussing resource allocation. If on the basis of these rates of return a given amount of resources were to be spent on schooling, the ranking of the marginals from high to low is as follows: Grades 7–8, 15–16, 3–6, 11–12, 9–10, 0–2, and 13–14.[22] At an alternative rate of return to society of, say, 10 per cent, investment in all grade levels except the last three would be justified. Were the alternative rate, say, 7 per

[22] It is interesting to note that most states require compulsory school attendance at least to age fourteen (in effect, to the end of Grade 8).

cent, only the last level would be excluded.

Viewing the matter in this fashion would be quite satisfactory if the rates of return declined steadily as we moved to successively higher increments of schooling, but because the marginal rates fluctuate some averaging is required. If we look at marginal rates for broader increments of schooling, for example, eight years of elementary school, four years of high school, and four years of college, then the rates of return to additional investment quite clearly decline, as shown by the respective figures: 15.0 per cent (col. [1], row [3]), 11.4 per cent (col. [4], row [5]), and 10.2 per cent (col. [6], row [7]). At an alternative rate of return of 10 per cent, investing in all levels of schooling becomes profitable. But were the original rates considered independently of each other and an alternative rate of return of 10 per cent prevailed, it would not pay to permit any new enrollments, the schooling of those people in elementary school would be terminated at Grade 8, and of those people already in high school and college, only students in their last two years of each would be allowed to graduate. To allocate investment in schooling this way would obviously reflect a very short-run view of the implied economic opportunities.

However, it might be desirable to consider some longer time horizon instead, particularly if the alternative rate of return were expected to remain reasonably constant over time. Given an alternative rate of return of, say, 10 per cent, investment through the completion of college could easily be justified for each age group currently enrolled, since every rate of return figure in the bottom row (row [7]) of Table 3 exceeds 10 per cent. Understandably, this result is no different than that obtained earlier.

On the basis of even longer-run considerations only the rate of return to investment in the schooling of new school entrants may be relevant, especially if schooling is thought of as a good to be purchased in large, indivisible quantities, for example, schooling from Grade 1 through college, or schooling from Grade 1 through high school. In this case the rates of return shown in column (1) indicate yields of 13.6 and 12.1 per cent, respectively, and suggest the obvious advantages of seeing to it that everyone completes college or high school, as the case may be. In fact, this averaging of the marginal rates makes such investment attractive at an alternative rate as high as 12 per cent.

## B. The Return to Private Resource Investment

Internal rates of return to total resource costs of schooling are of undeniable importance in assessing the efficiency with which an economy's resources are allocated, but for individuals and/or their parents the relevant rates of return are those based upon private resource costs. These private rates of return both before and after tax are shown in Tables 4 and 5, respectively; the tables are to be read in the same fashion as Table 3.

For all levels of schooling under eight years, private rates of return have no real meaning (they are infinitely large) since opportunity costs are assumed to be zero, school-related costs are negligible, and tuition and fees are not charged. Above Grade 8, however, all private rates of return before tax are higher than the total rates of return shown in Table 3, with the greatest disparities appearing at the younger ages and lower levels of schooling, where individuals pay smaller proportions of total resource costs; private rates of return after tax are also higher than total rates of return with but two exceptions. Otherwise, the general configuration in both the columns and the diagonals appears to be about the same for both total and private rates, whether

TABLE 4. INTERNAL RATES OF RETURN TO PRIVATE RESOURCE INVESTMENT IN SCHOOLING, BEFORE TAX, UNITED STATES, MALES, 1949*

| To: | From: Age | Grade | (1) 6 1 | (2) 8 3 | (3) 12 7 | (4) 14 9 | (5) 16 11 | (6) 18 13 | (7) 20 15 |
|---|---|---|---|---|---|---|---|---|---|
| (1) | 7 | 2 | † | ... | ... | ... | ... | ... | ... |
| (2) | 11 | 6 | † | † | ... | ... | ... | ... | ... |
| (3) | 13 | 8 | † | † | † | ... | ... | ... | ... |
| (4) | 15 | 10 | 28.3 | 34.6 | 25.9 | 12.7 | ... | ... | ... |
| (5) | 17 | 12 | 25.6 | 29.4 | 23.3 | 15.3 | 18.6 | ... | ... |
| (6) | 19 | 14 | 18.1 | 18.7 | 14.8 | 10.4 | 9.5 | 6.2 | ... |
| (7) | 21 | 16 | 18.2 | 18.7 | 16.2 | 12.9 | 13.0 | 11.6 | 18.7 |

* All rate-of-return figures are subject to some error, since the estimation to one decimal place had to be made by interpolation between whole percentage figures.
† This indicates an infinite rate-of-return, given the assumption that education is costless to the individual to the completion of eighth grade.

before or after tax, though the levels do differ.

When individuals and/or their parents plan an investment program in schooling, the private rates of return justify securing more schooling than do the rates of return on total resource investment. For example, the marginal rates of return to elementary, high-school, and college schooling are infinite (col. [1], row [3]), 15.3 per cent (col. [4], row [5]), and 11.6 per cent (col. [6], row [7]), respectively. Thus, investment in schooling through college is still profitable even if the private alternative rate is as high as 11.5 per cent. But, on an after-tax basis, the alternative rate of 10 per cent just permits private investment at the college level (Table 5, col. [6], row [7]).

When schooling is viewed in large blocks, a somewhat different picture emerges. If the decision-making age is

TABLE 5. INTERNAL RATES OF RETURN TO PRIVATE RESOURCE INVESTMENT IN SCHOOLING AFTER TAX, UNITED STATES, MALES, 1949*

| To: | From: Age | Grade | (1) 6 1 | (2) 8 3 | (3) 12 7 | (4) 14 9 | (5) 16 11 | (6) 18 13 | (7) 20 15 |
|---|---|---|---|---|---|---|---|---|---|
| (1) | 7 | 2 | † | ... | ... | ... | ... | ... | ... |
| (2) | 11 | 6 | † | † | ... | ... | ... | ... | ... |
| (3) | 13 | 8 | † | † | † | ... | ... | ... | ... |
| (4) | 15 | 10 | 27.9 | 33.0 | 24.8 | 12.3 | ... | ... | ... |
| (5) | 17 | 12 | 25.2 | 28.2 | 22.2 | 14.5 | 17.5 | ... | ... |
| (6) | 19 | 14 | 17.2 | 17.5 | 13.7 | 9.4 | 8.5 | 5.1 | ... |
| (7) | 21 | 16 | 17.2 | 17.3 | 14.4 | 11.5 | 11.4 | 10.1 | 16.2 |

* All rate-of-return figures are subject to some error, since the estimation to one decimal place had to be made by interpolation between whole percentage figures.
† This indicates an infinite rate of return, given the assumption of costless education to the individual through the completion of eighth grade.

fourteen and the objective is to complete schooling through college, the alternative rate of return would have to exceed 12.9 per cent (col. [4], row [7]) on a before-tax basis and 11.5 per cent on an after-tax basis for the investment to be unprofitable. If the decision-making age is six and the objective is to complete schooling through college, the alternative rate would have to exceed 18.2 per cent (col. [1], row [7]) on a before-tax basis and 17.2 per cent on an after-tax basis, for the investment to be unprofitable.

A comparison of the total rates of return with the private rates of return after tax is of interest in suggesting the extent to which distortions in the private rates caused by federal income taxes are offset by the counter-distortion of subsidized schooling. An examination of the results in Tables 3 and 5 indicates that even though income taxes do substantially reduce the levels of private rates of return, public subsidization of schooling makes the private rates of return net of tax considerably more attractive than the rate of return earned on total resource investment. Only two exceptions appear (col. [6]); these suggest that the student pays more than his own way in securing schooling at the college level. This might indicate the need for a restudy of the assessment of the costs of college against the individual, unless the possible underinvestment in college training that would be produced is regarded as acceptable in some broader sense. But these exceptions aside, the fact that private rates of return after taxes exceed the total rates of return would, in the absence of restraints on sources of private financing, probably give rise to overinvestment in schooling by individuals. However, a fuller treatment of the effects of other forms of taxation and methods of financing schooling would be required before any definitive judgment could be reached.

\* \* \*

## IV. CONCLUSION

Estimates of the internal money rate of return to both total and private resource investment in schooling have been presented to provide a more complete picture of the costs of and returns to schooling. While the rates of return to private resource investment obviously exceed those to total resource investment, we find that the rates of return to the various increments of schooling also differ and have somewhat different implications for resource allocation at both the societal and individual level. Basically, the marginal rates of return rise with more schooling up to the completion of Grade 8 and then gradually fall off to the completion of college. We also find that private rates of return after tax almost invariably exceed the total rates of return, a situation that could presumably induce private overinvestment in schooling. Finally, the rate of return provides a superior method of ranking the economic returns to investment in schooling than do the more conventional additional lifetime income or present value of additional lifetime income methods currently used.

Thus, one might conclude that the high rates of return to investment in schooling go a long way toward explaining, or justifying, this society's traditional faith in education, as well as the desire of individuals to take advantage of as much schooling as they can. But clearly we need to know much more about the relationship between income and ability, the importance of on-the-job training, the significance of education in the home, and so forth. My own suspicion is that full adjustment for these factors would have the effect of reducing the relative rates of return, especially at the higher levels of schooling.

In addition, we have barely begun to consider the possible disparity between the rate of return to total resource investment and the "social" rate of return to investment in schooling that takes additional account of those returns that are produced indirectly. Intuition as well as the little evidence available suggests that these returns may be considerable, but a full accounting of the economic value of schooling will have to await further work.[23]

Table 3 offers interesting information on the economic wisdom of continuing education. The main lesson of the table, following Hansen's use of a 10 percent return on alternative investment, is that it pays to complete a level of schooling beyond the primary level, but it is costly to drop out.

The marginal rates show this. A 12-year-old sixth-grader would realize a 29.2 percent rate from finishing grade school. His average rate would fall to 16.3 percent if he quit at 16 after two years of high school. This rate is still well above the 10 percent level, but the economic basis for further schooling rests on marginal returns. At 9.5 percent returns for the first two years of schooling, it would "pay" society if the average student quit after eighth grade than to continue on for only the first two years of high school.

Note further, that if the 12-year-old continued on through high school his average rate would fall still further, to 15.3 percent. But this would be economically beneficial to society,* since the overall, average, high school return is 11.4 percent raised above 10 percent by the high return for the last two years.

The high marginal rates for the last two years of high school (13.7 percent), and for college (15.6 percent), suggest that there are special earnings benefits from receiving a diploma or degree. If these benefits stem from the application of what Bowen calls "conspicuous production," discussed above, it is questionable whether the high returns for these terminal years actually measure the social benefit. Are graduates paid above their marginal product because they have a certificate of achievement, or are they paid their marginal product reflecting abnormal increases in productivity resulting from terminal year education? If the former, then the rate of return exaggerates society's economic gain from the years of education in question.

Table 5 shows a private, after tax, rate of return from college education of only 10.1 percent. (Note the severe economic loss from dropping out after two years of college.) This makes college education, if completed, barely worthwhile. From a different viewpoint, it indicates equilibrium in private investment decisions with the rate of return on college just about equal to the rate of return on alternative investments.

This rate is much below what Becker considers his best estimate for 1949, close to 13 percent. But Becker's rate allows for a (1 percent annual) growth in differential incomes over time, which accounts for about 1 percentage point of the difference in the two estimates. Furthermore, Becker raises the Census data by 10 percent, to account for their tendency to underestimate earnings,

* Hansen differentiates between the total resource rate and the "social" rate in that he uses the latter return to include immeasurable indirect economic returns.

[23] For an excellent analysis of some of the conceptual differences between private and social returns see Mary Jean Bowman, "Social Returns to Education," *International Social Sciences Review* (forthcoming), and Burton Weisbrod, "Education and Investment in Human Capital," *Journal of Political Economy: Supplement*, LXX (October, 1962), 106–23.

explaining an additional part of the difference in the estimate. Finally, however, Becker includes student earnings as an offset to foregone earnings—a practice that was questioned in the previous discussion—further explaining why his calculated rate was higher than Hansen's. All this suggests that the most appropriate rate would lie between Hansen's and Becker's estimates, yielding a slight economic advantage for private decisions to invest in college rather than in physical capital, at the margin.

Hansen accepts social constraints against child labor as the basis for considering private returns on primary schooling infinite. That is, direct costs are negligible and there are no foregone earnings because children cannot work. In his footnote 5, Becker holds that the same constraints that force children to attend school also force resources to be directed toward this education. This would make the opportunity cost of direct resources applied to education equal to zero, and raise the social, as well as the private, rate of return to infinity.

This confusion over correct treatment of opportunity costs does not alter the fact that rates of return are highest for the last years of any schooling level. In fact, with rates for the first two years of college, for example, so far below the rates on alternative investments, and the rates on the last two years so high, a facetious policy recommendation would be to skip the first two years. But, of course, this cannot be done since the first two years are required before the last years can be attended.

### The Option Value of Education

If the first years cannot be skipped, at least it should be recognized that their marginal rate of return understates their economic benefits in that they serve as the prerequisite for further, profitable study. The maginal rate should be raised to take this factor into account.

Just such an adjustment is made by Weisbrod in his upward correction of rates for lower levels of education to include the value of the financial option to continue to higher, and more profitable years of schooling.

# Education and Investment in Human Capital

## by Burton A. Weisbrod

### FINANCIAL OPTION RETURN

. . . Given our interest in resource allocation, we should like to know what financial return from additional education a
person can expect. I suggested above that
earnings differentials associated with edu-
cation-attainment differentials would have
to be adjusted for differences in ability,
ambition, and other variables before we
could isolate the education effects; and
that an adjustment for systematic differences between earnings and productivity
would also be required. Let us assume
that these adjustments have been made
and that we have computed the present
values of expected future earnings of an
average person with $J$ and with $K$ years
of education, *ceteris paribus;* it is my contention that this would be an erroneously
low estimate of the gross return which
may be expected from the additional education. The value of the additional education may be thought of as having two
components: ($a$) the additional earnings
resulting from completion of a given level
of education (properly discounted to the
present, of course) and ($b$) the value of
the "option" to obtain still further education and the rewards accompanying it. It
is ($b$) which I wish to elaborate upon
here.

In formula (1) below, the first term
represents the rate of return over cost for
education unit $j$, as computed in the usual
manner; it is the difference between the
present value of expected future earnings
of a person who has attained, but not exceeded, level $j$, and the present value of
expected future earnings of a person without education $j$, as a percentage of the
additional cost of obtaining $j$. This is the
rate of return as computed heretofore.

SOURCE Reprinted with permission from *Journal of Political Economy,* Vol. 70, Supplement, October
1962, pp. 106–123.

Subsequent terms in the formula measure the option value of completing $j$ and should be understood as follows: each of the $R^*$ are rates of return on incremental education $a$, computed in the manner described in the paragraph above. $R$ is the opportunity cost of expenditure on education in terms of the percentage return obtainable from the next best investment opportunity, so that $R^*â - R$ indicates any "supernormal" percentage return. $C_a =$ the marginal social cost of obtaining the incremental education $a$ (where each cost ratio, $C_a/C_j$, is a weighting factor, permitting the percentage returns on the costs of various levels of education to be added), and $P_a$ is the probability that a person who has attained level $j$ will go on to various higher levels.

$$R_j = R_j^* + (R_k^* - \overline{R})\frac{C_k}{C_j} \cdot P_k$$
$$+ (R_l^* - \overline{R})\frac{C_l}{C_j} \cdot P_l + \ldots$$
$$+ (R_z^* - \overline{R})\frac{C_z}{C_j} \cdot P_z = R_j^* \qquad (1)$$
$$+ \sum_{a/k}^{z} (R_a^* - \overline{R})\frac{C_a}{C_j} \cdot P_a .$$

Thus, for example, a decision to obtain a high-school education involves not only the likelihood of obtaining the additional earnings typically realized by a high-school graduate but also involves the value of the opportunity to pursue a college education.[1] The value of the option to obtain additional education will tend to be greater the more elementary the education. For the "highest" level of formal education, the value of the option is clearly zero,[2] except insofar as the education provides the option to pursue independent work.

The option-value approach attributes to investment in one level of schooling a portion of the additional return over cost which can be obtained from further education—specifically, that portion which is in excess of the opportunity cost rate of return. Although part of the return from college education is indeed attributed to high-school education, there is no double-counting involved. In fact, the procedure is the same as that involved in the valuation of any asset, where the decision to retain or discard it may be made at various times in the life of the asset. Consider the following case: a machine is offered for sale. The seller, anxious to make the sale, offers an inducement to the buyer in the form of a discount on the purchase of a replacement machine when the present one wears out. Analyzing the prospective buyer's current decision, we see that he is being offered a combination of (1) a machine now, and (2) a discount (or option) "ticket" for possible future use. Both may have value, and both should be considered by the prospective buyer.

Let us assume that the machine has been purchased and used, and the owner is now deciding whether he should buy a replacement. Needless to say, the rate of return expected from the prospective machine will be a function of its cost net of the discount. The profit-maximizing buyer will compare the rate of return on the net cost and compare it with the opportunity cost of capital. Thus, in a real sense, the discount ticket has entered into two decisions: to buy the original machine and to buy the replacement. But this is not equivalent to any erroneous double-counting.

[1] Research by Jacob Mincer suggests that additional schooling also provides opportunities to obtain additional on-the-job training (see his "On-the-Job Training: Costs, Returns, and Some Implications," Table 1, in this Supplement). The value of this opportunity should be included in the financial option approach developed here.

[2] Thus, for estimating the return from college or graduate education, omission of the value of the option may not be quantitatively significant. At the same time, since the return from higher education as previously estimated seems to be close to the return on business investments, recognition of the value of the option might tip the balance.

The machine discount-ticket analogy also makes clear the point that the value of the option (or discount) cannot be negative. If a greater rate of return (or discount) is available elsewhere, the value of the option merely becomes zero, as long as it need not be used. Thus, as long as a high-school graduate need not go on to college the value of the option to go on cannot be negative. It is formally conceivable, however, that a positive option value of elementary-school education could consist of a negative value for the high-school component and a larger, positive value for the college component.

Formula (1) indicates that the value of the option to pursue additional schooling depends upon (1) the probability of its being exercised and (2) the expected value if exercised. Without further information, factor 1 may be estimated by the proportion of persons completing a particular level of education who go on to a higher level. The expected value of the option if exercised, factor 2, is any excess of the return on that increment of education over the return obtainable on the best comparable alternative investment, where the latter may be assumed to equal, say, 5 per cent. Actually, the "excess" returns should be discounted back to the decision

date from the time the higher education level would begin, but to illustrate the point simply I shall disregard this, at least to begin with.

According to some recent estimates reported elsewhere, the return to the individual on total high-school costs (including foregone earnings) for white urban males in 1939[3] was approximately 14 per cent and the return on college costs for those who graduated was estimated at 9 per cent.[4] We might assume the return to be somewhat lower—say, 8 per cent—for those who did not complete their college training.[5] Then with approximately 44 per cent of high-school male graduates beginning college at 24 per cent graduating,[6] the a priori expected return on a social investment in high-school education in 1939 was, substituting in equation (1) above, 17.4 per cent, as shown in equation (2) (see bottom of following page).

To reiterate, the first term, 14, is the estimated percentage return to high school education. In subsequent terms the first element is an estimate of the return in excess of alternatives, obtainable on additional education; the second element is the total cost of the additional education as a proportion of the cost of high-school education;[7] the third element is the pro-

---

[3] T. W. Schultz, "Education and Economic Growth," *Social Forces Influencing American Education* (hereinafter cited as "Economic Growth") (Chicago: National Society for the Study of Education, 1961), chap. iii, referring to G. S. Becker's work. H. H. Villard has seriously disagreed with these estimates. See His "Discussion" of Becker's "Underinvestment in College Education?" in *American Economic Review, Proceedings,* May, 1960, pp. 375–78. See also W. L. Hansen, "Rate of Return on Human versus Non-human Investment" (draft paper, October, 1960).

[4] Schultz, "Economic Growth," p. 78.

[5] While this paper deals with education benefits; quantitative comparison of benefits with costs are made to help assess the relative magnitudes of benefits. In doing this I do not intend to imply complete satisfaction with the cost estimates. The appendix of this paper presents some of the issues involved in defining and measuring social costs.

[6] Computed from 1960 data for males of ages 25–29, in United States Bureau of the Census, *Current Population Reports: Population Characteristics, Projections of Educational Attainments in the United States, 1960–1980* (hereinafter cited as "*Educational Attainments*") (Series P-20, No. 91 [January 12, 1959, p. 8, Table 2]).

[7] Computed from data in Schultz, "Economic Growth," p. 79.

$$\underset{\substack{\text{High School}\\\text{Graduates}}}{14} + \underset{\substack{\text{College Graduates}\\(9\text{–}5)\,(2.70)\,(.24)}}{(9\text{–}5)\,(2.70)\,(.24)} + \underset{\substack{\text{Some College}\\(\text{Assumed}=2\text{ Years})\\(8\text{–}5)\,(1.35)\,(.20)}}{(8\text{–}5)\,(1.35)\,(.20)}$$

$$= 14 + 2.6 + 0.8 = 17.4 \text{ per cent} . \tag{2}$$

portion of high-school graduates who obtain the additional education. If the returns to college education were discounted back four years to the date at which high-school education was initiated, at a 5 per cent discount rate the expected return to high-school education would drop to $14 + 2.1 + 0.7 = 16.8$, instead of 17.4 per cent.

In the example above it was assumed that a decision to complete high school would be realized with certainty. Other assumptions could be fitted easily into the framework. And if knowledge existed regarding the prospective high-school student's college plans, then *average* probabilities of his continuation should not be used.

If the option value of education has been overlooked by parents as it has been by economists there would be a tendency toward underinvestment in education. If time horizons are short so that, for example, a prospective high-school student and his parents sometimes fail to consider that a few years later the child may wish he could be going on to college, there will be a systematic downward bias to the valuation of education by individuals. Even disregarding graduate education,

the option value of high-school education increased the rate of return on high-school costs from 14 to 17 per cent, considering only the "monetary" returns. For grade-school education, recognition of the value of the option to obtain additional education increases the expected 1939 return even more substantially above the previous estimate of 35 per cent[8] (see eq. [3] at foot of page).

The option turns out the be quite valuable indeed, increasing the return on elementary education from 35 to 54 per cent. It could be argued in this case that whether the return is 35 per cent or 54 per cent[9] is relatively immaterial for policy purposes, both being considerably greater than available alternatives. However, given the state of our confidence in the previously computed rates of return, it is comforting to see the estimates moved from the decision-making margin. Of course, in addition to these returns, assuming they are attributable solely to education, are the non-market returns to education, including the direct consumption value of learning and the opportunity to lead the "full life."

\* \* \*

Ignoring the fact that Weisbrod uses much higher values than Hansen for the basic rate of return for grade school education, and lower rates than either Becker or Hansen for the college graduate and the rate on alternative investments against which the returns on education are measured (all this in Equa-

| Grade-School Graduates | High-School Graduates | | College Graduates | | Some College (Assumed = 2 years) |
|---|---|---|---|---|---|
| 35 + | $(14-5)$ $(2.3)$ $(.67)$ | + | $(9-5)$ $(6.3)$ $(.16)$ | + | $(8-5)$ $(3.1)$ $(.13)$ |

$$= 35 + 13.9 + 3.8 + 1.2 = 53.9 \text{ per cent .} \tag{3}$$

[8] Again disregarding the discounting. The 35 per cent estimate is from Schultz, "Economic Growth," p. 81. Relative costs were estimated from the same source (p. 79), except that Schultz's elementary-school cost figure was doubled, since it applied to only four years of school. The proportions of children continuing on to higher education were estimated from *Educational Attainments*, p. 8.

In this paper I do not discuss any option value for college education; however, there may be a positive option value related to opportunities for graduate study and additional on-the-job training.

[9] Previous estimates of rates of return represented a discounting of costs and returns back to the beginning of that particular level of schooling; since our time bench mark is the beginning of grade school, the values of the high-school and college options should be discounted back to the beginning of grade school. Doing so, at a discount rate of 5 per cent, reduces the 54 per cent return to $35 + 9.5 + 2.1 + 0.7 = 47.3$. The return would almost certainly be larger if persons obtaining only some high-school education were considered.

tions 2 and 3), the essence of his method appears in Equation 1. The rate of return for any level of education equals the marginal rate for attaining that level over a previous lower one plus the expected net rate of return from future education that can be attained once the level in question has been reached. The size of this expected return is determined by the probability that each further education level will be reached and the net gain from each additional level measured as the rate for that level minus the rate for alternative investments. Each additional level's contribution to the corrected rate is further determined by its importance in the total investment; that is, it is weighted by its investment costs as a ratio of the costs of attaining the basic education level in question.

Weisbrod painstakingly explains why attributing the optional value of future education to the returns to a given level does not include double counting. Supporting his argument, it can be seen that including the option value of undertaking the last two years of college study in the returns of the first two years does not take part of the last years' returns and include them in those of the first years' as well. Using the values of Hansen's Table 5, if the average high school graduate decides to begin college, he should not estimate his returns on the first two years as 5.1 per cent. He should add to this amount the weighted net rate gain from the last two years, multiplied by the probability that he will complete them. If he is economically unwise enough not to take the option, then his returns from the first two years would be the unadjusted 5.1 percent. If he finishes school, then the return for the four years become 10.1 percent; the effect of the value of the option for the first two years, exercised, being subsumed in the overall return to a full college education.

An important area of application would be in the decision that many states are pondering regarding the establishment of two-year colleges. The data, at least Hansen's, indicate that in themselves these units would not yield as high returns as alternative public investments.* But if the option value of continuing education for two additional years at another college or university were included, the adjusted rate of return from the two-year unit would be raised, perhaps to a level above that on alternative investments.†

Although this review of rate of return studies reveals many uncertainties and problems of measurement and estimation, the purpose of the economic studies is clear. In the narrow sense of marginal decision making, the goal is to find whether additional education "pays," whether the direct measurable private and/or public returns to investment in education at the margin exceed the rate on "other" (physical capital) investments. In the broader sense of optimum resource allocation, comparison of the rates signals whether there is 'to much" or "too little" education, whether the capital market operates with competitive efficiency to allocate labor in various skill classifications so that differential incomes reflect the costs and normal profits on investment in acquiring skills through education and training.

* This abstracts from the gains that may accrue to graduates of these colleges over those calculated for two-years of a four-year college because of the value of a certificate or diploma in attaining better jobs through "conspicuous production." But this factor would only influence private, not social rates of return. It is assumed that the improvement in labor productivity is the same for two years of a two-year or four-year college.

† It is interesting to note that Hansen's data lead to the pessimistic conclusion that the two-year unit would "pay" only if almost all students continued on through four years.

## Related Readings

The literature on all aspects of the economics of education has expanded greatly in recent years. M. Blaug, *Economics of Education* (Pergamon Press, Oxford, 1966), presents a rich and varied annotated bibliography of almost 800 items. In his *Economics of Education I* (Penquin Books, 1968), Blaug collects many important papers on the human capital concept and cost-benefit analysis of investment in education.

Schultz's presidential address to the American Economic Association, "Investment in Human Capital" (*American Economic Review*, Vol. 51, March 1961, pp. 1–17), stimulated much of the recent research on the economic returns to education. His exchange with Harry G. Schaffer, "Investment in Human Capital: Comment" and "Reply" (by Schultz) (*American Economic Review*, Vol. 51, December 1961, pp. 1026–1039), contains a valuable discussion of the problems and purposes of studying education's economic returns.

D. S. Bridgman, "Problems in Estimating the Monetary Value of College Education," *Higher Education in the United States*, Seymour E. Harris, Ed. (Harvard University Press, 1960, pp. 180–184), and Edward F. Renshaw "Estimating the Returns to Education" (*Review of Economics and Statistics*, Vol. 42, August 1960, pp. 318–324), are well-known reviews of conceptual difficulties in the estimation process. Bridgman suggests the median may be a better measure than the mean of earnings data for estimating marginal gains to education. But Becker, n. 9, in the work included and Rudolph Blitz, "The Nation's Education Outlay"—and especially his appendix *Economics of Higher Education*, Selma Mushkin Ed., Department of Health, Education and Welfare, Washington, 1962—note that the mean is the appropriate statistic for measuring actual costs and gains from education.

Blitz derives much higher estimates than Schultz for foregone earnings for students in calculating the capital stock in education. Blitz estimates foregone earnings from direct evidence of a few local studies. He offers reasons for Schultz's low values, both in the paper included and in his "Education and Economic Growth," *Social Forces Influencing Education*, N. B. Henry Ed., University of Chicago Press, 1961, pp. 46–88. Blitz notes that Schultz's studies do not allow for the part-time nature—under 40 hours per week—of much of the earnings reported by the Census for student-age workers.

In an earlier study, Becker, "Underinvestment in College Education?" (*American Economic Review*, Vol. 50, May 1960, pp. 346–354), derives lower estimates for the rate of return on investment in college education than in the section of his book included above. In his paper, returns of about 9 percent are estimated for all college students, explaining the lower rate than for native-born white males, the group discussed above. Giora Hanoch, "An Economic Analysis of Earnings and Schooling" (*Journal of Human Resources*, Vol. 2, Summer 1967, pp. 310–329), also calculates low rates for college. Hanoch accepts Becker's method of offsetting foregone earnings by student earnings and notes that this offset about equals direct student costs.

There is an interesting "Discussion of Paper by Mary Bowman" [the paper included here], *Conference on the Economics of Education* (Macmillan, New York, 1966, pp. 689–708), especially on the differential effect of social constraints on the private and social rates of return. Edward F. Denison, *The Source of Economic Growth in the United States*, Committee for Economic Development, New York, 1962, Chapters 5–7, estimates the contribution of human capital to economic growth. Denison notes that public investments in education probably contribute more to growth than if they were not made, even if their rate of return were lower than on alternative investment, because investment in education is usually not a substitute for other investments but for consumption. But Denison does not claim that this tendency has any effect on the rate of return itself, nor on comparative returns if other investments were undertaken.

# CHAPTER 18

# The Economics of Poverty

Growing concern over poverty and the problems of the poor has been accompanied by a rapidly expanding literature, both popular and professional, on the issues involved. These writings deal with one or more of the many aspects of the problem—causes of income inequality; definition of poverty; identification of the poor; causes of poverty; methods to cure, eradicate, and alleviate poverty, and their effects on work incentives of the poor.

Poverty is both an economic and sociological condition. Economically, it is a level of income, or more precisely, spending power to include wealth as well as income, for a household below an impersonally measured subsistence level. Subsistence itself is an elusive concept, but one that certainly implies more than the economic command over goods and services to assure physical survival. In fact, however, the poverty line is determined by extrapolating the cost of an "adequate" daily diet—suggesting some variety in foods beyond minimum caloric intake for maintenance of health—to include expenses on other living items such as housing, clothes, medical care, etc. In the early 1960's, the poverty line food cost was estimated at $.70 per day per person, and on the assumption that expenses on food represented ⅓ of total costs for people at the poverty line, the much-cited poverty line income of about $60 per week and $3000 per year for a family of four was derived. Just as the food allotment represents a minimal diet, so too do the amounts allocated for other household needs yield a meager total living standard.

But this is just a basic functional economic definition of poverty. As Mollie Orshansky observes in her description of the calculations, they estimate "how much is too little" (for survival) but they do not measure "how much is enough"* (for social acceptance). This latter aspect acknowledges that poverty

---

* Mollie Orshansky, "Counting the Poor: Another Look at the Poverty Profile," *Social Security Bulletin*, Vol. 28, January 1965, pp. 3–4.

is a sociological concept reflecting a state of mind, both of the poor and the rest of the population. How low an income or spending power for those at the lower end of the economic ladder does society as a whole find acceptable? This level does not depend so much on the amount required to satisfy a little more than basic physical needs as it does on the income disparity among households.

As real income has grown over the years, the relative, and even absolute, number of poor families has declined. But at the same time the income gap between the poor and the majority of society has widened. Although the economic poverty line inches upward as the view of what constitutes an adequate diet, and consequently an adequate budget for minimal living, broadens, those concerned with the sociological aspect of poverty consider that the national problem of poverty grows more serious. To them, social well-being requires if not a narrowing of the income distribution, at least stability in the country's family economic level structure.

An extreme sociological position holds that whatever the average economic standard, those at the lowest levels, whether the bottom tenth, or third, etc., live in poverty. Tempering this thesis with the economic measurement of poverty, a more balanced viewpoint would consider both the income level and its distribution, with the budget study measure of the poverty line representing the lower limit of the poverty floor. For example, with this floor at $3000, those families with an income as high at $4000 might be considered poor, in the sociological sense, if the average family income rises to $10,000, but may be above the modified poverty level at an average income of, say, $7500.

Perhaps the widening of the income gap between the economically determined poor and society as a whole as average income has been rising contributes greatly to the growing interest in all aspects of the poverty problem. Another explanation may lie in our greater social consciousness of all phases of economic pathology; for example, as a nation we are more concerned over price increases of a given magnitude than we were twenty years ago, and a rise in the unemployment rate to, say, 6 percent, would generate as much, if not more, concern and action to remedy the situation today as arose thirty years ago with a rate some three or four times higher.

Perhaps our current preoccupation with the problem of poverty has been most stimulated by the aspects of modern poverty which differentiate it from that of the past, noted by Michael Harrington in his widely read, *The Other America*. Today, as he emphasizes, the poor are a distinct minority, hidden and isolated from the rest of society, and what is most important, centered chronically among a few specific groups—children, the aged, the unskilled, and Negroes.

## COUNTING THE POOR

In probably the best-known and most comprehensive detailed count of the poor, Mollie Orshansky, in the paper from which a large segment is included here, presents the grim data on the scope and concentration of poverty. It should be emphasized that the criterion for poverty in this study is the basic economic one. As Orshansky notes, the poverty index over the period 1959–

1966, which reflected only price changes for minimal needs, rose much less than average income, and as she hints, the widening of the poverty gap probably results in overstatement of the gains against poverty over the period. Expressed differently, use of a sociological standard to measure the poverty threshold would probably have revealed a much slighter reduction in the poor than the recorded count based on a constant real income standard of the poverty floor. But the poverty picture is dismal enough, using only the economic basis, and excluding the near poor from consideration.

Besides revealing the magnitude of poverty in our advanced economy, Tables 1 and 2 show its concentration among specific groups—those living alone,* those in large families, households headed by women, the aged, and nonwhites. The incidence of poverty is greatest for those with combinations of disadvantages; note the very high proportion of poverty among old women living alone, of large nonwhite families headed by women, etc. There are definable groups among whom almost 90 percent are poor.

* The emphasis of poverty among those living alone is evidenced by the fact that the percentage of households poor, including single units, is greater than the percentage of the population living in poverty—17.7% to 15.3%.

# The Shape of Poverty in 1966

## by Mollie Orshansky

### THE POVERTY INDEX

The index of poverty used as a reference criterion is a far from generous measure. It is the minimum income per household of a given size, composition, and farm-nonfarm status, as set by the Social Security Administration. In 1966 the Agriculture Department economy food plan, which is the core of the poverty index, provided for total food expenditures of only 75 cents a day per person (in an average four-person family). The index adds only twice this amount to cover all family living items other than food. It has not been adjusted for changes since 1959, except to allow for rising prices.[1]

Between 1959 and 1966 both the income received by consumers and the prices of what they bought continued to climb but income went up faster. Inevitably then, the poverty thresholds, adjusted only for price changes, were farther below general levels of income at the end of the period than at the outset. Median income of four-person families in 1966 was $8,340, according to the Bureau of the Census—just two and one-half times the nonfarm poverty threshold of $3,335. In 1959, by contrast, median income for four-person families was $6,070, about twice the poverty index cut-off line. In other words, the average income of four-person families had increased by 37 percent but the poverty line by only 9 percent or one-fourth as much.[2]

SOURCE Reprinted from *Social Security Bulletin,* Vol. 31, March 1968, pp. 3–32.

[1] The measure of near poverty—about one-third higher in cost—centers about the low-cost food plan.
[2] Bureau of the Census, *Current Population Reports,* Series P–60, No. 53, "Income in 1966 of Families and Persons in the United States," and No. 35, "Income of Families and Persons in the United States in 1959." See also the *Social Security Bulletin,* April 1966.

CHANGES IN POVERTY, 1959–66

In 1959, 24 percent of the Nation's households—counting as households both one-person units and families of two or more persons—had so little income as to be counted poor. Seven years later only 17.7 percent had too little money income to support the number dependent on them. What is perhaps of greater significance than the general improvement is that, as already indicated, more of the poor in 1966 were persons of limited earning capacity or those whom age, home responsibilities, race discrimination, or other factors kept out of the labor force altogether.

Children—particularly if they live in a home without a father—and old people are at a disadvantage, compared with persons aged 18–64, when it comes to earning. The number of children under age 18 being reared in poverty went down from 16.6 million in 1959 to 12.5 million in 1966, but the number near poor dipped by only 0.4 million to reach 6.6 million. All told, even in 1966, after a continued run of prosperity and steadily rising family income, one-fourth of the Nation's children were in families living in poverty or hovering just above the poverty line. [See Table 1.]

Though the poverty rate among all persons aged 18–64 or older declined by more than one-third in the 7-year period, for the aged as a group it dropped only 20 percent. Children in a family with a woman at the head were only 17 percent less likely to be poor in 1966 than in 1959; for children in a home headed by a man the risk of poverty was 40 percent lower in 1966 than it had been earlier.

As a group, persons aged 65 or older were even worse off than the youngsters. Those counted poor in 1966 numbered 5.4 million, the same number as the count of aged poor 2 years earlier, and only half a million less than the count in 1959. In that year, one-third of all aged couples were poor, and in 1966 only one-fourth

were so situated. But in 1966 the 1.2 million aged couples in poverty represented 1 in 5 of all families counted poor; in 1959 these couples had accounted for only 1 in 6 of the total. In similar fashion, the financial fate of the aged living alone was better than it once had been, but it still spelled poverty for the majority (55 percent). Moreover, compared with the situation in 1959 when aged unrelated individuals accounted for fewer than one-fifth of all households tagged poor, in 1966 every fourth household in poverty was that of an aged person living alone. Indeed, despite the overall drop in the number of poor of all ages, the number of elderly women living in solitary poverty was now 2.1 million, though it was only 1.8 million in the earlier year.

Such findings did not signify that these elderly persons as a group had less income than they used to have. It was rather that, thanks to social security and related programs, more of them had enough income to try going it alone—choosing privacy, albeit the privacy of poverty, rather than being an "other relative" in the home of their children. But despite spectacular improvement aided in large measure by increases in the number drawing OASDI benefits, and in the size of the checks, persons aged 65 or older remained the most poverty-stricken age group in the Nation.

Though the odds that households headed by women would have insufficient income were less than they used to be, the improvement was less marked than for units headed by men. In 1959, of all households counted poor, 5.4 million had a woman at the head and 8 million were headed by a man. By 1966 the number poor with a man at the head dropped 2.4 million, but the number poor and headed by a woman remained unchanged. (There was, to be sure, no telling how many were families who had been in poverty throughout the period and how many were replacing units elevated to better status or

TABLE 1.  THE POOR AND NEAR POOR, 1966: NUMBER AND PERCENT OF PERSONS IN HOUSEHOLDS BELOW SSA POVERTY LEVEL AND ABOVE THAT LEVEL BUT BELOW LOW-INCOME LEVEL, BY FAMILY STATUS AND SEX OF HEAD

[Numbers in thousands]

| Age and Family Status | All Households | | | | | With Male Head | | | | | With Female Head | | | | |
|---|---|---|---|---|---|---|---|---|---|---|---|---|---|---|---|
| | Total | Poor | | Near Poor | | Total | Poor | | Near Poor | | Total | Poor | | Near Poor | |
| | | Number | Percent | Number | Percent | | Number | Percent | Number | Percent | | Number | Percent | Number | Percent |
| All persons | 193,415 | 29,657 | 15.3 | 15,150 | 7.8 | 168,536 | 18,952 | 11.2 | 13,031 | 7.7 | 24,878 | 10,704 | 43.0 | 2,119 | 8.5 |
| Living alone [1] | 12,367 | 4,821 | 39.0 | 781 | 6.3 | 4,564 | 1,227 | 28.0 | 281 | 6.2 | 7,803 | 3,544 | 45.4 | 500 | 6.4 |
| Aged 14–21 | 690 | 378 | 54.8 | 43 | 6.2 | 280 | 141 | 50.4 | 27 | 9.6 | 409 | 237 | 57.9 | 16 | 3.9 |
| Aged 22–64 | 6,799 | 1,746 | 25.7 | 269 | 3.9 | 2,999 | 571 | 19.0 | 119 | 4.0 | 3,801 | 1,175 | 30.9 | 150 | 3.9 |
| Aged 65 and over | 4,878 | 2,697 | 55.3 | 469 | 9.6 | 1,285 | 565 | 44.0 | 135 | 10.5 | 3,593 | 2,132 | 59.3 | 334 | 9.3 |
| In families | 181,048 | 24,836 | 13.7 | 14,369 | 7.9 | 163,972 | 17,675 | 10.8 | 12,750 | 7.8 | 17,075 | 7,160 | 41.9 | 1,619 | 9.5 |
| Children under age 18 | 69,771 | 12,539 | 18.0 | 6,637 | 9.5 | 62,522 | 8,117 | 13.0 | 5,931 | 9.5 | 7,251 | 4,423 | 61.0 | 706 | 9.7 |
| Own children of head or spouse | 66,319 | 11,307 | 17.0 | 6,258 | 9.4 | 60,183 | 7,472 | 12.4 | 5,652 | 9.4 | 6,137 | 3,835 | 62.5 | 605 | 9.9 |
| Other related children | 3,452 | 1,232 | 35.7 | 379 | 11.0 | 2,339 | 645 | 27.6 | 279 | 11.9 | 1,114 | 588 | 52.8 | 101 | 9.1 |
| Under age 6 | 23,550 | 4,386 | 18.6 | 2,360 | 10.0 | 21,534 | 2,964 | 13.8 | 2,196 | 10.2 | 2,018 | 1,423 | 70.5 | 164 | 8.1 |
| Aged 6–13 | 32,303 | 5,904 | 18.3 | 3,167 | 9.8 | 28,816 | 3,767 | 13.1 | 2,829 | 9.8 | 3,487 | 2,140 | 61.4 | 338 | 9.7 |
| Aged 14–17 | 13,918 | 2,249 | 16.2 | 1,110 | 8.0 | 12,172 | 1,389 | 11.4 | 906 | 7.4 | 1,746 | 860 | 49.3 | 204 | 11.7 |
| Aged 18–54 [2] | 83,502 | 7,968 | 9.5 | 5,081 | 6.1 | 76,749 | 5,855 | 7.6 | 4,484 | 5.8 | 6,751 | 2,112 | 31.3 | 594 | 8.8 |
| Head | 34,304 | 3,748 | 10.9 | 2,177 | 6.3 | 31,043 | 2,337 | 7.5 | 1,877 | 6.0 | 3,260 | 1,411 | 43.3 | 299 | 9.2 |
| Wife | 33,202 | 2,549 | 7.7 | 1,990 | 6.0 | 33,202 | 2,549 | 7.7 | 1,990 | 6.0 | — | — | — | — | — |
| Never-married children aged 18–21 | 8,238 | 818 | 9.9 | 454 | 5.5 | 7,052 | 503 | 7.1 | 334 | 4.7 | 1,185 | 314 | 26.5 | 120 | 10.1 |
| Other relatives | 7,758 | 853 | 11.0 | 460 | 5.9 | 5,452 | 466 | 8.5 | 283 | 5.2 | 2,306 | 387 | 16.8 | 175 | 7.6 |
| Aged 55–64 | 14,716 | 1,653 | 11.2 | 854 | 5.8 | 13,487 | 1,403 | 10.4 | 762 | 5.6 | 1,230 | 251 | 20.4 | 92 | 7.5 |
| Head | 7,689 | 800 | 10.4 | 381 | 5.0 | 6,900 | 635 | 9.2 | 329 | 4.8 | 790 | 166 | 21.0 | 52 | 6.6 |
| Wife | 5,803 | 685 | 11.8 | 386 | 6.7 | 5,803 | 685 | 11.8 | 386 | 6.7 | — | — | — | — | — |
| Other relatives | 1,224 | 168 | 13.8 | 87 | 7.1 | 784 | 83 | 10.6 | 47 | 6.0 | 440 | 85 | 19.3 | 40 | 9.1 |

## TABLE 1 (Continued)

| Age and Family Status | All Households | | | | | With Male Head | | | | | With Female Head | | | | |
|---|---|---|---|---|---|---|---|---|---|---|---|---|---|---|---|
| | Total | Poor | | Near Poor | | Total | Poor | | Near Poor | | Total | Poor | | Near Poor | |
| | | Number | Per cent | Number | Per cent | | Number | Per cent | Number | Per cent | | Number | Per cent | Number | Per cent |
| Aged 65 and over | 13,059 | 2,675 | 20.5 | 1,798 | 13.8 | 11,215 | 2,300 | 20.5 | 1,572 | 14.0 | 1,844 | 375 | 20.3 | 227 | 12.3 |
| Head | 6,929 | 1,538 | 22.2 | 996 | 14.4 | 5,806 | 1,304 | 22.5 | 855 | 14.7 | 1,122 | 234 | 20.9 | 141 | 12.6 |
| Wife | 3,548 | 835 | 23.5 | 594 | 16.7 | 3,548 | 835 | 23.5 | 594 | 16.7 | — | — | — | — | — |
| Other relatives | 2,582 | 302 | 11.7 | 208 | 8.1 | 1,861 | 161 | 8.7 | 123 | 6.6 | 722 | 141 | 19.5 | 86 | 11.9 |
| Poor by own income | 2,007 | 292 | 14.5 | — | — | 1,448 | 157 | 10.8 | — | — | 559 | 135 | 24.2 | — | — |
| Not poor by own income [3] | 573 | 10 | 1.7 | — | — | 412 | 4 | 1.0 | — | — | 163 | 6 | 3.7 | — | — |

[1] Excludes children under age 14 who live with a family to no member of which they are related. Income normally not reported for persons under 14.

[2] Includes heads, wives, and other ever-married relatives under age 18.

[3] An additional 100,000 of those not poor nevertheless had income below the near poor level. Thus the total number of aged other relatives with own income below the near poor level was 2.1 million; only 0.5 million lived in a poor or near poor family.

SOURCE: Derived by the Social Security Administration from special tabulations by the Bureau of the Census from the Current Population Survey for March 1967.

disbanded as families.) Accordingly, in 1966 households headed by a woman accounted for nearly one-half of all units tagged poor rather than the two-fifths they represented in 1959. And if there were children in the home making it difficult for the mother to work, the disadvantage was especially striking.

The number of poor families with a man at the head and children under age 18 went from 3.8 million to 2.4 million in 1966. But the 1½ million poor families headed by a woman with children numbered almost as many as those poor in 1959. Thus, though the total count of children in poverty was one-fourth less than it had been 7 years earlier, the number poor in families with a woman at the head was actually one-tenth higher.

The peril of poverty for the child with several brothers and sisters remained high: The family with five or more children was still three and one-half times as likely to be poor as the family raising only one or two, and, just as in earlier years, almost one-half the poor children were in families with five or more children. The number of poor families with five or more children remained almost unchanged— 0.9 million in 1966, compared with 1.1 million in 1959—with the added disadvantage that 29 percent of them now were headed by a woman, instead of 18 percent as in 1959. What is more, the economic deprivation associated with a father's absence was more common than it used to be: from 1959 to 1966 the proportion of all children under age 18 who were in a family headed by a woman rose from 9 to 11 percent; and in parallel fashion it was 1 in 3 of all poor children in 1966 who were minus a father, not 1 in 4 as in 1959. To make matters worse, the poverty rate among children in families headed by a woman was now four and one-half times as high as in families headed by a man; in 1959 it was only three and one-third times as high. [See Table 2.]

There was other evidence that eco-nomic growth had not helped all population groups in equal measure. The non-white population generally had not fared as well as the white during the 1959–66 upswing, though by the end of the period it was making greater strides than at the beginning. To be sure, in 1966 it was 1 in 3 nonwhite families who were poor compared with 1 in 10 white families, and back in 1959 it was 1 in 2 nonwhite families and 1 in 7 white families who were poor. It is also a fact that the nonwhite made up about one-third of the Nation's poor in 1966, compared with just over one-fourth in 1959—a widening disadvantage explained only in small part by the greater population growth among the nonwhite.

The farm population, though still poorer than the nonfarm, had reduced the incidence of poverty by nearly one-half, a rate of improvement twice that registered by the nonfarm population. But with the nonfarm population growing while the farm population steadily declined, it was likely that many families had merely exchanged a farm address for a city one at which they might be even worse off than before.

Though in comparison with the situation in 1959 the poverty roster now included fewer poor families headed by a regularly employed man and more headed by men who encountered trouble finding and holding a job or by those out of the labor force altogether, the difficulty of the low-paid worker with a large family to support was growing more striking. In 1959, among families of a fully employed worker in poverty, one-half included one to three children under age 18 and 30 percent had more than three; 19 percent had none. Among the corresponding group in poverty in 1965, 37 percent had at least four children, 46 percent had from one to three, and only 16 percent had none.

It is clear that in the period since 1959, poverty, which never was a random afflic-

TABLE 2. INCIDENCE OF POVERTY AND LOW-INCOME STATUS, 1966: NUMBER AND PERCENT OF HOUSEHOLDS BELOW SSA POVERTY LEVEL AND ABOVE THAT LEVEL BUT BELOW LOW-INCOME LEVEL, BY NUMBER OF CHILDREN UNDER AGE 18 AND SEX AND COLOR OF HEAD

[Numbers in thousands]

| Type of Household | All Households | | | | | With Male Head | | | | | With Female Head | | | | |
|---|---|---|---|---|---|---|---|---|---|---|---|---|---|---|---|
| | Total | Poor Number | Poor Per-cent | Near Poor Number | Near Poor Per-cent | Total | Poor Number | Poor Per-cent | Near Poor Number | Near Poor Per-cent | Total | Poor Number | Poor Per-cent | Near Poor Number | Near Poor Per-cent |
| **All Households** | | | | | | | | | | | | | | | |
| Total | 61,291 | 10,906 | 17.7 | 4,334 | 7.1 | 48,314 | 5,552 | 11.5 | 3,341 | 6.9 | 12,977 | 5,354 | 41.3 | 993 | 7.7 |
| Unrelated individuals | 12,367 | 4,821 | 39.0 | 781 | 6.3 | 4,564 | 1,277 | 28.0 | 281 | 6.2 | 7,803 | 3,544 | 45.4 | 500 | 6.4 |
| Under age 65 | 7,489 | 2,124 | 28.4 | 312 | 4.2 | 3,279 | 712 | 21.7 | 146 | 4.5 | 4,210 | 1,412 | 33.5 | 166 | 3.9 |
| Aged 65 and over | 4,878 | 2,697 | 55.3 | 469 | 9.6 | 1,285 | 565 | 44.0 | 135 | 10.5 | 3,593 | 2,132 | 59.3 | 334 | 9.3 |
| Families | 48,924 | 6,085 | 12.4 | 3,553 | 7.3 | 43,750 | 4,275 | 9.8 | 3,060 | 7.0 | 5,174 | 1,810 | 35.0 | 493 | 9.5 |
| With no children | 20,332 | 2,204 | 10.8 | 1,436 | 7.1 | 18,118 | 1,874 | 10.3 | 1,247 | 6.9 | 2,214 | 330 | 14.9 | 189 | 8.5 |
| With children | 28,593 | 3,877 | 13.6 | 2,118 | 7.4 | 25,634 | 2,399 | 9.4 | 1,814 | 7.1 | 2,959 | 1,478 | 49.9 | 304 | 10.3 |
| 1 child | 9,081 | 843 | 9.3 | 433 | 4.8 | 8,034 | 491 | 6.1 | 331 | 4.1 | 1,047 | 352 | 33.6 | 102 | 9.7 |
| 2 children | 8,491 | 869 | 10.2 | 454 | 5.3 | 7,665 | 503 | 6.6 | 359 | 4.7 | 826 | 366 | 44.3 | 95 | 11.5 |
| 3 children | 5,416 | 694 | 12.8 | 458 | 8.5 | 4,949 | 406 | 8.2 | 411 | 8.3 | 467 | 288 | 61.7 | 47 | 10.1 |
| 4 children | 2,923 | 543 | 18.6 | 361 | 12.4 | 2,629 | 342 | 13.0 | 323 | 12.3 | 294 | 201 | 68.4 | 38 | 12.9 |
| 5 children | 1,396 | 387 | 27.7 | 206 | 14.8 | 1,262 | 281 | 22.3 | 195 | 15.5 | 134 | 106 | 79.1 | 11 | 8.2 |
| 6 or more | 1,286 | 541 | 42.1 | 206 | 16.0 | 1,095 | 376 | 34.3 | 195 | 17.8 | 191 | 165 | 86.4 | 11 | 5.7 |
| **White Households** | | | | | | | | | | | | | | | |
| Total | 54,801 | 8,402 | 15.3 | 3,644 | 6.6 | 43,826 | 4,272 | 9.7 | 2,808 | 6.4 | 10,975 | 4,130 | 37.6 | 836 | 7.6 |
| Unrelated individuals | 10,786 | 4,026 | 37.3 | 677 | 6.3 | 3,820 | 1,007 | 26.4 | 224 | 5.9 | 6,996 | 3,019 | 43.3 | 453 | 6.5 |
| Under age 65 | 6,296 | 1,626 | 25.8 | 241 | 3.8 | 2,688 | 510 | 20.1 | 110 | 4.1 | 3,608 | 1,086 | 30.1 | 131 | 3.6 |
| Aged 65 and over | 4,490 | 2,400 | 53.5 | 436 | 9.7 | 1,132 | 467 | 41.3 | 114 | 10.1 | 3,358 | 1,933 | 57.6 | 322 | 9.6 |

# TABLE 2 (Continued)

| Type of Household | All Households | | | | | With Male Head | | | | | With Female Head | | | | |
|---|---|---|---|---|---|---|---|---|---|---|---|---|---|---|---|
| | Total | Poor | | Near Poor | | Total | Poor | | Near Poor | | Total | Poor | | Near Poor | |
| | | Number | Per-cent | Number | Per-cent | | Number | Per-cent | Number | Per-cent | | Number | Per-cent | Number | Per-cent |
| Families | 44,026 | 4,373 | 9.9 | 2,967 | 6.7 | 40,006 | 3,265 | 8.2 | 2,684 | 6.5 | 4,013 | 1,111 | 27.7 | 383 | 9.5 |
| With no children | 18,759 | 1,863 | 9.9 | 1,268 | 6.8 | 16,823 | 1,607 | 9.6 | 1,111 | 6.6 | 1,936 | 256 | 13.2 | 157 | 8.1 |
| With children | 25,257 | 2,509 | 9.9 | 1,701 | 6.7 | 23,182 | 1,656 | 7.1 | 1,476 | 6.4 | 2,075 | 853 | 41.1 | 225 | 10.8 |
| 1 child | 8,164 | 616 | 7.5 | 340 | 4.2 | 7,337 | 372 | 5.1 | 258 | 3.5 | 827 | 244 | 29.5 | 82 | 9.9 |
| 2 children | 7,721 | 599 | 7.8 | 373 | 4.8 | 7,114 | 373 | 5.2 | 303 | 4.3 | 607 | 226 | 37.2 | 70 | 11.5 |
| 3 children | 4,865 | 461 | 9.5 | 394 | 8.1 | 4,533 | 278 | 6.1 | 358 | 7.9 | 332 | 183 | 55.1 | 36 | 10.8 |
| 4 children | 2,498 | 336 | 13.5 | 280 | 11.2 | 2,321 | 235 | 10.1 | 252 | 10.9 | 177 | 101 | 57.1 | 28 | 15.8 |
| 5 children | 1,125 | 217 | 19.3 | 165 | 14.7 | 1,063 | 175 | 16.5 | 159 | 15.0 | 62 | 42 | 67.7 | 6 | 9.7 |
| 6 or more | 884 | 280 | 31.7 | 149 | 16.9 | 814 | 223 | 27.4 | 146 | 17.9 | 70 | 57 | 81.4 | 3 | 4.3 |
| Total | 6,448 | 2,506 | 38.6 | 690 | 10.6 | 4,487 | 1,281 | 28.5 | 533 | 11.9 | 2,001 | 1,225 | 61.2 | 157 | 7.8 |
| Unrelated individuals | 1,584 | 796 | 50.3 | 105 | 6.6 | 744 | 270 | 36.3 | 58 | 7.8 | 840 | 526 | 62.6 | 47 | 5.6 |
| Under age 65 | 1,196 | 499 | 41.7 | 72 | 6.0 | 592 | 172 | 29.1 | 37 | 6.3 | 604 | 327 | 54.1 | 35 | 5.8 |
| Aged 65 and over | 388 | 297 | 76.5 | 33 | 8.5 | 152 | 98 | 64.5 | 21 | 13.8 | 236 | 199 | 84.3 | 12 | 5.1 |
| **Nonwhite Households** | | | | | | | | | | | | | | | |
| Families | 4,898 | 1,712 | 34.9 | 585 | 11.9 | 3,743 | 1,011 | 27.0 | 475 | 12.7 | 1,161 | 699 | 60.2 | 110 | 9.5 |
| With no children | 1,568 | 341 | 21.7 | 166 | 10.6 | 1,293 | 267 | 20.6 | 134 | 10.4 | 275 | 74 | 26.9 | 32 | 11.6 |
| With children | 3,333 | 1,371 | 41.1 | 421 | 12.6 | 2,449 | 746 | 30.5 | 341 | 13.9 | 884 | 625 | 70.7 | 80 | 9.0 |
| 1 child | 916 | 228 | 24.8 | 94 | 10.3 | 696 | 119 | 17.1 | 73 | 10.5 | 220 | 109 | 49.5 | 21 | 9.5 |
| 2 children | 770 | 270 | 35.1 | 82 | 10.6 | 551 | 130 | 23.6 | 57 | 10.3 | 219 | 140 | 63.9 | 25 | 11.4 |
| 3 children | 550 | 231 | 42.0 | 64 | 11.6 | 416 | 128 | 30.8 | 53 | 12.7 | 134 | 103 | 76.9 | 11 | 8.2 |
| 4 children | 424 | 209 | 49.3 | 82 | 19.3 | 308 | 108 | 35.1 | 72 | 23.4 | 116 | 101 | 87.1 | 10 | 8.6 |
| 5 children | 271 | 170 | 62.7 | 43 | 15.9 | 198 | 107 | 54.0 | 38 | 19.2 | 73 | 63 | 86.3 | 5 | 6.8 |
| 6 or more | 402 | 263 | 65.4 | 56 | 13.9 | 280 | 154 | 55.0 | 48 | 17.1 | 122 | 109 | 89.3 | 8 | 6.6 |

SOURCE: Derived by the Social Security Administration from special tabulations by the Bureau of the Census from the Current Population Survey for March 1967.

tion, has become even more selective, and some groups initially vulnerable are now even more so. There is still no all-embracing characterization that can encompass all the poor. Some are poor because they cannot work; others are poor even though they do. Most of the poor receive no assistance from public programs; others remain poor because they have no resources but the limited payments provided under such programs. And public programs to help the poor are in the main geared to serve those who cannot work at all or are temporarily out of a job. The man who works for a living but is not making it will normally find no avenue of aid.

\* \* \*

THE WORKING POOR

In our society it is a truism that work is the key to economic security. Yet though a job is usually necessary if one is to keep out of poverty, having ones does not guarantee it.

With all the interest in more jobs for the poor, the statistics reveal that for many it is not more jobs that are needed but better ones. In 1966, 1 in 4 of all poor families was headed by a man who had worked throughout the year. The families of these working men included 8 million persons, or one-third of all the poor who were not keeping house by themselves. To put it more directly, of the 3 million families headed by a man under age 65— leaving out families headed by an aged person or by a woman, persons who might have difficulty getting any work at all— half were "fully employed" in terms of time spent on the job. Seven out of 10 of these men were white and so presumably not subjected to discrimination in the hiring hall. Though a number of these men had large families, many had earnings so low they would have been poor with only two or three children to support. Overall, there was an average of 2.8 children un-

der age 18 per family. Indeed, in 1965— the latest year for which such details are available—of the men under age 65 heading a family in poverty despite their "full employment," three-fifths had no more than three children to support.

For many of the poor, particularly in households headed by women, it was the inability of the family breadwinner to find a job or keep one that accounted for their plight. When the family head did not work at all in 1966, 1 out of 3 families was counted poor, compared with only 1 in 17 when the family head was on a job every week in the year. But 9½ million persons were poor though they were in the family of a breadwinner who did have a job throughout 1966. To be sure, many families were poor because the head was unemployed part of the year. Families in poverty included 1 out of 4 of all those with the head looking for a job in March 1967, and 1 out of 5 of those whose family head had lost some weeks' pay in 1966 because of unemployment. Among men who were family heads and in the labor force in 1966, one-sixth of the poor had been out of work and actively seeking a job sometime during the year—an unemployment rate nearly three times that for the heads of nonpoor families. In families headed by women, the unemployment rate reported by the poor was about 12 per cent, or twice that in nonpoor families (Table 3).

All told, among poor families headed by men under age 65, 5 out of 6 of the heads worked some time in 1966, and the majority of those who didn't were disabled.

As one would expect, the kind of job held was intimately related to the risk of poverty. The most poverty-prone calling for men was farming or unskilled labor; for women workers it was domestic service. Indeed, among women family heads employed as household workers in March 1967, nearly 3 in 5 reported family income for 1966 below the poverty line. Most of

## TABLE 3. INCIDENCE OF POVERTY AMONG FAMILIES IN 1966 BY WORK EXPERIENCE AND SEX OF HEAD

| Work Experience of Head in 1966 | All Families | | | | With Male Head | | | | With Female Head | | | |
|---|---|---|---|---|---|---|---|---|---|---|---|---|
| | Total | Head Under Age 55 | Head Aged 55–64 | Head 65 or Over | Total | Under Age 55 | Aged 55–64 | 65 or Over | Total | Under Age 55 | Aged 55–64 | 65 or Over |
| **All Families (in thousands)** | | | | | | | | | | | | |
| Total¹ | 48,922 | 34,301 | 7,689 | 6,929 | 43,750 | 31,043 | 6,900 | 5,806 | 5,171 | 3,260 | 790 | 1,122 |
| Didn't work | 6,893 | 1,468 | 966 | 4,459 | 4,743 | 535 | 691 | 3,516 | 2,149 | 931 | 275 | 942 |
| Ill, disabled | 1,757 | 357 | 493 | 906 | 1,433 | 276 | 434 | 721 | 324 | 80 | 58 | 185 |
| Other | 5,136 | 1,111 | 473 | 3,553 | 3,310 | 259 | 257 | 2,795 | 1,825 | 851 | 217 | 757 |
| Worked part year | 7,805 | 5,418 | 1,353 | 1,033 | 6,615 | 4,499 | 1,168 | 948 | 1,189 | 919 | 186 | 85 |
| Unemployed | 2,858 | 2,313 | 430 | 116 | 2,626 | 2,117 | 400 | 108 | 232 | 195 | 30 | 6 |
| Other | 4,917 | 3,105 | 923 | 917 | 3,989 | 2,382 | 768 | 840 | 957 | 724 | 155 | 79 |
| Worked all year | 33,389 | 26,582 | 5,370 | 1,437 | 31,555 | 25,173 | 5,040 | 1,342 | 1,834 | 1,410 | 330 | 95 |
| **Poor Families (in thousands)** | | | | | | | | | | | | |
| Total¹ | 6,086 | 3,748 | 800 | 1,538 | 4,276 | 2,337 | 635 | 1,304 | 1,810 | 1,411 | 166 | 234 |
| Didn't work | 2,418 | 855 | 353 | 1,299 | 1,465 | 212 | 256 | 997 | 953 | 643 | 98 | 212 |
| Ill, disabled | 719 | 171 | 207 | 349 | 575 | 120 | 172 | 282 | 144 | 50 | 35 | 59 |
| Other | 1,699 | 684 | 146 | 869 | 890 | 92 | 84 | 715 | 809 | 593 | 63 | 153 |
| Worked part year | 1,653 | 1,243 | 221 | 189 | 1,132 | 777 | 180 | 175 | 521 | 466 | 41 | 14 |
| Unemployed | 573 | 467 | 76 | 31 | 471 | 372 | 69 | 29 | 102 | 93 | 7 | 1 |
| Other | 1,080 | 776 | 145 | 158 | 661 | 405 | 111 | 146 | 419 | 373 | 34 | 13 |
| Worked all year | 1,943 | 1,577 | 226 | 140 | 1,606 | 1,275 | 199 | 132 | 337 | 302 | 27 | 8 |

## TABLE 3 (Continued)

Percent of Families in Poverty

| Work Experience of Head in 1966 | All Families | | | | With Male Head | | | | With Female Head | | | |
|---|---|---|---|---|---|---|---|---|---|---|---|---|
| | Total | Head Under Age 55 | Head Aged 55–64 | Head 65 or Over | Total | Under Age 55 | Aged 55–64 | 65 or Over | Total | Under Age | Aged 55–64 | 65 or Over |
| Total [1] | 12.4 | 10.9 | 10.4 | 22.2 | 9.8 | 7.5 | 9.2 | 22.5 | 35.0 | 43.3 | 21.0 | 20.9 |
| Didn't work | 35.1 | 58.2 | 36.5 | 27.1 | 30.9 | 39.6 | 37.0 | 28.4 | 44.3 | 69.1 | 35.6 | 22.5 |
| Ill, disabled | 40.9 | 47.9 | 42.0 | 37.5 | 40.1 | 43.5 | 39.6 | 39.1 | 44.4 | 62.5 | 60.3 | 31.9 |
| Other | 33.1 | 61.6 | 30.9 | 24.5 | 26.9 | 35.5 | 32.7 | 25.6 | 44.3 | 69.7 | 29.0 | 20.2 |
| Worked part year | 21.2 | 22.9 | 16.3 | 18.3 | 17.1 | 17.3 | 15.4 | 18.5 | 43.8 | 50.7 | 22.2 | 16.5 |
| Unemployed | 20.0 | 20.2 | 17.7 | 26.7 | 17.9 | 17.6 | 17.3 | 26.9 | 44.0 | 47.7 | 23.3 | 16.7 |
| Other | 21.8 | 25.0 | 15.7 | 17.2 | 16.6 | 17.0 | 14.5 | 17.4 | 43.8 | 51.5 | 21.9 | 16.5 |
| Worked all year | 5.8 | 5.9 | 4.2 | 9.7 | 5.1 | 5.1 | 3.9 | 9.8 | 18.4 | 21.4 | 8.2 | 8.4 |

[1] Includes heads in Armed Forces in March 1967, not shown separately; work experience in 1966 but asked for such heads.

SOURCE: Derived by the Social Security Administration from special tabulations by the Bureau of the Census from the Current Population Survey for March 1967.

these women were nonwhite. Some women who go out to work achieve a better standard of living for their own family, but the families of some of the women who keep house for them are likely to remain on a substandard one.

* * *

It is somewhat heartening that the overall incidence of poverty fell significantly over the better part of a decade, from 1959 to 1966. But as Orshansky's text reports, it is very disturbing that the subgroups most susceptible to poverty are those who have experienced the least economic advance over the period, and who therefore constitute a larger and more pronounced segment of the poor. Thus, while poverty is gradually becoming a less serious problem when measured by global statistics, it is becoming relatively more serious for the particular groups at the bottom of the economic ladder.

The data on work status of the poor point out that poverty is not necessarily a result of absence of labor income, whether because of illness, age, or unemployment. The working poor constitute a significant number to the poverty count. Although the percentage of poor families with heads working full time is small, their share of the poverty population is large because of the preponderance of families with full-time working heads.

The fact that there are 9.5 million people in the 1.9 million poor households with full-time working heads, while there are 24.8 million poor in all 6.1 million poor families indicates that larger-than-average family size contributes to the economic weakness of the working poor. In any case, somewhat startling figures to people who see the easy elimination of poverty in the attainment of full employment are the data of Table 3, which show that of the 6.1 million poor families, 1.9 million, or almost one-third were headed by a full-time worker and, as Orshansky notes, in 1.5 million, exactly one-half the 3.0 million poor families headed by a male, the head works full time.

These facts on the working poor point out the low earnings of those at the bottom end of the income ladder. Furthermore, they substantiate the argument offered in an earlier chapter that if structural unemployment were to be eliminated or reduced by wage flexibility, in practice the process would be inflationary. In theory, a widening of the wage, and income, differential between those workers in short supply (high-wage workers) and those in surplus fields or areas (low-wage workers) could be achieved by a fall in wages of the latter as well as by a rise in wages of the former. But with so much poverty among low-wage, full-time workers, and with probably a large number just over the edge of the poverty barrier, the move toward full employment through the path of reduced wages for low-wage, surplus, workers would do little to alleviate the problem of poverty and might conceivably even increase the incidence of poverty. On the other hand, however, efforts to reduce the number of the working poor by pushing up their earnings levels through, say, minimum wage increases, runs the risk of raising unemployment among groups in weak labor markets.

Two general approaches to the problem of poverty can be classified as measures to prevent and measures to cure the condition. Prevention requires steps to increase the earning power of those who would otherwise be poor by raising the value of their productivity above poverty levels. Better education, training, improved health and housing, elimination of discrimination by law and hopefully by attitude, would all singly and in combination reduce the chances for poverty by increasing investment and/or fully utilizing existing capital in the potentially poor and thereby raising the odds that their earning power will put them above the poverty line.

These same measures can also be applied to eliminate poverty among the existing poor. But their effect on raising earning power takes time, and the economic problems of the poor require more immediate attention. Furthermore, although the benefits to the existing poor adults of improved productivity are obvious, the returns from investment in the older poor are necessarily that small to make it politically difficult to appropriate the investment costs to increase their productivity. At least the meager funds allocated under current retraining and older-worker programs indicate this.

### Causes of Poverty

In order to prevent poverty and thus eliminate it in the long run, it is extremely important to know something about the relative importance of various factors accounting for poverty. Using a regression equation, Lester Thurow has isolated the importance of seven variables that account for poverty; he also makes some suggestions for the relative importance of the kinds of things that must be done to reduce poverty.

# The Causes of Poverty

## by Lester C. Thurow

From 1947 to 1963 the percentage of families with incomes of less than $3000 fell from 31.4 per cent to 18.5 per cent (in 1963 dollars).[1] Acceleration of this decline requires an analysis of the different factors which contribute to the incidence of poverty. Since many of the possible explanations are interrelated, both their qualitative and quantitative importance are difficult to determine from descriptive classifications of those living in poverty.

\* \* \*

Since the explanatory variables used in the poverty model are not completely independent of each other and since many other variables are closely related to those

actually used in the model, principal component analysis is used to isolate the independent dimensions which are present among the various explanatory factors. This technique allows a further reduction in the number of factors necessary to explain the incidence of poverty, identifies the basic dimensions which are present, and permits a ranking of their relative importance.

### THE POVERTY MODEL

The independent variables used in the model are: (1) the percentage of families on farms, (2) the percentage of families

SOURCE Reprinted with permission from *Quarterly Journal of Economics*, Vol. 81, February 1967, pp. 39–57.

[1] This paper accepts but does not attempt to defend the use of the $3000 poverty line. Data availability limits the usefulness of more sophisticated definitions on a state-by-state basis. While only families are considered in this paper, the same techniques could be used for unrelated individuals.
All of the data in the paper came from the following sources: U.S. Department of Commerce, Bureau of the Census, *Current Population Reports*, Series P–60 and Series P–50; and *1960 Census of Population, Characteristics of the Population*, Vol. 1, Part 1, *U.S. Summary*.

headed by a Negro,[2] (3) the percentage of families with no one in the labor force, (4) the education of the family head, (5) the percentage of the population working full time, (6) the industrial structure of the state, and (7) a dummy variable necessary to correct for the particular circumstances of Alaska and Hawaii. The model for 1960 is specified by the following equation:

(1)
$$P = a + bF + cN + dL + eE - fW - gI - hD + u$$

where $P$ = percentage of families in poverty (income less than $3000),

$F$ = percentage of families living on farms;

$N$ = percentage of families headed by a nonwhite,

$L$ = percentage of families with no one in the labor force,

$E$ = percentage of family heads with less than eight years of school completed,

$W$ = percentage of population fourteen years old and above who worked 50–52 weeks per year,

$I$ = an index of the industrial structure of the state,[3]

$D$ = dummy variable for Alaska and Hawaii,

$u$ = error term.

In this equation the incidence of poverty is explained without having explicit recourse to state median incomes or wage levels. Differences in median incomes explain õver 90 per cent of the variance in the incidence of poverty by state, but median incomes and poverty are partially measuring the same phenomenon. To explain poverty by median incomes is to introduce a near tautology. The two variables undoubtedly move together and could be used in forecasting, but this is due to the fact that the same causes are influencing the behavior of both.[4] While equation (1) is an attempt to explain poverty, the same variables could equally well be used to explain median incomes (though the parameters would differ). The poverty model is designed to determine some of the factors influencing both poverty and median incomes.

Although the poverty model partially escapes from the problems of relating poverty and median incomes, the escape is not complete by any means. The industrial structure (farming is also part of the complete industrial structure) and the number of full-time workers both have a very direct connection with median incomes since they are two of the component elements that go into determining a state's median income. What the model does avoid is having to use the observed differences in state wage levels within a particular industry. This is significant, since wage scales in most industries have a range of 2 to 1 from the highest wage state to the lowest wage state, but this procedure does not eliminate the problem. The model uses explanatory variables more basic than median incomes, but it

---

[2] All data in this paper actually refer to the category which is officially called nonwhite. Since this group is 92 per cent Negro, the text will use Negro and nonwhite interchangeably.

[3] The index is defined as follows:

$$I = \sum_{i=1}^{n} X_i W_i$$

where $X_i$ = percentage of the state's labor force in industry $i$,

$W_i$ = the ratio of the U.S. median income in industry $i$ to the general U.S. median income. This index measures the prevalence of high-wage industries in the state.

[4] Gallaway has shown that changes in poverty are strongly related to changes in median family incomes over time. In his simplest formulation a $100 increase in real median family incomes reduces poverty by about 0.5 percentage points. L. E. Gallaway, "The Foundations of the 'War on Poverty'," *American Economic Review*, LV (Mar. 1965), 127.

has not answered the question as to why some regions have a poor industrial structure and few full-time jobs. Ideally, these factors should be represented in the model.[5]

Given our current theoretical and empirical knowledge of poverty, equation (1) cannot be considered a structural model since causation presumably does not move solely from independent to dependent variables. Low education levels and a poor industrial structure lead to a high incidence of poverty, but poverty also leads to low education levels and to a poor industrial structure. Eliminating this circle is difficult, both conceptually and from a policy standpoint.

Using equation (1) in a weighted regression gives the following results:[6]

(A)
$$P = 96.5125 + .2978\ F + .1133\ N + .5410\ L$$
$$(23.1516)\ (.0978)\ (.0544)\ (.1677)$$
$$** \qquad ** \qquad * \qquad **$$
$$+ .4345\ E - .5368\ W - .7600\ I - 10.3777\ D$$
$$(.0480)\ (.1117)\ (.1978)\ (4.8210)$$
$$** \qquad ** \qquad ** \qquad **$$

$*$ = significant at 5 per cent level
$**$ = significant at 1 per cent level
$$d.f. = 43$$
$$S_c = 2.3$$
$$\bar{R}^2 = .98$$

The poverty regression indicates that most of the variance in the incidence of poverty from state to state can be explained in terms of these seven variables (see Table 1). All, but one of the explanatory variables is significant at the 1 per cent level and it is significant at the 5 per cent level. All of the coefficients have the signs that would be expected theoretically.

While regression (A) gives impressive cross-sectional results, these results need to be tempered with the knowledge that the various explanatory variables are so closely related to each other that a wide variety of variables could be used to do an equally good job of explaining poverty. Thus the variables in the poverty model need to be interpreted with caution since they may be serving as proxies for a set of related variables.

FARMERS

Part of the significance and size of the coefficient of farmers in the poverty model (see regression A) occurs because the $3000 poverty line does not allow for income in kind, but adjusting for this problem does not eliminate the importance of farm poverty. If the average farmer had $500 worth of income in kind, the incidence of poverty among farm families would have fallen only from 47.6 per cent to 41.2 per cent in 1963.

\* \* \*

The positive coefficient for farmers in the poverty model indicates that reducing the number of farmers and thus the amount of farm poverty does not result in an equivalent increase in urban poverty. Reducing rural poverty by moving people into urban jobs reduces the general level of poverty as well as rural poverty.

FAMILIES WITH NO ONE
IN THE LABOR FORCE

Since 70 per cent of the 4.8 million families with no one in the labor force in

---

[5] Probably the factors that are missing in the equation are those factors which determine location decisions after adjustments have been made for the quality of the human labor force (education, etc.). If locational factors were known, they could probably be substituted for the industrial index of a region.

[6] A regression using equation (1) needs to be weighted by the population of each state since the dependent variable and most of the independent variables are in percentage terms. Since a large state provides more of the total number of families living in poverty, it needs to have a larger weight in the regression.

The large intercept term is a scaling factor in the weighted regression. It does not indicate anything about the incidence of poverty.

TABLE 1. RANGE OF DATA USED IN POVERTY REGRESSION

(Percentages)

|  | United States | High | Low |
|---|---|---|---|
| Percentage of families living on farms | 7.4 | 31.3 | 0.0 |
| Percentage of families headed by a nonwhite | 9.4 | 64.2 | 0.1 |
| Percentage of families with no one in the labor force | 10.7 | 24.7 | 7.5 |
| Percentage of family heads with 0–7 years of school completed | 21.9 | 45.0 | 8.0 |
| Percentage of population 14 and above who worked 50–52 weeks per year | 34.8 | 47.4 | 28.2 |
| Index of industrial structure | 98.9 | 103.1 | 83.9 |
| Incidence of poverty | 21.4 | 51.6 | 9.8 |

SOURCE: U.S. Census, 1960

1960 were accounted for by families headed by females or by persons over sixty-four years of age, these two variables were used as substitutes for the percentage of families with no one in the labor force in the poverty model (equation 1), but they proved to be poor substitutes, that is of lesser statistical significance. Other factors such as job opportunities, played an important role in bringing individuals into the labor force.

The importance of job opportunities can be seen both over time and across states. After accounting for demographic factors, a one percentage point rise in the number of full-time workers lowers the percentage of families with no one in the labor force by 0.4 percentage points across states, and a one percentage point decline in unemployment reduces the number of families with no earner by by 0.2 percentage points over time.[7]

* * *

While the coefficient of the percentage of families outside of the labor force (0.54) is very large in the poverty model (Regression A), both time series and cross-sectional results indicate that a major proportion of the families headed by females or by persons over age sixty-four are unable to benefit directly from general economic progress, though they are able to benefit from rising pensions and welfare payments made possible by economic growth. The same point is emphasized by the rising importance of this group in the total incidence of poverty. From 1950 to 1963, the proportion of poverty-stricken families accounted for by those with no one in the labor force rose from 29.3 per cent to 48.9 per cent. The number of families permanently outside of the labor force could be reduced by special training programs and by tailoring jobs to their specific capabilities, but many still could not or should not be in the labor force. For example, from society's point of view it is not at all obvious that mothers with young children should

[7] Two different economic variables and two slightly different dependent variables have to be used since the percentage of full-time workers and the percentage of families with no one in the labor force are not available annually for the full postwar period. The percentage of families with no one in the labor force differs from the percentage of families with no earner since the labor force figure refers to a survey week while the earner figure refers to the whole year.

have jobs or that older workers should be forced to work in their old age.

All of these factors indicate that if the United States is serious about eliminating poverty, and not just reducing it, a program of income redistribution will have to become a central part of the attack on poverty among those now outside of the labor force.

## EDUCATION

If the coefficient of education in the poverty model (Regression A) is correct, improvements in education are one of the most effective ways of eliminating poverty. According to the most optimistic projections of the Census Bureau, the percentage of family heads with less than an eighth-grade education will fall from 21.9 per cent in 1960 to 15.9 per cent in 1970 and to 11.1 per cent in 1980. This suggests that education alone will reduce the incidence of poverty to 18.8 per cent in 1970 and to 16.8 per cent in 1980, if the economy is able to generate enough capital to equip a more highly educated labor force.

Accelerating the decline of poverty by improving education levels will be difficult, however, since low educational attainments are concentrated among older workers. Reducing high-school dropouts might be an excellent investment in the war on poverty, but this program will not have a big impact on the number of poorly educated family heads in the short run. Any dramatic additional reduction in the number of poorly educated workers will depend on the establishment of efficient adult education programs.

While the largest reductions in poverty would occur by improving the lower end of the educational spectrum, the percentage of family heads with less than an eighth-grade education should be partially regarded as a proxy for all levels of education.[8] Since the incidence of poverty progressively falls as education rises (see Table 2), improvements in the entire structure of education should be important in eliminating poverty.

## FULL-TIME EMPLOYMENT

State unemployment rates were substituted for the percentage of the population aged fourteen and above who worked 50–52 weeks per year in the poverty model (equation 1), but proved to be statistically insignificant with regression coefficients close to zero. Many of those living in poverty are not unemployed, but are work-

TABLE 2.   EDUCATION AND POVERTY

(Percentages)

| Education of Head of Family | | Incidence of Poverty in 1963 |
|---|---|---|
| Elementary: | less than 8 years | 43.9 |
| | 8 years | 25.1 |
| High School: | 1 to 3 years | 17.9 |
| | 4 years | 10.1 |
| College: | 1 to 3 years | 9.3 |
| | 4 years or more | 4.7 |

SOURCE: Bureau of Census, Low Income Families, Series P-60, No. 65, 1964.

[8] The median number of school years completed was substituted for the percentage of family heads with less than an eighth-grade education, but proved to be a much less effective variable. Other more complex variables (such as the percentage of family heads with less than an eighth-grade education minus those with a college education) were just as effective but were not included since they did not improve on the results of the simpler index in the poverty regression.

ing on part-time jobs or are not in the labor force. In 1963 families with an unemployed head accounted for 4.5 per cent of those in poverty, but families with a head employed part time accounted for 23.1 per cent and families without a head in the labor force accounted for 48.9 per cent. Since the percentage of full-time workers takes into account the number of unemployed workers, the number of part-time workers, and the labor force participation rates of the region, it is a much broader measure of the employment characteristics of a labor market than the unemployment rate and consequently a better explanatory factor.

In the poverty regression, the coefficient for full-time workers is large (0.54), but rising productivity leading to higher wages also means that full-time work is becoming increasingly effective as a means of escaping poverty. The incidence of poverty among families with a head employed full time dropped from 12.2 per cent in 1956 to 6.9 per cent in 1963 (1963 dollars).

While the proportion of full-time workers is a better explanatory variable of the incidence of poverty than state unemployment rates, the same economic factors influence both. (The simple correlation between these two variables is 0.81.) In the five states with the lowest unemployment rates in 1960, the average percentage of the population who were full-time workers was 9.5 percentage points higher than in the five states with the highest unemployment rates. Over time the same relationship appears, but changes in the age-sex composition of the labor force also have to be considered. Increases in female participation rates increase the proportion of full-time workers in the population, even if they decrease the proportion of full-time workers in the labor force, while increases in the teenage population decrease the proportion of full-time workers.

* * *

## NONWHITES

The coefficient for the percentage of families headed by a nonwhite is relatively small in the poverty model (see regression A). If this variable were the only factor in the equation which was responsible for Negro poverty, it should account for 4.3 percentage points of the total incidence of poverty; yet it actually accounts for only 1.0 percentage points. Since many of the other regression coefficients are also important determinants of Negro poverty, the coefficient for Negroes primarily represents the sheer handicap of being a Negro. Negroes are poor in part because they suffer from a lack of equal opportunities, but they are also poor since they have low education levels, are more apt to be outside of the labor force, and are crowded into part-time jobs and into the lowest occupations. Consequently, the coefficients of the other variables in the regressions include many of the long-run effects of discrimination that would have to be eliminated before Negroes achieve true equality.

The hypothesis that the different variables in the poverty regression have a homogenous effect across race as well as across states could be tested by calculating the same poverty regression with data for Negroes and then for whites. If the regression coefficients were the same, the hypothesis would be substantiated. Lacking this test because the data are not available, an alternative is to insert national data for Negroes and whites into the poverty regression (regression A) and see how the actual and predicted incidences of poverty differ. The actual and predicted values could be similar due to offsetting errors among the different explanatory factors, but agreement would create a presumption that the effects were similar. Most of the explanatory variables have very different values for Negroes and whites (see Table 3), but the equation does a very good job of projecting the incidence of both Negro and white poverty. The projected and actual rates are identical for whites and differ by only 0.1 percentage points for Negroes (48.0 per cent versus 47.9 per cent), despite the fact that the incidence of Negro poverty is more than twice as high as that for whites. Both qualitatively and quantitatively the same variables seem to explain Negro and white poverty. Most of the difference between the incidence of white and Negro poverty is explained by the handicaps of being a Negro and low education levels (see Table 3).

\* \* \*

## IMPLICATIONS

The variables used in the poverty regression are essentially the standard economic factors for explaining why particular workers have low marginal produc-

tivities. The variables can be interpreted as proxies for the amount of capital per worker (farmers and the industrial structure), the amount of human investment per worker (education and outside of the labor force), and the adequacy of government policies in translating potential productivity into actual productivity by fully utilizing the available human and capital resources (full-time work and outside of the labor force). The real productivity from these factors is distorted by subjective evaluations of productivity which interfere with market adjustments (discrimination against Negroes).

Both the regression and principal component analysis reveal that the incidence of poverty can be explained with the use of very few general explanatory variables. These are basically the same variables that have been selected on the basis of a priori knowledge and descriptive classifications

TABLE 3.  POVERTY REGRESSION FOR WHITES AND NONWHITES

(Percentages)

|  | Data | | Contributions to Difference between White and Nonwhite Poverty |
|---|---|---|---|
|  | Whites | Nonwhites | Nonwhite minus White |
| Percentage of families living on farms | 7.5 | 6.6 | −0.3 |
| Percentage of families headed by nonwhite | 0.0 | 100.0 | 11.3 |
| Percentage of families with no one in the labor force | 10.5 | 12.9 | 1.3 |
| Percentage of family heads with 0–7 years of school completed | 19.2 | 48.5 | 12.7 |
| Percentage of population 14 and above who worked 50–52 weeks per year | 35.5 | 28.9 | 3.6 |
| Index of industrial structure[1] | 98.8 | 97.8 | 0.8 |
| Incidence of poverty— Projected Actual | 18.6 18.6 | 48.0 47.9 | 29.4 |

SOURCE: *U.S. Census, 1960.*

[1] The index of industrial structure is calculated by weighting the index of each state by the number of white and nonwhite families living in that state.

of families living in poverty. The numerical values of the parameters from the poverty equation are also comforting. They indicate that investment in human resources, equal rights for Negroes, and the push towards full employment can potentially make significant reductions in the number of families living in poverty.

Potential reductions do not become actual reductions, however, unless deliberate policy actions can effect the explanatory variables and through them the incidence of poverty. Some of the factors are relatively easily affected. The unemployment rate was 5.6 per cent in 1960, but if a more expansionary fiscal policy had resulted in a 4.6 per cent rate of unemployment and if the parameters from the poverty model are accurate, the incidence of poverty would have been approximately 0.7 percentage points lower through the effects of a tighter labor market on the number of farmers, the number of families outside the labor force, the number of full-time workers, and the industrial structure. A 3.6 per cent unemployment rate would have reduced poverty by 1.4 percentage points.

Other variables such as education and discrimination have large potential effects, but the cost of changing these variables has not yet been determined. Preschool classes which result in fewer school dropouts will not increase education levels among family heads for fifteen years. Adult education programs will have to convince all individuals that they do need to learn and can successfully do so. Both of these things may take time. This paper indicates that many of the expected results and benefits do occur, but it does not attempt to determine whether government programs can effect these variables or at what cost.

Eliminating poverty by accelerating the rate of growth of family income will depend on the ability of the economy to accelerate the growth of productivity and to utilize fully the available labor and capital resources. This is true for both Negroes and whites. After full employment is reached, an accelerated growth of productivity will not eliminate the gap between white and Negro incomes (though it will make training programs and the elimination of discrimination easier and more effective), but this fact would seem to be no reason for sacrificing the large (and equal) gains that would accrue to both whites and Negroes from a faster rate of growth.

All but one of the seven independent variables used by Thurow to explain the percentage of families in poverty are statistically significant at the one percent level; the one, percentage of families headed by nonwhites, is significant at the five percent level. The results of Thurow's analysis indicate that poverty can be explained mainly by: (1) the quality of the labor force "as viewed through discriminatory eyes," (2) the presence or absence of farming and often low-income industry in the economy, and (3) labor force participation. Improvement in the quality of the work force could come through education and training, but, as Thurow emphasizes, education, although one of the most effective ways of eliminating poverty, cannot apply uniformly to all groups in the economy because "low educational attainments are concentrated among older workers." It therefore will be necessary to improve the availability of adult education as well as reduce high school dropouts. Efforts therefore must be made to improve the quality of education and to eliminate some of the differences in the quality of education available to ghetto and farm youths in many areas. However, statistics on levels of educational attainment do not reflect the differences in educational achievement that has been validated by a number of studies. (See *Equality of Educational Opportunity*, U.S. Office of Education 1966.)

The quality of industry is related to the qualifications of the labor force available. Higher wage industry therefore can be generated by manpower and education programs that upgrade the work force. Poverty also can be reduced by making it possible for people to move from farm to nonfarm occupations. However, since poverty also can be reduced by increasing labor force participation rates, some people would improve their conditions by getting even low-income jobs in such marginal industries as farming or low-wage manufacturing industries. Of course, whether efforts should be made to get people to take marginal jobs depends on the ages, motivations, and levels of education of the people involved. Younger, better-educated people could benefit more by mobility programs to upgrade their occupations, but older people might wish to remain in farming rather than accept marginal nonfarm employment. The programs adopted must therefore be geared to the characteristics of the people they are supposed to help.

As Thurow points out, poverty also can be reduced by measures to maintain full employment, which not only facilitate upgrading of those already in the workforce, but increases labor force participation; ". . . a one percentage point rise in the number of full-time workers lowers the percentage of families with no one in the labor force by 0.4 percentage points across states, and a one percentage point decline in unemployment reduces the number of families with no earner by 0.2 percentage points over time."

At first glance, it is perhaps surprising that the race variable accounts for only one percentage point of the total incidence of poverty. However, as Thurow emphasizes, Negroes suffer lower incomes not only because they are black but also because they suffer all of the disadvantages reflected in his other independent variables. In some cases it becomes impossible to extract the influence of the race factor from these other variables. Education, for example, reflects the impact of segregation which causes Negroes to have inferior housing, limited job opportunities, and low incomes. Poverty among Negroes can be reduced and their general economic level upgraded, by effective education, manpower and training, welfare, and economic (full employment and growth to create adequate job opportunities) and antidiscrimination programs.

The kind of analysis undertaken by Thurow provides some insight into the causes of poverty by quantifying the relationships involved. But, as Thurow emphasizes, it has certain technical and data deficiencies. It is unfortunate, for example, that he and other researchers must use obsolete data or must use substitutes for significant variables because direct data on those variables is not available. Moreover, as he emphasizes, his equation is not a structural model because it cannot trace the flow of causation from independent to dependent variables. Nevertheless, it is possible to establish this kind of causation through logic; analyses of the type undertaken by Thurow thus help to establish functional relationships between variables as well as to quantify the relative importance of those relationships.

While Thurow's analysis of the underlying causes of poverty may lead to policy recommendations for corrections and prevention, until they are undertaken and found successful, attention must be paid to the treatment of existing poverty.

More immediate cures simply arbitrarily raise the purchasing power of the poor above the poverty level. One device is to increase the minimum wage. Apart from the fact that in itself this measure does nothing for the nonworkers who are the majority of the poor, as has been discussed above, raising the labor cost to employers of workers whose productivity has not increased may lift the earnings of those who retain their jobs above the poverty floor but in the process may also exacerbate the poverty problem by expanding unemployment among those with the lowest earnings capacity.

The more conventional assault on poverty uses subsidies to the poor to raise their purchasing power if not their wages and salary earnings. Current general assistance or welfare payments and categorical programs add to the income of the poor but, as the statistics show, are inadequate in eliminating poverty. In addition, the current system of benefits tends to destroy work incentives of the poor creating or at least perpetuating a poverty class. The negative income tax, a measure much discussed and even tested, is currently under governmental consideration. Its advantages over other programs are its broader scope, size of benefits and, most important, its attempt to maintain work incentives of recipients.

### Reducing Poverty

Before studying aspects of the negative tax program, efforts to cure poverty deserve closer attention. These are summarizd and analyzed in Lampman's paper presented here.

# Approaches to the Reduction of Poverty

## by Robert J. Lampman

### COUNTERING "EVENTS"

Approaches to the reduction of poverty can be seen as parallel to the causes or bases for selection recounted above. The first approach, then, is to prevent or counter the events or happenings which select some persons for poverty status. The poverty rate could be lessened by any reduction in early death, disability, family desertion, what Galbraith referred to as excessive procreation by the poor, or by containment of inflation and other hazards to financial security. Among the important events in this context the one most relevant to public policy consideration at this time is excessive unemployment. It would appear that if the recent level of over 5 percent unemployment could be reduced to 4 percent, the poverty rate would drop by about one percentage point.[1] Further fall in the poverty rate would follow if—by retraining and relocation of some workers—long-term unemployment could be cut or if unemployment could be more widely shared with the nonpoor.

To the extent that events are beyond prevention, some, e.g., disability, can be countered by remedial measures. Where neither the preventive nor the remedial

SOURCE Reprinted with permission from *American Economic Review*, Vol. 55, (May 1965, pp. 521–529.

[1] Unemployment is not strikingly different among the poor than the nonpoor. Nonparticipation in the labor force is more markedly associated with poverty than is unemployment. However, it seems that about 1 million poor family heads experience unemployment during the year. (*Census Population Reports*, P–60, No. 39, Feb. 28, 1963, Tables 15 and 16.) If half of this group were moved out of poverty by more nearly full employment, then the poverty rate would be one percentage point lower. Another way to estimate this is as follows: The national income would be $30 billion higher than it is if we had full employment. And a $30 billion increase in recent years has generally meant a full percentage point drop in the percent of families in poverty.

approach is suitable, only the alleviative measures of social insurance and public assistance remain. And the sufficiency of these measures will help determine the poverty rate and the size of the poverty income gap. It is interesting to note that our system of public income mainten- ance, which now pays out $35 billion in benefits per year, is aimed more at the problem of income insecurity of the mid- dle class and at blocking returns to pov- erty than in facilitating exits from poverty for those who have never been out of poverty. The nonpoor have the major claim to social insurance benefits, the levels of which in most cases are not adequate in themselves to keep a family out of poverty. Assistance payments of $4 billion now go to 8 million persons, all of whom are in the ranks of the poor, but about half of the 35 million poor receive neither assistance nor social insurance payments. One important step in the campaign against poverty would be to reexamine our insurance and assis- tance programs to discover ways in which they could be more effective in helping people to get out of poverty. Among the ideas to be considered along this line are easier eligibility for benefits, higher mini- mum benefits, incentives to earn while re- ceiving benefits, ways to combine work- relief, retraining, rehabilitation, and relo- cation with receipt of benefits.

Among the several events that select people for poverty, the ones about which we have done the least by social policy are family breakup by other than death and the event of being born poor. Both of these could be alleviated by a family al- lowance system, which the U.S., almost alone among Western nations, lacks. We do, of course, have arrangements in the federal individual income tax for personal deductions and exemptions whereby fam- ilies of different size and composition are ranked for the imposition of progressive rates. However, it is a major irony of this

system that it does not extend the full force of its allowances for children to the really poor. In order to do so, the tax system could be converted to have nega- tive as well as positive rates, paying out grants as well as forgiving taxes on the basis of already adopted exemptions and rates. At present there are almost $20 billion of unused exemptions and deduc- tions, most of which relate to families with children. Restricting the plan to such fam- ilies and applying a negative tax of, say, 20 percent, to this amount would "yield" an allowance total of almost $4 billion. This would not in itself take many people out of poverty, but it would go a consider- able distance toward closing the poverty income gap, which now aggregates about $12 billion.

It would, of course, be possible to go considerably further by this device with- out significantly impairing incentive to work and save. First, however, let me reject as unworkable any simple plan to assure a minimum income of $3,000. To make such an assurance would induce many now earning less than and even some earning slightly more than $3,000 to forego earnings opportunities and to ac- cept the grant. Hence the poverty income gap of $12 billion would far understate the cost of such a minimum income plan. However, it would be practicable to en- act a system of progressive rates articu- lated with the present income tax sched- ule.[2] The present rates fall from 70 percent at the top to 14 percent at income just above $3,700 for a family of five, to zero percent for income below $3,700. The average negative tax rates could move, then, from zero percent to minus 14 per- cent for, say, the unused exemptions that total $500, to 20 percent for those that total $1,000 and 40 percent for those that total $3,700. This would amount to a min- imum income of $1,480 for a family of five; it would retain positive incentives

2 Cf. Milton Friedman, *Capitalism and Freedom* (1962), pp. 192–93.

through a set of grants that would gradually diminish as earned income rose.

The total amount to be paid out (interestingly, this would be shown in the federal budget as a net reduction in tax collections) under such a program would obviously depend upon the particular rates selected, the definition of income used, the types of income-receiving units declared eligible, and the offsets made in public assistance payments. But it clearly could be more than the $4 billion mentioned in connection with the more limited plan of a standard 20 per cent negative tax rate. At the outset it might involve half the poverty income gap and total about $6 billion. This amount is approximately equal to the total federal, state, and local taxes now paid by the poor. Hence it would amount to a remission of taxes paid. As the number in poverty fell, the amount paid out under this plan would in turn diminish.

## BREAKING DOWN BARRIERS

The approaches discussed this far are consistent with the view that poverty is the result of events which happen to people. But there are other approaches, including those aimed at removing barriers which keep people in poverty. Legislation and private, volunteer efforts to assure equal educational and employment opportunities can make a contribution in this direction. Efforts to randomize unemployment by area redevelopment and relocation can in some cases work to break down "islands of poverty." Public policy can prevent or modify the forming of a poverty subculture by city zoning laws, by public housing and by regulations of private housing, by school redistricting, by recreational, cultural, and public health programs. It is curious that medieval cities built walls to keep poverty outside. Present arrangements often work to bottle it up inside cities or parts of cities and thereby encourage poverty to function as its own cause.

## IMPROVING ABILITIES AND MOTIVATIONS

The third broad approach to accelerated reduction of poverty relates to the basis for selection referred to above as limited ability or motivation. The process of economic growth works the poverty line progressively deeper into the ranks of people who are below average in ability or motivation, but meantime it should be possible to raise the ability and motivation levels of the lowest. It is interesting that few children, even those of below average ability, who are not born and raised in poverty, actually end up in poverty as adults. This suggests that poverty is to some extent an inherited disease. But it also suggests that if poor children had the same opportunities, including preschool training and remedial health care, as the nonpoor (even assuming no great breakthroughs of scientific understanding), the rate of escape from poverty would be higher. Even more fundamentally, we know that mental retardation as well as infant mortality and morbidity have an important causal connection with inadequate prenatal care, which in turn relates to low income of parents.

A belief in the economic responsiveness of poor youngsters to improved educational opportunities underlies policies advocated by many educational theorists from Bentham to Conant. And this widely shared belief no doubt explains the emphasis which the Economic Opportunity Act places upon education and training. The appropriation under that Act, while it seems small relative to the poverty income gap, is large relative to present outlays for education of the poor. I would estimate that the half-billion dollars or so thereby added increases the national expenditure for this purpose by about one-seventh. To raise the level of educational expenditure for poor children—who are one fifth of the nation's children but who consume about a tenth of educational outlay—to equal that of the average would cost in the neighborhood of $3 billion. Such an emphasis upon education and training is justified by the fact that families headed by young adults will tend, in a few years, to be the most rapidly increasing group of poor families.

## SUMMARY

Past experience provides a basis for the belief that poverty can be eliminated in the U.S. in this generation. The poverty rate has been reduced at the rate of one percentage point a year; the poverty income gap is now down to 2 percent of GNP.

Preventing and countering the "events" which select people for poverty can help to maintain or accelerate the rate at which we have been making progress against poverty. For example, by returning to the 4 percent "full employment" rate of unemployment, we would instantaneously reduce the poverty rate by one percentage point. For another example, we could make a great stride toward early closing of the poverty income gap by modifying the income tax to pay out family allowances.

Another broad approach to the elimination of poverty is to break down the social barriers which restrict opportunities for the poor. Examples of this are legislating against practices of discrimination and making plans to bring the poor into the mainstream of community life.

The third approach is to make progressively greater investment in improving the abilities and motivations of the poor. Substantial increase in outlays for education and training is a promising example of this approach.

Reduction of poverty hinges on the attainment of other goals such as economic growth, full employment, income security, and equal opportunity. But it also turns upon the reduction of poverty itself since poverty to an important degree causes itself. Hence, any favorable break in the circle makes the next step easier. More nearly full employment makes barriers less meaningful; lower barriers shrink differences in motivation. Similarly, higher incomes for the poor work to reduce both acquired and at birth limitations of ability.

But any one of the approaches will involve costs, and it would be valuable to know their comparative cost-benefit ratios. It is on this that, by theoretical and empirical research, including intercountry study, social scientists can make a distinctive contribution to the long-dreamed-of, but now explicitly stated, goal of eliminating poverty.

In the early part of his paper Lampman expresses optimism over the future reduction of poverty through the natural consequences of economic growth. As average income rises, the number of poor declines and the "poverty gap" as he defines it, becomes a smaller and smaller percentage of GNP. But, as Lampman acknowledges, there are some subgroups in the poverty population who are immune to the beneficial family income effects of economic growth. Then, too, economic growth leads mainly to a reduction of an unchanged poverty level. Assuming the poverty line as a sociological concept, rising with average income, the decline in the number of poor, as Lampman is aware, would be much less than estimated by a static subsistence standard.

In enumerating the "external events" that cause poverty, Lampman notes the high incidence of poverty among large families. Orshansky's data show the marked relative growth in poverty with increases in number of children per family. It is not that poor families tend to be large but that large numbers of dependents, with income of the head not related to family size, except for the small tax concession based on number of dependents, tend to lead many low-income families under the poverty line.

Lampman notes that many of the existing welfare programs are "aimed more at the problem of income insecurity of the middle class" than at helping the poor out of poverty. Social security and unemployment insurance represent such programs. But perhaps the most glaring example of social income support that misses the poor entirely is our system of tax deductions.

At the time of his paper, Lampman estimates unused exemptions and deductions at almost $20 billion. Tax offsets aid the disposable income of the middle and upper income groups but do nothing for those with no income. In fact, coincidentally, for a family of four at the poverty line of about $3000, with no extraordinary deductible expenses, the current income tax formula just permits full application of standard deductions and exemptions. Thus for all 4-member families in poverty there is some amount of unused deductions or exemptions, down to those with zero income who, of course, have nothing to write off.

### The Negative Income Tax

Lampman makes the short step from noting the inability of the poor to make full or, in some cases, partial use of tax offsets to suggesting some form of negative tax whereby instead of paying lower taxes as do those of higher income, the poor may receive positive subsidies from the government. The idea of a negative income tax, though not new, has only recently received wide publicity and serious consideration as practical public policy. Milton Friedman in the chapter of his *Capitalism and Freedom* included here, is credited with stimulating much of the current interest in the negative income tax.

# Capitalism and Freedom

## by Milton Friedman

The extraordinary economic growth experienced by Western countries during the past two centuries and the wide distribution of the benefits of free enterprise have enormously reduced the extent of poverty in any absolute sense in the capitalistic countries of the West. But poverty is in part a relative matter, and even in these countries, there are clearly many people living under conditions that the rest of us label as poverty.

One recourse, and in many ways the most desirable, is private charity. It is noteworthy that the heyday of laissez-faire, the middle and late nineteenth century in Britain and the United States, saw an extraordinary proliferation of private eleemosynary organizations and institutions. One of the major costs of the extension of governmental welfare activities has been the corresponding decline in private charitable activities.

It can be argued that private charity is insufficient because the benefits from it accrue to people other than those who make the gifts—again, a neighborhood effect. I am distressed by the sight of poverty; I am benefited by its alleviation; but I am benefited equally whether I or someone else pays for its alleviation; the benefits of other people's charity therefore partly accrue to me. To put it differently, we might all of us be willing to contribute to the relief of poverty, *provided* everyone else did. We might not be willing to contribute the same amount without such assurance. In small communities, public pressure can suffice to realize the proviso even with private charity. In the large impersonal communities that are increasingly coming to dominate our society, it is much more difficult for it to do so.

Suppose one accepts, as I do, this line of reasoning as justifying governmental

SOURCE Reprinted with permission from *Capitalism and Freedom,* Chicago, University of Chicago Press, 1962 Chapter XII.

action to alleviate poverty; to set, as it were, a floor under the standard of life of every person in the community. There remain the questions, how much and how. I see no way of deciding "how much" except in terms of the amount of taxes we—by which I mean the great bulk of us—are willing to impose on ourselves for the purpose. The question, "how," affords more room for speculation.

Two things seem clear. First, if the objective is to alleviate poverty, we should have a program directed at helping the poor. There is every reason to help the poor man who happens to be a farmer, not because he is a farmer but because he is poor. The program, that is, should be designed to help people as people not as members of particular occupational groups or age groups or wage-rate groups or labor organizations or industries. This is a defect of farm programs, general old-age benefits, minimum-wage laws, pro-union legislation, tariffs, licensing provisions of crafts or professions, and so on in seemingly endless profusion. Second, so far as possible the program should, while operating through the market, not distort the market or impede its functioning. This is a defect of price supports, minimum-wage laws, tariffs and the like.

The arrangement that recommends itself on purely mechanical grounds is a negative income tax. We now have an exemption of $600 per person under the federal income tax (plus a minimum 10 per cent flat deduction). If an individual receives $100 taxable income, i.e., an income of $100 in excess of the exemption and deductions, he pays tax. Under the proposal, if his taxable income minus $100, i.e., $100 less than the exemption plus deductions, he would pay a negative tax, i.e., receive a subsidy. If the rate of subsidy were, say, 50 per cent, he would receive $50. If he had no income at all, and, for simplicity, no deductions, and the rate were constant, he would receive $300. He might receive more than this if he had

deductions, for example, for medical expenses, so that his income less deductions, was negative even before subtracting the exemption. The rates of subsidy could, of course, be graduated just as the rates of tax above the exemption are. In this way, it would be possible to set a floor below which no man's net income (defined now to include the subsidy) could fall—in the simple example $300 per person. The precise floor set would depend on what the community could afford.

The advantages of this arrangement are clear. It is directed specifically at the problem of poverty. It gives help in the form most useful to the individual, namely, cash. It is general and could be substituted for the host of special measures now in effect. It makes explicit the cost borne by society. It operates outside the market. Like any other measures to alleviate poverty, it reduces the incentives of those helped to help themselves, but it does not eliminate that incentive entirely, as a system of supplementing incomes up to some fixed minimum would. An extra dollar earned always means more money available for expenditure.

No doubt there would be problems of administration, but these seem to me a minor disadvantage, if they be a disadvantage at all. The system would fit directly into our current income tax system and could be administered along with it. The present tax system covers the bulk of income recipients and the necessity of covering all would have the by-product of improving the operation of the present income tax. More important, if enacted as a substitute for the present rag bag of measures directed at the same·end, the total administrative burden would surely be reduced.

A few brief calculations suggest also that this proposal could be far less costly in money, let alone in the degree of governmental intervention involved, than our present collection of welfare measures. Alternatively, these calculations can be regarded as showing how wasteful our present measures are, judged as measures for helping the poor.

In 1961, government amounted to something like $33 billion (federal, state, and local) on direct welfare payments and programs of all kinds: old age assistance, social security benefit payments, aid to dependent children, general assistance, farm price support programs, public housing, etc.[1] I have excluded veterans' benefits in making this calculation. I have also made no allowance for the direct and indirect costs of such measures as minimum-wage laws, tariffs, licensing provisions, and so on, or for the costs of public health activities, state and local expenditures on hospitals, mental institutions, and the like.

There are approximately 57 million consumer units (unattached individuals and families) in the United States. The 1961 expenditures of $33 billion would have financed outright cash grants of nearly $6,000 per consumer unit to the 10 per cent with the lowest incomes. Such grants would have raised their incomes above the average for all units in the United States. Alternatively, these expenditures would have financed grants of nearly $3,000 per consumer unit to the 20 per cent with the lowest incomes. Even if one went so far as that one-third whom New Dealers were fond of calling ill-fed, ill-housed, and ill-clothed, 1961 expenditures would have financed grants of nearly $2,000 per consumer unit, roughly the sum which, after allowing for the change in the level of prices, was the income which separated the lower one-third in the middle 1930's from the upper two-thirds. Today, fewer than one-eighth of consumer units have an income, adjusted for the change in the level of prices, as low as that of the lowest third in the middle 1930's.

Clearly, these are all far more extravagant programs than can be justified to "alleviate poverty" even by a rather generous interpretation of that term. A program which *supplemented* the incomes of the 20 per cent of the consumer units with the lowest incomes so as to raise them to the lowest income of the rest would cost less than half of what we are now spending.

The major disadvantage of the proposed negative income tax is its political implications. It establishes a system under which taxes are imposed on some to pay subsidies to others. And presumably, these others have a vote. There is always the danger that instead of being an arrangement under which the great majority tax themselves willingly to help an unfortunate minority, it will be converted into one under which a majority imposes taxes for its own benefit on an unwilling minority. Because this proposal makes the process so explicit, the danger is perhaps greater than with other measures. I see no solution to this problem except to rely on the self-restraint and good will of the electorate.

\* \* \*

Friedman makes a strong argument for the negative income tax, but he overstates his case in comparing the costs of alleviating and eliminating poverty through this program with those of our existing measures, which cost so much more and leave so many poor. As Friedman and many others point out,

[1] This figure is equal to government transfer payments ($31.1 billion) less veterans' benefits ($4.8 billion), both from the Department of Commerce national income accounts, plus federal expenditures on the agricultural program ($5.5 billion) plus federal expenditures on public housing and other aids to housing ($0.5 billion), both for year ending June 30, 1961 from Treasury accounts, plus a rough allowance of $0.7 billion to raise it to even billions and to allow for administrative costs of federal programs, omitted state and local programs, and miscellaneous items. My guess is that this figure is a substanial underestimate.

existing programs—in particular farm price supports, social security benefit payments, and much of public housing—give little assistance to the poor. In fact, Friedman's arithmetic merely confirms this fact. Much of our current transfer payments aid the middle and even upper economic classes, so that a single program designed only to aid the poor is bound to cost less than "the present rag bag of measures." But contrary to Friedman's assumption, these are not necessarily "directed at the same end" of the elimination of poverty, as is the negative tax.

Thus the negative tax is not a true substitute for all existing transfer payments. A more accurate comparison of costs would entail measurement of the funding required for the negative tax relative to that of the poverty-reducing aspects of the existing programs. Expressed differently, even with the negative tax we may still want to continue transfer payments which admittedly give direct benefits to the nonpoor.

One advantage of the negative tax program is its easy flexibility in changing benefits should the poverty line be raised, to at least maintain the current income structure as economic growth continues. A simple adjustment downward in the marginal tax rate, the ratio of the reduction in subsidy, or negative tax, to a rise in market earnings, and an increase in the maximum subsidy—at zero earnings—would serve to raise the poverty floor and expand the range of subsidies to higher incomes.

Among the negative tax's many advantages over existing programs, even the categorical ones that aid the poor, the most important is its quality of at least partially maintaining work incentives. As a whole, current measures could not be designed more effectively to perpetuate poverty by their twin faults of inadequate benefits and destruction of work incentives. The typical welfare or general assistance program supplements income up to a fixed minimum level, usually well below the poverty line. Thus, if this minimum is, say, $1500 per year, or $125 per month, any earnings up to that level would result in a dollar-for-dollar reduction in the general assistance subsidy.

Thus, in effect, these programs impose a 100 percent marginal tax rate for the welfare recipient. Such a tax eliminates the incentive to work for all those earning less than the minimum standard, except those few for whom work is preferred to not working, and those who feel a strong stigma from receiving welfare benefits—in short, those who would work to receive no more income than what they would get if they did not work. Furthermore, it would greatly reduce or perhaps eliminate work incentive of those whose full-time market earnings were above but close to the minimum standard but still kept them in poverty, those who could receive almost as much if they did not work as from market earnings. The effect of the 100 percent tax discourages the poor from working.

A welfare program could be designed with a marginal tax rate below 100 percent, so that the negative tax plan is not intrinsically superior in that regard, although a marginal tax rate such that "an extra dollar earned always means more money available for expenditure" forms a basic aspect of a negative tax system. Reluctance to reduce the tax rate on welfare payments is probably based on an attitude that the negative tax must overcome if it is to be implemented in this country, that public funds should not be used to supplement incomes of those not in need. It is illogical that this attitude applies to direct income subsidies when, as has been mentioned above, many current programs give assistance to the nonpoor. Perhaps that the aid to the nonpoor in the form of direct income supplements is more visible than, say, the farm price support program makes this aspect of a negative tax program unpopular with a tax-conscious legislature and public. Perhaps it is that most people do not wish aid to the nonpoor to be associated with an antipoverty program.

A simple hypothetical example can explain why a negative tax plan with a marginal tax rate less than 100 percent must grant subsidies to those whose market earnings are above the support level. Assume a maximum negative tax for a family of four with no family earnings at the poverty floor of $3000. With a marginal tax rate of 50 percent, total income at market earnings of $1000 would be $3500, comprised of $1000 earnings and $2500 subsidy. Negative taxes would be received for earnings up to $6000. A policy of not subsidizing earnings above $3000 would lead to the strange condition under which a family would receive a higher total income by earning, and working, less.

Expressed in a different way, whatever the subidy maximum, the only way subsidies could be limited to those whose earnings did not exceed this margin, if the marginal tax rate were less than 100 percent for low earners, would be for the rate to rise above 100 percent for those earning closer to the subsidy maximum. Even our current plans are not that illogical. Then there is a need to educate the public to the fact that subsidies to the nonpoor do not introduce a new concept into our transfer payment formulas, although admittedly they would add a new aspect to an antipoverty program.

On the issue of work incentive, though many have noted the discouraging side effects of a negative tax plan on individual labor supply, what needs more emphasis is that these effects are weaker than those associated with the destructive 100 percent marginal tax rates of current general assistance programs. If we are going to eliminate poverty by direct income supplements to the poor, then the negative tax, with a marginal tax rate below 100 percent will damage work incentives less than our present welfare formulas.

To understand why, at first view, a negative tax will somewhat reduce individual labor supply, it may help to compare the work incentive effects of negative taxes on low, or nonexistent incomes, with those of our positive taxes on higher incomes. Economists have long studied the effect of (positive) taxes on incentives and have reached inconclusive results. Theoretically, a rise in the positive tax rate has an uncertain effect on work incentives.

This can be seen either by studying the effect on labor supply of a rise in the rate as income rises or a rise in the rate for a given earnings potential. Figure 18-1 depicts both changes graphically.

*OA* is the original wage ray, or work income line. If there were no increase in the tax rates,* a rise in wages would put the worker on wage ray *OB*. But the rise in the tax rate shifts the ray downward to *OC*. Note that *OC* must lie above, or be steeper than *OA*, because positive marginal tax rates do not reach 100 percent.

---

* For the sake of simplicity, rates are assumed constant over the income range. This lack of realism keeps the graph neater without altering qualitative conclusions.

*Figure 18-1. Effect on labor supply of a rise in tax rates.*

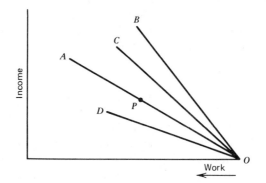

If there is no change in wages, but a rise in tax rates, then the wage ray falls to *OD*. What is important in the present discussion, however, is that no matter what the shift in the wage ray, whether to *OC* or *OD*, the effect on labor supply is uncertain. Whether equilibrium labor supply on the new wage ray will move to the left or right, show an increase or decrease, depends only on whether the labor supply schedule is positively or negatively sloped. If it is positively sloped, that is, if the substitution effect outweighs the income effect from a change in net wages, labor supply would increase from a rise in wages even though the marginal tax rose with income, and the equilibrium supply point along *OC* would lie to the left of *P*. At any given wage, an increase in the tax rate would reduce labor supply. The equilibrium point along *OD* would lie to the right of *P*. Opposite results would, of course, prevail if the labor supply schedule were negatively sloped.

This uncertainty over the direction of labor supply from the establishment or change of a tax does not arise in the case of the negative income tax on low incomes. For the negative tax, income and substitution effects impose compatible forces on labor supply no matter what marginal tax rate above zero is levied, nor what the nature of the labor supply schedule, whether positively or negatively sloped. Figure 18-2 shows these relationships.

*OA* represents the subsidy at zero income, which falls until it reaches earned income of *B*. Without the negative tax equilibrium labor supply is at *OC* with earnings at *CP*. The subsidy program in effect leads to a new wage

*Figure 18-2. Effect of negative tax on labor supply.*

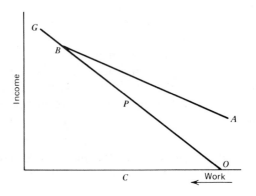

ray *ABG* which meets the nonsubsidy income opportunity line at *B*, the income level at which the subsidy becomes zero.

Equilibrium labor supply will lie to the right of *P* on the subsidy-plus-earnings income path because, in this case, unlike that of the positive tax, income is higher and marginal net wage lower. Thus, under the usual assumption of leisure as a normal good, both the substitution and income effects operate to reduce labor supply.

But there is debate over whether leisure is actually an inferior good for low-income recipients. Some argue that added income from higher wages, or as in this instance, subsidies, stimulates the economic appetite for higher consumption standards and so raises income aspirations to lead to income effects contrary to the conventional assumptions of leisure as a normal good. If leisure is an inferior good, then the effect of the subsidy program on work incentives would become uncertain. In any case, the question of the direction of work incentive effects merits empirical testing; however, the experiments that have been made on the issue are too recent for definite results to be reached.

Even if it is found that a subsidy program of the negative income tax type reduces work incentives, the proponents of the plan should emphasize that if the poor are to be lifted out of poverty, their work incentives would be hurt less than under existing programs, which have not had their harmful effects on labor supply publicized enough.

Referring to Figure 18-2, the case studied was for the worker whose equilibrium labor supply without subsidy was below the zero subsidy income level. Obviously, all those in poverty would have such an equilibrium earned income-subsidy relationship. That is, they would be eligible for subsidies. But, as has been mentioned above, many workers above the poverty line, that is, at an income from earnings along wage ray *OBG* greater than *OA*, would receive benefits.

In addition, those with earnings greater than those of point *B*, the income level at which subsidies disappear, might have their labor supply adversely affected by the introduction of a subsidy plan. The paper by Green, included here, analyzes the effect on work incentives of a negative income tax plan for the two groups—those whose presubsidy income lies below the zero-subsidy level and those whose income lies above it.

# Negative Taxes and Monetary Incentives to Work: The Static Theory

## by Christopher Green

*The note examines how negative income taxation may influence incentives to work. The model indicating the income-leisure trade-off is used in both graphical and algebraic forms. The analysis indicates that if both income and leisure are "normal" goods, and if preference patterns are not changed as a result of implementation of a negative income tax plan, utility maximizing individuals will choose to work less in the presence of negative tax payments than in their absence. How much less depends on the level of the income guarantee, the negative (marginal) tax rate, and the shape of the utility function.*

The purpose of this note is to show in simple theoretical terms how a negative income tax may affect the work-leisure choice. In recent years several proposals have been made to place a floor under family income and to supplement the meager income of low income families. One method which has found many sup-

porters is to use the income tax system as a vehicle for making cash payments to household units with incomes below some specified income level. For example, Friedman proposes making payments to taxpaying units whose income is less than the value of the exemptions and standard deductions allowed them under income tax law. [2] Another proposal is to pay poor families some percentage of their poverty income gap, i.e., the negative difference between a family's income and the official poverty line. [4] Still another proposal is that of Tobin which specifies a basic per capita allowance in lieu of personal exemptions for every dependent on a taxpayer's return if the taxpayer chooses the Tobin tax schedule. [9] A taxpayer's decision to choose either the present tax schedule and personal exemptions or Tobin's basic allowance and a flat 33 1/3 percent tax rate on pre-allowance income depends

SOURCE Reprinted with permission from *The Journal of Human Resources*, Vol. 3, Number 3 (© 1968 by the Regents of the University of Wisconsin), pp. 280–288.

on which schedule would saddle him with the lowest net tax liability. A proposal similar to Tobin's is that of Rolph who would substitute a tax credit for the present system of personal exemptions. [6] A taxpayer whose tax credit exceeds his gross tax liability[1] would receive cash payments from the government corresponding to the excess of tax credits over income tax liabilities. Taxpayers with a positive net tax liability would pay the government. Rolph would finance his plan and other government expenditures normally financed by individual income taxes with a flat rate income tax on a broadened tax base (Rolph would abandon progressive marginal tax rates in the income tax schedule).

## EFFECT ON PERSONS BELOW BREAK-EVEN INCOME LEVEL

The imposition of an income tax, it is widely recognized, may affect the supply of work effort.[2] Likewise, the introduction of an income guarantee in combination with a tax rate(s) on earnings and other income may have an impact on an individual's or a family's decision to work or not to work. Figure 1 is the time-honored diagram used by economists to describe the work-leisure decision. Income is measured on the ordinate and leisure on the abscissa. Line $Y_M T$ is the "budget" constraint with varying numbers of working hours and a fixed wage rate $W_0$. Given a set of indifference curves, the consumer is in equilibrium at point $A$ where he consumes $(OL^0)$ hours of leisure and $(OY^0)$ income. (For the purpose of simplicity only, I assume a consumer unit's income before receipt of negative tax payments consists solely of earnings.) Now assume the adoption of a negative income tax plan which guarantees an income equal to $OY_G$. That is, when a family has no other in-

come, it receives a negative tax payment equal to $OY_G$. Assume further that the basic minimum income paid to applicants who qualify for payments is reduced 50 cents for each dollar of earnings. Assume, finally, that the consumer unit's income-leisure decision depends on his total money income including negative taxes and not just upon his net earnings. Then the new budget constraint is $TBDY_M$. The segment $DB$ represents the 50 percent "tax rate" provision. Negative income tax payments are not reduced to zero until the consumer unit's total income is $Y_B$. At $Y_B$ the consumer unit's income consists only of earned income. Geometrically $OY_G = \frac{1}{2}OY_B$.

In algebraic terms, the budget equation applicable to consumer units who are eligible to receive negative tax payments is:

$$(1) \quad \begin{aligned} Y &= w(T - L) + \\ &\quad a[Y_B - w(T - L)] \\ &\qquad \text{if } Y_B > w(T - L) \text{ and} \\ Y &= w(T - L) \\ &\qquad \text{if } Y_B < w(T - L) \end{aligned}$$

where:

$Y =$ consumer unit's total income (earnings plus negative income payments).

$Y_G =$ the income guarantee or lump sum part of the plan.

$Y_B =$ the break-even level of income— i.e., the level of income below which a consumer unit is eligible for negative income tax payments and above which a consumer unit is no longer eligible for negative income tax payments. $Y_B = Y_G/a$.

$w =$ average annual hourly wage rate.

$a =$ negative income tax rate.

$T =$ available budget of hours in a year within which work and leisure may be substituted for each other.

[1] Gross tax liability is found by applying the income tax schedule to taxpayer income.
[2] In fact, the evidence available indicates that the work effort supplied by individuals facing nominally high tax rates is only negligibly affected by those rates.

$L$ = number of available hours which are taken in the form of leisure during the year. Then, substracting $L$ from $T$ gives hours of work.

Further, negative income taxes, $N_T$, may be defined as:

$$N_T = a[Y_B - w(T - L)],$$
$$\text{where } Y_B > w(T - L)$$

Thus, equation (1) may be rewritten as:

(2) $\quad Y = w(T - L) + N_T$ or
(2a) $\quad Y = Y_G + w(T - L)[1 - a]$

In Figure 1, $Y_G$ is the income guarantee portion of the budget constraint and $w(T - L)[1 - a]$ represents the segment, $DB$, of the budget constraint. The

slope of $DB$ depends on the wage rate, $w$, and the negative income tax rate, $a$. The higher the $a$, the smaller the slope of $DB$. If $a$ is increased toward unity, $DB$ approaches a horizontal position and the probability increases that the highest attainable indifference curve will touch the budget constraint at point $B$ (a "corner" solution).

If $a < 1$, say $a = 50$ percent, and earnings remain below the break-even level, the consumer unit's total income $Y$ depends on $w$ and $(T - L)$ as well as $N_T$. See equation (2). Thus, even though a consumer unit is receiving negative tax payments, it still "pays" in monetary terms to look for a better job (higher $w$) and/or to increase the supply of work effort (a greater $T - L$).

If, however, $a = 100$ percent and the constraint $Y_B - w(T - L) > 0$ applies, then equation (1) reduces to $Y = Y_B = Y_G$. Thus, over some range of work effort, neither the wage rate nor the amount of work effort will affect the consumer unit's total income. This, in essence, is the problem that arises under the categorical and general public assistance programs.[3] These programs utilize an implicit 100 percent "tax rate" in determining payments to potential welfare recipients.[4] Such an expropriatory "tax rate" is likely to induce persons whose earning potential is low to substitute leisure for work and earned income, and to convert many potential earners (those with non-zero wage alternatives) into "relief" cases. However, a lower penalty rate on increased earnings, say 50 percent, is likely to reduce the impact of public assistance on a potential recipient's work–leisure choice and, in particular, is less likely to induce a potential

*Figure 1*

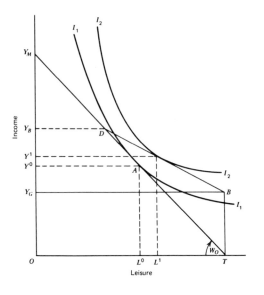

[3] These comments are relevant to the recent study of the demand for general assistance payments made by Professors Brehm and Saving. [1]

[4] The "tax rate" may exceed 100 percent since there is a waiting period to get back on the rolls and the relief recipient may also lose medical and housing benefits when his earnings disqualify him from receiving assistance. However, a recent (1967) amendment to the public assistance section of the Social Security Act is designed to reduce the marginal rate to 66⅔ percent for AFDC recipients.

relief recipient to give up work altogether.[5]

## EFFECT ON PERSONS ABOVE BREAK-EVEN INCOME LEVEL

The preceding analysis can also answer some questions about the potential reaction to a negative income tax by consumer units whose earnings are somewhat above the break-even level of income. Suppose, in Figure 1, the consumer unit's indifference curve, $I_1$, is tangent to the $Y_mD$ portion of the budget line. Now consider three possible relationships between indifferent curve $I_1$ and the $DB$ portion of the budget line. (a) $I_1$ is tangent to $Y_mD$ and always lies above the $DB$ portion of the budget line; (b) $I_1$ is tangent to $Y_mD$ but cuts $DB$ from above; (c) $I_1$ is tangent to both the $Y_mD$ and $DB$ portions of the budget line.[6]

Negative income taxation will have no effect on the work incentives of the consumer unit whose preferences are adequately reflected by case (a). However, if indifference curve $I_1$ cuts $DB$ from above, case (b), the utility maximizing consumer unit which was not supposed to be affected by a negative income tax will react by reducing its work effort. How much of a reduction will take place? If the indifference curve which cut $DB$ from

above cuts $TB$ with a slope steeper than $DB$ and if leisure is a normal good (i.e., higher indifference curves become steeper reflecting a rising marginal rate of substitution of income for leisure as income rises with *given* levels of leisure), then the highest attainable indifference curve will be reached at point $B$ in Figure 1. The consumer unit stops work altogether. This is not, however, an altogether reasonable case. The minimum income guarantee may be below what our leisure-loving worker considers to be a subsistence income. In this case the indifference curve which is tangent to $Y_mD$ may first cut $DB$ from above and then recut $DB$ from below. In this case there will be some indifference curve $I_2$ (higher than $I_1$) which is tangent to $DB$. The consumer unit reduces, but does not end, its work effort. The consumer unit's total income falls, but its total satisfaction rises because of its increased consumption of leisure.

The last case, (c), involves the special situation where the highest attainable indifference curve turns out to be tangent to both the $Y_mD$ and $DB$ portions of the budget line $Y_mDBT$. The effect of the negative tax plan is to make the consumer unit indifferent between being unaffected by the plan or going on the plan by substantially reducing its work effort.

Which of these cases (a), (b), or (c),

---

[5] If the tax rate were closer to 50 percent than to 100 percent, Brehm and Saving might not have found "that nearly one-half of all [general] assistance recipients are not on assistance due to zero wage alternatives" [1, pp. 1017–18]. (Does this mean these recipients are not working at all?) Professors Stein and Albin [7] dispute the findings of Brehm and Saving because the latter's findings are based on general assistance case data (mistakenly defined as recipients by Brehm and Saving). Stein and Albin use recipients instead of cases in order to avoid the problem of interstate variations in the average number of persons per case. They find that there is *no* positive significant relationship between the number of recipients and the benefit level. However, it seems to me they are on weak theoretical grounds in using data showing recipients rather than cases even though it is necessary to correct for state-to-state differences in the average size of general assistance cases. The consumer unit will usually be the case, and it is this unit which budgets its income and makes the income-leisure decision. The use of cases instead of recipients should be especially clear when the assistance program's "tax rate" is 100 percent (or more). With a 100 percent rate, the question that the consumer unit must answer is whether its nonassistance income (presumably mainly earnings) can exceed its maximum assistance grant. If the answer is "no," there will be no *monetary* reward from (and thus no monetary incentive to) work.

[6] Professor Richard Perlman of the University of Wisconsin–Milwaukee suggested to me the usefulness of distinguishing between these three cases. Note that the analysis (1) assumes no shift in the consumer unit's income utility function, and (2 ignores the possible reaction of consumer units to higher (positive) income taxes that may be required to finance negative income taxation.

seems most likely to best represent the typical low-to-middle income consumer unit's reaction to a negative income tax? If, as seems likely, the average worker has a target level of earnings which he only reluctantly alters, then case (a) seems most typical. The negative income tax perhaps produces some grumbling but no reduction in work effort.

\* \* \*

## SUMMARY OF EFFECTS

The purpose of a negative income tax plan is to raise the money income of low income families. Even if the lump sum guarantee and the tax rate induce some substitution of leisure for income, it is presumed that a negative income tax plan will increase the consumer unit's income. It is, of course, conceivable that payment of negative income taxes would result in a reduction in work effort so great as to actually reduce the consumer unit's total money income.[7] Receipt of negative income taxes might induce a reduction in total consumer unit income if a very powerful substitution effect is produced by negative marginal tax rates at or near 100 percent. (See the earlier discussion of 100 percent rates and "corner" solutions.) Assuming, however, that negative marginal tax rates are kept well below 100 percent, this extreme reaction to receipt of negative income tax payments seems no more likely than its polar opposite: a reduction in leisure upon receipt of negative taxes. Leisure might be reduced if leisure is an inferior good, if transfer payments, by increasing recipient income, changed "life styles" in such a way as to increase the consumer unit's "taste" for income relative to leisure, or if the assumption that the consumer unit makes

no distinction between earnings and negative tax payments is relaxed. With respect to the last possibility, suppose that in making its income-leisure decision the consumer unit takes only its wage rate into account. Then the lump sum income effect of a negative income tax plan vanishes and the consumer unit reacts solely to the tax rate part of the plan. In these circumstances, whether the consumer unit increases or decreases its work effort depends on the relative weights of the substitution and "pure" income effects produced by the negative tax rate.

These comments illustrate the large number of possible reactions to a negative income tax plan—or any other scheme designed to guarantee a minimum income. Casual observation might lead us to doubt the plausibility of the "extreme" reactions cited in the preceding paragraph. Nevertheless, there is a real need for empirical research in this increasingly important area of public policy.

## REFERENCES

1. C. T. Brehm and T. R. Saving. "The Demand for General Payments," *American Economic Review*, 54 (December 1964), pp. 1002–18.
2. Milton Friedman. *Capitalism and Freedom*. Chicago: University of Chicago Press, 1962.
3. Lowell E. Gallaway. "Negative Income Tax Rates and the Elimination of Poverty," *National Tax Journal*, 19 (September 1966), pp. 298–307.
4. Christopher Green and Robert J. Lampman. "Schemes for Transferring Income to the Poor," *Industrial Relations*, 6 February 1967), pp. 121–37.
5. Richard A. Musgrave. *The Theory of Public Finance*. New York: McGraw-Hill Book Co., 1959.

[7] A recent paper by Lowell Gallaway suggests this may happen [3, pp. 303–307]. Also see Michael Taussig [8] for a critique of the Gallaway paper. If income is treated as an inferior good, in which case the income consumption curve would be downward sloping to the right, receipt of negative income taxes would result in a reduction in total consumer unit income.

6. Earl Rolph. "The Case for a Negative Income Tax Device," *Industrial Relations,* 6 (February 1967), pp. 155–65.
7. Bruno Stein and Peter S. Albin. "The Demand for General Assistance Payments," *American Economic Review,* 57 (June 1967), pp. 575–85.
8. Michael K. Taussig. "Negative Income Tax Rates and the Elimination of Poverty: Comment," *National Tax Journal,* 20 (September 1967).
9. James Tobin. "On Improving the Economic Status of the Negro," *Daedalus* (Fall 1965), pp. 878–98.

Green exhausts the possibilities of labor supply adjustments to a negative income tax formula. His conclusions apply mainly to the standard theoretical assumption of leisure as a normal good, although he points out the uncertainties that arise if leisure is an inferior good.

Green's clear graphical and algebraic exposition lead to the inevitable result of weakened work incentives for those who would receive benefits, those with market earnings less than twice the maximum subsidy in his use of a 50 percent negative tax rate. Many in this group with incomes above the poverty level would receive benefits, as part of a workable antipoverty formula, and would also have reduced work incentives.

As for those with income above the subsidy range, although Green painstakingly analyzes the factors that affect their work incentives, he reaches the optimistic conclusion that typically "the negative income tax perhaps produces some grumbling but no reduction in work effort." More technically he suggests that those with equilibrium earnings and work effort before subsidy in the $Y_M D$ portion of their income opportunity path in his Figure 1 would be unaffected by the subsidy program; their indifference curve tangent to the equilibrium point would be relatively flat to the right of this point, never cutting the $BD$ segment.

Green's conclusion is based on the argument that "the average worker has a target level of earnings which he only reluctantly alters." But the idea of a target income usually refers to a low-income worker. Those with incomes above $D$, assuming a $3000 maximum subsidy and a 50 percent tax rate have incomes over $6000, well into the economic middle class. Speculating on the effect on a subsidy program's effect on their work incentive, in the absence of empirical studies, a strong theoretical position can be held that many of them will take advantage of a program designed to aid the poor, by sacrificing some income for a great deal more leisure.

Apart from the harmful effect on labor supply, the negative income tax may retard general improvement in labor force quality by reducing the incentive to upgrade skills. Subsidies to low-income earners have the effect of reducing income differentials based on skill, lowering the returns on investment in education and training. This influence applies regardless of whether work incentives are weakened for the current labor force in its present employment. But this is just another example of a shortcoming of a negative tax program that applies just as forcefully to existing measures, which do so much worse a job toward the central goal of eliminating poverty.

## Related Readings

Alan B. Batchelder, *The Economics of Poverty*, New York, Wiley, 1966, *Inequality and Poverty*, Edward C. Budd (ed.), New York, Norton, 1967, and *The Economics of Poverty*, Burton A. Weisbrod (ed.), Engelwood Cliffs, N.J., Prentice-Hall, 1965, offer general background to the demography, causes, and suggested cures of poverty. Oscar Ornati, "The Poverty Band and the Count of the Poor," in the Budd book, treats the issue of the sociological concept of the poverty floor as a changing standard.

Problems of poverty among older workers are treated comprehensively in *The Aged Population of the United States*, Social Security Administration, Department of Health, Education and Welfare, Washington, 1967, and by Lowell E. Gallaway in *The Retirement Decision*, Social Security Administration, 1965. In this essay, and in "Negative Tax Rates and the Elimination of Poverty" (*National Tax Journal*, Vol. 19, September 1966), Gallaway concludes that Social Security benefits greatly discourage work incentives of the aged, in some cases even leading to a chance of lower total income than would have been derived from work alone. Gallaway's methods and conclusions are challenged by Michael E. Taussig, "Negative Tax Rates and the Elimination of Poverty: Comment" (*National Tax Journal*, Vol. 20, September 1967, pp. 328–337). Burton A. Weisbrod and W. Lee Hansen, "An Income–Net Worth Approach to Measuring Economic Welfare" (*American Economic Review*, Vol. 58, December 1968, pp. 1315–1329), find that modification of the poverty concept to include wealth holdings as well as income, greatly reduces the incidence of poverty among those over 65, compared to other age groups, because older people, even those with low incomes, tend to have relatively more assets than younger groups at the same income level.

Reliance on economic growth to eliminate poverty, even in the narrow sense of a constant real income poverty threshold, receives pessimistic evaluation from Gallaway, "The Foundations of the 'War on Poverty'" (*American Economic Review*, Vol. 55, March 1965, pp. 122–131), and W. H. Locke Anderson, " 'Trickling Down': The Relationship Between Economic Growth and the Extent of Poverty Among American Families" (*Quarterly Journal of Economics*, Vol. 78, November 1964, pp. 511–524). They find that with rising average income, the reduction in poverty tends to decline as general economic improvement cuts only lightly into the economic misery of the hard-core poor.

In "The Demand for General Assistance Payments" (*American Economic Review*, Vol. 54, December 1964, pp. 1002–1018), C.T. Brehm and T. R. Saving conclude that general assistance payments have a strong work disincentive effect on the poor that carries over to those with higher incomes, with the number of recipients in different states closely correlated to the size of payments. Hirschel Kasper, "Welfare Payments and Work Incentive: Some Determinants of the Rates of General Assistance Payments" (*Journal of Human Resources*, Vol. 12, Winter 1968, pp. 86–110), on the other hand, finds the number of recipients in a state more dependent on labor market conditions, especially the level of unemployment.

On the effect of taxation on work incentive, Richard Musgrave, *The Theory of Public Finance* (McGraw-Hill, New York, 1959, Chapter 11), gives a thorough theoretical treatment of the influence of both positive and negative taxes, reaching the conclusion that the direction of the effect of positive taxes is uncertain, while negative taxes unequivocally reduce individual labor supply, provided leisure is not an inferior good. In an interesting survey of high-income English businessmen and professionals, George E. Break, "Income Taxes and

Incentives to Work: An Empirical Study" (*American Economic Review*, Vol. 47, September 1957, pp. 529–549), found no increase in work disincentive with rising taxes.

Regarding the negative tax plan for alleviating poverty, Christopher Green, *Negative Taxes and the Poverty Problem*, The Brookings Institution, Washington, examines all aspects of these proposals. Richard Perlman, *Labor Theory*, Wiley, New York Chapter III, offers a negative tax plan, with benefits based on labor effort, that would lead to less work disincentive effects than plans with a constant tax rate. Green and Lampman, "Schemes for Transferring Income to the Poor" (*Industrial Relations*, Vol. 6, February 1967, pp. 121–137) analyze various negative tax plans with respect to their costs, benefits and effects on work incentives. In the same issue containing a symposium on the negative tax, Earl R. Rolph, "The Case for Negative Income Tax Device," pp. 155–156 and George H. Hildebrand, "Second Thoughts on the Negative Income Tax," pp. 138–154, take pro and con positions on the effectiveness of a negative tax in helping solve the poverty problem. William A. Klein, "Some Basic Problems of Negative Income Taxation" (*Wisconsin Law Review*, Vol. 3, Summer 1966, pp. 1–25), points out complexities in implementing any negative tax plan, such as the appropriate definition of income, treatment of assets, and the accounting period to be used in calculating benefits. James Tobin, Joseph A. Pechman, and Peter M. Mieszkowski, "Is a Negative Income Tax Practical?" (*Yale Law Journal*, Vol. 77, November 1967, pp. 1–27), detail alternative tax plans as to costs and benefits for the poor, arriving at the view that the most feasible plan would require supplementary support from other assistance programs to pull all households above the poverty line. In fact, most payment proposals including the one now before congressional consideration do not suggest that the negative tax in itself have an income guarantee at the poverty floor.

# CHAPTER 19

# Negro Employment and Income

There can be little doubt that the race issue is one of the country's most important domestic problems. Although race is usually treated as a social rather than an economic problem, it is extremely important for human resource development because underutilization and underdevelopment not only deprives Negroes of opportunities to improve their material welfare but also deprives the nation of the economic contributions that would be made by programs that encouraged blacks to develop in accordance with their abilities and desires. Moreover, most of the manpower and poverty programs discussed in previous sections had strong racial overtones and were stimulated in large measure by the civil rights movement of the 1950's and 1960's. It was readily apparent to black leaders that civil rights meant very little without adequate incomes and better job opportunities.

This chapter deals primarily with the Negroes' economic status as measured by incomes and employment patterns and evaluates some of the recommended programs for improving the economic position of black workers.

## THE OCCUPATIONAL POSITION OF NEGROES

Becker, in the chapter on changes in discrimination over time in his *Economics of Discrimination*, presents the data on long-run stability in the low occupational status of the Negro male. There may be some question of his emphasis on occupational level as an accurate measure of discrimination, but the data do deny any noticeable long-run improvement in the Negro's relative position in the labor force.

Becker found no noticeable change in the Negro occupational level over the 40-year period 1910–1950. Adding the only slight improvement over the period found in other studies, leads to the stark conclusion that despite world wars, depression, boom, the New Deal, etc., over half a century, advances in the Negro's occupational status were mainly in the minds of well-wishers or in the imagination of believers in our society's inevitable tendency toward equality, regardless of facts to the contrary.

# Changes in Discrimination over Time

## by Gary Becker

The passage of time has been accompanied by changes in other variables, which may have changed the amount of discrimination. An important secular increase in real income per capita has occurred in the United States during the last hundred years, and it would be interesting to know whether this increased or decreased the "consumption" of discrimination. The continual rise in the educational attainments of the United States population would be relevant if there were a significant correlation between discrimination and educational level.[1]

There has been a secular increase in the activities of organizations dedicated to eliminating discrimination, and this may have affected tastes. The rapid growth of the federal government may have had important consequences for discrimination against minority groups. In the last fifty years the United States has passed through two major wars, one major depression, and several periods of expansion and contraction, and these, too, may have left their mark on the extent and direction of discrimination. Other changes, such as in the regional distribution of different groups, in the amount of immigration, or in the underlying technology, may also be relevant for a study of discrimination.

The almost total lack of income data for minority groups before the 1930's prevents any real study of the separate influence of each of these changes.[2] It is possible however, to learn something about the

SOURCE Reprinted with permission from *The Economics of Discrimination*, Chicago, University of Chicago Press, 1957.

[1] . . . discrimination in 1940 was greater against non-whites in higher education categories, but this does not imply greater discrimination by whites in higher categories.

[2] The one important exception is the rather substantial time series on male and female wage rates and incomes. No attempt has been made to analyze these differentials here because they are being studied in detail by a student at the University of Chicago.

secular change in discrimination. Probably the best statistics for this purpose are those in the United States Census reports giving, for each census year since 1890, the occupations of persons gainfully employed (or in the labor force), with a sex and color breakdown. These occupational statistics contain important information about the absolute and relative changes in the economic position of Negroes.

Our knowledge of the absolute and relative occupational distribution of Negro slaves is extremely limited. Since slaves were one form of capital, investment in them was carried to the point at which marginal costs equaled marginal gains; this view offers no reason to expect the occupational position of slaves to have been inferior to that of free Negroes and whites. On the other hand, slaves differed from other capital, since they could work with varying degrees of intensity; this often

made slave labor unsuitable for certain occupations, especially the more skilled ones. Very few (if any) Negro slaves received training for occupations requiring much formal education, such as medicine and law. This is not surprising if formal education was accompanied by aspirations for freedom, which, in turn, would reduce the productivity of educated slaves. Indeed, in many southern states there were laws prohibiting whites from teaching their slaves how to read and write.

The earliest detailed and inclusive occupational statistics for Negroes and whites located for this study were those in the 1890 Census; the data for this year are presented in Table 1 in the two categories of skilled and unskilled workers.[3] By 1890, the proportion of Negroes in skilled occupations was substantially less than that of whites. Although it is possible that this

TABLE 1. RELATIVE NUMBER OF NEGRO AND WHITE MALES IN DIFFERENT OCCUPATIONAL CATEGORIES FOR THE UNITED STATES 1890–1950

| Year | Relative Number in Skilled Occupations† | | | Relative Number in Semiskilled Occupations† | | | Relative Number in Unskilled Occupations† | | |
|---|---|---|---|---|---|---|---|---|---|
| | White | Negro | White Divided by Negro | White | Negro | White Divided by Negro | White | Negro | White Divided by Negro |
| (1) | (2) | (3) | (4) | (5) | (6) | (7) | (8) | (9) | (10) |
| 1950 | 0.597 | 0.193 | 3.093 | 0.230 | 0.249 | 0.923 | 0.174 | 0.558 | 0.311 |
| 1940 | .528 | .129 | 4.084 | .218 | .159 | 1.368 | .255 | .712 | .358 |
| 1930 | .531 | .118 | 4.486 | .174 | .115 | 1.512 | .295 | .767 | .385 |
| 1920 | .501 | .109 | 4.579 | .168 | .098 | 1.803 | .333 | .798 | .417 |
| 1910 | .461 | .092 | 4.999 | 0.146 | 0.064 | 2.301 | .393 | .844 | .466 |
| 1900 | .431 | .071 | 6.065 | ‡ | ‡ | ‡ | .569 | .929 | .613 |
| 1890 | 0.443 | 0.071 | 6.279 | ‡ | ‡ | ‡ | 0.557 | 0.929 | 0.599 |

† The "relative number" of Negroes in a particular occupational category means the number of Negro males in this category divided by the total number of gainfully occupied Negro males (excluding farmers and farm tenants); a similar definition is used here for whites.
‡ Combined with unskilled.

3 Semiskilled workers were not separated from unskilled before the 1910 Census. In deriving the figures in Table 1 the census occupation called "farmers and farm tenants" was omitted. It is extremely difficult to compare or classify the skills of whites and Negroes in this occupation, since most Negroes in it are farm tenants and most whites are farm owners (see U.S. Bureau of the Census, *United States Census of Agriculture, 1950, Color, Race, Tenure of Farm Operators* [Washington, D.C.: Government Printing Office, 1952], p. 924).

difference can be completely explained by the changes between 1865 and 1890, a more plausible inference would be that the proportion of slaves in skilled occupations was much less than that of whites. This would support the previous statement that slave labor is relatively unproductive in the more skilled occupations.

It is clear from columns 2 and 3 that there were relatively fewer skilled Negroes than whites in each census year from 1890 to 1950; it is also clear from columns 5 and 6 that there were relatively fewer semiskilled Negroes from 1910 to 1940 and slightly more in 1950. These data show that Negroes have been lower in the occupational hierarchy than whites. The average occupational level of Negroes has, however, been rising steadily over time; for example, in 1950, 19 per cent of all Negroes were skilled and 25 per cent were semiskilled, as against only 7 per cent skilled in 1890 and 6 per cent semiskilled in 1910.

Some might conjecture that this advance resulted from the steady movement of Negroes out of the South (see Table 2), since the occupational distribution of Negroes is higher in the North. Table 3 gives the occupational distribution of whites

and Negroes in the North and South in 1910, 1940, and 1950. Columns 3 and 6 show that the proportion of Negroes in skilled and semiskilled occupations has been consistently higher in the North than in the South. These columns also show that the average occupational position of Negroes has risen over time within both the North and the South. However, comparisons of column 2 with column 3 and of column 5 with column 6 show conclusively that in both regions Negroes have always had a much lower position on the occupational ladder.

It can be seen from columns 2 and 5 that the average occupational position of whites has also risen over time, and this leads to the question whether the average Negro position has risen primarily because of the impact of such forces as a general increase in education, which increases the position of all groups, or because of such forces, as a decrease in discrimination, which increases the relative position of Negroes. A numerical measure of occupational position is needed in order to determine the relative change in the position of Negroes.

Occupational position can probably be measured best by the average wage and

TABLE 2.  NUMBER OF NEGROES AND WHITES IN THE NORTH AND SOUTH, 1890–1950*

| Year | South | | | North | | |
|---|---|---|---|---|---|---|
| | Whites (in Millions) | Negroes (in Millions) | Negroes Divided by Whites | Whites (in Millions) | Negroes (in Millions) | Negroes Divided by Whites |
| 1950 | 36.8 | 10.2 | 0.28 | 98.1 | 4.8 | 0.049 |
| 1940 | 31.7 | 9.9 | .31 | 86.6 | 3.0 | .034 |
| 1930 | 28.4 | 9.4 | .33 | 81.9 | 2.5 | .031 |
| 1920 | 24.1 | 8.9 | .37 | 70.7 | 1.6 | .022 |
| 1910 | 20.5 | 8.7 | .43 | 61.2 | 1.1 | .018 |
| 1900 | 16.5 | 7.9 | .48 | 50.3 | 0.9 | .018 |
| 1890 | 13.2 | 6.8 | 0.51 | 41.9 | 0.7 | 0.017 |

* SOURCE: 1890–1910, U.S. Bureau of the Census, *Negro Population, 1790–1915* (Washington, D.C.: Government Printing Office, 1918), p. 43; 1920–40, U.S. Bureau of the Census, *Statistical Abstract of the United States, 1952* (Washington, D.C.: Government Printing Office, 1952), p. 32; 1950, U.S. Bureau of the Census, *Census of Population, 1950* (Washington, D.C.: Government Printing Office, 1953), II, 1–106.

TABLE 3.

TABLE 3.  RELATIVE NUMBER OF NEGRO AND WHITE MALES IN DIFFERENT
OCCUPATIONAL CATEGORIES FOR THE NORTH AND SOUTH
1910, 1940, 1950

| Year | Relative Number in Skilled Occupations† | | | Relative Number in Semiskilled Occupations† | | | Relative Number in Unskilled Occupations† | | |
|---|---|---|---|---|---|---|---|---|---|
| | White | Negro | White Divided by Negro | White | Negro | White Divided by Negro | White | Negro | White Divided by Negro |
| (1) | (2) | (3) | (4) | (5) | (6) | (7) | (8) | (9) | (10) |
| | North | | | | | | | | |
| 1950 | 0.597 | 0.245 | 2.433 | 0.237 | 0.297 | 0.798 | 0.167 | 0.458 | 0.364 |
| 1940‡ | .538 | .181 | 2.973 | .232 | .214 | 1.083 | .230 | .605 | .381 |
| 1910 | 0.472 | 0.135 | 3.504 | 0.162 | 0.136 | 1.195 | 0.366 | 0.730 | 0.501 |
| | South | | | | | | | | |
| 1950 | 0.597 | 0.162 | 3.683 | 0.208 | 0.221 | 0.942 | 0.195 | 0.617 | 0.316 |
| 1940‡ | .513 | .097 | 5.304 | .195 | .151 | 1.296 | .292 | .753 | .388 |
| 1910 | 0.411 | 0.080 | 5.126 | 0.071 | 0.043 | 1.657 | 0.518 | 0.877 | 0.591 |

† The relative number of Negroes or whites in a particular occupational category is defined in Table 1.

‡ The relative number of skilled Negroes is probably slightly understated and the relative number of semiskilled Negroes slightly overstated for 1940.

salary income received by whites in each skill category. Zeman estimated the incomes received by whites in 1940 in different census occupational categories in the North and South; these estimates suggest that the relative position of skilled, semiskilled, and unskilled occupations can be represented by 2.34, 1.44, and 1.00 in the North and by 2.69, 1.49, and 1.00 in the South.[4] The application of these weights to the distribution data in Table 3 yields the occupational indexes of Table 4. The indexes in columns 2, 3, 5, and 6 show that in both regions the average occupational position of Negroes and whites rose between 1910 and 1940 and between 1940 and 1950. However, the relative position of Negroes (given in columns 4 and 7)

TABLE 4.  AN INDEX OF THE OCCUPATIONAL POSITION OF NEGROES AND WHITES
IN THE NORTH AND SOUTH FOR 1910, 1940, AND 1950

| Year | North | | | South | | |
|---|---|---|---|---|---|---|
| | Whites | Negroes | Negroes Divided by Whites | Whites | Negroes | Negroes Divided by Whites |
| (1) | (2) | (3) | (4) | (5) | (6) | (7) |
| 1950 | 1.90 | 1.46 | 0.77 | 2.11 | 1.38 | 0.65 |
| 1940 | 1.82 | 1.34 | .74 | 1.96 | 1.24 | .63 |
| 1910 | 1.70 | 1.24 | 0.73 | 1.73 | 1.16 | 0.67 |

[4] Zeman's estimates can be found in "A Quantitative Analysis of White–Non-white Income Differentials in the United States in 1939" (unpublished Ph.D. dissertation, Department of Economics, University of Chicago, 1955), Appendix D. The average wage and salary income of white professional workers, proprietors and officials, clerical and sales workers, and foremen and craftsmen was used as the average income of skilled whites; the wage and salary income of white operatives as the income of semiskilled whites; and the wage and salary income of white laborers as the income of unskilled whites.

has been remarkably stable over time.[5] In both the North and the South the maximum deviation from the average was less than 6 per cent. In the North there was very little change from 1910 to 1940 and a 4 per cent increase between 1940 and 1950; in the South there was a 6 per cent decrease from 1910 to 1940 and a 4 per cent increase between 1940 and 1950. Thus, in comparing 1950 with 1910, Negroes in the North had about a 5 per cent higher relative occupational position and in the South about a 2 per cent lower position.[6]

In answer to the earlier question, it seems that almost all the increase in the absolute occupational position of Negroes was caused by forces increasing the position of whites as well. Changes in variables affecting the relative position of Negroes presumably either were minor or offset one another. A large secular decrease in discrimination against Negroes could have occurred only if changes in other variables offset its effect.[7] Since it is difficult to think of individual changes that could have greatly lowered their relative position, it seems probable that a large secular decrease in discrimination did not occur; yet it is possible that the combined effects of many small changes, such as a decrease in the number of unskilled whites immigrating from abroad, were great enough to offset a large decrease in discrimination.[8]

Table 1 shows that the average occupational level of Negroes rose steadily over the period 1910–1950. The percentage of Negroes in the skilled and semi-skilled occupations rose while the percentage in the unskilled jobs fell. But with reference to the relative position of the Negro, the white work force went through the same upgrading. In fact, the relative share of whites fell in all three occupational classifications. This occurred because the occupational change, for both groups, was from a classification, the unskilled, for which the white share was relatively much smaller than the nonwhite's to the labor groups where the white representation was relatively large, i.e., the skilled.

[5] Dewey, in "Negro Employment in Southern Industry," *Journal of Political Economy*, LX (August, 1952), *passim*, argues that in the last forty or fifty years Negroes have advanced little relative to whites in the occupational hierarchy in the South. These data not only support Dewey's observations but also show that the same is true for the North.

[6] For some purposes it would be preferable to use the weights obtained for the North in constructing occupational indexes for the South as well, since northern white incomes were less affected by discrimination. When this is done, the absolute and relative occupational position of Negroes and Whites are as in the accompanying table. Negroes had a consistently lower position in the South than in the

| | 1910 | 1940 | 1950 |
|---|---|---|---|
| Whites | 1.581 | 1.772 | 1.890 |
| Negroes | 1.126 | 1.195 | 1.314 |
| Negroes divided by whites | 0.713 | 0.675 | 0.695 |

North; whites had a lower position in the South in 1910 and 1940 and the same position in both areas in 1950. These weights imply a somewhat higher relative occupational position of southern Negroes than those used in Table 16, but the percentage changes in this position from 1910 to 1940 and from 1940 to 1950 are about the same.

[7] A decrease in discrimination could increase merely the relative income of Negroes within an occupational category and not change their relative occupational distribution. However, since discrimination against Negroes has been greater in the more skilled occupations, a large decrease in discrimination would probably also increase their opportunities in these occupations.

[8] The same considerations apply when estimating the likelihood that there was a large secular increase in discrimination.

Table 3 shows the same tendency of movement up the skill ladder for both races by region, North and South. To find a relative racial occupational index by regions, Becker weights the racial occupational ratios by 1940 average white wage levels for each class. The indexes, which appear in columns (4) and (7) of Table 4, show negligible regional changes over time in the Negro's relative position.

The influence of the weights in determining the index can be seen by examination of columns (4) and (10) of Table 3, which show the relative share of whites and Negroes among the skilled and unskilled. In the north from 1910 to 1950, the ratio of percentage white unskilled to Negro unskilled fell from .501 to .364 or to 73 percent of its 1910 level. The decline in the relative white share of the skilled fell a little more, from 3.504 to 2.433 or to 70 percent of its 1910 level. Thus the Northern index for Negroes, as shown in Table 4, rose from 1910 to 1950 both because of the growth in Negro share of the skilled, a more heavily weighted class, and because the relative growth in the Negro share of the skilled was greater than in the unskilled. For the 1910 to 1940 period, note that the index rose, albeit by only one point, even though the white relative decline in the unskilled was greater than for the skilled, to 76 and 84 percent of 1910 levels, respectively. In the South, both for the 1910–1940 and 1910–1950 period, there was much greater decline in the white share of the unskilled than in the skilled. But the negro position fell only slightly, supported as it was by the increase in the Negro share of skilled jobs.

Changes in the index for the nation as a whole for the period can be estimated by Becker's method, using 1940 white male income ratios for the three occupational classifications. The relative position of the Negro improved because of the greater relative decline in the white share of the skilled than in the unskilled, to 62 and 67 percent of the 1910 level, respectively, and because of the relative increase, itself, of Negroes among the skilled. But the calculated national index change from .68 in 1950 to .72 in 1960 hardly suggests that the total improvement did much to raise the low economic status of the Negro.

Becker's pessimistic findings on relative occupational improvement of the Negro have been questioned by Rayack who criticizes Becker's statistical techniques. Rayack claims that small gains are derived for the Negro's occupational position because of the use of constant (income) weights.

# Discrimination and the Occupational Progress of Negroes

## by Elton Rayack

Writing in 1942 in the preface to his monumental study, *An American Dilemma*, Gunnar Myrdal stated ". . . not since Reconstruction has there been more reason to anticipate fundamental changes in American race relations, changes which will involve a development toward the American ideal."[1]

How far has American society gone since the time of Myrdal's statement toward achieving a basic element of that "American ideal" of which he wrote, the provision of equal job opportunities irrespective of race? Two recent major studies concerned with the economic impact of racial discrimination in the United States have given sharply conflicting answers. Professor Ginzberg found that:

*The present position of the Negro in American society is far better than . . . his most optimistic friends could have predicted fifteen years ago. . . In addition to the increase in the availability of non-farm jobs, Negro workers made equally important gains by virtue of new opportunities to obtain preferred jobs in the urban economy . . . the Negro has made truly spectacular gains in the civilian economy, both in the North and South. . . .*[2]

Conversely, Professor Becker held that:

*The average occupational position of Negroes . . . relative to whites has been remarkably stable [since 1910] . . . a very tentative conclusion from this stability would be that neither striking increases nor striking decreases in discrimination against Negroes have occurred during the last four decades.*[3]

SOURCE Reprinted with permission from *Review of Economic Statistics,* May 1961.

[1] Gunnar Myrdal, *An American Dilemma* (New York, 1944), xix.
[2] Eli Ginzberg, *The Negro Potential* (New York, 1956), 5 and 11.
[3] Gary S. Becker, *The Economics of Discrimination* (Chicago, 1957), 125.

The purpose of this paper is to answer two questions raised by the above statements: (1) Has there been an advancement in the occupational position of Negroes since 1940? (2) If so, can that advancement be attributed to a reduction in discrimination?

## PROFESSOR BECKER'S OCCUPATIONAL INDEX

Certainly one of the most striking conclusions in Professor Becker's pathbreaking study on the economics of discrimination[4] is that there has been relatively little change in discrimination between 1910 and 1950. He points out that since the average occupational position of whites as well as Negroes has risen over time in both the North and the South (Table 1), the question arises as to "whether the average Negro position has risen primarily because of the impact of such forces as a general increase in education, which increases the position of all groups, or because of such forces, as a decrease in discrimination, which increases the relative position of Negroes."[5]

To determine the change in the position of Negroes relative to whites, Professor Becker constructs a numerical measure of occupational positions as follows: Negro and white workers are placed in one of three occupational classes—skilled, semiskilled, and unskilled (Table 1). He then applies weights reflecting the relative income position in 1939 of skilled, semiskilled, and unskilled workers to the percentage of workers of each race in each occupational class. The application of the income weights to the occupational distribution data yields the occupational indexes of Table 2 (see the source in Table 2 for an example of the calculations).

TABLE 1. RELATIVE NUMBER OF NEGRO AND WHITE MALES IN DIFFERENT OCCUPATIONAL CATEGORIES FOR THE NORTH AND SOUTH, 1910, 1940, 1950

| | Relative Number in Skilled Occupations | | Relative Number in Semiskilled Occupations | | Relative Number in Unskilled Occupations | |
|---|---|---|---|---|---|---|
| | White | Negro | White | Negro | White | Negro |
| A. North | | | | | | |
| 1950 | .597 | .245 | .237 | .297 | .167 | .458 |
| 1940 | .538 | .181 | .232 | .214 | .230 | .605 |
| 1910 | .472 | .135 | .162 | .136 | .366 | .730 |
| B. South | | | | | | |
| 1950 | .597 | .162 | .208 | .221 | .195 | .617 |
| 1940 | .513 | .097 | .195 | .151 | .292 | .753 |
| 1910 | .411 | .080 | .071 | .043 | .518 | .877 |

SOURCE: Becker, "The Economics of Discrimination," op. cit., Table 15, 112 and 115. Becker computed the figures from U.S. Bureau of the Census data. Included in the "skilled" classification are professional persons, proprietors, managers and officials, clerks and kindred workers, and skilled workers and foremen. Farmers and farm tenants are excluded.

[4] Ibid. The references to Professor Becker's study in this paper relate to one section of his work—chapter 9. The major portion of his book is devoted to developing a theory of discrimination in the marketplace.

[5] Ibid., 111 and 112. Many of the data in this paper are from publications of the U.S. Bureau of Labor Statistics and the U.S. Bureau of the Census. The data collected by these agencies usually are for "nonwhites" rather than for "Negroes." However, since Negroes make up more than 95 per cent of the "nonwhite" classification, the paper describes the characteristics of Negroes on the basis of those data, and the term Negro will be employed rather than nonwhite. U.S. Bureau of Labor Statistics, Negroes in the United States, Bulletin 1119 (Washington, 1952), 1.

| Year | North | | | South | | |
|------|-------|------|-----------------------------------|-------|------|-----------------------------------|
| | Whites (1) | Negroes (2) | Negroes Divided by Whites (3) | Whites (4) | Negroes (5) | Negroes Divided by Whites (6) |
| 1950 | 1.90 | 1.46 | 0.77 | 2.11 | 1.38 | 0.65 |
| 1940 | 1.82 | 1.34 | 0.74 | 1.96 | 1.24 | 0.63 |
| 1910 | 1.70 | 1.24 | 0.73 | 1.73 | 1.16 | 0.67 |

SOURCE: Becker, "The Economics of Discrimination," op. cit., 113. Becker calculated the indexes as follows: The relative income position of skilled, semiskilled, and unskilled workers in the North in 1939 was estimated as 2.34, 1.44, and 1.00, respectively. Multiplying the percentage of whites in each occupational class by the corresponding income weights and summing the resulting products yields an occupational index of 1.90 for Northern whites in 1950. The same procedure was followed for calculating the remaining indexes.

In comparing 1950 with 1910, Negroes in the North had about a 5 per cent higher relative occupational position and in the South about a 2 per cent lower relative occupational position (columns 3 and 6 of Table 2). Since the indexes reveal little change in the occupational position of Negroes *relative* to whites, Professor Becker draws the "very tentative conclusion . . . that almost all the increase in the absolute occupational position of Negroes was caused by forces increasing the position of whites as well" and that there have been "neither striking increases nor striking decreases in discrimination against Negroes . . . during the last four decades."[6]

## OCCUPATIONAL INDEX ADJUSTED FOR CHANGES IN INCOME DIFFERENTIALS

There is, however, a serious error in Professor Becker's construction of an occupational index. His index employs *constant* weights of relative income for the three classes of skills and thus does not take into account the sharp narrowing of income differentials which has occurred since 1940. Since Negroes are much more heavily concentrated in semiskilled and unskilled occupations than are whites, the relative improvement of the Negroes is seriously understated when constant relative income weights are used.

Census data are available which make it possible to take into account the effect of narrowing income differentials and thereby to improve on Professor Becker's index. From these data, using a classification substantially similar to Becker's, it was possible to calculate the relative income position for skilled, semiskilled, and unskilled workers; for 1939 the figures are 2.33, 1.50, and 1.00; and for 1951 they are 1.73, 1.41, and 1.00.[7] When these 1939 and 1951 relative income figures are applied as weights to the occupational distribution

[6] *Ibid.*, 114 and 125.

[7] The relative income position for the various skills was calculated from data on median wage and salary income of males for 1939 and 1951 presented in Herman P. Miller, *Income of the American People,* a volume in the Census monograph series (New York, 1955), 105. The income of "Laborers, except farm and mine" was used as the income of the "unskilled" class and employed as a base equal to 1.00. The incomes of the semiskilled and the skilled were then expressed as relatives to that base. "Operatives and kindred workers'" income was used as the income of the "semi-skilled," and the incomes of the following were weighted by the percentage each was of the total number of employed persons to obtain the income of the "skilled": professional, technical, and kindred workers; managers, officials, and proprietors, excluding farm; clerical and kindred workers; sales workers; craftsmen, foremen, and kindred workers.

TABLE 3. INDEX OF THE OCCUPATIONAL POSITION OF NEGROES AND WHITE MALES, 1940 AND 1950 (BASED ON CHANGES IN RELATIVE INCOME WEIGHTS FOR DIFFERENT SKILLS)

| | North | | | South | | |
|---|---|---|---|---|---|---|
| Year | Whites (1) | Negroes (2) | Negroes Divided by Whites (3) | Whites (4) | Negroes (5) | Negroes Divided by Whites (6) |
| 1950 | 1.53 | 1.30 | .85 | 1.52 | 1.21 | .80 |
| 1940 | 1.83 | 1.35 | .74 | 1.78 | 1.21 | .68 |

SOURCE: See source of Table 2 of this paper for the method of calculating the occupational index. Data used to calculate indexes are from Becker, "The Economics of Discrimination," op. cit., 112, for the percentage of workers in each class, and from the source discussed in footnote 7 of this paper for the relative income weights.

for 1940 and 1950, respectively,[8] in the manner employed by Becker, they yield the indexes of occupational position shown in Table 3.

Becker's indexes, based on constant income weights, show a meager improvement in the relative position of Negroes between 1940 and 1950 of 4 per cent in the North and 3 per cent in the South (columns 3 and 6 of Table 2). However, when income weights which reflect the narrowing of income differentials are used, the indexes show a very substantial improvement in the relative position of Negroes between 1940 and 1950—a rise of 15 per cent in the North and 18 per cent in the South (columns 3 and 6 of Table 3). The relatively smaller increase in the North may be explained by the large shift of

Negroes from the South, discussed later in this paper.

As an additional check, and also in order to carry the analysis forward to recent years, the indexes of the occupational position of Negro and white males were reconstructed and are shown in Table 4. These indexes are for the United States as a whole for 1940, 1950, and 1958, and employ income weights, which reflect the narrowing of income differentials among the three skill classes. These data indicate about a 20 per cent advance in the occupational position of Negroes relative to whites between 1940 and 1950 (column 3 of Table 4). They also show that since 1950 there has been a slight decline in the occupational position of Negroes relative to whites.

TABLE 4. AN INDEX OF OCCUPATIONAL POSITION OF NEGRO AND WHITE MALES FOR THE UNITED STATES, 1940, 1950, 1958

| | Whites (1) | Negroes (2) | Negroes Divided by Whites (3) |
|---|---|---|---|
| 1958 | 1.62 | 1.30 | .80 |
| 1950 | 1.52 | 1.24 | .82 |
| 1940 | 1.82 | 1.25 | .68 |

SOURCE: U.S. Bureau of the Census, Current Population Reports—Consumer Income, Series P-60, for the relative income position of skilled, semiskilled, and unskilled workers. Becker, "The Economics of Discrimination," op. cit., 110, for the percentage of workers in each race in each occupational class. See source in Table 2 of this paper for method of calculating the occupational indexes.

[8] Comparable income data are not available for earlier years.

| | White | Nonwhite | Nonwhite as a Per Cent of White |
|---|---|---|---|
| 1939 | $1,112 | $ 460 | 41.4 |
| 1947 | 2,357 | 1,279 | 54.2 |
| 1948 | 2,711 | 1,615 | 59.6 |
| 1949 | 2,735 | 1,367 | 50.0 |
| 1950 | 2,982 | 1,878 | 61.3 |
| 1951 | 3,345 | 2,060 | 61.6 |
| 1952 | 3,507 | 2,038 | 58.1 |
| 1953 | 3,760 | 2,233 | 59.4 |
| 1954 | 3,754 | 2,131 | 56.8 |
| 1955 | 3,986 | 2,342 | 58.8 |
| 1956 | 4,260 | 2,396 | 56.2 |
| 1957 | 4,396 | 2,436 | 55.4 |

SOURCE: U.S. Bureau of the Census, *Current Population Reports—Consumer Income,* Series P-60.

Wage and salary income data for Negroes and whites also raise doubts concerning Becker's conclusion that the occupational position of Negroes relative to whites has changed little since 1940. Between 1939 and 1950 the median wage and salary income of Negroes relative to whites rose from 41.4 to 61.3, and although it declined to 55.4 by 1957, it was still about 34 per cent higher than in 1939 (Table 5). It is significant that the wage and salary data support the conclusion drawn from the preceding discussion of occupational indexes—that the occupational position of Negroes relative to whites rose substantially between 1940 and 1950 and then declined slightly down through 1958.

FACTORS CONTRIBUTING
TO OCCUPATIONAL
ADVANCEMENT OF NEGROES

Although the evidence presented must lead to a rejection of Professor Becker's statement that "the average occupational position of Negroes . . . relative to whites has been remarkably stable," it cannot be inferred that the improvement in the relative position of Negroes resulted from striking decreases in discrimination with respect to employment.

Rather than resulting from a reduction

in discrimination, the improved position of Negroes relative to whites was essentially a product of severe labor shortages between 1940 and 1948; the labor shortages opened up a wider range of job opportunities for Negroes, making possible for them substantial occupational shifts as well as large-scale movements from the South to other regions and from rural to urban areas.

It might be argued that the improved occupational position of Negroes and their greater mobility does in fact reflect a reduction in "discrimination." It is necessary, however, to distinguish between discriminatory attitudes, which are subjective, and the actual ability to discriminate, which is a function of the objective environmental situation, in this case the peculiar and transitory condition of the labor market. Thus employers may continue to have the same subjective attitude toward discrimination yet be unable or unwilling to act accordingly because of extreme shortages in the labor market which make it difficult to hold or attract workers. Under such conditions the employer may suppress his subjective desires in favor of maintaining a stable labor force. For a real reduction in discrimination in the attitudinal (and socially significant) sense, employers would have to continue to pursue the same hiring policies with respect to race even after the labor shortages disappeared. The following evidence indicates that there probably has not been a significant real reduction in discrimination in this sense between 1940 and 1958.

After 1948, with the exception of the Korean War period, the extremely tight labor markets of the World War II and postwar years disappeared. The three recessions since 1948 contributed considerably to the reduction in labor market pressures. With the disappearance of severe labor shortages the movement of Negroes, and consequently their occupational advancement (as shown by occupation and income data already discussed), slowed down considerably and actually declined somewhat after 1950. Since their improved position materialized, for the most part, between 1940 and 1948, it seems highly unlikely that the improvement can be explained by a reduction in discrimination during just those years. The decline in the occupational position of Negroes after 1950 also indicates that a reduction in discrimination was not the basic force improving the position of the Negro, unless one is willing to argue that the subjective desire to discriminate fell between 1940 and 1950 and then rose in subsequent years. The following discussion shows that the major occupational shifts for Negroes

occurred between 1940 and 1948, that during that period their geographic mobility relative to whites was greatest, and that subsequently their mobility declined significantly—all indicating the primary role played by labor shortages in making possible the occupational advancement of Negroes relative to whites.

Table 6 shows the percentage of Negro males employed in various occupations in 1940, 1944, 1947, and 1957. The occupational classes shown include about 80 per cent of the employed Negro males and are the ones into and out of which substantial movement of Negroes took place between 1940 and 1957. The major decreases in Negro employment took place in the two farm classifications and the major increases occurred in four classifications— clerical and sales; craftmen, foremen, and kindred workers; operatives and kindred workers; and laborers, except farm and mine. About 50 per cent of the decline in Negro employment in the farm classifications occurred during the first four years of the seventeen-year period, and more than 70 per cent of the decline had taken place by 1947. For the group of occupations which had substantial increases in Negro employment, about 50 per cent of the increase occurred by 1944 and about two-thirds by 1947.

TABLE 6. PERCENTAGE OF EMPLOYED NEGRO MALES IN VARIOUS OCCUPATIONS, 1940, 1944, 1947, 1957

| Occupation | 1940 | 1944 | 1947 | 1957 |
|---|---|---|---|---|
| Farmers and farm managers | 21.4 | 14.0 | 14.4 | 6.2 |
| Farm laborers and foremen | 20.3 | 14.9 | 8.3 | 8.6 |
| Total | 41.7 | 28.9 | 22.7 | 14.8 |
| Clerical and sales workers | 1.7 | 2.8 | 3.6 | 5.9 |
| Craftsmen, foremen, and kindred workers | 4.4 | 6.8 | 6.2 | 8.9 |
| Operatives and kindred workers | 12.5 | 22.3 | 23.0 | 25.2 |
| Laborers, except farm and mine | 21.0 | 20.3 | 24.0 | 25.5 |
| Total | 39.6 | 52.2 | 56.8 | 65.5 |

SOURCE: For 1940, 1944, and 1947 the figures were calculated from U.S. Bureau of the Census data presented in Seymour Wolfbein, "Postwar Trends in Negro Employment," *Monthly Labor Review*, 65 (December, 1947), 664. The 1957 figures are also Census data and were presented in U.S. Department of Labor, Bureau of Labor Statistics, *Notes on the Economic Situation of Negroes in the United States*, revised May 1958, 6.

|  | Per Cent of Nonwhites | Per Cent of Whites |
|---|---|---|
| 1935–40 | 3.9 | 5.6 |
| 1940–47 | 14.1 | 9.7 |
| 1948–49 | 1.9 | 3.1 |
| 1949–50 | 1.7 | 2.7 |
| 1950–51 | 2.0 | 3.7 |
| 1951–52 | 2.1 | 3.5 |
| 1952–53 | 2.0 | 3.8 |
| 1953–54 | 2.4 | 3.3 |
| 1954–55 | 2.2 | 3.2 |
| 1955–56 | 2.2 | 3.2 |
| 1956–57 | 2.5 | 3.2 |
| 1957–58 | 3.0 | 3.4 |

SOURCE: U.S. Bureau of the Census, *Current Population Reports—Population Characteristics,* Series P-20. The figures were compiled by the Bureau between April and March of the various years cited.

Interstate migration data also support the conclusions that the major portion of the relative improvement in the economic position of the Negro occurred during 1940–48 and may be attributed to the labor shortages of those years (Table 7). For all years since 1935, *except for 1940–47*, the percentage of whites migrating between states exceeded the percentage of Negroes migrating between states.[9] Between 1940 and 1947 the Negro migration percentage exceeded that of the white by 45 per cent. Since 1948 there was a complete reversal of the mobility pattern of the World War II and postwar years. Annual figures reveal that after 1948 the percentage of whites migrating between states was, on the average, fully 50 per cent higher than the percentage of Negroes migrating.[10]

While movements from the South to other regions and from rural to urban areas do not necessarily mean shifts into higher skill categories, those movements surely resulted in occupational advancement for the Negroes since their incomes relative to that of the whites are much higher in urban and non-Southern areas than they are in rural areas and the South. Even though the Negroes may have moved from one unskilled job to another in leaving rural and Southern areas, they undoubtedly found higher paying jobs within the unskilled class.[11]

Between 1940 and 1950 the urban white population increased 17.2 per cent while the Negro urban population rose 43.2 per cent, or at a rate more than two and one hilf times as fast. The decline in the percentage of Negroes in rural farm areas was more than 30 percent greater than the decline in the percentage of whites in those areas (Table 8).

The significance of the relatively greater rural to urban migration of Negroes for their occupational advancement relative to whites is a product of the fact that Negro-white income differentials were (and are) substantially greater in rural areas than in urban areas. In 1945, during

[9] As stated by Taeuber and Taeuber, "Since it is primarily young adults who move, the influence of migration on labor supplies is understated by such figures [as those in Table 7]." Conrad Taeuber and Irene Taeuber, *The Changing Population of the United States,* a volume in the Census monograph series (New York, 1958), 111.

[10] Bailer points to the close correlation between the centers classified as "Labor shortage areas" and the rate of non-white population increase during the 1940's. Lloyd H. Bailer, "The Negro Labor Force of the United States," *Journal of Negro Education,* XXII, No. 3, 303.

[11] Professor Becker's occupational index discussed previously further understates the improved position of the Negro relative to the white since it does not reflect the impact of the relatively larger migration of Negroes from the South and from rural areas.

TABLE 8.   PERCENTAGE CHANGE IN POPULATION BETWEEN 1940 AND 1950 IN URBAN, RURAL NONFARM, AND RURAL FARM AREAS, BY COLOR

|  | White | Negro |
|---|---|---|
| Urban | 17.2 | 43.2 |
| Rural nonfarm | 43.4 | 38.0 |
| Rural farm | −22.5 | −29.8 |
| United States Total | 14.1 | 16.9 |

SOURCE: Donald J. Bogue, *The Population of the United States* (Glencoe, Illinois, 1959), 126. Figures compiled by Bogue from *U.S. Census of Population,* 1950, Volume II, Part 1, Table 36, and estimates prepared for Bogue's study.

the period when the mobility of Negroes was greatest, the median income of Negroes in rural areas was only 37 per cent of the median income of whites in those areas, while in urban centers Negro income was 60 per cent of white income.[12] Thus the nature of the rural-urban migration was bound to advance the occupational position of Negroes relative to whites. Lending further support to this conclusion is the fact that fully ". . . four-fifths of the decrease in rural farm population [between 1940 and 1947] can be accounted for by the movement of non-white households, mostly southern Negro sharecroppers and their families, from the farm to nonfarm areas."[13] In addition, the "increases in the Negro population were especially marked in the largest cities,"[14] and it is in those cities that the income differential between Negroes and whites is smallest.[15]

The relatively greater movement of Negroes from the South,[16] which also contributed to their relative occupational advancement, is shown in Table 9 and 10. The Negro population as a percentage of the total population declined in the three southern regions while it increased in all non-southern regions. In the South, the

TABLE 9.   NEGRO POPULATION AS A PER CENT OF TOTAL POPULATION, BY REGION, 1940 AND 1950

|  | 1940 | 1950 |
|---|---|---|
| New England | 1.3 | 1.6 |
| Middle Atlantic | 4.7 | 6.4 |
| East North Central | 4.1 | 6.1 |
| West North Central | 3.0 | 3.5 |
| Mountain | 4.1 | 4.5 |
| Pacific | 3.7 | 5.2 |
| South Atlantic | 26.5 | 24.3 |
| East South Central | 25.8 | 23.6 |
| West South Central | 19.1 | 17.2 |

SOURCE: U.S. Bureau of Labor Statistics, *Negroes in the United States,* Bulletin No. 1119 (Washington, 1952), 36. The source for the BLS data was the U.S. Bureau of the Census.

[12] U.S. Bureau of the Census, *Current Population Reports—Consumer Income,* Series P–60.
[13] Miller, op. cit., 36.
[14] Taeuber and Taeuber, op. cit., 124 and 140.
[15] Miller, op. cit., 39.
[16] Clearly, there is some overlapping in the use of data on rural-urban migration and migration from the South. However, the two must be separated for analytical purposes since much of the movement from the rural South was not to other regions of the United States but to southern urban centers. Irene B. Taeuber, "Migration, Mobility, and the Assimilation of the Negro," *Population Bulletin,* XIV, No. 7, 129.

TABLE 10.    Percentage distribution of negro population by region, 1930–50

|      | South | Northeast | North Central | West |
|------|-------|-----------|---------------|------|
| 1950 | 62.5  | 18.9      | 14.8          | 3.8  |
| 1940 | 72.0  | 15.6      | 11.0          | 1.4  |
| 1930 | 74.1  | 14.3      | 10.6          | 1.0  |

Source: *U.S. Census of Population,* 1950, Series P-B.

Negro population declined sharply in the decade of the 1940's while it increased in all other regions of the United States. Since the median income of Negro males relative to whites was (and is) markedly lower in the South than in all other regions, the relatively larger shift of Negroes from the South contributed to raising their relative occupational position. In 1949 the median income of Negroes relative to whites was a low 45 per cent in the South, while in the other regions of the United States it ranged from 68 to 77 per cent.[17] Adding force to the point being made is the fact that of the sixteen states and the District of Columbia included in the "Southern" classification of Table 9, in only three did the Negro population hold its own relative to the white—in Delaware, Maryland, and the District of Columbia— all three of which are relatively high wage areas.[18]

## SUMMARY AND CONCLUSION

As Professor Ginzberg has held and as Professor Becker did not perceive because of the statistical procedure he employed, the present occupational position of the Negro relative to the white is substantially better than it was prior to World War II. However, it would be incorrect to infer that this change necessarily reflects a significant reduction in discrimination. On the contrary, evidence was presented which indicated that the relative rise in the position of the Negro was a product of the acute labor shortages which persisted throughout the war and postwar period of 1940–48, shortages which opened up a wider range of job opportunities for Negroes. The disappearance of severe labor shortages after 1948 slowed down considerably the occupational advancement of Negroes relative to whites and, in fact, contributed to a slight decline in the Negroe's relative position since 1950. Thus the ability of the Negro to hold or advance his occupational position is, substantially, a function of the tightness of the labor market.

It is conceivable that the continuous high levels of employment for the economy as a whole since 1941 might have permitted the Negro to sufficiently consolidate his occupational position so that it would not decline greatly relative to that of the whites even in the face of a prolonged and severe depression. Only the future can provide a test of this hypothesis.

Using varying weights, that is, the income prevailing in each period for the three occupational classifications of unskilled, semiskilled, and skilled, Rayack calculates substantial 1940–1950 gains for the Negro, recorded in Table 3.

[17] U.S. Bureau of the Census, *Census of Population,* 1950, Vol. II, Part 1 (Washington, 1953), Table 175.

[18] U.S. Bureau of Labor Statistics, op. cit., 36.

These results follow because of the narrowing skill differential for the period, with the Negro heavily represented in the unskilled ranks.

Becker, in his rebuttal to Rayack's method, presented here, points out that varying weights result in an incorrect measurement of the index of changes in job status in that they include changes in income level for each classification as well as the changes in occupational position that may take place.

# Discrimination and the Occupational Progress of Negroes: A Comment

## by Gary S. Becker

In my book on discrimination I tried to determine the secular trend during the first half of this century in the market discrimination against American Negroes.[1] Since readily available income data before the late thirties were lacking, secular changes in occupational distributions were examined. A secular decline in discrimination probably occurred if there was a large increase in the relative number of Negroes in the more skilled and prized occupations. Data brought together for 1910, 1940, and 1950 clearly revealed that Negroes had significantly advanced their occupational position in both the North and South. The data also revealed, however, a significant advance by whites, and therefore, a qualitative examination of this evidence could not indicate whether Negroes had advanced more than whites. My

problem paralleled many long solved by economists with index numbers and by demographers and others with standardized averages. Outputs, prices, birth rates, etc. in different periods or areas are made comparable through aggregate indexes, which usually are fixed weighted averages of the individual components, as in a Laspeyres or Paasche index.[2] So I proceeded to construct "indexes of occupational position" for the different years, which were fixed weighted averages of the proportion of Negroes or whites in different skill categories, the weights being the relative wages paid to whites in 1939.

These occupational indexes seemed as relevant in determining the advance of Negroes as price and output indexes are in determining the advance of prices and outputs. Yet Professor Rayack in a recent

SOURCE Reprinted with permission from *Review of Economics and Statistics,* Vol. 44, May 1962.

[1] See *The Economics of Discrimination* (Chicago, 1957), Ch. 9.
[2] Sometimes several fixed weighted indexes are chained together into a single more complicated index.

article[3] takes vigorous exception, arguing that "There is . . . a serious error in Professor Becker's construction of an occupational index."[4] The "serious error" is simply that I used fixed weights instead of current year weights.[5] Would Professor Rayack also claim that there is a serious error in the BLS Consumer Price Index because it uses fixed base year quantity weights instead of current year weights? I doubt it, for if current weights were used, the index would not measure movements in prices alone but that combined with movements in quantities. In the same way Rayack's indexes of occupational position —which use current year weights and are shown in his Tables 3 and 4—do not measure entry into the more skilled occupations alone, but that combined with changes in earnings differentials. Perhaps this argument can be made clearer with an example. Suppose the relative number of Negroes and whites in different occupations remained absolutely constant over time. Surely an index which alleges to measure entry into skilled occupations should not show any change. The fixed weighted indexes I used would not, while the weighted indexes preferred by Rayack would change whenever there was any change in earnings differentials.

It appears, therefore, that my indexes do and Rayack's do not correctly measure occupational position. His discussion does, however, indirectly raise the question of whether the patterns suggested by fixed weighted indexes are very sensitive to the weights used. To test this I computed indexes using the 1951 weights derived by Rayack. The results, shown in Table 1, strongly confirm those obtained with 1939 weights: both indicate little net change in the relative occupational position of Negroes from 1910 to 1950. So the impression of a rather striking stability in the relative occupation position of Negroes does not greatly depend on the weighting system used.

Since my study was concerned with the overall secular trend during the first half of the century I did not pay much attention to changes within sub-periods. I now believe, however, that I was amiss in not pointing out that from the viewpoint of contemporary or future events a more sanguine interpretation might be given to the rise from 1940 to 1950. Although small by absolute standards it is very large rela-

TABLE 1.  INDEX OF THE OCCUPATIONAL POSITION OF NEGROES AND WHITES, 1910, 1940, AND 1950 (1952 WEIGHTS)

| Year | North | | | South | | |
|---|---|---|---|---|---|---|
| | Whites | Negroes | Negroes Divided by Whites | Whites | Negroes | Negroes Divided by Whites |
| 1950 | 1.53 | 1.30 | .85 | 1.52 | 1.21 | .79 |
| 1940 | 1.49 | 1.22 | .82 | 1.45 | 1.13 | .78 |
| 1910 | 1.41 | 1.16 | .82 | 1.33 | 1.08 | .81 |

SOURCE: Rayack, op. cit., 210 and Becker, op. cit., Table 15.

[3] Alton Rayack, "Discrimination and the Occupational Progress of Negroes," this *Review*, XVIII (May 1961).

[4] *Ibid.*, 210.

[5] "His index employs *constant* weights of relative income for the three classes of skills and thus does not take into account the sharp narrowing of income differentials which has occurred since 1940. Since Negroes are much more heavily concentrated in semiskilled and unskilled occupations than are whites, the relative improvement of the Negroes is seriously understated when constant relative income weights are used." (*Ibid.*, 210).

tive to the per decade change from 1910 to 1940. 1940 may have marked the turning point when Negroes began entering skilled occupations on a much larger scale than they had previously. It should be noted, though, that Negroes apparently advanced only slightly during the fifties.[6]

In conclusion, let me note that Rayack is wrong in suggesting[7] that there is an inconsistency between indexes showing a modest improvement in the occupational position of Negroes during the forties and indexes showing a large rise in their relative incomes. Indeed, their divergent movement only demonstrates again the advantage of a fixed weighted occupational index, or more generally, of an index separating an advance into skilled occupations from other changes. A comparison of his Tables 4 and 5 indicates that a good part of the income rise resulted from a general narrowing of earning differentials among occupations. Surely the presumed change in discrimination against Negroes is very different if their relative incomes rose because of their advance into skilled occupations than if they rose because relative earnings in unskilled occupations, where Negroes are heavily represented, rose.[8] The similarity between the movement in relative incomes and in Rayack's occupational index and the divergent movement shown by my index is not, therefore, testimony to the value of his and the error in mine (as alleged by Rayack . . .) but, on the contrary, strikingly shows the advantage of a fixed weighted index in discovering the sources of a change in relative incomes as well as in measuring occupational position.

What is under measurement is the change in job station, as contrasted to or as a contributer to changes in income, but what results from the use of varying weights is mainly the influence of income changes. Job discrimination is not reduced, although the relative income level for the Negro rises because of a relative increase in unskilled wages, if the Negro occupational distribution remains unchanged.

By the same reasoning, the slight worsening of Rayack's index for the period 1950–1958 may not reflect a deterioration in the Negro's occupational status, but the reduction in his relative wage and salary income over the period, recorded in Table 5, accompanying the probable slight widening of the occupational wage structure and sluggish economic conditions of the period.

Rayack presents a strong case for the view that there has been no basic change in the intensity of economic discrimination, at least until the end of the 1950's, even if his methods of measuring variations in job status over time are questionable. It certainly does not reflect a movement toward fair attitudes if the Negro's economic status is tied to the business cycle, as his relative income position rises and falls with the economy and the strength of the unskilled job market, in a framework of rigid and low occupational status. Perhaps the recent improvement in the Negro's relative income level, hailed by many as a sign of slackening discrimination, really reflects relative strength in

[6] Their relative occupational position in the country as a whole went from .816 in 1950 to .822 in 1958 (if 1951 weights are used). Rayack's occupational indexes declined during this period presumably because earnings differentials widened.

[7] "Wage and salary income data for Negroes and whites also raise doubts concerning Becker's conclusion that the occupational position of Negroes relative to whites has changed little since 1940." (*Ibid.*, 211.)

[8] Neither Rayack's nor my occupational indexes try to measure the effect of a rise in the relative incomes of Negroes *within* a given occupation (see my comment, *Economics of Discrimination*, 114, n. 7).

the unskilled labor market that will be wiped out by a later weakening of the economy. This would tend to happen if, as is likely when business falters, the market for the unskilled declines the most, and the persent rise in the Negro's earnings is not a result of an improvement in his job status.

However, the measurement of discrimination, though highly desirable for policy purposes, is a difficult undertaking even when one uses a residual approach that attempts to account for everything except race as the authors discussed above have done. If we take a gross approach, and use later data, as Fein and the authors discussed in the remainder of this chapter tend to do, the Negro's economic position shows more improvement, although we still have little insight into the weights to be attached to different factors in the constellation of forces responsible for the economic status of blacks relative to whites.

Of course, except conceptually, it is difficult to assign a precise numerical value to discrimination because the term has no precise and universally accepted meaning; to blacks, it tends to mean institutionalized racism, but to whites discrimination is more likely to refer to specific, overt acts of discrimination. From a policy standpoint, therefore, it is important to attempt to create conditions that improve Negro employment patterns relative to whites rather than to rely exclusively on measures to combat overt discrimination.

### Negro Employment Patterns

In "The Negro Job Situation: Has It Improved?" Claire C. Hodge argues that there was a "marked improvement" in the kinds of jobs held by black Americans between 1957 and 1967, although the statistics presented here also show that "the Negro today still holds a disproportionate share of the jobs at the lower end of the occupational ladder and is underrepresented in the higher-skilled, better paying jobs."

Between 1962 and 1967, Negroes made considerable progress in medicine, health services, the construction trades, mechanics, repair services, and the protective service occupations. However, very little progress was made in managerial and sales fields. Hodge does not attempt to account for the net effect of race on Negro employment patterns.

# The Negro Job Situation: Has It Improved?

## by Claire C. Hodge

The past decade has seen a marked improvement in the number and kinds of jobs held by black Americans. Some of this occupational upgrading occurred between 1957 and 1962, but the trend accelerated sharply in the 1962–67 period, as nearly 1.1 million Negroes moved into jobs offering higher pay and status. Furthermore, during the past 5 years, the employment growth has been concentrated among full-time workers, while the number involuntarily on short workweeks—one measure of underemployment—has declined sharply.

Despite these recent substantial gains, however, the Negro today still holds a disproportionate share of jobs at the lower end of the occupational ladder and is underrepresented in the higher-skilled, better-paying jobs. In 1967, nearly half the employed Negroes were in unskilled, service, or farm jobs, compared with a fifth of the white workers. Conversely, nearly half of the employed whites held white-collar jobs, but less than one-fourth of the Negroes. Nevertheless, over the past decade, there has been improvement in the occupational configuration of Negro employment, with a concomitant increase in pay, status, and security.

## EMPLOYMENT-UNEMPLOYMENT TRENDS

In 1967, employment of Negroes[1] age 16 and over averaged 8 million, a 20-percent increase over a decade earlier. The number of Negroes employed increased by about 400,000 from 1957 to 1962 (5.4 percent) and by 1 million from 1962 to 1967 (14.4 percent)—in both periods a faster rate of growth than that of white

SOURCE Reprinted with permission from *Monthly Labor Review*, Vol. 92, No. 1, January 1969.

[1] Statistics for nonwhite workers are used to indicate the situation for Negro workers. Negroes constitute about 92 percent of all nonwhites in the United States.

| Occupation Group | 1957 [1,2] | 1962 [1] | 1967 | Change 1957 to 1962 (Percent) | Change 1962 to 1967 (Percent) |
|---|---|---|---|---|---|
| Total, 16 years of age and over | 6,647 | 7,004 | 8,011 | 5.4 | 14.4 |
| Total, 14 years of age and over | 6,749 | 7,097 | — | 5.2 | 12.9 [3] |
| Professional, technical, and kindred | 246 | 373 | 592 | 51.6 | 58.7 |
| Medical and health | 42 | 72 | 120 | 71.4 | 66.7 |
| Teachers, excluding college | 88 | 138 | 202 | 56.8 | 46.4 |
| Other | 116 | 163 | 271 | 40.5 | 66.3 |
| Managers, officials, and proprietors | 140 | 188 | 209 | 34.3 | 11.2 |
| Salaried | 35 | 77 | 115 | 120.0 | 49.4 |
| Self-employed, retail trade | 61 | 59 | 51 | −3.3 | −13.6 |
| Self-employed, excluding retail trade | 44 | 52 | 43 | 18.2 | −17.3 |
| Clerical | 401 | 512 | 899 | 27.7 | 75.6 |
| Stenographers, typists, and secretaries | 80 | 95 | 163 | 18.8 | 71.6 |
| Other | 321 | 417 | 736 | 29.9 | 76.5 |
| Sales | 78 | 115 | 138 | 47.4 | 20.0 |
| Retail trade | 62 | 77 | 99 | 24.2 | 28.6 |
| Other | 16 | 38 | 39 | 137.5 | 2.6 |
| Craftsmen and foremen | 380 | 427 | 617 | 12.4 | 44.5 |
| Carpenters | 35 | 44 | 52 | 25.7 | 18.2 |
| Construction excluding carpenters | 92 | 111 | 157 | 20.7 | 41.4 |
| Mechanics and repairmen | 119 | 133 | 192 | 11.8 | 44.4 |
| Metal craftsmen excluding mechanics | 35 | 36 | 69 | 2.9 | 91.7 |
| Other craftsmen | 76 | 76 | 100 | 0.0 | 31.6 |
| Foremen, not elsewhere classified | 23 | 27 | 49 | 17.4 | 81.5 |
| Operatives and kindred workers | 1,411 | 1,412 | 1,882 | 0.1 | 33.3 |
| Drivers and deliverymen | 314 | 303 | 354 | −3.5 | 16.8 |
| Other | 1,097 | 1,110 | 1,528 | 1.2 | 37.7 |
| Durable goods manufacturing | 342 | 359 | 575 | 5.0 | 60.2 |
| Nondurable goods manufacturing | 286 | 306 | 484 | 7.0 | 58.2 |
| Other industries | 469 | 445 | 409 | −5.1 | 5.4 |
| Nonfarm laborers | 1,007 | 962 | 899 | −4.5 | −6.5 |
| Construction | — | 225 | 197 | — | −12.4 |
| Manufacturing | — | 264 | 285 | — | 8.0 |
| Other industries | — | 473 | 416 | — | −12.1 |
| Service workers | 2,159 | 2,326 | 2,353 | 7.7 | 1.2 |
| Private households | 1,008 | 1,040 | 835 | 3.2 | −19.7 |
| Service workers, excluding private household | 1,151 | 1,286 | 1,519 | 11.7 | 18.1 |
| Protective service workers | 32 | 37 | 67 | 15.6 | 81.1 |
| Waiters, cooks, bartenders | 239 | 253 | 304 | 5.9 | 20.2 |
| Other service workers | 880 | 996 | 1,149 | 13.2 | 15.4 |
| Farm workers | 927 | 782 | 423 | −15.6 | −45.9 |
| Farmers and farm managers | 276 | 195 | 107 | −29.3 | −45.1 |
| Farm laborers and foremen | 651 | 587 | 317 | −9.8 | −46.0 |
| Paid | 463 | 444 | 281 | −4.1 | −36.7 |
| Unpaid family workers | 188 | 143 | 36 | −23.9 | −74.8 |

[1] Beginning in 1967, occupational data cover persons 16 years of age and over. Prior to 1967, occupational data have not been revised to exclude persons 14–15 years of age except for the figures on total employment shown here for comparison with 1967 total employment.

[2] 1957 averages based on observations for January, April, July, and October: 1962 and 1967 are based on 12-month averages.

[3] Based on change between 1962 including persons 14 years of age and over, and 1967 including persons 16 years and over.

Note: Dashes indicate data not available.

workers. Major factors contributing to these gains included an exceptional increase in the total number of job opportunities provided by the rapid economic expansion of most of the decade, new and expanded programs for restraining the existing workforce and for tr ining prospective new entrants to the labor force, higher levels of educational attainment, and the decline in discrimination in hiring. Some of this, of course, can also be attributed to increases in the Negro labor force and the fact that in 1962 unemployment among Negroes was very high, thus providing an ample supply of workers for employers.

The 1-million gain in the past 5 years was accompanied by a sharp drop in the Negro unemployment rate—from 10.9 percent in 1962 to 7.4 percent in 1967—which, even so, was about double the white rate, a differential that has persisted for more than a decade. For most color and age-sex groups, unemployment rates have fallen sharply since 1962, but the rate for Negro teenagers has remained between 25 and 30 percent.[2]

One encouraging development has been the decline in long-term unemployment of Negro workers. In 1962, 300,000 Negroes, or about one-third of the Negro unemployed, were out of a job 15 weeks or more. By 1967, the number of long-term unemployed had been cut significantly, and an average of only 100,000 Negroes (about one-sixth of total Negro unemployment) were jobless 15 weeks or more—about the same proportion as among white workers.

The 1962–67 period was also marked by a concentration of employment growth among full-time workers and a substantial decline in the number of workers who were on short workweeks for economic reasons. Over 90 percent of the increase in the total number of Negroes at work was in those on full-time job schedules (35 hours or more a week). By 1967, 5.8 million Negro nonagricultural workers were on full-time schedules, compared with 4.7 million 5 years earlier. During the same period, the number of nonagricultural Negro workers employed part time for economic reasons—such as slack work, material shortage, inability to find full-time work, and so forth—fell from 615,000 to 475,000.

Still another encouraging aspect during the past 5 years was the expansion of Negro employment into those industries considered to offer the best jobs in terms of pay, advancement, security, and status. Negro employment grew especially rapidly—by one-third or more—in the fields of education, public administration, and durable-goods manufacturing. The number of Negroes at work in these industries rose from 1.3 million in 1962 to 2.1 million in 1967, a pickup of nearly 60 percent, compared with an increase of about 25 percent for whites. Meanwhile, substantial reductions in Negro employment were noted in two lower-paying fields of work in which Negro workers have been concentrated in the past—agriculture and private household work.

MOVEMENT TOWARD BETTER JOBS

An evaluation of Negro occupational employment changes during the past decade points up clearly the significant upgrading of the black worker and his movement toward better jobs. As table 1 illustrates, the Negro made substantial gains between 1957 and 1962 but there was a sharp acceleration of this trend in the 1962–67 period.

From 1962 to 1967, the number of Negroes moving into better jobs reached sizable proportions among professional and technical workers, clerical workers, craftsmen and foremen, and operatives in

[2] See "The Employment Situation for Negroes," *Employment and Earnings and Monthly Report on the Labor Force,* September 1967; and *Recent Trends in Social and Economic Conditions of Negroes in the United States* (BLS Report 347, 1968).

the steel, automobile, and other durable goods manufacturing industries.[3] In total (including small increases in management, sales and protective service positions), there was an increase of nearly 1.1 million jobs in fields that generally offer higher pay and status, 3 times the increase in the previous 5 years. In addition, there was a substantial increase in the employment of Negro operatives in non-durable-goods manufacturing and non-manufacturing industries. Many of these semiskilled jobs (truck and taxi drivers, deliverymen, assemblers, etc.) offer good pay and steady work.

In the less attractive, lower paying, and less secure occupations, Negro employment declined about 600,000 from 1962 to 1967. There was a drop of about 200,000 private household workers, 60,000 industrial (nonfarm) laborers, and 360,000 farm workers. In the remaining occupational group—which consists of a diverse group of service-worker occupations that are difficult to classify according to quality—Negro employment increased by about 230,000.

The rise in Negro professional and technical workers has been about equally divided between men and women. The increase in clerical and service jobs (except protective services) has been greatest among women. On the other hand, the advance in salaried managerial, crafts, durable goods operatives, and protective service occupations has been mostly among men.

One way of evaluating the extent to which Negro workers have succeeded in gaining entry into higher status or better paying occupations is to examine the changes that have taken place in the proportion of such jobs held by black workers in relation to the total proportion of Negroes in the labor force. In 1967, Negroes constituted 10.8 per cent of total employment; therefore, while their share of white-collar jobs, for example, increased from 4.0 percent in 1962 to 5.4 percent in 1967, they were still underrepresented in the white-collar jobs. It is significant, however, that in this 5-year period they moved at least part of the distance between the 4-percent level of 1962 and the 10.8 percent that would equal their proportion in the employed labor force. The gain of 1.4 percentage points represents about one-fifth of the distance they would have had to gain to move from 4.0 to 10.8 percent.

This way of evaluating occupational gains is illustrated in table 2. The computation, of course, is useful only to provide a rough measure of relative gains in different occupations. There is no reason to expect the members of any one ethnic group to be distributed among occupations exactly like every other group; even if all racial discrimination in employment and all inequalities in educational and training opportunity were removed, the traditional interests, personal preferences, and geographic location of various ethnic groups might lead to a somewhat different mix of occupations. Keeping these qualifications in mind, however, one can compare the Negroes' proportion of jobs in each occupation with their proportion of total employment to give a rough measure of progress.

As noted above, Negroes made substantial progress in white-collar jobs in the 5-year period 1962 to 1967. Most noteworthy are their gains in medical and health occupations and clerical occupations—in each case they moved about

---

[3] Employment data by occupation and color for 1967 are not exactly comparable with data for years prior to 1966. Data prior to 1967 have not been revised to exclude persons 14 and 15 years of age. However, Negro 14- and 15-years-olds have little impact on specific occupations or on the occupational distribution, since they make up less than 2 percent of total Negro employment. In 1966, this group of 93,000 Negro teenagers was composed of farm workers (30 percent), nonfarm laborers (18 percent), service workers except in private households (16 percent), private household workers (15 percent), salesworkers (12 percent), operatives (6 percent), and clerical workers (3 percent).

TABLE 2.   NONWHITE WORKERS AS A PROPORTION OF ALL WORKERS IN HIGHER STATUS OCCUPATIONS

| Occupation | Nonwhite workers as a proportion of all workers in the occupation | | | Increase in proportion of nonwhite workers required to reach 10.8 percent of all workers in occupation [1] (Percentage points) | Actual increase, 1962–67, as a percent of the increase required to reach 10.8 percent (Percent) |
| | Percent | | Increase, 1962–67 (Percentage points) | | |
| | 1962 | 1967 | | | |
|---|---|---|---|---|---|
| Professional, technical and kindred workers | 4.6 | 6.0 | 1.4 | 6.2 | 23 |
| Medical and health | 5.3 | 7.6 | 2.3 | 5.5 | 42 |
| Teachers, except college | 8.1 | 9.4 | 1.3 | 2.7 | 48 |
| Others | 3.3 | 4.4 | 1.1 | 7.5 | 15 |
| Managers, officials, and proprietors | 2.5 | 2.8 | 0.3 | 8.3 | 4 |
| Salaried | 1.9 | 2.2 | 0.3 | 8.9 | 3 |
| Self-employed, retail trade | 3.7 | 4.7 | 1.0 | 7.1 | 14 |
| Self-employed, other | 2.9 | 3.8 | 0.9 | 7.9 | 11 |
| Clerical and kindred workers | 5.1 | 7.3 | 2.2 | 5.7 | 39 |
| Stenographers, typists and secretaries | 3.8 | 5.1 | 1.3 | 7.0 | 19 |
| Others | 5.5 | 8.0 | 2.5 | 5.3 | 47 |
| Sales workers | 2.6 | 3.0 | 0.4 | 8.2 | 5 |
| Retail trade | 3.0 | 3.6 | 0.6 | 7.8 | 8 |
| Other | 2.1 | 2.2 | 0.1 | 8.7 | 1 |
| Craftsmen, foremen, and kindred workers | 4.9 | 6.3 | 1.4 | 5.9 | 24 |
| Carpenters | 5.4 | 6.2 | 0.8 | 5.4 | 15 |
| Construction craftsmen except carpenters | 6.5 | 8.2 | 1.7 | 4.3 | 40 |
| Mechanics and repairmen | 6.2 | 7.6 | 1.4 | 4.6 | 30 |
| Metal crafts except mechanics | 3.4 | 5.5 | 2.1 | 7.4 | 28 |
| Other craftsmen | 4.3 | 5.4 | 1.1 | 6.5 | 17 |
| Foremen, not elsewhere classified | 2.2 | 3.4 | 1.2 | 8.6 | 14 |
| Protective service workers | 4.6 | 7.0 | 2.4 | 6.2 | 39 |

[1] Difference between 1962 level and 10.8 percent (the proportion of Negroes in the employed labor force in 1967).

NOTE: Operatives and kindred workers are not included in this table because the nonwhite proportion was greater than 10.8 percent of all workers in the occupation in 1967. (See table 4.)

two-fifths of the way toward the theoretical goal of 10.8 percent. Already relatively well-represented in the teaching profession, Negroes covered nearly half of the distance in teaching jobs. The slowest upgrading, and the smallest relative progress, was found in the managerial and sales occupations, in which Negroes moved less than 5 percent of the distance.

In the skilled crafts, Negroes also made substantial gains, moving nearly one-quarter of the way toward the 10.8 figure. Notable gains were made in the construction trades (where a modest gain among carpenters was far outdistanced by progress in other trades), mechanics and repairmen, and metal crafts. Notable progress was made in protective service occupations, which include policemen, firemen, guards, and watchmen. Negroes increased their share of these jobs sharply in the 5-year period, moving nearly two-fifths of the distance toward a proportionate number of jobs.

Negroes thus have made substantial progress in a relatively short period toward better representation in some of the major higher status, better paid occupational fields. This is a significant record, even if it has to be qualified in two major respects: First, within any of the broad occupation groups for which data are available there are occupations with a wide range of earnings levels and status, and Negroes may have entered the lower levels in greater proportions than the higher levels; second, differences in pay and status exist even within a specific occupation, and this, too, could result in a greater degree of occupational inequality than is apparent from the broad occupational group data.

## CHANGES IN PATTERNS

The changes in Negro occupational patterns are summarized in chart 1 and described in greater detail below.

About two-thirds of the net increase in employment of all Negro workers from 1962 to 1967 was in professional and technical, managerial, clerical, and sales occupations. As a result, the proportion of all Negro workers who were employed in

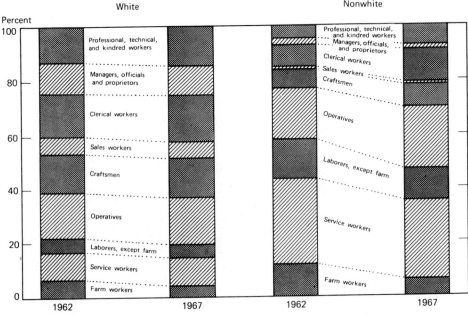

Chart 1. Change in distribution of workers, by occupational group, 1962–1967.

white-collar jobs rose substantially, from 16.7 percent in 1962 to 22.9 percent in 1967. Nevertheless, Negroes still represented only 5.4 percent of all white-collar workers in 1967, a moderate rise from the 4.0 percent in 1962.

The most substantial gains in Negro employment were among professional and technical workers (an increase of 59 percent) and clerical workers (76 percent).

Black workers in professional and technical occupations numbered 600,000 in 1967, a gain of 200,000 jobs since 1962. The proportion of all Negro workers who were employed in such jobs advanced significantly during this period, from 5.3 to 7.4 percent.

Within the professional fields, teaching remained a primary field of employment for Negro college graduates, and, as a result, Negroes made up a relatively large proportion of all teachers—8.1 percent in 1962 and 9.4 percent in 1967. Negroes have also made substantial advances in medical and health jobs.

Negro employment opportunities grew even more rapidly in the clerical occupations. From 1962 to 1967, Negro clerical worker employment grew by 400,000 to 900,000. Although these are fast-growing occupations for whites as well as for Negroes, the proportion of Negro workers nonetheless increased sharply, both as a percent of their total employment and within the occupational group. The largest part of the gain occurred in clerical occupations other than stenographers, typists, and secretaries, in jobs such as cashiers, shipping and receiving clerks, stock clerks and storekeepers, mail carriers, postal clerks, and so forth.

## MANAGERS AND SALESWORKERS

In managerial and sales occupations, little occupational improvement occurred in the 1962–67 period. There were increases of less than 25,000 each in the number of Negroes in these two fields, and the proportion of all Negro workers who were employed in these occupations remained virtually unchanged.

One reason for so little progress in these two groups is that it is easier to gain access to faster growing fields, where openings are more plentiful, than to move into relatively stable occupations such as managers or more slowly growing occupations such as sales workers.

A second reason may be educational and skill requirements that make it difficult for many Negroes to qualify for these jobs. In 1966, the median educational attainment for persons employed in these two groups was about 12.5 years, higher than for any other group except professional workers. Another reason may be that Negroes often lack the experience that would permit upgrading or, as in the case of managers of small businesses, the financial resources to start their own enterprises. Also, the fact that a large proportion of sales jobs offer only part-time work and its corresponding low income may have discouraged Negro workers from entering sales jobs. Many qualified Negroes, women in particular, may prefer to seek full-time jobs elsewhere because they need the added earnings to augment their generally low family incomes.

One encouraging recent development is the progress of Negroes into salaried managerial positions, often in large companies or in government. The number of Negro salaried managers rose by about 40,000 from 1962 to 1967, nearly a 50-percent increase. This is a rapidly growing field (the exception within this major group) for both Negro and white workers, and the Negro proportion of all such jobs edged up only from 1.9 to 2.2 percent. (See tables 3 and 4.)

In the self-employed group of managers, on the other hand, the number of Negroes declined, as did the number of white workers in the occupation. These self-employed managerial positions differ

[Numbers in thousands]

| Occupation Group | 1962 [1] | | | | 1967 | | | |
|---|---|---|---|---|---|---|---|---|
| | White | | Nonwhite | | White | | Nonwhite | |
| | Num-ber | Per-cent | Num-ber | Per-cent | Num-ber | Per-cent | Num-ber | Per-cent |
| Total | 60,749 | 100.0 | 7,097 | 100.0 | 66,361 | 100.0 | 8,011 | 100.0 |
| Professional, technical and kindred | 7,667 | 12.6 | 373 | 5.3 | 9,287 | 14.0 | 592 | 7.4 |
| Managers, officials, and proprietors | 7,220 | 11.9 | 188 | 2.6 | 7,287 | 11.0 | 209 | 2.6 |
| Clerical | 9,594 | 15.8 | 512 | 7.2 | 11,435 | 17.2 | 899 | 11.2 |
| Sales | 4,231 | 7.0 | 115 | 1.6 | 4,387 | 6.6 | 138 | 1.7 |
| Craftsmen and foremen | 8,250 | 13.6 | 427 | 6.0 | 9,229 | 13.9 | 617 | 7.7 |
| Operatives and kindred | 10,629 | 17.5 | 1,412 | 19.9 | 12,002 | 18.1 | 1,882 | 23.5 |
| Nonfarm laborers | 2,597 | 4.3 | 962 | 13.6 | 2,635 | 4.0 | 899 | 11.2 |
| Service workers | 6,476 | 10.6 | 2,326 | 32.8 | 6,971 | 10.5 | 2,353 | 29.4 |
| Private household | 1,301 | 2.1 | 1,040 | 14.7 | 934 | 1.4 | 835 | 10.4 |
| Service, excluding private household | 5,175 | 8.5 | 1,286 | 18.1 | 6,037 | 9.1 | 1,519 | 19.0 |
| Farm workers | 4,084 | 6.7 | 782 | 11.0 | 3,130 | 4.7 | 423 | 5.3 |
| Farmers and farm managers | 2,400 | 4.0 | 195 | 2.7 | 1,862 | 2.8 | 107 | 1.3 |
| Farm laborers and foremen | 1,684 | 2.8 | 587 | 8.3 | 1,268 | 1.9 | 317 | 4.0 |

[1] Beginning in 1967, occupational data cover persons 16 years of age and over. Prior to 1967, persons 14 years of age and over are included.

greatly from salaried jobs. Many self-employed managers (both white and Negro) are proprietors of small marginal businesses. Moreover, opportunities in this type of work have been declining rapidly; the number of self-employed managers fell by about one-third from 1962–67.[4] However, special new programs designed to assist Negro small businessmen to remain in operation and the push for Negro-owned and managed businesses in ghettos may offset some of these recent declines.

## CRAFTSMEN AND OPERATIVES

Two blue-collar groups—craftsmen and foremen, and operatives and kindred workers—have also provided additional well-paying higher status jobs for Negroes over the last 5 years. The number of Negro craftsmen and operatives increased about 35 percent, and the proportion of all Negro workers who were employed in these occupations also rose, equaling the propor-

tion of all white workers in these occupations. However, the bulk of the employment gain occurred in the operative group, where Negroes were already employed in large numbers.

In the higher skilled craftsmen group, Negro employment rose 45 percent. Because of large gains for white workers, however, Negro workers still remain underrepresented in craftsmen jobs. Nevertheless, progress in the occupational group has kept pace with the proportionate increase in professional and technical occupations.

The picture differs sharply among individual craftsmen occupations, however. The most improved situation was for construction workers (except carpenters), mechanics and repairmen, and metal craftsmen (except mechanics). The occupations of construction craftsmen and mechanics and repairmen provided the largest number of additional opportunities for Negro job seekers—an increase of more

[4] In 1967 the Current Population Survey tightened its definition of self-employed, which had the effect of shifting many self-employed workers to the wage and salary group. However, it appears likely that even without this change the number of self-employed Negroes would have declined.

[Numbers in thousands]

| Occupation Group | 1957 [1,2] | | 1962 [1] | | 1967 | |
|---|---|---|---|---|---|---|
| | Total Employment | Percent Nonwhite | Total Employment | Percent Nonwhite | Total Employment | Percent Nonwhite |
| Total | 65,100 | 10.4 | 67,846 | 10.5 | 74,372 | 10.8 |
| Professional, technical, and kindred | 6,476 | 3.8 | 8,040 | 4.6 | 9,879 | 6.0 |
| Medical and health | 1,157 | 3.6 | 1,353 | 5.3 | 1,578 | 7.6 |
| Teachers, excluding college | 1,351 | 6.5 | 1,713 | 8.1 | 2,159 | 9.4 |
| Other | 3,968 | 2.9 | 4,974 | 3.3 | 6,143 | 4.4 |
| Managers, officials, and proprietors | 6,705 | 2.1 | 7,408 | 2.5 | 7,495 | 2.8 |
| Salaried | 3,045 | 1.1 | 4,053 | 1.9 | 5,284 | 2.2 |
| Self employed—retail trade | 1,835 | 3.3 | 1,583 | 3.7 | 1,074 | 4.7 |
| Self employed, excluding retail trade | 1,825 | 2.4 | 1,773 | 2.9 | 1,137 | 3.8 |
| Clerical | 9,172 | 4.4 | 10,107 | 5.1 | 12,333 | 7.3 |
| Stenographers, typists, and secretaries | 2,170 | 3.7 | 2,511 | 3.8 | 3,190 | 5.1 |
| Other | 7,002 | 4.6 | 7,596 | 5.5 | 9,144 | 8.0 |
| Sales | 4,137 | 1.9 | 4,346 | 2.6 | 4,525 | 3.0 |
| Retail trade | 2,495 | 2.5 | 2,529 | 3.0 | 2,761 | 3.6 |
| Other | 1,642 | 1.0 | 1,817 | 2.1 | 1,765 | 2.2 |
| Craftsmen and foremen | 8,663 | 4.4 | 8,678 | 4.9 | 9,845 | 6.3 |
| Carpenters | 899 | 3.9 | 812 | 5.4 | 840 | 6.2 |
| Construction, excluding carpenters | 1,673 | 5.5 | 1,705 | 6.5 | 1,923 | 8.2 |
| Mechanics and repairmen | 2,032 | 5.9 | 2,145 | 6.2 | 2,539 | 7.6 |
| Metal crafts, excluding mechanics | 1,182 | 3.0 | 1,046 | 3.4 | 1,260 | 5.5 |
| Other craftsmen | 1,709 | 4.4 | 1,751 | 4.3 | 1,858 | 5.4 |
| Foremen, not elsewhere classified | 1,168 | 2.0 | 1,218 | 2.2 | 1,427 | 3.4 |
| Operatives and kindred | 12,542 | 11.3 | 12,041 | 11.7 | 13,884 | 13.6 |
| Drivers and deliverymen | 2,330 | 13.5 | 2,352 | 12.9 | 2,511 | 14.1 |
| Other | 10,212 | 10.7 | 9,689 | 11.5 | 11,372 | 13.4 |
| Durable goods manufacturing | 3,805 | 9.0 | 3,611 | 9.9 | 4,751 | 12.1 |
| Nondurable goods manufacturing | 3,458 | 8.3 | 3,314 | 9.2 | 3,761 | 12.9 |
| Other industries | 2,949 | 15.9 | 2,764 | 16.1 | 2,861 | 16.4 |
| Nonfarm laborers | 3,682 | 27.3 | 3,559 | 27.0 | 3,533 | 25.4 |
| Construction | N.A. | N.A. | 747 | 30.1 | 732 | 26.9 |
| Manuacturing | N.A. | N.A. | 1,017 | 26.0 | 1,107 | 25.7 |
| Other industries | N.A. | N.A. | 1,796 | 26.3 | 1,694 | 24.6 |
| Service workers | 7,653 | 28.2 | 8,802 | 26.4 | 9,325 | 25.3 |
| Private household | 2,108 | 47.8 | 2,341 | | | |
| Service workers excluding private household | 5,545 | 20.8 | 6,461 | 44.4 | 1,769 | 47.2 [3] |
| | | | | 19.9 | 7,556 | 20.1 |
| Protective service workers | 742 | 4.3 | 805 | 4.6 | 954 | 7.0 |
| Waiters, cooks, bartenders | 1,593 | 15.0 | 1,774 | 14.3 | 2,061 | 14.8 |
| Other service workers | 3,210 | 27.4 | 3,882 | 25.7 | 4,541 | 25.3 |
| Farm workers | 6,070 | 15.3 | 4,866 | 16.1 | 3,554 | 11.9 |
| Farmers and farm managers | 3,326 | 8.3 | 2,595 | 7.5 | 1,970 | 5.4 |
| Farm laborers and foremen | 2,744 | 23.7 | 2,271 | 25.8 | 1,584 | 20.0 |
| Paid | 1,495 | 31.0 | 1,382 | 32.1 | 1,049 | 26.8 |
| Unpaid family workers | 1,249 | 15.1 | 889 | 16.1 | 536 | 6.7 |

[1] Beginning in 1967, occupational data cover persons 16 years of age and over. Prior to 1967, persons 14 years of age and over are included.

[2] 1957 averages based on observations for January, April, July, and October.

[3] The change in definition of employment eliminating persons 14 and 15 years of age affects comparisons of white-nonwhite employment in this category. If allowances are made for these changes, the proportion of Negroes in this occupation would be slightly lower in 1967 than in 1962.

N.A.—Not available.

Negro Employment and Income    883

than 100,000 workers, or 43 percent, during the 5-year period.

Negro operatives had increased opportunities in both durable and nondurable-goods manufacturing, a rise of about 200,-000 jobs in each. Operative jobs in steel, automotive, and other durable-goods manufacturing offer better pay and status than operative jobs in nondurable goods, and are usually filled by men. Between 1962 and 1967, Negroes in operative jobs increased from 1.4 to 1.9 million. By 1967, nearly one-quarter of all Negroes were employed as operatives.

Despite the gains enumerated above, in 1967 41 percent of all Negro workers were still employed in unskilled or service jobs. This compared with only 15 percent of all white workers.

In the nonfarm labor group, Negro employment declined between 1962 and 1967. The proportion of all Negro workers who were in this occupational group also fell, as declines in the number of Negro laborers in construction and other industries offset an increase in the number of Negro laborers in manufacturing. However, because manual labor is a declining occupation for both whites and Negroes, the proportion of Negro workers to the total in the occupation was practically unchanged between 1962 and 1967.

SERVICE WORKERS

Declines in the number of Negro service workers in private households and farm workers have made a further contribution to the overall upgrading of Negro workers. It would appear that most workers leaving these fields during the last 5 years have found better opportunities elsewhere, since their numbers were at least not added to the unemployed rolls.

The number of Negro service workers (not including private household workers) rose by nearly 250,000 in the 1962–67 period, to a total of 1.5 million, keeping pace with the overall increase in service-worker employment. As a result, Negro employment as a proportion of the occupational group was unchanged from 1962 to 1967. Because there are a variety of jobs in the group with different rates of pay, hours of work, benefits, security and status, these developments are difficult to evaluate in terms of upgrading.

There are several tentative conclusions that can be drawn, however. Negro workers continue to be concentrated in the desirable service occupations. For example, the latest available data (1966) show that black workers made up 30 percent or more of the employment of chambermaids and maids and janitors and sextons. On the other hand, Negroes constituted less than 10 percent of those more desirable service occupations—bartenders, hairdressers, firemen, policemen, and guards. Negro workers have nonetheless made gains in these better jobs durings the last 5 years. For example, job opportunities have been good in the protective service category—policemen, firemen and guards—and the number of Negroes employed has increased from less than 40,000 to nearly 70,000. Except for the protective service group, the rise in service-worker employment has been among women.

The largest Negro job increase in the service occupations (150,000) was in the less favorable "other service workers" category. Typically, Negro men in these jobs were janitors and sextons, porters, and kitchen workers. Negro women held more than half of all jobs in this category, typically as hospital attendants, chambermaids and maids, kitchen workers not elsewhere classified, and practical nurses. Except for practical nurses, most of these jobs pay very low wages and offer little in the way of advancement. Thus, increased employment in these occupations does not necessarily reflect an upgrading of the Negro worker.

During the past 5 years, both whites and Negroes have been leaving domestic service jobs in large numbers. Employment of Negro private household workers (nearly all women) fell by 200,000. However, the number of white workers in this category also declined, and the proportion of Negro workers to the total in the occupation was basically unchanged.[5]

The number of Negro farm workers continued to decline, dropping by more than 350,000 between 1962 and 1967, with Negroes leaving the farms at twice the white rate. As a result, the proportion of all Negro workers employed as farm workers was halved by 1967, and farm work now accounts for about the same proportion of black as white employment. However, Negro farm workers were primarily farm laborers and foremen, while three-fifths of all white farm workers were farmers and farm managers.

### Negro Unemployment

There is overwhelming evidence that Negroes and other minorities suffer higher unemployment rates than whites. Moreover, during the 1960's nonwhite-white unemployment ratios generally were over 2:1. However, we are not at all sure about the reasons for these differentials. The easy answer is "discrimination," but this term is difficult to define or to measure. In its most general and meaningful sense, discrimination refers to the pervasive, institutional forces that cause Negroes to be at a disadvantage in incomes, housing, education, and other aspects of life. In another sense, discrimination means the specific overt acts that cause Negroes or other minorities to be discriminated against because of their race. Since institutional discrimination is captured by education, skill, and other variables, it becomes very difficult to measure the importance of these factors in accounting for differentials in income or employment. In other words, we know that unemployment differentials vary by occupation, education, and skill level, but if we try to standardize for these variables, we have difficulty because skill and education levels are themselves influenced by institutional discrimination.

In "Economic Discrimination and Unemployment," Harry J. Gilman attempts to account for the racial differences in unemployment rates by standardizing for such factors as education, age, occupation, and region. He shows that a sizable amount of the racial differences in male unemployment rates can be accounted for by standardization.

However, Gilman recognizes that the residual differences might be due in part to insufficient standardization. In examining this problem, he notes that standardization reduces a much larger proportion of the racial unemployment differential in the South than it does in the non-South. The pattern of unemployment differentials reveals lower rates at the extremes of the occupational differentials, with higher rates in the craftsman category. Indeed,

> . . . in most major occupations, nonwhite males with low levels of education had . . . lower unemployment rates than white males with similar

[5] Changes in definitions of employment and unemployment instituted in 1967 eliminated 14- and 15-year-olds from the employment totals. As indicated previously, this did not affect the occupational composition of Negro employment, However, since this change eliminates 300,000–350,000 white baby-sitters from the total, it does affect comparisons of white-nonwhite employment in this category. If allowances are made for these changes, the proportion of Negroes in the occupation would be slightly lower in 1967 than in 1962.

education, increased for groups with one to three years of high school education, and declined for high school graduates and for groups with college education.

Moreover,

> . . . the unemployment differentials for the lower-skilled groups are small or negative for the South but positive and substantial for the North and West.

Gilman concludes,

> . . . the patterns among the residual unemployment-rate differences . . . are inconsistent with the hypothesis that they are due to incomplete control over the skill factor.

Gilman then examines the differential wage-rate-rigidity hypothesis.

> The existence of economic discrimination against nonwhite workers need not lead to higher unemployment rates for nonwhite than for white workers. Under complete wage flexibility, for instance, the majority's preference for discrimination will result in higher wages for white than for nonwhite workers.

However, if wages are rigid or equalized by law or collective bargaining, employers who prefer white workers may reduce

> employment opportunities of nonwhite relative to white workers. Thus we would expect a greater effect of such factors as statutory and union minimum wages on the employment opportunities of nonwhite than of white workers; employment opportunities should fall more for nonwhite than for white workers.

However, this factor could not explain the unemployment differential of the highest occupational groups, because these are not influenced directly by minimum wages. Moreover, according to Gilman, unions are weaker in the South than in the non-South, and therefore this might have weakened their ability to reduce wage differentials. He also assumes minimum wage coverage to be smaller in the South, although there is less evidence for this assumption. If anything, minimum wages probably have had a relatively greater impact on the South than on the non-South because the South has had much higher proportion of workers below the legal minimum. Gilman notes, moreover, that the differential unemployment rates would exist whether or not wages were inflexible because of the greater range of occupational choices open to whites.

An alternative hypothesis, not explored by Gilman, might explain his inverted U-shaped racial wage differential pattern, which means that the greatest differentials are in the middle occupational ranges. Nonwhites might suffer relatively greater unemployment rates in those markets in which they have the greatest competition with whites and the least in labor markets where nonwhites are more isolated from white competition. Since most black professionals probably have black clients, racial segregation protects their market. At the other end of the occupational scale, blacks might be "protected" from competition by prevailing employer prejudices that Negroes are "better suited" for low-wage, hot, dirty, and menial jobs than whites. These attitudes and segregation are stronger in the South than the non-South. In all regions, racial competition in the labor market is probably greater in the middle occupational ranges, which are heavily influenced by the manufacturing sector in which Negroes have very limited managerial control of job opportunities.

The wage-rigidity hypothesis probably has much less explanatory power than would a broader model that includes institutional forces. It is perhaps true that employers' discriminatory preferences manifest themselves in wage discounts, but prejudices are not uniform throughout the occupational structure. In other words, some employers have preferences for black workers for some jobs. This probably is particularly true of black employers. Moreover, other factors, particularly the supply of white and black labor, because of institutional barriers to entry, may not be responsive to wage differentials. Similarly, job status, influenced by such factors as whether a particular job leads to promotion into higher-level jobs, also is important and might not be revealed in comparative wage rates. (For evidence on this point, see David P. Taylor, "Discrimination and Occupational Wage Differentials," *Industrial and Labor Relations Review*, April 1968.)

# Economic Discrimination and Unemployment

## by Harry J. Gilman

The proposition that members of minority groups are "the last to be hired and the first to be fired" has gained wide acceptance. This proposition will be interpreted here as saying that the burden of short-time layoffs and unemployment will fall disproportionately on workers, such as nonwhite workers, who are members of minority groups. Given this interpretation, the aggregate unemployment rates for white and nonwhite workers support the proposition in two respects: (a) the level of unemployment has been persistently greater for nonwhite than for white workers, and (b) the absolute cyclical variability of unemployment rates has been greater for nonwhite than for white workers.

However, differences in aggregate unemployment rates are not necessarily the result of differential hiring and firing of nonwhite workers. Instead, such differences may be accounted for by some characteristics of the nonwhite labor force which also produce higher unemployment rates for subgroups of the white labor force. Nonwhite workers, for instance, are employed disproportionately in the occupations in which unemployment rates for white workers are highest in level and in the absolute size of the cyclical swings. Also, within occupations nonwhite workers have lower levels of education (see Table 3) and less on-the-job training[1] than do white workers.

Moreover, although there is ample evidence of economic and political discrimination against nonwhite persons in the United States, it is important to distinguish the effects of discrimination on, for example, the level of training and the occupational distribution from its effects

SOURCE Reprinted with permission from *American Economic Review*, December 1965.

[1] See Jacob Mincer's estimates of investment in "On-The-Job Training" [8].

on unemployment rates, given the level of skill. The cure for discrimination at the points of hiring and firing may be quite different from the cure for higher unemployment rates due to low levels of skill.

This paper examines only the difference in levels of unemployment rates between white and nonwhite experienced male workers.[2] The 1940 and 1950 census data show a greater impact of unemployment on nonwhite than on white workers. This differential impact continues into the 1960's. For instance, in the period October, 1953-October, 1961, the average unemployment rates for white and nonwhite male wage and salary workers were 5 and 10.4 per cent, respectively. The two questions for which this paper attempts to provide answers are these:

1 To what extent can the persistently higher level of the unemployment rate for nonwhite than for white male workers be accounted for by differences between the two groups in their distributions by occupation, education, age, industry, region, and like characteristics?

2 Are the residual differences—those that remain after standardization for such differences as skill—related to other aspects of market discrimination against nonwhites that have been revealed in other studies [3] [29] [5] [10]?

The first of these questions is examined in Part I, the second in Part II. Part III is a summary of findings.

## I. MEASUREMENT OF THE NONWHITE-WHITE UNEMPLOYMENT-RATE DIFFERENTIALS [3]

The purpose of this section is to estimate the effect of the characteristic "color" on the level of unemployment rates. This is achieved through standardization, e.g., by removing that part of the difference in unemployment rates which is attributable to factors that make for high unemployment rates for whites as well as for nonwhites. For example, the aggregate data are adjusted for differences between white and nonwhite workers in their educational attainment, age composition, and occupational, industrial, and regional distributions.

The analysis is based mainly on unpublished unemployment data from the monthly sample for the Current Population Survey by the Bureau of the Census. The study also uses data from the 1940 and 1950 decennial censuses.[4]

Columns (3) and (6) of Table 1 show the excess of the nonwhite unemployment rates over those for white workers in 1950 and in the average for October, 1953-October, 1961. In both April, 1950, and in

---

[2] Comparisons between the "color" unemployment rate differentials during peaks and troughs of business cycles reveal that nonwhite workers are neither laid off earlier nor in greater proportion than are comparable white workers. But such comparisons merely show that the observed excess in nonwhite over white unemployment is independent of the level of business activity. For a report on several tests of the cyclical behavior of the nonwhite-white unemployment-rate differential, see Gilman [6] [7, Ch. 3].

[3] The term "differential" is used throughout this paper to denote the absolute difference ($NW$-$W$) in unemployment rates. The absolute rather than the relative differential ($NW/W$) is used because the former measure seems better able to detect differential hiring and firing. This comment has particular relevance for comparisons of unemployment rate differentials between two or more periods of time. If nonwhite workers had a higher unemployment rate than did white workers in some initial period, proportionate increases in the two rates would not have affected their ratios. However, under this assumption, the absolute increase in unemployment would have been greater for nonwhite than for white workers. At any rate, the conclusions reached in this paper would have been the same had I used the relative differentials instead. The patterns among the absolute differentials discussed below are observed also among the relative differentials [7, Tables 3, 5, and 8].

[4] The decennial census data (April, 1940 and April, 1950) are not strictly comparable to those for 1953–61 because of the change of definition in unemployment that occurred in January of 1957 and because of the difference in sources. For a discussion of the comparability of CPS and decennial census data see [19, p. xiii] [1, pp. 72–84] [21]. See also note 5.

TABLE 1. UNEMPLOYMENT RATES BY COLOR FOR BOTH SEXES AND FOR MALES BY
CLASS OF WORKER 1950 AND AVERAGE OF OCTOBER 1953–OCTOBER 1961

(In per cent)

| Workers Covered | 1950 | | | October 1953–October 1961 [a] | | |
|---|---|---|---|---|---|---|
| | NW (1) | W (1) | NW—W (3) | NW (4) | W (5) | NW—W (6) |
| Both sexes | 7.9 | 4.5 | 3.4 | 9.8 | 4.8 | 5.0 |
| All males | 7.8 | 4.7 | 3.1 | 10.2 | 4.6 | 5.6 |
| Male, experienced labor force | 7.7 | 4.6 | 3.1 | 9.4 | 4.2 | 5.2 |
| Male, experienced wage and salary workers only | | | | 10.4 | 5.0 | 5.4 |

[a] This is an average of the January, April, July, and October observations for each year beginning October, 1953. The series has been adjusted for the change in the definition of unemployment that occurred in January of 1957. The adjustment was made by linking the two periods on the basis of the two January, 1957 observations.

SOURCES: The 1950 entries were computed from the 1950 U.S. Census of Population, Bulletin PC-1 *U.S. Summary*, Table 118, and Special Report, PE-1B, *Occupational Characteristics*, Table 3; the 1953–61 averages were computed from U.S. Census, *Current Population Reports*, Series P-50 and P-57, and from unpublished BLS tabulations, "CPS Tabulation Specifications (Univac I)," September 1953–February, 1959, Tables 18 and 21; "CPS Univac 1105 Tabulation Specifications" (Beginning March, 1959), Table 23.

1953–61, nonwhites had higher unemployment rates than whites, both in the aggregate and for males alone. This was also true in April of 1940, though the differentials have increased over time. The absolute differences in unemployment rates in April, 1940, were only 2.7 per cent and 2.9 per cent for both sexes and for males, respectively.

These positive differentials, however, are not surprising, given that nonwhites are concentrated in low-skill occupations which have a high incidence of unemployment for whites as well as for nonwhites. For instance, the percentage of nonwhite males in the unskilled or semiskilled major occupation groups is more than twice the percentage for white males (74.3 per cent to 35.7 per cent).

The figures in Table 2 are the unem-

TABLE 2. NONWHITE-WHITE MALE UNEMPLOYMENT DIFFERENTIALS, BY MAJOR OCCUPATIONAL GROUPS
FOR 1940, 1950, AND AVERAGE OF OCTOBER 1953–OCTOBER 1961

| Major Occupation Group | 1940 | 1950 | October 1953–October 1961 |
|---|---|---|---|
| | NW—W | NW—W | NW—W |
| Professional and kindred workers | 7.5% | 1.4% | 1.9% |
| Managers and proprietors, exc. farm | 1.3 | 1.4 | 1.4 |
| Clerical and kindred workers | 6.1 | 3.4 | 3.8 |
| Sales workers | 4.3 | 3.2 | 3.9 |
| Craftsmen, foremen, and kindred workers | 8.6 | 4.4 | 5.3 |
| Operative and kindred workers | 2.7 | 2.1 | 3.6 |
| Private household workers | 1.2 | 1.0 | −0.5 |
| Service workers, exc. private household | 4.0 | 1.5 | 3.7 |
| Farm laborers and foremen | −6.9 | −0.8 | 1.9 |
| Laborers, exc. farm and mine | −2.7 | 1.0 | 2.4 |

SOURCES: The 1940 entries were computed from the 1940 U.S. Census of Population, the Labor Force, *Usual Occupation*, Table 4; the 1950 entries were computed from the source given in Table 1; the entries for October, 1953–October, 1961 were computed from Tables 23 and 31 and from Table 24, respectively, of the unpublished sources given in Table 1.

ployment differentials for males by major occupation group, for 1940, 1950, and the average for the period October, 1953, to October, 1961 (four observations per year). In all periods, the differentials tend to be smaller for the unskilled or semi-skilled than for the skilled or white-collar occupation groups. For laborers and domestics they are frequently negative. The differentials are consistently highest for craftsmen. The patterns among these differentials will be discussed in greater detail in Part II. It is important to note here that the average effect of standardization of the data by major occupation groups is to reduce the excess in the aggregate nonwhite male unemployment rate by roughly 100 per cent in 1940, by 42 per cent in 1950, and by about 38.5 per cent in the average figures for October, 1953, to October, 1961. Thus, in recent periods, the inequality in the occupational distributions (major occupations) between nonwhite and white male workers accounts for less than half of the difference in their unemployment rates.

However, nonwhite males have lower levels of educational attainment than white males within each of the major occupation groups [7, Tables 2 and 4]. For white males there is an inverse relationship between their educational attainment and their level of unemployment. This suggests that differences in education may partly account for the generally positive unemployment differentials within major occupations shown in Table 2. The correlations between the unemployment differentials and the differences in educational attainment (see Table 3), however, are small.

Similarly, within major occupation groups, nonwhite males are concentrated in the detailed occupations that are relatively less skilled; occupations with high unem-

ployment rates for whites as well as for nonwhites [7, Table 6].

Another factor that may be partly responsible for the excess nonwhite unemployment is that nonwhite males of given major occupations may be concentrated, more than white males, in industries with high levels of unemployment. Unfortunately employment or unemployment data are not available simultaneously by color, occupation, and industry, and thus this hypothesis cannot be fully tested. However, some of the occupation groups in the intermediate occupation classification are heavily concentrated in particular industry groups. Thus some standardization for the unequal distribution by skill and industry within major occupation groups can be achieved by comparing white and nonwhite male unemployment rates in the intermediate occupation groups. The unemployment differentials for these groups are reported in Table 3.[5]

The pattern of the differentials revealed here is similar to that for the major occupation groups: the differentials are positive but low for the unskilled, higher for the higher-skilled or white-collar workers, and then lower for professional workers. Standardization by intermediate occupation groups reduces the excess in the nonwhite male unemployment rate by roughly 58 per cent in April, 1950, and 45 per cent in 1957–61.

In an effort to achieve a greater degree of control over unemployment factors other than color, I have computed several multiple regressions involving these factors simultaneously. The regressions, which cover only male workers, were run separately for all occupations in the intermediate-occupation-groups classification, and within them for higher- and lower-skill occupation groupings. The dependent variable is the average unemployment

[5] The samples for the nonwhites in the high-skill occupations are very small. Data for 1950 are based on a sample of 3⅓ per cent of the population. The CPS data are based on a sample of 35,000 households. However, the CPS data presented here are averages of 20 observations: January, April, July, and October observations for the period 1957–61.

TABLE 3. NONWHITE-WHITE MALE UNEMPLOYMENT AND EDUCATION DIFFERENTIALS BY INTERMEDIATE OCCUPATION GROUPS FOR 1950 AND AVERAGE OF 1957–1961

| Intermediate Occupation Group | Unemployment Differentials | | Education |
|---|---|---|---|
| | Average 1957–1961 | 1950 | 1950 |
| | NW-W | NW-W | W-NW |
| | (Percentage points) | (Percentage points) | (Years) |
| Technical engineers | 0.4 | 3.8 | ? [b] |
| Medical, salaried only | 2.6 | 1.7 [a] | ? |
| Other professional, salaried only | 2.5 | 1.7 | 2.3 |
| Managers, salaried only | 2.9 | 2.5 | 2.5 |
| Stenos, secretaries, and typists | 3.8 | 4.5 | −0.2 |
| Other clerical workers | 4.3 | 3.4 | 0.2 |
| Salesmen, retail trade | 5.2 | 3.0 | 2.6 |
| Salesmen, other trade | 4.3 | 3.4 | 2.5 |
| Machinists and metal craftsmen | 4.6 | 3.1 | 2.1 |
| Mechanics and repairmen | 3.7 | 2.2 | 1.5 |
| Construction craftsmen | 6.0 | 3.8 | 2.1 |
| Other craftsmen | 4.1 | 8.3 | 1.2 |
| Foremen | 1.8 | 1.6 | 1.4 |
| Drivers and deliverymen | 3.4 | 1.8 | 1.8 |
| Mine and durable-goods operatives | 5.3 | 1.9 | 1.8 |
| Nondurable-goods operatives | 4.7 | 3.1 | 1.9 |
| Nonmanufacturing operatives | 2.3 | 2.1 | 1.9 |
| Private household workers | 1.8 | 1.0 | 1.7 |
| Protective service workers | 3.9 | 0.4 | 1.0 |
| Waiters, cooks, and bartenders | 0.6 | 0.8 | 0.7 |
| Other service workers | 4.4 | 1.0 | 0.5 |
| Paid farm laborers | 1.3 | −0.9 | 3.4 |
| Construction laborers | 3.4 | 2.4 | 2.7 |
| Manufacturing laborers | 2.2 | 1.3 | 2.6 |
| Other laborers | 3.3 | 0.2 | 2.7 |

[a] The 1950 differentials for the medical and the other professional groups are not comparable to the average differentials for 1957–61. The 1950 figures will be smaller in part because they include self-employed.

[b] The median number of school years completed was 16+ for both white and nonwhite engineers and medical personnel.

SOURCES: The unemployment differentials for 1957–1961 and 1950 were computed from the sources given in Table 1. Education differentials were computed from the 1950 U.S. Census of Population, Special Report P.E. No. 1B, *Occupational Characteristics,* Tables 10 and 11.

rate (in per cent) for an occupation $(U)$.[6] The independent variables are color $(C)$, industry $(I)$, education $(E)$, per cent of workers between the age of 25 and 55 $(A)$, and the per cent of wage and salary worker $(WS)$.

The color variable is a "zero" or "one" dummy variable with "one" assigned to all nonwhite observations.

The industry variable is the "expected"

unemployment rate for each occupation group. For each occupation group it was computed by weighting the average white male unemployment rates $Wi$, in the 22 major industry groups[7] by the percentage, $P_i$, of employees in the given occupation group who were in the industry groups. The "expected" unemployment rate for each occupation group on the basis of its industrial distribution is then:

[6] It is an average for 1957–61.

[7] The average industry unemployment rates are for periods that parallel those for the average occupation unemployment rates.

$$\sum_{i=1}^{22} \frac{P_i W_i}{100}.$$

A rise of 1 per cent in this variable should result in a rise of approximately 1 per cent in the occupational unemployment rate. Since there are no data available on the the occupational distribution between industries by color, I have assigned to both white and nonwhite males the weights of their combined industrial distributions.

The preliminary findings suggest that for the intermediate occupation breakdown this procedure will not bias the results significantly.[8]

The education variable is the median number of school years completed by occupation group and color in 1950.[9] The age variable is the percentage, in 1950, of those employed in a given occupation group, by color, who were 25-55 years of age. The "wage and salary" variable is the percentage, in 1950, of those employed in a given occupation group, by color, who were wage and salary workers (rather than self-employed or unpaid family workers).

I expected negative signs for the coefficients of education $(E)$, and age $(A)$, and positive signs for those of industry $(I)$, and "wage and salary" $(WS)$. The size and sign of the "color" variable are of most interest, of course. The coefficient of this variable is an estimate of the average (over the occupational groups covered) absolute unemployment differential, NW-W, attributable to color.

The results of these regressions are re-ported in Table 4. All of them show a positive coefficient for color. The color coefficient across all occupations in the intermediate occupation classification is large (2.9 per cent) and statistically significant at the 1 per cent level or better. This coefficient, however, is the result of combining higher- and lower-skill occupation groups. This is shown in the results for regressions (2) and (3). For the higher-skill occupations, the color coefficient is even larger (3.17 per cent) and statistically significant at the 1 per cent level or better, while for the unskilled or semi-skilled groups it is substantially smaller (.84 per cent) and is statistically not significant at the 30 per cent level.[10]

The coefficients for the industry variable $(I)$ are approximately unity[11] and are highly significant statistically.

The coefficients for the education $(E)$ variable have the expected sign and except in the case of the regression across low-skill occupations they are statistically significant. The coefficients for the other variables—age and wage and salary distributions—generally have the expected signs; however, their statistical significance typically is low.

*In summary:* the available evidence indicates that much of the apparent excess in the nonwhite male aggregate unemployment rate is eliminated with standardization. For the averages for 1957–61, standardization by major occupation groups, intermediate occupation groups, and the regression across all intermediate occupations removed roughly 40, 45, and 50 per cent, respectively, of the NW-W

---

[8] See [7, Table 7].

[9] I computed several regressions in which I had introduced (full-time) income and education as proxies for "skill." Income for given years of schooling was meant to measure at least roughly the skill not accounted for by years of schooling. However, owing to the high degree of intercorrelation between these two variables, their statistical significance was low. Moreover, the inclusion of the income variable had little effect on the "color" coefficient or on $R^2$.

[10] Relative to the mean unemployment rates for whites and nonwhites combined, the coefficient for the higher-skill occupations is 63.0 per cent, whereas for the lower-skill groups it is only 8.9 per cent.

[11] The difference between the observed and expected size (1.0) of this coefficient may be the result of (a) weighting the 1957-61 average unemployment rates with 1950 weights, and (b) using the same weights for white and nonwhite workers (see the discussion on the industry variable above.)

TABLE 4. MULTIPLE REGRESSIONS OF AVERAGE UNEMPLOYMENT RATES IN OCCUPATIONS ON COLOR AND LABOR DEMAND AND SUPPLY VARIABLES

| Regression Number and Dependent Variable | Independent Variables | | | | | | Number of Observations |
|---|---|---|---|---|---|---|---|
| | $C$ | $I$ | $E$ | $A$ | WS | $R^2$ | |
| 1) $U_{io}$ | 2.90 (.84) | 1.21 (.19) | −.58 (.16) | −.14 (.05) | .083 (.078) | .725 | 50 |
| 2) $U_{hs}$ | 3.17 (.76) | .87 (.28) | −.33 (.16) | −.12 (.08) | −.04 (.08) | .762 | 26 |
| 3) $U_{ls}$ | .84 (2.54) | 1.20 (.29) | −1.16 (.83) | −.02 (.10) | .05 (.19) | .666 | 24 |

Symbols:
$C$ = color variable, 0–1 shift, 1 for nonwhite observations
$I$ = expected unemployment on the basis of the industry distribution (per cent)
$E$ = number of school years completed (years)
$A$ = per cent between the ages of 25 and 55 (per cent)
WS = per cent wage and salary employees (per cent)
$U_{io}$ = unemployment rates in all occupations (per cent)
$U_{hs}$ = unemployment rates in the occupations craftsmen through professionals (percent)
$U_{ls}$ = unemployment rates in low skill occupations, laborers through operatives (percent)
SOURCES: Average unemployment rates were computed from the source quoted in Table 1. The occupational distribution among industries were computed from the 1950 U.S. Census of Population, Special Report, *Occupation by Industry*, Table 2. Age was computed from the 1950 U.S. Census of Population, Special Report P-E No. 1B, *Occupational Characteristics*, Tables 6 and 7. Per cent wage and salary employees was computed from the same source, Tables 12 and 13.

male unemployment-rate differential for the United States. In earlier periods standardization reduced the male unemployment-rate differential by an even larger fraction. Thus, in 1950, standardization by major and intermediate occupation groups removed roughly 42 and 58 per cent of the differential, respectively, and in 1940 standardization by major occupation alone eliminated all of the gross unemployment differential in the U.S. average figure [13].

Regional standardization reveals that the inequality in occupational distribution is responsible for a larger fraction of the NW-W male unemployment-rate differential in the South than elsewhere. Thus, standardization by major occupations reduced the 1960–61 differential by roughly 68 and 43 per cent for the South and non-South respectively. However, in both regions much of the differential remains. Whether the residual differences are due to insufficient standardization for differences in skill or to some other causes

is a question that is discussed in Part II of this paper.

## II. THE DISPERSION OF UNEMPLOYMENT DIFFERENTIALS

The amount of standardization achieved in Part I reduced the recent NW-W male unemployment-rate differentials by about 50, 43, and 68 per cent for the U.S. average figures, the non-South, and South, respectively. But these figures show the average effect of standardization across all major or intermediate occupation groups. We saw earlier (Tables 2 and 3 and regressions (2) and (3)) that standardization reduced the apparent excess in nonwhite unemployment in low-skill occupations by more than it did in the high-skill occupations. Also, standardization by major occupations had a greater impact on the unemployment differentials in the South than in the non-South. This part of the paper examines the patterns among the unexplained differences in light of two alternative, though not necessarily competing, hypotheses about them.

## A. The Differential-Skill Hypothesis

The first hypothesis examined is that the residual differences in NW-W male unemployment rates are due to incomplete statistical control over the skill factor. In particular, the residual differences within occupation groups (major or intermediate) may be due to differences in either the quantity or quality of education or to differences in the amounts of specific on-the-job training received by white and nonwhite workers [4] [10] [8]. This hypothesis implies, however, that the differences in unemployment rates should be directly related to differences in either of the above-named skill factors. It implies, for instance, the following: (1) Since differences in the quality of education are cumulative with respect to time spent in education, the NW-W unemployment differentials ought to be highest for groups in the highest-skill occupations or levels of education. (2) Since for each year of job experience nonwhites receive less on-the-job training than whites, we should observe a greater skill differential and hence a greater unemployment-rate differential for older than for younger groups of workers. (3) Since education differential (years of schooling in an occupation group for whites minus those for nonwhites) are greatest in the South, we should find higher unemployment-rate differentials in the South than in the non-South. (4) Since the educational differentials have declined over time, we should observe a secular decline in unemployment-rate differentials.

The observed patterns among the differentials will be discussed in the remaining paragraphs of this section. It is important to note here that except for some isolated observations the data contradict the hypothesis.

1. *Occupational and Educational Cross Sections* Several pieces of evidence in support of the differential-skill hypothesis are, in my opinion, misleading because they are based on the pattern among the NW-W unemployment differentials across occupations or levels of education for the United States as a whole. . . .

The further reduction of the differential may be inferred from the low color coefficient in the regression (3) across the unskilled and semi-skilled occupation groups. For it can be argued that had the regressions been run for a more detailed occupational breakdown, the color coefficient for the high-skill groups would have become as small as that for the low-skill groups. This argument is partly supported by evidence showing that within major occupation groups nonwhite males tend to be concentrated in detailed occupations that are relatively less skilled, and that this inequality in occupational distributions is greater, the higher the average of level of skill of the major occupation group [7, Table 2]. It can be assumed that intermediate occupation groups still have wide dispersions of skill and that the dispersions are wider within the higher-skill intermediate occupations than within the lower-skill intermediate occupations.

However, on the basis of the rising inequality in the occupational distributions of white and nonwhite males with increasing average levels of skill of occupations, we would expect the highest unemployment differentials for the highest-skill occupations. Instead we find (Tables 2 and 3) that the absolute unemployment differentials are consistently highest for craftsmen. Separate regressions for the upper- and middle-skill groups of the intermediate occupation classification would have revealed the same pattern; they would have revealed a larger color coefficient (than the present 3.17 per cent of regression (2)) for the middle groups and a lower one for the highest-skill groups. This is suggested by the residuals for the professional and managerial groups and for clerical, sales, and craftsmen groups separately. The nonwhite minus white residuals are negative $(-2.02)$ for professional and managerial groups, but are positive $(0.91)$ for the clerical, sales, and craftsmen groups.

For the United States data the inverted U-shaped patterns among the NW-W male unemployment-rate differentials are observed in 1940, 1950, and in the average figures for 1953–61 or 1957–61.[12] They are observed across major and intermediate occupations as well as across levels of education within occupations. Thus, in most major occupations, nonwhite males with low levels of education had (in April, 1940) lower unemployment rates than white males with similar education. The differentials generally became positive for groups with seven-to-eight years of education, increased for groups with one-to-three years of high school education, and declined for high school graduates and for groups with college education [7, Table 5].

A somewhat similar pattern was observed by Jacob Mincer in data for April, 1950, classified by age and education. Mincer observed that "Negro unemployment rates are higher in almost all classifications; the difference is negligible at the lowest education levels, and generally increases with education. The differentials remain positive, but decrease at the highest educational level" [8, p. 71].

Thus, even for the U.S. average figures, the differential-skill hypothesis may, in part, explain the rising unemployment differentials from the lowest-skill occupation groups through the craftsmen groups or from low to medium levels of education. It will not explain the lower differentials for the highest-skill groups or the highest-education levels.

Moreover, the rising unemployment differentials through the craftsmen groups are the result of combining the data for the South and non-South. This is apparent from the figures reported in Table 5, which are the 1960–61 average unemployment levels[13] and the differences in these levels, NW-W, separately for the South and non-South. These figures show that the unemployment differentials for the lower-skilled groups are small or negative for the South, but positive and substantial for the North and West. Indeed, there is a possibility that a separate regression for the North and West would show the opposite relationship between the level of skill and the size of the color coefficient.

The same conclusions can be drawn from the occupation data for April, 1940, and for data for April, 1950, by region and age-education classes [7, Tables 10 and 11]. For the lower-education groups, the differentials are small or negative for the South, but are positive and substantial in the non-South.

2. *Age Cross Sections* The "differential skill hypothesis" is similarly deficient in explaining the behavior of the unemployment-rate differentials across age groups. The effect of differences in the amounts of on-the-job training received by whites and nonwhites of given levels of education should be to increase the unemployment-rate differentials with age. Instead Mincer's data show the opposite to be true [8, Table 7].

3. *Regional Cross Sections* The regional data in Table 5 are surprising in the light of the common conception of greater discrimination in the South than elsewhere. Column (7) of Table 5 shows the NW-W unemployment-differentials in the non-South minus the differentials in the South. All except one of the figures are positive, indicating consistently greater

---

[12] The patterns are somewhat weaker, but are present among the relative differentials as well. See also note 3.

[13] This is an average of eight observations.

| Major Occupation Group | South | | | Non-South | | | Non-South Minus South | Education |
|---|---|---|---|---|---|---|---|---|
| | (1) W | (2) NW | (3) (2)–(1) | (4) W | (5) NW | (6) (5)–(4) | (7) (6)–(3) | (8) a |
| Professional workers | 1.4 | 2.2 | 0.8 | 1.9 | 4.6 | 2.7 | 1.9 | b |
| Managers and proprietors, exc. farm | 1.4 | 2.3 | 0.9 | 1.5 | 4.5 | 3.0 | 2.1 | 1.4 |
| Clerical workers | 2.9 | 6.3 | 3.4 | 4.0 | 9.4 | 5.4 | 2.0 | 1.2 |
| Sales workers | 3.2 | 8.6 | 5.4 | 2.9 | 5.5 | 2.6 | −2.8 | 2.6 |
| Craftsmen and foremen | 6.1 | 10.2 | 4.1 | 5.5 | 10.5 | 5.0 | 0.9 | 1.5 |
| Operatives | 6.4 | 9.2 | 2.8 | 7.5 | 12.2 | 4.7 | 1.9 | 1.7 |
| Service workers exc. private household | 5.4 | 8.0 | 2.6 | 5.7 | 10.2 | 4.5 | 1.9 | 1.1 |
| Farm laborers and foremen | 6.9 | 6.3 | −0.6 | 5.6 | 22.9 | 17.3 | 17.9 | |
| Laborers, exc. farm and mine | 12.7 | 12.9 | 0.2 | 12.9 | 21.2 | 8.3 | 8.1 | 0.7 |

a Median number of school years completed, W-NW, in the South minus the difference in these medians, W-NW, in the non-South.

b Both white and nonwhite workers had 16+ years of education.

SOURCES: Unemployment rates were computed from the unpublished sources quoted in Table 1. Median number of school years completed were computed from the 1950 U.S. Census of Population, Special Report, P-E, No. 5B, *Education,* Table 11.

unemployment differentials, NW-W, in the non-South than in the South. The consistently greater unemployment differentials for the non-South than for the South are also revealed in the 1950 data classified by age and education, in 1940 data classified both by occupation and by age and education, and in 1940 data classified by city size.[14]

Even without taking account of regional differences in discrimination, we would expect greater unemployment differentials, by occupation, in the South than non-South. We expect this because both the education and income differentials [29, Table 16] are greater there than in the non-South and the regression coefficients for these two variables are negative. The absolute education differentials are reported in Column (8) of Table 5. The excess of white over nonwhite years of schooling is consistently greater in the South than in the non-South.[15]

4. *Trend* The rising unemployment-rate differentials over time (see Tables 1, 2, and 3) also contradict the hypothesis. These have occurred, notwithstanding the narrowing of the W-NW educational differentials within occupations.[16]

Thus, the patterns among the residual

[14] This last finding is based on unpublished unemployment data compiled by Rosanne Coale of the National Bureau of Economic Research.

[15] In a recent article on the decline in relative income of Negro men, A. B. Batchelder speculates [2, p. 538] that in the decade of the 1950's "the average quality of a year of school completed by Negroes living in the North and West was reduced." It is his guess that "the quality dilution exceeded quantitative gains for Negroes in the North and West." I would doubt that he would be equally willing to guess that the average difference in the quality of education is greater in the non-South than in the South. But if that were the case, we might observe higher unemployment-rate differences in the non-South, notwithstanding the greater difference in the number of school years completed in the South than in the non-South.

[16] Moreover, we observe over time a greater increase in expenditures for the instruction of nonwhite than of white students. For instance, between 1939 and 1954, the increase in expenditures, per pupil, in the South has been more than double for Negro than for white public elementary and secondary school students [26, Table 21].

unemployment-rate differences described in the four preceding tests are inconsistent with the hypothesis that they are due to the incomplete control over the skill factor.

## B. *The Differential-Wage-Rigidity Hypothesis*

The second hypothesis examined is that the residual differences in NW-W unemployment rates are due, at least in part, to the existence of greater wage rigidity for nonwhite workers in the presence of discrimination against them. The implications of this hypothesis for the behavior of these differences among occupations or regions will be discussed after a brief review of the market forces that operate differentially against nonwhite workers in the United States.

The existence of economic discrimination against nonwhite workers need not lead to higher unemployment rates for nonwhite than for white workers. Under complete wage flexibility, for instance, the majority's preference for discrimination will result in higher wages for white than for nonwhite workers [3].

However, if there are legal or quasi-legal pressures towards nonwhite-white wage equality, discrimination may take the form of reducing the employment opportunities of nonwhite relative to white workers. Thus, we would expect a greater effect of such factors as statutory and union minimum wages on the employment opportunities of nonwhite than of white workers; employment opportunities should fall more for nonwhite than for white workers.

If unemployment differentials are related to the difference between equilibrium and actual wages, the excess of nonwhite over white unemployment will vary among occupation groups, education classes, or regions. Because of differences in degrees of discrimination against groups in different occupations or levels of education, the equilibrium wage ratio, $NW/W$, will be different for different levels of skill [3, pp. 71–74, 88–90, 124]. Similarly, the extent to which maxima are effectively imposed on discriminatory wage differentials will vary among occupation groups or regions, depending on such factors as the degree of applicability of legal minimum wages and the degree of unionization. Given a preference for discrimination, the greater the pressure in an occupation or region for nonwhite-white wage equality, the greater will be the gap between equilibrium and actual wages, and the greater will be the reduction in employment opportunities for nonwhite relative to white workers.

1. *Occupational Cross Sections* The consistently lower unemployment-rate differentials (in both the South and non-South) for the highest-skill groups are probably the result of the greater ability to discriminate on the wage side for these groups than for other groups of workers. Clearly, statutory and union minimum wages are less applicable to the highest-skill groups. And, generally, there is more individual wage-bargaining for professional than, say, for craftsmen or factory workers.

2. *Regional Cross Sections* These considerations are equally applicable to the differences in the nonwhite-white unemployment differentials between the South and non-South. Because of the lower wages for nonwhite workers in the South, federal minimum-wage legislation and union-wage standardization, if equally applicable to the South and non-South, would tend to raise nonwhite wages more in the South than in the non-South. This effect by itself would tend to make the unemployment-rate differentials greater in

the South than elsewhere.[17] However, the coverage of these minima is probably significantly smaller in the South. This is clearly true for the degree of unionization.[18] There is some evidence that it is true for federal statutory minima as well. Such minima [did] not apply to agricultural workers, and the unemployment-rate differential for these workers is very low or even negative in the South.[19]

\* \* \*

3. *Trend* It is not clear whether there has been an increase in differential-wage rigidity over time, but such an increase would tend to reduce the employment opportunities of nonwhites and widen the unemployment differential over time. Clearly there has been a secular increase in the activities of organizations dedicated to the elimination of discrimination.[20] If such activities do not parallel changes in tastes for discrimination, they will tend to make market adjustment more difficult; they may thus limit rather than increase the employment opportunities of nonwhites. Increased effectiveness or coverage of minimum wages or unions would tend to have the same effect.

The preceding pages have emphasized what I have called "differential wage rigidity" as a factor making for higher unemployment rates for nonwhite workers in the presence of discrimination. It may be that even in the absence of such differential-wage rigidity, discrimination would produce higher unemployment rates for nonwhite workers. For discrimination has the effect of restricting the range of employment opportunities more for nonwhite than for white workers. I would expect this, unless it is offset by increased knowledge to nonwhites about jobs available to them, to create a nonwhite-white unemployment differential.

When discrimination is quite openly practiced, however, as it is in the South, information regarding the identity of employers who do hire nonwhite workers, at least in specified occupations, may be more widespread in the nonwhite labor force than in areas where discrimination, though practiced, is strongly frowned upon. This aspect of discrimination may also create regional differences in the nonwhite-white unemployment differential.

Another factor that may be involved is a higher fraction of recent migrants in the nonwhite labor force in the non-South than in the Southern nonwhite labor force.[21]

---

[17] Indeed, most studies of the impact of minimum wages show a greater effect of such minima on employment in the South than in the non-South. However, these studies measured the regional employment effects in covered industries only. The effect of such minima on total employment in a region depends on the fraction of the total labor force in covered industries as well as on the magnitude of the change in wages effected by minimum wage legislation. The latter is also a function of the degree of compliance and enforcement of such legislation. BLS surveys indicate that the degree of compliance, at least, is significantly smaller in the South than in the non-South.

[18] See Leo Troy's estimates of regional differences in the extent of union organization [12, pp. 17–22].

[19] The positive differential for this occupation group in the non-South is based on an extremely small sample.

[20] This would be the case if, and only if, such groups were more effective in getting equal pay than in getting equal employment opportunities. It might be argued that this has not been the case since civil rights groups have concerned themselves with equal employment opportunities. It is clear, however, that these groups have worked toward increasing the employment opportunities of nonwhite workers at the same rather than at lower wages than those for white workers. Concentration on employment opportunities may thus produce a greater effect on wages than on employment if wage discrimination—unequal pay for equal work—is the more apparent of the two forms of discrimination.

[21] One must keep in mind, however, that unemployment is related to rural-urban population movements as well as to regional migration. In the non-South, the rural-urban flows take place largely within the white labor force. Also, the greater regional migration of nonwhites may be offset, at least in part, by equally greater nonwhite rural-urban flows in the South. Thus, the net effect of migration on the regional differences in the unemployment-rate differentials is likely to be small. Partial evidence for

## III. SUMMARY

This paper attempts to estimate the effect of the characteristic "color" on the level of unemployment rates. The characteristic "color" was given a narrow definition to separate differences in unemployment rates attributable to differences in levels of skill from the effects of discrimination on hiring and firing practices, given the level of skill. This study has not attempted to measure the total effects of discrimination on unemployment, for the lowel levels of education or on-the-job training of nonwhite than of white male workers are probably themselves the results of discrimination.

With this limitation in mind, the degree of standardization achieved here removed roughly half of the difference between white and nonwhite unemployment rates that appears in the U.S. averages for these two groups in 1950 and 1957–61 (see Tables 2, 3, and 4). In the South the nonwhite-white unemployment differential appears to be small or even negative at both ends of the skill distribution, but is substantial in the middle levels of skill. In the non-South the excess of the nonwhite over the white unemployment rate by skill level declines as skill increases. However, the excess is consistently greater than in the South. These differences by skill and region in the unemployment differential also appear in the data for April, 1940. However, in that month standardization for skill accounted for all of the gross unemployment differential in the U.S. average figures.

The differences in the excess of nonwhite over white unemployment rates by skill level, region, and date (trend?) need further study. It may be that these differences are partly the result of incomplete control over the skill factor, including specific on-the-job training. I suspect, however, that a considerable part of the unexplained differentials is not due to such inadequate control, but rather is the result of differential-wage rigidity in the presence of discrimination against nonwhite workers. Such differential rigidity, as I pointed out in Part IIB, may produce moment-of-time difference in the nonwhite-white unemployment rates.

## REFERENCES

1. G. Bancroft, "Current Unemployment Statistics of the Census Bureau and Some Alternatives," in *The Measurement and Behavior of Unemployment,* a Conference of the Universities National Bureau Committee for Economic Research, Princeton 1957, pp. 63–122.
2. A. B. Batchelder, "Decline in the Relative Income of Negro Men," *Quart. Jour. Econ.,* Nov. 1964, 78, 525–48.
3. G. S. Becker, *The Economics of Discrimination.* Chicago 1957.
4. ————, "Investment in Human Capital: A Theoretical Analysis," *Jour. Pol. Econ.,* Oct. 1962 (Supp.), 70, 9–49.
5. D. Dewey, "Negro Employment in Southern Industry," *Jour. Pol. Econ.,* Aug. 1952, 60, 279–93.
6. H. J. Gilman, "The White/Non-White Unemployment Differential," in *Human Resources in the Urban Economy,* Resources for the Future, Inc., Baltimore 1963, pp. 75–113.
7. ————, *Discrimination and the White-Nonwhite Unemployment Differentials.* Unpublished doctoral dissertation, Univ. Chicago, 1963.
8. J. Mincer, "On-the-Job-Training: Costs, Returns; And Some Implications," *Jour. Pol. Econ.,* Oct. 1962 (Supp.), 70, 50–73.
9. NPA Committee of the South, Report No. 6, *Selected Studies of Negro Employment in the South,* National Planning Association, Washington, D.C. 1955.
10. W. Y. Oi, "Labor as a Quasi-Fixed Factor," *Jour. Pol. Econ.,* Dec. 1962, 70, 538–55.

---

this proposition is provided by the results of Leonard Rapping's study of the effect of migration on the white-nonwhite unemployment differential [11].

11. Leonard Rapping, "Unionism, Migration, and the White-Nonwhite Unemployment Rate Differential." Unpublished paper, Carnegie Institute of Technology, 1965.
12. Leo Troy, *Distribution of Union Membership among the States, 1939 and 1953.* Nat. Bur. Econ. Research Occas. Paper 56, 1957.
13. R. H. Turner, "Foci of Discrimination in the Employment of Nonwhites," *Am. Jour. Soc.,* Nov. 1952, 58, 247–56.
14. U.S. Bureau of the Census, *Sixteenth Census of the United States: 1940 Population.* The Labor Force, Vol. 3, Pt. 1, *U.S. Summary.* Washington 1943.
15. ———, *Sixteenth Census of the United States: 1940. Population.* The Labor Force. *Usual Occupation.* Washington 1943.
16. ———, *Sixteenth Census of the United States: 1940. Population.* The Labor Force. *Occupational Characteristics.* Washington 1943.
17. ———, *U.S. Census of Population: 1950. Education.* Special Report P-E, No. 5B. Washington 1953.
18. ———, *U.S. Census of Population: 1950. Occupational Characteristics.* Vol. 4. Special Report P-E, No. 1B. Washington 1956.
19. ———, *U.S. Census of Population: 1950. U.S. Summary.* Bull. PC-1. Washington 1953.
20. ———, *U.S. Census of Population: 1950. Occupation by Industry.* Special Report. Washington 1954.
21. ———, *Current Population Reports.* Series P-23, No. 5, May 1958.
22. ———, *Current Population Reports. Labor Force.* Series P-50 and P-57, 1948–1959.
23. U. S. Congress, *Unemployment: Terminology, Measurement, and Analysis,* Joint Economic Committee, Subcommittee on Economic Statistics, 87th Cong., 1st sess., 1961.
24. U.S. Department of Labor, *Negroes in the United States: Their Employment and Economic Status,* Bull. 1119. Washington 1952.
25. ———, *Notes on the Economic Situation of Negroes in the United States.* May 1957; revised May 1958 and August 1959.
26. ———, *The Economic Situation of Negroes in the United States,* Bull. S-3, October 1960.
27. ———, *Employment and Earnings.* 1959–1961.
28. U.S. Senate, *Studies in Unemployment,* 86th Cong., 2nd sess., 1960.
29. M. Zeman, *A Quantitative Analysis of White-Nonwhite Income Differentials in the United States in 1939.* Unpublished doctoral dissertation, Univ. Chicago, 1955.

## The Causes of Negro Income Differentials

Although he does not make the distinction between overt and institutional discrimination, James Gwartney, in "Discrimination and Income Differentials," has some of the same problems Gilman faced in trying to account for differences in "productivity" and "discrimination" factors. The "productivity" factors themselves reflect institutional discrimination, as Gwartney recognizes. Gwartney also makes the assumption, which is questioned in connection with Gilman's article, that "white employees of similar employability would be preferred if the wage rates were identical for both whites and nonwhites." Although Gwartney recognizes that things other than wage rates affect the "terms and conditions" of the sale of labor, his analysis is restricted to "money income differentials between white and nonwhite urban and nonfarm occupations for males, 25 years of age and over, in 1960." He also considers regional differences in these variables.

After adjustment for differences in education, scholastic achievement, age, region, and city size, the nonwhite median income is estimated between 81 and 87 percent of the white for urban males and 77 and 86 percent for males in nonfarm occupations.

A large proportion of the white-nonwhite income differential is accounted for by differences in the quantity of education and scholastic achievement. Scholastic achievement reflects the quality of education as contrasted with the absolute years of education. One-third to three-fifths of the income differential remains unaccounted for after Gwartney adjusts for income differentials, ". . . and this residual may result from employment discrimination." However, this residual might also result from data limitations that prevent Gwartney from disaggregating sufficiently to account for differences between racial, industrial, and occupational compositions within urban areas. Moreover, the residual could result from important variables that are not accurately measured or not measured at all by Gwartney's variables. For example, the amount of on-the-job training differs significantly by race and could be the most important cause of racial income differentials for workers in the craftsman and operative classifications. Since workers are selected on the basis of education, which is measurable, income differences attributed to education might really reflect differences in the amount of on-the-job training, native ability, family or social connections, or other variables that are difficult to measure.

# Discrimination and Income Differentials

## by James Gwartney

Income differentials between whites and nonwhites may result from several factors. The two populations differ in educational attainment, age distribution, geographic distribution, and rural-urban distribution; all of which are related to income and are, in some cases, determinants of it. When measuring employment discrimination, the relevant comparison is between individuals of similar productive capacity who differ only in color.[1]

This study seeks to break down the income differential between whites and nonwhites into two categories: (a) a differential resulting from differences in productivity factors not directly related to employment discrimination, and (b) a residual unaccounted for by differences in productivity factors and which may result largely from employment discrimination. Assuming homogenous preferences and standardizing the white and nonwhite populations for all differences in productivity factors that affect income, we could reasonably infer that any remaining income differential approximates income differences resulting from color discrimination in employment.

It should be noted that differences between whites and nonwhites in productivity factors may be the result of color discrimination in areas other than employment. The magnitude of the income differences resulting from differences in productivity factors will give some indication of the possible intensity of color discrimination in education and in other areas not related to employment discrimination.

SOURCE Reprinted with permission from *American Economic Review,* June 1970.

[1] The terminology of this paper includes locational factors such as regional and city-size distribution among "productivity factors." While locational factors are not often considered productivity factors, they do affect earnings capacity, and have the potential of contributing to income differentials between individuals and/or groups.

If there were employment discrimination against nonwhites, they would be expected to receive lower incomes than whites of similar employability. If an employer had a preference for white labor relative to nonwhite labor purely because of color, he would be indifferent between white and nonwhite employees of similar employability only if the nonwhite employees were paid lower wages. White employees of similar employability would be preferred if the wage rate were identical for both whites and nonwhites. The greater the intensity of employment discrimination against nonwhites, the lower the nonwhite wage rate, and thus earnings, relative to that of whites of similar employability.

Employment discrimination could be present however, even if the money-wage rates were identical. The terms and conditions of the sale of labor by an employee include not only wages and related monetary compensation, but also working conditions and other nonpecuniary benefits. Individuals have some trade-off between preferred working conditions and additional money income. They would be willing to take less money income if the employment had offsetting nonpecuniary benefits. Since these factors result in a difference between money income and "total" income, the total income of a white could be greater than for a nonwhite, even if their money incomes were identical, assuming the white received greater nonpecuniary job benefits.[2] Since all of the data of this paper are money income or earnings data, we can investigate only the consistency of those data with employment discrimination.[3] But money income is a sizeable component of total income, and where discrimination resulted in a significant total income differential between whites and nonwhites, we would expect to observe a money income differential as well.

In the following discussion, Section I estimates the importance of various factors in explaining the money income differential between white and nonwhite urban males, 25 years of age and over, in 1960.[4] Section II contains similar estimates using both mean and median earnings data for males in nonfarm occupations. Section III considers regional differences in earnings differentials between white and nonwhite males.

After adjustment for differences in education, scholastic achievement, age, region, and city size, the nonwhite median income is estimated between 81 and 87 percent of the white for urban males and 77 and 86 percent for males in nonfarm occupations. When mean income data are used, the estimated adjusted nonwhite/white income ratio is only slightly smaller than in the case of medians.

The adjusted nonwhite/white earnings ratio is estimated to be greater in the North than in the South. In the North for nonfarm occupations, the adjusted nonwhite/white earnings ratio is estimated between .83 and .88, compared to .68 and .74 for the South.

The results indicate that a large portion

[2] For example, a Negro might prefer to be a filling station attendant rather than a garbage collector. Strong employment discrimination might result in his becoming a garbage collector. His money income may be as great or greater, but his total income is less because he would have preferred employment as a filling station attendant.

[3] Wage and salary income, were it available, would be more appropriate than income data reflecting income from other assets in addition to earnings from labor. If there is proportionality between the two income measures, the relative incomes will be unaffected. On the assumption that relative income from other assets is a positive function of income level, the income data for whites may overstate their wage and salary income relative to nonwhites. However, if as seems likely, nonwhite income from labor is affected more by discrimination than their non-labor income, the bias will be in the opposite direction.

[4] M. Zeman estimated the significance of various factors in explaining income differences between whites and nonwhites in 1939. Due to data limitations, Zeman did not standardize for a number of factors considered in this paper.

of the income differential between white and nonwhite urban males is the result of differences in quantity of education and scholastic achievement. Differences between whites and nonwhites in these two education-related factors are estimated to have accounted for nonwhite urban males receiving between 23 and 27 percent less income than white urban males in 1959. The size of these estimates indicate that unless differences between the two poulations in these two factors can be reduced substantially, the median income of nonwhite males is unlikely to increase to more than 70 to 80 percent that of whites, even if employment discrimination is substantially reduced.

However, the unexplained differential in income between the two populations was estimated between 14 and 25 percent for nonfarm occupations and 13 to 19 percent for urban areas in the United States. This indicates that one-third to three-fifths of the nonwhite-white income differential remained unaccounted for after adjustment for the productivity factors of this paper and this residual may result largely from employment discrimination.

## I. INCOME DIFFERENCES BETWEEN WHITE AND NONWHITE URBAN MALES IN 1959

The median income of nonwhite urban males was 58.3 percent of white urban males in 1959. The income differential between white and nonwhite urban males is partially due to distributional differences in productivity factors.

This section seeks to estimate the income ration of nonwhite to white urban males after correction for income differences resulting from differences in productivity factors. These factors include quantity of education, level of scholastic achievement, regional, age, and city-size distributions.

Three criteria were used in choosing productivity factors relevant to the explanation of income differentials between whites and nonwhites. First, only factors generally recognized as determinants of money income, or as closely correlated with income, were used in this study. Second, the factors chosen are *not* directly related to employment discrimination as such. For example, the median income of nonwhites in the United States is less than that of whites partially because of the overrepresentation of nonwhites in the low-income South—a situation which is not the result of employment discrimination.[5] By contrast, occupational distribution according to color is related to employment discrimination. Therefore, no adjustment was made for differences in occupational structure. Third, factors were either considered simultaneously, or chosen where the apparent relationship with other factors was one of independence. Thus even though low earnings are associated with youth, the factor of age is utilized in explaining the income differential only if the relatively low incomes are not the result of such other factors as size of cities or the regional distribution of population, with which both low earnings and age might also be correlated.

Standardization could either increase or decrease the magnitude of the observed income difference between whites and nonwhites. Factors with positive (negative) signs are those which tend to make the differential larger (smaller) than it would have been in the absence of those factors.

The income differential between whites and nonwhites is disaggregated by constructing indexes of *income* and *distributional* differences. *Distributional* differences in income result from differences in

---

[5] The intensity of discrimination in the South has, if anything, resulted in migration from the South which tends to decrease the magnitude of the regional distribution factor.

productivity factors between whites and nonwhites. *Income* differences result from differences in income between whites and nonwhites after adjustment for the productivity factors considered.

The Laspeyres index of *income differences* is the hypothetical ratio of the median income of nonwhite to white males, assuming both color groups were distributed among productivity categories as whites actually were. The Paasche index of income differences is a similar hypothetical ratio under the assumption that both color groups had the productivity distribution of nonwhites.[6] The index of income differences is essentially an estimate of the ratio of nonwhite to white income after adjustment for differences in the productivity factors considered.

The indexes of *distribution differences* represent the hypothetical ratios of nonwhite to white income if whites and nonwhites had the same income *within* productivity categories.[7] The index of *distribution differences* is essentially an estimate of income differences that result from differences in the distribution of productivity factors. The index of *income differences* multiplied by the index of distribution differences yields an index of "total" money income differences, which closely approximates the actual ratio of nonwhite to white income.[8]

The index of *income differences* will be less than unity if the median income of nonwhites is less than whites *within* productivity categories. The index of *income differences* is an estimate of the income ratio of nonwhites to whites if the two populations were similarly distributed among the adjusted productivity categories.

The index of *distribution differences* will be less than unity if nonwhites are overrepresented relative to whites in low income productivity categories. Such an index is an estimate of income differences resulting from differences in productivity capacity between the two populations. We proceed to adjust the data for the effects of differences in productivity factors that influence the ratio of nonwhite to white income.

### 1. *Quantity of Education Adjustment*

White urban males have a greater quantity of education than nonwhites. Since income is positively related to education, whites would be expected to receive larger incomes than nonwhites on this basis. In isolating the "quantity of education" ef-

---

[6] The mathematical form of the index of income differences is:

$$\frac{\Sigma\,(Y_n \cdot D_w)}{\Sigma\,(Y_w \cdot D_w)}\ \text{(Laspeyres) and,}\ \frac{\Sigma\,(Y_n \cdot D_n)}{\Sigma\,(Y_w \cdot D_n)}\ \text{(Paasche)}$$

where,

$Y$ is the median income of those with income within a productivity category (e.g. age, education or region) according to color.

$D$ is the percent of population according to color with income within the productivity category, and

$n$ and $w$ are subscripts denoting nonwhite and white population groupings.

[7] The form of the index of distribution differences is:

$$\frac{\Sigma\,(Y_n \cdot D_n)}{\Sigma\,(Y_n \cdot D_w)}\ \text{(Laspeyres) and,}\ \frac{\Sigma\,(Y_w \cdot D_n)}{\Sigma\,(Y_w \cdot D_w)}\ \text{(Paasche)}$$

Since the distributional categories are in percent form, the estimates for those with income are not affected by differences in the size or participation rates of the two labor forces. One could construct an index of distribution differences assuming both color groupings had the median income of the total population within productivity categories. Since whites compose a large percentage of the total population, such an index would closely approximate the Paasche index.

[8] Also the inverse of the index of distribution differences multiplied by the ratio of total money income differences yields the index of income differences.

908 Human Resource Development

fect, the 1960 Census data indicating the median income of white and nonwhite urban males for each of eight different educational levels were utilized, (Table 223 of the *Final Report*, "Characteristics of the Population.") Both indexes of income and distribution differences were calculated. The Laspeyres and Paasche indexes of income differences were 67.0 and 69.9 percent, respectively, after correction for differences in the quantity of education distributions between white and nonwhite urban males.[9] The adjustment indicates that the income of nonwhite urban males was just over two-thirds the income of white urban males with similar quantity of education in 1960.

## 2. *Scholastic Achievement Adjustment*

Whites and nonwhites differ not only in quantity of education, but also in what we shall term scholastic achievement level. National education tests show that nonwhites with the same number of years of formal schooling perform at a significantly lower level than whites. Some of the income differential between whites and nonwhites is the result of this lower achievement level.

The outlay funds per pupil is often less for nonwhites than for whites, hence the lower achievement of nonwhite students may be the result of attending schools of inferior quality. Days of attendance vary among those with equal number of years of education. Nonwhites with equal quantity of education have fewer days of attendance than whites because of their overrepresentation in schools (largely in the South) with a six- to eight-month term

and a seven-year elementary degree requirement. In addition, even if nonwhites have a similar attendance record in schools of comparable quality, they may do less well than whites because cultural and environmental factors may hinder their taking advantage of educational programs reflecting white cultural standards, values, and traditions. Thus even when whites and nonwhites attend the same schools, it is possible, even probable, that a differential in achievement will result.

A recent study for the U.S. Office of Education by James Coleman, *et al.*, estimates differences in scholastic achievement between whites and nonwhites in terms of quantity of education (years of schooling) for three different grade levels in metropolitan areas.[10]

\* \* \*

Using the maximum scholastic achievement differential of the *Coleman Report* for grades 6, 9, 12, a maximum estimate of the scholastic achievement differential was projected under the assumptions that (a) the differential is linear, and (b) whites and nonwhites are of the same scholastic achievement level before entrance to school.[11] Under the same assumptions, plus the further assumption that the scholastic achievement differential for grade levels beyond twelve remained constant at the level of grade 12, a minimum estimate of the scholastic achievement differential was projected, using the minimum estimates of the scholastic achievement differential of the *Coleman Report*.

The income ratio of nonwhites to whites after adjustment for both quantity of education and scholastic achievement was estimated by comparing the actual income

[9] The data and specific calculations for all estimates of this paper are contained in an Appendix that is available from the author on request.

[10] This study will subsequently be referred to as the *Coleman Report*.

[11] Recent studies indicate that nonwhites are, in fact, already behind whites upon entrance to school. The results of the *Coleman Report* (p. 20) indicated scores of minority pupils are as much as one standard deviation below the majority pupils' scores in the first grade. No adjustment was attempted for this differential because comparative income data for whites with no education and low achievement would not be available. Failure to make adjustment for this factor will tend to understate the ratio of nonwhite to white income after correction for the scholastic achievement factor.

of nonwhites urban males in an education cell with the income of white urban males equal in achievement level with the nonwhites of the education cell.[12] The results indicate that in 1960 the income of white urban males was between 12.2 (Paasche) and 18.1 (Laspeyres) percent greater than nonwhite urban males because of the lower achievement level of nonwhites.[13] Cumulatively, the adjusted nonwhite/white income ratio was estimated between 82.1 and 85.1 (Table 1).[14]

c. *State Distribution.*

Nonwhites are overrepresented in southern states. This reduces their income relative to whites because (a) incomes of both whites and nonwhites are lower in southern states than northern states and (b) the income differential is greater in southern states.

*   *   *

After adjustment for both quantity of education and state distribution, nonwhite urban males are estimated to receive incomes between 72.3 (Paasche) and 72.9 (Laspeyres) percent as large as incomes of white urban males. Comparing these indexes with the indexes when only quantity of education was adjusted for, the data indicate the income of nonwhite urban males increased between 2.4 (Paasche) and 5.9 (Laspeyres) percent relative to that of white urban males as the result of the marginal effect of the state distribution adjustment. The Laspeyres adjustment, which assumes that both populations had the distributional characteristics of whites, is greater than the Paasche estimate because of a smaller income differential in the North—the area where whites are relatively overrepresented. Cumulating the adjustments for (a) quantity of education, (b) scholastic achievement, and (c) state distribution, the income of nonwhite urban males is estimated be-

[12] The form of the adjusted index of income differences between whites and nonwhites is:

$$\frac{\Sigma\,(Y_w \cdot E_w)}{\Sigma\,(Y_w' \cdot E_w)} \text{ (Laspeyres) and, } \frac{\Sigma\,(Y_n \cdot E_n)}{\Sigma\,(Y_w'' \cdot E_n)} \text{ (Paasche)}$$

where, $Y_n$ is the median income of nonwhite urban males with income in 1959 for each of the eight different quantity of education cells,

$Y_w'$ and $Y_w''$ are respectively, maximum and minimum estimates of the incomes of white urban males of equal achievement level with the nonwhites of the education cell, and

$E_w$ and $E_n$ represent the percent of white and nonwhite urban males within each education cell with income in 1959.

It is possible, using both the maxmum and minimum estimates of income adjusted for scholastic achievement differences within an education cell, to make two estimates of the Laspeyres and Paasche indexes of income differences.

[13] The data used are from 1960 Census of Population, "Characteristics of the Population" Table 223. The income data for white males of equal achievement level with nonwhites of a given education cell were derived by interpolation, using the achievement level differentials of the *Coleman Report* and the assumptions stated in the text of this paper. The data of the *Coleman Report* were not disaggregated according to sex, thus the achievement level differences were assumed to be the same for males as for the total.

[14] The data of the *Coleman Report* were obtained in September 1965. Since those covered by the 1959 income data completed their education anywhere from several years to a half century or more before 1965, the differential in level of scholastic achievement is assumed constant over time. Increased expenditures on nonwhite education relative to white and Supreme Court decisions on desegregation suggest a possible narrowing of achievement differentials in recent years inasmuch as they are related to differences in the quality of schools. If there has been a narrowing of the achievement level differentials over time, the estimate of the adjusted nonwhite/white income ratio is biased downward. However, the little evidence existing on comparative test scores over time does not confirm a narrowing of achievement level differentials, but indicates there has been little change (see John Miner and A. M. Shuey). In any case, there would not seem to be any a priori reason to suggest a smaller scholastic achievement differential for the adult population in 1959 than was the case for the school age population of 1965.

TABLE 1.  INCOME OF NONWHITES AS A PERCENTAGE OF WHITES, ADJUSTED FOR VARIOUS
DETERMINANTS OF INCOME DIFFERENTIALS BETWEEN WHITE AND NONWHITE
URBAN MALES FOR THE UNITED STATES IN 1959

| | Index of Income Differences [a] | | Marginal Effect of Factor | |
|---|---|---|---|---|
| | Laspeyres | Paasche | Laspeyres | Paasche |
| Unadjusted Income Ratio (Nonwhite/White) | 58.3 | 58.3 | — | — |
| *Explanatory Factors* | | | | |
| A. Quantity of Education | 67.0 | 69.9 | 8.7 | 11.6 |
| B. Scholastic Achievement | 85.1 | 82.1 | 18.1 | 12.2 |
| C. State Distribution | 91.0 | 84.5 | 5.9 | 2.4 |
| D. City Size | 89.3 | 83.3 | −1.7 | −1.2 |
| E. Age Distribution | 86.5 | 80.9 | −2.8 | −2.4 |

[a] Since both a maximum and minimum scholastic achievement differential was used from the *Coleman Report*, it is possible to calculate two Paasche and Laspeyres indexes of income differences when adjusting for this factor. The above estimates of the scholastic achievement factor "bracket" the other two estimates that could be calculated. Therefore, the procedure yields both a maximum and minimum estimate of the nonwhite/white income ratio adjusted for the five productivity factors. The same procedure was also followed for the estimates of Tables 2 and 3.

SOURCE: Estimates are derived from U.S. Census data, "Characteristics of the Population," Tables 219 and 223; *Subject Report, Size of Place*, Tables 2, 3, 4, and 5; *Detailed Characteristics*, Tables 47 and 138.

tween 84.5 and 91.0 percent of white urban males (Table 1).

### 4. City-Size Distribution

Nonwhites are overrepresented relative to whites in the larger cities. Median income differs among cities of different size, tending to increase as the size of the city increases. Nonwhite overrepresentation in the larger cities would therefore result in the income of nonwhites being greater than if they were distributed among cities in the same manner as whites.

Data from the 1960 Census gives the median income of the total population and of nonwhites according to size of city by region, as well as the percentage of the white and nonwhite population residing in cities of each size, (see Tables 2, 3, 4, and 5, *Subject Report, Size of Place*). Thus, both a Laspeyres and Paasche index of distribution differences can be constructed to estimate the amount by which nonwhite income exceeds white income because of the overrepresentation of nonwhites in large cities. The indexes are calculated by

region, thus minimizing interaction with the state distribution factor.

The results of the adjustment indicate that the incomes of nonwhite urban males were between 1.2 (Paasche) and 1.7 (Laspeyres) percent higher relative to white males because of this factor. Adjusting for the city-size factor increases the white/nonwhite income differential— hence the index of distribution differences is greater than one and the sign of the factor is negative. The Laspeyres index, which assumes both populations were distributed among cities in the same manner as whites, is greater than the Paasche index because the city-size differential is greater in the North. After the adjustment for city size in addition to the three previous factors, the nonwhite/white income ratio for urban males is estimated between 83.3 and 89.3 percent.

### 5. Age Distribution

Nonwhite urban males were overrepresented in the prime earning age categories in the United States in 1959. While whites are overrepresented in older age categories, particularly those over 65, nonwhites are overrepresented among the young. However, the larger percentage of the white urban male population among those past the years of prime earnings more than offsets of the youth of the nonwhite population.[15]

Data are available to calculate both the Laspeyres and Paasche indexes of distribution differences ("Characteristics of the Population," Table 219). The results indicate that if the age distribution of white urban males in 1959 had been the same as that of nonwhite urban males, the income of nonwhites relative to whites would have been between 2.4 (Paasche) and 2.8 (Laspeyres) percentage points lower than the observed ratio (i.e. negative in explaining the income differential).

*Summary of Estimates for Urban Males*

Table 1 consolidates the separate estimates of the magnitude of various factors upon the earnings differentials between white and nonwhite urban males. While the unadjusted income of nonwhites was only 58.3 percent as great as whites, the income of nonwhite urban males is estimated between 81 and 87 percent of the white income after adjustment for the five factors of Table 1. An income differential of between 13 and 19 percent remains unexplained.

## II. EARNINGS DIFFERENTIALS BETWEEN WHITES AND NONWHITES IN NONFARM OCCUPATIONS IN 1959

The estimates of Section I might be in error because it was not always possible to adjust for all factors simultaneously.[16] In addition, only median income data were used, and mean income estimates would be useful for purposes of comparison.

Mean and median earnings data for males according to color, age, education, and region were obtained for nonfarm occupations from 1960 Census data, *Subject Report, Occupation by Earnings and Education*. This data will allow for the simultaneous adjustment for all factors of Section I, except city-size.

The data used in this section differ from that of Section I in four respects. First, the data used are for earnings rather than income. Earnings data, unlike the income data used in Section I, include only wage and salary and self-employment income.[17] Second, they are for males with income between 25 and 64 years of age in nonfarm occupations, rather than males 25 and over in urban areas. Third, the quantity of education data used in Section I was more refined, having eight education categories rather than only six.[18] Fourth, estimates of the previous section were based on adjustment for state distribution of the populations, while data of this section will allow for only a North-South regional adjustment.

The adjustment techniques used in this

[15] Since the data cover those over age 25 with income, the youth of the nonwhite population is less important than if the data were for all with income. Census data used contained six age classes: 25–34, 35–44, 45–54, 55–64, 65–74, and 75 years of age and over.

[16] Obvious interaction between such factors as region and quantity of education was avoided by estimating their effect simultaneously.

[17] Income data includes, in addition to earnings, income from Social Security, pensions, Veterans payments, rents, interest or dividends, unemployment insurance and welfare payments.

[18] The data used in this section classifies those with 0 to 7 years of education as one group, rather than the 0, 1–4, 5–7 year classes previously used. This important since a large percentage of the nonwhite population is in this class. The impact of using the broader educational class will result in an under-estimation of (a) the quantity of education adjustment and (b) the adjusted nonwhite/white income ratio.

| | Index of Income Differences | | Index of Distribution Differences | |
|---|---|---|---|---|
| | Median | Mean | Median | Mean |
| Unadjusted Income Ratio (Nonwhite/White) | 60.1 | 54.6 | — | — |
| *Explanatory Factors* | | | | |
| A. Region | | | | |
|     Laspeyres | 68.1 | 59.9 | 88.3 | 91.2 |
|     Paasche | 63.7 | 55.6 | 94.3 | 96.8 |
| B. Region-Age | | | | |
|     Laspeyres | 66.5 | 58.9 | 91.8 | 92.7 |
|     Paasche | 62.1 | 55.6 | 98.2 | 98.2 |
| C. Region-Education | | | | |
|     Laspeyres | 72.0 | 64.4 | 84.4 | 84.8 |
|     Paasche | 71.0 | 64.8 | 85.7 | 84.3 |
| D. Region-Age-Education | | | | |
|     Laspeyres | 71.2 | 65.4 | 84.3 | 83.5 |
|     Paasche | 70.8 | 67.1 | 84.8 | 81.3 |
| E. Region-Age-Education-Scholastic Achievement | | | | |
|     Laspeyres | 85.6 | 83.6 | 70.2 | 65.3 |
|     Paasche | 77.2 | 75.2 | 77.8 | 72.6 |

SOURCE: The data used in calculating the estimates of this table were derived from U.S. Census data, *Subject Report, Occupation by Earnings and Education,* Tables 1, 2 and 3.

section are identical to those of Section I: the Laspeyres (Paasche) index calculated assuming both whites and nonwhites are distributed among productivity categories in the same manner as whites (nonwhites). Table 2 summarizes the results.

After simultaneous adjustment for the four factors considered in Table 2, the median earnings of nonwhite males in nonfarm occupations is estimated between 77 and 86 percent of the earnings of whites. For means, the adjusted earnings ratio is estimated between 75 and 85 percent, 2 percent less than for the medians.

The estimates are consistent with those of Section I. Adjustment for age had little effect after the region-education adjustment was considered. The failure of age to have the negative impact estimated in Section I results from the exclusion of those over 65 from the data used in this section. Since whites are highly overrepresented in the over-65 group, their inclusion increased the observed nonwhite/white income ratio and resulted in the negative contribution of age found in Section. I. Table 2 estimates that adjustment for region-education differences would increase the income of nonwhites by between 10 and 12 percent relative to whites. This is between 2 and 4 percent less than the estimates of Section I. Since this adjustment was made by exactly the same techniques in both cases, the difference between the two estimates must be attributable to the use of broader educational and regional classes in this section.

The median earnings estimate of the scholastic achievement factor of Table 2 is slightly less than the estimate of Section I. When mean earnings data are used, the estimated importance of the scholastic achievement factor increases. The magnitude of the scholastic achievement factor is greater for means than medians because the rate of change in the education-income relationship is greater for means than medians. Thus even though the unadjusted differential was 5 percent greater for means than medians, after adjustment for the four factors of Table 2 the difference was reduced to only 2 percent.

\* \* \*

The estimates of the adjusted ratio of nonwhite/white income of Section I are consistent with the estimates of this section. Due to the factors referred to in footnote 22 we might have expected these estimates to be slightly less. Considering the expected downward bias, the results of this section reenforce our estimates of Section I.

III. REGIONAL DIFFERENCES IN THE NONWHITE/WHITE EARNINGS RATIO FOR NONFARM OCCUPATIONS

Previously we indicated the importance of the regional (state) distribution factor on the nonwhite/white relative income for the United States. Now, we investigate *regional* differences in these income differentials. The South is generally believed to be more inclined toward employment discrimination than the North. Census data indicate the median income of nonwhite males in 1959 was 47 percent that of white males in the South and 73 percent in the North. The relative income of nonwhites to whites in the South was only 65 percent of the same ratio in the North.

At least three factors unrelated to employment discrimination, although not necessarily unrelated to other forms of color discrimination, result in making the income data of the South appear very unfavorable relative to the North. First, the quantity of education of nonwhites relative to whites is much less favorable in the South. Second, the nonwhite population in the North is significantly overrepresented in urban areas. Third, the nonwhite population in the North is not only overrepresented in urban areas, but specifically in large urban areas with high money income.

Table 3 disaggregates the estimates of Section II by region. After simultaneous adjustment for the four factors of Table 3, the median earnings ratio of nonwhites to whites is estimated between .83 and .88 in the North and .68 and .74 in the South. Similar differences in the adjusted mean earnings ratio exist between the two regions. The adjusted relative earnings estimates of the nonwhite/white income ratio

TABLE 3. EARNINGS OF NONWHITES AS A PERCENTAGE OF WHITES ADJUSTED FOR VARIOUS DETERMINANTS OF EARNINGS DIFFERENTIALS BY REGION FOR NONFARM OCCUPATIONS IN 1959

| | Index of Median Income Difference | | Index of Mean Income Difference | |
|---|---|---|---|---|
| | North | South | North | South |
| Unadjusted Income Ratio (Nonwhite/White) | 72.7 | 52.1 | 63.7 | 47.1 |
| *Explanatory Factors* | | | | |
| A. Age | | | | |
| Laspeyres | 72.8 | 52.2 | 63.4 | 47.2 |
| Paasche | 72.4 | 52.2 | 63.8 | 47.2 |
| B. Education | | | | |
| Laspeyres | 65.1 | 58.9 | 68.0 | 53.9 |
| Paasche | 67.1 | 61.9 | 70.8 | 58.2 |
| C. Age-Education | | | | |
| Laspeyres | 75.8 | 58.6 | 68.4 | 54.6 |
| Paasche | 79.5 | 62.1 | 72.2 | 59.7 |
| D. Age-Education-Scholastic Achievement | | | | |
| Laspeyres | 87.9 | 73.9 | 86.0 | 72.5 |
| Paasche | 83.6 | 67.9 | 81.3 | 66.5 |

SOURCE: See Table 2.

for nonfarm occupations (Table 3) for the South are 82 and 83 percent of similar estimates for the North.[19] Standardization for differences in the productivity factors between the two populations reduces, but does not eliminate, the North-South differential for relative income of nonwhites to whites.

Estimates similar to those of Table 3, using the same data can be derived by regression analysis. When the logarithm of income is the dependent variable and a dummy variable (white 1 and nonwhite 0) is used for color, the regression coefficient of color is the antilogarithm of the white/nonwhite income ratio.[20] Table 4 presents such regression equations by region, using median earnings as the dependent variable. In addition to the color variable, adjustment was made for differences in education ($X_4$), age ($X_1$, $X_2$, $X_3$), and scholastic achievement ($X_5$). The regression was run using both the maximum and minimum estimates of the scholastic achievement differential between whites and nonwhites.

Nonwhite earnings are estimated between 83.9 and 92.8 percent of the white earnings in the North, and 68.4 and 78.1 percent in the South. The color variable is significant at the 0.90 level in all cases. The results also indicate that even after correction for age, education, and scholastic achievement differences, the adjusted nonwhite/white earnings ratio is greater in the North than the South.

\* \* \*

The estimates of Table 4 reenforce our previous estimates that after adjustment for the productivity factors of this paper,

an unexplained income differential between white and nonwhite males still remains and the unexplained differential is larger in the South than in the North.

## REFERENCES

G. Becker, *The Economics of Discrimination.* Chicago 1957.

S. Bowles and H. M. Levin, "The Determinants of Scholastic Achievement—An Appraisal of Some Recent Evidence," *J. Hum. Resources,* spring 1968, 3, 1–24.

J. S. Coleman, et al., *Equality of Educational Opportunity.* Washington 1966.

R. A. Dentler, "Equality of Education Opportunity: A Special Review," *Urban Rev.,* Dec. 1966, *1,* 27–29.

J. B. Miner, *Intelligence in the United States.* New York 1957.

D. P. Moynihan, "The Crisis of Confidence," presented to the Subcommittee on Executive Reorganization of the U.S. Senate Committee of Government Operations, Dec. 13, 1966.

R. C. Nichols, "Schools and the Disadvantaged," *Science,* Dec. 9, 1966, *154,* 1312–14.

A. M. Shuey, *The Testing of Negro Intelligence.* New York 1966.

M. Zeman, "A Quantitative Analysis of White-Nonwhite Income Differential in the United States in 1939," unpublished doctoral dissertation, Univ. Chicago 1955.

U.S. Census of Population: 1960, *U.S. Summary, Final Report,* "Characteristics of the Population."

———, *Subject Report, Size of Place,* PC (3)–1B.

———, *Subject Report, Occupation by Earnings and Education,* PC (2)–7B.

———, *Detailed Characteristics, Final Report,* PC(1) Series.

[19] The North-South differential is slightly overstated because of the greater city-size contribution in the North. The city-size factor in the North is estimated between 1.5 and 1.8—in the South 0.9 and 1.6. In both cases it is negative, indicating the actual nonwhite/white income ratio is overstated because of the failure to adjust for this factor. In addition, it is usually argued that less money per head is spent on the education of southern Negroes as compared to northern Negroes, resulting in an inferior quality of education for the former. However, the *Coleman Report* indicated the white/nonwhite scholastic achievement differential for a given grade level was nearly as great in the North as the South. The existence of a greater scholastic achievement differential in the South would decrease the adjusted North-South differential.

[20] The regression coefficient for color is $log\ Y^w - log\ Y^n$, or $log\ (Y^w/Y^n)$. The nonwhite/white earnings ratio ($Y^n/Y^w$) contained in Table 4 is the inverse of the anti-logarithm of the color coefficients.

TABLE 4. REGRESSION EQUATIONS ESTIMATING THE NONWHITE/WHITE EARNINGS $(Y^n/Y^w)$ RATIO AFTER ADJUSTMENT FOR VARIOUS PRODUCTIVITY FACTORS

(t-ratios in parentheses)[b]

| Logarithm of Median Earnings[a] | $b_0$[c] | $X_1$ | $X_2$ | $X_3$ | $X_4$ | $X_5$ | $X_6$ | $R^2$ (df) | $Y^n/Y^w$ |
|---|---|---|---|---|---|---|---|---|---|
| 1. North | 3.461 | .060 (4.78) | .057 (4.52) | .034 (2.71) | .022 (14.99) | −.042 (4.10) | .0326 (1.32) | .791 (41) | .928 |
| 2. North | 3.430 | .060 (4.22) | .057 (4.04) | .034 (2.42) | .021 (11.99) | −.017 (2.30) | .0760 (3.10) | .776 (41) | .839 |
| 3. South | 3.232 | .069 (4.56) | .063 (4.23) | .020 (1.34) | .031 (17.51) | −.056 (4.58) | .1072 (3.60) | .817 (41) | .781 |
| 4. South | 3.190 | .069 (3.99) | .063 (3.70) | .020 (1.18) | .029 (13.78) | −.023 (2.56) | .1645 (5.43) | .806 (41) | .684 |

$X_1$ = dummy—35–44 age group
$X_2$ = dummy—45–54 age group
$X_3$ = dummy—55–64 age group

$X_4$ = years of education of those with income in the age education cell
$X_5$ = scholastic achievement differential between whites and nonwhites
$X_6$ = dummy for color (white 1 and nonwhite 0)

[a] Odd (even) numbered equations are for data containing the maximum (minimum) estimate of the scholastic achievement differential from the *Coleman Report*.

[b] Critical values for t are approximately ±2.42 for 99 percent, ±1.68 for 95 percent, ±1.30 for 90 percent, ±1.05 for 85 percent.

[c] The coefficient $b_0$ is an estimate of the median earnings of nonwhite males in the 25–34 age group. The interpretation of the last column $(Y^n/Y^w)$ is given in fn. 24.

A factor of considerable importance in explaining white and nonwhite employment differentials not considered by either Gilman or Gwartney is housing segregation. Housing segregation is important because of the postwar trend for industry to move to the outer rings of cities or to rural areas while blacks are concentrating increasingly in the central cities. The availablity and costs of transportation in time and money therefore become more important in determining job opportunities for blacks.

To test the importance of industry location and residence of blacks in Detroit and Chicago, Kain, in "Housing Segregation, Negro Employment, and Metropolitan Decentralization," presents results from a series of multiple regression models using the percentage of Negro employment in each of 98 work places (areas) as the dependent variable and a series of proxy variables representing the factors causing Negroes to be underrepresented in distant work places as explanatory variables. These proxies include: (1) the percentage of Negro employed residents in each work place zone as a proxy for the employer's propensity to discriminate and (2) as a proxy for transportation costs, "airline distance from the work place to the nearest Negro residence area" and "the airline distance to the nearest point of a major ghetto." Kain's regression explained only 40 percent of the variance for Detroit and over 70 percent for Chicago, a difference that he attributes to greater segregation in Chicago.

Kain concludes that

> Housing market segregation clearly affects the distribution of Negro employment. Its effect on the level of Negro employment and unemployment is a more complex question and, consequently, the answer is less certain.

Moreover, while Kain's estimates are admittedly highly tentative,

> . . . they nonetheless suggest that housing market segregation may reduce the level of Negro employment and thereby contribute to the high unemployment rates of metropolitan Negroes.

It was possible for Kain to obtain an empirical test for Chicago "of the impact of employment dispersal on Negro job opportunities." However,

> This is an even more complex issue than that discussed above, and the conclusions must be more guarded. Even so, the empirical findings do suggest that postwar suburbanization of metropolitan employment may be further undermining the position of the Negro, and the continued high levels of unemployment in a full employment economy may be partially attributable to a rapid and adverse (for the Negro) shift in the location of jobs.

Kain's article clearly deals with a very important problem. However, his analysis and conclusions are limited by the data and specification difficulties and deficiencies of all of those who use regression models to explain racial income and employment differentials. Regression analysis does not make it possible to assign causation and tends to attribute "discrimination" to the residual not explained by specific independent variables. The researcher must therefore be sure he has selectd the right explanatory variables and that some of the variables used might not really reflect other important causal factors not measured. Kain, for instance, has to use proxies for his main independent variables, and it is not at all clear that the percentage of Negro employed residents in a work place zone is a satisfactory proxy for employer discrimination. Many factors influence the demand side of the employment equation other than discrimination, especially the employer's skill requirements, and there are many other factors on the supply side of the equation other than discrimination, especially the skill attainments of work forces. Moreover, transportation probably has much greater significance for low-wage jobs than it does for high-wage ones. Thus, using Kain's model, we might demonstrate discrimination against whites who live in suburbs and therefore must commute long distances into central cities where they do not live, but where the white-collar jobs are concentrated. Clearly, however, people are more willing to incur the costs in time and money to commute to high-wage jobs than to low-wage jobs. Transportation probably is more important for Negroes because they are concentrated in low-wage jobs as well as because they are black. Similarly, housing segregation is highly correlated with income, education, and factors other than race, making it difficult to measure the net effect of race.

# Housing Segregation, Negro Employment, and Metropolitan Decentralization

## by John F. Kain

This paper investigates the relationship between metropolitan housing market segregation and the distribution and level of nonwhite employment.[1] Numerous researchers have evaluated the effects of racial discrimination in the housing market. . . .[2] Hypotheses evaluated in this paper are that racial segregation in the housing markets (1) affects the distribution of Negro employment and (2) reduces Negro job opportunities, and that (3) postwar suburbanization of employment has seriously aggravated the problem. These hypotheses are tested empirically using data on place of work and place of residence obtained from the home

SOURCE Reprinted with permission from *Quarterly Journal of Economics*, Vol. 82, No. 2, May 1968.

[1] The terms Negro and nonwhite are used interchangeably in this paper. Since Negroes are 99 per cent of all Chicago nonwhites in 1960 and 97 per cent of all Detroit nonwhites in 1960, the distinction has little practical significance.

[2] Davis McEntire, *Residence and Race: Final and Comprehensive Report to the Commission on Race and Housing* (Berkeley: University of California Press, 1960); Eunice and George Grier, *Privately Developed Interracial Housing: An Analysis of Experience* (Berkeley: University of California Press, 1960); Nathan Glazer and Davis McEntire, *Studies in Housing and Minority Groups* (Berkeley: University of California Press, 1960); Luigi Laurenti, *Property Values and Race: Studies in Seven Cities* (Berkeley: University of California Press, 1960); Chester Rapkin and W. C. Grigsby, *The Demand for Housing in Racially Mixed Areas: A Study of the Nature of Neighborhood Change* (Berkeley: University of California Press, 1960); O. D. Duncan and Beverly Duncan, *The Negro Population of Chicago* (Chicago: University of Chicago Press, 1957); Morton Grodzins, *The Metropolitan Areas as a Racial Problem* (Pittsburgh: University of Pittsburgh Press, 1958); Beverly Duncan and P. M. Hauser, *Housing a Metropolis—Chicago* (Glencoe, Illinois: The Free Press, 1960); J. F. Kain, "Commuting and the Residential Decisions of Central Business District Workers," National Bureau of Economic Research, Special Conference Series, 17, *Transportation Economics* (New York: Columbia University Press, 1965); J. R. Meyer, J. F. Kain, and Martin Wohl, *The Urban Transportation Problem* (Cambridge, Mass.: Harvard University Press, 1965).

interview surveys of the Detroit Area Traffic Study in 1952 and the Chicago Area Traffic Study in 1956.[3]

## I. NEGRO RESIDENTIAL SEGREGATION

To understand how housing segregation affects the distribution and level of Negro employment, it is necessary to comprehend the location and growth of Negro ghettos in metropolitan areas. The means by which racial segregation in housing has been maintained are amply documented.[4] They are both legal and extra-legal; for example: racial covenants; racial zoning; violence or threats of violence; preemptive purchase; various petty harassments; implicit or explicit collusion by realtors, banks, mortgage lenders, and other lending agencies; and, in the not-so-distant past, the Federal Housing Administration (FHA) and other Federal agencies.

The existence, extent, and persistence of residential segregation in American cities is even better documented. Negro residential segregation indexes have been calculated by Karl and Alma Taeuber from block statistics for 207 cities in 1960 and 109 cities in 1940 and 1950.[5] These segregation indexes assume values between zero and 100. A value of zero indicates that every block has the same proportion of Negroes. A value of 100 indicates segregated distribution wherein each block contains only whites or Negroes, but not both. Values for the 207 cities in 1960 range from 60.4 to 98.1 with only a few cities having values in the lower range of observed scores—only eight cities have values below 70. Similar results were obtained for the twelve metropolitan areas completely tracted in both 1950 and 1960. If block indexes had been computed for entire metropolitan areas the measured degree of Negro segregation would have been even higher since virtually all urban Negroes reside in the larger cities for which block statistics are available. By contrast, the remaining portions of metropolitan areas are virtually all white.[6] Moreover, urban Negroes are highly segregated in all regions of the country and the patterns of Negro segregation show very great stability, having existed for at least thirty-five years.[7] The experience of Negroes has been remarkably different from that of other ethnic and racial groups in this respect. Stanley Lieberson has shown that Negroes are far more segregated than any other ethnic or racial group in American cities and that while segregation of immigrants and other groups has generally declined, the segregation of Negroes has increased over time.[8]

Analyses by Karl and Alma Taeuber, Anthony Pascal, and others suggest that very little of this observed residential seg-

---

[3] Detroit Area Traffic Study, *Report of the Detroit Metropolitan Area Traffic Study: Part 1—Data Summary of Interpretation* (Lansing, Michigan, July 1955); *Chicago Area Transportation Study,* Vol. 1 (Chicago, 1959).

[4] G. S. Becker, *The Economics of Discrimination* (Chicago: University of Chicago Press, 1957); Robert Weaver, *The Negro Ghetto* (New York: Harcourt, Brace, 1948); Glazer and McEntire, *op. cit.;* Grodzins, *op. cit.;* McEntire, *op. cit.;* T. J. Woofter, Jr., *Negro Problems in Cities* (Garden City, N.Y.: Doubleday, Doran and Company, 1928); Rapkin and Grigsby, *op. cit.;* Laurenti, *op. cit.*

[5] Karl E. and Alma F. Taeuber, *Negroes in Cities* (Chicago: Aldine Publishing Co., 1965). Similar results were obtained by Donald Cowgill for 109 cities in 1940 and 1950 using a slightly different segregation index. D. O. Cowgill, "Trends in Residential Segregation of Nonwhites in American Cities, 1940–50," *American Sociological Review,* Vol. 21 (Feb. 1956), pp. 43–47.

[6] Central city and metropolitan area indexes are not directly comparable, since those for central cities are based upon city blocks while those for metropolitan areas are based on census tracts. For a detailed discussion of the methodological differences arising from use of census tracts and blocks as well as from alternative segregation indexes see: Taeuber and Taeuber, *op. cit.,* Appendix A. "The Measurement of Residential Segregation," pp. 195–245.

[7] *Ibid.,* pp. 37–40.

[8] Stanley Lieberson, *Ethnic Patterns in American Cities* (Glencoe: The Free Press, 1963), pp. 120–32.

regation of Negroes can be explained by economic factors.[9] Similar conclusions about the inadequacy of nonwhite/white socioeconomic differences as an explanation of residential segregation have been reached by the author. Estimates published elsewhere suggest that as many as 40,000 nonwhite workers might move from Detroit's central ghetto to outlying residence areas, and that as many as 112,000 nonwhite workers might move away from Chicago's South Side, if racial barriers to nonwhite housing choices were removed.[10]

## II. SEGREGATION IN DETROIT AND CHICAGO

Chicago and Detroit nonwhites are highly segregated. The central city (block) segregation index for Chicago exceeds 92.0 in all three decades and the metropolitan area (tract) indexes are only marginally lower. Segregation scores indicate Detroit Negroes are slightly less segregated in every year; but they all are still highly segregated.[11]

Nonwhite ghettos in Detroit and Chicago, as in most other U.S. metropolitan areas, lie within the central city near the Central Business District (CBD). Small secondary ghettos are sometimes found in the central parts of older suburbs and in previously rural areas. Both kinds of outlying Negro residential areas may importantly affect the distribution of nonwhite employment and the job loss that may result from housing segregation.

Detroit's principal ghetto, which houses approximately 93 per cent of Detroit's nonwhite work force, but only about 29 per cent of its whites, lies within the central city and has a slight sectoral pattern. Nearly all of the remaining 7 per cent of nonwhites live in one of three small outlying nonwhite residence areas.[12]

Most Chicago Negroes live in the notorious South Side, although fingers of the ghetto extend due west and due north from the Loop. Chicago's principal ghetto houses a larger percentage of its nonwhite work force than does Detroit's: 96 per cent of Chicago's nonwhite workers reside there, but only 20 per cent of its white

[9] Pascal, using multiple regression techniques, is able to explain a maximum of 46 per cent of the variation in the proportion of all households headed by Negroes among 100 residence areas in metropolitan Chicago. The proportion of explained variance for 100 Detroit residential areas is even smaller, 33 per cent. Anthony H. Pascal, "Summary: The Economics of Housing Segregation," paper presented at the RAND Conference on Urban Economics, The RAND Corporation (Santa Monica, California, August 24–25, 1964), pp. 6–7. Karl and Alma Taeuber make several estimates of the proportion of residential segregation by cenus tracts that can be explained by economic factors in several cities. The most satisfactory of these, for fifteen cities in 1940, 1950, and 1960 (including Detroit but not Chicago), are also obtained from multiple regression models. Using census tract variations in tenure, median value, and contract rent of occupied dwelling units as explanatory variables, the Taeubers are able to explain less than 5 per cent of the variation in the nonwhite percentage among Detroit census tracts in all three years. The largest amount of variation that can be attributed to these three variables in any of the fifteen cities and in any of the three years is less than one-third. Moreover, the amount of residential segregation explained by these three socioeconomic variables is generally lower in more recent years. Taeuber and Taeuber, op. cit., pp. 23 and 24.

[10] Meyer, Kain, and Wohl, op. cit., pp. 163–66.

[11] Chicago city (block) segregation indexes are: 1940, 95.0; 1950, 92.1; and 1960, 92.6. The metropolitan (tract) indexes are 1950, 88.1 and 1960, 89.7. Detroit city segregation indexes (block) are 89.9 in 1940, 88.8 in 1950, and 84.5 in 1960, and the metropolitan area indexes (tract) are 83.3 in 1950 and 86.7 in 1960.

[12] By comparison with other U.S. metropolitan areas, Detroit and Chicago have a large number of relatively large outlying Negro residential areas. Detroit possesses three and Chicago possesses two of the thirty suburban communities with 1,000 or more nonwhite households. Only the metropolitan areas of New York and San Francisco-Oakland have a larger number. Moreover, nonwhites are highly segregated within these suburbs; the 1960 indexes for Chicago are: Evanston, 87.2 and Joliet, 90.2. Those for Detroit suburbs are: Highland Park, 7.4; Inkster, 95.0; Pontiac, 90.5. Taeuber and Taeuber, op. cit., p. 59.

workers. The only other significant nonwhite settlement in the Chicago area straddles the suburbs of Evanston and Skokie to the north of the Loop and houses about 1,900 nonwhite workers, or just under 1 per cent of the nonwhite labor force.[13]

## III. THE DISTRIBUTION OF NEGRO EMPLOYMENT

There are several reasons why housing market segregation may affect the distribution and level of Negro employment. The most obvious are: (1) The distance to and difficulty of reaching certain jobs from Negro residence areas may impose costs on Negroes high enough to discourage them from seeking employment there. (2) Negroes may have less information about and less opportunity to learn about jobs distant from their place of residence or those of their friends.[14] (3) Employers located outside the ghetto may discriminate against Negroes out of real or imagined fears of retaliation from white customers for "bringing Negroes into all-white residential areas," or they may feel little pressure not to discriminate. (4) Similarly, employers in or near the ghetto may discriminate in favor of Negroes.

To test the hypothesis that the central location of the Chicago and Detroit ghettos and limitations on Negro residence outside these areas affect the location of Negro employment, a series of multiple regression models have been fitted for Chicago and Detroit using the Negro percentage of total employment in each of 98 workplace areas as the dependent variable and a series of proxy variables representing the factors causing Negroes to be underrepresented in distant workplaces as explanatory variables.

The Negro percentage of population residing in each of the 98 workplace zones is a proxy for the employers' propensity to discriminate in favor or against nonwhite workers because of real or imagined attitudes of the resident population toward the employment of Negroes. Businesses located in the ghetto, and particularly those selling predominately to ghetto residents, would be expected to hire disproportionate numbers of Negroes. Similarly, retailers and others located in all white suburbs and having few or no Negro customers may feel some reluctance to employ Negroes in sales and other contact jobs. The Negro percentage of population residing in each workplace zone is unavailable. Therefore, the Negro percentage of employed residents of the workplace zone, hereafter referred to as the residence ratio, is used to measure the impact, if any, of neighborhood racial composition on the employment of Negroes in each workplace zone.

Transportation costs from the workplace area to the ghetto and the effect of distance on knowledge of job opportunities are proxied by two variables: the airline distance from the workplace to the nearest Negro residence area (the nearest zone having more than 2 per cent Negro residents), and the airline distance from the workplace to the nearest point in the major ghetto. (The residence zones used in the analysis have the same boundaries as the workplace zones.)

[13] Otis and Beverly Duncan conclude that the spatial outline of the Negro community in Chicago had been established by 1920, if not by 1910; that further expansion of the Negro community occurred within areas which already had been accommodating a nucleus of Negro residents in 1920; and that what expansion there has been of the Negro residential areas has consisted of adding areas contiguous to existing Negro concentrations. Duncan and Duncan, op. cit., pp. 87–107.

[14] Labor mobility studies show that few jobs are located from newspaper advertisements, employment offices, and the like. Workers most frequently learn of jobs from friends, by passing the place of work and seeing help wanted signs, and by other casual associations. Since nonwhites have few associations with white areas distant from the ghetto and since few of their friends and neighbors are employed there or make frequent trips there, the chances of their learning of distant job opportunities may be significantly lessened.

Distance from Negro residence areas to outlying workplaces may seriously understate transportation costs between the ghetto and many workplaces because of the indirectness or complete absence of public transit services from ghetto residential areas to outlying or suburban workplaces. Public transit systems invariably focus on the central business district and are usually badly oriented for making trips from the ghetto to outlying workplaces. Historically the principal function of these systems was to transport workers from outlying residental areas to centrally located high density workplaces, and their specialization in this regard has increased as the automobile has become increasingly competitive for off-peak and nonradial travel. As car ownership among ghetto Negroes is relatively low, the difficulty or impossibility of using public transit systems to reach outlying workplaces may severely restrict their ability to seek or accept employment there. Because of housing segregation, low skilled Negroes are unable to move close to suburban workplaces or perhaps even to live near a direct transit line serving current or potential workplaces as do must low skilled whites.[15]

Frequently ghetto Negroes may be forced to choose between buying a private automobile and thus spending a disproportionate share of their low incomes on transportation, making a very long and circuitous trip by public transit (if any service is available at all), or foregoing the job altogether. Where the job in question is a marginal one, their choice may frequently be the latter. More often they will not even seek out the job in the first instance because of the difficulties of reaching it from possible residence locations.

Three equations are fitted for each city. The residence ratio ($R$) is included in all three. In addition, the first equation for each city, (1) and (4), includes distance from the nearest ghetto, $d^n$; equations (2) and (5) include distance from the major ghetto, $d^m$; and equations (3) and (6) include both distance variables, $d^n$ and $d^m$. Since distance from the major ghetto and distance from the nearest ghetto are highly intercorrelated, including both in the regression equation does not add much to the explained variance and greatly reduces the statistical significance of their coefficients.[16] This is especially true for the Chicago models. When only one distance proxy is used, the coefficients of all variables are highly significant.

## Equations

Chicago $\hspace{6cm}$ $R^2$

(1) $\quad W = 9.18 + 0.458R - 0.521\ d^n$
$$0.78$$
$\hspace{2cm}(10.7)\quad(15.6)\quad\ \ (4.3)$
$\hspace{3cm}$ ($t$ ratios in parentheses)

(2) $\quad W = 9.28 + 0.456R - 0.409\ d^m$
$$0.782$$
$\hspace{2cm}(10.5)\quad(15.4)\quad\ \ (4.2)$

(3) $\quad W = 9.36 + 0.455R - 0.324\ d^n$
$$0.785$$
$\hspace{2cm}(10.6)\ (15.4)\quad\quad(1.2)$
$\hspace{4.5cm}- 0.176\ d^m$
$\hspace{4.8cm}(0.8)$

Detroit $\hspace{6cm}$ $R^2$

(4) $\quad W = 12.78 + 0.091R - 1.141\ d^n$
$$0.359$$
$\hspace{3cm}(2.9)\quad\ \ (4.4)$

(5) $\quad W = 12.64 + 0.100R - 0.758\ d^m$
$$0.382$$
$\hspace{3cm}(2.9)\quad\ \ (4.7)$

---

[15] Meyer, Kain, and Wohl, *op. cit.*, Chap. 7; John F. Kain, "The 'Big Cities' Big Problem," *Challenge*, Vol. 15 (Sept./Oct. 1966), pp. 5–8.

[16] The simple correlation coefficients between distance from the major ghetto and distance from the nearest ghetto are $R = 0.91$ for Chicago and $R = 0.75$ for Detroit.

$$(6) \qquad W = 13.45 + 0.082R - 0.563 \ d^n$$
$$0.400$$
$$(2.3) \qquad (1.7)$$
$$- 0.52 \ d^m$$
$$(2.5)$$

$W =$ Employment ratio, per cent of zones $i$'s workers who are Negroes = $\dfrac{\text{Negro workers employed in } i}{\text{Total workers employed in } i}$ $\times$ 100.

$R =$ Residence ratio, per cent of zone $i$'s resident workers who are Negroes = $\dfrac{\text{Negro workers residing in } i}{\text{Total workers residing in } i}$ $\times$ 100.

$d^n =$ Distance from the nearest ghetto, airline distance in miles to nearest boundary point of a Negro residence area.

$d^m =$ Distance from the nearest ghetto, airline distance in miles to nearest boundary point of the major ghetto.

The most obvious difference between the Detroit and Chicago models is the proportion of total variance explained. All three Chicago regressions explain more than seven-tenths of the variance in the dependent variable, while the Detroit regressions explain only about four-tenths. This difference is attributed to Chicago's greater racial segregation.[17] Detroit's major ghetto is larger and more dispersed than Chicago's, and Detroit also has more and better located outlying Negro residential areas. Thus, it is reasonable that the model explains less about the spatial distribution of nonwhite employment in Detroit, where Negro residences are not

so concentrated geographically.[18] These differences are indicated by the mean distance to the ghetto in Chicago and Detroit. Mean distance from the 98 Chicago workplace areas to the major ghetto is 5.4 miles while the mean distance for Detroit is only 4.3 miles. Similar relationships hold for distance to the nearest ghetto.

The regression coefficients also differ considerably for the two cities. Coefficients of the residence ratio in the Chicago equations are much larger than those for the Detroit equations. A 1 per cent increase in the number of Negro workers living in a Chicago residence area is associated with nearly a .5 per cent increase in Negro employment. By contrast, a 1 per cent increase in the residence ratio is associated with only a .1 per cent increase in employment in Detroit. However, the distance coefficients are much larger in the Detroit models. In Detroit the percentage of Negroes employed in a workplace area declines by .8 per cent with each one mile increase in distance from the major ghetto. The decline is only .4 per cent in Chicago (equations (2) and (5)). There is a similar correspondence for the distance from the nearest ghetto coefficients in equations (1) and (4), and when both distance variables are included in equations (3) and (6).

If the previously discussed evidence of severe restriction of Negro residential choice is accepted, these findings would seem to suggest that housing market segregation does strongly affect the location of Negro employment. However, if this evidence on housing market discrimination is not accepted, these findings could be construed as demonstrating the opposite causal hypothesis; that the location of Negro jobs strongly affects the distribu-

[17] It should be noted that the variance of the dependent variable is considerably smaller in Detroit.
[18] This is not to deny the possible importance of other differences between the two cities, such as the nondiscriminatory behavior of the United Auto Workers in Detroit and the importance of the auto industry there.

tion of Negro residences.[19] Some further tests of these alternative causal hypotheses are presented below.

## IV. NEGRO EMPLOYMENT BY OCCUPATION AND INDUSTRY

Since Negroes typically have less skill and less education than whites, an unequal spatial distribution of skill requirements might lead to results like those obtained for Detroit and Chicago, if the average skill level requirement of jobs increased with distance from the ghetto. Such a distribution of skill requirements could occur by chance or for historical reasons. Similarly, firms demanding many low skilled workers might locate near the ghetto because of the plentiful supply of low skilled workers available there. No direct evidence on the education or skill requirements of the labor force by distance from the ghetto, which would permit direct evaluation of this hypothesis, is available. However, data are available on white and Negro employment in each Chicago workplace zone by one-digit occupation and industry classifications and these permit some indirect tests. Relationships, like those given in equations (1)–(6) are estimated for each occupation and industry group for Chicago. Insofar as these industry and occupation groups have different education and skill requirements, the estimates thereby obtained will reflect differences in labor force racial composi-

tion attributable at least in part to these differences.

Equations (7)–(22) are regression equations obtained for eight one-digit occupational and eight one-digit industry groups. The overall consistency and goodness of fit of these sixteen equations is rather remarkable given the small number of nonwhites employed in some of these occupation and industry groups and the very large sampling errors that must exist.[20] The proportion of explained variance ranges from a low of 53 per cent for wholesaling to a high of 80 per cent for retailing.[21]

The regression coefficient's generally have high statistical significance (as indicated by the $t$ ratios given in parentheses) and have the correct sign. Regression coefficients for the distance from ghetto variables, $d^n$ or $d^m$, are negative and those for the residence ratios $R$, are positive in all sixteen equations. The problem of multicollinearity between the two distance variables remains and only the most significant relationship is presented here. Neither distance variable differs significantly from zero at the 5 per cent level in equations (7)–(10) (the first four occupational groups—professional, managerial, clerical and sales) and both are omitted. Significantly these four occupation groups are those for which prejudice in favor of or against employment of

19 Findings published elsewhere indicate that the location of Negro employment does affect the location of Negro residences within the constraints imposed by housing market segregation. However, the location decisions of Negroes appear irrational and inconsistent, if the hypothesis of significant restriction on their choice of residence is not accepted. Meyer, Kain, and Wohl, op. cit., pp. 144–77.

20 These data are based upon a one and thirty sampling rate. Thus, for some occupations and industries with either relatively few workers or relatively low nonwhite proportions the number of nonwhite workers is very small. The sample included only 241 nonwhites employed in wholesale trade; 671 employed in finance, insurance, and real estate; and only 740 employed in public administration. Even fewer nonwhites were sampled within several occupation groups. There were only 170 nonwhite sales workers; 316 nonwhite private household workers; 287 nonwhite managers, officials, and proprietors; and 370 nonwhite professional, technical, and kindred workers.

21 A much poorer fit was obtained for private household workers. That equation (not reported above) explains only 15 per cent of the total variance. The poor statistical fit obtained for domestics is hardly surprising. Private household workers include an especially small number of workers and thus the sampling variability is especially great. Moreover, because of "living in" their behavior would be expected to be much different than hypothesized by the above model.

| Occupation | | Equations | |
|---|---|---|---|
| Professional, technical, and kindred workers | (7) | $W = 0.83 + 0.392\,R$ <br> $(1.3)\ (14.1)$ | $R^2 = 0.68$ |
| Managers, officials, and proprietors | (8) | $W = 0.04 + 0.416\,R$ <br> $(-0.06)\ (16.0)$ | $R^2 = 0.73$ |
| Clerical and kindred workers | (9) | $W = 1.25 + 0.526\,R$ <br> $(1.8)\ (17.2)$ | $R^2 = 0.76$ |
| Sales workers | (10) | $W = 0.48 + 0.469\,R$ <br> $(0.65)\ (14.6)$ | $R^2 = 0.69$ |
| Craftsmen, foremen, and kindred workers | (11) | $W = 5.68 + 0.330\,R - 0.256d_m$ <br> $(7.6)\ (13.1)\quad (-3.1)$ | $R^2 = 0.72$ |
| Operatives and kindred workers | (12) | $W = 15.5 + 0.479\,R - 0.820d_m$ <br> $(11.0)\ (10.1)\quad (-5.3)$ | $R^2 = 0.67$ |
| Service workers except in private houses | (13) | $W = 15.4 + 0.680\,R - 0.803d_n$ <br> $(8.8)\ (11.3)\quad (-3.2)$ | $R^2 = 0.66$ |
| Laborers and farm workers | (14) | $W = 34.9 + 0.421\,R - 1.87d_m$ <br> $(16.7)\ (6.02)\quad (-8.13)$ | $R^2 = 0.62$ |
| Industry | | | |
| Manufacturing, durable goods | (15) | $W = 10.8 + 0.291\,R - 0.54d_m$ <br> $(9.2)\ (7.4)\quad (-4.2)$ | $R^2 = 0.53$ |
| Manufacturing, nondurable goods | (16) | $W = 9.7 + 0.367\,R - 0.62d_m$ <br> $(8.7)\ (9.8)\quad (-5.0)$ | $R^2 = 0.64$ |
| Transportation, communication and other | (17) | $W = 5.8 + 0.317\,R - 0.36d_m$ <br> $(6.3)\ (10.2)\quad (-3.5)$ | $R^2 = 0.63$ |
| Retail trade | (18) | $W = 4.07 + 0.645\,R - 0.264d_n$ <br> $(3.8)\ (17.8)\quad (-1.8)$ | $R^2 = 0.80$ |
| Finance, insurance, real estate, professional, services, etc. | (19) | $W = 2.73 + 0.552\,R$ <br> $(3.2)\ (14.9)$ | $R^2 = 0.70$ |
| Wholesale trade | (20) | $W = 4.86 + 0.341\,R - 0.256d_m$ <br> $(4.2)\ (8.8)\quad (-2.0)$ | $R^2 = 0.53$ |
| Business, repair, personal, services, etc. | (21) | $W = 18.2 + 0.582\,R - 0.805d_n$ <br> $(9.5)\ (8.9)\quad (-3.0)$ | $R^2 = 0.55$ |
| Public administration | (22) | $W = 10.5 + 0.562\,R - 0.581d_m$ <br> $(7.3)\ (11.6)\quad (-3.6)$ | $R^2 = 0.68$ |

Negroes on the basis of the racial composition of the residential area would be expected to be greatest.

Virtually no Negroes hold jobs in these four occupational groups outside of non-white residence areas, and within the ghetto their representation is disproportionately large. Nonwhites were an estimated 4.6 per cent of all Chicago clerical workers in 1956. Yet they were 78 per cent of all clerical workers employed in ghetto workplace zone 24 and 77 per cent of these employed in zone 13 (Table 1); Negroes were an estimated 98 per cent of all Chicago workers tresiding in zone 24 in 1956 and 96 per cent of those residing in zone 13. As the data in Table 1 indicate, this very large overrepresentation of non-white employees in ghetto workplace zones is characteristic of all occupation and industry groups. By contrast, 41 of the 98 workplace zones used in the anal-

| | Per cent Nonwhite | | | | | | | |
|---|---|---|---|---|---|---|---|---|
| | Mean [a] of 98 Work-place Zones | Entire [b] Area | Selected | Ghetto Workplace | | | Zones [c] | Number of [d] Areas With no Nonwhites |
| | | | 3 | 4 | 12 | 13 | 24 | |
| Professional, technical | 4.4 | 6.0 | 12.2 | 8.1 | 45.3 | 35.3 | 69.1 | 50 |
| Managers, officials, and proprietors | 3.7 | 4.2 | 4.6 | 4.6 | 37.0 | 59.9 | 60.1 | 55 |
| Clerical | 6.0 | 9.6 | 26.7 | 14.5 | 35.0 | 76.9 | 78.4 | 41 |
| Sales | 3.7 | 4.6 | 5.2 | 4.5 | 28.0 | 70.0 | 70.6 | 69 |
| Craftsmen | 7.3 | 9.3 | 10.4 | 15.4 | 28.6 | 45.9 | 54.4 | 20 |
| Operatives | 15.4 | 21.6 | 23.8 | 32.1 | 46.0 | 80.7 | 58.1 | 24 |
| Service workers | 18.3 | 30.2 | 41.2 | 39.4 | 79.1 | 95.8 | 95.5 | 25 |
| Laborers | 28.6 | 41.5 | 44.4 | 56.3 | 67.5 | 81.7 | 79.9 | 21 |
| Durable manufacturing | 10.4 | 12.9 | 16.0 | 23.3 | 32.5 | 42.1 | 49.8 | 24 |
| Nondurable manufacturing | 9.8 | 18.5 | 20.9 | 24.7 | 40.5 | 56.8 | 43.2 | 40 |
| Transportation | 6.7 | 11.0 | 13.1 | 19.1 | 26.0 | 38.1 | 41.4 | 45 |
| Retailing | 8.8 | 13.5 | 21.0 | 31.3 | 56.9 | 76.6 | 90.5 | 33 |
| Finance, insurance, real estate | 7.7 | 10.1 | 27.0 | 18.7 | 48.4 | 51.6 | 84.3 | 47 |
| Wholesaling | 6.5 | 10.1 | 10.0 | 19.7 | 41.1 | 48.4 | 50.0 | 58 |
| Business services | 20.2 | 26.7 | 23.6 | 30.8 | 71.6 | 94.4 | 92.3 | 23 |
| Public administration | 12.4 | 24.8 | 47.1 | 22.3 | 48.4 | 87.8 | 74.0 | 40 |
| All workers | 11.2 | 14.6 | 21.2 | 23.1 | 45.8 | 64.4 | 71.5 | 11 |
| Employed residents | 9.0 | 14.6 | 32.9 | 29.0 | 87.1 | 96.3 | 98.1 | 35 |

[a] Unweighted mean of the per cent of nonwhites for the 98 Chicago analysis zones used in the analysis.

[b] Per cent nonwhite for the entire area = number of Chicago nonwhites employed in industry or occupation group $K$ divided by total Chicago employment in group $K_1$.

[c] Per cent nonwhite for selected individual analysis zones.

[d] Number of the 98 analysis zones used in the analysis having no sampled nonwhite workers.

ysis have no nonwhite clerical workers.[22] The number of zones with no reported Negro workers is even greater for the professional, technical and kindred; the manager, official, and proprietor; and sales groups. The Negro proportion of all craftsmen in ghetto areas is generally lower than the Negro proportion in the more visible occupations, even though Negroes are a larger proportion of all Chicago area craftsmen. Negro craftsmen were employed in all but twenty workplace zones and Negro laborers in all but twenty-one.

Differentiation by industry group is less great. This finding might be expected, since all industries have some jobs, such as janitors and laborers, in which Negro employment is traditionally accepted. Even so, the data in Table 1 indicate that nonwhites are most overrepresented in those ghetto industries having the greatest amount of customer contact—retailing; finance, insurance and real estate; business services; and public administration. They are least overrepresented in those ghetto industries having the least customer con-

[22] In interpreting the data in Table 2 on the number of analysis areas or workplace zones having no nonwhite workers, it should be remembered that these data are based on a one and thirty sample. Thus, the number of analysis zones having no nonwhite workers in a given industry or occupation group will generally be smaller than the number of areas having no sampled workers in a given occupation or industry group. Moreover, eleven analysis areas have no sampled nonwhite workers whatsoever and this thereby is a lower bound for any given occupation or industry group.

|  | $R$ | $d^m$ | $R^2$ | $R$ | $d^c$ | $R^2$ |
|---|---|---|---|---|---|---|
| Occupation |  |  |  |  |  |  |
| Professional | 0.8 | 0.0 [a] | 0.68 | 0.8 | −0.2 [a] | 0.68 |
| Managerial | 1.0 | 0.1 [a] | 0.73 | 1.0 | −0.0 [a] | 0.72 |
| Clerical | 0.8 | 0.0 [a] | 0.76 | 0.8 | −0.2 [a] | 0.76 |
| Sales | 1.2 | 0.2 [a] | 0.69 | 1.1 | −0.1 [a] | 0.69 |
| Craftsmen | 0.4 | −0.2 | 0.72 | 0.4 | −0.4 | 0.75 |
| Operatives | 0.3 | −0.3 | 0.67 | 0.3 | −0.4 | 0.69 |
| Service | 0.3 | −0.2 | 0.65 | 0.3 | −0.4 | 0.70 |
| Laborers | 0.1 | −0.4 | 0.63 | 0.1 | 0.5 | 0.64 |
| Industry |  |  |  |  |  |  |
| Durable manufacturing | 0.2 | −0.3 | 0.53 | 0.3 | 0.4 | 0.72 |
| Nondurable manufacturing | 0.3 | −0.3 | 0.64 | 0.3 | −0.5 | 0.65 |
| Transportation | 0.4 | −0.3 | 0.63 | 0.4 | −0.4 | 0.64 |
| Retailing | 0.7 | −0.1 | 0.80 | 0.7 | −0.2 | 0.80 |
| Finance, insurance, real estate | 0.6 | −0.1 | 0.70 | 0.6 | −0.2 | 0.71 |
| Wholesaling | 0.5 | −0.2 | 0.53 | 0.5 | −0.5 | 0.56 |
| Business services | 0.3 | −0.1 | 0.52 | 0.3 | −0.3 | 0.59 |
| Public administration | 0.4 | −0.3 | 0.68 | 0.4 | −0.4 | 0.70 |
| All | 0.4 | −0.2 | 0.78 | 0.4 | −0.4 | 0.82 |

[a] Not significantly different from zero at the 5 per cent level.

tact—durable and nondurable manufacturing, wholesaling, and transportation. The converse seems to hold for Negro employment in all white areas.

Table 2, which gives the elasticities at the sample means for (1) $d^m$, distance from the major ghetto, and (2) $R$, the residence ratio for each industry and occupation group, provides additional information about the relative impact of the racial residential composition of a workplace area and its distance from the ghetto. Also included in Table 2 are elasticities calculated from regression equations in which air line distance from the ghetto centroid ($d^c$) is used as the distance measure. Distance from the ghetto centroid ($d^c$) is included because of the suspicion that the size of the workplace and residence zones used in the analysis may cause distance from the ghetto boundaries to some workplace zones to be understated. Insofar as distance proxies labor-market information loss and similar concepts, these may be more closely related to the centroid of the distribution of the nonwhite population than to the ghetto's boundaries, particularly when the

boundaries are as grossly measured as those used in this analysis.

Elasticities of the residence ratio variable are generally larger in those occupations and industries with frequent customer contact. Among occupations the largest residence ratio elasticity is obtained for sales (1.2) and the smallest is obtained for laborers (0.1). Similarly, among industry groups, retailing and finance, insurance, and real estate have the largest residence ratio elasticities, 0.7 and 0.6, and durable manufacturing and business services have the smallest, 0.2 and 0.3.

In addition to increasing slightly the proportion of total variance explained for most occupation and industry groups, substitution of the distance from the ghetto centroid ($d^c$) for distance from the major ghetto ($d^m$) generally increases the distance elasticities and reduces slightly the residence ratio ($R$) elasticities. Of the nine occupation groups the residence ratio elasticity is larger in the distance from the ghetto centroid model only for laborers; of the eight industry groups, it is larger only for durable manufacturing, although the elasticities are the same for three other industry groups. Similarly, the distance elasticities are larger using distance from the ghetto centroid for all industry and occupation groups and the differences are generally larger than for the residence ratio. The regression coefficients for distance from the ghetto centroid differ significantly from zero at the 5 per cent level or better for professional, managerial, clerical, and sales occupation groups. It will be recalled that for these four residential serving occupation groups the distance coefficients did not pass the test of statistical significance using either distance from the major or nearest ghetto.

## V. THE LEVEL OF NONWHITE EMPLOYMENT

This section investigates the second of the paper's three hypotheses—that racial discrimination in housing markets reduces Negro employment opportunities. Estimates of Negro job loss caused by housing segregation are obtained by assuming the proportion of Negro workers living in every residence zone is the same. This assumption is computationally convenient and provides a smaller estimate of Negro job loss than would most other plausible assumptions. For example, it provides a lower estimate than if Negro workers were allocated to the 98 residence zones according to their income or occupational characteristics and those of the residence zones.

Solving equations (1)–(6) (assuming the residence ratio is identical for each zone) provides three estimates each for Chicago and Detroit of what the area-wide Negro percentage of employment might be, assuming that there were no racial segregation. Since all zones under these assumptions have identical racial characteristics, and distance from the major and nearest ghettos would be zero, the expected proportion of nonwhite employment is the same for every workplace zone. The expected nonwhite proportion of workplace employment is shown in Table 3. Once these percentages are obtained, alternative estimates of "expected" Negro employment are derived by multiplying them by the total labor force in each metropolitan area. The loss of Negro jobs is then the difference between the actual and "expected" numbers of Negro jobs. For Chicago, the estimated losses range from 22,157 to 24,622.[23] The estimated losses in Detroit are much smaller, ranging from a low of 3,863 to a high of 9,113. Actual total employment, actual Negro employment, "expected" Negro employment, and the estimated job loss for equations (1)–(6) are shown in Table 3. Part of the differences undoubtedly are due simply to the fact that Chicago's labor force is nearly twice as large as Detroit's. In addition, the much smaller estimated losses for Detroit, like the smaller explanatory power of the Detroit models, are consistent with the lesser degree of racial segregation there. Since Detroit's ghetto is larger and more extensive and there are more and better-located secondary ghettos, housing constrains Negro job choices less than in Chicago. Thus, the larger estimates of non-white job losses obtained for Chicago are entirely reasonable.

While these estimates must be considered highly tentative, they do suggest that housing market segregation and discrimination may significantly affect the level of Negro employment in metropolitan areas. If this is true, it has grave welfare implications since the costs that housing segregation impose on Negroes may be even larger than is generally believed. The constraint placed upon job opportunities by housing market discrimi-

---

[23] These estimates for Chicago are lower than those reported in an earlier paper by the author (see fn. 15, p. 923). These differences are due to a data correction that affected the estimates obtained in equations (1)–(3).

| | | Metropolitan Area Employment | | | | | |
|---|---|---|---|---|---|---|---|
| | | Actual | | | Estimate | | |
| Equation Variables | | Total Number | No. Nonwhite | Per cent Nonwhite | Per cent Nonwhite [a] | No. Nonwhite [b] | Nonwhite Job Loss [c] |
| Chicago | | | | | | | |
| 1 | $R, d^n$ | 1,760,148 | 257,178 | 14.61 | 15.87 | 279,335 | 22,157 |
| 2 | $R, d^m$ | 1,760,148 | 257,178 | 14.61 | 15.94 | 280,568 | 23,390 |
| 3 | $R, d^n, d^m$ | 1,760,148 | 257,178 | 14.61 | 16.01 | 281,800 | 24,622 |
| Detroit | | | | | | | |
| 4 | $R, d^n$ | 937,555 | 127,395 | 13.59 | 14.01 | 131,351 | 3,956 |
| 5 | $R, d^m$ | 937,555 | 127,395 | 13.59 | 14.00 | 131,258 | 3,863 |
| 6 | $R, d^n, d^m$ | 937,555 | 127,395 | 13.59 | 14.56 | 136,508 | 9,113 |

[a] Obtained by solving equations (1)–(6) assuming $R$ equals either 14.61 (Chicago) or 13.59 (Detroit) and $d^m$ or $d^n$ equals zero.

[b] Obtained by multiplying estimated per cent nonwhite times total number employed in Chicago (1,760,148) or Detroit (937,555).

[c] Obtained by subtracting estimated nonwhite employment from actual.

nation may also partly explain the much higher unemployment rates of Negroes. Part of what is usually charged to employment discrimination may be an indirect effect of housing discrimination. This illustrates how pervasive various types of discrimination may be and how the indirect costs of discrimination may greatly exceed the direct costs.

## VI. SUBURBANIZATION AND NEGRO EMPLOYMENT

Suburbanization of employment and population has been one of the most discussed facets of postwar metropolitan development. Between 1950 and 1960 population declines occurred in over half of the central cities (based on 1950 boundaries) of the forty largest metropolitan areas.[24] Moreover, census tract data indicate that these declines were greatest in the central parts of these central cities.

Employment dispersal is less well documented because of the unavailability of time series data on the location of employment within metropolitan areas. Even so, the fragmentary evidence strongly suggests a rapid dispersal of employment.[25] This employment dispersal is significant to this paper for two reasons. Jobs traditionally held by Negroes appear to be suburbanizing at an equal, and very possibly at an above-average rate, while there is only token suburbanization of Negro households.

❖    ❖    ❖

## VII. POSTWAR DISPERSAL OF EMPLOYMENT AND POPULATION IN CHICAGO

Sufficient data exist for Chicago to make rough quantitative estimates of the effects

[24] U.S. Bureau of Census, *1960 Census of Population*, Vol. I, *Characteristics of the Population*, Part I, *U.S. Summary* (Washington, D.C.: U.S. Government Printing Office).

[25] The central cities of twenty-four of the forty largest metropolitan areas lost manufacturing employment in the 1947–58 period using constant 1950 boundaries. Retailing employment declined in thirty and wholesaling employment in thirteen of these central cities during the 1947–58 decade. If anything these trends appear to have accelerated during the period 1958–63. John F. Kain, "The Distribution and Movement of Jobs and Industry," paper prepared for the Task Force on Economic Growth and Opportunity of the United States Chamber of Commerce. Also available as Discussion Paper No. 8, Harvard Program on Regional and Urban Economics, November, 1966.

of postwar populations and employment shifts on nonwhite employment. Good estimates of white and nonwhite resident populations by small areas are available for census years and some data, although much less, are available on intrametropolitan employment locations. The cumulative distribution of manufacturing employment in 1950 and 1960, arrayed by distance from the ghetto centroid, is presented in Figure 1.[26] These 1950 and 1960 employment distributions were obtained by aggregating employment data for 54 postal zones within the city of Chicago and 87 suburban communities and their surrounding unincorporated areas outside. While the precision of these estimates can be questioned, their general dimensions cannot. From Figure 1 it is apparent that Chicago Negroes were competing for an approximately constant number of jobs in

1950 and 1960, but that in 1960 the jobs were on the average located further from the ghetto. The effect of these job shifts on Negro manufacturing employment would appear very serious at first glance. But there was an offsetting trend. Despite rapid employment dispersal in the postwar period, a disproportionate number of jobs remain located at central parts of the city. With the expansion of the ghetto between 1950 and 1960 many whites moved further away from these centrally located jobs. Thus, total population within fifteen miles of the ghetto centroid remained approximately constant between 1950 and 1960, but its composition changed markedly. During the decade the Negro population within fifteen miles of the ghetto centroid increased by 319,000, while the white population declined by 261,000. These outward shifts of the white resident population would be expected to improve the labor market position of Negroes relative to whites at central locations.

*Figure 1. Cumulative manufacturing employment by distance from the ghetto centroid, 1950 and 1960.*

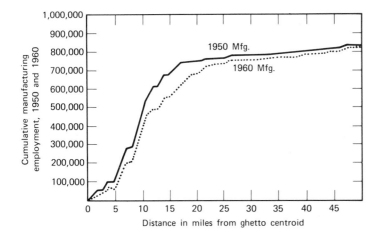

[26] The manufacturing employment estimates were obtained by interpolation and extrapolation of employment data contained in: Northeast Illinois Planning Commission, *Metropolitan Planning Guidelines, Phase One: Background Documents* (Chicago: The Commission, 1965); Center for Urban Studies, *Mid-Chicago Economic Development Study, Volume III: Technical Supplement, Economic Development of Mid-Chicago* (Chicago: University of Chicago, 1966); Illinois State Employment Service, *Employed Workers Covered by the Illinois Unemployment Compensation Act, 1955–1964* (Chicago: Illinois State Employment Service, 1965); and U.S. Bureau of Census, *Census of Manufactures,* Vol. III, *Area Statistics,* 1954, 1958, 1963. A detailed discussion of the way in which these estimates were prepared is available on request from the author.

| | Distance from the | | | | | |
| --- | --- | --- | --- | --- | --- | --- |
| | Ghetto Centroid | | | Major Ghetto | | |
| | 1950 | 1960 | 50–60 | 1950 | 1960 | 50–60 |
| Total Actual (thousands) | 838 | 835 | −3 | 838 | 835 | −3 |
| Estimated Negro (thousands) | 93 | 89 | −4 | 86 | 79 | −7 |
| Per cent Estimated Negro | 11.1 | 10.6 | − .5 | 10.3 | 9.5 | − .8 |

To provide a crude indication of how these offsetting trends net out, regression equations were obtained for total manufacturing employment and were solved using 1950 and 1960 values of the residence ratio for the 141 geographic areas (54 postal zones and 87 suburban communities). Equations 30 and 31 are the estimates for all manufacturing.

$$(30) \quad W = 12.3 + 0.30R - 0.29d^c$$
$$\quad\quad (11.1) \quad (9.3) \quad (5.9)$$
$$R^2 = 0.65$$

$$(31) \quad W = 11.0 + 0.30R - 0.61d^m$$
$$\quad\quad (11.3) \quad (9.0) \quad (5.6)$$
$$R^2 = 0.64$$

These estimated manufacturing employment ratios ($W$'s) were then multiplied by total manufacturing employment in each of the 141 areas to obtain two estimates of Negro manufacturing employment, one for each distance variable in each year. Both the units of aggregation and the sources of data used in estimating 1950 and 1960 Negro manufacturing employment are different from those used in estimating equations 30 and 31; and not all of these differences can be reconciled. Still the resulting estimates are suggestive of the impact of these population and employment shifts on Negro employment opportunities.

Estimates of Negro manufacturing employment in 1950 and 1960 obtained from equations 30 and 31 are presented in Table IV. As these data indicate, total manufacturing employment declined by about 3,000 between 1950 and 1960. Negro employment declined even more: an estimated 4,000 using equation 30 and an estimated 7,000 using equation 31. As a result the ratio of Negro to all manufacturing employment declined during the ten-year period.

*  *  *

VIII. CONCLUSIONS

This paper has examined the relationship between housing market segregation and the distribution and level of Negro employment. The investigation was prompted by concern that racial segregation in metropolitan housing markets may further reduce the employment opportunities of Negroes who are already handicapped by employer discrimination and low levels of education. In addition, it seems possible that the extensive growth of metropolitan areas and the rapid postwar dispersal of employment, accompanied by no reduction and perhaps even an increase in housing market segregation, may have placed the Negro job seeker in an even more precarious position.

Support for the paper's hypotheses is obtained from analyses of data for the Chicago and Detroit metropolitan areas. Housing market segregation clearly affects the distribution of Negro employment. Its effect on the level of Negro employment and unemployment is a more complex question and, consequently, the answer is less certain. While the estimates presented in this paper of Negro job loss due to housing market segregation are highly tentative, they nonetheless suggest that housing market segregation may reduce the level of Negro employment and thereby contribute to the high unemployment rates of metropolitan Negroes.

For the Chicago area it is possible to obtain an empirical estimate of the impact of employment dispersal on Negro job opportunities during the 1950–60 decade. This is an even more complex issue than that discussed above, and the conclusions therefore must be even more guarded. Even so the empirical findings do suggest that postwar suburbanization of metropolitan employment may be further undermining the position of the Negro, and that the continued high levels of Negro unemployment in a full employment economy may be partially attributable to the rapid and adverse (for the Negro) shifts in the location of jobs.

### Related Readings

In his article on "Decline in the Relative Income of Negro Men," (*Quarterly Journal of Economics*, November 1964, pp. 525-548) Alan Batchelder examines racial income differentials in considerable detail with the latest—though limited —data available to him. Although his emphasis is on the relative income of Negro men, he also makes comparisons with white men and Negro and white women.

At the outset, Batchelder raises the important question of the meaning of income improvement for Negroes and then examines the question of whether Negro incomes have improved relative to whites. The common assumption that the Negro's conditions have improved rests primarily on the evidence concerning increases in absolute incomes through time. The importance of secular improvements rests on the assumption that Negroes should be pleased with higher levels of income as compared with their own earlier earnings or those of their parents. Batchelder is skeptical of the significance of the secular approach, although he presents evidence concerning absolute as well as relative income changes; he feels that income comparisons with whites are more important. As in the case of many conflicts, however, both absolute and relative income changes, especially of Negro men, are important for race relations. Of course, one's satisfaction with improvements depends upon whether he looks at the distance traveled or whether he looks at the distance that remains between the ideal and reality.

Batchelder discusses the need for an index to measure the extent of changes in the Negro's economic position. He first discusses the occupational indexes constructed by Becker and Rayack, treated more fully above. Becker compared 1910, 1940, and 1950 and found substantial advances during the tight labor market period of the 1940's, and losses during the 1920–1940 period. Using different (current year) weights for his index, Rayack comes to essentially the same conclusion as Becker with respect to the changes, although he found improvement from 1940–1950 to be greater than that revealed by Becker's index.

The differences between Rayack and Becker show the importance of different weights, only one of many problems associated with the construction of any index. Avoiding these index number problems, Batchelder uses income rates for Negroes and whites between 1949 and 1959 to show that the incomes of Negro men remained about the same for the United States, but declined by varying amounts for each of the major regions. The low relative position of Negro men in the South, where most Negroes lived during this period, is significant. Batchelder then contrasts the relative position of Negro and white women and finds considerable improvement in the position of Negro women. Comparing women and men, the data show a consistent decline for Negro males relative to whites; the Negro ratios declined in the West but especially in the South. Batchelder concludes: "First, the 'changing role' of American women in the 1950's was different for Negro than for white women. Second, the income of Negro women became increasingly important during the 1950's relative to the income of Negro men, first . . . because Negro women in the South and West earned more relative to Negro men and, second, . . . because a substantially larger per cent of Negro women worked in 1960 than had worked in 1950." In view of the traditional matriarchy among Negroes, and the increasing relative income of Negro women relative to the income of Negro men, "One is left to speculate upon the social implication of this trend."

In attempting to analyze the reasons for the relative decline of Negro men, Batchelder considers changes in the quality of the labor force, the number of Negro males in the labor force, and increased discrimination.

Using median education and age levels to measure changes in the quality of the labor force, Batchelder finds increases in both the Negro male and female positions relative to whites. Comparisons of the 1950–1960 changes in relative educational positions in the regions are not possible because the data is not comparable. He also discusses the effects of educational inequalities of Negroes in the South in view of heavy migration to other regions from the South, where Negro schools have been markedly inferior to those attended by whites. "Although assurance on this score must wait upon further research, it is the author's guess that, in educational attainment, quality dilution exceeded quantitative gains in the North and West."

The Negro work force is considerably younger than that of whites, especially for women. "Thus the greater aging of white than nonwhite women might have tended, *ceteris paribus*, to increase the Negro-white income differences for women. However, the changes in the average age of the employed white and nonwhite male populations were so nearly the same that the age factor, as measured by medians, cannot be credited with having had any part in causing the decline in the relative economic status of Negro men."

Using data that are inadequate for the purpose, Batchelder finds that the Negro proportion of the work force increased outside the South, but declined in the South and the nation as a whole. He hypothesizes that the increase in Negro proportion of the work force might have depressed wages for black workers outside the South.

Unemployment increased much more for Negroes than for whites between 1949 and 1959, especially for Negro men. Although the ratios of Negro to white unemployment rates are lower in the South, for Negro men this ratio increased substantially in the South between 1949 and 1959, while declining in the South for Negro women and for Negro men and women in all other regions. The greater increase in unemployment among Negro men in the South might have accounted for their relative income losses, unless this greater unemployment rate is a statistical delusion because hidden unemployment in agriculture was simply translated into counted unemployment when Negroes moved out of agriculture. Since there was no increase in the Negro male relative unemployment rate outside the South, this could not have accounted for their relative income losses.

The relative income losses also might be accounted for by changes in part-time employment, but the limited evidence available shows little differential in this variable.

Since the 1959 or 1960 data are obsolete, Batchelder relies on later sources to update the relative income data. When this is done, the ratio of Negro to white income for males declined during the 1950's, falling from .50 in 1958–1960 to .49 in 1962. However, Rashi Fein's data shows an increase to .52 in 1963 and .58 in 1964. For females, the ratio has increased steadily from .61 in 1958–1960, .67 in 1962 and 1963 and .71 in 1964. ("Relative Income of Negro Men: Some Recent Data," *Quarterly Journal of Economics*, May 1966). Although we do not know whether these improvements were a result of tight labor markets, civil rights legislation, or exhortation, tight labor markets probably were most important.

In his book *Jobs and Income for Negroes* (a joint publication of the National Manpower Policy Task Force and the Institute of Labor and Industrial Relations, The University of Michigan-Wayne State University, May 1968), Professor Charles Killingsworth, in keeping with the structuralist position discussed in Part II, takes strong exception to the arguments advanced by Tobin and others that increasing aggregate demand is "the single most important approach" to counteracting Negro job problems. (James Tobin, "On Improving the Economic Status of the Negro," *Daedalus*, Fall, 1965.) It is Killingsworth's position that the aggregate demand position rests on wartime experience, which he feels was very unusual because drastic labor shortages required considerable job redesign in order to facilitate the employment of unskilled workers. Killingsworth makes it clear that he does not believe these wartime experiences are likely to be repeated during peacetime. Killingsworth also contends that the aggregate demand position is based on unrealistic assumptions about labor markets. He is particularly concerned about the assumption that the labor market is a great "homogenizer" of labor that tends to reduce employment and wage differentials between workers within the labor market, although Killingsworth points out that we know very little about the extent to which the labor is a homogenizer. In addition, Killingsworth presents statistics covering the period 1964–1967 to counteract claims that an increase in the level of aggregate demand would cause nonwhite unemployment rates to fall faster than average unemployment rates. In relative terms, the 1964 tax cuts were accompanied by declines in unemployment for whites that were greater than those for nonwhites. Indeed, the level of unemployment for nonwhite teenagers actually increased during this period.

Moreover, Killingsworth is not willing to concede that even the improvements in unemployment that did take place after the 1964 tax cut can be attributed entirely to increases in aggregate demand. In his opinion, military inductions and expenditures on manpower and poverty programs probably accounted for much of the reduction in unemployment of the disadvantaged.

Killingsworth also questions the advisability of the negative income tax proposed by Tobin. Proponents of the negative income tax assume, erroneously in Killingsworth's judgment, that " 'the market' is generally the most responsive and accurate apparatus for providing things that people really want and that the poor will be better off getting what they want through the market instead of having it prescribed for them by social workers. . . ." Killingsworth also objects to Moynahan's proposal for family allowances, arguing that child allowances would perhaps meet the criterion of providing incentives for people but would not be adequate or economical.

Killingsworth argues for a mix of aggregate demand, manpower and welfare programs in order to overcome the job problems of Negroes, but he is not prepared to say what the appropriate mix should be. He also points out that there is considerable consensus on this question, but feels that those who argue for the aggregate demand position place too much emphasis on general measures and give inadequate attention to specific programs to overcome the imperfections in the market. In general, however, structuralists like Killingsworth and generalists like Tobin agree that both the general and specific programs need to be adopted.

On the special case of the Negro, Marion Hayes, "A Century of Change: Negroes in the U.S. Economy, 1860–1960" *Monthly Labor Review*, December 1962, pp. 1359–1365), finds most of the economic gains of the Negro attributable to migration. A well-known, early study by Donald Dewey, "Negro Employment in Southern Industry" (*Journal of Political Economy*, Vol. 60 August 1962, pp. 279–293), takes a pessimistic view regarding the future of Negro occupational advancement in the South. Dale L. Hiestand, *Economic Growth and Employment Opportunities for Minorities* (New York, Columbia University Press, 1964), calculates similar stability in the relative occupational status of Negroes for the 1910–1960 period to that found by Becker, even after expanding the number of occupational classifications.

Dale Hiestand's *Discrimination in Employment: An Appraisal of the Research* (A Joint Publication of the Institute of Labor and Industrial Relations, The University of Michigan-Wayne State University and the National Manpower Policy Task Force, February 1970) presents an analysis of research on Negro employment with special emphasis on concepts of discrimination, employment patterns, and remedial programs. He concludes with some suggestions for further research; in his view, "the highest priority should be given to analyzing implications for minorities of the structure and operations of labor markets, including those internal to the firm." Hiestand's book also contains a very good bibliography on discrimination in employment.

The most comprehensive and up-to-date analyses of Negro employment by industry are the *Racial Policies of American Industry* and the *Studies of Negro Employment* published by the Industrial Research Unit, Wharton School of Finance and Commerce, University of Pennsylvania, 1968–1971. Louis A. Ferman's *The Negro and Equal Employment Opportunities* (New York, Praeger, 1968), contains an analysis of the racial employment practices of twenty companies based on detailed interviews.

In "The Black Revolution and the Economic Future of Negroes in the United States," a commencement address at Tennessee A. & I. University, June 8, 1969, Andrew Brimmer, a Negro member of the Board of Governors of the Federal Reserve System, reviews the extent of economic progress Negroes have made in the 1960's, projects these trends into the future, and flags "several of the deceptively inviting digressions which are luring some of our most promising young people with false hopes of progress through separate development along racial lines."

Brimmer's main theme is that Negroes benefited more than whites from economic expansion during the 1960's, although the greatest gains have been made by blacks with the highest levels of education and the disadvantaged in the black community are lagging behind. Moreover, in the 1970's Brimmer expects the black community to benefit more than whites, primarily because of expansion in the national economy, but also because of improvements in education. However, Brimmer is concerned that black separatist programs will impede the economic progress of Negroes by diverting them from the achievement of technical competence.

Brimmer cites statistics to show that Negroes gained relative to whites in total employment, occupational distribution, median incomes, and education during the 1960's. In Brimmer's view, these trends are likely to continue during the 1970's.

However, in spite of these encouraging trends, Negroes still lag considerably behind whites in these indicators and there are some disturbing trends. For one thing, although black men gained in income relative to white men during the 1959–1967 period, the income gap widened in the Negro community because the greatest black gains were at the higher educational and income levels.

But Brimmer's chief concern is that the "black studies" movement will divert students from the "technical underpinnings" of their majority fields, "some degree of understanding of mathematics and other so-called hard sciences," and "some acquaintance with the social sciences—especially . . . economics, sociology and political science."

In "Negro Participation in Apprenticeship Programs," (Journal of Human Resources, Winter 1967), Ray Marshall and Vernon Briggs discuss underrepresentation in apprenticeship programs, which lead to many higher-paying jobs and supervisory positions in the skilled trades. This article first discusses some of the reasons for the civil rights movement's interest in the apprenticeship question and some of the reasons for so few black apprentices. Most of the reasons can be attributed to institutionalized discrimination. The authors take the view that although general programs like antidiscrimination laws, tight labor markets, and improved education facilitate the flow of Negroes into apprenticeship programs, these general measures must be supplemented by specific programs like the apprenticeship outreach programs (AOP's) if they are to do much to cause many Negro youngsters to move into apprenticeship programs. The authors' appraisal of the outreach programs seem to have been confirmed by subsequent developments because the AOP's had resulted in the admission of about 6000 minorities to apprenticeship programs by the end of 1969.

# CHAPTER 20

## The Status of White Blue-Collar Workers

As is typical of public opinion in the United States, concern seems to focus on particular problems for a time and then swing, pendulumlike, to others. During the 1950's and 1960's, considerable attention was devoted to the problems of Negroes and other minorities, with very little apparent concern for white manualists. However, now that white blue-collar workers have given evidence at the polls and in public demonstrations that they are dissatisfied with public policies, including those espoused by their unions, government officials have become concerned for this group.

A major point of conflict between black and white manual workers has been the control of jobs by unions. Historically, labor organizations have been controlled mainly by whites, except for a few all- or predominantly black organizations such as the Brotherhood of Sleeping Car Porters. Moreover, since most immigrants were workers seeking to establish themselves in the American system, white ethnics have given strong support to the American labor movement. Historically, these white-controlled unions have been used to ration scarce job opportunities to particular groups of white workers, particularly the better jobs in the railroads, printing, and construction crafts.

However, as noted in other chapters in this part, as Negroes migrated out of the rural South, they began to challenge the unions' racial restrictions. Negro demands for job opportunities became particularly strong during World War II and resulted in a steady series of government programs to improve their lot, culminating in the Civil Rights Act of 1964 and the antipoverty and manpower legislation of the 1960's. Many white unionists now think the government has gone too far in promoting job opportunities for Negroes at the expense of whites. Since they are a strong political force, some observers are afraid that white reactions to equal employment opportunities programs will impede additional progress in this area and will aggravate race conflicts, which will split the Negro-labor political coalitions formed during the 1930's. Some even see a danger of a hard swing to the right in the American labor movement.

The first selection in this chapter is a memorandum from Assistant Secretary of Labor Jerome M. Rosow on "The Problem of the Blue-Collar Worker." Mr. Rosow emphasizes the common economic and social problems confronting all blue-collar workers, regardless of race. He discusses the economic squeeze confronting these workers, a problem unrelieved by government tax, welfare, and other government measures. Similarly, blue-collar workers are "bugged" by a number of social problems which cause them to feel like "forgotten" people. Mr. Rosow concludes with some suggestions for programs to help blue-collar workers.

# The Problem of the Blue-Collar Worker

## by Jerome M. Rosow

The social and economic status of blue-collar workers has become a subject of increasing concern in the last few years. Recent reports have identified the economic insecurity and alienation which whites in this group have felt. What such reports have failed to note is that there are some two million minority-group males who are skilled or semi-skilled blue-collar workers who are full-time members of the work force and who share many of the same problems as whites in their income class. This non-white group also shares the same concern as white workers for law and order and other middle-class values. Many have moved from subemployment to low-income entry-level jobs, but they now feel blocked from further opportunity.

In 1968, 34 percent of all minority-group families were in the $5,000 to $10,000 income category. Of course, on the average, most black families are still not anywhere as well off as white families: The median income of all Negro families was $5,590; that of all white families $8,937. But the point is that both these groups have essentially "working-class" economic and social problems related to wage, tax and government benefit structure for the nonpoor—a fact not given adequate recognition by the media, which, to the extent it emphasizes only the black ghetto, perpetuates a stereotype.

We should recognize:

1. The common *economic* problem which many blue-collar workers have, of both races (mostly white, of course, in numbers); and

2. The common *social* problems concerned with housing, education, jobs and

SOURCE Reprinted with permission from Memorandum from the Assistant Secretary of Labor, Washington, D.C. (April 16, 1970).

personal safety which are related to income class but also are a function of the close proximity of the blue-collar workers to disadvantaged people.

These two points are worth further consideration.

## I. THE ECONOMIC SQUEEZE

Forty percent of American families—including 70 million family members—have incomes between $5,000 and $10,000 a year and might be termed "lower-middle-income." The head of the household is usually a vigorous, fully employed blue-collar worker with heavy family responsibilities although many of this group are also in white-collar or service jobs. It is precisely when his children reach their teens and family budget costs are at their peak that two things happen to the bulk of such male breadwinners:

> They reach a plateau in their capacity to earn by promotion or advancement;
>
> Their expenses continue to rise, as the last family members are born, as they become homeowners, as car and home equipment pressures mount, as the children may become ready for college, or support is needed for aging parents.

The American wage and salary structure does not respond directly to this situation, since it is based on the ethic of "equal pay for equal work." It does not provide additions for either growing family size or age (except as it may reflect job seniority); payment is exclusively for work done—the same pay is given to everyone in the same job; and, unlike the situation in many other countries, the wage structure is not supplemented by public payments based on family size, although income tax exemptions give some recognition:

> Income needs for a growing family

rise faster than are normally provided by advancement. Family budget costs for a two-child family are three times the needs of a single individual, according to BLS, while a typical semi-skilled steelworker's increase in job level results only in a wage rise of somewhat less than one and a half times.

The result is illustrated by the accompanying table, which portrays the case of a typical steelworker. The worker has some margin beyond his budget needs when he is young, but only if he saves and does not acquire a living standard commensurate with his pay. If he does not anticipate later family needs by adequate early savings—and usually he does not—he begins to be squeezed in his later thirties, and finds himself in deeper straits as his children reach their teens.

Many other industries have even fewer promotion opportunities than steel. A study of 11 major industries estimated that one-third of all non-supervisory jobs were "dead-end." The lack of an adequate adult education system geared to workers hinders movement out of these jobs. Relatively few firms have work-site education and few community colleges direct courses for upgrading purposes to blue-collar workers.

Upward job mobility is also hindered by age discrimination against older workers; by lack of detailed, free information about other jobs; and by the high costs of private employment agencies (which often have job openings which the Employment Service does not have).

The result for semi-skilled blue-collar workers as a whole is that, when general wage rate increases are added to increased individual earnings due to promotion, real income has somewhat less than doubled in the past two decades, which is still not enough to meet the cost of the same standard of living throughout the period. Males aged 45 to 54 years in

TABLE 1. COMPARISON OF FAMILY BUDGET COSTS AND STEELWORKERS' EARNINGS

(1967 Budget Costs and Wage Rates)

| Age | Family Status | Family Budget Costs | | Pay Grade | Estimated Annual Earnings | |
|-----|---------------|---------|-------|-----------|---------|-------|
| | | Dollars | Index | | Dollars | Index |
| 22 | Single | $3,358 | 100 | 2 | $5,747 | 100 |
| 23 | Married, no children | 4,538 | 135 | 2 | 5,747 | 100 |
| 28 | One child, under 6 | 5,627 | 168 | 7 | 6,629 | 115 |
| 38 | 2 children, older 6–15 | 9,076 | 270 | 12 | 7,510 | 131 |
| 41 | 2 children, older 9–18 | 10,347 | 308 | 15 | 8,039 | 140 |

NOTES

Budget costs and wage rates as of 1967.

Annual earnings are based on hourly rates, with no further adjustments for effect of seniority on immunity from layoffs and opportunities for more overtime and no allowance for the value of fringes.

Grade 15 in the chart is approximately the midpoint of the U.S. steel job evaluation wage structure and is at beginning point of skilled craftsmen wage scales.

Family budget costs are based on BLS Moderate Living Standard for a 4-person family, spring 1967, and include occupational expenses, gifts and contributions, life insurance, social security payments, and Federal, State and local income taxes, in addition to the goods and services for family consumption. For equivalence scale appropriate for total budget—see Table A–1, p. 14, BLS Bulletin 1570–2.

1968 who had one to three years of high school—the educational level typical of blue-collar workers in that age group—had increased their incomes by only 84 percent between 1949 and 1968.

The worker who established his standard of living when he was single or first married thus finds that he can maintain it only by:

1. Having saved when he was younger (which he didn't do); or

2. Moonlighting on a second part-time job; or

3. Having his wife work even in spite of the obstacles to doing so; or

4. Continued pressure for wage increases.

If a younger worker has no opportunity for advancement, the entire annual productivity-related rise in wages, about three percent, is needed just to *keep up* with his increasing family needs. If such a worker wants to improve his standard of living he must be able to move up the ladder. The pressure on wages promises to increase as those born in the post World War II baby boom move into their late twenties and early thirties, and thus assume family responsibilities in the next

five years. Workers in the 25–34 age group will represent 25 percent of the labor force in this decade.

This problem is intensified by inflation. Since 1965 money wages have advanced *20 percent, but* real earnings measured in true purchasing power remained almost static. These men are on a treadmill, chasing the illusion of higher living standards. Thus their only hope seems to be continued pressure for higher wages. Their only spokesmen seem to be union leaders spearheading the demand for more money wages. They are overripe for a political response to the pressing needs they feel so keenly.

The *tax* structure offers little relief to this worker since it gives only small recognition to family size considerations. Even the Tax Reform Act of 1969 does not provide adequate relief to these families:

A married couple with an $8000 income who has two children will pay $263 less under the new law—which doesn't fully take effect until 1973 —than under the old one. This fails to bridge the budget gap described above;

Deductions for family members are token in character, even under the new tax law, and provide more at higher income levels than at lower or moderate levels (the $750 deduction is a tax savings of $125 for the person in the 16 to 17 percent bracket and $300 for the person in the 40 percent bracket). Moreover, the size of the tax deduction has no relation to the age of the children, even though budget costs for older children are more than for younger.

There is no provision for tax relief as family education costs rise, either in terms of the $100 a year that it costs to send a child to school or the additional cost of going to college.

Regressive State and local taxes also hit heavily at this group. Average State and local taxes are almost $700, and have increased rapidly in recent years. Moreover, in at least some states income is redistributed from lower-income to higher-income groups to subsidize higher education for the children of the latter.

Government policies on child care designed to enable the wife to work also give little relief. At present, families with income of $6900 or above cannot deduct child care expenses. This figure was set in the Internal Revenue Act of 1964 and is now unrealistically low. Adjusted to current prices the ceiling would be about $8200. Government child care centers under Headstart and WIN are for the "poor," and do not help this group. Their costs for child care (when not provided by other family members) may run from $25 to $40 a week. The Family Assistance Act of 1970 will aggravate this problem. Welfare mothers will receive subsidized child care to facilitate their move from welfare to work. Lower income mothers who seek work and are outside the welfare system will incur the full cost or be unable to add to family income.

Finally, high transportation costs, wage discrimination and lack of education and training also discourage many blue-collar wives from working or minimize their contribution to family income. Yet it is precisely working wives who make very meaningful contributions to the family income, and who have the potential to make even more: In the 40 percent of husband-wife families where wives do work, median income in 1968 was $10,700, compared to $8200 where they didn't. Part-time employment has almost doubled since 1956 and provides a new opportunity for more women to combine work with family responsibility.

The problem of restricted economic opportunity for the blue-collar worker also spreads into the next generation. The children of this group in our society are not "making it" to the same degree as are children in the middle and upper-middle classes.

Despite the broadening base of college enrollments, we still find marked evidence that the lower-income groups have a much smaller proportion of their children continuing beyond high school. Only one-fourth of the youth in college are from the half of the families with a below-median income. Worse yet, the great majority of high school dropouts are not from the disadvantaged ghetto population. Many white and black school dropouts are from this lower-middle-income group; in some of the urban areas the dropout rate for this group runs about 30 percent. Here we sense the stirrings of a new type of unfortunate cycle, as some of the children of these blue-collar workers are unable to achieve a reasonable entry into productive society. Twenty percent are unemployed in the fall following the year they drop out of school. Present efforts to reduce youth unemployment (e.g., Neighborhood Youth Corps) are geared to disadvantaged youth—not these people.

*Other Government Aids* minimum wage, training, welfare payments—are not for this group because they have presumably "made it," and whatever the government may have done to keep employment and jobs up generally has faded or is overwhelmed.

Economic insecurity is compounded by the fact that blue-collar workers are often the first to feel the effects of an increase in unemployment, feel most threatened by automation, and are also more dependent on sheer physical health for their livelihood than white-collar workers. Yet there is inadequate protection for temporary or permanent disability under State workmen's compensation laws.

There are other dimensions to the problem too: the shortage and high cost of housing; the high cost of medical and legal services, the lack of inexpensive entertainment and recreation facilities (e.g., few summer camps for the worker's children).

All these factors add up to an economic squeeze and insecurity for the working man. We have no package of solutions to deal with this problem. However, in fashioning any attack, certain things should be recognized: (1) that government aid being given to the disadvantaged is sorely needed, and (2) that it would be impossible and undesirable to try to modify the American wage structure; and (3) that almost anything which could be done by the government would cost money.

## II. THE SOCIAL SQUEEZE

People working and living close to the margin of economic needs are under constant pressures. These pressures have an economic base but find other outlets, other frustrations of a social nature.

People in the blue-collar class are less mobile, less organized, and less capable of using legitimate means to either protect the status quo or secure changes in their favor. To a considerable extent, they feel like "forgotten people"—those for whom the government and the society have limited, if any, direct concern and little visible action.

Some of the problems which "bug" the blue-collar class include:

*Fear of violent crimes.* This is a growing fear of crime in the inner cities and this fear is spilling over to the outer ring of the metropolis— primarily areas where they live. Economic immobility blocks a flight from these conditions.

*Class status.* Many of these workers are immigrants or sons of immigrants, they feel unsure about their place in the "mainstream" of American society. Some live in mixed neighborhoods—feeling the pressure of constant succession by lower status groups, especially minorities. As the minorities move up a bit, they squeeze these people. Minority inroads in housing, schools, and jobs create fears. They worry over merging of seniority lists, changing entrance requirements for jobs, and lower admissions standards for public schools.

*Feeling of being forgotten.* These people are most exposed to the poor and the welfare recipients. Often their wages are only a notch or so above the liberal states' welfare payments. Yet they are excluded from social programs targeted at the disadvantaged—medical aid, housing, job training, headstart programs, legal aid, and the like. As taxpayers, they support these programs with no visible relief—no visible share.

*Educational level.* Since most blue-collar workers have barely completed formal high school education, they have limited leverage to change occupations, and they have limited mobility to use their education as a lever to escape from their economic and social problems. Overt hostility between ethnic and racial groups is probably greater between less educated groups than betwen more educated groups. Thus, the blue-collar worker is more prone to transfer his economic and social frustrations to racial and ethnic prejudices, and of late to overt hostilities.

*Low status of blue-collar work.* The American working man has lost relative class status with the growth of higher education. Changes in the nature of the labor force have dramatized the professional and technical experts to the relative detriment of the skilled worker. Skilled workers also have hostility toward those below them at semi-skilled and unskilled levels and the feeling is mutual. But all blue-collar workers, skilled or not, have been denigrated so badly—so harshly—that their jobs have become a last resort, instead of decent, respected careers. Manual and skilled occupations have become almost invisible in terms of the propaganda of today. Fathers hesitate —and even apologize—for their occupations instead of holding it up as an aspiration for their sons. This attack has been so strong, so emotional and so unfounded that the workers have suffered a loss of self respect and the nation is suffering a loss of future manpower.

Low status also derives from the working conditions and nature of much unskilled and semiskilled work. Much of it is oppressively tedious, noisy, and mind numbing, with little room for human contact. Research has found a significant relation between poor mental health and such types of work.

Let us examine the problem of the low status of blue-collar work further.

According to union leaders, the blue-collar worker increasingly feels that his work has no "status" in the eyes of society, the media, or even his own children.

While the nation has, in recent years, sold the importance of science and technology to our younger people, it has neglected to communicate the importance of some ten million skilled blue-collar workers who are responsible for transforming the ideas of scientists and the plans of engineers into tangible goods and services. These workers make and maintain the models, tools and machines without which industrial processes could not be carried out. They exercise considerable independent judgment and are responsible for extremely valuable equipment and products.

A good auto mechanic, for example, must know hydraulics, pneumatics, electricity, and some chemistry and other skills. Yet many youth learn that status accrues to the white-collar job (and so "prefer" it) even though a job in coveralls, such as mechanic, may pay better. The average mechanic working for a metropolitan auto dealer earns nearly $10,000, yet there is a short supply of them due to lack of interested youth. A recent survey showed that only one out of four male high school seniors wished to work as blue-collar workers, even though almost half of all jobs in the economy are blue-collar jobs.

Schools tend to reinforce this tendency, since most teachers know little about blue-collar work. So do the media; the only publicity given to workers is when they are out on strike and there they are often shown in a bad light.

Adding to the problem is that fact that the long-term narrowing of manual skill wage differentials (temporarily halted) has relatively worsened the position of semi- and skilled blue-collar workers compared to the unskilled. At the same time, high-skilled white-collar workers have been making substantial and publicized improvements in their economic position, with salary increases often far higher than wage increases. Furthermore, the educated workers with college and advanced degrees have been getting the biggest pay gains.

The result is chronic and inflationary shortages in many skilled blue-collar fields; a feeling of "failure" for the many youth who won't get white-collar jobs; exacerbation of racial friction when black youth refuse to take "dirty" blue-collar jobs offered them "by a white society," even when they may be good-paying; and a general resentment by blue-collar workers which is translated into wage demands.

Resentment is likely to worsen with any increase in unemployment, together with a continued push for opportunities for the disadvantaged, plus the addition of returning veterans to the labor force.

### III. POSSIBLE DIRECTIONS FOR ACTION

Our attention has been focused on an analysis of the economic and social situation faced by the blue-collar worker and not on private or public steps that might be taken to relieve the pressures he faces. Still, the analysis itself identifies several specific areas of concern:

> *Upgrading.* What can be done to assist the worker in moving out of a dead-end job?
>
> *Income.* Upgrading will provide more income, but this may need to be augmented by a job for the wife, and perhaps in other ways.
>
> *Expenses.* The workingman's budget squeeze can be relieved through subsidized housing, transportation, recreation, and education and various kinds of tax relief.
>
> *Social Issues.* Such things as low status of blue-collar work, poor urban environment, and inadequate medical facilities contribute to a feeling of neglect and should be addressed.

Again, though we have not developed a specific action program, some ideas appear worthy of consideration by the Nixon Administration to reach out and come to grips with many of the basic needs:

### Job Upgrading

The JOBS program is placing a new emphasis on upgrading for both disadvantaged and others but even more manpower services could be provided the blue-collar worker. Much authority exists but imaginative proposals are needed for such things as instruction in plants, community college courses designed to meet specific skill shortages, worker leave of absences, and loans for non-instruction expenses. The Employment Service could do more to help the blue-collar worker get ahead—through such steps as counseling and upgrading, soliciting jobs for experienced workers and opening its offices nights and Saturdays to serve the employed as well as the unemployed.

### 2. Child Care

The Nixon Family Assistance Plan will provide child care facilities for welfare mothers who go to work. Child care facilities might next be provided to slightly higher income groups on a partial fee basis. This would enable many more mothers to work and relieve the costs of child care for those who already work. Steady expansion of part-time employment opportunities can open new avenues for wives to work without neglecting their family role. Tax relief for child care is now limited to families earning less than $6,900 and this could be raised to $10,000 with deductions increased to $900 for the first child and $1,200 for two or more children. This change can be made with little revenue loss. The public pressure for action in this area is expected to mount.

### 3. Education for Adults

The Vocational Education Act of 1968 is already financing evening courses for about three million adults. However, this meets only a fraction of the need. Moreover, above and beyond vocational education, there is a need to allow workers to study for high school diplomas and for two-year community college degrees. For many blue-collar workers and their wives, the result should be new or better jobs and promotions. Increased education also frequently leads to less racial hostility.

### 4. Higher Education for the Worker's Children

The right to higher education implicit in the President's Higher Education Message for college loans and grants where families are earning less than $10,000 is a significant promise to the blue-collar workers. The President also proposed a $100 million program for training in critical occupations in community colleges. This should be the first step in a steady thrust toward increased Federal support of these colleges which are of such importance to the blue-collar worker's children. These opportunities should be targeted to these people.

### 5. Tax Policy

The Tax Reform Act will give a tax reduction to families earning $5,000 to $10,000. However, this does not go very far in alleviating the squeeze on this group. Revenue sharing should be emphasized since it will tend to help them by raising taxes through the progressive Federal tax system rather than through the regressive local and State systems. In addition, a review should be made of possible further ways to relieve the tax burden on this group, including possibly increasing the amount of the tax exemption for older children, since budget costs for them are greater.

### 6. Higher Status for Blue-Collar Work

Efforts should be made to enhance the status of blue-collar work. Public relations work would help, as would more effective guidance and placement in blue-collar jobs by secondary schools (including more visits by workers to the schools). Other possibilities are National awards for outstanding craftsmen; portrayal of various skilled trades on postage stamps; a series of vocational guidance films for youth, on skilled trades; programs for school teachers to visit plants and offices; training for foremen and supervisors; Federal standards for decent working conditions and/or establishing a Job Environment Subcommittee of the Environmental Quality Council, to investigate oppressive noise, heat, air pollution, and the like.

### 7. Recreation Facilities

Recreation and vacations, a major problem for the blue-collar worker and his family, might be made more available through vest-pocket parks, more development of public lands near metropolitan areas, and mortgage guarantees for low-income recreation facilities.

### 8. Transportation

Automobile expenses are a major expense item to the blue-collar worker. Moderate budget costs for the U.S. automobile owner are more than $900 yearly for replacement, insurance, and maintenance. More mass transit is part of the answer. If "no-blame" auto insurance would reduce costs as much as has been claimed, it might also be helpful.

## 9. Housing

Action has been taken to pump more mortgage money into the housing market which should increase the houses available to low-income workers and reduce their cost. The most significant potential for reducing housing costs is probably in Operation Break-through and offer efforts to increase productivity in construction. HUD and the Domestic Council are obvious focal points for policy direction.

## 10. Disability Protection

On the job and off the job accidents are still a major hazard for the working population. New attempts should be made to develop modern temporary disability insurance and workmen's compensation systems.

## 11. The Federal Government as a Model Employer of Blue-Collar Workers

The Federal Government should continue its policy of wages comparable with private employment. But it could go beyond this on non-wage matters. It could become a model employer by careful attention to such things as upgrading possibilities, subsidized child care, part-time employment for women, and particularly subsidized recreation and vacation facilities for low-income Federal workers.

The White House working group under your chairmanship could develop feasible ways by which to meet the needs of blue-collar workers in some or all of these areas.

In the final selection in this part, Gus Tyler, a staff member of the International Ladies' Garment Workers Union, analyzes the mood and plight of white ethnics, whom he considers to be on a collision course with nonwhites.

Tyler emphasizes that the working class earning between $3000 and $15,000 a year are not affluent. Indeed, the median income of this class was about $1000 below the amount needed for a "modest but adequate" budget. Moreover, "whether we look at white or dark America in 1947 or 1968, the maldistribution of income remains constant."

Tyler attributes the restlessness of blue-collar workers at the beginning of the 1970's not to the maldistribution of income but to the quantitative erosion of income, a qualitative erosion of living, and "a frightening erosion of social order," all of which he discusses in some detail. He concludes that these forces are producing serious social and economic pressures.

Tensions between workers of various ethnic and racial groups undoubtedly will persist throughout the 1970's and will require special efforts to prevent serious physical conflict and social disruption. There is, therefore, an urgent need to understand as clearly as we can the nature of the frustrations, values, fears, and motives involved in these conflicts. It is especially important for higher-income groups, whose wealth and income might give them temporary immunity from conflict, to recognize the dangers involved in simplistic policies or attitudes that stereotype groups and intensify what Tyler calls "tribalization."

Public officials and other opinion molders can moderate conflict between black and white manualists by recognizing a number of realities. The first of these is that hostile racism, whether black or white, must consistently be challenged. The second is the need for programs that pay careful attention to the legitimate interests of the various groups involved while counteracting demands that are radically motivated. Third, many of the doubts and frustrations of various racial and ethnic groups are based on fear; others are based on myth. Perhaps the myths can be overcome by presenting factual evidence. But whether or not this is possible, efforts should be made to avoid appealing to the racist attitudes of blacks or whites. It is extremely shortsighted, in our opinion, for higher-income groups to think they can solve the nation's domestic problems by playing off one group of workers against the other.

Because public opinion swings like a pendulum from one problem area to another, there is perhaps some danger that the present concern about white manualists might cause us to ignore the interests of minorities. There is a growing realization by policy makers that our concentration on the problems of blacks and other disadvantaged persons during the 1960's caused many programs to ignore the problems of white manualists. Indeed, in the South, too many programs had difficulty attracting whites because they were regarded as "black" and therefore "inferior" programs. Legislatures also ignored the white manualists in their failure to reform the tax system and to take measures to provide beter law enforcement and protection from "block-busting" in working-class neighborhoods. Even those who saw the need for black pride and identity were not concerned about ethnic pride and identity.

Now we are persuaded that it was entirely correct to give priority to black employment problems, because this was, and is, our most disadvantaged group. But public programs for the disadvantaged erred in not considering the legitimate concerns of white manualists, whose resistance to human resource development programs could seriously impede the development of much-needed public programs in this area. Of course, as indicated in Chapter 19, it is unnecessary either to ignore the white manualist or to adopt preferential treatment and quotas for blacks. Proper attention to program design can provide remedial efforts for all manualists similarly situated without threatening whites or taking a condescending attitude toward manual occupations. To fail to adopt these programs is to risk unnecessary racial conflict and to generate serious obstacles to social progress.

# The White Worker

## by Gus Tyler

White and non-white ethnics are on a collision course—not because they are so different but because they are so much alike. Both feel they are forgotten people —the invisibles in an affluent society; both are driven by expanding expectations; both feel that their future is frustrated; both sense a potential power that, for lack of militant assertion, lies powerless.

Consequently, both the white and non-white ethnics are raring to make their presence visible, to spell out their expectations, to make themselves a future, and to gird their potent loins (group by group) to end their powerlessness.

Unfortunately, all these tribal ambitions are proliferating on a limited piece of turf: limited economically and geographically. Hence, the coming crisis—the clash of conflicting cultures in the American society.

The peril is dual: first, a direct resort to violence to resolve social conflicts; second, a rising clamor for a strong man to restore order. At one and the same time, America drifts toward anarchy and dictatorship.

To cool it by talk has little appeal at this moment. As tensions mount, pure reason will have even less appeal. The turf is too tight to let tempers untense.

If there is a hope for the days ahead it lies in expanding that turf—economically and geographically. The foregoing is the thesis of this paper.

Who are the main actors in this tightening tragedy?

### WHO ARE THE ETHNICS?

In present parlance, the word "ethnic" has become a kind of genteel way of saying "black." In one respect, such an interpretation has some validity for, in the

SOURCE Reprinted with permission from ILGWU.

United States, it was the black revolution —the reassertion of negritude—that sparked the rediscovery of active ethnicity among many other groups. Among non-whites, there are new active ethnic movements of Indians; Mexican-Americans; Hispanics, mainly Puerto Ricans.

Vital as these movements are, they are not—in this paper—our point of prime focus. We intend to take a look at the white ethnic who, rightly or wrongly, feels that in our national preoccupation with the blacks we have neglected the white sibling in our national family.

Who are the white ethnics? In a sense, they are everyone who is white. If ethnicity is defined by race, religion, national origin, or by traits peculiar to a group that has long lived in isolation from the general culture, then everybody is an ethnic.

Perhaps we should redefine this to refer, more narrowly to those ethnics who suffered discrimination. But who didn't?

The Pilgrims came here because they could find no other place to salve their persecuted souls. As soon as they got established, however, they turned, in persecution, against their own, driving Roger Williams, Ann Hutchinson and Thomas Hooker into the wilds of Connecticut and Rhode Island.

The Huguenots and Walloons came here fleeing persecution, only to find, on arrival, that they were promptly placed on the rims of the established colonial lands as a buffer against the Indians and a reserve against slave revolts.

The Scotch-Irish were known as the "white savages," whose Methodism made them theologically dedicated to disorder.

The Germans, according to Benjamin Franklin, were those "Palatine boors."

The Irish were lazy, drunken, criminal "micks" and—worse—Papists. For work, "no Irish need apply."

The Slavs were "hunkies," a term of denigration now transmigrated to the word "honkie."

The Jews were kikes, sheenies, and Christ-killers.

The Italians were dagos, guinees, and wops. Said one mine owner, explaining why he had no safety props in his mine, "Wops are cheaper than props."

Everybody has had and, in the fitting locale, still has his turn at discrimination —as hater or hated. In the Twin Cities, a Lutheran can look down his long nose at a Catholic in Minneapolis, and a Catholic can turn up his short nose at a Lutheran in St. Paul.

Perhaps we ought to redefine white ethnic, for our purposes, to refer to those groups that have not been fully assimilated in the American culture. But who has been?

Recently I heard a sixth generation corporate head explain his financial policy by reference to his "Scotch" genes. The Pennsylvania Dutch still wear their habit and practice their habits as if tomorrow were yesterday. In NYC, Woodside is Irish, Ridgewood is German, Sunset Park is Scandinavian, and Mosholu Parkway is Moishele's Parkway.

America is less a melting pot than a casserole with solid chunks of ethnic ingredients flavoring one another while holding on to their distinctive textures.

Who then are the white ethnics of whom we speak in our current context? That is, the white ethnics on the collision course?

By class, they are working people—employees who wear bule collars or who, if the collar is white or grey, might as well be blue.

By income, they make between $3,000 and $15,000 a year—reaching out to include many who make less than $3,000 and a few who make more than $15,000.

By locale, they live in metropolitan areas or in small cities outside metro-America.

By ethnicity, they are the more recent immigrant stock, here from one to three generations, reaching out to include several added millions who come from older stock but, who, in our upwardly mobile society, still have not escaped their economic clan, their ethnic neighborhood, or their urban entrapment.

This is an arbitary, yet sufficiently flexible definition to include those whites who, like their darker siblings, feel forgotten, frustrated, fearful, and furious. In the Twentieth century, they have been called the proletariat by radicals; the forgotten man by Roosevelt; the common man by Henry Wallace; the white ethnic by the *Wall Street Journal;* the urban villager by sociologists; the affluent American by economists; the middle-class by the media; the middle-American by columnists; the silent majority by Nixon pundits. He is the American worker—our very own yeoman who, after a generation of quietude, is about to shatter the stillness.

## WHITE WORKERS DO EXIST

Now a few facts about this class:

The first fact to be recorded is that *it does exist—and in great number.* For about a decade—the Sixties—it was the fad to depict "the worker" as the vanishing American. Automation would make him obsolete. His numbers would decline. His unions would disappear. His voice in the nation's politics would become an echo of an echo.

This theory was based on a vision of a post-industrial society in which work would be an anachronism. This conclusion was reached by taking a truth and then extrapolating and exaggating it into an untruth.

The fuller *truth* is that of the 77,902,000 gainfully employed in 1969, 28,237,000 wore blue collars; that is, 36%. But others might as well have worn the same colored collar. Of the 36,844,000 "white collar" workers, about 18 million were in clerical and sales—an added 22% of the employed. In addition, there were another 9,528,000 engaged in service trades—a

category that earned less than the blue collar, clerical or sales people. The total in theses blue and bluish jobs comes to sixty-nine percent of the employed.

Who is not included, beside farm workers? There is the class listed as Professional Technical, Managerial, Officials, and Proprietors. They make up about a quarter of the employed. But—despite their lofty title—millions of these belong with our worried white ethnics. Consider, for instance, that Italian "professional" who teaches in Franklin K. Lane High School or that Jewish "proprietor" who owns a candy store in Harlem.

*     *     *

The following Table A shows the breakdown of the employed 16 years and over by occupation and color.

## THE WORKER IS NOT AFFLUENT

The truth is that these people are not affluent—not even near affluent. The median family income in 1968 was $8,632, about a thousand dollars short of what the Bureau of Labor Statistics considered to be a "modest but adequate" income. Half the families earned less than this half-way figure—and about 80% of these were white. Put bluntly, most white families have not "made it." They don't make enough to live on a "modest but adequate" level.

This fact—that the median family in America can not meet the American standard of living—is but one of a constellation of facts that refute the mischievous myth that, in this country, poor means black and white means affluent. This myth is mischievous because it turns an ethnic difference into a class struggle. It is doubly mischievous because it implies and, in some cases outrightly states, that the way to end poverty is to end racism. This myth—like that of the vanishing American worker—is based upon a truth that extrapolated and exaggerated becomes an untruth.

While it is true that a much higher percentage of non-whites than whites is officially poor, it is equally true that in 1968 two-thirds of the poor were *white*. This white poverty, moreover, is not limited to Appalachia. In New York City, the poor are 60% white and 40% non-white.

\* \* \*

The next fact is that families with incomes above the $3,000 poverty line are not rich. Twelve percent of the families in America have an income between $3,000 and $5,000. (A recent Labor Department study found that an urban family of four needed at least $5,895 a year to meet its demands. If $6,000 a year were used as a cut-off poverty line, then 29.3% of the families in America are living in poverty.) A high fifty-two percent of the families had an income of less than $9,000 a year—a figure still below the official "modest but adequate" income. Seventy-two percent of the families have an income below $12,000 a year—a sum just above what the BLS considers adequate for a family of four in New York City. In toto, about three of four families struggle along.

This seventy-five percent even includes those mythically merry gentry: the professionals and the suburbanites.

In 1968, the median salary of professional and technical workers was, by sex, $10,151 a year for men and $6,691 for women. If that median man wanted to raise a family of four in New York City, he would have to send his wife out to work—which is exactly what he does.

\* \* \*

That's why among the families in America that have an income of between $7,000 and $10,000, fifty-six percent have two earners. Ten percent have three or more.

## WHERE DOES THE MONEY GO?

If so many Americans are non-affluent, who gets the money in this affluent society? That depends on the quintile, decile or percentile within which you live. If we list the American people by fifths (quintiles) and then look into what share of the nation's income (or wealth) goes to each fifth, we will quickly discover that the reason why four-fifths of the nation is not rich is due, in no small measure, to the fact that one-fifth of the nation—the top quintile—is super-rich. If we take that top fifth (the richest) and break it into deciles—tenths—we will find that the top tenth has an income about double that of the next-to-the-top tenth. If we then take the top *one* percent —percentiles—we will really begin to find out where the money goes.

Here are the facts on income distribution in America:

In 1968, the bottom fifth of the nation's families received 5.7% of the country's income; the top fifth received 40.6%. The middle three fifths were bunched between 12 and 23%.

These figures come from the U. S. Department of Commerce publication, "Consumer Income" (December 1969). These statistics actually understate the great gap between the top and the bottom. In calculating income, the Department of Commerce excludes certain types of income; namely, "money received from the sale of property, such as stocks, bonds, a house, or a car . . . gifts . . . and lump sum inheritances or insurance payments." If these items were included, the income of the top fifth would be appreciably increased—and, by the inclusion of these receipts in the total calculation of income, the income of the other fifths would be automatically decreased as a percentage of the whole.

\* \* \*

In sum, whether we look at white or dark America in 1947 or 1968, the maldistribution remains almost constant. Put bluntly, what this means is that if we bleached everybody in America an albino white and brainwashed away every ethnic memory, we would end up—under our present system—with a lower fifth getting about 5% of the income and a top fifth with about 40% of the income.

\* \* \*

BUT—WHY NOW?

If, however, the maldistribution of income is an inequity of ancient origin, whose persistent presence we have noted for this whole century, why, then, is the white worker turning restless at this particular moment? The reasons are triple: (1) a quantitative erosion of income; (2) a qualitative erosion of living; (3) a frightening erosion of social order.

Although the white worker has not been living in affluence, he was better off in the '60s than at any other time of his life. In the recovery years following the Great Depression (early 1930s), he and his family were enjoying an ever rising standard of living. Real income was going up and, so were his expectations.

In 1947, the median family income (in constant 1968 dollars) was $4,716; by 1967, it rose to $8,318, an increase of about $4,000—after allowing for inflation.

\* \* \*

The rise in income was reflected in a life-style based on rising expectations. You mortgaged your life for a home, because you expected to earn more in the days to come. You bought on the installment plan, everything from baby carriage to auto. You planned a future for your kids: a nice neighborhood, a good school, a savings plan to put the kids through one of the better colleges—maybe even Harvard or Vassar. You were out to "make it," no matter how hard you worked, how much you scrimped, how often you bor-

rowed, how late you moonlighted. You had hope!

You didn't even mind paying an ever higher tax, so long as your take-home pay was bigger. The tax was an investment in the future—a town or a country where things were better. You would enjoy it tomorrow and the kids would enjoy it for generations. You were future-minded.

As a result, this numerous class became the mass base of social stability in America. It was not status quoish in the sense that it would be happy to have its present frozen forever; it was constantly pushing for change. But it sought change within a system that it felt was yielding more and could continue to yield more.

To keep moving, this class joined unions for direct economic advance and voted Democratic for socio-economic legislation.

Sometime in the mid-60s, however, this presumed social structure began to fall apart. The institutionalized dream, like almost every other institution of our times, began to wobble. Hope was suddenly halted.

Almost unnoticed by the media was the decline in the real income of the non-supervisory employee. Between 1965 and 1969, the take-home buying power of the worker was in steady decline—despite sizeable wage and salary increases. The pay envelope was being chewed up by inflation and taxation.

The date—1965—was the first year of the escalated involvement in Vietnam, an effort that imposed a triple burden on the American worker. First, he had to pay a greater tax to help finance the war. Second, he had to pay more for consumer goods because this war—like any other—automatically increases demand without increasing supply. Third, he supplied his sons for the military: the affluent found ways to escape in schools and special occupations; the poor were too ill or illiterate. The great irony is that these white workers are also the nation's patriots, its loyal yeomanry who, by and large, support the war.

1965 is also the mid-point of a decade that saw America discover and respond to poverty and discrimination. The Johnson years produced a spate of national legislation to provide income and open opportunities to the poor, especially the Negroes. Simultaneously, local governments were trying to cope with their accumulating crises. At all levels, America began to spend public money to resolve pressing problems.

The American worker voted for these social measures. His unions and his Democratic Party spearheaded these efforts. Individually and institutionally, he saw these bits and pieces of socio-economic legislation as a continuation of his upward effort.

What was not apparent to these same workers was the upside-down system of taxation in the United States that placed the cost of these measures on the shoulders of that huge middle sector—not poor nor rich enough to escape taxes. Although the Federal income tax is supposed to be graduated to make the wealthy pay at a higher rate, this expressed intent is reversed by the many loopholes for those who derive their income from sources other than wages or salaries. At the local level, it is the small homeowner who pays the tariff through ad valorem property taxes and the small consumer who pays through the nose for city, county and state sales taxes.

The worker feels that he is paying triple; he pays for his own way; he pays for the poor; he pays for the rich. He is ready to do the first; he resists doing the extra chores for the others.

Finally, this same worker has been squeezed by a system of private taxation, operated through monopoly pricing. Everything from electricity to eggs is manipulated in closed and increasingly enclosed markets. As buying power goes up (current dollars in income) the response of dominant sectors of the economy is not to *increase* supply but to *limit* production (or distribution) to keep the consumer on the same level while increasing profits to the seller.

\* \* \*

The result is that millions of workers feel that they are paying more and more for less and less. They are paying for a war—with their sons, their taxes, and their overcharged purchases—only to feel that they are losing the war. They are paying more for what they buy—and get more cars doomed for early obsolescence, phones that ring wrong numbers, trains that collapse and collide, homes that are jerry built, doctors who make no home visits. They pay more and more in local taxes for education and welfare—and feel that they are subsidizing crime and riot.

Hard work seems to have brought on nothing but hard times. After Federal taxes are taken out of the pay, after local taxes are paid, and then the rest is used to buy debased goods and services at inflated prices, the worker knows—and his wife knows—better: that he is no longer moving up.

## THE MALDISTRIBUTION OF POPULATION

The worker in urban America, however, is not only the victim of income maldistribution (especially as it has hit him in the last half of the '60s) but is also the victim of *population maldistribution*. The latter is a catastrophe whose impact he can not stand and whose origin he does not understand. Indeed very few city dwellers even suspect that much of their urban crisis started down on the farm.

Since World War II, about a million Americans a year have moved from a rural to an urban culture. This massive shift of about 25 million people in one generation has been described as the most gigantic migration in the history of man

—comparable to the invasion of the Holy Roman Empire by the Goths and Vandals, but on a larger scale.

Such a collision of cultures has always meant crowding, crime and conflict. It was so with settlers and Indians, Protestants and Catholics, Nativists and European laborers, Jews and Gentiles, blacks and whites. In the 1960s, history repeated itself—except that the immigrant was invisible because he was an in-migrant.

What set this wave in motion? Two contradictory national policies toward agriculture: to increase productivity and to restrict production. Subsidized science found ways to make four stalks grow where one grew before. Subsidies to farmers, then, reversed the process by rewarding growers for non-production. The result was less and less need for labor on the soil. Farm workers went jobless; small farm owners went bankrupt or were bought out. Like the old British yeomanry who were driven from their lands by sheep walks, the rural Americans were driven from their familiar farms into the unfamiliar cities, from the warm earth to the cold concrete.

This rural push-urban-pull has been in motion ever since the turn of the century, but what was once a drift became a flood in the 1960s. The discomfort and disorder that followed set another dynamic in motion: the urban-push-suburban-pull.

In many ways, man, when jam-packed, behaves like lesser orders of animals. When rats are packed tight, they secrete adrenalin, filling them with the need to seek flight or a fight. When cats are crammed, they restructure their society: amidst constant hissing and spitting one cat becomes the tyrant and the weakest cats become pariahs. Judging from man's behavior in our crowded cities, he acts like both the rat and the cat.

Like the rat, his adrenalin urges him to flee or fight. If he can afford it, he generally flees—to outskirts and suburbs. He does so if he is black or white. (Between 1964 and 1969, 600,000 blacks fled the central cities for other parts of the metropolitan areas.) Those who can not flee, stay and get ready for the fight.

A current myth holds that the central cities are black and the suburbs are white, dividing metros into separate but unequal societies in geographic separation. Again this is half truth that, if totally true, might well lessen social conflict. The truth is many whites can not move, because they can not afford to move. Typically, they are the white-ethnics of more recent stock: economically unmonied and geographically immobile. Often, their neighborhoods abut black ghettos where—after the flight of the more affluent blacks—there are left, according to James Q. Wilson, "only the most deprived, the least mobile, and the most pathogical."

Through the '60s, the crush became a crunch—not simply because there were more bodies in the central cities but also because there were fewer places to put them. By public action, we have torn down about twice as many housing units as we have put up. Private builders have bulldozed slums to erect luxury highrisers. Hundreds of thousands of units are abandoned annually by their landlords, because the rotting property is all pain and no profit. As decay sets in at the ghetto core, rats and rain and fleas and fire take over to deprive even the most deprived of their turf. So these newly dispossessed become the latest in-migrants, driven from their holes into the surrounding neighborhoods, spreading panic in their path.

Under the pressures, the ethnics—white and black—move from economic frustration and personal fear to political fury. They begin to restructure like the crammed felines: the human cats spit and hiss; demand a strong leader; seek pariahs.

\* \* \*

## THE EROSION OF SOCIAL ORDER

In the 1970s fury comes easily to the white ethnic. It's stylish. He sees it everywhere. In the form of common crime—in the subway, on the street, at his doorstop. In the form of riots in the last summers of the sixties. In the form of confrontations in academia: clashes of gangs in the high schools; pummeling of professors and presidents; burning of books, bombing of buildings, bloodying of heads. In the form of kids throwing rocks at pigs and police swinging clubs at kids. In the form of raw rhetoric pouring from Panthers, Weathermen, Yippies, threatening overthrow while brandishing guns and mixing explosives.

The present generations of white ethnics have grown up in an age of war: World War II, Korea, Vietnam. For these decades, they have lived with mass violence, directly and vicariously.

Retribalization reawakens ancient feelings, a primitive recall of tribal origins. The white ethnic has always had this sense of belonging to some special groups. There were constant reminders of ethnicity in neighborhood names, groceries, bars, funeral parlors, holidays, language papers, ward politics, gang leaders, subtle prides and prejudices. But in an America that was devoted to the mythos of the melting pot and in a period dedicated to the ethos of one world, the white ethnic tucked his ethnicity up his sleeve. Now, in a retribalized world, he displays his ethnicity on his sleeve—as a pennant to carry into battle.

The young among the white ethnics, like the young everywhere, add their special stridency to the clamor. The youth who have affected our campuses, politics, sex, music, and hair style have their very sizeable quota of young workers. Like the young blacks and the young campus radicals and the young separatists of French Canada, Belgium, Scotland, the young workers are high on expectations and low on boiling point. In the teen grades, they form their ethnic gangs to battle for their turf. The fighting spills over on to the streets. In the police and fire-fighting forces, it is the young who are ready to wild-cat strike against government and who, when bated in their line of duty by radicals, are ready to strike out against their tormentors. To a civilizational distemper, the young add their hot tempers, turning ethnic salvation into the moral justification for ruthless violence.

## WHO IS THE ENEMY?

Our white ethnic is ready for battle. But he does not quite know against whom to declare war.

As a child of toilers, the white ethnic holds the traditional view of those who labor about those who don't. He feels that those inflated prices, those high taxes, those inadequate wages are all part of a schema for fattening up the fat. While he rarely, if ever, uses the words "Establishment" or "System," he instinctively assumes that there is an Establishment that exploits him through a devilishly devised system.

Part of the System, his experience teaches, is for the rich to use the poorest to keep the once-poor and the possibly-poor as poor as possible. For generations, employers who demanded protection against foreign imports were importing foreigners to depress wages and break strikes. Out of this arose the Known-Nothing Party that threatened within a matter of a couple of years, to become a major national movement. In the mid-nineteenth century, Irish workers (themselves recent immigrants) feared that the Emancipation Proclamation would end chattel slavery for the blacks and intensify wage slavery for the whites. Out of this fear arose the sadistic Draft Riot of 1863 with its beating, lynching and burning of Negroes. In the 1920s, the white ethnics opted for immigration legislation to stem the flow of cheap hands on to the labor market.

And now, as we move into the '70s, many workers fear that Class is using Underclass to undermine the Working Class. The way these workers hear it, this is what the rich are saying: "We must fight poverty and discrimination to the last drop of *your* blood. Share *your* job; share *your* neighborhood; pay *your* taxes." These moral exhortations come from Hohenheeren, economically ensconced in tax havens and personally residing far from the madding crowd.

In protest against this Establishment, the worker turns to strikes for higher wages and to revolt against taxes. But, in the last half dozen years, neither remedy works. Wage gains are offset by higher prices. Lower taxes mean lower services— schools, streets, travel, sanitation, police, medical care. What looked like a direct way out turns out to be a maze ending in a blind alley.

The reason these simple devices fail is the closed character of our complex society. The society is in the iron grip of income maldistribution. The wage gain usually follows the price (profit) rise and is generally followed by a new price rise, a process that can be manipulated easily so long as the key points in the economy are oligopolized. The tax revolt ends up, if successful, in fewer services because the revolt lacks the needed reform to get at the income of the top brackets. Hence, the easy answer ends up as no answer.

Since our worker does not know how to deal with the system, he tries to do the next best thing: to act within the system to protect his own skin. And in our torn and turbulent cities, it is too often his "skin" that determines his mood.

This mood is generally called the "backlash," the implication being that this is a reawakening of an ancient prejudice directed against Negroes because they have dared to raise their heads and voices. But to explain the growing tension simply as "backlash" is once more to create a mischievous myth out of partial truth. To deny that prejudice exists is naive. But to ascribe rising racial clash as a simple proliferation of prejudice is equally naive. The white ethnic feels economically threatened, personally imperiled, politically suckered. He feels socially and physically crowded (as he is). His mood turns ugly.

Racial suspicion turns into tribal war when peoples—no matter their ethnics— are oppressed by their economic and ecological circumstances. Maldistribution of income and people must multiply strife.

\* \* \*

The further irony is the innocence of those on top who are, in a depersonalized way, responsible for the turmoil on the shrinking turf. The uppest one percent rarely suspects that its incredible wealth is the prime reason the lesser peoples, without urging, are at one another's throats. As they see their role, these wealthiest are the great creators: investing, employing, making. They are the great givers, turning tax exempt funds to do God's work.

In short, there is no Devil: those at the top merely move their money around in a depersonalized way through impersonal channels (corporations) to multiply their money so they may do man's and God's work better; those in the middle (our white ethnic) merely move to lift their real income so they and their family can live—better; those at the bottom merely want what man needs to stay alive and kicking. Yet somehow they all end up in a fight with the top acting genteely with finances and the lesser people resorting intemperately to fists.

## Related Readings

Herman Miller of the U.S. Bureau of the Census in "A Profile of the Blue-Collared American," in Sar Levitan, Ed., *Blue Collar Blues: A Symposium on Middle America*, New York, McGraw-Hill, 1971, presents a profile of the blue-collar American based on census data. These data present several significant conclusions:

1. As compared with those who earned between $8000 and $12,000 in 1968, a significantly higher percentage of the wives of blue-collar men who earned $4000 to $8000 worked.

2. White males in each of the occupational groups had about the same relative gain in real earnings between 1960 and 1969. "The result suggests that there was no increase in the differential between whites in blue-collar jobs and those who were higher paid. However, nonwhite men overall averaged a 55 percent gain during the same period, and those employed in blue-collar jobs had gains of 44 percent. The changes were very similar in the South and in the northern and western parts of the country, with the exception that the relative gains for nonwhites were greatest in the South."

3. In the craftsman and operative category, nonwhites increased by about 40 percent between 1960 and 1969 as compared with only 7 percent for whites.

4. Miller concludes that ". . . the typical white craftsman or operative encountered many more nonwhite men on the job in 1969 than he did nine years earlier and . . . these men were making more money than ever before. . . . On the basis of this evidence and in light of continued pressure by the Federal Government and civil rights groups to break down barriers to employment and, particularly, to get more blacks into craft unions, there is reason to believe that the expressed attitudes of white union members are in part, at least, inspired by the fear of economic competition from blacks."

# Index